AUTOMOTIVE BODY REPAIR AND REFINISHING

William H. Crouse
and
Donald L. Anglin

McGRAW-HILL BOOK COMPANY
Gregg Division

New York
St. Louis
Dallas
San Francisco
Auckland
Bogotá
Düsseldorf
Johannesburg
London
Madrid
Mexico
Montreal
New Delhi
Panama
Paris
São Paulo
Singapore
Sidney
Tokyo
Toronto

Library of Congress Cataloging in Publication Data
Crouse, William Harry, (date)
Automotive body repair and refinishing

Includes index.
1. Automobiles—Bodies—Maintenance and repair.
I. Anglin, Donald L., joint author. II. Title.
TL255.C69 629.2′6′028 78-23532
ISBN 0-07-014791-4

Automotive Body Repair and Refinishing

Editors / D. Eugene Gilmore
Mary Levai
Design Supervisor / Judy Grossman
Art Supervisor / George T. Resch
Cover Designer / Caryl V. Spinka
Production Supervisor / Frank P. Bellantoni
Cover Photographer / Eric J. Barrick
Technical Studio / Fine Line, Inc.
Set in Helvetica by Waldman Graphics.

ABOUT THE AUTHORS

William H. Crouse

Behind William H. Crouse's clear technical writing is a background of sound mechanical engineering training as well as a variety of practical industrial experience. After finishing high school, he spent a year working in a tinplate mill. Summers, while still in school, he worked in General Motors plants, and for three years he worked in the Delco-Remy Division shops. Later he became Director of Field Education in the Delco-Remy Division of General Motors Corporation, for which he prepared service bulletins and educational literature.

Mr. Crouse has contributed numerous articles to automotive and engineering magazines, and has written many books about science and technology. He was the first Editor-in-Chief of the 15-volume *McGraw-Hill Encyclopedia of Science and Technology.* In addition, he has authored more than 50 technical books, including *Automotive Mechanics,* which has sold over a million copies. His books have been widely translated and used in automotive mechanics training throughout the world.

William H. Crouse's outstanding work in the automotive field has earned for him membership in the Society of Automotive Engineers and in the American Society of Engineering Education.

Donald L. Anglin

Trained in the automotive and diesel service field, Donald L. Anglin has worked both as a mechanic and as a service manager. He has taught automotive courses in high school, trade schools, community colleges, and universities. He has also worked as curriculum supervisor and school administrator for an automotive trade school. Interested in all types of vehicle performance, he has served as a racing-car mechanic and as a consultant to truck fleets on maintenance problems.

Currently, he serves as editorial assistant to William H. Crouse, visiting automotive instructors and service shops. Together they have coauthored a number of magazine articles on automotive education, as well as several books in the McGraw-Hill Automotive Technology Series.

Donald L. Anglin is a Certified General Automotive Mechanic, a Certified General Truck Mechanic, and he holds many other licenses and certificates in automotive education, service, and related areas. His extensive work in the automotive service field has been recognized by membership in the American Society of Mechanical Engineers and the Society of Automotive Engineers.

CONTENTS

PREFACE

Courses in automotive body repair and refinishing are being offered in more schools every year. One challenge faced by the instructor of these programs has been to find a textbook and related materials that cover today's car. With the emphasis on new materials and serviceability, teaching the student metal work and spray-gun operation simply is not enough. Most textbooks concentrate on one of these two subjects, but this fails to train today's student for tomorrow's jobs in fixing and refinishing real cars.

This new textbook, *Automotive Body Repair and Refinishing,* is comprehensive. It provides complete and current coverage of the practices used in the field. It is oriented to the hands-on activities required to perform practical shop jobs and contains a minimum of theory.

Starting with an overview to place the job in perspective, the book covers automobile construction and progresses through how each part of the car is repaired and refinished. Included is the related shop knowledge and skills that a technician must have in welding, soldering, frame straightening, plastics and fiberglass, trim and upholstery, glass, and overlay and decal service. The chapters on painting cover painting equipment, spray guns, surface preparation, matching and mixing paints, typical paint jobs, and avoiding, recognizing, and correcting paint problems.

To round out the student's experiences in the shop, the basics of estimating are discussed. To help the student quickly grasp the words and phrases of the field, a glossary is included at the back of the book.

Automotive Body Repair and Refinishing covers the subjects included in the National Institute for Automotive Service Excellence (NIASE) certification tests *Body Repair* and *Painting and Refinishing.* These NIASE tests are used for certifying specialists under the NIASE voluntary testing and certification program.

The *Workbook for Automotive Body Repair and Refinishing* is available for use in the shop. This workbook has been especially developed to provide the student with specific instruction in 36 shop jobs. These jobs are considered basic requirements for the auto body and paint technician.

Also available, to instructors only, is the *Instructor's Planning Guide for Automotive Body Repair and Refinishing.* It contains several articles of interest to the instructor and the answer key for the written exercises at the end of each job in the workbook.

These materials add up to an instructional program that will fit any type of teaching situation whose purpose is to train automotive body repair and refinishing technicians. The instructor's planning guide explains how the various materials can be used, either alone or with others, to satisfy different curriculum requirements.

The authors are grateful to the many people, both in the industry and in education, whose contributions and comments helped shape this book. Special thanks must go to Albert Conner, instructor in auto body repair at the Richmond Technical Center (Richmond, VA), and to his students. Special thanks are also due to the following: Jim Jackman, Clifford Lutz, Edward Skutt, John Paul Poppell, Alan Keene, E. H. Hendley, Karla Hunter, and Fred Meador, Jr. They share with the authors a hope that this program will help achieve the aims of all who work in the field of automotive education: to train high-caliber automotive technicians who are capable of taking their proper place in the automotive-servicing profession.

William H. Crouse
Donald L. Anglin

ACKNOWLEDGMENTS

During the preparation of *Automotive Body Repair and Refinishing,* the authors were given invaluable aid and inspiration by many, many people in the automotive industry and in the field of education. The authors gratefully acknowledge their indebtedness and offer their sincere thanks to these people. All cooperated by providing accurate, complete information that is useful in training automotive technicians.

Special thanks are owed to the following organizations for having supplied information and illustrations: Allstate; American Motors Corporation; Applied Power, Inc.; Avdel Corporation; Binks Manufacturing Company; The Black & Decker Manufacturing Company; Buick Motor Division of General Motors Corporation; Cadillac Motor Car Division of General Motors Corporation; Channellock, Inc.; Chevrolet Motor Division of General Motors Corporation; Chicago Pneumatic Tool Company; Chrysler Corporation; Dana Corporation; Delco-Remy Division of General Motors Corporation; DeVilbiss Company; Ditzler Automotive Finishers, PPG Industries, Inc.; Du Pont; Fisher Body Division of General Motors Corporation; Ford Motor Company; General Motors Corporation; Guy Chart; Harris Calorific; Lenco, Inc.; The Lincoln Electric Company; Lincoln St. Louis Division of McNeil Corporation; 3M Company; Motor Vehicle Manufacturers Association; Novus, Inc.; Oldsmobile Division of General Motors Corporation; Pontiac Motor Division of General Motors Corporation; Proto Tool Company; Rego Company; Rinshed-Mason Company; Rockwell International; Snap-on Tools Corporation; Society of Automotive Engineers, Inc.; Stanley Tool Company; Toyota Motor Sales Company, Ltd.; Union Carbide Corporation; United Delco Division of General Motors Corporation; and Waldes Kohinoor, Inc. To all these organizations and the people who represent them, sincere thanks.

TO THE STUDENT

Automotive Body Repair and Refinishing is one of the books included in the McGraw-Hill Automotive Technology Series. These books cover the construction, operation, inspection, and maintenance of automotive vehicles. They are designed to give you the background you need to become successful in the automotive-service business. These books satisfy the recommendations of the Motor Vehicle Manufacturers Association–American Vocational Association Industry Planning Council, the Automotive Mechanics Certification, State Vocational Educational Programs, and the Automotive Trade Apprenticeship Training Program. The full coverage of the subject matter makes the books valuable additions to the library of anyone interested in automotive engineering, manufacturing, sales, service, or operation.

Meeting the Standards

The books meet the standards set by the Motor Vehicle Manufacturers Association (MVMA) for an associate degree in Automotive Servicing and in Automotive Service Management. These standards are described in the MVMA booklet "Community College Guide for Associate Degree Programs in Auto and Truck Service and Management." The books also cover the subjects recommended by the American National Standards Institute in their detailed standard D18.1-1972, "American National Standard for Training of Automotive Mechanics for Passenger Cars and Light Trucks."

In addition, the books cover the subject matter tested by the National Institute for Automotive Service Excellence (NIASE). These subject-matter tests are used for certifying General Automotive Mechanics and Automotive Technicians working in specific areas of specialization under the NIASE voluntary mechanic testing and certification program.

Getting Practical Experience

As you study, you should be getting practical experience in the shop. That is, you should handle automotive parts, automotive tools, and automotive servicing equipment. You should perform actual servicing jobs. To assist you in your shop work, there is a *Workbook for Automotive Body Repair and Refinishing* that includes 36 jobs covering basic servicing procedures required in the body and paint shop. If you do every job covered in the workbook, you will have had "hands-on" experience that will provide you with skill and confidence.

If you are taking a regular course in a school, you have an instructor to guide you in your classroom and shop activities. But even if you are not taking a regular course, the workbook can act as an instructor. It tells you, step by step, how to do the various jobs. Perhaps you can meet others who are taking a regular school course in automotive body repair and refinishing. You can talk over any problems you have with them. A local body and paint shop is a good source of practical information. If you can get acquainted with the automotive technicians there, you will find that they have a large amount of practical information. Watch them at their work if you can. Make notes of important points and file them in your notebook.

Service Publications

While you are in a shop, study the various publications they receive. Automobile manufacturers and suppliers publish shop manuals, service bulletins, and parts catalogs. They are published to help service technicians do a better job. In addition, automotive magazines deal with the problems and methods of automotive service. Paint manufacturers have excellent magazines on automotive and truck refinishing. These publications will be of great value to you. Study them carefully.

Such activities will help you get practical experience. Sooner or later, this experience plus the knowledge you gain in studying *Automotive Body Repair and Refinishing* will permit you to step into the automotive shop on a full-time basis. Or, if you are already in the shop, they will equip you for a better and a more responsible job.

Checking up on Yourself

Every few pages, this book gives you the chance to check your progress by answering a series of questions. Many of the answers are given at the back of the book. Each progress quiz should be taken just after you have completed the pages preceding it. The quizzes allow you to check yourself. Because they are review tests, you should review the entire chapter by rereading it, or at least checking the important points, before trying a test. If any of the questions stump you, reread the pages that give you the answer. This type of review is valuable because it helps you remember the information you will need when you go out into the automotive shop.

Keeping a Notebook

Keeping a notebook is a valuable part of your training. Start it now, at the beginning of your studies. Your notebook will help you in many ways. It will be a record of your progress. It will become a storehouse of valuable information that you will refer to time after time. It will help you learn. It will help you organize your training program to do you the most good.

When you study a lesson in the book, have your notebook open before you. Start with a fresh notebook page at the beginning of each lesson. Write the lesson title or textbook page number at the top of the page, along with the date. As you read your lesson, jot down the important points.

In the shop, make your notes on a small scratch pad or on cards. Transfer these notes to your notebook as soon as possible.

Make sketches in your notebook. Save articles and illustrations from technical and hot-rod magazines. File them in your notebook. Also, save the instruction sheets that come with new parts. Paste or tape these to sheets of paper, and file them in your notebook.

Your notebook will become one of your most valuable possessions. It will be a permanent record of how you learned about automotive body repair and refinishing.

Glossary and Index

There is a glossary (a list of definitions) of automotive body repair and refinishing terms in the back of the book. If you are not sure about the meaning of a term, or the purpose of a part, refer to the glossary. There is also an index at the back of the book. This index will guide you to the page in the book where you can find the information you need.

And now, good luck to you. You are studying a fascinating art—automotive body repair and refinishing. Your studies can lead you to success in the automotive field, a field where opportunities are nearly unlimited. It is the person who knows—the person who can do things—who moves ahead. Let this person be you.

PART 1
THE AUTOMOTIVE BODY SHOP

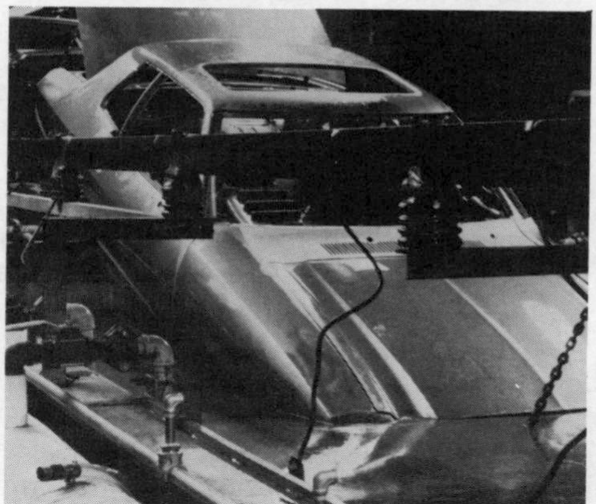

In this part, we discuss opportunities in the automotive body-repair business. Then we introduce you to a typical automobile body, describe its component parts and accessories, and explain how everything is put together. This is important information, because the body-repair technician must know the car body inside and out to work successfully on it. The body includes not only the sheet metal that you can see but also the underbody and the frame. In addition, the glass (called the glazing), grills, trim, molding, bumpers, doors, door latches and locks, windows and window controls, upholstery, seats and seat controls, and safety equipment such as seat belts and air bags are all considered part of the body and are included in this book.

Part 1 of this book also includes discussions of the tools and materials used in the body shop. In addition, Part 1 covers safe operating practices that will help prevent anyone getting hurt in the shop. There are nine chapters in Part 1, as follows:

1 OPPORTUNITIES IN AUTOMOTIVE BODY REPAIR

Estimates show that more than 30 million paint and body jobs go through body shops every year. Total bill for all this work runs into many billions of dollars. This means that it takes hundreds of thousands of men and women working in body-repair shops to handle all these jobs.

○ 1-1 Why More Auto Body Technicians Are Needed

There are about 63,000 auto body and paint shops and about 200,000 body technicians and paint technicians working in these shops. But this is not enough. Walk down the street in any city and look at the cars passing and parked at the curb. You will see many cars in need of body and paint work. Many of the owners of these cars would like to have this work done. However, the owners are often put off by being told to come back to the shop in a few days or weeks. The shops they check with may be booked up a long time in advance.

There is a great deal of body work to be done. However, body shops and body-repair technicians are not always available to do the work when the car owner wants it done. This means that there are opportunities in the auto-body-repair field for anyone who wants to work on automobiles. Body-repair work is more than simply removing and replacing parts, using hand tools. The auto body technician gets great personal satisfaction from taking a car that has been damaged and restoring it to its original condition.

○ 1-2 Jobs in the Auto Body Shop

Many people think in terms of two jobs when they talk about auto body repair. These are metalwork and painting. But there are many more jobs than these performed in the auto body shop. In the body shop (Fig. 1-1) which handles complete vehicle rebuilding, you might see the following:

1. Manager (who may be the owner)
2. Foreman
3. Estimator
4. Body-repair technicians
5. Power-equipment operators (such as frame and alignment specialists)
6. Painting and refinishing technicians
7. Upholsterers
8. Glass technicians
9. Office staff

In smaller shops, some of these separate jobs are combined. For example, the manager or owner may also be the foreman and the estimator. Body-repair technicians, who repair or replace body panels, may also operate the power equipment. The painter may also work on the sheet metal, sanding and filling in preparation for painting. Some shops may not have an upholsterer or glass technician. These jobs may be sent out, or sublet, to other shops specializing in this work. The office staff may be one person who handles all the paperwork, such as billing insurance companies, ordering parts and materials, answering the phone, and paying the bills. This job also may include writing the paychecks. Now, let's look at each of these jobs.

FIGURE 1–1. A typical automotive body shop.

○ 1-3 Manager

Usually the body-shop manager or owner (Fig. 1-2) started out as an apprentice metalworker, working for someone else. Gradually, he or she learned all aspects of the job and moved up to become foreman, estimator, or body-shop manager. Later, this person decided to open an auto-body-repair shop. Today, about one out of every eight body-repair technicians is self-employed. In many of these small shops, the owner does it all.

The manager is responsible for everything that the shop does or does not do. During the day-to-day operation of the shop, the manager hires, trains, and fires workers, as required. Also, it is the job of the manager to see that a steady flow of body repair and paint work

FIGURE 1–2. The body-shop manager is a busy person, especially if estimating also is part of the job.

is coming into the shop. Once a job is in the shop, the manager makes sure that the parts needed are received by the body technician within a reasonable time. In addition, the manager checks that each worker is skilled and productive. Those who are slow or find certain jobs difficult receive instruction or are sent to school for training. Some managers try to personally meet each customer who brings in a car for repair.

This description does not cover all the things that a manager has to do. But in the body shop, the manager is "the boss."

○ 1-4 Foreman

The foreman runs the shop. Duties include assigning jobs to the workers, checking on when jobs will be completed, making sure materials and parts are available, determining that all workers are productive, and observing that quality jobs are being turned out. In the smaller shops, the manager is also the foreman. Larger shops have a separate foreman. In other shops, the estimator may share some of these responsibilities with the manager.

○ 1-5 Estimator

The estimator (Fig. 1-3) gets the repair jobs for the body shop. In the smaller shop, the manager or owner is also the estimator. Larger body shops have one or more specialists to handle this essential job. Estimating requires a knowledge of automobile construction. Personal experience in body repair is an asset for the estimator.

When a car is damaged or wrecked, the estimator looks over the car—inside and out, top, sides, and bottom. Then it is the estimator's job to prepare a written estimate of the cost of repair. A good estimate must cover the shop expenses in doing the job, plus a profit for the shop. This is especially difficult on cars that have had considerable damage, particularly to the underbody or frame. On these cars, additional serious damage may not be obvious. However, the experienced estimator knows what to look for.

FIGURE 1–3. The estimator prepares an estimate of slight front-end damage to a new car.

As the cost of repairing a wrecked car goes up, the chances that the car will be repaired decrease. If the repair costs are too high, the car may be declared a "total." This means that the car is damaged so much that it is not worth repairing. The cost of making the repairs would be higher than the value of the car. For example, insurance companies and most owners would not want to spend $1000 to repair a wrecked car that was worth only $500 on the used car market. This makes the car a total loss. Such a car usually is sold to an automobile junkyard, salvage dealer, or dismantler. Useful and undamaged parts then can be removed for installation on other cars of the same model.

The estimator must walk a narrow path between making too low an estimate and making too high an estimate. If the estimate is too low, the shop loses money on the job. If the estimate is too high, the shop can lose the job to another shop that offers to do it cheaper. Chapter 40 covers estimating in detail.

○ 1-6 Body-Repair Technician

The sheet-metal worker or body-repair technician (Fig. 1-4) straightens or replaces the various sheet-metal and fiberglass parts on the car. If a part is not too badly damaged, it can be straightened or repaired satisfactorily. Usually, this means restoring the original contour and filling the low spots with plastic or solder. Then the repair is smoothed by filling and sanding so it will be ready to accept the primer and final paint coats.

If a metal panel or part is too badly damaged to straighten, it is cut out. A new part is welded or riveted in its place. The welds or rivets are pounded down below the contour and the low spots filled and finished in preparation for painting.

○ 1-7 Power-Equipment Operator

Power equipment uses compressed air, chains, clamps, and fasteners to pull or push on bent parts so they are brought back to their original shape. Figure 1-5 shows a car with power equipment attached. When the technician operates the air switch or switches, the power cylinders expand or telescope. This applies pressure or pull that will straighten the bent parts. In many shops, the front-end technician operates the frame-straightening equipment.

FIGURE 1–4. Body-repair technician straightening a damaged right quarter panel.

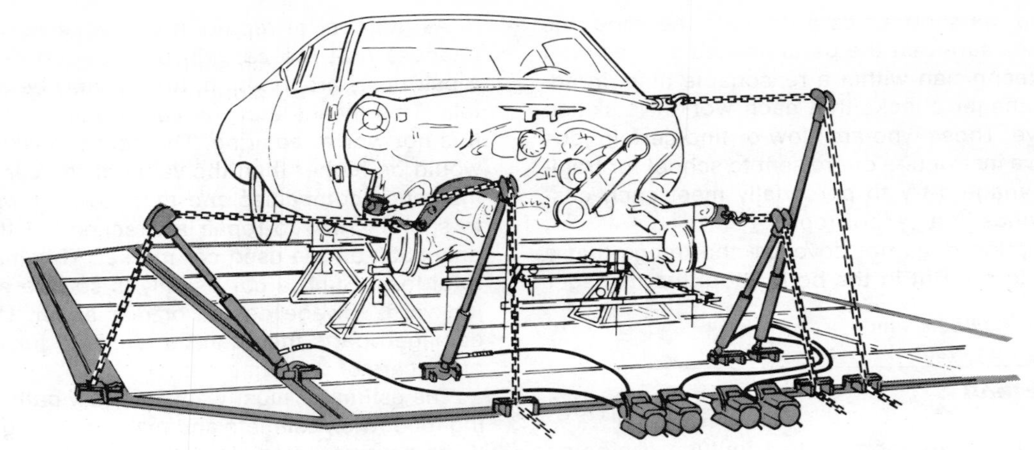

FIGURE 1–5. Hydraulic frame-and-body straightener making pulls on a car to straighten the frame and body. (*Blackhawk Division of Applied Power, Inc.*)

○ 1-8 Painting and Refinishing Technician

After the body panels, doors, roof, hood, and trunk lid—whatever part was damaged—have been restored to their original contours, the sheet-metal surfaces are smoothed by sanding. This job is started with coarse sandpaper and finished with very fine sandpaper. Then the painter applies a coat of primer, followed by the final coats of paint, as shown in Fig. 1-6. Painting is an exacting job and takes some time to learn. The paint must be mixed in the right proportions to match the color of the original paint. If this is not done, the paint patch will dry to a different color. Then the customer will not be happy with the job.

Before the paint job is started, all parts that are not to be painted must be covered with paper and tape. You can see these protected areas in Fig. 1-6. Often the painter has a helper who does this job. It is called masking. The car is then ready for painting. This is often done in a special paint booth. It is very important to keep dust out of the air in the painting area. Dust on the freshly painted car will show up, and the job may have to be done over. After the fresh paint is on, heat may be applied by heat lamps to speed the drying process.

FIGURE 1–6. A painter spraying a door. Note that a respirator is worn to prevent the inhaling of dangerous fumes.

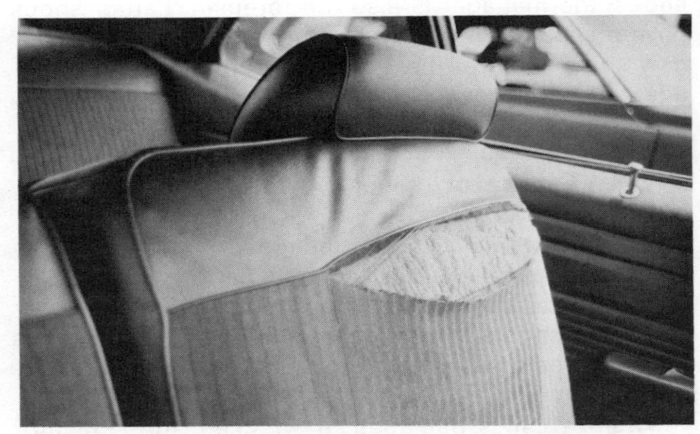

FIGURE 1–7. A car with seat in need of new upholstery.

○ 1-9 Upholsterers

The upholsterer removes worn upholstery from the seats and replaces it with new material to restore the original look to the interior of the car (Fig. 1-7). The upholsterer also installs new headliner (the cloth lining that is the inside "roof" of the car), and new carpet. In other words, the upholsterer's job is to maintain and repair the car interior. Some customers may want a custom interior. This means that the upholsterer will use special materials and patterns for the seats, headliner, and carpet.

○ 1-10 Glass Technician

The glass technician installs new glass in the car. This may require two people, as for example, when installing a new windshield (Fig. 1-8). Some shops specialize in this work, because it is easy to chip or crack the new glass during installation. Many body shops send, or sublet, their glasswork to a local glass shop.

○ 1-11 Office Staff

The size of the body shop determines the size of the office staff. Except for writing the estimate and the repair order, the office staff handles all paperwork in the shop.

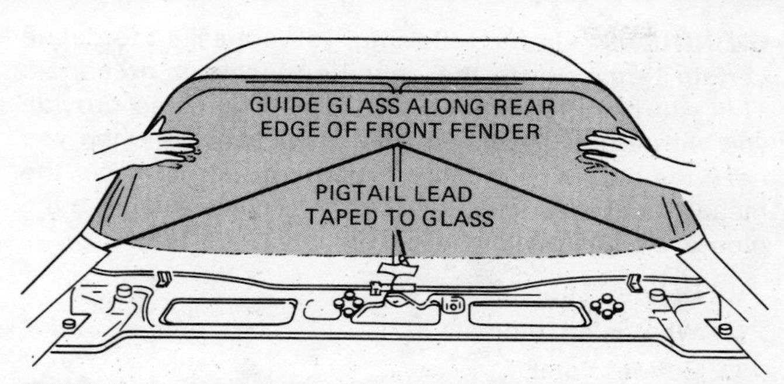

FIGURE 1–8. Installing a windshield. ***(Fisher Body Division of General Motors Corporation)***

This includes billing, paying bills, and keeping records. In some shops, it also includes ordering parts, checking parts in when received, and charging the parts to the job being worked on.

○1-12 The Successful Body Shop

Success in a body shop starts with good management. A steady flow of repair jobs must come in. Then they must go out finished on time. The manager must see that all sections of the body shop operate as they should. The shop must be kept clean, both inside and out. There must be spaces where customers can park, a drive-in area where the customers may get an estimate, and a clean customer lounge or waiting room.

In particular, records must be properly kept so that the manager will know at all times how the shop is doing financially. More business failures are caused by poor record keeping than by any other single problem.

CHECK YOUR PROGRESS[1]

PROGRESS QUIZ 1-1 The following exercises will help you find out how well you understand what you are studying. If you have trouble answering any of the questions, study the chapter again. Most successful students read and study their assignments several times, to make sure they understand them. Don't be discouraged if you cannot answer all the questions the first time. The material you are studying is not as easy to remember as the plot of a novel or a movie. So, if you run into trouble as you do the exercises, restudy the chapter and try the questions again. As you practice this technique of read and restudy, you will learn how to pick out the important facts you should know. The book will then become much easier to read and understand. You will be better able to sort out and retain the essential facts. This will mean that you are becoming a successful student. And the successful student, the person who knows the facts, is headed for success as an automotive body-repair technician.

COMPLETING THE SENTENCES The sentences below are incomplete. After each sentence there are several words or phrases. Only one of them correctly completes the sentence. Write each sentence in your notebook, ending it with the one word or phrase that completes it correctly.

1. The auto body includes the (*a*) wheels, tires, and brakes; (*b*) hood, engine, and battery; (*c*) trunk, fuel tank, and exhaust pipe; (*d*) sheet metal, underbody, and frame.
2. Each year paint and body-repair jobs are performed on more than (*a*) several billion vehicles, (*b*) 30 million vehicles; (*c*) 10,000 vehicles, (*d*) 1 million vehicles.
3. The "boss" in a big body shop is the (*a*) manager, (*b*) glass technician, (*c*) painter, (*d*) upholsterer.
4. Checking on the quality of work put out by the shop is one duty of the (*a*) foreman, (*b*) office staff, (*c*) front-end technician, (*d*) painter.
5. Figuring out how much it will cost to profitably repair a wrecked car is the job of the (*a*) glass technician, (*b*) painter, (*c*) estimator, (*d*) metalworker.
6. Filling in low spots with plastic or solder is done by the (*a*) office staff, (*b*) manager, (*c*) foreman, (*d*) metalworker.
7. Masking a car for painting may be done by the painter or the (*a*) painter's helper, (*b*) foreman, (*c*) estimator, (*d*) glass technician.
8. Repairing a torn seat is the job of the (*a*) glass technician, (*b*) metalworker, (*c*) upholsterer, (*d*) foreman.
9. Figuring the amount due in each employee's paycheck is the job of (*a*) each employee, (*b*) the office staff, (*c*) the estimator, (*d*) the painter.
10. Most businesses such as body shops fail because of (*a*) high parts prices, (*b*) poor record keeping, (*c*) low labor rates, (*d*) poor location.

JOBS AND JOB DESCRIPTIONS The following questions ask you to explain various jobs in the automotive body shop as discussed in this chapter. Write the answers in your notebook. If you have any difficulty, turn back in the chapter and reread the pages that give you the answer. Then write the required explanation. Do not copy directly from the book. Instead, try to tell it in your own words. This is a good way to fix the explanation firmly in your mind.

1. Why is some type of office staff needed in most body shops?
2. Why do many body shops send their glasswork to glass shops?
3. Who repairs vinyl tops and convertible tops?
4. What job can be ruined if there is too much dust in the air?
5. Who works mostly with plastic and solder?
6. Who has to meet and talk with each customer?
7. Who runs the shop?
8. What is the job of the manager?
9. Who is included in the category of "power-equipment operators"?
10. What is the difference between a body-repair technician and a painting and refinishing technician?

[1]Answers to questions in the quizzes and chapter checkups are given at the end of the book.

CHAPTER 1 CHECKUP

NOTE: Since the following is a chapter review test, you should review the chapter before taking the test.

MATCHING In the left column below are 10 words or phrases used in the chapter you just studied. In the right column are 10 other words or phrases. Each of these tells about or completes a word or phrase in the left column. Match each item in the right column with an item from the left column. Then write the combined list in your notebook. When you have finished, turn to the answers at the end of the book to check your work. If you missed any, restudy the pages in the chapter that give you the correct answer.

about 200,000	paint and body repairs each year
foreman	looks over wrecked car
dismantler	cuts out badly damaged parts
one out of every eight	hires, trains, and fires
body-repair technician	uses lots of sand-paper
upholsterer	auto body technicians
estimator	maintains and repairs interiors
painter	buys "totaled" cars
manager	runs the shop
more than 30 million	self-employed body-repair technicians

DEFINITIONS In the following, you are asked to define certain terms. Write the definitions in your notebook. This will help you remember them. It will also provide you with a quick way to locate the meanings when you need the information again. If you cannot remember the meanings of the terms, look them up in the text or in the glossary at the back of the book.

1. Define "sublet."
2. What is an estimate?
3. Define "total."
4. What is an apprentice?
5. Define "foreman."
6. What is an estimate?
7. Define "estimator."
8. What is masking?
9. Define "upholsterer."
10. What are shop records?

SUGGESTIONS FOR FURTHER STUDY

Auto body repair and painting occasionally receive publicity in newspapers and magazines and on radio and television. When you see an informative article dealing with the subject (or with a related subject such as experimental safety vehicles), cut out the article and add it to your notebook. Also, if you have a chance, talk about automotive body and paint work with your friends, local body-repair and paint technicians, and your instructor. Many professionals have had experience at customizing, striping, and other skilled techniques.

2
AUTOMOBILE BODY CONSTRUCTION

There are two main types of automotive body construction:

1. Body-and-frame construction
2. Unitized-body, also called unibody and unit, construction

The body-and-frame construction is the most common today. The unibody construction is used largely on the smaller, or compact, cars. Let us look at each type of construction.

○2-1 Body-and-Frame Construction

The body-and-frame type of construction uses a separate frame such as shown in Fig. 2-1. The frame is designed to support all body and engine parts and is, in turn, supported by the front-and rear-wheel springs. The frame is usually made of specially formed channel or U-shaped steel members that are riveted or welded together. Note, in Fig. 2-1, how the frame members are shaped to take the various parts that are attached to it. Figure 2-2 shows a frame on which the wheels and springs, engine, brakes, and steering system have been mounted. This subassembly of the complete automobile is often called the *chassis*. The chassis shown in Fig. 2-2 is ready for the attachment of the body.

○2-2 Body

The body includes more than the body panels. It also includes the doors and their window-operating mechanisms, the seats and their adjusting mechanisms, floor carpet, headliner (lining overhead), trim, lights, bumpers, windshield washers and wipers, grills, instrument panel with instruments, and so on. In other words, the body has just about everything, except the chassis parts, that is required to make a complete automobile.

Figure 2-3 shows a body, in phantom view, on a complete chassis. The body is fastened to the chassis by a series of body bolts. These large bolts use rubber washers or body mounts to isolate the body from the metal of the chassis. This prevents the transfer of noise and vibration from the chassis to the body. Figure 2-4 shows how the body bolts fasten the body to the frame while isolating vibration in the frame from the body.

○2-3 Unitized-Body Construction

This type of body does not have a separate one-piece frame, such as shown in Fig. 2-1. Instead, the floor pan serves as the center part of the frame, with all body panels being welded together to form the body, as shown in Fig. 2-5. Figure 2-6 shows this same basic body with the front fenders, doors, hood, and trunk lid added.

Some types of unibody construction require partial frames, called *stub frames,* as shown in Fig. 2-7. These are required to provide support of and attachment points for the front and rear suspension systems.

○2-4 Body Sheet Metal

Figure 2-8 shows a car with the major body panels named. These are only the exterior main panels. Under-

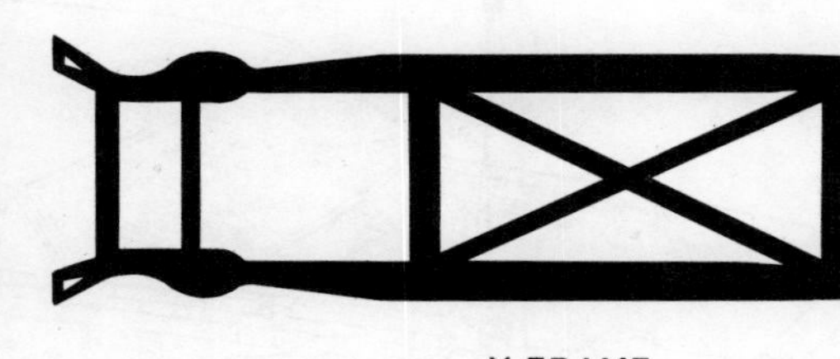

FIGURE 2–1. Various types of automobile frames. (*Blackhawk Division of Applied Power, Inc.*)

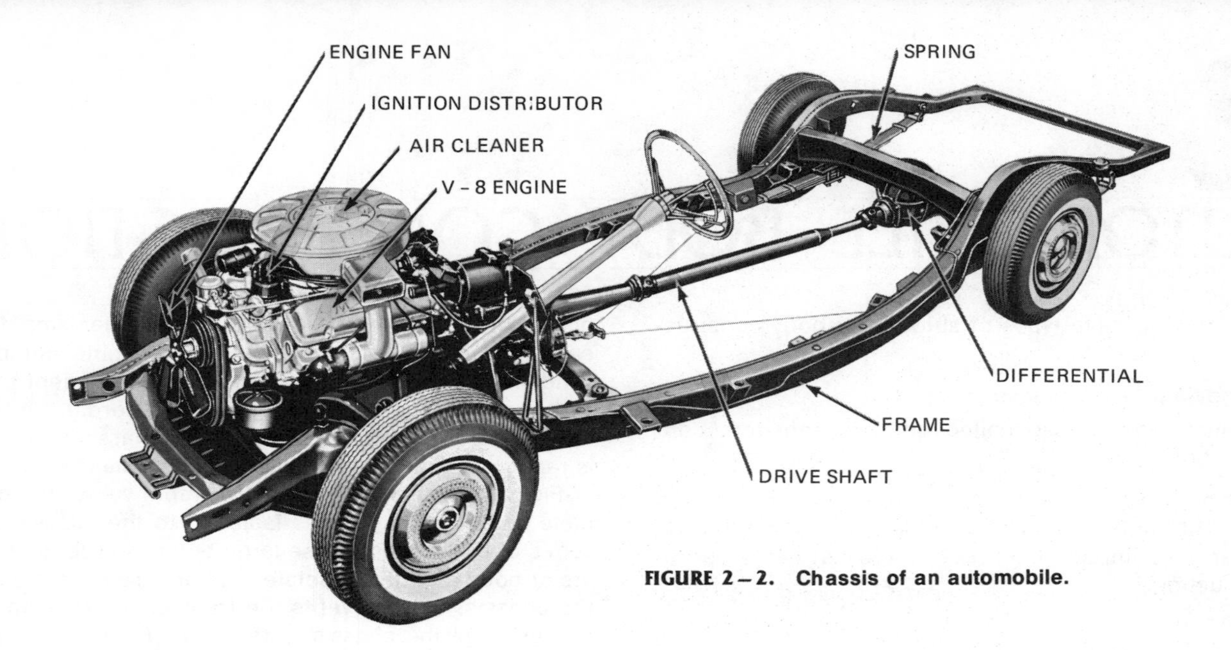

FIGURE 2 – 2. **Chassis of an automobile.**

FIGURE 2 – 3. **The body, in phantom view, mounted on complete chassis.**

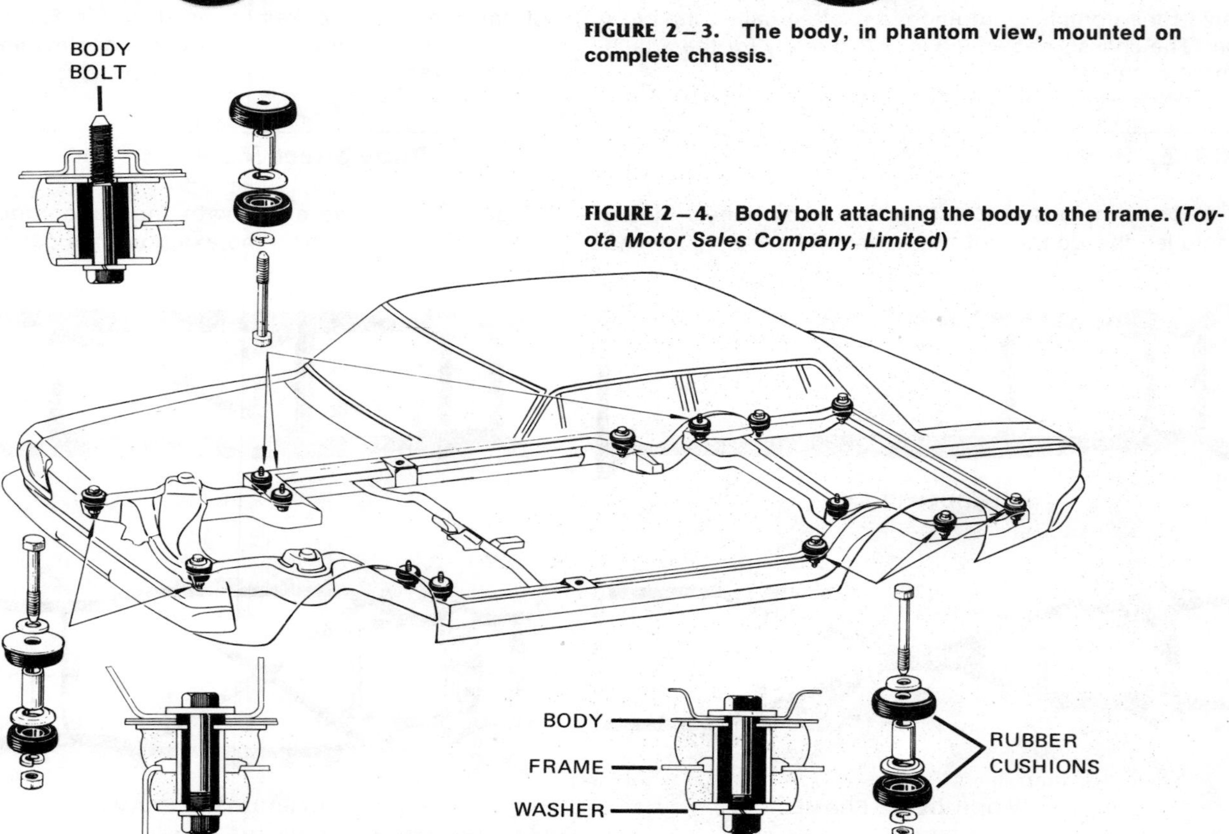

FIGURE 2 – 4. **Body bolt attaching the body to the frame. (*Toyota Motor Sales Company, Limited*)**

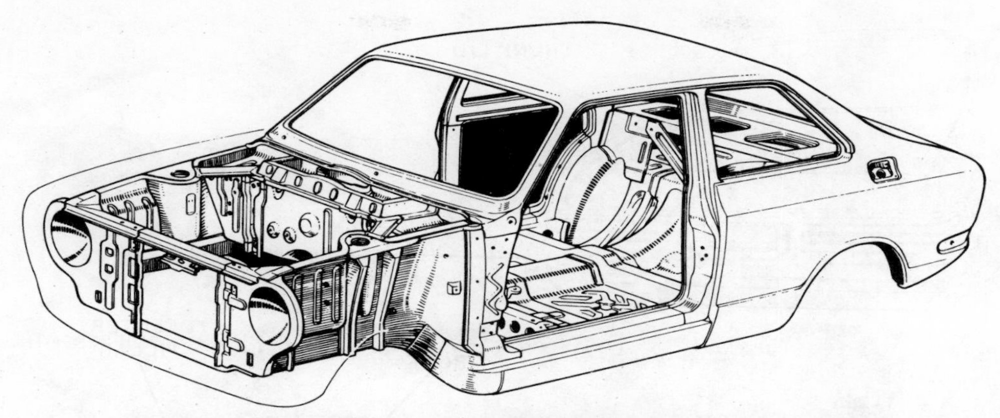

FIGURE 2–5. A unitized body. (*Toyota Motor Sales Company, Limited*)

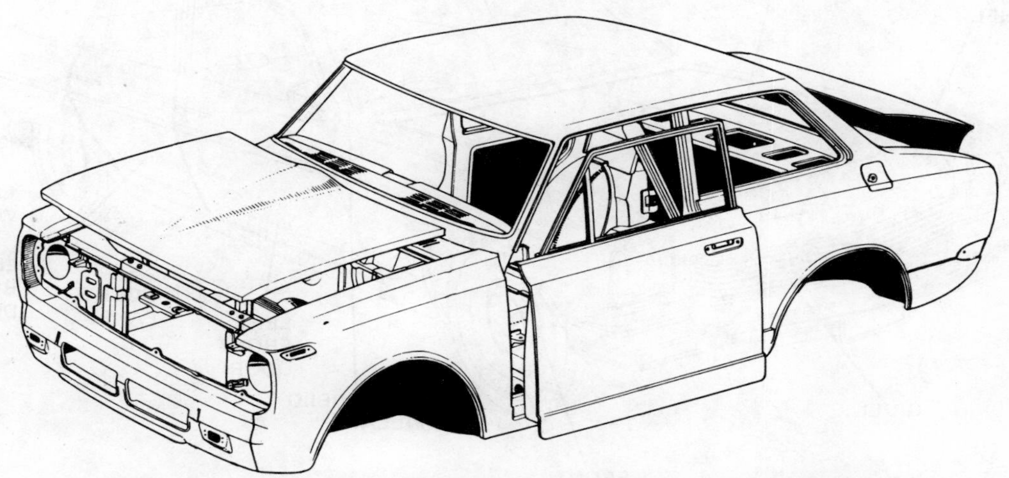

FIGURE 2–6. The unitized body shown in Fig. 2-5 with hood, trunk lid, and doors added. (*Toyota Motor Sales Company, Limited*)

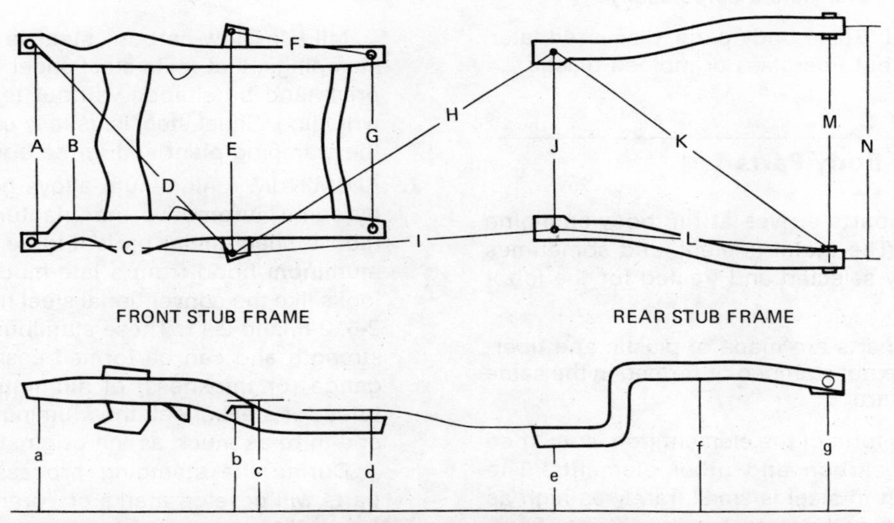

FIGURE 2–7. Horizontal and vertical checking dimensions on stub frames on a vehicle with unitized construction. (*Fisher Body Division of General Motors Corporation*)

neath are a number of smaller sheet-metal stampings that are welded together to form the underbody. These parts can be seen in Fig. 2-9. Each of these parts is stamped out from rolls of sheet metal, as explained later. The individual parts are then assembled into the basic body by welding them together.

After the underbody parts shown in Fig. 2-9 are welded together, the assembly is cleaned in a chemical bath. Then it is given a rust-preventive coating, as shown in Fig. 2-10.

Other parts that are attached to the basic body assembly include fenders, doors, hood, trunk lid, and so on. The body assembly includes brackets and attachment plates to accept these parts. Figure 2-11 shows the sheet

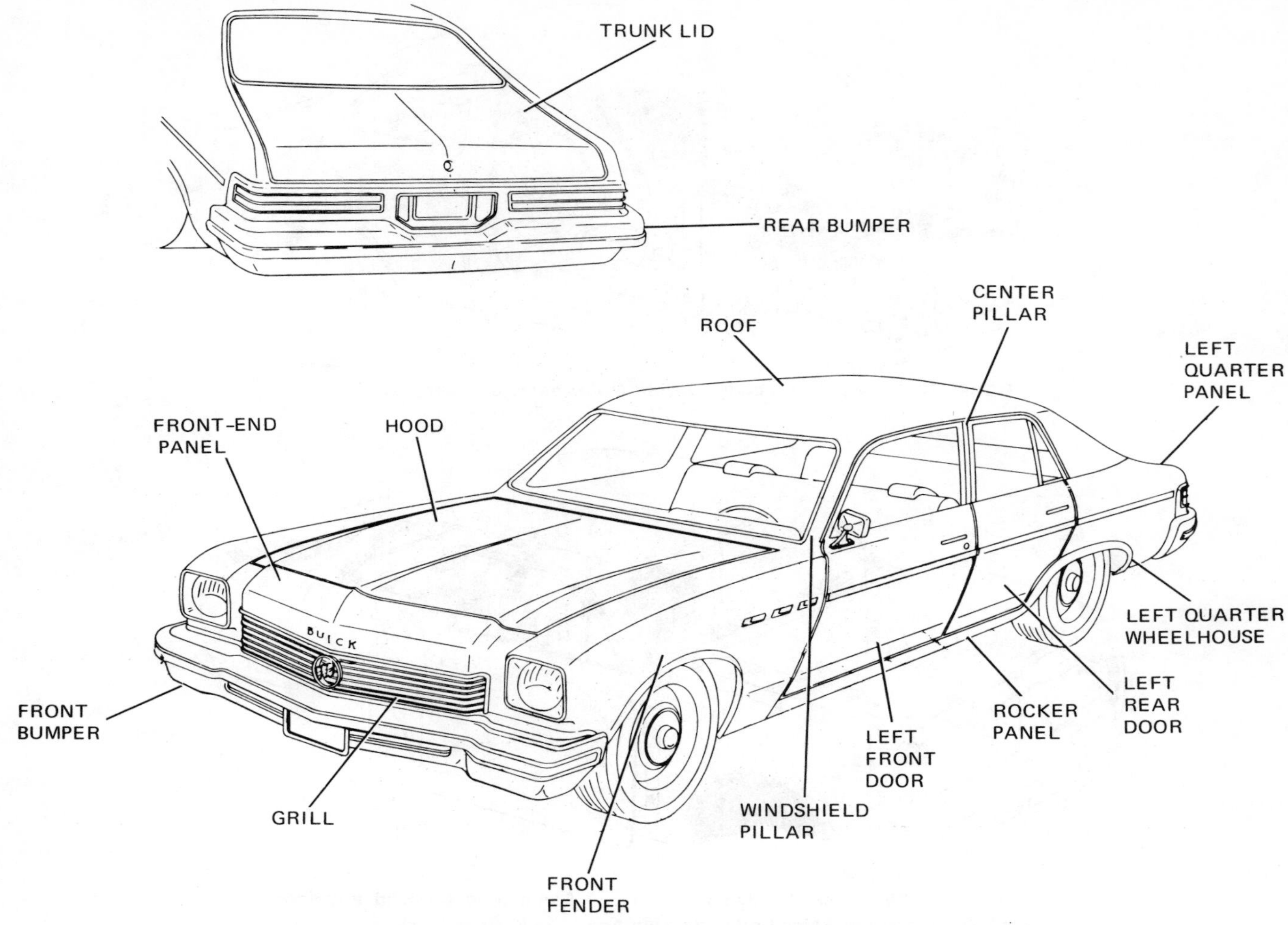

FIGURE 2-8. Car with major body panels named. (*Buick Motor Division of General Motors Corporation*)

metal for a front end. Some body parts, discussed later, are not sheet metal but fiberglass or molded plastic.

○2-5 Metal for Body Parts

The metal for body parts arrives at the body-stamping plant in large rolls. The metal is steel, and sometimes aluminum, especially selected and treated for the job it has to do.

NOTE: Some body parts are made of plastic and fiberglass. These parts are not stamped or formed in the same way as metal body parts.

1. STEEL Steel is a form of the element iron, combined or alloyed with carbon and other elements. The amount of carbon in steel is small, rarely as high as 2 percent. A high-carbon steel is a relatively hard, strong steel. A low-carbon steel is relatively soft and less strong. Low-carbon steel, also called mild or soft steel, has less than 0.25 percent carbon. This is the type of steel used for body panels. The metal must be relatively soft so it can be bent and shaped easily.

   For special purposes, other elements are added to steel to give it toughness, hardness, corrosion resistance, and wear resistance. Such steel may be used to fabricate other automobile parts such as axles, drive shafts, and engine valves.

   Mild, or low-carbon, steel is required for body stampings. Flat, mild-steel sheet can go through the press and be shaped without tearing, breaking, or wrinkling. Sheet steel is usually called *sheet metal* in the stamping plant and in the body shop.

2. ALUMINUM Aluminum alloys now are being used by some automotive manufacturers to make automotive sheet-metal parts. Figure 2-12 shows an all-aluminum hood from a late-model car. Note that it looks like the conventional steel hood, shown in Figs. 2-6, 2-8, and 2-11. These aluminum alloys have good strength and can be formed easily. When the same gauge (or thickness) of aluminum sheet is substituted for steel sheet, the aluminum parts weigh only one-third as much as the original steel parts.

   During the stamping process, some aluminum parts will develop marks or "orange peel." This surface roughness can be removed, but usually these parts are nonvisible and so the surface roughness can be ignored.

   The metal aluminum does not occur in nature. As a result, all aluminum must be produced. Most aluminum comes from bauxite, a very plentiful aluminum ore which may contain as much as 45 percent aluminum oxide. The bauxite is processed to remove the aluminum oxide. Then the aluminum oxide is smelted to produce aluminum.

   Aluminum and its alloys have good resistance to

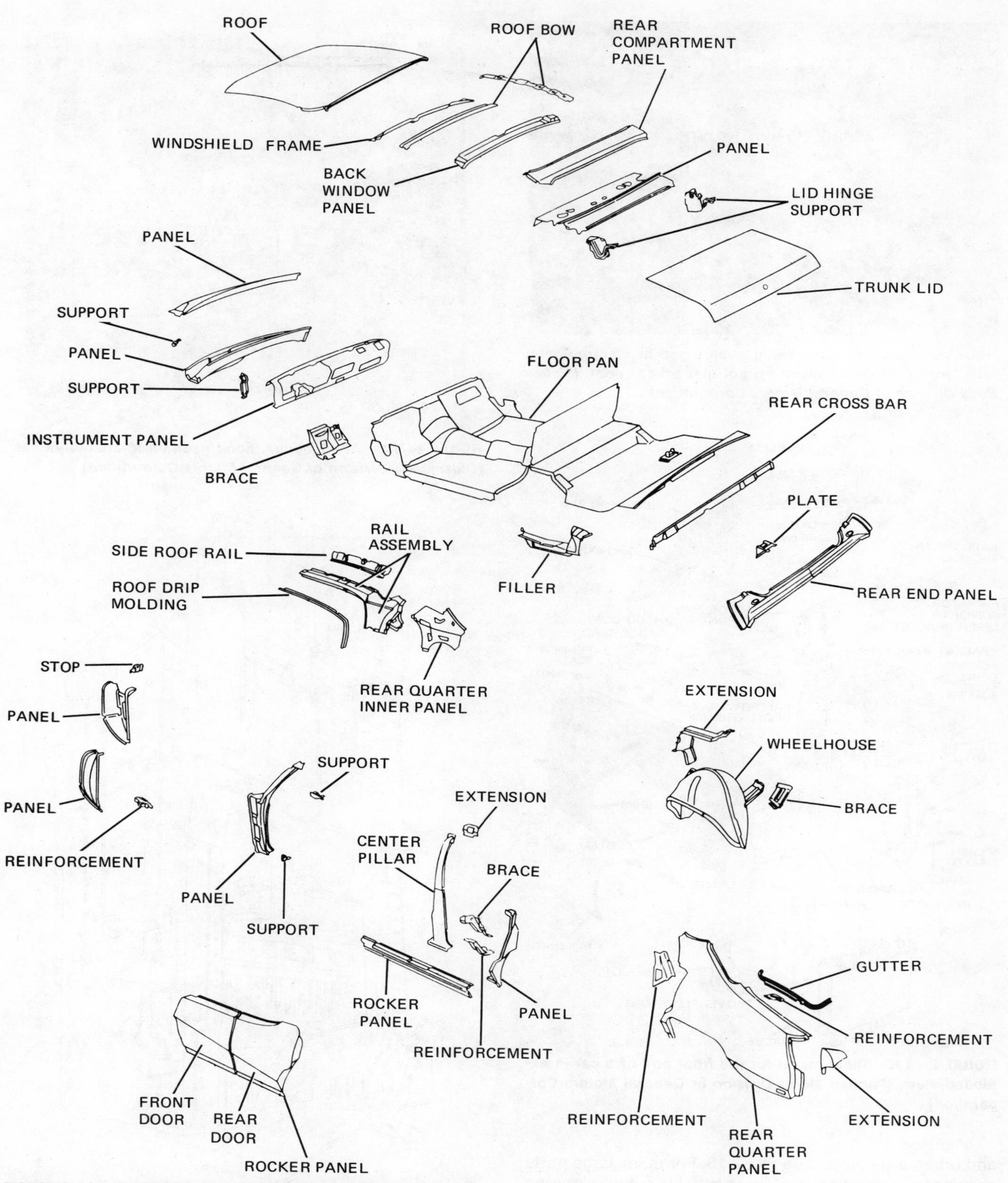

FIGURE 2 – 9. Exploded view of a car body, showing the underbody parts. (*General Motors Corporation*)

corrosion. Also, they are nonferrous metals. This means that they are not attracted by a magnet. Anytime you think a body panel or other part may be made of iron or steel, check it with a magnet. If the magnet is *not* attracted and if the part is made of a dull silvery-white metal, it probably is aluminum.

○2-6 Stamping Body Parts

Stamping is carried out in stamping presses. These presses vary from small units for stamping out small parts to the large presses used to form the car roof panel

FIGURE 2 – 10. Car body being submerged in electroplating tank, where it will be given an antirust primer coat. (*Fisher Body Division of General Motors Corporation*)

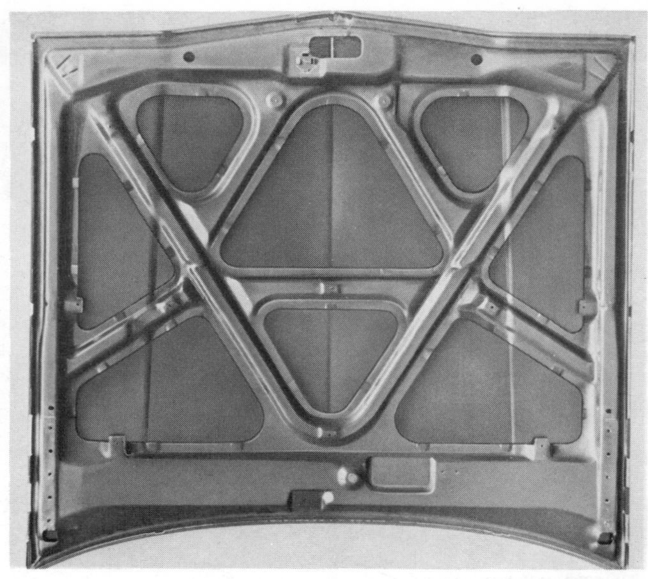

FIGURE 2 – 12. All-aluminum hood used on a late-model car. (*Oldsmobile Division of General Motors Corporation*)

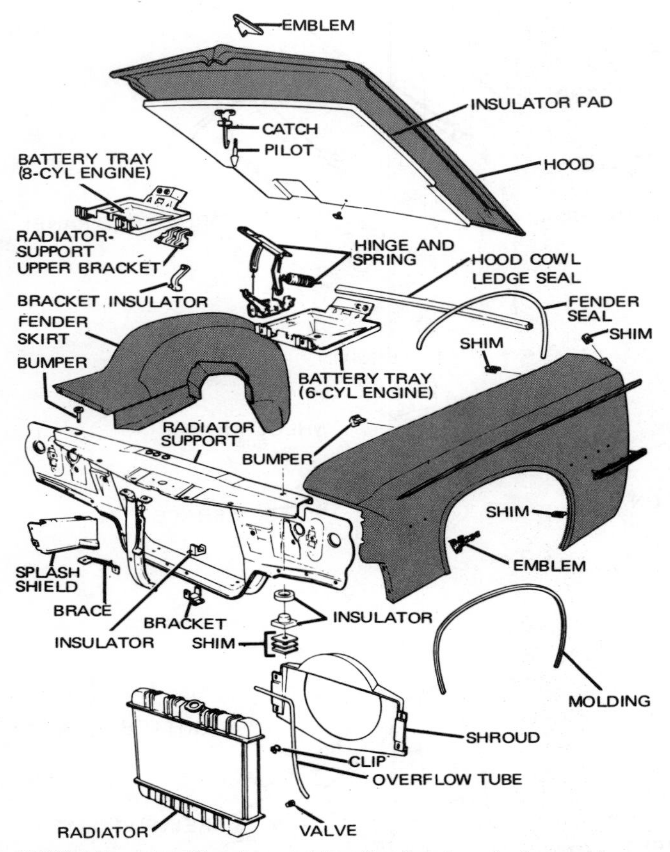

FIGURE 2 – 11. Sheet metal for the front end of a car in exploded view. (*Pontiac Motor Division of General Motors Corporation*)

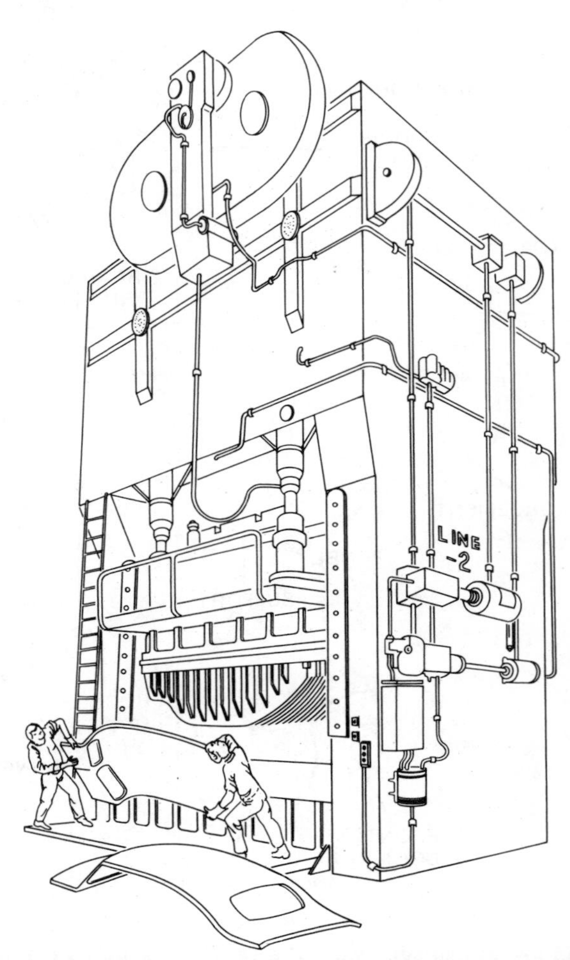

FIGURE 2 – 13. Large stamping press which blanks out steel roofs for automobiles.

and other large parts. See Fig. 2-13. For many large parts such as the roof panel, the sheet metal is cut into lengths of suitable size. These sheets are fed individually into the press.

The press uses a pair of dies, a male die and a female die, such as shown in Fig. 2-14. The sheet metal is placed between the dies, and they are then pressed together. This forces the metal to take the shape of the die faces. Figure 2-14 illustrates this. The male die is in the up position in Fig. 2-14A. The sheet-metal blank is positioned between the dies. When the press is operated, the movable die moves down (Fig. 2-14B). This forces the sheet-metal blank down so it takes the shape of the dies. Any excess metal on the formed part is cut off after the part is removed from the press. The new part may be given further treatment to remove sharp or uneven edges and to clean it.

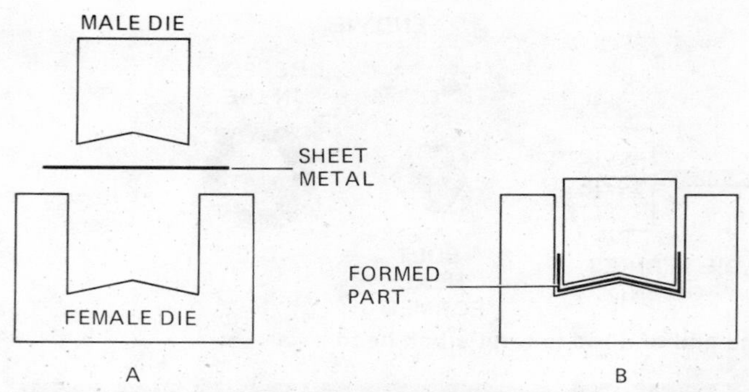

FIGURE 2 – 14. A simple die set to stamp metal parts.

○2-7 Effect of Stamping on Sheet Metal

Whenever sheet metal is worked—that is, whenever its shape is changed—it gets harder. The effect is called *work hardening.* You can prove this for yourself by taking a piece of sheet metal and bending it a few times. You can feel that the metal in the bend becomes harder to bend. You get the same effect by laying a piece of sheet metal on a flat surface and hitting one section of it with a hammer several times. To do this, let the hammer blows fall on a line along one section of the sheet metal, as shown in Fig. 2-15. Then try to bend it at this spot. You will find it bends more easily on either side of the hammered area.

When a sheet-metal part is formed in a press, different areas will be bent different amounts. Consider a fender, for example. When it comes out of the press, varying curvatures have been stamped into it. See Fig. 2-16. Where the sheet metal has been given a great amount of curvature, that area is said to have a high crown. Where the curvature is slight, the metal has a low crown. This ties in with what we said previously about work hardening. The more that sheet metal is bent, the harder it gets. Therefore, the fender shown in Fig. 2-16, which has varying amounts of curvatures or crown, varies considerably in its hardness. The high-crown area is considerably harder than the low-crown area. This is important to the body-repair technician. The amount of hardness an area of sheet metal has determines how the area will be distorted when damaged in a collision. Also, the hardness determines how the distortion must be treated to restore the original contour of the sheet metal. All this is covered in detail in later chapters.

Hardness can be relieved by heating the metal to just a little under the melting point, as we will explain later. The heat changes the crystal structure of the metal. This relieves the internal strains that have caused the hardness. Working metal and then heating it is a routine procedure in the body shop.

○2-8 Properties of Sheet Metal for Stamping

As we mentioned earlier, mild, or low-carbon, steel is used for most body parts. This steel must have the proper chemical composition to permit it to be shaped in the stamping press without wrinkling, cracking, or otherwise failing.

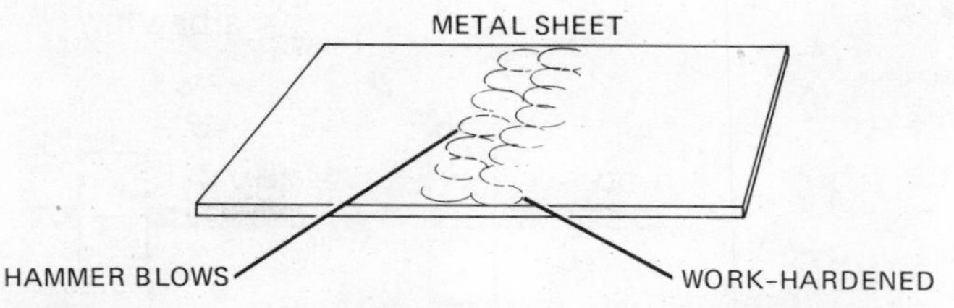

FIGURE 2 – 15. Hammering on sheet metal work-hardens it.

FIGURE 2 – 16. Low- and high-crown areas of a fender.

The composition of the steel may be different for the outer panels that show than for the inner panels and parts that are hidden. An internal part may be required to be stronger, and the importance of its surface finish is not so great. Therefore, a higher-carbon steel might be used for an internal part. If you examine internal body parts, you may see wrinkling and roughness. These mean nothing so far as strength is concerned. But such roughness could not be tolerated on outside body panels. The sheet metal for outside body panels must be such as to allow it to come out of the press smooth and clean. Also, the metal must take welding and painting with minimum problems.

The basic property of metal that permits it to be pressed into different shapes is called its *plasticity.* A mild steel is much more plastic than a high-carbon, or hard, steel. When flat sheet metal is shaped in a press, it is said to have undergone *plastic deformation.* That is, it has been deformed from a flat surface because it is *plastic.* It may be hard to think of steel as being plastic, because you may think of modeling clay or silicone when you hear the word "plastic." However, steel can be made to flow under pressure. If the steel is soft enough, it will do this without breaking, provided its yield point is not reached. *Yield point* is the point at which the metal actually breaks rather than continues to flow and become deformed.

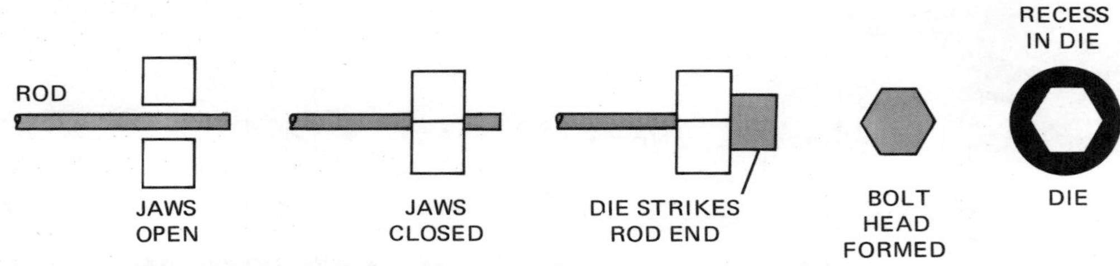

FIGURE 2 – 17. Sequence of upsetting the end of a rod to form a bolt head.

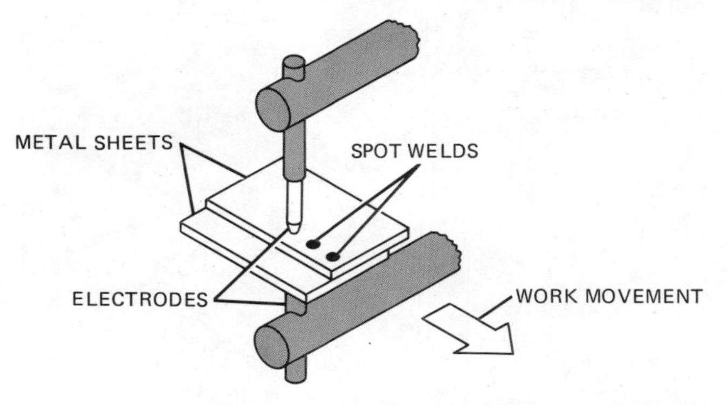

FIGURE 2 – 18. Principle of electric spot welding. Two metal sheets are overlapped, and two electrodes close on them to send current through the sheets. This melts the metal so a spot weld is formed.

FIGURE 2 – 19. Body assembly line in a modern assembly plant. Machines with electronic memories push electrodes onto the body panels, automatically welding them together. (*Fisher Body Division of General Motors Corporation*)

Plastic deformation can result from a pull or a push on the metal. If you pull on metal, it is under tension and it will elongate, or stretch. This stretchability is called *ductility.* If the metal is subjected to a push that tends to compress it, and if it does change shape, the metal has *malleability.* An example here would be the metal used in the machines that form bolts. The metal enters the machine as a round rod. It is gripped, and a die with a recess shaped like a bolt head hits the end. Figure 2-17 shows the process. With the jaws open, the rod is positioned between the jaws. The jaws close, leaving the proper length of rod sticking out. The die then strikes the end of the rod. This forces the protruding rod to flow into the shape of a bolt head. This process is called *upsetting.* The material is forced to flow in compression. The ease with which it flows, or can be upset, is called malleability.

○2-9 Putting the Parts Together

As you can see from Fig. 2-19, many parts must be put together to make up the body. These parts are welded together. Electric welding is used. Electric welding uses a flow of electric current to heat the parts where they are touching each other. The metal gets so hot that it melts. Then, when the current flow stops and the metal cools, the parts have become attached by welds.

Figure 2-18 shows the principle of electric welding. The parts to be joined are positioned between two electrodes. The electrodes are brought into contact with the two sides of the two metal sheets that are to be joined. A high current flows, and the metal between the two electrodes becomes so hot that it melts. When the electrodes are withdrawn and the spot cools, we have a spot weld. Now picture this on a large scale, with special machines welding the body parts together. A modern version of this is shown in Fig. 2-19. The parts are positioned by clamps so they are held in place in readiness for the welds. Then the machines automatically extend electrodes that contact the parts and weld them together.

The surfaces on outside body panels are then given further treatment to eliminate weld marks. Next, the body is given a chemical treatment, as already explained (Fig. 2-10), and painted. It is then attached to the frame or stub frames for unibody construction.

○2-10 Streamlining

The car body is designed to reduce its resistance to moving through air. This is called streamlining (Fig. 2-20). Streamlining makes use of curves and sloping surfaces rather than sharp angles and flat surfaces. This allows the air to move smoothly up and around the car as it moves forward and reduces the amount of engine power required to overcome air resistance.

○2-11 Doors

There are two general types of doors: closed style (with upper frames) and hardtop or convertible style (without upper frames). Doors contain a variety of devices (Fig. 2-21), including window regulators (opening and closing mechanisms), locks, cigarette lighters, windshield-wiper controls, seat-adjustment controls, rearview mirror and control, and door reinforcing strips. Window regulators can be mechanical, with a hand crank, or electric, with a reversible electric motor. Door locks can be mechanical with a hand-operated button or electric with a two-way solenoid. Cigarette lighters and ashtrays may be

FIGURE 2–20. **Streamlining the car means shaping it so that the air flows smoothly over and around it, rather than forming eddies that hold the car back and use up power.**

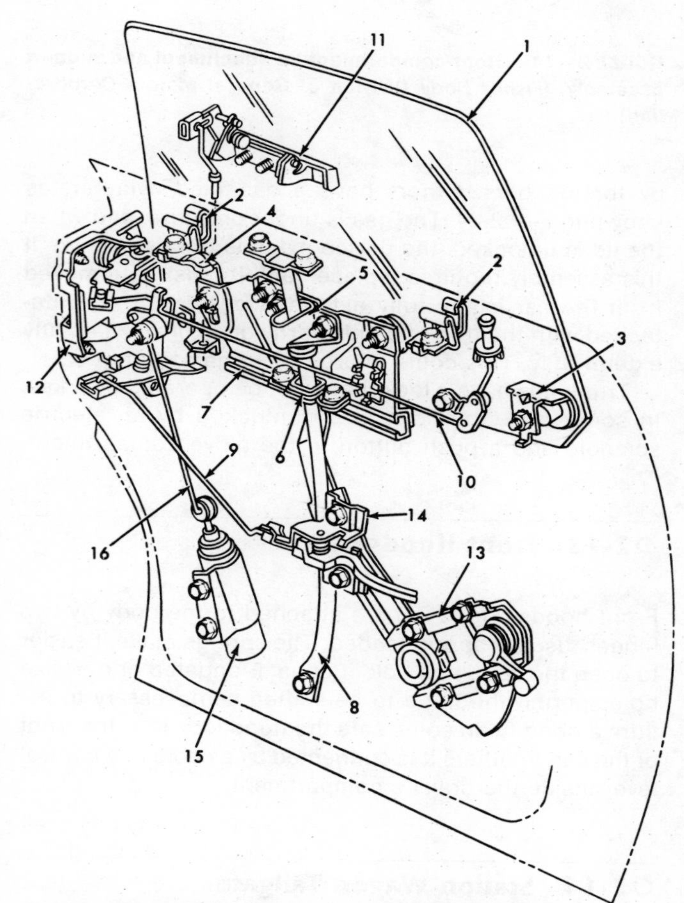

1. **Window assembly**
2. **Belt trim support retainers**
3. **Front up-travel stop**
4. **Rear up-travel stop**
5. **Lower-sash upper guide**
6. **Lower-sash lower guide**
7. **Lower-sash guide plate assembly**
8. **Guide-tube assembly**
9. **Remote control to lock-connecting rod**
10. **Inside locking rod**
11. **Door outside lift-bar handle**
12. **Door lock**
13. **Window regulator (electric)**
14. **Door-lock remote-control handle**
15. **Door-lock solenoid**
16. **Rod inside locking to solenoid**

FIGURE 2–21. **Rear-door hardware. (*Fisher Body Division of General Motors Corporation*)**

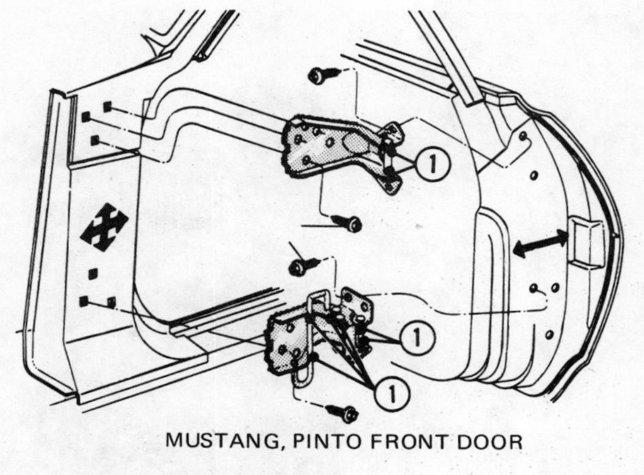

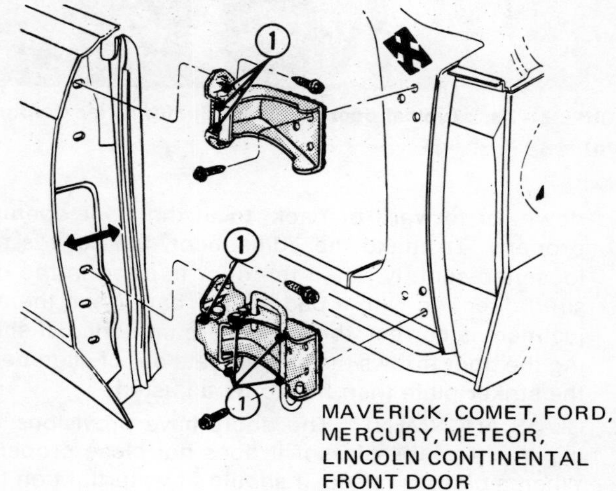

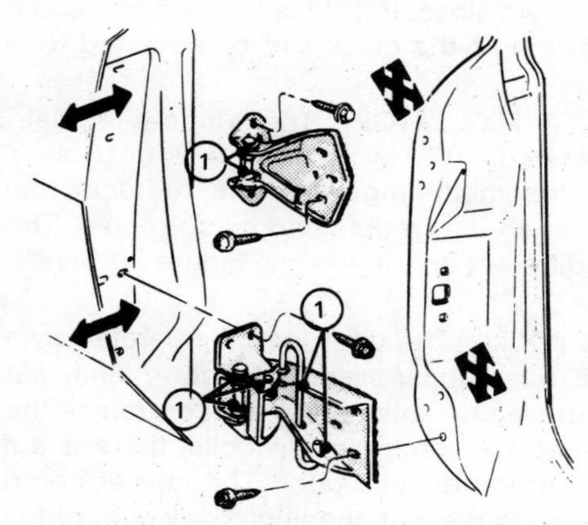

FIGURE 2–22. **Side-door hinge adjustments on various car models. (*Ford Motor Company*)**

found in many doors. On some cars, the windshield-wiper control is located in the front left-hand door, as are the rearview mirror and its remote control. This location permits the driver to operate the controls as necessary.

1. DOOR ADJUSTMENT Many doors have provisions for adjustment (Fig. 2-22). The holes in the hinges and the hinge-attachment points are enlarged or elongated. These allow the door to be shifted up or

FIGURE 2 – 23. Typical door weatherstrip. (*Chrysler Corporation*)

down, or forward or back, to fit the door opening properly. To make the adjustment, the screws are loosened slightly. Then the door is pried in the desired direction with a padded pry bar. When the adjustment is correct, the screws are tightened. If shifting the door throws the striker plate out of alignment, the striker plate then has to be adjusted.

2. GLASS ALIGNMENT The doors have provisions for alignment of the glass if it does not close properly. When a glass is raised, it should fit watertight on the top and two sides. If it does not, the two supports at the bottom of the glass can be adjusted to correct the fit.
3. WINDOW REGULATOR The window regulator may be operated either by a hand crank or by an electric motor. If something goes wrong, the door trim must come off so the trouble can be corrected. There are many different arrangements. Figure 2-21 shows only one.
4. DOOR LOCK The door lock is operated by a push button in the upper sash of the door. Many cars also have an electric solenoid to lock or unlock the door. If the car has electric door locks, there is a master control in the driver's door. The master control can be flipped to prevent opening of any door or to permit any of the doors to be individually controlled by the passengers.
5. TRIM AND WEATHERSTRIPPING Doors must have weatherstripping to seal them against the entrance of rain or outside air (Fig. 2-23). The weatherstripping seals at all joints. Door trim includes handles and embellishment strips, attached by screws or locking catches.

○2-12 Trunk Lid

The trunk lid, or rear-compartment lid, is attached at the forward end by two hinges. Most cars have some type of lid support assembly to assist in opening the lid (Fig. 2-24). Many trunk lids are supported in the open position

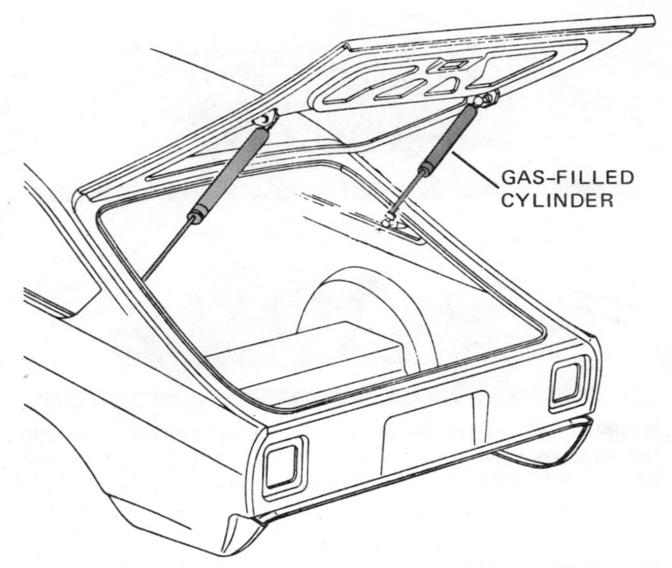

FIGURE 2 – 24. Rear-compartment-lid attachment and support assembly. (*Fisher Body Division of General Motors Corporation*)

by torsion bars. Others have a gas-filled cylinder, as shown in Fig. 2-24. The gas is under pressure, and when the lid is unlocked, the device extends to raise the lid. If this assembly requires replacement, it must be removed from the car in the fully extended position. If it is detached with the trunk lid only partly open, it will instantly extend fully. This could injure you or damage the car.

Trunk lids have a lock that must be operated by a key. In some cars, the lid may be unlocked by an electric solenoid and a push button in the glove compartment.

○2-13 Front Hoods

Front hoods (Fig. 2-25) are attached to the body by two hinges, usually spring-loaded. The springs make it easier to open the hood and hold it open. Elongated or oversize holes permit the hood to be shifted as necessary to secure a good fit. In some cars the hood lock is at the front of the car. In others it is connected by a cable to a control lever inside the driver's compartment.

○2-14 Station-Wagon Tailgate

There are several styles of tailgate. In one, the tailgate is in one piece with a fixed window. With this arrangement, the tailgate is hinged at the top, just like the trunk lid. It is similar to the rear-compartment lid shown in Fig. 2-24. Another arrangement has the glass separate from the rest of the tailgate, which is hinged at the bottom. The glass can be retracted into the roof of the car by an electric motor. In some vehicles, the tailgate is hinged to swing down or to swing to one side. The tailgate can contain a variety of devices: lock-release solenoid, defogger, blower, and counterbalance support assemblies. In addition, it may have a warning system that turns on a warning light on the instrument panel if the gate is not closed when the ignition switch is turned on.

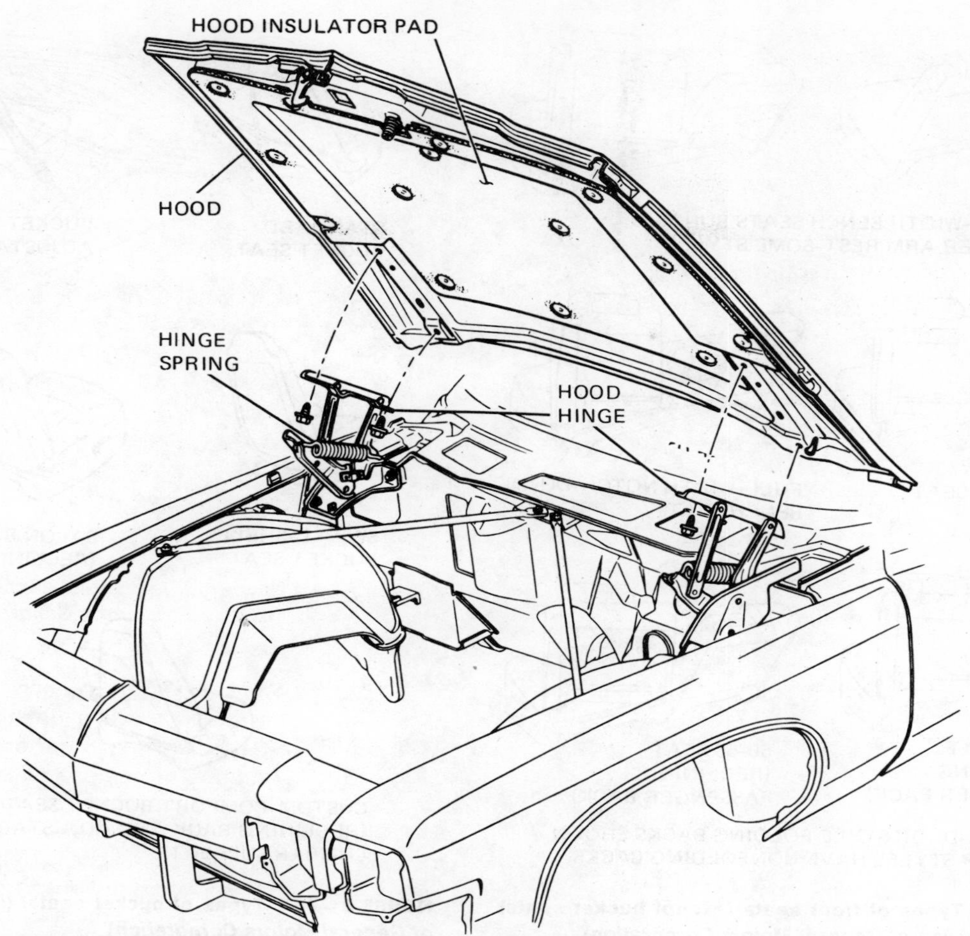

FIGURE 2–25. Details of front-hood attachment. (*Buick Motor Division of General Motors Corporation*)

○2-15 Sun Roof

The sun roof is a metal panel in the roof of the car that slides back and forth on guide rails in the roof (Fig. 2-26). When it is slid back, the sun can shine down through the opening onto the passengers. On some cars the sun panel is operated by a two-way electric motor; on other cars it is operated by a hand crank.

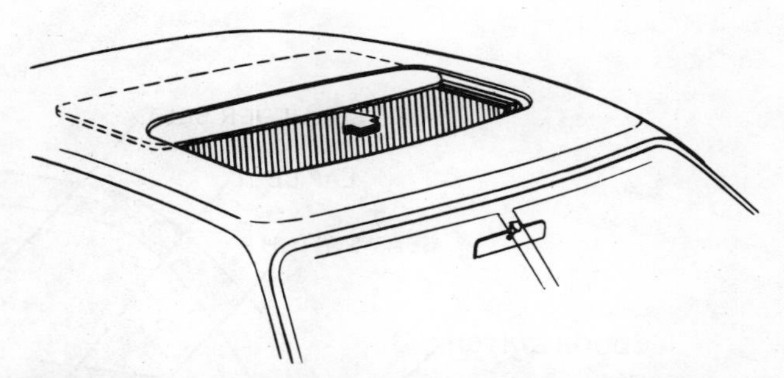

FIGURE 2–26. Sun roof, partly open. (*Fisher Body Division of General Motors Corporation*)

○2-16 Seats

Seats come in a variety of designs (Figs. 2-27 and 2-28). Some have a manual forward-and-back adjustment. Others have electric motors to move them back and forth or up and down. The latter are called four-way seats. Some seats are six-way. These have an additional control that changes the tilt of the seat.

○2-17 Seat Belts

The purpose of seat belts (Fig. 2-29) is to restrain the driver and passengers if there is an accident. During a front-end crash, for example, the car is brought to a sudden stop. But everything inside the car continues to move forward until it hits some solid object. An unrestrained passenger would continue to move forward until he or she hit a part of the car such as the windshield or the instrument panel. It is these so-called second collisions that hurt and kill people. However, if the passengers and driver are wearing seat belts, they will be restrained. They will not continue to move forward and will not hit some solid object in the car.

There are two different kinds of seat belts: lap belts and shoulder belts. Both of these are shown in Fig. 2-29.

○2-18 Air Bags

Air bags are a passive safety device to protect the driver (Fig. 2-30) and passengers in an accident. "Passive"

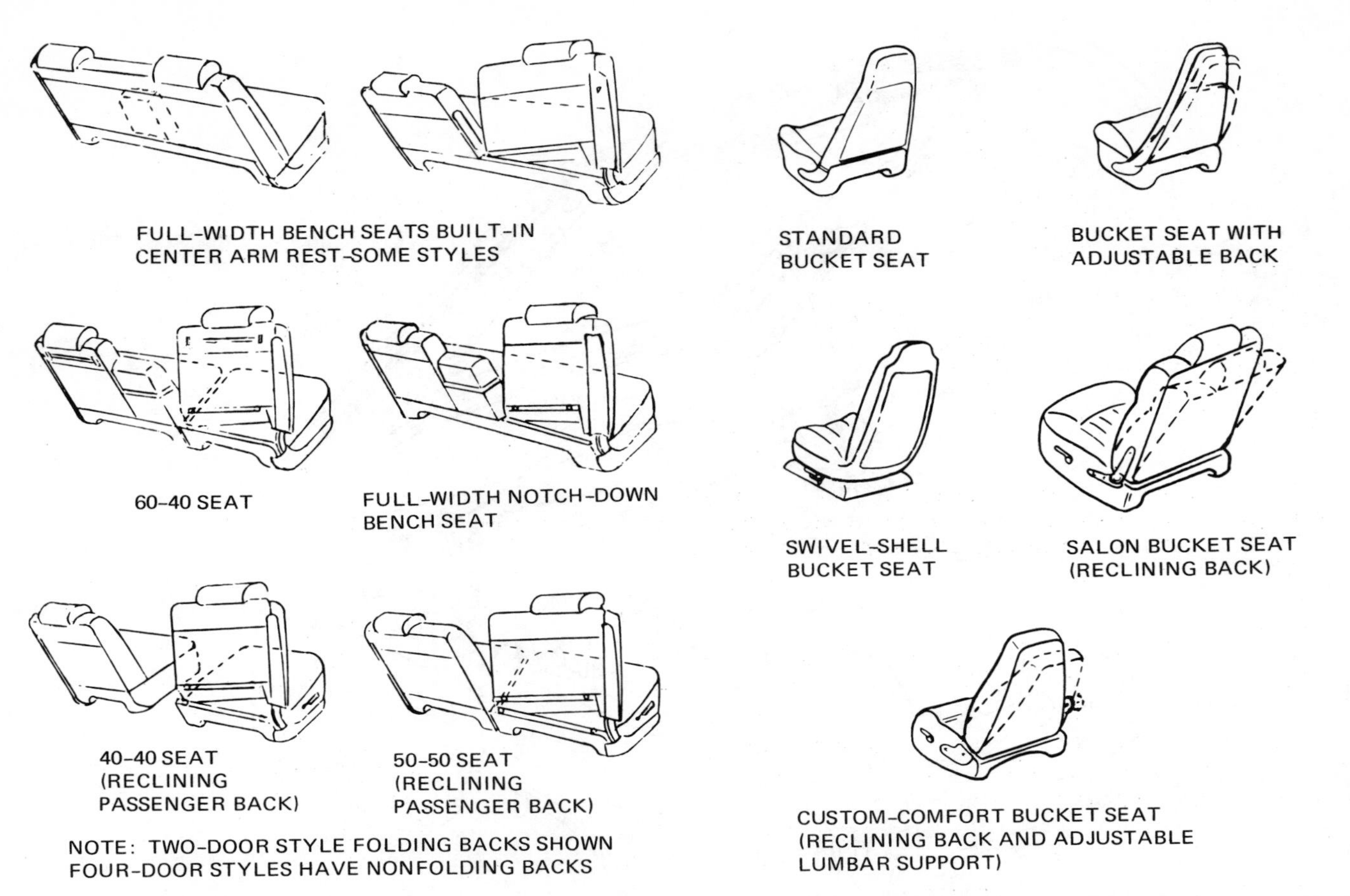

FIGURE 2–27. Types of front seats (except bucket seats). (*Fisher Body Division of General Motors Corporation*)

FIGURE 2–28. Types of bucket seats. (*Fisher Body Division of General Motors Corporation*)

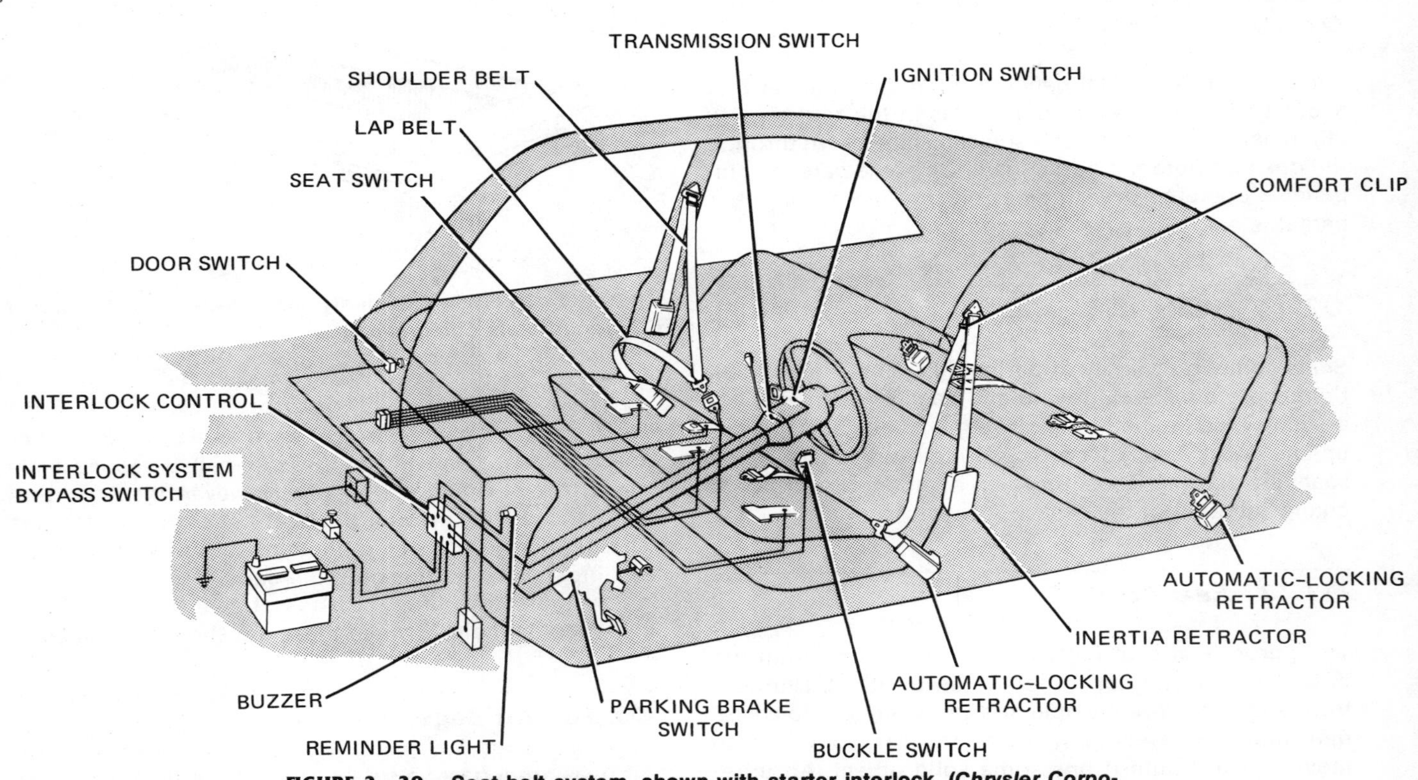

FIGURE 2–29. Seat-belt system, shown with starter interlock. (*Chrysler Corporation*)

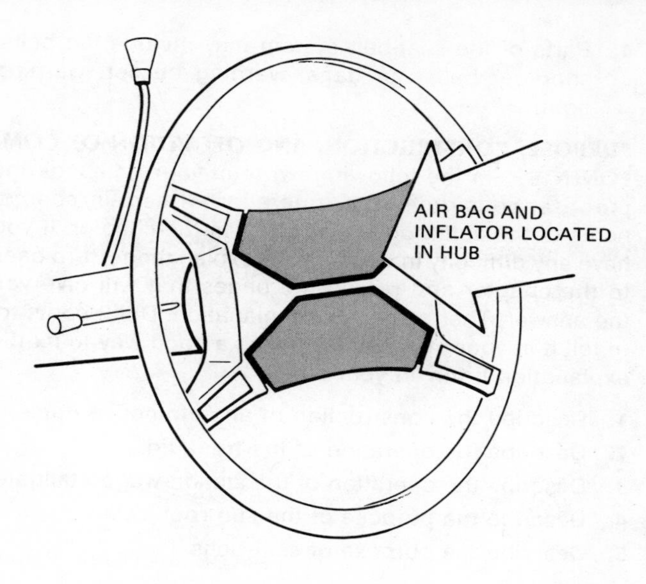

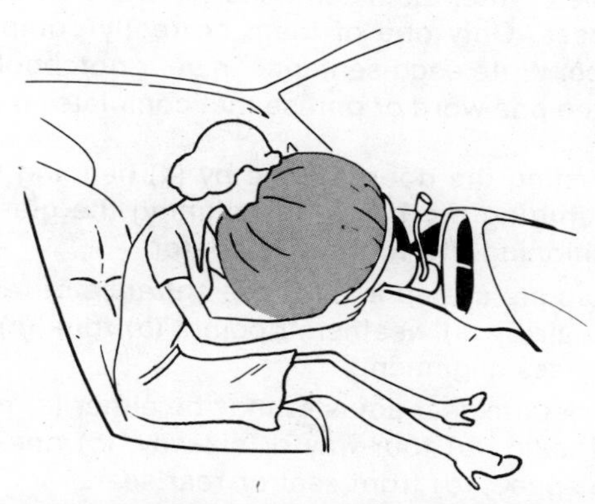

FIGURE 2–30. Location of the air bag in the steering wheel. The lower picture shows the action when the air bag is inflated and the driver is thrown forward into it. (*General Motors Corporation*)

means that the driver and passengers do not have to do anything to be protected by the air bags. This is in contrast with seat belts, described above, that require an action—buckling up. Many people do not bother to buckle up because it is "too much trouble." As a result, there are far more highway injuries and deaths than there need be. Air-bag advocates believe that the air bag will save many lives and prevent many injuries.

The principle is simple. At the instant that a crash occurs, the air bags are blown up. They then give the driver and passengers a cushion into which to move, as shown in Fig. 2-30. The air bags absorb the forward motion of the occupants and save them from hitting anything hard that could injure them.

○2-19 Energy-absorbing Bumpers

The energy-absorbing bumper is required by law on late-model cars. It will withstand collisions at low speed without damage to the bumper or car. Most of these bumpers resume their original position after the collision. There are several types, used at both the front and the rear of

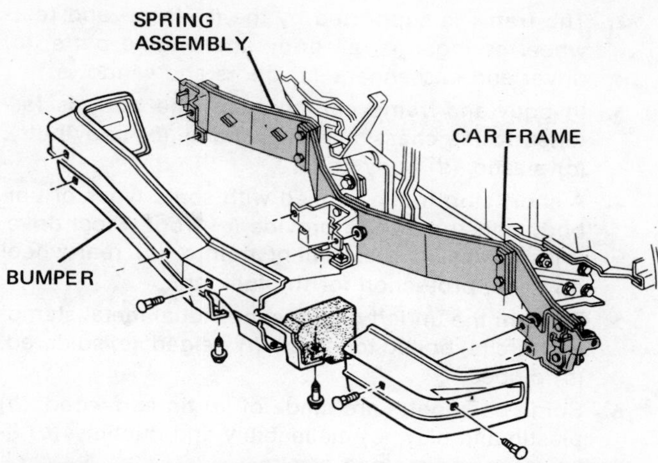

FIGURE 2–31. Front-bumper system using a leaf-spring assembly to absorb the energy of a front-end impact. (*Chevrolet Motor Division of General Motors Corporation*)

late-model cars. One uses a leaf-spring assembly which supports the bumper, as shown in Fig. 2-31. On impact, the spring gives and absorbs the blow. It then returns to its original position, if the impact was within the designed limits. If the impact was greater than the designed limits, damage may have occurred and repair may be required.

○2-20 Body Electric Equipment

The body carries a considerable amount of wiring connecting the various electrically operated body devices. We have covered some of these—door locks, window regulators, sun-roof motors, seat adjusters, seat-belt-starter interlock systems, and so on. In addition, the body carries several lights—headlights, taillights, turn-signal lights, and interior lights. Several other electrical devices include the open-door warning buzzer and the security alarm system. These are covered in a later chapter.

CHECK YOUR PROGRESS

PROGRESS QUIZ 2-1 This chapter on automobile body construction covers a lot of material. Here is a chance for you to check up on yourself and find out how well you are understanding the material being discussed. There are two reasons for these progress quizzes. One is to help you review and understand the important points covered in the book. The other is to let you check yourself on the progress you are making.

COMPLETING THE SENTENCES The sentences below are incomplete. After each sentence there are several words or phrases. Only one of them correctly completes the sentence. Write each sentence in your notebook, ending it with the one word or phrase that completes it correctly.

1. The two main types of automotive body construction are (*a*) unibody-and-unit, (*b*) body-and-frame, (*c*) body-and-frame and unitized-body, (*d*) compact and intermediate.

2. The frame is supported by the (*a*) front- and rear-wheel springs, (*b*) all body and engine parts, (*c*) driver and passengers, (*d*) doors and windows.
3. In body-and-frame construction, the body is fastened to the chassis by (*a*) welding, (*b*) body putty, (*c*) plastic, (*d*) body bolts.
4. A short stub frame is used with some types of unibody construction to provide (*a*) front-wheel drive, (*b*) suspension attachment points, (*c*) rear-wheel drive, (*d*) protection for the fuel tank.
5. To form the underbody, the individual metal stampings are (*a*) bolted together, (*b*) welded, (*c*) soldered, (*d*) dipped.
6. Some body parts are made of (*a*) tin and wood, (*b*) plastic and clay, (*c*) malleability and ductility, (*d*) fiberglass and molded plastic.
7. The steel used for body panels is (*a*) low-carbon steel, (*b*) high-carbon steel, (*c*) cast iron, (*d*) stainless steel.
8. When the shape of sheet metal is changed, it gets (*a*) hot, (*b*) cold, (*c*) harder, (*d*) softer.
9. Hardness in sheet metal can be relieved by (*a*) soaking in acid, (*b*) freezing the metal, (*c*) heating the metal, (*d*) grinding.
10. The point at which metal breaks instead of flowing and deforming is its (*a*) yield point, (*b*) malleability, (*c*) plasticity, (*d*) ductility.

CHAPTER 2 CHECKUP

NOTE: Since the following is a chapter review test, you should review the chapter before taking it.

The following questions will help you determine how well you remember what you have been reading. If you have any trouble answering the questions you should reread the chapter. Don't be discouraged if questions stump you. That simply means you should review the chapter. As you do this and take the tests in the book, you will be able to pick out the important facts you should remember. This is because you are improving your studying habits and learning what is most important in the material you are reading. Answering the questions helps you by pointing out the important facts to remember.

CORRECTING PARTS LISTS The purpose of this exercise is to give you practice in spotting unrelated items in a list. For example, in the sentence "Parts of the automobile include engine, frame, filling station, brakes, wheels," you can see that "filling station" does not belong in the list, because it is the only thing named that is not part of an automobile. In each of the lists, one item is named that does not belong. Write each sentence in your notebook, but do not write the item that does not belong in the list.

1. Parts of the chassis include frame, springs, shock absorbers, windshield, steering system, brakes, engine.
2. Parts of the door may include window regulator, lock, rearview mirror, cigarette lighter, ignition switch.
3. Parts of the station-wagon tailgate may include backup lights, window, defogger, OPEN warning light, lock.
4. Parts of the seat-belt system may include lap belts, shoulder belts, air bags, warning buzzer, warning light.

PURPOSE, CONSTRUCTION, AND OPERATION OF COMPONENTS In the following, write in your notebook the purpose, construction, or operation of certain components of the automobile discussed in the chapter. If you have any difficulty in writing your explanations, turn back to the chapter and reread the pages that will give you the answer. Then write your explanation. Don't copy; try to tell it in your own words. This is a good way to fix the explanation firmly in your mind.

1. Describe the construction of an automotive frame.
2. Describe the operation of the trunk lid.
3. Describe the operation of the station-wagon tailgate.
4. Describe the purpose of the sun roof.
5. Describe the purpose of seat belts.

COMPLETING THE SENTENCES The sentences below are incomplete. After each sentence there are several words or phrases. Only one of them correctly completes the sentence. Write each sentence in your notebook, ending it with the one word or phrase that completes it correctly.

1. Adjusting the door is done by (*a*) bending the door, (*b*) shifting the hinge, (*c*) aligning the glass, (*d*) repositioning the window regulator.
2. Doors are sealed against the entrance of rain or outside air by (*a*) weatherstripping, (*b*) trim, (*c*) chrome, (*d*) glass alignment.
3. An electric seat adjuster may be either (*a*) manual or hydraulic, (*b*) four-way or six-way, (*c*) one-speed or two-speed, (*d*) front seat or rear seat.
4. Body panels may be stamped from (*a*) wood and glass, (*b*) steel and lead, (*c*) plastic and aluminum, (*d*) aluminum and steel.
5. Passive safety devices include (*a*) seat belts, (*b*) automatic transmissions, (*c*) air bags, (*d*) safety glass.

DEFINITIONS In the following, you are asked to define certain terms. Write the definitions in your notebook. This will help you remember them. It will also provide you with a quick way to locate the meanings when you need the information again. If you cannot remember the meanings of the terms, look them up in the text or in the glossary at the back of the book.

1. Define "body-and-frame construction."
2. Define "unitized-body construction."
3. Define "frame."
4. Define "chassis."

SUGGESTIONS FOR FURTHER STUDY

To be sure that you understand this material and that you understand the various parts and systems used in automobile body construction, here is a suggestion. Locate a late-model car that you can examine in detail. Then, using the chapter as a guide, determine if the car has body-and-frame construction or unibody construction. Next, following the illustrations in the chapter, identify each panel and part of the body.

3

SAFETY IN THE SHOP

Shopwork is varied and interesting. In the body shop you learn how to handle sheet-metal repair and replacement, how to straighten frames, and how to repair or replace glass, doors, hoods, trunk lids, and other body parts.

But before you work in the shop, you should know about safety. Safety in the shop means protecting yourself and other workers from possible danger and injury. This chapter describes the rules you should follow in the shop to protect yourself and others. When everybody obeys the rules, the shop is a much safer place to work than your home! Many more people are hurt in the home than in the shop.

○ 3-1 Safety Is Your Job

Yes, safety is your job. In the shop, you are "safe" when you protect your eyes, your fingers, your hands—all of you—from danger. And just as important is looking out for the safety of those around you.

The rules of safety are listed and discussed in the next few pages. Follow the rules for your protection and for the protection of your fellow workers.

○ 3-2 Shop Layouts

The term "shop layout" means the locations of benches, car lifts, machine tools, and so on. Shop layouts vary.

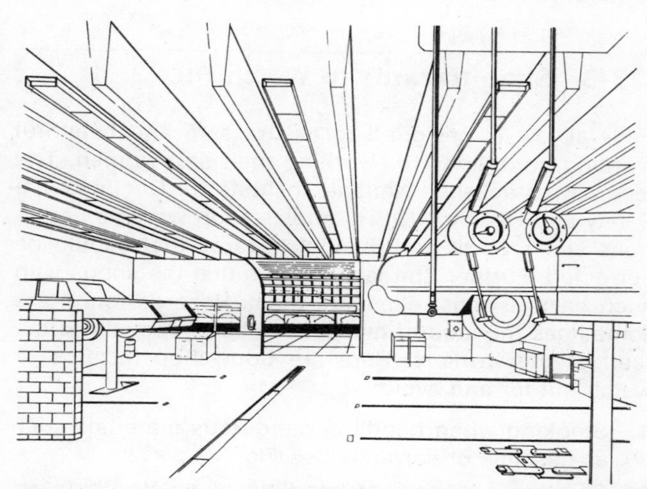

FIGURE 3-1. Typical shop layout. (*Motor Vehicle Manufacturers Association*)

Figure 3-1 shows the layout of a typical general automotive repair shop. Figure 3-2 shows the layout of a body shop. These are only two of many possible variations. So the first thing you should do in a shop is to find out where everything is located. This includes the different machine tools and the workbenches, car lifts, and work areas. Many shops have painted lines on the floor to mark off work areas. These lines guide customers and

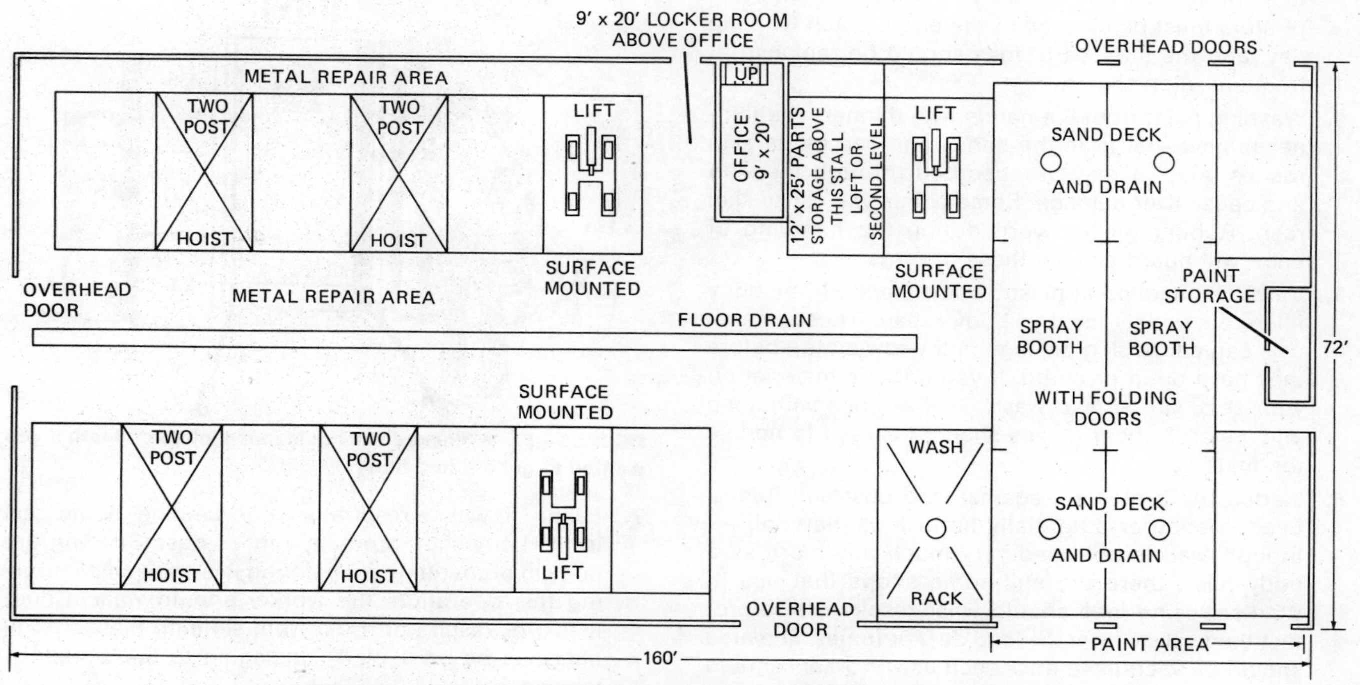

FIGURE 3-2. Floor plan for a body shop with a dozen body and paint technicians. (*Fisher Body Division of General Motors Corporation*)

workers away from danger zones where machines are being operated. The lines also remind workers to keep their tools and equipment inside work area lines.

Many shops have warning signs posted around machinery. These signs are there to remind you and other workers about safety and about how to use the machines safely. Follow the posted instructions at all times. The most common cause of accidents in the shop is failure to follow instructions.

○3-3 Shop Hazards to Watch For

Federal law is designed to assure safe and healthful working conditions for working men and women. The federally established National Institute for Occupational Safety and Health (NIOSH) studies shop working conditions and reports on potential hazards that should be corrected. Further, the law requires that the shops with such hazards must eliminate them. Hazards found are sometimes the fault of management and sometimes the fault of the workers. Here are body-shop hazards to watch out for and avoid:

1. Smoking when handling dangerous materials such as gasoline or solvents. See Fig. 3-3.
2. Careless or incorrect handling of paints, thinners, solvents, and other flammable substances. As an example of safe handling, Fig. 3-4 shows the correct way to pump a flammable liquid from a large container into a small one. Note the bond and ground wires. Without these, a spark might jump from the nozzle to the small container, causing a disastrous explosion and fire.
3. Failure to wear the proper respirator (Fig. 1-6) when handling thinners and paints. The thinners used in most paints may cause liver and lung damage if the vapors are inhaled over a long period of time. Proper ventilation of the work area and wearing of respirators will reduce this hazard to a minimum. The respirators must be cleaned at the end of each working day, and the filter cartridges should be replaced at frequent intervals.
4. Washing paint from the hands with thinner. The thinner removes fat from the hands and can cause skin rashes. Also, it may be absorbed through the skin and cause liver damage. Some paints will cause skin rash. Rubber gloves worn during the handling of paint will guard against these hazards.
5. Careless handling of plastic body fillers. Plastic body fillers are widely used in body repair. These chemicals can cause skin damage in the raw state—before they have dried or cured. It you get this material on your skin, you should wash it off at once with soap and water. Rubber gloves should be used to handle the material.
6. Inadequate protection against lead dust and fumes. Lead is another potentially hazardous material. Although lead is not used very much any more as a body filler, there are still some shops that use it. Workers using lead should wear respirators to protect themselves from the lead dust or fumes. The area should be vacuumed after each use. Workers should not eat or smoke after using lead until they have washed their hands.

FIGURE 3–3. Do not smoke or have open flames around combustibles such as gasoline or solvents.

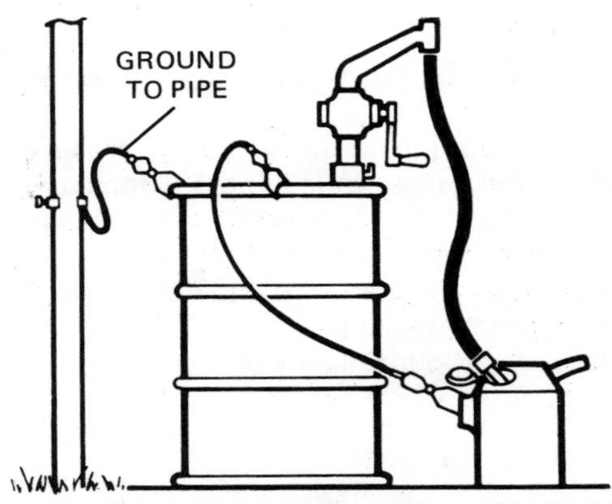

FIGURE 3–4. Setup for pumping a flammable liquid from a large to a small container. Note that if the hose is nonconducting, a ground wire should be connected as shown.

FIGURE 3–5. A blocked exit could mean injury or death if you wanted to get out in a hurry.

7. Failure to wear a respirator when sanding. Some jobs in the body shop produce a lot of dust. Sanding the body in preparation for painting it is an example. During this operation, the worker should wear a dust mask, or respirator. Dust from sanding plastic body filler can be particularly damaging to the worker, if inhaled.
8. Blocked exits (Fig. 3-5). Areas around exit doors and

passageways leading to exits must be kept free of all obstructions. If you wanted to get out in an emergency—as, for example, in a fire or explosion—a blocked exit could mean serious injury or even death.

○3-4 Equipment Hazards to Watch Out For

Safety inspectors have found that the following are the most common equipment hazards to watch out for:

1. Incorrect safety-guarding of moving machinery. For example, fans should have adequate guards, as shown in Fig. 3-6. Air compressors are sometimes found without a guard over the belts and pulley. See Fig. 3-7. These should be covered with a guard.
2. Misuse of flexible electric cords. Cords that are worn or frayed, or have been spliced poorly, should not be used. Flexible cord should not be run through holes in the wall or tacked onto the wall. See Fig. 3-8. Any of these practices could cause a fire or electrocute someone.
3. Improper storage of compressed gas cylinders. These cylinders should not be stored near radiators or other sources of heat. They should be kept well away from combustible materials, stairs, and elevators. They should not be kept in unventilated enclosures such as lockers and closets. There should be at least 20 feet [6.1 meters (m)] between stored oxygen cylinders and stored acetylene cylinders. Or else the cylinders should be separated by a fireproof barrier. Cylinders should not be allowed to stand free but should be secured with a chain or lashing to keep them from toppling over. See Fig. 3-9. Cylinders should be plainly marked to identify their contents. Later, we will have more to say about the proper handling and storage of compressed gas cylinders.
4. Poorly maintained gas-welding hose. The hose must be in good condition and not have leaks, burns, or worn places. See Fig. 3-10. During gas-welding or cutting operations, the area must be protected with screens, and all combustibles should be kept well away—and this includes fuel and solvent vapors.
5. Carelessness in handling oil and grease. Oil and grease must be kept away from the gas-welding equipment. If high-pressure oxygen hits oil or grease, an explosion and fire can result. Never allow oil or grease to get on oxygen tanks. Never wear greasy or oily clothing or gloves when working with gas-welding equipment.
6. Improper use of hydraulic car lifts. Do not allow passengers to remain in the car when it is lifted. Make

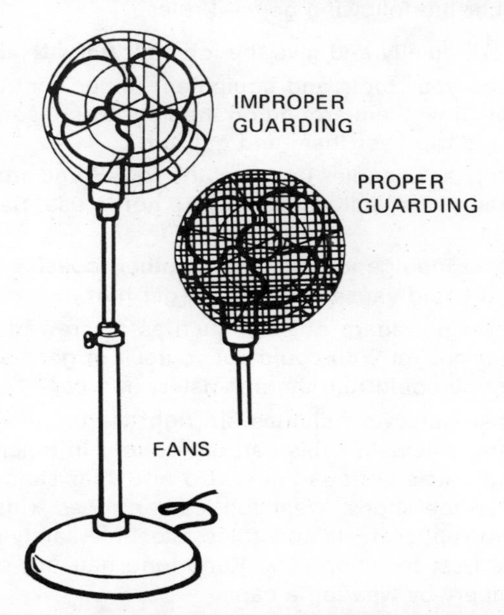

FIGURE 3–6. A fan, improperly and properly guarded.

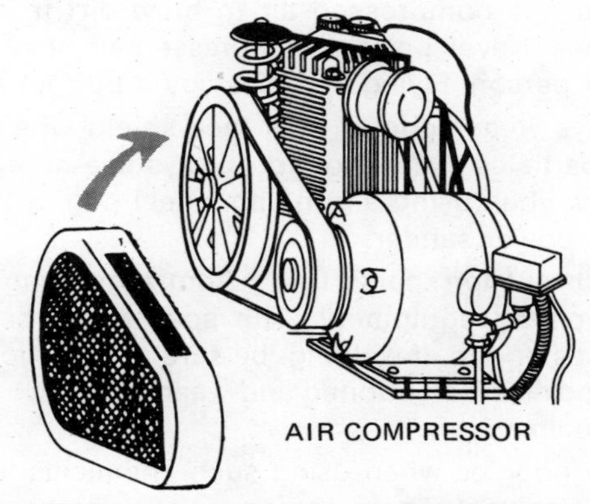

FIGURE 3–7. Belts and pulleys should always be protected with guards.

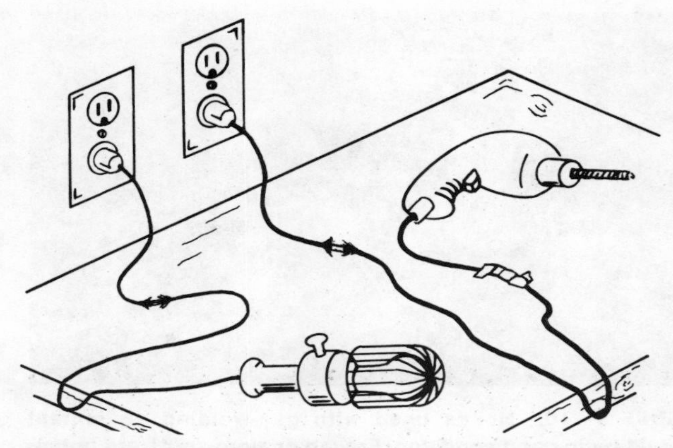

FIGURE 3–8. All electrical appliances should be used carefully. Plugs should be grounded and appliances stored neatly. What safety rules are violated here?

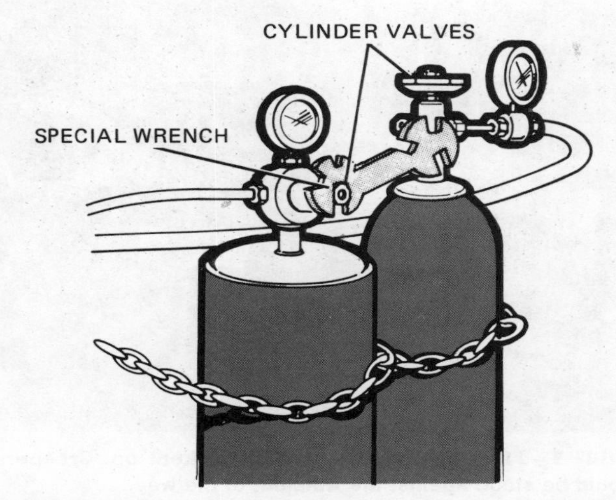

FIGURE 3–9. Gas cylinders should not be allowed to stand freely but should always be secured with chain or lashing.

FIGURE 3-10. **Hoses used with gas-welding equipment should be in good condition. Frayed or worn spots are potentially dangerous and could let gas leak out, with disastrous results.**

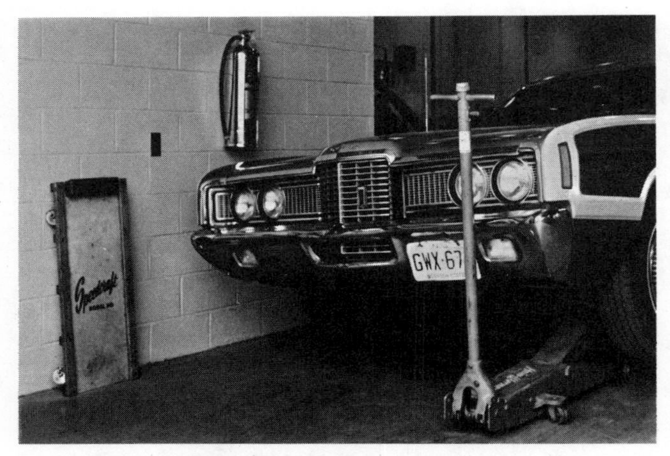

FIGURE 3-11. **Jack handles should be kept up. Creepers should be stood against the wall, out of the way.**

sure that all doors, hoods, and trunk lid are closed. Otherwise, they might be ripped off or damaged as the car is lifted. If the lift has a mechanical locking device, it should be engaged before you go under the lift. Do not use a lift that is not working properly: that jerks or jumps when raised, slowly settles when it should not, rises or settles too slowly, blows oil out of the exhaust line, or leaks oil at the packing gland.

7. Inadequate precautions in using hand-held electric tools. Hand-held drills, grinders, and so on must have a separate ground lead or have double insulation to guard against shocks.
8. Insufficient worker protection in electric arc or gas welding. Welding should be done in a protected area, and the worker must wear a welding helmet or use a face shield. Arc welders should wear fire-resistant gloves and clothing with the collar and sleeves buttoned. Fire-extinguisher equipment should be kept handy. The air must be free of any flammable vapors or gas. The arc-welding cable should be spread out and not coiled. It should never be coiled around the body of the welder. Hot material should be marked to prevent someone from trying to handle it.
9. Misuse of oxygen cylinders. These cylinders must never be used as a support or as rollers to move another object. Such treatment could cause the cylinder to explode with terrible effect on anyone standing nearby. Those closest could be killed.

○3-5 Hand-Tool Hazards to Watch Out For

Hand tools should be kept clean and in good condition. Greasy and oily tools are hard to hold and use. Always wipe them before trying to use them. Do not use a hardened hammer or punch on a hardened surface. Hardened steel is brittle and it can shatter from heavy blows. Slivers may fly out and enter the hand, or, worse, the eye. Hammers with broken or cracked handles, chisels and punches with mushroomed heads, and broken or bent wrenches are other tool hazards that should be avoided.

Never use a tool that is in poor condition or that does not fit the job. Either situation can cause you to get hurt.

○3-6 General Safety Rules

Some people say, "Accidents will happen!" But safety experts do not agree. They say, "Accidents are caused. They are caused by careless actions, by inattention to the job at hand, by using damaged or incorrect tools. And sometimes accidents are caused by just plain stupidity!"

To keep accidents from happening, remember what we have just discussed on the previous pages. And also, remember the following general rules:

1. Work quietly and give the job your full attention.
2. Keep your tools and equipment under control. Do not strew them around on the floor where someone could trip over them and get hurt.
3. Keep jack handles up out of the way. Stand creepers against the wall when they are not in use. See Fig. 3-11.
4. Never indulge in horseplay or other foolish activity. You could cause someone to get hurt.
5. Never put sharp objects, such as a screwdriver, in your pocket. You could cut yourself or get stabbed. Or you could ruin the upholstery in a car.
6. Make sure your clothes are right for the job. Dangling sleeves or ties can get caught in machinery and cause serious injury. Do not wear sandals or open-toe shoes. Wear full leather shoes with non-skid rubber heels and soles. Steel-toe safety shoes are best for shopwork. Keep long hair out of machinery by wearing a cap.
7. If you spill oil, grease, or any liquid on the floor, clean it up at once so that no one will slip and fall.
8. Never use compressed air to blow dirt from your clothes. Never point a compressed-air hose at another person. Flying particles could put out an eye.
9. Always wear goggles or a face shield when there are particles flying around. Always use an eye protector when using a grinding wheel (Fig. 3-12) or a body power sander.
10. Watch out for sparks flying from a grinding wheel or welding equipment. The sparks can set your clothes on fire. If welding, be sure to keep your collar and sleeves buttoned and wear protective gloves and helmet.
11. Wear goggles when using such chemicals as thinner or solvent. These can cause eye damage. If you get a chemical in your eyes, wash them out at once

FIGURE 3 – 12. **Always wear safety glasses, goggles, or a face shield when using a bench grinder. (*Ford Motor Company*)**

FIGURE 3 – 13. **If solvent or some other chemical splashes into your eye, immediately wash your eye with water.**

with water (Fig. 3-13). Then see the school nurse or doctor as soon as possible.

12. When using a car jack, make sure it is centered so it won't slip. And never, *never* jack up a car while someone is working under it! People have been killed when the jack slipped and the car fell on them. Always use car stands or supports, properly placed, when going under a car. See Fig. 3-14.

13. Always use the right tool for the job. The wrong tool, or a defective tool, could damage the part being worked on and could cause you to get hurt.

14. Never run an engine in a closed garage that does not have a ventilating system. The exhaust gases contain carbon monoxide, a deadly gas that is colorless, odorless, and killing! In a closed one-car garage, enough carbon monoxide to kill you can collect in only 3 minutes. Use proper exhaust equipment. See Fig. 3-15.

FIGURE 3 – 14. **Safety stands should be properly placed before you go under a car.**

FIGURE 3 – 15. **When running an engine in an enclosed garage, always use the exhaust equipment so the exhaust gases will be sent outside.**

○3-7 Using Power-Driven Equipment

Always read the instructions carefully before attempting to use a piece of power equipment. Have your instructor check you out on the equipment to make sure you know how to use it. Be sure you are wearing the proper clothes for using the equipment. Remember that dangling ties, sleeves, and hair are serious hazards and should be avoided. If they were caught in moving machinery, you could be pulled in and seriously injured. Keep your hands out of the way when using any cutting device, such as a lathe. Do not attempt to feel the finish while the lathe is running. There may be slivers of metal that could cut your hand badly. When using pneumatic (air-driven) chisels, make sure the chisel is tight in the tool. Never attempt to adjust or oil moving machinery unless the instructions tell you this should be done.

○3-8 Driving Cars in the Shop

Cars have to be moved in the shop. They must be brought in for service, and they have to be moved from one work area to another. When the job is finished, they have to be moved out of the work area. You must be extremely careful when driving a car in the shop. Make sure the

FIRES
A CLASS *A* FIRES ORDINARY COMBUSTIBLE MATERIALS SUCH AS WOOD, PAPER, TEXTILES AND SO FORTH. REQUIRES. . .COOLING-QUENCHING
B CLASS *B* FIRES FLAMMABLE LIQUIDS, GREASES, GASOLINE, OILS, PAINTS AND SO FORTH. REQUIRES. . .BLANKETING OR SMOTHERING
C CLASS *C* FIRES ELECTRICAL EQUIPMENT, MOTORS, SWITCHES AND SO FORTH. REQUIRES. . .A NONCONDUCTING AGENT

EXTINGUISHERS TYPE	USE		OPERATION
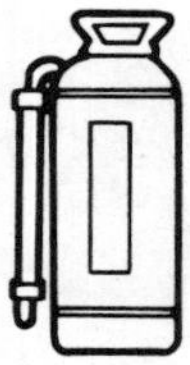 **FOAM** SOLUTION OF ALUMINUM SULPHATE AND BICARBONATE OF SODA	OK FOR A B NOT FOR C		*FOAM*: DON'T PLAY STREAM INTO THE BURNING LIQUID. ALLOW FOAM TO FALL LIGHTLY ON FIRE 
 **CARBON DIOXIDE** CARBON DIOXIDE GAS UNDER PRESSURE	NOT FOR A OK FOR B C		*CARBON DIOXIDE*: DIRECT DISCHARGE AS CLOSE TO FIRE AS POSSIBLE. FIRST AT EDGE OF FLAMES AND GRADUALLY FORWARD AND UPWARD 
 **DRY CHEMICAL**	MULTI-PURPOSE TYPE OK FOR A B C	ORDINARY BC TYPE NOT FOR A OK FOR B C	*DRY CHEMICAL*: DIRECT STREAM AT BASE OF FLAMES. USE RAPID LEFT-TO-RIGHT MOTION TOWARD FLAMES 
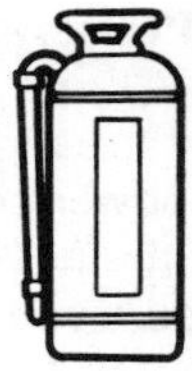 **SODA-ACID** BICARBONATE OF SODA SOLUTION AND SULPHURIC ACID	OK FOR A NOT FOR B C		*SODA-ACID*: DIRECT STREAM AT BASE OF FLAME 

FIGURE 3-16. Chart showing types of fire extinguishers and the classification of fires. (*Ford Motor Company*)

way is clear. Make sure no one is under a nearby car. Someone might suddenly stick out an arm or a leg. Also, make sure that there are no tools on the ground that you could run over.

CAUTION: Always fasten your safety belt in a moving car whether you are the driver or a passenger. Seat belts save lives; your seat belt could save yours.

○ 3-9 Tow-Truck Operation

Driving a tow truck and doing emergency work at the scene of a collision takes experience. Each collision is a special problem. But there are some general comments that can be made about the tow truck:

1. Make sure the fire extinguisher is properly serviced, in good working condition, and securely mounted on the truck.
2. Do not exceed the maximum hoisting capacity of the unit.
3. Make sure the truck floodlights are in good working condition.
4. Wheel chocks and flares should be available on the truck.
5. The control mechanism for the hoist should be in-

THINK
OSHA REQUIRES EMPLOYEES TO WEAR GOGGLES WHERE EYE INJURY HAZARDS EXIST & FACE MASKS WHEN PAINTING
ACT IN A SAFE MANNER

FIGURE 3 – 17. Type of sign found in many automotive service shops, and other shops as well, reminding employees to obey the rules.

spected periodically to make sure that it is in good operating condition and that the cable, hooks, drum, and other parts are in working order.

○3-10 Fire Extinguishers

Note the locations of the fire extinguishers (Fig. 3-16) in the shop. Make sure you know how to use them. Figure 3-16 is a chart showing different types of fires and the types of fire extinguishers used to fight them. Remember that the quicker you get at a fire, the easier it is to control it. But you have to use the right kind of fire extinguisher and use it correctly. The chart explains this. If you have any questions, ask your instructor.

○3-11 Warning Signs

Warning signs, such as shown in Fig. 3-17, are posted in shops to warn against hazards. They should be obeyed at all times to avoid injury and promote safety.

CHAPTER 3 CHECKUP

NOTE: Since this is a chapter review test, you should review the chapter before taking the test.

Safety in the shop is a subject that you cannot know too much about. Every year some people are injured in accidents that happen while they are working on cars. In this chapter, we try to point out some of the danger areas in automobile service work. As you learned from the chapter, you must be very careful when working on, around, and under the car.

Now find out how well you understand safety in the shop by taking the test that follows. If you cannot answer all the questions, or if you are confused about the proper action to take in any situation, study the chapter again. If you still are not sure about something, ask your instructor for further safety instructions.

COMPLETING THE SENTENCES The sentences below are incomplete. After each sentence there are several words or phrases, but only one of them correctly completes the sentence. Write each sentence in your notebook, ending it with the one word or phrase that completes it correctly.

1. Safety in the shop means protecting, from danger or harm, yourself and (*a*) no one else, (*b*) those around you, (*c*) your boss.
2. One of the most common causes of accidents in the shop is (*a*) failure to follow instructions, (*b*) following instructions, (*c*) following wrong instructions.
3. If there is an accident in the shop, you should (*a*) ignore it, (*b*) notify your parents, (*c*) notify your instructor at once.
4. One liquid that is used so much in the shop that people forget it is very dangerous if not handled properly is (*a*) engine oil, (*b*) carburetor cleaner, (*c*) gasoline.
5. You should never store gasoline in (*a*) an approved safety container, (*b*) a glass jug, (*c*) a metal tank.
6. Oily rags must be stored in (*a*) a closed metal container, (*b*) piles under the workbench, (*c*) the corner of the shop.
7. A compressed-air hose must never be (*a*) used in the automotive shop, (*b*) pointed at someone else, (*c*) left pressurized overnight, (*d*) kept on a reel.
8. The right time to jack up a car is when (*a*) someone is working under it, (*b*) never, (*c*) you are working under it, (*d*) no one is working under it.
9. Before you get under a car to work on it, you must be sure that (*a*) the jack handle is up, (*b*) you use a creeper, (*c*) the tires are inflated, (*d*) the car is supported on stands.
10. Safety goggles should be worn (*a*) when doing any job that could endanger your eyes, (*b*) when you are told to wear them by the instructor, (*c*) only if you do not wear glasses, (*d*) while welding.

QUESTIONS Write each of the following questions, and then the answer, in your notebook. If you have trouble recalling the answer to a question, turn back to the pages that cover the material and study them again.

1. What is "shop safety"?
2. What do the lines painted on the shop floor mean?
3. What should you do if someone nearby is injured in the shop?
4. What is the proper procedure to follow when you walk into a shop and smell a strong odor of gasoline?
5. Explain why horseplay is forbidden in the shop.

DEFINITIONS In the following, you are asked for several definitions. Write them in your notebook. The act of writing the definitions does two things: It tests your knowledge, and it helps fix the information more firmly in your mind. Turn back into the chapter if you are not sure of a definition, or look it up in the glossary at the back of the book.

1. Define "safety."
2. What are safety glasses? Goggles?
3. Define "approved safety container."
4. What is carbon monoxide?
5. Define "power-driven equipment."

SUGGESTIONS FOR FURTHER STUDY

Study the various safety charts, posters, and signs placed around the shop. Then make a safety inspection of your shop and your work area. Notice the locations of the fire extinguishers, first-aid kits, telephones, and fire exits. Inspect each fire extinguisher to be sure that it has been checked recently. Make sure the pressure gauge shows it is still charged and ready for use.

4 FASTENERS

The automobile is held together by soldering, welding, brazing, adhesives, and a variety of fasteners such as screws, nuts, and clips. We cover welding and brazing in later chapters. Now, in this chapter, we discuss the fasteners, with special emphasis on the fastening devices used on automobile bodies.

○4-1 Threads

Before we talk about screws, bolts, studs (Fig. 4-1), and nuts, let's find out about threads. Screws, bolts, and studs all have external threads, that is, threads on the outside. Nuts and threaded holes have threads on the inside. As you know, nuts and bolts come in many sizes, from very small to very large. Large nuts and bolts have coarse threads, which means that there are only a few threads per inch. You can count the number of threads on a bolt, as shown in Fig. 4-2. You just measure 1 inch from the end of the bolt and count the number of threads. There are also other measurements, as shown in Fig. 4-2. These include the length of the bolt, diameter of the bolt, length of the thread, and size of the wrench required to turn the head. Figure 4-3 is a table showing how threads are classified.

SCREW | BOLT (WITH NUT) | STUD (WITH NUT)

FIGURE 4–1. Screw, bolt, and stud. (Top) The attaching parts are shown separated but aligned for assembly. (Bottom) The parts are shown together, in sectional view.

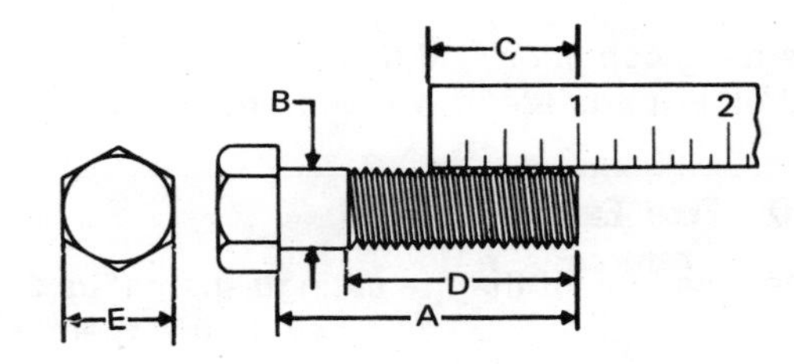

FIGURE 4–2. A hex-head bolt with its parts named: (A) length, (B) diameter, (C) pitch, or threads per inch, (D) length of thread, (E) size of wrench required to fit head.

		Threads per Inch		
Size	Diameter (Decimal)	Coarse (UNC or NC)	Fine (UNF or NF)	Extra-fine (UNEF or NEF)
0	0.0600	. . .	80	
1	0.0730	64	72	
2	0.0860	56	64	
3	0.0990	48	56	
4	0.1120	40	48	
5	0.1250	40	44	
6	0.1380	32	40	
8	0.1640	32	36	
10	0.1900	24	32	
12	0.2160	24	28	32
1/4	0.2500	20	28	32
5/16	0.3125	18	24	32
3/8	0.3750	16	24	32
7/16	0.4375	14	20	28
1/2	0.5000	13	20	28
9/16	0.5625	12	18	24
5/8	0.6250	11	18	24
3/4	0.7500	10	16	20
7/8	0.8750	9	14	20
1	1.0000	8	12	20
1 1/8	1.1250	7	12	18
1 1/4	1.2500	7	12	18
1 3/8	1.3750	6	12	18
1 1/2	1.5000	6	12	18

FIGURE 4–3. Table of screw-thread sizes and pitches. UNC, NC, UNF, NF, UNEF, and NEF stand for special features of the threads. UNC means Unified National Course, NC means National Course, UNF means Unified National Fine, NF means National Fine, UNEF means Unified National Extra Fine, and NEF means National Extra Fine.

○4-2 Pitch

Pitch is the number of threads per inch (Fig. 4-2). In addition to using a ruler to count the number of threads per inch, you can also use a thread gauge, as shown in Fig. 4-4. To use the gauge, find the blade that has the proper number of teeth to fit the threads. The blade is marked with the pitch, or number of teeth per inch.

NOTE: Screw threads are puzzling, but you should know about them. A screw that is ¼ inch in diameter can have 20, 28, or 32 threads per inch. The difference is important. You cannot put a ¼-inch 20-thread nut on a ¼-inch 24-thread bolt.

○4-3 Thread Series

There are three thread series: coarse, fine, and extra-fine. By "coarse," "fine," and "extra-fine," we mean the pitch, or number of threads in an inch. A ½-inch bolt, for example, could have coarse threads (13 threads per inch). Or a ½-inch bolt could have fine threads (20 threads per inch) or extra-fine threads (28 threads per inch). A coarse thread shortens the disassembly and reassembly time, because fewer turns are required to remove or install it. The fine and extra-fine threads are smaller than the coarse threads. The fine and extra-fine threads are used where greater bolt strength and additional accuracy of assembly are required.

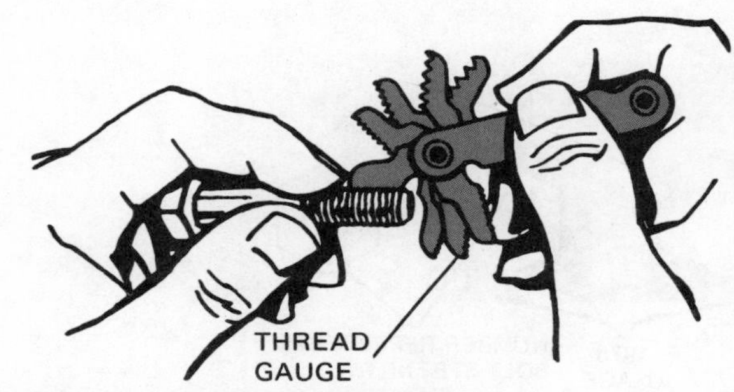

FIGURE 4–4. Using a thread gauge.

○4-4 Bolt Strength

Bolts and hex-head screws are made of materials of different strengths. The table in Fig. 4-5 shows the head markings that tell the quality of the bolt or screw. The minimum tensile strength is the pull, in pounds, that a round rod with a cross section of 1 in² [6.45 cm²] can stand before it tears apart or breaks. Stronger screws are more expensive; they are used only where added strength is necessary.

○4-5 Thread Classes

There are three thread classes. The difference is in the closeness of fit. Class 1 has the loosest fit and is easiest to remove and install, even when the threads are dirty and somewhat battered. Class 2 has a tighter fit. Class 3 has a very close fit. An external thread, used on a bolt, screw, or stud, is called an A thread. An internal thread, used in a nut or threaded hole, is called a B thread.

○4-6 Complete Thread Designation

A thread is designated by size, pitch, series, and class. For example, suppose you have a ¼-20 UNC-2A bolt. This means that the bolt is ¼ inch in diameter, that it has coarse threads (20 threads per inch), and that the thread is an external Class 2 thread. Now you can see why it is important to know about threads. You cannot use a ¼-28 UNF-2A bolt with a ¼-20 UNC-28 nut, because the threads don't match. Not only the bolt size but also the thread pitch must be the same for a bolt or screw to fit a nut or a threaded hole.

○4-7 Metric Fasteners

The two most widely used measuring systems are the U.S. Customary System and the metric system. The U.S. Customary System (USCS) uses inches, feet, miles, pints,

USAGES IN VEHICLES	SOME USED	MUCH USED	FOR SPECIAL EQUIPMENT	CRITICAL POINTS	COMPETITION MAXIMUM REQUIREMENTS
TYPICAL APPLICATIONS	FENDERS	BELL HOUSINGS	HEAD BOLTS	BEARING CAPS	RACE CARS
MINIMUM TENSILE STRENGTH PSI	64,000	105,000	133,000	150,000	160,000
MATERIAL	LOW-CARBON STEEL	MEDIUM-CARBON STEEL	MEDIUM-CARBON STEEL	ALLOY STEEL	SPECIAL ALLOY STEEL
QUALITY	INDETERMINATE	MINIMUM COMMERCIAL	MEDIUM COMMERCIAL	BEST COMMERCIAL	BEST QUALITY
HEAD MARKINGS					

FIGURE 4–5. Meaning of bolt-head markings.

quarts, gallons, and so on. This is the system of measurement we worked with above in describing thread designation. The United States is the only major country still using the USCS. Most countries already use the metric system or are in the process of switching to it.

Cars, trucks, and motorcycles imported into the United States are dimensioned in the metric system. Also, some engines built in the United States are already completely metric. This means that all measurements, all nuts and bolts, are in metric units. If you work on imported cars you will need an extra set of tools—metric tools. Also, you will need to understand metric fasteners.

Many metric fasteners are very close in dimension to "inch" fasteners in the U.S. Customary System. You must not mix metric and customary fasteners. Mismatched or incorrect fasteners can result in vehicle damage, malfunction, or possible personal injury. Fasteners removed from the vehicle should be saved for reuse whenever possible. When fasteners are not reusable, you should select a replacement fastener that matches the original.

In general, the American automotive manufacturers are using certain metric fastener sizes as defined by the International Standards Organization (ISO). This reduces the number of fastener sizes used while retaining the best strength characteristics in each thread size. For example, the customary ¼-20 and ¼-28 screws are replaced by the metric M6.3 × 1 screw. It has nearly the same diameter and 25.4 threads per inch. The thread pitch is between the customary coarse and fine thread pitches.

The designations for customary thread and for metric thread differ. Figure 4-6 illustrates the difference. Metric fasteners generally are identified by markings on the bolt head and nut face. Figure 4-7 shows some of the different types of metric-fastener identification. There are exceptions to this marking system, and in some cases metric fasteners are not identified. Bolt strength, in the metric system, is embossed on the head of the bolt (Fig. 4-8). The two most commonly used classes are 9.8 and 10.9

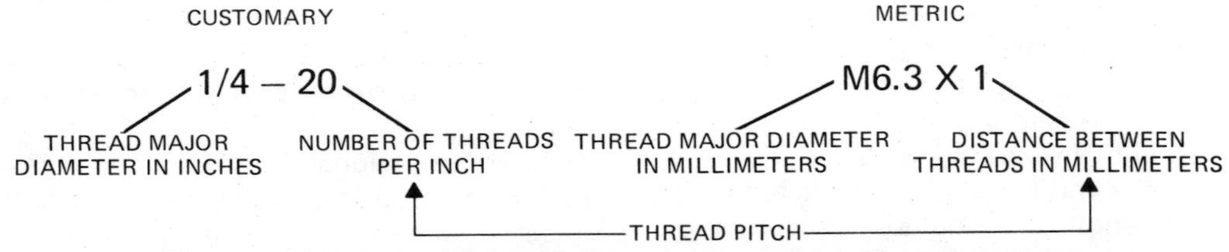

FIGURE 4–6. Difference in customary and metric thread designation. (*General Motors Corporation*)

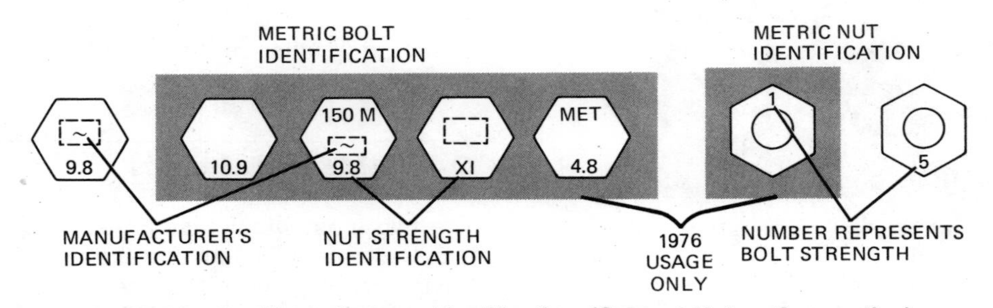

FIGURE 4–7. Metric fastener identification. (*General Motors Corporation*)

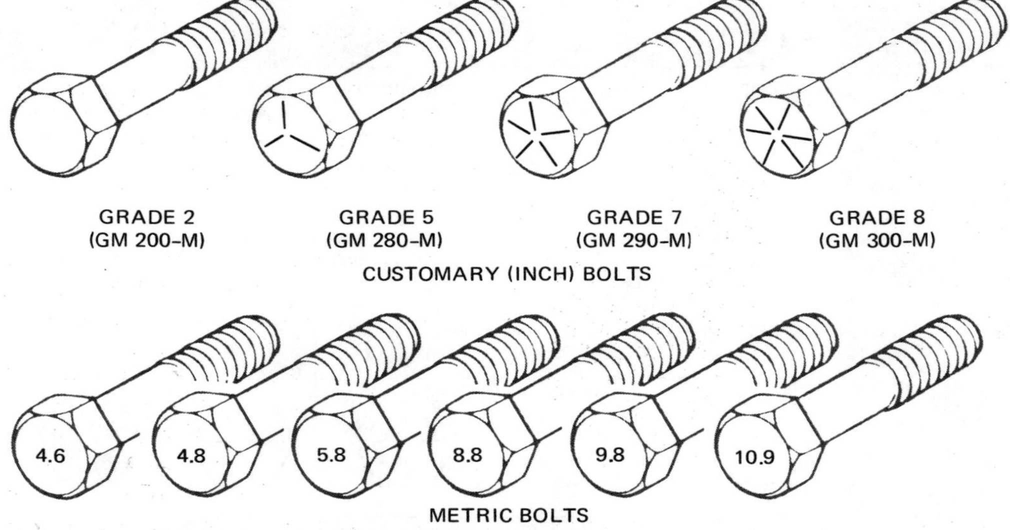

FIGURE 4–8. Bolt strength markings. (*General Motors Corporation*)

In the customary system, as shown in Figs. 4-5 and 4-8, bolt-strength classes range from 2 to 8, with line identification embossed on each bolt head. Markings correspond to two lines less than the actual grade. That is, in the customary system a grade 7 bolt will have five lines embossed on the bolt head. This is shown in Fig. 4-8.

Some metric nuts are marked with a single number on the nut face, as shown in Fig. 4-7. In both systems, increasing numbers represents increasing bolt strength.

Some cars have both customary-thread fasteners and metric-thread fasteners. When working on these cars, be sure that metric and inch nuts and bolts are not interchanged. This could result in cross-threading and dangerous loosening of the fastener.

When buying and installing metric fasteners, be sure that the new fastener is the equivalent of the original fastener in dimensions, strength, and pitch of threads. If equivalent metric fasteners are not available from your local fastener supplier, the proper fasteners can be obtained from the dealer for the car you are repairing. Listed below are the metric-thread diameters and pitch combinations that are most commonly used on automobiles.

M4 × .7	M8 × 1.25	M14 × 2
M5 × .8	M10 × 1.5	M16 × 2
M6.3 × 1	M12 × 1.75	M20 × 2.5

Note that all pipe-plug threads are the same in both the customary and metric systems.

○4-8 Screws and Bolts

Screws enter threaded holes. Bolts are used with nuts. However, screws and bolts are alike in appearance. The main difference is in the head and the type of screwdriver or wrench that is used to turn them. A great variety of screws and bolts are used in automobiles. Figure 4-9 shows various screws and bolts and the types of screwdrivers and wrenches required to turn them. The most common bolts have hexagonal (six-sided), or "hex," heads. The most common screws have slotted heads. But many Phillips-head screws are also used. Find these screws in Fig. 4-9.

○4-9 Setscrews

The setscrew is a special type of screw (Fig. 4-10). Its purpose is to fasten a collar or gear to a shaft. The setscrew is turned down into a threaded hole in the collar or gear until the point "bites" into the shaft. This holds the collar or gear in position.

○4-10 Self-Tapping Screws

Self-tapping screws cut their own threads. Figure 4-11 shows one type of self-tapping screw. The end of the screw is smaller and has slots cut in it. These slots form cutting edges. When the self-tapping screw is turned into a hole, threads are cut in the hole. Another type of screw, the drill-and-tap screw, shown in Fig. 4-12, not only cuts its own threads but also drills the hole. The point of the screw is formed into a drill, as you can see. When this

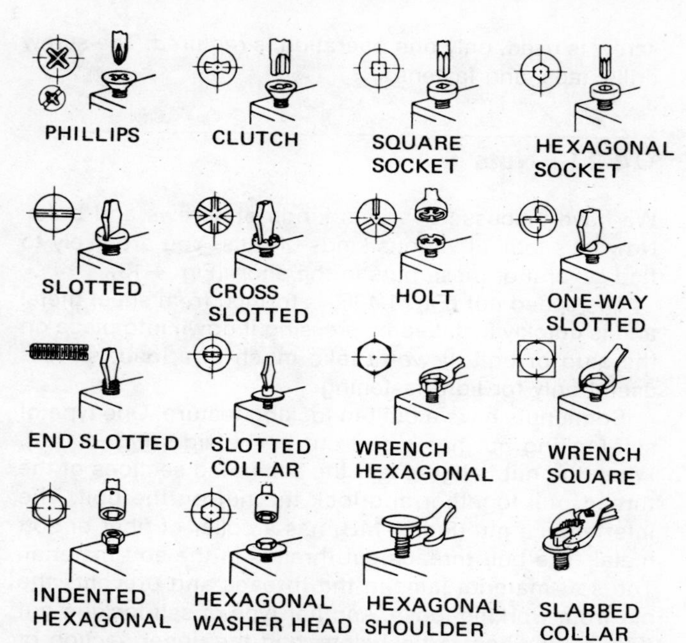

FIGURE 4–9. Screwdrivers and wrenches required to drive various types of screws and bolts.

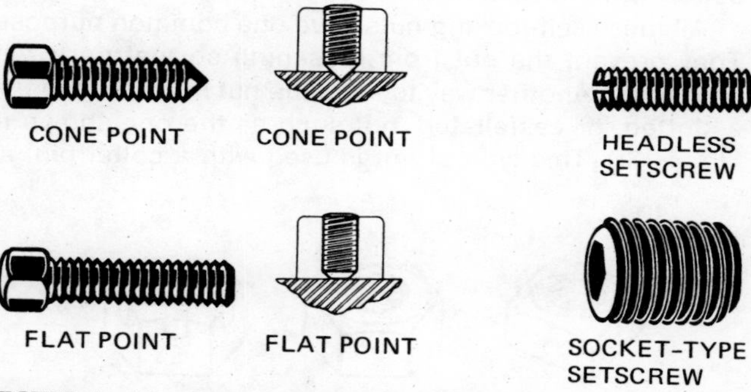

FIGURE 4–10. Types of setscrew points.

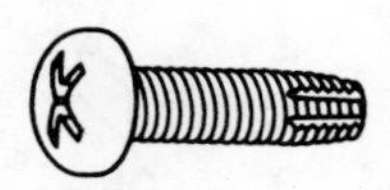

FIGURE 4–11. A self-tapping screw.

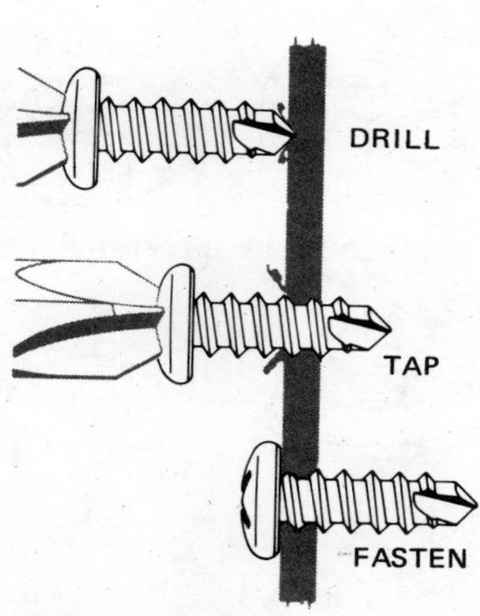

FIGURE 4–12. A drill-and-tap screw.

screw is used, only one operation is required. The screw drills, taps, and fastens.

○4-11 Nuts

We have discussed various kinds of screws and bolts. Now let's look at various kinds of nuts. You are likely to find several of these nuts in the shop (Fig. 4-13).

The speed nut (Fig. 4-13F) is formed from sheet metal and is quickly installed by pressing it down into place on the stud or bolt. It won't take much of a load; so it is useful only for light fastening.

Some nuts have a built-in locking feature. One type of self-locking nut has a slot cut in the side (Fig. 4-14A). When the nut is tightened, the separated sections of the thread pull together and lock the nut on the bolt. The interference nut (Fig. 4-14B) has a collar of fiber or soft metal. The bolt threads cut threads in the soft material. The soft material jams in the threads and prevents the nut from working loose. Another type of self-locking nut (Fig. 4-14C) has vertical slots, and the upper section of the nut is somewhat smaller in diameter than the lower section. Thus the upper threads jam tightly against the bolt threads to lock the nut into place. The Palnut (Fig. 4-14D) is a single-thread nut that provides some locking action when turned down on the nut.

All these self-locking nuts have one common purpose. They prevent the nut from loosening so that parts will not fall off. Another way to keep the nut in place is to use a slotted, or castellated, nut such as the one shown in Fig. 4-13D. This type of nut is used with a cotter pin, as shown in Fig. 4-15. The cotter pin is made of soft steel. After the nut is tightened properly, the pin is inserted through a hole in the bolt and two slots in the nut. The two ends of the pin are then bent around the nut, as shown.

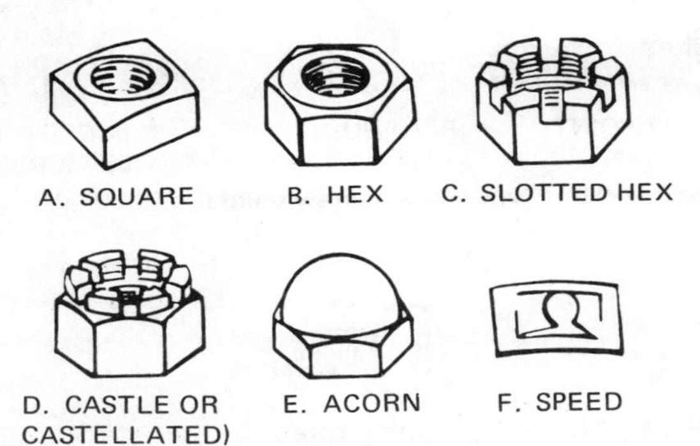

FIGURE 4–13. Several common nuts.

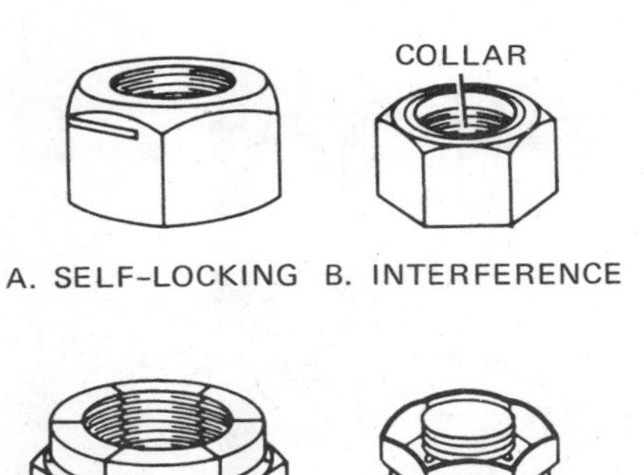

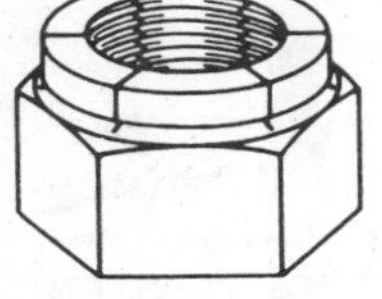
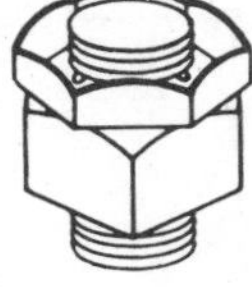

FIGURE 4–14. Self-locking nuts.

FIGURE 4–15. Cotter pin before installation (top), and after installation through the hole in the bolt and the slot in the nut.

Another way to lock a nut on a bolt is to use a second nut tightened against the first. The second nut is called a jam nut.

○4-12 Lock Washers

A common way to lock a nut in place is to use a lock washer. Lock washers are placed between the nut or screw head and a flat washer, as shown in Fig. 4-16. The edges left by the split or by the teeth in the lock washer bite into the metal and keep the screw or nut from turning. In some assemblies, the flat washer is not used. The lock washer is then placed directly against the part.

○4-13 Snap Rings

There are two types of snap rings: external and internal (Fig. 4-17). External snap rings are used on shafts to prevent the endwise movement of a gear or collar on the shaft. Internal snap rings are used in housings to keep shafts or other parts in position. Snap-ring pliers must be used to install and remove snap rings.

Figure 4-18 shows several kinds of Truarc retaining rings. This type has two lips with holes into which the pin ends of a special snap-ring pliers fit (Fig. 4-17). With this design, there is less chance for the pliers to slip off the snap ring during removal or installation.

○4-14 Keys and Splines

Keys and splines are used to lock gears, pulleys, collars, and other, similar parts to shafts so that they will rotate together. Figure 4-19 shows a typical key installation. The key is wedge-shaped and fits into slots, called keyways, cut in the shaft and collar (or other part being installed). The key locks the shaft and collar together.

Splines (Fig. 4-20) are internal and external teeth cut in both the shaft and the installed part. When the gear,

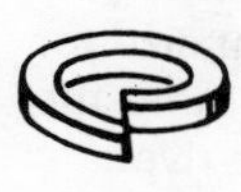

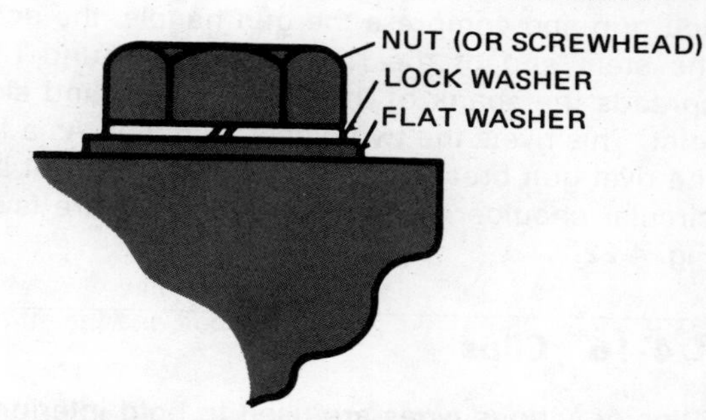

FIGURE 4–16. (Top) Lockwashers. (Bottom) A plain lockwasher installed between a flat washer and a nut or bolt head.

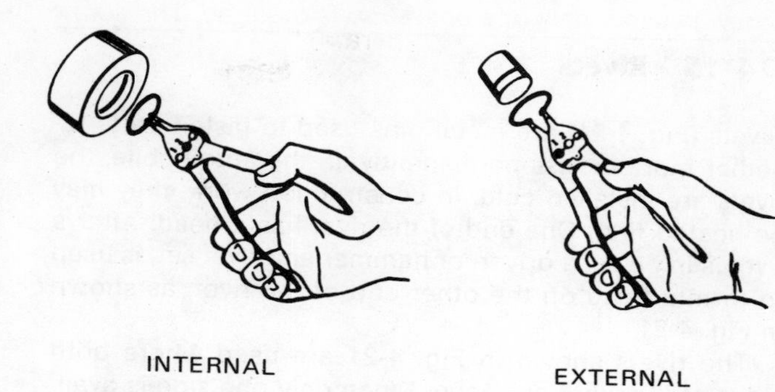

FIGURE 4–17. Using Truarc retaining-ring pliers to install internal and external retaining rings. ***(Waldes Kohinoor, Inc.)***

END-PLAY TAKE-UP	INTERNAL BOWED FOR HOUSINGS AND BORES	EXTERNAL BOWED FOR SHAFTS AND PINS	INTERNAL BEVELED FOR HOUSINGS AND BORES	EXTERNAL BEVELED FOR SHAFTS AND PINS	EXTERNAL BOWED E-RING FOR SHAFTS AND PINS	EXTERNAL PRONG-LOCK® FOR SHAFTS AND PINS
AXIAL ASSEMBLY	INTERNAL BASIC FOR HOUSINGS AND BORES	EXTERNAL BASIC FOR SHAFTS AND PINS	INTERNAL INVERTED FOR HOUSINGS AND BORES	EXTERNAL INVERTED FOR SHAFTS AND PINS	EXTERNAL HEAVY-DUTY FOR SHAFTS AND PINS	EXTERNAL HIGH-STRENGTH FOR SHAFTS AND PINS

FIGURE 4–18. Various types of internal and external Truarc retaining or snap rings. ***(Waldes Kohinoor, Inc.)***

pulley, or collar is installed on the shaft, it is the same as having a great number of keys between the two parts. In many machines, the splines fit loosely so that the gear or other part is free to move back and forth on the splines. The splines, however, force both parts to rotate together. Splines may be straight or curved, as shown in Fig. 4-20.

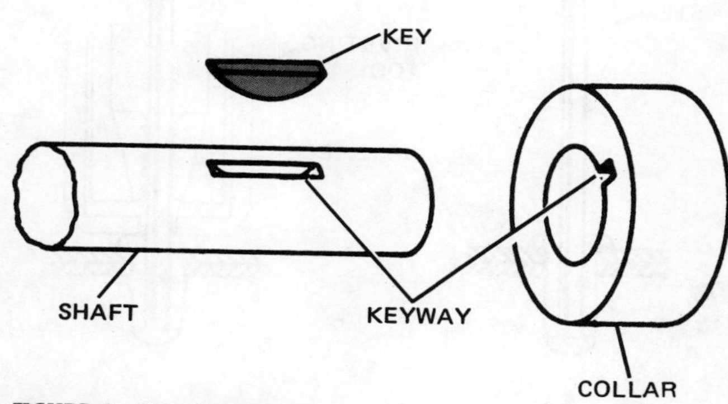

FIGURE 4–19. Using a key.

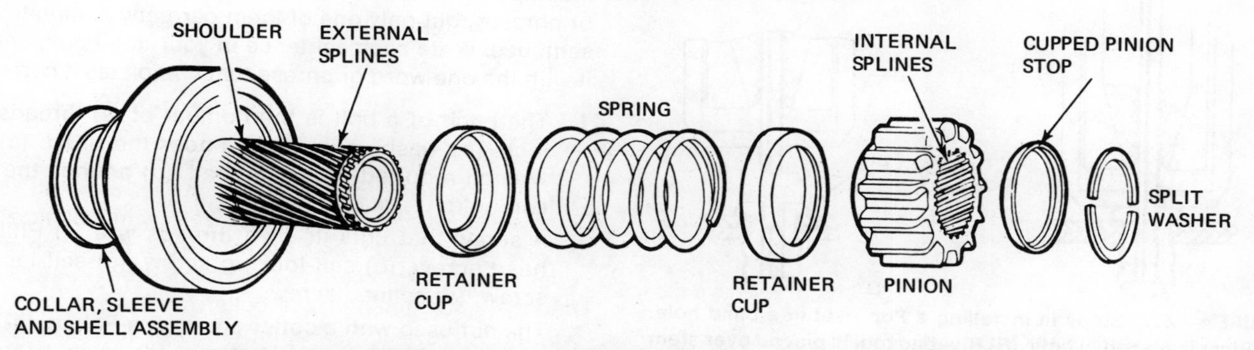

FIGURE 4–20. Disassembled starting-motor drive, showing internal and external splines. ***(Delco-Remy Division of General Motors Corporation)***

○4-15 Rivets

Rivets (Fig. 4-21) are metal pins used to fasten parts together more or less permanently. In the automobile, the rivets are installed cold. In construction work, they may be heated first. One end of the rivet has a head. After a rivet is in place, a driver, or hammer and rivet set, is used to form a head on the other end of the rivet, as shown in Fig. 4-21.

The rivets shown in Fig. 4-21 are used where both sides of the work are open. When only one side is available, a special type of rivet called a Pop[R] rivet (Fig. 4-22) and a rivet gun or riveter are used. The rivet gun has nosepieces of different sizes to take different size rivets.

To use the Pop rivets, you first drill a hole through both pieces of metal to be joined. Then you select a rivet of the size to fit the hole and insert it into the rivet gun. The gun nosepiece, of course, must be the right size for the rivet. You insert the pointed end of the rivet into the gun nosepiece, and you are ready to install the rivet.

You push the blunt end of the rivet with the ball head into the drilled holes in the two metal sheets. Now, when you grip and compress the gun handle, the action pulls the stem end of the rivet out. The round rivet head spreads the shank of the rivet on the blind side of the joint. This rivets the two pieces together. As a final step, the rivet gun breaks off (or pops off) the rivet below the circular shoulder. The complete procedure is shown in Fig. 4-22.

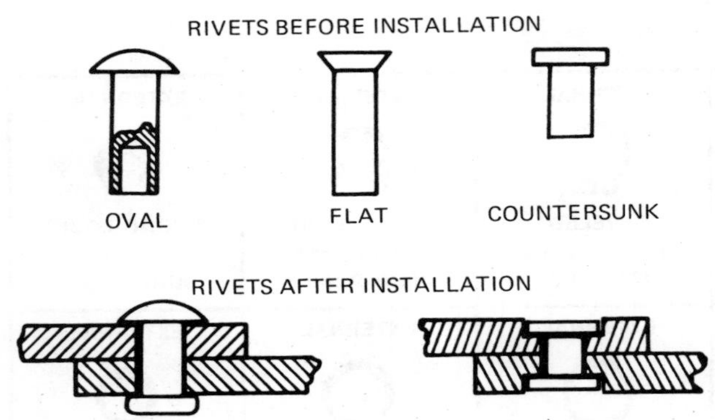

FIGURE 4–21. Rivets before installation (above) and after installation (below).

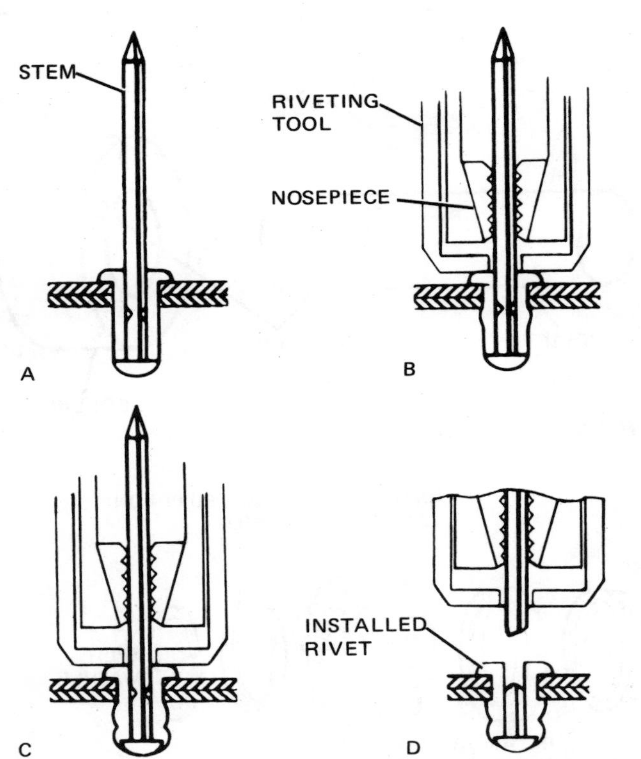

FIGURE 4–22. Steps in installing a Pop rivet in a blind hole. (A) Rivet is placed in hole. (B) Riveting tool is placed over stem of rivet. (C) Rivet head compresses. (D) Stem "pops" or snaps off. (*Avdel Corporation*)

○4-16 Clips

Clips of various types are used to hold interior trim and trim panels and exterior molding in place. For example, Fig. 4-23 shows the molding and clips used on one model of the Lincoln Continental. The clips are installed in holes in the body panels, and the molding is snapped onto the clips. Some molding is attached by adhesive.

Figure 4-24 shows an assortment of fasteners that are used in various cars to attach trim panels, as, for example, on the inside of doors and on quarter panels. Note that many of these are simply U-shaped brackets onto which the trim panels are slid. Trim panels also are held in place by screws. The screws may or may not be covered by plates that snap into place.

CHAPTER 4 CHECKUP

NOTE: Since this is a chapter review test, you should review the chapter before taking the test.

Working with fasteners is a job that the auto body-repair technician does almost all the time. Parts must be removed and installed in order to perform many of the different body-repair tasks confronting the technician. A knowledge of fasteners is more than knowing the difference between a nut and a bolt. The technician must know the tools required to remove and install each fastener and know the type of fasteners to use for any job.

Now find out how well you understand fasteners by taking the test that follows. If you cannot answer all the questions, or if you are unsure of which fastener to use in any repair, study the chapter again. If you still are not sure about something, ask your instructor for further information.

COMPLETING THE SENTENCES The sentences below are incomplete. After each sentence there are several words or phrases, but only one of them correctly completes the sentence. Write each sentence in your notebook, ending it with the one word or phrase that completes it correctly.

1. The pitch of a bolt is the number of (*a*) threads per inch, (*b*) washers required under the head, (*c*) the wrench required to fit the head, (*d*) pounds the bolt can hold.
2. A screw that cuts its own threads is a (*a*) Phillips-head screw, (*b*) self-locking screw, (*c*) self-tapping screw, (*d*) splined screw.
3. The nut used with a cotter pin is (*a*) a Palnut, (*b*) self-locking nut, (*c*) castellated nut, (*d*) an interference nut.

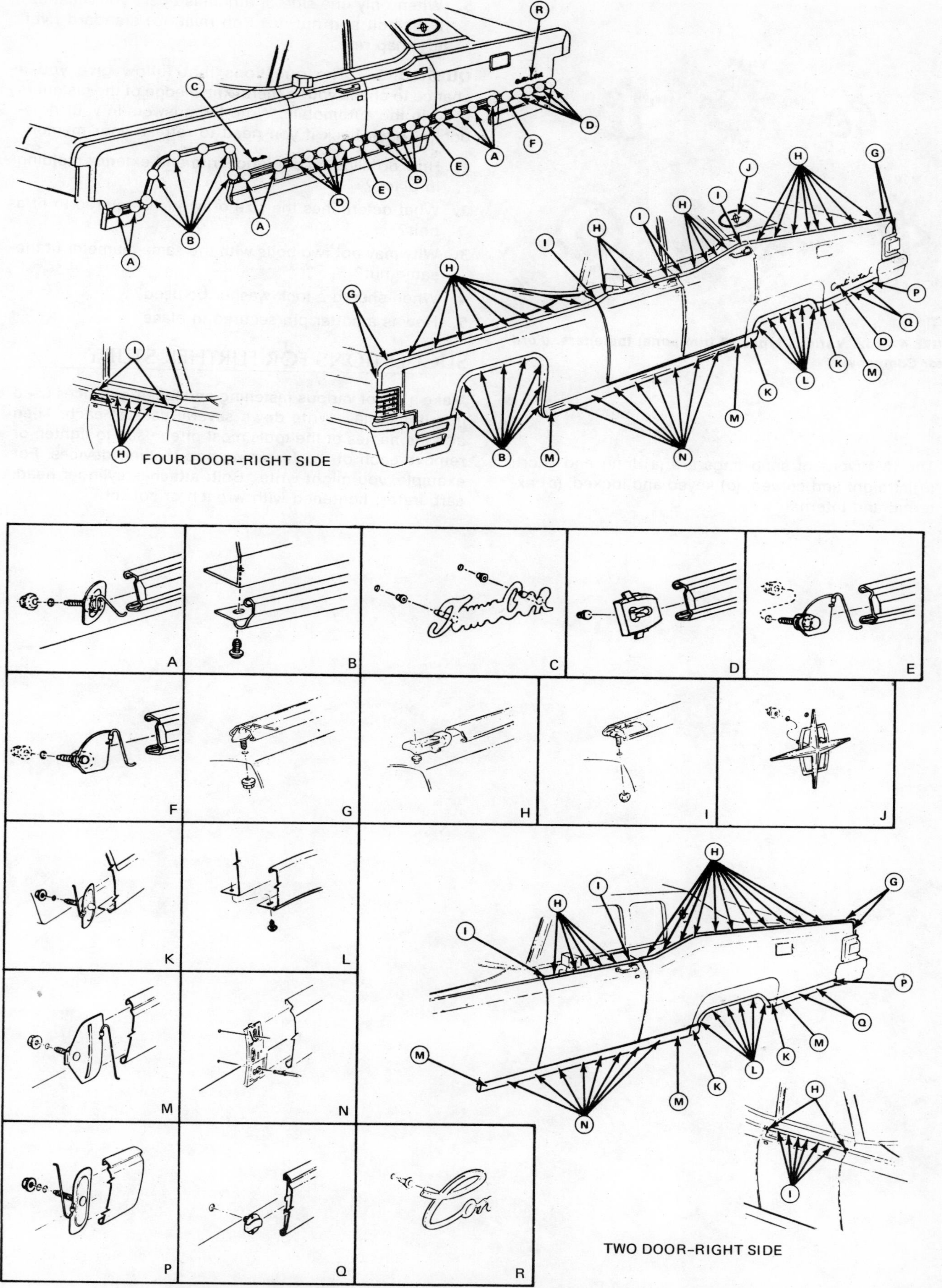

FIGURE 4–23. Moldings and clips used on one model car. (*Ford Motor Company*)

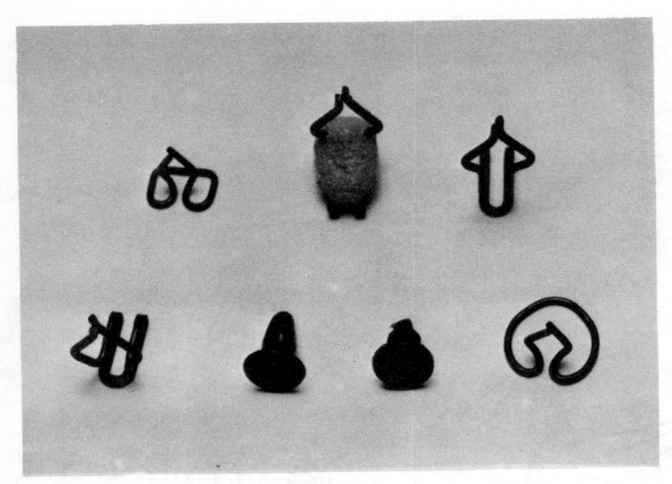

FIGURE 4–24. Various types of trim-panel fasteners. (*Ford Motor Company*)

4. The two types of snap rings are (*a*) long and short, (*b*) straight and curved, (*c*) keyed and locked, (*d*) external and internal.

5. When only one side of a hole is open, you must use a (*a*) bolt and nut, (*b*) Pop rivet, (*c*) standard rivet, (*d*) snap ring.

QUESTIONS The questions that follow give you a chance to check your general knowledge of the fasteners used in the automobile. Write the answers in your notebook. Check back if you need to refresh your memory.

1. How do clips hold interior trim and exterior molding in place?
2. What determines the size of wrench required to fit a bolt?
3. Why may not two bolts with the same diameter fit the same nut?
4. When should a lock washer be used?
5. How is a cotter pin secured in place?

SUGGESTIONS FOR FURTHER STUDY

Make a list of various fastening and locking devices used in automobiles. Write down several uses of each. Then add the names of the tools most often used to tighten or remove each of the fastening and locking devices. For example, you might write "Bolt: attaches cylinder head, carburetor; tightened with wrench or socket."

5 HAND TOOLS

The auto body technician needs a variety of hand tools. The professional body expert usually has a tool chest, as shown in Fig. 5-1, filled with the hand tools required to do the job. Although there are hundreds of tools in the chest shown, the expert knows where every one is because they are all neatly arranged in the drawers. But the body technician does not acquire these tools all at once. He or she starts out with a basic set and then gets new tools as they are required. Note that the body shop is normally equipped with such power tools as pneumatic or electric lifts, hydraulic floor lifts, and pneumatic frame and body straighteners. Power tools are discussed in a following chapter. In this chapter we look at the common hand tools used in automotive shops and then at the special hand tools used in the body shop.

○5-1 Screwdrivers

The common screwdriver is used to drive or turn screws with slotted heads. Figure 5-2A shows a typical slotted-head screwdriver. The screwdriver tip fits into the slot in the head of the screw. When the screw is turned one way, it goes into the workpiece. When it is turned the other way, it is removed from the workpiece.

Some screws have what seem to be two slots at right angles. The Phillips screw is one of these. The Reed and Prince screw is another. Each requires a special screwdriver with a tip that fits the crossed slots (Fig. 5-3). The Phillips screw is widely used on automobile trim and molding. It reduces the chances that the screwdriver will slip out of the slots and damage the finish.

Figure 4-9 shows a variety of screwheads and the special kinds of screwdrivers needed to turn them. Some of these screws do not have slotted heads at all, but have hexagonal (six-sided) heads. These "hex-head" screws require wrenches to turn them.

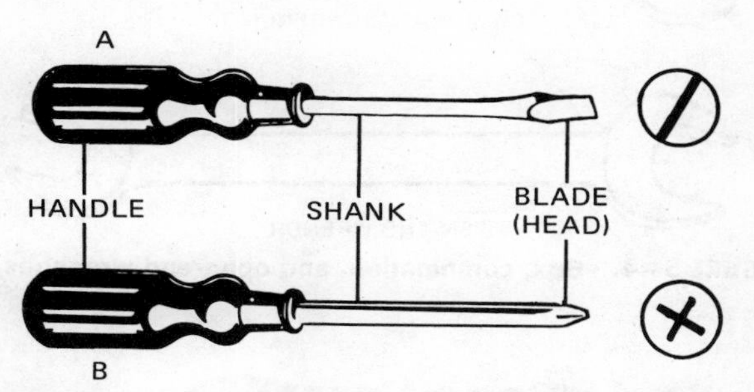

FIGURE 5-2. (A) Typical slotted-head screwdriver. (B) Phillips-head screwdriver.

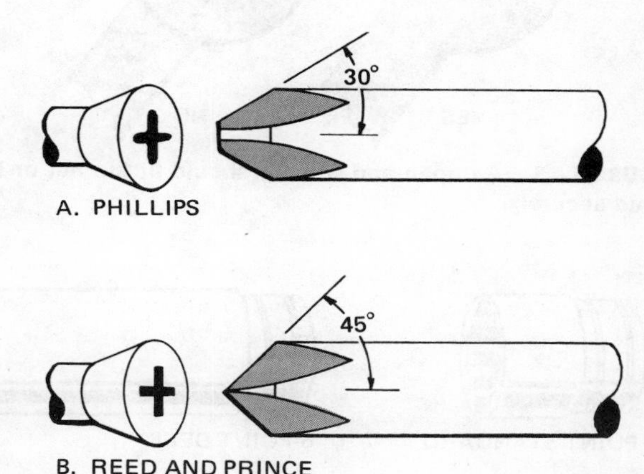

FIGURE 5-3. Difference between the Phillips and the Reed and Prince screwdrivers.

FIGURE 5-1. The professional body technician owns a large tool chest filled with the special tools of the trade.

Always be sure to pick the right screwdriver for the job. For example, when choosing a common screwdriver, make sure to pick one with a tip that properly fits the screw slot.

○5-2 Wrenches

Wrenches are used to turn screws or bolts that have hexagonal (six-sided) heads. They are also used to turn nuts that are hexagonal. Bolts with six-sided heads are called *hex-head bolts.* Nuts with six sides (hexagonal) are called *hex nuts.* A stud goes into a threaded hole, and a nut is turned down on the other end. Figure 4-1 shows you the differences among screws, bolts, and studs.

The simplest wrench to use is the open-end wrench (Fig. 5-4). Select the proper size wrench to snugly fit the bolt head or nut, as shown in Fig. 5-5. Then pull or push the wrench to turn the nut or bolt.

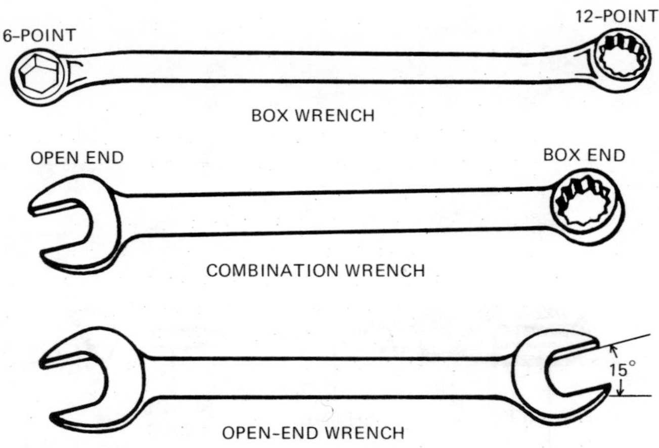
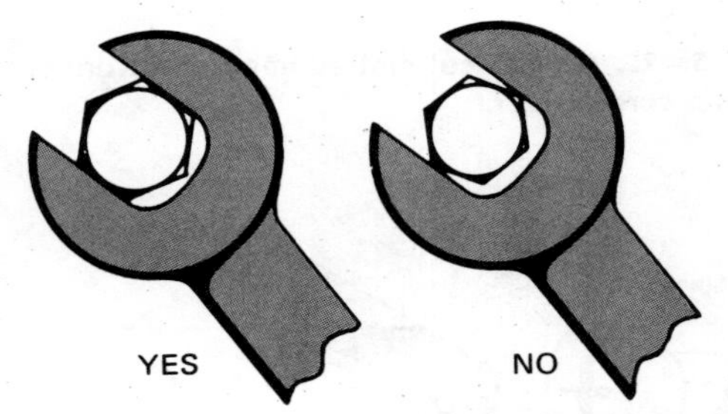

FIGURE 5–4. Box, combination, and open-end wrenches.

FIGURE 5–5. An open-end wrench should fit the nut or bolt head securely.

FIGURE 5–6. Various types of sockets.

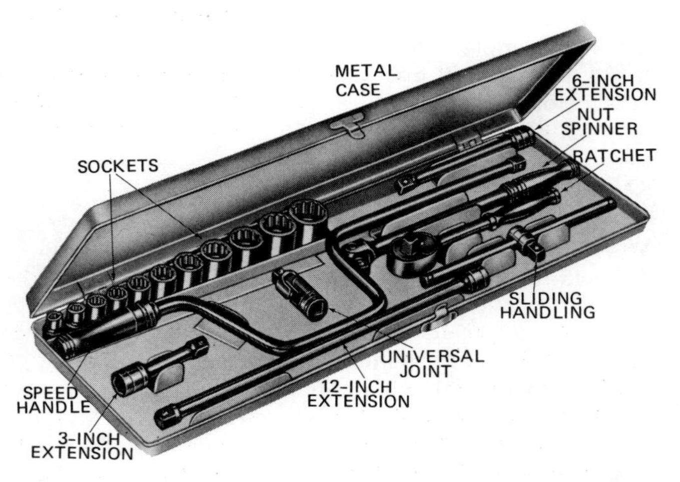

FIGURE 5–7. Set of sockets with handles, extension, and universal joint. (*Snap-on Tools Corporation*)

○5-3 Box Wrenches

The box wrench (Fig. 5-4) has an opening into which the bolt head or nut fits. The advantages of this wrench are that it will not slip off the bolt head or nut and that it can be used in restricted spaces because of the thinness of the wrench head. The typical box wrench has 12 notches in the head. Using this wrench, you can install a nut or bolt in an area where the wrench can be swung only about 15°. Figure 5-4 also shows a combination wrench that has the advantages of both the open-end and the box wrenches.

○5-4 Socket Wrenches

The socket wrench is the same as the box wrench except that the head, or socket, is detachable. Figure 5-6 shows different types of sockets. To use a socket wrench, first select a handle. There are several types of handles, as shown in Fig. 5-7. Select the socket that will fit the bolt head or nut. Next snap the socket onto the handle. Finally, place the socket over the bolt head or nut and push or pull the handle.

The ratchet handle (Fig. 5-7) has a ratcheting device that releases in one direction but catches in the other. When you want to tighten a nut, just flip the lever on the ratchet-handle head to make the ratchet catch the socket only in the tightening direction.

The speed handle (Fig. 5-7) lets you spin a nut on or off very quickly.

If you are going to work on imported cars and trucks, you will need a set of metric sockets. USCS-sized tools will not fit some nuts and bolts on imported vehicles. Study Fig. 5-8 to familiarize yourself with the difference between metric and USCS sizes of sockets.

When you work with metric nuts and bolts, remember that the bolt-head sizes are expressed in millimeters. But the drive lugs on socket drivers are measured in inches throughout the world. That is, the drive end of a socket is always made to accept ¼-inch, ⅜-inch, or ½-inch drive lugs (Fig. 5-9).

○5-5 Torque Wrenches

In automobiles nuts and bolts must be tightened properly, otherwise they will come loose and something may fall apart. This could cause great trouble, damage to the car, and possibly a serious accident. If nuts or bolts are tightened too much, they would be strained excessively and could break later, again with disastrous results.

To assure proper tightening of nuts and bolts, you must use torque wrenches. For example, a specification might call for tightening a bolt to "20–24 lb-ft." This means that you have to put a 20- to 24-pound (lb) torque (or twist) 1 foot (ft) from the bolt. The torque wrench (Fig. 5-10) lets you do this accurately. You snap the correct socket on the torque wrench, fit the socket on the bolt head, and pull the wrench handle. Watch the indicator needle on the wrench as you gradually increase your pull. When it registers somewhere between 20 and 24, you know you have tightened the bolt correctly. This procedure is called *torquing* the bolt.

SOCKET	METRIC SIZE	DECIMAL EQUIVALENT IN INCHES		USCS SIZE	SOCKET	METRIC SIZE	DECIMAL EQUIVALENT IN INCHES		USCS SIZE
	3 mm	0.118	0.125	1/8 INCH		16 mm	0.630	0.625	5/8 INCH
	4 mm	0.157	0.187	3/16 INCH		18 mm	0.709	0.687	11/16 INCH
	6 mm	0.236	0.250	1/4 INCH		19 mm	0.748	0.750	3/4 INCH
	9 mm	0.354	0.312	5/16 INCH		20 mm	0.787	0.812	13/16 INCH
	10 mm	0.394	0.375	3/8 INCH		22 mm	0.866	0.875	7/8 INCH
	12 mm	0.472	0.437	7/16 INCH		24 mm	0.945	0.937	15/16 INCH
	13 mm	0.512	0.500	1/2 INCH		25 mm	0.984	1.00	1 INCH
	15 mm	0.590	0.562	9/16 INCH					

FIGURE 5–8. Comparison of metric and USCS sizes of sockets. (*Dana Corporation*)

NOTE: Threads must be clean and in good shape. Dirty or damaged threads put a drag on the threads as the bolt is turned down, and this prevents proper tightening of the bolt. Therefore, when assembling the various components, make sure that the threads are clean and in good condition.

On some torque wrenches, the amount of torque is registered on a dial or by a pointer as the handle is pulled (Fig. 5-10). On other types of torque wrenches, the specified torque is set by turning the handle (Fig. 5-10). A loud click is heard when that torque is reached. This type of torque wrench is called a micrometer or clicker torque wrench. Figure 5-10 shows how the specified torque is preset into the micrometer torque wrench by adjusting and locking the handle. This type of torque wrench per-

FIGURE 5–9. The drive end of a socket is always made for the U.S. Customary System.

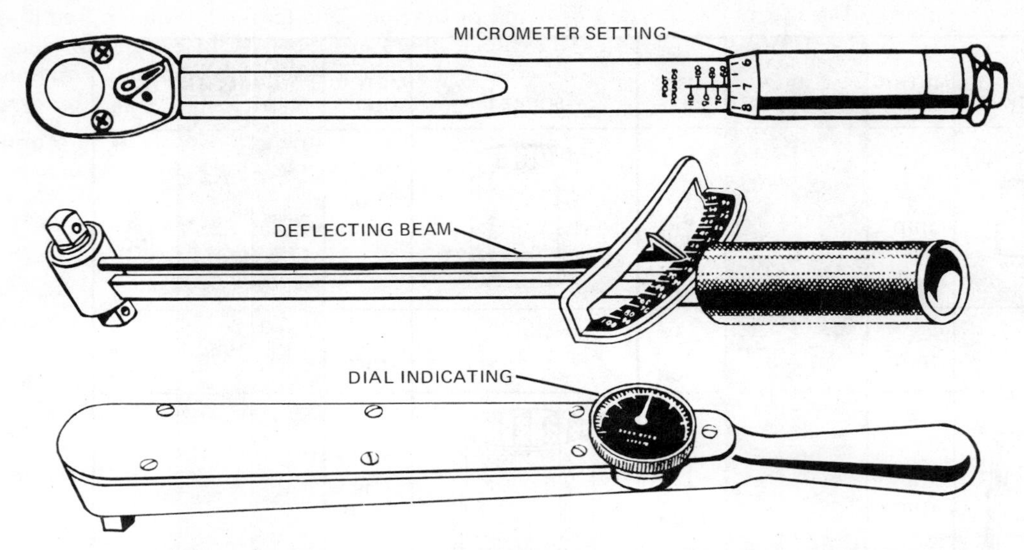

FIGURE 5–10. Various types of torque wrenches. (*General Motors Corporation*)

mits very accurate tightening of nuts and bolts.

Regardless of their type, most torque wrenches measure torque in pound-feet (lb-ft). However, some torque wrenches (mainly those used for more accurate readings on smaller nuts and bolts) measure torque in pound-inches (lb-in). Twelve pound-inches equals one pound-foot. To convert pound-feet to pound-inches, multiply the pound-feet by 12. To convert pound-inches to pound-feet, divide the pound-inches by 12 (Fig. 5-11).

$$\text{Pound-inches} = \text{pound-feet} \times 12$$

$$\text{Pound-feet} = \frac{\text{pound-inches}}{12}$$

$$\text{Pound-feet} = \frac{\text{kilogram-centimeters}}{13.8}$$

$$\text{Pound-inches} = \frac{\text{kilogram-centimeters}}{1.15}$$

$$\text{Kilogram-meters} = \text{pound-feet} \times 0.138$$

$$\text{Pound-feet} = \text{kilogram-meters} \times 7.233$$

$$\text{Kilogram-centimeters} = \text{pound-inches} \times 1.15$$

$$\text{Kilogram-centimeters} = \text{pound-feet} \times 13.8$$

FIGURE 5–11. Chart showing the formulas for converting torque specifications between the U.S. Customary System and the metric system. (*Proto Tool Company*)

In the metric system, torque wrenches are scaled in kilogram-meters (kg-m) and in kilogram-centimeters (kg-cm). To convert pound-feet to kilogram-meters, multiply the pound-feet by 0.138. To convert pound-inches to kilogram-centimeters, multiply the pound-inches by 1.15. Several torque conversion formulas are shown in Fig. 5-11.

○5-6 Pliers

Pliers (Fig. 5-12) are a special type of adjustable wrench. The jaws are adjustable because the two legs move on a pivot. Thus, pliers can be used to grip or turn an object. But pliers must not be used on nut or bolt heads. They will round off the edges of the hex and roughen the flats so that a wrench will no longer fit properly.

Some pliers have a side cutter, which can be used to cut wires. There are also regular nippers which have cutting edges instead or jaws. These are used to cut wire, thin sheet metal, small bolts, and so on.

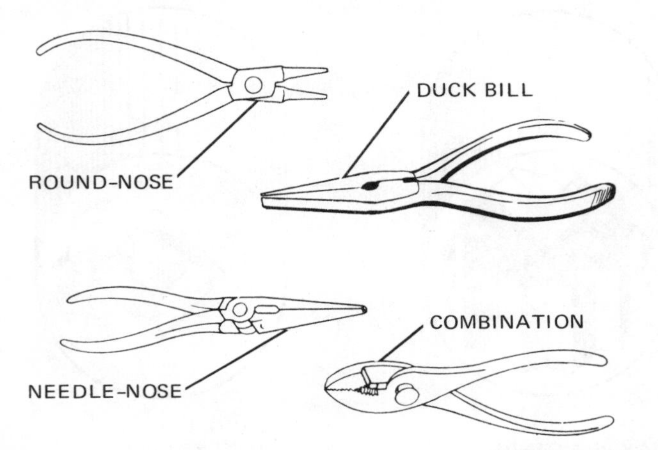

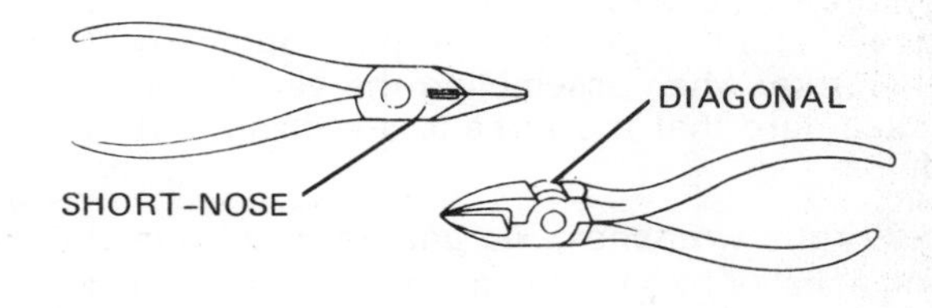

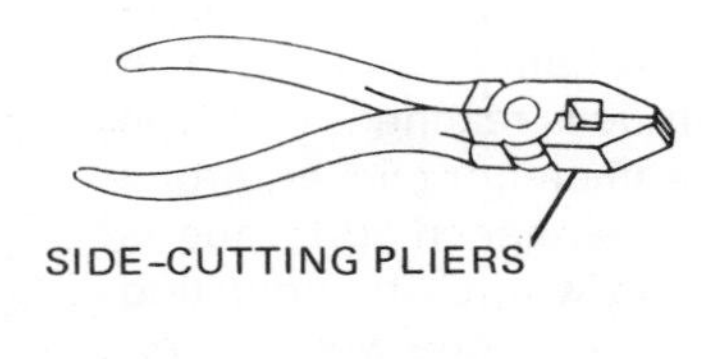

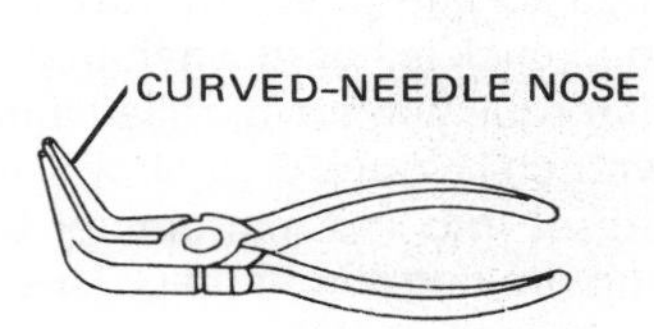

FIGURE 5–12. Various types of pliers.

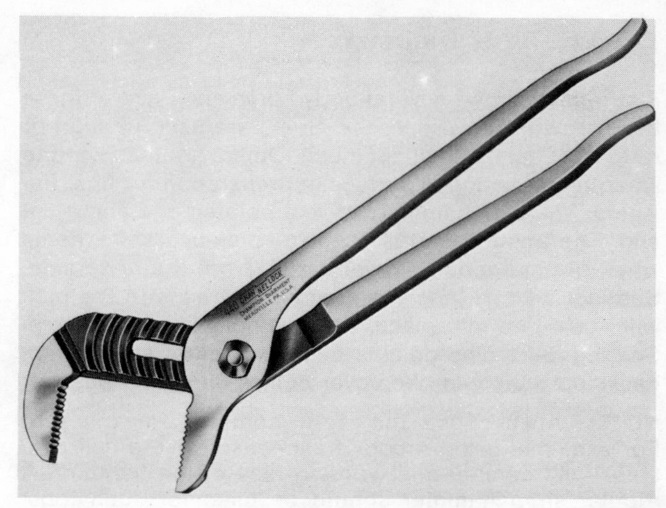

FIGURE 5–13. **Channellock pliers have grooves and lands which permit changing the distance between the gripping jaws. (*Channellock, Inc.*)**

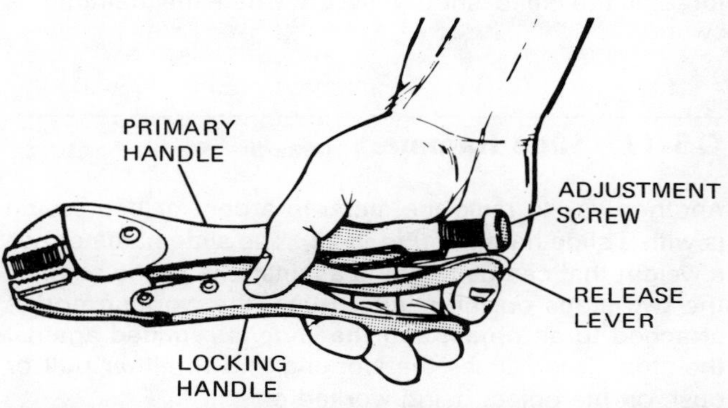

FIGURE 5–14. **Vise-Grip, or locking jaw, pliers. (*Ford Motor Company*)**

○5-7 Channellock Pliers

These pliers (Fig. 5-13) are similar to the other pliers shown in Fig. 5-12. However, they have extra-long handles which make them a very strong gripping tool. These pliers have grooves on one jaw and lands on the other. To change the amount the jaws can open, the relative positions of the grooves and lands are changed. The groove-and-land design permits the jaws to be parallel to each other at any setting. This makes the pliers less likely to slip when gripping an object.

○5-8 Vise-Grip Pliers

These pliers (Fig. 5-14) are locking-jaw pliers. That is, they can be locked onto an object. The screw at the end of the handle is used to adjust the size of the jaw opening. When the jaws are adjusted to grip an object, closing the handles will lock the jaws in place. They are released by pulling on the release lever.

A variety of locking-jaw pliers are used in the body shop. They are available in lengths from 6 to 12 inches. Some have flat jaws, as shown in Fig. 5-14. Another type has curved jaws and is used to grip pipe and other round objects. One special locking-jaw pliers has smooth jaws and is used to hold sheet-metal panels together for welding or brazing. This leaves the hands free to do the job. These pliers are also useful on an upholstery job, because they permit the cloth material to be pulled as necessary without damage.

NOTE: All pliers and other tools should be kept clean and, when not in use, returned to your toolbox or the toolroom. If properly cared for, tools will last a long time. But if they are abused, their life will be short. Take care of your tools.

○5-9 Sheet-Metal Cutters

Sheet-metal cutters are used to cut thin sheet metal of the type used for body panels and trunk lids. To cut out a damaged area of a body panel—for example, part of a fender—special panel cutters are used. Figure 5-15 shows one of these. They are thin so they can be easily worked around on the body panels needing repair.

Regular metal cutters are shown in Fig. 5-16. These are sometimes called tin snips. Metal cutters have sharp-edged jaws that produce the cutting action—just like scissors—as the jaws are moved past each other. They must be treated with care: cleaned and oiled periodically and stored in a clean, dry place. They should never be used to cut anything but sheet metal. Cutting bolts or rod stock will ruin the cutting edges.

NOTE: Generally, the professional body technician owns and uses an air-driven cutting tool that can cut out damaged sheet metal very quickly and neatly. We describe this tool in Chapter 7.

○5-10 Shop Hammers

A variety of hammers are used in the automotive shop. Figure 5-17 shows some of the more common types. The soft-face hammers, tipped with plastic or rawhide or made of brass, are used on metal that has been dented or otherwise damaged. Figure 5-18 shows the wrong and right way to use a hammer. Note that the handle should be gripped on the end and that the blow should bring the face of the hammer down flat on the surface.

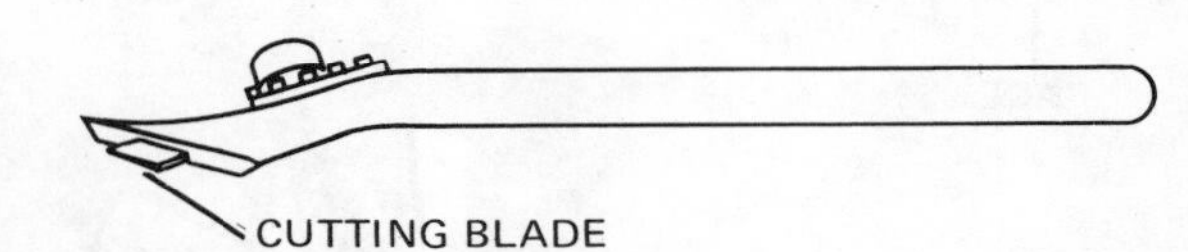

FIGURE 5–15. **Panel cutter.**

FIGURE 5–16. **Cutting sheet metal with snips.**

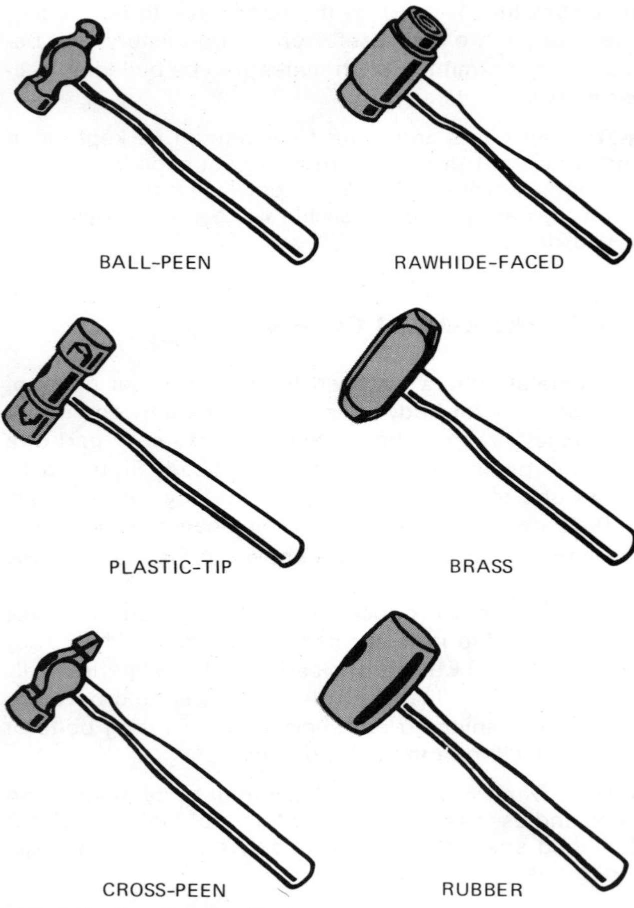

FIGURE 5-17. Types of hammers.

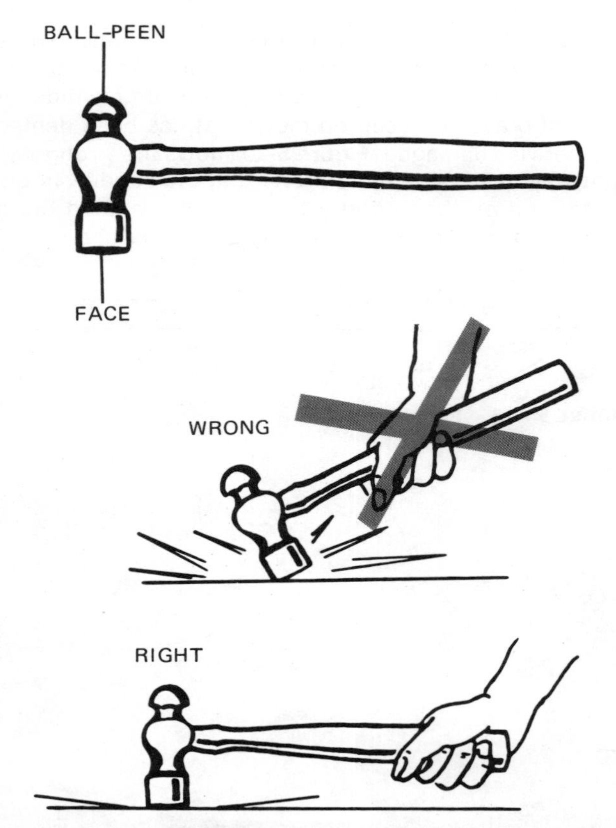

FIGURE 5-18. Ball-peen hammer, showing wrong and right way to grip and use it. (*General Motors Corporation*)

○5-11 Body Hammers

Figure 5-19 shows several body hammers. Each of these has its own special purpose. Some are used to align or rough out damaged sheet metal. Others are then used to smooth the damaged surface in preparation for final finishing. The pick hammers have a pointed end and a flat end. The pointed end is used to "pick-up" small dents when the metal can be worked on from the underside. See Fig. 5-20. Hitting the depressed area with the pick will push it up into place. Often, a dolly is used to help. See Fig. 5-21. The dolly is a solid block of steel which backs up the panel. We cover dollies on a later page.

NOTE: Always use the right hammer for the job. For example, using a body hammer to drive a nail or a chisel will damage the working face of the hammer. A regular shop hammer should be used for such jobs. Check the head of the hammer occasionally to make sure it is firmly on the handle. A wedge or screw is used to spread the handle and tighten it in the eye of the hammerhead. Make sure it is tight. Someone could be injured if the head should fly off when the hammer is swung.

○5-12 Slide Hammer

Another way to raise the metal in a dent or depression is with a slide hammer (Fig. 5-22). The slide hammer has a weight that can be rammed against one or the other of the two stops on the shaft. In use, the working end is attached to an object and the slide is rammed against the stop. This causes the working end to either pull or push on the object being worked on.

For example, let us see how a slide hammer would be used to raise a depressed area on a fender. First, holes are drilled in the depressed area (Fig. 5-22A). Then a sheet-metal screw is screwed into one of the holes. The slide hammer is then hooked onto the end of the screw, as shown. Careful operation of the slide hammer will then bring the sheet metal out into its approximate original contour. The technician moves the screw from one hole to another as necessary to do the job. Proper use of the slide hammer in this manner will get the sheet metal ready for the next steps—filing, filling, finishing, and painting.

Note that using the slide hammer as described does not require any work from the inside of the panel. It is all done from the outside. Figure 5-22A, B, C, and D show various uses of the slide hammer.

○5-13 Pull Rods

Pull rods (Fig. 5-23) are another type of tool that can be used to pull dents out. They will not work on larger dents or depressed areas as effectively as the slide hammer. To use a pull rod, a hole is drilled in the center of the dent. The hook end of the pull rod is then pushed through the hole and hooked on the back side of the sheet metal. This enables the technician to pull the dent out. Often, the technician will use a body hammer to tap lightly around the dent to help the metal spring back to its original contour.

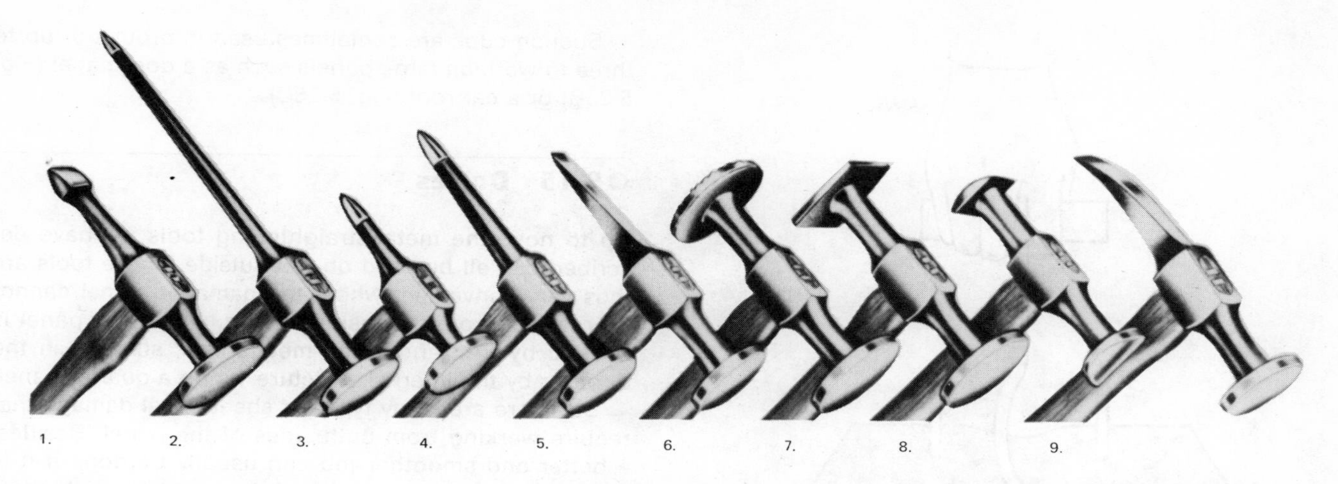

FIGURE 5–19. Body hammers.

NOTE: Some body technicians prefer not to use pull rods or slide hammers to pull out dents and do not use them unless there is no other way to work out the dents. The reason for this is that a pull rod or slide hammer is apt to leave a raised rim around each hole (Fig. 5-24). This then has to be worked down or filed off.

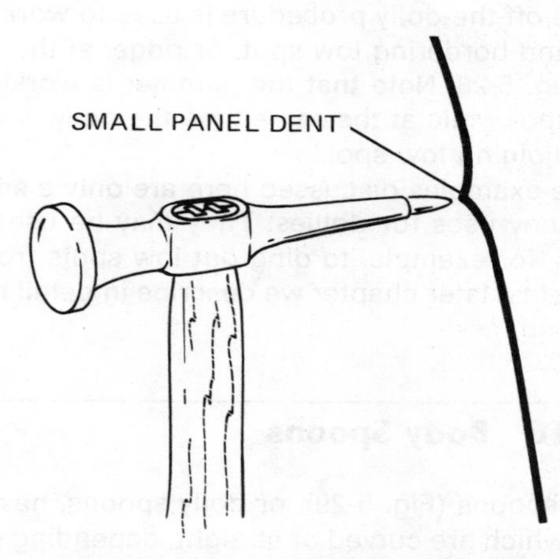

FIGURE 5–20. The pick hammer is used to pick up, or flatten, dents in sheet metal, working from the reverse side.

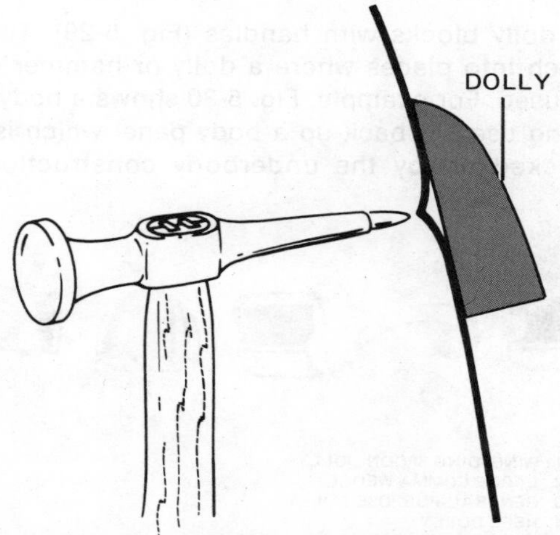

FIGURE 5–21. The dolly block is used to back up the metal when the hammer is being employed to straighten the metal.

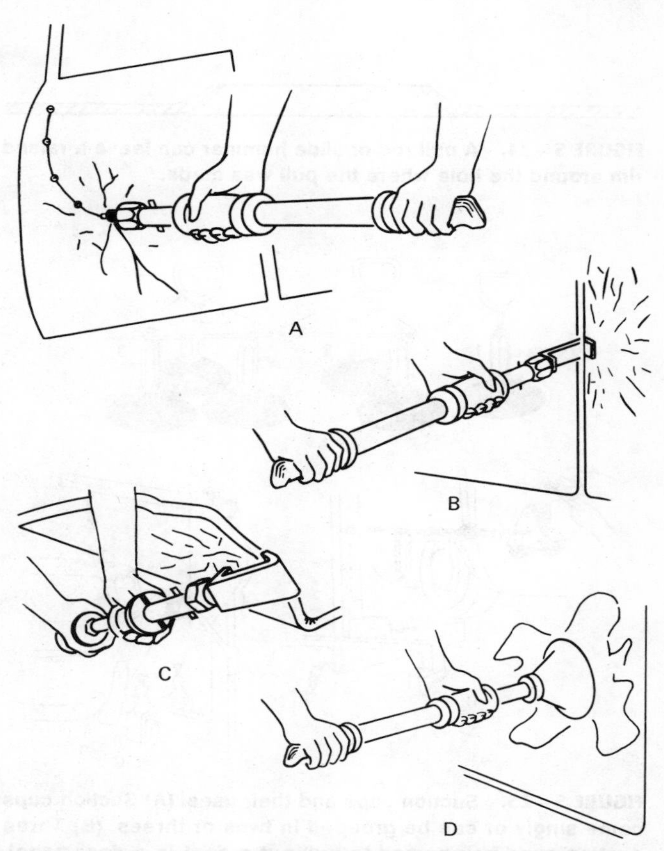

FIGURE 5–22. Using a slide hammer. In A it is being used to pull out a crease, or buckle, in a body panel. B shows it being used to pull out the edge of the panel. C shows it pulling against the edge of the fender. D shows it being used with a vacuum cup (described later) to pull out a dent in a panel. (*Guy Chart*)

○5-14 Suction Cups

The rubber suction cup (Fig. 5-25A) is another tool that can be used to pull out larger, but shallow, dents. For example, suppose a car door has been bumped so that a large area has been pushed in. If the metal has not

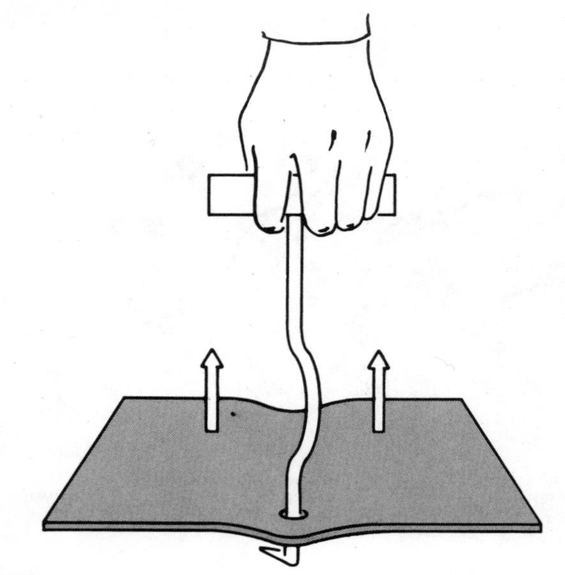

FIGURE 5–23. Using a pull rod to straighten a dent.

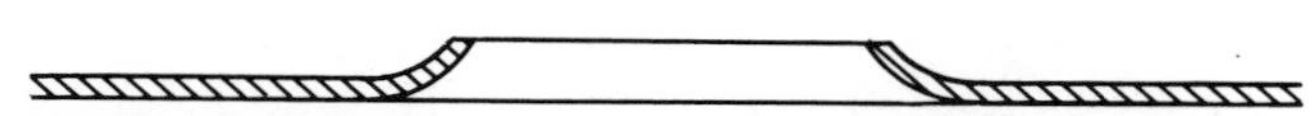

FIGURE 5–24. A pull rod or slide hammer can leave a raised rim around the hole where the pull was made.

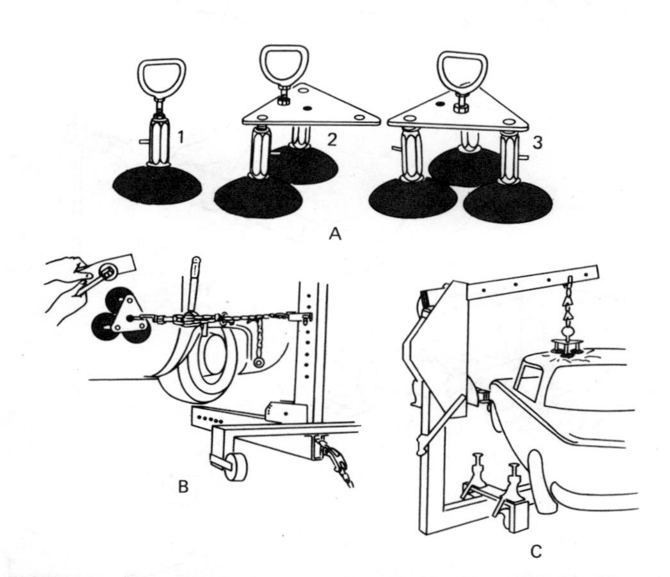

FIGURE 5–25. Suction cups and their uses. (A) Suction cups come singly or can be grouped in twos or threes. (B) Three suction cups being used to pull out a dent in a door panel. Note that the technician is tapping the area above the dent to relieve the tension in the metal. (C) Using suction cups to pull up on a dent in a car roof. (*Guy Chart*)

been actually buckled (the metal upset), a suction cup can often be used to pull the metal out to its original contour. Figure 5-22D shows how this is done, using a slide hammer. The panel must be clean and wet. The cup should also be wet. It is pushed in at the center of the depression so that the air is expelled from the cup. The vacuum will then hold the cup against the panel. Now the cup can be pulled out, and if the operation is successful, the panel will snap back to its original contour.

Suction cups are sometimes used in groups of up to three to work on large panels such as a door panel (Fig. 5-25B) or a car roof (Fig. 5-25C).

○5-15 Dollies

Up to now, the metal-straightening tools we have described can all be used on the outside. These tools are thus very convenient where the damaged panel cannot be reached from the inside, that is, where the panel is backed by trim and some mechanism, such as in the door, or by the internal structure, as on a quarter panel.

But there are many types of sheet-metal damage that require working from both sides of the panel. Besides, a better and smoother job can usually be done if it is possible to get a hand back of the panel. In such case, a dolly is used. Figure 5-26 shows several dollies.

The dolly is held in one hand either directly under the dent or off to one side. A body hammer is used to hammer against the other side of the sheet metal. There are two procedures called hammering *off the dolly* and hammering *on the dolly.* The general name for the procedure is called *dinging.*

For example, Fig. 5-27 shows a dolly and body hammer being used to work out a small dent in sheet metal by the on-the-dolly process. The dolly provides the backing needed to counter the hammer blows.

The off-the-dolly procedure is used to work out a high spot and bordering low spot, or ridge, at the same time. See Fig. 5-28. Note that the hammer is working down a high spot while at the same time the dolly is working up the adjoining low spot.

The examples discussed here are only a small part of the many uses for dollies. They may be used by themselves, for example, to ding out low spots from inside a panel. In a later chapter we describe in detail how dollies are used.

○5-16 Body Spoons

Body spoons (Fig. 5-29), or dolly spoons, have flattened ends which are curved or straight, depending on the purpose of the spoon. There are three general types, varying considerably in their size and shape. Here is how body spoons are used:

1. As dolly blocks with handles (Fig. 5-29). They can reach into places where a dolly or hammer cannot be used. For example, Fig. 5-30 shows a body spoon being used to back up a body panel which is partly blocked off by the underbody construction. The

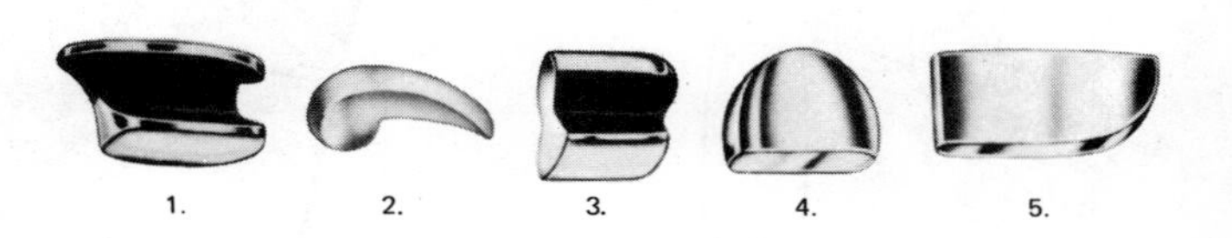

1. WING-DING SPOON DOLLY
2. LARGE COMMA WEDGE
3. GENERAL-PURPOSE DOLLY
4. HEEL DOLLY
5. TOE DOLLY

FIGURE 5–26. Dollies.

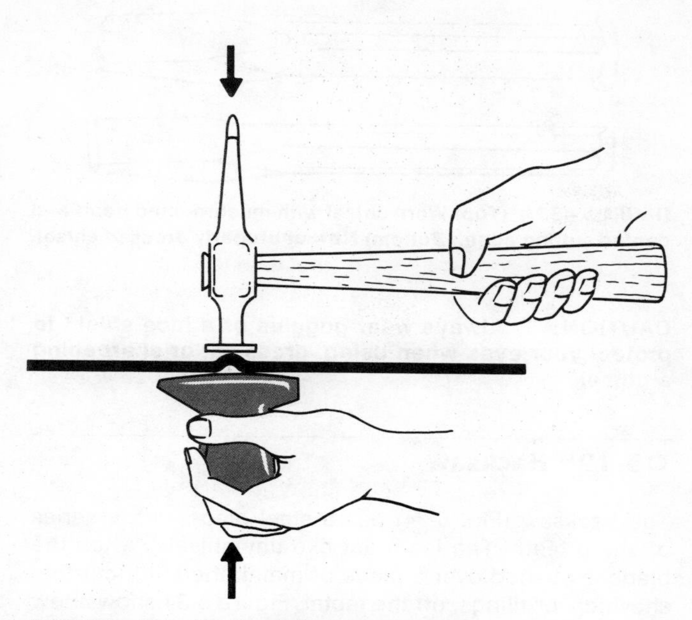

FIGURE 5–27. On-the-dolly hammering.

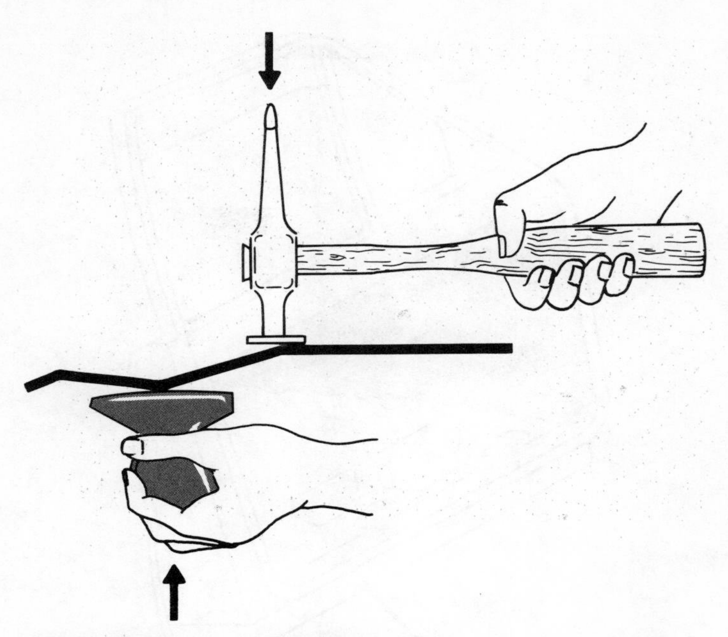

FIGURE 5–28. Off-the-dolly hammering.

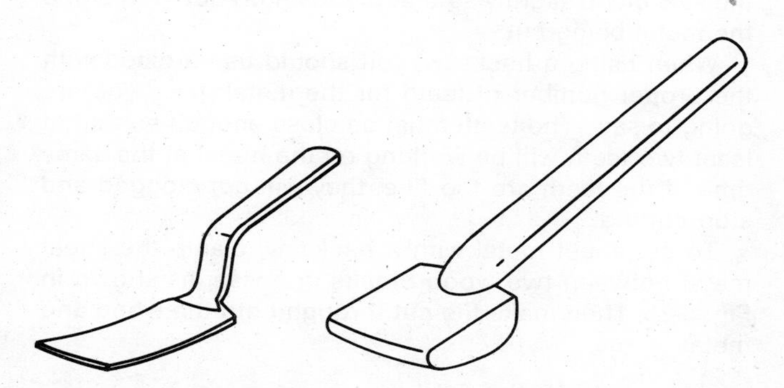

FIGURE 5–29. Two of the many shapes of body spoons. (*Snap-on Tools Corporation*)

spoon here acts as a dolly with the hammering being on-the-dolly.

2. To spread the blows of the hammer over a large area. For this purpose a flat body spoon can be laid down along a ridge. Hammering is done on top of the spoon to work the ridge down.
3. As a heavy-duty prying or driving tool. That is, the spoon itself is used to pry or drive against low spots to work them out. For example, this type of tool might be used to separate an outer panel from the inner construction when the two have been crushed together. We describe various uses of spoons in later chapters.

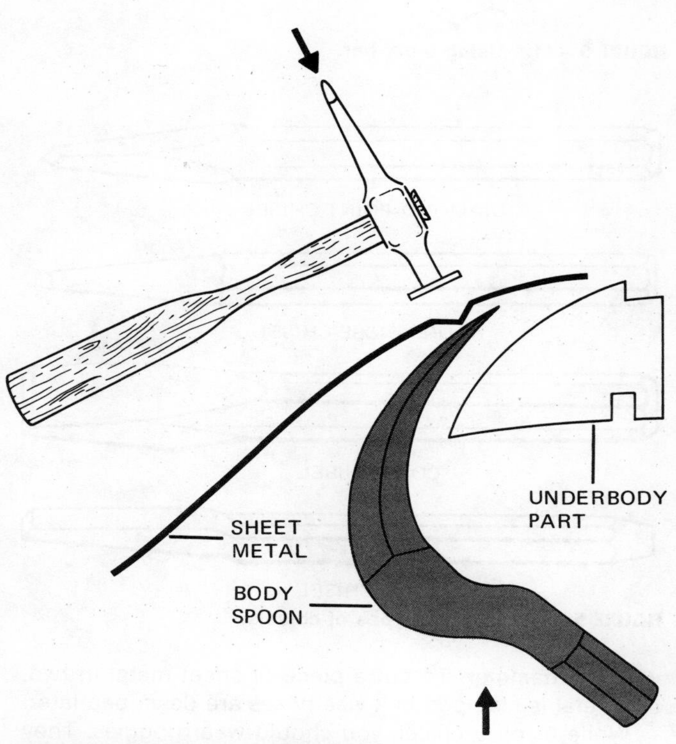

FIGURE 5–30. Using a dolly spoon.

If this operation is a success, the low spot can be taken care of without removing the door trim and internal mechanism.

○5-17 Pry Bars

Pry bars (Fig. 5-31) are available in various sizes and shapes. They are used to pry against low spots that are inaccessible unless other parts are removed. For example, Fig. 5-31 shows a pry bar being used to work out a low spot in a door panel. Note that the pry bar has been inserted through a drain hole in the bottom of the door.

○5-18 Chisels

The chisel has a single cutting edge and is driven with a hammer to cut metal. Figure 5-32 shows different kinds of chisels. You hold the chisel in your left hand and the hammer in your right hand. (Of course, if you are left-handed, you hold the chisel in your right hand and the hammer in your left hand.) Strike the end of the chisel

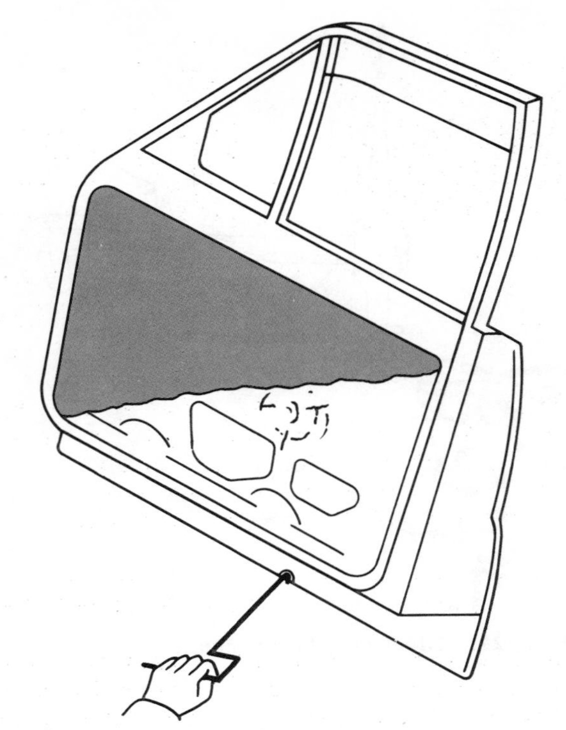

FIGURE 5–31. Using a pry bar.

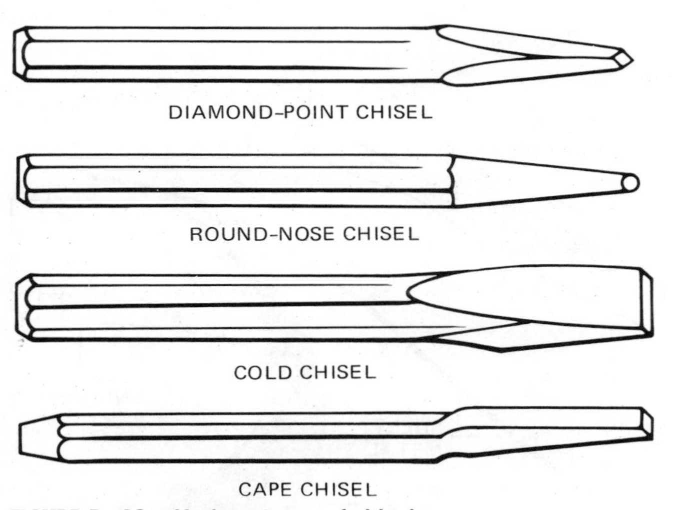

FIGURE 5–32. Various types of chisels.

with the hammer. To cut a piece of sheet metal in two, the metal is clamped in a vise. Vises are described later.

While using a chisel, you should wear goggles. They protect the eyes from flying chips that could put out an unprotected eye.

After a chisel has been used for a while, the cutting edge gets dull and the head tends to mushroom (Fig. 5-33). The mushroom must be ground off on a grinding wheel, as discussed in a later chapter. Grinding off the mushroom from the head of the chisel protects you from getting hurt. The turned-over metal could break off when the head is struck, and a piece of it could fly into your hand and cut you. Figure 5-33 also shows how the chisel should look after it is ground.

NOTE: The professional auto body technician uses an air-operated chisel or cutter to cut out damaged sheet metal in preparation for a patch or replacement job. These tools are discussed in Chapter 7.

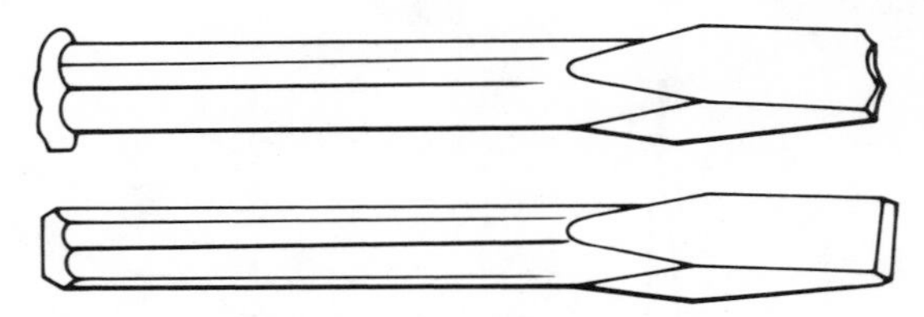

FIGURE 5–33. (Top) Worn chisel with mushroomed head and dented cutting edge. (Bottom) New or properly dressed chisel.

CAUTION: Always wear goggles or a face shield to protect your eyes when using, dressing, or sharpening a chisel.

○5-19 Hacksaw

The hacksaw (Fig. 5-34) has a steel blade with a series of sharp teeth. The teeth act like tiny chisels. When the blade is pushed over a piece of metal, the teeth cut fine shavings, or filings, off the metal. Figure 5-34 shows how to hold and use a hacksaw. Each forward stroke should be full and steady and not jerky. On the back stroke, lift the saw blade slightly so that the teeth do not drag along the metal being cut.

When using a hacksaw, you should use a blade with the proper number of teeth for the metal piece you are going to saw. The teeth must be close enough so that at least two teeth will be working on the metal at the same time. If the teeth are too fine, they will get clogged and stop cutting.

To cut sheet metal with a hacksaw, clamp the sheet metal between two wood blocks in a vise, as shown in Fig. 5-35. Then make the cut through both the wood and metal.

○5-20 Files

The regular shop file (Fig. 5-36) is a cutting tool with a large number of cutting edges, or teeth, each like a tiny chisel. There are many types and shapes of files. The flat file is the most common. Files range in coarseness, or size of individual teeth, from "rough" or "coarse-cut," through "bastard" and "second-cut," to "smooth" or "dead-smooth." See Fig. 5-37.

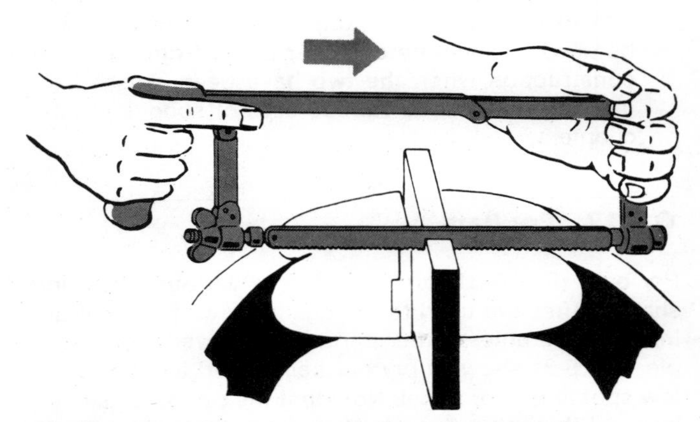

FIGURE 5–34. How to hold and use a hacksaw.

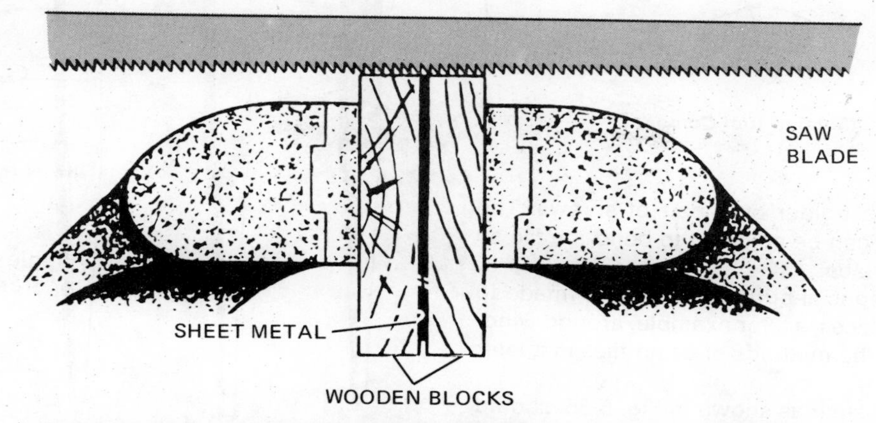

FIGURE 5–35. To cut sheet metal with a hacksaw, clamp the sheet metal between two wood blocks in a vise. Saw through both wood and metal.

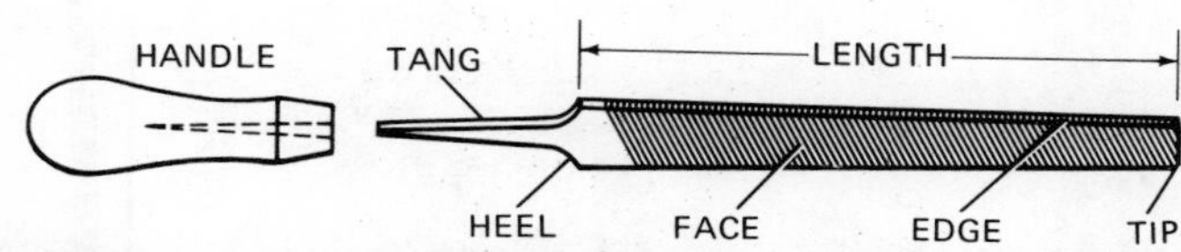

FIGURE 5–36. Typical file and handle, with the parts named. (*General Motors Corporation*)

Files also can be single-cut and double-cut. The single-cut file has a series of teeth, like knife blades, that are parallel to one another. The double-cut file has two sets of cuts on the face of the file that are at an angle to each other. The teeth on the double-cut file are pointed.

To use a file, strokes should be steady and the right amount of pressure should be used. Excessive pressure will clog the file teeth, and it could break the file. Insufficient pressure will not cut the metal, and it can cause the file to chatter or vibrate.

○5-21 Body Files

Body files are usually single-cut and come in a variety of sizes and shapes (straight, curved, round). The most common body file is used to semifinish a damaged area of sheet metal. The teeth are curved, as shown in Fig. 5-38. This allows better cutting and also easier cleaning of the teeth. Note that the file cuts in one direction only.

File holders are of two types: fixed and adjustable. The fixed holder (Fig. 5-38) is usually made of wood. It has a pair of holes that match the holes in the file. The

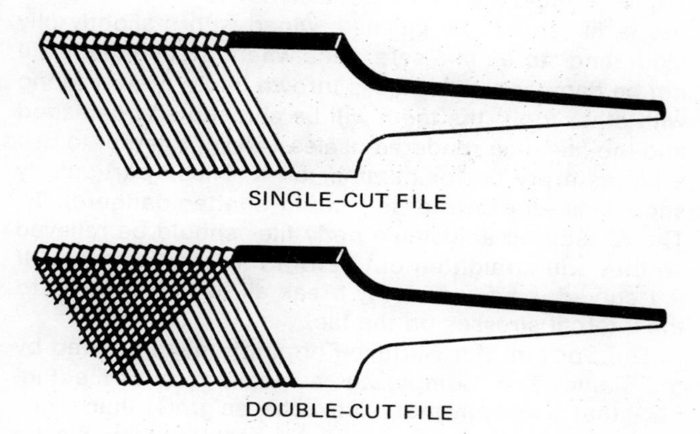

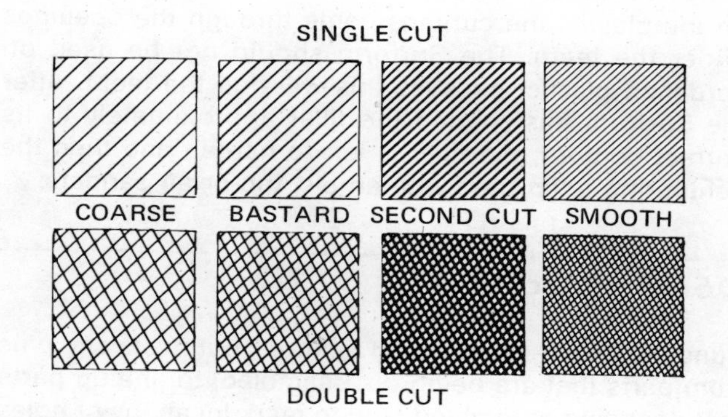

FIGURE 5–37. Types of files and file cuts.

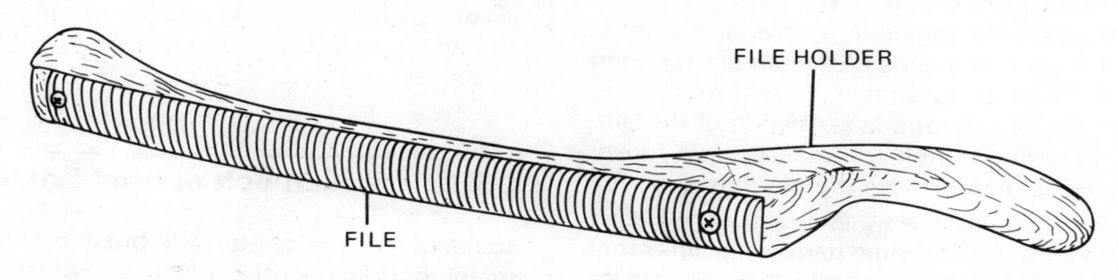

FIGURE 5–38. Body file in a wood holder.

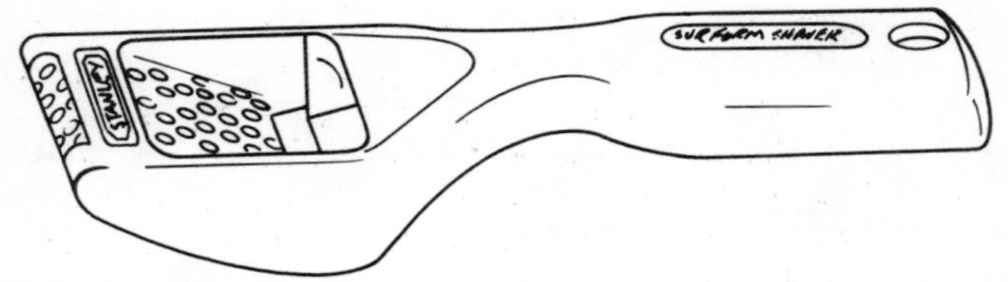

FIGURE 5–39. **Surform.** (*Stanley Tool Company*)

file is attached to the holder by a pair of screws. The adjustable file holder can be adjusted to bend the file so it will fit a curved surface.

There are several special-purpose body files, made to fit and work in tight places, as, for example, around windshields. We describe the methods of using files in a later chapter.

Regular shop files, such as shown in Fig. 5-36, should be used with a handle, as shown. The handle is tightened on the file tang by tapping the end of the handle on the bench.

Files should always be treated with care. When not in use, a file should be cleaned, wiped with a slightly oily cloth, and stored in a safe place where the file teeth will not be damaged. If the file is thrown into a drawer along with other tools, the teeth will be chipped and damaged and the file soon rendered useless. Never attempt to use a file as a pry bar or hammer on it. Files—particularly shop files—are brittle and could shatter dangerously. The tension on adjustable body files should be relieved so they will straighten out before they are put away. If left curved, a body file may break all by itself, owing to the internal stresses on the file.

The Surform (for Surface Forming), manufactured by the Stanley Tool Company, is a special form of file (Fig. 5-39) that is actually more like a cheese grater than a file. It has a series of open teeth, and is used to shape plastic body filler while the body filler is still soft. When it is used on the plastic, the cuttings come through the openings under the teeth. The Surform should not be used on hardened plastic, because this will dull the teeth. After the Surform has shaped the filler approximately to its correct contour, the filler is left to harden and then the contouring is finished with an electric or air sanders.

○5-22 Punches

Punches (Fig. 5-40) are used to knock out rivets and pins from parts that are being disassembled, to line up parts that are being assembled, and to mark locations of holes to be drilled. Let's take a look at the different kinds of punches and how they are used for these jobs.

1. Knocking out rivets and pins. A starting punch and a pin punch are used to knock out rivets and pins. Some parts are held together by rivets and pins. When a pin is used, the ends of the pin are rounded off, or peened over, by a hammer. To remove the pin, first file off one of the rounded-off ends of the pin. Next, use a starting punch to break the pin loose. Then use a pin punch to drive the pin out.
2. Lining up machine parts. An aligning punch is used to line up, or align, parts. Some parts have holes that must align when the parts are assembled. To ensure proper alignment, place the aligning punch through each hole in each part. Then it will be easy to install a bolt or screw through the holes.

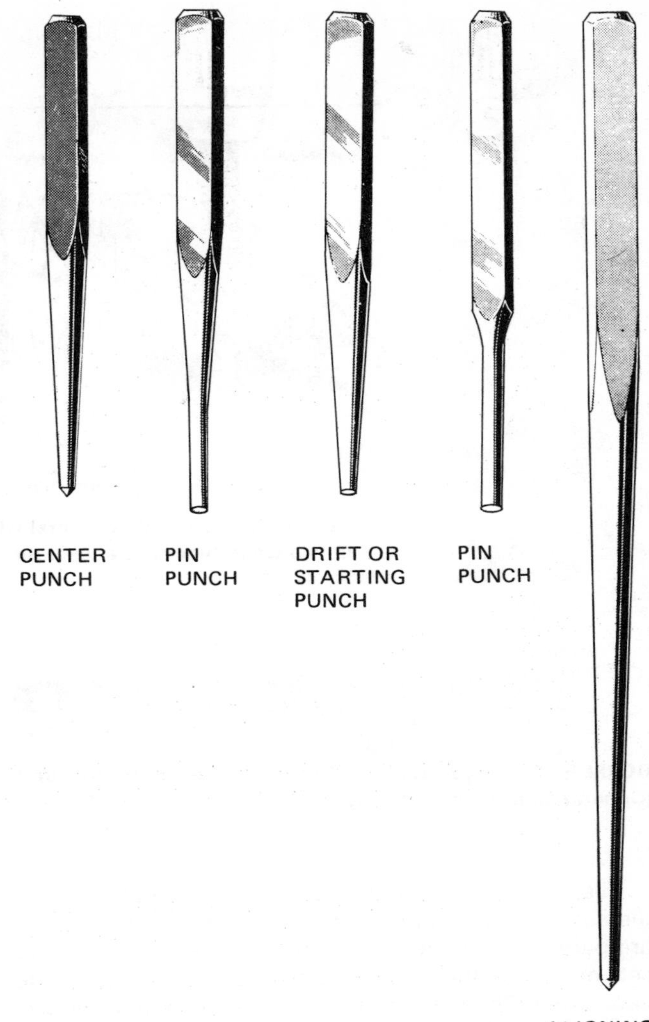

FIGURE 5–40. **Various kinds of punches.** (*General Motors Corporation*)

3. Marking locations of holes to be drilled. A center punch is used to mark locations of holes to be drilled. Marking the location of the hole gives the drill a place to start. This prevents it from wandering on the surface of the workpiece (Fig. 5-41).
4. Marking parts before disassembly. The center punch is also used for this purpose so that the parts can be put back together correctly. For example, suppose a cover plate could be put back on a housing in two positions, one right and one wrong. Before taking the cover plate off, put punch marks next to each other on the housing and the cover plate. Now there can be no question about which way the parts are to be reassembled.

○5-23 Broken Bolt or Stud Extractor

Sometimes a bolt or stud will break off and you have to get the bottom part out. If this part is rusted in, put some penetrating oil around the bolt and leave it in for a while.

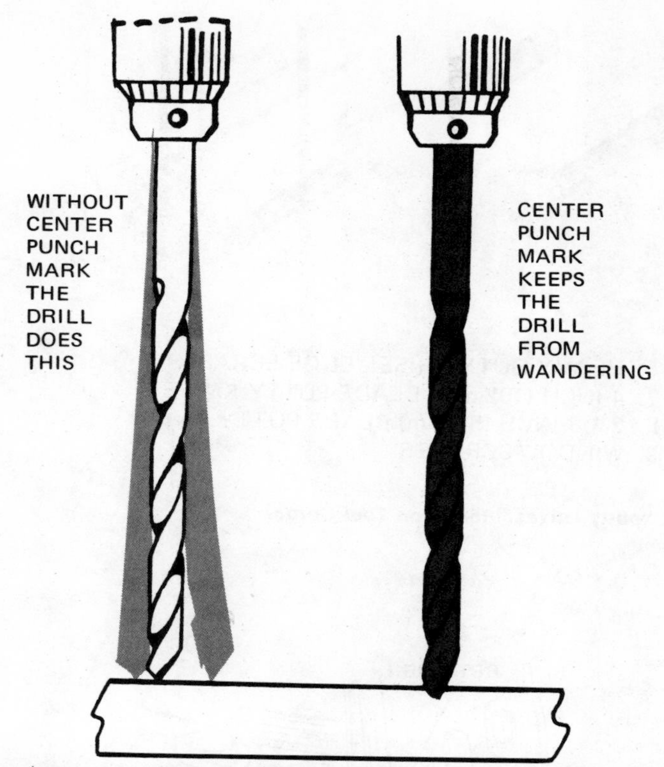
WITHOUT
CENTER
PUNCH
MARK
THE
DRILL
DOES
THIS
CENTER
PUNCH
MARK
KEEPS
THE
DRILL
FROM
WANDERING

FIGURE 5–41. **How center-punching a hole location keeps the drill from wandering. (*General Motors Corporation*)**

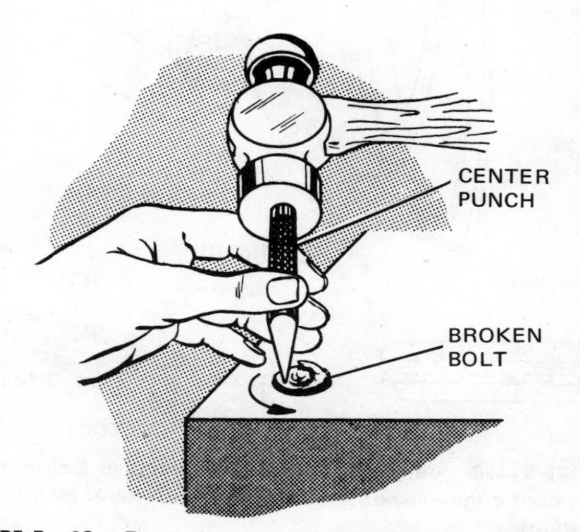
CENTER
PUNCH
BROKEN
BOLT

FIGURE 5–42. **Removing a broken bolt with a center punch.**

Then you may be able to remove the bolt with a center punch, as shown in Fig. 5-42. If this doesn't work, drill a hole down through the center of the broken bolt, as shown in Fig. 5-43. Then drive a stud extractor of the right size down into this hole. Next, use a wrench to turn the stud extractor, as shown in Fig. 5-43 to back the bolt out.

○5-24 Tape Measure

A tape measure, or steel tape (Fig. 5-44), is often required in the body shop. It is needed to make measurements when aligning body or frame parts and cutting sheet metal for patching damaged panels.

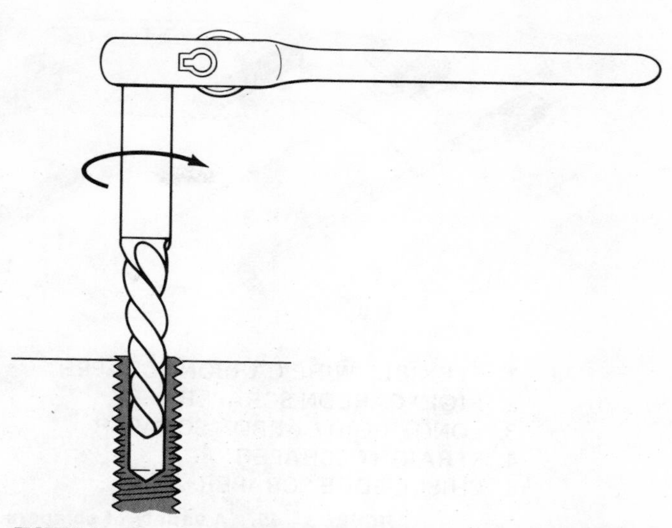

FIGURE 5–43. **Using a stud extractor to remove a broken bolt. (*General Motors Corporation*)**

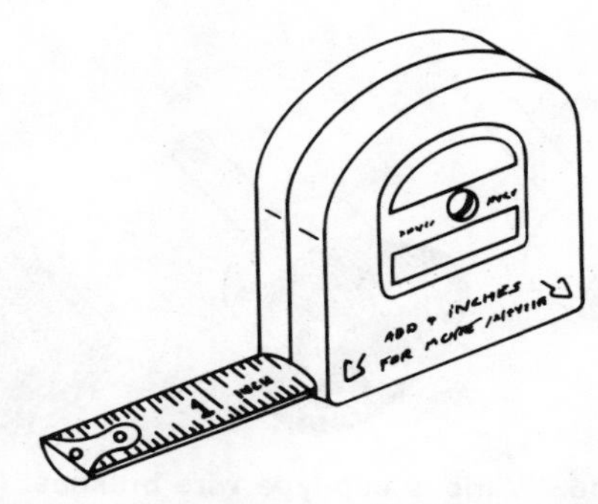

FIGURE 5–44. **A tape measure is used for checking frame dimensions and making other measurements.**

○5-25 Scrapers

Scrapers (Fig. 5-45) are used in the body shop for such jobs as scraping off paint, undercoating, applying plastic filler, and caulking. A variety of scrapers are used by the body technician.

○5-26 Brushes

Brushes are needed in the body shop to remove rust and old paint. The type of brush required depends on the job to be done. To remove dirt, for example, use a bristle brush. On rust, use a stiff wire brush.

Some wire brushes are made to be used with an air or electric drill. Figure 5-46 shows a cup-type wire brush for cleaning off rust spots and paint in depressions which are to be filled with body solder or plastic filler. Wear goggles when using wire brushes in drills. These brushes can throw off particles at high speed, and such particles could injure your eyes.

○5-27 Trim-Panel Tool

This tool (Fig. 5-47) is used to remove upholstery trim panels (also called trim pads) from the insides of doors and quarter panels. The tool is slipped under the trim at

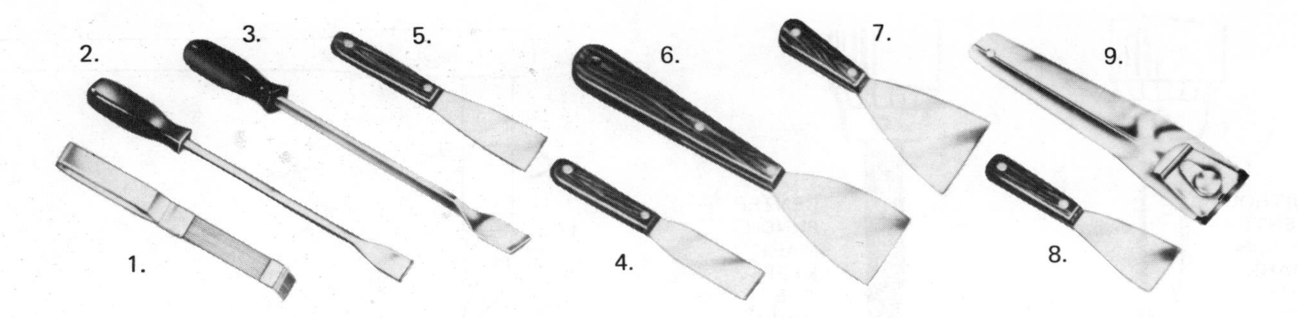

1. FLEXIBLE WIRE CARBON SCRAPER
2. RIGID CARBON SCRAPER
3. LONG, RIGID CARBON SCRAPER
4. STRAIGHT SCRAPER
5. CHISEL-EDGE SCRAPER
6. HEAVY-DUTY CHISEL-EDGE SCRAPER
7. 4-INCH (102-mm) BLADE PUTTY KNIFE
8. 2 1/8-INCH (54-mm) BLADE PUTTY KNIFE
9. WINDOW SCRAPER

FIGURE 5–45. A variety of scrapers and "putty knives." (*Snap-on Tool Corporation*)

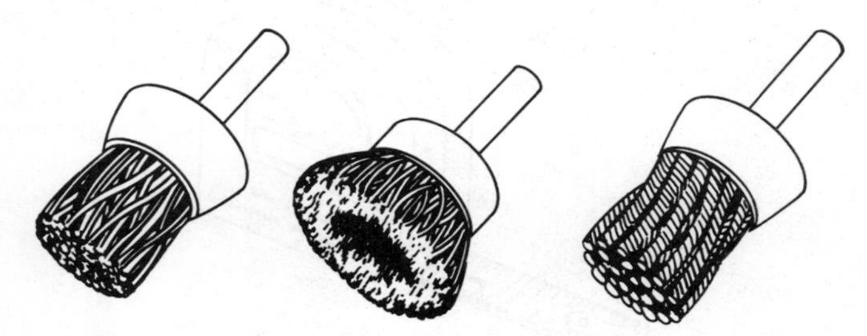

FIGURE 5–46. Various cup-type wire brushes. (*Ford Motor Company*)

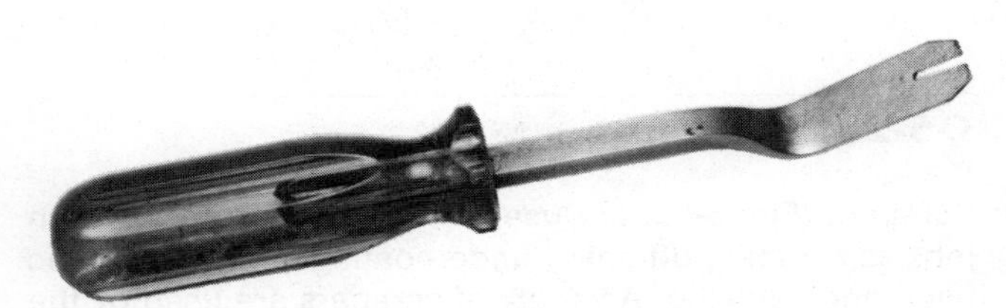

FIGURE 5–47. Panel trim tool.

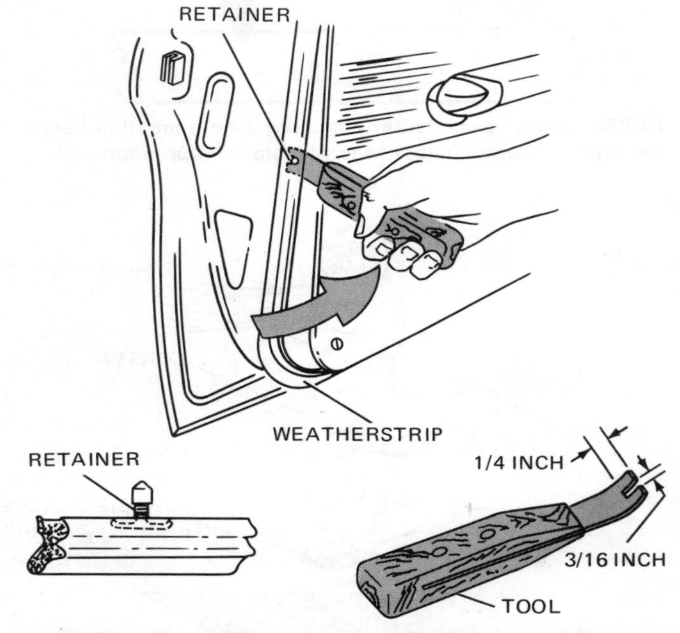

FIGURE 5–48. Using a special tool to remove weatherstrip from door edge. (*Fisher Body Division of General Motors Corporation*)

the points where it is attached, and the trim panel is then pried loose from the door. Properly done, the trim panel will come off with no damage.

○5-28 Door Weatherstrip Tool

This tool (Fig. 5-48) is used to disengage the door weatherstrip from the fasteners which are hidden under the trim assembly.

○5-29 Masking Stand

Just before the car is rolled into the paint shop for painting, all parts that should not be painted are masked. That is, they are covered with masking tape and paper. A handy portable masking stand, such as shown in Fig. 5-49, makes this job easier and more quickly completed. The masking stand is on wheels so it can be moved to the place where it is needed. Note that the masking tape and paper are dispensed together, with the tape attached to the edge of the paper.

○5-30 Vise

The bench vise (Fig. 5-50) is used to hold objects that are being worked on. When the handle is turned, a screw in the base of the vise moves the movable jaw toward or away from the stationary jaw. To protect objects that could be easily marred, "soft jaws" are put on the vise, as shown. These are caps made of a soft metal such as copper. They are less likely to scratch or dent the object being gripped.

FIGURE 5–49. Masking-tape dispenser, or masking stand. *(3M Company)*

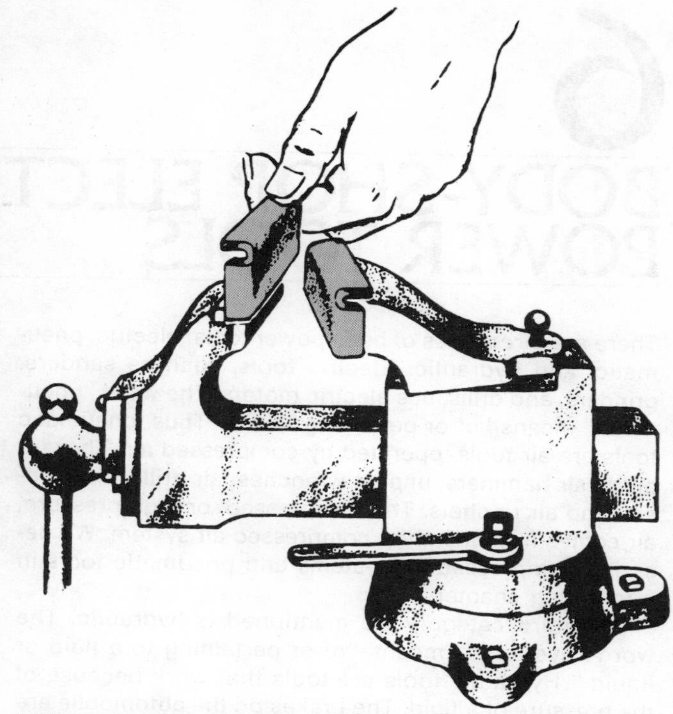

FIGURE 5–50. Bench vise, showing soft jaws being installed on the vise jaws.

CHAPTER 5 CHECKUP

NOTE: Since this is a chapter review test, you should review the chapter before taking the test.

In this chapter, we have studied about hand tools. For the body technician, these include the hand-powered cutting tools such as chisels and files. These are very important tools in body repair. You must know when and how to use each one properly. Before you start any repair work, you should have a good understanding of what each tool will help you to do.

The checkup that follows tests your understanding of hand tools discussed in the chapter you have just finished. If you have any trouble answering the questions, read the chapter again.

COMPLETING THE SENTENCES The sentences below are incomplete. After each sentence there are several words or phrases, but only one of them correctly completes the sentence. Write each sentence in your notebook, ending it with the one word or phrase that completes it correctly.

1. Hand tools include screwdrivers, wrenches, sockets, and (*a*) bench vise, (*b*) welders, (*c*) electric drills, (*d*) pliers.
2. To tighten nuts to specifications, you should use a (*a*) screwdriver, (*b*) torque wrench, (*c*) open-end wrench, (*d*) Channellock pliers.
3. A slide hammer can be used to (*a*) lower metal, (*b*) raise metal, (*c*) cut metal, (*d*) weld metal.
4. A dolly is used with a (*a*) file, (*b*) punch, (*c*) chisel, (*d*) body hammer.
5. A tool with a flattened end that is curved or straight is called a (*a*) body spoon, (*b*) body hammer, (*c*) body file, (*d*) body putty.

Purpose and Operation of Tools In the following, you are asked to write the purpose of certain tools and to describe their operation. If you have any difficulty in writing your explanations, turn back to the chapter and reread the pages that will give you the answer. Don't copy from the book. Try to answer the question in your own words. This is an excellent way to fix the explanation firmly in your mind. Write each question and then your answer to it in your notebook.

1. What is the purpose of the combination wrench?
2. Describe how to use the ratchet handle in a socket set.
3. When is a torque wrench used?
4. What is the purpose of body hammers?
5. Describe how to use suction cups.
6. What is the purpose of a dolly?
7. Describe three ways to use body spoons.
8. What is the purpose of a body file?
9. Describe four ways to use punches.
10. Describe how to use a stud extractor.

SUGGESTIONS FOR FURTHER STUDY

Make a list of the various tools contained in the set of basic hand tools with which you will be working. Opposite the list of tools, write down the major use you will have for each tool.

6
BODY-SHOP ELECTRIC POWER TOOLS

There are three types of body power tools: electric, pneumatic, and hydraulic. Electric tools, such as sanders, grinders, and drills, use electric motors. The word "pneumatic" means "of or pertaining to air." Thus, pneumatic tools are air tools, operated by compressed air. They include air hammers, impact wrenches, air drills, air sanders, and air ratchets. The compressed, or high-pressure, air comes from the shop compressed-air system. We describe compressed-air systems and pneumatic tools in a following chapter.

The third category we mentioned is hydraulic. The word "hydraulic" means "of or pertaining to a fluid or liquid." Hydraulic tools are tools that work because of the pressure of a fluid. The brakes on the automobile are hydraulic. Operation of the brake pedal sends brake fluid at high pressure to the wheel-brake mechanisms, causing the brakes to apply. The hydraulic tools used in the body shop include car lifts, power jacks, and body-panel and -frame straighteners. They are powered either by a hand pump, by a pump driven by an electric motor, or by an air-driven pump. We discuss hydraulic tools in a later chapter.

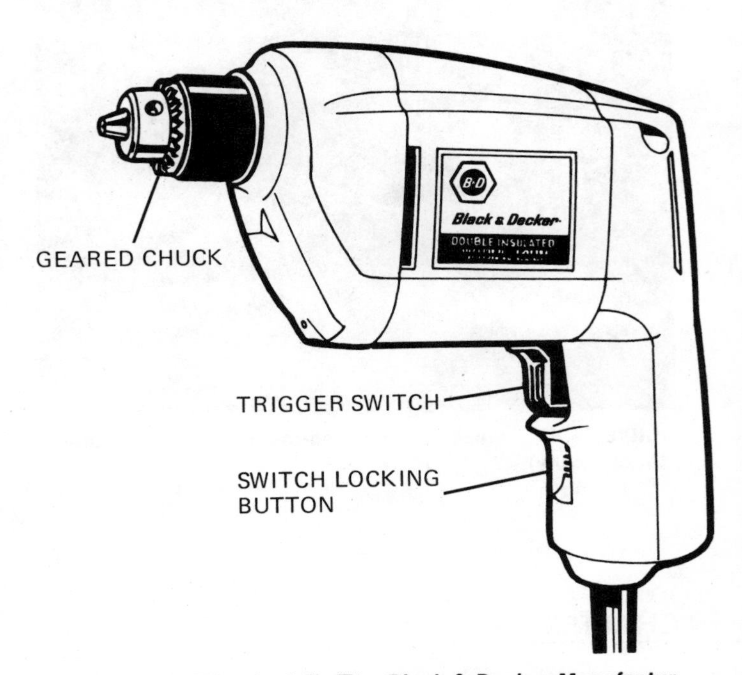

FIGURE 6–1. Electric drill. (*The Black & Decker Manufacturing Company*)

○6-1 Using Power Tools Safely

When you use a power tool, you must use common sense, too, if you want to work safely. Common sense tells you that electricity can give you a severe and possibly fatal shock, that high-pressure air can cause serious injury if it is not used properly, and that you must respect moving parts and power tools when they are operating. In our descriptions of the various power tools in this chapter, we include safety cautions to observe when using these tools. The cautions are based on common sense, but we stress them in our discussions because we do not want you to get hurt. You will remember that we devoted an entire chapter to safety (Chapter 3). You should read that chapter again and again until everything in it becomes second nature to you when you are working in the shop. Safety is as much a part of your job as dinging out fenders or painting a quarter panel.

○6-2 Electric Drill

The electric drill (Fig. 6-1) has an electric motor that drives a chuck. The chuck has jaws that can be opened to accept a drill and then closed to grip it (Fig. 6-2). Note that a special chuck key is used to turn the chuck collar and operate the chuck jaws. The electric drill uses twist drills, such as shown in Fig. 6-3. The twist drill has two cutting edges, as shown. Chips that these edges cut from metal pass up through the two helical grooves and away from the working area.

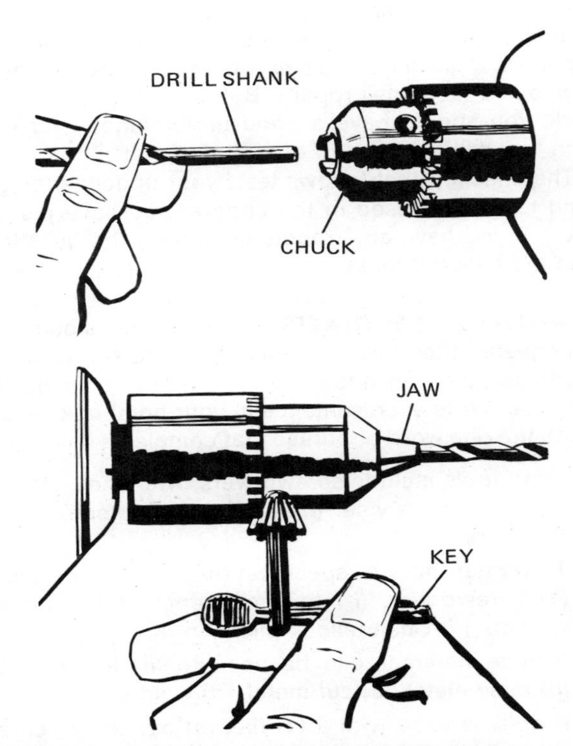

FIGURE 6–2. Installing a twist drill in a drill chuck.

To cut larger holes in sheet metal, a large-hole cutter such as shown in Fig. 6-4 is used. The drill goes into the metal first and then holds the hole cutter on center so the hole it cuts is smooth and round. A smaller version of this tool, shown in Fig. 6-5, is used to drill out spot welds. Drilling out spot welds is necessary to remove some body panels without major damage to them or to the underbody part to which the panel is spot-welded. Figure 6-6 shows how spot welds have been cut out with the tool.

NOTE: The electric drill can be used for small sanding jobs using a small sanding disk or with a wire brush, such as shown in Fig. 5-46.

NOTE: Many body-shop technicians prefer to use pneumatic or air-powered drills and other tools because they are lighter and more easily manipulated than electric tools. Body shops all have a compressed-air system to supply air to operate air tools.

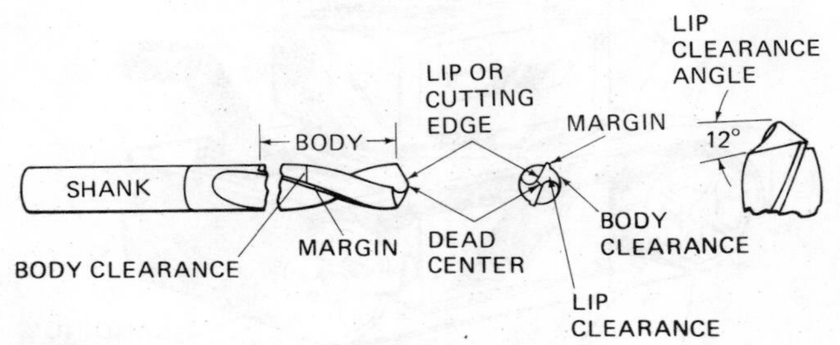

FIGURE 6–3. Parts of a twist drill.

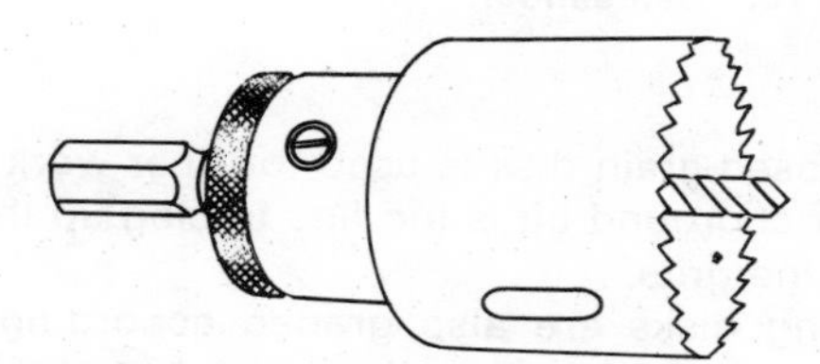

FIGURE 6–4. Large-hole cutter.

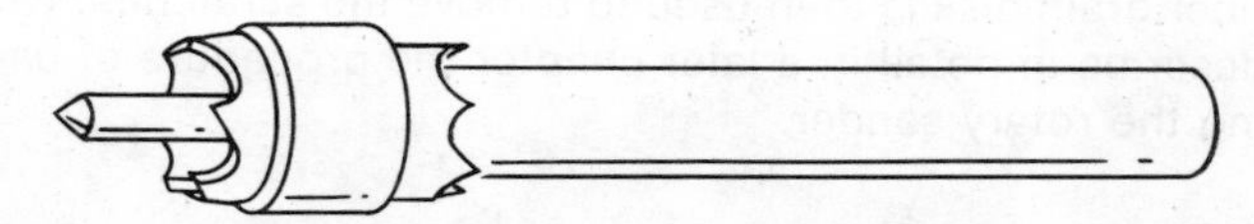

FIGURE 6–5. Small "large-hole" type cutter, called a spot-weld cutter. It is used to cut out spot welds.

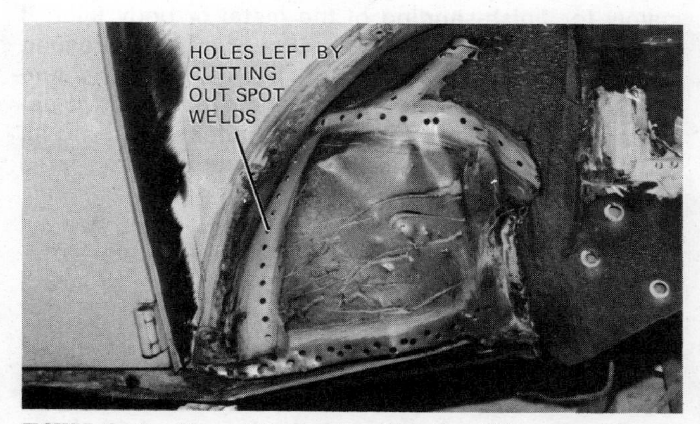

FIGURE 6–6. Use of the spot-weld cutter. When used, it cuts out the metal in the spot weld, thus separating the sheet metal.

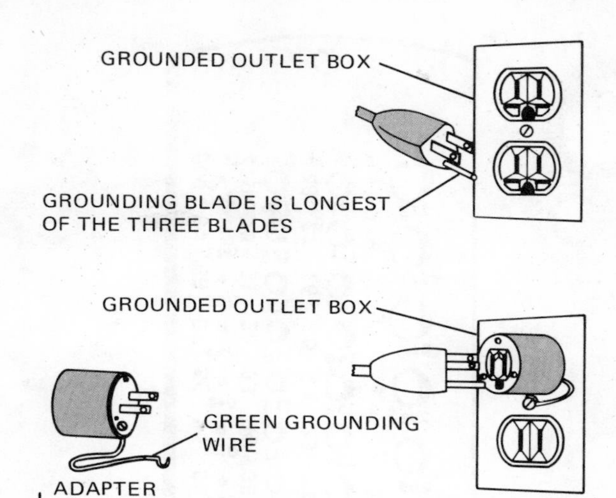

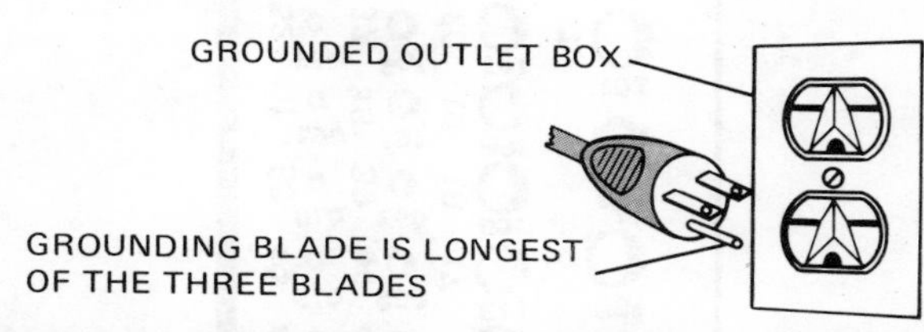

FIGURE 6–7. Various methods of grounding electric tools. *(The Black & Decker Manufacturing Company)*

Here are some precautions to observe when using an electric drill:

1. Make sure that the drill is properly grounded (Fig. 6-7), with the third blade on the plug, or that the drill is double-insulated.
2. Make sure the cord is in good condition. Do not kink it or allow anyone to step on it or run a machine over it. Do not drag the drill around by its cord. Doing any of these things can damage the insulation so that someone could be shocked when using the drill.
3. Keep your hands and clothing away from the moving parts of the drill.
4. Do not drag electric tools around by their cords.
5. Keep a firm grip on the drill and be ready to shut it off if it jams. When a drill is about to break through metal, it sometimes tends to jam. Be prepared for this.
6. If a drill jams, do not try to break it free by turning the switch on and off. This can damage the drill. Instead, pull back on the drill to loosen it.
7. Do not leave the drill lying around on the floor or bench. When you are through with it, put it away where it belongs. The drill should be wiped clean and oiled occasionally if it is the type requiring oiling. Some drills have preoiled bearings and require no additional oil.

If you want to check the size of a twist drill, use a drill gauge (Fig. 6-8). Find the gauge hole in which the drill fits snugly and then note the drill size as marked on the side of the hole.

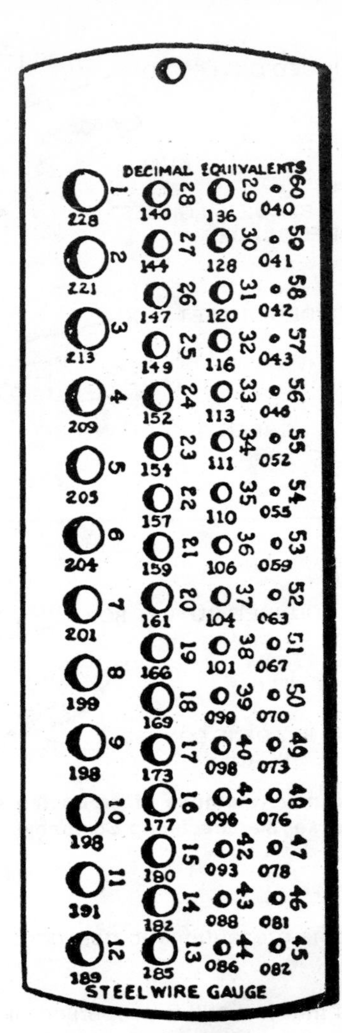

FIGURE 6-8. Drill gauge. The number and size of the drill are shown beside the hole in which the drill fits snugly.

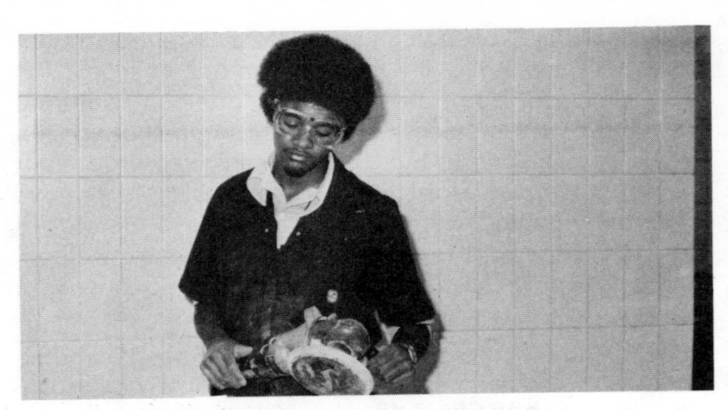

FIGURE 6-9. Electric-powered disk sander.

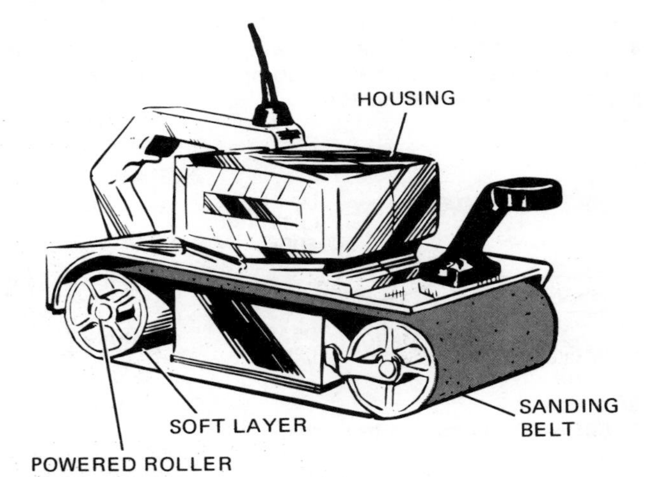

FIGURE 6-10. Belt sander.

○6-3 Power Sanders

There are four types of power sanders used in the body shop: rotary (Fig. 6-9), reciprocating, orbital, and belt. They are powered either by electric motors or by compressed air. We discuss these various types later. First, let us look at the grinding disks or sandpaper the rotary sanders use.

Grinding disks are used in preparing car sheet metal for painting. They come in various sizes up to 9 inches [228.6mm] in diameter. Grinding disks are made by applying grit, which is very hard, sharp-edged pieces of aluminum oxide, to a fiber backing. The size of the particles, or grit, determines the coarseness of the disk and the speed with which it will cut. In the manufacturing process, the grit is graded by being passed through a series of screens. The grit is passed down through the screens, each screen being finer than the one above it.

There are two types of grinding disks: open-grain and closed-grain. On the open-grain disk, the abrasive particles are separated, with some space between them. This type of disk is used to remove old paint and rust and to cut down solder or welds. Because the grits have space around them, the disks do not clog up. That is, the paint or other material that is removed will not fill in the spaces and thus reduce the cutting ability of the disk.

The closed-grain disk is used for finer work in which the material ground off is too fine to clog up the spaces between the grits.

Grinding disks are also graded according to their coarseness, as we mentioned previously. In the finishing process, the grinding is started with a coarse grain. This removes material rapidly but leaves heavy scratches. A finer grain disk is then used to remove the scratches. We describe in detail in a later chapter the procedure of using the rotary sander.

○6-4 Reciprocating Sander

The electric reciprocating, or straightline, sander is used mainly for finish-sanding of the metal or body filler. It uses a pad on which is mounted a strip of sandpaper. The sander moves this sandpaper back and forth. In general, the electric reciprocating sander is similar in appearance to the air reciprocating sander shown in Fig. 7-10. The air reciprocating sander is more widely used today.

○6-5 Orbital Sander

This sander is similar to the reciprocating sander except that the sandpaper moves in a circular or oval pattern. Some sanders have a switch that allows the technician to select the sanding action desired. Figure 7-12 shows an air-powered orbiting-reciprocating sander.

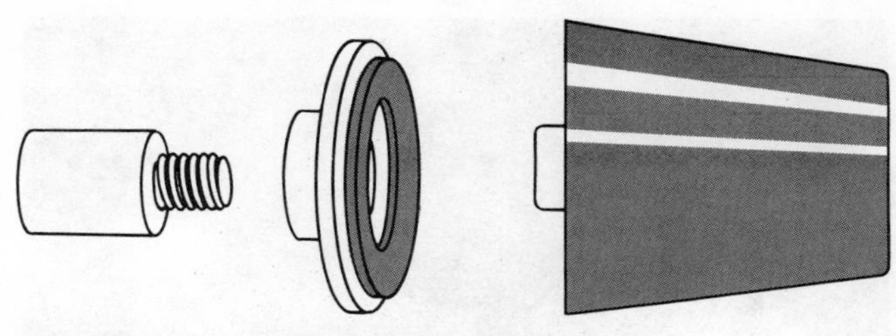

FIGURE 6–11. Cone mandrel. (*3M Company*)

○6-6 Belt Sander

This sander (Fig. 6-10) uses an abrasive belt. It does the same job as the other sanders. It is usually equipped with a vacuum device that draws off most of the dust produced by the sanding operation. Which sander the body technician uses often depends on personal preference.

○6-7 Abrasive Cones

In addition to disks, pads, and belts, some body jobs require abrasive cones for getting at sharp curves around moldings, reveals, and curved areas of doors and hoods. Figure 6-11 shows an abrasive-cone mandrel which is mounted on a disk grinder. The abrasive cone is then mounted on the mandrel.

○6-8 Cautions on Using Sanders

We have discussed safety and safe operating procedures (in Chapter 3), but there are certain hazards in using sanders that should be stressed here. First, a sander raises dust, and this dust can be irritating to the throat and lungs. Therefore, a respirator is desirable. This is especially important when plastic body filler is being sanded, because this material is toxic to the human body; it can cause lung and liver damage.

Goggles or a face protector should be worn to protect the eyes from particles thrown off by the disk sander.

Before laying the sander down on the floor, make sure it is turned off and has stopped running. The electric disk grinder pulls air through it to keep it from overheating. If the grinder is laid on the floor while it is still running, it will pull dust in from the floor and this can cause fast dust buildup and damaging overheating.

In addition to the above, the precautions outlined in ○6-1 and ○6-2 also apply to electric sanders.

○6-9 Grinding Wheel

The bench grinder (Fig. 6-12) has one or more grinding wheels made of abrasive material bonded together. When the wheel is rotated by the electric motor, objects held against the wheel are ground down. Thus, the grinder can be used to shape and sharpen tools.

There are many different sizes and grades of wheels. For coarse work, the abrasive particles are relatively large; they cut material rapidly. An example might be the grinding wheels used to take the rough edges off castings. For fine work, such as sharpening small tools, a relatively fine grinding wheel is used.

FIGURE 6–12. Bench grinder. (*Rockwell International*)

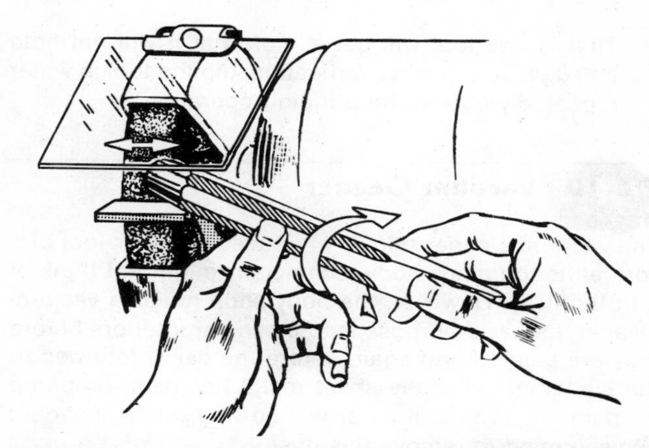

FIGURE 6–13. Grinding the mushroom from the head of a chisel.

As an example of how to use the grinding wheel, see Fig. 6-13, which shows how to grind the mushroomed head from a chisel. Figure 5-33 shows the chisel before and after it is ground.

Certain special cautions should be observed when using a grinding wheel, as follows:

1. Do not hammer on the wheel or put excessive pressure on it.
2. When installing a wheel, do not hammer on it or tighten the spindle nut too much.
3. Do not apply excessive pressure on the wheel.
4. Be alert against the danger of the heavy stream of sparks that often flies off the wheel during the grinding of metals. These sparks are hot and can set fire to your clothing or burn you.
5. Do not attempt to make adjustments of the tool rest when the grinder is running. Turn it off first.
6. Do not touch the rotating wheel with your hand. It can take skin and flesh off in an instant.
7. Always wear safety goggles, even though the wheel is equipped with an eye shield.
8. When grinding a tool, do not allow the metal to get overheated. This will draw the temper out of the tool.

FIGURE 6–14. Heavy-duty vacuum cleaner. (*Rockwell International*)

FIGURE 6–15. Paint shaker.

That is, the tool will get so soft that it will not hold an edge. To prevent overheating, dip the tool in water repeatedly during the grinding operation.

○6-10 Vacuum Cleaner

The vacuum cleaner (Fig. 6-14) is also a power tool of a sort, although many body technicians might not think of it in that way. However, the body shop needs a vacuum cleaner. Its basic purpose is to clean car interiors before they are painted and again before the car is returned to the customer. After the sheet metal has been prepared for painting, the car interior will be very dusty. It should be vacuumed to remove this dust.

A good heavy-duty vacuum cleaner is also very handy for cleaning the shop floor. Even though the floor is dampened to hold down the dust, or floor-sweeping compound is sprinkled around, using a broom will raise dust. This is always troublesome. The vacuum cleaner will clean up the dust without raising it.

The vacuum cleaner should have a long hose so it can reach into the car interior and trunk. It should have the proper accessories to get at corners and other places hard to reach. Some shops use a small, hand-held vacuum cleaner to clean car interiors. These do a good job even though they are not as powerful as the heavy-duty units.

○6-11 Paint Shaker

When a can of paint sits on the shelf, the heavy materials in the can settle to the bottom. In order to mix the paint, the can should be shaken vigorously. Therefore, most body shops that do car painting have a paint shaker (Fig. 6-15). The can of paint is clamped in the shaker, and the shaker is turned on. An air or electric motor then drives an eccentric that shakes the clamp and can to assure thorough mixing of the paint. This is necessary, because if the paint is not properly mixed, the paint job will be defective.

Painters in shops that do not have a paint shaker take sufficient time, when they open a can, to stir the paint thoroughly.

CHAPTER 6 CHECKUP

NOTE: Since this is a chapter review test, you should review the chapter before taking the test.

A power tool is a tool whose power source is not muscle power. In automotive work, the two power sources most often used for power tools are electricity and air. In this chapter, we have discussed power-tool safety and the most frequently used body-shop electric power tools. As you increase your knowledge of the tools and equipment that you will be working with in the automotive body shop, you become better prepared for the work that you are learning about. The checkup below will help you check yourself on how well you understand electric power tools. If any of the questions are difficult to answer, study the chapter again.

COMPLETING THE SENTENCES The sentences below are incomplete. After each sentence there are several words or phrases, but only one of them correctly completes the sentence. Write each sentence in your notebook, ending it with the one word or phrase that completes it correctly.

1. The jaws on an electric drill are adjusted with (*a*) an ignition key, (*b*) a woodruff key, (*c*) a chuck key, (*d*) a square key.
2. To cut a large hole in sheet metal, use a (*a*) twist drill, (*b*) chisel, (*c*) hole cutter, (*d*) sander.
3. Four types of power sanders are orbital, reciprocating, belt, and (*a*) disk, (*b*) rotary, (*c*) square, (*d*) dished.
4. When sanding plastic body filler, you should wear (*a*) a coat, (*b*) rubber boots, (*c*) a hair net, (*d*) a respirator.
5. The machine that mixes paint after it has been stored on the shelf is a (*a*) vacuum cleaner, (*b*) electric drill, (*c*) abrasive cone, (*d*) paint shaker.

DEFINITIONS In the following, you are asked to define certain terms. Write the definitions in your notebook. This will help you remember them. It will also provide you with a quick way to locate meanings when you need the information again. If you do not know the meanings of the terms, look them up in the text or in the glossary at the back of the book.

1. What is an electric power tool?
2. Which part of an electric drill holds the twist drill?
3. What are the precautions to observe when using an electric drill?
4. What is a grinding disk?
5. Explain the basic difference between the four types of power sanders.
6. Define "abrasive cone."
7. What is a respirator?
8. List the safety cautions to observe when using a power sander.
9. Explain the different sizes and uses of grinding wheels.
10. Explain the uses of a vacuum cleaner in an automotive body shop.

SUGGESTIONS FOR FURTHER STUDY

Take your notebook, and on a clean sheet of paper write the heading "Body Shop Electric Power Tools." Then make a tour of your school body shop, listing each electric power tool in the shop. As you list each one, write down the following: (1) its location in the shop, (2) the location of the operating instructions, (3) the safety cautions to be observed for that piece of equipment.

7 PNEUMATIC TOOLS

Pneumatic tools are operated by compressed air. The compressed air comes from the compressed-air system in the body shop. We describe the compressed-air system later in the chapter. The compressed air, as it enters the pneumatic tools, spins a rotor or causes a piston to move in a cylinder. The pneumatic, or air, tools used in the body shop include impact wrenches, impact chisels, sanders, drills, floor jacks, and spray guns for painting cars. The air must be supplied at high pressure to the air tools, and it must be clean and dry. Dirt or moisture in the air would damage pneumatic tools and would ruin paint jobs.

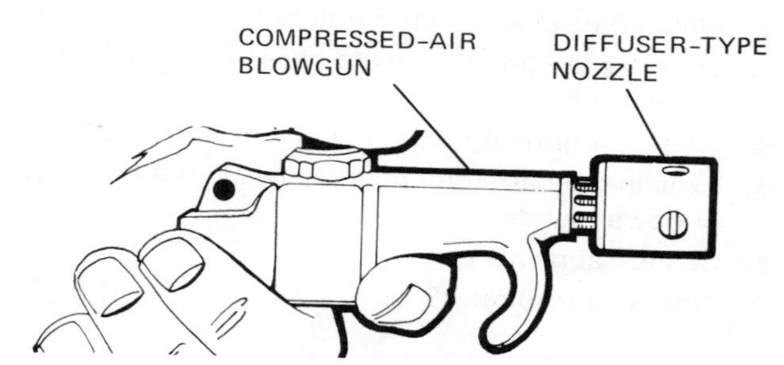

FIGURE 7-1. Approved type of diffuser nozzle on a compressed-air blowgun. The maximum allowable discharge pressure is 30 psi [2.1 kg/cm²]. (*Ford Motor Company*)

7-1 Using Air Tools Safely

Air tools are safe and reliable if they are properly and sensibly used. Never forget, however, that compressed air can be dangerous, even deadly, when misused. Here are the rules you must obey when using any compressed-air tool in the shop:

1. Body shops have air nozzles—often called blowguns—used to blow parts dry and clean (Fig. 7-1). Never point this blowgun at yourself or anyone else. Do not use it to blow dust off your clothes. Dirt particles, driven at high speed by the compressed air, can penetrate the flesh or the eyes, causing serious trouble. If high-pressure air is directed toward an open wound, it can send air into the blood stream with fatal results.
2. Do not look into the air outlet or nozzle of any compressed-air tool.
3. Do not operate air impact chisels without a chisel installed. This can damage the tool.

7-2 Basic Types of Air Tools

There are two basic types of air tools, aside from spray guns: (1) rotary and (2) reciprocating. The rotary type includes sanders, drills, and impact wrenches. The reciprocating type includes air hammers and chisels. The rotary type has a rotor that is driven by the compressed air. The reciprocating type has a piston that is moved back and forth in a cylinder by the air pressure. We will now look at these various types of air tools.

7-3 Quick Coupler

Air tools are connected to the air hose through a quick coupler (Fig. 7-2). Note that the quick coupler is not connected to the air tool, but is connected at the end of the leader hose that leads away from the tool. The connection is made by pulling back the collar on the coupler,

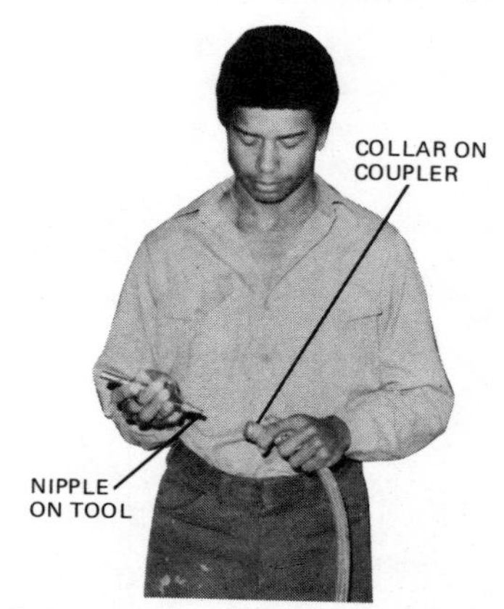

FIGURE 7-2. Quick coupler to connect air hose.

inserting the nipple into the coupler, and then releasing the collar. The collar holds the coupler onto the nipple. Air pressure seals the connection.

7-4 Air Chisel

The air chisel, or air hammer (Fig. 7-3) as it is also called, uses reciprocating motion to drive a cutting or hammering tool. Figure 7-3 shows an air hammer being used to cut a nut that has rusted onto a stud. The air hammer repeatedly and rapidly drives a chisel against the nut. Air hammers can be used with a variety of tools—cutters, chisels, and punches—to do many jobs. Figure 7-4 shows an air hammer equipped with a chisel being used to cut away the damaged part of a body panel. This is done when the part is considered too damaged to be repaired with body hammers and dollies. After the damaged area is cut away, a patch will be riveted or welded on and the panel is then refinished.

7-5 Air Nibbler

The air nibbler (Fig. 7-5) works like a pair of scissors with one movable blade and two stationary blades. The two

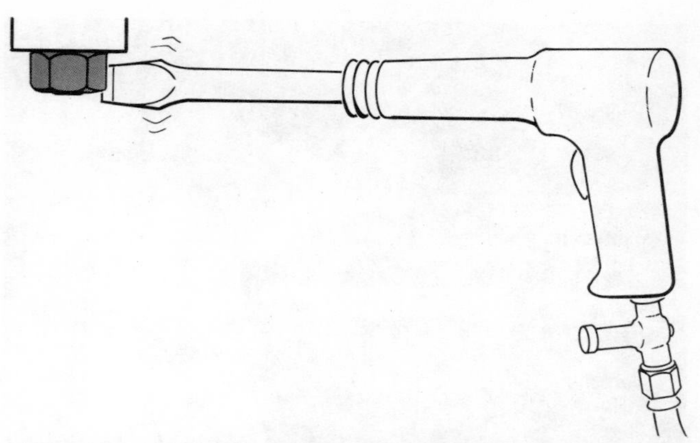

FIGURE 7–3. Air hammer in operation, driving a chisel to cut a nut that has frozen onto a stud. (*Chicago Pneumatic Tool Company*)

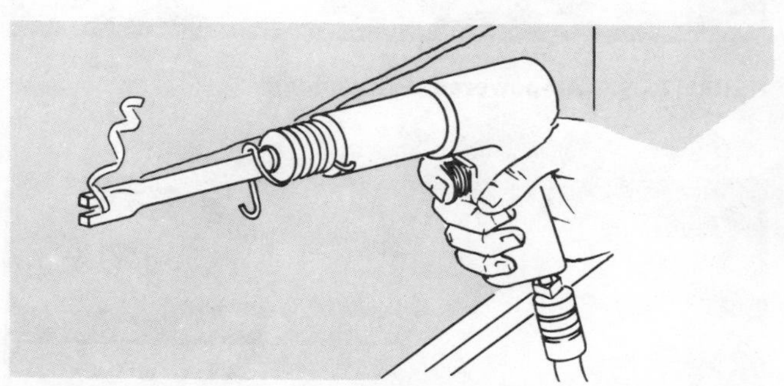

FIGURE 7–4. Air hammer equipped with a panel-cutting chisel being used to cut out damaged part of a panel. (*Snap-on Tool Corporation*)

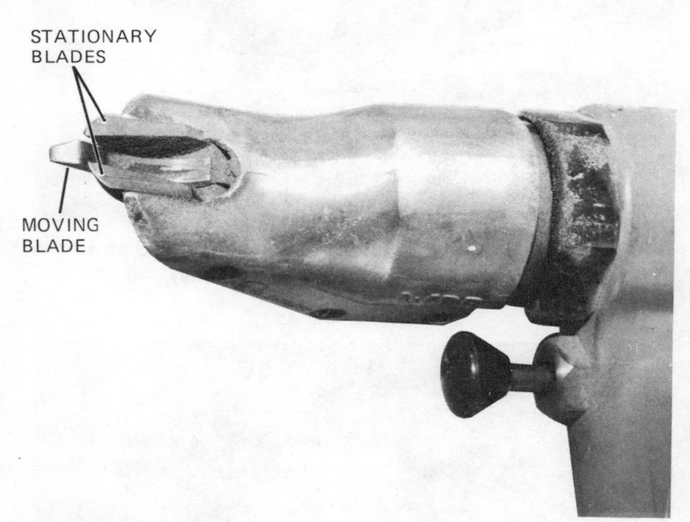

FIGURE 7–5. Nibbler.

outer blades are stationary, and the center blade moves up and down between them. As the center blade moves up between the stationary blades, it cuts out a thin ribbon of metal, as shown in Fig. 7-6. The name "nibbler" comes from the action of the tool. The nibbler takes small bites from, or it nibbles, the metal. To use the nibbler on a body panel, a hole large enough to get the nibbler started is first drilled in the metal. Then the movable blade is inserted in the hole, and the air valve is opened to start the nibbler. The tool is easily controlled and easy to use so that a clean, accurate cut can be made. When a patch is being cut out for a panel from flat sheet metal, the cut is started from the edge of the sheet.

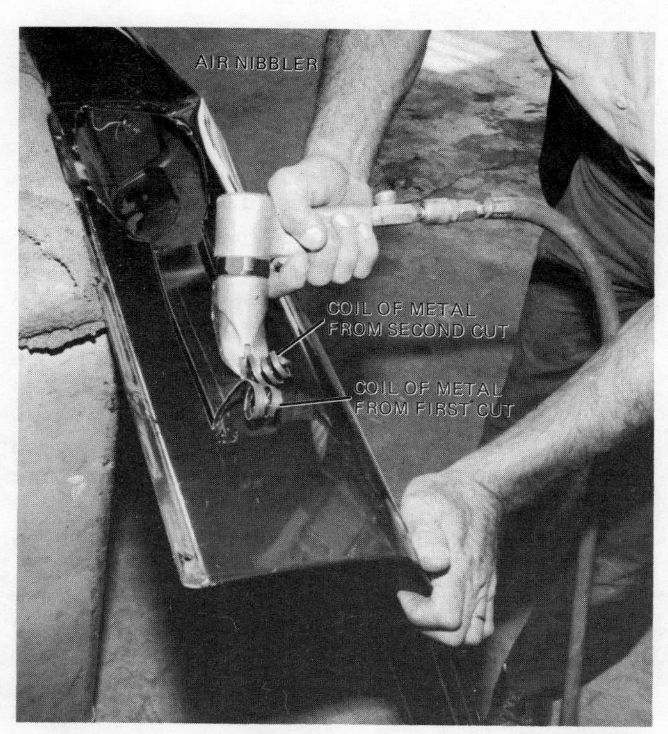

FIGURE 7–6. Air nibbler cutting out a strip of metal from a discarded fender. The technician will use this strip to patch a body panel on a car.

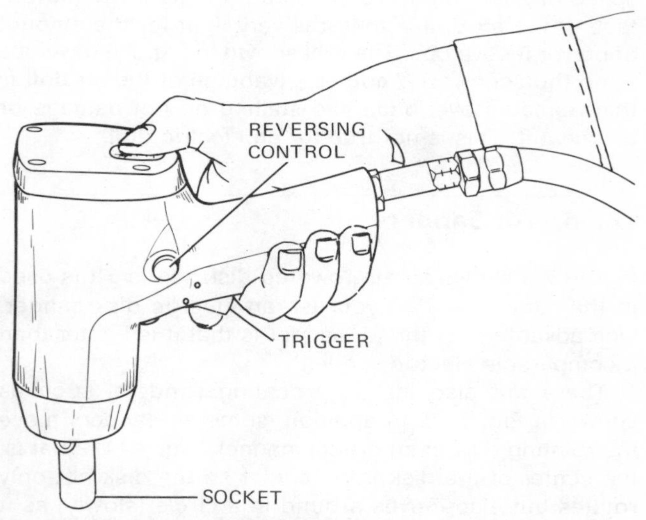

FIGURE 7–7. Using an impact wrench.

○7-6 Air Impact Wrenches

Air impact wrenches (Fig. 7-7) use a pounding or impact force to loosen or tighten nuts or bolts. They do the job very rapidly and so are widely used in the shop. The direction of rotation can be changed by operating a reversing control on the wrench.

Most shop impact wrenches have a standard ½-inch [12.7mm] socket drive. Only special impact sockets should be used with the impact wrench. Standard sockets will crack and round out when used on an impact wrench. Impact sockets are often black in color.

NOTE: Some impact wrenches are electric. These have an electric motor. They are usually larger and bulkier than a comparable air impact wrench. You must be careful in using an electric impact wrench—in fact, any electric tool—to avoid damage to the electric cord.

Here are some rules for using an air impact wrench:

1. Always use impact sockets with an impact wrench.
2. Use only the correct size socket for the bolt or nut.
3. Use the simplest possible assembly of sockets, extensions, and universal joint.
4. Use a deep socket, where possible, rather than a standard-length socket and extension.
5. Hold the wrench so the socket fits squarely on the bolt or nut. Apply a slight forward pressure to hold the socket in place before you operate the wrench.
6. Once a nut or bolt tightens, never impact it beyond an additional one-half turn. Continued impacting might strip the threads or break the bolt.
7. For accurate tightening of a bolt or nut to a specified tension, you must use a torque wrench. (See Fig. 5-10.)
8. Soak large rusty nuts or bolts with penetrating oil before impacting them.

○7-7 Air Drill

Figure 7-8 shows an air drill with hose and coupling. This drill has a ¼-inch [6.35-mm] chuck capacity and a free speed of 2800 rpm (revolutions per minute). One advantage of the air drill is that it is very light for the amount of power it develops. The drill shown in Fig. 7-8 develops ½ hp (horsepower). Another advantage of the air drill is that repeated overloads and stalling do not damage or overheat it. This is not true for an electric drill.

○7-8 Air Sanders

Figure 7-9 shows an air-powered disk sander. It is used in the same way that you use an electric disk sander. One advantage of the air sander is that it is lighter than a comparable electric sander.

There are also air reciprocating sanders, such as shown in Fig. 7-10. In addition, some air sanders move the rotating disk in an orbital manner (Fig. 7-11). That is, the center of the disk is off center so the disk not only rotates but also moves around in a circle (slowly) as it does so. Another type of orbital sander (Fig. 7-12) is an orbiting-reciprocating type. Some sanders are equipped

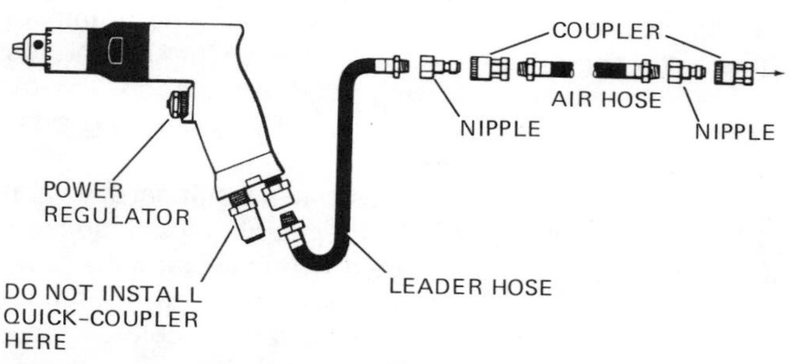

FIGURE 7–8. Air drill with hose and couplings. (*Chicago Pneumatic Tool Company*)

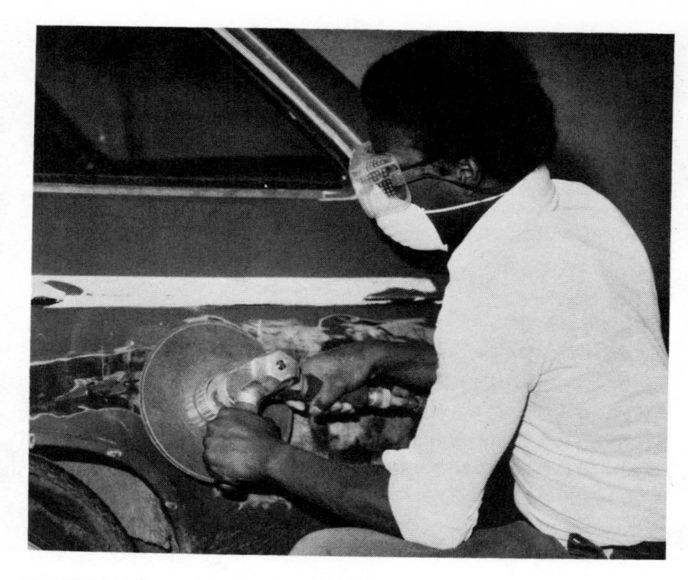

FIGURE 7–9. Air-powered disk sander.

FIGURE 7–10. Air reciprocating sander, also called an *air file* in the shop. (*Chicago Pneumatic Tool Company*)

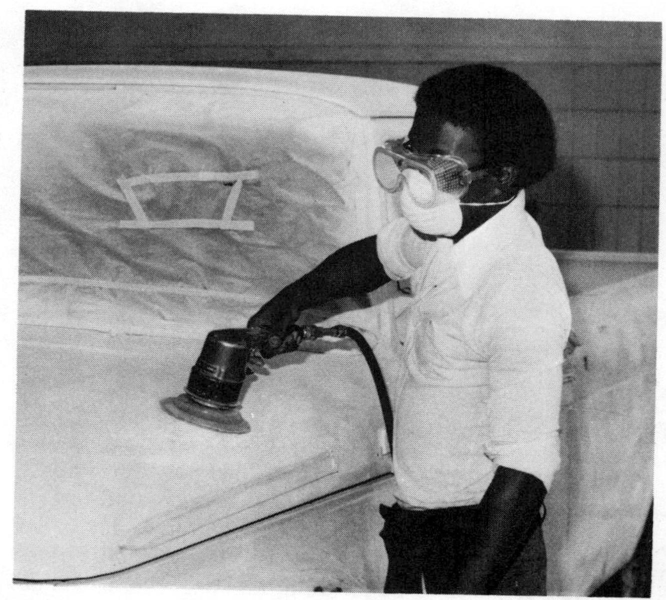

FIGURE 7–11. Random orbital sander.

FIGURE 7 – 12. Orbiting-reciprocating sander. (*Chicago Pneumatic Tool Company*)

with a vacuum device to suck up dust from the sanding operation.

○7-9 Pneumatic Floor Jack

Many types of pneumatic jacks are used in the automotive body shop. The pneumatic floor jack, or bumper-type end lift (Fig. 7-13), uses compressed air to jack up one end of the car. When the air valve is actuated, compressed air flows into the jack cylinder, causing the ram to extend and raise the car. When the lever position is reversed, the air is released and so the car settles back to the floor. The jack is very handy. It does its job quickly.

CAUTION: Never go under a car that is supported only by the jack. Always use safety stands placed under the car to support it safely before working under a car. The pneumatic jack could slip or release, allowing the car to come down on you. This could seriously injure or kill you. Don't take chances!

○7-10 Ratchet

The air ratchet (Fig. 7-14) is usually supplied with a ⅜-inch [9.53-mm] drive and can use the sockets and attachments from a standard socket set. Since air ratchets do not apply quite as much force on impact, special impact sockets are not required.

○7-11 Paint Spray Guns

There are two basic types of paint spray guns (Figs. 7-15 and 7-16): suction-cup and pressure-pot. The suction-cup spray gun is easier to move in the body shop and is the most widely used, particularly for touch-up work and painting body panels that have been repaired. The suction-cup spray gun has a "cup" or container into which the paint is poured. Then, when the operating lever is pulled, compressed air passes through the gun, picking

FIGURE 7 – 13. Bumper-type end lift, or air jack.

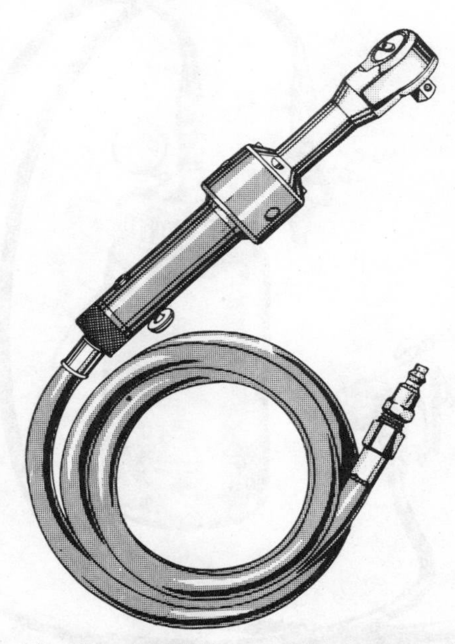

FIGURE 7 – 14. Air ratchet. (*Snap-on Tool Corporation*)

up paint from the container. The amount of paint picked up and the pattern that issues from the gun can be changed by adjustments on the gun to produce the spray needed for the job. We describe this further in a later chapter.

The pressure-pot spray gun (Fig. 7-16) is handy for larger jobs such as repainting a complete car. The container holds considerably more paint than the cup on the suction-cup spray gun. Note that the pressure-pot spray gun uses compressed air in the container to force paint through a hose to the spray gun.

A later chapter discusses vehicle painting and explains how spray guns are used and the care they require.

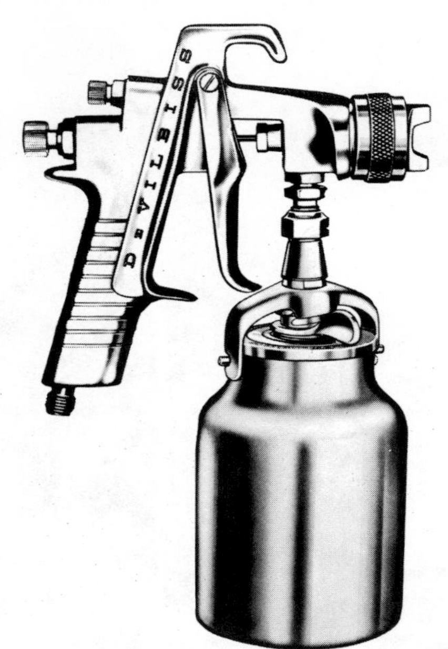

FIGURE 7–15. Suction-cup paint spray gun. (*DeVilbiss Company*)

FIGURE 7–16. Pressure-pot paint spray gun. (*DeVilbiss Company*)

○7-12 Care of Air Tools

Air tools should be given the same care as any other power tool. They should not be dropped on the floor or dragged around by the air hose. When not in use, they should be put on the workbench or on the designated shelf so they will not be carelessly handled. Every day, before using an air tool, apply three or four squirts of flushing oil to the air-tool inlet (Fig. 7-17). Then connect and operate the tool. This flushes out any dirt or moisture from the air motor and lubricates the moving parts. Any deposits are flushed out through the air exhaust.

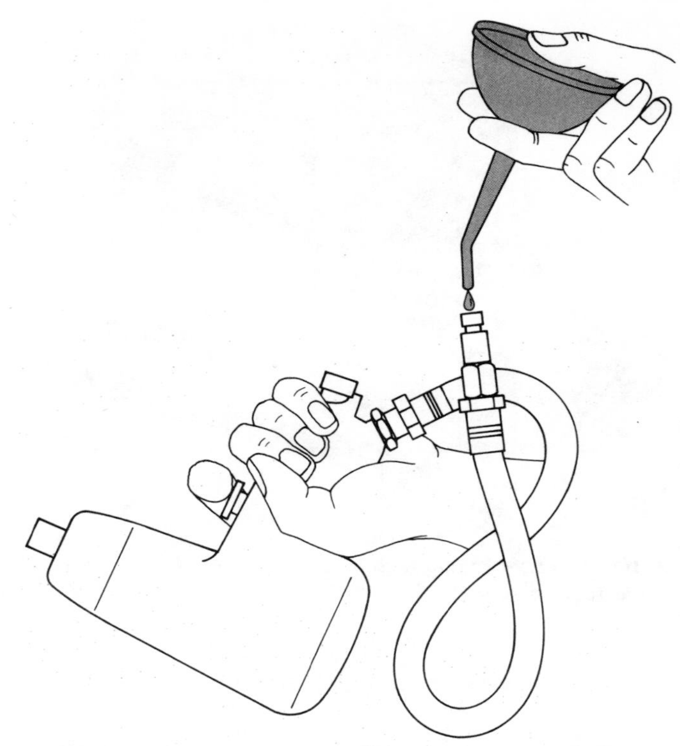

FIGURE 7–17. Squirting a few drops of flushing oil into an impact-wrench air line. (*Chicago Pneumatic Tool Company*)

CAUTION: Do not flush the wrench around an open flame. The mist coming out, which contains flushing oil, is flammable. Always point the tool air exhaust away from your body.

○7-13 Air Supply

The auto body shop needs an adequate supply of compressed air to operate the various pneumatic tools used in the shop. Also, compressed air is needed to operate the spray guns used to paint cars. The air must be supplied at the correct high pressure. In addition, the air must be clean and dry. As we said previously, dirt or moisture in compressed air can damage pneumatic tools and will ruin paint jobs.

○7-14 The Compressed-Air System

Figure 7-18 shows schematically a complete compressed-air system. It includes an electric motor that drives an air pump. The air pump draws air in from the surrounding space, compresses it, and forces it into the air tank. When the air pressure in the tank reaches a predetermined level, a switch automatically turns off the motor. The air tank is connected by pipes and flexible hoses to the various pneumatic tools and to the spray guns in the paint booths.

Note that there are drains in the tank and pipe lines. These are to drain out the water in the system. When air is compressed, the moisture in the air condenses into water. This water must be drained out so it will not get to the tools or spray guns.

In addition, the system has air filters to clean the air and a regulator to regulate the air pressure going to the

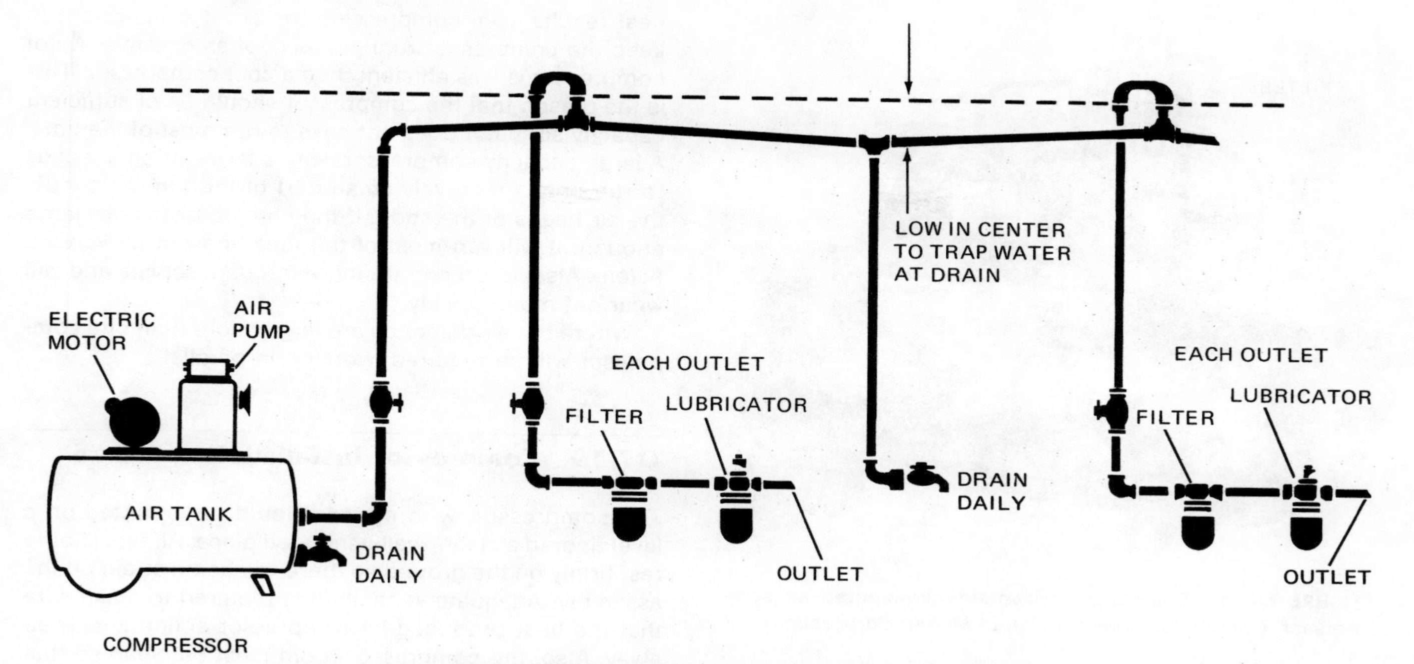

FIGURE 7 – 18. Schematic diagram of a shop compressed-air system. (*Chicago Pneumatic Tool Company*)

spray guns. Regulating the air pressure to the pneumatic tools is not important so long as the pressure is within the general tool-operating range. But the air pressure at a spray gun is critical. If it is not correct within a very narrow range, the paint job will be bad.

We will now look at each of these components of the system.

○7-15 Compressor

The compressor (Fig. 7-19) is a little like a gasoline engine. It uses one or two pistons, moving up and down in cylinders, to compress the air and deliver it to the air tank. Each piston is attached by a connecting rod to a crank on a crankshaft, as shown in Fig. 7-19. The crankshaft is rotated by an electric motor. When the crankshaft is driven, it pushes and pulls on the connecting rod so the piston moves up and down.

On the down stroke, a partial vacuum is created above the piston. This allows atmospheric pressure to push the inlet valve down so that air can enter to fill the partial vacuum. At the same time, atmospheric pressure on the outlet valve holds it closed.

Then, on the up stroke of the piston, the air pressure increases above the piston as the air is compressed. This increasing pressure forces the inlet valve closed and the outlet valve open. The high-pressure air flows into the air tank. There is a check valve in the line from the compressor to the tank that prevents any back flow of air.

When the pressure in the tank reaches the proper value, a pressure switch is pushed open. This opens the electric circuit to the motor so the motor and compressor stop. Now the high-pressure compressed air is available for any pneumatic tools or spray guns in the shop. When the pressure falls sufficiently as compressed air is used by the tools, the pressure switch closes and the motor starts again to bring the air pressure up to full again.

FIGURE 7 – 19. Cutaway view of air-cooled air compressor showing two-stage model with a large piston and bore and with a smaller piston to boost pressure still higher. (*Lincoln St. Louis Division of McNeil Corporation*)

The actual pressure in the air tank varies according to the setting of the pressure switch. In a typical shop, the air pressure will run around 100 to 150 pounds per square inch (psi) [7.03 to 10.55 kg/cm^2]. As we mentioned previously, this pressure is satisfactory for most pneumatic tools but is excessive for spray-gun work. Therefore, a regulator is used to reduce this pressure, as we explain later.

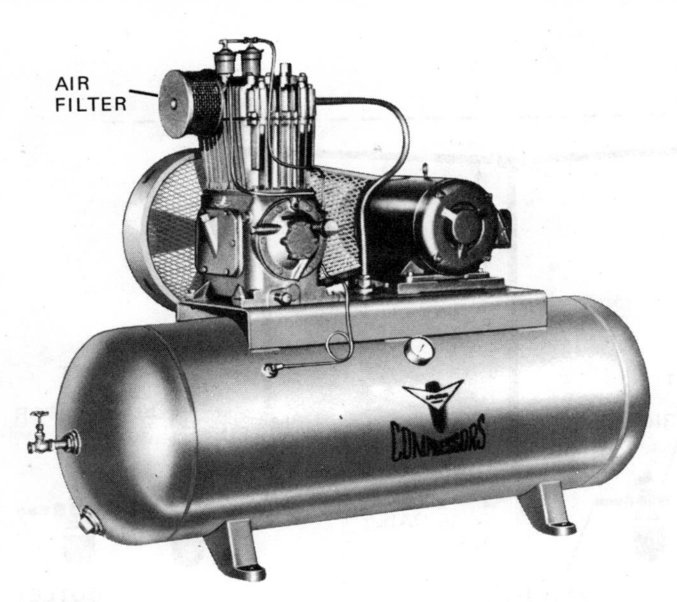

FIGURE 7–20. Two-stage horizontal-tank-mounted air compressor. (*Lincoln St. Louis Division of McNeil Corporation*)

○7-16 Single-Stage and Two-Stage Compressors

A single-stage compressor has a single piston working in a single cylinder. It is satisfactory for small shops with limited compressed-air requirements.

The two-stage compressor (Figs. 7-19 and 7-20) has two cylinders, one considerably larger than the other. Both work off a common crankshaft. The larger piston compresses the air to an intermediate pressure. This partly compressed air then enters the smaller cylinder, where it is further compressed to the final pressure. It then flows into the air tank.

○7-17 Air Filter

The air entering the compressor must first pass through an air filter. Figure 7-20 shows the location of the air filter on a compressor. The purpose of the filter is to remove dust and dirt particles from the air so they do not enter the compressor. Dust particles in the compressor could scratch the piston, rings, and cylinder wall and ultimately ruin the compressor. Also, if dust gets into the system, it can cause trouble. Pneumatic tools can be damaged, and the spray gun will clog up and stop working properly.

The filter should be cleaned or changed periodically. The service intervals depend on the type of filter and the amount of dirt in the air. Compressor manufacturers supply instructions which include recommendations on how often the filter should be cleaned or changed. These instructions should be carefully followed to protect the compressor and the system.

○7-18 Compressor Cooling

Most compressors are air-cooled. A few are water-cooled. Air-cooled compressors have cooling fins on the cylinder block and head to help dissipate the heat. The heat results from compressing the air. It is important to keep the compressor running as cool as possible. A hot compressor is less efficient than a cool compressor. This is the reason that the compressor should be of sufficient capacity so that it does not have to run most of the time. A large capacity compressor, with a large air tank, needs to run only a relatively small part of the time to supply the air needs of the shop. If the compressor is not large enough, it will run most of the time and not be very efficient. Also, it will require more frequent service and will wear out more quickly.

Where the air demands are large, more than one compressor will be required, working in parallel.

○7-19 Compressor Installation and Care

The compressor, with motor, should be mounted on a level floor in a clean, well-ventilated place. All feet should rest firmly on the ground so there will be no strain on the assembly. Adequate ventilation is required to make sure that the heat produced by compressor action is carried away. Also, the compressor room must be clean so that the air going into the compressor is relatively free of dust particles.

All pipe connections from the main line should be taken off the top of the line, as shown in Fig. 7-20. This is to prevent water in the system from flowing to the tools or spray guns. When air is compressed, not only does it get hot but also moisture in the air condenses into water. As previously mentioned, water flowing into pneumatic tools or spray guns can cause trouble. The air system and air tank are equipped with drains which should be opened daily to drain out any water that has accumulated.

NOTE: Some compressors have an automatic device that opens a valve every cycle (starting and stopping of compressor), releasing any water that has accumulated.

Once a week, the belt should be checked for wear, tightness, and alignment. At the same time, oil the electric-motor bearings (if they are of the type requiring oil).

CAUTION: When checking the belt and oiling the motor, open the main switch to the motor so it will not start while you are working on the belt and motor.

The oil level in the compressor crankcase should be checked weekly. If it is low, add the type of oil prescribed by the compressor manufacturer. At longer intervals, as recommended by the manufacturer, the oil should be drained and fresh oil put into the crankcase.

Blow the dust off the compressor cooling fins periodically. Dirty fins will not transmit heat as easily, causing the compressor to run hotter.

○7-20 Transformer

The transformer (Fig. 7-21) is actually a pressure regulator-separator assembly and is connected in the line to the spray guns. Some transformers have a main-line pressure gauge and one or more regulated-pressure gauges. The main-line gauge indicates the pressure in the main-line air tank. The regulator-pressure gauge or gauges indicate the pressure going to the spray guns. As previously mentioned, this pressure must be correct or the paint will not spray properly.

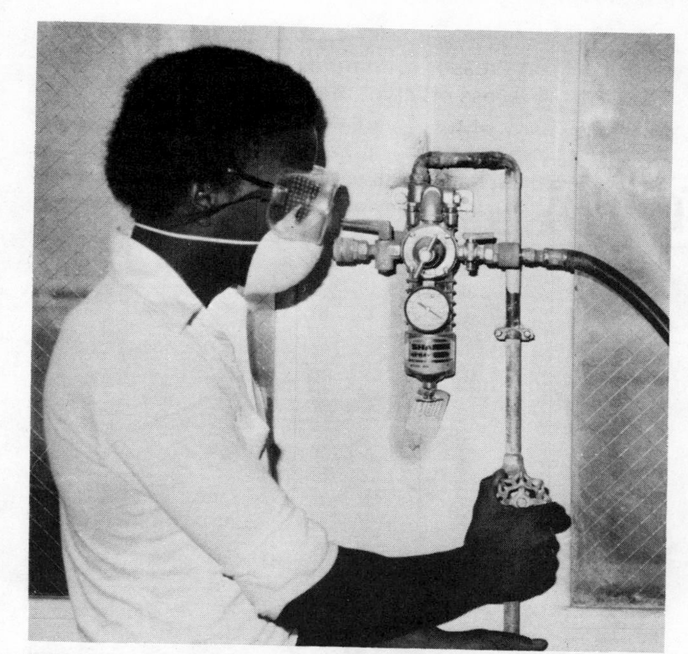

FIGURE 7-21. Air transformer for cleaning and regulating compressed air.

The pressure is regulated by a regulator valve. Turning the valve knob or handle one way or the other changes the air pressure going to the spray guns. Thus, the paint technician can adjust the pressure to suit the requirements of the job.

The transformer also has a separator system to filter the air and remove any dust or water that has remained in the air. There is a drain valve at the bottom of the regulator to drain off any water that has collected.

○7-21 Transformer Installation

The transformer should be mounted conveniently close to the paint technician so the pressure can be adjusted as needed. One recommendation is that it should be installed at least 25 feet [7.6 m] from the compressor. The takeoff should be from the top of the air line. The line should slope down and away from the takeoff so as to minimize the possibility of water entering the transformer.

○7-22 Hoses

The proper size hose should be used. The equipment manufacturer makes the recommendations for hose types and sizes, and these recommendations should be followed. Quick-disconnect couplings are used to connect and disconnect the tools to the air line. See Fig. 7-2.

CHAPTER 7 CHECKUP

NOTE: Since this is a chapter review test, you should review the chapter before taking the test.

A pneumatic tool is a tool powered by compressed air. These tools are great labor-saving devices, but they must be properly maintained and used with care. Here are some questions that will help you to better understand the types and uses of pneumatic tools discussed in this chapter. If you don't know the answer to any of the questions, reread the section about that tool.

COMPLETING THE SENTENCES The sentences below are incomplete. After each sentence there are several words or phrases, but only one of them correctly completes the sentence. Write each sentence in your notebook, ending it with the one word or phrase that completes it correctly.

1. In the shop, the source of compressed air is (*a*) the shop air compressor, (*b*) bottles of compressed air.
2. Air tools provide either (*a*) rotary or circular motion, (*b*) rotary or reciprocating motion, (*c*) rotary or rotating motion, (*d*) reciprocating or back-and-forth motion.
3. An impact wrench provides (*a*) rotary motion, (*b*) reciprocating motion, (*c*) back-and-forth motion.
4. An advantage of an air drill is that it is undamaged by (*a*) use under water, (*b*) lack of service, (*c*) water in the air line, (*d*) stalling.
5. Most air tools require an air pressure of about (*a*) 60 psi [4.22 kg/cm^2], (*b*) 100 psi [7.03 kg/cm^2], (*c*) 150 psi [10.55 kg/cm^2], (*d*) 250 psi [17.58 kg/cm^2].

MATCHING TOOLS AND USES When the two lists below are unscrambled and combined, you will have matched up the tool with one of its uses. To unscramble the lists, take one item at a time from the Tool list, and then find the item in the Use list that goes with it. Write the correct tool and use combination in your notebook.

Tool	Use
air chisel	cuts thin ribbon of metal
air nibbler	stalls without damage
impact wrench	spins a rotating disk
air drill	cuts rusted nuts
air sander	turns bolts and nuts

SUGGESTIONS FOR FURTHER STUDY

Inspect the shop air compressor. Note how to turn it on and off and how to drain it. Locate the compressor pressure gauge, and note the reading. Then write down in your notebook the compressor start-up and servicing procedure.

CAUTION: The compressor is automatically controlled and may start running at any time. Keep your hands and clothing away from the motor and drive belts.

8 HYDRAULIC BODY TOOLS

The word "hydraulic" means "of or pertaining to liquid or fluid." Thus, hydraulic tools are tools that are operated by the pressure on a liquid. The brakes on automotive vehicles are operated by hydraulic pressure. When the brake pedal is pushed down, brake fluid at high pressure is sent to the wheel-brake mechanisms. This applies the brakes. The hydraulic tools used in the body shop include car lifts, power jacks, and body-panel and -frame straighteners. Lifts are powered by electric motors. Power jacks and straighteners are powered by a hand pump, by a pump driven by an electric motor, or by an air-driven pump.

○8-1 Car Lifts

Car lifts are either single- or double-post. Figures 8-1 and 8-2 show two types. Both have lift pads which can be positioned under lift points on the car frame or suspension. There is also the drive-on type, which has parallel tracks onto which the car is driven. The drive-on type is convenient for such jobs as draining the engine oil and work on the differential, clutch, and transmission. However, the type with lift pads is preferred for the body shop, because it can be adjusted to handle any size of car with any kind of damage.

The lift is actuated by an air or electric motor that drives a hydraulic pump. The pump sends fluid to the cylinder or cylinders that form the post or posts. A piston or pistons are forced upward in the cylinder or cylinders by the fluid pressure, thus raising the lift and the car.

FIGURE 8–2. Two-post lift. The post under the front wheels can be moved forward or backward, as shown by the arrows, to accommodate vehicles of different lengths. (*Lincoln St. Louis Division of McNeil Corporation*)

CAUTION: Do not allow passengers to remain in a car that is being lifted. Make sure all doors, hood, and trunk lid are closed; otherwise, they might get ripped off when the car is lifted. If the lift has a mechanical locking device, make sure it is engaged before you go under the lift. If a lift is not working properly, don't use it. Evidence of improper operation include the following: the lift may jerk or jump when raised, settle slowly when it should not, work too slowly, blow oil out of the exhaust line, or leak oil around the packing gland on the cylinder.

FIGURE 8–1. Single-post lift. The four lifting arms can be swiveled. They can also be extended or telescoped to fit a wide variety of cars and light trucks. The arms are positioned so the lift pads are directly under the lift points on the vehicle frame. Then the technician moves a lever which directs oil under pressure into the cylinder. This raises the piston and the vehicle. (*Lincoln St. Louis Division of McNeil Corporation*)

○8-2 Hydraulic Floor Jack

The hydraulic floor jack (Fig. 8-3) is operated by pumping the handle. This raises the lifting saddle. A lever on the handle releases the hydraulic pressure so that the saddle and load on it will settle back down. When using the jack, be sure the saddle is firmly placed under the proper lift point on the car. If the saddle should slip, the car could drop and be damaged.

CAUTION: Never work under a car that is supported only by a jack. If it should slip, the car could fall on you.

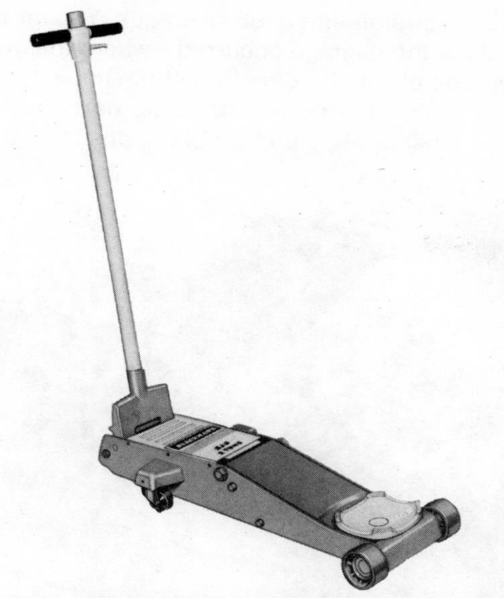

FIGURE 8–3. Hydraulic floor jack. *(Blackhawk Division of Applied Power, Inc.)*

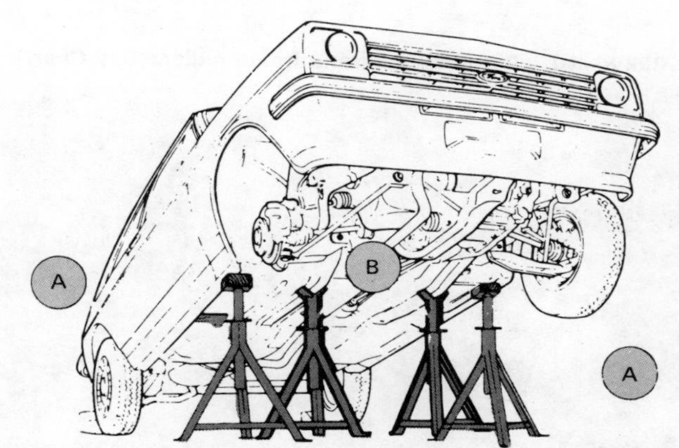

FIGURE 8–4. Always place safety stands under a car at the proper lift points (A or B) before going under a car. *(Ford Motor Company)*

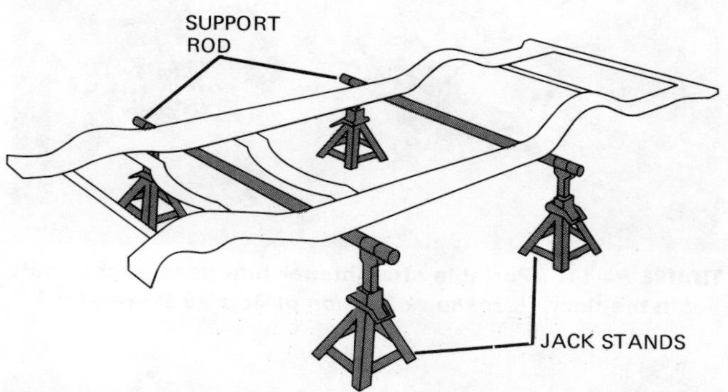

FIGURE 8–5. Frame supported by support rods and stands. The body is omitted here so you can see how the rods and stands are placed to support the car. *(Bear Division of Applied Power, Inc.)*

Put safety stands under the car at the proper lift points and allow the car to rest on them before you go under the car. See Fig. 8-4. For some body and frame work, you will use special support rods and stands, as shown in Fig. 8-5. This illustration shows the frame supported only on the stands. The body has been omitted in the picture so that you may see how the frame of the car rests on the support rods.

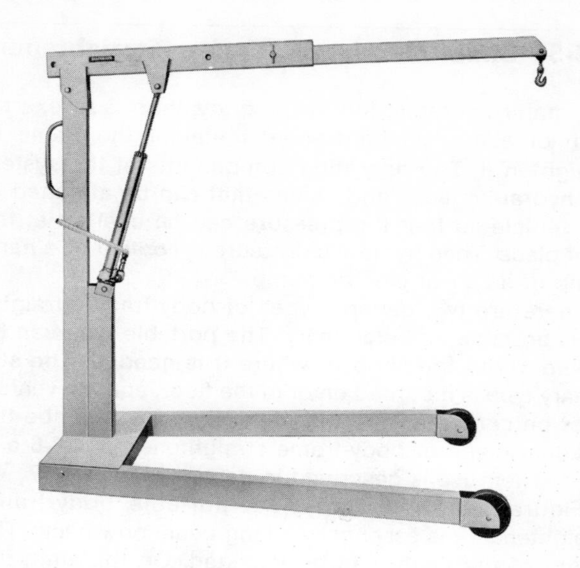

FIGURE 8–6. Portable crane. *(Blackhawk Division of Applied Power, Inc.)*

○8-3 Portable Crane

The portable crane (Fig. 8-6) is used to lift the engine out of the car. It is operated hydraulically by a hand pump. The crane can be used for other jobs where a heavy object must be lifted and transported.

CAUTION: When using the portable crane or other lifting equipment, stand clear of the part that is being lifted. That way, you would not be injured if the part should slip or if the lift should topple. Never work on a part that is suspended in the air (engine, transmission, etc). Instead, lower the part onto your workbench or into a support stand before working on it.

○8-4 Hydraulic Power Jack

This jack works on hydraulic pressure that is supplied by operating the handle on the pump (Fig. 8-7). Hydraulic fluid from the pump is forced into the jack, extending the piston. Some jacks of this type have an air-hydraulic pump that operates when the technician presses the treadle. See the Caution above (○8-2 Hydraulic Floor Jack) about working under a car not properly supported.

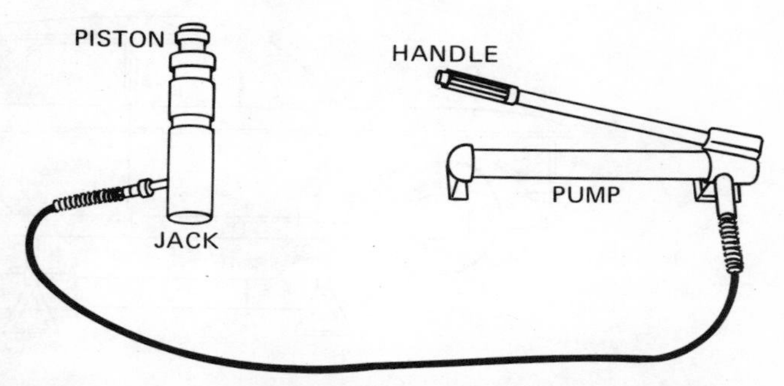

FIGURE 8–7. A hydraulic power jack operated by a hand pump.

○8-5 Sheet-Metal and Frame Straighteners

The major hydraulic job in the body shop is to exert a push or a pull on bent sheet metal or the frame to straighten it. The operating components of the system are hydraulic jacks and chains that can be attached to the vehicle so that the pressure can be exerted at the right place. Then hydraulic pressure is applied by a hand pump or an air or electric pump.

There are two general types of body-frame straightener: portable and stationary. The portable type can be moved about the shop to where it is needed. The stationary type is mounted on or in the floor, and the vehicle must be centered in the straightener. We describe the stationary type of body-frame straightener in ○8-6 and ○8-7. Their use is described in detail in Chapter 17.

Figure 8-8 shows a typical portable body-frame straightener. It is essentially a long beam on wheels. The length of the beam can be adjusted. On this unit, the hydraulic pressure is developed by a hand pump. Figure 8-9 shows how the rear end of a car, pushed in by a rear-end collision, can be pulled out with the straightener.

Figure 8-10 shows a similar portable body-frame straightener. The major difference is that this unit uses an air pump to drive the hydraulic pump that furnishes the operating hydraulic pressure to the jack.

Another type of portable straightener is shown in Fig. 8-11. This unit uses anchor pots set in the floor to hold the mobile cart. The chain is then attached to the car, as shown, and pull is exerted when the operator pushes the treadle. This extends the ram, causing the pull on the car.

No two collisions are identical, and thus the damages to the cars are never the same. This means that you must look at each straightening job as unique. You must figure out just how the damage occurred—where the impact or impacts took place, the direction of the impact, and how the push forced the body and frame parts out of line. Then you must apply a pull that is opposite to the push

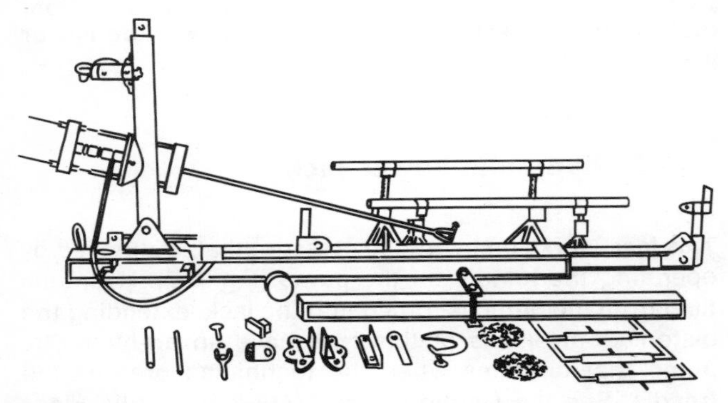

FIGURE 8–8. Portable body-frame straightener. (*Bear Division of Applied Power, Inc.*)

FIGURE 8–10. Portable body and frame puller. (*Guy Chart*)

FIGURE 8–11. Portable straightener that uses anchor pots set in the floor. (*Blackhawk Division of Applied Power, Inc.*)

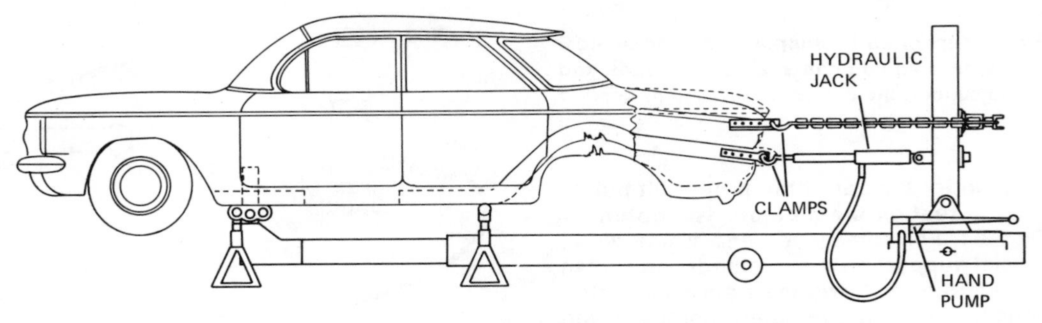

FIGURE 8–9. Using power equipment to pull the rear end of a car back into shape. (*Bear Division of Applied Power, Inc.*)

that caused the damage. Most straighteners use pull to correct damage. We describe the procedure in detail in a later chapter.

NOTE: The body panels and frame are not straightened by pull alone. As the pull is exerted, the body technician uses body tools to help the metal move back to its original contour. The combination of pull and hammering on or off the dolly, for example, will usually simplify the straightening of a buckled body panel. Note that the instructions call for pulling a little beyond the original shape and then releasing the pull. There will be some spring-back when the pull is released, and pulling slightly beyond will allow the metal to spring back to its approximate original shape. Sometimes the body technician applies heat from a gas torch (Chapter 10) to the damaged area to help relieve the "set" of the metal.

○8-6 Anchor Pots

Anchor pots set into the floor at properly located spots (Fig. 8-12) can be used in connection with chains and hydraulic equipment to exert pulls in almost any direction on body and frame parts. Figure 8-13 shows how an anchor pot can be set into an existing floor. Figure 8-14 shows the installation in a new floor. Note that paper or cloth is stuffed into the anchor pot when the concrete is poured to keep the concrete from getting down into the pot.

Figure 8-11 shows how one anchor pot and a portable hydraulic ram can be used to pull on a car body.

Figures 8-15, 8-16, and 8-17 show how the pulling forces are absorbed by the pot. Figure 8-18 shows var-

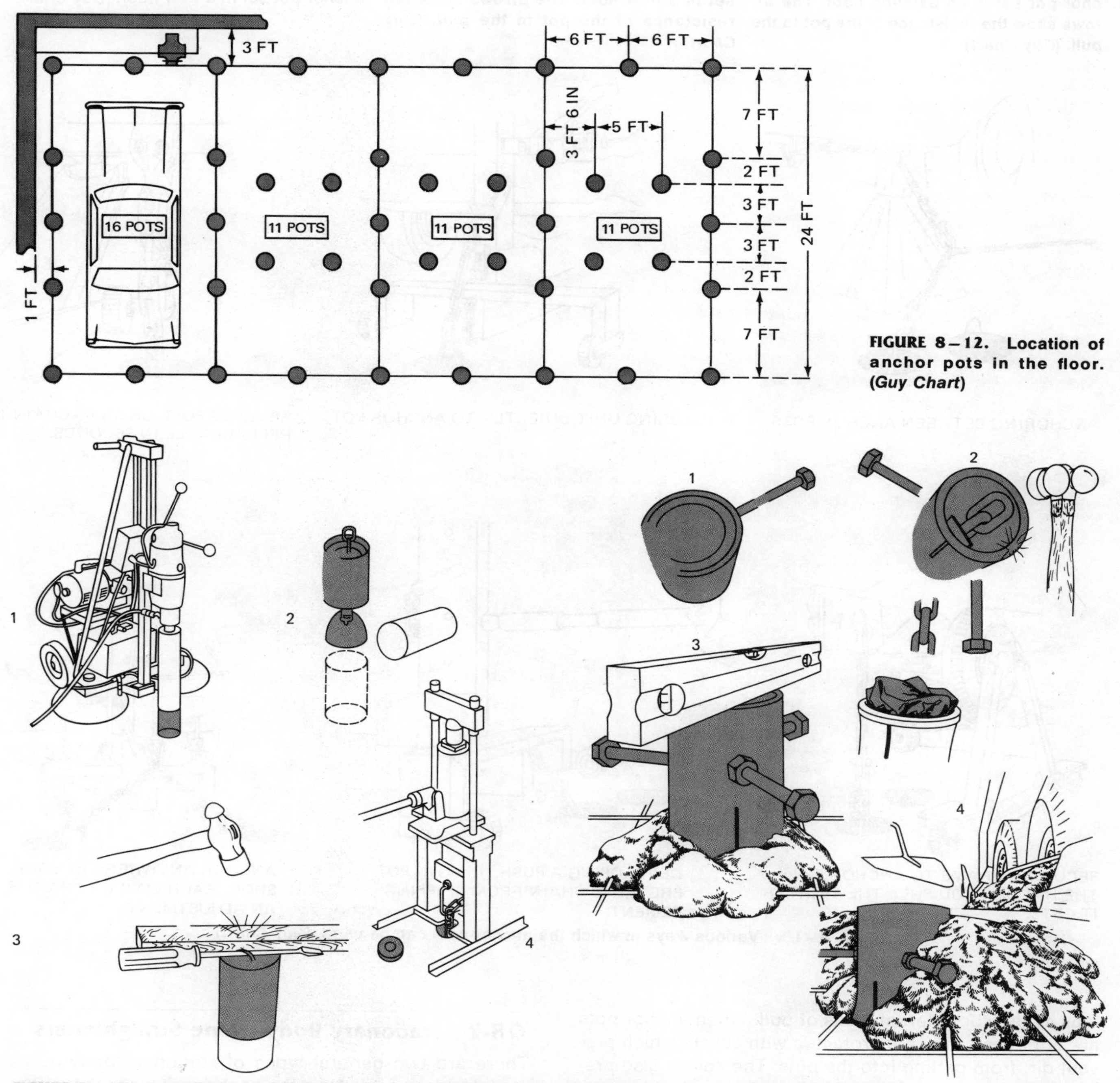

FIGURE 8-12. Location of anchor pots in the floor. *(Guy Chart)*

FIGURE 8-13. Installing an anchor pot in an existing floor. *(Guy Chart)*

FIGURE 8-14. Installing an anchor pot in a new floor. *(Guy Chart)*

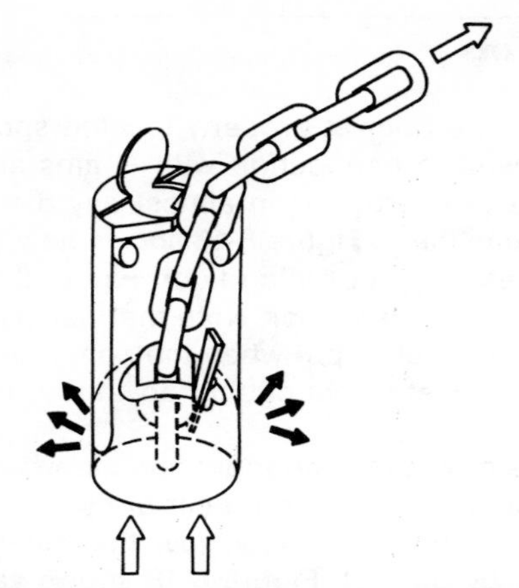

FIGURE 8–15. **The pull on a standard anchor pot set in an existing floor. The arrows show the resistance of the pot to the pull. (*Guy Chart*)**

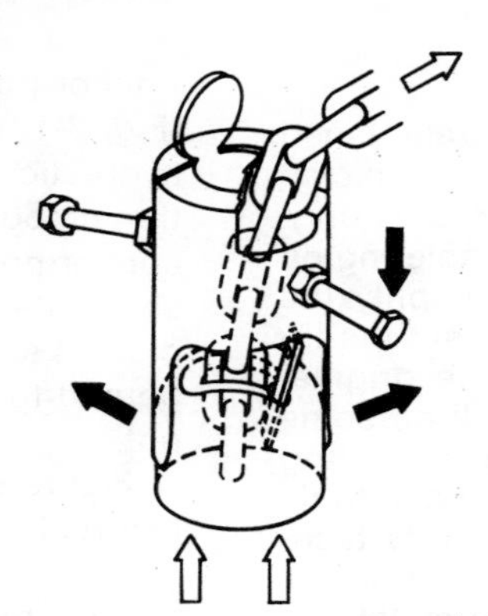

FIGURE 8–16. **The pull on an anchor pot set in a new floor. The arrows show the resistance of the pot to the pull. (*Guy Chart*)**

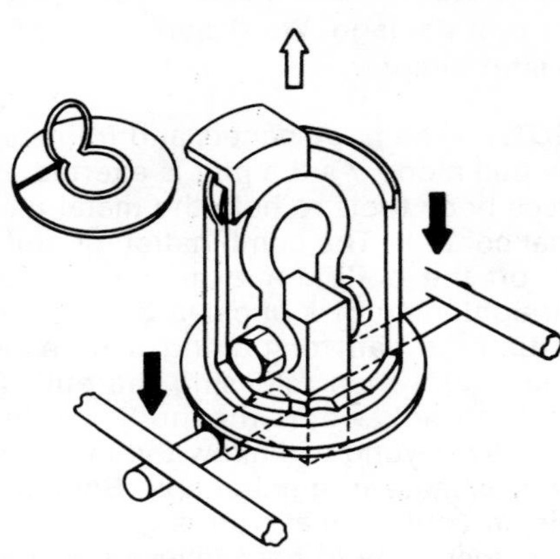

FIGURE 8–17. **The pull on a heavy-duty anchor pot set in a new floor. (*Guy Chart*)**

ANCHORING BETWEEN ANCHOR POTS.

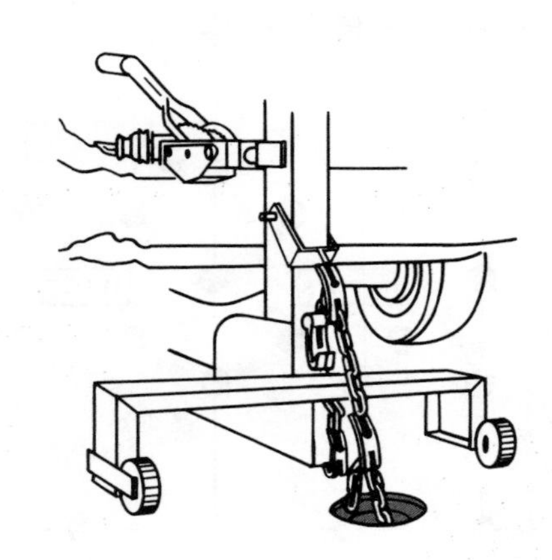

ANCHORING UNIT DIRECTLY TO ANCHOR POT.

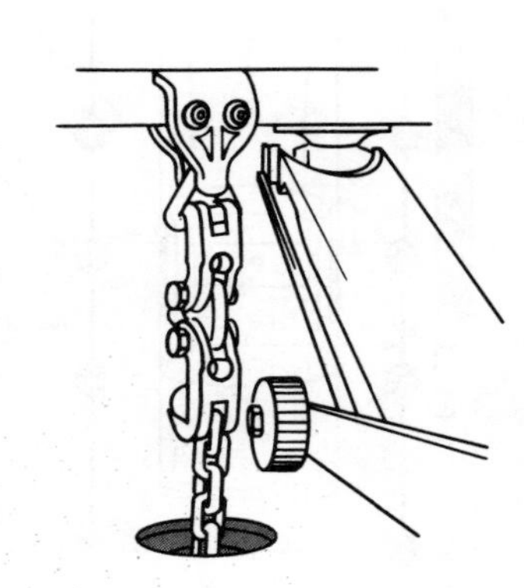

REVERSE PULL ON SILL. CHAIN IS REPLACEABLE IN SECONDS.

SECURING FRAME TO ANCHOR POT. THE HARDER YOU PULL THE TIGHTER IT GETS.

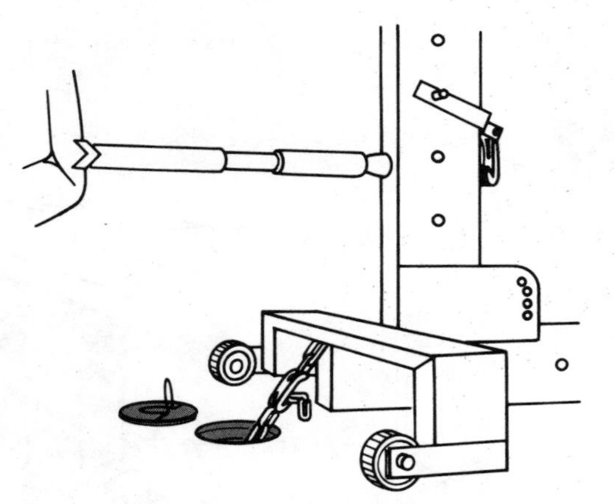

DEVELOPING A PUSH. RING IN POT PREVENTS CHAIN FROM CHIPPING CEMENT.

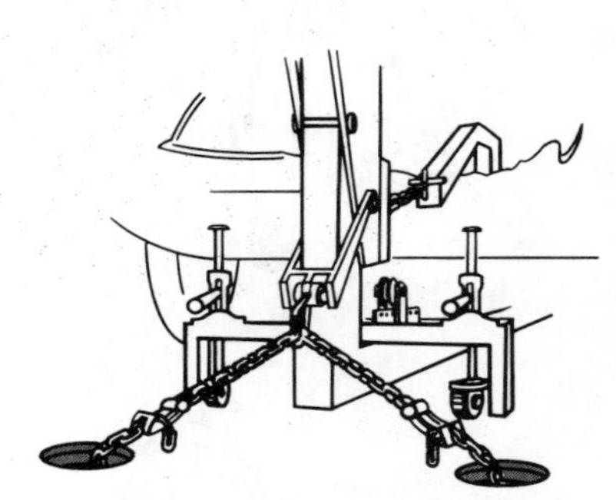

ANCHOR ANYWHERE IN YOUR SHOP. EACH LINK OF CHAIN IS AN ADJUSTMENT.

FIGURE 8–18. **Various ways in which the anchor pots can be used. (*Guy Chart*)**

ious setups for different kinds of pull. When anchor pots are not in use, they are protected with covers which prevent dirt from getting into the pots. The covers also prevent jack or creeper rollers from getting caught in the pots.

○8-7 Stationary Body-Frame Straighteners

There are two general types of stationary body-frame straighteners, aside from the anchor pot type: above-the-floor and in-the-floor. Figure 8-19 shows an above-the-

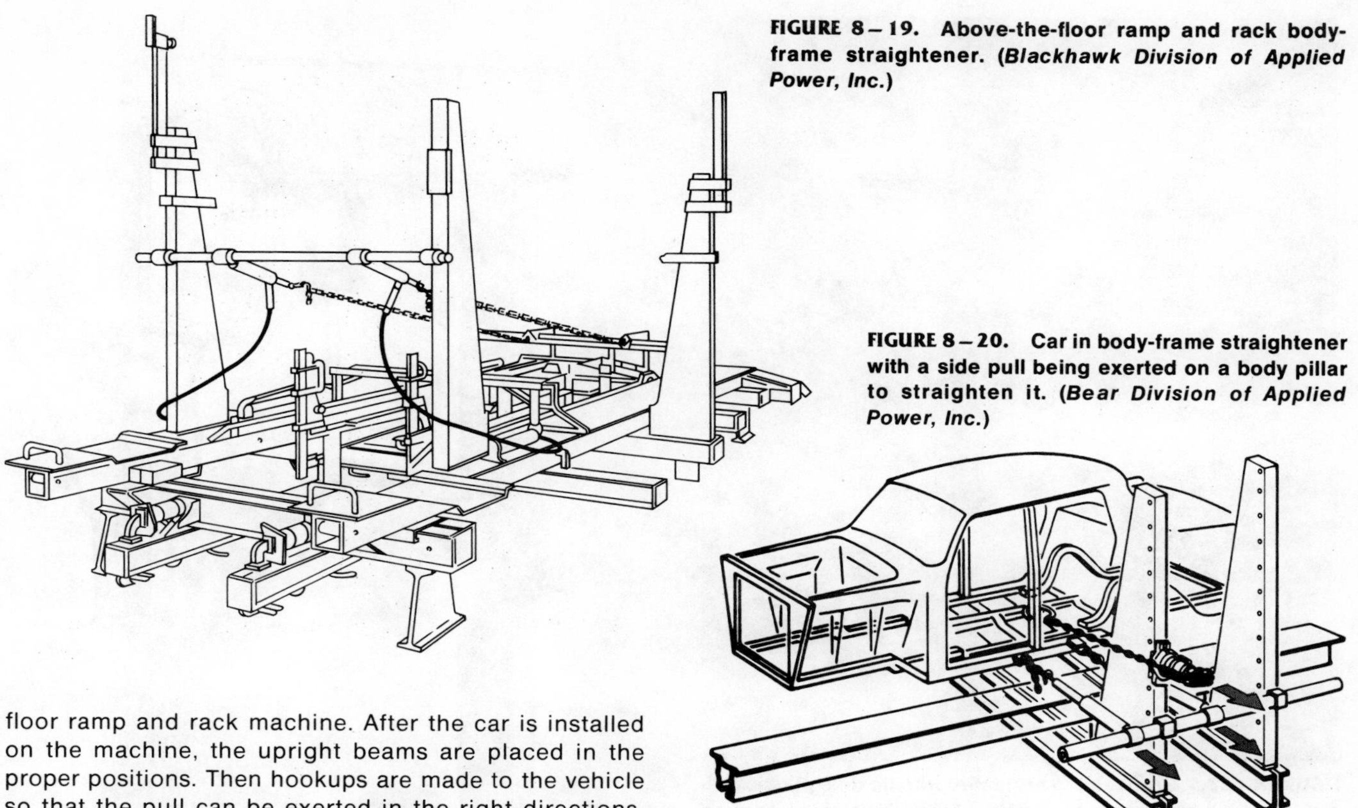

FIGURE 8 – 19. Above-the-floor ramp and rack body-frame straightener. (*Blackhawk Division of Applied Power, Inc.*)

FIGURE 8 – 20. Car in body-frame straightener with a side pull being exerted on a body pillar to straighten it. (*Bear Division of Applied Power, Inc.*)

floor ramp and rack machine. After the car is installed on the machine, the upright beams are placed in the proper positions. Then hookups are made to the vehicle so that the pull can be exerted in the right directions. For example, Fig. 8-20 shows a side pull being exerted on a body pillar to straighten it.

Figure 8-21 shows an in-the-floor body-frame straightener. This unit has a series of anchor rails embedded in the floor. The chain anchors can be slid along in the slots in the anchor rails to achieve any position required. Note that, in the installation shown in Fig. 8-21, there are three power rams in use and each has its own air-hydraulic pump. Three separate and independently controlled pulls can be exerted at the same time. We describe the system in detail in Chapters 19 to 21.

NOTE: As the pulls are exerted, body tools should be used to help the parts move back into shape.

When the tracks are not in use, the grooves can be filled with flexible plastic rail-slot covers, as shown in Fig. 8-22. These covers keep dirt and other foreign matter out of the slots. They also prevent jack and creeper wheels from getting caught in the slots.

In the in-the-floor body-frame straightener shown in Fig. 8-21, the tracks are embedded in the floor. This is the system installed when a new concrete floor is being poured. The same company also supplies an above-the-floor system with the tracks set on the existing concrete floor and anchored to the floor with anchor pots (Fig. 8-23).

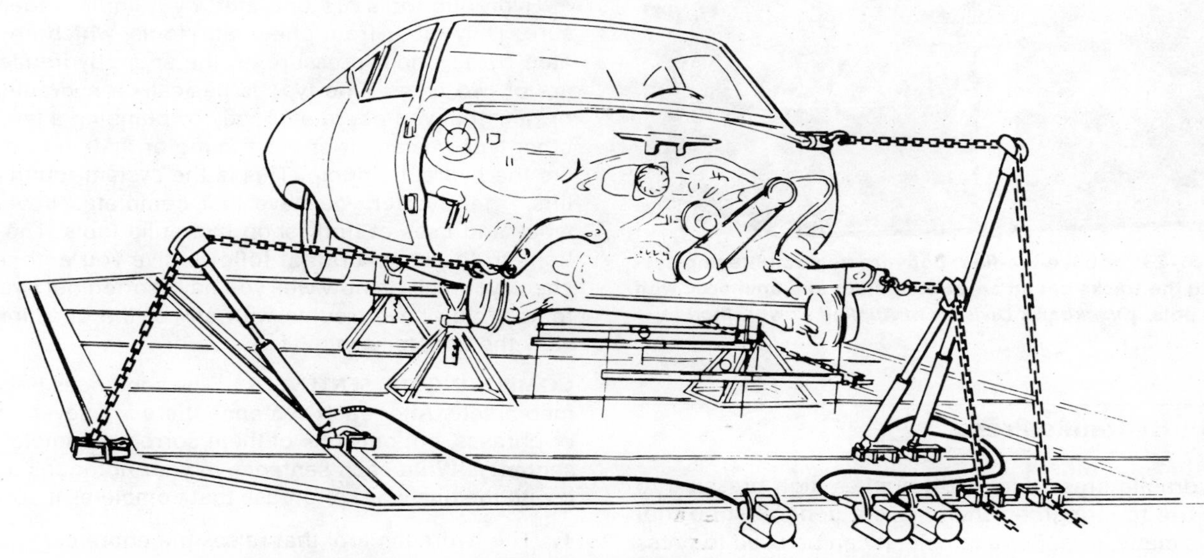

FIGURE 8 – 21. In-the-floor body-frame straightener in use making pulls on the front end of a car. (*Blackhawk Division of Applied Power, Inc.*)

FIGURE 8–22. **Grooves are protected with flexible plastic rail-slot covers when not in use. (*Blackhawk Division of Applied Power, Inc.*)**

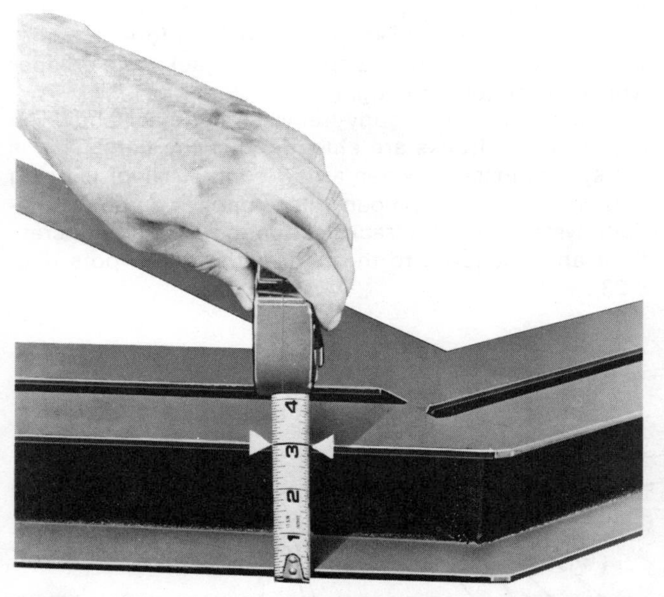

FIGURE 8–23. **Above-the-floor body-frame straightening system with the tracks set on an existing floor and anchored with anchor pots. (*Blackhawk Division of Applied Power, Inc.*)**

○8-8 Hydraulic Press

The hydraulic press (Fig. 8-24) applies high pressure to bent parts to straighten them. It is a general shop tool that has many uses. For example, it can be used to press bushings in or out, to press out rivets, and to straighten bent braces and brackets.

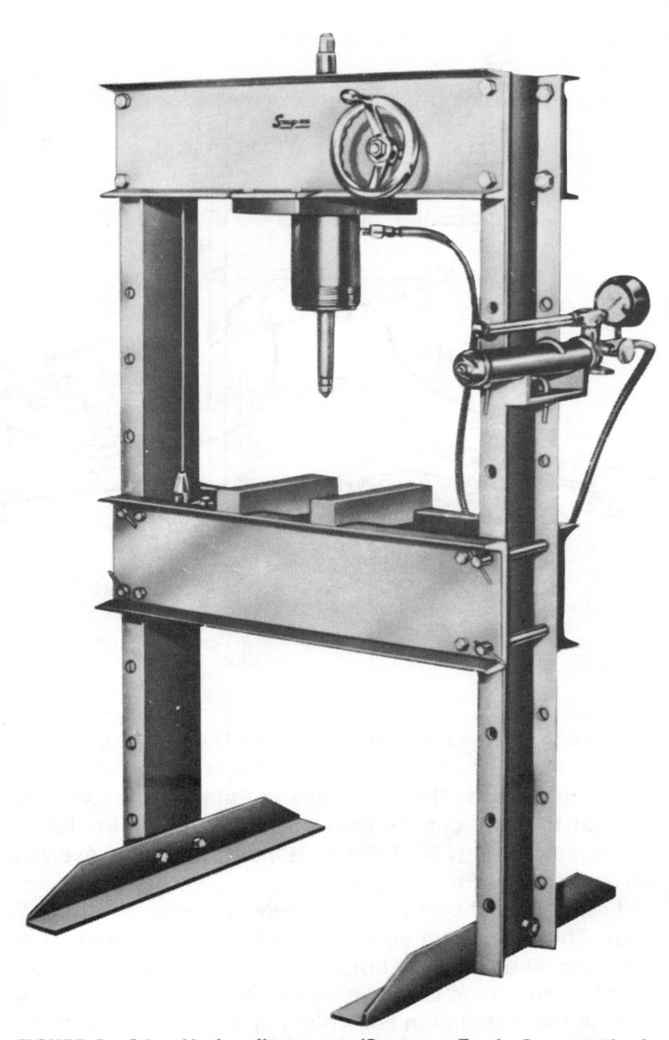

FIGURE 8–24. **Hydraulic press. (*Snap-on Tools Corporation*)**

CHAPTER 8 CHECKUP

NOTE: Since this is a chapter review test, you should review the chapter before taking the test.

Hydraulic tools are operated by a liquid under pressure. They differ from pneumatic tools, which are operated by air under pressure. In the shop, hydraulic tools are of two types. One type is basically a hydraulic jack, or ram, that you operate directly by pumping a lever. The other type has an air or electric motor that, in turn, powers the hydraulic pump. This is the system found in car lifts. The chapter you have just completed covers the types and uses of body-shop hydraulic tools. The questions in the checkup that follows give you a chance to check yourself on how well you have sorted out hydraulic tools. If you have trouble with any of the questions, review the chapter again.

COMPLETING THE SENTENCES The sentences below are incomplete. After each sentence there are several words or phrases, but only one of them correctly completes the sentence. Write each sentence in your notebook, ending it with the one word or phrase that completes it correctly.

1. The hydraulic tool that raises the entire car is the (*a*) floor jack, (*b*) portable crane, (*c*) car lift, (*d*) power jack.

2. To remove an engine, you would use a (*a*) car lift, (*b*) floor jack, (*c*) portable crane, (*d*) frame straightener.
3. In the body shop, the major hydraulic job is to (*a*) straighten frames and sheet metal, (*b*) remove engines, (*c*) lift cars, (*d*) align wheels.
4. Two types of body-frame straighteners are (*a*) air and electric, (*b*) portable and stationary, (*c*) hydraulic and pneumatic, (*d*) lift and crane.
5. Anchor pots are used with (*a*) floor jacks, (*b*) car lifts, (*c*) portable cranes, (*d*) body-frame straighteners.

QUESTIONS Write each of the following questions and then the answer in your notebook. If you have trouble recalling the answer to a question, turn back to the pages that cover the material and study them again.

1. How does a car lift work?
2. When should safety stands be used?
3. Why is each straightening job on a car body or frame unique?
4. What is the reason for pulling a body or frame a little beyond its original shape?
5. What body-repair jobs can be done on a hydraulic press?

SUGGESTIONS FOR FURTHER STUDY

Make a tour of your body shop and locate each hydraulic tool in it. In your notebook, write down the name of the tool, where it is located, and the types of jobs that it is used for. Locate the operating instructions for each tool and learn how to operate each hydraulic tool. Also, in the instructions there probably are illustrations that call out the name of each attachment that can be used with the basic tool. In your notebook, finish your study of each hydraulic tool by listing the additional attachments available for it.

9 THE AUTO BODY SHOP

All body shops have seven basic operational areas:

1. Office
2. Estimating
3. Metal straightening
4. Painting preparation
5. Painting and drying
6. Storage
7. Rest rooms and employee lockers

In the smaller shops, some of these areas and jobs are combined. For example, the technician who is straightening metal may also sand and fill to get the car ready for painting. This technician might also do the actual painting. In small shops, each technician may be required to handle several different operations. Let us look at each of these areas in detail. Then, later in the chapter, we will discuss several shop layouts.

FIGURE 9-2. An essential part of the office is the library, which contains crash-estimating manuals, paint-color books, factory shop manuals, and other literature.

○9-1 Office

The office is an essential part of the auto shop. It should be separated by partitions and doors from the rest of the shop. The office serves several functions. All records are kept there—inventories of parts and materials, time schedules for all employees, time and materials required to complete each job that goes through the shop, payroll information including Social Security and other benefits, insurance records, profit and loss statements, and tax data. The office should be equipped with one or more typewriters, a calculator, filing cabinets, desks and chairs, and chairs or a sofa for customers (Fig. 9-1).

The employees should not use the office as a lounge or lunch room.

FIGURE 9-1. The office should be clean, neat, and equipped with chairs or sofas for customers to sit on while discussing repairs to their car.

The office should have a place for the body-shop library (Fig. 9-2). The library should contain collision estimating and service manuals for various cars, frame-measurement manuals, body-repair estimating manuals, paint-color manuals, and other literature important to the body shop. Larger shops are equipped with microfiche equipment which uses microfilm and a viewer. Great amounts of information can be stored in a small space with this equipment.

A properly run office is the key to a profitable body shop. Without accurate records, an efficient billing and collection procedure, and a good parts and materials purchasing program, the business can fail.

A clean, neat office and a clean, orderly shop will impress customers favorably. When a customer comes in, try to have your discussions in a place where the doors can be closed to shut out the body-shop noises and dust. Often a customer will get more than one estimate, and will not necessarily choose the lowest bid. If a shop creates an unfavorable impression, the customer might give the job to a shop that looks more professional and makes the customer feel more comfortable.

○9-2 Estimating

The estimator may or may not have a special place to work. Estimating may be done on a car that a customer has driven in to the shop, on a car that a wrecker has deposited in the storage space outside, or sometimes on a car at the scene of an accident. The main point is that the estimator must have enough time to make the estimate (Fig. 9-3). This may mean putting the car on a lift so the estimator can assess damage on the underbody and frame. The estimator may be an employee or the owner or manager of the shop.

FIGURE 9–3. Every repair job, large or small, requires a detailed, expert examination and estimate of repair costs.

○9-3 Metal Straightening

Metal straightening falls into two categories: straightening or replacing sheet metal (body panels, doors, trunk lid, hood) and straightening or replacing frame components. These two jobs are closely related, but they require different tools and procedures.

The first step in working on a major repair job is straightening the body and frame with hydraulic and hand tools. These procedures are described in previous chapters. We cover body and frame straightening and sheet-metal work later in the book. We mention them here in connection with the shop layout. For these procedures there has to be a special place where the tools are available and the space is adequate to permit free access to all sides, top, and bottom of the car.

○9-4 Preparation for Painting

In the smaller shop, this work is done in the metal-straightening area. The same worker who straightens the metal probably also does the preparation for the paint job. In the larger shop, the car is moved out of the metal-straightening area into a special place used for the paint preparation work. This work includes final smoothing, filling, and sanding. Then all areas of the car not to be painted, such as wheels, tires, windows, and headlights, are covered with masking tape and paper. Since the sanding operation raises a great deal of dust, particularly if vacuum exhaust devices are not used, some shops partition off the paint preparation area from the rest of the shop. As a health measure, technicians in this enclosed area are then required to wear some sort of dust mask or respirator so they do not breathe the dusty air. This is particularly important when some of the plastic fillers are used. Dust from these is particularly dangerous to breathe. It can cause lung and liver damage.

○9-5 Paint Area

Painting is usually done in an enclosed booth which can be sealed off from the rest of the shop. Any dust in the air can ruin a paint job, so the air in the booth must be

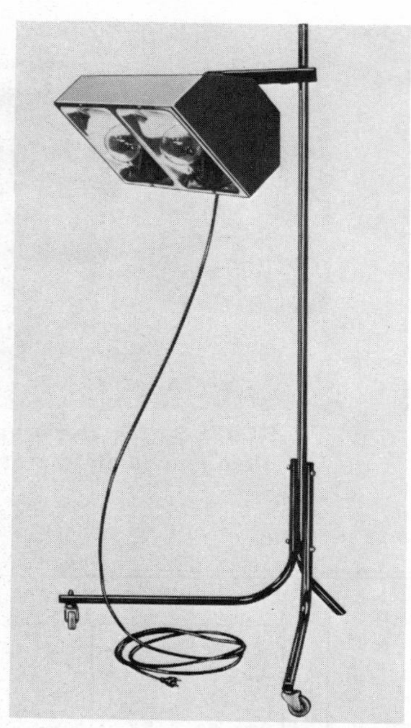

FIGURE 9–4. Portable drying unit for speeding up of paint drying. (*DeVilbiss Company*)

clean. Painters working in the paint booth should always wear respirators. The paints and thinners used are toxic and can cause serious liver and lung damage. One design of car-painting booth includes a paint compartment and a drying compartment. Filtered and heated air is pumped into the spray-paint compartment to replace the air taken out by the exhaust system. The drying chamber has a traveling oven which moves from one section to the next as needed to dry the paint.

Smaller shops may not have enough room for a separate drying area. Instead, they may use portable infrared drying units such as shown in Fig. 9-4. These smaller units are especially handy for drying spot and panel repairs.

○9-6 Storage

There must be adequate storage space for cars awaiting repair and also for customers driving in. Usually, this area is fenced in to protect it from thieves and vandals (Fig. 9-5). It is very important to have a parking area that is easy to get into and out of. Customers do not like to park in difficult places that risk damage to fenders and doors.

○9-7 Rest and Locker Rooms

Rest rooms are essential. It makes sense for them to be cleaned every day and to be kept clean. In larger shops, there are separate rest rooms for customers.

Each employee should have a locker in which to keep uniforms, personal effects, and street clothes. To prevent theft, each locker should be equipped with a lock. In the locker room, some shops have showers available for the employees.

FIGURE 9–5. The area surrounding the body shop, where cars are stored, is often fenced off to protect the cars and the shop from vandals.

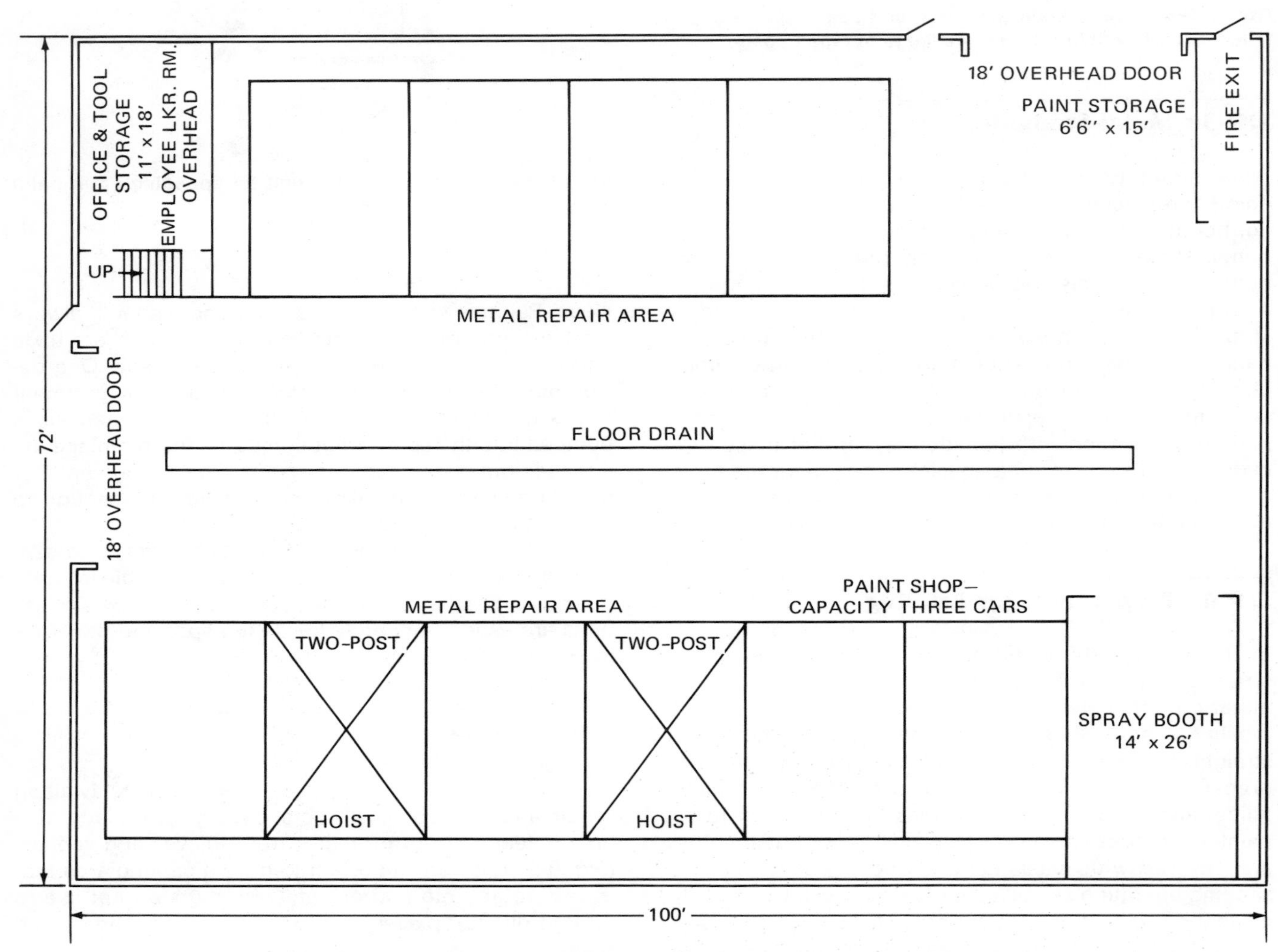

FIGURE 9–6. Floor plan for a shop with 6 employees which has 11 stalls. (*Fisher Body Division of General Motors Corporation*)

○9-8 Auto-Body-Shop Floor Plans

A great variety of floor plans for an auto body shop are possible. All of these floor plans follow a pattern: one or more hoists, stalls along the sides where metal repair is done, a spray booth in one corner or along one side, and the office. If a new auto body shop is being planned, room for expansion should be considered. For example, look at Fig. 9-6. This is a shop for 6 employees that is equipped with 11 stalls including the paint booth. It can be expanded into a 12-employee shop with 18 stalls by the addition of a 32-foot [9.75-m] area, as shown in Fig. 9-7.

○9-9 Stall Sizes

The general rule for stall size is 5 feet [1.52 m] in front of the vehicle for tools and work space (Fig. 9-8). Note

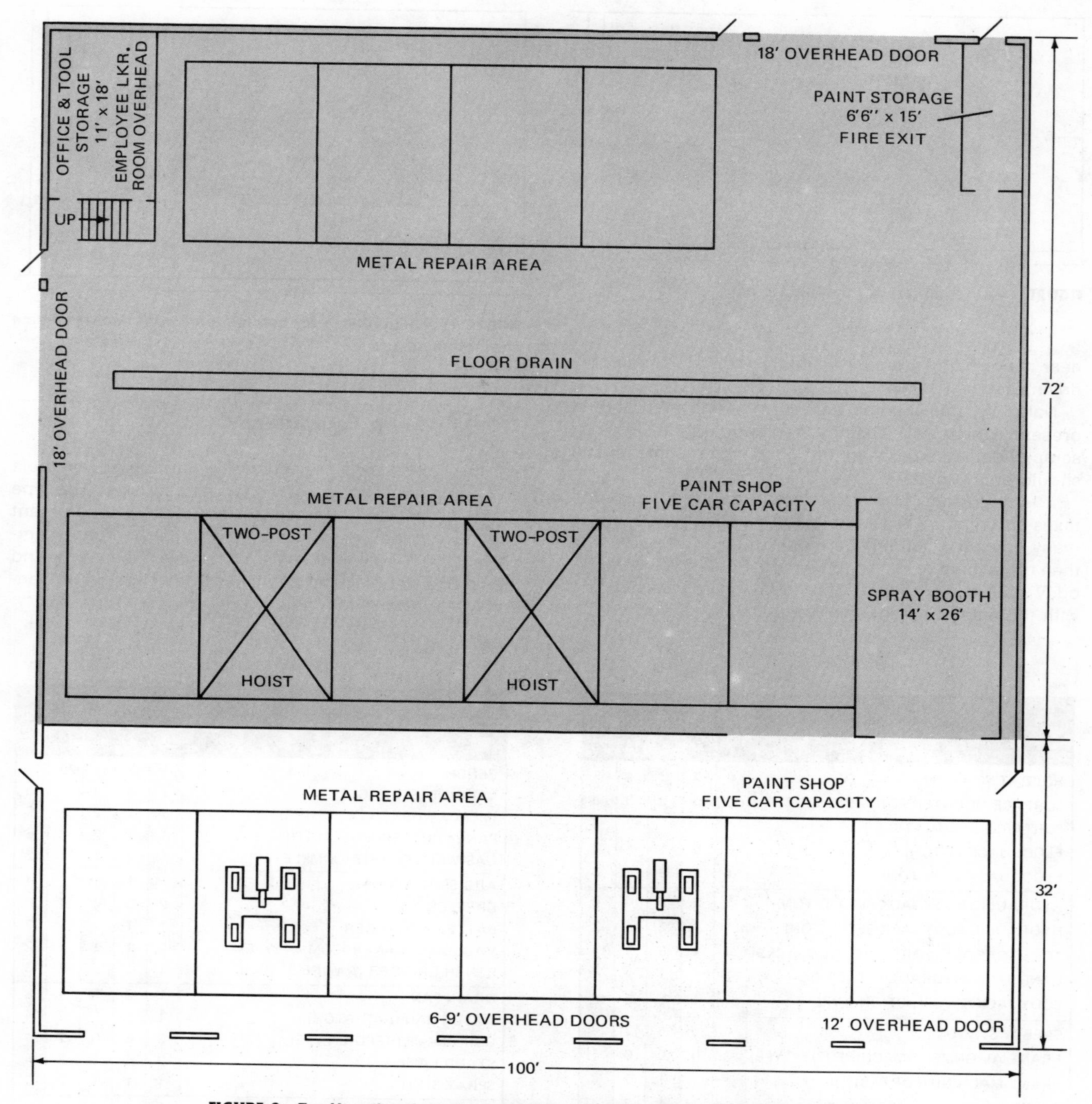

FIGURE 9–7. How the shop shown in Fig. 9-6 can be expanded by the addition of 7 stalls to make it a 12-employee shop. (*Fisher Body Division of General Motors Corporation*)

that this requires a 24-foot [7.32-m] overall space, front to back of the vehicle. Normally, 12 feet [3.66 m] from side to side is desirable, but this distance may be decreased if many compact cars are handled by the shop.

For heavy metal work where frame straightening is done, the side-to-side distance must be greater. Fourteen feet [4.27 m] is a recommended distance (Fig. 9-9). If the body-straightening equipment is permanently mounted or installed in the floor, sufficient space is required around it to allow room to work.

○9-10 Auto-Body-Shop Location

Location of an auto body shop is less important than the location of a drug or food store. Stores that customers go to every few days should be conveniently close. The auto body shop is a place that a customer may visit only once or twice in a lifetime. Yet, it should be reasonably convenient to get to.

Also, it is very important to have plenty of parking space for customers and for cars awaiting repair. The building should be easily seen and, if possible, located

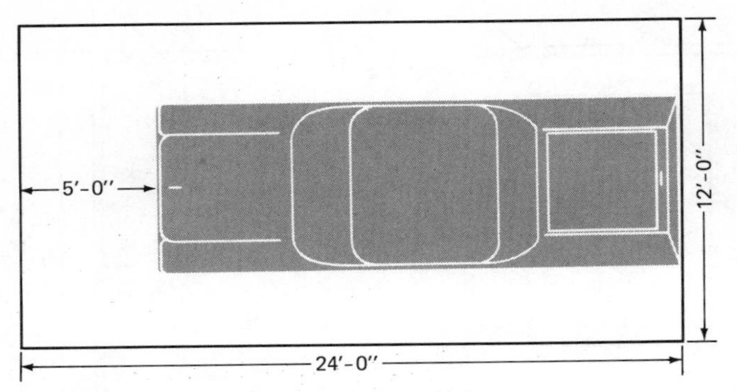

FIGURE 9–8. Stall size for a standard car.

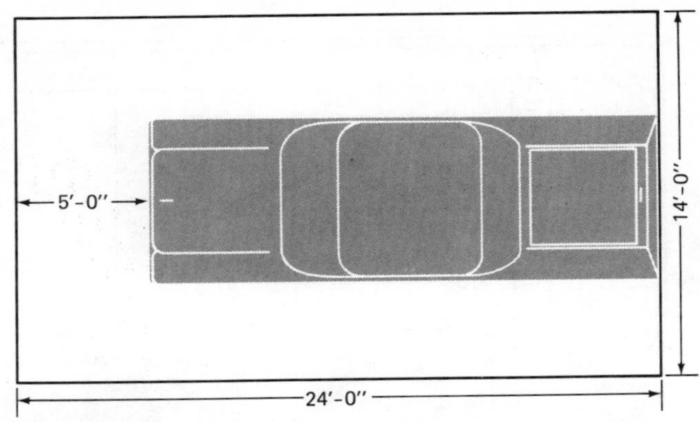

FIGURE 9–9. Stall size for heavy metal work such as frame straightening.

near major highways so it is highly visible to the people driving by.

Naturally, the building and surrounding area should present a neat and businesslike appearance. Piles of scrap and junked parts are not good advertisements and should be avoided.

It is important, also, to locate in an area where the taxes and rent are reasonable. We mention rent because many times the buildings are put up by an investor who then rents them to the shop owners. Sometimes an auto-body-shop owner may be able to finance a new building with the help of a bank mortgage.

○9-11 Shop Equipment

We have described previously the various power tools and equipment that a body shop should have. The type of equipment and number of each piece of equipment depends on the size of the shop and the number of employees working in it. Many studies have been made, and the results of one done by Fisher Body Division of General Motors Corporation is listed in Fig. 9-10.

DESCRIPTION	SIZE OF SHOP (NO. OF EMPLOYEES)				
	2	4	6	13	25
HOIST (TWO-POST)	0	2	3	4	8
SURFACE MOUNTED PORTABLE LIFT	0	0	0	3	5
PORTABLE PNEUMATIC LIFT	1	1	1	2	3
FLOOR JACK (4-TON)	0	0	1	1	2
FLOOR JACK (1-½-TON)	1	2	3	4	8
HYDRAULIC BODY JACK SET (10-TON)	1	2	2	4	6
HYDRAULIC BODY JACK SET (2-TON)	1	1	2	4	7
TOOL BOARDS (HYDRAULIC BODY JACKS)	3	4	5	9	14
HAND JACK, HYDRAULIC (5-TON)	1	1	1	2	4
BODY JACK SET (FRICTION-TYPE)	1	1	1	3	6
SAFETY STANDS	4	6	8	12	24
FRAME ALIGNMENT MACHINE (PIT-TYPE)	0	0	0	0	1
FRAME MACHINE (PORTABLE)	1	1	1	2	4
CENTER LINE GAUGE SET	1	1	1	2	4
TRAM GAUGE	1	1	1	2	4
AIR COMPRESSOR (7.5 hp–2-STAGE)	0	0	1	1	1
AIR COMPRESSOR (5 hp–2-STAGE)	0	1	0	0	1
AIR COMPRESSOR (3 hp–1-STAGE)	1	0	0	0	0
MOISTURE TRAP AND REGULATOR	1	2	4	8	10
DISC SANDER (PORTABLE)	2	3	4	6	12
DISC CUTTER	1	1	1	2	4
DRILL MOTOR (¼")	1	1	2	3	6
DRILL MOTOR (¼" OFFSET)	1	1	1	1	1
DRILL MOTOR (⅜")	0	1	1	1	2
DRILL MOTOR (½")	1	1	1	1	1

DESCRIPTION	SIZE OF SHOP (NO. OF EMPLOYEES)				
	2	4	6	13	25
BENCH	5	7	11	20	40
CABINET (STORAGE)	2	3	4	5	10
IMPACT WRENCH (½" DRIVE)	1	1	2	3	6
PANEL CUTTER (PNEUMATIC)	1	1	2	3	6
GAS-WELD OUTFIT (COMPLETE)	1	2	3	*1	*2
ARC-SPOT WELDER	1	1	1	2	4
CREEPER	2	3	4	4	8
BATTERY CHARGER	1	1	1	1	2
VACUUM CLEANER (COMM.-TYPE)	0	1	1	2	2
BENCH GRINDER (W/WIRE BRUSH)	1	1	1	2	3
DRAIN PAN	1	2	2	4	8
WATER CAN (RADIATOR)	1	1	2	2	4
CORD LAMP (RECOIL TYPE)	3	6	10	12	24
STAND LAMP	2	4	6	8	14
SPRAY BOOTH	1	1	1	2	2
PAINT SHAKER	1	1	1	2	2
SPRAY GUN (SIPHON)	2	2	3	6	10
SPRAY GUN (PRESSURE–2 QT)	1	1	1	1	2
SIPHON CUP	4	4	6	9	13
AIR HOSE (5/16" I.D.–25 FT)	2	2	3	15	25
AIR HOSE (5/16" I.D.–50 FT)	2	3	5	8	12
AIR TRANSFORMER	1	2	2	4	4
SPRAY GUN (TOUCH-UP)	1	1	2	2	2
PAINT POLISHER	1	1	2	2	4
DRYING LAMP (QUARTZ-TYPE)	2	2	2	3	4
BANK OF DRYING LAMPS	0	0	0	0	1
SANDER (PNEUMATIC)	1	1	2	3	6
MASKING UNIT (PORTABLE)	1	1	1	2	4

*MANIFOLD SYSTEM RECOMMENDED FROM A CENTRAL GAS SUPPLY WITH OUTLETS FOR EACH THREE METAL REPAIR STALLS.

FIGURE 9–10. Recommended equipment for automotive body shops of varying size. (*Fisher Body Division of General Motors Corporation*)

CHAPTER 9 CHECKUP

NOTE: Since this is a chapter review test, you should review the chapter before taking the test.

Automotive body shops differ in size from small one-person operations to large, highly departmentalized operations with many employees. But regardless of size, a body shop has seven basic operational areas. In this chapter, we have discussed and taken a look at several recommended body-shop layouts. For a complete understanding of the automotive body-repair business, you should understand why each of the seven operational areas is necessary. The information in the chapter provides you with this knowledge. Now the questions that follow will help you to review the information and to find out how well you understand it.

COMPLETING THE SENTENCES The sentences below are incomplete. After each sentence there are several words or phrases, but only one of them correctly completes the sentence. Write each sentence in your notebook, ending it with the one word or phrase that completes it correctly.

1. All records such as completed estimates and repair orders should be kept in the (*a*) technician's stall, (*b*) office, (*c*) locker room, (*d*) paint area.
2. When a wrecker tows in a wrecked car, the first step is to (*a*) write an estimate, (*b*) straighten the metal, (*c*) prepare for painting, (*d*) paint the car.
3. Masking a car is part of (*a*) estimating, (*b*) metal straightening, (*c*) painting, (*d*) preparation for painting.
4. In a body-shop layout, the storage area is for (*a*) storing cars, (*b*) storing records, (*c*) storing supplies, (*d*) dirty laundry.
5. As a general rule, the technician's work space in front of a vehicle should be (*a*) 12 feet [3.66 m], (*b*) 24 feet [7.32 m], (*c*) 5 feet [1.52 m], (*d*) 14 feet [4.27 m].

QUESTIONS Write each of the following questions and then the answer in your notebook. If you have trouble recalling the answer to a question, you should then turn back to the pages that cover the material and study them again.

1. What are the seven basic operational areas in a body shop?
2. Who uses the collision-estimating manuals?
3. Why should painters working in the paint booth wear a respirator?
4. What are the dimensions for a typical body-shop stall?
5. Where should the automotive body shop be located?

SUGGESTIONS FOR FURTHER STUDY

Take a close look at the body shop you will be working in. In addition to the seven basic operational areas discussed in this chapter, your school body shop may also have a separate classroom area. On a page in your notebook, draw a rough sketch of the body shop and classroom areas. Then, identify and label each of the areas.

PART 2

WELDING

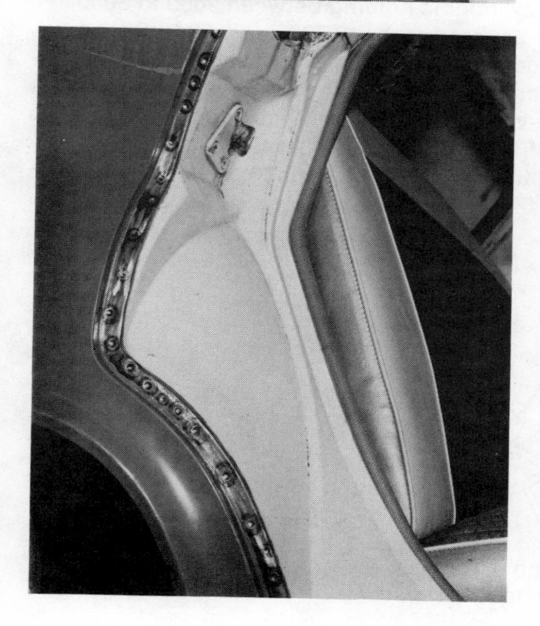

Welding is a very important part of auto body activity. There are two general types of welding equipment used in the body shop: gas and electric. The gas-welding equipment uses two gases – oxygen and acetylene – which are mixed and burned to produce a very hot flame. In addition to welding, gas-welding equipment is used for brazing, heat shrinking, and cutting metals.

There are two types of electric welding: spot and arc. Spot welding sends a high electric current at one spot through two overlapping metal sheets to weld that spot together. Electric arc welding uses an electric arc to weld. The arc is formed between an electrode and the metal parts to be joined. The heat from the arc is so intense that the electrode and the metal melt at the point where the arc strikes the metal. The melted metal fuses to form the weld.

We describe both types of welding in this part. Part 2 consists of three chapters, as follows:

10 OXYACETYLENE WELDING AND CUTTING

The oxyacetylene torch has several uses in the body shop. It is used for welding metal parts together, as shown in Fig. 10-1. It also is used for cutting metal, heating metal to normalize or shrink it, brazing, and applying body solder. We explain gas welding and cutting in this chapter and describe the various ways in which oxyacetylene-welding equipment is used. Note that the equipment is also called acetylene or gas-welding equipment. It uses two separate gases, oxygen and acetylene, to produce the flame. Following chapters describe brazing and body soldering with the torch.

○ 10-1 What Is Welding?

Simply stated, welding is a permanent type of metal-joining process that uses heat to form the bond. When sheet metal is heated to a high enough temperature, it melts. In gas welding, the heat comes from a hot burning flame at the tip of the torch. (The torch is discussed in detail later in this chapter). As the temperature rises, the heat fuses, or melts together, the two adjoining pieces of sheet metal. When the liquid metal cools, the two pieces have been joined together to form a single sheet.

Two types of joining can be done with gas-welding equipment. These are welding, similar to the procedure discussed above, and brazing. Both processes are covered in Chapter 11.

In electric or arc welding, which we discuss in Chapter 12, the heat from an electric arc melts the metal.

○ 10-2 Oxyacetylene-Welding Equipment

The oxyacetylene-welding process uses highly flammable acetylene gas and burns it in pure oxygen to produce a flame with temperatures up to 6300°F [3482°C]. The temperature reached depends on the percentages of oxygen and acetylene delivered to the torch.

The oxyacetylene-welding equipment includes the following (see Fig. 10-2):

1. Oxygen cylinder with regulator
2. Acetylene cylinder with regulator
3. Cart or hand truck with safety chains for cylinders
4. Fire extinguisher, often mounted on the hand truck
5. Hoses
6. Torch ("blowpipe") with handle, mixing chamber, check valves, and tip
7. Eye shield or goggles for the technician
8. Torch lighter

Before we describe each of these and put them all together to explain the various ways the equipment can be used, we want to emphasize safety precautions that must be followed.

○ 10-3 Safety

As we mentioned in Chapter 3, there are certain special precautions that must be observed when gas-welding equipment is used. See Figs. 3-9 and 3-10. Remember that the mixture of oxygen and acetylene is highly explosive. The flame is very hot. The materials worked on will reach high temperatures. All hose connections must be tight and leakproof. Hoses must be in good condition. Any leakage could result in a disastrous explosion and fire.

The cylinders must be treated with respect. Remember that the oxygen cylinder is holding between 2000 to 3000 psi (pounds per square inch) [13,790 to 20,684 kPa] of pressure. Cylinders are supplied with valve-protection caps, or safety caps (Fig. 10-3). The purpose of the cap is to protect the valve during transit. The cap should not be removed until after the cylinder is safely mounted on and chained to the cart or truck. If the cap is removed

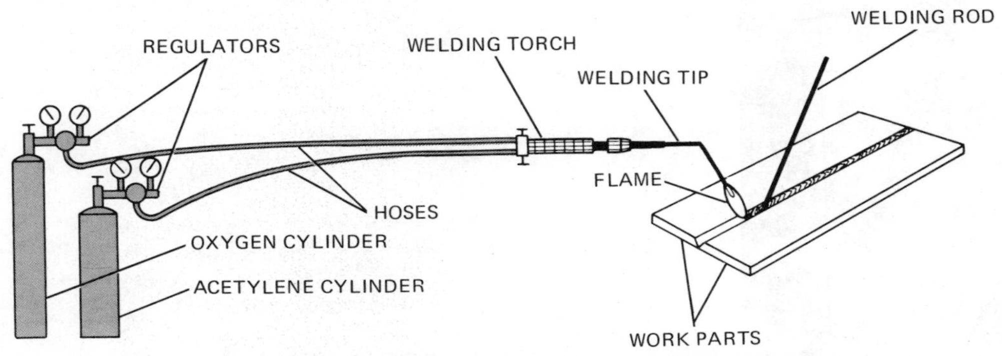

FIGURE 10-1. Using gas-welding equipment. (*General Motors Corporation*)

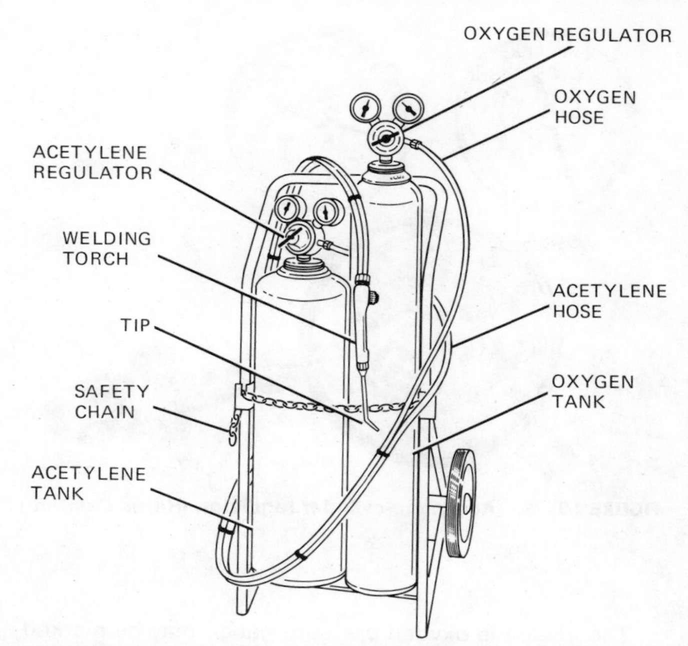

FIGURE 10–2. Oxyacetylene-welding equipment mounted on cart. Note chains that secure the cylinders of acetylene and oxygen to the cart.

and the cylinder falls over, the valve might break off. If the cylinder contains oxygen, the compressed gas will be released at such high pressure it can turn the cylinder into a deadly missile which can actually ram through brick walls. Anyone in the way could be injured or killed. If the gas is acetylene, release of the gas by the breaking off of the valve could cause an explosion and fire.

CAUTION: Sometimes sheet metal is treated with rust-resistant zinc. When it is heated, as for example by gas welding, toxic zinc-oxide fumes are released. Adequate ventilation should be provided or respirators should be worn by technicians.

○10-4 Oxygen Cylinder

The oxygen cylinder (Fig. 10-3) is a high-strength steel tank capable of holding pressures of 3000 psi [211 kg/cm²]. Oxygen cylinders are painted either yellow or green so they can be easily identified. The cylinder has two valves: a safety valve and the operating valve. The safety valve is designed to open and release the gas in case the pressure goes so high as to cause the cylinder to explode. For example, in case of a fire, the cylinder might get so hot that the gas pressure inside would cause the cylinder to explode. The safety valve releases the pressure so as to prevent this. Release of the oxygen in this manner is much less hazardous than by a cylinder explosion.

The operating valve at the top of the cylinder is a double-acting valve. That is, when it is turned all the way in, it seals the cylinder. When it is turned all the way out, it opens the cylinder to allow oxygen to flow to the regulator. Also, in the out position, the valve seals against the valve head to prevent any leakage of oxygen around the valve stem. When you use gas-welding equipment, turn the oxygen cylinder valve all the way on in the open position to get this sealing effect.

Oxygen cylinders are filled to a pressure of 2200 psi

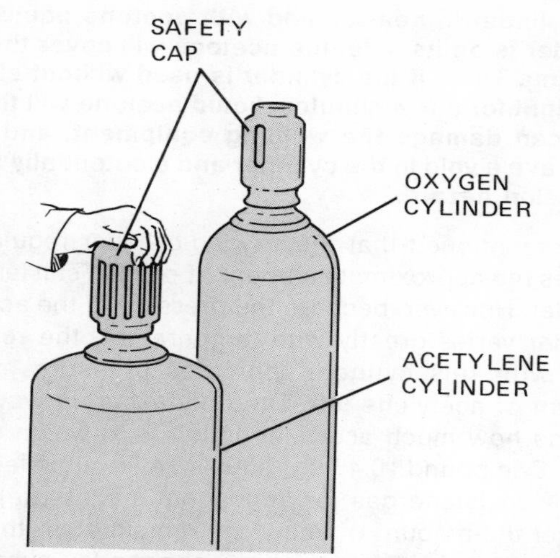

FIGURE 10–3. Oxygen and acetylene cylinders with safety caps in place. (*Rego Company*)

[155 kg/cm²] at 70°F [21°C]. As we indicated previously, pressure will go up as temperature increases. It will also go down as pressure decreases. For example, a fully filled cylinder at 0°F [−17.8°C] will have a pressure of only about 1780 psi [125 kg/cm²]. If the cylinder is heated to 120°F [48.9°C], the pressure will go up to 2500 psi [176 kg/cm²].

Oxygen cylinders are supplied in three sizes for most purposes. The large size used in auto body shops holds about 244 cubic feet [4.088 m³] of oxygen (if released at atmospheric pressure) at 70°F [21.1°C]. The two-stage oxygen regulator, described later and illustrated in Fig. 10-5, indicates the approximate amount of oxygen still left in the cylinder.

○10-5 Acetylene Cylinder

Acetylene gas is produced by the action of a solid chemical, calcium carbide, when immersed in water. The gas is collected and stored in cylinders. The acetylene cylinder is somewhat different in construction from the oxygen cylinder (Fig. 10-2). Like the oxygen cylinder, the acetylene cylinder is made of steel. However, it is lighter in construction because it does not have to contain such high pressures.

Actually, free acetylene gas is very unstable at any pressure above 15 psi [1.08 kg/cm²]. When the gas is put under pressure, it will explode. Thus, a special process has been developed to store acetylene. The acetylene tank is filled with a porous substance such as charcoal, asbestos, or balsa wood. This material is saturated with the liquid acetone. Acetone has the peculiar property of being able to absorb large amounts of acetylene gas. Acetylene stored in this manner is safe, provided normal precautions are taken, as we explain below.

There are two general kinds of acetylene cylinders. One has a safety cap similar to the one for the oxygen cylinder to protect the cylinder valve. This type is shown in Fig. 10-3. The other type has the cylinder valve recessed so that a safety cap is not necessary.

CAUTION: Never store an acetylene cylinder on its side. Always store it upright. The reason for this is that

the cylinder is nearly filled with acetone liquid. If the cylinder is on its side, the acetone will cover the valve opening. Then, if the cylinder is used without standing it upright for a few minutes, liquid acetone will flow out. This can damage the welding equipment, and also it will leave a void in the cylinder and a potentially serious explosion hazard.

We mentioned that the oxygen-cylinder regulator indicates the approximate amount of oxygen still left in the cylinder. However, because the pressure in the acetylene cylinder varies greatly with temperature, the regulator used with this cylinder indicates pressure, not the amount of acetylene left. The only accurate way to determine how much acetylene is left is to weigh the cylinder. One pound [0.45 kg] equals 14.74 cubic feet [0.42 m^3] of acetylene gas (at atmospheric pressure). Thus, you get the amount of acetylene remaining in the cylinder (in cubic feet) by weighing it (pounds), subtracting the cylinder weight empty (pounds), and multiplying the result by 14.74. Empty cylinder weight is stamped on the cylinder.

The acetylene cylinder has safety fuse plugs at top and bottom. These fuses will melt at a few degrees above the boiling point of water to release the internal pressure and thus prevent an explosion.

○ 10-6 Regulators

Each cylinder must be equipped with a regulator to reduce the internal pressures in the tanks to the low pressures required at the torch tip. Figures 10-4 and 10-5 show regulators for the oxygen cylinder and the acetylene cylinder. The oxygen-cylinder regulator, shown in Fig. 10-4, has two gauges. The gauge connected to the inlet side shows the tank pressure. The other gauge shows the outlet or working pressure that goes to the torch. Turning the valve handle in increases this outlet pressure. That is, this lets more of the tank pressure through the regulator. Turning the valve out reduces the pressure at the outlet.

FIGURE 10–4. Two-stage oxygen-cylinder regulator. (*Harris Calorific*)

FIGURE 10–5. Acetylene-cylinder regulator. (*Harris Calorific*)

The inlet-side oxygen pressure gauge may be marked to indicate both actual pressure and the amount of oxygen still remaining in the cylinder (based on the volume it would occupy if released at atmospheric pressure).

The acetylene regulator, shown in Fig. 10-5, also has two gauges. One shows the cylinder pressure, and the other shows the outlet pressure that goes to the torch. The outlet pressure can be changed by changing the valve setting.

○ 10-7 Regulator Threads

It could be disastrous to accidentally install the wrong regulator on a cylinder—an oxygen regulator on an acetylene cylinder, or an acetylene regulator on an oxygen cylinder. To prevent this, the two regulator connections have different threads. The connecting nut of an oxygen regulator has right-hand threads to fit the right-hand threads on the oxygen-cylinder valve. The connecting nut on the acetylene regulator has left-hand threads that fit the left-hand threads of the acetylene-cylinder valve. In addition, some oxygen regulators are coded in green and acetylene regulators in red for easy identification.

○ 10-8 Handling Cylinders

Compressed-gas cylinders provide safe and convenient sources of oxygen and acetylene. However, they must be treated with respect and handled with care. Cylinders must always be chained to the welding cart, to the wall, or to a post so they cannot fall. Always use the cylinders when they are in the vertical or upright position. Never use gas from cylinders that are lying on their side.

Many body shops have several sets of gas-welding equipment in use and do not store extra cylinders of oxygen or acetylene. When a cylinder is low, the shop foreman calls the local gas distributor, who sends over a truck with the required new cylinders. The truck driver then exchanges cylinders (Fig. 10-6).

Some shops keep extra oxygen and acetylene cylinders in reserve. Here is how to store and exchange them.

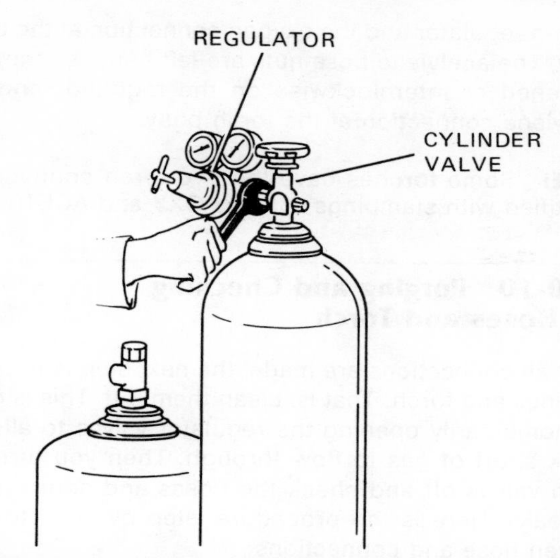

FIGURE 10-6. Exchanging cylinders on the cart requires removal of the regulator from the empty tank and reconnecting it to the full tank. *(Rego Company)*

We have already noted, in Chapter 3, that compressed-gas cylinders are sometimes found by safety inspectors to be improperly stored. They should not be stored near radiators or other sources of heat. They should be kept far away from combustible materials, stairs, or elevators. They should not be stored in unventilated enclosures such as lockers or closets. There should be at least 20 feet [6.1 m] between stored oxygen and acetylene cylinders. Or, the cylinders should be separated by a fireproof barrier.

Cylinders should never be allowed to stand free but should be secured with a chain or lashing to keep them from toppling over. See Fig. 3-9. Cylinders should always be plainly marked or painted to identify their contents.

Now, let's discuss the procedure of taking an empty cylinder off the cart and putting a new cylinder in its place. As a first step, turn off the cylinder valve on the empty cylinder and disconnect the regulator. Then install a safety cap on the cylinder (Fig. 10-3). Next, unhook the chain holding the cylinder to the cart. Tip the cylinder on edge and roll it off the cart and to the place where cylinders of its type are stored. Chain it in place upright. Mark it "E" or "Empty" with a piece of chalk.

NOTE: Always handle "empty" cylinders the same as full cylinders. The empty ones may still have some gas in them.

Next, unchain the new cylinder, tip it on edge, and roll it to the cart. After you have put it on the cart, install the chain. Next, remove the safety cap. Before installing the regulator, "crack" the cylinder valve slightly to blow any dirt out of the valve opening (Fig. 10-7). To do this, stand to one side of the cylinder as shown in Fig. 10-7. Open the cylinder valve slightly, until you hear the hiss of escaping gas. Then immediately close the valve completely, but not too tightly.

CAUTION: Do not crack the acetylene cylinder valve in a small or closed room or close to any open flame. For safety, roll the cart into an open area where no flame is present.

Now attach the regulator (see Fig. 10-6). Use an open-end wrench and turn the regulator attaching nut in the

FIGURE 10-7. Cracking the cylinder valve. *(Rego Company)*

proper direction (clockwise for oxygen, counterclockwise for acetylene). Before you tighten the nut, position the regulator so the gauges are easy to read.

If the regulator connection leaks after you have applied the proper torque to the wrench, shut off the valve and remove the regulator. Carefully clean the threads and seat on the regulator and on the cylinder valve. Should you find cross-threading, nicks, cracks, or other damage, do not use the damaged equipment. Call your welding-equipment supplier for service.

CAUTION: Never lubricate the threads of the regulator nuts or cylinder valves. If high-pressure oxygen hits oil or grease, an explosion and fire can result. Technicians doing gas welding should not wear greasy or oily gloves or clothes while working with the gas torch. Oil and grease should be kept away from the gas cylinders and hoses.

○ 10-9 Setting Up to Weld

We will now go through the procedure of setting up the gas-welding equipment and preparing to do a job. First, you connect the regulators if they are not already connected to the cylinders, as outlined above.

Next, you select the torch body and tip that you need to do the job. There are two basic types of torch bodies, one for welding and the other for cutting. See Figs. 10-8 and 10-9. The basic difference is in the oxygen control. The welding torch has two rotary-type valves, one for oxygen and one for acetylene. They are adjusted to give the steady flame needed for welding or brazing.

The cutting torch has four valves, three for oxygen and one for acetylene (Fig. 10-9). The torch oxygen valve (at the back of the torch) is opened to admit oxygen at the regulator pressure to the torch body. The second valve, the preheat oxygen valve, is used to adjust the amount of oxygen in the preheat flame. The third valve, operated by a lever, releases additional oxygen at full regulator pressure into the flame. This produces an oxygen-rich flame which reacts with the white-hot metal to cut through it.

There are various types of welding and cutting tips, as shown in Figs. 10-10 and 10-11. The thicker the metal to be welded or cut, the larger the tip. Once the proper

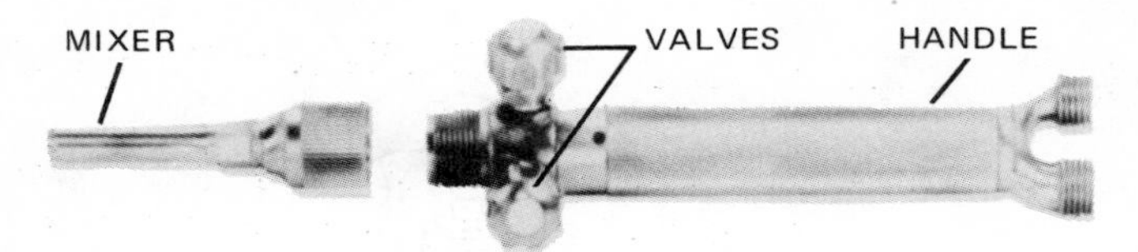

FIGURE 10–8. Welding torch. (*Harris Calorific*)

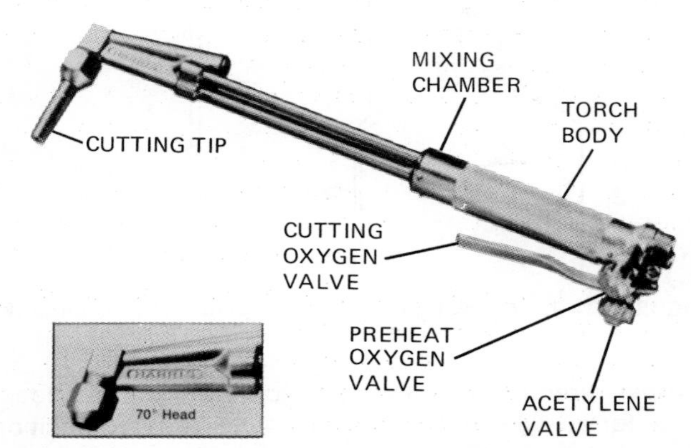

FIGURE 10–9. Cutting torch, showing both straight and 70° heads. (*Harris Calorific*)

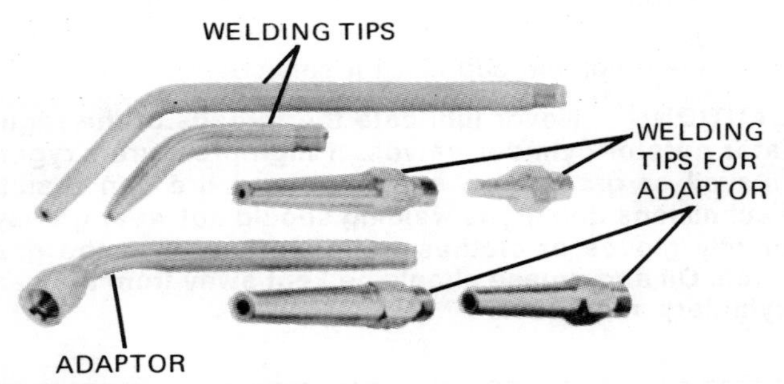

FIGURE 10–10. Welding tips. (*Harris Calorific*)

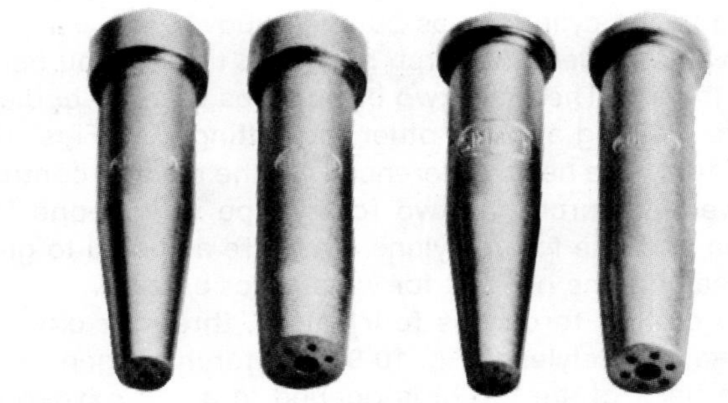

FIGURE 10–11. Cutting tips. (*Harris Calorific*)

torch body and tip have been selected and assembled, the torch is ready to be connected to the cylinders. Hoses of the proper type and length are used. Both ends of the hoses have nuts, which are screwed onto the regulator and torch threads. Remember that the oxygen hose nuts are right-hand, so they are tightened clockwise on the oxygen regulator and the oxygen connection at the torch body. The acetylene hose nuts are left-hand, so they are tightened counterclockwise on the regulator and the acetylene connection at the torch body.

NOTE: Some torches have the two torch connections identified with stampings such as OXY and ACET.

○ 10-10 Purging and Checking the Hoses and Torch

After all connections are made, the next step is to purge the lines and torch. That is, clean them out. This is done by momentarily opening the regulator valves to allow a quick spurt of gas to flow through. Then you turn the torch valves off and check the hoses and connections for leaks. Here is the procedure, step by step, for the oxygen hose and connections:

1. Loosen the regulator valve by turning it counterclockwise until the handle is loose. The valve is now closed. Open the cylinder valve. Oxygen will now enter the regulator, and the cylinder pressure will be indicated on the cylinder pressure valve of the regulator.

NOTE: Open the oxygen-cylinder valve *all the way.* This is a double-seating valve, and opening it all the way allows it to backseat in the open position. This prevents oxygen leakage around the valve stem.

2. Check to make sure the oxygen valve on the torch is open. Then slowly turn the pressure-regulator valve in until oxygen begins to come out of the torch tip. Now shut off the torch oxygen valve.
3. There is now pressure in the hose and connections. To check for leaks, brush soapy water over the regulator, hose, and connections. Leaks will cause bubbles to form. Any leaks should be fixed before proceeding further.
4. If all is in order, turn the cylinder valve off. This shuts off the oxygen flow to the regulator and torch. Now back off the regulator valve to close it. This is a double assurance that gas will not be escaping from the cylinder.

NOTE: Whenever finishing a welding job or stopping for a while, *always* make it a habit to shut off *both* valves—the cylinder valve *and* the pressure-regulator valve.

5. The procedure for the acetylene regulator, hose, and torch is the same except for one thing. You turn the acetylene cylinder valve only *one* turn (some authorities say one-half turn). This is not a backseating valve. The lower pressure in the acetylene cylinder can be retained by the packing around the valve stem, and the backseating arrangement is not required.

CAUTION: Do not purge the acetylene hose and torch in an area where there are open flames or other conditions that could ignite the acetylene. Remember: acetylene gas is highly explosive.

○ 10-11 Torch Lighter

The torch lighter (Fig. 10-12) has a striker bar and a lighter flint to produce a spark which will ignite the torch.

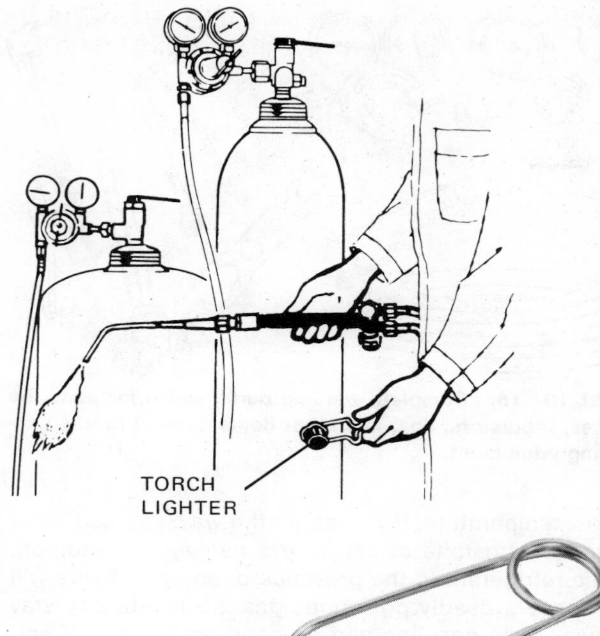

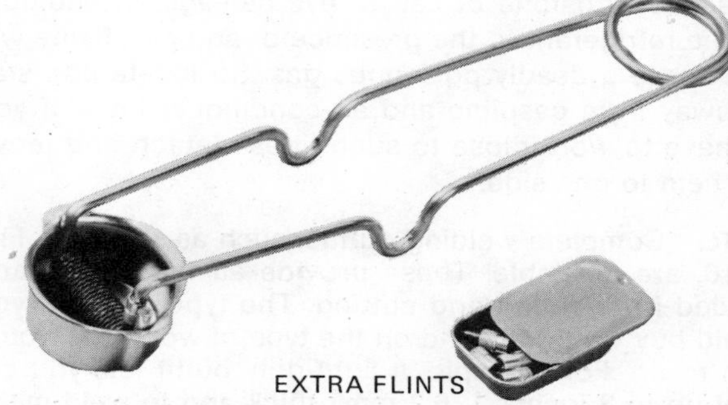

FIGURE 10–12. (Top) Using a torch lighter. *(Rego Company)* (Bottom) Torch lighter with extra flints. *(Harris Calorific)*

This is much like a cigarette lighter but larger and heavier, with a long handle so the hand can be kept safely away from the flame. The procedure of using the lighter is as follows:

Hold the lighter cup under the torch tip, and open the acetylene valve on the torch just a little. (The cylinder and regulator valves must be open, also). The acetylene, being heavier than air, will fill the cup. Now squeeze the lighter handle. This strikes the flint on the bar and produces a spark that ignites the acetylene. You now have an acetylene flame which will be yellow and smoky. We explain how to add oxygen and adjust the flame for welding in a following section.

CAUTION: Never try to light the torch with a match or cigarette lighter. You may get badly burned.

○ 10-12 Gas Pressure for Welding

The pressures of the gas (oxygen and acetylene) as released by the regulators must be increased as the thickness of the metal being welded is increased. Thick metal requires more pressure. For example, Union Carbide recommends 5 psi [0.35 kg/cm²] pressure for both the oxygen and acetylene when welding sheet metal up to ¼ inch [6.35 mm] thick. For metal from ¼ to ⅜ inch [6.35 to 9.53 mm] thick, the pressure should be 6 psi [0.42 kg/cm²]. Then, ⅜-inch [9.53-mm] or thicker metal should have pressures of around 9 psi [0.63 kg/cm²] for proper welding.

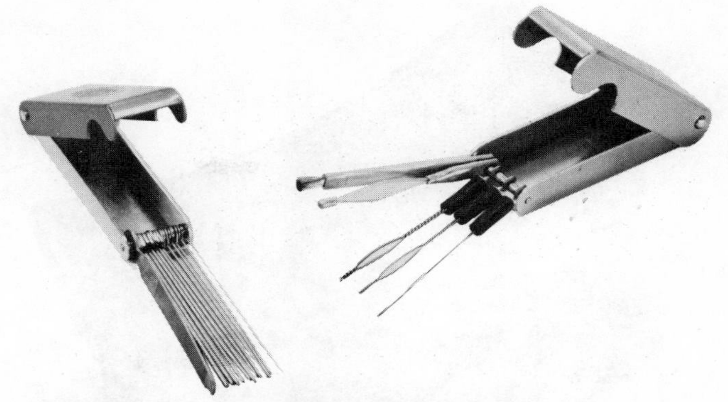

FIGURE 10–13. Tip cleaners. *(Harris Calorific)*

○ 10-13 Tip Cleaners

Tips must be kept clean. Two different kinds of cleaners are used (Fig. 10-13). One is a file that can be used to clean off the outside of the tip and reshape the tip if it has become damaged. The other type is a wire, or two wires twisted together, which are inserted into the tip hole or holes to clean them out. Wire of the correct size should be selected for the tip to be cleaned. If the wire is too small, it will not clean out all the soot that has formed. If the wire is too large, it might enlarge the tip hole or holes too much.

CAUTION: Tips must be kept clean. If a tip becomes clogged, it can cause a flashback. That is, the flame can back up inside the tip. This is potentially dangerous because it can result in an explosion.

○ 10-14 Welding Safely

While there are certain hazards in gas welding, it is just as safe a job as anything in the shop if the proper precautions are taken. We have already given you a number of general safety rules to follow (see Chapter 3). Here are the safety rules that apply particularly to gas welding:

1. Wear special dark welding safety goggles (Fig. 10-14). These goggles protect the eyes from flying sparks and from the powerful light given off by the flame. This light can damage the eyes if they are not

FIGURE 10–14. Gas-welding goggles. *(Harris Calorific)*

FIGURE 10–15. Leather welding gloves. (*Marquette Division of Applied Power, Inc.*)

protected. The special welding safety goggles have dark lenses that filter out the harmful rays from the flame.

2. Wear leather gloves with wrist protectors (Fig. 10-15). They protect the hands and wrists from the white-hot sparks that the torch produces, particularly when cutting metal. Do not use cloth gloves. They can burn if a spark hits them.
3. Clothes should be worn that protect the arms, legs, and feet. A professional welder will wear heavy "leathers" or a jacket that is closed at the neck and a cap to protect the hair. A spark down the neck can be very painful. Hair can catch fire, especially if it is long.
4. Keep oil and grease away from the welding equipment. Never lubricate the threads on the nuts that attach the hoses. If oxygen hits a spot of grease or oil, it will burst violently into flame. For this reason, the welder's gloves and clothes must be free of grease or oil.
5. Welding should be done in a safe area, behind a shield of some sort that will protect others in the shop from sparks or from the strong light given out by the flame. There should be no flammable substances in the vicinity.
6. Keep the fire extinguisher handy and make sure it is in good working order.
7. If a flashback occurs—that is, if the flame backs up into the mixing chamber of the torch—*shut off the torch valves at once.* Otherwise, the tip will get too hot. Also, there is always the danger that the flame will back up into the hoses and cause an explosion.
8. When welding a frame or other internal part of a car, stay away from gasoline and air-conditioner lines. If a gasoline line is broken, gasoline could spurt out and create a serious fire before you could do anything about it. If an air-conditioner line or component, such as the condenser, is overheated, it could burst, releasing refrigerant. This is a potentially dangerous situation. The refrigerant comes out at a very low temperature. If you are in the way, you could get serious frostbite or severe eye damage. In addition, the refrigerant in the presence of an open flame will release a deadly poisonous gas. So locate and stay away from gasoline and air-conditioner lines. If you have to work close to such lines, detach and move them to one side.

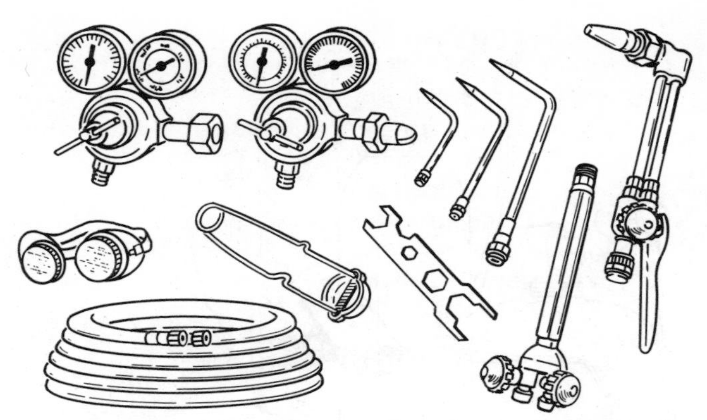

FIGURE 10–16. Complete welding outfit, which includes the torches, regulators, tips, and other items needed to use gas-welding equipment.

NOTE: Complete welding outfits, such as shown in Fig. 10-16, are available. These provide all the basic parts needed for welding and cutting. The type of outfit you would buy would depend on the type of work you would plan to do. For example, a light-duty outfit lets you cut steel up to 3 inches [76.2 mm] thick and to weld metal ¼ inch [6.35 mm] thick. The heavy-duty outfit shown in Fig. 10-16 lets you cut steel up to 6 inches [152.4 mm] thick and weld metal up to 1 inch [25.4 mm] thick. Both outfits will also heat and braze.

○10-15 Practicing Gas Welding

In the shop, you will be given some practice jobs before you will get to work on actual cars. Let us now discuss typical practice jobs, starting with lighting the torch and adjusting the flame. First, however, we will look at the various kinds of welds to be made. There are six basic types. Figure 10-17 shows these various types. Let us look at each. In a later section we will go through the welding procedure in detail.

1. Butt weld. This weld (Fig. 10-17A) is made between two pieces of metal placed side by side, with or with-

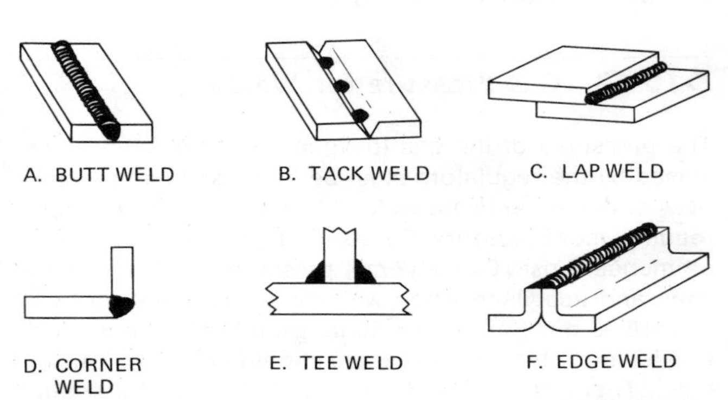

FIGURE 10–17. Six basic types of welds. (*General Motors Corporaticn*)

out a gap between them. In actual practice on car sheet metal, the butt weld is used to repair cracks or tears in a body panel or fender.

2. Tack weld. This is not an actual weld but a preliminary weld made before the complete weld is started. Figure 10-17B shows a tack weld. The purpose of the tack weld is to hold the two pieces in place while the actual weld is being made. As you can see from Fig. 10-17B, welds are made in several spots to tack the two pieces together. This assures that the two pieces will not move out of position during the actual welding job.
3. Lap weld. This weld (Fig. 10-17C) is made by placing the edge of one piece on top of the other, as shown, and then welding the edge of the upper piece to the flat surface of the lower piece. This is used when a patch is being applied to a body panel or when a replacement panel is being installed. Note that the weld is made on the outside and not on the underside. After the weld is completed, it must be hammered down to a level with the surrounding sheet metal. The irregularities are then smoothed down and filled, as noted later.
4. Corner weld. The corner or fillet weld (Fig. 10-17D) is made to join two metal pieces at an angle. This type of weld is not often used in auto-body sheet-metal work. However there may be occasions when it is necessary to use angle welding to repair frame and pillar members.
5. Tee weld. This weld (Fig. 10-17E) joins one part to another to form an upside-down capital letter T. It is not often used in sheet-metal body work. The joint is stronger if the weld is made on both sides. To make this weld, as to make the corner weld, some means of holding the parts in position must be used—with a vise or clamps, for example.
6. Edge weld. This weld (Fig. 10-17F) joins two pieces along one edge. While this method can be used to join two body panels, it is more convenient and quicker to use electric-spot-welding equipment to do the job, spot-welding through the two sides rather than along the edges. Spot welding is described in Chapter 12.

○10-16 The Welding Flame

Before we describe the actual welding procedures to make the various joints, let us see how to adjust the torch to give a welding flame. This type of flame is called a neutral flame and results from a mixture of about equal parts of oxygen and acetylene coming out of the torch tip. The flame picks up some oxygen from the air so the flame is composed of about one part of acetylene to about two parts of oxygen.

The proper proportions of the two gases are required to achieve a good welding flame. Too much acetylene will produce a carbonizing flame that has unburned carbon in it. This carbon will deposit on the pieces to be welded, and they will not weld properly. Too much oxygen will produce an oxidizing flame that will burn or oxidize the metal. The resulting weld, even if successful, may be too hard, so that it would crack later.

The flame is adjusted by turning the two valves at the back end of the welding torch. To start with, when the torch is first lighted (Fig. 10-12), only the acetylene valve is opened (about one-quarter turn). The torch is then burning acetylene only. This gives a yellowish flame which is not hot enough for welding (Fig. 10-18). Note that this flame is wavy and sooty. To adjust the acetylene gas flow, gradually turn the acetylene valve on the torch, increasing the gas flow, until the flame just leaves the end of the tip. Then close the valve just enough to allow the flame to settle back onto the tip.

FIGURE 10–18. Acetylene flame immediately after lighting.

NOTE: The actual adjustment of the acetylene valve depends mainly on the size of the welding tip. A large tip will pass more gas, and thus the valve would have to be opened wider to make the correct adjustment.

Next, slowly open the oxygen valve on the torch. This causes the flame to sharpen and change color (Fig. 10-

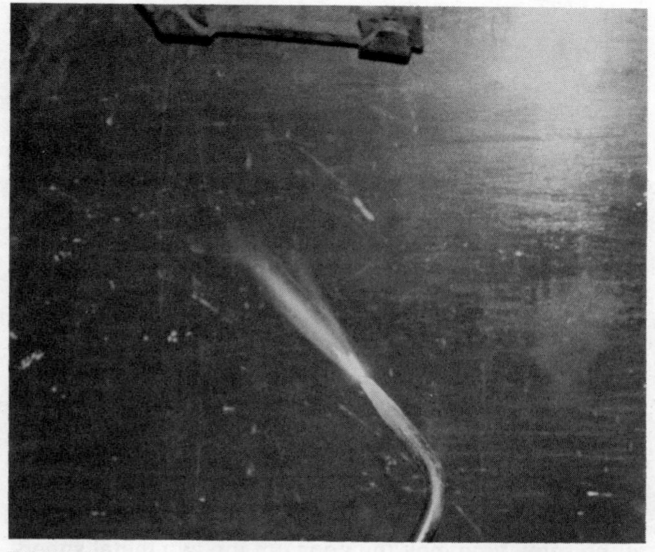

FIGURE 10–19. Acetylene flame with some oxygen in it. Note that the flame has sharpened and shortened and that an inner blue cone has formed.

FIGURE 10–20. Welding flame. The yellow flame has vanished and the inner blue cone has sharpened.

19). The flame takes on a bluish tinge. Also, the flame stops wavering and sharpens into a steady flame. As the oxygen valve opens further, when the flame is neutral, the yellow flame will have vanished into the blue inner cone of the flame, as shown in Fig. 10-20. This is the flame you need for welding.

NOTE: When a sheet-metal body panel needs to be heat-shrunk, a flame slightly heavy with acetylene is used. This is not as hot or as pointed a flame and can heat a fairly large area without danger of burning the metal.

If there is too much oxygen in the flame, the inner cone will shrink and almost vanish. This flame makes a hissing noise. It is not a good welding flame because it can cause the molten metal to bubble and spark, resulting in a poor weld. The extra oxygen also changes the chemical composition of the metal and causes it to become harder.

○ 10-17 Making a Butt Weld

To make any weld, including a butt weld (Fig. 10-17), you need the gas-welding equipment and welding rods, as shown in Fig. 10-1. Welding rods are made of metal and are melted by the heat so the molten metal flows into the joint and becomes part of it. For practice in making butt welds, two pieces of metal are laid out on the special firebricks set on the welding bench, as shown in Fig. 10-21.

Then you put on your goggles, cap, and gloves, and light the torch. Adjust the torch valves to get a neutral flame. Next you hold the torch and welding rod at about the angles shown in Fig. 10-22. Start at one edge of the two pieces of sheet metal. Bring the torch down until the tip of the inner core of the flame is about touching the welding rod and sheet metal. Back up the torch flame a little on the rod. You want to melt the end of the rod and at the same time melt the edges of the two metal sheets. As soon as the metal begins to puddle—which should take only a few seconds—you start the weld.

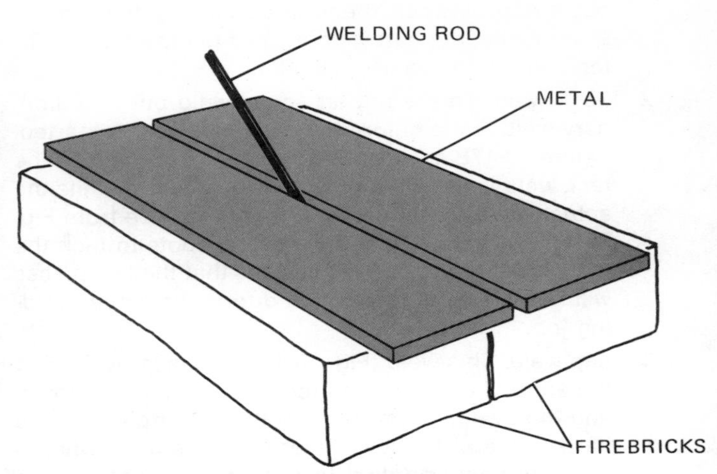

FIGURE 10–21. Setup to make a butt weld.

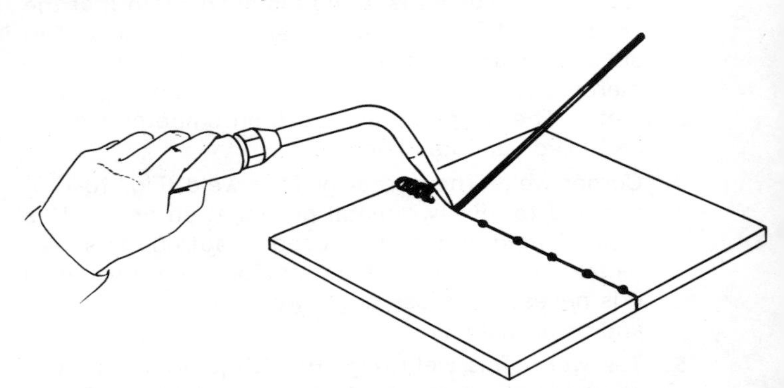

FIGURE 10–22. Positions of torch and welding rod to start a weld.

Keep the torch flame moving up and down the welding rod, so the rod melts, and at the same time moving across the gap between the two pieces of metal. Make sure you are melting the edges of the metal sheets and at the same time melting enough rod to fill the gap. It takes practice to make a uniformly smooth weld across the metal sheets. Make several butt welds until you learn to control the torch and rod. Move the torch flame up from the end of the rod just a small amount—just enough to melt the end of the rod. At the same time, you swing the flame a little from side to side so the edges of the metal sheets also melt.

The welding process we just described is called *running a bead,* because you run a bead across the weld. The weld metal, which rises above the level of the surrounding metal, is ground, hammered, or sanded down during the final finishing procedure on the car.

Figure 10-23 shows some good and bad welds. The bad welds are caused by not enough or too much heat or by failure to move the torch flame uniformly across the metal pieces as the weld is being made. What often happens when a person is just starting to learn welding is that the torch is moved in a jerky fashion. That is, it is held in one spot a little too long and then moved too quickly, held more or less stationary for a few moments and then again moved too fast. Keep the torch moving smoothly up and down the end of the welding rod, and at the same time from side to side to heat the metal pieces. Continue to work smoothly across and along the joint being welded.

FIGURE 10–23. A and D show good welds. B and C show bad welds. ***(Union Carbide Corporation)***

After the work has cooled, turn it over and examine the back side. See if the weld has penetrated properly and if you have uniform welding all along the seam between the two metal pieces. Sometimes a weld looks good from the top but when you turn it over you find there are places where the undersides of the workpieces are not properly joined; that is, the weld is not filled in.

NOTE: On your first butt welds, you may wish to tack-weld the two pieces, as shown in Fig. 10-17B, to hold them in position.

○ 10-18 Tack Welding

In tack welding, you want to weld the two metal pieces together in several spots. This means you select a spot and heat it and the welding rod so you get a puddle of molten metal. You repeat this in two or more spots along the joint. Later, when you make the weld, these spots will blend in with the rest of the joint.

○ 10-19 Lap Welding

This weld (Fig. 10-17C) is made the same way as you make a butt weld. However, when you are working with relatively thin sheet metal, you must be careful not to blow holes through the bottom sheet. That is, stay close to the joint as you move the flame from side to side. This joint can be made without using a welding rod if the metal pieces are not too thin. To do this, you apply most of the heat to the lower piece so the puddle starts to form there. It takes more heat to puddle the flat surface than to puddle the edge of the upper piece.

○ 10-20 Other Welds

The other welds—corner, tee, edge—are all made in about the same way as the butt and lap welds. With these other welds, jigs or clamps are required to hold the parts in place while the welds are being made. You should practice making these various welds until you can complete them properly.

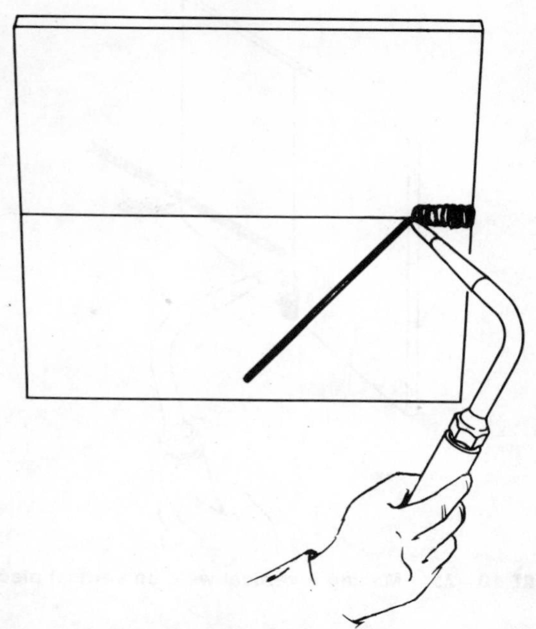

FIGURE 10–24. Making a horizontal weld on vertical pieces.

○ 10-21 Welding Positions

Up to now, we have been describing welding of metal pieces that are lying flat on a workbench. In other words, the pieces are horizontal and the torch flame and welding rod are pointed down. On the car, however, most welding jobs must be done on metal that is upright or even overhead. These require that the torch flame and welding rod be pointed up.

Figure 10-24 shows how to hold the torch and rod to weld a horizontal joint in sheet metal that is in a vertical position. This is the sort of job you might be doing to fix a horizontal tear in the side of a fender, for example. In this type of job, you would first straighten the metal and bring the two torn edges together. Then you would run a bead along the edges to make the weld. The reason you hold the torch and rod pointed upward, as shown in Fig. 10-24, is to control the puddle so it will not dribble down.

If you are welding a vertical joint between two vertical metal pieces, hold the torch and rod, as shown in Fig. 10-25. Note that the flame is again pointed upward to control the puddle so it does not run down. Move from bottom to top in making the weld. The welding rod is pointed downward toward the puddle. With this type of weld, the rod requires less heating from the flame because the heat from the puddle rises toward the rod.

Overhead welding (Fig. 10-26) is the most difficult and most hazardous. An example of this type of job might be going under a car on the rack to weld a broken joint in the car frame. In doing this type of weld, keep to one side so that molten metal or sparks will not drop on you. Gloves with protective cuffs are a must, and a cap and a welding jacket that is fastened tightly around the neck should be worn.

Point the torch flame up at about a 45° angle, with the rod pointed up at about the same angle. See Fig. 10-26.

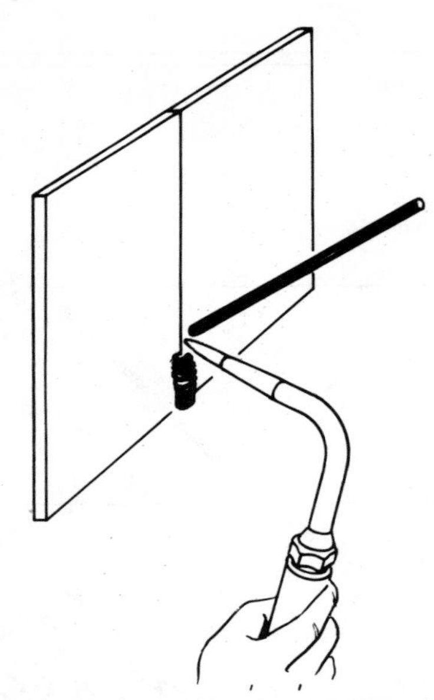

FIGURE 10-25. Making a vertical weld on vertical pieces.

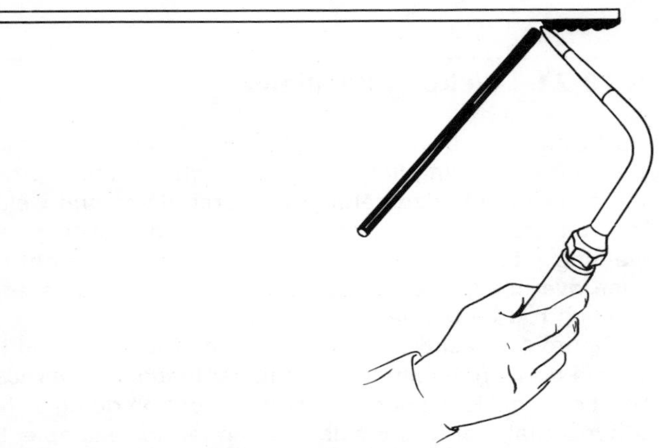

FIGURE 10-26. Making an overhead weld.

○ 10-22 Learning to Weld

In order to become an expert welder, you must practice making the various joints. Also, you should practice making horizontal and vertical welds on work that is held upright, that is, in a vertical position. See Figs. 10-24 and 10-25. Practice making welds on overhead work, as shown in Fig. 10-26. Once you have mastered the technique, you will be able to make smooth, even, perfect welds every time. Later, you will make welds on actual cars. This will enable you to see how the proper welds contribute to restoring cars to their original condition.

○ 10-23 Shutting Down

When you finish a weld, turn off the torch. You close the acetylene valve on the torch first. Then you turn off the torch oxygen valve. If you are stopping for a short time, also turn off the oxygen and acetylene regulator valves. Then open and close the oxygen and acetylene valves

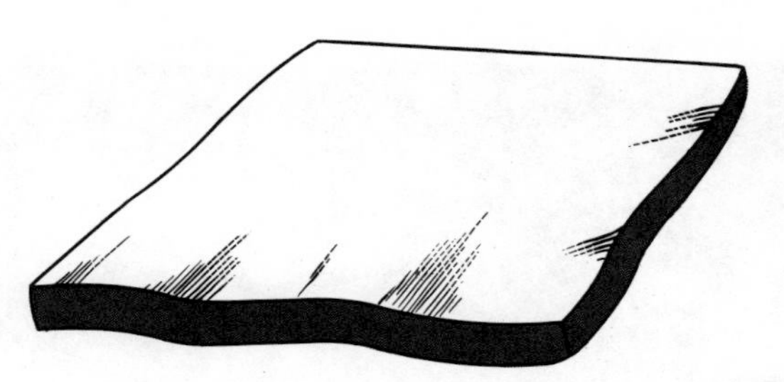

FIGURE 10-27. Effect of heating one edge of a metal sheet. It expands when hot and then, when it cools, it warps and wrinkles.

on the torch to release any pressure in the torch and hoses.

If you stop work for a longer time or at the end of a welding session, you should also close the cylinder valves on the oxygen and acetylene cylinders. You should then close the regulator valves. Finally, open and close the torch valves to release all gas in the hoses and torch. When you leave the job, all valves should be closed—cylinder, regulator, torch.

○ 10-24 Effect of Welding on Metal

Whenever metal is heated, by a torch or otherwise, it undergoes certain changes. For one thing, it expands. If you heat one edge of a piece of sheet metal, for example, it will expand and warp, as shown in Fig. 10-27. The reason for this is that the metal along the edge, as it expands, has to go someplace. So the warp, or ripple, develops to take care of this expansion.

This can be a problem in welding body sheet metal, as for example, when you are welding a patch onto a damaged fender. To guard against the ripple, you would first tack the patch to the fender in several places. This would then tend to hold the two pieces being joined in place so warping would not occur.

NOTE: This expansion of the metal with heat is one reason that body technicians prefer other methods of patching body sheet metal and repairing rips in the metal. Expansion caused by heating the metal must be taken care of to bring the surface back to contour. Thus, you will find body technicians using electric spot welding (○12-18), screws, or Pop rivets (○4-15) to attach patches.

Heating sheet metal to near its melting point changes its crystal structure so it becomes softer. You will recall our discussions (in Chapter 2) of how sheet metal is formed into body panels. We mentioned that when sheet metal is bent, it becomes hard; that is, it work-hardens. The more it is bent, the harder it becomes. The same thing happens when sheet metal is hammered. The hammered area gets harder. It also tends to expand as the metal is pushed out and away from the hammer blows.

The two effects, work hardening and expansion, result whenever body sheet metal is straightened and aligned. The two conditions—hardening and expansion—can be eliminated by heating the metal with a torch. Heating the area not only softens the metal but also, if the area is then worked with a hammer and dolly, shrinks it. Cooling the area with water is part of this procedure. Heat shrinking is one of two procedures used to take care of the expansion or stretching of sheet metal. We describe the procedure in detail in a later chapter.

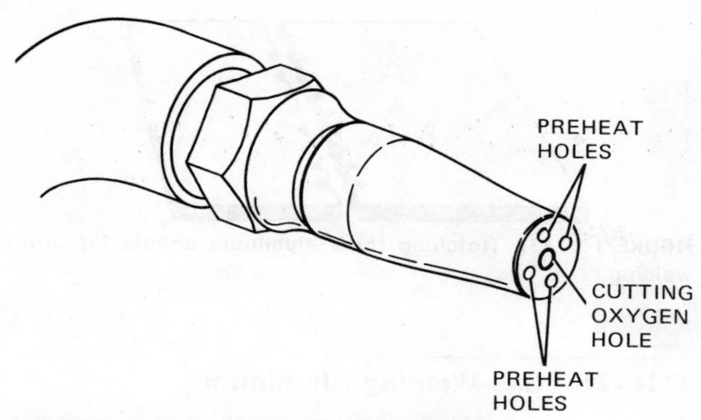

FIGURE 10–28. Construction of cutting tip.

○10-25 Cutting Metal

To cut metal, a special cutting torch and tip are required. See Figs. 10-9 and 10-11. The cutting torch has four valves, one for acetylene and three for oxygen. See Fig. 10-9 to locate these valves. The acetylene valve, when open, admits acetylene to the torch. The torch oxygen valve admits oxygen to the torch when it is open. It should be opened all the way when the torch is in use. The preheat oxygen valve admits oxygen to the preheat flame. The cutting oxygen valve is operated by a lever and sends oxygen through the center hole of the torch tip. See Fig. 10-28.

The outside holes in the tip release a mixture of oxygen and acetylene which forms the neutral flame for preheating the metal to be cut. When the metal turns dark red and is close to the melting point, the cutting oxygen lever is pressed to release oxygen from the center hole of the tip. This produces the cutting action. We now describe the procedure.

NOTE: The cutting torch is not often used in the body shop. Body technicians do not like to use it to cut sheet-metal panels because the resulting heat causes the panels to warp. This then requires additional work to relieve the expansion and warpage. Instead, body technicians use chisels or nibblers to cut body panels (Figs. 7-3 to 7-6). If a frame member needed to be cut out so a new member could be welded into the frame, the cutting torch would be used for this job. But this is a comparatively rare procedure.

○10-26 Setting Up to Cut

Follow the procedure outlined for setting up to weld, except that you attach a cutting torch with the appropriate tip to the oxygen and acetylene hoses. The size of tip you select is determined by the thickness of the metal you are to cut. A thick piece requires a larger tip, which can deliver more preheat and more cutting oxygen than a thin piece. Likewise, a thick piece requires more gas pressure than a thin piece. For example, Union Carbide recommends the pressures shown in Fig. 10-29, for metal of various thickness.

The metal to be cut should be marked to indicate the line where the cut is to be made. The mark can be made with chalk or soapstone. It should be clear because the dark goggles make faint lines harder to see.

METAL THICKNESS inch (mm)	OXYGEN PRESSURE psi (kPa)	ACETYLENE PRESSURE psi (kPa)
1/8 [3]	15-20 [1.05-1.41]	3-5 [0.21-0.35]
1/4 [6]	20-35 [1.41-2.46]	3-5 [0.21-0.35]
3/8 [10]	20-35 [1.41-2.46]	3-5 [0.21-0.35]
1/2 [13]	30-40 [2.11-2.81]	3-5 [0.21-0.35]
1 [25]	40-50 [2.81-3.51]	3-5 [0.21-0.35]
2 [50]	60 [4.22]	3-5 [0.21-0.35]

FIGURE 10–29. Recommended oxygen and acetylene pressures to cut metal of various thicknesses. (*Union Carbide Corporation*)

After you have the torch set up and have the piece to be cut marked and on the workbench, put on your goggles, cap, and gloves. Adjust the regulators to the required pressures. Open the torch oxygen valve all the way. This admits oxygen to the torch. Depress the cutting oxygen valve momentarily to purge the torch. Release the lever.

Open the torch acetylene valve about a quarter turn and use the torch lighter to light the acetylene. Gradually open the acetylene valve until the flame moves off the tip. Then close the acetylene valve just enough so the flame backs up to the tip again. The torch is now feeding the proper amount of acetylene.

Next, turn the preheat oxygen valve to admit oxygen to the preheat flames. These are the flames produced by the gas coming out of the outside or preheating holes in the tip (see Fig. 10-29). These separate flames more or less blend into a single, fairly broad flame suitable for preheating the metal to be cut. If any of the smaller flames coming from one of the preheating holes is small or missing, that hole is clogged. The torch should be shut off and, after it has cooled, the tip should be cleaned or replaced.

When the right amount of oxygen is feeding to the preheating holes, the combined flame will be neutral. That is, the yellowish acetylene flame will have practically disappeared into the central blue cone.

Now squeeze the operating lever momentarily to make sure cutting oxygen will flow out of the cutting oxygen hole in the tip. The flame will now change to an intense blue and will become longer and narrower. Release the cutting-oxygen-valve lever.

You are now ready to cut.

○10-27 Cutting

Many technicians rest their goggles on their forehead so they can see what they are doing while getting ready to cut. Then, when ready, they pull the goggles down over their eyes and start cutting. Here is the procedure:

Find the cutting line on the workpiece. Direct the preheating flame at the cutting line on the edge of the workpiece. Hold the preheating flame at this point until the metal becomes dark red and is ready to melt. See Fig. 10-30. Note that the torch is tilted so the flame hits the metal at an angle. The flame points toward the edge of the workpiece.

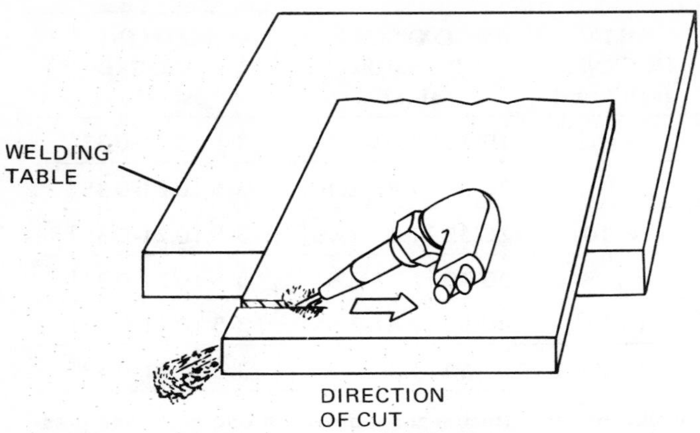

FIGURE 10–30. Starting the cut. (*Rego Company*)

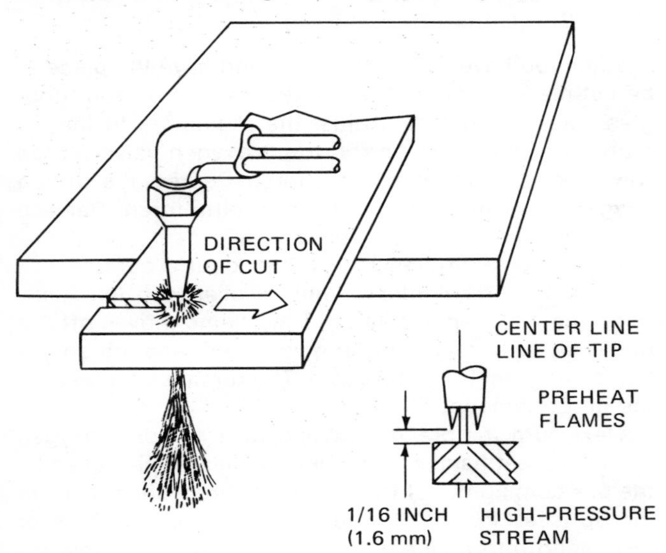

FIGURE 10–31. Cutting-torch action in making the cut. (*Rego Company*)

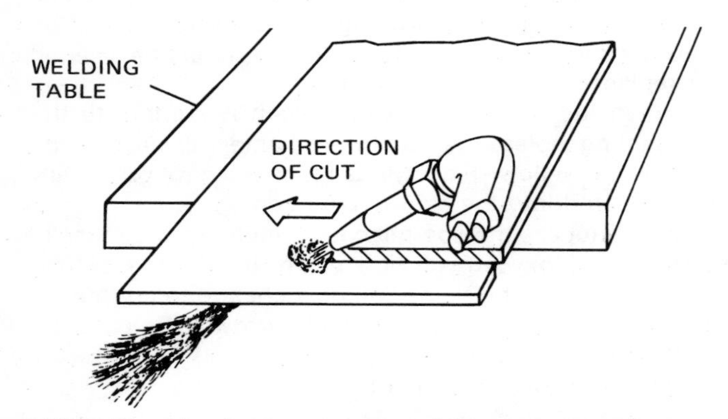

FIGURE 10–32. Cutting sheet metal. (*Rego Company*)

Squeeze the cutting-valve lever to release cutting oxygen. This additional oxygen starts the cutting action. As the metal cuts through, move the torch slowly along the cutting line to continue the cut. As the cut starts, straighten the torch so the cutting flame hits the metal more nearly straight on, as shown in Fig. 10-31. This reduces the thickness of metal that the flame must cut through. However, when cutting sheet metal, tilt the torch so the flame strikes the metal at an angle of up to 30°, as shown in Fig. 10-32. This blows away slag and makes a cleaner cut.

To cut a rivet or bolt head, preheat the head until hot and then hit it with the cutting flame.

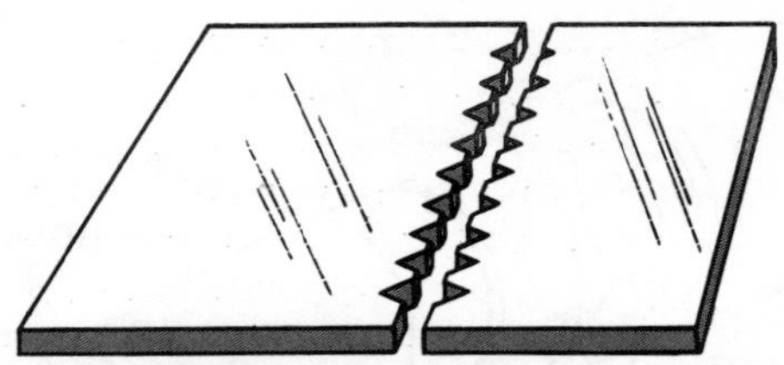

FIGURE 10–33. Notching thick aluminum sheets for butt welding.

○ 10-28 Gas-Welding Aluminum

Welding aluminum is somewhat trickier than welding steel. Aluminum does not give any warning that it is hot enough to weld, by changing color. Instead, it will suddenly collapse, because it becomes very weak when it nears its melting temperature. Also, aluminum has a very high degree of heat conductance. This means much more heat must be directed to the joint. The heat is conducted away from the hot area very rapidly by the aluminum itself.

As the aluminum get hot, it oxidizes. This oxide can form a coating that prevents a good weld. However, all these problems can be overcome if the right technique is followed. Now let's discuss a typical aluminum welding job.

Some body technicians who work with aluminum recommend goggles with blue-tinted lenses. These enable you to see the actions at the weld. The flame is slightly acetylene rich. The inner cone should be a little fuzzy. This flame will appear rather yellow with ordinary welding goggles, and so you can't see the metal under the flame. Wearing goggles with blue lenses enables you to see the metal.

The aluminum surfaces to be welded must be absolutely clean. Oxide forms readily on aluminum, and it must come off, along with any dirt. Chemical cleansers are available, but new wire brushes will do the job. Flux is necessary to prevent the accumulation of aluminum oxide at the weld. The flux floats the oxide away. You can use aluminum welding rods which are coated with flux, or have the flux available so you can dip the rod into it before the weld starts. The rod should be heated and dipped into the flux. Flux will cool the rod and adhere to it.

Thin sheets of aluminum can be butt-welded. For thicker aluminum sheets, notching is recommended, as shown in Fig. 10-33. Aluminum sheets thicker than ½ inch [12.7 mm] should be both notched and beveled on the edges to be joined.

Preheat the surfaces to be welded and apply flux on both sides. The flux prevents formation of oxide on the surfaces. Now hold the welding rod at the work. Start at one edge of the aluminum sheets. Heat the rod and sheets at the same time, keeping the torch flame moving in a small circle to distribute the heat. Remember that aluminum does not change color as it reaches melting temperature. Instead, it just gets mushy all at once. Be prepared for this so you can run the bead at just the right moment and temperature. Hold the rod and torch at a flatter angle than when welding steel. Also, the flame should be directed more toward the unwelded part of the joint to preheat the metal.

CHAPTER 10 CHECKUP

NOTE: Since the following is a chapter review test, you should review the chapter before taking the test.

Knowing how and when to use the gas torch for cutting and welding is a skill that the automotive body-repair technician must have. In this chapter, we have introduced the oxyacetylene torch and discussed how it is set up for use on sheet metal and aluminum. To find out how well you understand the chapter, answer the questions that follow.

COMPLETING THE SENTENCES The sentences below are incomplete. After each sentence there are several words or phrases, but only one of them correctly completes the sentence. Write each sentence in your notebook, ending it with the one word or phrase that completes it correctly.

1. The cylinder with the highest pressure is the (*a*) oxygen, (*b*) acetylene, (*c*) air, (*d*) water.
2. The oxygen-cylinder regulator has (*a*) one gauge, (*b*) three gauges, (*c*) two gauges, (*d*) four gauges.
3. On the acetylene regulator, the connecting nut has (*a*) left-hand threads, (*b*) right-hand threads, (*c*) an interference fit, (*d*) ¼ × 20 thread.
4. The regulator sets and cylinder valves must never be touched by (*a*) oxygen or acetylene, (*b*) a wrench, (*c*) grease or oil, (*d*) air.
5. Oxygen-hose nuts have (*a*) left-hand threads, (*b*) cotter pins, (*c*) right-hand threads, (*d*) lock washers.

QUESTIONS Write each of the following questions, and then the answer, in your notebook. If you have trouble recalling the answer to a question, turn back to the pages that cover the material and study them again.

1. How do you purge the hoses and torch?
2. Describe the proper way to light a torch.
3. When are tip cleaners used?
4. Name the six basic types of welds.
5. Why must you always wear goggles when welding?

DEFINITIONS In the following, you are asked for several definitions. Write them in your notebook. The act of writing the definitions does two things. It tests your knowledge, and it helps fix the information more firmly in your mind. Turn back into the chapter if you are not sure of a definition, or look it up in the glossary at the back of the book.

1. Define "running a bead."
2. What is tack weld?
3. What is a vertical weld?
4. Define "sheet metal."
5. What is the difference between cutting and welding?

SUGGESTIONS FOR FURTHER STUDY

Learning to use the torch is a must for the student in auto body repair. Examine closely the oxyacetylene-welding equipment in your shop. Following the illustrations in this chapter, note the name and location of each part. Determine the different types of torch and tips that are available. In your notebook, list the tips. Then write down the use for each tip.

11 BRAZING AND BODY SOLDERING

Brazing and body soldering are much like oxyacetylene welding. The same gas-welding equipment is used and the procedure is similar. However, when brazing or soldering, the metal to be joined is not heated to the melting point. Also, the rods used usually are made of brass or lead. They have a lower melting point than the steel welding rods used for welding. If the filler rod melts above 840°F [450°C], the process is defined as brazing. If the filler rod melts below 840°F [450°C], the process is called soldering. Both processes are sometimes referred to as low-temperature welding. We will now discuss in detail the brazing and body-soldering processes.

○ 11-1 What Is Brazing?

Brazing is a process that requires the use of a filler material (a brazing rod). The metals to be joined are heated along with the filler rod. At a temperature above 840°F [450°C] but below the melting temperature of the metals being joined, the rod melts. The joint is formed as shown in Fig. 11-1. In brazing, the metals being joined do not melt. Instead, the rod melts and then solidifies to hold the two pieces in position. As you can see in Fig. 11-1, the brazed joint made this way is similar to the joining together of two pieces of wood with glue. The strength of the joint is determined by the strength of the filler material. Some brazed joints can be very strong, often depending on the material in the filler rod used.

○ 11-2 Brazing Rods

A brazing rod is a convenient form in which to handle the brass filler material. Actually, brazing rods are classified and sold as types of gas-welding rods. Like welding rods, brazing rods are usually 36 inches [914 mm] long. They are available in various diameters. Popular sizes of brazing rods are 1/16 inch [1.59 mm], 3/32 inch [2.38 mm], and 1/8 inch [3.18 mm]. Gas-welding rods (including brazing rods) are sold by the pound. Brazing rods are very expensive compared to steel gas-welding rods. Also, some flux-coated brazing rods are available. Flux is discussed in the following section.

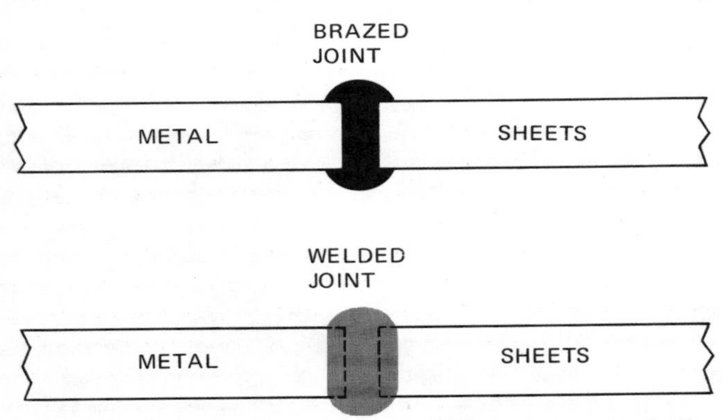

FIGURE 11-1. (Top) A brazed joint. Note that the two metal sheets being joined did not melt. (Bottom) A welded joint. Note that the two metal sheets have been melted together.

○ 11-3 Brazing Flux

When brazing, a flux must be used to produce a clean, strong joint. A flux is a special powder or paste that is melted with the rod to dissolve any oxides and to help remove any dirt that may be on the surfaces. However, the surfaces should be cleaned before brazing begins. Also, the flux promotes the free flow of the melted rod.

Most fluxes are mainly borax or boric acid. Probably the most frequently used flux in the body shop comes in 1-pound [0.454-kg] cans. However, many shops order and use flux-coated brazing rods. These rods have a flux coating the length of the rod. No additional flux normally is necessary when they are used.

○ 11-4 Advantage of Brazing

Many body technicians prefer brazing to welding when repairing body brackets and underparts. One reason is that less heat is required. Therefore, there is less distortion of the metal. The more distortion, the more additional body work that will be required. Also, brazing is a faster procedure because the work does not have to be heated to as high a temperature. Brazing is seldom used on body sheet metal.

NOTE: By definition, brazing usually means the use of a brass (copper and zinc) filler rod. You can identify a brazed joint because of its color, which is brassy or yellowish. Figure 11-2 shows a braze on a front fender underbracket.

○ 11-5 Brazing Sheet Metal

Thin sheet metal can be brazed in an overlapped or butt joint. Thick metal is not overlapped but brazed in a butt joint. The edges of the thick metal must be beveled first to form a vee in which the brazing will be made. This process is covered in a following section.

The size of the torch tip and the gas pressures are determined by the thickness of the metal to be brazed. The major difference from welding is in the type of flame used. In welding, a neutral flame is required. In brazing, a slightly oxygen-starved flame is used. This is a carbonizing flame. The acetylene flame does not quite disappear into the central cone as in the welding flame.

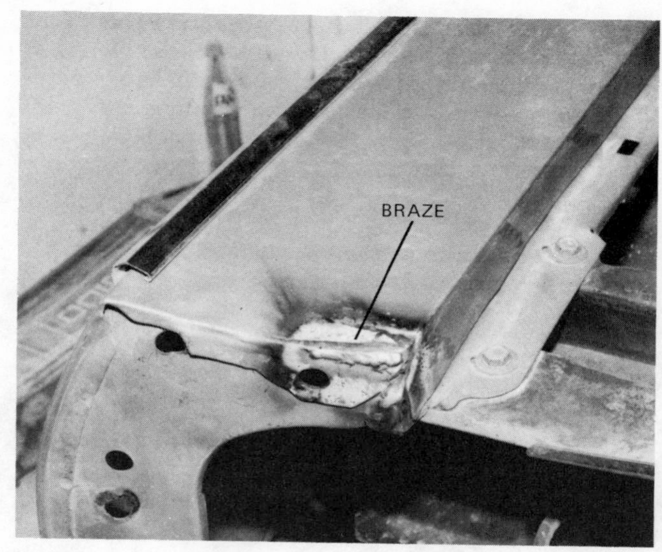

FIGURE 11–2. Brazing job on a bracket on a fender underbody.

NOTE: In many body shops, brazing of body sheet metal is seldom done. Instead, other methods of attaching patches or sheet-metal parts are used, such as riveting or electric spot welding. Electric welding is covered in the following chapter.

○11-6 Brazing Other Materials

Brazing can be used to fasten together two different metals, such as sheet steel and aluminum. (In welding, you fasten together two pieces of the same metal.) Softer metals such as brass or copper can be brazed. These metals cannot be welded easily, because they melt at relatively low temperatures and are not as easy to handle as steel. Cast iron can also be brazed. Cracked cylinder blocks are sometimes repaired by brazing the cracks. This process can be used successfully on cast iron, because extremely high temperatures are not required. If cast iron is heated too much, it will crack.

○11-7 Brazing Thin Sheet Metal

Thin sheet metal can be brazed in an overlapping or butt joint. Let us see how to braze an overlapping joint (Fig. 11-3). First, make sure the surfaces to be joined are clean. In brazing, the brass melts and penetrates into the heated surfaces of the metal being joined. These surfaces must be free of any oxide or other material that would prevent this penetration.

The surfaces should be scrubbed with a very clean or new wire brush (to avoid putting grease or dirt on the surface from a used brush). Position the two pieces of sheet metal. Use flux-coated brazing rods. If these are not available, you can coat the rods with flux when the job begins. This is done by heating the rod and dipping it into a container of flux. The flux helps clean the metal being brazed and prevents the brass and other metal from oxidizing. The flux floats to the surface of the braze. There it protects the brass from the oxygen in the air, which could otherwise form a film of oxide. This could prevent good adhesion of the brass to the metal surfaces.

Now put on your goggles, cap, and gloves and make sure your clothing is right for the job. Light the torch and adjust the flame so it is slightly oxygen-starved. This is a carbonizing flame which is not quite as hot as a neutral welding flame. Fairly low regulator gauge pressures are used. Around 6 psi [0.42 kg/cm^2] for both oxygen and acetylene is about right for most brazing jobs.

NOTE: The size of torch tip depends on the job, particularly on the thickness of the metal and the brazing rod.

When brazing, you do not hold the torch as close to the work as in welding. If you hold it too close, the flame could blow the melted brass away and it would be hard to get a good braze.

Heat the edges of the sheet metal, at the same time holding the brazing rod just above the joint. Move the flame up and down and in a circular pattern to distribute the heat over the sheet metal and rod. Only the brass rod melts, not the metal. When the metal and rod are heated enough, the rod starts to melt and it flows into the joint. As it cools, it solidifies and forms the brazed joint.

For larger patches and panels, you should tack-braze the sheet metal in several places so it will hold its position during the complete job.

○11-8 Brazing Thick Metal

Thick metal should be butt-brazed, not lap-brazed. The edges to be joined should be beveled at about a 45° angle (Fig. 11-4). When heating the vee, be careful not to

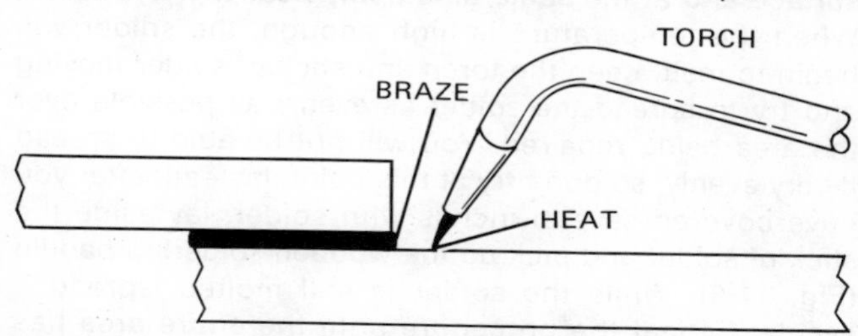

FIGURE 11–3. Brazing an overlapped joint.

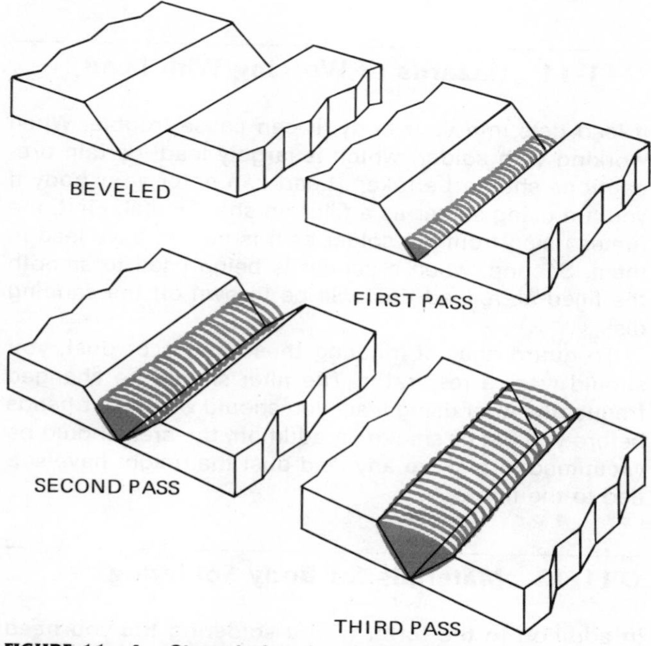

FIGURE 11–4. Steps in brazing thick metal.

overheat the top edges. Keep the flame pointed directly down and do not move it from side to side too much. When the metal is hot enough, the brass rod will melt and flow onto it. You may need to run several beads, one on top of the other, if the metal is very thick (Fig. 11-4). The first bead just fills the bottom of the vee. The final pass over the joint should just fill the vee with a little extra so there will be no voids. The extra may then be ground off if a smooth surface is desired.

○11-9 Cleaning the Braze

After a braze is completed, it will be covered with soot and flux. The soot comes from the oxygen-starved brazing flame. The soot and flux will have to be cleaned off and the braze leveled and smoothed before the area is finished.

○11-10 Body Soldering

Solder is an alloy or mixture of tin and lead. It is widely used for making electrical connections. At one time, it was the preferred way to fill in damaged body-panel spots. Today, however, it has been largely replaced by plastic fillers which go on faster and are more easily worked. Nevertheless, we include body soldering (or body leading, as it is also known) because some technicians consider it is still the best repair for good custom jobs, even though it takes longer and costs more than plastic.

Solder can be painted in the same way as other metal surfaces. It will adhere to the metal if properly applied and will not crack, peel, or flake off. It will last as long as the panel to which it has been applied. The disadvantage is that it takes longer, is messy, and is harder to work with. However, unlike other metals, solder does not change from a solid to a liquid at a certain temperature. Instead, as heat is applied, it becomes soft and plastic. This characteristic makes solder useful as a body filler.

○11-11 Hazards of Working With Lead

If lead gets into your body, it can cause trouble. When working with solder, which is largely lead, certain precautions should be taken. Lead can enter your body if you are using solder as a filler on sheet metal. First, the fumes rising from the solder as it is melted have lead in them. Second, when a sander is being used to smooth the filled area, lead dust will be thrown off the sanding disk.

To guard against inhaling these fumes or dust, you should wear a respirator. The filter should be changed frequently. After using lead, you should wash your hands before you eat or smoke. In addition, the area should be vacuumed to pick up any lead dust that might have settled to the floor.

○11-12 Materials for Body Soldering

In addition to the torch with a soldering tip, you need several sticks (or bars) of body solder, a roll of acid-core solder, some clean rags, a wooden soldering paddle, and lacquer thinner (to remove acid from the soldered area). See Fig. 11-5.

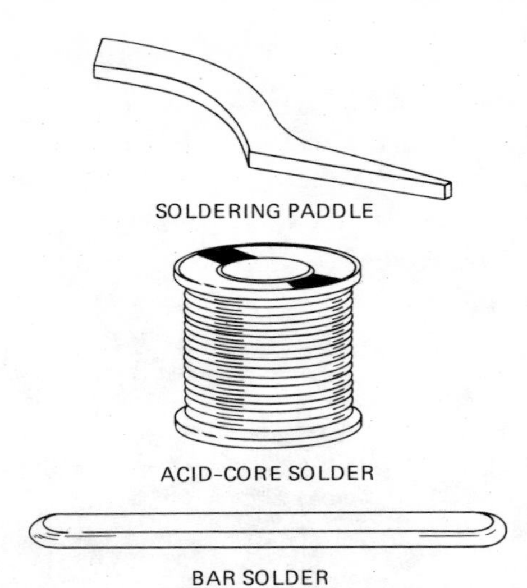

FIGURE 11–5. Materials for body soldering.

○11-13 Body-Soldering a Panel

Let us now go through the procedure of preparing a damaged body panel for body solder and then applying the solder. As a first step, the area on the body panel must be cleaned of all paint and dirt. The metal must be clean or the solder will not stick to it. The cleaning can be done with a power grinder or sander or with a new and clean wire brush.

Next, the area to be soldered must be tinned. For small areas, the tinning can be done with acid-core solder. For larger areas, the tinning may be done with acid while a preliminary coat of solder is applied. The purpose of the tinning is to put a clean coat of solder over the surface so it is protected until the actual soldering job can be done. The solder will adhere to the tinned surface much more easily.

To tin the area with acid-core solder, first heat the area with the torch. The torch should be equipped with a soldering tip, and the flame adjusted to be heavily carbonizing. That is, it should have an excess of acetylene. This gives a fairly cool flame, which is good because high temperatures are not needed for soldering.

As the area is heated, the end of the acid-core solder is applied to the metal under the flame. The solder will melt if the temperatures are right and will tend to spread over the prepared surface. Once the whole area is properly tinned, application of solder can begin.

Hold the end of the stick of body solder onto the metal surface and at the same time apply heat with the torch. When the temperature is high enough, the solder will begin to melt. Keep the torch and stick of solder moving and try to spread the solder as evenly as possible over the area being repaired. You will not be able to spread it very evenly, so don't try at this point. Instead, after you have covered several inches with solder, lay aside the stick of solder and pick up the wooden soldering paddle (Fig. 11-6). While the solder is still molten, spread it evenly. Repeat the procedure until the entire area has been filled in and is reasonably smooth.

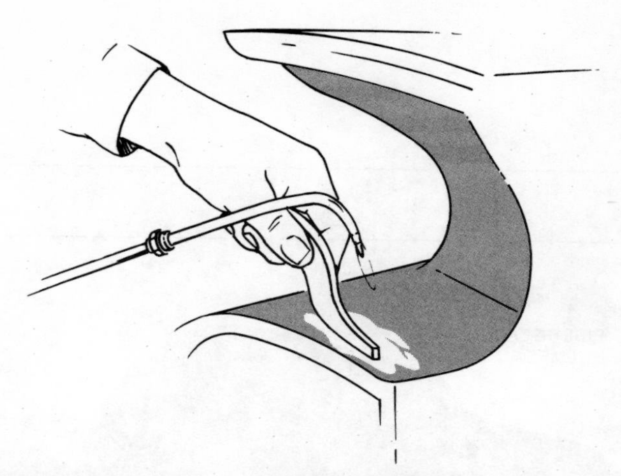

FIGURE 11-6. Using the soldering paddle.

○11-14 Finishing the Soldered Area

After the soldered area has cooled, it must be finished with a metal body file. Edges should be featheredged with a fine grade of sandpaper. Next, the area must be treated to neutralize the acid used in the flux. Unless the acid is removed, it will cause the paint job to fail. Even a trace of acid will soon cause the new paint to peel. The area can be cleaned of acid with lacquer thinner. Be careful when wiping the area with thinner. Do not get any of it on surrounding painted areas. It will spot and damage the old paint. After the lacquer thinner has evaporated, the area is ready for priming and painting.

CHAPTER 11 CHECKUP

NOTE: Since the following is a chapter review test, you should review the chapter before taking the test.

In this chapter, we have discussed brazing and body soldering. Although how often a body technician may use these processes varies greatly, you must know what they are and how to do them. In the body shop, you may be assigned a job demanding several different welding processes.

COMPLETING THE SENTENCES The sentences below are incomplete. After each sentence there are several words or phrases, but only one of them correctly completes the sentence. Write each sentence in your notebook, ending it with the one word or phrase that completes it correctly.

1. In brazing, the metals being joined (*a*) melt together, (*b*) are riveted together, (*c*) do not melt, (*d*) are soldered together.
2. A brazing rod is made of (*a*) steel, (*b*) brass, (*c*) lead, (*d*) solder.
3. Brazing can be used to fasten together (*a*) two pieces of the same metal, (*b*) two different metals, (*c*) a crack in cast iron, (*d*) all of the above.
4. Solder is a mixture of (*a*) copper and tin, (*b*) copper and zinc, (*c*) lead and copper, (*d*) tin and lead.
5. To smooth the molten solder, you use a (*a*) torch, (*b*) sandpaper, (*c*) solder paddle, (*d*) grinder.

DEFINITIONS In the following, you are asked for several definitions. Write them in your notebook. The act of writing the definitions does two things. It tests your knowledge, and it helps fix the information more firmly in your mind. Turn back into the chapter if you are not sure of a definition, or look it up in the glossary at the back of the book.

1. Define "brazing."
2. What is flux?
3. Define "body soldering."
4. What is leading?
5. Define "acid-core solder."

SUGGESTIONS FOR FURTHER STUDY

In Chapter 10, you learned the basics of how to use a torch. Now in this chapter, you have studied two specific welding processes, brazing and body soldering. To develop the skill necessary to use these techniques, practice each one in the shop until you can braze and body-solder quickly and correctly. Have your instructor check your work. Be sure to follow all safety cautions.

12
ELECTRIC WELDING

There are two basic types of electric welding: spot and arc. In spot welding, two sheet-metal panels are overlapped and a flow of current is sent through them at one spot. The current heats the metal at that spot, causing it to melt. The metal from the two panels, being liquid, mix together, or fuse. Now, when the metal cools, the two panels are spot-welded together. In the actual job, the spot welder repeats the spot at many places along the joint where the two metal pieces overlap. In arc welding, an electric arc is struck between a metal rod, called the *electrode,* and the work. The intense heat produced by the arc melts both the work and the electrode so that a weld is formed. This process is somewhat like gas welding, but there are many differences, as we shall see.

○ 12-1 Arc Welding and Safety

There are certain special safety hazards that must be kept in mind when welding with electricity. For example, arc-welding sparks may fly (see Fig. 12-2B). These sparks are white-hot molten metal. They can burn your skin or clothing, put out an eye, or cause a fire if they land on nearby flammable materials.

In addition, the light from an electric arc is very intense and can seriously damage the eyes in only a few seconds if you look directly at it. It is much more intense than the light from a gas-welding flame. The electric arc emits ultraviolet light, which acts much like sunlight. That is, it can cause a severe "sunburn" on skin exposed to it for only a few minutes.

CAUTION: You can even get "sunburned" from the arc through light, thin clothing. A thin cotton shirt is not adequate protection for heavy arc welding.

These two hazards are the reason that full-time arc welders do a complete "cover-up" when on the job. Anytime you are arc welding, you must wear a helmet or face shield that completely covers the face, as shown in Fig. 12-1. The helmet has a window of special tinted glass. The tint filters out the harmful ultraviolet and thus protects the eyes. In front of this special glass is a window of ordinary glass which serves to protect the special glass. Metal splatters when arc welding is in progress. The ordinary glass, which can be cheaply replaced, guards the more expensive special tinted glass against damage.

Helmets have hinges which permit the technician to swing the helmet up when welding is not in progress, as when getting the work ready to weld (Fig. 12-2A). It is difficult to see things in ordinary light through the special tinted glass. Then, just before striking an arc, the technician swings the helmet down (Fig. 12-2B).

NOTE: Helmets are made in different styles and with various features. A deluxe helmet model has a hinged window which can be swung up to give the welder a clear view of the work before starting to weld. When welding is about to begin, the window is swung down to protect the eyes.

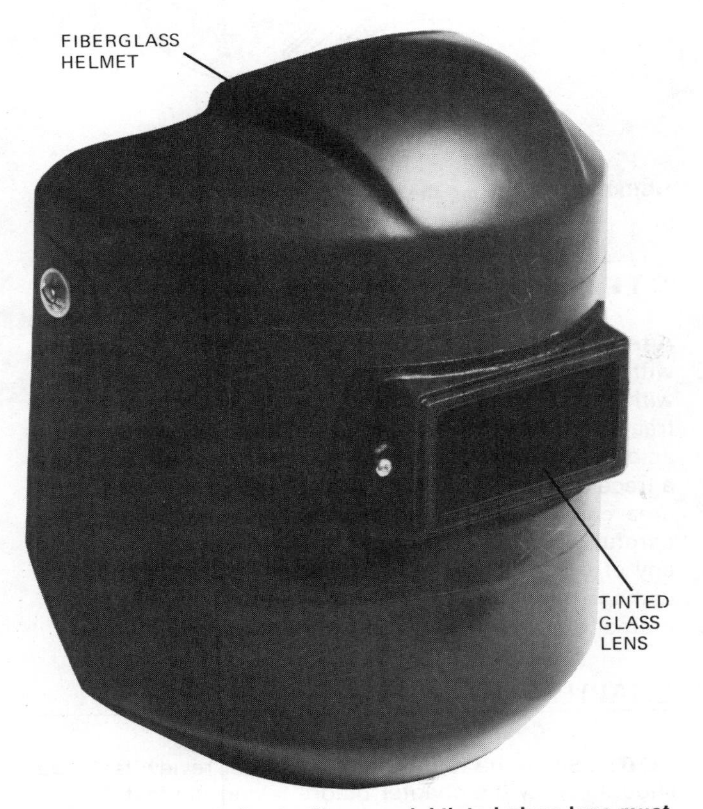

FIGURE 12 – 1. A helmet with a special tinted-glass lens must be worn anytime you are arc-welding. (*Marquette Division of Applied Power, Inc.*)

In addition to the helmet, the arc welder wears leather gloves with cuffs (Fig. 10-15). Also, a complete set of leathers may be worn to protect the arms, neck, and chest. Some technicians, when arc welding, wear leather aprons which provide adequate cover for the front of the body. Leather is preferred because it will not burn or catch fire as some clothing materials might. The degree of cover-up a technician uses when arc welding depends on how heavy a job is being done. For relatively light jobs, such as welding sheet-metal panels, fairly light protection might be appropriate. But for heavy-duty welding, such as welding a truck frame, full body protection is best.

CAUTION: If another person is helping you weld, the assistant must have adequate protection also. It is sometimes believed that the assistant, being several feet further away from the arc than you, does not need as much protection. However, the assistant should

A

B

FIGURE 12 – 2. How the helmet is used. At A, the technician has swung the helmet up so he can adjust the welder. At B, the technician is welding and the helmet has been swung down to protect his face and eyes.

have a face shield or helmet, gloves, and clothing that provides complete coverage of the skin.

In addition, welding in the shop should be done in an area away from other technicians. When an arc-welding job is in progress, shields should be erected around the area and signs posted warning of the danger. Otherwise, a customer, child, or anyone passing by might suffer eye damage from casually looking at the arc.

○ 12-2 Spot-Welding Hazards

During spot welding (Fig. 12-3), sparks will fly, just as with arc welding. The amount of sparking depends on the size of the job being done. With the spot welders found in the usual body shop, the sparking is not as severe as when an arc welding job is in progress. Thus, you may find spot welders being used in body shops by technicians not wearing any protection. This is wrong, because a single stray spark can put out an eye. As a minimum, goggles and gloves should be worn. Clothing should be buttoned or zipped up around the neck.

Since no arc is formed with spot welding, there is no hazard from the light. However, there are hazards from the sparks.

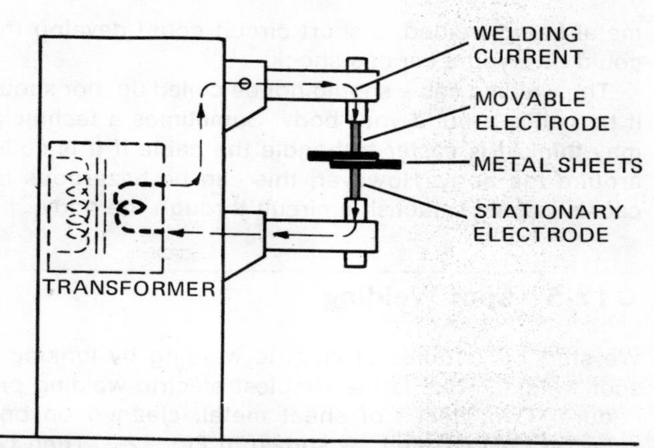

FIGURE 12 – 3. The basic principle of spot welding is illustrated by this floor-type spot-welding machine. Current flows through two overlapped metal sheets, from one electrode to the other, causing the metal to fuse in the spot. (*General Motors Corporation*)

○ 12-3 Fire Hazard

The welding area should be free of any flammable materials. One spark hitting a pile of oily rags can cause it to burst into flames. All flammable materials should be cleared away before welding begins. As an added safety precaution, position a fire extinguisher nearby.

When welding a frame or other internal part of a car, stay away from gasoline and air-conditioner lines. If a gasoline line is broken, gasoline could spurt out. Then you would have a serious fire before you could do anything about it. If an air-conditioner line or component part such as a condenser is overheated, it could burst, releasing refrigerant. This can be very dangerous. The refrigerant comes out at a very low temperature. If you are in the way, you could get serious frostbite or severe eye damage. In addition, the refrigerant, in the presence of an open flame or arc, will release a deadly poison gas. So before welding, locate the gasoline and air-conditioning lines and stay away from them. If you have to work close to such lines, detach and move them to one side.

○ 12-4 Electric Shock Hazard

Although spot and arc welding require a heavy flow of current, sometimes amounting to several hundred amperes, the voltage is very low. Voltage is what furnishes the "push" that sends the amperes through the circuit. In the spot welder, the circuit is through the two metal sheets being welded. In the arc welder, the circuit is through the electric arc.

This low voltage is not ordinarily dangerous, because it is not high enough to give you a shock. The voltage needed for arc welding is only a few volts, not enough to present any hazard. However, there is always some risk in operating and handling any electrical equipment. Thus, you should always make sure that the cable is in good condition and that the insulation is intact. If you are using a portable machine which has a long power cable, make sure the cable is not damaged by being stepped on or run over. If the power-cable insulation is bad and if the cable is on a wet floor or in contact with metal being welded, a short circuit could develop that could give you a serious shock.

The welding cable should not be coiled up, nor should it be coiled around your body. Sometimes a technician may think it is easier to handle the cable if it is coiled around the body. However, this can be hazardous because it could establish a circuit through the body.

○ 12-5 Spot Welding

We start our studies of electric welding by looking at spot welding. This is the simplest electric welding procedure. Two pieces of sheet metal, cleaned on both sides, are overlapped, as shown in Fig. 12-3. Then two electrodes are brought up against the two sheets. A heavy electric current at low voltage flows from one electrode to the other, through the sheet metal. This melts the metal at the spot. When the electrodes are withdrawn and the spot cools, the metal has fused to form a spot weld. The metal must be clean, because any dirt, paint, rust, or grease can prevent a good weld.

A great variety of spot welders are available (Fig. 12-4). They all operate in a similar manner. The typical spot welder has a transformer which steps down the shop 220 voltage to only a few volts. The spot welder includes a pair of heavy conductors on the ends of which are attached electrodes. The electrodes are copper, which offers low resistance and can pass a high current. The current is 100 amperes or more. This can produce almost instantaneous heating and fusing of the metal clamped between the two electrodes.

○ 12-6 Faulty Spot Welds

Technique does not enter into spot welding. You simply press the two electrodes to the two sides of the metal

FIGURE 12-4. A spot welder. (*Lenco, Inc.*)

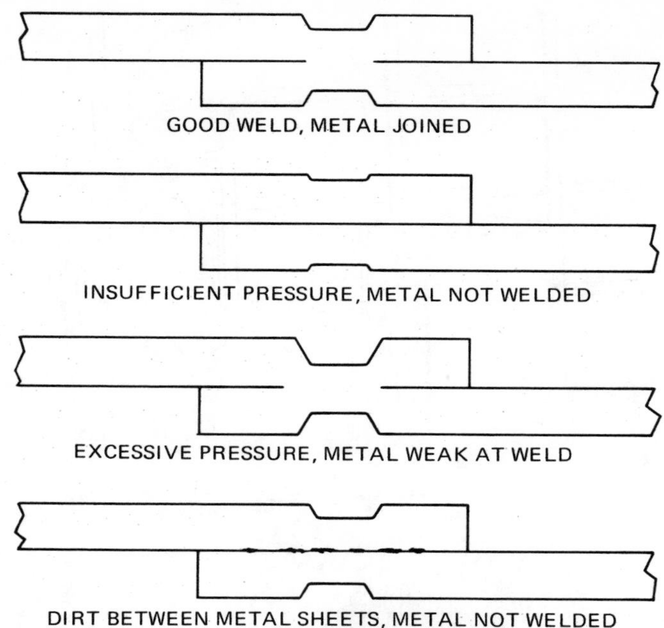

FIGURE 12-5. Good and bad spot welds.

panels and close the switch that is located on one of the electrodes. The current flow does the rest. Faulty spot welds will result if the pressure is not correct or if the areas to be welded are not clean. Figure 12-5 shows good and faulty spot welds.

○ 12-7 Arc Welding

In arc welding, the welder supplies a high amperage at low voltage. The current may run up to several hundred amperes. The arc welder used in the typical body shop can weld body sheet metal and frames. It does not have to be as heavy-duty as arc welders used in factories.

The heavy current flows through an electrode to the work (Fig. 12-6). The end of the electrode is held a small distance away from the work so that an arc is formed. The heat from this arc melts both the end of the electrode and the immediate area of the work. As the electrode is moved along the work, the melted area cools and solidifies, thus forming the weld. This is called *running a bead*.

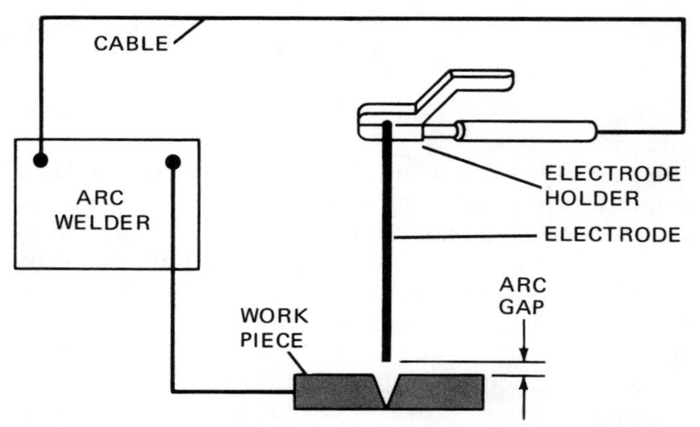

FIGURE 12-6. Principle of arc welding, shown in simplified form. (*General Motors Corporation*)

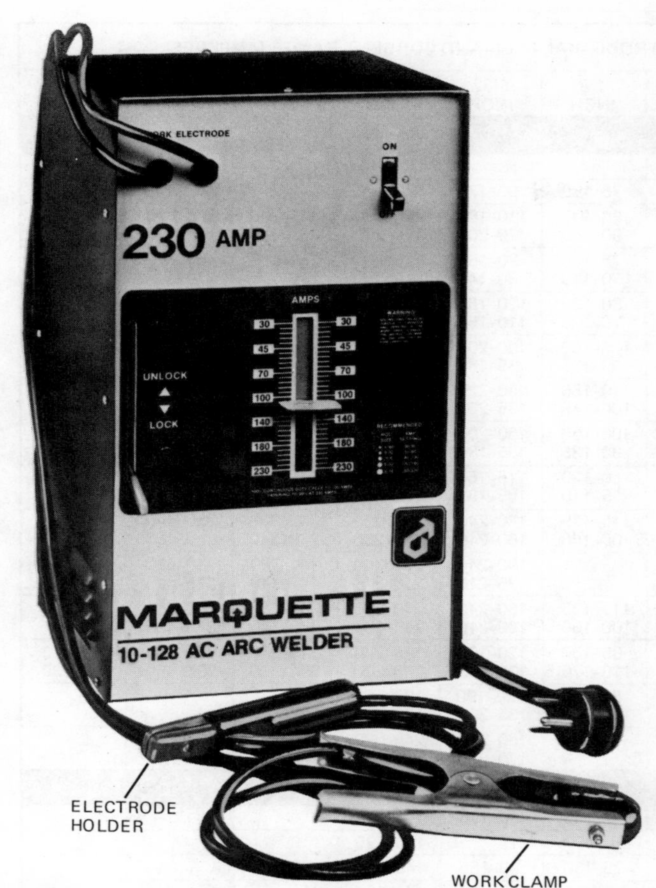

FIGURE 12–7. **An arc welder.** ***(Marquette Division of Applied Power, Inc.)***

There are two basic types of arc welders: alternating-current (AC) (Fig. 12-7) and direct-current (DC). The AC welder uses a transformer to reduce, or step down, the 220 shop voltage to just a few volts. This is like the automotive ignition coil in reverse. The ignition coil takes the 12-volts of the battery or alternator and steps it up to the thousands of volts needed to jump the gaps at the spark plugs. The arc-welder transformer reduces the 220 shop voltage to a few volts. Only a few volts are needed to maintain the arc after it is started. A hundred or more amperes may flow in the arc. This is what produces the high welding temperature.

The DC arc welder has a means of stepping down the 220 AC voltage and also converting it into DC. The voltage reduction is produced by either a transformer or a motor-generator set. If a transformer is used, there is also a converter, much like the rectifier used in the automotive alternator. The converter uses electrical check valves that change the AC to DC. If a motor generator is used, the shop AC runs the motor, which then drives the DC generator. The generator produces the DC directly. DC welders usually have a polarity switch. This switch can change the direction of the current flow. When current flows from the electrode to the work, it is called straight polarity. But when the polarity switch is thrown, the current flows from the work to the electrode. This is called reverse polarity.

Welders have either a current-adjustment rheostat or several plug-in jacks so that the correct amperage for the job can be selected.

The most common body-shop arc welder is the AC type (Fig. 12-7). It is available in various sizes. The larger sizes produce more current. For example, one make of AC arc welders includes a 100-ampere, a 230-ampere, and a 295-ampere welder. All of these are portable, and many can be equipped with wheels.

There are also engine-powered arc welders. On these, a gasoline engine drives the generator.

○ 12-8 Comparing AC and DC Arc Welders

As we mentioned, the AC arc welder is the one most commonly used in the body shop. It is simpler, lighter, costs less, and is satisfactory for body and frame work. The only disadvantage is that the arc is formed by alternating current. That is, the current flows momentarily from the electrode to the work, and then the next moment it flows from the work to the electrode. It alternates, or changes directions, 120 times a second. This is 60-cycle AC, the kind used throughout the United States.

The current can flow easily from the very hot electrode to the work, but it meets with much greater resistance in attempting to flow from the cooler work to the hotter electrode. However, this is no problem with the usual welding jobs on steel body panels and frame members. It can be a problem with some other metals, however, because the reverse current flow prevents a good weld from being formed.

Many stainless steels, low-alloy high-tensile steels, and nonferrous metals such as aluminum cannot be easily welded with AC. AC is usually slower than DC, especially on thin metal. Arc blow (tendency for the arc to bounce back) is reduced when welding in corners with AC.

○ 12-9 Types of Electrodes

The arc between the electrode and the work melts both the electrode and the work. There are many types of electrode, each designed to be used on a specific metal at a specific thickness (Fig. 12-8). The electrodes are usually heavily coated with a flux, as shown. The purpose of this flux is to provide a gas shield around the molten pool of metal so the gases in the atmosphere cannot react with it and spoil the weld. See Fig. 12-9. Here we show welding being done with a bare electrode. The nitrogen and oxygen are free to get to the molten metal and react with it. These gases form chemicals, such as iron oxide, that combine with the molten metal so that the weld will be very weak.

Now look at Fig. 12-10. Here we see welding being done with a coated electrode. The coating is melting and forming a gaseous shield over the molten pool. In addition, the coating floats up to the top of the weld, carrying with it impurities in the metal so that a purer and stronger weld is formed. After the weld is completed and cooled, this slag must be chipped off with a chipping hammer (Fig. 12-11).

NOTE: Also, when a weld is interrupted, as, for example, when you stop to put a new electrode in the holder, you should chip off the slag at the point where you stopped. This assures a good union at that point when you start to weld again.

COATING COLOR	AWS CLASS	ELECTRODE POLARITY (+) = REVERSE (–) = STRAIGHT	ELECTRODE DIAMETER AND CURRENT RANGE (AMPERES)							
			5/64 INCH	3/32 INCH	1/8 INCH	5/32 INCH	3/16 INCH	7/32 INCH	1/4 INCH	5/16 INCH
ELECTRODES FOR MILD STEEL										
LIGHT TAN	E6010	DC (+)						200–275	250–325	280–400
BRICK RED	E6010	DC (+)		40–75	75–130	90–175	140–225			
TAN	E6012	DC (–) AC			80–135 90–150	110–180 120–200	155–250 170–275	225–290 250–320	245–325 275–360	
LIGHT TAN	E6011	AC DC (+)			75–120 70–110	90–160 80–145	120–200 110–180	150–260 135–235	180–300 170–270	
RED BROWN	E6011	AC DC (±)			80–130 70–120	120–160 110–150				
DARK TAN	E6013	AC DC (±)		75–105 70–95	100–150 90–135	150–200 135–180	200–260 180–235			
GRAY-BROWN	E7014	AC DC (–)			110–160 100–145	150–225 135–200	200–280 180–250	260–340 235–305	280–425 260–380	
BROWN	E6013	AC DC (±)	45–80 40–75	75–105 70–95	100–150 90–135	150–200 135–180	200–260 180–235	250–310 225–280	300–360 270–330	360–460 330–430
BROWN	E6011	AC DC (+)		40–90 40–80	60–120 55–110	115–150 105–135				
GRAY	E7024	AC DC (±)		65–120 60–110	115–175 100–160	180–240 160–215	240–300 220–280	300–380 270–340	350–440 320–400	
BROWN	E6027	AC DC (±)				190–240 175–215	250–300 230–270	300–380 270–340	350–450 315–405	
GRAY	E7024	AC DC (±)			115–175 100–160	180–240 160–215	240–315 215–285	300–380 270–340	350–450 315–405	450–600
GRAY	E7018	DC (+) AC		70–100 80–120	90–150 110–170	120–190 135–225	170–280 200–300	210–330 260–380	290–430 325–440	375–500 400–530
GRAY	E7018	DC (+) AC		70–100 80–120	85–150 100–170	120–190 135–225	190–260 180–280			
GRAY-BROWN	E7028	AC DC (+)				180–270 170–240	240–330 210–300	275–410 260–380	360–520	
ELECTRODES FOR LOW ALLOY, HIGH-TENSILE STEEL										
PINK	E7010-A1	DC (+)		50–90	75–130	90–175	140–225			
PINK	E7010-A1	DC (+)					140–225			
TAN	E7010-G	DC (+)			75–130	90–185	140–225	160–250		
TAN	E7010-G	DC (+)			75–130	90–185	140–225			
WHITE	E8010-G	DC (+)			75–130	90–185	140–225			
GRAY-BROWN	E8018-C1	DC (+) AC			90–150 110–160	120–180 140–200	180–270 200–300		250–350 300–400	
GRAY-BROWN	E8018-C3	DC (+) AC			90–150 110–160	120–180 140–200	180–270 200–300	210–330 250–360	250–350 300–400	
GRAY	E8018-B2	DC (+) AC			90–150 110–160	110–200 140–230	160–280 200–310			
GRAY	E11018-M	DC (+) AC			95–155 115–165	120–200 145–230	160–280 200–310	190–310 240–350	230–360 290–410	
ELECTRODES FOR STAINLESS STEEL										
PALE GREEN	E308-15	DC (+)		30–70	50–100	75–130	95–165		150–225	
GRAY	E308-16	DC (+); AC	20–45	30–60	55–95	80–135	115–185		200–275	
GRAY	E308L-16	DC (+); AC		30–65	55–100	80–140	115–190			
GRAY	E309-16	DC (+); AC		30–60	55–95	80–135	115–185		200–275	
PALE GREEN	E310-15	DC (+)		30–70	45–95	80–135	100–165			
GRAY	E310-16	DC (+); AC		30–65	55–100	80–140	120–185		200–275	
GRAY	E316L-16	DC (+); AC		30–65	55–100	80–140	115–190			
PALE GREEN	E347-15	DC (+)		30–70	50–100	75–130	95–165			
GRAY	E347-16	DC (+); AC		30–60	55–95	80–135	115–185			
ELECTRODES FOR BRONZE AND ALUMINUM										
PEACH	E-CuSn-C	DC (+)			50–125	70–170	90–220			
WHITE	Al-43	DC (+)		20–55	45–125	60–170	85–235			

, ELECTRODES FOR CAST IRON						
			1/8″ SIZE	5/32″ SIZE	3/16″ SIZE	1/4″ SIZE
LIGHT TAN	ESt	DC (+); AC	80–100			
BLACK	ENi-CI	DC (±) AC	60–110 65–120	100–135 110–150		
ELECTRODES FOR HARDSURFACING						
BLACK		DC (±) AC	40–150 50–165	75–200 80–220	110–250 120–275	150–375 165–410
BLACK		DC (+); AC			60–150	
BLACK		DC (+); AC			60–150	
DARK GRAY		DC (±) AC		145–210 155–225	180–280 200–290	230–360 255–375
DARK GRAY		DC (±) AC		120–180 135–230	160–260 165–285	200–350 220–385
DARK GRAY		DC (+) AC			110–275 125–275	150–400 200–400

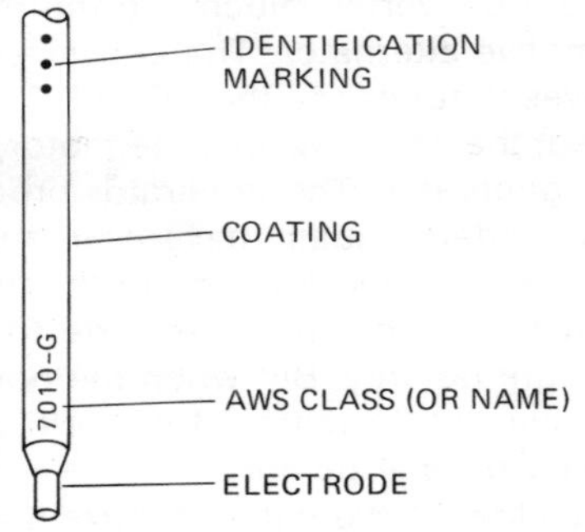

IDENTIFICATION MARKING

COATING

7010-G

AWS CLASS (OR NAME)

ELECTRODE

FIGURE 12–8. Types of electrodes.

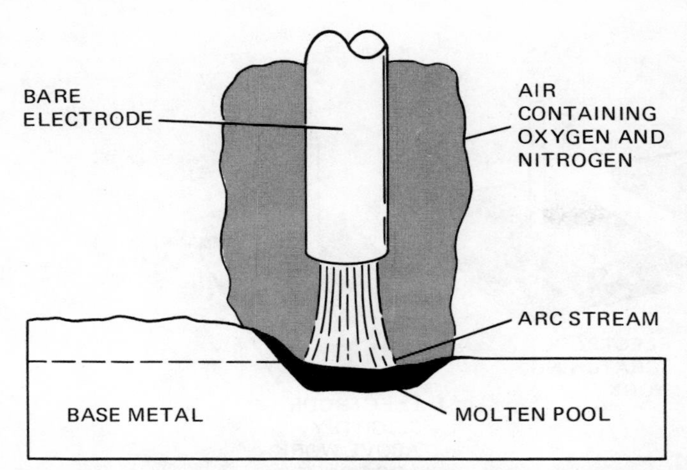

FIGURE 12 – 9. When arc welding is done with a bare electrode, the molten metal reacts with the oxygen and nitrogen in the air to cause a poor weld.

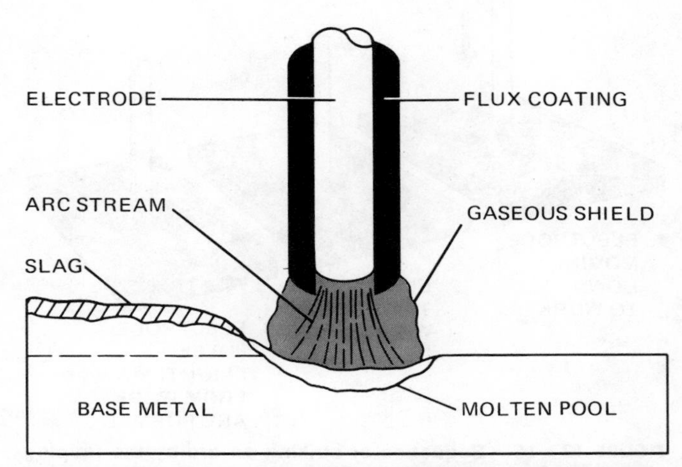

FIGURE 12 – 10. When the arc welding is done with a flux-coated electrode, the coating melts and forms a gaseous shield over the molten metal, protecting it from the oxygen and nitrogen in the air.

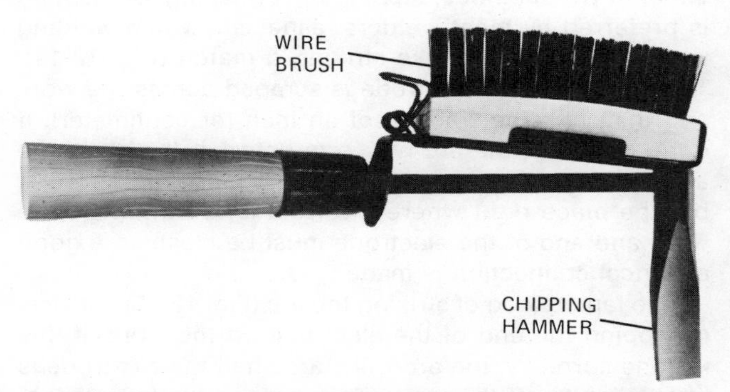

FIGURE 12 – 11. Combination chipping hammer and wire brush for cleaning arc welds. (*Marquette Division of Applied Power, Inc.*)

○12-10 Types of Arc Welds

Figure 12-12 illustrates a variety of welds that can be made by electric arc. Note that the electric arc welder can make the same welds as gas-welding equipment—butt, lap, edge, tack, and tee.

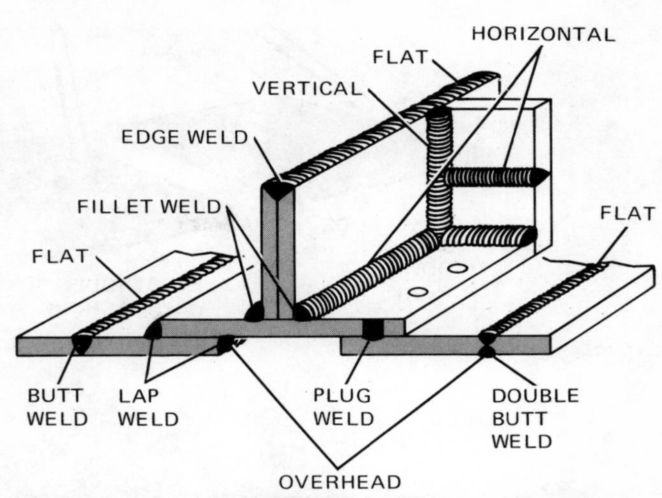

FIGURE 12 – 12. Types of weld made with an arc welder.

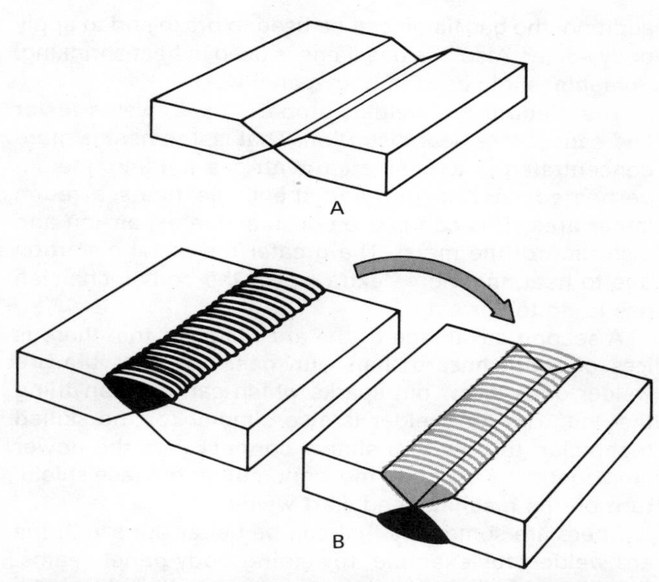

FIGURE 12–13. Double-vee butt weld. In A, the pieces are ground to form a vee on both sides. When the weld is made on one side, then the piece is turned over to weld the other side as shown at B.

It is rather difficult to make butt welds on thin metal, particularly if the two edges are not perfectly aligned. The arc is so hot that it can quickly burn holes in the work if it is thin. In butt-welding thicker materials, the edges should be beveled so a vee is formed. A double-butt weld is often used on thick materials. See Fig. 12-13. The two pieces are ground on both edges to form a vee on both sides (A in Fig. 12-13). One side is then welded, and the piece is turned over so the other side can also be welded, as shown in B in Fig. 12-13.

○12-11 Comparing Gas and Arc Welding

The type of welding done in a shop depends on the preferences of the shop owner and the technicians. There are advantages and disadvantages to both types of welding.

The gas welder is more versatile in many ways, because it can be used for cutting as well as welding.[1] In

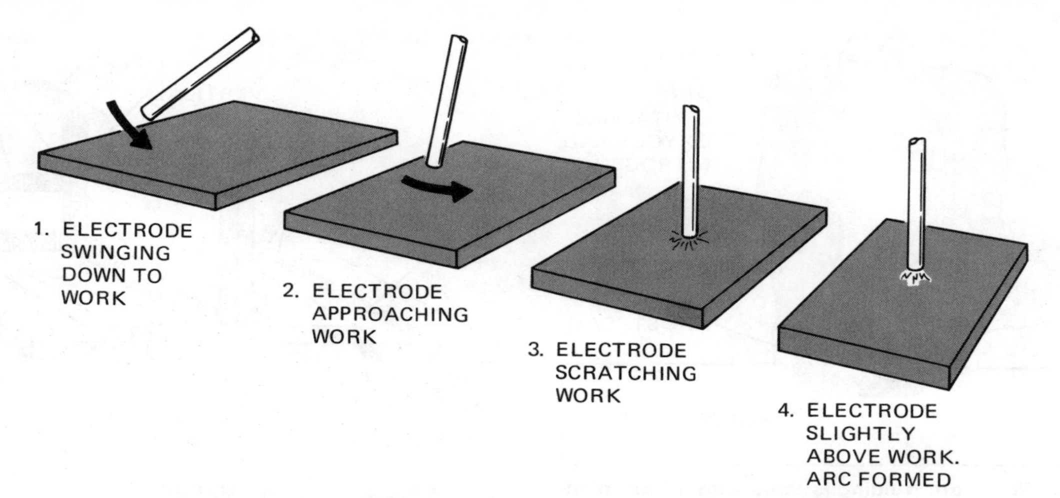

FIGURE 12 – 14. Sequence of striking an arc by the scratch method.

addition, the gas flame can be used to braze and to apply body solder. Also, the gas flame is used in heat shrinking. Sometimes it is used in body-panel work.

The electric arc welder, properly used, welds faster and causes less heat distortion. That is, the heat is more concentrated in a small area. With gas welding, the superheated gas surrounding the flame heats a much larger area. This can cause considerable expansion and distortion of the metal. The greater the metal distortion due to heat, the more "extra work" the body technician has to do to correct it.

A second advantage of the arc welder is that there is less of a fire hazard than with gas. However, the arc welder does throw out sparks which can burn anything they hit. The arc welder is also simpler for the skilled technician to use. You simply connect it to the power line, connect a clamp to the work, put on the face shield, turn on the machine, and start welding.

There are some jobs that can be better done with the arc welder, for example, rewelding body-panel seams. But where heat is needed to straighten parts and to weld, the gas welder is better.

○ 12-12 Arc Welding

Let us now look at a typical arc-welding job, butt-welding two metal plates. First, the plates are beveled along the edges to be welded. They are then placed on the workbench and clamped so they will be held in position during the welding operation.

Next, the equipment is set up for the job. Plug the machine into the 220-volt shop circuit. Connect the welding cables to the machine and the ground clamp to the workpiece or worktable. Select the correct electrode for the job and put it into the electrode holder.

Now turn on the welder, adjust it to the correct amperage,[2] put on your gloves and face shield, and lower the shield to protect your face. Be sure that you are completely covered and that your shirt is buttoned up to protect your neck. Refer to ○ 12-1 for a discussion of arc welding and safety.

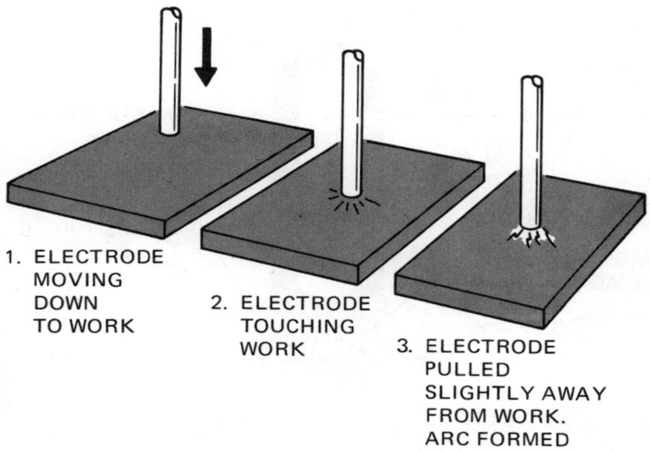

1. ELECTRODE MOVING DOWN TO WORK
2. ELECTRODE TOUCHING WORK
3. ELECTRODE PULLED SLIGHTLY AWAY FROM WORK. ARC FORMED

FIGURE 12 – 15. Sequence of striking an arc by the tapping method.

You are now ready to strike an arc. This is done by either of two methods, tapping or scratching. Scratching is preferred by most welders, especially when welding with AC. This is just like striking a match (Fig. 12-14). The tip end of the electrode is scraped across the work and then raised a fraction of an inch (or centimeter). If done correctly, the arc will form between the electrode and the work. Do not scratch just any place on the work, but the place right where the weld is to be made. The work and end of the electrode must be clean so a good electrical connection is made.

The tap method of striking the arc (Fig. 12-15) consists of tapping the end of the electrode on the work. If this is done correctly, the arc will start when the electrode is lifted slightly off the work. This method works satisfactorily with DC but not as well with AC. If the electrode is raised from the work just as the current alternates and starts to flow from the work to the electrode, no arc will form. However, repeating the tapping procedure several times should start the arc.

[1]Heavy duty arc welders can cut metal, but higher voltage and amperage are required. The arc welders found in body shops are not normally used to cut metal.

[2]Amperage, or *heat* as it is usually called in the body shop, varies with the thickness and type of metal. The thicker the metal, the higher the amperage, or heat, required. Instruction manuals supplied with the welders give you specific instructions on the correct adjustments for different thicknesses of metal.

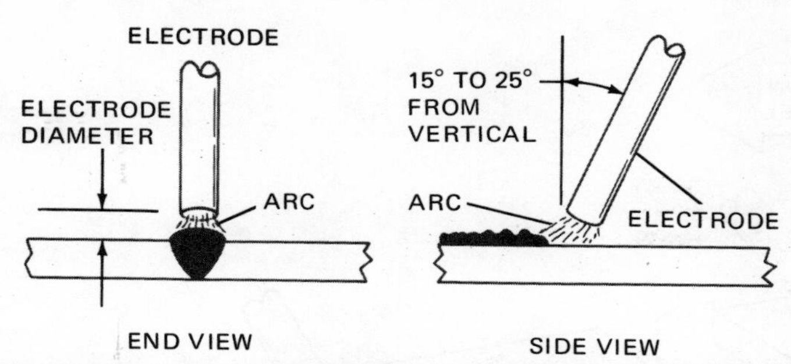

FIGURE 12–16. Correct positioning of the end of the electrode above the work.

Once the arc is started, you are ready to run a bead. Hold the electrode at a slight angle with its end at a distance from the work about equal to the diameter of the electrode (Fig. 12-16). The electrode should be tilted in the direction that it is moving.

There are two things to remember when running a bead. First, keep the electrode moving steadily. Second, maintain the same air gap between the end of the electrode and the work. If you move jerkily, the weld will be jerky—too much metal in one place, not enough in another. Likewise, if you vary the length of the arc, you will have poor welding action in some places. See ○ 12-13, which explains the "sound" way of determining whether or not the length of the arc is correct.

○ 12-13 Sound of a Good Arc

When the electrode is held at the proper distance from the work, the arc will give off a sharp crackling sound which some technicians call the "frying-egg" sound. Actually, it is a sort of sputtering or frying sound that is a little sharper than you would get frying eggs. If the arc is too long, which means poor welding, you would get not the frying sound but rather a more subdued humming noise. Have a welding expert strike an arc; if you listen carefully, you should be able to distinguish the difference between the sound from an arc of the right length and the sound from an arc that is too long. If the electrode is moved too far away from the work, the arc will not be able to jump the gap, and so it will die.

CAUTION: Do not look at the arc without your helmet on and your eyes protected by the lens!

○ 12-14 Stringer and Weave Beads

Stringer and weave beads are the two basic types of bead. See Fig. 12-17. The stringer bead (Fig. 12-17A) is made by moving the electrode in a straight line across the work at a steady pace. After striking the arc, the electrode should be held momentarily at the starting point to assure good melting of the metal and good fusion. Then the electrode should be moved smoothly and at a steady pace along the joint being welded. The correct length of arc should be maintained, as has been previously described.

The stringer bead is satisfactory for most welding around the shop, except where a wider bead is needed. A wider bead might be needed to join two slightly irregular edges, for example, or to finish off a closed vee-butt weld, as shown in Fig. 12-13B. To make the weave bead, you weave the end of the electrode from one edge of the space to be filled to the other, as shown in Fig. 12-17B. You continue this weaving motion at the same time that you move forward along the bead. You should hesitate momentarily at each edge of the weave. This supplies as much heat to the edges as at the center.

Figure 12-18 shows the procedure of butt welding on thick metal. We show four beads being laid here. Bead 1 runs along the bottom of the vee. Then you add beads 2 and 3 along the two sides of the vee, as shown. Finally, you make a weave bead to finish off the weld.

NOTE: After each bead is completed, you must chip off the slag from the top of the bead before starting the next bead. If you do not do this, you will get a poor weld, because the upper weld will not fuse satisfactorily through the layer of slag.

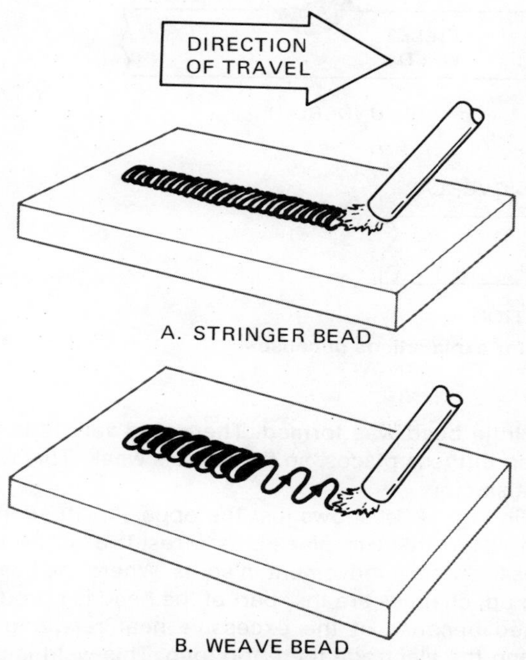

FIGURE 12–17. Stringer and weave beads.

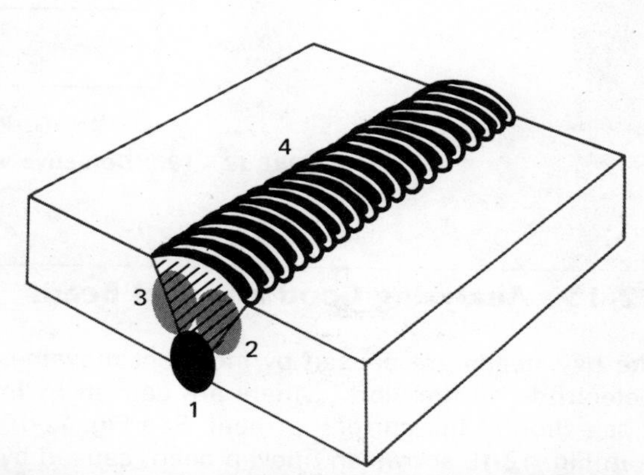

FIGURE 12–18. Procedure of making a vee butt weld on thick metal. Four beads are shown, and they should be made in the numbered sequence.

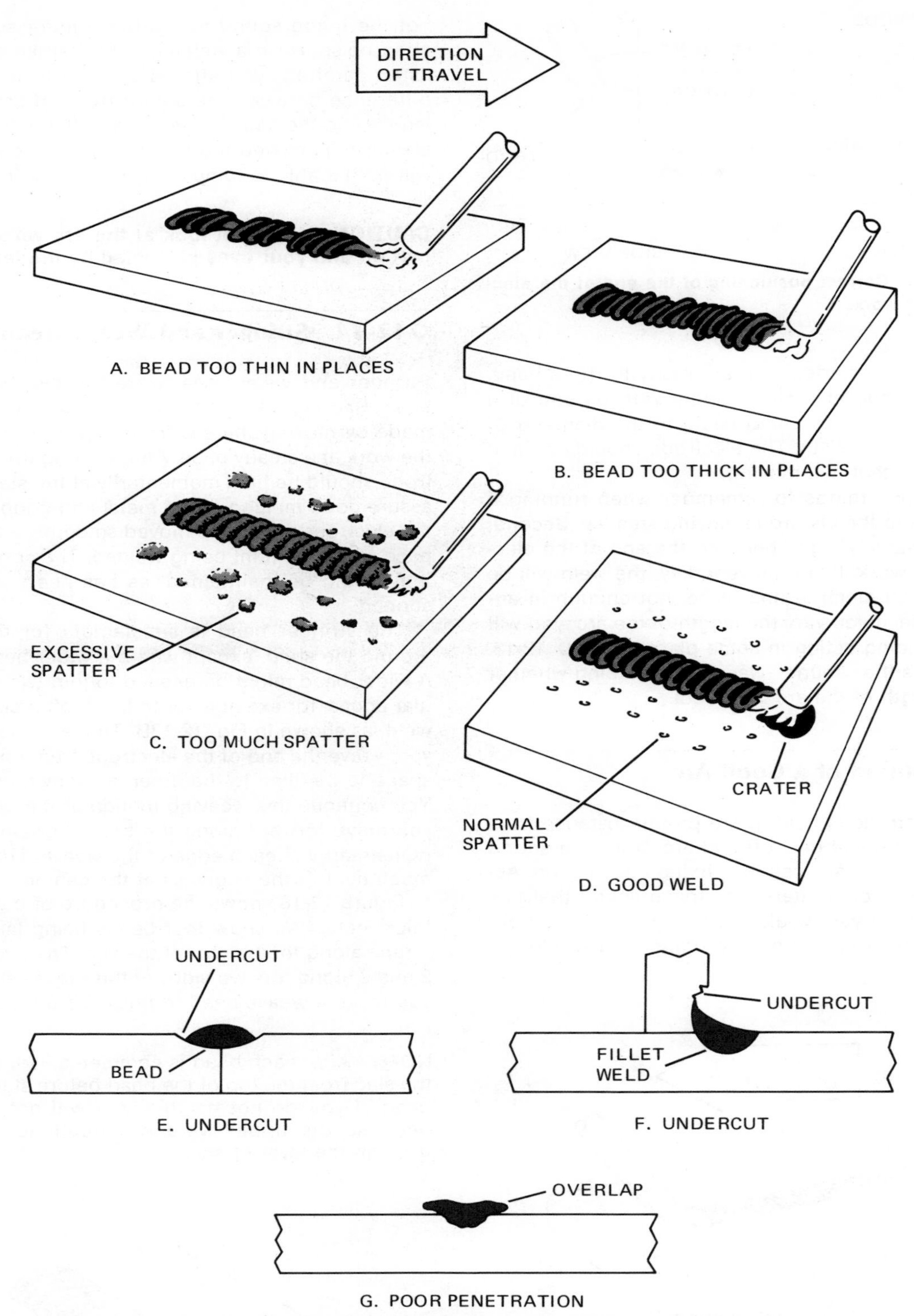

FIGURE 12–19. Defective welds. See text for explanations of causes.

○12-15 Analyzing Good and Bad Beads

Some bad beads are caused by incorrect movement of the electrode on the work. Others are caused by incorrect selection of the current, or heat. See Fig. 12-19.

A in Fig. 12-19 shows an uneven bead, caused by uneven speed of movement across the work. In some places, the technician moved slowly and a good bead was formed. Then the technician moved too fast, and so very little bead was formed. There was very little penetration in these places, so the weld is weak. This weld is unsatisfactory.

B in Fig. 12-19 shows just the opposite situation. The bead is too thick in places, as a result of uneven and excessively slow movement in spots. Where the bead has piled up, chances are that part of the bead is porous and burned because of the excessive heat resulting from holding the electrode there too long. This weld is unsatisfactory.

C in Fig. 12-19 shows too much spatter. That is, the metal "splashes" away from the bead. The usual cause is an arc that is too long. The length of the arc should be about the thickness of the electrode being used. An excessively long arc gives off more of a humming sound than a crackling sound. See ○ 12-13.

D in Fig. 12-19 shows a good weld being made. The bead is uniform and there is only a little spatter.

E and F in Fig. 12-19 show the same defect. This is called undercutting and is due to failure to fill the depression created by the arc. This is caused by moving the arc too rapidly along the work so that there is not enough time for the electrode to melt and fill the crater.

G in Fig. 12-19 shows another kind of defective weld, called overlap. The edges of the bead overlap the base metal beyond the sides of the crater. This overlap does not fuse to the work. There are several possible causes of this condition, including too low a welding current (heat), too long an arc, or excessive travel. To avoid overlap, try a higher heat, a shorter arc, and slower electrode movement.

There is one other condition that sometimes causes a beginner trouble, and this is that the electrode sticks to the work. The cause of this condition is allowing the electrode to remain in contact with one area for too long. When this happens, the electrode welds to the base metal. To release the electrode, bend it from side to side to break it free. The instant an arc is struck, move the electrode away from the spot—that is, along the joint to be welded.

○ 12-16 Practicing Welding

Now, having noted what can happen if incorrect technique or current is used, let us see how we can perfect our technique. Try welding with the welder turned off. That is, practice holding the electrode the proper distance from the work and moving it smoothly along the joint you want to weld. Some technicians find that using both hands helps to steady the electrode. Also, keeping the elbows close to the body reduces the tendency to weave the electrode as you move it. Do this practice with your face shield up so you can see what you are doing. There will be no arc with the welder turned off, so there is no danger. When practicing, try to keep the end of the electrode only about 1/16 to 1/8 inch [1.59 to 3.18 mm] from the work as you move it along the weld.

In actual welding, the electrode melts away, so you must keep moving the electrode holder down toward the work in order to maintain the proper length of arc. See Fig. 12-20.

CAUTION: Always have the helmet down to protect your eyes and face before striking the arc and welding.

○ 12-17 Making Different Kinds of Welded Joints

After you have mastered the basic welding technique and have made a good butt weld on two metal plates on the bench, try other types of welds. See Fig. 12-12. As you develop skill, you should begin performing the basic welds on actual cars.

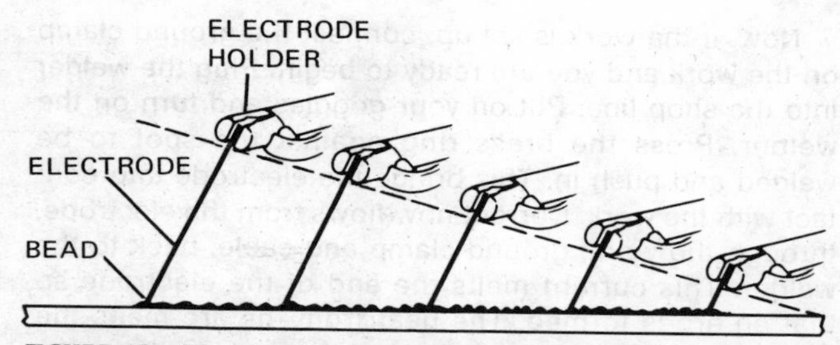

FIGURE 12-20. As the electrode is used up when running a bead, you must move the handle steadily downward in order to maintain the same length of arc.

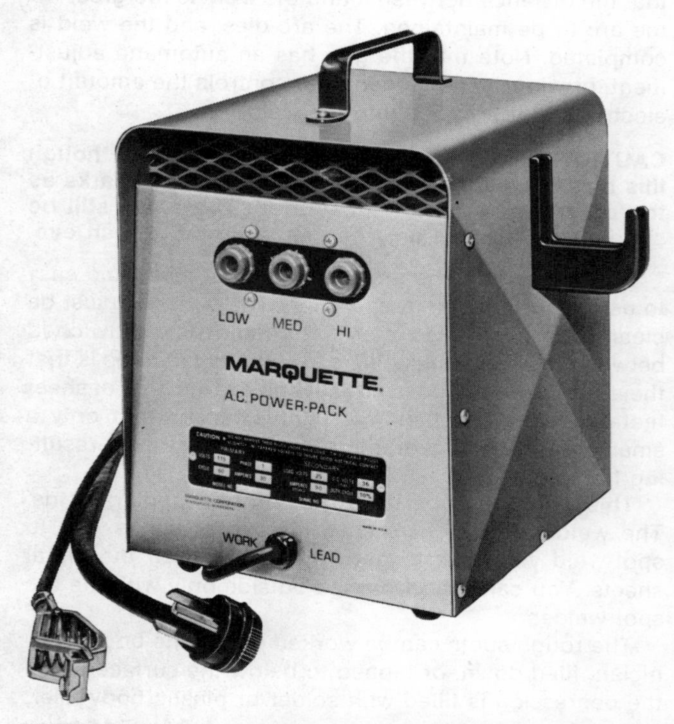

FIGURE 12-21. An arc spot welder with three receptacles for low, medium, and high heat. (*Marquette Division of Applied Power, Inc.*)

○ 12-18 Arc Spot Welding

Figure 12-21 shows an arc spot welder. This is a semiautomatic machine that makes arc welds in spots. A typical job would be to spot-weld two overlapping panels together. The arc spot weld is similar in many ways to the resistance spot weld discussed in ○ 12-5. However, the arc spot weld adds filler metal to the weld so that a small bump is left.

Here is how this welder is used. First, the arc-spot-welding gun is plugged into the proper receptacle in the welder. There are three receptacles—low, medium, and high—in the unit shown in Fig. 12-21. Which one is selected depends on the type and thickness of material being welded. The "high" receptacle supplies more current and is used for heavier material. Then the electrode is inserted through the brass ring on the end of the gun and into the gun. Its end should be flush with the brass ring. Next, the adjusting knob on the gun should be turned to set the electrode feed, that is, to set the amount of electrode that will be fed into the weld. This determines the size of the bump of metal left on the weld.

Now, if the work is set up, connect the ground clamp on the work and you are ready to begin. Plug the welder into the shop line. Put on your goggles and turn on the welder. Press the brass ring against the spot to be welded and push in. This brings the electrode into contact with the work. Current now flows from the electrode, through the work, ground clamp and cable, back to the welder. This current melts the end of the electrode so that an arc is formed. The heat from the arc melts the spot in the work where the arc is formed. At the same time, metal is added to the surface of the weld. After a few moments, the electrode has melted away enough so that the distance between it and the work is too great for the arc to be maintained. The arc dies, and the weld is completed. Note that the gun has an automatic adjustment, previously mentioned, that controls the amount of electrode that will feed into the weld.

CAUTION: Goggles should be worn even though this type of welding does not throw as many sparks as the other types already described. There will still be sparks, and it takes only one spark to put out an eye.

As you can see, the arc spot welder is quick and easy to use, requiring little preparation. The surfaces must be clean, and no foreign material should be sandwiched between the two metal sheets. Another advantage is that the arc spot welder does not heat up a large area of sheet metal. To the body technician this means that only a small area must be worked to remove expansion resulting from heat.

This welder can be used only on overlapping welds. The welds are much rougher than spot welds, but to spot-weld you have to get on both sides of the metal sheets. You can weld from the outside only with the arc spot welder.

The rough spots can be worked out by the body technician, filed down, or tapped to below the surface. Then the depression is filled with solder or plastic body filler.

○ 12-19 Panelspotter®

The Panelspotter® (Fig. 12-4) does spot welding with two electrodes applied to only one side of a panel or metal sheet. Figure 12-22 shows the principle. The electric current flows into the metal from one electrode, through the metal, and out through the other electrode. The two

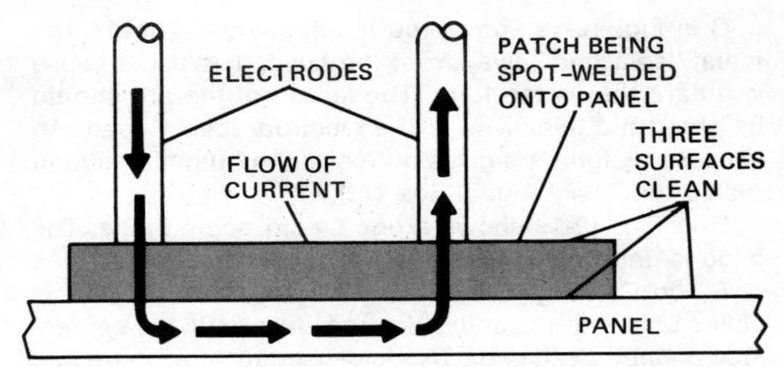

FIGURE 12–22. Principle of operation of Panelspotter®.

spots where the electrodes are applied become hot enough for welding to take place.

NOTE: The manufacturer of the Panelspotter® now makes another model called the Lencospot®. It has a solid-state timer and switch. Both models operate the same way.

Figure 12-23 shows a patch being applied to a rear deck which has rusted out along the edge of the back window. To make a weld, the surfaces to be welded must be clean. The rusted-out area on the car, shown in Fig. 12-23, was first sandblasted to remove all old rust and expose clean metal. Then the sheet-metal patch was cut to fit, cleaned, and spot-welded to the old metal.

To make a weld, the machine must be plugged in and turned on. Then the two electrodes are pressed against the patch, as shown in Fig. 12-23. Next, the electrode handle is pressed. This turns on the current. It flows from one electrode, through the work, to the other electrode. The heat produced at the two electrodes produces two welds. The amount of time that the current flows is automatically controlled by a setting on the machine. After this time has lapsed (only a few seconds), the machine shuts off the current and the welds are completed.

The Panelspotter® is a very handy welder for installing replacement panels. To start with, the parts have to be cleaned so that there is clean metal-to-metal contact between the edge of the sheet metal on the car and the edge on the replacement panel. Then, the replacement panel should be held in position, either by tacking in several places or by clamps. Next, the machine is used to make as many welds as necessary to secure the replacement panel in place.

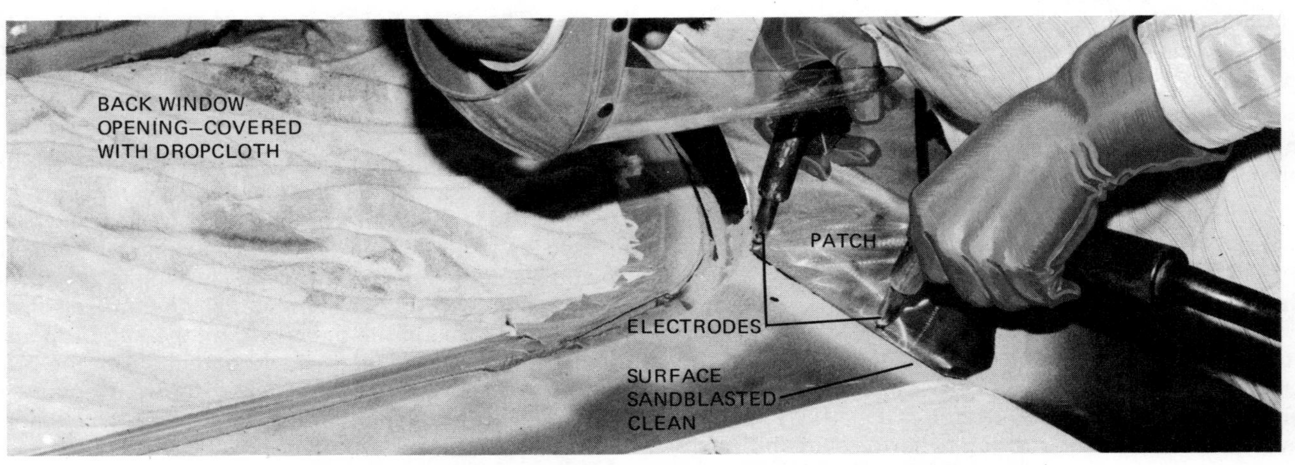

FIGURE 12–23. Using the Panelspotter® to weld a patch on rear deck.

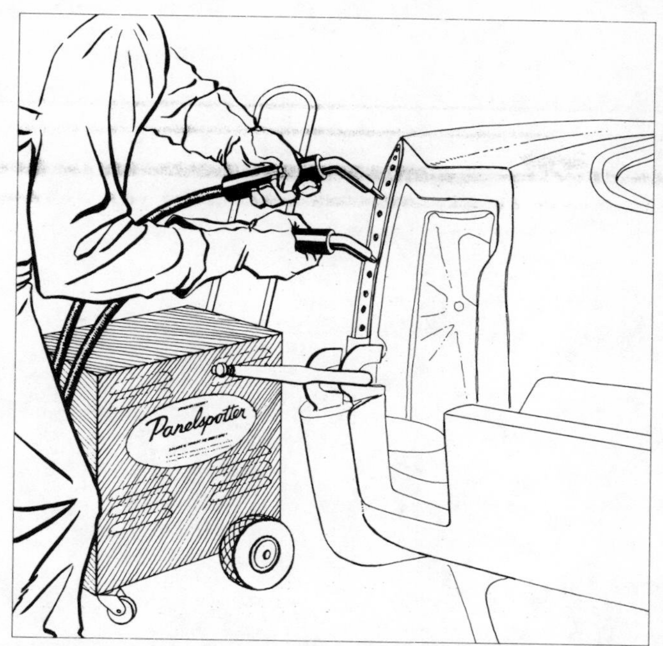

FIGURE 12–24. Welding rear end of a left quarter panel to the underbody. (*Lenco, Inc.*)

FIGURE 12–25. Front end of a right quarter panel welded to underbody. (*Lenco, Inc.*)

Many other uses will be found for the Panelspotter®. Figure 12-24 shows it being used to weld the crimped-over rear end of a left quarter panel to the underbody. Figure 12-25 shows how the front end of a right quarter panel was welded to the underbody.

CHAPTER 12 CHECKUP

NOTE: Since the following is a chapter review test, you should review the chapter before taking the test.

COMPLETING THE SENTENCES The sentences below are incomplete. After each sentence there are several words or phrases, but only one of them correctly completes the sentence. Write each sentence in your notebook, ending it with the one word or phrase that completes it correctly.

1. Two types of electric welding are (*a*) oxygen and acetylene, (*b*) brazing and soldering, (*c*) heating and cutting, (*d*) arc and spot.
2. When arc welding you *must* always wear (*a*) shoes, (*b*) gloves, (*c*) leather pants, (*d*) a helmet.
3. Arc-welding electrodes are coated with flux to (*a*) prevent air from reaching the molten metal, (*b*) provide more oxygen for better burning, (*c*) add nitrogen for stronger welds, (*d*) allow the use of lower "heats."
4. Striking an arc is done by (*a*) matches or a torch lighter, (*b*) tapping or scratching, (*c*) adding flux, (*d*) breaking away the slag.
5. The machine that adds filler metal to the spot weld is (*a*) an arc spot welder, (*b*) a resistance spot welder, (*c*) an AC welder, (*d*) a DC welder.

QUESTIONS Write each of the following questions, and then the answer, in your notebook. If you have trouble recalling the answer to a question, turn back to the pages that cover the material and study them again.

1. What safety precautions do you take when arc welding?
2. Describe the difference between arc welding and spot welding.
3. What is the difference between a DC arc welder and an AC arc welder?
4. How does a good arc sound?
5. Describe how to use a spot welder.

DEFINITIONS In the following, you are asked for several definitions. Write them in your notebook. The act of writing the definitions does two things. It tests your knowledge, and it helps fix the information more firmly in your mind. Turn back into the chapter if you are not sure of a definition, or look it up in the glossary at the back of the book.

1. Define "ultraviolet light."
2. What is the "heat" setting on a welder?
3. Define "spot welding."
4. What is an arc-welding electrode?
5. Define "striking an arc."

SUGGESTIONS FOR FURTHER STUDY

Tour your shop, and make a list of all the different electric welders. You may find only an arc welder, or you may find several types of electric welders. In your notebook, write down the types of welders and the operating procedure for each.

PART 3

CORRECTING SHEET-METAL AND FRAME DAMAGE

In this part, we discuss sheet-metal and frame damage and describe the tools and their use to correct such damage. The purpose of such work is to restore the frame and body to their original alignment and body contours. Our discussions include methods of removing and replacing such damaged parts as trim, bumpers, air-conditioning components, engine radiator, and battery. Often these parts must be removed so that work can commence on the damaged sheet metal and frame. Following this, we describe sheet-metal repair and frame straightening. Part 3 consists of five chapters, as follows:

Chapter 13	Basic Operations in Collision Repair
Chapter 14	Methods of Sheet-Metal Repair
Chapter 15	Repairing Sheet Metal
Chapter 16	Fundamentals of Body and Frame Straightening
Chapter 17	Using the Body and Frame Straightener

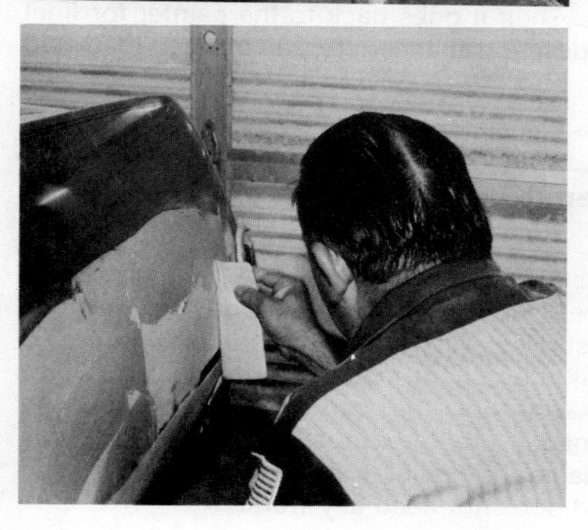

13
BASIC OPERATIONS IN COLLISION REPAIR

In this chapter, we describe the preliminary work required before actual work begins on sheet metal and the frame. This preliminary work can include removing such parts as moldings, grills, headlight assemblies, bumpers, air-conditioning components, cooling system radiator, and battery. For example, the car shown in Fig. 13-1, suffered a right-front collision. The right fender was so badly damaged it had to be replaced. There was also damage to the frame. The first thing the body technician did was remove all the front-end parts that were damaged and pile them to one side for later examination. The only part that could be saved was the radiator. It was repaired and reinstalled. The grills, headlight assemblies, front panel, fender marker lights, and trim were so badly damaged they were junked. However, the bumper was sent to a bumper recycler, where it was straightened and rechromed so it could be reused.

The chapter also explains how to reinstall the various components that have been removed during a body-frame repair job, after the body and frame have been repaired.

FIGURE 13–1. Car damaged by a right-front collision. It has been set up on car stands, and damaged front-end parts have been removed.

○ 13-1 Sequence of Operations

A vehicle that has been in an accident is given a preliminary estimate to determine whether or not it is worth repairing. Generally, if the cost of repair exceeds 75 percent of the value of the vehicle, it is declared a "total." This means that the vehicle is not repaired, but is sold for salvage, usually to a salvage yard. If the preliminary estimate of the cost of repair falls below this percentage and the insurance adjuster agrees, then a detailed estimate is made. This written estimate lists every new part needed and every labor operation required to repair the vehicle. When the vehicle owner or the insurance company agrees to pay the repair costs on the estimate, the car is ready to become a job in process.

The parts needed to repair the car are ordered. The car is assigned to a body technician and brought into the body shop. The body technician then takes the following steps:

1. Analyzes the damage and determines the course of action.
2. Removes damaged parts that are in the way of assessing the job and making necessary alignment checks.
3. Makes alignment check.
4. Straightens sheet metal and frame, as required.
5. Checks and corrects the fit of doors, hoods, trunk lids, and other parts.
6. Fills damaged areas of sheet metal with plastic body filler or fiberglass.
7. Sands off the plastic body filler in preparation for priming and painting.
8. Sends the vehicle to the paint shop.

If the damage is extensive, there may be additional steps in the procedure. For example, if the windshield or rear glass requires replacement and if door pillars have been repaired, the car may make two trips between the body shop and the paint shop. It will go to the paint shop for painting of door pillars, interior of the trunk, and other interior parts that will show. At the same time, the painter may put on primer coats. Next, the car is returned to the body shop for installation of the glass and other exterior parts. Then it goes back to the painter for final painting. We describe all these steps in this and following chapters.

○ 13-2 Removing Molding

Molding is installed by various methods. Some is put on with adhesive. Other molding is attached to the body panels with screws, nuts, or plastic studs. Figure 13-2 shows typical attachment methods. The molding is removed by special tools that can be inserted under the molding to snap it free. Care must be used in doing this to avoid damaging the paint if the body panel is in good condition and does not need any work.

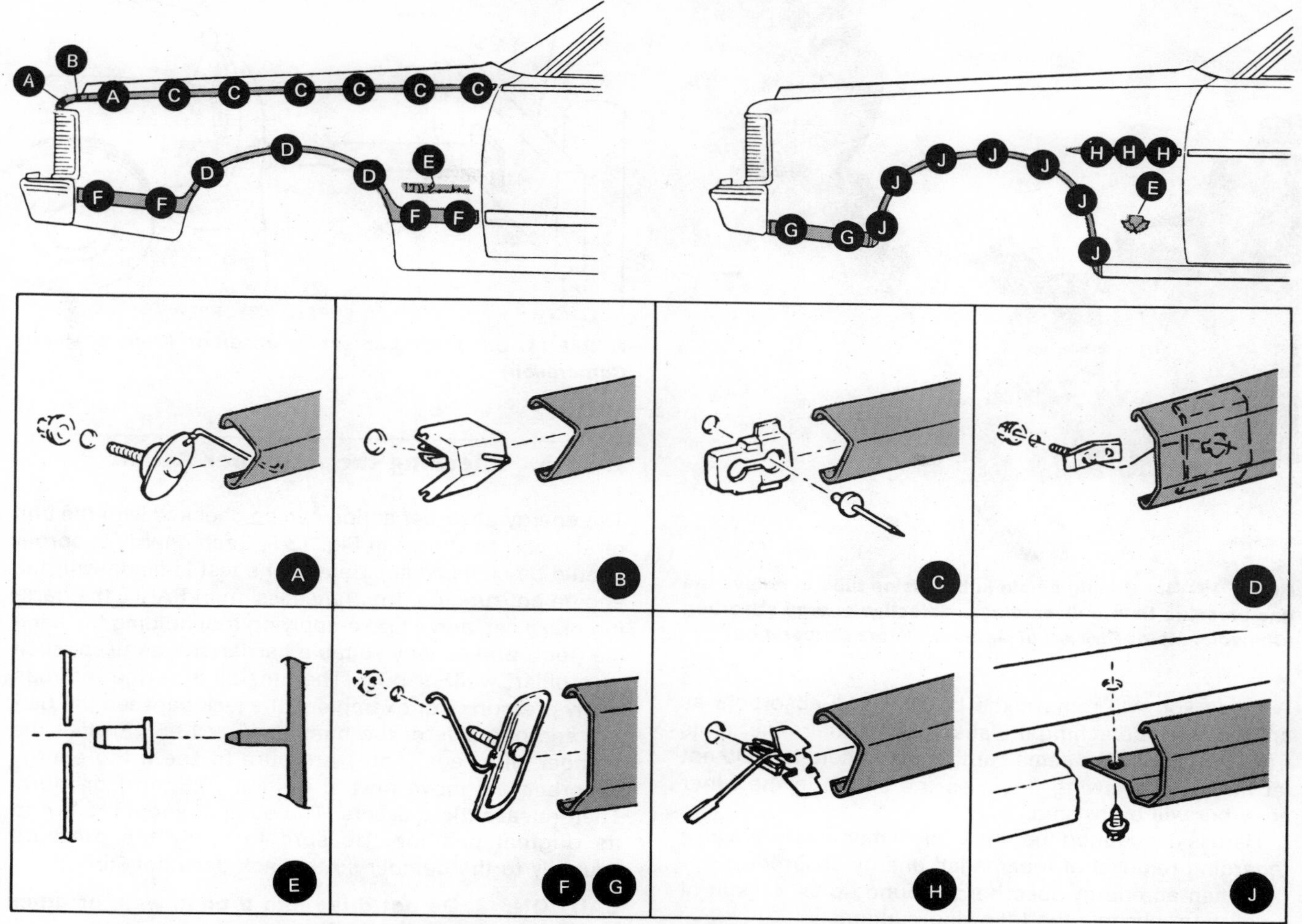

FIGURE 13–2. **Methods of attaching front exterior side molding. (*Ford Motor Company*)**

○ 13-3 Removing Bumpers

Bumpers have energy-absorbing components. We described these in Chapter 2. These energy absorbers (also called isolators) are often hydraulic shock absorbers very similar to the shocks used in suspension systems. Figure 13-3 shows how the hydraulic units are fitted to the front bumpers. Their purpose is to permit the bumpers to withstand collisions at low speeds without damage to the bumper or car. That is, the energy absorbers will shorten in length during the impact. Then they will resume their original length after the collision. At high speeds, the energy absorbers will probably be damaged and require replacement. In any event, you must use care in removing and handling these absorbers, regardless of whether they are in good condition or not. If they are to be junked, the gas-filled type must have a hole drilled in it, as we explain later, so the gas pressure will be released. This renders the absorber harmless. Unless this is done, someone could be severely injured if a compressed absorber suddenly extended or if it were heated and exploded.

The gas-filled energy absorber is shown in one model in Fig. 13-3. A typical energy absorber, using a spring instead of gas to provide the return force, is shown in Fig. 2-31.

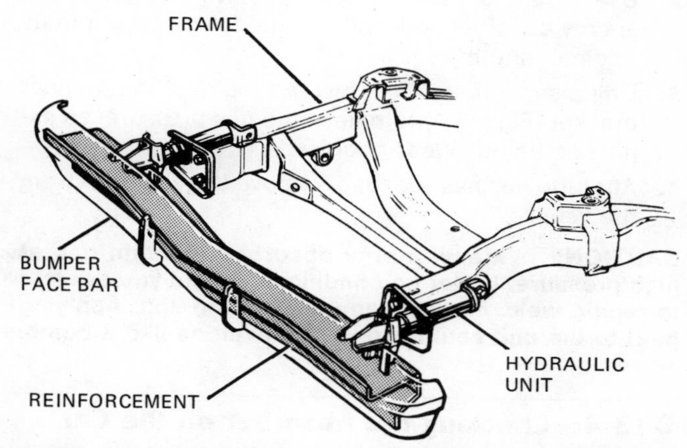

FIGURE 13–3. **Energy-absorber installation on front bumper. (*Chrysler Corporation*)**

When starting work on a car that has had a front or rear collision, use care when removing the bumper and energy absorbers. You should not disconnect the bumper from one absorber and then let the bumper swing down to the floor. This twists the piston in the other absorber and damages the seal. Instead, support the bumper until you detach it from the other absorber.

FIGURE 13–4. Drilling a hole in the piston tube to relieve the gas pressure before discarding a defective energy absorber. (*Chevrolet Motor Division of General Motors Corporation*)

Often you will remove the bumper and absorbers as an assembly, detaching the absorbers at their inner ends from the frame. The same caution holds here too. Do not let the bumper swing down so the piston in the other absorber will be twisted.

Here is the caution that the vehicle manufacturers give regarding removal of a damaged energy absorber:

"When an energy absorber is bound up as a result of a collision, observe the following cautions:

1. Stand clear of the bumper. The absorber might release and snap the absorber out suddenly.
2. Use a chain or cable to apply positive restraint to the energy absorber so it will not suddenly pop out to its original length.
3. Drill a small hole in the piston tube near the bumper bracket (Fig. 13-4) to relieve the gas pressure, as explained below. Wear goggles!
4. After the gas has escaped, remove the absorber from the vehicle."

CAUTION: Many energy absorbers contain gas at high pressure. Under no conditions should you attempt to repair, weld, or apply any heat to the unit. Applying heat to the unit could cause it to explode like a bomb.

○ 13-4 Checking the Absorber on the Car

First, examine the energy absorber for leakage around the seal between the cylinder tube and the piston tube. A stain or trace of oil on the piston tube near the seal is normal. But if oil is dripping from the seal or stud end of the unit, it should be replaced.

Examine the bumper bracket, piston tube, frame bracket, and cylinder tube for evidence of visible distortion. Scuffing of the piston tube, if the unit has been stroked, is considered normal. If there is obvious damage, the unit and associated damaged parts should be replaced.

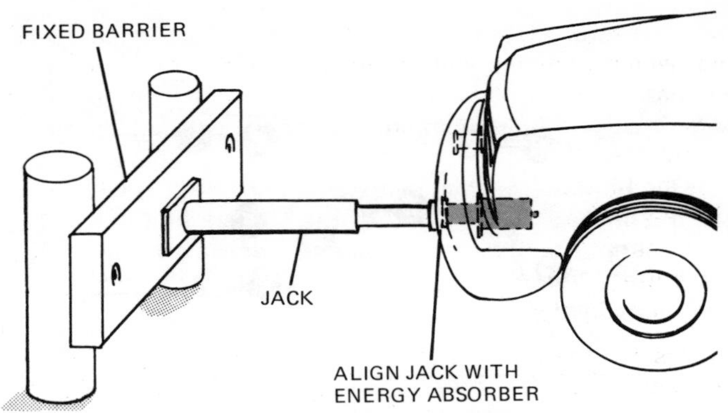

FIGURE 13–5. Testing an energy absorber. (*General Motors Corporation*)

○ 13-5 Checking the Absorber Action

The energy-absorber action can be checked with the unit on the car, as shown in Fig. 13-5. Each energy absorber should be checked separately. The test is made with the engine not running, the transmission in PARK, the parking brake set, and a brake-applying tool holding the service (foot) brakes. Any suitable barrier can be used, such as a pillar, wall, or post. Then install a device that can apply pressure. For example, put a jack between the barrier and one side of the bumper (Fig. 13-5). Protect the bumper with rags. Apply pressure to see if the energy absorber will move inward ⅜ inch [9.5 mm] or more. Then release the pressure. The bumper should return to its original position. Be sure to apply the pressure squarely to the bumper so the jack does not slip off.

CAUTION: Do not drive into a post, wall, or other barrier to perform the test!

A bench check can also be made of the energy absorber in a suitable arbor press. The unit should compress at least ⅜ inch [9.5 mm] and then return to its normal length when the pressure is released. If the unit does not, discard it.

○ 13-6 Scrapping an Energy Absorber

If an energy absorber is to be scrapped, the internal gas pressure must be released. Put the energy absorber in a vise. Drill a small hole in the piston tube, as shown in Fig. 13-4. Use the caution label as a locator for drilling. Drill either in front of or through the label.

CAUTION: Wear safety glasses when drilling the hole. The gas, when released, can drive metal chips at high speed. One of these could enter an eye and put it out.

○ 13-7 Removing Battery

If the accident to the vehicle has pushed metal in enough to press against the battery, you will need to remove the battery. Even if the metal has not been pushed in that much, you may still want to remove the battery so you can work on the metal. The first thing you must do is examine the battery to see whether its case has been damaged. If the case has been damaged, the battery liquid (called the electrolyte) may have leaked out. This liquid, which contains sulfuric acid, is highly corrosive. It will eat holes in your clothes, give you severe burns if it gets on your skin, and can injure your eyes if it gets into them.

If the battery case has been damaged and the electrolyte has leaked out, the battery must be junked. Battery cases cannot be repaired. Proceed as follows to remove the battery, regardless of whether or not the case has been damaged:

1. First disconnect the grounded-battery-terminal cable from the battery-terminal post. This guards against accidental shorting across the battery when the insulated battery-terminal cable is being disconnected. If the grounded terminal is not disconnected first and the battery is still charged, there can be sparks if the wrench accidentally touches metal. The wrench would be shorting directly across the battery.

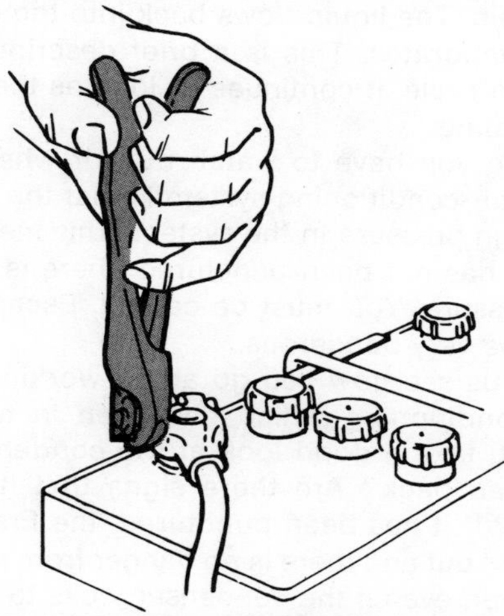

FIGURE 13-6. Using battery-cable pliers to loosen a nut-and-bolt type of battery cable. (*United Delco Division of General Motors Corporation*)

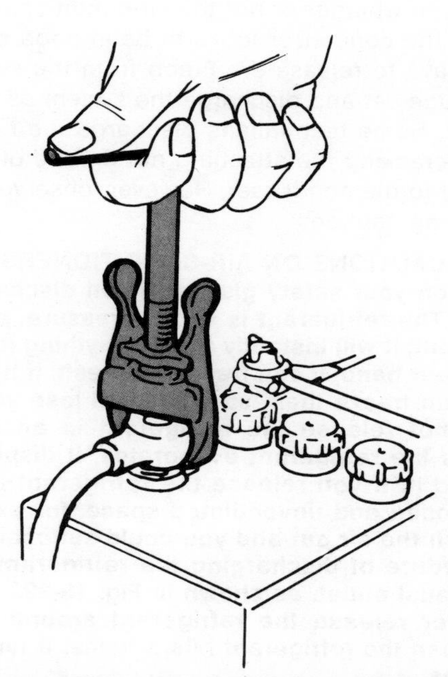

FIGURE 13-7. Using a clamp puller to pull the cable from a battery terminal. (*United Delco Division of General Motors Corporation*)

2. There are various types of battery connectors. Some have a cable clamp that is attached to a terminal on top of the battery (Fig. 13-6). If the clamp is of the nut-and-bolt type, as shown, loosen it with battery pliers. If you use an open-end wrench or ordinary pliers, you may break the battery top. As you turn the wrench or pliers, the jaw could swing around and hit the top, breaking it. Use a battery-terminal puller, as shown in Fig. 13-7, to pull the clamp off if it sticks. Do not try to pry the clamp off, as this can damage the battery.
3. The spring-ring type of battery connector (Fig. 13-8) is loosened with pliers, as shown.
4. The side-terminal battery connector (Fig. 13-9) requires a wrench to disconnect the screws.
5. Some batteries have stainless-steel screw-type terminals. These take nuts which require wrenches to loosen them.

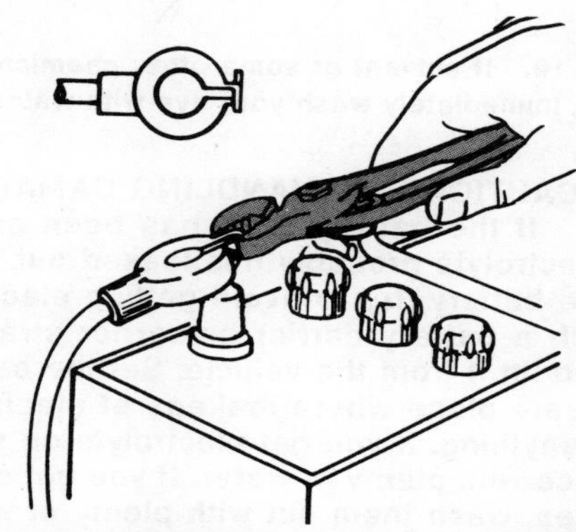

FIGURE 13-8. Using pliers to loosen a spring-ring type of cable clamp from a battery terminal. (*United Delco Division of General Motors Corporation*)

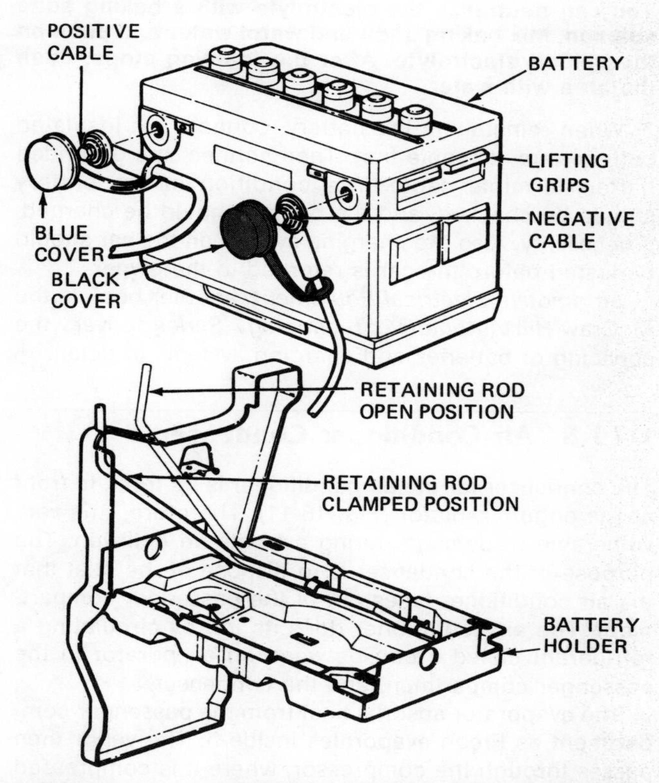

FIGURE 13-9. Cable connection and battery mounting arrangement. (*Cadillac Motor Car Division of General Motors Corporation*)

FIGURE 13-10. If solvent or some other chemical splashes in your eye, immediately wash your eye with water.

SPECIAL CAUTIONS ON HANDLING DAMAGED BATTERIES: If the battery case has been cracked or broken, electrolyte probably has leaked out. When removing the battery, try to avoid getting electrolyte on you. Attach a battery carrier or carrier straps to the battery and lift it from the vehicle. Set the battery outside in a safe place where leakage of electrolyte will not harm anything. If you get electrolyte on you, wash it off at once with plenty of water. If you get electrolyte in your eyes, wash them out with plenty of water (Fig. 13-10). Then see a doctor right away.

Remember, also, that the electrolyte will eat the paint on the car and also eat away vinyl and upholstery. You can neutralize the electrolyte with a baking soda solution. Mix baking soda and warm water and put it on the spilled electrolyte. After the foaming stops, flush the area with water.

When reinstalling the battery, connect the insulated battery-terminal cable first. Then connect the grounded battery-terminal cable. The condition of the battery should be checked, and the battery should be charged, if necessary. Also the charging system on the car should be tested before the car is returned to the owner.

Automotive Electrical Equipment, another book in the McGraw-Hill *Automotive Technology Series*, covers the servicing of batteries and charging systems in detail.

○13-8 Air-Conditioner Condenser

The condenser for the air conditioner is up front, in front of the engine radiator (Fig. 13-11). Therefore, it is very vulnerable to damage during a front-end collision. The purpose of the condenser is to dispose of the heat that the air conditioner takes out of the passenger compartment. The air conditioner does its job by circulating a refrigerant called Freon between an evaporator in the passenger compartment and the condenser.

The evaporator absorbs heat from the passenger compartment as Freon evaporates inside it. The vapor then passes through the compressor, where it is compressed to a high pressure. This increases the temperature of the compressed vapor. When the vapor passes through the condenser, it gives up this heat and condenses back into

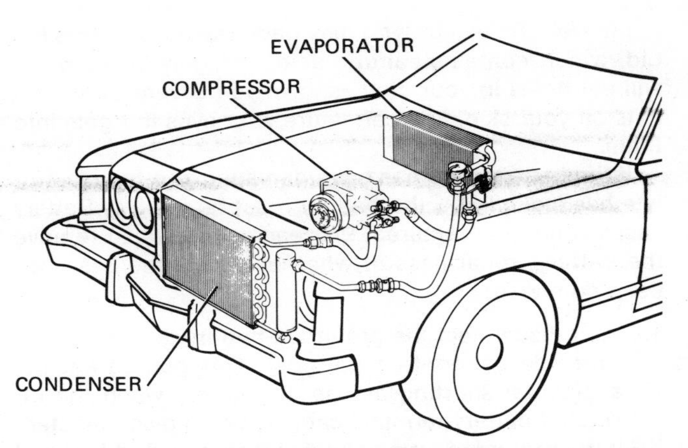

FIGURE 13-11. Components of the air conditioner. (*Ford Motor Company*)

a liquid again. The liquid flows back into the evaporator where it evaporates. This is a brief description of the refrigeration cycle. It continues as long as the compressor is operating.

The thing you have to watch out for when working around an air-conditioning system is that the refrigerant is under high pressure in the system. This means that, if the system has not been punctured, there is gas inside at high pressure. You must be careful. Escaping refrigerant can be very dangerous.

Now let us see how you go about working on a car with air conditioning which has been in a front-end crash. First, take a good look at the condenser. Has it been pushed back? Are there signs that it has been punctured? If it has been punctured, the Freon has already leaked out and there is no danger from pressurized gas. However, even if the condenser looks to be in good condition, a connecting tube may have been damaged or twisted so leakage has occurred.

If the front end has been pushed in, you may have to take the condenser off so you can work on the metal, regardless of whether or not the air-conditioning system is okay. If the condenser looks to be in good condition, you will have to release the Freon from the system. Attach a gauge set and discharge the system as shown in Fig. 13-12. Some technicians discharge the refrigerant by barely cracking the attaching nut on one of the lines connected to the condenser. However, observe carefully the following cautions:

SPECIAL CAUTIONS ON AIR-CONDITIONERS:

1. Put on your safety glasses when discharging refrigerant. The refrigerant is under pressure, and when it comes out, it will instantly freeze anything it touches. If it hits your hand, it can freeze the flesh. If it hits your eyes, it can freeze them so you could lose your sight!

2. Do not release the refrigerant in an enclosed space. As the refrigerant evaporates, it displaces the air around it. If you release the refrigerant in a completely closed and unventilated space, for example, it could push the air out and you could suffocate. Follow the procedure of discharging the refrigerant into the shop exhaust outlet, as shown in Fig. 13-12.

3. Never release the refrigerant around an open flame. When the refrigerant hits a flame, it turns into a deadly gas.

4. Heat in any form must never be applied to any refrigerant line or any component of the air-conditioning system. The refrigerant is under pressure. Heating

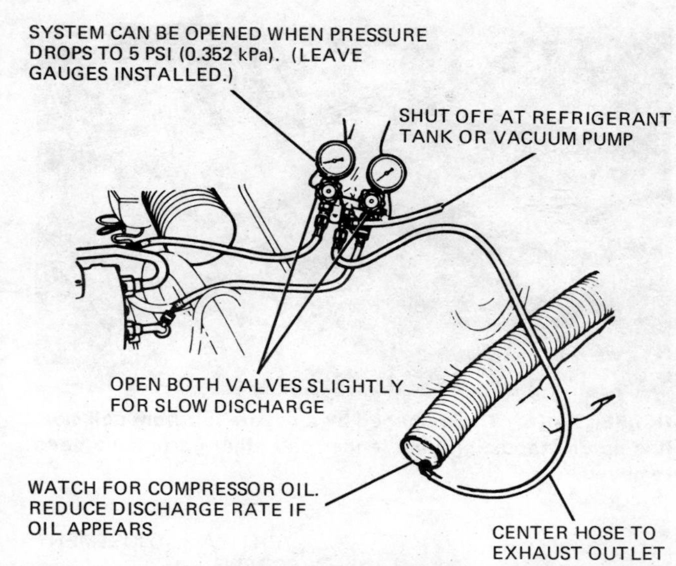
SYSTEM CAN BE OPENED WHEN PRESSURE
DROPS TO 5 PSI (0.352 kPa). (LEAVE
GAUGES INSTALLED.)
SHUT OFF AT REFRIGERANT
TANK OR VACUUM PUMP
OPEN BOTH VALVES SLIGHTLY
FOR SLOW DISCHARGE
WATCH FOR COMPRESSOR OIL.
REDUCE DISCHARGE RATE IF
OIL APPEARS
CENTER HOSE TO
EXHAUST OUTLET

FIGURE 13–12. Using a gauge set to discharge the refrigerant. (*Ford Motor Company*)

the refrigerant could increase the pressure enough to cause an explosion. Thus, never steam-clean any air-conditioner component or line. When welding, remove these components and move refrigerant lines out of the way.

A special refrigerant oil that lubricates the compressor circulates with the refrigerant. If the refrigerant escapes slowly, little oil will be lost. See Fig. 13-12. However, if the refrigerant escapes rapidly, it will carry most of the oil out with it. This oil must be restored to the system when it is repaired or the compressor will fail from lack of lubrication.

○ 13-9 Installing Condenser and Recharging System

Installing a condenser, or any other component of the air-conditioning system, is a job for the trained technician. You must connect the condenser and attach it to the car. When a new condenser is installed, a specified amount of fresh, clean refrigerant oil must be added to it. After the condenser is installed, a gauge set, a vacuum pump, and a container of refrigerant must be connected to the system. Then the system must be purged and recharged. *Automotive Air Conditioning,* another book in the McGraw-Hill *Automotive Technology Series,* covers the servicing of air conditioners in detail.

○ 13-10 Cooling-System Radiator

Check the coolant level in the radiator. If it is still full, then the radiator has not been damaged, even though it may have been pushed back. What often happens is that the radiator is shoved back into the engine fan and the fan cuts into the radiator before the engine stalls. In this case, the radiator may be so badly damaged that it must be replaced. However, if the damage is slight, the radiator can be repaired and used again.

You may have to remove the radiator to straighten the front-end metal, even though the radiator is not damaged. In such case, you must decide whether or not to save the coolant. Generally, if the coolant has been in the system for a year or longer, it probably should be replaced anyway. In that case, you drain out the coolant and discard it. You can then disconnect the hose clamps and remove the attaching nuts or screws holding the radiator to the car.

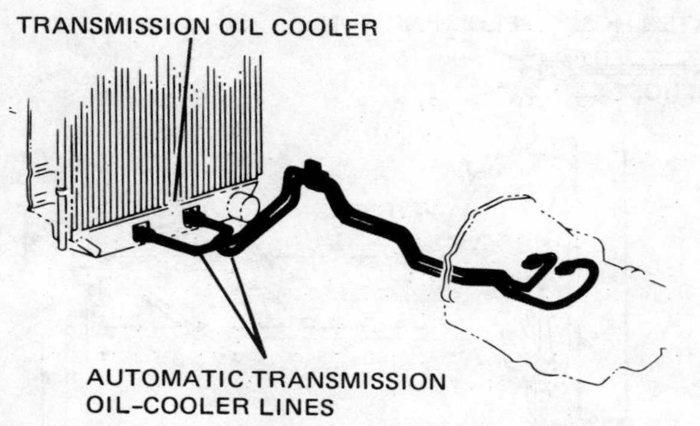
TRANSMISSION OIL COOLER
AUTOMATIC TRANSMISSION
OIL-COOLER LINES

FIGURE 13–13. Automatic-transmission oil cooler and lines. (*Ford Motor Company*)

○ 13-11 Transmission Oil Cooler

On some cars, the radiator has a special section that cools the automatic-transmission oil (Fig. 13-13). That is, the automatic transmission is connected by oil-cooler lines to this special section in the bottom of the radiator. When the engine is running, transmission oil flows through the tubes to the radiator, where the oil is cooled. It then flows back to the transmission. If the radiator is damaged so that oil has been lost, or if the radiator has to be removed, oil must be added to the transmission. This is done after the radiator has been reinstalled and reconnected. The procedure varies with different vehicles. *Automotive Transmissions and Power Trains,* another book in the McGraw-Hill *Automotive Technology Series,* covers the procedure in detail.

○ 13-12 Installing Radiator and Filling the System

If the vehicle has high mileage, it may be desirable to flush out the engine water jackets while the radiator is off. (However, this is not a job routinely performed by the auto body technician.) This is done with the thermostat removed, as shown in Fig. 13-14. Sending water through the water jackets in the reverse direction helps to remove scale.

After the radiator is reinstalled and the hoses are reconnected (including the transmission oil lines if used), the cooling system should be filled. Add the proper amount of antifreeze to get adequate protection against freezing at the lowest temperature expected in your area. Then add water. This mixture is called the *coolant.* Note, in Fig. 13-15, that the thermostat will be closed when water and antifreeze are added. This prevents instant filling of the cooling system. The thermostat has a small hole in it that permits the air to leak out, but this takes some time. You may have to wait and refill the radiator a couple of times. The engine can be started and run for

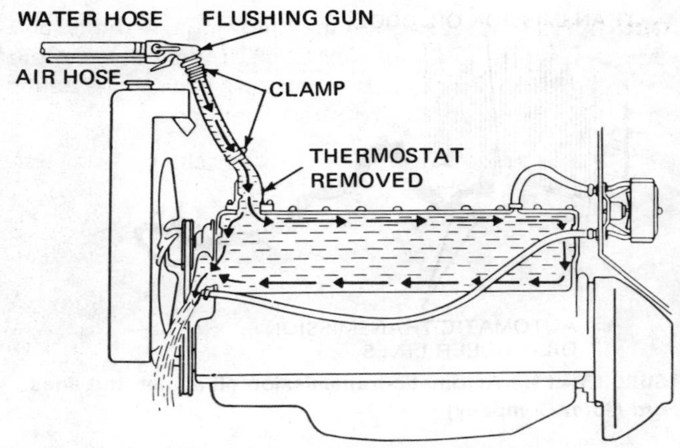

FIGURE 13-14. Reverse flushing the engine water jackets.

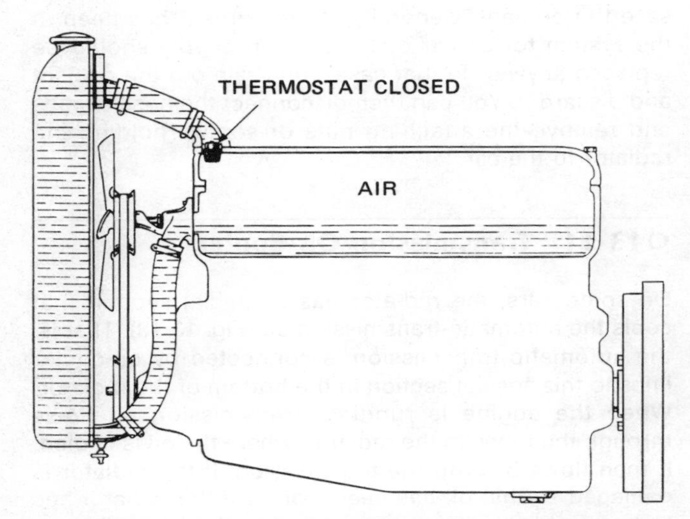

FIGURE 13-15. Air trapped in back of a closed thermostat as the engine cooling system is filled.

a few moments until the thermostat heats up and opens. Then the system can be completely filled.

Install the radiator cap. Run the engine for a few minutes to check for leaks. The complete servicing procedure for engine cooling systems is covered in detail in *Automotive Fuel, Lubricating, and Cooling Systems,* another book in the McGraw-Hill *Automotive Technology Series.*

○ 13-13 Suspension System

If a front end has suffered a relatively severe impact, the damage might extend back into the front suspension. For example, the vehicle shown in Fig. 13-16 got a stiff blow on its left front. The body technician has removed all parts that might get in the way of checking alignment. Note that extensive straightening has already been done. The underfender, for example, has been straightened. The left door panel has been straightened and plastic body filler has been added to it.

While checking the suspension on the left front, the technician found that the lower arm had been bent back. Therefore, a new lower arm was installed. You can see the label on the new arm in Fig. 13-16. It may be that the

FIGURE 13-16. Car damaged by a severe left-front collision. It is up on stands, and the fender and other parts have been removed.

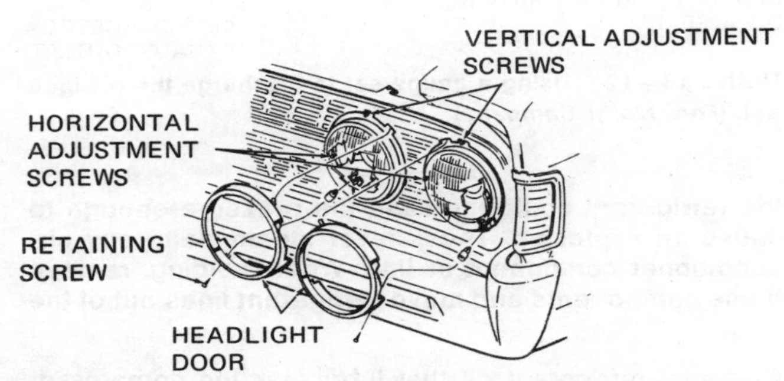

FIGURE 13-17. Left front headlights with bezels (doors) removed so the adjustment screws can be seen. (*Ford Motor Company*)

upper arm was also bent, but it showed no evidence of this. However, after the car has gone through the body and paint shop, it will be taken to the alignment rack. There, front alignment will be checked. These checks may show that the upper arm is also bent and it will also be changed.

Front suspension service is covered in detail in *Automotive Chassis and Body,* another book in the McGraw-Hill *Automotive Technology Series.*

○ 13-14 Headlight Aiming

After any front-end collision, regardless of whether the headlight assemblies are replaced, the aiming of the headlights must be checked. Aiming is checked with a special aiming device and adjusted by turning screws (Fig. 13-17). Each headlight has two screws, one for vertical adjustment and one for horizontal adjustment. Aiming of headlights is covered in detail in *Automotive Electrical Equipment,* another book in the McGraw-Hill *Automotive Technology Series.*

CHAPTER 13 CHECKUP

NOTE: Since the following is a chapter review test, you should review the chapter before taking the test.

There are certain basic operations that must be performed in almost every collision repair job. In this chapter, we have discussed the sequence in which the body technician performs these operations. Also, we have covered the safety cautions that must be observed when working on cars with energy-absorbing bumpers, damaged batteries, and air conditioners. To test your understanding of the chapter, answer these questions:

COMPLETING THE SENTENCES The sentences below are incomplete. After each sentence there are several words or phrases, but only one of them correctly completes the sentence. Write each sentence in your notebook, ending it with the one word or phrase that completes it correctly.

1. The strips that run along the outside of the body are called (*a*) pillars, (*b*) posts, (*c*) louvers, (*d*) moldings.
2. You should never attempt to repair, weld, or apply heat to a (*a*) fender, (*b*) energy absorber, (*c*) door panel, (*d*) molding.
3. After a front-end collision, always check the battery for (*a*) overcharging, (*b*) shorts, (*c*) cracks, (*d*) overheating.
4. The part of the air conditioner that is frequently damaged in front-end collisions is the (*a*) compressor, (*b*) condenser, (*c*) evaporator, (*d*) drive belt.
5. After you have checked the cooling system and radiator for leaks, fill the radiator with (*a*) water, (*b*) antifreeze, (*c*) oil, (*d*) coolant.

QUESTIONS Write each of the following questions, and then the answer, in your notebook. If you have trouble recalling the answer to a question, turn back to the pages that cover the material and study them again.

1. What is an estimate and how does the body technician use it?
2. How are body side moldings removed?
3. Why must the bumpers on a wrecked car be considered dangerous?
4. Describe the procedure for scrapping a gas-filled energy absorber.
5. Why must goggles be worn when you are working on or around an air conditioner?

SUGGESTIONS FOR FURTHER STUDY

Locate a car with front-end damage. Carefully examine the damage to reconstruct how it occurred. Then in your notebook, write down the steps that you think are necessary to repair the damage. With each step, list the damaged parts to be removed, classifying them into "Repair" or "Replace." In automotive work the word "replace" means that a part is removed and a new or different part is reinstalled.

14 METHODS OF SHEET-METAL REPAIR

In this chapter we introduce you to the various methods of sheet-metal repair. Which repair method or methods are used on a particular job depends on the quality of job required, the equipment available, and the type of damage that has been done. For small dents or ridges you would select one repair method. If the damage is extensive, you would select another repair method, perhaps three or four. Also, the value of the car must be considered. If the car is relatively new and expensive, the owner might insist on the most expensive methods of repair. If it is an older car being reconditioned for resale, you would probably use less expensive repair methods. We list these various methods in this chapter and discuss them in detail in following chapters. Also, later chapters take you through the repair procedures on specific damages, such as a damaged door panel or front end.

○ 14-1 Working Sheet Metal

When sheet metal arrives at the stamping plant, the sheet metal is uniform in thickness and softness (or ductility). But when it goes through a press and is shaped into a body part—a fender, for example—its hardness is changed in some places. Whenever sheet metal is bent, it becomes harder. This is called work hardening, and we discussed it earlier in Chapter 2. See Fig. 2-16. The area where the metal has been bent considerably (the high-crown area) has become harder than the area which has been bent very little (the low-crown area).

Pounding on sheet metal with a hammer will also work-harden the metal. Heating the metal, as with a gas torch, will relieve the hardness, regardless of whether the hardness resulted from bending or hammering. This is one method used in straightening sheet metal. First, the damage is dinged out with a body hammer and dolly. Then the area is heated to soften and also shrink the metal so it is restored to approximately its original contour. We describe the procedure later.

When a body panel is bent in a collision, the part that is bent is work-hardened. It has bent beyond its elastic limit. The elastic limit is the limit to which the metal can be bent and not be deformed. The bottom of an oil can, for example, can be bent (pushed in) and it will return to its original contour when the pressure is relieved. The metal has not been bent to its elastic limit. If it had been, it would not return to its original shape.

Often, when a body panel has been damaged by an impact, part of the sheet metal will be bent beyond its elastic limit. But other areas, even though pushed out of shape, may not. That is, they have simply "oil-canned." When you straighten the area that has been bent beyond its elastic limit, this other part often will spring back to its original contour. On the other hand, if you should start your work on the "oil-can" area, you could *add damage to* instead of *remove damage from* the panel.

○ 14-2 Methods of Sheet-Metal Repair

There are at least 12 methods of repairing damaged sheet metal. On some jobs you will use only one method. Other types of damage might require you to use two or more of the basic methods. Which method and how many you use depend upon the damage that is to be corrected. Here we list the 12 methods. We discuss them in detail later in the chapter. We have described the tools to be used in Chapter 5 and discuss their use in later chapters on specific jobs you will meet in the shop.

NOTE: Although it is desirable to restore the sheet metal as nearly as possible to its original contour, this is a practical impossibility for many jobs. Your aim should be to restore the sheet metal to *near* its original shape and then fill it with plastic body filler.[1] The plastic is then finished to the final contour, and the panel is painted.

NOTE: We say "at least 12 methods of repairing damaged sheet metal" because new tools and straightening methods are being developed all the time. However, if you learn the basics, you will be able to use any new tool or procedure that comes along.

Here are the 12 repair methods. We describe them in detail later in the chapter.

1. Pulling out an "oil-can" dent with vacuum cups. This procedure can often be used on a panel which has been pushed in but has suffered little or no bending beyond its elastic limit.
2. Pulling out a crease or dent with pull rods or a slide hammer. This method might be used on a panel which cannot be easily worked on from the inside. Such metal has been bent beyond its elastic limit and must be pulled out working from the outside only.
3. Using pull tabs. When pull rods or a slide hammer are used to pull out a crease or dent, there are two ways of doing the job. One is to drill holes into the panel so the pull rods or slide hammer can have someplace to hook onto. The other is to weld a series of pull tabs to the panel. The pull tab is a small steel tab (Fig. 14-1) one end of which is welded to the body panel at the point where it needs to be pulled out. As many of the tabs as necessary can be welded to the panel (Fig. 14-2). With pull tabs, no holes need be drilled or inner panels cut to get to the back side of the body panel. We describe the procedure of using pull tabs later.
4. Pulling out a panel from two sides to straighten the sheet metal. This is like straightening a sheet of

[1]Body solder can also be used to fill low spots in body panels. However, very few body technicians use body solder any more. This was discussed in Chapter 12.

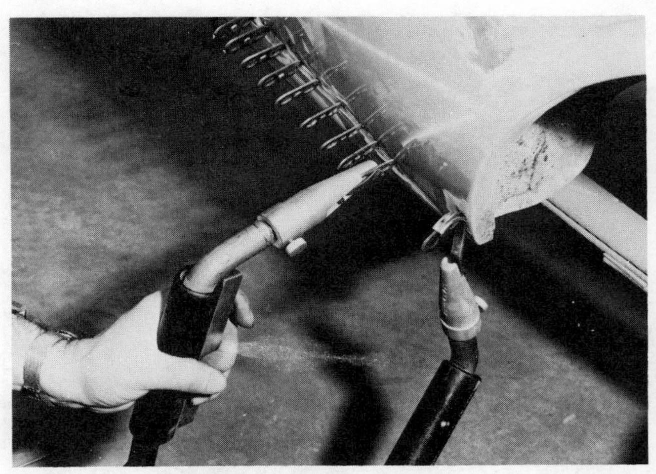

FIGURE 14–1. **Pull tabs being welded to a crease in a panel. (*Guy Chart*)**

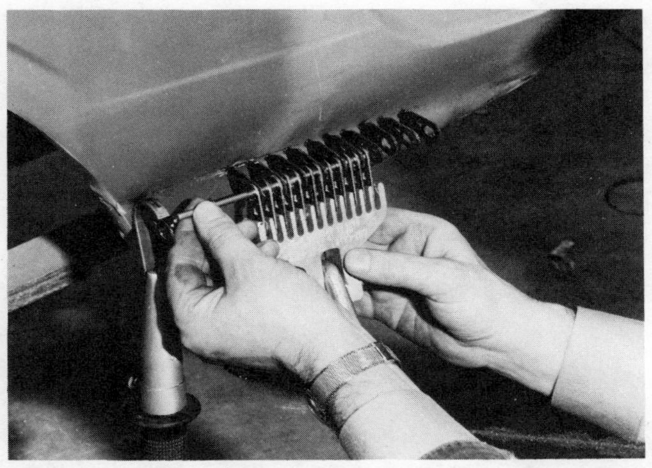

FIGURE 14–2. **After the pull tabs are welded to the crease, a rod is threaded through the holes in the tabs so a puller can be attached to them. (*Guy Chart*)**

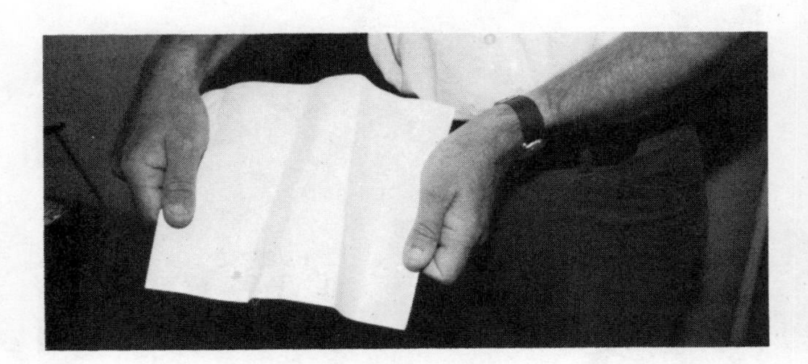

A

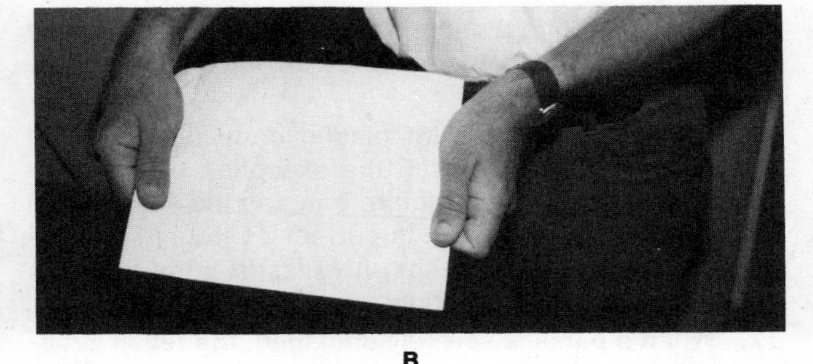

B

FIGURE 14–3. **A sheet of paper which has been wrinkled, as at A, can be partly straightened out by pulling on the two ends, as at B.**

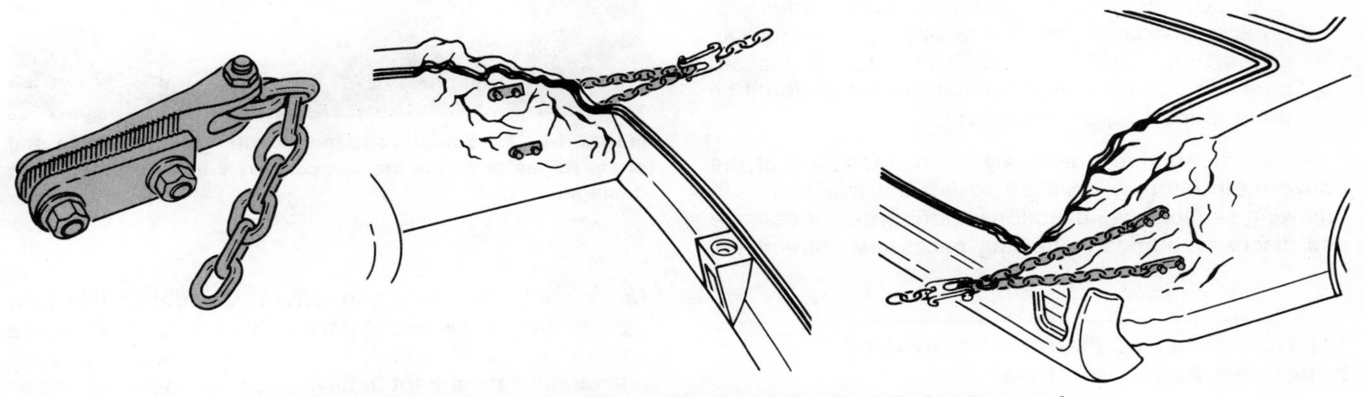

FIGURE 14–4. **The clamp shown requires that holes be drilled in the panel so the clamp can be firmly attached. Then the pull can be made, as shown. (*Guy Chart*)**

paper which has wrinkles in it, by pulling on two edges, as shown in Fig. 14-3. The pull can be done by attaching appropriate clamps or solder pads[2] to the sheet metal and then exerting the pull with a power ram. Figure 14-4 shows a body clamp and methods of attachment of the clamp to sheet metal. The holes drilled in the sheet metal to attach the clamps are filled later. Some body clamps do not require drilled holes but can be clamped onto the edge of the metal (Fig. 14-5).

5. Using a pry bar to get behind a dent and push it out.
6. Using a spread ram.
7. Using a hammer and dolly where both sides of a damaged panel are accessible.
8. Using a hammer, dolly, and body file where both sides of a damaged panel are accessible. This method, called the *pick and file* procedure, prepares the metal for painting. No filling is necessary.
9. Using a bumping spoon.

[2]Solder pads are almost never used today because they are messy, cumbersome, and cause heat distortion of the panel where they are applied.

FIGURE 14–5. Pulling out a door with body clamps and hydraulic equipment. (*Guy Chart*)

10. Heat-shrinking a panel which has been stretched by the impact and by the work of straightening the panel.
11. Filling low areas with plastic body filler. All the above procedures, with the exception of the pick-and-file procedure, require bringing the sheet metal out to approximately its correct contour. Then the irregularities are filled with plastic body filler, as described in a following chapter.
12. When a panel is severely damaged, the repair probably would be to install a new or salvaged panel in its place. Whether to repair or replace is a matter of materials and labor cost. With severe damage, the labor cost required to make a correction would approach or exceed the cost of buying a new or salvaged panel and installing it in place of the old panel. In that case, replacement probably would be the preferred repair procedure.

As we mentioned previously, more than one of the above methods may be used to correct a damage. In following sections, we describe various types of damage and discuss methods of making necessary corrections.

FIGURE 14–7. Sculptured fenders with reverse curves and sharp ridges or bends are comparatively hard to repair after damage.

○ 14-3 Effect of Plain vs Sculptured Panels on Repair Method

Many earlier cars had fenders and other body panels that were fairly simple in design. That is, they had relatively smooth curves, going from flat surfaces to curved surfaces gradually (Fig. 14-6). When a fender of this type was damaged, it was comparatively easy to work out the damage to approximately the original contour. However, late model cars are apt to have what are known as *sculptured* body panels. These are body panels with reverse curves leading to ridges or to raised accents or ridges around the wheel openings. See Fig. 14-7. Not only does this sculpturing effect add style to the car, but also the curved panels are stronger than flat panels would be. Because of this and because automotive manufacturers must make cars lighter, thinner sheet metal can be used for many body panels. Another factor permitting the use of thinner sheet metal for body joints is that the sheet metal used today, although lighter, also is stronger and tougher.

FIGURE 14–6. A fender with relatively smooth curves is comparatively easy to repair.

The combination of curves with thinner and tougher metal makes it more difficult for the body technician to straighten damaged panels. As a result, it has become more common in recent years to replace damaged parts rather than attempt to repair them.

○ 14-4 Classifying Damage

Damage to a panel can be analyzed in terms of collision-caused bends, tears, or holes which have occurred to the panel. Tears or holes have to be patched or filled. Bends can be of several types, requiring several types of repair. Let us analyze just what a simple bend is, and then look at the more complex bends that actually occur.

Take a strip of sheet metal and bend it over the edge of the workbench, as shown in Fig. 14-8. Figure 14-9 shows what happens. The top area has been stretched. The bottom area has been pushed together or shrunk. Both areas have been work-hardened.

In common shop talk, the metal has buckled, and the area which has bent is called a *buckle.* Figure 14-9 is a simple buckle which you will not find in car body damage. The reason is that there are no perfectly flat sheet-metal panels on the car. When curved panels buckle, the buckles are more complicated.

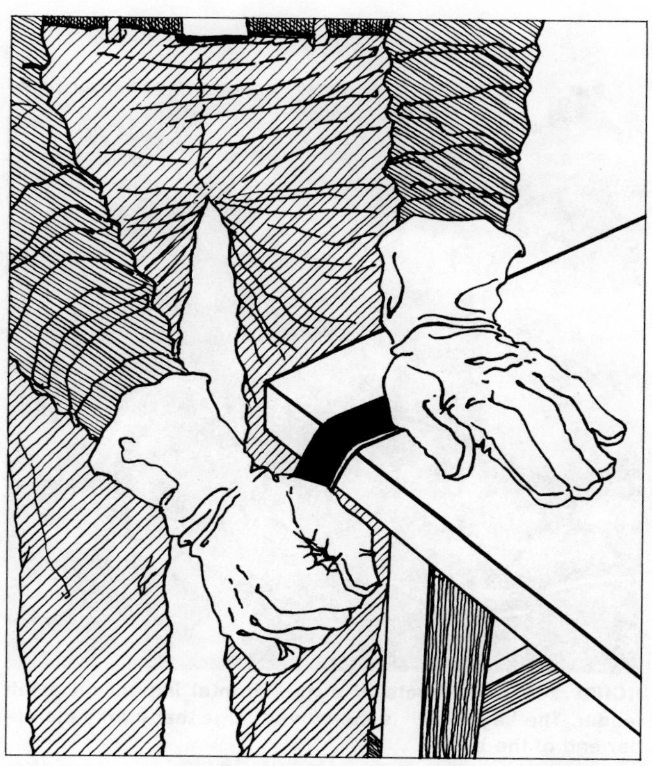

FIGURE 14–8. Bending a strip of sheet metal work-hardens it at the bend.

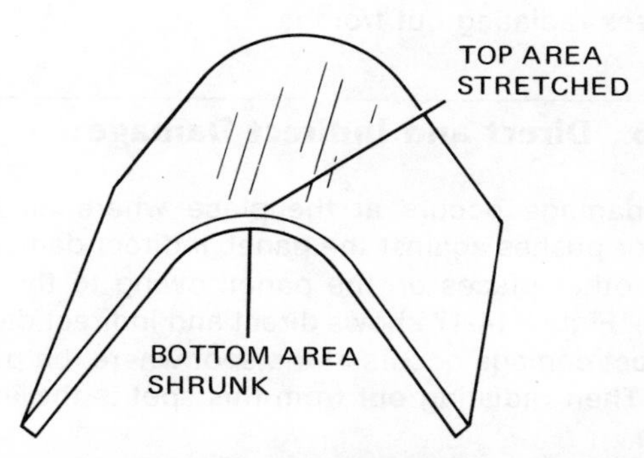

FIGURE 14–9. What happens to a strip of sheet metal that is bent.

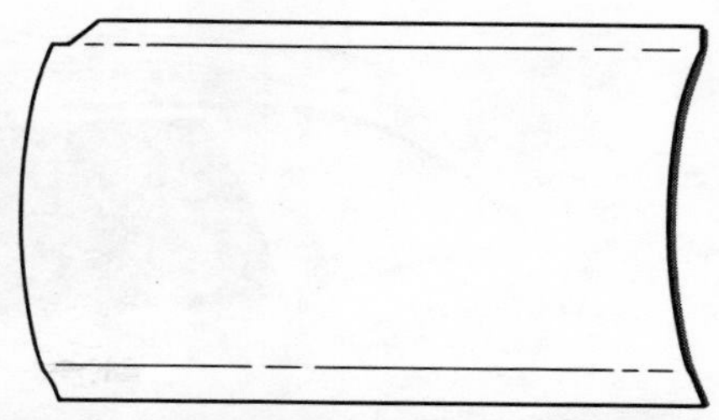

FIGURE 14–10. Door panel typically has a curve from top to bottom. (*Ford Motor Company*)

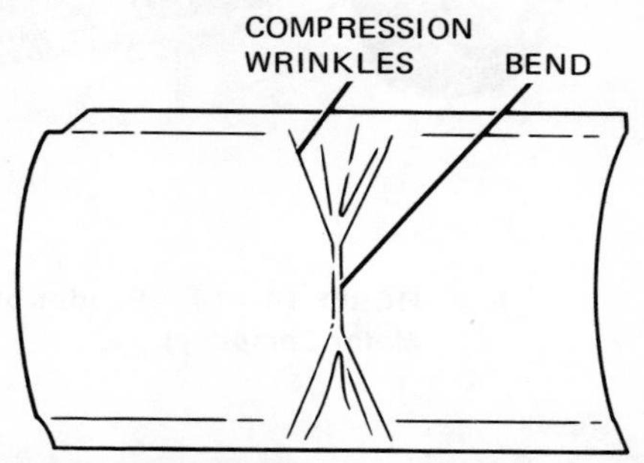

FIGURE 14–11. What happens when a curved panel, such as a door panel, is bent at the middle in a vertical direction.

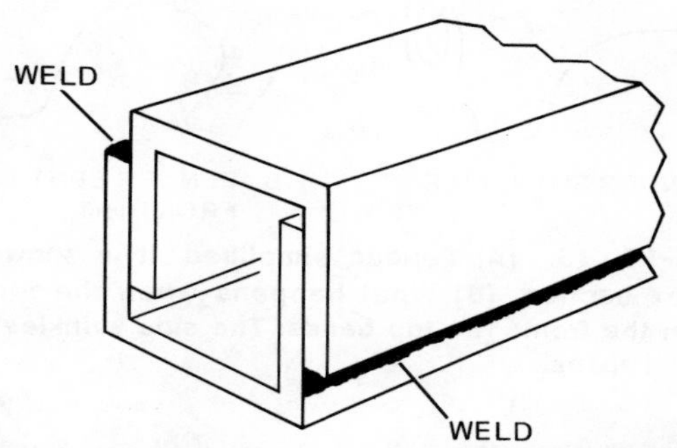

FIGURE 14–12. Box section made by welding together two U-shaped members.

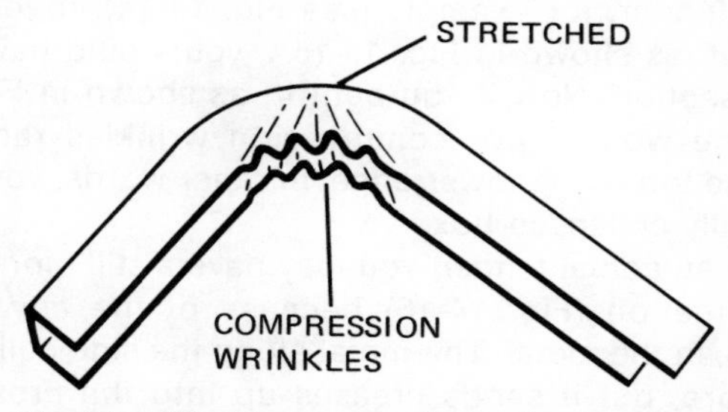

FIGURE 14–13. What happens when a box section is bent.

For example, let us look at the curved panel on a car door (Fig. 14-10). If you tried to bend this panel along its vertical centerline, as shown in Fig. 14-11, you would get a much more complex bend. The upper and lower edges would wrinkle, because the metal, under compression, has to go someplace.

Another example will make this clear. Look at Fig. 14-12 which shows a box section similar to those used in car frames. If this box section is bent, the top part will be stretched and the bottom will be compressed and wrinkled (Fig. 14-13). This type of damage is called a *collapsed box* and is more typical of what occurs in col-

FIGURE 14–14. Fender of car is a modified form of a half box section. (*Ford Motor Company*)

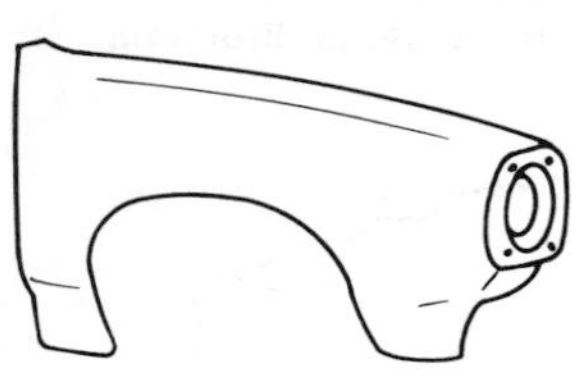

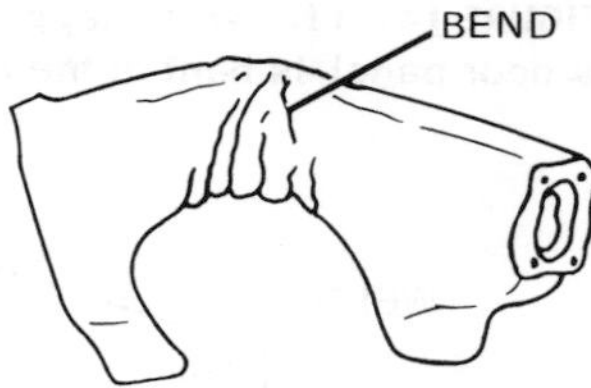

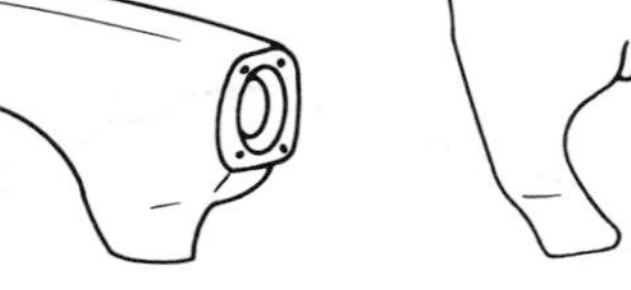

FIGURE 14–15. (A) Fender, simplified. It is shown as a semibox section. (B) What happens when the fender is hit from the front: The top bends. The side wrinkles as the metal collapses.

lision accidents. The reason is that many of the body sheetmetal parts are in the form of partial boxes. Let us take a fender, for example (see Fig. 14-14). If you simplified it, as shown in Fig. 14-15A, you would have half a box section. Now if you bent it, as shown in Fig. 14-15B, you would have compression wrinkles radiating from the top to the lower edge. In other words, you have a partially collapsed box.

With an actual fender, you may have a still more complex situation (Fig. 14-16) because of the curves, or crowns, in the metal. The metal along the side collapses, as before, but it sends creases up into the crown, as shown. These creases are known as *rolled buckles.* They tend to end at some point in the crown with a sharp dent. The ridge above is called an *eyebrow.* The metal all along the creases has been shrunk. When correction is made, the metal not only must be straightened but also must be expanded.

○ 14-5 Visualizing How Damage Occurred

If you were able to watch, in slow motion, just what happens to body panels when they are damaged, you would know exactly how the metal came to be bent and the order in which the bending occurred. For example, suppose you hit the side of a door panel a heavy blow (Fig. 14-17). The sequence of pictures shows the resulting deep dent in the panel and, as this is being made, a series of creases radiating out from it.

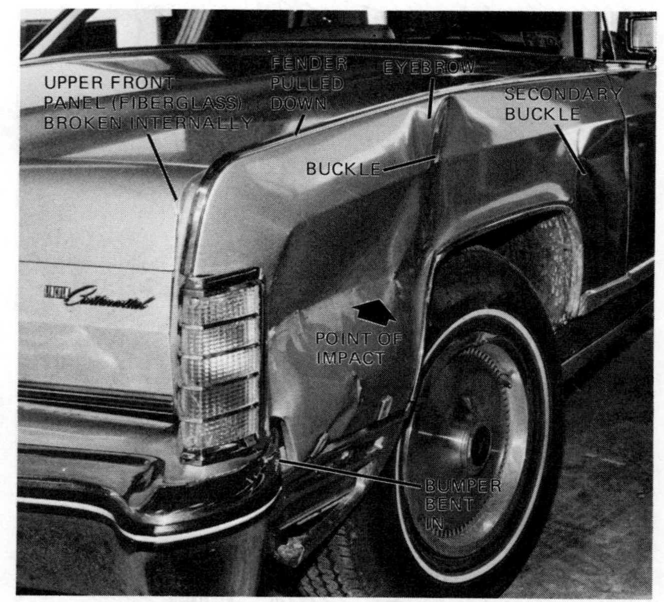

FIGURE 14–16. Effects of a near frontal impact on a left fender. The "eyebrow" is the curved ridge that marks the upper end of the buckle.

○ 14-6 Direct and Indirect Damage

Direct damage occurs at the place where an object strikes or pushes against the panel. Indirect damage occurs at other places on the panel, owing to the direct damage. Figure 14-17 shows direct and indirect damage. The direct damage occurs at the spot where the panel is struck. Then radiating out from this spot is the indirect damage.

It is important to recognize direct and indirect damage. Normally, you start work on the indirect damage

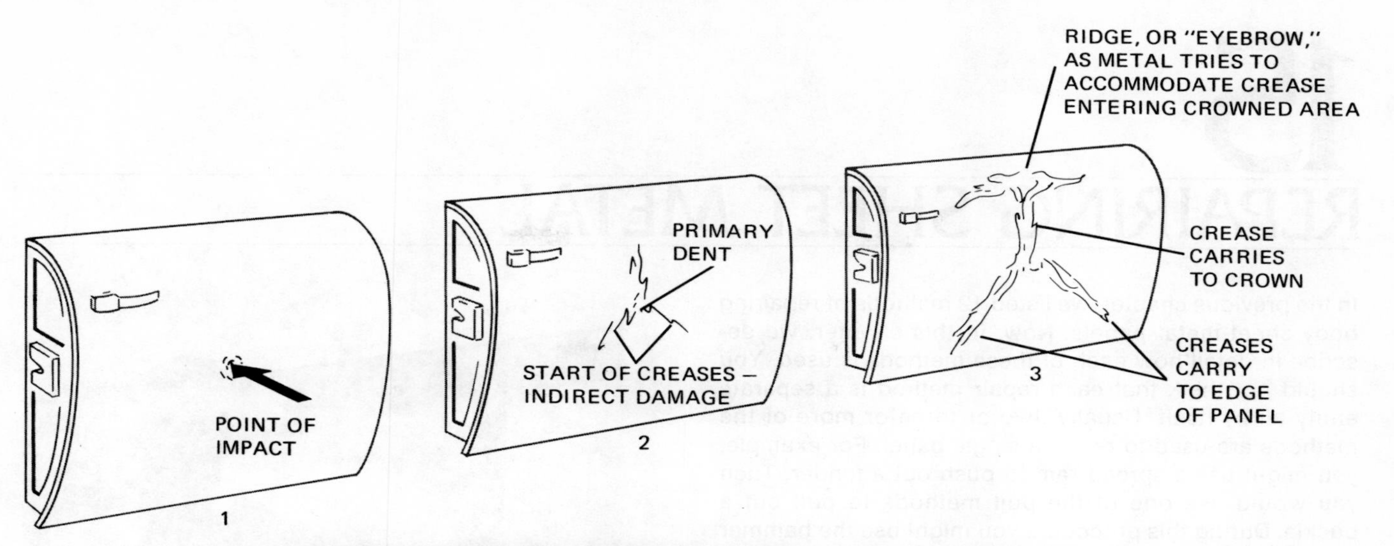

FIGURE 14–17. Sequence of events following an impact on a door panel.

first, working back to the direct damage. Going the other way, from the direct to the indirect damage, would probably make the situation worse. Many times, the technician will work out the indirect damage and then fill the direct-damage spot with plastic body filler. Using filler eliminates a lot of expensive time-consuming labor, because direct damage is sometimes difficult to completely work out.

CHAPTER 14 CHECKUP

NOTE: Since the following is a chapter review test, you should review the chapter before taking the test.

As you know, there is more than one way to wreck a car. There is also more than one way to repair a wrecked car. In this chapter, we have discussed these basic methods of sheet-metal repair. To find out how well you understand everything in this chapter, answer the questions that follow.

COMPLETING THE SENTENCES The sentences below are incomplete. After each sentence there are several words or phrases, but only one of them correctly completes the sentence. Write each sentence in your notebook, ending it with the one word or phrase that completes it correctly.

1. On sheet metal, the area that bends gets (*a*) harder, (*b*) softer, (*c*) rusted, (*d*) shorter.

2. An "oil-can" dent can be pulled out with (*a*) a hammer and dolly, (*b*) vacuum cups, (*c*) a ram, (*d*) a bumping spoon.

3. Compared to flat panels, sculptured panels are (*a*) weaker, (*b*) thicker, (*c*) stronger, (*d*) cheaper.

4. A fender is similar to a (*a*) half box, (*b*) half circle, (*c*) round bar, (*d*) square frame.

5. Indirect damage is caused by (*a*) the tow truck, (*b*) the direct damage, (*c*) hitting a stationary object, (*d*) hitting another moving vehicle.

DEFINITIONS In the following, you are asked for several definitions. Write them in your notebook. The act of writing the definitions does two things. It tests your knowledge, and it helps fix the information more firmly in your mind. Turn back into the chapter if you are not sure of a definition, or look it up in the glossary at the back of the book.

1. Define "working sheet metal."

2. What is a high-crown area?

3. What is a low-crown area?

4. Define "buckle."

5. What is the difference between direct damage and indirect damage?

SUGGESTIONS FOR FURTHER STUDY

Write down, in your notebook, the various methods of sheet-metal repair. Under each method, list the tools and equipment that each method requires. Then note the most common types of damage that can be repaired by each method.

15
REPAIRING SHEET METAL

In the previous chapter, we listed 12 methods of repairing body sheet-metal panels. Now, in this chapter, we describe in detail how each of these methods is used. You should not think that each repair method is a separate entity all by itself. Usually, two or three or more of the methods are used to repair a single panel. For example, you might use a spread ram to push out a fender. Then you would use one of the pull methods to pull out a buckle. During this procedure you might use the hammer to relieve the stresses in the metal. Finally, you would sand and fill the damaged area with plastic body filler. Now let us look at each of these methods in detail.

○ 15-1 Using Vacuum Cups

Vacuum cups can be used to correct oil-can damage to sheet metal. If the paint has not been damaged and if the metal has not been bent beyond its elastic limit, the depression often may be pulled out without damaging the paint. Under ideal conditions, this would be a repair job that would take only a few minutes. However, if there is paint damage and direct damage to the metal (metal bent beyond elastic limit), then the pull-out is only the first step in the repair job.

To use a vacuum cup, first make sure that the body panel is clean. All dirt should be washed off so the paint will not be scratched when the vacuum cup is used. Wet the cup and press it in against the panel, at the center of the depression (Fig. 15-1). When the air has been squeezed out of the cup, it will grip the metal. Pull out steadily to bring the metal out to its original contour. Sometimes the use of a slide hammer, as shown in Fig. 15-1, is necessary to apply adequate force. This procedure will work if the metal has not been buckled or bent beyond its elastic limit. It will not work on crowned surfaces, because the cup will not be able to grip the curved surface. Also, if there is a depression on a crown, the metal probably has been stressed beyond its elastic limit. When this has occurred, another repair method will be required.

For working on large areas, such as a damaged roof, vacuum cup assemblies with three cups are available (see Fig. 5-25). They are attached to a plate which has a

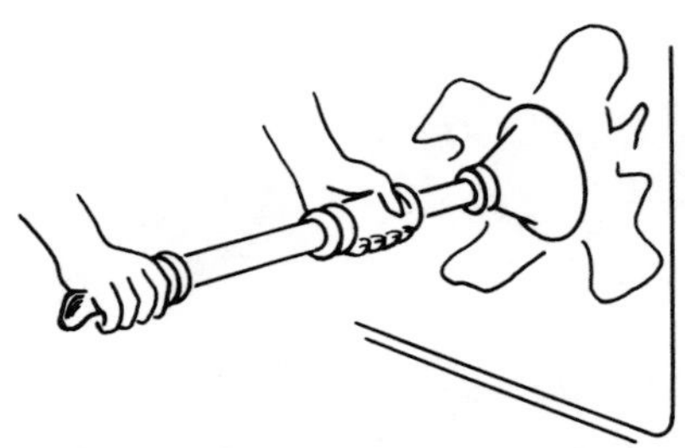

FIGURE 15 – 1. Using vacuum cup to pull out a dent in a panel. (*Guy Chart*)

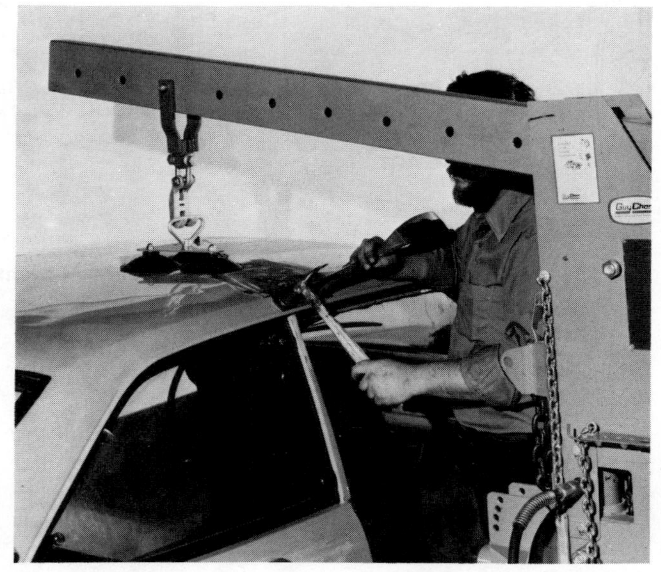

FIGURE 15 – 2. Using vacuum cups to pull up on a dent in a car roof. At the same time, the technician is using a body spoon and hammer to tap down the ridge at the edge of the roof. (*Guy Chart*)

handle that can be pulled out by hand or by a crane. Figure 15-2 shows a roof panel being repaired by this method. Note that the technician is using a body spoon and hammer to work out a ridge while the pull is being made.

○ 15-2 Using Pull Rods and Slide Hammers

If the dent has sharp edges or is too deep or irregular, the vacuum cup will not work. If it is also difficult to get behind the panel, then the pull has to be made from the outside. This requires pull rods or a slide hammer.

There are two ways of attaching the pull rods or slide hammer to a panel. These are to drill into the panel or to weld pull tabs onto the panel. If holes are drilled, they must be filled later. If pull tabs are used, they must be twisted off later.

Let us first discuss the use of a slide hammer with holes drilled or punched in the panel. Screw a sheet-metal screw into a hole near one end of the crease. When it takes hold, hook on and operate the slide hammer (Fig. 15-3). This will create enough force to pull the crease out. To operate the slide hammer, hold the hammer handle in one hand and slam the slide against the stop. Be careful not to use excessive pull because the screw might pull out. Go from one hole to the next until you have pulled the dent out. Use a body hammer to tap around the outside of the damage while the pull is being exerted. This helps to release the tension that was intro-

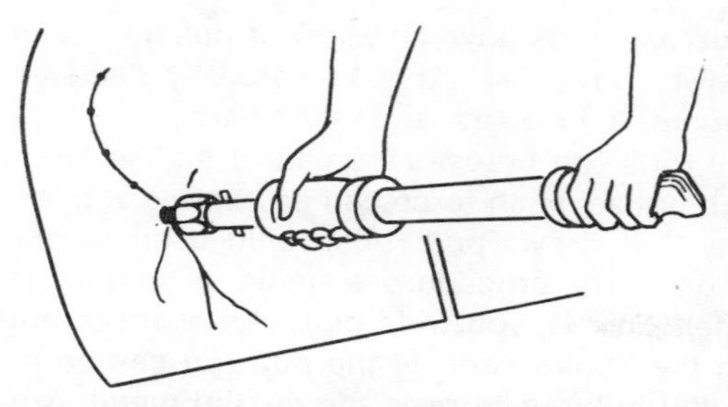

FIGURE 15–3. Using a slide hammer to pull out a crease, or buckle, in a body panel. (*Guy Chart*)

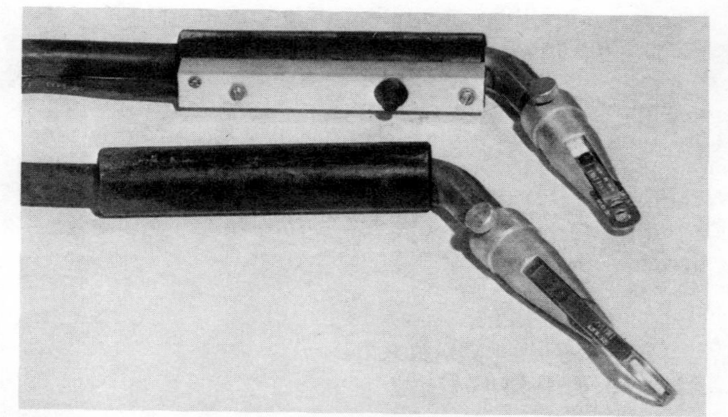

FIGURE 15–4. Special attachments for electrodes when pull tabs are to be welded onto a panel. (*Guy Chart*)

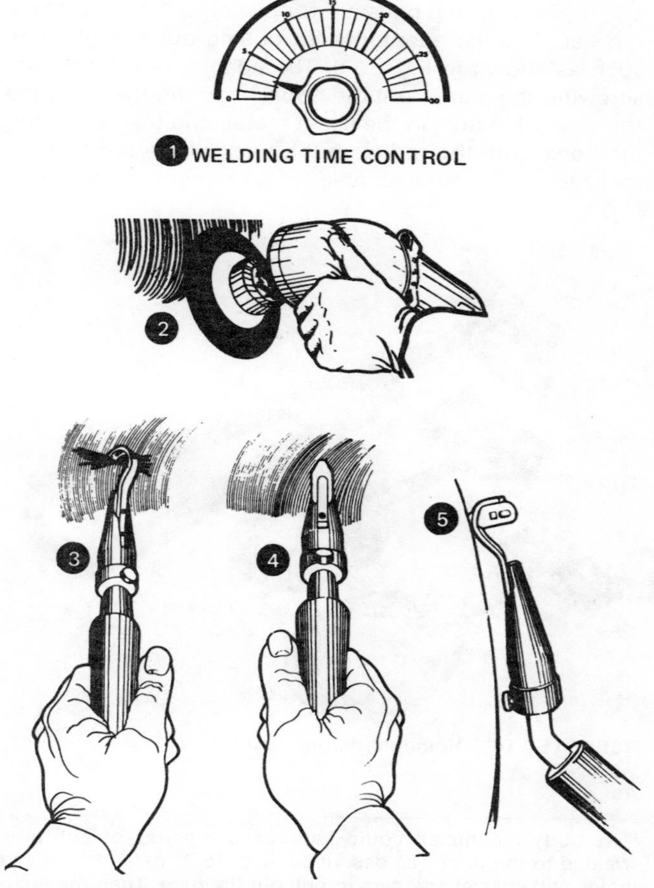

FIGURE 15–5. Sequence of actions to weld pull tabs onto a panel. See text for explanation of steps 1 to 5. (*Guy Chart*)

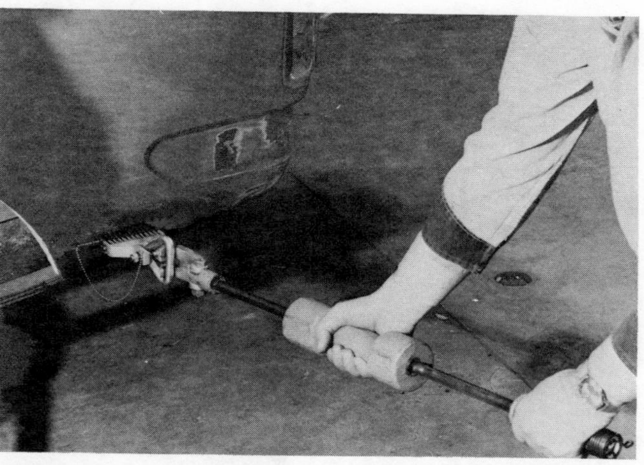

FIGURE 15–6. Using a slide hammer to pull on the pull tabs. (*Guy Chart*)

duced by the impact. As this tension is released, the dent can be raised more easily.

Now let us describe the procedure of using pull tabs (Figs. 14-1 and 14-2). The pull tab is used with a spot welder, which we described in Chapter 12. The welding electrodes are fitted with special attachments to take the pull tabs (Fig. 15-4). One of these is for the ground tip. It has a slot so it can be hooked over the first pull tab to be welded onto the panel. The other holds the pull tabs, which are then welded onto the panel. Here is the procedure:

Install the spot-tip pull tab holders over the spot-welder electrodes. Adjust welder to a low setting (1 in Fig. 15-5). Grind a small area of about a square inch (or a few square centimeters) to clean metal (2 in Fig. 15-5). This assures good contact for the first pull tab to be welded on. Put a pull tab in the clip on the welding electrode. Hold the ground tip and pull tab close together on the bare area, and pull the trigger to weld the first pull tab to the panel. See 3 and 4 in Fig. 15-5. Now hook the ground tip onto the first pull tab, as shown at 5 in Fig. 15-5. Be sure the back side of the ground tip makes good contact with the panel. You can now proceed to weld additional pull tabs to the panel (see Fig. 14-1). The edges of the pull tabs are sharpened and will cut through paint with a little pressure. So the whole area does not need to be sanded to use pull tabs.

After the necessary number of pull tabs have been welded on, a pull-plate assembly is attached by interlocking the pull tabs with the tabs on the pull plate, as shown in Fig. 14-2. Then the slide hammer is attached so the pull can be made, as shown in Fig. 15-6. The number of pull tabs to be used varies with the size and type of damage to the panel. During the pull, tap with a body hammer on the high spots around the crease to relieve the set of the metal and help it settle down to contour. After the pull is completed, the pull tabs can be twisted off, as shown in Fig. 15-7. Only a small mark will be left, which can then be touched up and refinished (if the panel has been brought back to contour).

NOTE: Any pull equipment in the shop, including the hydraulic body-frame straighteners (Chapter 17), can be hooked onto the pull tabs. When the pull tabs are welded in a series, as described above, you can pull up to 2 tons [1850 kg].

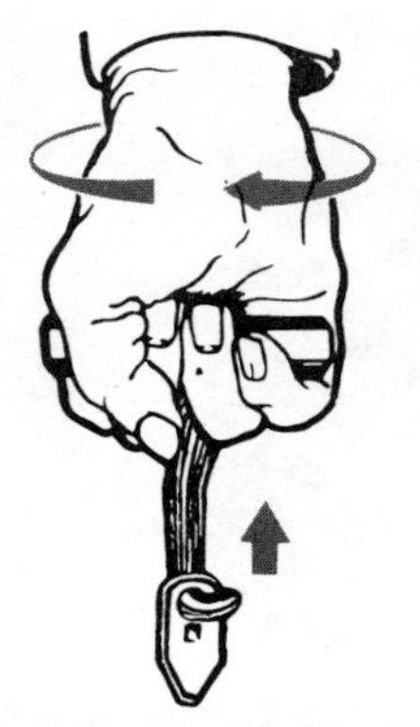

FIGURE 15–7. **Twisting off a tab. (*Guy Chart*)**

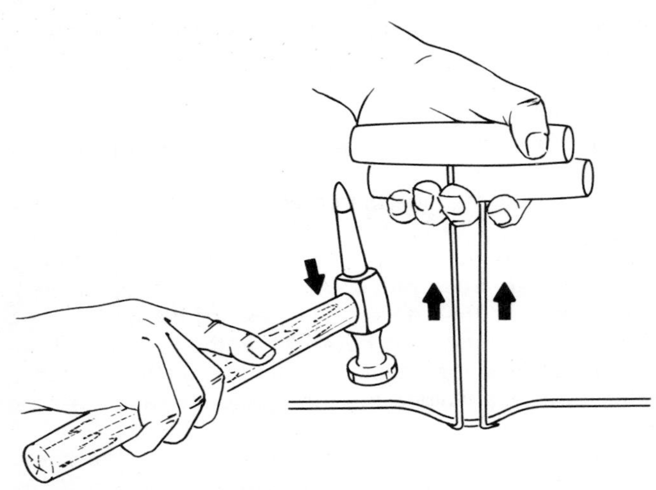

FIGURE 15–8. **When pulling on a panel, a body hammer is often used to tap on the high spots near the dent being pulled out.**

FIGURE 15–9. **Left quarter panel damaged by an impact from the side.**

Slide hammers have a variety of pulling attachments, as shown in Fig. 5-22, to take care of pulling on edges of fenders, door posts, and other parts.

Pull rods can be used instead of a slide hammer, although not as much force can be exerted with pull rods. Figure 15-8 shows pull rods being used to pull out a small dent. The procedure is similar to that for the slide hammer. That is, you weld pull tabs or make holes into which the hooked end of the pull rod can be inserted. Then you pull out to raise the dented metal. A hammer can be used here, too, to tap around the damaged area and release the tension that has locked the dent into the metal (Fig. 15-8). Sometimes, with larger dents or creases, more than one pull rod can be used in adjacent holes. With three or more pull rods hooked to the metal, the pull can be exerted over a larger area.

The holes left after using a slide hammer or pull rods are later filled with plastic body filler. Some body technicians do not like to drill holes and use pull rods or slide hammers. Sometimes these tools can raise ridges around the holes (Fig. 5-24), which then require additional work to correct.

○ 15-3 Using Hydraulic Ram to Pull Out Dent

If the dent is too big to be pulled out with a slide hammer or pull rods (see Fig. 15-9), a hydraulic ram can be used. To pull out the large dented area shown, the body technician drilled holes[1] and used a special adapter (Fig. 15-10). Three special home-made adapters are shown in Fig. 15-10. The two thin ones are for placement behind sharp creases. The flat adapter is for pulling out a large dent, such as shown in Fig. 15-9. The adapter is used by unscrewing the plate from the hook, inserting the threaded rod through a hole in the sheet metal, and then screwing the hook onto the rod from the back of the panel. Note that the technician was able to get behind the panel by

FIGURE 15–10. **Home-made pull tools.**

[1]The body technician could have used a series of pull tabs welded to the panel, as described in ○ 15-2, instead of drilled holes and special adapters to pull out the dent. Then the technician would not have needed to remove the rear seat and interior trim to get behind the panel.

FIGURE 15–11. Using hydraulic equipment to pull out the damage.

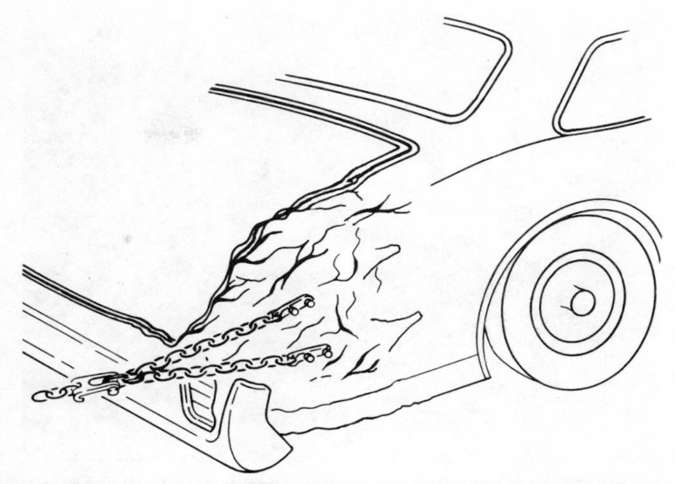

FIGURE 15–13. Right quarter panel shortened by a rear-end impact. A pull in the reverse direction will pull out much of the damage. (*Guy Chart*)

FIGURE 15–12. Panel restored to its approximate contour in readiness for sanding, filling, and painting.

removing the rear seat and trim. This permitted the technician to attach the plate to the threaded rod.

Figure 15-11 shows the hookup for making the pull. The chain was attached to the hook at one end and to the hydraulic pull mechanism at the other. (This mechanism is described in Chapter 17.) The technician actuated the hydraulic pump, and the dent was pulled out. Actually, the procedure was a little more complicated than this. The technician used a hammer at certain points on the panel to relieve stress. Also, an additional hole was drilled to pull out from a different point. In addition, the technician worked from behind the panel with a hammer and pry bar. Figure 15-12 shows the panel restored approximately to its correct contour. Note the two pull holes have been welded closed. The panel can now be filled, sanded, and filed in readiness for painting.

○ 15-4 Using Pull to Straighten a Panel

If a panel has been crushed or shortened by an impact, it can often be straightened by a combination of pulling and working with a hammer and dolly or other tools. As we mentioned previously, this is somewhat like straightening a crumpled sheet of paper by pulling on two edges (Fig. 14-3). For example, the right quarter panel shown in Fig. 15-13 has been shortened by a rear-end impact. If the pull is exerted in a line vertical to the wrinkles and in line with the shortening, most of the damage can be pulled out. In other words, a force is exerted in a direction exactly opposite to the impact force that caused the damage.

There are two methods of applying the pull to a panel: with clamps and a power jack or ram and with solder plates and a power jack or ram. Solder plates are almost never used today because they are messy, slow, and cause heat distortion of body panels. Where clamps can be used, it is the preferred method because it is much quicker and less messy. The clamps are attached by welding on pull tabs (Fig. 15-5) or by boring holes in the sheet metal so the clamps can be attached. Tightening the nuts tightens the hold of the clamps on the metal. The clamps are large enough to spread the pull so there is less chance of tearing the metal. Figure 14-4 shows a typical clamp. Some clamps do not require bored holes to take hold (Fig. 14-5).

Sometimes the pull has to be made in a direction about vertical to the sheet metal so that clamps cannot be used. In such case, a hole can be drilled in the panel so that a special adapter can be fitted to transfer the pull to the panel. Figure 15-14 shows the setup for pulling out a right fender of a Volkswagen which has been crumpled by a front-end impact. The adapter being used is homemade and is one of the thin adapters shown in Fig. 15-10. The thin adapter is lined up in back of the crease so it is resting squarely on the back of the crease in the metal.

While the pull is being exerted on a panel by the power ram, a body hammer is used to tap against high spots (Fig. 15-15). If a dolly, pry bar, or pick bar can be worked behind the panel, it can work on high spots on the un-

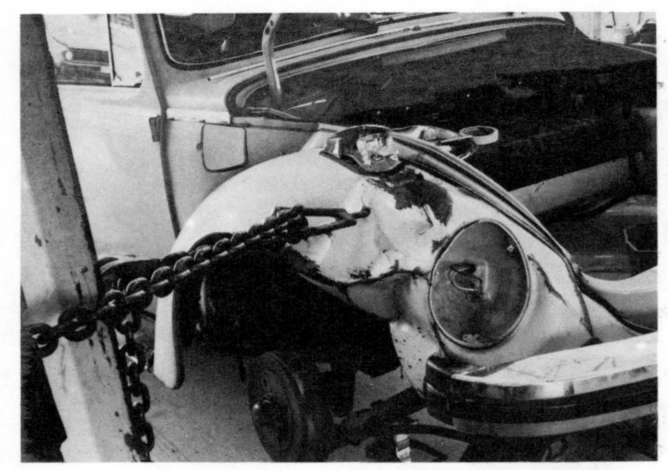

FIGURE 15–14. Pulling out a right fender of a Volkswagen.

FIGURE 15–15. Pulling a body hammer to tap on high spots while a pry bar inserted in the hole for the quarter-panel marker light works on low spots from the inside.

derside (which would be low spots on the outside). Sometimes the torch is also used to relieve work hardening in the damaged area and make the metal more plastic so the area can be worked down to contour more easily.

NOTE: The power ram does not do all the work. It merely puts the panel in tension. It cannot pull out all the damage. The damage must be worked out with hammer, dolly, pick or pry bar, and torch. As the damage is worked out, the panel will elongate. This means that the hydraulic ram must be adjusted so as to maintain adequate tension on the panel as the damage is worked out.

NOTE: Care must be used when pulling against sheet metal with the hydraulic ram. Excessive pull can tear the sheet metal and present you with a very difficult repair job.

Although solder plates are hardly ever used today, we cover their use here so you will have a complete picture of all methods, old and new, of repairing sheet metal. The solder plates are soldered onto the body panel at the proper spots so the pull can be exerted in the right direction. To use solder plates, you first sand off the paint from the two spots, and then the plates are soldered to those spots. We described the procedure of preparing a body panel for the application of body solder in Chapter 11. The area is cleaned and tinned, and then solder is applied, using the oxyacetylene torch to supply the heat. At the same time, the face of the solder plate is tinned. With hot solder on both and the temperature right, the plate is pressed to the panel. After a few seconds, the solder cools and you have a solid joint. With two solder plates soldered to the panel in this manner, the power ram has something to work on. The ram, when installed between the plates and activated, subjects the panel to a pull which is the reverse of the force that damaged the panel.

While the pull is being exerted, the area to be straightened should be worked on with a body hammer and dolly or with other tools. At the same time it should be heated with the torch, as previously explained.

After a panel is straightened, the solder plates are removed by heating them with the torch. Then the panel is heated enough to melt the solder, and the solder is wiped off. That part of the panel is then ready for final finishing after you have wiped it with lacquer thinner to remove any trace of acid. Don't get lacquer thinner on the paint!

NOTE: The heat injected into the sheet metal by the soldering and unsoldering operation can distort the metal and change the contour. When this happens, additional work will be required to correct the problem. This is another reason most body technicians don't use solder plates.

○15-5 Using a Pry Bar

Damage in some places is hard to get at from the inside. For example, a dent in a door panel. We have described various means of working out this type of damage by using a vacuum cup, pull rods, or a slide hammer. Pull rods or a slide hammer leave holes that must be filled. An alternative is to use a pry bar inserted into drain holes (or holes drilled) in the bottom edge of the door, as shown in Fig. 5-31. It is often possible to put the end of the bar on the spots that have to be pushed out. In such case, the pry bar is used to pry the spots out to approximately restore the original contour.

○15-6 Using a Spread Ram

The spread ram (Fig. 15-16) is like a pair of pliers in reverse. The two jaws are placed between a damaged panel

FIGURE 15–16. A spread ram. When the ram is operated, the jaws of the spread ram open.

and the underbody. The ram is then activated and the two jaws are spread, thus exerting pressure on the damaged panel. Note that the jaws of the ram are covered with ridged rubber so they will not slip.

For example, the spread ram can be used to apply pressure to a fender that has been crushed inward. The spread ram forces the damaged area outward approximately to its original contour. After this operation, a hammer and dolly can be used to work out the major irregularities still left. Before the spread ram is used, there may not be enough room to get a hand with a dolly up behind the fender.

○15-7 Using a Hammer and Dolly

The right hammer and dolly must be used to ding out sheet metal. On low-crown surfaces, a dolly with a fairly flat face is used. On high-crown surfaces, a dolly with a curved face is used. The curvature of the dolly should be slightly greater than the final contour of the surface being worked on (Fig. 15-17).

Figure 15-18 shows the proper way to hold the hammer and dolly. Note that the dolly is held rather loosely with the palm exerting the pressure on it. The hammer should be gripped fairly loosely close to the end of the handle. The dolly is held on one side of the metal, and the hammer strikes the other side (Fig. 15-19). There are two basic techniques: hammer-on-dolly and hammer-off-dolly. It is essential that you learn both techniques and that you practice both on scrap sheet metal until you have mastered them. We describe them in following paragraphs, and this may give you some clues as to how each is done. But you must practice them, repeatedly, to become an expert body technician.

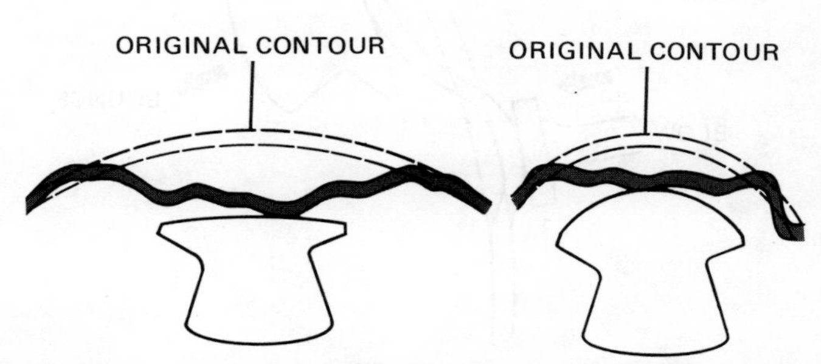

FIGURE 15–17. Curvatures of dollies for working on areas with low crowns and high crowns. Curves should fit the final contours.

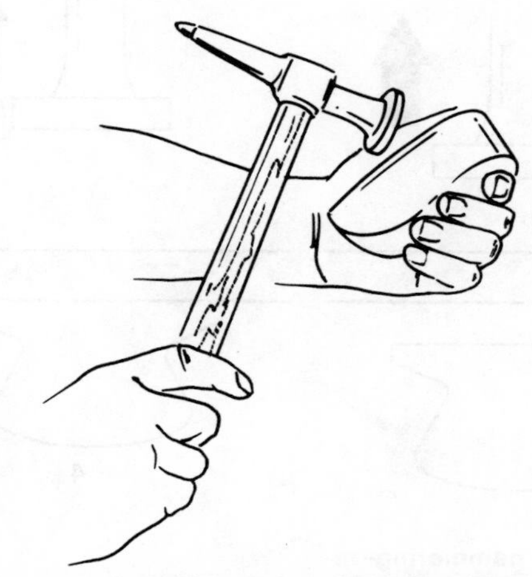

FIGURE 15–18. Proper way to hold dolly and hammer.

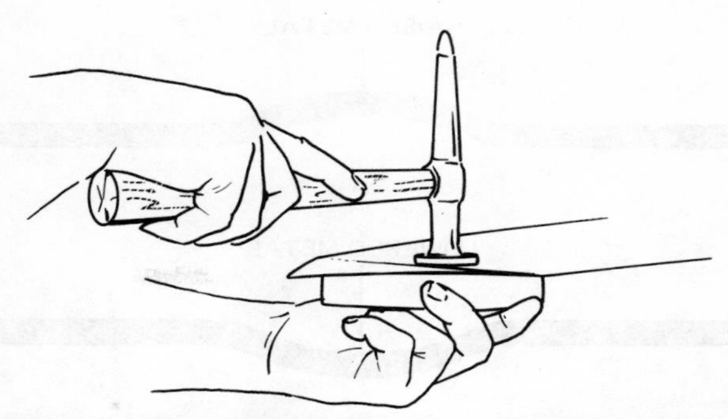

FIGURE 15–19. The dolly is held on one side of the sheet metal, and the hammer strikes the other side.

○15-8 Hammer-on-Dolly

This is the simpler of the two techniques, and we discuss it first. The hammer blows fall on the metal under which the dolly is held, as shown in Fig. 15-20. The metal, in effect, is squeezed between the hammer and dolly. This can lower raised metal, as shown. The action also spreads the metal, and this action is resisted by the metal surrounding the point where the hammer blows fall. The result is a slight bubble raised in the metal, as shown in Fig. 15-21A. There is no way that further hammering will flatten this bubble. In fact, additional hammering will spread the metal still more and increase the size of the bubble. There are two ways of dealing with this problem. One is to tap the bubble and drive it below the surface of the original contour (Fig. 15-21B) and then to fill the depression with plastic body filler.

The second way of removing the bubble, at least partly, is to heat it with a gas torch and then cool it. The process is called heat shrinking. After the heat shrinking is completed, there will still be some irregularity which must be filled with plastic body filler. Later we cover both methods of taking care of the problem shown in Fig. 15-21. (See also ○15-14 Handling Larger Areas of Damage.)

Here are some hints on how to hammer-on-dolly that will help you learn the technique: First, hold the dolly out in front of you so you can see it. Then tap the dolly face

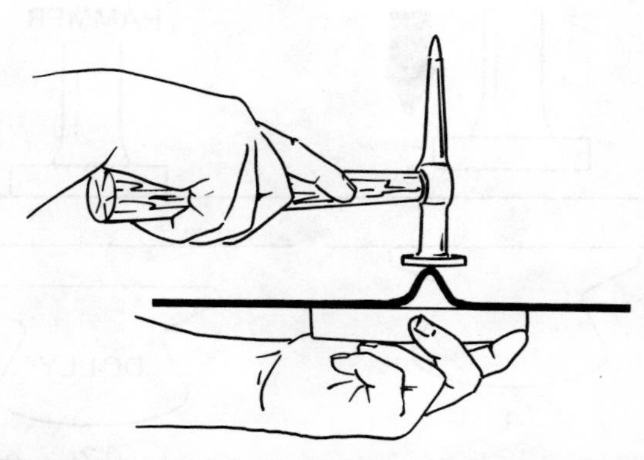

FIGURE 15–20. How to work down a raised dent in sheet metal. Hold the dolly under and tap the center of the dent with the hammer.

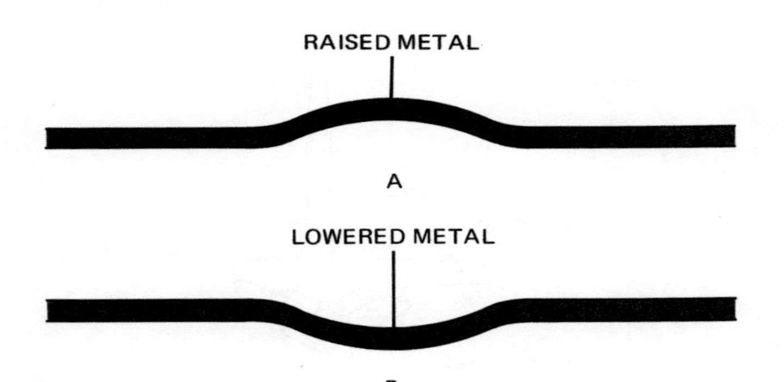

FIGURE 15–21. Driving down the dent expands the metal and leaves a bubble of raised metal as shown at A. At B, the metal has been driven down below the surface so the surface can be sanded and filled in preparation for painting.

lightly with the hammer (Fig. 15-18). This helps you learn how to guide the hammer so it will strike the center of the dolly face. Once you move the dolly behind a panel, you cannot see it. Therefore, you must sense exactly where it is so you can strike the metal that is directly above the dolly. You must have a good feel for exactly where your hidden hand and the dolly are. Hold the dolly out in front of you again and, with your eyes closed, tap the center of the dolly face with the hammer. Practice this until you can tap the center of the dolly face every time.

Hold the hammer lightly, as explained earlier. Swing the hammer from the elbow, with only enough force to strike the metal lightly. Hard blows will spread the metal and work-harden it too much.

Now let's work on a dent, such as is shown in Fig. 15-20. Make a dent in a discarded body panel by hitting it with a pick hammer. Hold the dolly firmly against the lower side of the panel. Swing the hammer, allowing the flat face of the hammer to fall squarely on the metal. See Fig. 15-20. If you cock the hammer, the edge of the face will make small dents in the metal and these will be hard to work out. When the hammer strikes the metal, the force of the blow goes through the metal and into the dolly. This momentarily drives the dolly away from the metal. See Fig. 15-22. At almost the same instant, the springiness of the metal causes the hammer to bounce up from the metal surface. Then the hand pressure on the dolly pushes it upward so it strikes a blow on the underside of the metal.

Note the sequence in Fig. 15-22 carefully. The metal is struck twice, once from above with the hammer, and once from below with the dolly. The effect of these two blows is determined by the amount of force back of them. For example, when working a fairly large depressed area, the dolly is held with heavy pressure against the metal. Now, after the dolly is driven down by the hammer blow, it snaps back up against the metal with that heavy pressure. This action is effective in raising the metal as the blows are repeated over the surface of the metal.

○ 15-9 Hammer-off-Dolly

Now let us look at the hammer-off-dolly technique. Figure 15-23 shows the procedure on a large dent that has been made in a low-crown area. The metal has been pushed down at the point of impact. The metal above and below has been raised as a result of the impact. The metal on the two sides of the impact has not been moved to any extent. Figure 15-24 is a top view of a section through the dent. The contour of the metal allows the

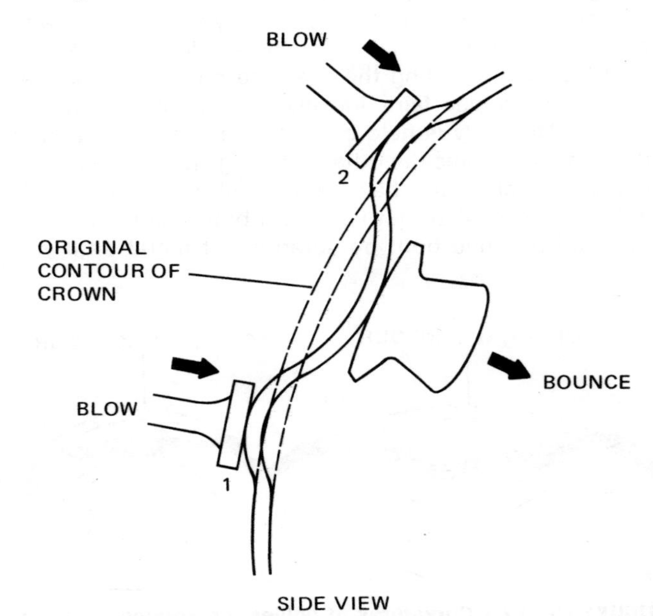

FIGURE 15–23. Side view of a panel which has been pushed in, showing the hammering-off-dolly technique to bring the metal back to contour.

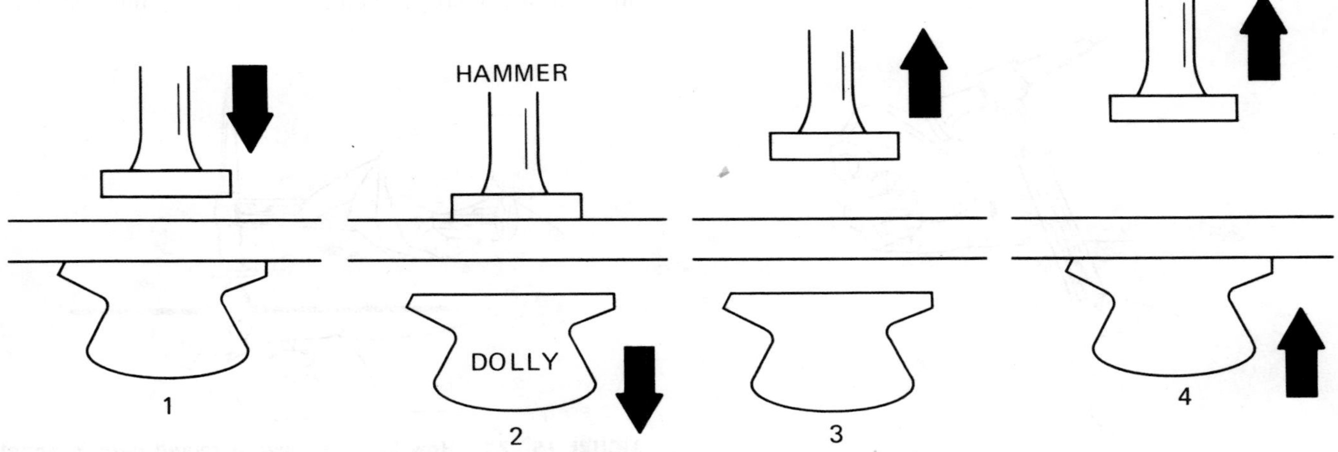

FIGURE 15–22. Sequence of events when hammering-on-dolly. See text for explanation of what is happening.

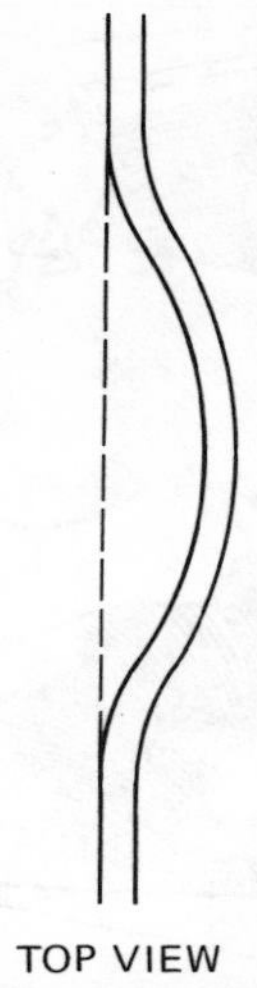

FIGURE 15–24. Top view of panel shown in Fig. 15–23. Note that the metal has not been distorted on the two sides of the dent. The distortion of metal has taken place above and below the dent owing to the crown in the metal.

metal to expand horizontally from the effect of the blow. But the crown resists the expansion and causes the ridges ("eyebrows") that appear above and below the point of impact. You will recall that bending the metal produces work hardening. The crown shown in Fig. 15-24 was made by bending the metal in a vertical direction. Therefore, it is harder above and below the dent. This is why the metal resists expansion from the impact.

Now, to work the dent up and the ridges down, you hold the dolly in the center of the dent and hammer on the two ridges above and below the dent, as shown at 1 and 2 in Fig. 15-23.

The action is different from the hammer-on-dolly procedure. When the hammer strikes a ridge, it drives the ridge down. The spot is not supported by the dolly. The movement of the metal carries the force of the blow to the dolly, causing it to bounce off the metal. Even before this happens, the springiness of the metal bounces the hammer back off the metal. The hand pressure on the dolly carries the dolly back up to the metal, striking a blow in the center of the dent. The sequence is as follows: (1) hammer strikes ridge, (2) hammer rebounds, (3) dolly rebounds, (4) dolly strikes center of dent.

Once the metal has been worked back fairly close to its original contour, hammer-on-dolly work can start to complete the hammer-on-dolly job. Note that the metal will have expanded as a result of this work and also will have been work-hardened. The expansion can be taken care of by heat shrinkage and filling with plastic body filler. (See also ○15-14 Handling Larger Areas of Damage.)

Note that the metal on the two sides of the dent is not touched. This metal has been pushed below the original level. Working on this metal would expand it further and act against bringing the dented metal out toward its original contour.

Here are two general rules to remember when using the hammer-off-dolly process:

1. Start the hammer blows on the raised metal that is farthest from the dent. Work inward from this point, alternating from one side to the other.
2. Never strike metal that is below the original level, only that which has been raised above the original level.

○15-10 Using the Body File

The body file (see Fig. 5-38) has a series of curved teeth. When the file is pushed across a body panel, it will remove thin shavings of metal. The body file must be used with a file holder.

In the typical body shop today, the body file is normally not used if the body technician is planning to fill a panel after straightening the metal. However, if the technician is going to bring the metal itself out to its original contour and then, with no further work, prime and paint it, the body file is an essential tool. The procedure of using the file in this manner is called the *pick-and-file* method.

Sometimes the body file is also used on plastic filler after it has hardened or set up. For example, some body panels, such as a hood or trunk lid, are fairly flexible. Suppose damage to such a panel has been repaired and filled with plastic body filler. Next, the filler has set and requires sanding, as explained in a following chapter. If an oscillating air or electric sander is used, the weight might cause the panel to flex while the sanding is going on. This would prevent a smooth and level panel finish. In such case, the body technician may use the body file to bring the plastic to contour and then finish the job by hand-sanding the plastic (see Chapter 18).

○15-11 Using the Body File on Metal

At one time, fenders and other body panels were of heavier metal and were simpler in contour. In addition, they were often more accessible from the inside than they are today. Thus, it was easier to work from both sides of the panel, using hammers, dolly, and picks, to restore the metal to approximately its original contour. At the same time, the body file was used to check the panel being worked on for low spots. The combination of tools brought the metal back to its original shape, ready for finishing and painting.

The body file is still used to some extent today for this same purpose. Let's assume that the right quarter panel on a car is damaged by a rear-end impact that put a crease or buckle in the panel. Working from the inside, the technician has succeeded in pushing and bumping the crease out.

Once the metal is about where it should be, sanding and filing begin. Figure 15-25 shows the start of the sanding operation with an air-powered disk sander. We describe the sanding operation in detail in Chapter 18. After the sander has removed most of the paint and has exposed raw metal, the file is used. Figure 15-26 shows the technician stroking the file across the bare metal. Note that he is looking at a sharp angle at the surface. Any place the file does not remove metal is low and should be worked up. Note for example in Fig. 15-27 that there is a spot at the top of the panel where no paint has been removed. This is the top of the crease. Figure 15-28 shows the technician, working from inside the panel, using a pick hammer to work the low spot out.

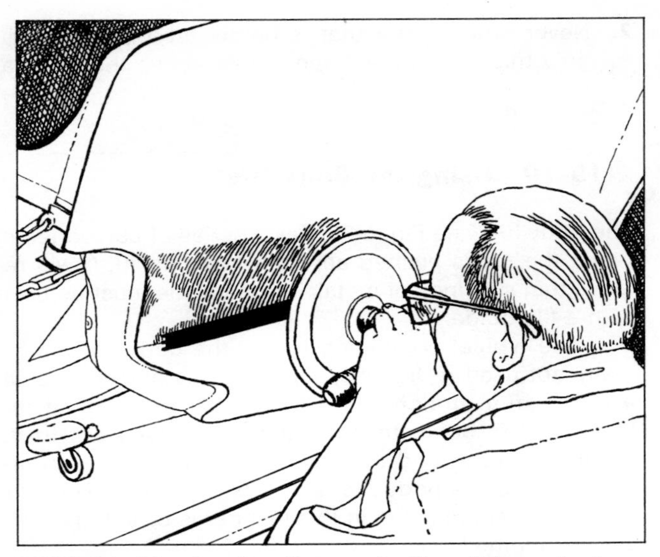

FIGURE 15–25. Sanding the panel with a disk sander to remove paint.

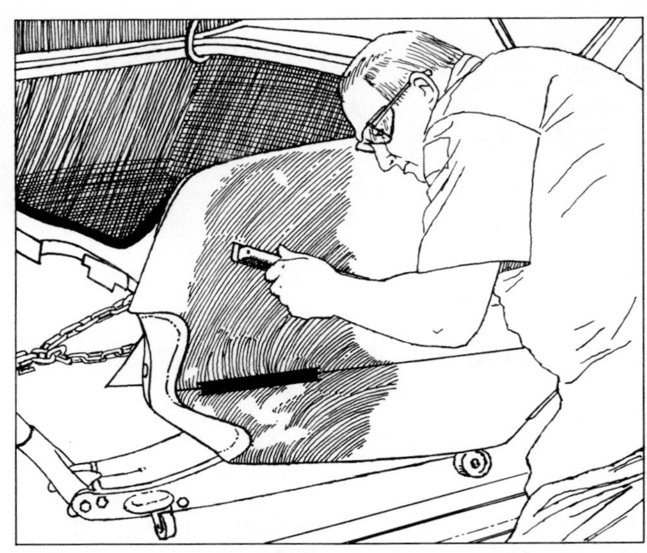

FIGURE 15–26. Stroking the body file across the previously sanded area.

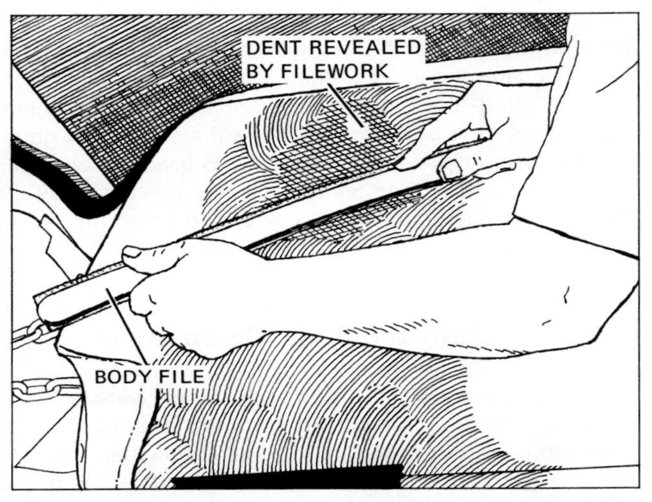

FIGURE 15–27. The body file has revealed a low spot in the metal.

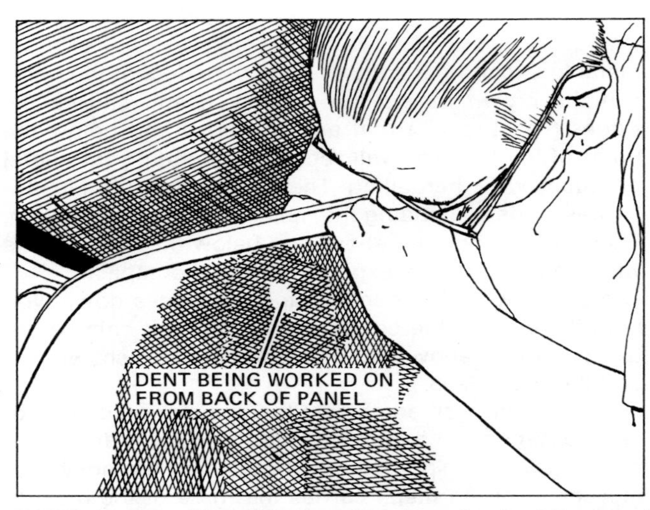

FIGURE 15–28. Technician working from back of the panel with a pick hammer to raise the low spot.

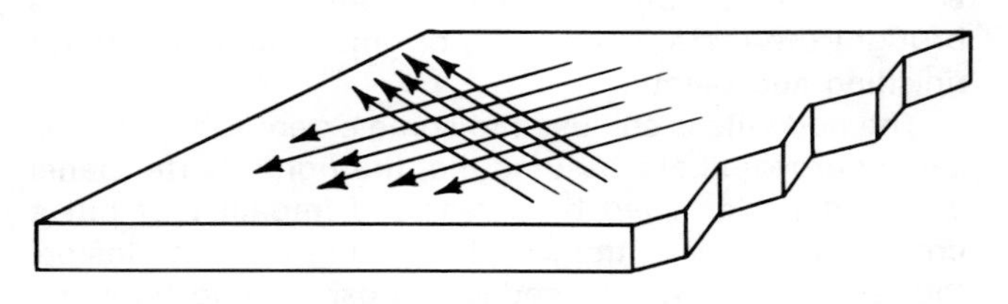

FIGURE 15–29. Directions of file strokes on a panel.

The file is used in an "X," or crossing, pattern, as shown in Fig. 15-29. The file therefore crosses the metal surface in two or more directions, and this reveals the low spots. If the file were used in only one direction, low spots might not be revealed.

NOTE: As we said, the body file is generally used today on unfilled body panels only when the body technician is bringing the metal out to its original contour and no filling with plastic body filler is planned.

○ 15-12 Using the Body File on Plastic

As we mentioned previously, the weight of the air or electric sander on some body panels can cause the panel to flex. This prevents a smooth and level finish. Therefore, on such surfaces, the plastic filler is smoothed off with a body file. The pressure on the file can be controlled accurately so that the body panel is not flexed as the file is moved across its surface.

○ 15-13 Filing or Filling

Sometimes new body panels arrive slightly damaged in transit. That is, the replacement part has a dent or crease in it, put there by careless handling during shipping. The body technician can fill this with plastic body filler or straighten it with hammers, dollies, picks, and body file, as previously described. Since the new body panel is off the car, it is relatively easy to work on it from both sides. Thus, the preferred repair method is to use the body file.

○15-14 Handling Larger Areas of Damage

We have looked at how a dolly and hammer can treat simple dents in body panels. At the end of the procedure, you will still be left with an area that must be filled with plastic body filler. This is standard practice.

If the area is larger and includes several dents, ripples, or creases, there may be considerable stretching of the metal as a result of the damage. You add to this stretch as you work the area down (or up) to near its original contour. As a result, you could end up with a large bulge or depression. This can be removed, at least partly, by heat shrinking, as described later. Another and more practical way, used by experienced body technicians, is to put a series of small ripples into the expanded area. These, in effect, absorb the expansion. Figure 15-30 shows you what we mean. The small depressions that form the ripples are not too deep and can be filled sat-

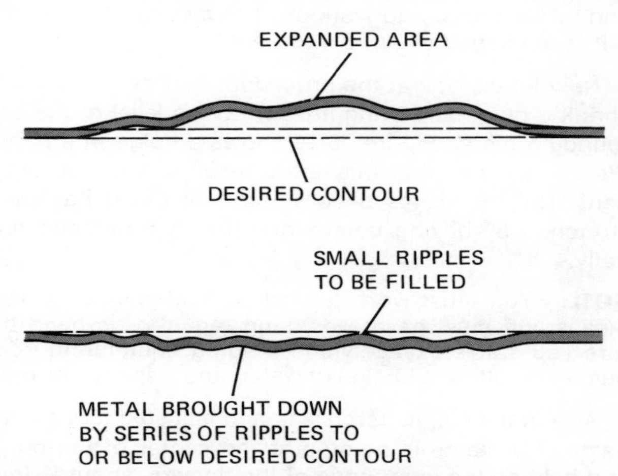

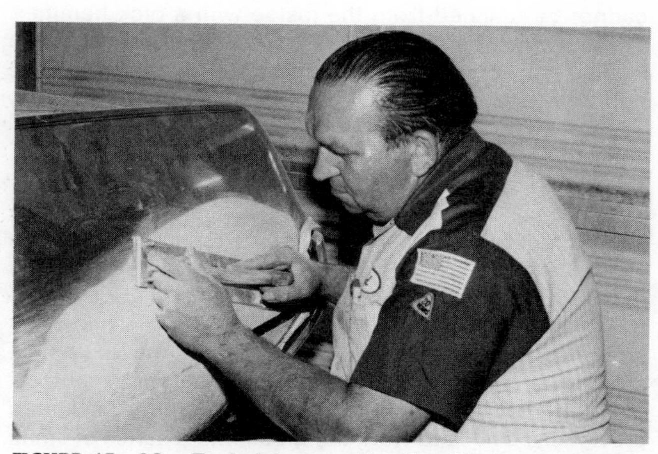

FIGURE 15–30. How to bring the expanded area down to and below contour by producing a series of small ripples to be filled.

isfactorily. Figure 15-31 shows a body technician using plastic body filler to fill a left quarter panel which has been treated this way. Figure 15-32 shows the technician sanding the hardened plastic in preparation for painting. Using plastic body filler is covered in a following chapter.

NOTE: Another method of shrinking sheet metal, used by some body technicians, is to work the expanded area with a shrinking hammer (Fig. 15-33). This is described in ○ 15-17 Heat Shrinking.

○15-15 Bumping Spoon

The bumping spoon (Fig. 15-34) is held between the damaged metal and the hammer. The hammer blows fall on the bumping spoon. This distributes the force of the blows over a larger area than does the use of the hammer alone. The bumping spoon is effective in working down long ridges or buckles that are not too large. These ridges could be reduced with a hammer, but it would take longer. Also there is always the chance that you would leave hammer marks, which would then require additional work.

Bumping spoons come with flat faces or with faces of various contours. Figure 15-34 shows a bumping spoon in use.

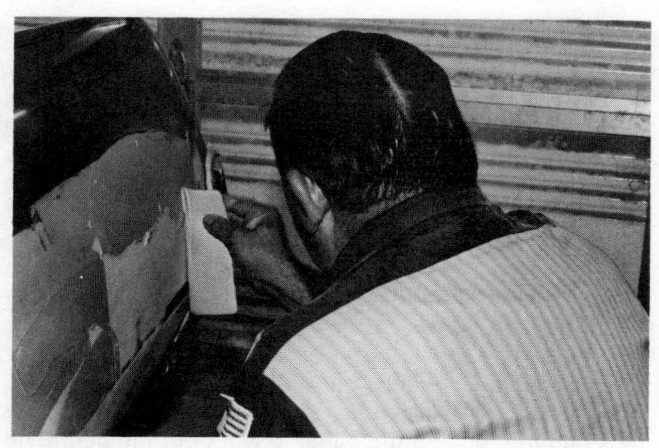

FIGURE 15–31. Body technician filling a left quarter panel.

FIGURE 15–32. Technician sanding the filled area down to contour.

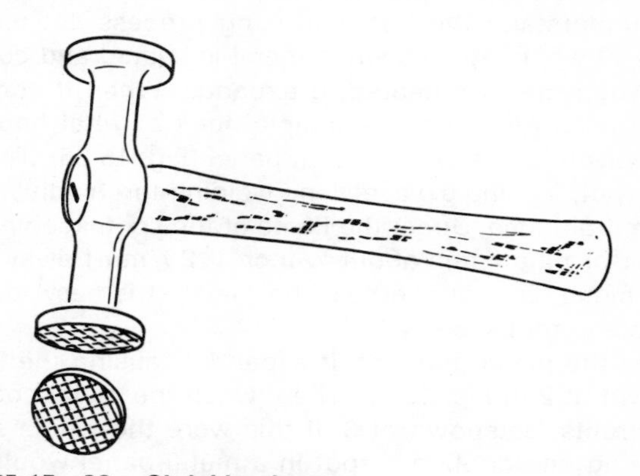

FIGURE 15–33. Shrinking hammer.

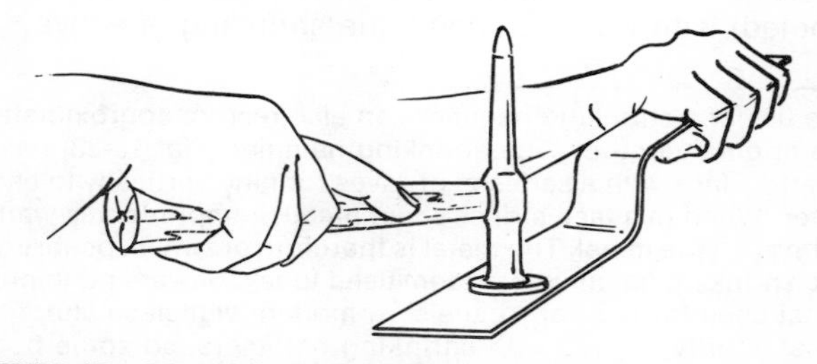

FIGURE 15–34. Using a bumping spoon.

○15-16 Picking Small Dents

Small dents can be picked up with a pick hammer, as shown in Fig. 5-20. You must be careful when using the pick end of the pick hammer. The pointed end can easily punch holes in the metal or push dents in it. Make sure the point hits the center of the dent and strike only light blows.

Figures 15-27 and 15-28 show a practical application of the procedure discussed above. In Fig. 15-27, the body technician has showed up a dent by using a body file which files the metal that is level. The paint on the dent is untouched, showing clearly that there is a significant dent or low spot. In Fig. 15-28 the technician is using a pick hammer behind the panel to work out the dent. The hammer and the technician's hand are hidden behind the panel.

Small dents can often be raised with a pry bar if they cannot be reached from the inside with a pick hammer. For example, a small dent in a door panel can often be leveled with a pry bar stuck through a drain hole in the bottom of the door.

○15-17 Heat Shrinking

Most impact forces will cause metal to stretch. The two examples we used in discussing hammer-on-dolly and hammer-off-dolly procedures (Figs. 15-20 and 15-23) both result in stretched metal. Hammering on the metal stretches it. In other words, there is too much surface area for the metal to settle back into the original contour. There are two ways to correct this, as we have explained previously. One is to work the metal into a series of small ripples, as shown in Fig. 15-30.[2] The other way is to heat-shrink the area. By either method, the metal will still have irregularities that must be filled with plastic body filler.

Now, we look at the process known as heat shrinking. To understand the heat-shrinking process, let us first look at what happens when metal is heated and cooled.

When metal is heated, it expands. When it cools, it contracts. As a simple example, look at what happens when you heat a spot in a flat panel (Fig. 15-35). To heat the spot, use the oxyacetylene welding torch adjusted to a neutral flame. Direct the flame at the spot, keeping the inner or blue flame about ½ inch [12.7 mm] away from the metal. Do not overheat the metal. It is easy to burn a hole in thin sheet metal.

As the metal gets hot, it expands, causing the bulge shown at 2 in Fig. 15-35. Then, when the metal cools, it contracts, as shown at 3. If this were the whole story, heating and cooling a spot in a metal panel would not be helpful because you would be left with a slight sag, as shown at 3 in Fig. 15-35. However, the hot metal can be worked with a hammer and dolly, and then quenched (cooled) with water, to make the shrinking effective.

[2]The use of a shrinking hammer can also restore approximately the original contour. The shrinking hammer (Fig. 15-33) has a "waffle" face with a series of grooves running vertically to each other. When this face strikes sheet metal, it imprints this waffle pattern on the metal. The metal is therefore drawn in, or shrunk. The shrinking hammer is seldom used today. Newer and thinner metal used for the body panels on modern vehicles cannot be satisfactorily treated with shrinking hammers, so some body technicians say. Other shrinking methods are preferred.

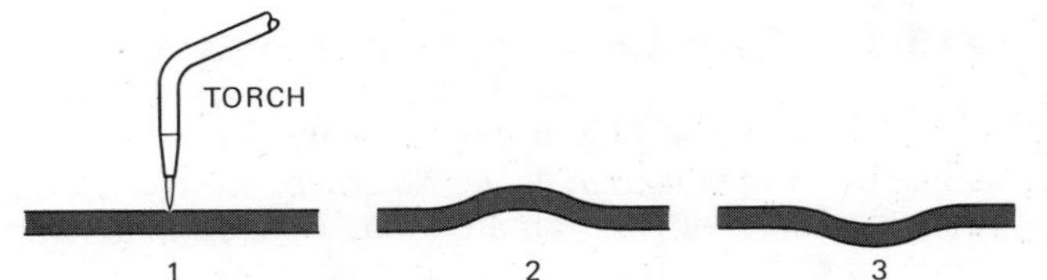

FIGURE 15–35. Sequence of actions when a sheet-metal panel is heated. At 1, a gas torch is applying heat. This causes the metal to expand and form a bulge as shown at 2. When the metal cools, it shrinks some and forms the depression as shown at 3.

NOTE: Some body technicians believe that the only reason for water quenching—that is, cooling—the heated metal is to cool the surface quickly so they can feel the surface to determine how much bulge remains. They believe that the quick quenching can crystallize the metal and make it harder to work on. The metal will crystallize if it is quenched when it is too hot.

Now let us look at the procedure that can be used to shrink a bulge and bring it down to the level of the surrounding metal. Figure 15-36 shows a bulge in a panel. We can assume that this is the result of working out a dent. The metal has been smoothed, but it has been stretched by having been worked with a hammer and dolly.

NOTE: You must work fast when heat-shrinking. This means you must have everything required on hand before you start—oxyacetylene-welding equipment, body hammer, dollies, a bucket of water, and a sponge or rags.

As a first step, the torch is lit and adjusted to a neutral flame. The flame is pointed at the center of the bulge and held so the inner cone of the flame is about ½ inch [12.7 mm] away from the metal (see Fig. 15-36). Heat a small area about the size of a dime until it is cherry red. Do not overheat it! You can burn a hole in the metal very quickly.

As soon as the area turns cherry red, put aside the torch and pick up the hammer and dolly. The dolly should have a face of the correct curvature for the panel. In the example, we are assuming the panel is flat.

Hit the center of the heated area with the body hammer, as shown in Fig. 15-37. Hit it several times to drive the center down, as shown. Note that this produces a ridge around the center. Quickly bring the dolly (a body

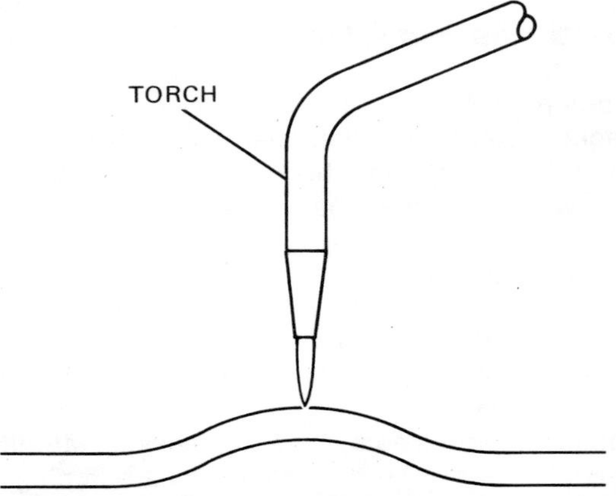

FIGURE 15–36. Heat the center of the bulge with a torch.

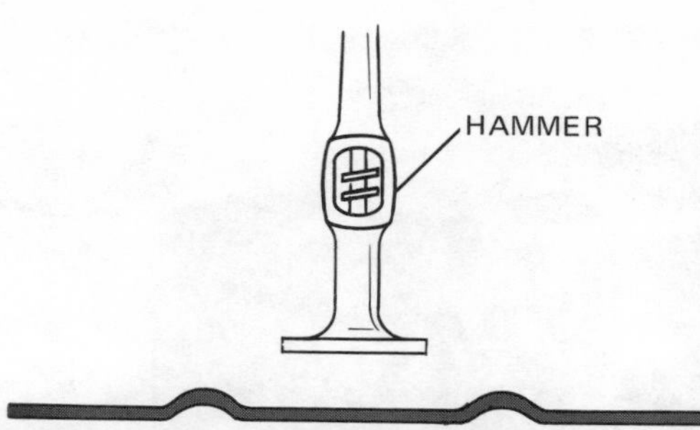

FIGURE 15–37. Hit the center of the heated area to drive it down.

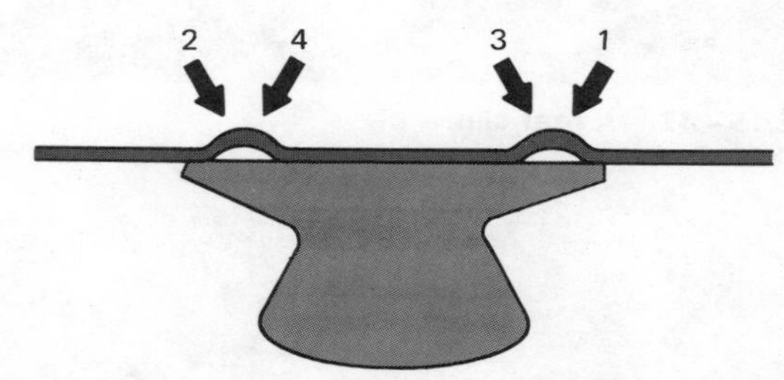

FIGURE 15–38. With dolly under, strike blows as shown and in the numbered sequence.

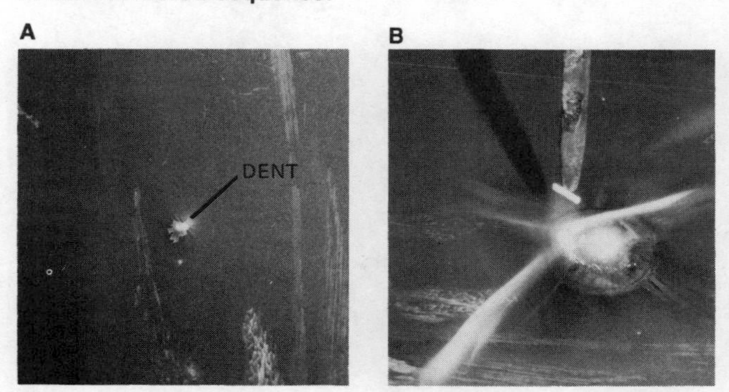

FIGURE 15–39. (A) Dent in a panel. (B) Heating the dent as the first step in heat shrinking.

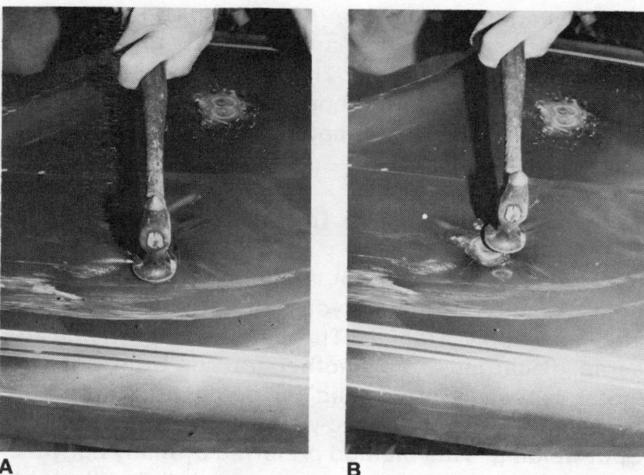

FIGURE 15–40. (A) Hitting the center of the heated area with a body hammer. (B) Working around the heated area which has been driven in.

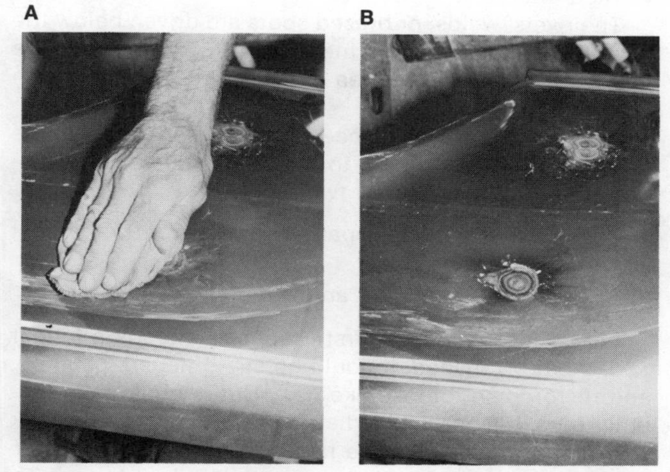

FIGURE 15–41. (A) Quenching the heated area. (B) Area flattened.

spoon can also be used) up under the work area, as shown in Fig. 15-38. Strike blows, as shown at 1, 2, 3, and 4 in Fig. 15-38. This brings the ridge down. Striking the ridges pushes the ridge metal toward the heated spot. The heated spot, being soft, can accept this metal without any great tendency to bulge. That is, the heated metal becomes thicker. There will be a tendency for a bulge to occur, and this is where the quenching with water comes in. Figures 15-39 and 15-40 show a body technician working down a dent in a panel by heating and hammering.

After the area has been worked so it is smooth except for a slight bulge, it should be quenched to flatten it. This is done by running a wet sponge or rag over the heated area, as shown in Fig. 15-41. If the area does not level completely, it will require reheating, further working, and quenching.

NOTE: Quench only after the color has left the metal and it has turned black. If you quench the metal when it is too hot (has some color), the steel will become very hard. It will be difficult to file and sand in preparation for painting. If the metal is very hot when it is quenched, it could actually crack.

The preceding explanation covers the theory of heat shrinking. In actual practice, the procedure can become somewhat more complicated. For example, when heat-shrinking a large panel, such as the quarter panel of a car, you do not heat the whole panel. Instead, you heat a number of small spots, quenching each before going on to the next. The spots should be fairly widely spaced so that there will be strong metal between them. If this is done properly, the panel will be brought down to contour. If the hot spots are too closely spaced, they can cause wrinkles, because a large area will be shrunk. Heating one spot after another is sometimes called sequence shrinking.

○15-18 Filling

Filling can be done with body solder or with plastic body filler. We have already described the application of body solder (in Chapter 11). However, body solder is seldom used today. As you know, body solder is put on hot. Plastic filler is put on cold. The surface preparation for the application of plastic filler is similar to that for body solder. The surface must be clean and sanded down to bare metal. Then the plastic material is mixed and applied with a putty knife or squeegee. After the plastic has set up (hardened), it can be filed and sanded in preparation for painting, just as for metal. The use of plastic filler, which is the generally preferred body-filling method, is covered in detail in a following chapter.

○ 15-19 Patching or Installing a Panel

If an area of damage is not too large but is severe (tears, holes, rusted-out metal), you can cut out the damaged area and apply a patch. The patch can be made from scrap discarded from another job, or from flat sheet metal especially purchased for patch work. The patch may be riveted, spot- or arc-welded, or brazed into place. Spot welding is the method preferred by many body technicians, because it is fast and does not distort the metal. Arc welding and brazing can heat and distort the sheet metal and produce expansion, which must then be worked out.

The rivets, welds, or brazed spots are driven below the level of the surrounding metal, and the low areas are filled with plastic. The area is then filed and sanded in preparation for painting.

If a major damage has been done to a body panel, the decision will probably be to replace it entirely. The decision is usually based on two factors:

1. The cost of making repairs as compared to the cost of replacing the panel.
2. The general condition and value of the car.

Let us look at item 1 first. Suppose there is a fender that is badly crushed. It could be straightened, patched, and restored so it looks like new. But it would take several hours. If labor is billed at $10.00 an hour and it took 8 hours to do the job, the labor cost would be $80.00. And the result would still be an old, repaired fender. To buy and install a new fender might cost only a little more and would be the preferred way to do the job.

Now let us look at item 2. Here we have an unknown factor—the owner's desires. The owner may be proud of the car and want only the best. So you install a new fender. On the other hand, if the car is fairly old or is for sale, the owner will not want to put too much money in it. So if the damage can be repaired at less cost than by replacement, the old panel is repaired.

If a replacement panel is called for, the shop might get a new replacement part or a part that comes from a salvage yard. As previously mentioned, these car "graveyards" are places where cars damaged in collisions are brought. Generally, these cars have been "totaled," which means that it would have cost more to fix them than they were worth. The rule of thumb in some localities in deciding whether or not a car is totaled is that if it costs 75 percent of the assessed value of the car to repair it, it is totaled. For example, if a car is worth $2000 on the market and would require $1500 to fix up, it would be considered totaled.

Totaled cars, however, are not necessarily completely junked. They usually have many still usable parts on them. Alternators, air conditioners, engines, undamaged body panels, and many other parts can be salvaged and reused. The operator of the salvage yard removes these parts and stores them in readiness for resale. Or the operator merely leaves the junked cars in rows in the yard.

FIGURE 15-42. A rear clip.

FIGURE 15-43. A side clip.

When you need a part, you search out the model car for which the part is needed. Then if that car has the part you need undamaged, you remove it yourself.

Some of the larger parts the salvage yard may remove and store in readiness for resale include front clips and rear clips. These are substantial parts of the car body. Figure 15-42 shows a rear clip. When a rear clip is used, the car being repaired has the rear part of its body removed so the replacement rear clip can be installed in its place.

The front clip is sometimes called the *doghouse*. It includes all the front and body parts. Sometimes a side clip (Fig. 15-43) is also used.

Often, when a salvage part is used, it is not from a car exactly identical to the car being repaired. That means the part must be adapted by cutting and fitting.

○ 15-20 Selecting the Right Repair Procedure

In this chapter we have described a variety of sheet-metal-repair procedures. Which method you select to work on a specific job depends on several factors: first, what kind of damage has been done; second, what equipment you have available; third, the quality of job which is required.

It takes experience to be able to determine which way to go when you are confronted with a sheet-metal repair job. But as long as you know the various repair methods covered in this chapter, you will be equipped to handle any job that comes along.

CHAPTER 15 CHECKUP

NOTE: Since the following is a chapter review test, you should review the chapter before taking the test.

Earlier chapters covered the tools used in auto body repair. In this chapter, we put those tools to work and began making simple repairs to damaged panels. Probably you found that many of the tasks appeared easy, but when you tried them, you found you needed more practice. To find out how well you understand everything in this chapter, answer the questions that follow.

COMPLETING THE SENTENCES The sentences below are incomplete. After each sentence there are several words or phrases, but only one of them correctly completes the sentence. Write each sentence in your notebook, ending it with the one word or phrase that will complete it correctly.

1. Many tools in the body shop can be used to (*a*) cover dents, (*b*) push the dents in, (*c*) pull the dents out, (*d*) shrink the dents.
2. To pull out a dent, pull in the direction (*a*) of the impact force, (*b*) above the impact force, (*c*) opposite the impact force, (*d*) below the impact force.
3. Straightening metal by hammering on a dolly will cause the metal to (*a*) shrink, (*b*) bubble, (*c*) tear, (*d*) rust.
4. A body file can be used to (*a*) ding out dents, (*b*) hammer on, (*c*) prepare primer for painting, (*d*) locate low spots.
5. The process of restoring stretched metal to its original contour is (*a*) hammering-on-the-dolly, (*b*) hammering-off-the-dolly, (*c*) pulling, (*d*) heat shrinking.

QUESTIONS Write each of the following questions, and then the answer, in your notebook. If you have trouble recalling the answer to a question, turn back to the pages that cover the material and study them again.

1. When would you use vacuum cups?
2. Describe the procedure for using the slide hammer.
3. When should a hydraulic ram be used?
4. Why must you determine the direction of the impact force?
5. How would you determine if a panel had a small low spot?

DEFINITIONS In the following, you are asked for several definitions. Write them in your notebook. The act of writing the definitions does two things. It tests your knowledge, and it helps fix the information more firmly in your mind. Turn back into the chapter if you are not sure of a definition, or look it up in the glossary at the back of the book.

1. What is the difference between filing and filling?
2. Define "bumping spoon."
3. What is "quenching"?
4. What is "patching a panel"?
5. Define "salvage yard."

SUGGESTIONS FOR FURTHER STUDY

In this chapter, we discussed the use of many body tools. Go through your shop, toolroom, and toolbox. Make a list, on a page in your notebook, of all the various body tools that are available to you. Divide your list into three parts: "Shop," "Toolroom," and "Toolbox." Beside the name of each tool, write down where it is located. Referring to this list will save you time as you learn your way around the body shop.

16

FUNDAMENTALS OF BODY AND FRAME STRAIGHTENING

In previous chapters, we looked at procedures and equipment used to straighten body sheet metal. We did not consider the possible damage to the frame members in our previous discussions. However, whenever a car has been damaged by a collision, roll-over, or other accident, the alignment of the frame and body should be checked. This should be done even though damage appears light. For example, a car that struck a large animal, such as a horse or cow, may appear to suffer only light damage. Because the animal was large and the impact took place over a large area of the car, very little visible damage may be seen. However, since the impact was heavy, the shock could have carried back into the frame and underbody, causing misalignment that should be worked out. Even a glancing blow on one fender can throw the frame out of line. Therefore, it is very important to always check frame alignment whenever any possibility exists of frame misalignment.

○ 16-1 Frame and Body Alignment Comes First

Before you attempt to do any work on body sheet-metal panels, you should check alignment and make whatever corrections are required. Actually, straightening the frame (or body members in unitized cars) also straightens, at least to some extent, the body sheet metal.

There is no use to work on sheet metal before the frame and body have been properly realigned. Suppose you did straighten some sheet metal. Then, when you put the power equipment to work on the car to align the frame, you would probably pull the sheet metal out of line again.

In this and following chapters, we discuss various types of frame damage that can occur. Then we explain how hydraulic equipment can be used to realign the frame. We also cover realignment of unibody vehicles. We take specific examples of damage and explain how the damage was worked out and alignment restored. In Chapter 6, various frame- and body-straightening equipment was discussed. This equipment and its uses are covered in detail in this and the following chapter.

○ 16-2 Types of Full Frames

Before we discuss frame- and body-straightening equipment, let us look at various types of frames used in cars having full frame (see Fig. 2-1). With this construction, the major resistance to twist or other body-frame distortion is offered by the frame itself (Fig. 16-1). The frame is somewhat flexible, but it is made of steel beams of various shapes that provide great strength. In recent

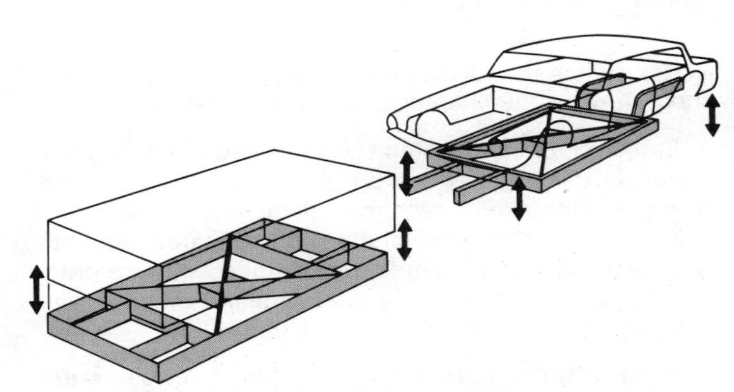

FIGURE 16–1. Major resistance to twist is offered by the frame. (*Bear Division of Applied Power, Inc.*)

years, the tendency has been to reduce weight. However, at the same time, steels of greater strength, and scientific design of the structural parts of the frame, have improved the impact resistance and basic strength of the frame. Figure 16-2 shows the intricate shapes into which the frame parts are formed. This frame illustrates the scientific principles of getting strength from relatively light weight.

○ 16-3 Frames for Unitized Bodies

In the fully unitized body, the body itself forms the support for the engine, suspension, and drive train. Figure 16-3 shows a fully unitized body. Note that the body includes heavy structural sills, box-section rails, and lower-body reinforcing members to add strength to the assembly and provide support for the engine and suspension system. Figure 2-5 shows another unitized body.

Many cars use stub frames at the front. Figure 16-2 shows one of these. It is attached to the body by bolts through isolators, as shown. These isolators absorb road and suspension vibration and prevent it from carrying up to the body.

Figure 16-4 shows a similar stub frame. Note again how the structural parts are intricately formed to provide strength and support for the engine and other parts.

With these various unitized and semi-unitized bodies, the body itself provides the structural strength. This is illustrated in Fig. 16-5, where the body is shown as part of a structural box section. This contrasts with the full-frame assembly, shown in Fig. 16-1, where the body itself does not greatly add to the basic strength of the assembly. In the full-frame car, the body is dropped onto the frame and the frame is the supporting and strength member. Figure 16-6 shows a frame with the basic parts named.

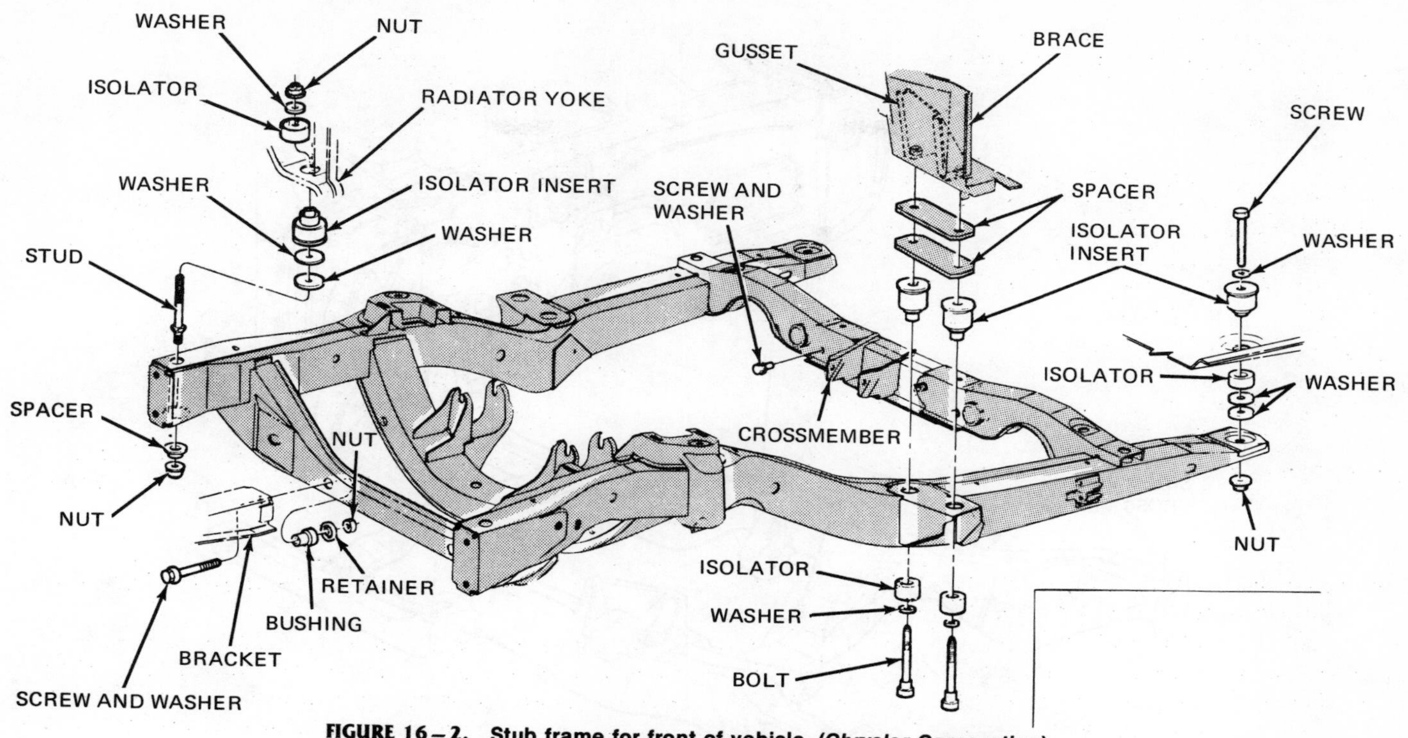

FIGURE 16–2. Stub frame for front of vehicle. (*Chrysler Corporation*)

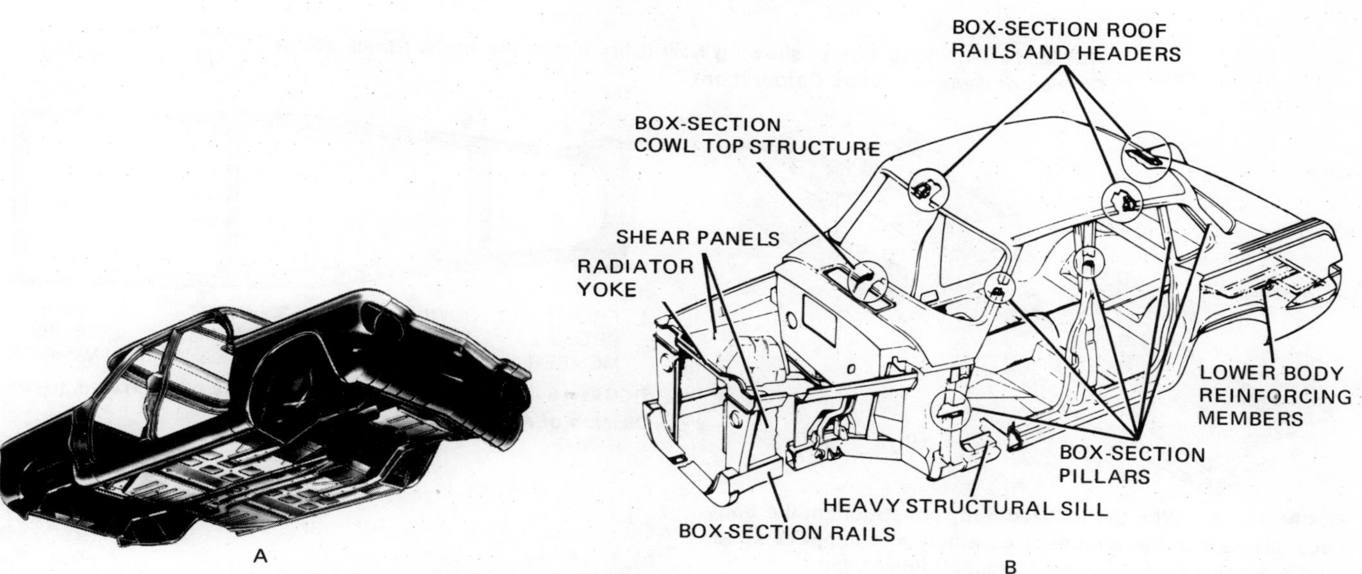

FIGURE 16–3. Unitized construction of car body and frame (A) as seen from underneath and (B) in partial cutaway view to show details of the separate parts that are welded together. (*Chevrolet Motor Division of General Motors Corporation and Chrysler Corporation*)

○16-4 The Controlling Points

There are four controlling points in body-frame straightening, as shown in Fig. 16-7. These are as follows:

1. The front cross member
2. The cowl cross member
3. The cross member at the rear-door area
4. The rear cross member

These are the four reference points for any checks and straightening operations. The frame, in effect, is divided into three sections: the front or engine section, the center or passenger section, and the rear or trunk section. Each section is bordered by a cross member or controlling point. Hookups of straightening equipment are usually applied at or near any of the controlling points.

Even though the unitized car has no frame, as such, the same general principle applies. The car can be divided into three sections with four controlling points. As we describe various impact damage conditions, we will demonstrate what we mean.

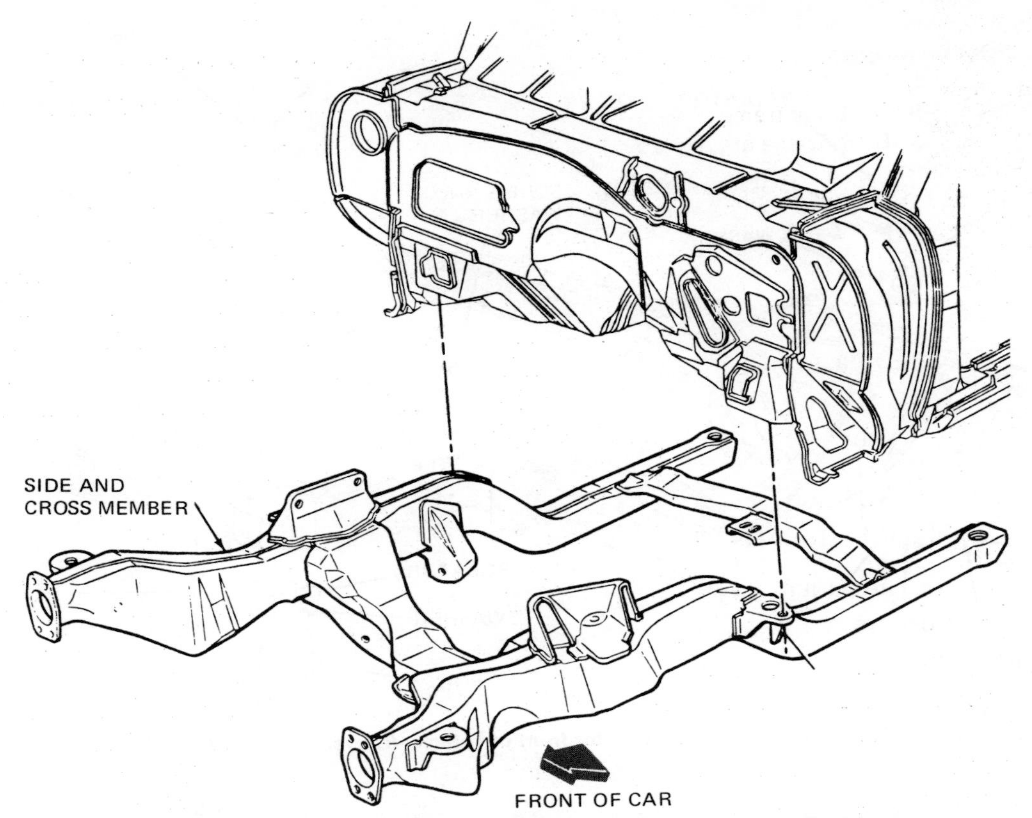

FIGURE 16–4. **Stub frame, showing how it fits under the body. (*Buick Motor Division of General Motors Corporation*)**

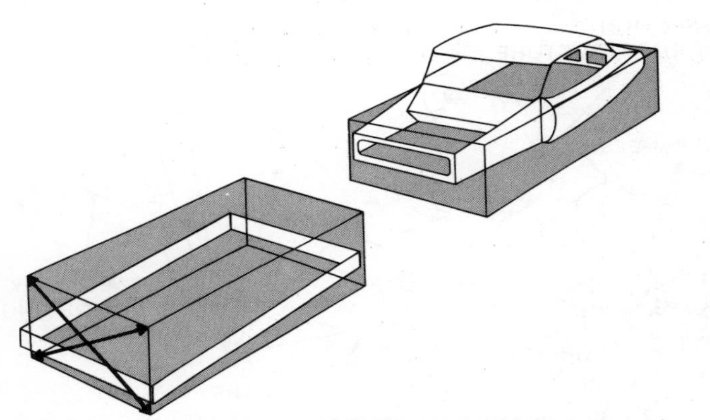

FIGURE 16–5. **With the unitized body construction, the body becomes part of the structural assembly and supplies structural strength. (*Bear Division of Applied Power, Inc.*)**

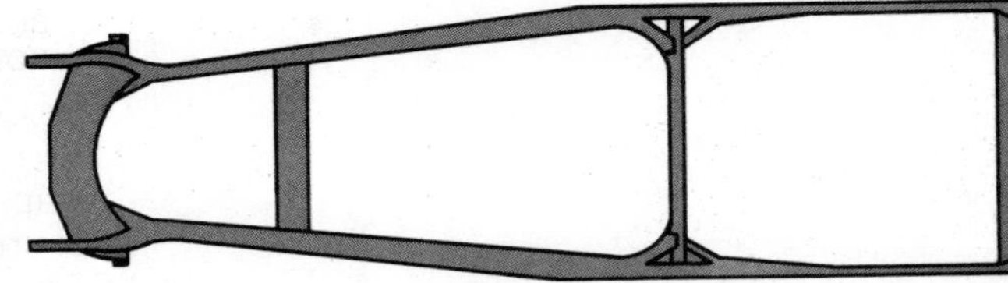

FIGURE 16–7. **The four controlling points of the frame. (*Bear Division of Applied Power, Inc.*)**

FIGURE 16–6. **Frame of a car.**

○16-5 Basic Types of Body-Frame Misalignment

There are five basic types of body-frame misalignment, as shown in Figs. 16-8 to 16-16. These are sidesway, sag, mash, diamond, and twist.

Three basic kinds of sidesway are shown in Figs. 16-8 to 16-10. In Fig. 16-8, the sidesway has resulted from a front-end collision which has pushed the front of the frame to the left and buckled the side rails. In Fig. 16-9, the sway has resulted from the car's being hit from one side. Figure 16-10 shows sway from a rear-end collision.

Figure 16-11 shows side-rail sag from a front-end collision, and Fig. 16-12 shows side-rail sag from a rear-end collision.

Figures 16-13 and 16-14 show frames mashed and buckled from a front-end and a rear-end collision. Side-rail sag, as shown in Figs. 16-11 and 16-12, is similar to mashed and buckled frame damage, as shown in Figs. 16-13 and 16-14. In side-rail sag, the collision impact was just great enough to push the body and frame in so the frame has buckled and dropped at one point. During mash, the impact is harder and therefore the rails, as well as the car body, suffer more damage. As shown in the two examples in Figs. 16-13 and 16-14, the frame side rails not only sag at some point but also are forced upward at a related point. There are buckles at these two points.

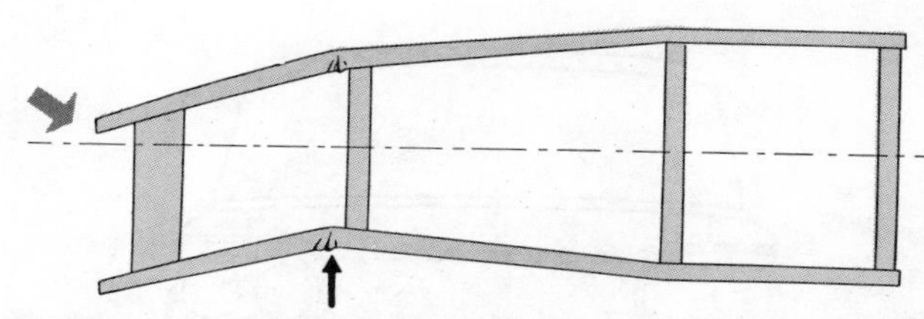

FIGURE 16-8. Sidesway from front-end collision. *(Bear Division of Applied Power, Inc.)*

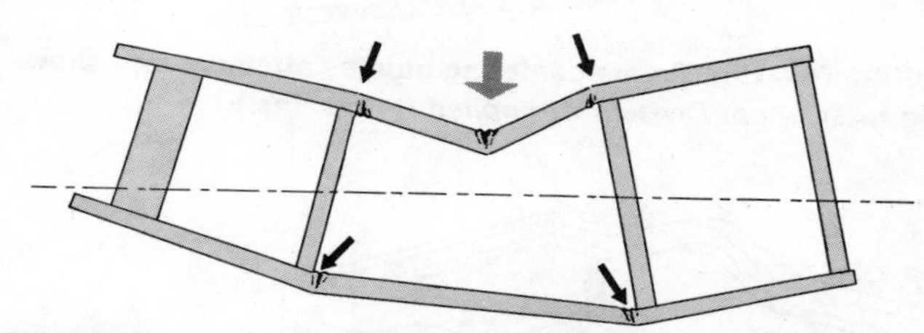

FIGURE 16-9. Sidesway from impact at center. *(Bear Division of Applied Power, Inc.)*

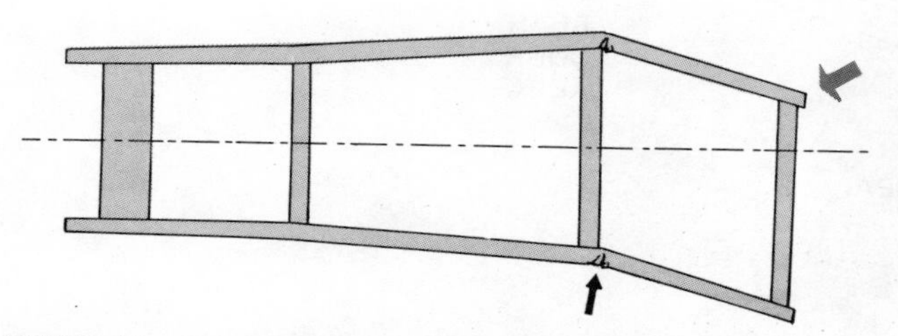

FIGURE 16-10. Sidesway from rear-end impact. *(Bear Division of Applied Power, Inc.)*

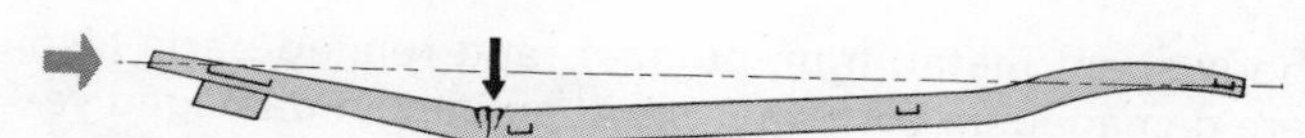

FIGURE 16-11. Side-rail sag from front impact. *(Bear Division of Applied Power, Inc.)*

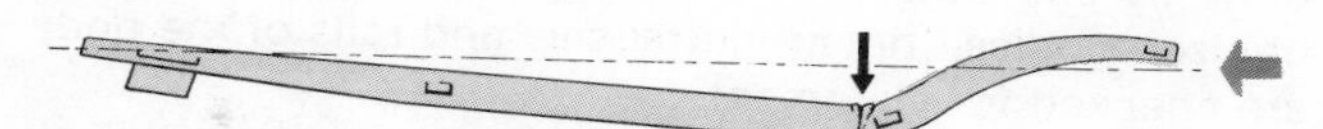

FIGURE 16-12. Side-rail sag from rear impact. *(Bear Division of Applied Power, Inc.)*

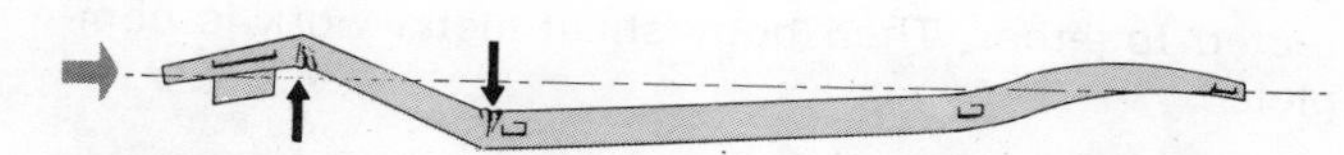

FIGURE 16-13. Frame mashed and buckled from front-end impact. *(Bear Division of Applied Power, Inc.)*

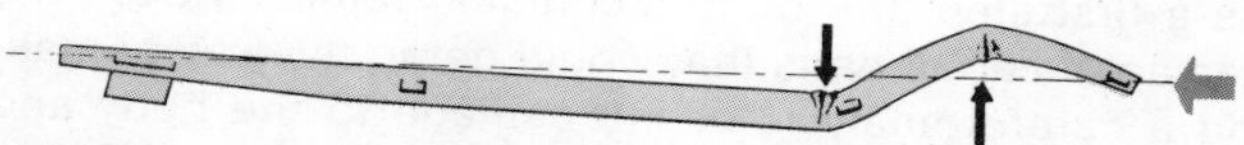

FIGURE 16-14. Frame mashed and buckled from rear-end impact. *(Bear Division of Applied Power, Inc.)*

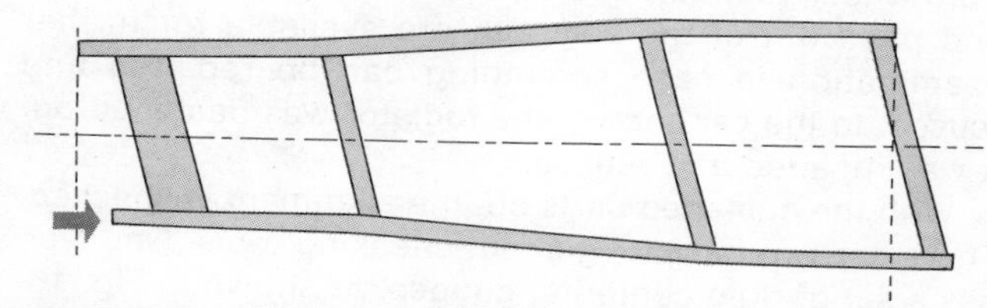

FIGURE 16-15. Diamond misalignment. *(Bear Division of Applied Power, Inc.)*

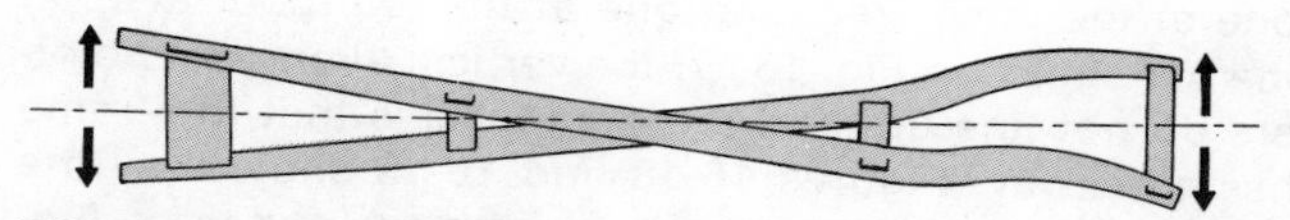

FIGURE 16-16. Twisted frame. *(Bear Division of Applied Power, Inc.)*

Figure 16-15 shows a frame that has suffered an impact at one corner great enough to push the cross members out of right angles with the side rails. This is called a diamond frame.

Figure 16-16 shows a twisted frame. This can result from a roll-over where uneven loads at any of the four points, shown by the arrows, cause the frame, and body, to twist.

You must view the illustrations showing the five types of body-frame misalignment (Figs. 16-8 to 16-16) with caution. A severe impact may produce a combination of the basic conditions shown. Regardless of the type of damage, the expert body technician must size up the condition of the body and frame. As a first step, the technician must figure out where the impact came from. Then the technician applies a pull or push, using hydraulic equipment, which will reverse the force. This "undoes" the impact. We describe the procedure in following sections.

○16-6 Preparing to Correct Body-Frame Damage

In the previous section, we described the various types of frame damage. Whenever a frame is damaged, the body sheet metal, trim, bumper, and related parts also are damaged. In your analysis of an impact-damaged vehicle, you look at the frame first to determine whether the impact has been severe enough to penetrate through the body and underbody and reach the frame. This is done by checking the frame alignment. Or, in case of unitized bodies, the structural sills and rails of the body are checked for alignment.

You do not loosen body bolts attaching the body to the frame or stub frame when checking and correcting alignment. Alignment of the frame and body are corrected together. Then body sheet-metal work is completed.

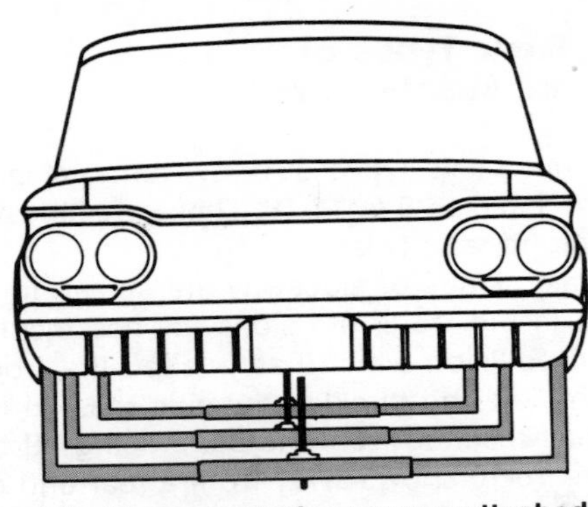

FIGURE 16–17. Frame centering gauges attached and showing sidesway. (*Bear Division of Applied Power, Inc.*)

○16-7 Diagnosing Body-Frame Damage

As a first step, the body technician removes from the damaged car all parts that would get in the way of making a careful analysis of the damage to the body and frame. Figure 13-1, for example, shows a car which has suffered a right-front-end collision. The front grill, right-front wheel, radiator, and other parts have been removed and piled out of the way, but are available for further examination in case something can be repaired and reused. In the car shown, the radiator was damaged but it was repaired and reused.

With the damaged parts off, the alignment is checked. There are two basic alignment-checking tools. One type has a set of rigid centering gauges, as shown in Fig. 16-17. These are placed at the three front controlling points, shown in Fig. 16-7; that is, one at the front cross member, one at the cowl area, and one at the rear-door area. In the car shown in Fig. 16-17, the vertical alignment pointers do not line up, and the diagnosis is that the frame has sidesway. Figures 16-18 and 16-19 show how the centering gauges line up on cars with sag and twist. Figures 16-20 and 16-21 show various methods of attaching the centering gauges to the frame or underbody.

The second type of alignment-checking tool uses chains and a pendant with vertical rod, as shown in Fig. 16-22. Three of these are hung from the reference points noted above. As you can see in Fig. 16-22, the frame has sidesway. This is the same car shown in Fig. 13-1.

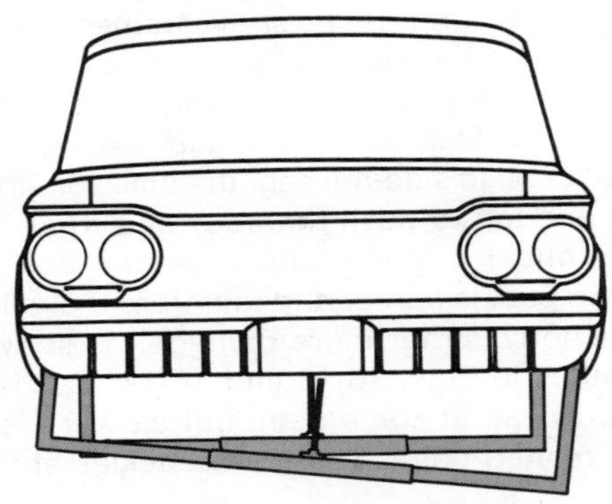

FIGURE 16–18. Frame centering gauges attached and showing sag. (*Bear Division of Applied Power, Inc.*)

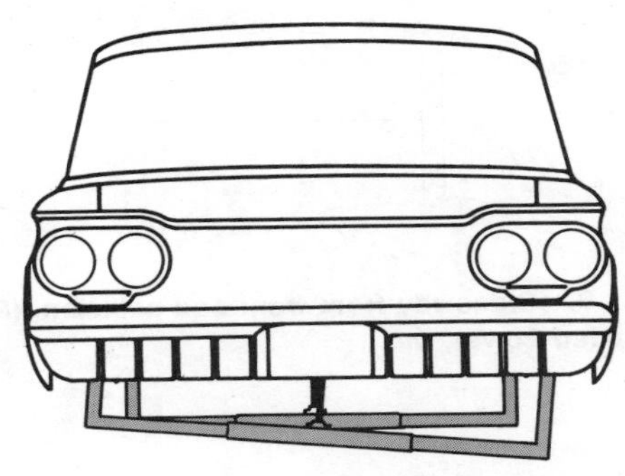

FIGURE 16–19. Frame centering gauges attached and showing twist. (*Bear Division of Applied Power, Inc.*)

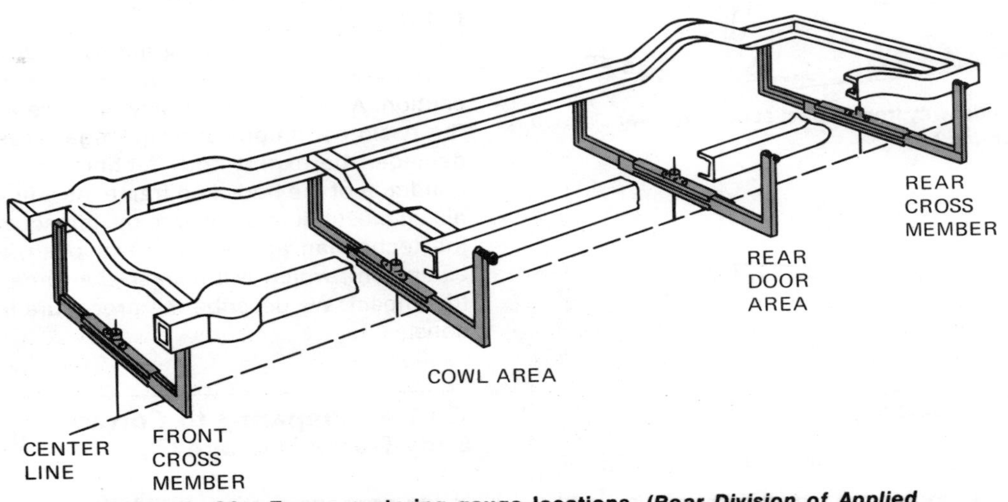

FIGURE 16–20. Frame centering gauge locations. (*Bear Division of Applied Power, Inc.*)

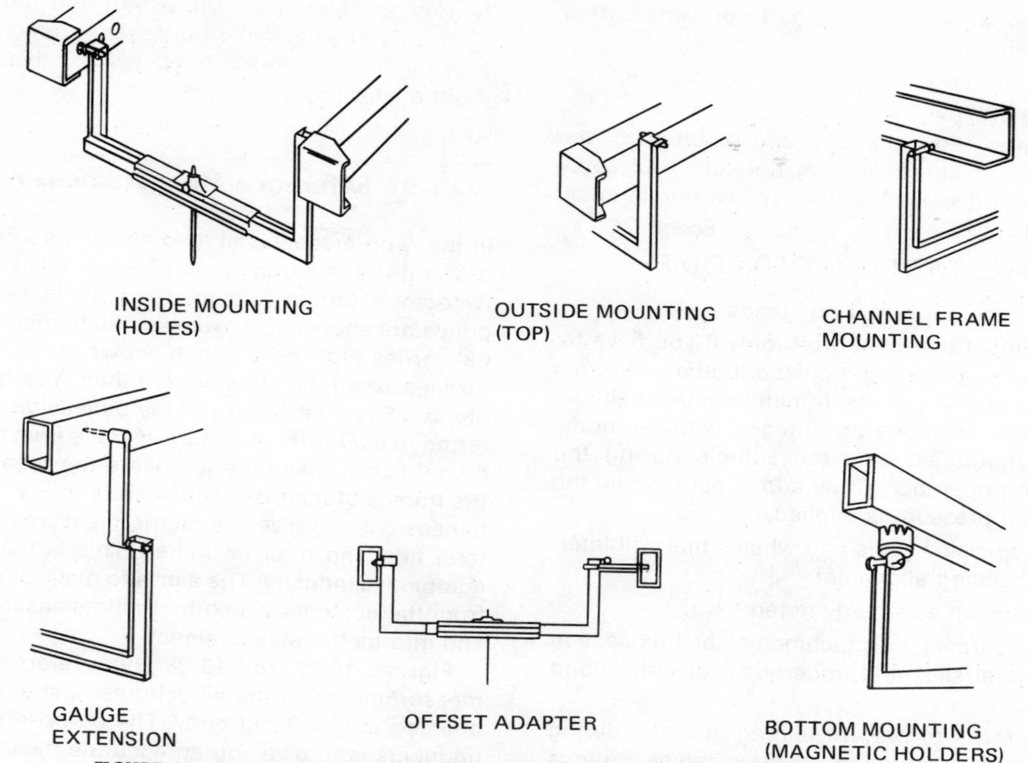

FIGURE 16–21. Methods of attaching centering gauges to frame. ***(Bear Division of Applied Power, Inc.)***

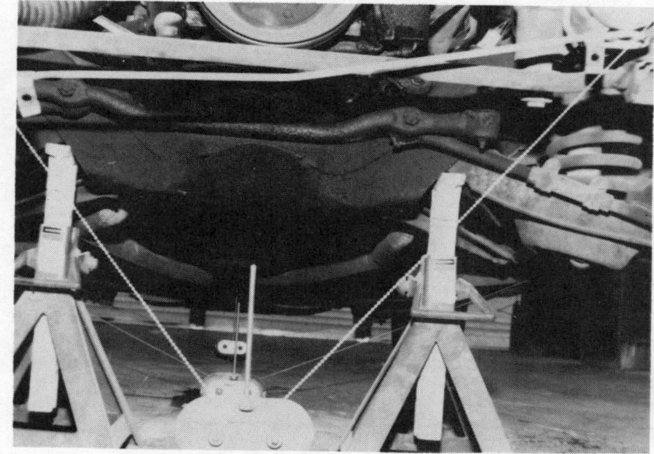

FIGURE 16–22. Type of alignment-checking tool using pendants and vertical rods. The rods, being out of line, show that the frame has sidesway.

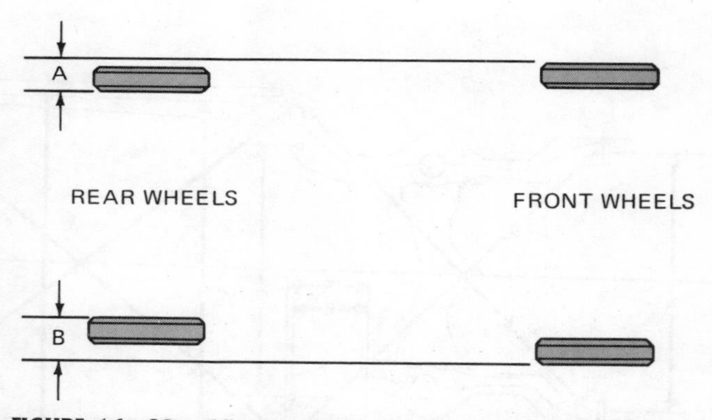

FIGURE 16–23. Alignment check of the rear suspension. A should equal B. ***(Ford Motor Company)***

○16-8 Preparing the Car for Straightening

Where collision damage has been light, the body technician may not use the alignment gauges to check the frame alignment. However, if there is the slightest doubt, check the frame alignment. Failure to check and correct frame alignment is the reason you occasionally see a car going down the highway with wheels that do not track.

Tracking is the following of the rear wheels in proper alignment behind the front wheels (Fig. 16-23). If the rear wheels do not follow properly, that is, if they do not track as they should, the frame is probably out of line. A car that fails to track properly after a body-frame repair job has not been properly repaired. The technician who did the job did not take the time to check and correct frame alignment. This is the reason we stress the necessity of checking alignment, as explained in ○ 16-7, whenever there is the possibility of damage. While not all collision jobs are the same, the following steps are usually required. Cars with frames and cars with unitized bodies are listed separately.

FOR CARS WITH FRAMES

1. Jack up car and support it on stands.
2. Remove wheels, bumpers, and whatever metalwork might interfere with checking alignment.
3. DO *not* remove or loosen body bolts!
4. Remove suspension parts that might interfere.
5. Check alignment, as already noted.
6. Examine frame for buckles and breaks.
7. If frame is cracked or broken, weld it (○ 16-10). Observe the safety cautions outlined in Chapters 10 and

12. This step is necessary so as to prevent further damage to and tearing of the sheet metal.

8. If parts still on the car will interfere with straightening, remove them.
9. Having determined the extent and direction of the misalignment, make necessary hookups and apply straightening pressure. We discuss this step in detail in a later chapter.

FOR CARS WITH UNITIZED BODIES

1. Jack up car and support it on stands.
2. Remove bumper and metalwork only if you have to. Ordinarily, straightening unitized bodies requires that all component parts remain on the vehicle. These component parts are integral with the body, and they should stay on the vehicle during the straightening operation. They add support while the straightening pressure is applied.
3. Remove suspension parts and wheels that will interfere with checking alignment.
4. Check alignment, as already noted.
5. Examine stub frame, its attachments, the box-section rails, structural sills, and underbody for cracks and breaks.
6. Weld any breaks to prevent tearing of metal during the straightening operation. Observe safety cautions outlined in Chapters 10 and 12. See ○ 16-10.
7. Having determined the extent and direction of the misalignment, make necessary hookups and apply straightening pressure. We discuss this step in detail in a later chapter.

○ 16-9 Reference Measurement Points

In the shop manuals, all automotive manufacturers have drawings of the frames and bodies used in their cars. Reference points and measurements between these points are shown. For example, a late-model Buick manual carries Fig. 16-24, which shows the reference points for measuring the alignment of their A-series frame. Figure 16-25 is a tabulation of the dimensions in inches referred to in Fig. 16-24. Figure 16-26 is from the same late-model Buick manual and covers the measurements of the frames of their B-C series. Note in Fig. 16-26 that the dimensions are given in metric measurements (millimeters) first and then in inches. This is the trend in the automotive industry. The aim is to move completely away from the customary inch-foot-mile measurement system and into metric measurement.

Figures 16-27 and 16-28 show reference points for measurements of the wheelhouse panel and the trunk opening in a unitized body. The purpose of such measurements is to give you an accurate means of checking whether alignment is correct.

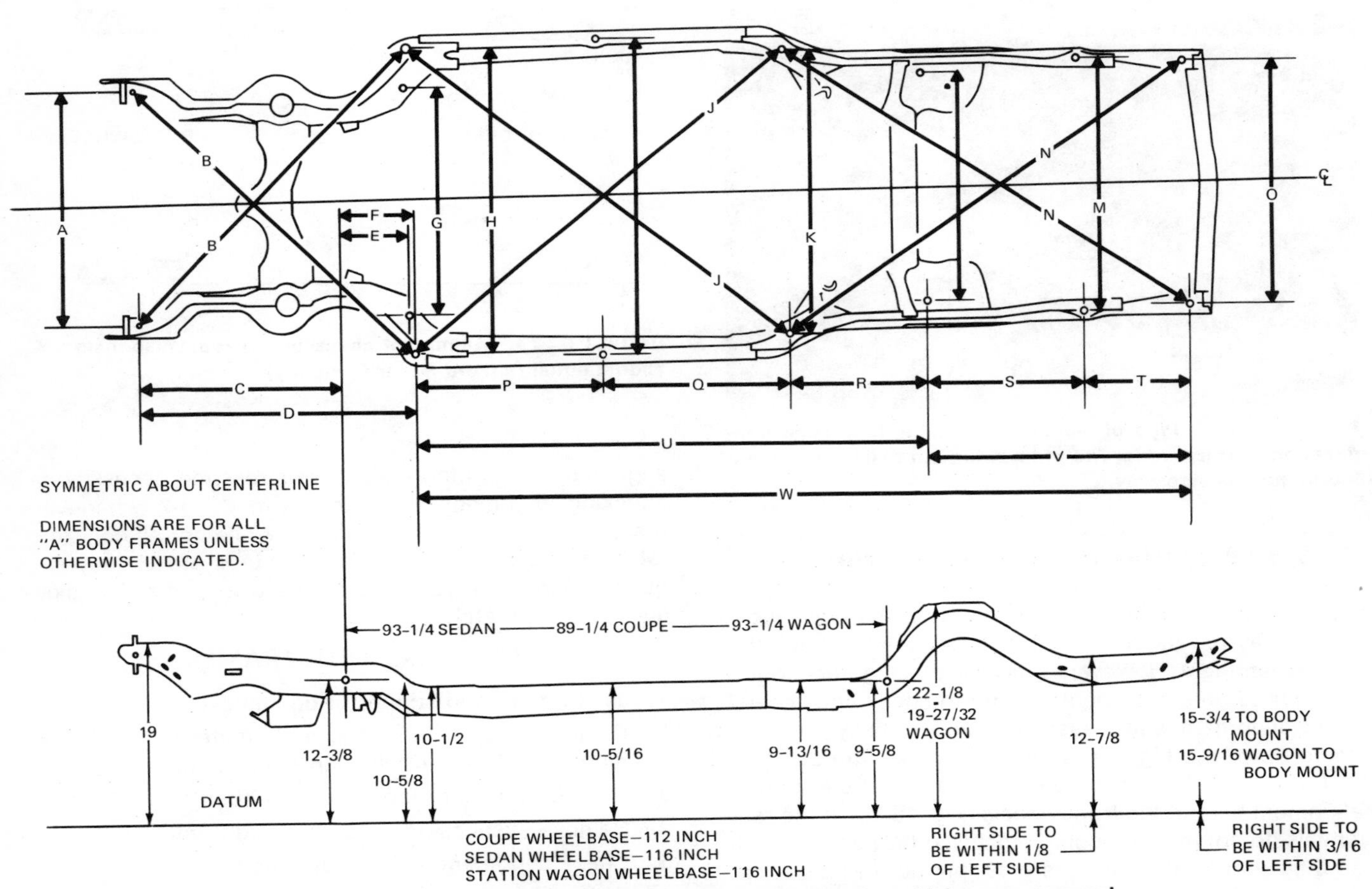

FIGURE 16-24. Dimensions for late-model Buick A-frame vehicles as measured from reference points indicated. Dimensions are in inches. (*Buick Motor Division of General Motors Corporation*)

A-SERIES FRAME DIMENSIONS
NOTE: All dimensions are from centerline to centerline. All dimensions in inches.

DIMENSION	2-DOOR	4-DOOR	STATION WAGON
A	40-3/4	40-3/4	40-3/4
B	64-29/32	64-29/32	64-29/32
C	32-5/32	32-5/32	32-5/32
D	44-29/32	44-29/32	44-29/32
E	12-3/16	12-3/16	12-3/16
F	12-3/4	12-3/4	12-3/4
G	39	39	39
H	53	53	53
I	54-1/2	54-1/2	54-1/2
J	80-21/32	83-25/32	83-25/32
K	49-1/4	49-1/4	49-1/4
L	39-7/16	39-7/16	39-7/16
M	43-5/16	43-5/16	40-9/32
N	79-7/32	79-7/32	84-13/16
O	38	38	34-21/32
P	31-1/2	31-1/2	31-1/2
Q	30-7/8	34-7/8	34-7/8
R	22-21/32	22-21/32	21-3/8
S	25-3/4	25-3/4	27
T	17-23/32	17-23/32	25-5/16
U	85-1/32	89-1/32	87-3/4
V	43-15/32	43-15/32	52-5/16
W	128-1/2	132-1/2	140-1/16

FIGURE 16–25. A-series frame dimensions. See Fig. 16–24 for reference points. (*Buick Motor Division of General Motors Corporation*)

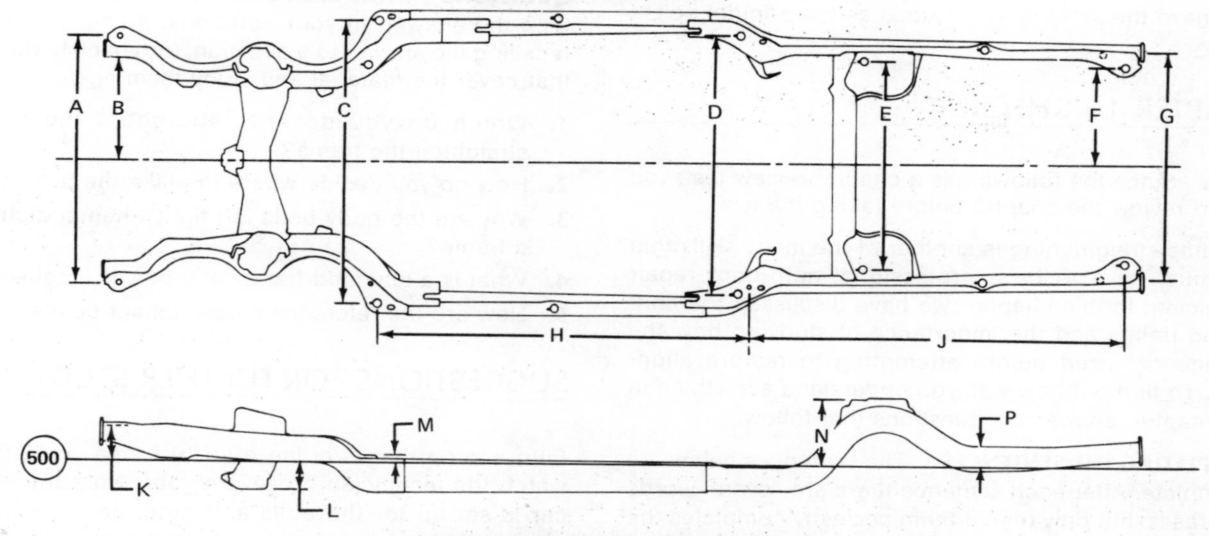

UPPER DIMENSIONS ARE IN MILLIMETERS
(LOWER DIMENSIONS ARE IN INCHES)

BODY STYLES	A	B	C	D	E	F	G	H	J	K	L	M	N	P
B–C SERIES EXCEPT STATION WAGON	1188.0 (46.77)	490.0 (19.29)	1364.0 (53.7)	1250.0 (49.21)	1002.0 (39.45)	472.0 (18.58)	1104.0 (43.46)	1726.5 (67.97)	1732.0 (68.19)	163.0 (6.42)	142.6 (5.61)	27.4 (1.08)	316.0 (12.44)	98.5 (3.88)
B SERIES STATION WAGON	1188.0 (46.77)	490.0 (19.29)	1364.0 (53.7)	1250.0 (49.21)	1080.0 (42.52)	500.0 (19.68)	1134.0 (44.65)	1726.5 (67.97)	1804.0 (71.02)	163.0 (6.42)	142.6 (5.61)	27.4 (1.08)	277.0 (10.9)	174.0 (6.85)

FIGURE 16–26. Frame measurements of Buick B–C series. Note measurements are given in both inches and millimeters. (*Buick Motor Division of General Motors Corporation*)

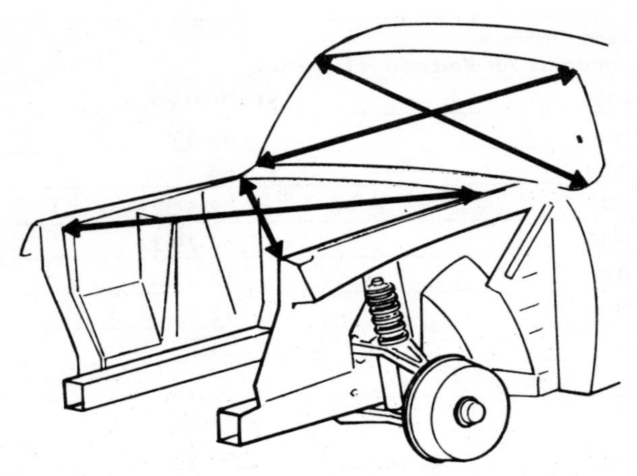

FIGURE 16–27. **Wheelhouse panel measurements.** (*Bear Division of Applied Power, Inc.*)

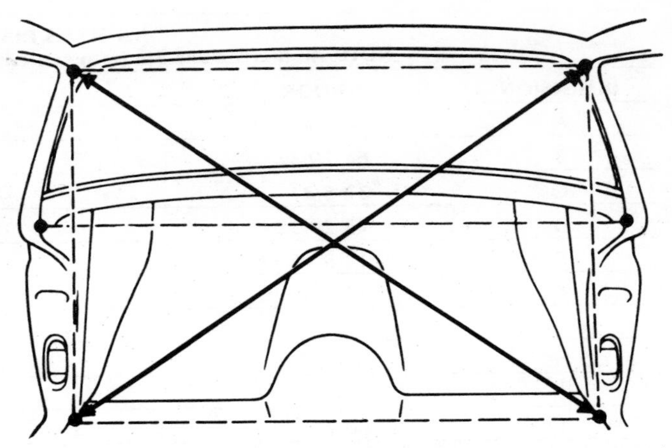

FIGURE 16–28. **Trunk opening measurements.** (*Bear Division of Applied Power, Inc.*)

○16-10 Frame Repair

If a frame is cracked or broken, it is often possible to weld the break. Ford cautions that electric-welding equipment should be used for all frame welding. Heat must be kept to a minimum so that the hardness of the metal will not be affected.

When a reinforcing plate is to be welded to a frame side member, run the welds lengthwise along the sides of the reinforcement. If a damaged frame member is to be replaced, use the same method of attachment as was used for the original frame member. Also, new bolts, required for reattachments of parts to the new member, must have the same specifications as the original bolts.

CHAPTER 16 CHECKUP

NOTE: Since the following is a chapter review test, you should review the chapter before taking the test.

Frame straightening is another of the many skills that you must have to be a professional auto-body-repair technician. In this chapter, we have discussed the controlling points and the importance of studying how the damage occurred before attempting to restore alignment. To find out how well you understand everything in this chapter, answer the questions that follow.

COMPLETING THE SENTENCES The sentences below are incomplete. After each sentence there are several words or phrases, but only one of them correctly completes the sentence. Write each sentence in your notebook, ending with the one word or phrase that will complete it correctly.

1. In the fully unitized body, the body itself supports (*a*) engine, (*b*) transmission, (*c*) wheels, (*d*) tires.
2. When straightening a frame, there are (*a*) three controlling points, (*b*) three reference points. (*c*) four sections, (*d*) four controlling points.
3. Sidesway, sag, and mash are types of (*a*) frame construction, (*b*) body-frame misalignment, (*c*) front-end collision, (*d*) body-frame assembly.
4. To check a unitized body for alignment, check the (*a*) frame, (*b*) door fit, (*c*) sills and rails, (*d*) glass and regulators.
5. A car that fails to track has a (*a*) flat tire, (*b*) bent frame, (*c*) broken spring, (*d*) defective shock absorber.

QUESTIONS Write each of the following questions, and then the answer, in your notebook. If you have trouble recalling the answer to a question, turn back to the pages that cover the material and study them again.

1. Which do you do first, straighten the body or straighten the frame?
2. How do you decide where to make the pulls?
3. Why are the body bolts left tight when straightening a frame?
4. What is a diamond frame, and how is it caused?
5. How are the reference measurement points used?

SUGGESTIONS FOR FURTHER STUDY

Find a shop that is doing a lot of frame work. Closely watch the technician do several jobs. Note the way the car is set up for the pulls and note the tools that are used. If you can, ask the technician if there are any other tools or setups that could be used to make the same correction. No two wrecked cars are exactly alike. As you watch, decide in your own mind how you would make each repair. Then check yourself as you see how the professional technician corrects the damage.

17 USING THE BODY AND FRAME STRAIGHTENER

After the preliminary work discussed in the previous chapters is completed, the body technician knows what must be done to straighten the body and frame and restore alignment. After this, the sheet metal must be repaired and painted. In this chapter, we discuss the various types of body-frame straighteners and how to use them. Earlier chapters described sheet-metal repair. Following chapters explain how to prime and paint automotive vehicles.

○ 17-1 Hydraulic Principles

Body and frame straighteners operate on hydraulic principles. The word "hydraulic" means of or pertaining to liquids such as water and oil. Our special interest, so far as body-frame straighteners are concerned, is in the pressure that can be developed in liquids. This is called *hydraulic pressure*.

Note first that movement can be transmitted from a piston in one cylinder to a piston in another cylinder (Fig. 17-1). As the piston in cylinder A is moved, the liquid flows through a tube to cylinder B, forcing the piston in cylinder B to move.

Pressure can be transmitted by a liquid (Fig. 17-2). If the piston shown in Fig. 17-2 has an area of 1 square inch, and if it is pushed with a force of 100 pounds, the pressure on the liquid is 100 pounds per square inch (100 psi). Regardless of where we take the reading, the pressure is the same throughout the hydraulic system.

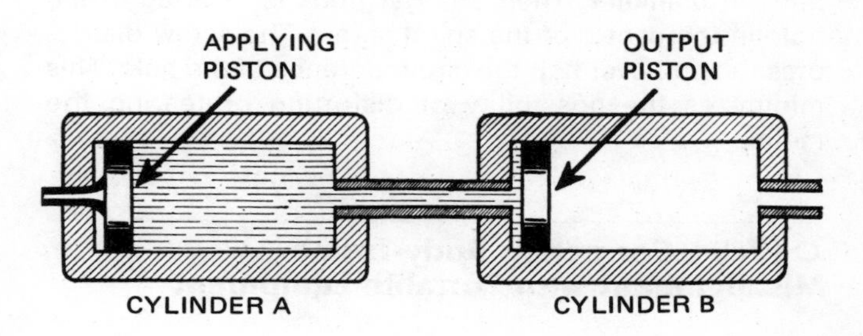

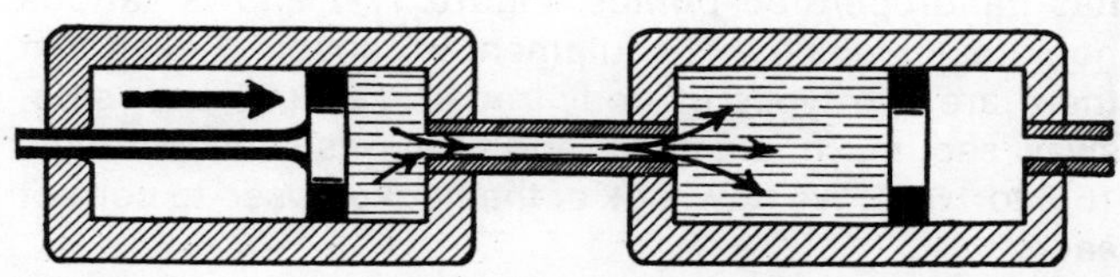

FIGURE 17-1. Motion can be transmitted through a tube from one cylinder to another by liquid, or hydraulic, pressure. (*Pontiac Motor Division of General Motors Corporation*)

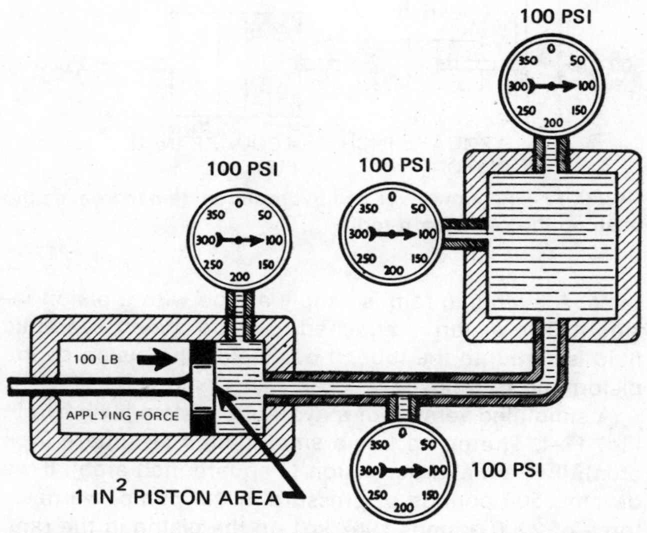

FIGURE 17-2. The pressure applied to a liquid is transmitted equally in all directions. (*Pontiac Motor Division of General Motors Corporation*)

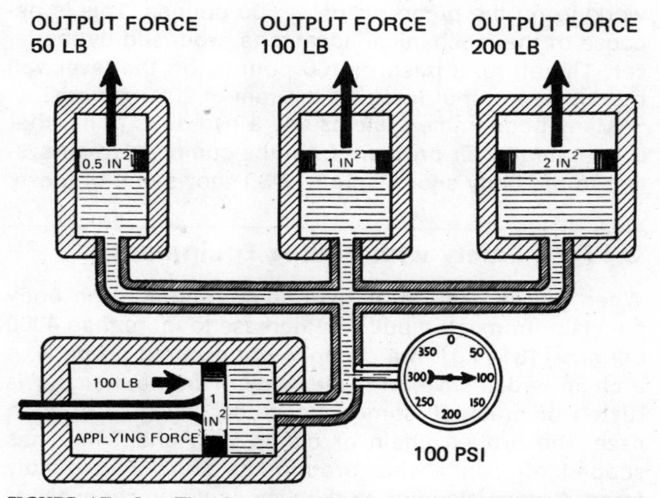

FIGURE 17-3. The force applied to the output piston is the pressure in the system in pounds per square inch (kg/cm^2) times the area of the output piston. (*Pontiac Motor Division of General Motors Corporation*)

Figure 17-3 shows how the same pressure can be used to produce different output forces. The bigger the output piston, the greater the output force. For example, the output piston to the right has an area of 2 square inches. Since the pressure is 100 pounds for each square inch, the total pressure on this piston is 200 pounds.

Now let us apply this to a hydraulic system used in body-frame equipment. This equipment uses hydraulic

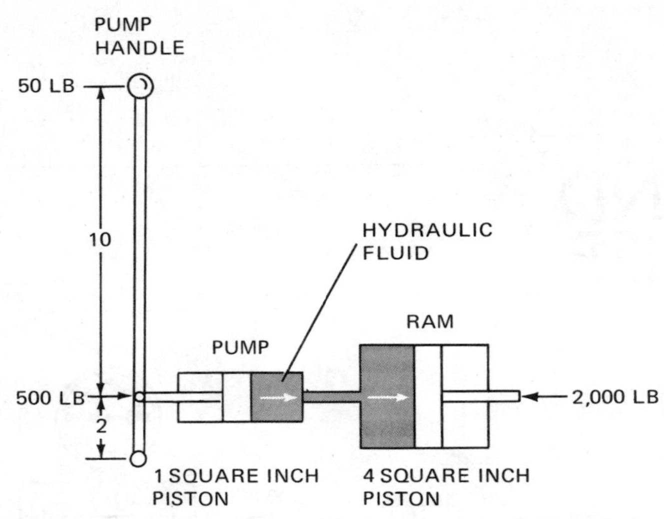

FIGURE 17–4. How lever and hydraulic system increases the push on the ram piston rod.

rams. A hydraulic ram is simply a tube with a piston inside it. The piston is attached to a rod. When hydraulic fluid is sent into the tube, it pushes on the piston so the piston and rod move.

A simplified version of a hydraulic system is shown in Fig. 17-4. The pump has a small piston (1 square inch area), the ram a larger piston (4 square inch area). If we develop 500 pounds of pressure in the pump, we get a force of 2000 pounds [907 kg] on the piston in the ram. First, let us consider the effect of the pump handle, or lever—or how we can get 500 pounds of force on the pump piston. If you push on the lever at the point, shown by the arrow, with a force of 50 pounds, the pressure working on the pump piston is 500 pounds. This is because of the mechanical advantage produced by the lever. Therefore, a push of 100 pounds on the lever will produce an output force on the ram of 2000 pounds.

Many body-frame systems use a hydraulic pump that is operated by air pressure from the compressed-air system in the body shop. Figure 17-30 shows one of these.

○ 17-2 Safety with Pulling Equipment

When pull is exerted by hydraulic equipment on body panels or frame, the pull can increase to more than 4000 pounds [1814 kg]. If a clamp is not secured properly, if a chain is defective, or if the body or frame member is rusted or cracked, something could "let go." In such case, the broken chain or clamp with chain that has slipped off could whip around the shop with deadly force. Anyone standing in the way could be seriously or fatally injured. For that reason, we list several special safety cautions you should observe when working with pulling equipment.

1. When using a clamp on a body part, make sure that the undercoating is removed so the clamp gets a firm hold on the metal and will not slip.
2. Make sure that the clamp teeth are clean and sharp so they will grip well. They should be cleaned periodically with a wire brush.
3. Check the clamps and chain for wear before each use. Worn clamps and chains with nicked or otherwise damaged links should be replaced.
4. Be careful about attaching a clamp to a rusted panel. The panel may be so weak it will pull apart with very little tension. You can help here by tack-welding a supporting brace across the weakened part.
5. If the vehicle is on a stand when it is pulled, make sure it is tied down securely so it will not roll off.
6. Double up on the chain, using two in parallel, for extra heavy pulls.
7. Cover the chain and clamp with a heavy blanket. If anything lets go, the blanket will help muffle the chain and clamp and prevent it from whipping.
8. Never stand in a direct line with chains.

○ 17-3 Types of Body-Frame Straighteners

There are two general types of body-frame straighteners: portable and stationary. They were illustrated and described in Chapter 8. See ○ 8-5 to 8-7 and Figs. 8-8 to 8-21 to review the two types and their possible uses.

In our discussions of body and frame straightening, we will first describe how the portable straightener is used. Then we will cover the use of the stationary type.

Note that sometimes the pull is on the sheet metal and sometimes it is on the frame.

○ 17-4 Types of Attachment

Most attachments for pulling body metal are clamps, such as shown in Fig. 14-4. These are usually attached by drilling holes in the sheet metal to accommodate the clamp bolts. (Some clamps attach without drilling holes.) Then the clamp is bolted to the metal and the pull applied.

Hooks are often used to pull on the frame. They can be inserted in reference or structural holes in the frame members. A variety of clamps that can be attached in various ways to body and frame parts are shown in Fig. 17-5. Figure 17-6 shows another type of hookup. Its components include finger hooks, spiral screws, wedge tips, and hook extensions. Note that the spiral screw can be screwed into a hole from 1 to 1½ inches [25.4 to 38.1 mm] in diameter. Then a finger hook is inserted in the hole in the center of the spiral screw. The screw distributes the pull over half the circumference of the hole. This minimizes the possibility of distorting or tearing the metal.

○ 17-5 Correcting Body-Frame Misalignment with Portable Equipment

Now let us look at alignment procedures using portable equipment, such as shown in Fig. 8-8. Note that this unit has hand-operated pumps. Figure 17-7 shows various hookups of which this equipment is capable. Recall that there are five types of body-frame misalignment—sidesway, sag, mash, diamond, and twist—as shown in Figs. 16-8 to 16-16. We now look at the hookup used to correct each.

As a general rule, you want to apply pull in a direction the reverse of the direction of the force that caused the damage. Visualize the damage and the impact that

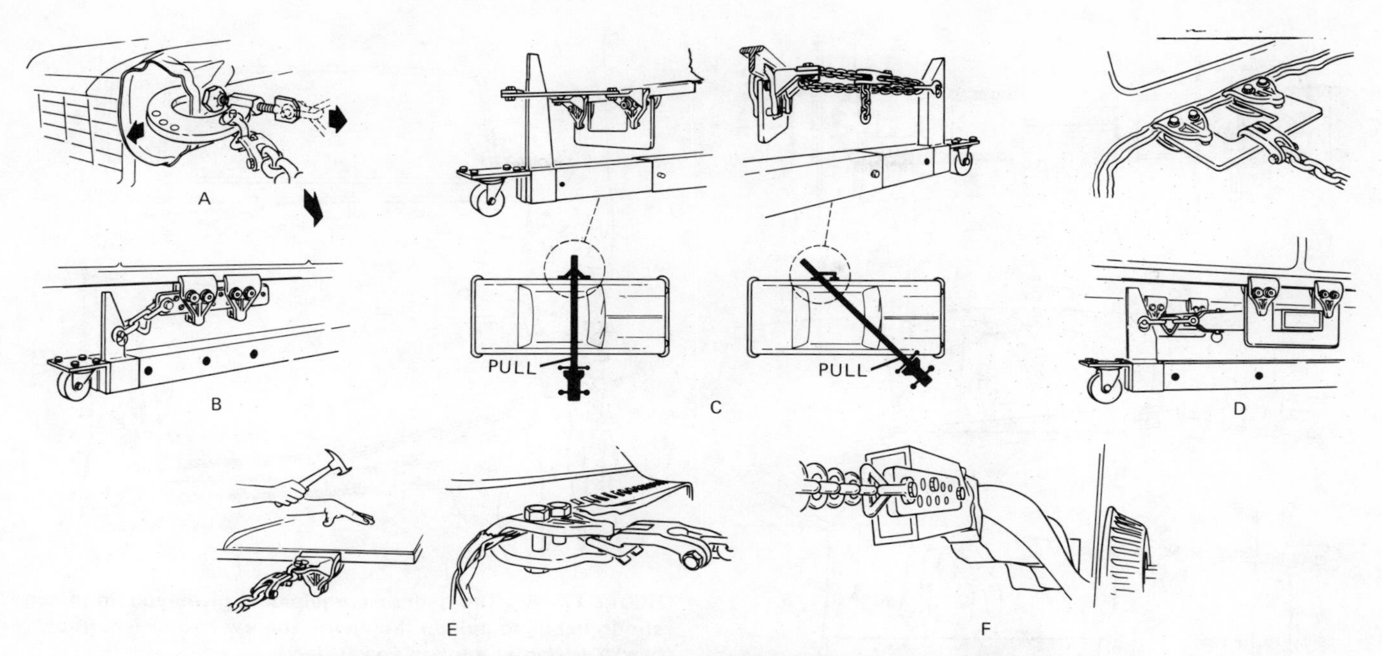

FIGURE 17–5. Various types of clamps and how they can be used. (A) "C" clamp, (B) rack clamp, (C) double-scott clamp with bars, (D) double-scott clamp, (E) single-scott clamp, (F) drawbar. (*Guy Chart*)

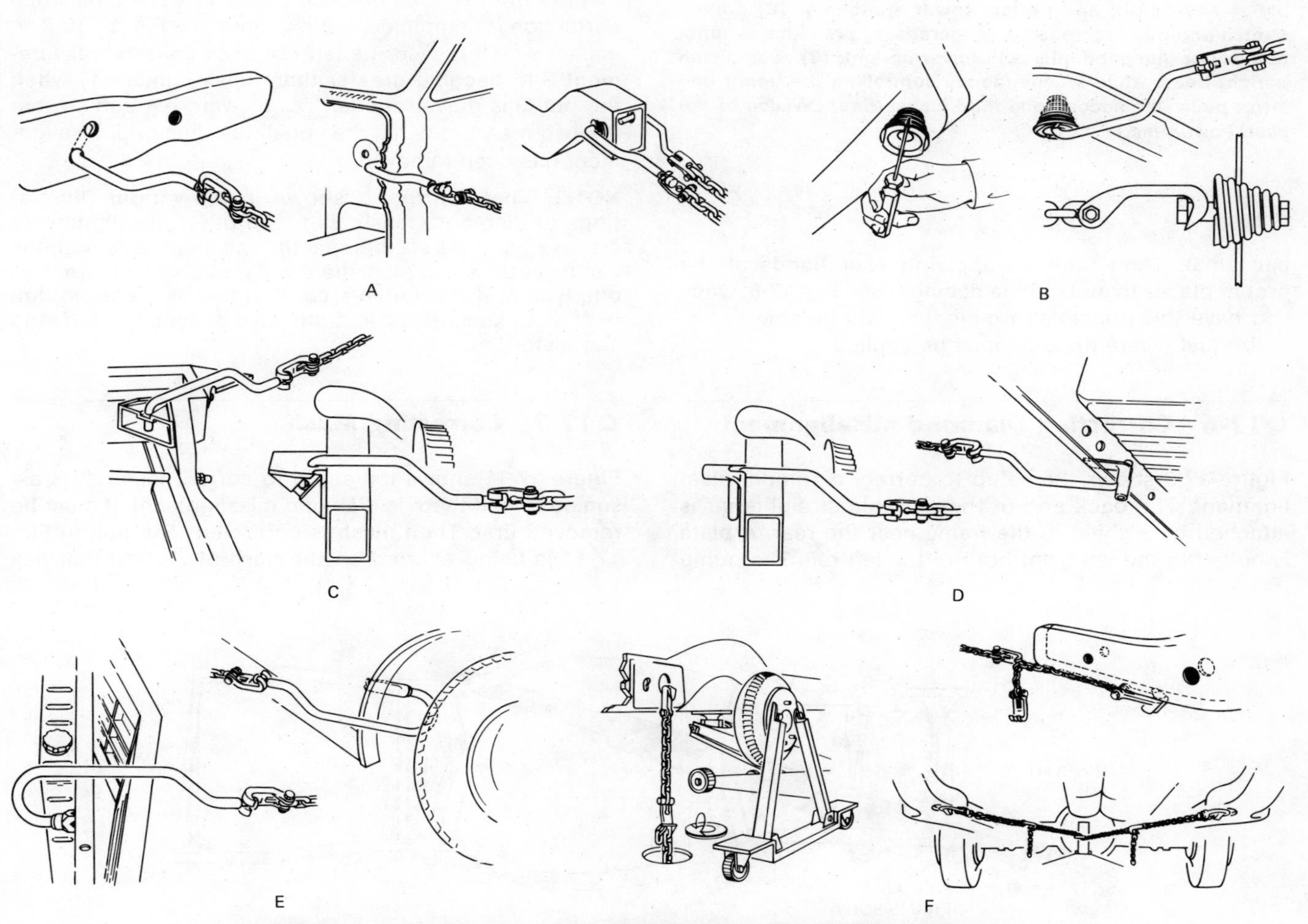

FIGURE 17–6. Another type of hookup for making pulls on body and frame. (A) finger hooks, (B) spiral screw, (C) wedge tip, (D) hook extension, (E) utility tip and extension wedge, (F) plug hook (anchor) assembly. (*Guy Chart*)

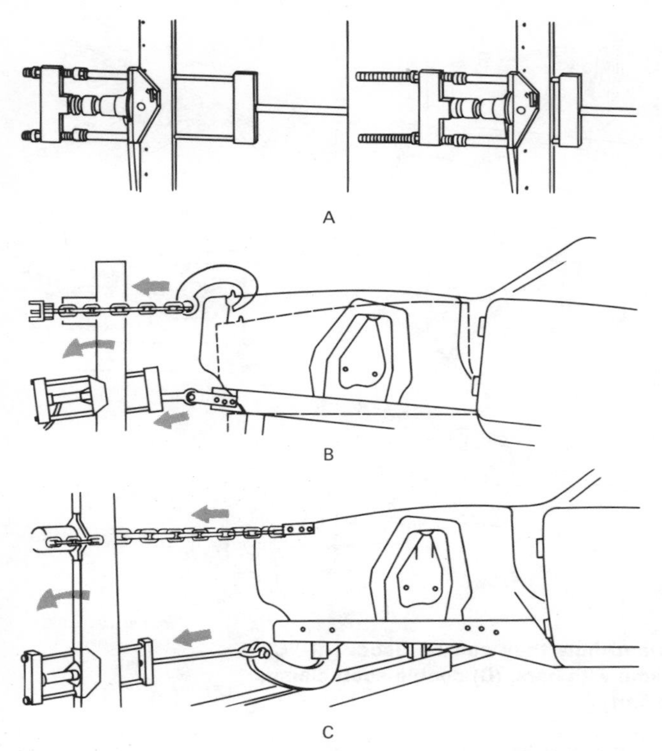

FIGURE 17–7. **Various pulls that can be made with portable equipment. (A) 10-inch [254-mm] pull at pull-yoke with assembly at any height and upright tower stationary; (B) double stretch-and-pull, decreasing or increasing pressure simultaneously or independently with tower upright; (C) pulling with upright beam while independently controlling the upper and lower pulls with second and third jacks. (*Bear Division of Applied Power, Inc.*)**

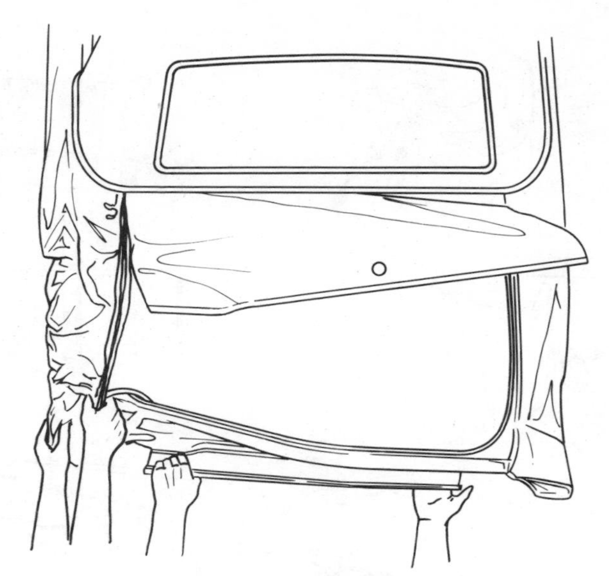

FIGURE 17–8. **The hydraulic equipment gives you, in effect, strong hands to pull on the metal wherever you wish. (*Blackhawk Division of Applied Power, Inc.*)**

caused it. Then think of applying your hands at the proper places to pull out the damage. See Fig. 17-8. Once you have this principle in mind, you will be able to visualize just where the pull must be applied.

○ 17-6 Correcting Diamond Misalignment

Figure 17-9 shows the setup to correct diamond misalignment. The back end of the portable straightener is attached by a chain to the frame near the rear. A plate is bolted to the left front horn of the left rail. The pump is then operated to exert a pull on the left side rail. This will generally pull the rail back into line. During the straightening procedure, you will be taking measurements from various reference points to determine when correction is completed. For example, see Fig. 17-10. The impact which moved the left rail back caused measurement 2 to become greater than measurement 1. When the pull has moved the left rail forward enough so that the two measurements are equal, the diamond misalignment has been removed.

NOTE: The distortions, shown in the various illustrations of diamond, mash, sag, and other misalignments are exaggerated so the specific misaligned conditions can be easily seen. Also, there will probably be more than one type of distortion in a car that has had a severe impact. For example, a car might have diamond, mash, and sag distortion.

○ 17-7 Correcting Mash

Figure 17-11 shows the setup to correct mash. It is assumed that, if there is diamond misalignment, it must be removed first. Then mash is corrected. The pull in Fig. 17-11 is being exerted on the horn of the rail that has

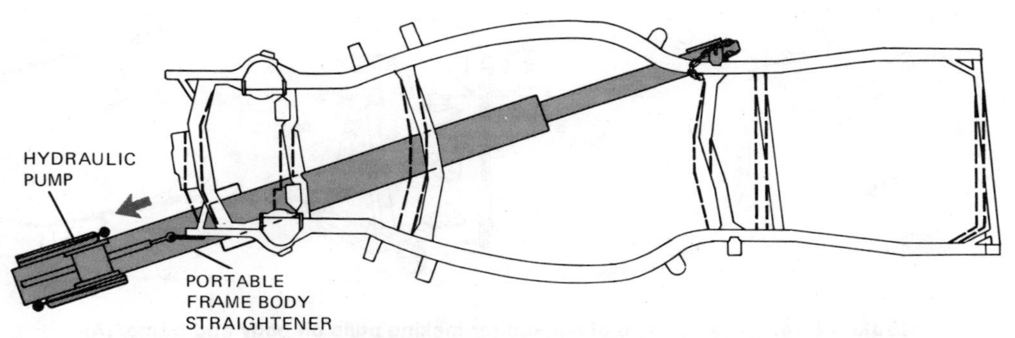

FIGURE 17–9. **Setup to correct diamond misalignment. (*Bear Division of Applied Power, Inc.*)**

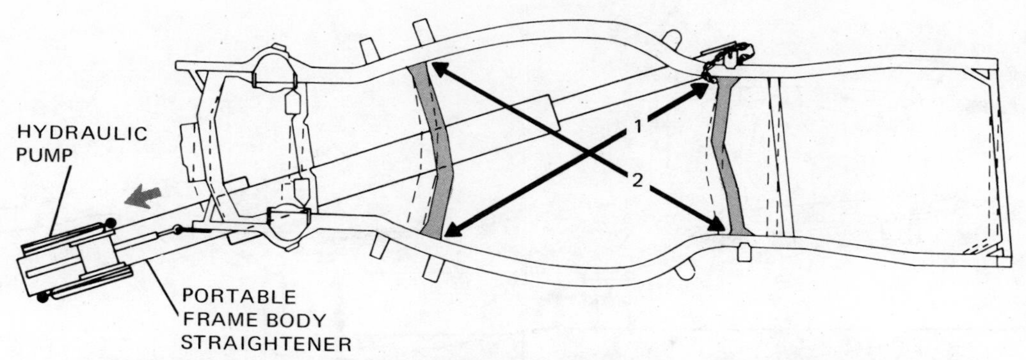

FIGURE 17–10. The impact that produced the diamond misalignment caused measurement 2 to become greater than measurement 1. When the two measurements are the same, the misalignment has been corrected. (*Bear Division of Applied Power, Inc.*)

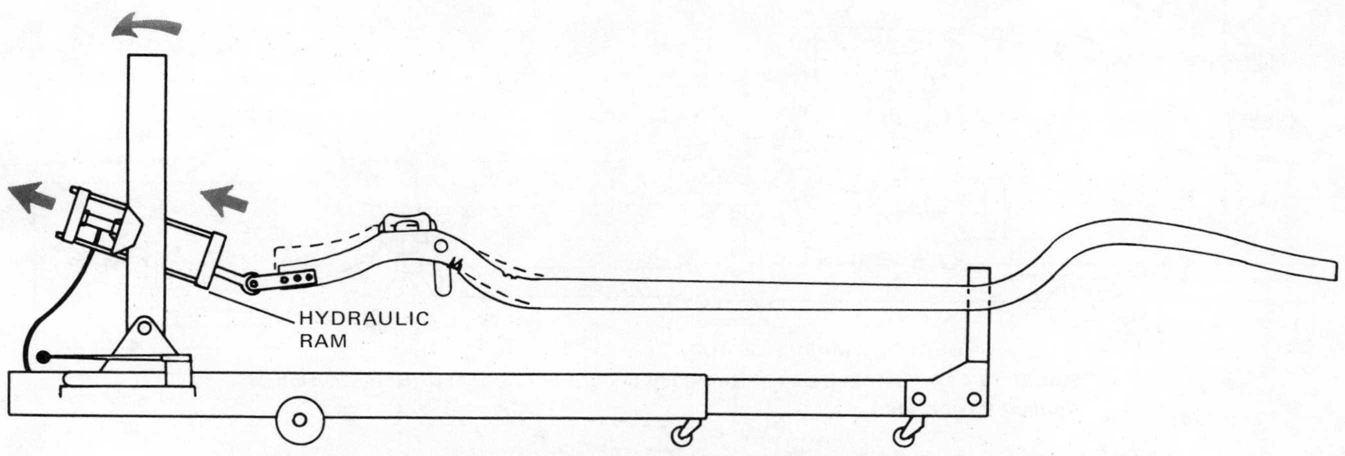

FIGURE 17–11. Pull to correct mash. (*Bear Division of Applied Power, Inc.*)

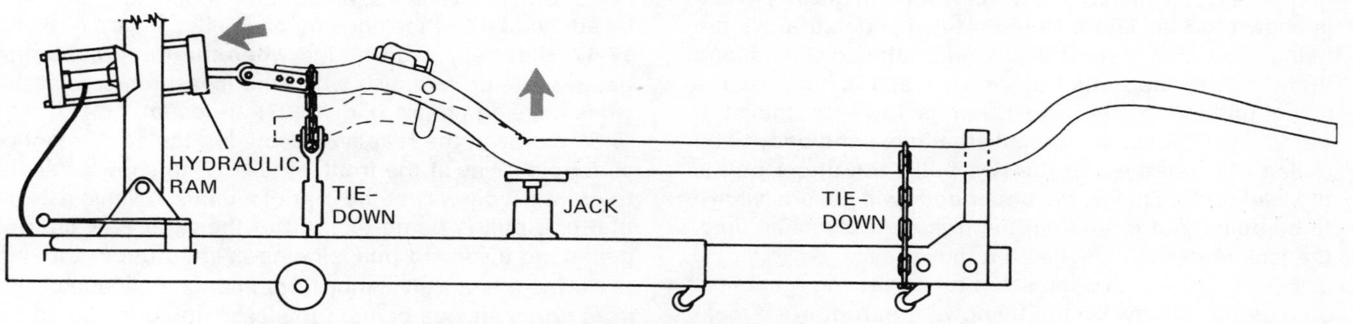

FIGURE 17–12. Pull to correct sag. (*Bear Division of Applied Power, Inc.*)

been mashed. When it is pulled out to the same dimension as the other rail, the mash has been corrected. Mash at the rear is corrected in the same manner, except that the connections are reversed. To correct mash on unitized cars, refer to ○ 17-8 Correcting Sag.

○ 17-8 Correcting Sag

Figure 17-12 shows the setup to correct sag. Generally, sag and mash occur together. As a rail is mashed in, it tends to sag at some point. Sag and mash are removed at the same time. The basic difference between the procedures for removing them is the direction in which the pull is exerted. Study Figs. 17-11 and 17-12. Note how an upward pull is used to correct mash and a downward pull is used to correct sag. Also, note in Fig. 17-12 that a jack has been placed under the rail at the cowl area. In addition, there is a tie-down at the front and another at the rear-door area. These are required to assure that, when the pull is exerted, the rail will be bent downward to the straightened position.

If heavy pressure is required, always use steel plates between the jack and chains and the frame. The plates

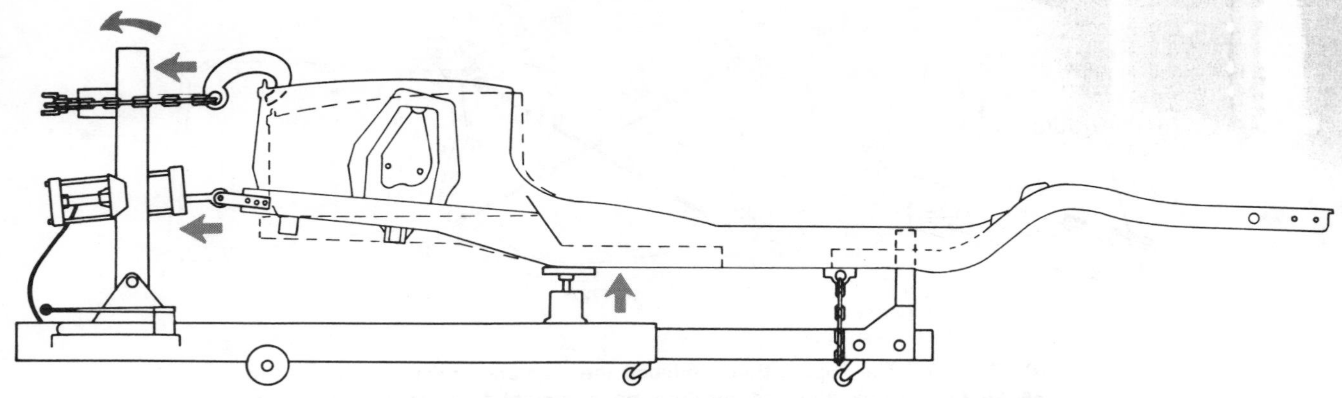

FIGURE 17–13. Hookup to correct front end mash and sag. (*Bear Division of Applied Power, Inc.*)

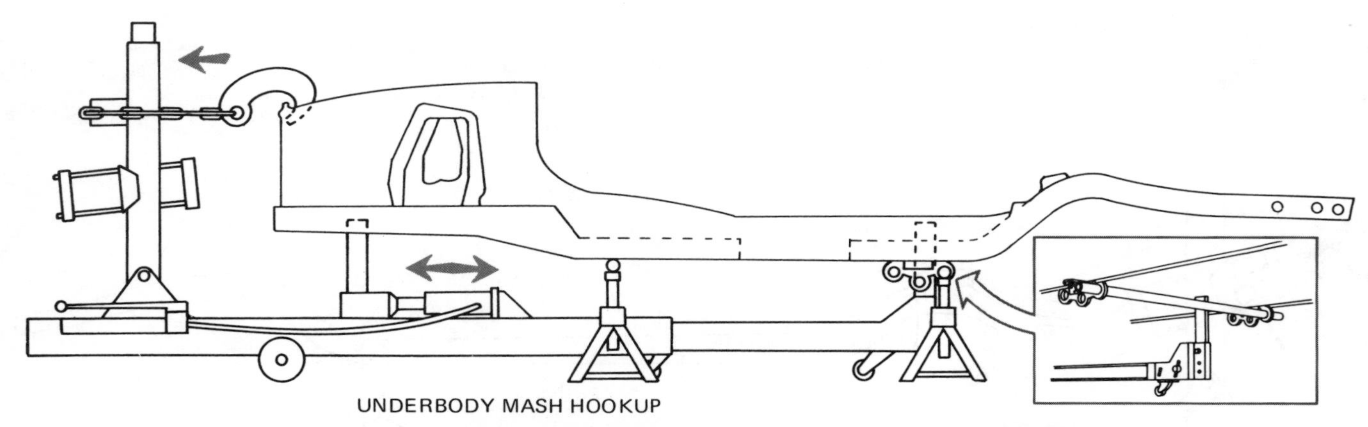

FIGURE 17–14. Hookup on unitized body to correct rear mash. (*Bear Division of Applied Power, Inc.*)

spread the pressure away from the center point and prevent the rail from being crushed at that point.

For unitized vehicles, sag and mash are treated together. A typical setup to correct front-end mash and sag is shown in Fig. 17-13. Note that two separate pulls are being used, that there is a jack under the cowl area, and that the rear end is tied down. One pull is high—at the wheelhousing panel. The other is low—on the stub frame. This double pull permits the frame and body to be pulled out together. Of the two pulls, the upper pull is the lead force. That is, the upper body will generally have to be pulled out more than the frame. At the same time, the jack under the cowl area removes sag.

Figure 17-14 shows the setup for correcting rear mash on a unitized body. Do not tie down the front when making this correction, because this could cause the roof to crease.

NOTE: Padding for unitized bodies should be wood blocks. Wood offers greater protection for body rails and sills when placed between tie-downs and jacks.

○ 17-9 Correcting Sidesway

Once diamond, sag, and mash misalignment have been corrected, sidesway should be eliminated. Figure 17-15 shows the setup to correct sidesway on a vehicle with a full frame. Note that the sidesway has affected the front part of the frame clear back to the cowl area.

The three centering gauges should be in place, as shown in Figs. 16-17 and 16-22. Sidesway is corrected when the three gauges line up.

For unitized vehicles, an additional pulling force must be added to the wheelhousing panel. See Figs. 17-16 and 17-17. Sidesway is corrected when the three centering gauges line up and also when the measurements at the wheelhousing panels (Fig. 16-27) are equal.

Sidesway at the rear is corrected in the same manner as for sidesway at the front. Figure 17-18 shows a setup to correct sidesway at the rear of a unitized vehicle. Note that one pull is being exerted at the right rear quarter panel and a second pull is being exerted under the car.

During a relatively minor front impact, only one of the front horns may be bent. In this case, the pull should be made against this horn alone to straighten it. Figure 17-19 shows pull being exerted on the right front horn. The rod stuck through holes in the horn is to prevent the chain from slipping back.

○ 17-10 Correcting Twist

If a frame has been twisted, as shown in Fig. 17-20 (exaggerated in the illustration), an untwisting force must be applied, as shown. In the setup, two jacks are used to apply pressure and bring the two rails back into alignment. The centering gauges should be installed (see Fig. 16-19), and the condition is corrected when they line up.

Figure 17-21 shows the setup for a unitized vehicle.

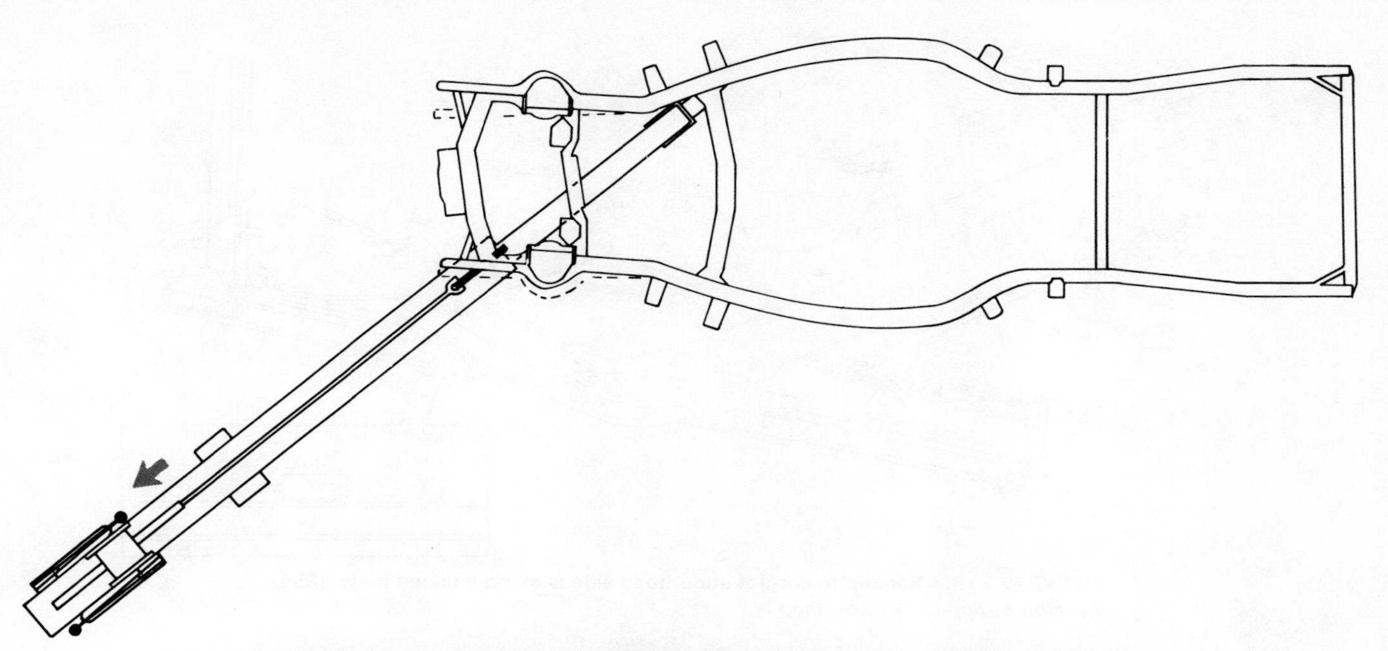

FIGURE 17–15. Hookup on car with frame to correct sidesway. (*Bear Division of Applied Power, Inc.*)

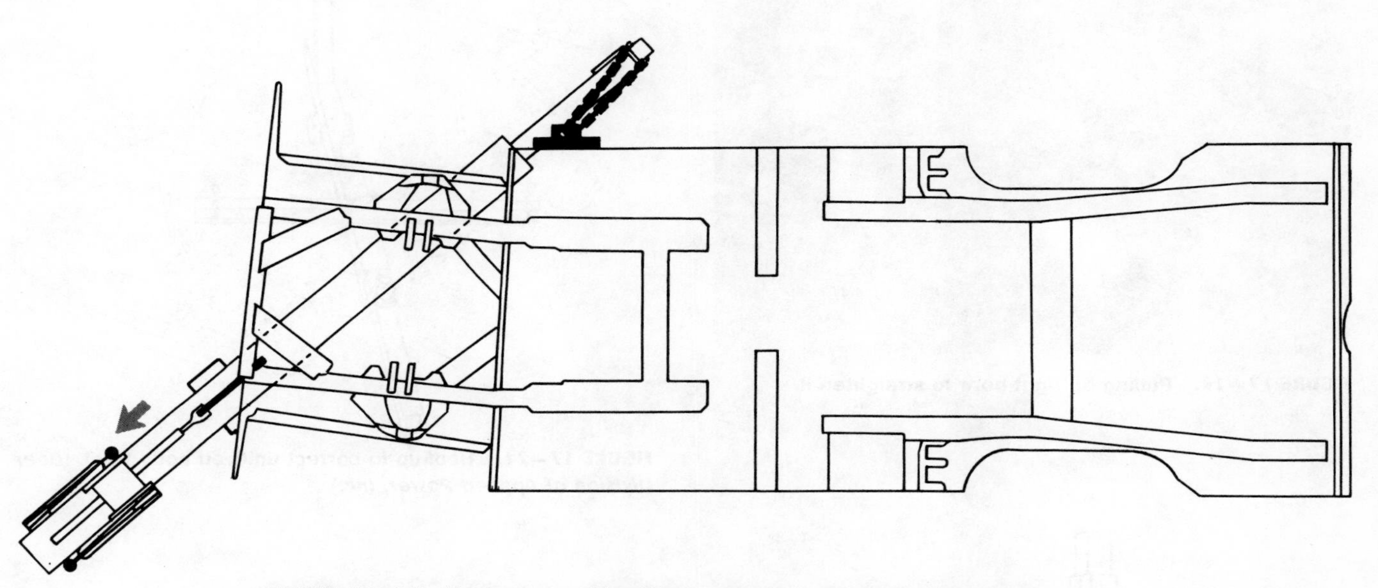

FIGURE 17–16. Hookup on unitized body to correct sidesway. (*Bear Division of Applied Power, Inc.*)

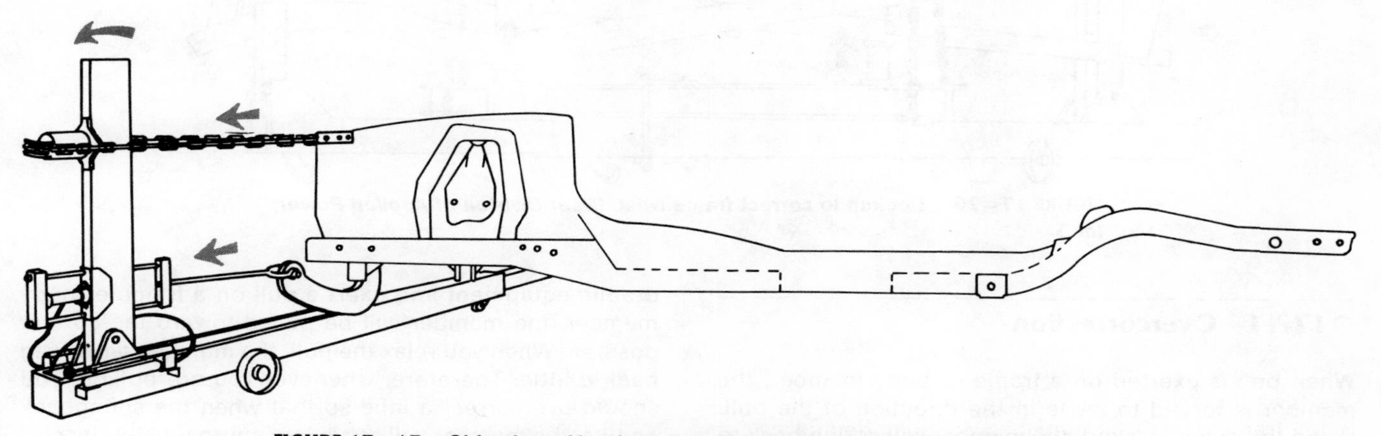

FIGURE 17–17. Side view of hookup on unitized body to correct sidesway. (*Bear Division of Applied Power, Inc.*)

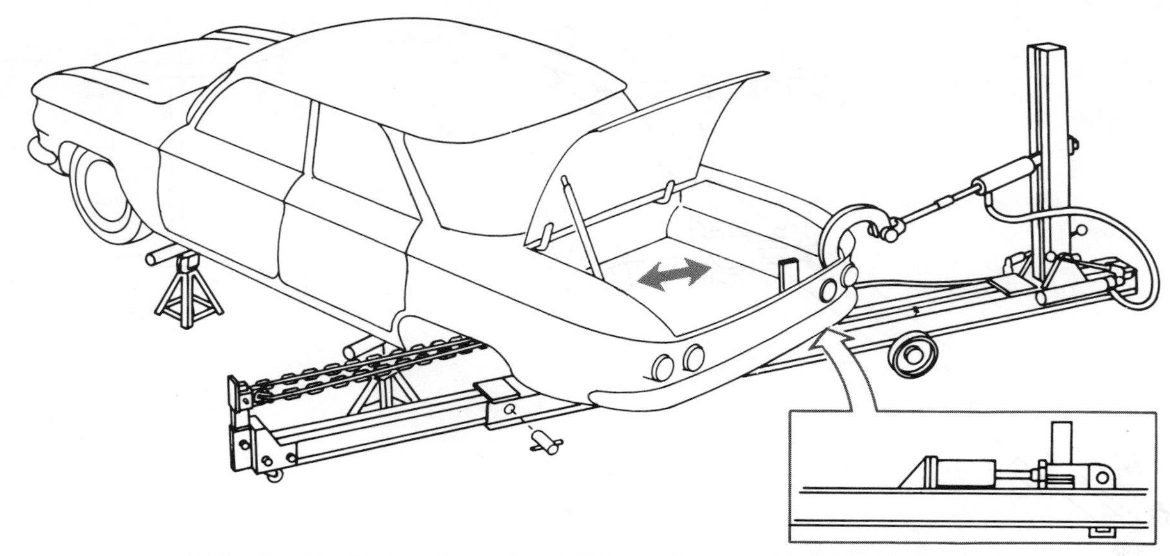

FIGURE 17–18. Hookup to correct underbody sidesway on unitized body. (*Bear Division of Applied Power, Inc.*)

FIGURE 17–19. Pulling on right horn to straighten it.

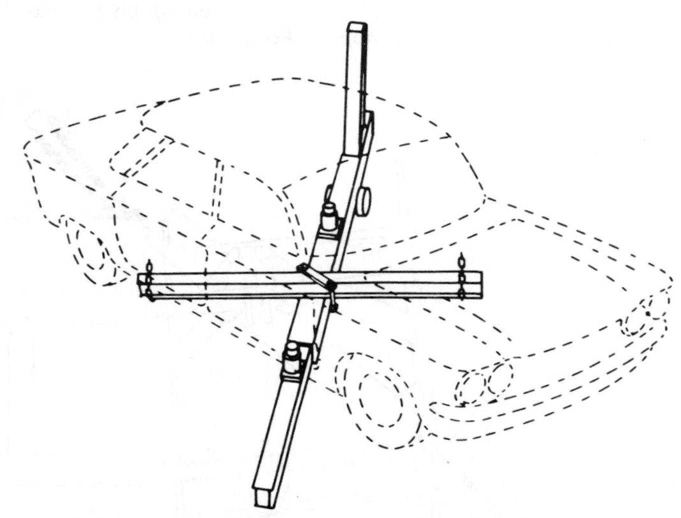

FIGURE 17–21. Hookup to correct unitized body twist. (*Bear Division of Applied Power, Inc.*)

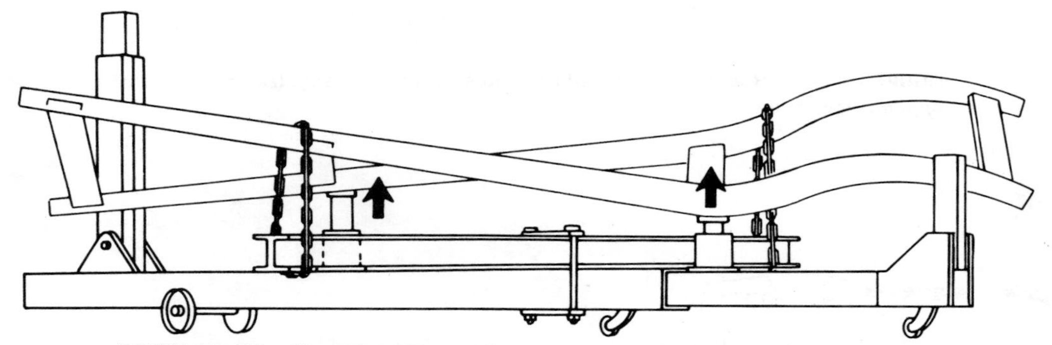

FIGURE 17–20. Hookup to correct frame twist. (*Bear Division of Applied Power, Inc.*)

○17-11 Overcorrection

When pull is exerted on a frame or body member, the member is forced to move in the direction of the pull. When the pull is relaxed, the member will spring back to some extent. This means that when you attach the hydraulic equipment and exert a pull on a frame or body member, the member will be pulled toward the correct position. When you relax the pull, the member will spring back a little. Therefore, whenever you are pulling, you should overcorrect a little so that when the springback occurs, the member will settle into approximately its correct position. The amount of overcorrection needed is something you have to learn from experience. If you don't pull quite enough, the springback will carry the member back too far. But if you pull too much, you are apt to damage or tear the metal.

○17-12 Upper-Body Pulls

Figures 17-22 and 17-23 show upper-body pulls. In Fig. 17-22, the pull is being made at the door post. In Fig. 17-23, the pull is being made at the front of the roof panel. Figure 17-24 shows a portable straightener which is able to hold in two places and pull in a third to straighten a door post.

○17-13 Types of Stationary Body-Frame Equipment

There are three basic types of stationary body-frame straightening equipment:

STATIONARY BODY-FRAME EQUIPMENT

1. Anchor pot. This type, shown in Figs. 8-11 to 8-18, provides stationary anchor pots in the floor. Anchor pots are positioned in the floor so that pulls can be exerted on the body or fender from many angles. The car must be maneuvered so it is properly located within the anchor pots. Then the proper hookups and directional pulls can be made. Actual pulls for various straightening operations are very similar to those made with the track-type system, which is described later.
2. Track. This type, shown in Figs. 8-21 to 8-23, has tracks set into or anchored onto the floor. The chain anchors can be slid along the tracks to provide pull at any point and in any direction desired. Then a hydraulic ram is brought into position, as shown in Fig. 17-25 in dotted line. As the ram is extended by hydraulic action, a strong pull is exerted on the chain, as shown. We describe the procedure for using this equipment later.

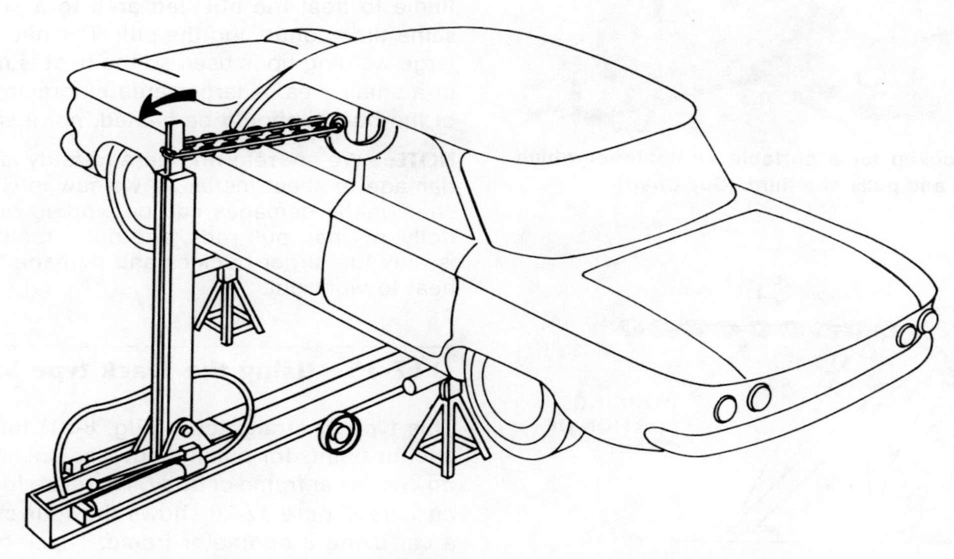

FIGURE 17–22. Hookup for door-post roof-panel pull. ***(Bear Division of Applied Power, Inc.)***

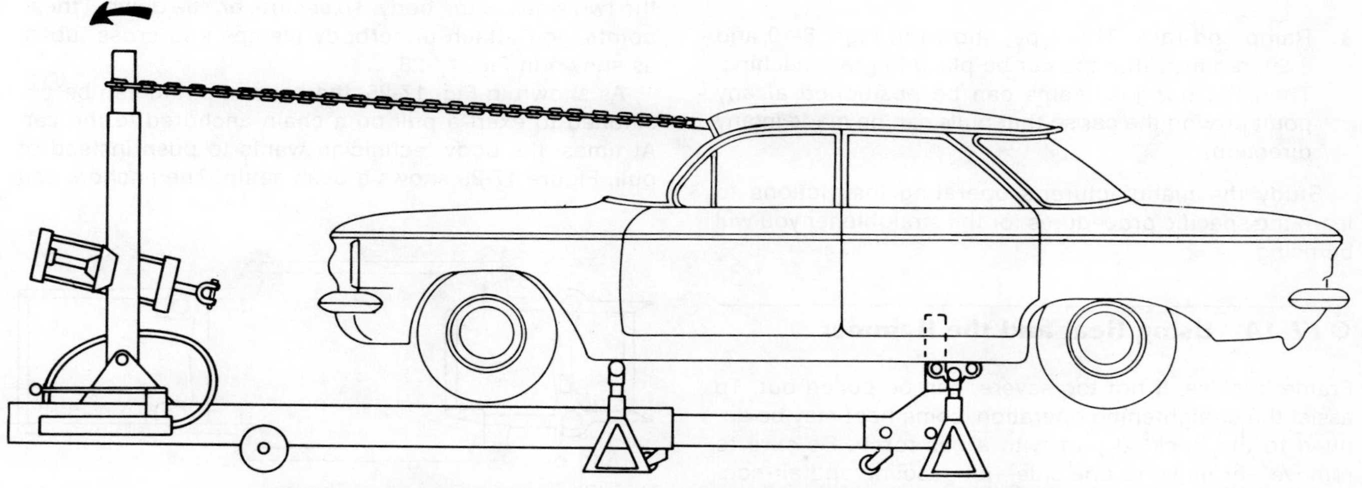

FIGURE 17–23. Hookup for roof pull at front. ***(Bear Division of Applied Power, Inc.)***

FIGURE 17–24. Hookup for a portable straightener which holds in two places and pulls at a third. (*Guy Chart*)

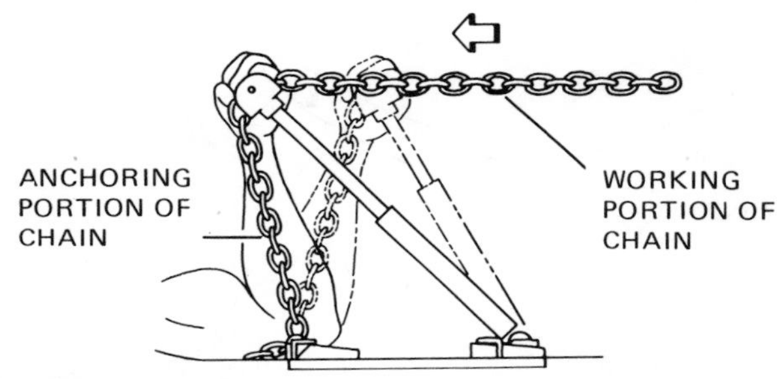

FIGURE 17–25. Showing the principle of the chain and ram action. As the ram extends, it pulls on the working portion of the chain. (*Guy Chart*)

3. Ramp and rack. This type, shown in Figs. 8-19 and 8-20, requires that the car be placed in the machine. Then the upright beams can be positioned at any point around the car so that pulls can be made in any direction.

Study the manufacturer's operating instructions to learn the specific procedures for the straightener you will be using.

○ 17-14 Using Heat and the Hammer

Frame buckles, if not too severe, can be pulled out. To assist the straightening operation, some heat may be applied to the buckled part with a gas torch. Be sure to remove—or move to one side—all gasoline and air-conditioning lines so they will not be heated. A fuel line heated by the torch could break, and you would have a serious gasoline fire. Likewise, an overheated air-conditioner line or component, if overheated, could burst, releasing refrigerant. The refrigerant, expanding as it is released, could freeze anything it touches—hands, face, eyes. Also, the refrigerant, in the presence of an open flame, turns into a deadly poisonous gas. So exercise caution regarding fuel and air-conditioner lines.

Ford Motor Company says that if heat is needed to straighten a frame member, the temperature of the metal should be kept below 1200°F [649°C]. Excessive heat can so weaken the metal that the member could fail later on the highway.

As the buckle is heated, further pull can be applied. The general rule is to pull the member somewhat beyond proper alignment, because it will tend to relax or spring back when the pull is released.

Sheet metal is often tapped with a body hammer when it is being pulled. This helps release the set of the metal. One recommendation (by Bear) is that while the pull is being exerted on the panel, tap around the buckle and continue to pull until a silver streak begins to appear in the heart of the buckle. Then apply heat from a neutral flame to heat the buckled area to a cherry red, at the same time continuing the pull. The neutral flame from a large welding tip is used so the heat is not concentrated in a small area. A larger area embracing the worst part of the buckle should be heated, not a small spot.

NOTE: We are referring here to fairly large buckles and damage to sheet metal. As we saw in Chapter 15, many sheet-metal damages can be worked out with hammer, dolly, pry bar, pull rods, and other tools without heat. It is only the larger buckles and damage that may require heat to work out.

○ 17-15 Using the Track-type Straightener

This type of straightener (Fig. 8-21) furnishes not only anchor points for pulling, but also anchor points to hold down the car frame or body. There are four anchor points on cars. Figure 17-26 shows the four anchor points on a car using a perimeter frame. These points are at the cowl and rear-door area. These are the four points at which hold-down chains can be attached. See Fig. 17-27.

In unitized cars, the four anchor points are at the ends of the rocker sills. These are the two sills that run along the two sides of the body. To secure, or "tie down," these points, you attach underbody clamps and cross tubes, as shown in Fig. 17-28.

As shown in Fig. 17-25, the hydraulic ram can be positioned to exert a pull on a chain anchored to the car. At times, the body technician wants to push instead of pull. Figure 17-29 shows a push setup. The anchors can

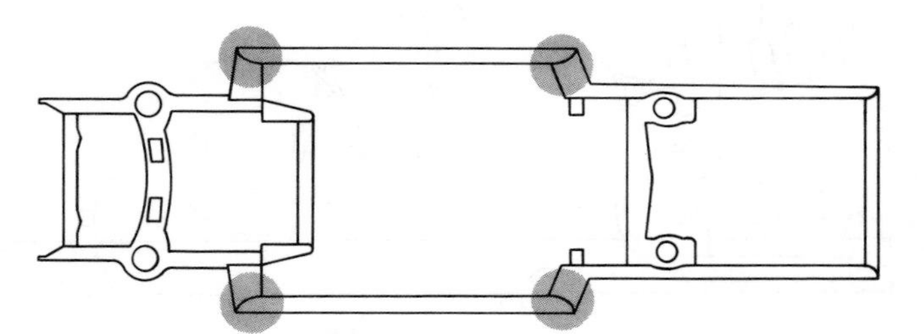

FIGURE 17–26. Four anchor points on a car with a perimeter frame. (*Blackhawk Division of Applied Power, Inc.*)

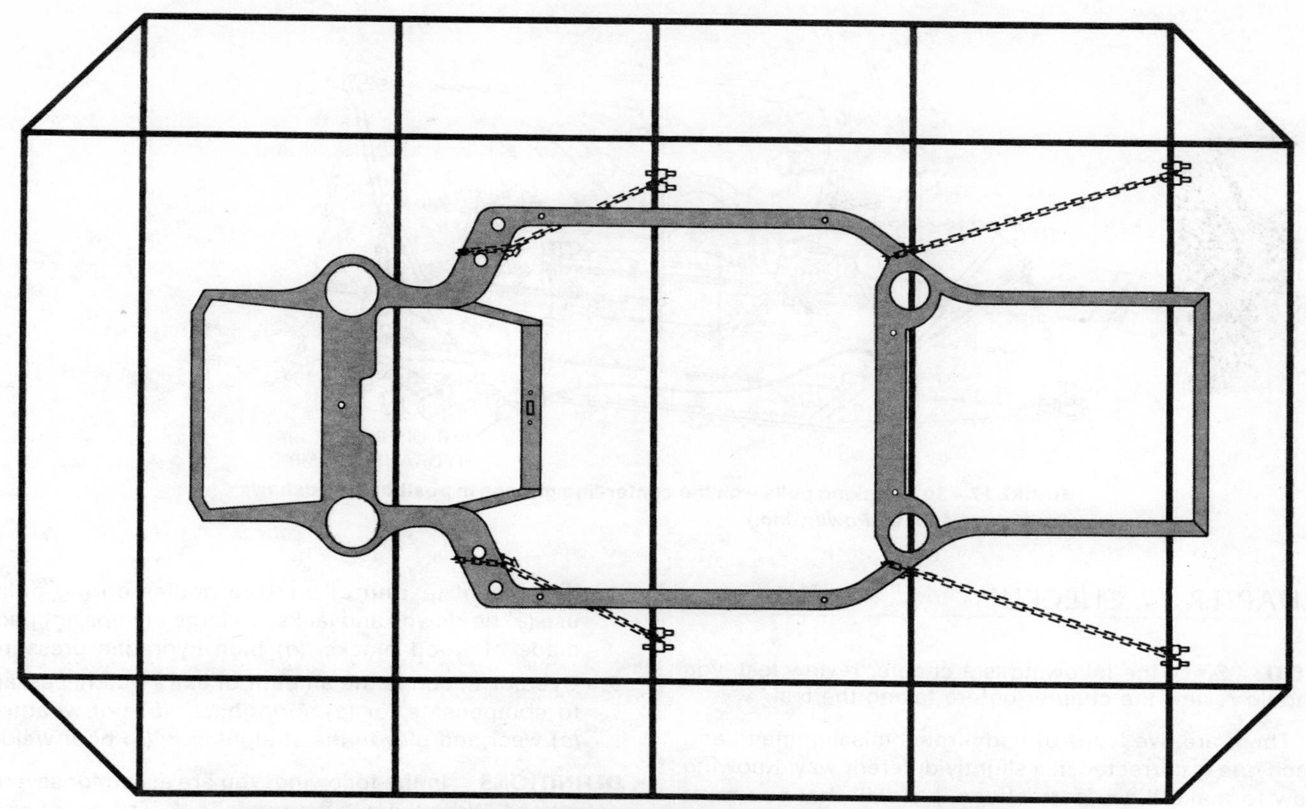

FIGURE 17–27. Attachment points for hold-down chains on a perimeter frame. ***(Blackhawk Division of Applied Power, Inc.)***

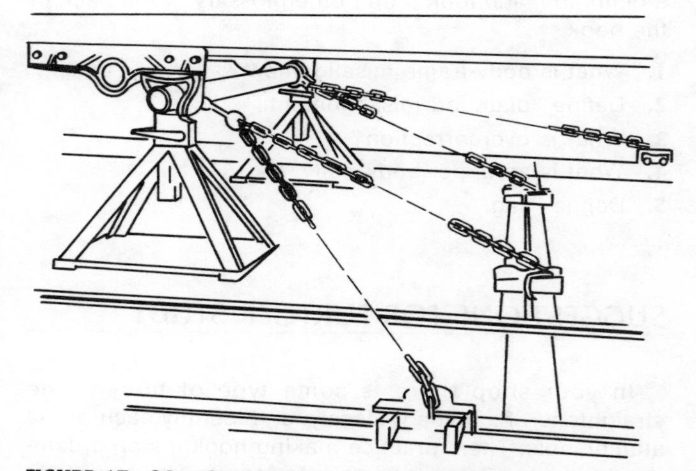

FIGURE 17–28. Attachment of underbody clamps and cross tube to get the necessary hold-downs on a unitized body. ***(Blackhawk Division of Applied Power, Inc.)***

be slid along the track into any position that gives the pull or push desired. Figure 17-30 shows a car being straightened. The center-line gauges are in place so the technician can observe the amount of straightening being done. When the pointers line up, *after the pull is relaxed*, the technician knows alignment has been achieved.

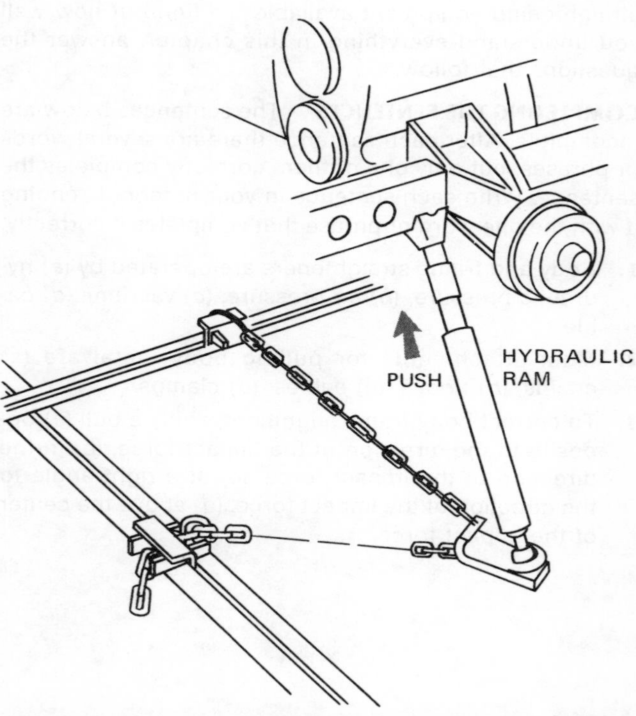

FIGURE 17–29. Setup for making a push from underneath the car. (*Blackhawk Division of Applied Power, Inc.*)

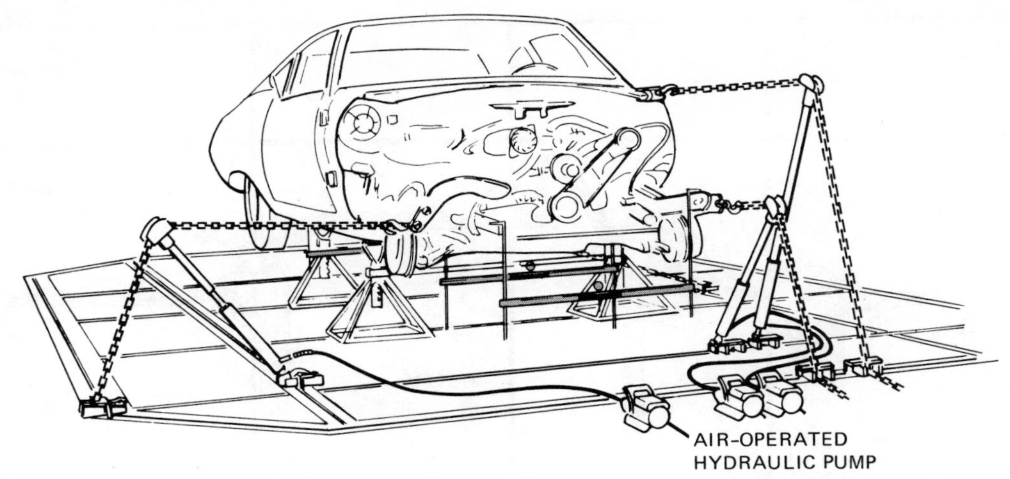

FIGURE 17-30. Making pulls with the center-line gauges in position. (*Blackhawk Division of Applied Power, Inc.*)

CHAPTER 17 CHECKUP

NOTE: Since the following is a chapter review test, you should review the chapter before taking the test.

There are five types of body-frame misalignment, and each one is corrected in a slightly different way. Knowing how to make these corrections is a skill that you must develop. Different manufacturers of body-frame straighteners have equipment that is very different in appearance. However, the repair job that needs to be done to the damaged vehicle is the same regardless of the straightening equipment available. To find out how well you understand everything in this chapter, answer the questions that follow.

COMPLETING THE SENTENCES The sentences below are incomplete. After each sentence there are several words or phrases, but only one of them correctly completes the sentence. Write each sentence in your notebook, ending it with the one word or phrase that completes it correctly.

1. Body and frame straighteners are operated by (*a*) hydraulic pressure, (*b*) air pressure, (*c*) vacuum, (*d*) cables.
2. Most attachments for pulling body metal are (*a*) chains, (*b*) hooks, (*c*) cables, (*d*) clamps.
3. To correct body-frame alignment, apply a pull (*a*) opposite to the direction of the impact force, (*b*) in the direction of the impact force, (*c*) at a right angle to the direction of the impact force, (*d*) above the center of the impact force.
4. To prevent tearing of unitized bodies during pulls, use (*a*) tie-downs and jacks, (*b*) large clamps, (*c*) pads made of wood blocks, (*d*) high hydraulic pressure.
5. Overcorrection is the amount of extra pull necessary to compensate for (*a*) springback, (*b*) hot weather, (*c*) wear and play in the straightener, (*d*) poor welds.

DEFINITIONS In the following, you are asked for several definitions. Write them in your notebook. The act of writing the definitions does two things. It tests your knowledge, and it helps fix the information more firmly in your mind. Turn back into the chapter if you are not sure of a definition, and look it up in the glossary at the back of the book.

1. What is body-frame misalignment?
2. Define "diamond misalignment."
3. What is overcorrection?
4. What is an upper-body pull?
5. Define "sag."

SUGGESTIONS FOR FURTHER STUDY

In your shop there is some type of body-frame straightener. Examine it closely, and identify each of the attachments. Then, practice making hookups on a damaged vehicle. Get your instructor to check your work, and if it is satisfactory, practice applying pressure and straightening the misalignment.

PART 4

PLASTIC BODY FILLER, FIBERGLASS, AND PLASTIC REPAIR

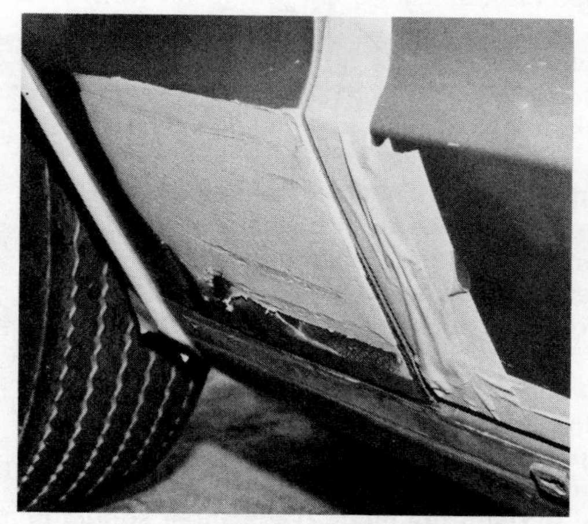

In this part, we discuss the preparation of sheet metal for filling, that is, for application of plastic body filler. We then describe the procedure of mixing and applying plastic body filler and explain how the filler is then sanded in readiness for priming and painting. We include a chapter in this part on the use of fiberglass and the procedure for making fiberglass repairs. There is also a separate chapter on plastic and plastic repairs. There are three chapters in Part 4, as follows:

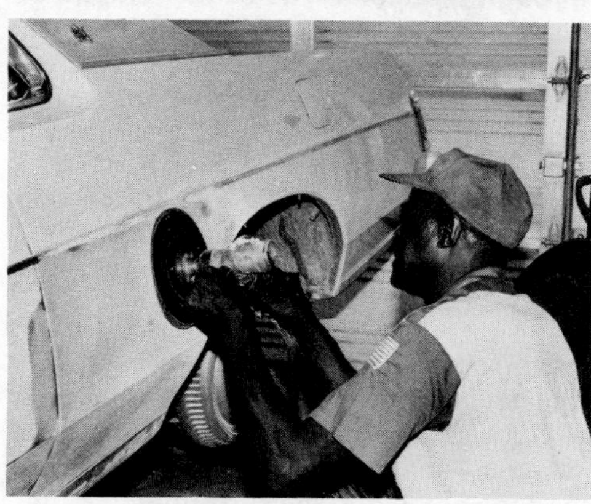

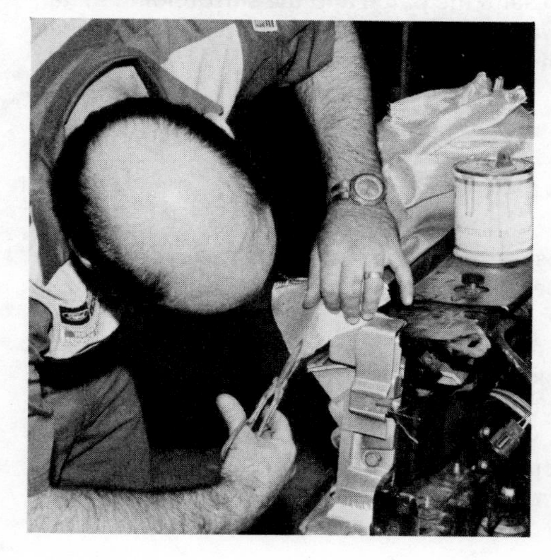

18
USING PLASTIC BODY FILLERS

In Chapters 14 and 15, we described the various methods of restoring damaged sheet-metal panels to an approximation of their original contours. We noted that the aim of the body technician is to bring the metal back, as nearly as possible, to its original shape. At the same time, the technician must keep the correction at the level of the original contour or slightly below. Various methods are used to accomplish this, including working on the original metal, patching the metal, and replacing complete body panels. In this chapter, we describe how to prepare a sheet-metal panel for filling and then how to use plastic body filler to fill it.

○ 18-1 Sanders

Chapters 6 and 7 describe and illustrate various electric and air sanders, including rotary, reciprocating, and orbital types. This purpose is to move abrasive disks or strips on metal and plastic body filler. This removes material (paint, metal, plastic), smoothing the surface and bringing it down to contour. Some sanders are operated by electric motors, others by air motors. Which type a body technician uses depends on personal preference. Some technicians say they prefer the air type, because this type is lighter and easier to maneuver.

○ 18-2 Preparing to Sand

After the body technician has straightened the damaged panel approximately to its original contour, the next steps are to check the fit of doors, hood, trunk lid, and sun roof. If everything fits properly, then clean the surface in preparation for sanding.

Checking and correcting the fit of doors, trunk lids, hoods, and sun roofs is covered in Part 5 and in Part 6. All of these must fit properly before work proceeds on the sheet metal. Sometimes an improper fit does not become apparent until the body sheet-metal and frame work begins. Then pulls must be made to correct the fit.

All such corrections must be made, as described elsewhere in the book, before sanding and filling. The area to be sanded should then be cleaned with a shop cloth and solvent to remove all grease and wax. These can clog the sanding disk and prevent its cutting properly.

○ 18-3 Using the Disk Sander

The disk sander (Fig. 18-1 shows an electric model) has a number of attachments, as shown. The attachments we are interested in now may be seen at the left in the illustration. They include the backup pad, the backing disk, and the abrasive disk.

To start sanding, the body technician selects a disk of the correct size and grit for the job. To sand fairly large areas, use a 9-inch [229-mm] disk. For smaller areas, a 7-inch [178-mm] disk would be used. Figure 18-2 shows a technician using a 9-inch [229-mm] disk on a station-wagon rear door. Figure 18-3 shows a 7-inch [178-mm] disk being used on a smaller area—the lower front of a right fender.

The grit selected depends on the preference of the technician. Some might use a 24-grit open-coat disk. Others might select a 16-grit open-coat disk. The coarser the grit, the deeper the scratches in the metal. The scratches do not mean much if they are in the area where filling is to be done. However, if they are at the edge of the area, where there is good painted metal, it is important not to leave scratches that would have to be removed as the repair is blended into the surrounding good paint.

Figure 18-4 shows the right and wrong ways of applying the rotating disk to the metal surface. It should be tipped, or applied at a slight angle, so that most of the face will be on the metal surface. If only the tip is applied, it is apt to cut through the metal. The sander should be moved back and forth in long, sweeping strokes that overlap. Do not hold the sander in one place or you will burn the metal. Do not move it in circles, because when you do this, some spots (where the circles overlap) will be sanded more than others.

○ 18-4 Sanding Smaller Spots

You will often have relatively small spots to sand. For example, the technician had to apply a patch to the lower front edge of the right quarter panel shown in Fig. 18-5. The technician used a 7-inch [178-mm] disk, as shown in Fig. 18-5, to sand the patch and the surrounding metal. The results were as shown in Fig. 18-6. Later, we will describe further how to apply plastic body filler to this patch.

○ 18-5 Octagonal Disks

The round disks cannot get into contoured surfaces—that is, surfaces with reverse curves. There are two ways of getting into these curved surfaces: with an octagonal (eight-sided) disk and with a zoom stick (○ 18-6). The octagonal disk (Fig. 18-7) can work into reverse curves, because the points are flexible and will bend to conform to the curves when the disk is fed into the curve. Many body shops cut old, discarded round 9-inch [229-mm] disks to an octagonal shape and thus get some more use out of them.

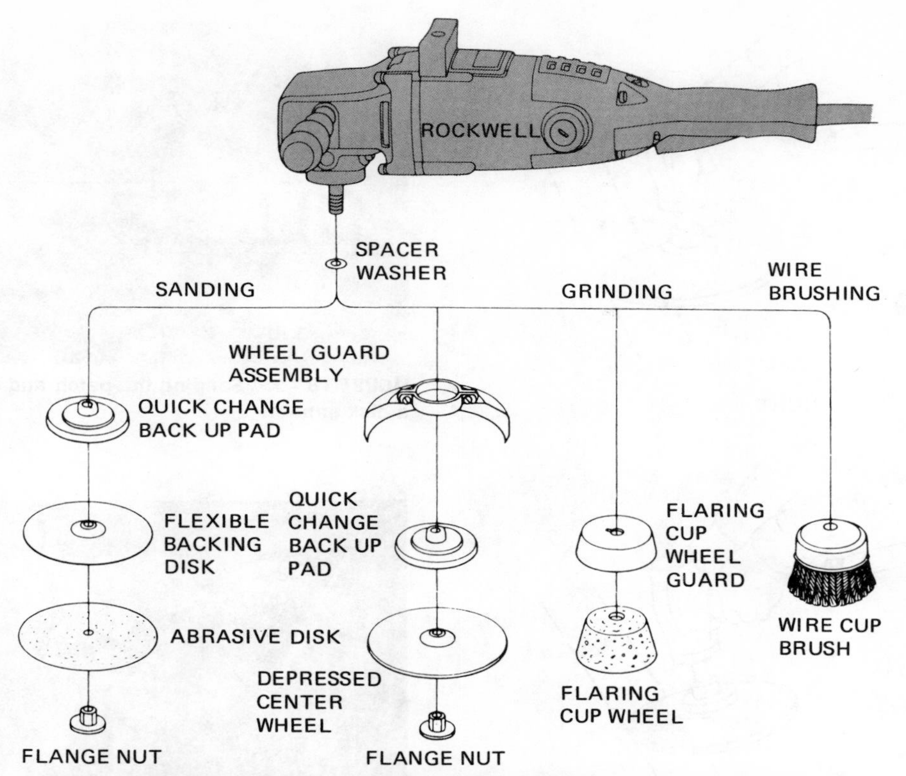

FIGURE 18–1. Electric disk sander with attachments (*Rockwell International*)

FIGURE 18–2. Sanding the damaged area of a station-wagon rear door with a 9-inch [229-mm] disk.

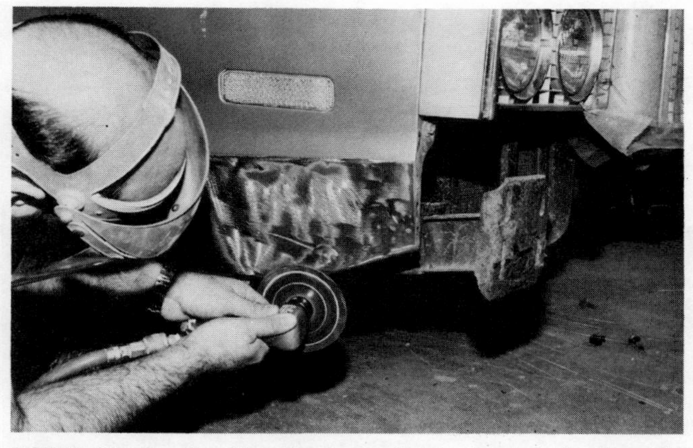

FIGURE 18–3. Sanding the lower front of a right fender with a 7-inch [178-mm] disk.

○ 18-6 Zoom Stick

The second way to get into reverse curves is to use a zoom stick (Fig. 18-8). The zoom stick (or rod or pole, as it is also called) is a cardboard tube with a strip of abrasive paper glued to it. It will fit into most curved areas. Working it back and forth will remove paint and metal and prepare the surface for filling. The zoom stick is also used to shape plastic body filler after it has hardened. Sometimes the technician will wrap a strip of fine sandpaper around the zoom stick to finish an area. Sandpaper applied by hand is also used in hard-to-get-at areas. Instead of a zoom stick, some body technicians wrap sandpaper around a piece of old radiator hose to work into curved areas.

○ 18-7 Cup Brush

The cup brush (lower right in Fig. 18-1) can also be used to get into difficult spots on a panel.

○ 18-8 The Reciprocating Sander

The reciprocating sander (Fig. 7-10) moves a strip of abrasive paper back and forth. To finish the preparation of the panel for filling, a strip of 40-grit open-coat abrasive paper is put into the sander. The sander is then used to rough up the edges of the paint, featheredging into the paint. This gives the plastic something to adhere to. The plastic will adhere to a rough surface much better than to a smooth surface.

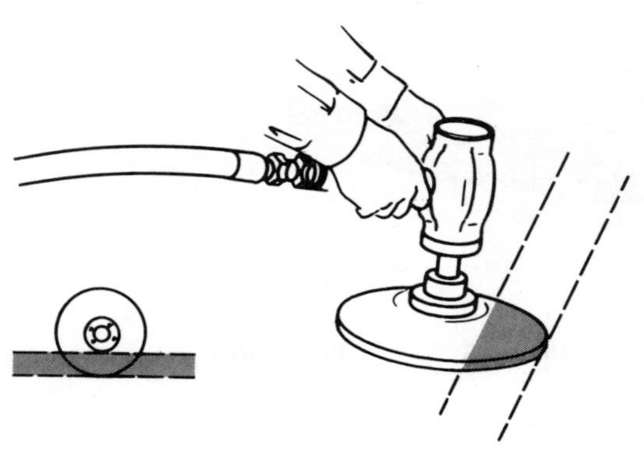

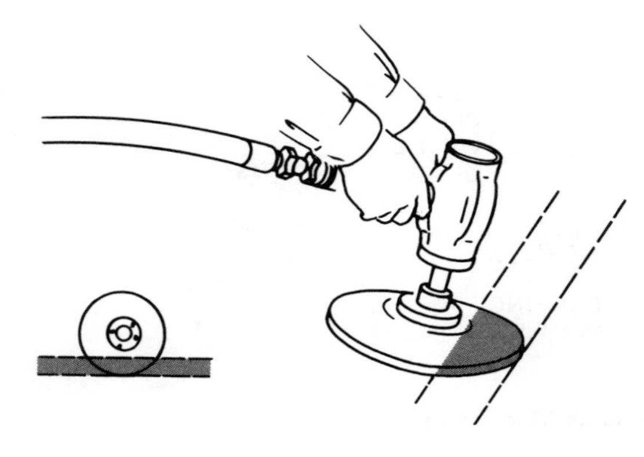

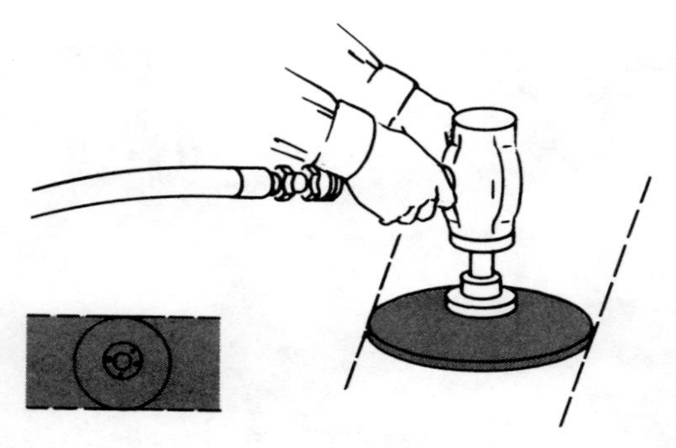

FIGURE 18–4. Correct and incorrect ways to apply the rotating disk to the metal.

NOTE: The air model of the reciprocating sander is sometimes called an *air file*.

○ 18-9 Preparing for Priming

Once the surface has been sanded as described above, it should be blown clean of dust. It is then ready for the paint shop, where it will be primed and painted, as described in the following sections. However, before we discuss painting, we must give further details about plastic body fillers and how to use them.

There are several different body fillers on the market, varying somewhat in the materials used to make them. Some have fibers in them, some have metal, as, for example, aluminum particles. These are claimed to provide added strength to the plastic when it is applied and sets up. The plastic body filler is supplied in two parts: the

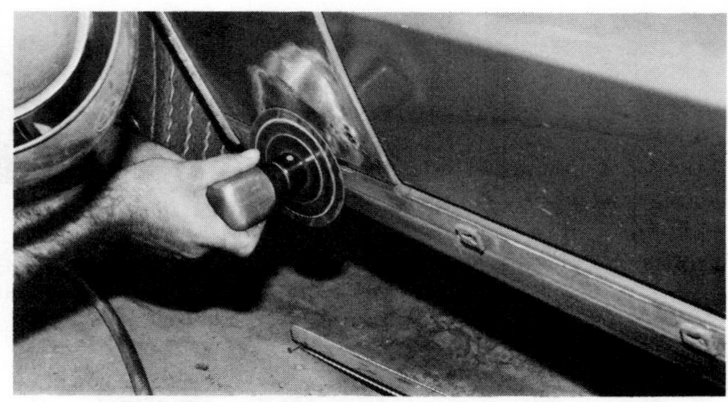

FIGURE 18–5. Sanding the patch and surrounding area with a disk sander.

FIGURE 18–6. Sanding completed, in readiness for filling.

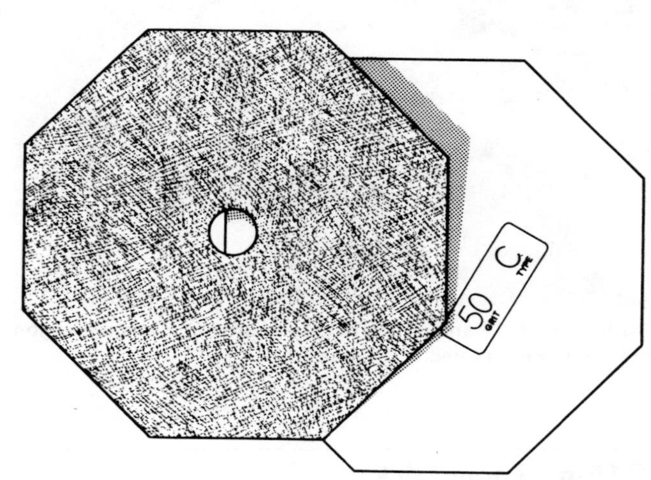

FIGURE 18–7. Octagonal disk.

basic material, in a can, and the catalyst, or hardener, usually in a tube (Fig. 18-9). When mixed, the plastic sets up, or hardens, in a few minutes. It can then be filed and sanded in preparation for painting.

NOTE: Plastic and fiberglass repair procedures are sometimes confused. Plastic body filler is a paste that is mixed with a liquid hardener. The fiberglass comes in mats or cloth; it requires the use of a liquid resin material and a hardener. Fiberglass is used primarily to repair fiberglass panels. However, it can also be used to patch metal panels by the same general procedure.

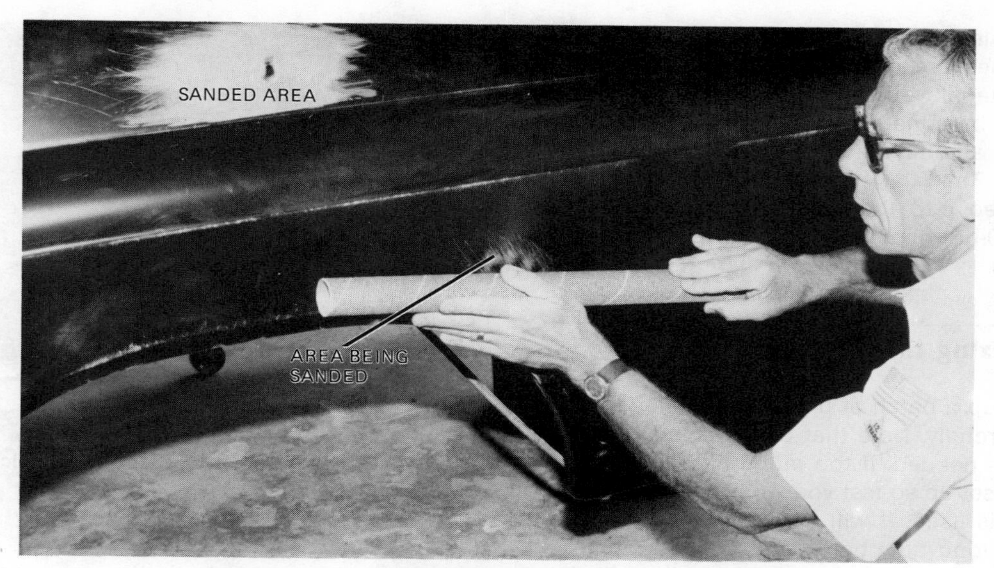

FIGURE 18–8. Zoom stick working into a reverse curve.

FIGURE 18–9. Can of plastic body filler and tube of cream hardener.

○18-10 Safety

When handling the plastic body filler, try not to get it on your hands. It can dry the hands. But most important, it can be absorbed through the skin and ultimately cause liver and other damage to your body. For this reason, a dust mask or respirator should be worn when filing and sanding the plastic. If you breathe the dust, it can cause lung trouble and liver damage. This applies especially to those body technicians who use the plastic filler every day. Occasional exposure will normally cause little harm. It is the day-after-day use that could cause the material to accumulate in the body and result in serious trouble. However, to be safe, always use a dust mask or respirator when sanding plastic body filler.

○18-11 Where Plastic Filler Can and Cannot be Used

Because plastic body filler is so easy to use, some technicians try to use it in places where it will not survive. The plastic material should be applied to relatively rough, but clean, metal surfaces. It should not be applied in thick coats to fill deep creases or dents. Nor should it be applied out to the edge of a panel. When it is used to build up an edge, it can soon break off or be knocked off. Here are the "dos and don'ts" about using plastic body filler:

1. It can be used to bring panels back to their original contour after they have been roughed out. Be careful not to leave any high spots in the metal, because these cannot be worked down after the plastic is applied.
2. It can be used to fill seams left when sheet metal has been repaired by welding or brazing, or where new sheet metal has been riveted, welded, or brazed on the panel.
3. It cannot be used satisfactorily to fill out to the edge of a panel. If it extends to the edge, moisture can work up under the edge between the metal and plastic, and the plastic will fall off. Also, bumping the edge can break off the plastic.
4. It should not be used to fill depressions deeper than about ¼ inch [6.35 mm]. Thicker fills can crack and break off.
5. The metal surface must be worked up to its final shape before the plastic is applied. After the plastic is on and is hardened, no further work on the metal should be done, as this would knock off the plastic. Plastic is not like body solder: after soldering, you can do some additional work to drive down high spots, for example, and then do further soldering on the panel.
6. Any flexing of the panel can cause the plastic to crack and ultimately fail. Plastic is not flexible like body solder: it is rigid when it sets up.

○18-12 Preparing the Surface for Filling

The surface to be filled should be prepared by first straightening the metal, as described in previous chapters. Then the fit of doors, hood, trunk lid, and sun roof should be checked and corrected as necessary (Part 5). When all metal is straight and everything fits, clean the surface to be filled with solvent to remove wax, oil, and road grime. Unless this is done, these materials could contaminate the bare metal as the sanding proceeds. That is, the material would stick to the sanding disk and smear onto the bare metal.

The surface should then be sanded with a 24-grit open-coat disk. Then the edges of the raw metal should be featheredged into the paint with a reciprocating sander using 40-grit paper. All this is covered in detail in earlier sections.

○ 18-13 Mixing the Ingredients

Before mixing up a batch of plastic body filler, read the instructions carefully. Note that only a small amount of the hardener is needed. If too much hardener is used, the plastic will set up so fast you won't be able to use it. If not enough is used, it will set up so slowly you will have to wait a long time before you can take the next step in the process—smoothing and sanding the filler surface in preparation for painting. You learn by experience just how much hardener to use. After doing several jobs, you will begin to get the feeling about the amount required. Remember that on a cold day, the plastic is slower to set up and so you would use more hardener. On a hot day, the plastic sets up faster and so you would use less hardener. Read and follow the instructions on the can (Fig. 18-10).

Here are the things to look out for:

1. On your first jobs, use less hardener rather than more, because this will give you more time to work the plastic onto the prepared sheet-metal surface.

Easy-To-Use Directions

Sand area to be repaired, using approximately 16 or 24 grit paper. Area must be clean, free of paint, oil, moisture. Do NOT wipe with oil or solvent-soaked rag. Place required amount of Plastic Body Filler on clean, hard surface. Using spatula or putty knife, mix in Creme Hardener: ¼ teaspoon for golf ball-size lump or 1 oz to every 3 lbs. Mix thoroughly and quickly. If Filler hardens too quickly, use less Hardener.
"Wipe" thin coat of mixed Plastic Body Filler on area to be repaired, assuring good bond, and then fill entire dent or hole with filler.
Mixed as directed, Plastic Body Filler will harden in approximately 10 minutes. For quicker hardening, add a little extra Hardener while mixing.
Never return mixed Filler to can: keep can closed and in a cool place. Under 85°F (29°C).

Caution:

Vapors harmful. Do not take internally. If taken internally, induce vomiting. Consult a physician. Wash hands after use and before smoking or eating. Keep away from heat and open flame. Use only with adequate ventilation. Avoid prolonged breathing of vapor. Avoid prolonged or repeated contact with skin. In case of contact, flush skin or eyes with plenty of water. KEEP OUT OF REACH OF CHILDREN.

FIGURE 18-10. Directions on a can of plastic body filler.

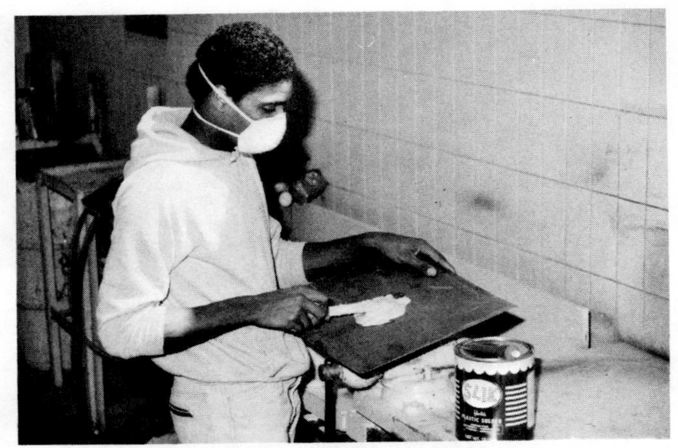

FIGURE 18-11. Mixing a batch of plastic body filler and hardener.

2. Never mix more plastic than you can apply in a few minutes. Properly mixed plastic sets up in 30 minutes or less. After about 10 minutes, however, it begins to set up and becomes harder to apply and work.
3. Never return mixed plastic to the container. It will contaminate the base material and cause it to set up.
4. Mix the ingredients on a clean sheet of safety glass or metal sheet (Fig. 18-11). A piece of cardboard will do in an emergency, but the glass or metal sheet is easier to use.
5. The base material is white. The hardener is colored. The purpose of this color difference is to assure thorough mixing. Mixing should continue until the mix is of a uniform color throughout.
6. Use a wide-bladed putty knife to mix the two ingredients. Make sure the putty knife and mixing board or glass are clean.
7. Mix the two ingredients by scooping the mixture up from the bottom and turning the putty knife over to press down on the mixture. Continue to mix until the mixture is smooth and creamy and of a uniform color throughout.
8. Do not whip the material, as this will create air bubbles which would cause you trouble later.
9. Always thoroughly clean the putty knife and mixing sheet in solvent after each use. Any old material remaining on these will put crumbs in your next mix which will prevent your doing a good job.

○ 18-14 Applying the Plastic Filler

Apply the plastic filler immediately after it is mixed. Use a wide-bladed putty knife or a squeegee. The squeegee, being soft, is preferred by some technicians, because it can follow the contours of the metal more easily. Skim a thin coat of filler on the area to be filled to assure good coverage and adherence. Then apply more filler with even strokes all in one direction, to work out any air bubbles that might appear. Use enough pressure to assure a good bond of the plastic to the metal. See Fig. 18-12.

If there is a gouge or crease to fill, or if it is going to take considerable filling to repair the area, don't try to do the complete job in one step. That is, do not apply the

FIGURE 18–12. Applying plastic body filler to a left fender.

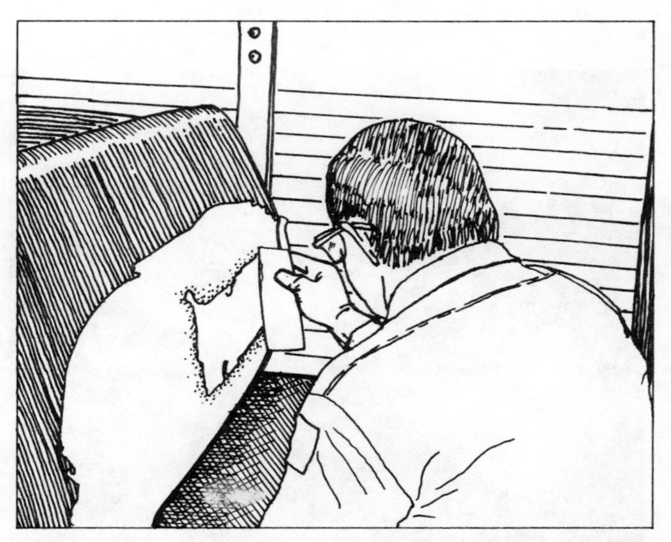

FIGURE 18–13. Applying a second coat of plastic body filler to a left quarter panel.

filler in a thick coat. It may take two or even three thin coats to bring the filler out far enough (Fig. 18-13). The surface should be finished as smoothly as possible but with enough plastic to raise the level above the final contour. There has to be enough filler to permit sanding it down to the actual final contour.

○18-15 Finishing the Plastic

Some body technicians like to use a "cheese grater" (Surform) to remove excessive plastic and bring the filler down to near the final contour. If you use a Surform, you do it while the plastic is still soft. Work it very lightly over the surface so you do not take off too much material. Do not gouge the surface.

Many body technicians do not use the Surform. They say it is too much trouble, that if they put the plastic on properly they do not need this preliminary smoothing. They let the sanding operation that follows take care of any irregularity.

After the plastic has set up hard enough to sand, the body technician starts the sanding operation with the rotary grinder, using a 50-grit open-coat abrasive disk.[1] See Fig. 18-14. After this sanding operation brings the filler down to near contour, the technician usually switches to a reciprocating sander, using 40-grit abrasive paper.[1] See Fig. 18-15. The job is then finished with 80-grit paper[1] to bring the filler down to contour and to featheredge out into the surrounding paint. The surface must be reasonably smooth to reduce the work in the paint shop. In the paint shop, the final smoothing is done with a fine grade of sandpaper (360- or 400-grit). The final surface preparation and application of primer and paint are covered in later chapters.

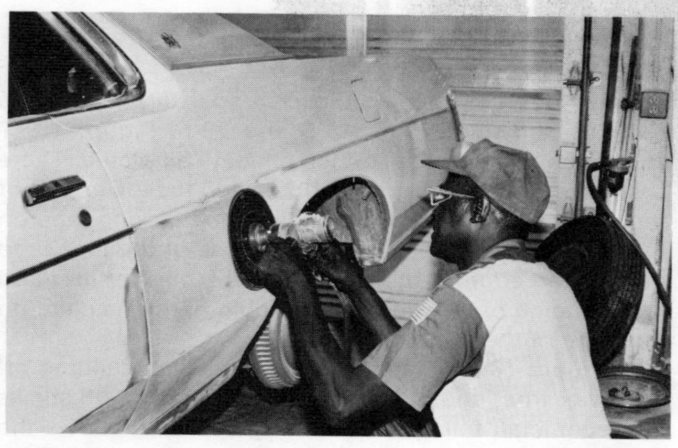

FIGURE 18–14. Sanding a filled area on a left quarter panel.

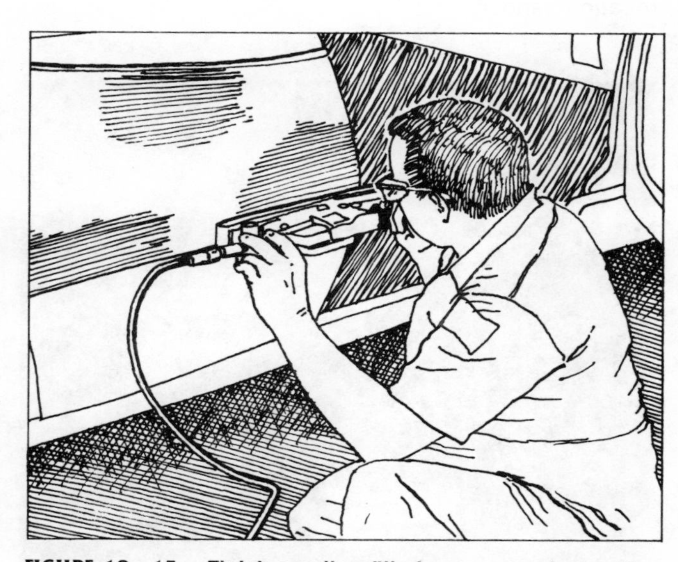

FIGURE 18–15. Finish-sanding filled area on a door with a reciprocating sander.

CAUTION: **Remember that the plastic is irritating to the skin. Some technicians who work with the plastic every day use rubber gloves to protect their hands. Remember also that the dust from sanding plastic is dangerous to breathe. You should wear a respirator if you are raising any dust while sanding. The area in which sanding of plastic is done should be cleaned with a vacuum cleaner every day.**

NOTE: Before applying a primer to plastic body filler, check that the primer is recommended for use on plastic. Some primers and paints do not work well with plastic.

[1]These grits are the recommendation of some technicians. Other technicians may use paper with different grades of coarseness. It is usually a matter of personal preference.

○ 18-16 Typical Jobs for Plastic Body Filler

Figure 18-16 shows the technician applying filler to the damage shown in Figs. 18-5 and 18-6. Figure 18-17 shows the filler-application job almost completed. There is still some smoothing to be done, and the lower part of the patch is yet to be filled. Notice the masking tape on the rear edge of the door. The purpose of the tape is to protect the edge of the door from the plastic filler and final sanding of the filler. These could harm the paint on the edge of the door.

In Figure 18-3 we showed the technician sanding off the lower front end of a right fender. Figure 18-18 shows the technician filling the area. Figure 18-19 shows the technician using a disk sander on the plastic filler. Then in Fig. 18-20 the technician may be seen using the reciprocating sander.

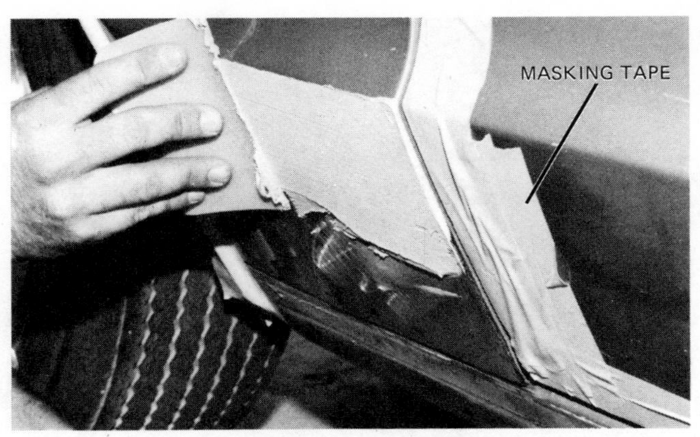

FIGURE 18 – 16. Applying plastic body filler over the patched area shown in Figs. 18–5 and 18–6.

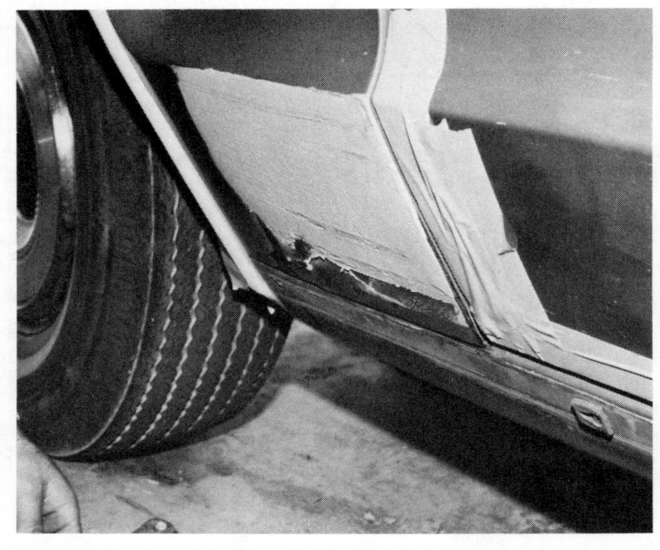

FIGURE 18 – 17. Job of applying plastic body filler nearly completed. Note the masking tape which protects the rear and bottom edges of the door.

FIGURE 18 – 18. Applying plastic body filler to the lower front of a right fender.

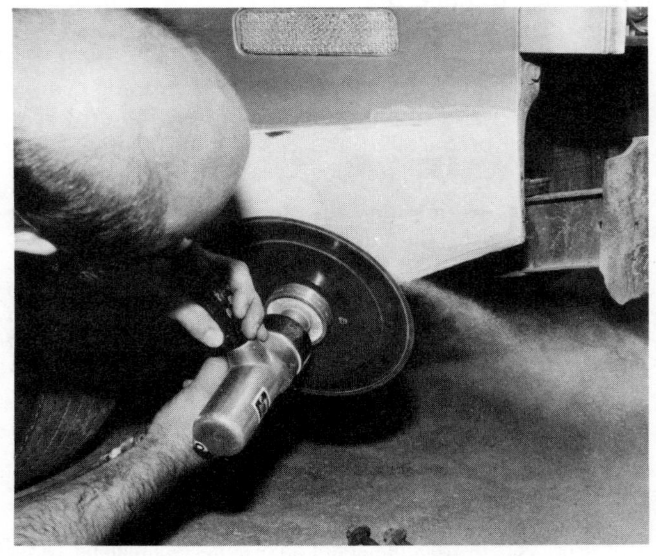

FIGURE 18 – 19. Sanding the filler with a disk sander.

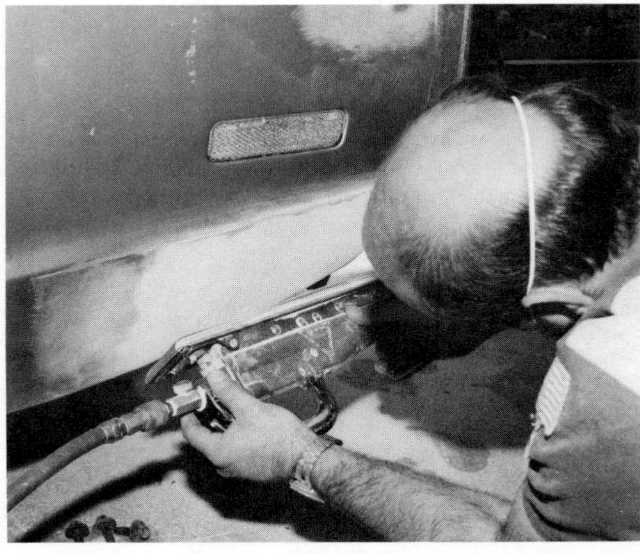

FIGURE 18 – 20. Finish sanding the area with a reciprocating sander.

○18-17 Causes of Plastic Filler Failure

Plastic filler can fail for a number of reasons:

1. Failure to prepare the metal surface properly. Oil, wax, or traces of paint on the metal surface will prevent proper adhesion of the plastic, which will therefore ultimately fail. That is, the plastic will break or flake off.
2. Putting the plastic on too thickly. Generally, ¼ inch [6 mm] is about the thickest the plastic should be applied to a panel. Of course, if you have a gouge or a weld that has been hammered below the surface, it is all right to fill the depression, provided the metal is clean and the fill is done in steps.
3. Trying to fill over holes or tears in the metal. It is all right to fill over small holes, as, for example, those left in pulling out a crease with pull rods. But the plastic will not bridge over larger holes or tears satisfactorily. It will soon crack or chip away. These holes should be closed by welding.
4. Trying to cover up rusted spots. You will not get good adhesion unless the metal is clean. Rusted spots should be patched. Sometimes a relatively small rusted area can be patched with fiberglass, as explained later in the chapter on working with fiberglass panels.
5. Trying to build up the edge of a panel with plastic, as, for example, the bottom edge of a door. Water will ultimately work up from under the edge of the door between the plastic and metal. This causes the plastic to fail. In addition, the door edge is vulnerable to bumps, and any bump can crack or break off plastic. It is all right to featheredge out to the edge of a panel, but the plastic should fade off into nothing at the edge. That is, there should be no filler at the edge.

CHAPTER 18 CHECKUP

NOTE: Since the following is a chapter review test, you should review the chapter before taking the test.

After the contour has been restored as nearly as possible to damaged sheet metal, a plastic body filler is applied to the worked area. Then the filler is finished-sanded, and the panel is ready for priming and painting. In this chapter, we have discussed how to prepare the panel for the filler and how to finish the filler. To find out how well you understand everything in this chapter, answer the questions that follow.

COMPLETING THE SENTENCES The sentences below are incomplete. After each sentence there are several words or phrases, but only one of them correctly completes the sentence. Write each sentence in your notebook, ending the sentence with the one word or phrase that completes it correctly.

1. To sand large areas, on the disk sander you would install (*a*) a 7-inch [178-mm] disk, (*b*) an octagonal disk, (*c*) a square disk, ((d) a 9-inch [229-mm] disk.
2. Compared to a fine-grit disk, a coarse-grit disk (*a*) scratches less, (*b*) moves in smaller circles, (*c*) moves in larger circles, (*d*) scratches deeper.
3. The hardener for plastic body filler usually is supplied in a (*a*) bottle, (*b*) can, (*c*) tube, (*d*) box.
4. To correct heavy damage, the body filler must be applied (*a*) in layers, (*b*) all at one time, (*c*) to painted panels, (*d*) to primed panels.
5. At the edge of a panel, you should (*a*) always have a layer of body filler, (*b*) never have body filler, (*c*) cover the damage with spot welds, (*d*) cover the damage with arc welds.

QUESTIONS Write each of the following questions, and then the answer, in your notebook. If you have trouble recalling the answer to a question, turn back to the pages that cover the material and study them again.

1. Why must you sand the body filler?
2. How can you remove paint or sand body filler on surfaces with reverse curves?
3. List the safety cautions that you must follow when working with body filler.
4. What happens when moisture gets between the panel and the body filler?
5. How do you mix body filler?

SUGGESTIONS FOR FURTHER STUDY

You will find that learning how to use plastic body filler is a very interesting experience. In the shop, watch a body technician mix and apply body filler. Then watch the technician work the surface of the filler until the original contour of the panel is restored. On a clean sheet of paper for your notebook, you should write down the steps in each operation. By doing so, when the time comes for you to try your hand at this job in the shop, you will be able to review the steps in the procedure.

19 FIBERGLASS REPAIR

In this chapter, we describe the procedures of repairing body parts with fiberglass. Fiberglass is a synthetic (manufactured) fiber, or thread, made from glass. Normally, we think of glass as a rigid pane that forms the transparent part of a window, or as a drinking glass. When someone mentions glass, we instantly think of how easy it is to break. However, if molten glass is squeezed into threads, the threads become very flexible and strong (for their size).

○ 19-1 Construction of Fiberglass Parts

When fiberglass thread is woven into cloth or made into a mat, the glass fibers form a strong, flexible material that can be used to make fiberglass panels or fiberglass car bodies (Fig. 19-1). The Chevrolet Corvette (Fig. 19-1) entered production in 1953. It was the first mass-produced car to have a fiberglass body. Today, fiberglass bodies are used on many limited-production vehicles, such as racing cars, sports cars, dune buggies, and recreational vehicles.

The way these bodies and other parts are made is very similar to the way you will use fiberglass to patch metal, plastic, and fiberglass panels. That is, the fiberglass material is laid in a mold which has the shape desired. Then resin with hardener is applied to the fiberglass. When this has set up (the setting process is also called curing, drying, or hardening), the panel is taken out of the mold. Now the new part is ready for finishing. Actually, the procedure is a little more complicated. The general idea is that fiberglass can be shaped as desired and then set permanently in that shape by the addition of the resin hardener. However, the fiberglass cannot be removed from the mold until the new part has set up. This means that manufacturing fiberglass parts is a very slow, expensive, labor-intensive process. When it is advantageous not to make a part of metal, plastic (not fiberglass) parts often can be made reasonably at a fairly high rate of production. Plastic parts and their repair are discussed in Chapter 20.

○ 19-2 Characteristics of Fiberglass Bodies

Body panels made of fiberglass have several advantages. They are very strong, highly resistant to fire and corrosion, and waterproof. When damaged by an impact, the damage does not spread over a large area as with sheet metal. Instead, the damage is usually confined to the immediate area of the impact. As you will recall, in severe impacts, sheet-metal parts crumble. However, similar fiberglass parts crack and tear badly. To repair severely torn fiberglass, the technician cuts off the damaged area and installs a new section. Fiberglass panels usually are easy to repair, as we will explain later in the chapter.

FIGURE 19–1. Car with fiberglass body. (*Chevrolet Motor Division of General Motors Corporation*)

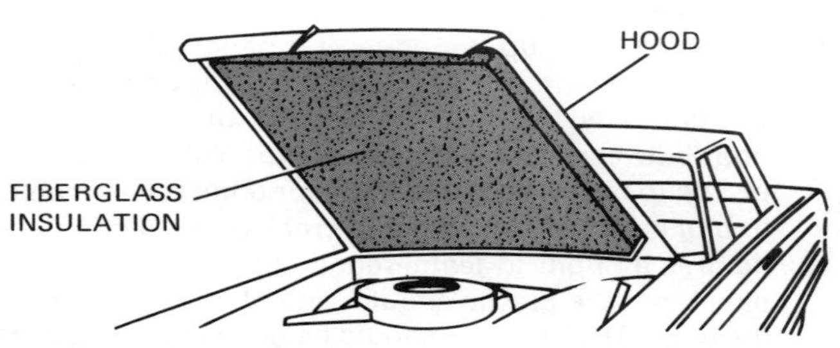

FIGURE 19–2. Fiberglass insulation is used under the hood of many cars to reduce engine noise.

For the automobile manufacturer, the major disadvantage of fiberglass as a body material is that making a body panel of this material is a slow process. With sheet metal, the parts are stamped out, sometimes hundreds an hour. They are then welded together quickly to form the body shell. With fiberglass, however, the fiberglass matting or cloth is laid in the mold, the resin with hardener is applied, and the material is left until cured. This is the reason why only a few specialty low-production cars, such as the Chevrolet Corvette, have all-fiberglass bodies. However, many body parts such as hoods, deck lids, and quarter-panel extensions on high-production cars now are made of fiberglass. Also, fiberglass insulation is used under the hood of many cars to reduce engine noise, as shown in Fig. 19-2.

○ 19-3 Fiberglass Repair Materials

Figure 19-3 shows the materials that are needed to repair minor damage, such as scratches and stone pits, with fiberglass. You will need a piece of fiberglass cloth, a can of resin, and a small tube of hardener. In a shop that does a lot of fiberglass work, these materials would be purchased in larger quantities than shown in Fig. 19-3.

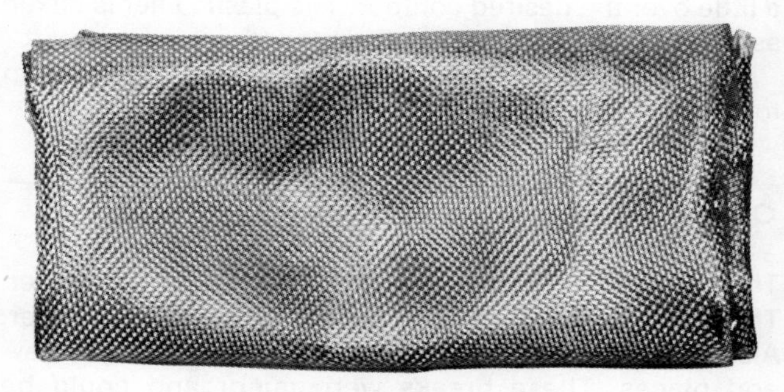

FIGURE 19–3. Materials required to make a fiberglass repair.

○19-4 The Fiberglass Repair Procedure

In the repair process, the purpose of the fiberglass cloth is to provide a strong reinforcement across the damaged area. The resin is a liquid that has little strength. However, when applied to the fiberglass cloth, the resin acts to bind the strands of glass together. Then, when the resin dries, the repaired area is ready for sanding.

But getting the resin to dry can be a problem. Applied by itself, the resin might not dry for days. This obviously is too long a time for practical purposes. The solution to the problem is the liquid hardener. When a few drops of hardener are added to the resin, curing time may be reduced to as little as 30 minutes.

Curing is a heat process brought about by mixing the hardener and resin. This causes a chemical action. As a result of the chemical action, the resin gets hot and largely dries itself. You can actually feel this heat with your hand. To aid in the drying and to reduce drying time even more, heat lamps can be turned on to the patched area. On very cold days, drying takes longer. One point to remember is that because the chemical action creates heat all through the fiberglass, it all is dry at the same time. That is, when the outside surface of the fiberglass is hard, it is hard all the way through.

○19-5 Repairing a Fiberglass or Plastic Panel

Figure 19-4 shows the sequence for repairing a crack in a body panel. Let's follow the sequence from A to H. Note that this is a surface panel which will show and must be painted to match the rest of the body.

In A you can see the crack. In B, the crack has been widened and smoothed with a file or knife. At C, a power sander with an 80-grit open-coat disk has been used to bevel the surface back from the crack for 2 to 3 inches [51 to 76 mm]. In D, the lower edges are beveled.

Before applying the patches, the surface is cleaned with lacquer thinner. Then in E, the application of the layers of fiberglass is begun. The usual recommendation is to apply three layers on top and two underneath, provided you can work from the inside of the panel. If you cannot work from under the panel, bevel out a little further on the surface so the fiberglass will have more area to bind to. To apply the patches as at E, cut each patch to the area. A good technique is to cut the outer ones a little larger than the ones underneath. When you apply the fiberglass patches, be sure that the layer you apply is completely saturated with the resin and that the surface to which you are applying the layer is coated with the resin. The resin, which is thick like heavy oil, is mixed with a small amount of the hardener. The amount you add depends on the temperature and the supplier's instructions. Here are some of the things to look out for when mixing and using the resin:

1. Make sure the cup in which you mix the resin and hardener is clean. Use a clean spatula or putty knife to mix the resin and hardener. Make sure they are mixed thoroughly.
2. Never mix any more resin and hardener than you can use in a few minutes.
3. Never return unused resin-hardener mix to the resin can. You will ruin the resin in the can.
4. When using fiberglass and resin, you should wear rubber gloves. The hardener-resin mixture is toxic, or poisonous. It can be absorbed through the skin and can cause liver damage.

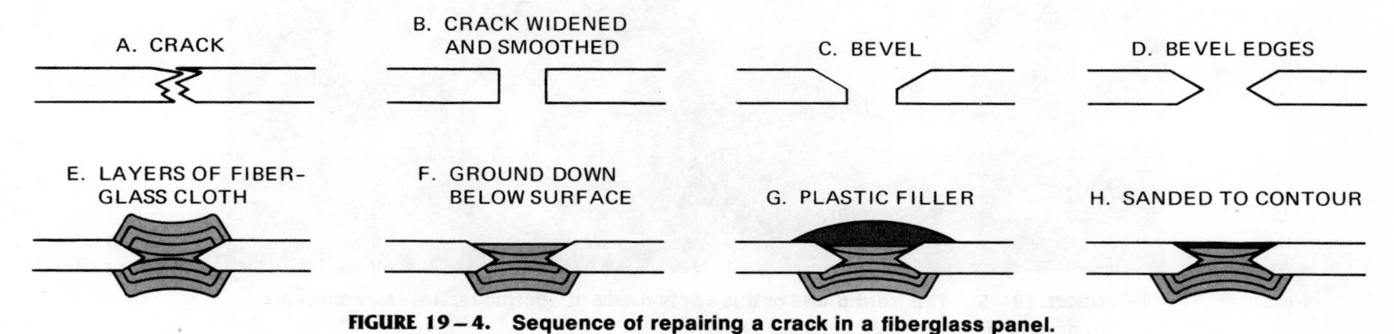

FIGURE 19–4. Sequence of repairing a crack in a fiberglass panel.

5. Work out all air bubbles as you apply the layers of resin-saturated fiberglass. Any bubble will show up later and can ruin an otherwise good job.
6. Make sure that the fiberglass layers are completely saturated with the resin-hardener mixture. One way to do this is to lay the fiberglass patch on cellophane or polyethylene film (food wrap). Then pour on or brush on the resin. Be sure the fiberglass is thoroughly soaked with the resin. Then pick up the patch and lay it face down across the prepared surface. Brush on additional resin to make sure the exposed side of the fiberglass is covered. Work out all air bubbles with a putty knife.
7. Put the brush and other tools in lacquer thinner to remove the resin remaining on them. If the resin hardens, it is difficult to get off; in fact, the brush will be ruined.
8. Make sure the area you are working in is well ventilated. Do not inhale the vapor any more than necessary. The vapor is toxic.
9. Use a respirator when sanding the finished patch. Fiberglass dust is also toxic.

Now let's get back to Fig. 19-4. After putting on the layers of fiberglass patches shown in E of Fig. 19-4, repeat the complete procedure as outlined in step 6 above. Make sure that each layer is thoroughly saturated with the resin. Work out all air bubbles as the layer is applied.

NOTE: Some body technicians, when making fiberglass patches, do not coat the patch with resin first. Instead they lay the fiberglass patch directly over the crack and saturate one side of the patch with resin. Then they remove the patch momentarily and coat the prepared surface of the panel with resin. Next, they turn the patch over and lay it, saturated side down, over the area to be repaired. Then they saturate the untreated side of the fiberglass patch. They repeat the procedure for each fiberglass layer.

After all the layers of fiberglass have been applied, allow the patch to dry. The time required varies with the amount of hardener added to the resin and with the temperature. Set-up time can be shortened by applying heat from a heat lamp. However, do not overheat the patch; do not let the temperature exceed 200°F [93.6°C]. Higher temperatures can cause vapor bubbles to form under the patch. The surface layers will set up too fast, and then, when the bottom layers start to harden and release vapor, bubbles will form.

Now, at F in Fig. 19-4, we show how the patch has been sanded down so there is a slight depression. Then, as at G, you apply the plastic body filler so it mounds up a little over the desired contour. The plastic filler is mixed as needed, as discussed in Chapter 18.

After the filler has hardened, it should be sanded down to contour as at H.

○ 19-6 Repairing a Fiberglass Front Panel

The car shown in Fig. 19-5 was hit on the left front fender. The damage was bad enough to require a new fender. Also, the impact broke the front panel (Fig. 19-5) in several places. These breaks were minor and could be patched. Figure 19-6 shows one break which becomes exposed when the fender is removed. Figure 19-7 shows the technician working on a second break, this one out in the open, where the repair must be perfect so it will not be seen. Note that, in Fig. 19-7, the technician has sanded the damaged areas in preparation for applying the fiberglass patches.

In Fig. 19-8, the technician is cutting fiberglass patches to repair the crack shown in Fig. 19-6. Note in Fig. 19-7, he is applying the resin-hardener mix to the

FIGURE 19–5. The front panel of this car is made of fiberglass. It was damaged in the collision that crumpled the fender.

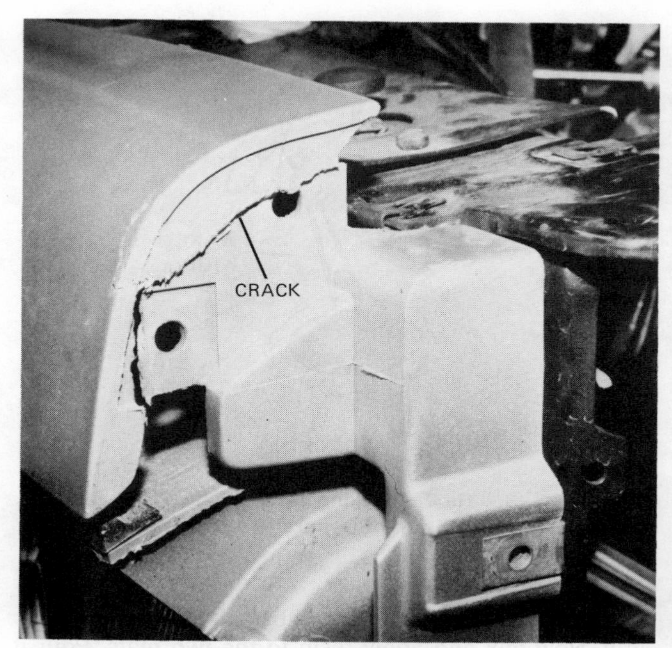

FIGURE 19–6. Crack in fiberglass panel.

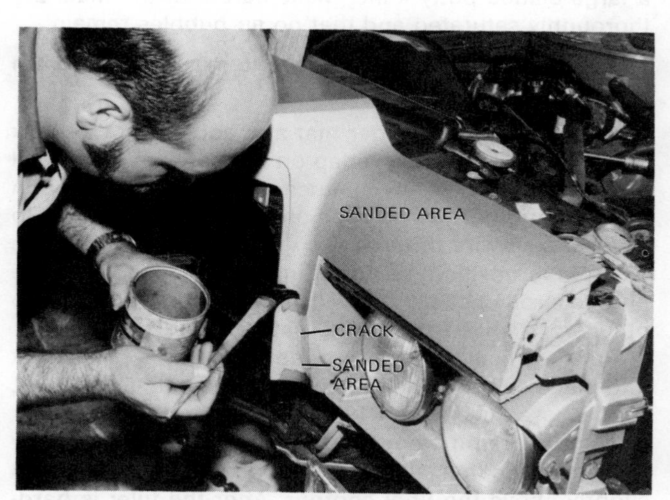

FIGURE 19–7. Applying resin to the damaged area in preparation for putting on a fiberglass patch.

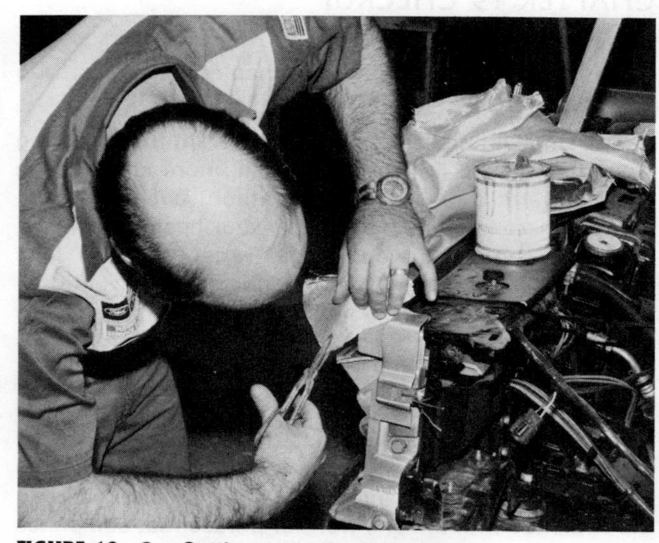

FIGURE 19–8. Cutting a patch of fiberglass.

FIGURE 19–9. Repaired area which has been patched with fiberglass and then filled with plastic filler.

prepared area. Next, the technician applies layers of fiberglass saturated with the resin-and-hardener mixture. Then, after the material has set up, he sands and applies plastic filler. After that has set up, the technician sands it down to prepare it for painting (Fig. 19-9).

○ 19-7 Larger Fiberglass Repair Jobs

So far, we have described the repair of cracks in plastic and fiberglass panels. Now we discuss what you do when you get larger jobs, such as a fiberglass fender with a piece broken out of it (Fig. 19-10). The first thing you do is try to find the piece or pieces that were broken out. If you can find the pieces, you may be able to fit them together like a jigsaw puzzle and cement everything together with a backing of fiberglass cloth and resin.

Suppose you can't find the pieces. You will have to fill in with fiberglass mat. This mat is much thicker and more loosely woven than the fiberglass cloth we described earlier.

There are two alternatives to using fiberglass mat as a patch. One of these is to cut out from a similar panel

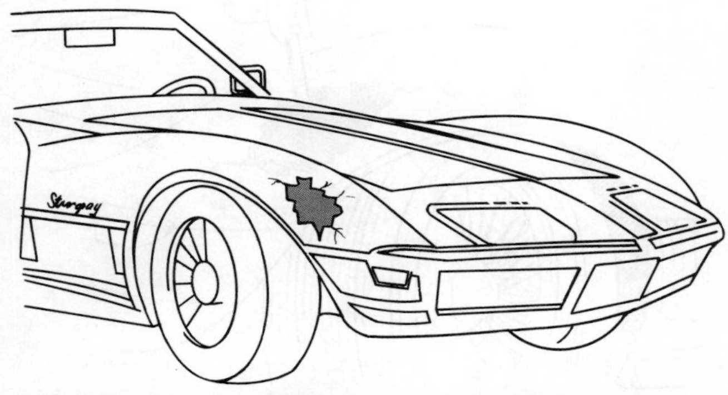

FIGURE 19–10. Fiberglass fender with a large hole in it.

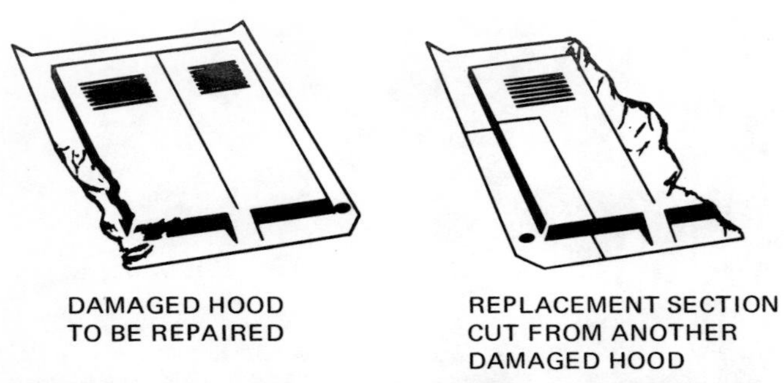

FIGURE 19–11. (Left) Cut out damaged area. (Right) Cut similar area from a replacement hood. (*Ford Motor Company*)

a patch that will exactly fit the hole and put it in place with fiberglass cloth from the back. Figure 19-11 shows how this procedure is done on a damaged fiberglass hood. The other alternative is to actually make a patch that will fit.

○ 19-8 Patching with Fiberglass Mat

Now let's see how to use fiberglass mat to repair the hole shown in Fig. 19-10. First, square up the hole or at least remove the irregularities around the edge (Fig. 19-12). As shown in Fig. 19-12, a power hacksaw can be used for this job. Next, sand off the paint around the hole out to about 2 inches [51 mm] beyond the hole. Bevel the edges, inside and out, at a 45° angle (Fig. 19-4).

Next, cut two pieces of fiberglass mat, one to exactly fit the hole and the other about 2 inches [51 mm] larger all around. The larger piece will go on the back side of the panel to support the smaller piece when it is installed to fill the hole.

Thoroughly clean the back surface of the panel around the hole with lacquer thinner to remove all grease and road dirt. Clean the front of the panel where it has been sanded.

Lay a strip of plastic film on the workbench and put the two pieces of fiberglass mat on it. The plastic bags

FIGURE 19–12. Removing the jagged edges from the hole.

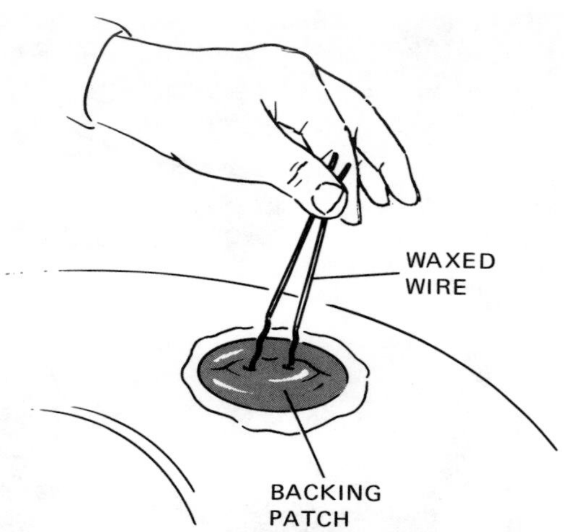

FIGURE 19–13. Tie the backing patch in place while it cures. (*Chevrolet Motor Division of General Motors Corporation*)

that dry cleaners use will be satisfactory for the plastic strip. Now mix and apply resin to the two mats. Pour it on liberally, and work it back and forth on the mats with a large-bladed putty knife. Make sure that the mats are thoroughly saturated and that no air bubbles remain.

CAUTION: Use rubber gloves to prevent resin from getting on your hands.

Now, pick up the larger mat and apply it to the back of the panel, letting it overlap on the panel evenly on all sides. Hold it for a few minutes until it sets up enough to stick. Another way to position the backing patch is to run a waxed wire through it (Fig. 19-13). Then, after the patch is in position, secure it in place by tying the wire around a rod or stick. This will allow you to continue with other work while the backing patch cures.

Put the smaller patch into the hole, firmly pressing it into place on the larger patch. Cure the patch with heat, as discussed in Section 19-5.

Then, working from the outside of the panel, apply filler to the patch, filling it enough to raise the patch slightly above the final contour. After the filler is hardened, it is sanded down and painted.

CHAPTER 19 CHECKUP

NOTE: Since the following is a chapter review test, you should review the chapter before taking the test.

Working with fiberglass is very different from working with sheet metal. For the technician, more chemistry is involved, and a lot less noise. Without adequate safeguards, there is greater danger to your health. However, fiberglass can permit you to do a variety of repair jobs more quickly than they can be done by conventional sheet-metal methods. To find out how well you understand everything in this chapter, answer the questions that follow.

COMPLETING THE SENTENCES The sentences below are incomplete. After each sentence there are several words or phrases, but only one of them correctly completes the sentence. Write each sentence in your notebook, ending the sentence with the one word or phrase that completes it correctly.

1. Fiberglass cloth is made of (*a*) plastic, (*b*) glass, (*c*) body filler, (*d*) lead.
2. Fiberglass can be used to repair fiberglass and (*a*) torn weatherstrip, (*b*) cracked windshields, (*c*) plastic and sheet metal, (*d*) ripped vinyl.
3. The purpose of the resin is to (*a*) provide strength, (*b*) bond glass threads together, (*c*) prevent overheating, (*d*) speed up the drying process.
4. To repair large holes, you must first apply (*a*) body putty, (*b*) wax paper, (*c*) fine wire mesh, (*d*) a backing patch.
5. Drying time can be reduced even more by use of (*a*) compressed air, (*b*) the gas torch, (*c*) heat lamps, (*d*) a fan.

DEFINITIONS In the following, you are asked for several definitions. Write them in your notebook. The act of writing the definitions does two things. It tests your knowledge, and it helps fix the information more firmly in your mind. Turn back into the chapter if you are not sure of a definition, or look it up in the glossary at the back of the book.

1. What is fiberglass?
2. Define "resin."
3. Define "hardener."
4. What is curing?
5. What is the difference between fiberglass mat and fiberglass cloth?

SUGGESTIONS FOR FURTHER STUDY

Fiberglass is a very interesting material to work with. Some body technicians specialize in fiberglass work, while others refuse to do it. Try to find a technician who does a lot of fiberglass work, and carefully watch what the technician does. Be especially watchful for the safety cautions that the technician takes. In a page of your notebook, write down the safety cautions that must be followed to work safely with fiberglass.

20
PLASTIC REPAIR

More and more car parts are being made of plastic. Fiberglass, which we studied in the previous chapter, is made by combining glass fiber and a plastic, or resin. Like fiberglass, plastics are synthetic (manufactured) materials. Many of the plastics used in automobiles today are made from petroleum. In this chapter we will learn more about the various types of plastics and how to repair them.

○ 20-1 Types of Resin

In Chapter 19, we discussed how a patch or a part was made with fiberglass. As you will recall, fiberglass cloth or mat was laid in the mold. Then the cloth or mat was soaked with a mixture of resin and hardener. The resin is a plastic in the form of a thick syrup. There are many types of resins, but we are interested in two main types. These are (1) thermoplastic resin and (2) thermosetting resin.

Before we discuss these types, let's define a few basic terms. The word "thermo" means of or pertaining to heat. "Plastic" means soft and pliable. "To set" means to harden. Now, with these definitions in mind, let's take another look at the names of the two types of resins.

"Thermoplastic" means heat soften. A thermoplastic resin is a material that softens when heat is applied to it. This occurs every time you heat it. Resins that are thermosetting have different characteristics. "Thermosetting" means heat hardens. Therefore, thermosetting resins are materials that harden the first time that heat is applied. Then, if heat is applied a second time, the thermosetting material is destroyed.

Now probably you can see why it is so important for the body technician to identify the type of plastic being worked on. If, for example, a piece of vinyl from a vinyl top is heated, the vinyl becomes soft and pliable. It is a thermoplastic resin, or a material that softens when heated. In fact, heat can be applied to vinyl many times to soften it without damaging it. This is a characteristic of thermoplastic resin.

Fiberglass, however, is a thermosetting material. To cure fiberglass, it is heated one time, usually from the chemical release of internal heat aided by heat lamps. This heat cures and hardens the resin. Should you apply high heat to fiberglass a second time, it does not soften or melt. Instead, the material is ruined. These two examples point out the importance of knowing the type of plastic you are working on. Using the wrong servicing procedure can ruin the part instead of repairing it. Also, as you will learn in a later chapter, the type of plastic determines the proper paint and painting procedure to use.

○ 20-2 Identifying Plastic Parts

Figures 20-1 and 20-2 show the exterior parts on one model of car which now are being made of plastic. It is difficult for even the most experienced body technician to be certain which plastic is used for each part.

The first step in repairing a plastic part is to find out which plastic it is made of. There are three basic types of plastics used for car parts. These are ABS plastic (the initials of the compound *a*crylonitrile-*b*utadiene-*s*tyrene), polypropylene plastic, and vinyl plastic. Polypropylene parts are hard, and vinyl parts are soft. However, the problem of identification arises because of the wide use of ABS. This plastic has several forms, and both hard parts and soft parts are made of it.

Here are two simple tests that will help you identify the type of plastic you are about to repair.

VINYL
FIBERGLASS
LEXAN

FIGURE 20–1. Front body parts on one model car that are made of plastic. (*Oldsmobile Division of General Motors Corporation*)

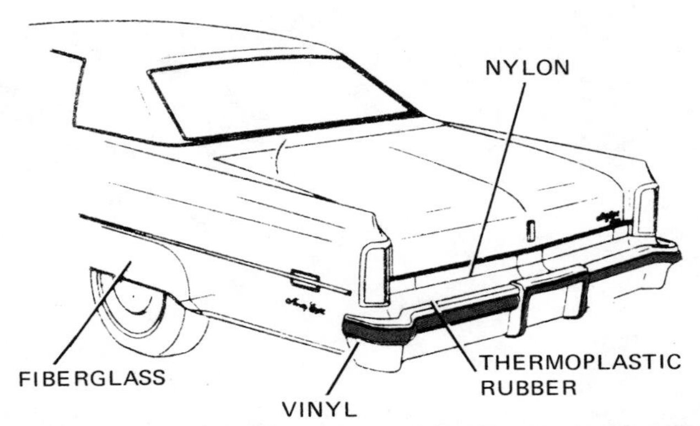

FIGURE 20–2. Rear body parts made of plastic. (*Oldsmobile Division of General Motors Corporation*)

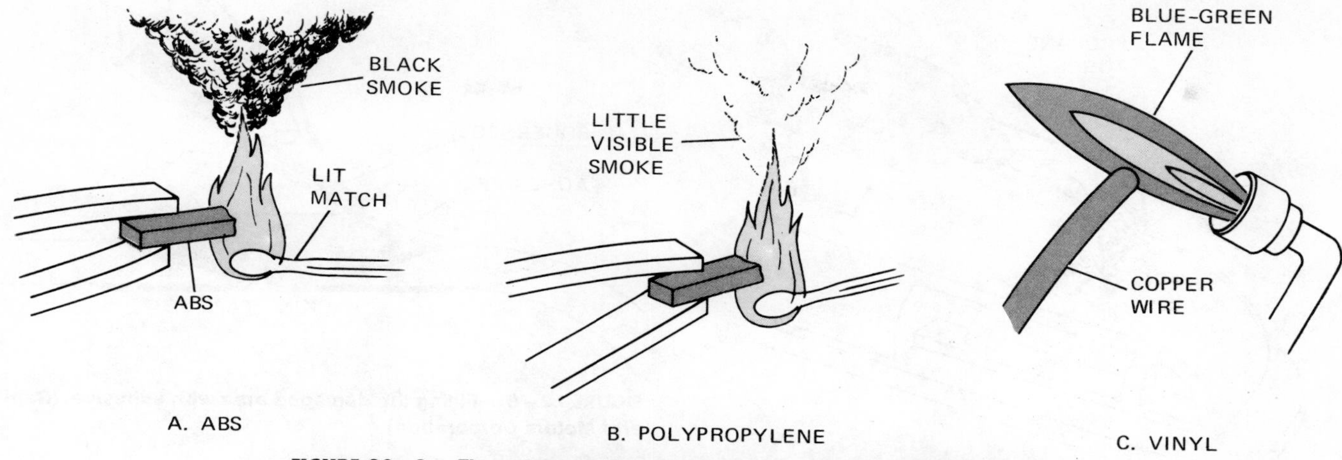

FIGURE 20–3. Flame test to identify the various types of plastic. (*Ditzler*)

○20-3 Identifying Polypropylene and ABS

From a hidden back-side portion of the plastic part, remove a sliver of the material with a sharp knife. Hold the sliver with tweezers and ignite it with a match (Fig. 20-3). Watch the burning plastic closely. Polypropylene burns with no readily visible smoke. ABS burns with a readily visible black smoke residue that hangs temporarily in the air.

○20-4 Identifying Vinyl

Heat a copper wire in the flame of a propane torch until the wire glows and turns red. Then touch the heated wire to the back side or hidden surface of the material being tested. Some of the material must stick on the wire.

Return the wire with the material on it to the flame (Fig. 20-3C). Look for a green-turquoise-blue flame. If the flame is in this color range, the material is vinyl.

○20-5 Plastic Repair Procedures

Hard parts made of ABS, nylon, Lexan, Noryl, and fiberglass can be repaired with fiberglass. Follow the fiberglass repair procedures as outlined in Chapter 19.

Soft parts made of ABS/vinyl, and vinyl tops and interior trim can be repaired with vinyl patching kits. This procedure is covered in Chapter 32. Other soft plastic materials can be repaired with Scotch Weld Structural Adhesive tape or similar patch material.

Repairs to thermoplastic materials can be made with the hot-air plastic welding technique. This is covered in a later section.

○20-6 Repairing Soft Plastic Parts

Soft plastic parts are being used more and more on the exterior of automobile bodies (see Figs. 20-1 and 20-2). Typical examples include front and rear bumper filler panels or sight shields, valance and end panels, quarter-panel extensions, front- and rear-bumper upper and lower covers, and bumper center moldings.

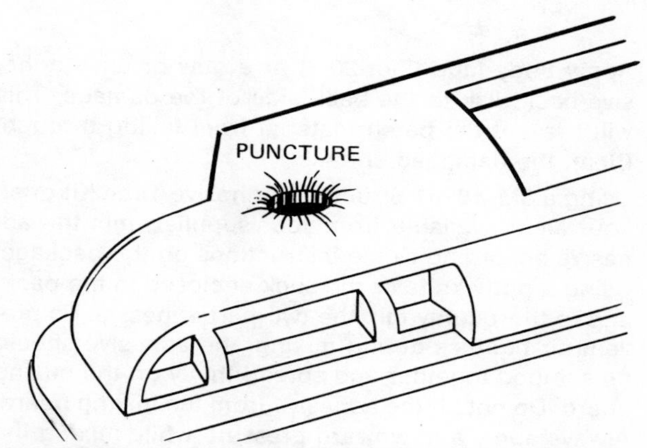

FIGURE 20–4. A punctured soft plastic panel that can be repaired. (*General Motors Corporation*)

Many of these plastic parts are replaced when they are damaged. However, a punctured, gouged, or torn plastic panel can be restored to its original appearance by following the procedure listed below. Figure 20-4 shows a punctured soft plastic panel that we will repair.

1. Clean the damaged area with a general-purpose adhesive cleaner and wax remover. If the damage is through the thickness of the part, clean both sides. Then grind away the damaged material with a 36-grit disk (Fig. 20-5). Featheredge the paint around the damage using a 180A-grit disk.
2. Lightly singe the repair area with a gas torch for approximately 15 seconds (Fig. 20-6). This will improve adhesion. Be careful not to burn the plastic!

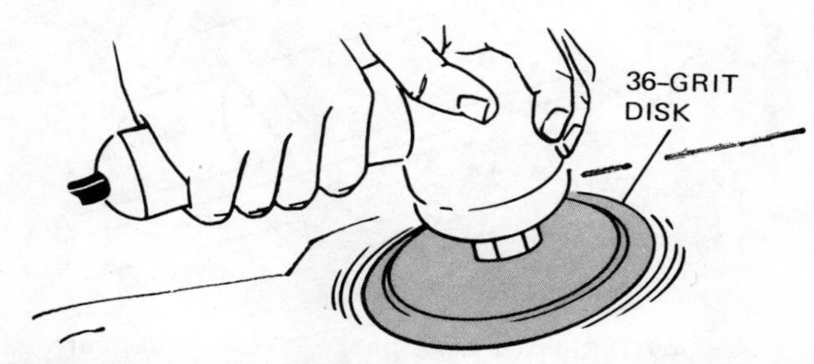

FIGURE 20–5. Grinding away the damaged material. (*General Motors Corporation*)

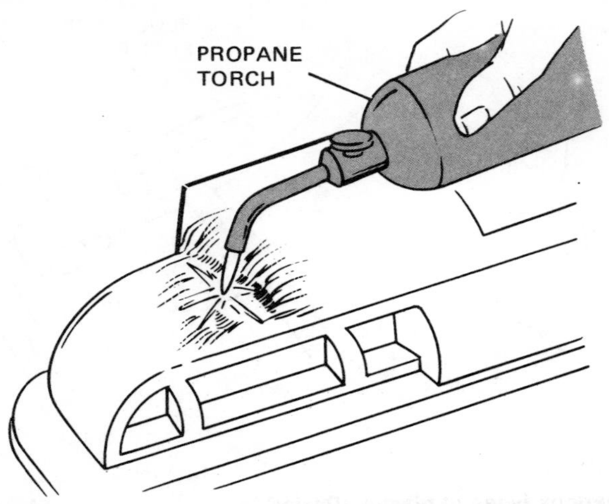

FIGURE 20–6. To improve adhesion, lightly singe the repair area with a torch. (*General Motors Corporation*)

3. Apply body tape (Fig. 20-7) or a new or used adhesive-back disk to the back side of the damage. This will prevent the patch material from falling through. Clean the damaged surface.
4. Using a 3M #8101 Structural Adhesive Tube Kit or an equivalent available from your supplier, mix the adhesive according to the instructions on the package. Using a putty knife or the stick enclosed in the package to thoroughly mix the two-part adhesive. To prevent air bubbles during mixing, the adhesive should be scraped together and spread thinly on the mixing board. Do not lift the adhesive from the mixing board. Always apply a downward pressure while mixing the two materials together.
5. Scrape the mixture from the board and apply a thin coat to the damaged area with a soft squeegee (Fig. 20-8). Heat for 15 minutes at approximately 180°F [82.2°C] with a heat lamp or heat gun. Temperature can be checked with an inexpensive cooking thermometer. Mix and apply a second coat of adhesive, as shown in Fig. 20-8. Follow the mixing procedure carefully.
6. Sand the patch level with the surrounding area using a 240A-grit disk. Check for pinholes and low areas.

FIGURE 20–7. Applying body tape to the back side of the damage. (*General Motors Corporation*)

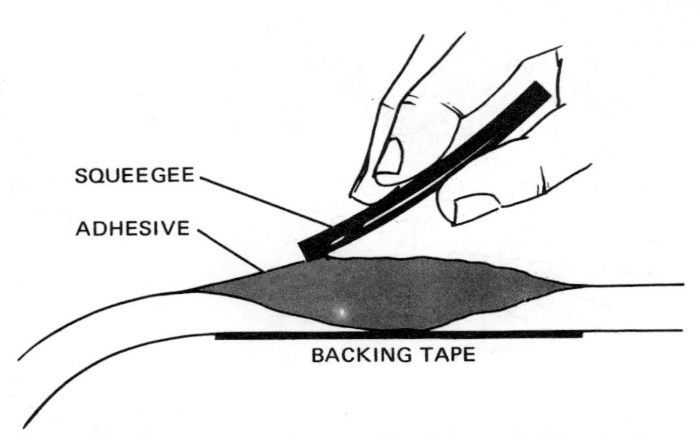

FIGURE 20–8. Filling the damaged area with adhesive. (*General Motors Corporation*)

If necessary, mix more adhesive and apply it to low areas.

7. Bake 15 minutes at 180°F [82.2°C]. Then sand, using a 320A-grit disk. Next, scuff-sand the entire panel with a 320-grit disk. Do this by hand or with a random orbital sander. Prime and paint the entire panel, using the Ditzler Elastromeric Lacquer paint system or an equivalent.

○20-7 Hot-Air Plastic Welding

Hot-air welding is a process available to fuse together or repair thermoplastics. (Thermoplastics, as you will recall, are plastics that soften when heat is applied.) The process utilizes a special welding torch that electrically heats low-pressure compressed air. Figure 20-9 shows some of the shapes of available welding torches. In general, these torches utilize compressed air at 2 to 3½ psi [0.14 to 0.24 kg/cm^2] and a 115-volt heating element in the 300-to-500-watt range. They heat the air to between 400 and 750°F [between 204 and 399 C]. This is hot enough to partially melt thermoplastic materials.

There is some variation in the torches, as you can see in Fig. 20-9. Follow the manufacturer's operating instructions. In operation, the barrel of the torch gets hot enough to burn you, should you touch it. Also, the low volume of hot air put out by these torches can cause burns if the hot air is directed against the skin long enough. However, accidental fanning of the torch-heated

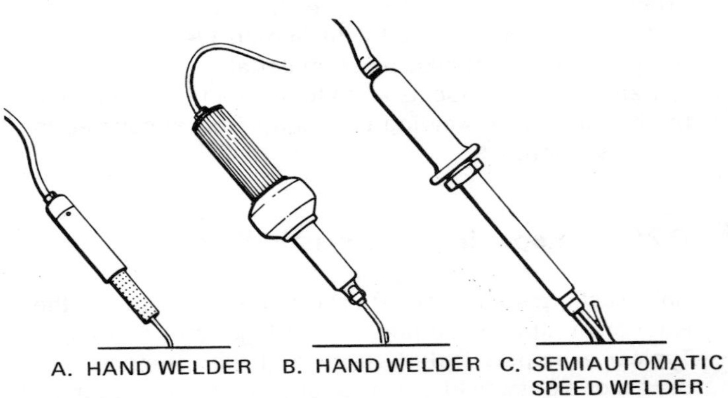

FIGURE 20–9. Various types of hot-air welding torches. (*General Motors Corporation*)

air over your hands produces a warm sensation with adequate warning to move the torch or your hand.

The torch is used with a plastic "welding rod" made from the same material as the plastic being repaired. By using a welding rod of the same material, the strength, hardness, and flexibility of the repair is the same as those of the original part. You can make your own welding rod from scrap material of the same type being repaired or from the underside of the piece you are repairing. However, the material may be stressed and may not produce a good weld. Various types of plastic welding rod may be obtained from your local plastics suppliers.

○20-8 The Plastic Welding Procedure

Good plastic welding requires the following:

1. Correct welding rod material
2. Correct temperature
3. Correct pressure
4. Correct angle between the welding rod and the part
5. Correct speed

In the welding of thermoplastics, the material is fused together by the application of heat and pressure. In hand welding, this is achieved by heating the rod and base material at the same time and pushing on the rod to get proper pressure. Too much pressure stretches and distorts the weld. Too much heat will char, melt, or distort the material. Too little heat or pressure results in poor welds.

Here is the repair sequence for hot-air plastic welding:

1. Prepare the damaged area.
2. Align the damaged area.
3. Weld.
4. Cool.
5. Sand. If pinholes or low spots are present, bevel the edges of the problem area and add another bead of weld. Then resand.
6. Paint.

○20-9 Preparing the Damaged Area

The tear or break should be trimmed to a vee shape with a knife or by sanding. As in metal welding, studied in earlier chapters, this provides a surface to heat and a space to fill with softened rod. Types of welds for plastics are shown in Fig. 20-10. Some tears can be heat-welded by melting the material along the crack. However, this usually does not provide complete bonding or any excess material to sand off for a smooth finish. Wipe any dust or shavings from the joint with a clean, dry rag. Solvents should not be used for cleaning damaged plastics, because they tend to soften the edges and cause poor welds.

○20-10 Operating the Hot-Air Welding Torch

This torch requires a source of clean compressed air. The compressed air always must be flowing before the torch is plugged into an electrical outlet.

To start the torch, turn on the compressed air. Adjust the air pressure to approximately 2½ psi [0.18 kg/cm^2]. The pressure needed depends on the type of plastic to be welded. The higher the air pressure, the lower the welding temperature. Conversely, the lower the air pressure, the higher the welding temperature.

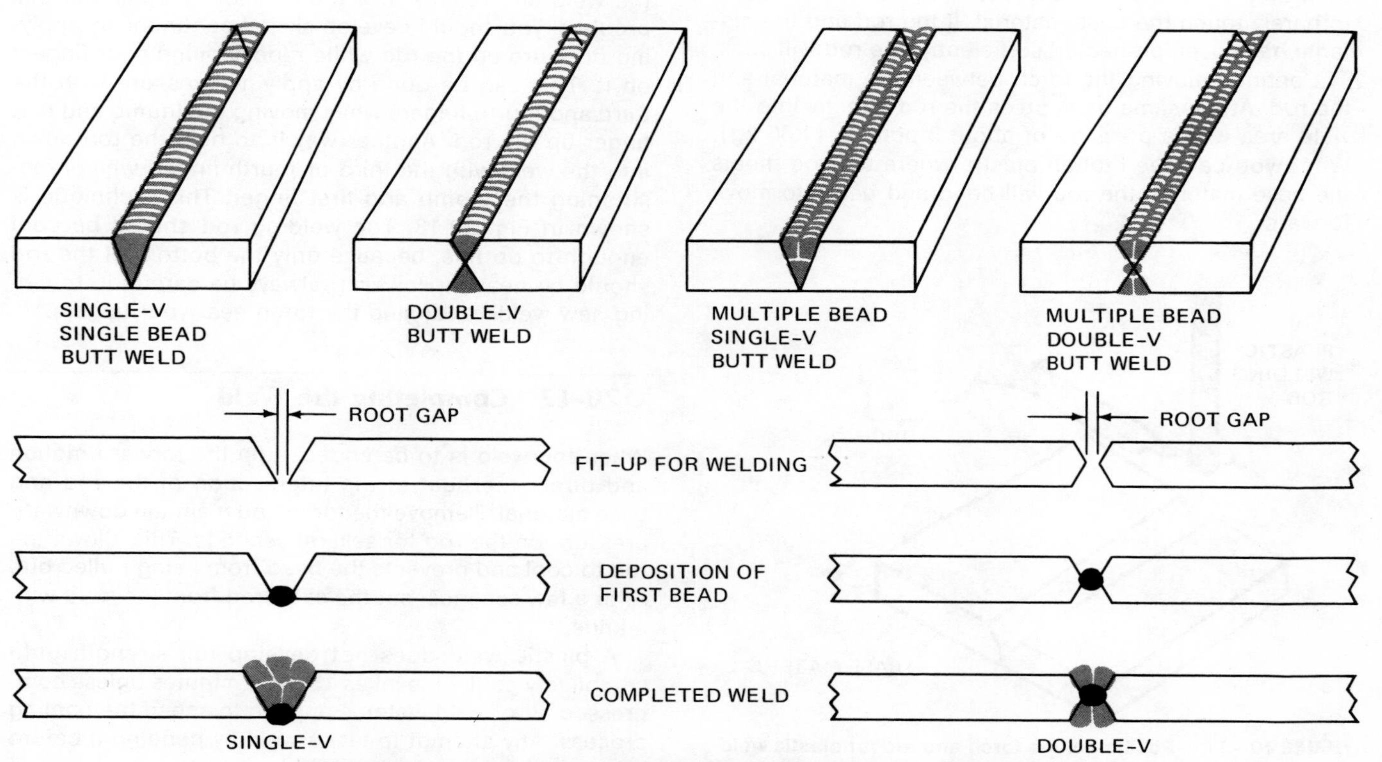

FIGURE 20–10. Various types of welds for plastic. (*General Motors Corporation*)

After the pressure is set and air is flowing, plug the torch into a 115-volt electrical outlet. Allow the torch to preheat for 5 to 10 minutes. Then check the hot-air temperature by holding a thermometer ¼ inch [6.35 mm] from the hot-air end of the torch. The temperature should be in the 400-to-750°F [204-to-399°C] range for most thermoplastics. Information supplied with the torch usually includes a chart of welding temperatures.

To shut off the torch, disconnect the electrical plug. Be sure to continue the compressed-air flow for approximately 10 minutes after unplugging the electrical cord. This cools the heating element in the torch before disconnecting the compressed air line.

○20-11 Welding Plastic Parts

The edges to be joined should be aligned as necessary (Fig. 20-10). If a tear is long and you have difficulty getting a backing strip on it, tack-weld it. Small tack welds can be made along the tear to hold the two sides in place while you are performing the finish weld. (Tack welding is discussed in ○10-15 and illustrated in Fig. 10-17B).

To tack-weld plastic, hold the damaged area in its correct position. Use clamps and other fixtures, as necessary, to hold the pieces in position. With the torch, apply hot air to each side of the damage until some material from each side melts together.

NOTE: Do not attempt to add new material at this time.

To start the weld, hold the torch ½ inch [12.7 mm] from the damaged area (Fig. 20-11). Hold the end of the welding rod at a 90° angle to the base material (that is, the welding rod should be pointed straight up). The welding rod also should be ½ inch [12.7 mm] from the torch. Move the torch back and forth between the rod and the material, as shown in Fig. 20-12, to evenly preheat both until they are shiny and tacky. Now move the rod down to barely touch the base material. If the rod and the material have been preheated sufficiently, the rod will stick.

Continue moving the torch between the material and the rod. At the same time, press the rod directly into the weld area with a pressure of about 3 pounds [1.36 kg]. When you can see molten plastic where the rod meets the base material, the rod will bend and begin to move forward.

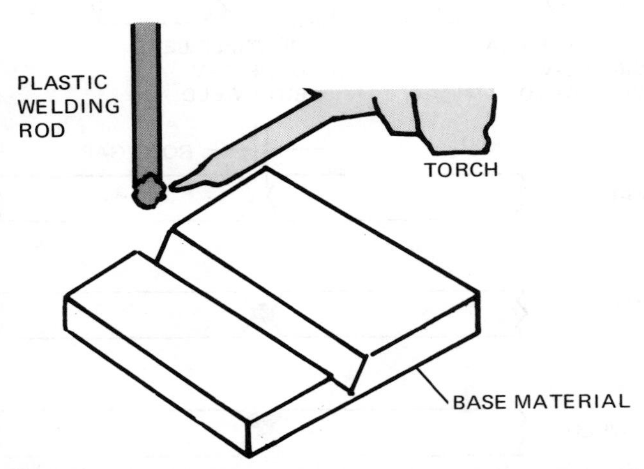

FIGURE 20–11. Position of the torch and rod for plastic welding. (*General Motors Corporation*)

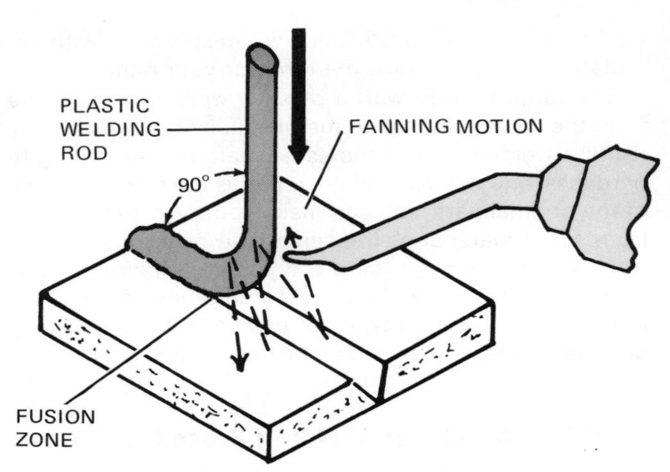

FIGURE 20–12. Welding plastic. (*General Motors Corporation*)

NOTE: Do not overheat the base material. It will char or melt.

In welding, a good start is essential, because this is where most plastic weld failures begin. For this reason, starting points on multiple-bead welds should be staggered whenever possible.

Once the weld has been started, you should continue to fan the torch from rod to base material, as shown in Fig. 20-12. Because the base material has greater bulk, a greater amount of heat must be directed at it than at the rod. Experience will help you to develop the proper technique.

In the welding process, the rod will gradually be used up. This makes it necessary for you to renew your grip on the shortened rod. Unless this is done carefully, the release of pressure may cause the rod to lift away from the weld bead. This allows air to become trapped under the weld and results in a weak weld. To eliminate this problem, you should develop skill at continuously applying pressure on the rod while repositioning your fingers on it. This can be done by applying pressure with the third and fourth fingers while moving the thumb and first finger up the rod. Another way is to hold the rod down into the weld with the third or fourth finger, while repositioning the thumb and first finger. This technique is shown in Fig. 20-13. The welding rod should be cool enough to do this, because only the bottom of the rod should be heated. However, always be careful in touching new welds or aiming the torch near your fingers.

○20-12 Completing the Weld

When the weld is to be ended, stop the forward motion and direct the heat at the intersection of the rod and base material. Remove the torch and maintain downward pressure on the rod for several seconds. This allows the rod to cool and prevents the bead from being pulled out. After a few seconds, cut the extra rod from the weld with a knife.

A plastic weld does not develop full strength until completely cool. This takes 15 to 30 minutes unless compressed air or cold water is applied to speed the cooling process. Any attempt to test a weld by bending it before it has cooled may result in weld separation.

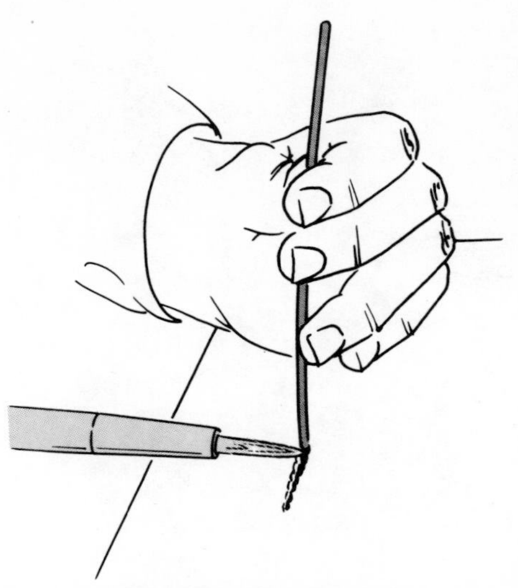

FIGURE 20 – 13. In plastic welding, you must keep a constant pressure on the rod. (*General Motors Corporation*)

○20-13 Smoothing the Weld

First, remove any excess plastic with a sharp knife. The welded area then can be smoothed by grinding it with a coarse 36-grit disk of emery or sandpaper. A 9-inch [229-mm] disk on a 5000-rpm air-powered polisher will remove large weld beads.

The weld area will soften from the heat generated by grinding it. Be careful not to allow the welded plastic to overheat. During grinding, you should frequently apply water to the weld area to cool it. This will speed up your work and prevent damage to the weld.

After rough grinding, the weld should be checked visually for defects. Bending the part across the welded area should not produce any cracks. The weld should be as strong as the original material. Any pinholes, low spots, or cracks make the weld unacceptable.

Finish sanding the welded area using 220-grit sandpaper, followed by 320-grit. Use a belt or an orbital sander, plus hand sanding as required.

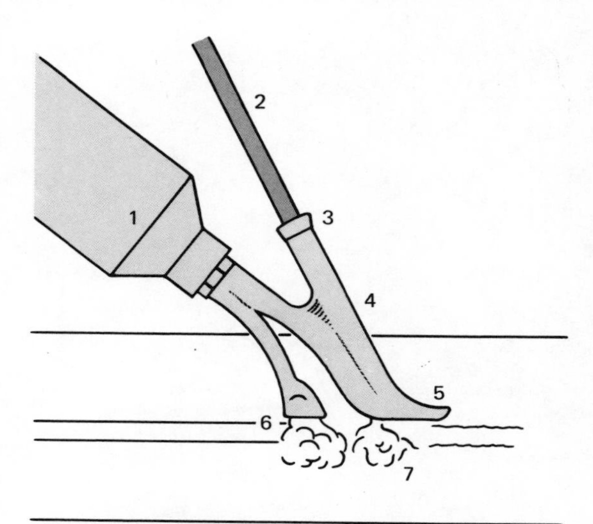

FIGURE 20 – 14. Semiautomatic speed-welding torch for plastic welding. (*General Motors Corporation*)

○20-14 Semiautomatic Speed Welding

Figure 20-14 shows a semiautomatic speed-welding torch. It has a special tip that allows you to control heat and pressure with one hand while the rod is fed automatically. The rod is preheated as it passes through the tube in the welding tip. The base material is heated by hot air coming out of the tip ahead of the rod tube. A shoe on the end of the tip applies pressure to the rod at the point of weld, and at the same time smooths the weld. The forward motion pulls the rod through the tip.

A good speed weld in a vee-joint will have a slightly higher crown than a hand weld and more uniformity. It will appear smooth and shiny with a slight bead on each side. For best results, the tip should be cleaned occasionally with a wire brush.

CHAPTER 20 CHECKUP

NOTE: Since the following is a chapter review test, you should review the chapter before taking the test.

COMPLETING THE SENTENCES After each incomplete sentence below there are several words or phrases, but only one of them correctly completes the sentence. Write each sentence in your notebook, ending the sentence with the one word or phrase that completes it correctly.

1. Two types of plastic are (*a*) hot and cold, (*b*) resin and glass, (*c*) plastic and resin, (*d*) thermoplastic and thermosetting.

2. A plastic that softens when heated is a (*a*) thermoplastic resin, (*b*) fiberglass, (*c*) thermosetting resin, (*d*) body filler.

3. Plastic parts can be identified by the (*a*) acid test, (*b*) way they tear, (*c*) flame test, (*d*) weight and color.

4. Punctured soft plastic panels (*a*) can be patched with adhesive, (*b*) must be replaced, (*c*) cannot be painted, (*d*) are repaired by hot-air plastic welding.

5. The welding rod used in hot-air plastic welding is made of (*a*) steel, (*b*) rubber, (*c*) the plastic being patched, (*d*) a special type of fiberglass.

QUESTIONS Write each of the following questions, and then the answer, in your notebook. If you have trouble recalling the answer to a question, turn back to the pages that cover the material and study them again.

1. What is the difference between fiberglass and plastic?

2. Describe how to identify the plastic used in a plastic part.

SUGGESTIONS FOR FURTHER STUDY

Locate a late-model car, and make a thorough examination of it to identify plastic parts. On a sheet of paper for your notebook, make two columns. The heading for one column is "Interior Parts." Label the other column "Exterior Parts." Write down the name of each part you find inside and outside the car under the proper heading.

[illegible]

[illegible] [illegible]

[illegible] remove [illegible] [illegible] [illegible] [illegible] a sharp knife. The welded [illegible] can [illegible] [illegible] [illegible] [illegible] [illegible] [illegible] coarse 36-[illegible] weld [illegible]

PART 5

ADJUSTING BODY PANELS

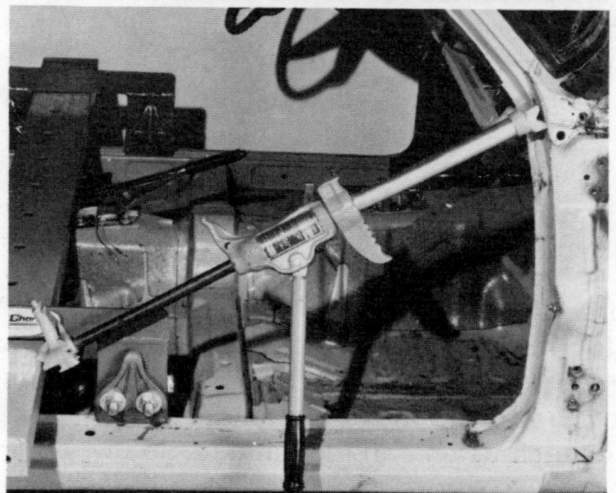

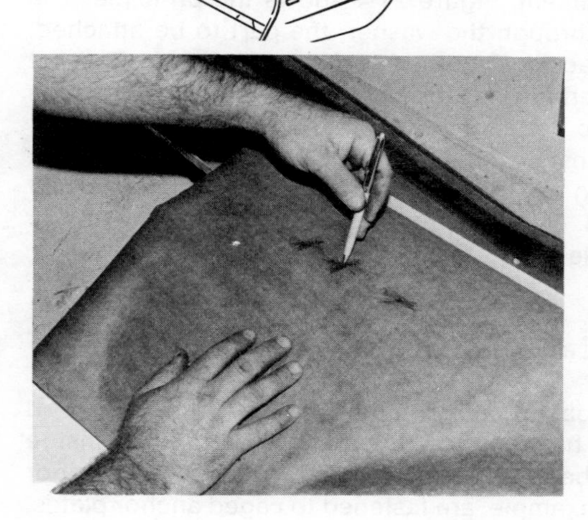

In this part, you will learn how certain body panels are adjusted. These include the fenders, doors, hoods, and trunk or luggage-compartment lids. All these panels are attached to the body with hinges.

Doors, hoods and trunk lids may be made of sheet metal, sheet aluminum, or fiberglass. Regardless of the material, the adjusting methods for each of these panels are the same. In general, part of the procedure is to reposition the panel hinges.

Fenders are securely fastened in place. However, the other panels are each a type of door that provides access to a compartment. The hood provides access to the engine compartment. The doors provide access to the passenger compartment. The trunk lid provides access to the luggage compartment.

Part 6 covers the servicing of doors, tailgates, lift gates, sun roofs, and the special mechanisms—such as door locks and window regulators—that they contain.

There are three chapters in Part 5. These are as follows:

21 ADJUSTING BODY PANELS

In this part, you will learn the various methods used to shift body panels with respect to the car body so that they will fit properly. Four mechanical devices are used:

1. Shims
2. Slotted holes
3. Caged or floating anchor plates
4. Adjustable stops

In addition, bending of metal is also used to secure a proper fit. We describe each of these methods of adjustment in this chapter.

FIGURE 21-1. A fender must line up with hood, door, and other parts. (*Ford Motor Company*)

○21-1 Reasons for Adjusting Body Panels

There are three reasons why body panels must fit and open and close properly:

1. SAFETY. Doors latch in two positions: the safety position and the closed or locked position. The door, when closed, should move past the safety latch position and into the fully closed position. If the door and latch are improperly positioned, only the safety latch will catch. This endangers the passenger sitting by the door. Hoods also have a safety latch position.
2. APPEARANCE. A fender that does not properly line up with the adjacent metal will look bad. The fender must fit on the sides, back, and front (Fig. 21-1). Likewise, misalignment of a door or trunk lid will show up and indicate poor workmanship.
3. SEALING. All openings but one into the car interior are closed by swinging panels—doors, hoods, trunk lids, tailgates, and lift gates. The one exception is the sun roof, which slides. These swinging or sliding panels must fit properly without binding and tightly enough to prevent the entrance of water, wind, or dust. There is one exception here also: sealing is not critical with the hood. With all other panels, however, the fit is completed with weatherstripping.

○21-2 Shims

Body shims are thin pieces of metal that can be placed between a part being attached and the car body (Fig. 21-2). Some shims are slotted. Others look like thick, flat washers.

Shims are available in various sizes and thicknesses. Frequently used thicknesses of body shims are 1/16 inch [1.59 mm], 1/8 inch [3.17 mm], and 3/16 inch [4.76 mm].

Installing a shim moves the part out from the body. If shims are present, removing a shim moves the part in. For example, Fig. 21-3A shows a part attached to the body with two shims between the part and body. Figure 21-3B shows the part attached with the shims removed. The part is moved closer to the body member. We explain later how shims are actually used. Note that the lower shims shown in Fig. 21-2 are slotted. Slotting permits them to be added or removed without taking the bolt out. That is, if the bolt or nut is loosened enough so there is space between the part and the body member, the shim can be slipped into place. It will be held there when the bolt or nut is tightened.

Where and how many shims to install are matters of judgment. If, for example, a fender fits too closely at the front edge, one or more shims can be installed between it and the body bracket to move the fender out. The experienced body technician can look and decide whether to install one, two, or more shims to make the adjustment.

○21-3 Slotted Holes

Slotted, or elongated, holes, either in the body bracket or post or in the part to be attached, can be used to secure alignment. Figure 21-4 shows the principle. The bolt is run through the washer, the part to be attached, the body bracket, the other washer, and the nut. The nut is not tightened until the part is moved up or down as necessary to get alignment. Then it is tightened.

In some installations, the holes are enlarged to permit movement in any direction so that proper alignment can be obtained. On these, there is no need to elongate the oversize holes.

○21-4 Caged or Floating Anchor Plates

Caged or floating anchor plates are much like oversized nuts which have tapped holes and are mounted inside the part to be attached or the body bracket. Some door hinges, for example, are fastened to caged anchor plates. Figure 21-5 shows the principle with a striker plate

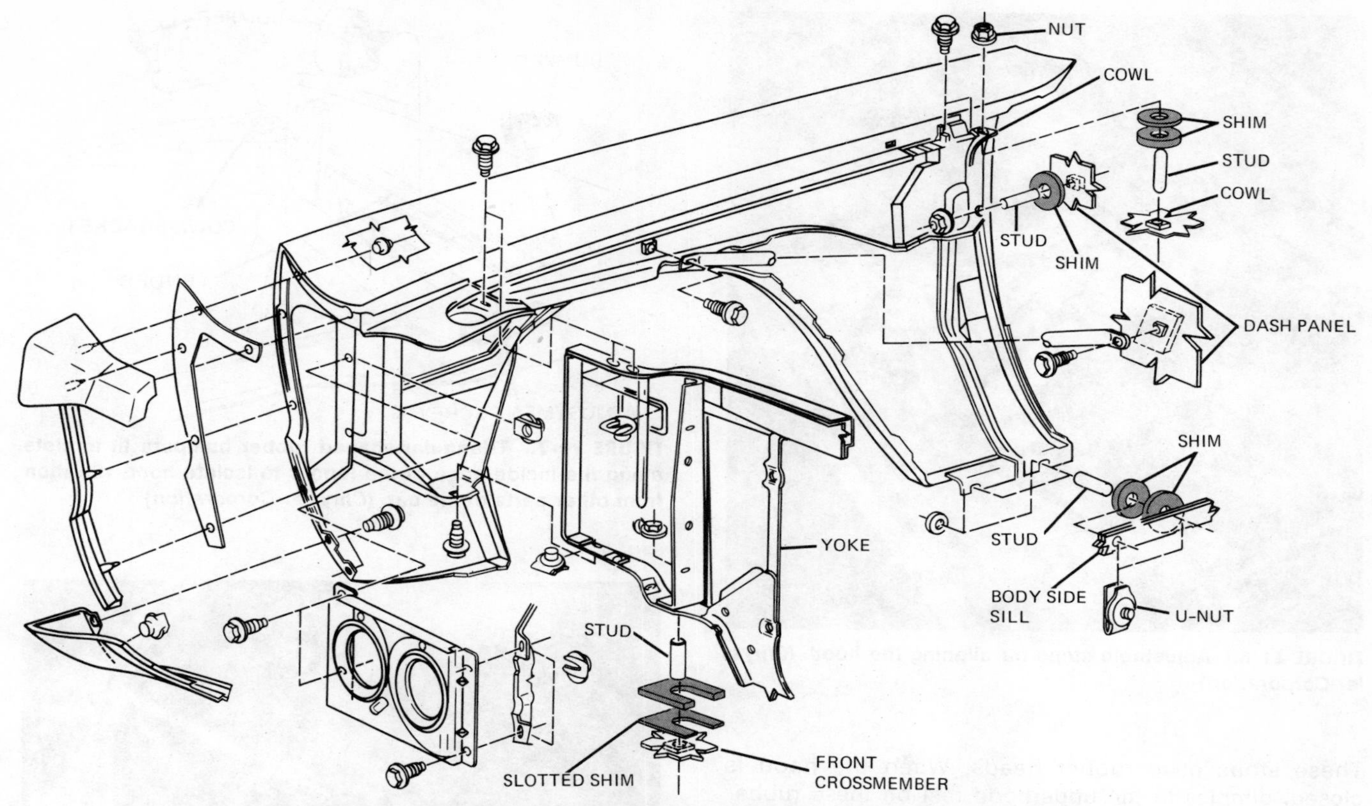

FIGURE 21-2. Shims are placed between the fender and the car body. ***(Chrysler Corporation)***

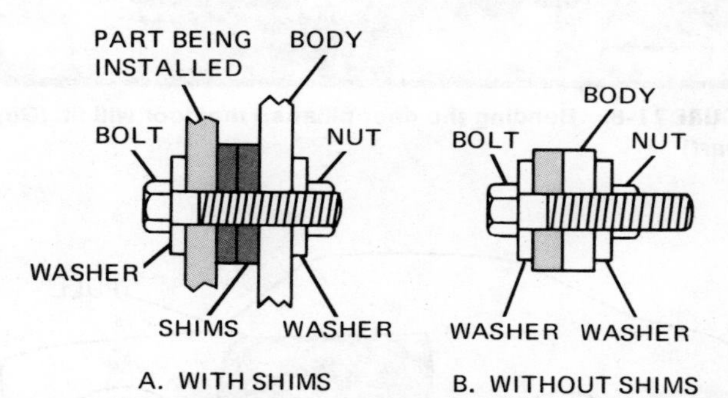

FIGURE 21-3. How shims position a part away from or closer to the car body.

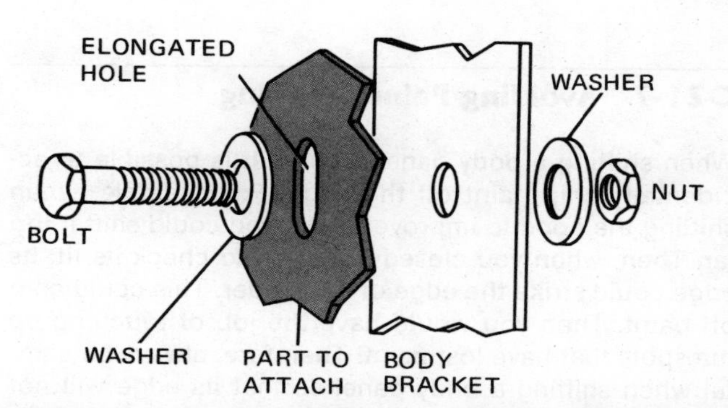

FIGURE 21-4. Elongated holes in some parts are used to secure alignment of attaching parts.

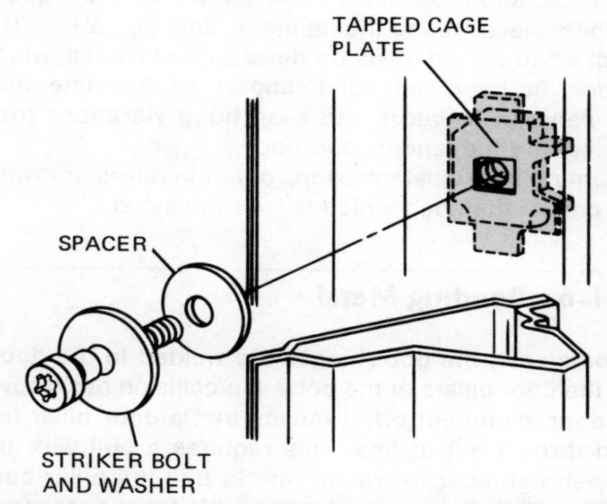

FIGURE 21-5. Tapped caged plate in the pillar does not fall when striker bolt is removed. ***(Fisher Body Division of General Motors Corporation)***

mounting. The anchor plate shown is in a pillar and is caged on the inside so it will not fall down when the bolt is removed. The hole in the pillar is enlarged so the plate can be shifted around as necessary. We describe the adjustment procedure later.

○21-5 Adjustable Stops

The body of many cars has several adjustable stops which position the hood when it is closed (Fig. 21-6).

FIGURE 21-6. Adjustable stops for aligning the hood. (*Chrysler Corporation*)

These stops have rubber heads. When the hood is closed, dimples in the underhood rest on these rubber heads. The stops properly position the hood when it is closed, and they also isolate the hood metal from the other metal of the car. This prevents any vibration of the hood from passing into other parts of the car. Assisting in this isolation, on many cars, are a series of rubber bumpers placed along the fender in slots (Fig. 21-7). The hood, when closed, rests on these rubber blocks, which provide the hood with solid support. At the same time, they serve as isolators and keep hood vibrations from passing into the fenders and body.

Turning the adjustable stops out or in raises or lowers that part of the hood which is over the stops.

○21-6 Bending Metal

In some cars, the door hinges are welded to the doors and the door pillars of the body. If a collision has thrown the door alignment off, it means that a door pillar has been thrown out of line. This requires a pull with the body-straightener hydraulic ram to pull the pillar back into line. Even on cars with adjustable hinges, door pillars may require pulling back into line. Figure 21-8 shows an example. This car suffered a heavy impact on its right front. During the repair operation, the technician found that even with the maximum adjustment allowable on the hinges, the right front door would not fit properly. The cowl and door pillar were bent back so that the door, in effect, sagged and did not fit the opening. Therefore, a correction was made as shown. Figure 21-9 shows the effect of the impact and what the pull did.

By exerting the pull, as shown, the technician pulled the cowl and pillar forward. This raised the door from its sagged position. In the following chapter we describe the procedure of checking and adjusting the fit of the door. This includes checking of the weatherstripping around the door and opening.

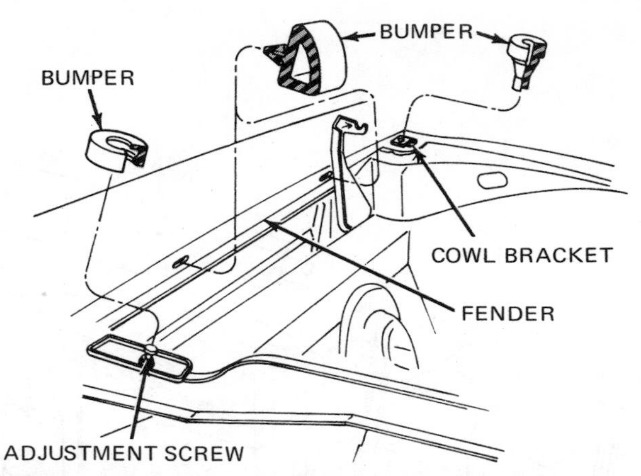

FIGURE 21-7. Triangular-shaped rubber bumpers fit in slots along the inside edge of the fender to isolate hood vibration from other parts of the car. (*Chrysler Corporation*)

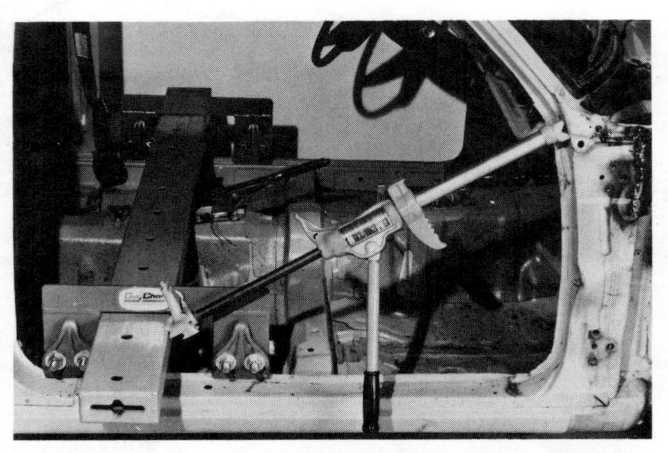

FIGURE 21-8. Bending the door pillar so the door will fit. (*Guy Chart*)

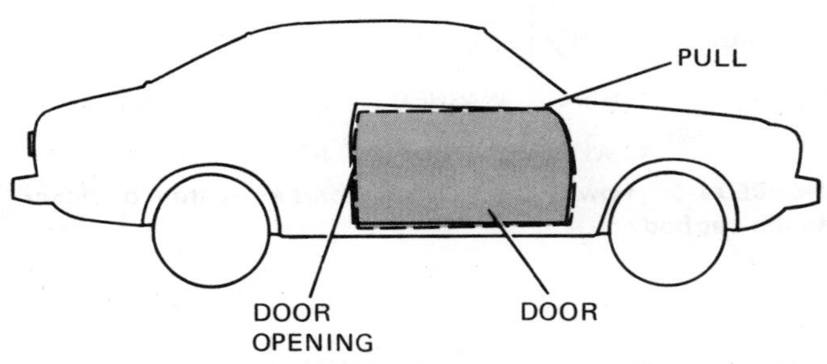

FIGURE 21-9. Door sag caused by impact to right front fender.

○21-7 Avoiding Paint Chipping

When shifting a body panel around, it is possible to accidentally chip paint off the edge. For example, when shifting the hood to improve the fit, you could shift it too far. Then, when you closed the hood to check its fit, its edge could strike the edge of the fender. This could chip off paint. Then you would have the job of touching up the spots that have lost paint. Therefore, always be careful when shifting a body panel so that its edge will not strike an adjacent stationary edge when the panel fit is tested.

CHAPTER 21 CHECKUP

NOTE: Since the following is a chapter review test, you should review the chapter before taking the test.

In this chapter we have discussed the various ways that body panels are adjusted for proper fit. Although most of the panels have some type of adjusting device, others do not. Occasionally you will have to use a body-frame straightener or a body jack to make the necessary push or pull to bring a pillar into alignment. To find out how well you understand everything in this chapter, answer the questions that follow.

COMPLETING THE SENTENCES The sentences below are incomplete. After each sentence there are several words or phrases, but only one of them correctly completes the sentence. Write each sentence in your notebook, ending the sentence with the one word or phrase that completes it correctly.

1. Four methods of panel adjustments are shims, slotted holes, caged anchor plates, and (*a*) welding, (*b*) adjustable stops, (*c*) brazing, (*d*) cotter pins.
2. Safety, appearance, and sealing are three reasons why (*a*) new cars are popular, (*b*) lower speeds are required today, (*c*) the car passes safety inspection, (*d*) body panels must fit properly.
3. Doors and hoods have (*a*) three hinges, (*b*) only torsion-bar springs, (*c*) a safety latch position, (*d*) no method of adjustment.
4. Body shims may be (*a*) slotted or adjustable, (*b*) slotted or washer type, (*c*) adjustable or rubber, (*d*) caged or anchored.
5. A caged anchor plate (*a*) is held in position by the cage, (*b*) falls when the screws in it are removed, (*c*) is welded in place, (*d*) is not used today.

QUESTIONS Write each of the following questions, and then the answers, in your notebook. If you have trouble recalling the answer to a question, turn back to the pages that cover the material and study them again.

1. Why is it necessary to adjust body panels?
2. What determines how many shims you use in positioning a body panel?
3. How do you adjust a door that has slotted holes in the body bracket?
4. When might you have to bend metal in order to secure alignment?
5. What is the purpose of the rubber head used on adjustable hood stops?

SUGGESTIONS FOR FURTHER STUDY

On a car, carefully examine how each body panel is fastened. Raise the hood, and locate the adjustable stops and the rubber bumpers. Also note how the fender is attached at the cowl and at the front. Look under the fender, and notice how it is fastened at the bottom. You will probably see a fender brace, which is used to prevent the sheet-metal panel from flapping. Next, open a door and see how the hinges are mounted to the door and to the body. Then examine the hinges to see if they are welded in place or if they have a provision for adjustment. Check the door pillar post, and find out how the door-latch striker plate is fastened in place and adjusted. Raise the trunk lid and make the same checks of the trunk-lid hinges.

22 FITTING FENDERS AND DOORS

In this chapter, you will learn how fenders that are bolted onto the car body are fitted. This includes adjusting the position of the fender fore and aft, up and down, and in and out. Also, you will learn how to adjust the fit of the car doors to the door openings in the car body. Chapter 24 covers door services other than adjusting fit.

○22-1 Fender Alignment

A fender must fit properly (Fig. 21-1) to avoid unsightly gaps that could cause air, dust, and water leaks. An even gap on each side, between the fender and hood and between the fender and door, usually is considered a good fit. Damage to the fender may result from a gap that is too small. If the fender is too far back (towards the door), it will be struck by the forward edge of the door as it opens. A fender too far in (towards the hood) may be hit by the hood as it closes. This can happen when sufficient space is not left for the hood to close into. Striking a misaligned fender with a hood or door probably will chip the paint on the fender, and it may cause dents.

Figure 22-1 shows how the fore-and-aft and the in-and-out adjustments are made. By using slotted holes, the attaching bolts are permitted some movement in the desired direction. Note that the slotted holes at the bot-

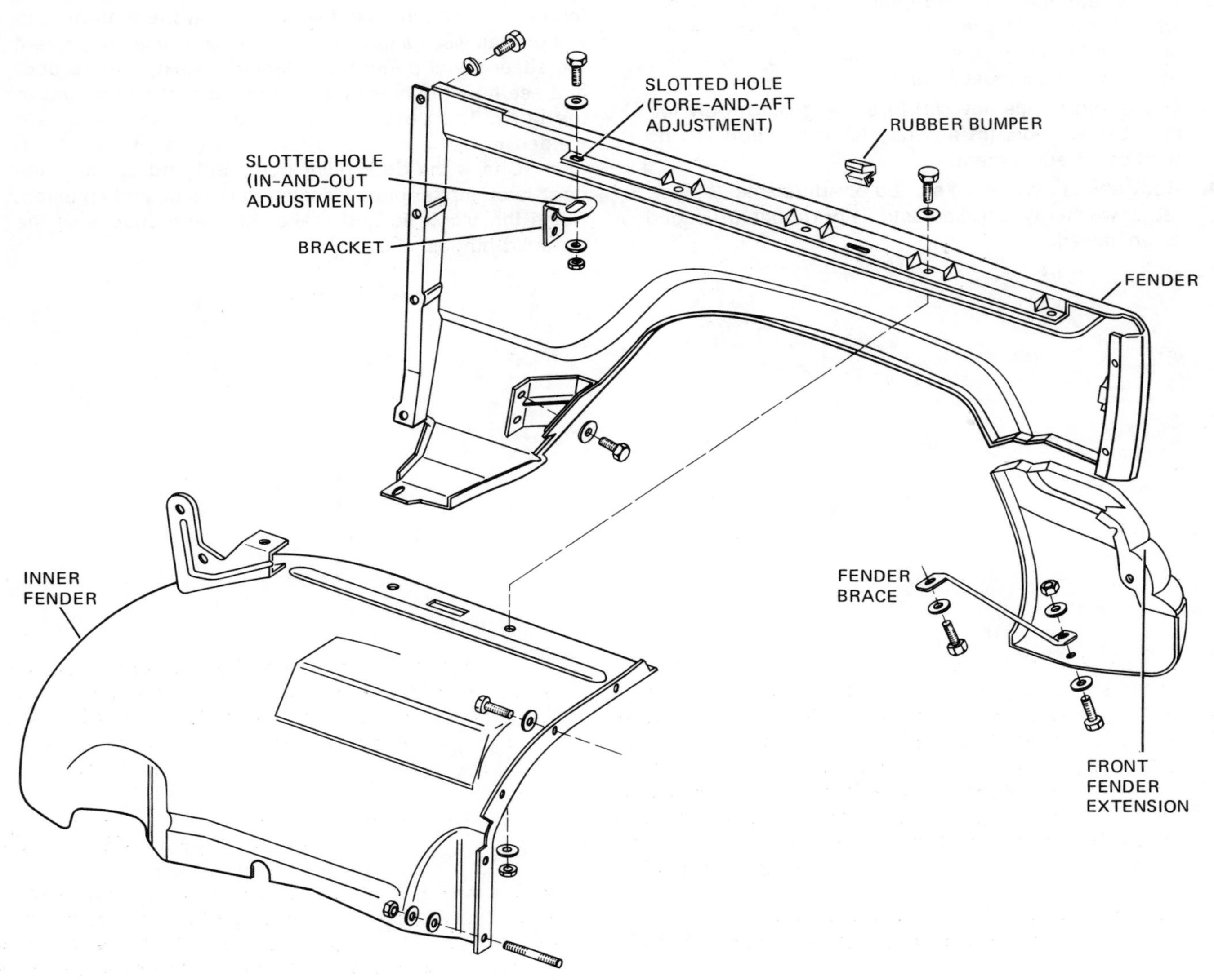

FIGURE 22-1. Slotted holes provide a method of adjusting the fender. (*American Motors Corporation*)

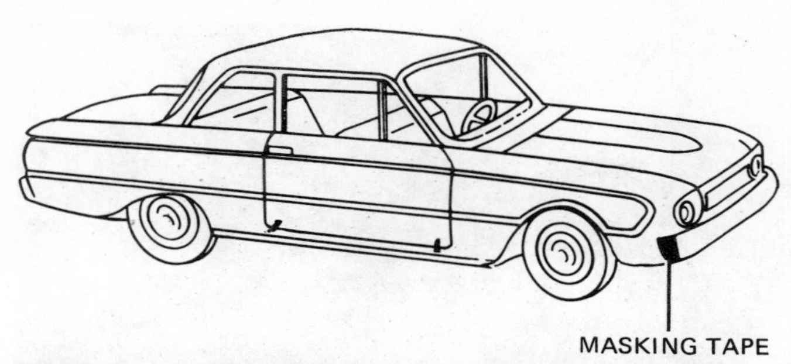

FIGURE 22-2. Mask the edge of the bumper to prevent damaging the paint on the fender.

tom of the fender allow a separate in-and-out adjustment for each end of the fender. Refer back to Fig. 21-2 to see how shims are used to make the up-and-down adjustment.

○22-2 Fender Removal

When a fender is removed, you must be very careful not to chip the paint on it. Also, care must be taken not to chip paint from the door. Removing a fender sometimes is like taking one piece out of a completed jigsaw puzzle without touching any of the other pieces. With wrap-around bumpers and with little space between the fender and other panels, it requires skill and proper masking to remove a fender without damaging the paint.

One way to avoid chipping paint on the fender is to apply several layers of masking tape over the edge of the bumper on its end, as shown in Fig. 22-2. This will prevent the rough edges of the bumper from damaging the paint should the fender drag against the bumper while being removed.

Disconnect the battery ground cable. If the radio antenna is mounted on the fender, the antenna must be removed. This is done by disconnecting the antenna wire from the radio in the dash. Tie a long string to the antenna wire, and then remove the antenna assembly from the fender. You will use the string to guide the antenna wire back into position when you reinstall the fender.

Place several layers of masking tape over the front edge of the door, as shown in Fig. 22-3. This will prevent paint damage should the fender strike the door during removal. If the fender has a wheel lip molding, you may have to remove it. Then turn the steering wheel in the same direction as the fender being removed. That is, if you are removing a right fender, turn the steering wheel to the right. This will allow you to get to the attaching screws more easily.

MASKING TAPE

FIGURE 22-3. Place masking tape on the front edge of the door.

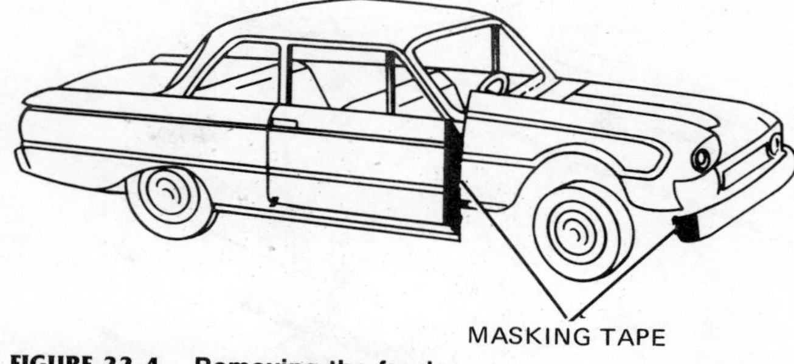

FIGURE 22-4. Removing the fender.

NOTE: Remember that the parts on a car are named by their position when you are sitting in the driver's seat and facing forward.

Remove the splash-guard or inner-fender (Fig. 22-1) mounting screws from inside the fender. You may have to hunt for these screws, as they often are covered with undercoating and dirt. Next, take out all other screws that attach the fender to another part. The screw holes shown in Fig. 22-1 are typical locations. In general, the fender fastens on all edges except around the wheel opening. This area of the fender is supported and protected by an attached splash guard or inner fender, as shown in Fig. 22-1.

Today the fenders on many cars contain headlamps, parking lamps, and side-marker lamps. On these, you must disconnect the wiring for each and then remove the lamp. Some fenders may have moldings that must be removed to prevent damage to them. When the fender is free of all attachments, you are ready to remove it.

To remove the fender, first tilt the top of the fender out at the front. Then lift the fender at the rear and remove it from the car, as shown in Fig. 22-4. Be careful not to scrape the paint or make dents while you are lifting and removing the fender.

○22-3 Fender Installation

To install the fender, tilt the rear of the fender up and carefully position it in place. Align the fender (○22-1) and install the attaching screws. Brush or spray undercoating onto the underside of the fender and the entire splash guard-to-fender contact area. This area must be sealed to prevent rust.

Install in the new fender any lamps, moldings, or other parts that were removed. Connect the wiring for the lights. Use the string attached to the radio antenna to pull the antenna wire back through the fender. Reconnect the antenna to the radio. Then install the antenna assembly on the fender. Connect the battery ground cable to the battery.

The fender should be adjusted to provide for equal spacing at the cowl, door front edge, and door top panel edge. On the fender shown in Fig. 21-2, these adjustments are made with shims in three areas: at the bottom of the body side sill, at the cowl top panel, and at the yoke.

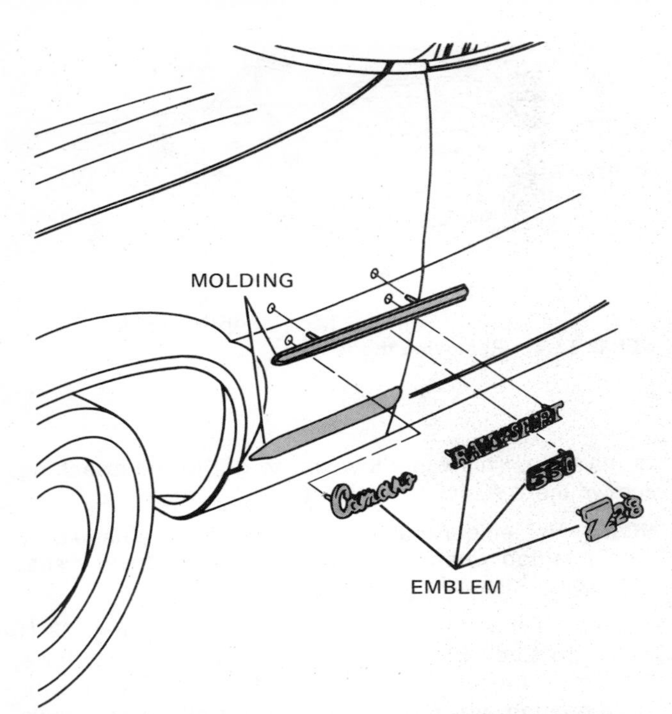

FIGURE 22-5. **Small moldings and emblems sometimes can be removed from the old fender and installed on the new fender.** *(Chevrolet Motor Division of General Motors Corporation)*

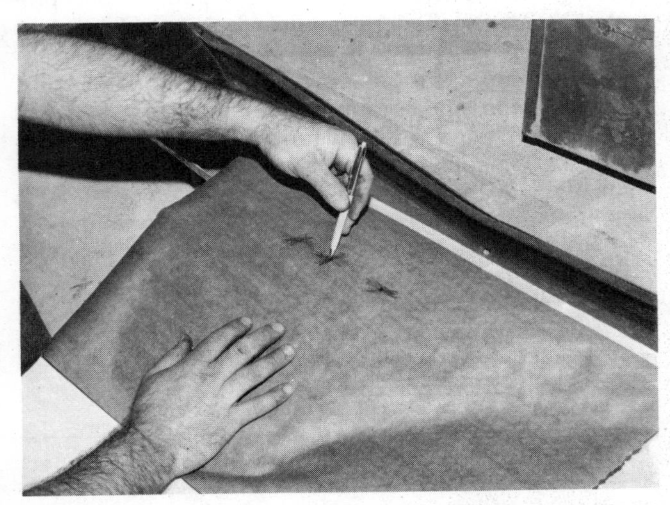

FIGURE 22-6. **The technician carefully positions the paper on the discarded fender and marks the exact location of the holes where the emblem was attached.**

○22-4 Locating the Emblem

Many cars have small moldings and names in fancy script or lettering attached to the fenders. Several examples of these emblems are shown in Fig. 22-5. When a damaged fender is removed, it is often possible to remove the emblem and install it on the new fender after the fender has been put in place. Figures 22-6 and 22-7 show the way to locate the emblem correctly. In Fig. 22-6, the technician carefully positions paper on the old fender after the emblem has been taken off. The exact locations of the holes are marked on the paper. Then the technician transfers the paper to the new fender. Now a punch and hammer are used to mark the locations of the holes to be drilled for the emblem in the new fender (Fig. 22-7).

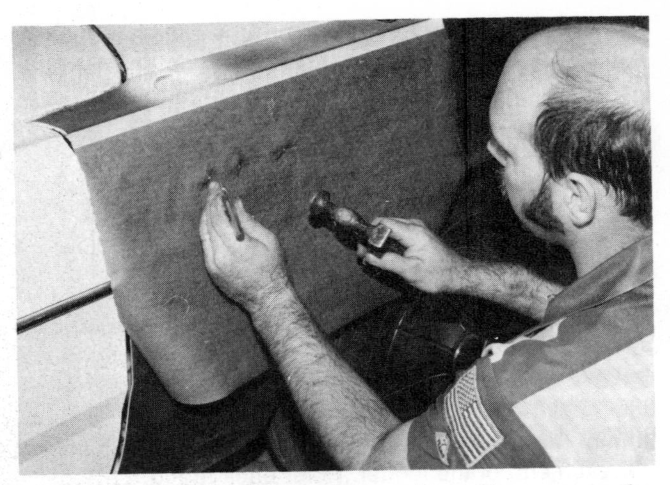

FIGURE 22-7. **The technician then positions the paper on the new fender after it has been installed and uses a punch to mark the locations of the holes for drilling.**

○22-5 Fitting Doors

As we mentioned in Chapter 21, the holes in which the hinge-attaching bolts go (in door or door pillar) are slotted or enlarged. This enables the technician to shift the hinges up or down, or sideways, to get proper door fit. In addition, the latch pin, or striker bolt as it is also called, may require adjustment to assure proper latching of the door when it is shut.

NOTE: Chapter 24 covers door services other than adjusting fit. These include servicing window regulators, latching and locking devices, and weatherstripping. In addition, Chapter 24 covers water-testing door seals for leaks and also locating and eliminating wind noise, air, and water leaks.

○22-6 Door Alignment

Proper alignment is achieved when the gaps between the edges of the door and the surrounding metal are uniform all the way around (Fig. 22-8). In addition, the door should open and close without binding. It should not move up or down as it latches. If it does, the latch and striker bolt are not properly aligned.

As the door closes, the latch should move through the safety latch position and into the fully latched or locked position. There are two latching positions on a car door. The first is the safety latch position. The second is the fully closed or fully latched position. Open and close a car door slowly to check this out for yourself. Sometimes, when adjustments have been made to the door and striker bolt, the door will latch in only the first, or safety latch, position. This creates a dangerous riding condition for the person sitting next to the improperly latched door. Correct adjustment allows the door to close into the full-latched, or locked, position.

If the door is shifted rearward during an adjustment, the switch on the door jamb which controls the dome light or interior courtesy lights may require adjustment. That is, the switch may have to be shifted rearward. If it is not adjusted, the switch might not open and turn off the courtesy lights in the car when the door is closed.

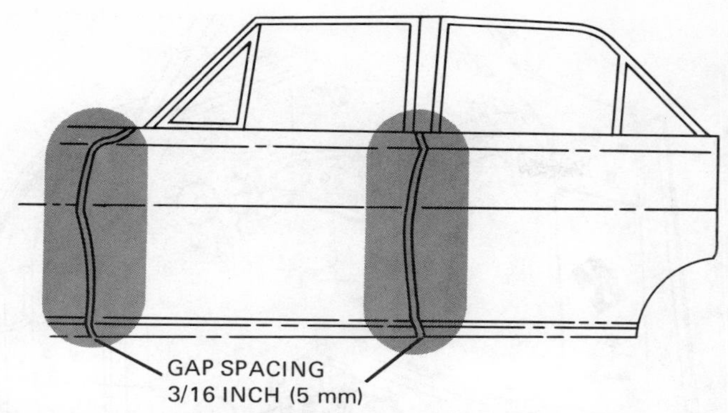

FIGURE 22-8. Typical gap spacing around a door.

Sometimes a hinge or striker plate is moved enough to expose unpainted metal. When this occurs, touch up the unpainted area with paint of the proper color.

NOTE: When rebuilding a wrecked car, it is especially important to achieve proper door fit, not only from the standpoint of safety. The customer often judges the quality of the body-repair job by the way the doors open, close, fit, and sound (when closing).

◯22-7 General Motors Door Adjustments

Some General Motors cars have the hinges welded onto the doors and door pillars. No adjustment is possible on these doors except by using the hydraulic pulling equipment to pull on the pillars supporting the doors. In Chapter 24, covering door service, we describe the procedure of drilling out the welds and removing the hinges from the door pillars and doors. Then we explain how to reinstall the doors.

The General Motors door-adjustment procedure for doors attached by bolts is described below. This procedure applies to all late-model General Motors cars using bolts to attach the hinges to doors and pillars.

1. Before checking door alignment and fit, and before making any adjustments, remove the striker bolt (Fig. 21-5) from the door pillar. This allows the door to hang freely on its hinges. When a front door is being adjusted, you may want to loosen the front fender so that it will not interfere.
2. The fit is checked by observing the variations in the gap between the edges of the door—at the top, sides, and bottom of the door—and the adjacent sheet metal of the body (Fig. 22-8). If the fit is not about the same all around, adjustment is required.
3. Adjust the door up or down, or fore or aft, at the body-hinges pillar attachments (Fig. 22-9). That is, the bolts attaching the hinges to the pillar are loosened so the door can be shifted up, down, fore, or aft. Use a pry bar padded heavily with shop cloths to avoid damaging the edge of the door. Loosen the bolts only enough to permit the door to be shifted with light pressure. Tighten the bolts when the adjustment is correct.
4. To move the door in or out, loosen the bolts attaching the hinges to the door. Then shift the door as required and tighten the bolts to the specified torque.

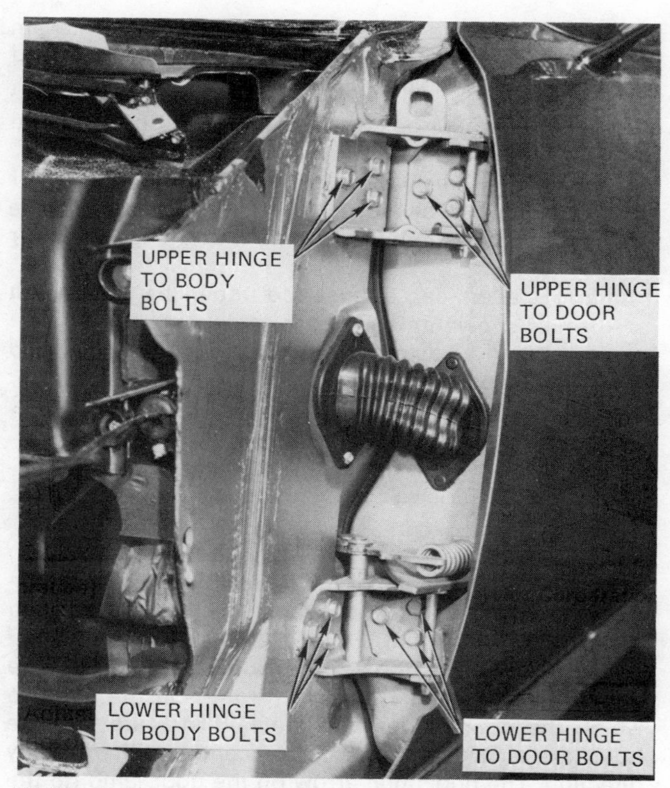

FIGURE 22-9. Hinge adjustment points on GM cars with bolt-on hinges. (*Fisher Body Division of General Motors Corporation*)

5. The striker bolt (Fig. 21-5) must be adjusted so that it is centered in the door latch when the door is closed. General Motors recommends checking this adjustment with a small amount of modeling clay or caulking compound (Fig. 22-10), as follows:
   a. Make sure door is properly aligned.
   b. Apply modeling clay or caulking compound to the lock-bolt opening as shown in Fig. 22-10.
   c. Close door only as far as necessary for the striker bolt to form an impression in the clay or caulking, as shown.

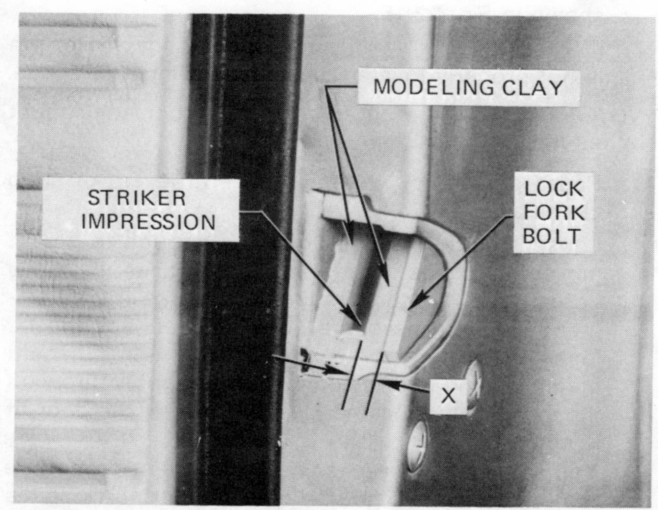

FIGURE 22-10. Checking striker-bolt adjustment with modeling clay. (*Fisher Body Division of General Motors Corporation*)

NOTE: Do not close the door completely or you will jam the clay or caulking compound into the door lock and give yourself a problem in removing it.

- **d.** The striker-bolt impression should be centered fore and aft, as shown in Fig. 22-10.
- **e.** The striker bolt can be shifted up or down, or sideways, by loosening it and moving it to make the adjustment. It screws into a caged anchor plate.
- **f.** Spacers can be inserted under the striker bolt as shown in Fig. 21-5 if necessary.
- **g.** When adjustment is correct, tighten the bolt to the specified torque.

6. Make sure the door fully latches and that the door-jamb switch is correctly adjusted (Section 22-6).

○22-8 Ford Door Adjustments

The holes in the hinges or the holes at the hinge-attaching points are either slotted (elongated) or enlarged to permit door alignment. Figure 22-11 shows the adjustments of the front door of the Bobcat and Pinto. The vertical and horizontal arrows (to left) on the pillar to which the door hinges are attached indicate that the holes are enlarged so the hinges can be shifted in any direction. The horizontal arrow on the door jamb (to the right) indicates that the hinges can be shifted only horizontally on the jamb.

Proper alignment is achieved when the gap between the edge of the door and the surrounding metal of the car body is uniform all around (Fig. 22-8). In addition, the door should open and close without binding. Also, the door should latch and hold closed.

Figures 22-12, 22-13, and 22-14 show the front- and rear-door adjustments on other Ford-built cars. Figure 22-15 shows the adjustments of the door-latch striker pin. The adjustments are made as follows:

1. Check the fit of the door to determine how it must be moved in order to achieve proper fit all around. Open and close the door and note whether the latch is working properly. The striker pin should center in the latch assembly. The latch should close around the pin at the proper distance from the end of the pin as shown in Fig. 22-15.
2. If the door does not fit properly or if the striker pin is not properly located, adjustments must be made.

NOTE: Do not try to cover up a poor door adjustment by readjusting the striker pin.

3. Pad a pry bar by wrapping several layers of shop cloths around it.
4. Loosen the door hinge bolts just enough to permit movement of the door. Use the pry bar to move the door in the direction required to make the adjustment. Tighten the hinge bolts and recheck the fit. Make sure there is no interference with adjacent metal. Making this adjustment will probably throw off the striker-pin adjustment. Check it after the door fit is corrected.
5. You may need to repeat the adjustment procedure more than once to get the correct door fit. Once the fit is correct, tighten the hinge bolts to the specified torque. Recheck the fit of the striker pin.

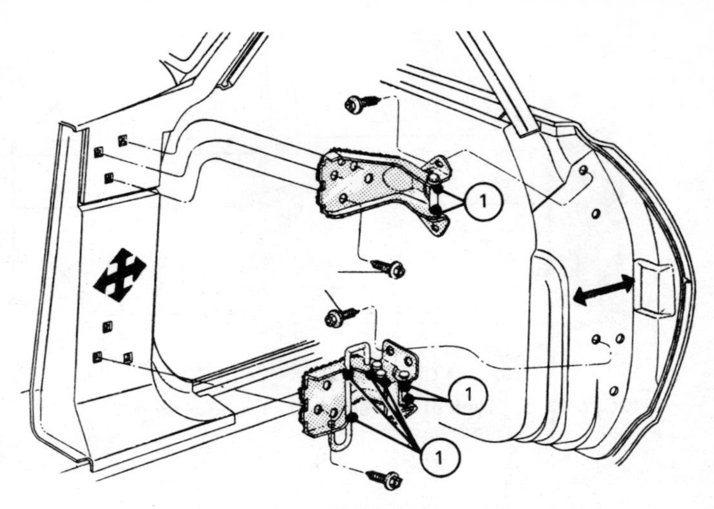

FIGURE 22-11. Front-door and adjustments on Ford-built Bobcat and Pinto models. (*Ford Motor Company*)

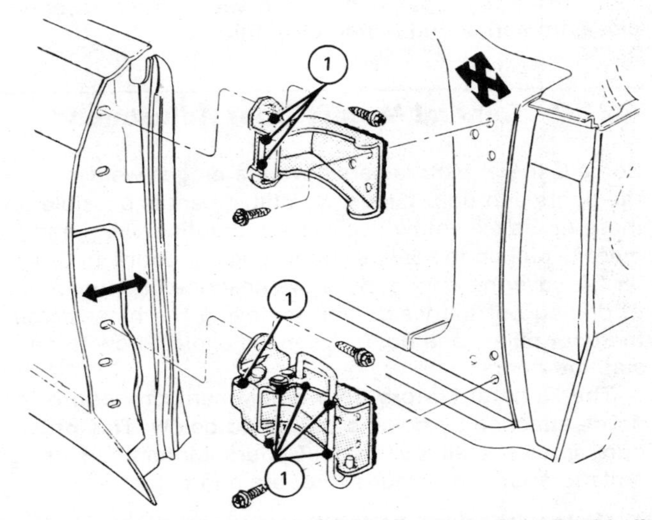

FIGURE 22-12. Front-door adjustments on other Ford-built cars. (*Ford Motor Company*)

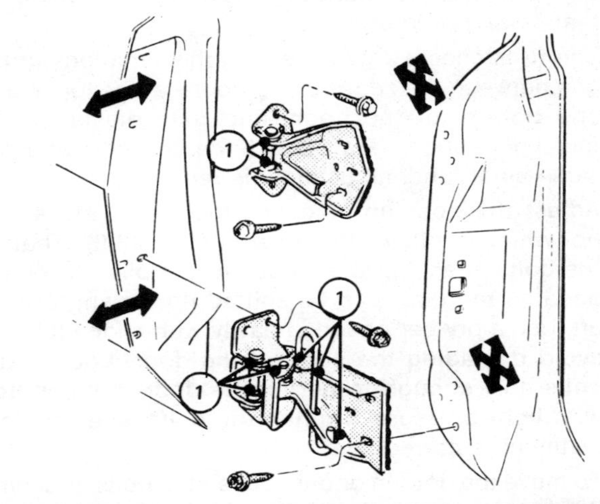

FIGURE 22-13. Rear-door adjustments on certain Ford cars. (*Ford Motor Company*)

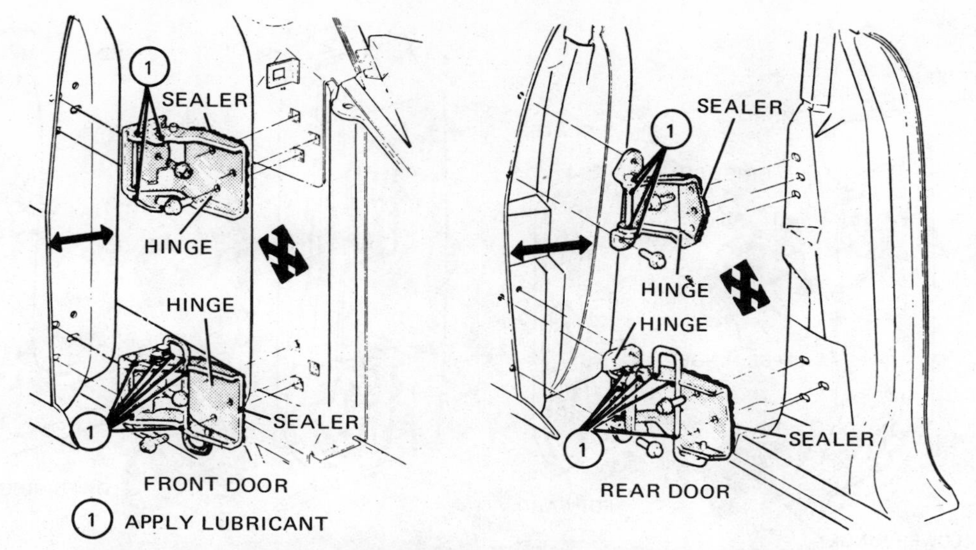

FIGURE 22-14. Door-hinge adjustments on Ford hardtop models. (*Ford Motor Company*)

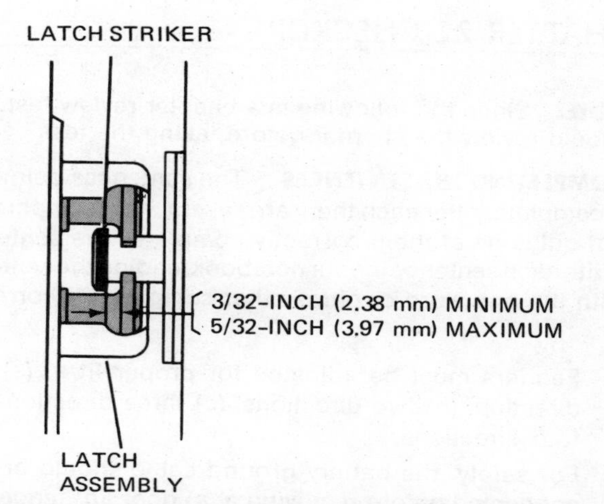

FIGURE 22-15. Proper adjustment of the door-latch striker pin. (*Ford Motor Company*)

6. The striker pin can be adjusted sideways and up and down. Its threaded end goes through an enlarged hole in the door pillar and into a threaded anchor plate behind the pillar. When the pin is loosened (with a Phillips screwdriver), it can be shifted in the direction required. The pin should be located so that it centers in the latch when the door is closed.

If the latch is not closing on the pin within the dimension range given in Fig. 22-15, you may have to add or remove shims (spacers) under the pin plate. To check the clearance, or the point at which the latch is contacting the pin, apply a thin coat of dark grease on the pin. Then close and open the door. Examine the marks in the grease to see where the latch has hit the pin. Shim as necessary. Wipe off the dark grease so it won't get on a customer's clothes.

When the adjustment is completed, the latch should close over the pin smoothly with no upward or downward movement of the door. The door should open smoothly without dragging on the pin.

7. Make sure that the door fully latches and that the door-jamb switch is correctly adjusted (Section 22-6).

○22-9 Chrysler Door Adjustments

Figure 22-16 shows the tool Chrysler recommends for loosening and tightening the door hinge bolts on automobiles they build. Figure 22-17 shows the arrangement for front-door hinges and striker pin. Figure 22-18 shows the rear-door hinges.

The doors can be shifted up and down on the door pillar, forward or backward, or in and out, as follows:

1. Up-and-down adjustment. This is made at either the pillar or door hinges. That is, the hinge bolts holding the hinge to the door can be loosened to make the adjustment. Or the hinge bolts holding the hinge to the pillar can be loosened to make the adjustment.

2. In-and-out adjustment. If the door panel is not flush with the surrounding metal, the door must be moved in or out. This adjustment is made at the door hinge half. Adjust only one hinge at a time. Raising the outer end of the door (door open) moves the upper part of the door into the door opening (when door is closed). Lowering the outer end of the door (door open) moves the lower part of the door into the door opening (when door is closed).

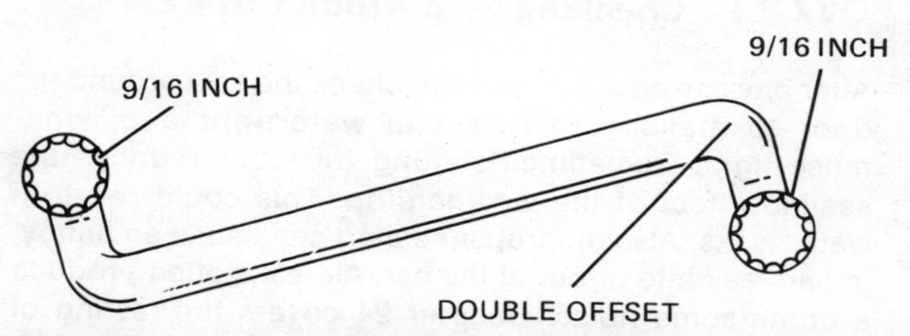

FIGURE 22-16. Front-hinge adjusting tool. (*Chrysler Corporation*)

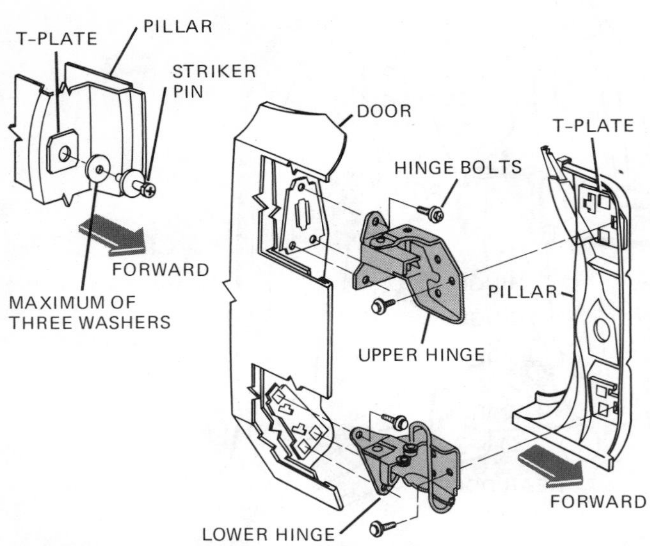

FIGURE 22-17. Front-door hinge and striker pin arrangement on Chrysler-built cars. (*Chrysler Corporation*)

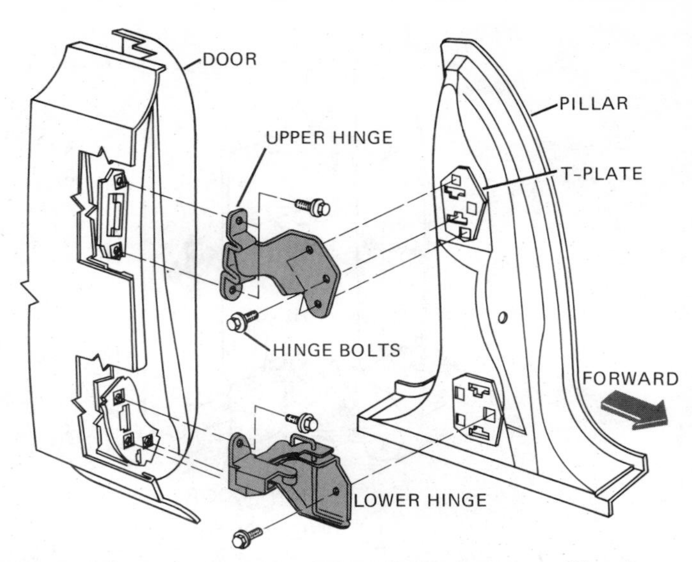

FIGURE 22-18. Rear-door hinge arrangement on Chrysler-built cars. (*Chrysler Corporation*)

3. Fore-and-aft adjustment. The fore-and-aft adjustment is made at the pillar hinge half. Adjust only one hinge at a time. Raising the outer end of the door (with door open) moves the upper part of the door forward (with door closed). Lowering the outer end of the door (with door open) moves the lower part forward (when door is closed).
4. Check the position of the striker pin as the door latches, and make the necessary adjustments to center the pin in the latch. Make sure the pin is entering the latch deeply enough. That is, the latch must close over a central part of the pin.
5. Make sure that the door fully latches and that the door-jamb switch is correctly adjusted (Section 22-6).

○22-10 AMC Door Adjustments

The adjustments on the doors of cars made by American Motors are similar to those described previously. The striker bolt should be removed and the fit of the door noted as the door hangs freely in the door opening. In-and-out adjustments are made by loosening the hinge bolts at the door. Up-and-down or fore-and-aft adjustments are made by loosening the hinge bolts at the door pillar. The striker bolt should be tightened after it is adjusted. Make sure that the door fully latches and that the door-jamb switch is properly adjusted (Section 22-6).

○22-11 Checking Seal Around Door

After any car-door adjustment, check the seal around the door to make sure it is still watertight and wind-noise–tight. Sometimes shifting the door reduces the sealing effect of the weatherstrip. This could result in water leaks. Also, improper sealing can cause an annoying air leak into or out of the car. Air leaks often produce a bothersome noise. Chapter 24 covers the testing of weatherstripping for water leaks and tells how to check for air noise and to correct the condition causing it.

CHAPTER 22 CHECKUP

NOTE: Since the following is a chapter review test, you should review the chapter before taking the test.

COMPLETING THE SENTENCES The sentences below are incomplete. After each there are several words or phrases, but only one of them correctly completes the sentence. Write each sentence in your notebook, ending the sentence with the one word or phrase that completes it correctly.

1. Fenders must be adjusted for proper fit in (*a*) one direction, (*b*) two directions, (*c*) three directions, (*d*) four directions.
2. For safety, the battery ground cable should be disconnected before removing a (*a*) door, (*b*) fender, (*c*) door hinge, (*d*) striker bolt.
3. As a general rule, the door fits properly when the gap (*a*) is narrower at the front, (*b*) is narrower at the rear, (*c*) does not exceed ¼ inch [12.7 mm], (*d*) is the same all around.
4. After adjusting a door, you may have to readjust the (*a*) headlights, (*b*) brake lights, (*c*) dome light switch, (*d*) glove-box light.
5. The door latch mechanism on a car door has (*a*) only one position, (*b*) two positions, (*c*) three positions, (*d*) four positions.

QUESTIONS Write each of the following questions, and then the answer, in your notebook. If you have trouble recalling the answer to a question, turn back to the pages that cover the material and study them again.

1. Name the three adjustments made to fit a fender.
2. Name the three adjustments made to fit a door.
3. How do you prevent paint damage while replacing a fender?
4. Describe how to change an emblem from an old fender to a new fender.
5. Why should the door seal be checked after adjusting the door?

23

FITTING HOODS AND TRUNK LIDS

In this chapter, you will learn how hoods are attached to the car body to cover the engine compartment. You will learn how to adjust the attachment points so as to get a good fit of the hood in relation to the fenders, cowl, and nose of the vehicle. Also, you will learn how trunk or rear-compartment lids are attached and how to adjust their fit. Various types of "hold-open" arrangements used to hold the lid open when it is raised are covered in this chapter. In addition, you will learn about weatherstripping and lid locks and how to replace them.

○23-1 Hood Hinge Locations

Most hoods are hinged at the back with the latch at the front of the car, above the radiator. Some are hinged at the front with the latch being at the cowl. The latch control is located inside the driver's compartment on many cars. This makes it harder for thieves to get into the engine compartment. That is, if the car is locked, you need a door key to gain easy access to the car and unlatch the hood.

○23-2 Adjusting Hoods

Hoods have two hinges, one on each side of the car. The opposite end of the hood has the latching arrangement (Fig. 23-1). The hood has bumpers which cushion the hood when it is closed and produces a tight and rattle-free fit. Some of these bumpers are adjustable (see Fig. 21-7).

Many times, you will be required to adjust the fenders along with the hood. For example, if one of the fenders is out of line, it will change the gap between the fender and hood and require adjustment. Figure 23-2 shows various types of misalignment and possible corrections. Chapter 22 covers fender adjustments. Hood hinges and hood latches have slotted holes which allow sufficient movement to correct the alignment. Shims may also be required to correct the fit. The adjustable bumpers are used not to secure alignment but to secure snug latching. This holds the hood tight at all four corners and along the sides so it will not rattle or flutter.

NOTE: The adjustable bumpers on the cowl (back of hood) must not be used to adjust the hood fit. The fit of the hood is adjusted by the slotted holes as explained above. *Only after this adjustment* is completed do you adjust the bumpers to take up any play and eliminate the possibility of rattles. To explain why this is the proper procedure, here is an example:

Suppose the right rear corner of the hood is too low. You could raise this by backing out the adjustable bumper. Then when the hood was closed, it would hit this bumper and be lifted up to align with the fender. However, every time the hood was closed the sheet metal would be bent up. You could end up with a bent hood that would require work to straighten it out. This would not happen if you adjusted the hood hinge first and *then* adjusted the bumper.

In many cars, the hinges have a special coil-spring arrangement that holds the hood up when it is raised (Fig. 23-4). The springs, in effect, go over center to produce the "hold-open" tension. Then as the hood is moved down to the closed position, the springs go back over center to produce a "hold-closed" tension. Without some such arrangement, a support is required to hold the hood open. Figure 23-1 shows a vehicle that uses a hood support rod.

Instead of coil-springs in the hinges, late-model cars made by Chrysler use torsion bars to produce the counterbalancing action. Figure 23-3 shows the torsion-bar arrangement.

○23-3 The Hood-Adjustment Procedure

First, check the hood fit at the back, front, and sides. If fenders are misaligned, adjust their fit as explained in Chapter 22. Then note hood alignment. Loosen the hinge screws as necessary to shift the hood fore and aft, or sideways, to secure proper alignment. Figures 23-3 to 23-5 show various attachment methods. As previously noted, the hinge screw holes are elongated or oversize

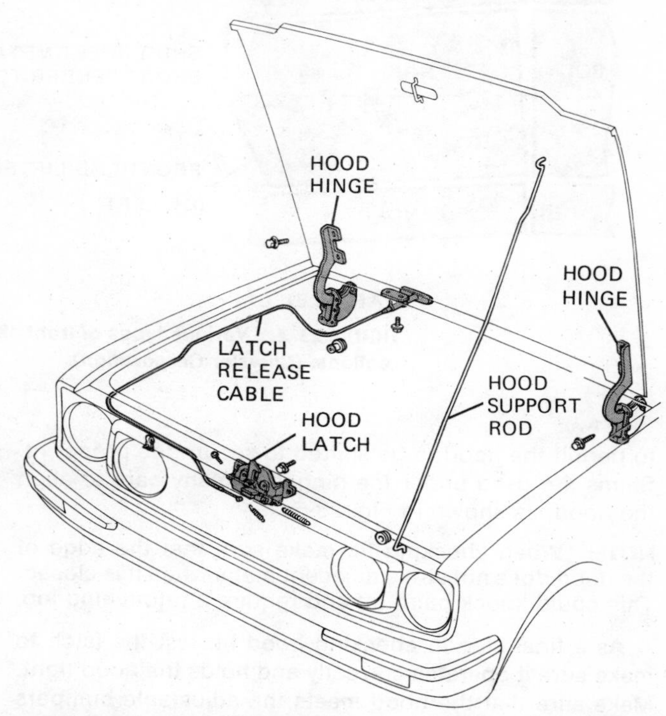

FIGURE 23-1. Hinges and latching arrangements on a hood. (*Toyota Motor Sales Co., Ltd.*)

A. POOR FENDER TO DOOR GAPS (FENDER FLUSH TO DOOR)

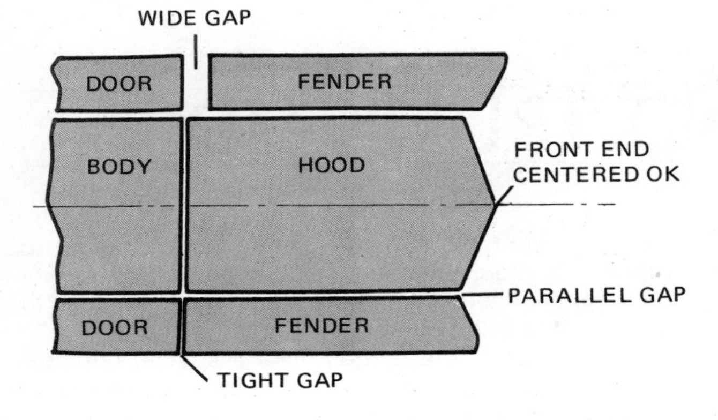

D. FENDERS OK BUT HOOD INCORRECTLY FIT (FENDERS SQUARE WITH PROPER DOOR ALIGNMENT)

DOOR
FENDER
BODY
HOOD
DOOR
FENDER

B. FENDER SET TO RIGHT OR LEFT AT DOORS (GAP OK)

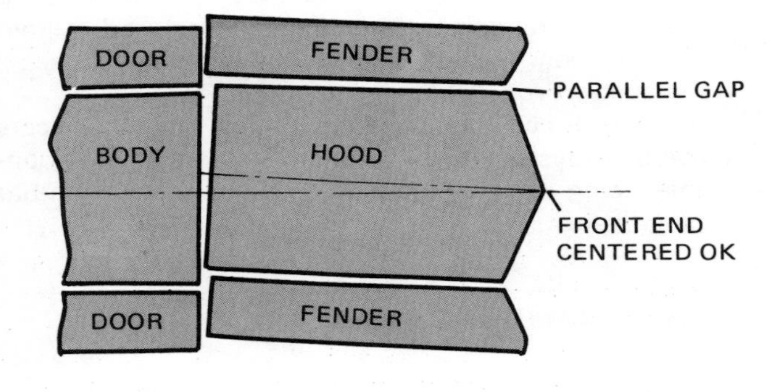

E. DOORS – ONE FOREWARD AND THE OTHER AFT (FENDER AND DOOR ALIGNMENT OK)

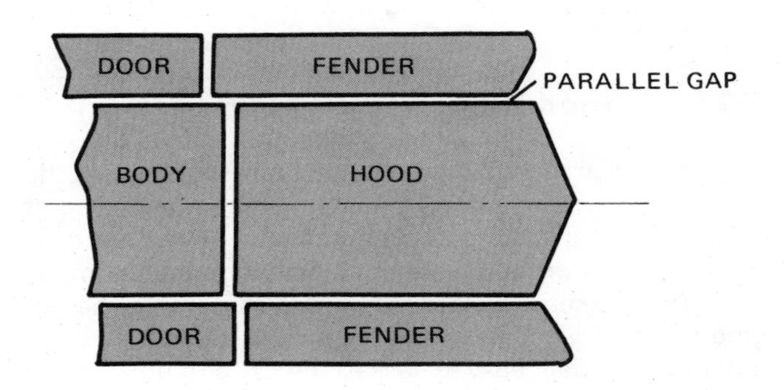

C. FENDERS OUT OF SQUARE (DOOR ALIGNMENT OK)

SKETCH SHOWING FENDER TO DOOR GAP NOT PARALLEL

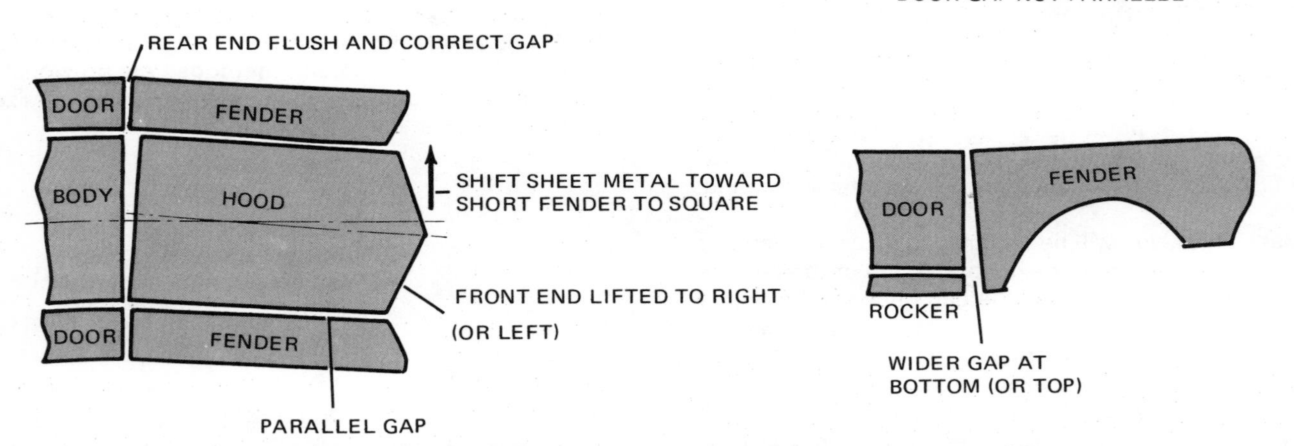

FIGURE 23-2. Various types of front sheet-metal misalignment and possible corrections. (*Chrysler Corporation*)

to permit the hood to be shifted to secure the proper fit. Shims are used under the hinges in many cars to align the hood, as shown in Fig. 23-5.

NOTE: When checking fit, make sure that the edge of the hood does not strike adjacent metal when it is closed. This could knock paint off and require a retouching job.

As a final step in checking hood fit, test the latch to make sure it operates correctly and holds the hood tight. Make sure that the hood meets the adjustable bumpers when it is closed. Also, see that all the bumpers along the sides of the hood (if used) are in place.

○23-4 Hood Latch

Hoods have two latches: the locking latch and the safety or auxiliary latch. When the hood release is operated, the locking latch releases, allowing the hood to pop up to the safety latch position. The safety latch is then released by reaching in under the hood and operating a lever by a finger. The hood release is located inside the passenger compartment in some cars (Fig. 23-6). In other cars, the hood release is located at the front of the car, as shown in Fig. 23-7. With either location, when the release

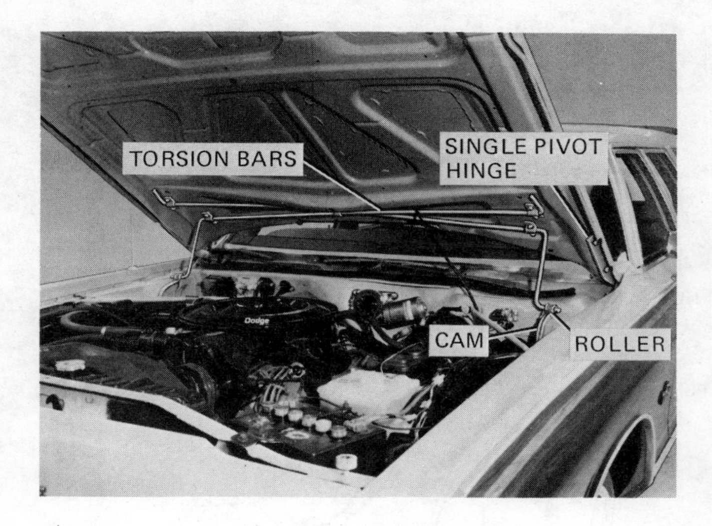

FIGURE 23-3. Torsion bars used to counterbalance the hood. (*Chrysler Corporation*)

FIGURE 23-4. Hood mounting on hinges using coil-springs for counterbalancing. (*Buick Motor Division of General Motors Corporation*)

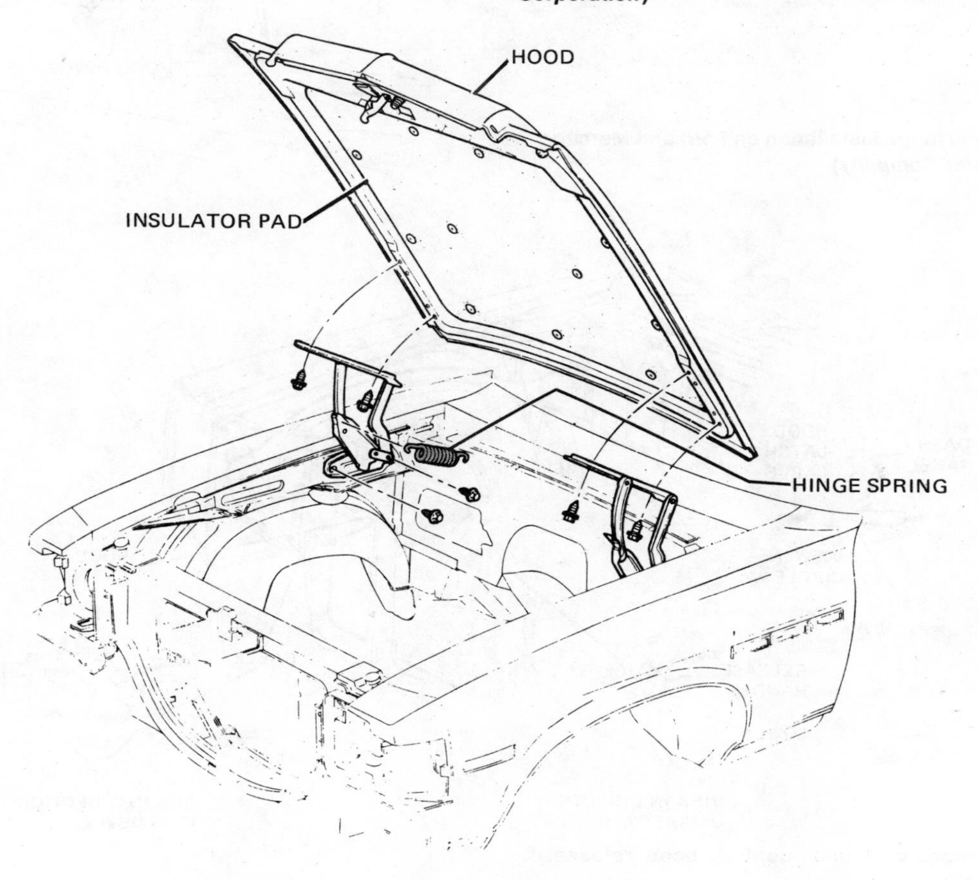

is pulled, a cable carries the movement to the latch, causing it to release. A pop-up spring (Fig. 23-8) then pushes the hood up to the safety latch position. The safety latch is released, as noted previously, by reaching in under the partly open hood.

○23-5 Adjusting Hood Latch

The hood latch can be moved from side to side, and up or down, to secure the proper fit. You must first make sure that the hood hinges are properly adjusted before attempting to adjust the latch. Then loosen the nuts or screws attaching the latch and make the adjustment. If an up or down adjustment must be made, first loosen the adjustable stop screws at the front and turn them in so they will not interfere with the adjusting procedure. Then adjust the latch so that the hood aligns along the sides and at the front. Tighten the hood-attaching screws. Then turn the adjustable stops up so they snug up against the hood when it is closed. Tighten the lock nuts.

Check the action of the safety latch (Fig. 23-8). Open and close the hood several times to make sure that the safety latch works.

○23-6 Trunk-Lid Adjustment

The trunk or rear compartment lid is attached at the forward end with hinges. A locking latch is centered at the

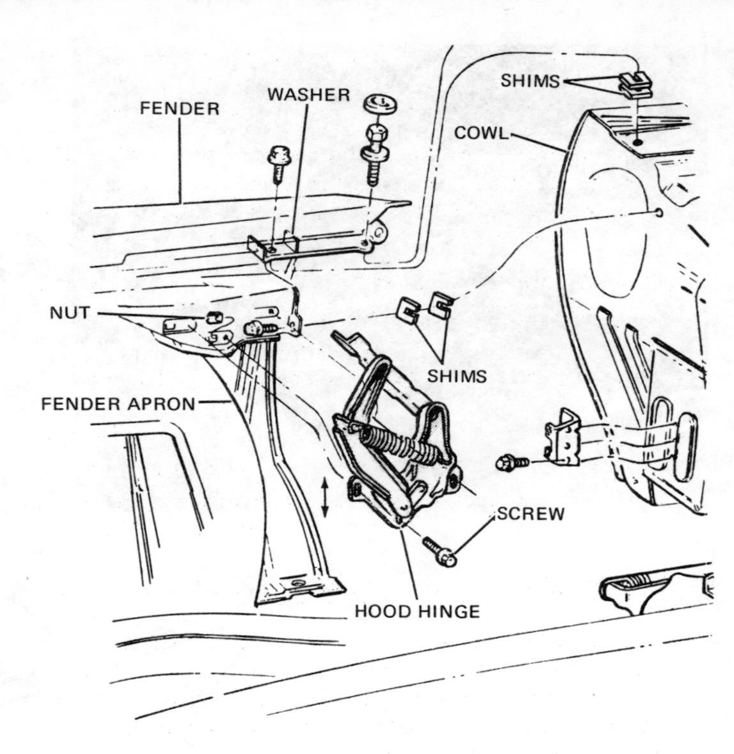

FIGURE 23-5. Hood hinge installation on Ford and Mercury models. (*Ford Motor Company*)

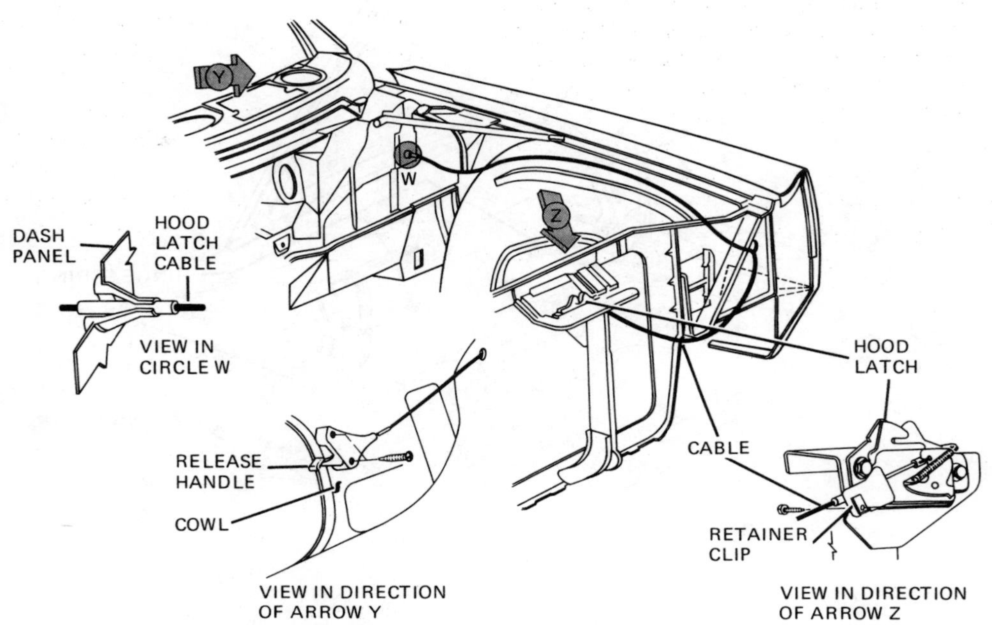

FIGURE 23-6. Inside, or remote-control, hood release. (*Chrysler Corporation*)

rear (Fig. 23-9). The hinge screw holes are elongated or enlarged so that the lid can be shifted one way or the other to get proper alignment. To make the adjustment, loosen the screws slightly and shift the lid as necessary. Then tighten the screws.

○23-7 Trunk-Lid Latch

The trunk lid latches in the locked position when it is closed. It is released by a key. When the key is turned, the lock is unlatched and the trunk lid opens. In some cars, the lid can also be unlocked by an electric solenoid and a push button in the glove compartment. (Ignition switch must be in the ON or accessory position.) The lid latch is adjusted by loosening the attaching screws and moving the latch up or down as required, or by moving the striker.

NOTE: When adjusting the electric lid latch, avoid placing excessive tension on the latch. This could prevent the solenoid from releasing the latch.

○23-8 Hold-open Springs

Two types of hold-open springs are used: torsion-bar (Figs. 23-9 and 23-10) and spiral (Fig. 23-11). Both work in the same way. When the lid is unlocked, the springs

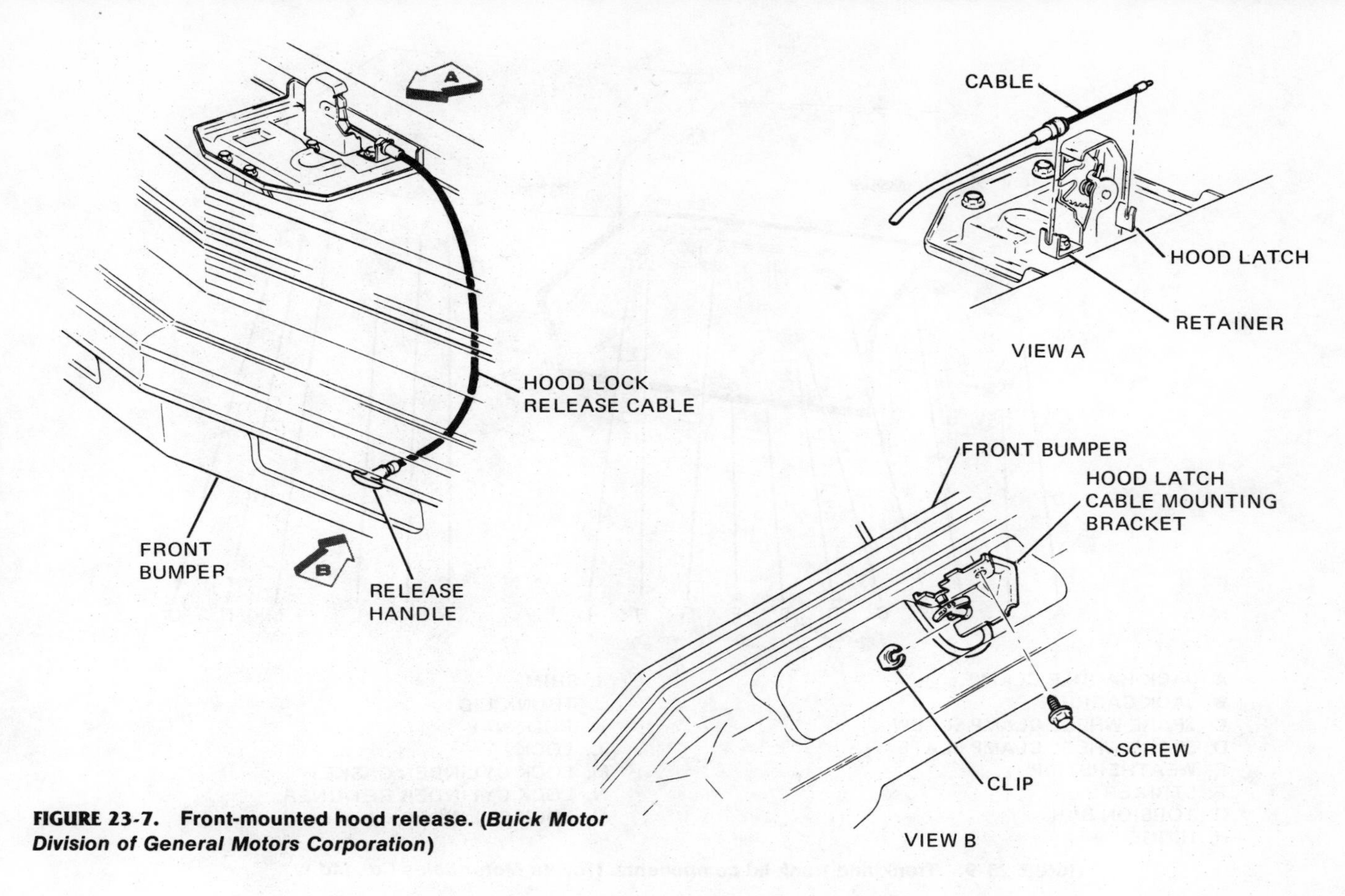

FIGURE 23-7. Front-mounted hood release. (*Buick Motor Division of General Motors Corporation*)

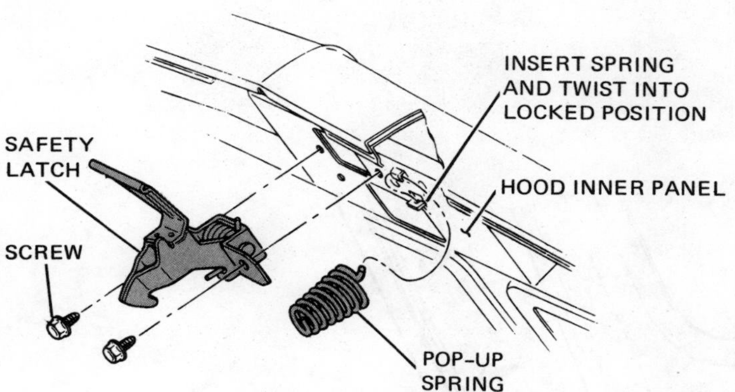

FIGURE 23-8. Location of the pop-up spring and safety latch. (*Buick Motor Division of General Motors Corporation*)

counterbalance the weight of the trunk lid. They supply most of the effort of moving the lid up to the fully opened position. The torsion bars can be adjusted if they do not supply sufficient tension to hold the lid open (Fig. 23-10).

○23-9 Adjusting Torsion Bars

If the lid does not open properly, the torsion bars are not supplying enough tension. This requires a readjustment that will increase the tension. Figure 23-10 shows the principle. The end of the torsion bar is lifted from one of the adjustment holes and moved to the next adjustment hole. Figure 23-12 shows the use of Vise-Grip pliers to make the adjustment. Note that in Fig. 23-10 the arrangement uses adjustment holes. In Figure 23-12 there is a series of adjustment slots. With either arrangement, moving the end of the torsion bar from one position to another changes the tension.

○23-10 Weatherstrip

The joint between the trunk lid and the surrounding metal is closed by a rubberlike weatherstrip (Figs. 23-9 and 23-13). The shape of the weatherstrip varies with the car, but its purpose is the same. When the lid closes, the weatherstrip mashes down to form a tight seal between the deck lid and the surrounding metal. Figure 23-14 shows another shape of weatherstrip.

To install weatherstrip, first make sure that all the old weatherstrip and cement have been removed from the trough into which the new weatherstrip is to be installed. Different manufacturers have different methods of installing the weatherstrip. For example, Chrysler recommends the following method: Apply an even, continuous coat of rubber cement to the weatherstrip-contact surface in the deck-lid opening and also to the contact surface of the weatherstrip (Fig. 23-13). Then install the

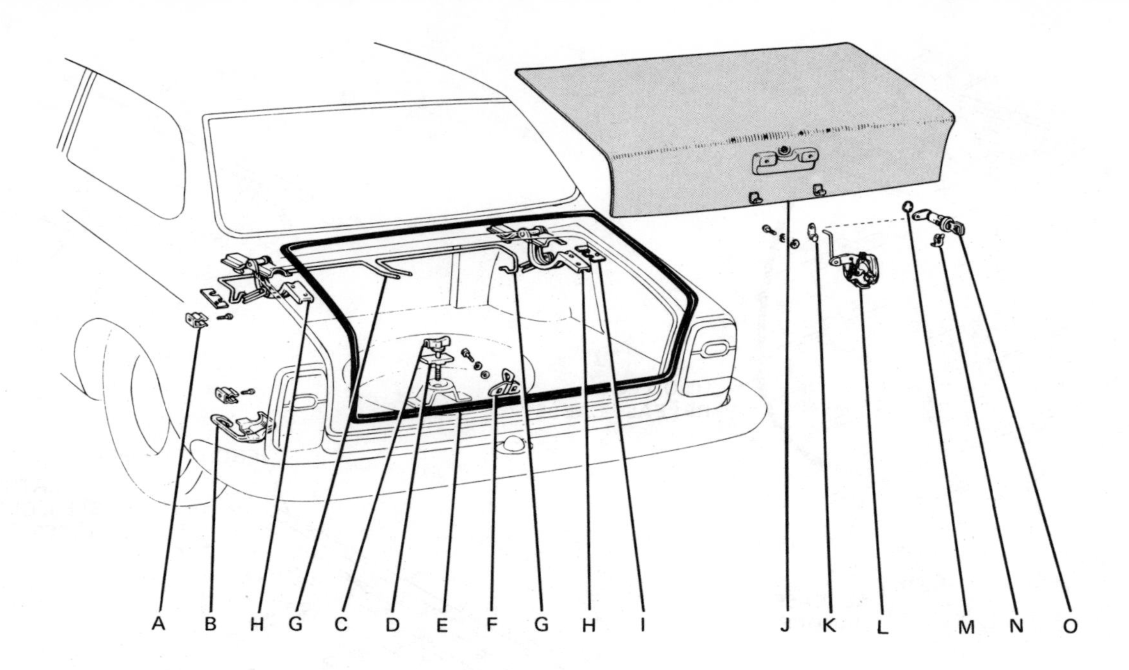

A. JACK HANDLE CLAMP
B. JACK CARRIER
C. SPARE WHEEL CLAMP SCREW
D. SPARE WHEEL CLAMP PLATE
E. WEATHERSTRIP
F. STRIKER
G. TORSION BAR
H. HINGE
I. SHIM
J. TRUNK LID
K. ROD SNAP
L. LOCK
M. LOCK CYLINDER GASKET
N. LOCK CYLINDER RETAINER
O. LOCK CYLINDER

FIGURE 23-9. Trunk and trunk-lid components. (*Toyota Motor Sales Co., Ltd.*)

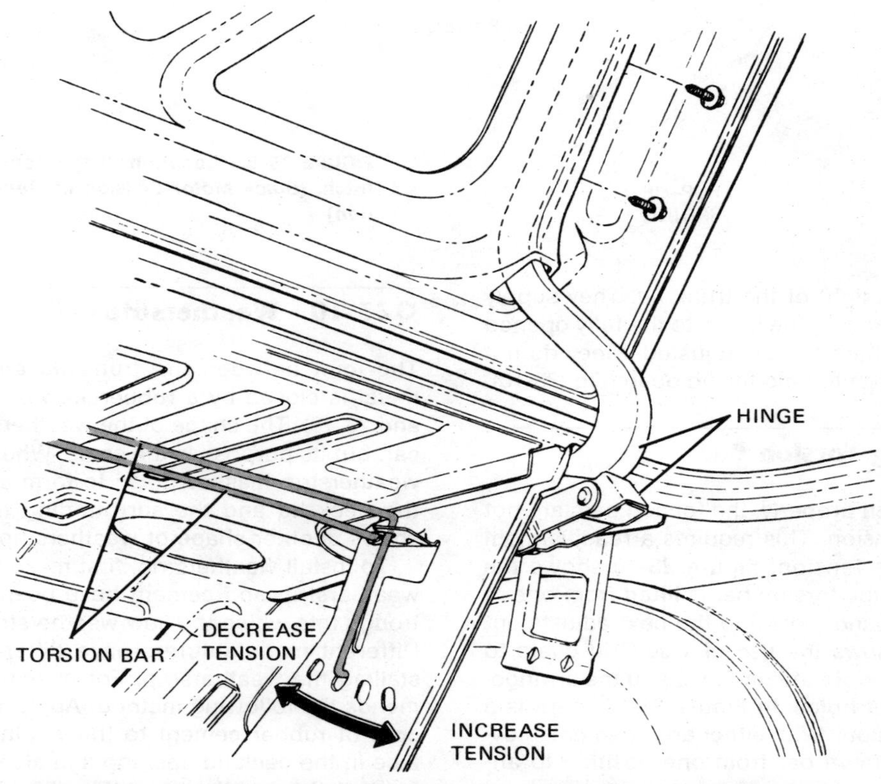

FIGURE 23-10. Adjustment of the torsion-bar springs. (*Ford Motor Company*)

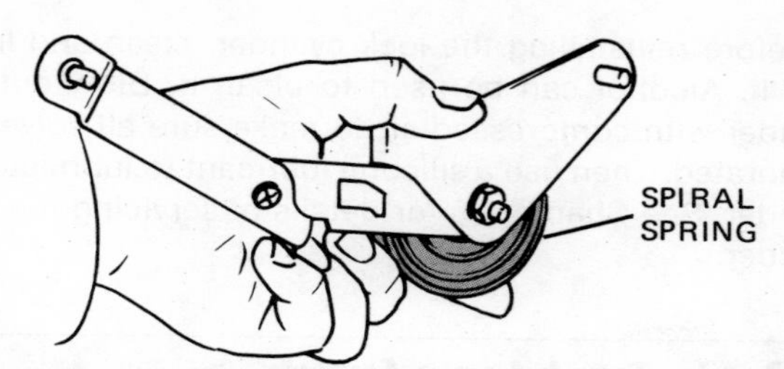

FIGURE 23-11. **Spiral type of counterbalancing spring. (*American Motors Corporation*)**

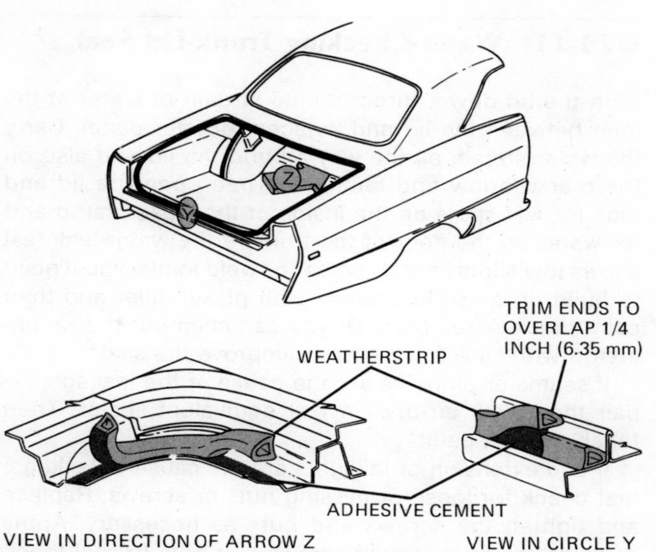

FIGURE 23-13. **Weatherstrip around trunk lid. (*Chrysler Corporation*)**

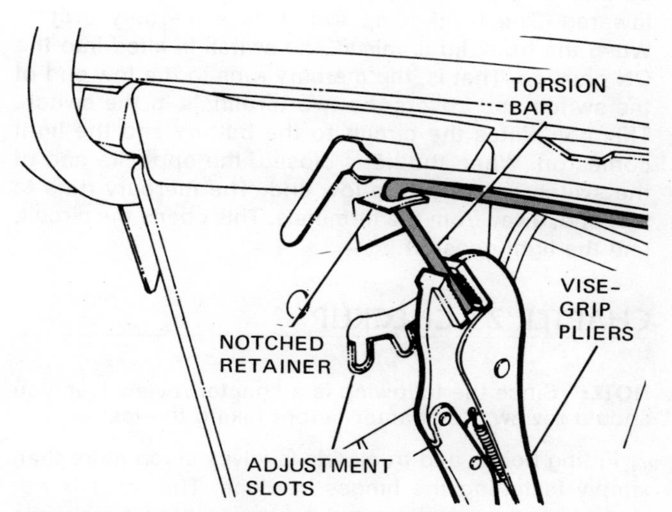

FIGURE 23-12. **Using Vise-Grip pliers to adjust the torsion bar. (*American Motor Corporation*)**

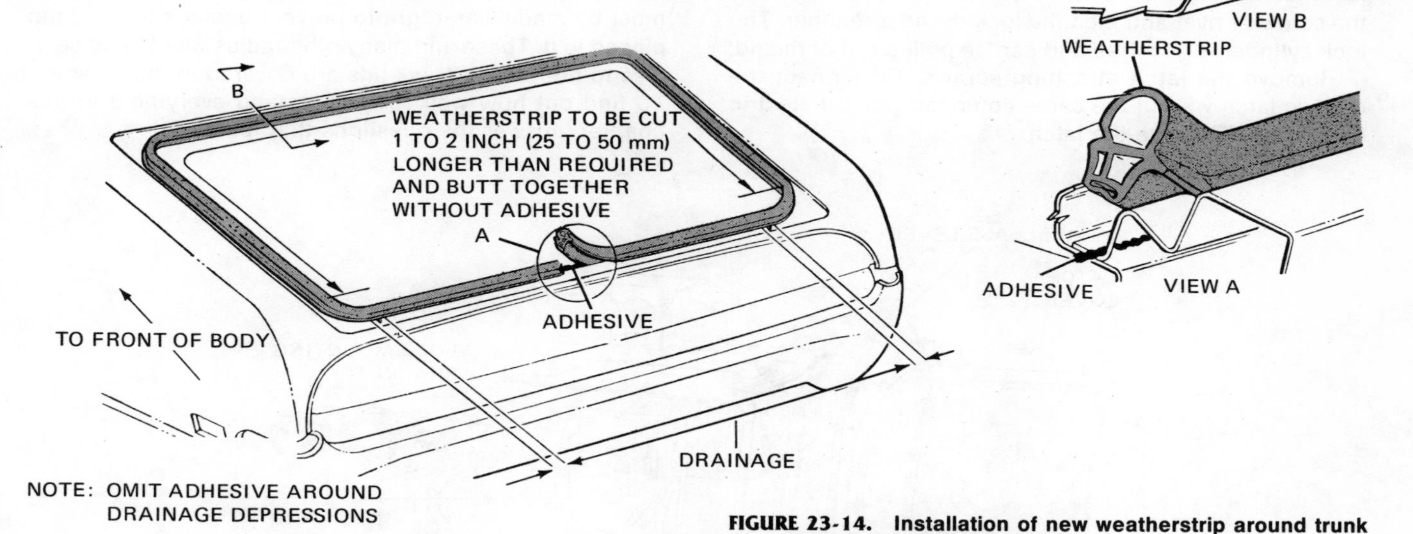

FIGURE 23-14. **Installation of new weatherstrip around trunk lid. (*Ford Motor Company*)**

weatherstrip. Locate the joint at the bottom as shown at Y in Fig. 23-13. Make sure that the weatherstrip molded corners are correctly positioned. Avoid puckering or stretching the weatherstrip around corners. Trim ends to overlap ¼ inch [6.35 mm]. Apply cement to the ends, and when it becomes tacky, compress the ends into position. Wipe off any excess cement with a cloth moistened with a suitable solvent.

Ford supplies these instructions (see Fig. 23-14): Apply a ¼-inch [6.35-mm] bead of rubber cement in the bottom of the weatherstrip trough except at the drainage depressions (see to right in Fig. 23-14). Position the new weatherstrip as shown in Fig. 23-14. Cut the weatherstrip about 1 to 2 inches [25 to 50 mm] longer than required and butt the two ends together without adhesive. Apply a 3/32-inch [2.38-mm] bead of rubber under the outboard lip of the weatherstrip between the points shown in Fig. 23-14.

○23-11 Water-Checking Trunk-Lid Seal

With the lid down, direct a mild stream of water at the joint between the lid and adjacent quarter panel. Carry the water stream all the way around the lid and also on the rear window and taillights. Then open the lid and look for wet spots on the inside of the weatherstrip and for water on the floor of the trunk. If the water-leak test shows low spots at body solder or weld joints, you'll need to build up these low points with plastic filler and then paint the repaired area. Or you can shim out the weatherstrip with vinyl foam strip to improve the seal.

If seams or pinholes are the cause of the leakage, repair them with air-dry vinyl or equivalent sealer. Then touch up with paint.

If end extension or taillights are the cause of leakage, first check for loose or missing nuts or screws. Replace and tighten the screws and nuts as necessary. Apply caulking material around screws and nuts to seal them.

If water leakage is found around the lower edge of the rear window, it will be necessary to replace the weather seal around the window. Servicing rear windows is covered in Chapter 28.

On vinyl-roof vehicles, check molding retainer studs for looseness or leaks at the upper deck panel.

○23-12 Lid Lock

The lid lock is held in position by a retainer which is attached with a rivet or screw (Fig. 23-15). To remove the lock, work from the inside of the lid (lid open). Remove the screw or rivet and then the lock cylinder retainer. The lock cylinder is now free and can be pulled out of the lid.

Remove the latch attaching screws. Disconnect the electric latch wire (if the car is equipped with an electric lid release). Remove the latch.

Before reinstalling the lock cylinder, clean and lubricate it. Alcohol can be used to clean it. Blow out the cylinder with compressed air to make sure all solvent is evaporated. Then use a silicone lubricant to lubricate the cylinder. See Chapter 25 for details of servicing the lock cylinder.

○23-13 Trunk-Lamp Switch

Some cars are equipped with a trunk lamp. It turns itself on and off automatically as the trunk lid is raised and lowered. The trunk-lamp switch is a mercury switch. When the trunk lid is raised, the switch is tilted into the ON position. That is, the mercury runs to the low end of the switch and covers the two terminals in the switch. This completes the circuit to the battery and the light comes on. When the lid is closed, the opposite end of the switch becomes the low end. The mercury runs to that end, away from the terminals. This opens the circuit, and the light goes off.

CHAPTER 23 CHECKUP

NOTE: Since the following is a chapter review test, you should review the chapter before taking the test.

Fitting hoods and trunk lids involves much more than simply fastening the hinges in place. The hood is not required to be watertight, but it must not blow open while the car is moving. Therefore, the hood latch must be checked in two positions. The luggage compartment must be made watertight to prevent damage to anything placed in it. These and many other adjustments and services to hoods and trunk lids are covered in this chapter. To find out how well you understand everything in this chapter, answer the questions that follow.

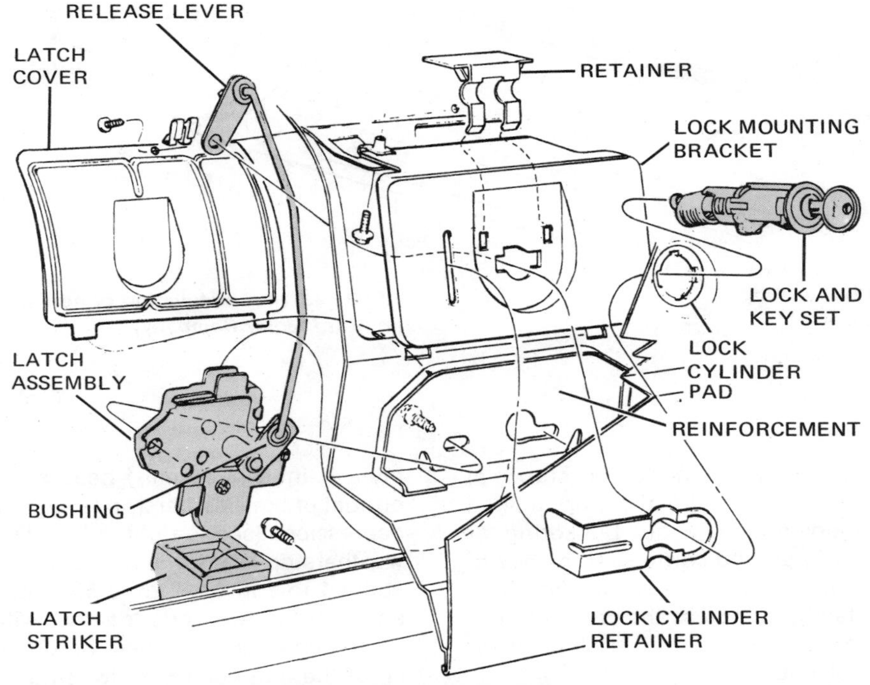

FIGURE 23-15. Trunk-lid latch and lock arrangement. *(Ford Motor Company)*

COMPLETING THE SENTENCES The sentences below are incomplete. After each sentence there are several words or phrases, but only one of them correctly completes the sentence. Write each sentence in your notebook, ending the sentence with the one word or phrase that completes it correctly.

1. Hoods may be hinged (*a*) only one way, (*b*) at the front or at the back, (*c*) at the front only, (*d*) at the rear only.
2. Adjustable bumpers on the hoods are used to (*a*) prevent rattle or flutter, (*b*) secure alignment, (*c*) prevent water leaks, (*d*) secure the proper gap.
3. To get proper alignment, hoods and trunk lids can (*a*) be shimmed, (*b*) have thicker weatherstrip added, (*c*) have strong springs added, (*d*) be shifted one way or the other.
4. The main purpose of weatherstrip around the trunk opening is to prevent (*a*) trunk-lid flutter, (*b*) water leaks, (*c*) wind noise, (*d*) rattles.
5. The trunk-lid seal can be checked with (*a*) shims, (*b*) an air hose, (*c*) a water hose, (*d*) a flashlight.

QUESTIONS Write each of the following questions, and then the answer, in your notebook. If you have trouble recalling the answer to a question, turn back to the pages that cover the material and study them again.

1. Describe how to adjust a hood.
2. How do you check the hood latch?
3. Describe how to adjust the trunk lid.
4. When should the trunk-lid torsion bars be adjusted?
5. Explain how to correct a water leak into the trunk.

SUGGESTIONS FOR FURTHER STUDY

Closely examine the hood and trunk-lid mounting and adjusting arrangements on a car. On a page for your notebook, list the steps in fitting the hood and in checking it. Then write down the steps in checking and adjusting the trunk lid. If the trunk-lid counterbalance is supplied by torsion bars, be sure to include how to check and adjust them.

PART 6

SERVICING DOORS, TAILGATES, LIFT GATES, AND SUN ROOFS

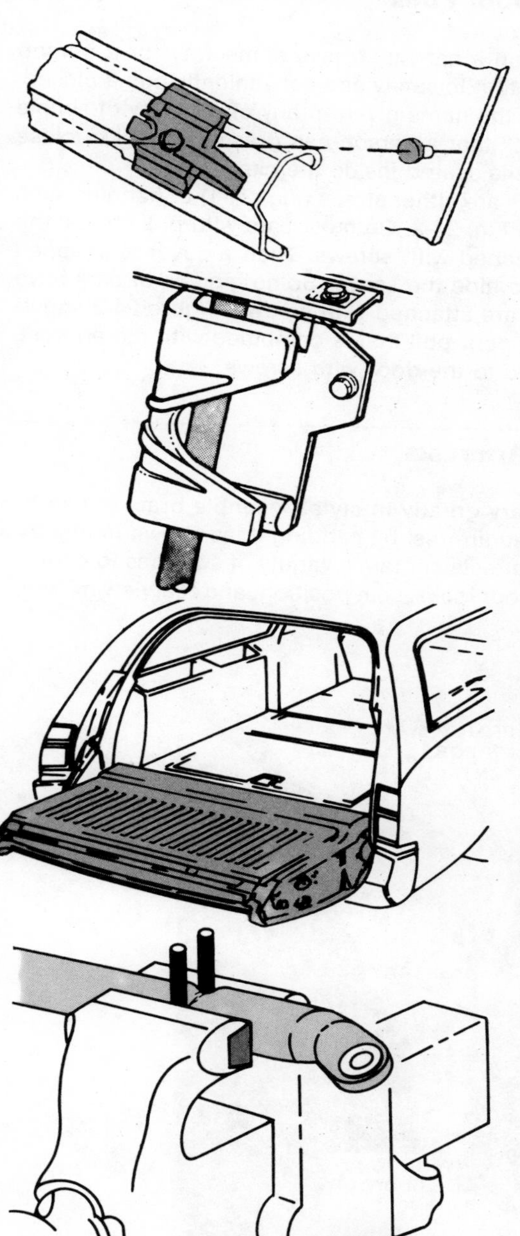

In this part, you will learn about the mechanisms inside doors, tailgates, and lift gates and how to service them. In addition, you will learn about sun roofs and possible services they may require.

Doors contain two basic types of mechanisms. One raises and lowers the windows, either mechanically with a crank or electrically with a motor. The second mechanism latches and unlatches the door. This includes a locking device that may be operated mechanically with a knob or electrically with a solenoid.

Front doors contain additional devices. The left front door on the driver's side has, on some late model cars, a rearview-mirror control trim, door pull, arm rest, electrical-door lock switch, window regulators, ashtray, cigarette lighter, and control switches for the electrically operated seat adjuster.

Tailgates can be still more complex than doors. They may contain a mechanical or electrical device for raising or lowering the back window. They also contain a handle and latching device that permits the tailgate to be lowered. The latching device includes a lock. In addition, dual-action tailgates have a second hinging arrangement that permits them to swing to one side like a door. Some tailgates also include a window wiper (like the windshield wiper) and a window heater to prevent the formation of frost or mist that could impede vision to the rear.

In contrast, lift gates are comparatively simple. The sun roof is also comparatively simple. It is a sliding cover that can be mechanically or electrically moved back to provide an opening in the roof. We cover all of these body panels in this part. There are three chapters in Part 6, as follows:

24

DOOR TRIM, MOLDINGS, AND WEATHERSTRIP

In this chapter, you will learn about the interior trim of a door, exterior moldings on the outside of a door, and the weatherstrip that seals the door. In addition, we explain how to replace weatherstrip around the door openings. The chapter also describes water testing of the seals around doors and finding and eliminating wind noise and water and air leaks.

○24-1 Door Components

The typical car door (Fig. 24-1) is a rather complicated assembly. It includes several items:

Door latch
Door lock
Window regulator
Weatherstrip
Interior trim
Exterior moldings

In addition, doors have armrests, door pulls, ashtrays (some with cigarette lighters), and litter bags. The door on the driver's side may contain additional devices such as rearview mirror control, seat adjuster switches (for electrically adjusted seats), a door lock switch for all doors, and separate master switches for each window regulator in the car. In this chapter we describe the door trim, molding, and weatherstrip. Door latch and lock mechanisms, and window regulators, are covered in Chapter 25.

○24-2 Door Pulls

Each door on a car must have some way for a person seated next to it to safely and conveniently pull it closed. *Door pull* is the name given to any of a variety of simple "hand-holds" that a person can grasp and pull to close the door while seated inside the car.

Door pulls are either straps (Fig. 24-1) or handles such as shown in Fig. 24-2. On most cars with pull straps, the strap is attached with screws. Then a cover is snapped into place to hide the screw. Some models of cars have covers that are attached with screws. Figure 24-2 shows a solid-type door pull that is combined with the armrest. It is fastened to the door with screws.

○24-3 Armrests

Armrests vary greatly in style. A simple bracket can be made into an armrest by padding it, as shown in Fig. 24-3. Some armrests contain a variety of switches to control windows, door locks, seat position, and rearview mirrors.

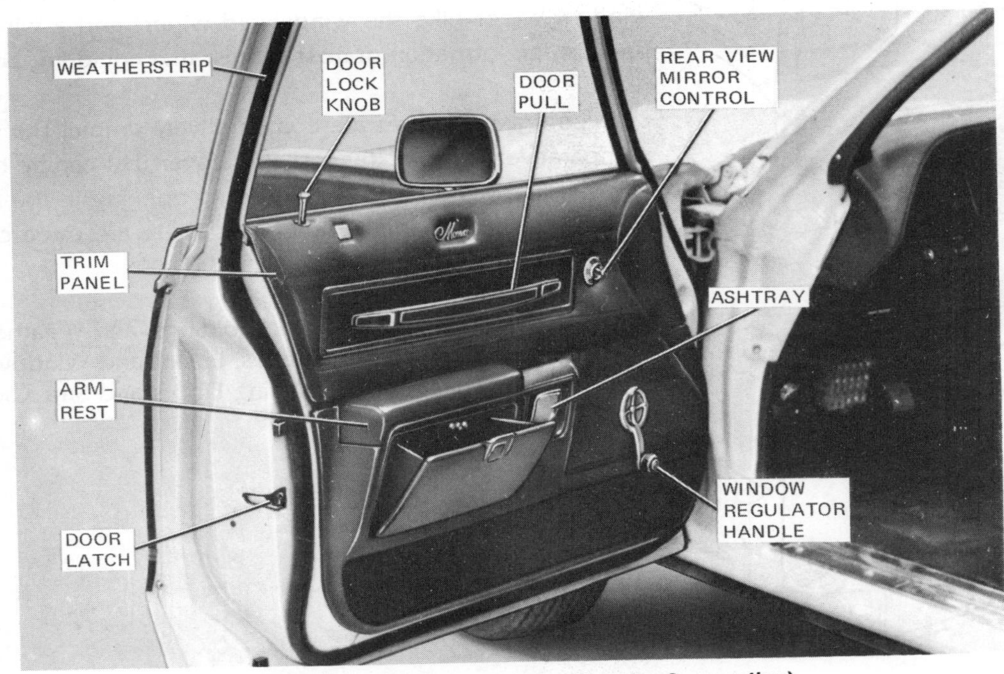

FIGURE 24-1. Typical car door. (*Chrysler Corporation*)

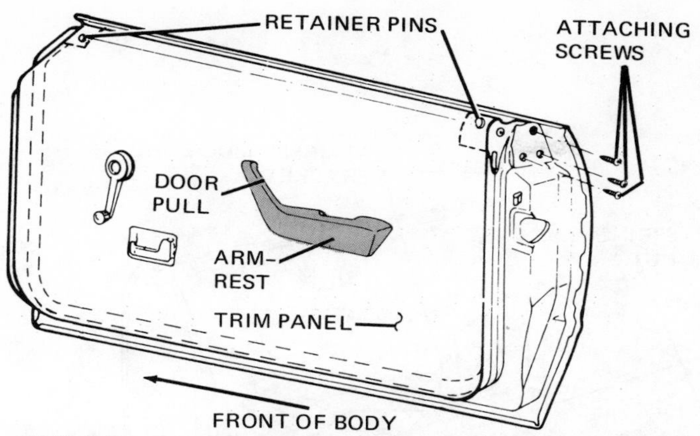

FIGURE 24-2. A solid-type door pull combined with the armrest. (*Ford Motor Company*)

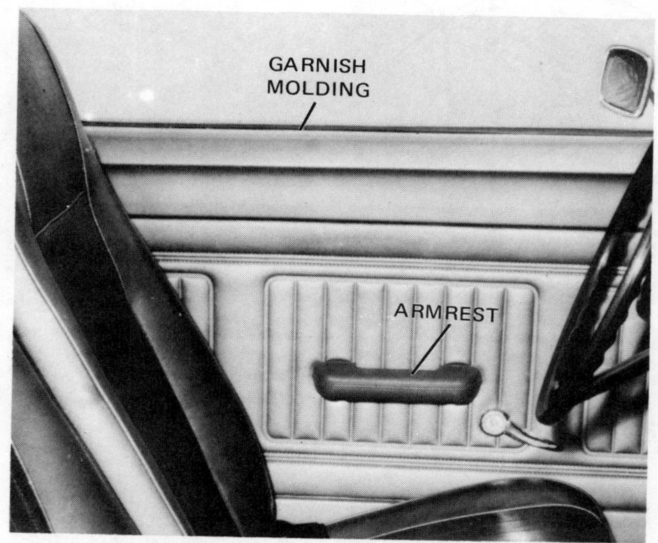

FIGURE 24-3. Armrest that is simply a padded bracket. (*Ford Motor Company*)

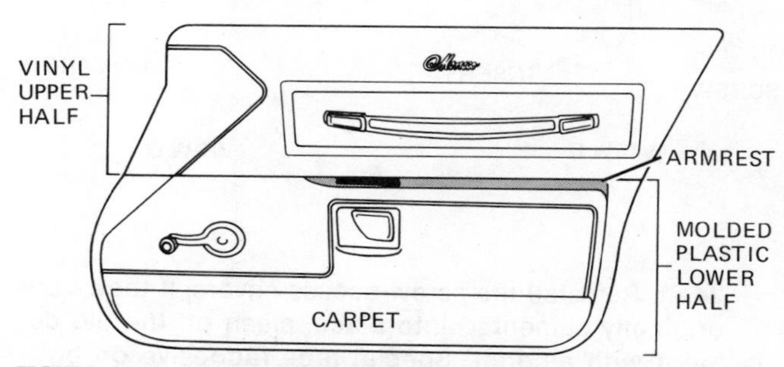

FIGURE 24-4. Armrest molded into the lower half of the trim panel. (*Chrysler Corporation*)

Figure 24-4 shows another type of armrest. It is molded into the lower half of the door trim panel and then covered with a pad.

○24-4 Door Trim

Any cloth or plastic material used to line the interior of a door is called door trim. Usually the various pieces of trim for a door are assembled into one-piece or two-piece "trim pads" or "trim panels." Figures 24-1 to 24-4 show different styles of door trim panels.

A variety of fastening methods are used to attach door trim to doors. Figure 24-5 shows a typical attachment method for a one-piece door trim panel. Others are similar, although various types of fasteners are used. We will now describe in detail the removal and installation of door trim panels on late-model Ford-built cars. This procedure will show you how to get into and out of a door. While these instructions apply in general to many similar vehicles, refer to the manufacturer's shop manual for the car you are working on.

NOTE: Some of the steps given below do not apply to all vehicles. If they do not, skip them and go to the next step. See Figs. 24-5 to 24-7 for details of attachment.

REMOVAL

1. Remove the door-lock knob and the garnish molding (see Fig. 24-3).
2. Remove the window-regulator handle and the door-latch handle (Fig. 24-6). These are attached in various ways. Sometimes there is a screw cover which is removed first. This exposes the screw (or screws) that attaches the handle.
3. Remove the armrest assembly. If the armrest contains electrical switches, disconnect the switch wiring before removing the armrest.
4. Remove the mirror remote-control bezel nut.
5. Remove the door-trim retaining screws (Fig. 24-5).
6. Use a putty knife or trim-panel clip remover and lift the trim-panel retaining clips from the door inner panel to disengage the panel (Fig. 24-7).
7. Disconnect all wiring as necessary to remove the trim panel.
8. If the trim panel or armrest requires replacement, transfer the pull-handle rivets and retaining screws, retaining clips, trim moldings, and other parts to the new assembly. If the watershield (also called water dam and water deflector) has been removed or damaged, replace it (see Fig. 24-8). Check that the watershield is positioned and sealed correctly (see ○24-5) before installing the trim panel.
9. Make sure the armrest screw U-nuts are properly positioned on the door inner panel. If they have been dislodged, they must be repositioned before the watershield is installed.

INSTALLATION

1. Position the trim panel on the door inner panel and connect wiring (if so equipped). Route the mirror control cable through the hole in the trim panel.
2. Replace any damaged trim-panel clips. Then push the trim panel and retaining clips into the holes in the inner door panel. See Fig. 24-5. Install the retaining screws.
3. Install the remote-control-mirror bezel nut.
4. Connect the wiring (if any) to the armrest, position the armrest on the trim panel, and install the retaining screws.
5. If the armrest has a finish panel or trim, install it.
6. Position the door-latch and window regulator handles and secure them with the attaching screws (Fig.

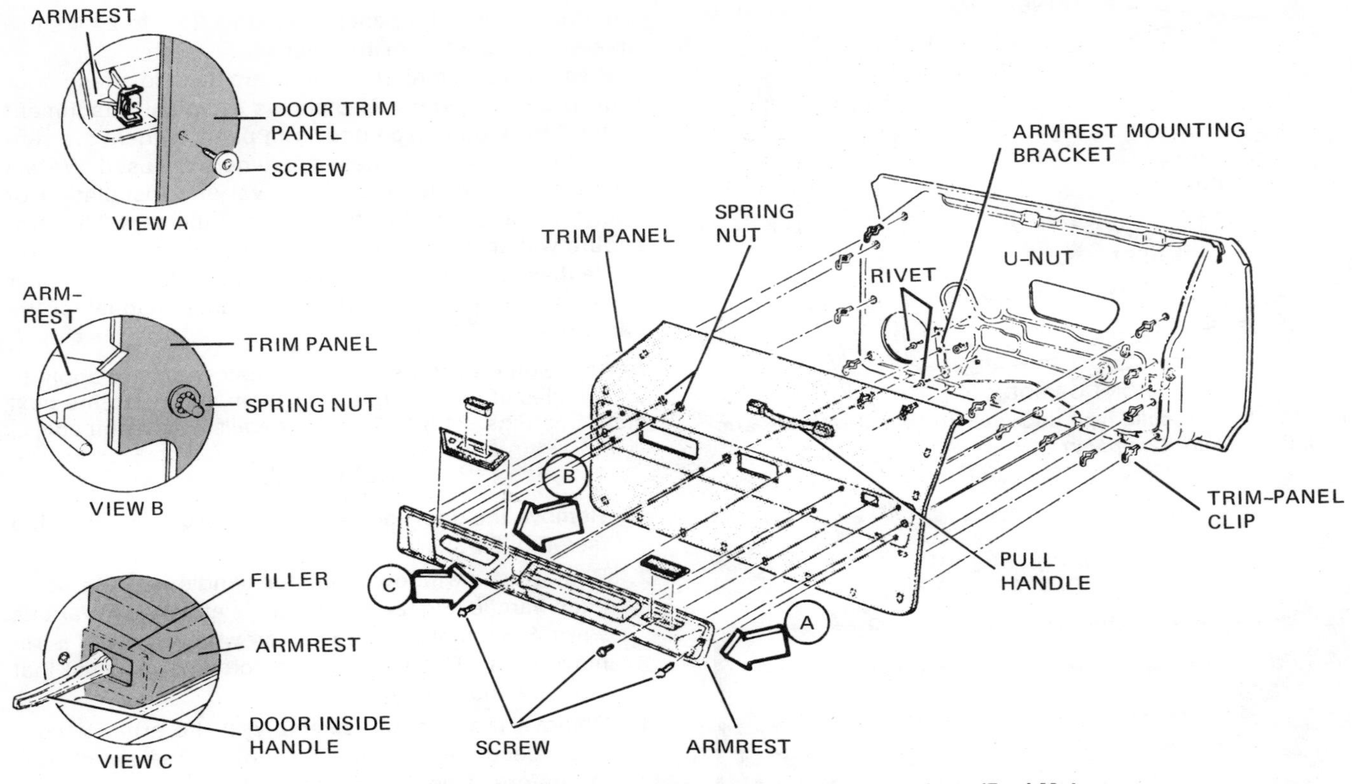

FIGURE 24-5. **Method of attaching one-piece trim panel to the door. (*Ford Motor Company*)**

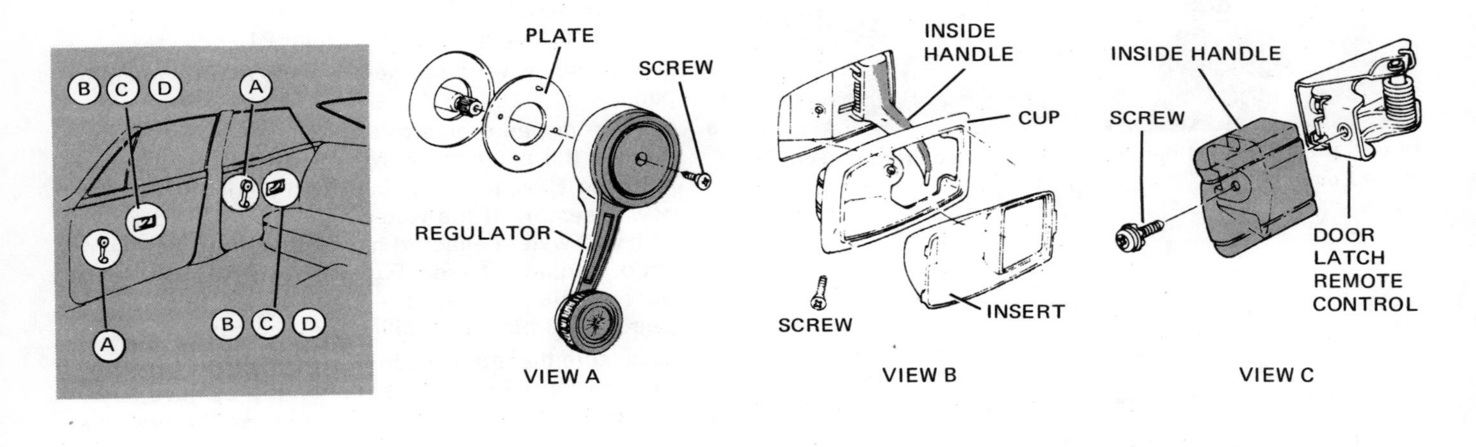

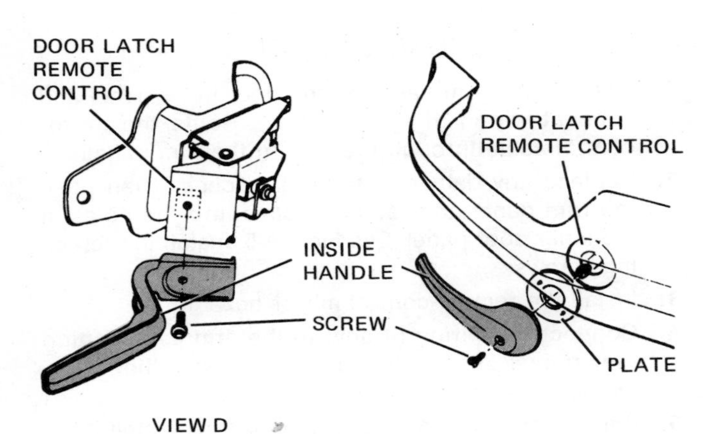

FIGURE 24-6. **Typical installations of door and window-regulator handles. (*Ford Motor Company*)**

24-6). Reinstall the screw-access covers. If they were originally cemented into place, clean off the old cement with alcohol. Special tape (adhesive on both sides) is required to tape the covers back into place.

7. Install the garnish molding and door-lock knob (Figs. 24-1 and 24-3).

○24-5 Water Deflector

The purpose of the water deflector (Fig. 24-8) is to seal the door inner panel and prevent the entry of water into the body. The deflector is attached by a sealing material that is loaded with string and by waterproof sealing tape. The deflector is made of tough waterproof paper. Whenever work is done on the doors that disturbs the deflec-

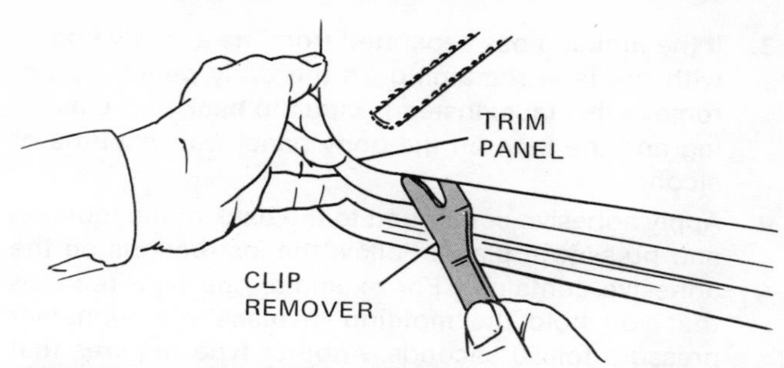

FIGURE 24-7. Removing trim-panel clips. ***(Ford Motor Company)***

tor, it must be reattached and resealed, as explained below, to prevent water leaks.

1. Put a bead of sealer on the deflector as shown in Fig. 24-8, making sure there are no gaps so water will be guided into the drain slots.
2. Make sure the sealing area on the door inner panel is clean and dry. Position the deflector on the door inner panel. Insert the lower edge of the deflector in the retaining slot. Then firmly press or roll the edges of the deflector to get a good seal between the door panel and deflector.

NOTE: If you are merely resealing the old deflector which you have only partly detached, you may need additional sealer. Use body caulking compound or strip caulking on the inner panel at the unsealed areas.

3. Seal the lower edge of the deflector with waterproof body tape.
4. On the doors that have inner-panel hardware attachments below or outside of the water deflector, seal the screwheads and panel holes with body caulking compound.

○24-6 Door Exterior Moldings

Door exterior moldings are attached in various ways. The following procedures cover the removal and replacement of the moldings used on the doors of General Motors cars. The procedures are similar for cars made by other manufacturers. If you run across a different sort of attachment, refer to the shop manual covering the specific model of car you are working on.

NOTE: See Sec. 24-7 for the procedure of removing and replacing moldings that are secured by adhesive tape.

If the deflector is damaged, it should be replaced. The material comes in rolls. To fabricate a new deflector, cut off a length of the paper, lay the old deflector on it, and cut out a new deflector of the same size and shape.

NOTE: The complete procedure of removal and replacement that follows may not be required if the deflector is only partly detached to get to the internal door mechanism.

REMOVAL

1. Remove the door-trim assembly and the waterproof body tape attaching the top of the water deflector to the door inner panel.
2. Use a putty knife to break the seal between the deflector and panel. Work down both sides of the deflector. Make sure the tool blade is between the inner panel and the string that is embedded in the sealer.
3. Remove the tape from the inner panel at the lower edge of the water deflector (Fig. 24-8). Disengage the deflector from inner-panel drain slot and remove it.

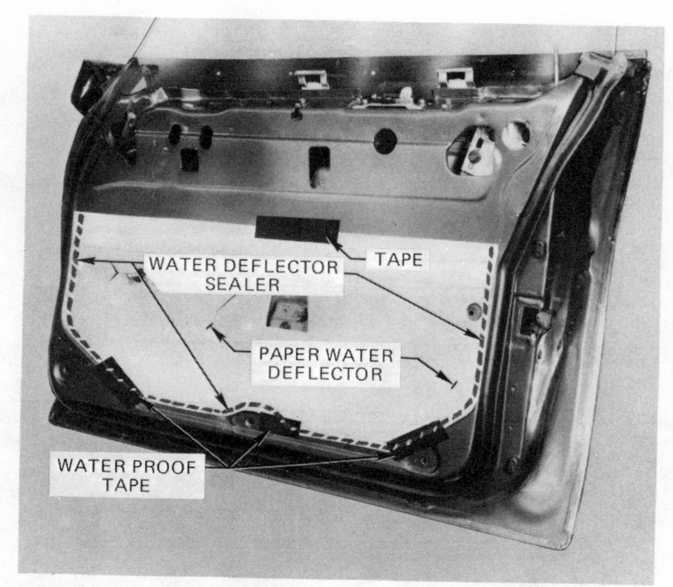

FIGURE 24-8. Watershield, or water deflector, sealed in place on door. ***(Fisher Body Division of General Motors Corporation)***

INSTALLATION

Inspect the deflector. If it is torn or has holes, repair it with waterproof body tape applied to both sides of the deflector. If the deflector is in bad shape, use it as a template to cut out a new deflector from the roll of special paper.

Refer to Figs. 24-9, 24-10, and 24-11. Figure 24-9 numbers the different moldings for reference when you look at the chart in Fig. 24-11. Figure 24-10 illustrates the various door molding attachments, as follows:

1. Weld stud retained plastic clip
2. Weld stud retained plastic clip with attaching screws and/or "T" bolt clip and nut retaining molding end or ends in the hem flange
3. Adhesive bonded with either tape or urethane sealant
4. Spring or clinch type (self-retained)
5. Attaching screw with integral or separate belt molding

To determine the removal procedure for any piece of molding, first refer to Fig. 24-9 to determine its reference number. Then refer to Fig. 24-11 to find this number in the vertical column to the left. To the right of this reference number you will find the molding described and also, in the right-hand column, the attachment reference. Use this reference to go back to Fig. 24-10 to find the illustration showing the attachment method.

POINTS TO WATCH

1. Protect the adjacent painted surface with masking tape to prevent damaging it.
2. Use the proper tools, and exercise care to avoid damaging the molding.

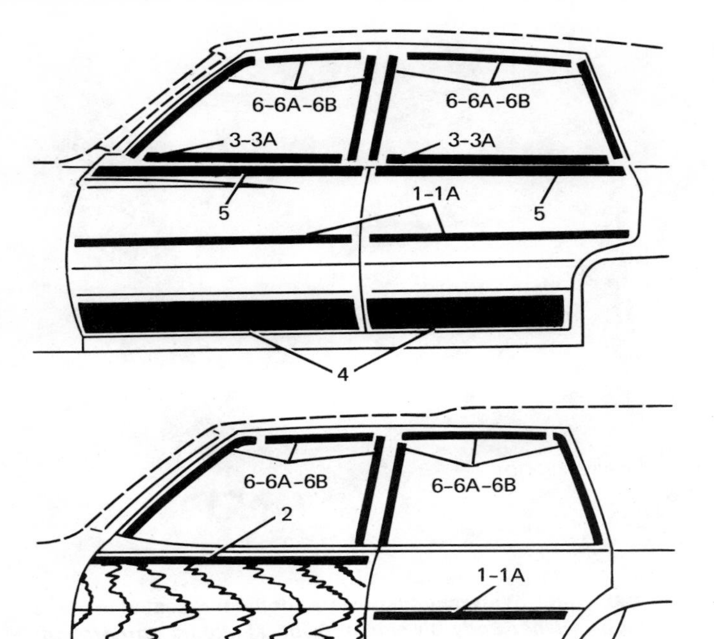

FIGURE 24-9. **Typical door exterior moldings. Numbers in the illustration refer to the usage (Fig. 24-11) and to the method of attachment (Fig. 24-10). (*Fisher Body Division of General Motors Corporation*)**

3. Holes in body panels for screws, bolts, or clips may allow water to leak into the body interior if they are not sealed off. Use body caulking compound or presealed screws, nuts, or clips.
4. If a weld stud on an outer panel becomes damaged or is broken off, drill a small hole in the panel next to the original weld-stud location. Insert a self-sealing screw through the original clip and into the outer panel. Or you can replace the damaged weld stud with a self-sealing screw-type weld stud.

○24-7 Adhesive Body Moldings

The procedure that follows applies to door moldings and to all moldings that are applied to body panels with adhesive tape. Separate procedures are included for reattaching loose ends of moldings and for completely removing and replacing moldings.

NOTE: The panel surface should be warm (70 to 90°F) [21.1 to 32.2°C] and free of any wax or oil film.

REATTACHING LOOSE ENDS

If only one end of the molding has come loose, proceed as follows:

1. Wash the panel area from which the molding has come loose with detergent and water. Wipe dry. Wipe the panel and adhesive side of the molding with oil-free naphtha or alcohol.
2. If you need a guideline, apply a length of masking tape to the panel. You can also use a straightedge.
3. If the molding has separated from the adhesive back, with the tape remaining on the body panel, do not remove this tape. Instead, wipe the back of the molding and the tape on the body panel with naphtha or alcohol.
4. Apply adhesive compound to the back of the molding and press it in place. Follow the instructions on the adhesive container. For example, one type requires that you hold the molding in place with constant pressure for 30 seconds. Another type requires that you tape the molding in place with masking tape for 15 minutes or longer, or until the adhesive sets.

REMOVING AND ATTACHING MOLDING

If the molding has to be completely removed or if it has come off, proceed as follows:

1. After removing the molding, wash the affected panel area with detergent and water and wipe it dry. Wipe the panel and adhesive side of the molding with alcohol.
2. If you need a guide, mark the position of the molding with masking tape as shown in Fig. 24-12. (Figures 24-12, 24-13, and 24-14 show the application of molding to a quarter panel. The principle is the same for doors.)

NOTE: If the adhesive tape has separated from the molding and remains on the body panel, do not remove it from the panel. Instead, wipe the tape and back of the molding with alcohol and proceed with step 3.

3. Temporarily attach the molding following with masking-tape strips applied every few inches as shown in Fig. 24-13.
4. If the body is cold—well below 70°F [21°C]—warm the body panel with a heat lamp or heat gun.
5. Loosen the top of the tape strips so the molding can be hinged downward as shown in Fig. 24-14. Then, using a circular motion, quickly apply a thin film of weatherstrip adhesive (GM recommends 3M Super Weatherstrip Adhesive) to the adhesive part of the molding.
6. Immediately align molding to previously installed tape guideline and firmly press it into place. Hold it there by reapplying the masking-tape strips as shown in Fig. 24-13. Allow it to set for at least 15 minutes. Then remove the masking-tape strips, using care to avoid detaching the molding.

NOTE: Although the adhesive cures sufficiently to hold the molding in place after about 15 minutes, it will not completely cure for at least 24 hours. Therefore, the car should not be washed by any high-pressure method for at least a day after the molding has been applied. If any adhesive has squeezed out, clean it off with a cloth dampened with alcohol.

○24-8 Weatherstripping

There are two basic types of doors, each requiring a somewhat different method of weatherstripping. The weatherstripping must be water-, wind-, and dust-proof. The two types of doors are the sedan type and the hardtop type. The sedan-type door (Fig. 24-15) has an upper

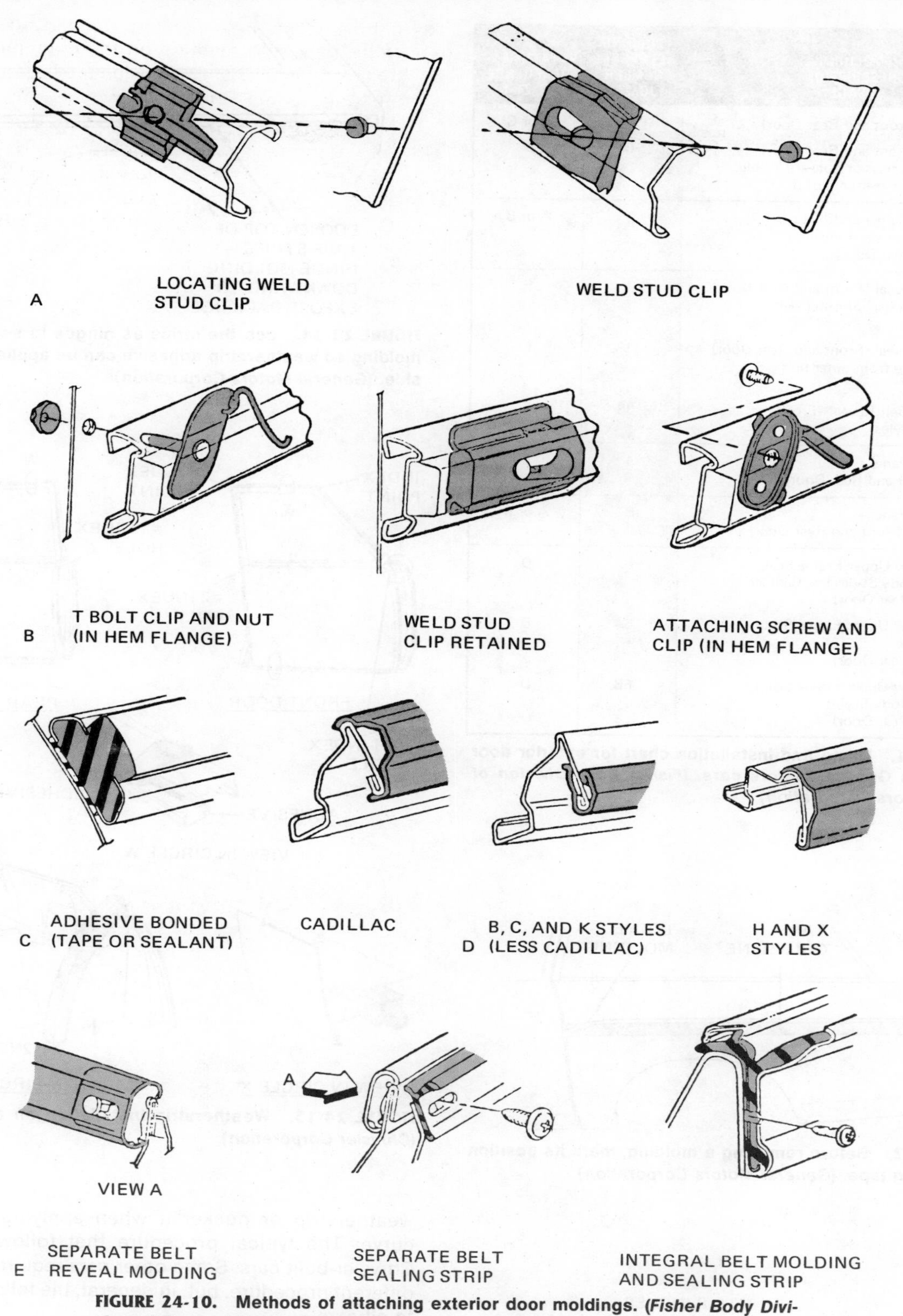

FIGURE 24-10. Methods of attaching exterior door moldings. (*Fisher Body Division of General Motors Corporation*)

frame which surrounds the glass when it is raised. The hardtop-type door (Fig. 24-16) has no upper frame. The sedan door has weatherstripping all the way around the edge, including the upper frame. On the hardtop door, the weatherstrip for the glass is in the roof rail. Following sections describe the removal and installation for this weatherstripping.

○24-9 Sedan-type Door Weatherstripping

This type of door and its weatherstripping are shown in Fig. 24-15. When new weatherstripping is required, remove all the old weatherstrip particles and cement before applying the new weatherstrip. Do not stretch the

MOLDING DESCRIPTION (USAGE)	MOLDING REFERENCE NUMBER (FIG. 24-9)	ATTACHMENT REFERENCE (FIG. 24-10)
Body Side (Front and Rear Door)	1	A or C
Body Side (Front and Rear Door) If attaching screws or nuts are visible in front and/or rear hem of door	1A	B
Body Side - Upper and/or Lower - Woodgrain Transfer Finishing (Front and Rear Door)	2	A or B
Door Belt Reveal (Front and Rear Door) When integral part of outer belt sealing strip	3	E
Door Belt Reveal (Front and Rear Door) When separate from outer belt sealing strip	3A	E
Front Door Belt Reveal -Front "A" Body Styles	3B	E
Door Outer Panel - Lower (Front and Rear Door)	4	B
Door Outer Panel - Upper Peak (Front and Rear Door)	5	A or B
Door Window Upper Frame Scalp "B, C, K" Body Styles less Cadillac (Front and Rear Door)	6	D
Door Window Upper Frame Scalp Cadillac Style (Front and Rear Door)	6A	D
Door Window Upper Frame Scalp "H and X" Body Styles (Front and Rear Door)	6B	D

FIGURE 24-11. Name and installation chart for exterior door moldings on General Motors cars. (*Fisher Body Division of General Motors Corporation*)

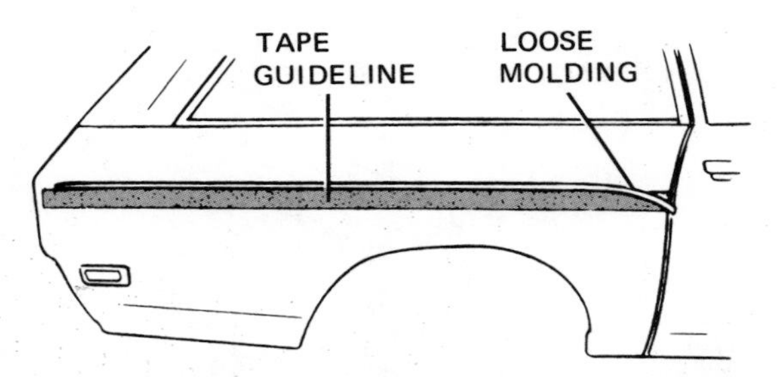

FIGURE 24-12. Before removing a molding, mark its position with masking tape. (*General Motors Corporation*)

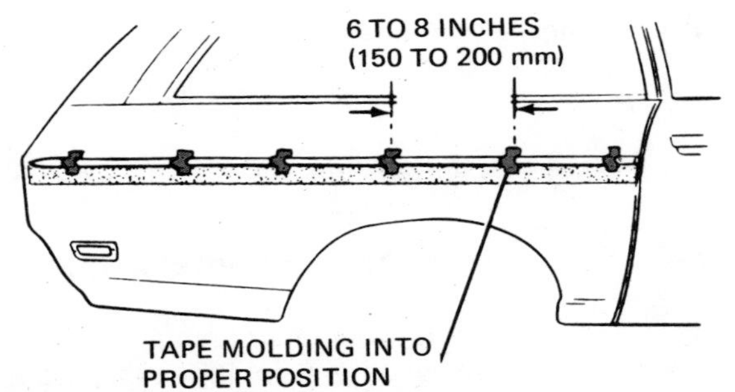

FIGURE 24-13. Hold the molding in place with strips of masking tape. (*General Motors Corporation*)

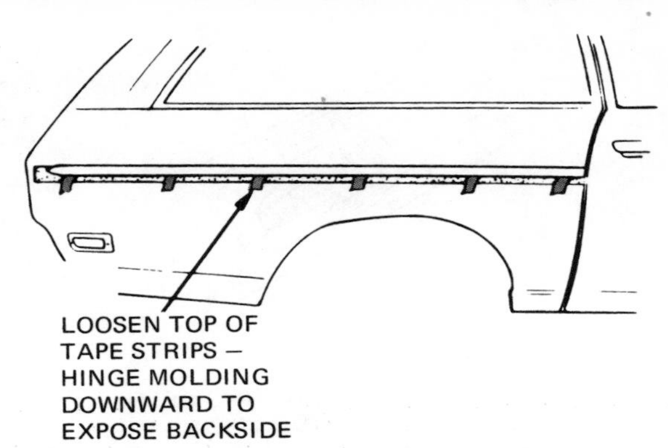

FIGURE 24-14. Use the strips as hinges to swing down the molding so weatherstrip adhesive can be applied to the back side. (*General Motors Corporation*)

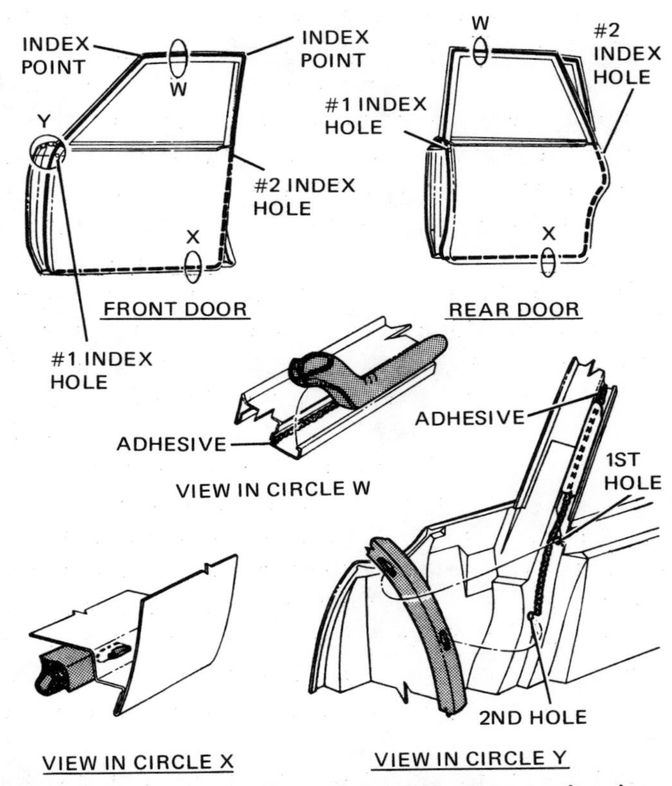

FIGURE 24-15. Weatherstrip installation on a sedan door. (*Chrysler Corporation*)

weatherstrip or pucker it when applying it around a curve. The typical procedure that follows applies to Chrysler-built cars. Some other cars require a somewhat different procedure, but, in general, the following applies to all cars.

1. Refer to Fig. 24-15. Apply the lower half of the weatherstrip, starting at the number 1 index hole and ending at the number 2 index hole. Use the fasteners on the weatherstrip to locate and attach the weatherstrip.
2. For the upper half of the weatherstrip, start by applying a ⅛-inch [3.18 mm] bead of cement to the weatherstrip seating area on the door upper half.
3. Install the upper half of the weatherstrip to the door, indexing it as shown in Fig. 24-15. Work the weath-

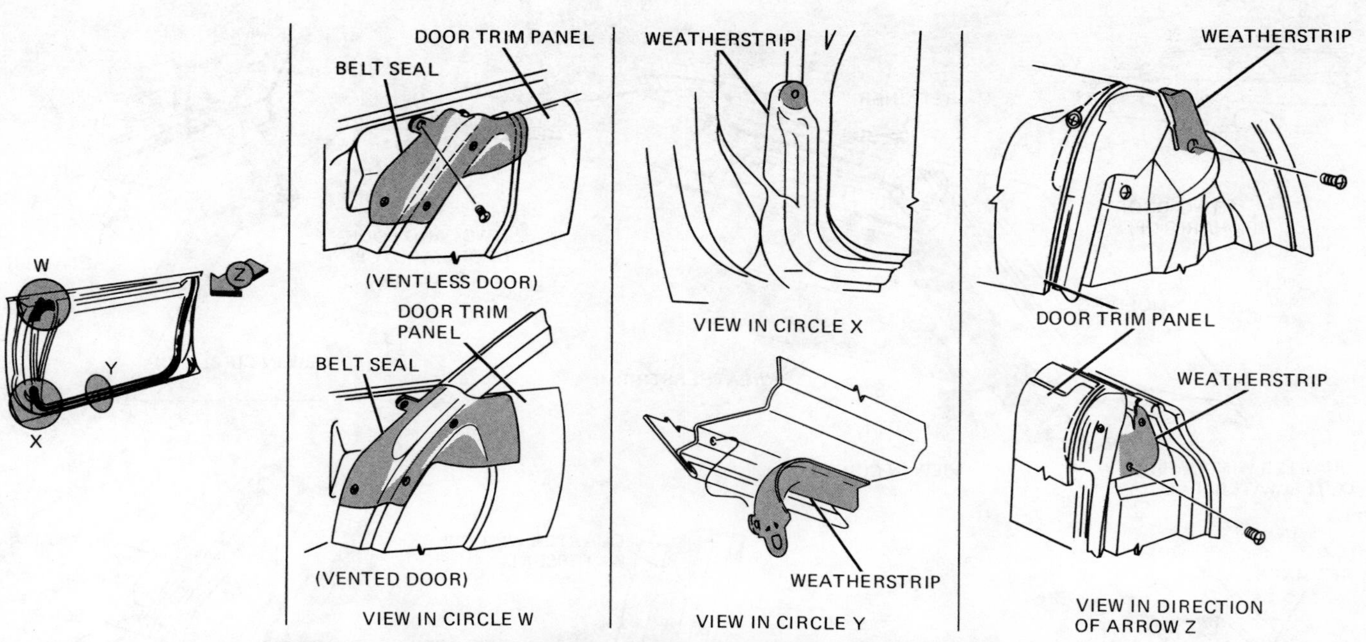

FIGURE 24-16. Weatherstrip installation on a hardtop door. (*Chrysler Corporation*)

erstrip from the index holes to points midway between, making sure that it is not stretched or puckered.

4. On Ford-built cars the weatherstrip is partly retained by pins inserted into holes in the door panel. Adhesive is also used where needed.

○24-10 Hardtop Door Weatherstripping

This type of door does not have the upper frame, and so the weatherstrip for the glass is installed in the roof rail. Figure 24-16 shows how the weatherstrip is installed in this type of door used on Chrysler-built cars. The procedure is as follows:

1. Position and attach the molded end of the weatherstrip with fasteners at the door-hinge pillar. See view X in Fig. 24-16.

2. Index and install the weatherstrip on the door, using fasteners at locating points. Work from the hinge-pillar side of the door completely around to the lock pillar.

3. Install lock-pillar seal on lock pillar with fasteners as shown in view Z in Fig. 24-16.

4. Install front-belt seal with screws as shown in view W in Fig. 24-16.

5. The hardtop roof-rail weatherstrips are attached to the weatherstrip retainers as shown in Fig. 24-17. The retainers are installed first. Then the weatherstrips are pressed into place. The quarter-window-belt outer water seal is held in place by screws. The weatherstrip retainers are adjustable. They have elongated attaching holes. Thus, the weatherstrip can be moved in or out as necessary to get the required sealing action.

NOTE: When the glass is up against its stop and the roof-rail weatherstrip and the glass are properly adjusted, the outer lip of the weatherstrip will seal along the top outer edge of the glass. The inner lip of the weatherstrip will seal along the top inside edge of the glass. See Fig. 24-18.

○24-11 Door Belt-line Weatherstrip

A weatherstrip is required at the door belt-line so that the door outer panel will seal against the glass regardless of its position (up or down). Figure 24-19 shows one way the glass belt-line weatherstrip is installed. By sealing between the glass and the outer door panel, the belt-line weatherstrip prevents water from running down the glass into the door.

○24-12 Water-Leak Test of Door Seals

Only a small stream of water is needed to find a leak. If you use too much water pressure, the water may be forced past even a good weatherstrip. Water with too much pressure also can splash over the suspected area so you could have trouble finding the source of the leak.

Hold the pressure down to get about a 3-inch [76-mm] stream (Fig. 24-20). Have an assistant sit inside ana watch for water coming in as you work the hose around the gap at the door edge on the outside. Start at the lower edge of the door and work upward. If you start at the top, the runoff will wet the untested area and make any leak harder to locate. If your assistant locates leaks, mark the leaky area with chalk or tape.

If you find a leak, take necessary steps to fix it. If the cause is low spots at body solder or weld joints or other places around the door opening, build up these low points. Use plastic filler and repaint the repaired area. Or you can shim out the weatherstrip with vinyl foam strip.

There might be more than one leaky point. Correct leaks you find at the lower places before proceeding with

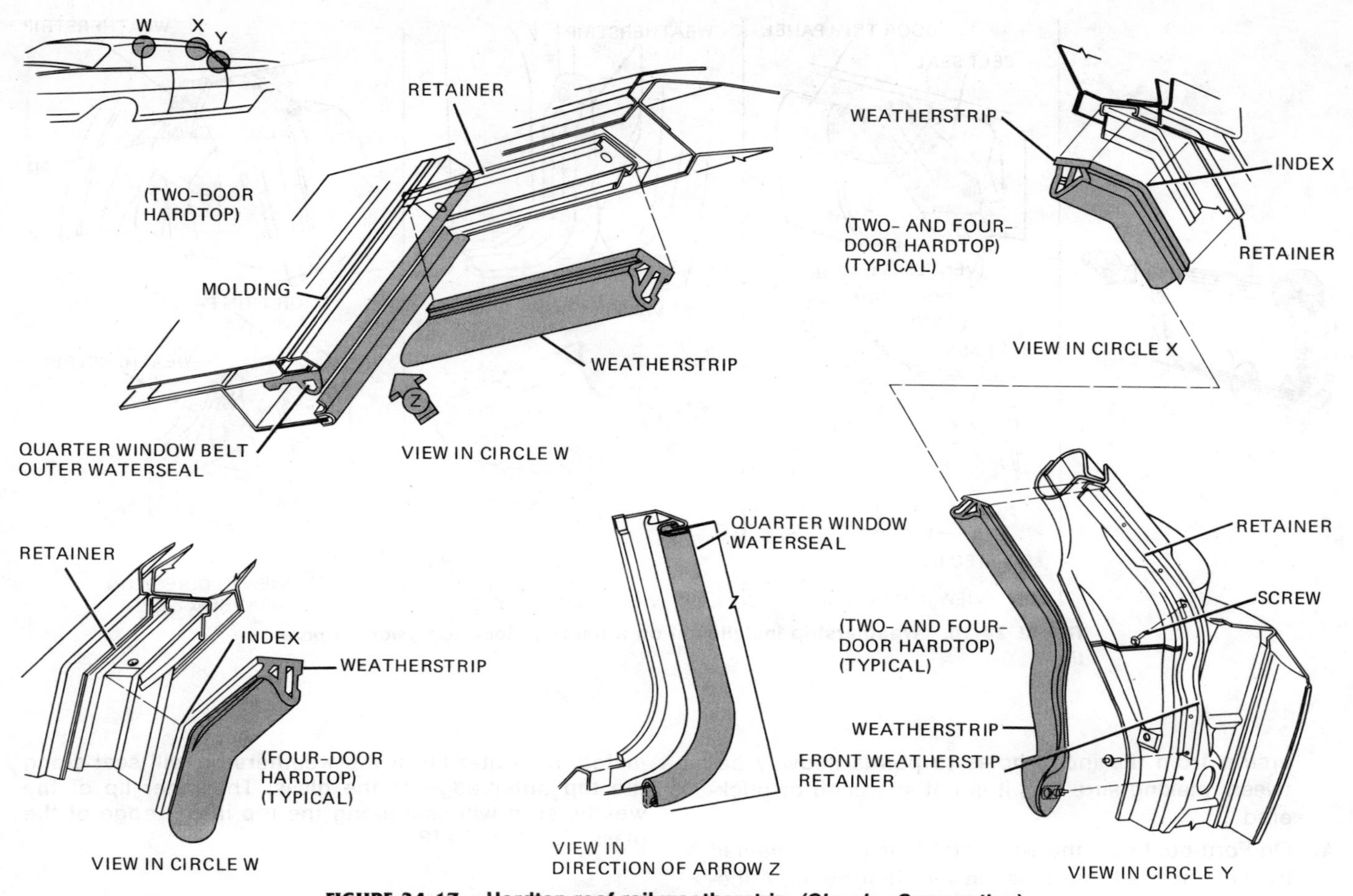

FIGURE 24-17. Hardtop roof-rail weatherstrip. (*Chrysler Corporation*)

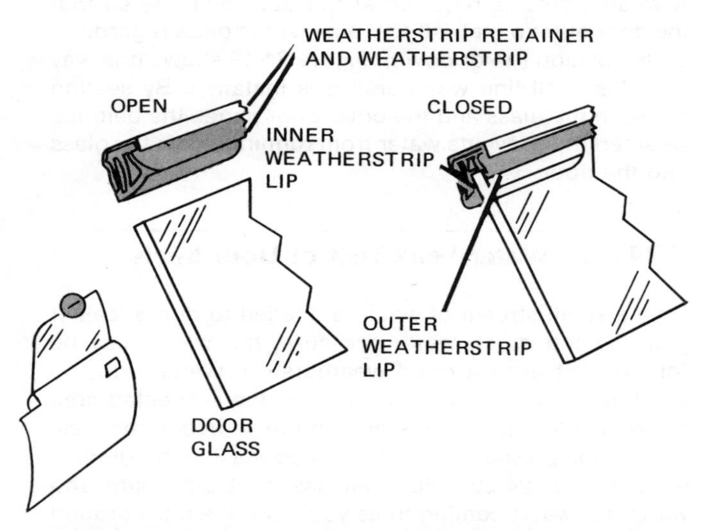

FIGURE 24-18. Action of the roof-rail weatherstrip with the door open and closed. (*Chrysler Corporation*)

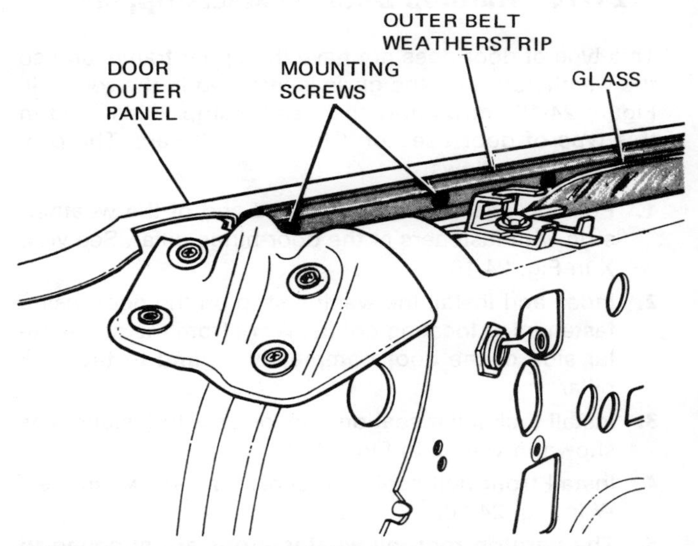

FIGURE 24-19. Typical installation of a door belt-line weatherstrip. (*Chrysler Corporation*)

the test above them. Make sure the areas to be fixed are dry before you try to apply plastic or cement.

Run water along the belt line and check the inside trim panels for dampness, especially at the bottom. If you find water there, it means the plastic watershield is damaged or has come loose. It should be fixed (Fig. 24-5).

○24-13 Checking Glass-to-Weatherstrip Fit

On hardtops, the door glass must make good contact with the weatherstrip, especially along the top. The upper edge of the glass should not be visible when the door is

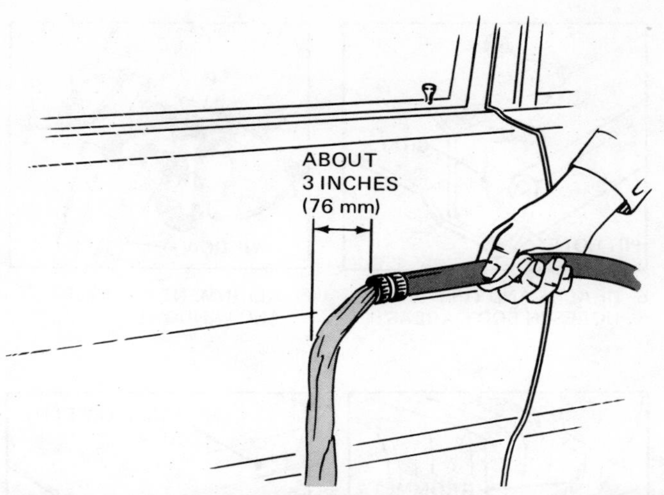

FIGURE 24-20. Proper water stream to use for locating body water leaks. (*Chrysler Corporation*)

closed. A quick test is to cut several strips of masking paper about 2 inches [50 mm] wide. Lay them across the top of the glass and close the glass. The paper strips should be clamped firmly between the top edge of the glass and the weatherstrip. Try pulling on them. If they pull out easily, the weatherstrip is not fitting tightly enough. Check further by the water test (○24-12).

If there is leaking between the glass and the weatherstrip, the glass may need adjustment. If leakage is occurring over the weatherstrip, the weatherstrip probably has come loose or has deteriorated. Examine it and repair or replace it as necessary. Adjust the glass in the door if required.

○24-14 Diagnosing Wind Noise

The source of wind noise is sometimes difficult to locate. The spot where the noise is heard may not be the place where the wind leakage is occurring. Wind leaking into or out of the vehicle can set up a whistling noise that is very annoying. Most wind-noise complaints are caused by air leaks in the upper area (Fig. 24-21).

Let's look at the causes of wind noise. The shape of the vehicle causes air to flow around the windshield and

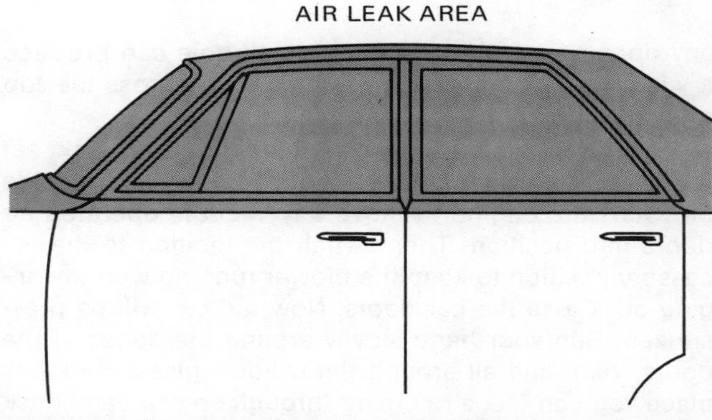

FIGURE 24-21. Most air leaks are in the upper area of the body. (*Chrysler Corporation*)

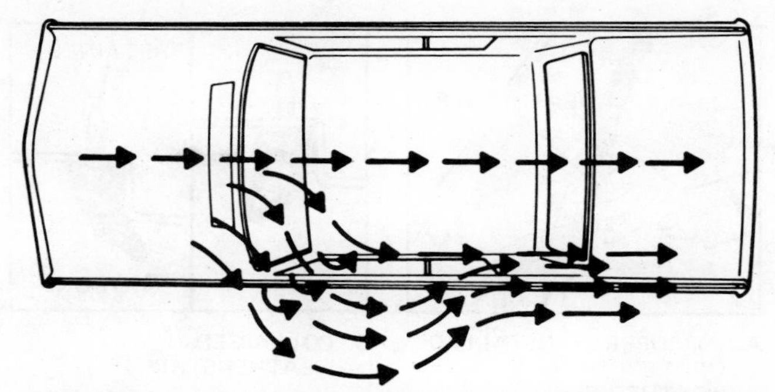

FIGURE 24-22. Air flow around vehicle as it moves forward. (*Ford Motor Company*)

FIGURE 24-23. Low-pressure area develops around window area of a moving car. (*Ford Motor Company*)

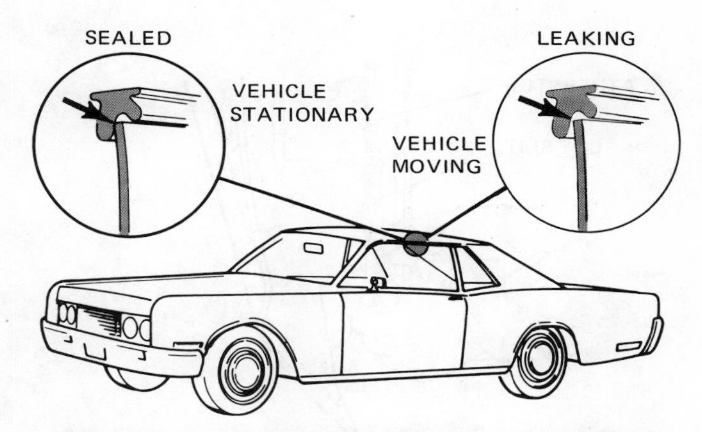

FIGURE 24-24. Actions of a defective seal when car is stopped and when car is moving. (*Ford Motor Company*)

alongside the vehicle as it moves forward (Fig. 24-22). This causes a low pressure area to develop outside the car, especially in the window areas (Fig. 24-23). Now, inside the car, the ventilating and air-conditioning or heating system build up pressure. So you have a combination of low pressure outside and high pressure inside the car. If the weatherstrip is loose fitting at any point, air will escape from the car around the loose weatherstrip. This can be a puzzler, because the seal may appear satisfactory when the car is standing still but may allow air leaks when the car is moving (Fig. 24-24). To the left, the circled drawing shows that the glass apparently fits against the weatherstrip. To the right, however, you can see that the fit is poor. When the car is moving, the internal pressure tends to push the glass out and this allows air leakage along the top of the glass.

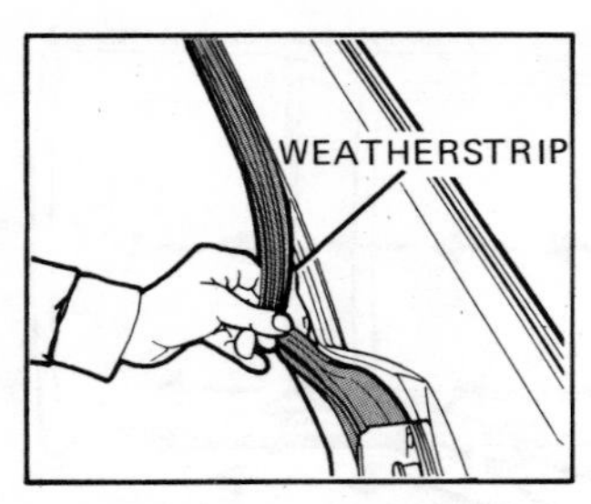

A. IMPROPERLY INSTALLED OR MISROUTED WEATHERSTRIPS

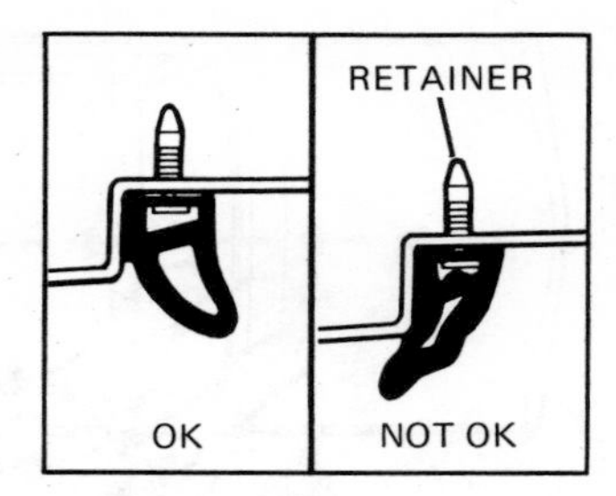

B. COLLAPSED WEATHERSTRIP

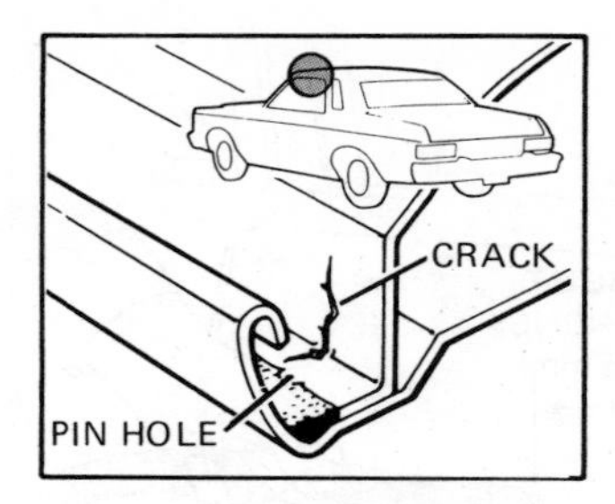

E. CRACKS AND/OR PIN HOLES IN BODY AREAS

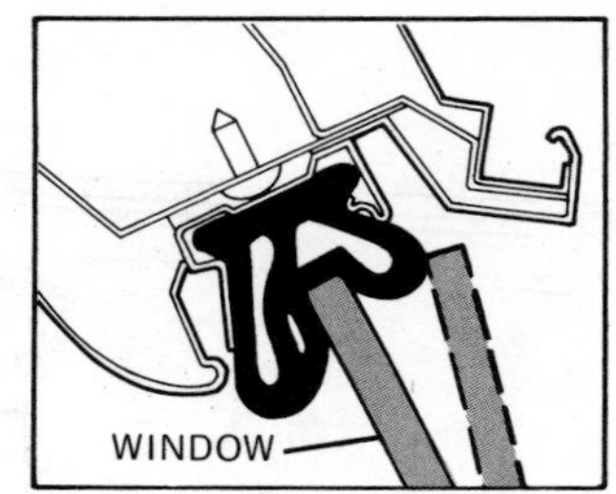

F. ALIGNMENT OF DOORS AND WINDOWS

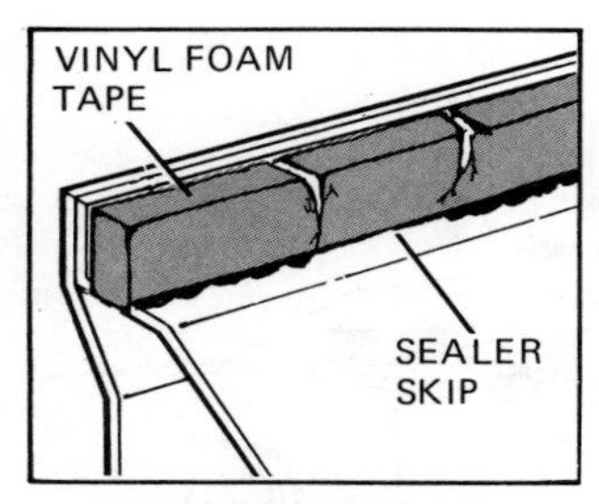

C. SEALER SKIPS AND VINYL FOAM TAPE TORN OR OMITTED

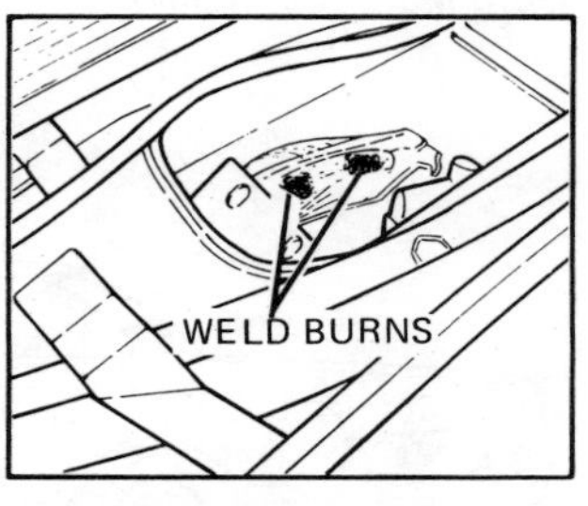

D. OMITTED WELDS OR WELD BURNS

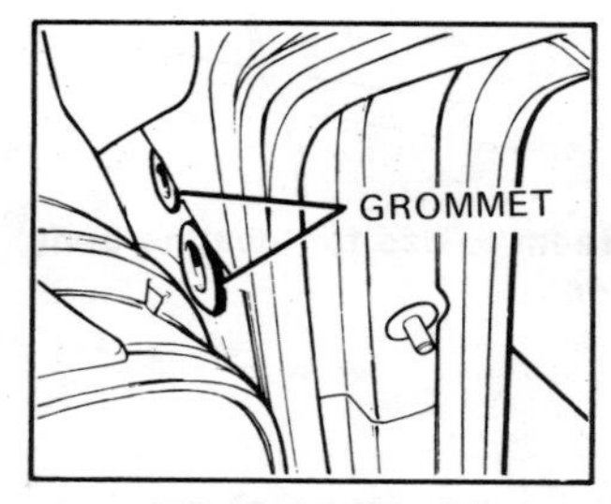

G. LOOSE, IMPROPERLY SEATED AND/OR MISSING GROMMETS AND BODY PLUGS

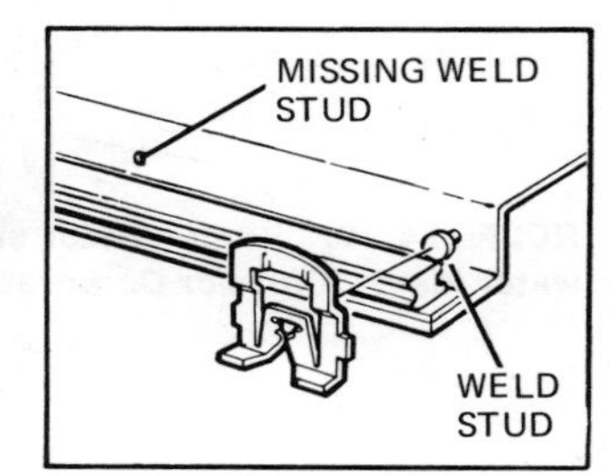

H. MISSING WELD STUD

FIGURE 24-25. Sources of wind and water leaks. (*Ford Motor Company*)

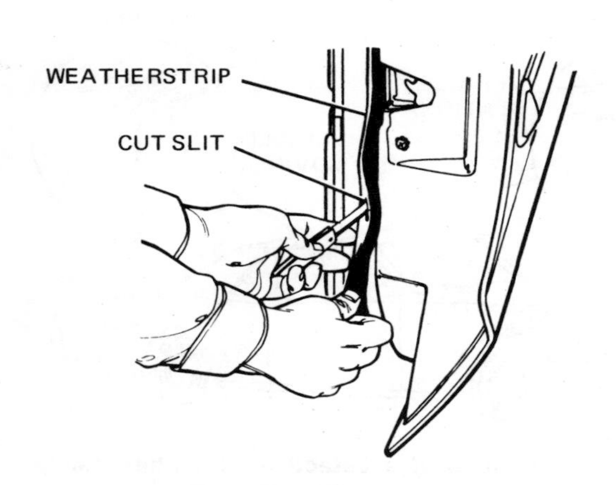

CAREFULLY SLIT REAR LIP OF WEATHERSTRIP

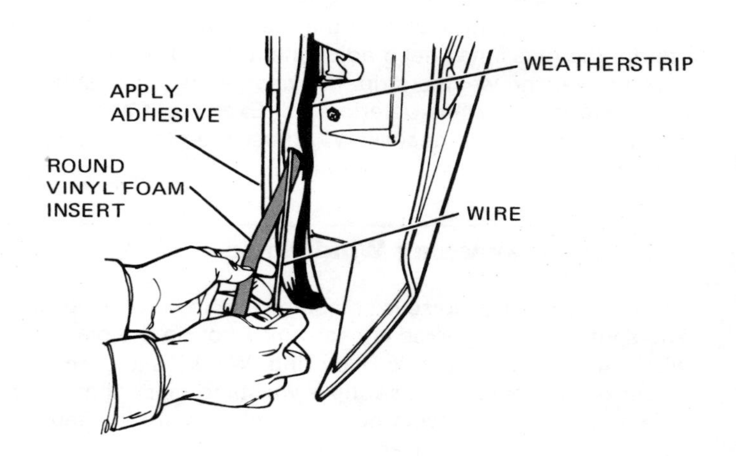

POSITION FOAM INSERT INTO CAVITY OF COLLAPSED WEATHERSTRIP USING A WIRE

FIGURE 24-26. Building up weatherstrip with vinyl. (*Ford Motor Company*)

○24-15 Checking Possible Causes of Wind Noise

First take a good look at the weatherstrip and adjoining metal around the doors and glass (Fig. 24-25). Often it is easy to spot the cause of wind noise because you can see where the poor fit is. If the cause is loose, torn, or distorted weatherstrip, you can usually fix it by repositioning, patching, or replacing the weatherstrip. Figure 24-26 shows one method of building up the weatherstrip at a weak point where it does not fit properly. Slit the weatherstrip and insert the vinyl, as shown. Vinyl should be coated with adhesive. Also look for holes in the sheet-metal joints on the front and rear faces of the door. Seal any openings you find. Even a small hole can produce a whistling or "pop-bottle" sound. Blow across the top of a soft-drink bottle to hear this sound.

If you don't see any obvious cause of wind leak, set the heater or air-conditioner controls to bring in outside air. Start the engine to move any vacuum-operated air doors into position. Then switch the ignition to the accessory position to keep the blower running with the engine off. Close the car doors. Now the car will be pressurized. Run your hand slowly around the edges of the doors, vent, and all around the window glass. Mark any place you can feel air coming through so you can check back at these points later. If you moisten your hand with water, you can feel the air leakage more easily.

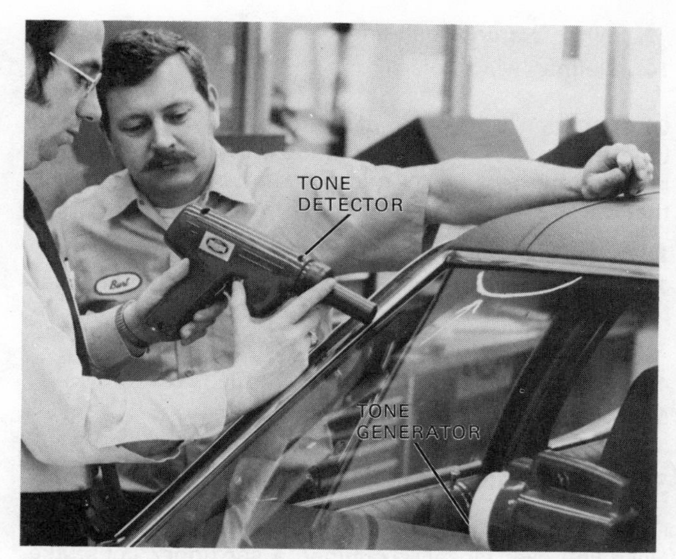

FIGURE 24-27. Electronic leak detector can locate the source of wind noise. (*Ford Motor Company*)

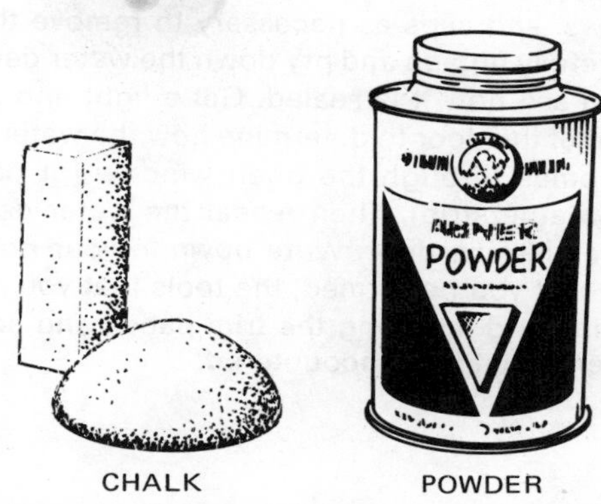

FIGURE 24-28. Materials for making a leak test. (*Chrysler Corporation*)

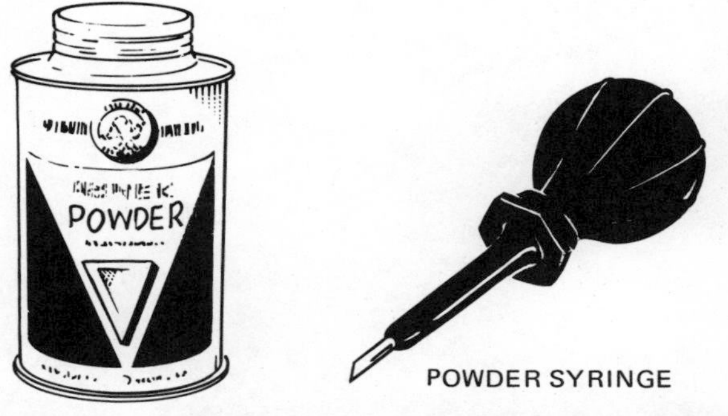

FIGURE 24-29. A powder syringe can be used to blow powder around the edge of the doors and windows. (*Chrysler Corporation*)

Listen for any hissing noise. You can improve your chances of hearing any hiss by using a short length of small-diameter hose. Hold one end of the hose to your ear and pass the other end slowly around the door and glass edges. Even a small leak will usually make enough noise for you to hear it through the hose.

If feeling and listening do not help you locate the source of the wind noise, you can use an electronic leak detector. This detector includes a tone generator and a tone detector (Fig. 24-27). The tone generator is placed inside the vehicle. It produces a high-pitched (ultrasonic) tone that is inaudible to the human ear but travels out through a leak. While the tone generator is operating, the technician moves the detector around the edges of the door and glass. A meter in the detector measures the strength of the signal being received. The signal will be strong if there is a leak.

If you do not have an electronic leak detector, there are two other tests to make. These tests use carpenter's chalk or tracing powder (Fig. 24-28). To make a chalk test, open the door and run chalk all around the weatherstrip. Gently close the door, holding the button so it does not latch. Then open the door and look around the door opening for chalk transfer. Where the weatherstrip has made good contact, you will find chalk on the door. Where there is poor contact, little or no chalk will transfer.

To use the tracing powder, you need a powder syringe (Fig. 24-29). Close the doors and windows. Load the syringe with powder. Blow powder around the edges of the doors and windows. Then open the doors and look for powder on the inside. There is loose weatherstrip at any point where powder has blown in.

As explained previously, correction of wind noise, once the source of trouble is located, requires sealing holes, building up low spots in the metal, shimming up the weatherstrip, or repositioning or replacing the weatherstrip.

NOTE: Some technicians will take the car out on the road to try to locate the cause. If you hear the noise while driving and can get a general idea of where it is coming from, pull over to the side of the road and seal the suspected area with masking tape. That is, actually apply tape over the joint between the door and adjoining body metal, or between the glass and adjoining metal. Then drive some more. If the tape kills the noise, you've pinpointed the source.

NOTE: *Always* recheck after having made any repair for wind noise. In addition, be sure to clean the car before returning it to the customer.

CHAPTER 24 CHECKUP

NOTE: Since the following is a chapter review test, you should review the chapter before taking the test.

A car door is a very complicated assembly. In addition to having a latch mechanism, lock mechanism, and window regulator, the door must have trim or upholstery on the inside, moldings on the outside, and seal against the car body around the edges. In this chapter, you studied about door trim, moldings, and weatherstrip and how to service and replace them. To find out how well you understand everything in this chapter, answer the questions that follow.

COMPLETING THE SENTENCES The sentences below are incomplete. After each sentence there are several words or phrases, but only one of them correctly completes the sentence. Write each sentence in your notebook, ending the sentence with the one word or phrase that completes it correctly.

1. Door pulls are used to (*a*) rest your arm, (*b*) lock the door, (*c*) close the door, (*d*) latch the door.
2. The materials lining the interior of a door are called the (*a*) door trim, (*b*) watershield, (*c*) weatherstrip, (*d*) moldings.
3. To prevent water from entering the body, between the door and the trim pad there is a (*a*) molding, (*b*) weatherstrip, (*c*) water deflector, (*d*) glass.
4. Some exterior moldings are attached by (*a*) gas welding, (*b*) soldering, (*c*) adhesive tape, (*d*) masking tape.
5. Two types of doors are the (*a*) two-door and four-door, (*b*) hardtop door and sedan door, (*c*) front door and back door, (*d*) hood and trunk.

DEFINITIONS In the following you are asked for the definitions of several words and phrases. Write them in your notebook. The act of writing the definitions does two things. It tests your knowledge, and it helps fix the information more firmly in your mind. Turn back into the chapter if you are not sure of an answer, or look up the definition in the glossary at the back of the book.

1. What is door trim?
2. Define "garnish molding."
3. What is a water deflector?
4. What is a door exterior molding?
5. Define "door pull."
6. What is adhesive compound?
7. Define "weatherstrip."
8. What is a roof rail?
9. What is a door belt line?
10. Define "wind noise."

QUESTIONS Write each of the following questions, and then the answer, in your notebook. If you have trouble recalling the answer to a question, turn back to the pages that cover the material and study them again.

1. What is the procedure for removing a trim panel?
2. List the exterior moldings that may be found on a car door.
3. Explain how to attach an adhesive body molding.
4. How do you test a door for water leaks?
5. Explain how to correct a wind noise.

SUGGESTIONS FOR FURTHER STUDY

Have you ever closely examined a car door? Let's take time now to study the door carefully. Open the door on a car. Locate and identify each part on the outer panel, inner panel, and around the edges. Then remove the handles, screws, and clips as necessary to remove the trim panel. Carefully untape and pry down the water deflector, so you can see how it is sealed. Get a light and look in the bottom of the door to determine how the water drains out if it comes through the open window (or past the belt-line weatherstrip). Then reseal the water deflector and reassemble the door. Write down in your notebook each step that you performed, the tools that you needed for removing and installing the trim panel, and any special problems that you encountered.

25

DOOR LATCHES, LOCKS, AND WINDOW REGULATORS

In this chapter, you will learn about various mechanisms in doors and how to service them. These include the window regulators that raise and lower the glass, the latching mechanism that holds the door closed but allows it to be opened when operated, and the locking device.

We covered, in Chapter 22, the fitting of the door and explained how the hinges can be moved in various directions to achieve proper fit of the door at front and back and at top and bottom. Now, in this chapter, we describe the internal mechanisms of doors and explain how to service them.

NOTE: The mechanisms and servicing procedures that follow are typical only. Specific door models vary somewhat from those described. When servicing a car door, refer to the manufacturer's shop manual that covers that specific model. If you do not have the shop manual available, make sketches of the mechanism as you take it apart. In your drawing, show just where the rod connects, how a lever is attached, and so on. If you run into trouble when trying to reassemble a mechanism, remove the trim from another similar door, or the door on the opposite side of the car, and note how it is assembled. This will give you a clue as to how to proceed.

○25-1 Door Internal Mechanisms

Inside the door are two mechanisms: one to raise and lower the window, called the window regulator, and a latching and locking mechanism. Figure 25-1 shows these mechanisms in a rear door. Note that the window regulator (item 13) is electric. Note also that the door lock uses a solenoid (item 15). Figure 25-2 shows a hardtop door with the parts named in considerably greater detail. This picture also shows, outside the door, the manual type of door lock and window regulator. Examine various car doors and note whether they have manual or electrical controls. We cover the service of these mechanisms in following sections.

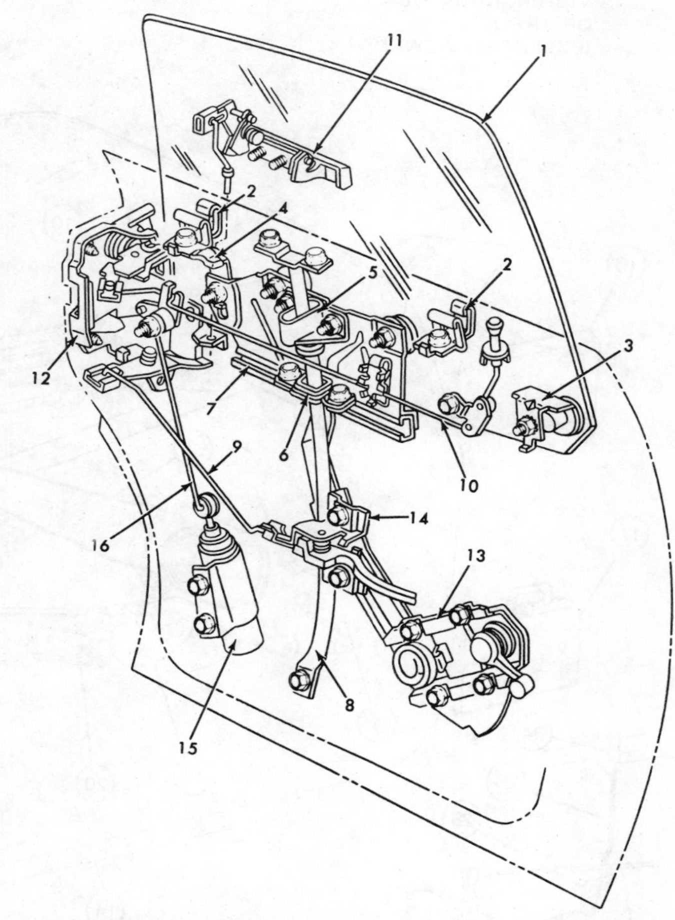

1. Window assembly
2. Belt trim support retainers
3. Front up-travel stop
4. Rear up-travel stop
5. Lower-sash upper guide
6. Lower-sash lower guide
7. Lower-sash guide plate assembly
8. Guide-tube assembly
9. Remote control to lock-connecting rod
10. Inside locking rod
11. Door outside lift-bar handle
12. Door lock
13. Window regulator (electric)
14. Door-lock remote-control handle
15. Door-lock solenoid
16. Rod inside locking to solenoid

FIGURE 25-1. Rear-door hardware. (*Fisher Body Division of General Motors Corporation*)

○25-2 Door Latch Mechanisms

The latch mechanism for a front door is shown in Fig. 25-3. Study the illustration as we explain how it works. When the door handle is operated, either from the inside or outside, a rod is moved. This causes the latch to release so the door can be opened. Then, when the door is closed, the latch operates to hold it closed. We described, in Chapter 22, how to adjust the latch and striker bolt.

The door lock is part of the latching mechanism. When the locking knob is pushed down (mechanical type) or when the solenoid is actuated (electrical type), the latch is disconnected from the operating handles. See Fig. 25-3 for the location and connections of the solenoid to the linkages.

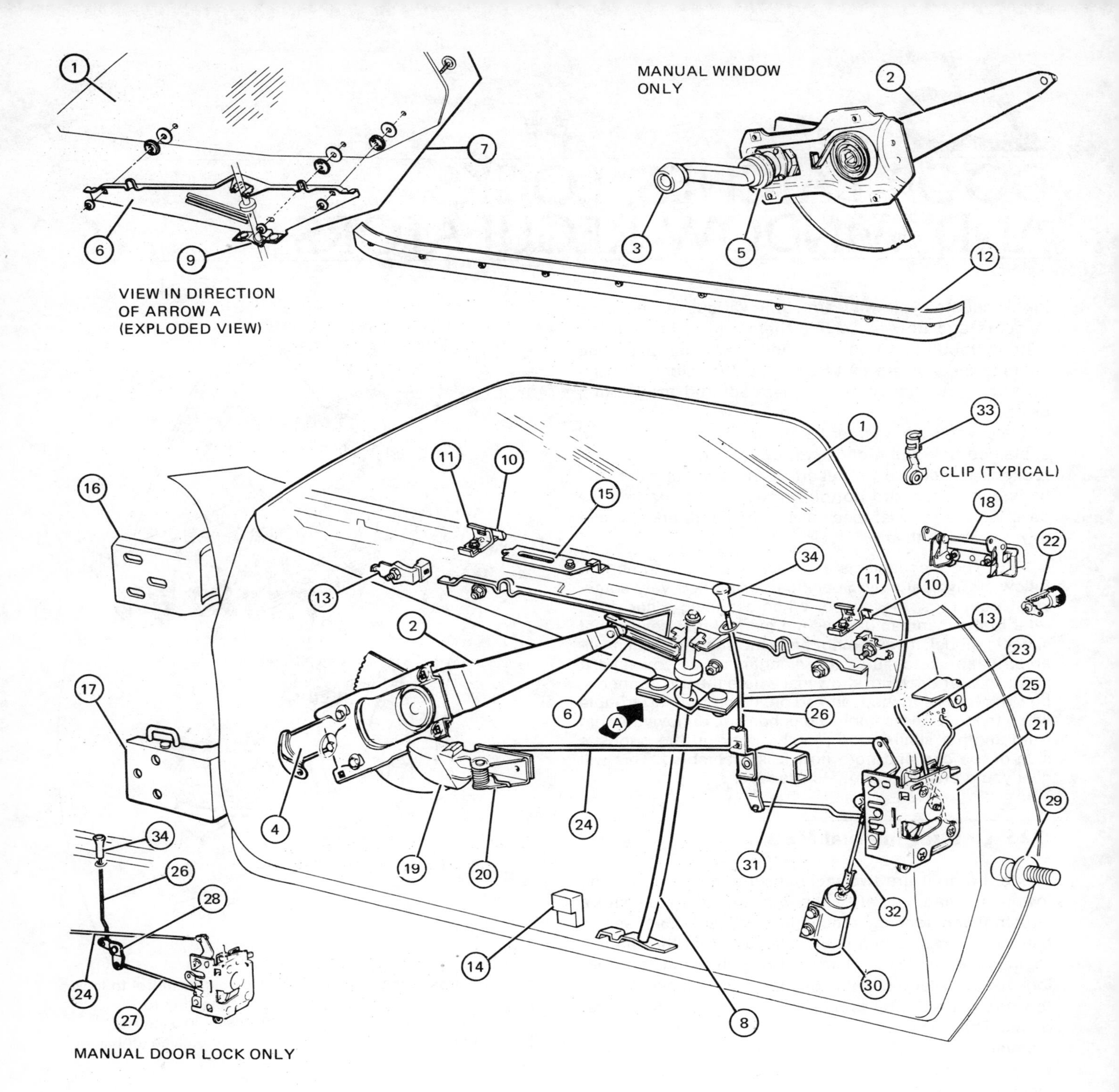

1. Door Glass
2. Rear Door Regulator
3. Regulator Handle
4. Motor
5. Regulator Handle Spacer
6. Glass Lift Channel
7. Glass Lift Channel Fastener
8. Track, Tube Type
9. Track Guide
10. Glass Stabilizer
11. Glass Stabilizer Trim Support Bracket
12. Outer Belt Weatherstrip
13. Upstop
14. Downstop Bumper
15. Lift Channel Stabilizer
16. Upper Hinge
17. Lower Hinge
18. Outside Door Handle
19. Inside Remote Handle
20. Remote Control
21. Door Latch
22. Door Lock Cylinder
23. Link, Outside Handle to Latch
24. Link, Remote Control to Latch
25. Link, Lock Cylinder to Latch
26. Link, Pushrod to Latch Lock Control
27. Link, Latch Lock Control to Latch
28. Latch Lock Control
29. Door Latch Striker
30. Lock Solenoid
31. Locking Switch Assembly
32. Link, Solenoid to Latch
33. Linkage Clips
34. Locking Knob

FIGURE 25-2. Details of the internal mechanisms in a door. (*Chrysler Corporation*)

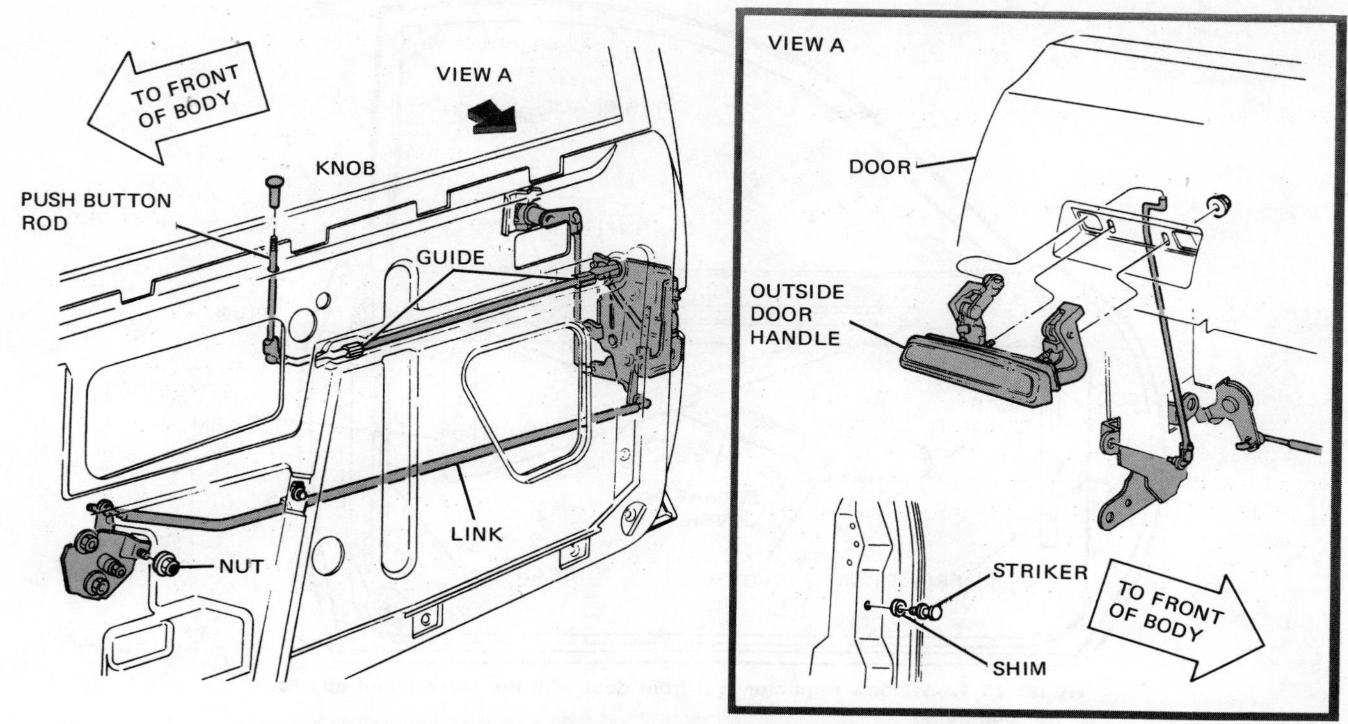

FIGURE 25-3. Latch mechanism for a front door. (*Ford Motor Company*)

○25-3 Door-Latch Service

All door latches are very similar in construction and linkage to the handles and lock. There are some variations from one car model to another. If you ever get stuck trying to reconnect the linkages inside a door, refer to the manufacturer's shop manual covering that model car. You will find detailed instructions and illustrations showing how to put everything back together. If a manual is not available, remove the trim from the opposite door in the car. This will give you a clue as to what needs to be done.

The first step in door-latch service is to remove the trim panel and watershield (deflector) as explained in Chapter 24. You can then get to the mechanism through the access holes in the inner door panel. Detach connecting rods and remove screws and nuts as necessary to take off defective parts and replace them. Before replacing the watershield and trim panel, work the door latch several times to make sure it is operating properly.

Servicing the lock cylinder is covered in detail in ○25-10.

○25-4 Window Regulator

Windows are raised and lowered either mechanically, by turning a crank, or electrically, with a motor. Both styles are shown in Figs. 25-1 to 25-3. The window regulators also differ in the glass guidance system. One system called the *dual U-run* type uses a U-shaped channel at the bottom of the glass and a pair of levers as shown in Figs. 25-2 and 25-4. The crank or electric motor (on electric units) has a gear which is meshed with the gear segment. When this gear turns, it causes the gear segment to turn. Let us see what happens when the window is being lowered. As the gear segment turns, the primary lever, which is part of the gear segment, pivots and moves downward. The roller in the end of the lever rolls in the channel. At the same time, the secondary lever is forced to pivot downward because it is fastened at the middle to the primary lever. The channel, therefore, is forced to move downward. The glass is attached to the channel so it moves down. The two runs, which are vertical channels, guide the glass as it moves down and up.

The second type of window regulator uses a tube, called the *tube run* or *glass run,* to guide the window as it moves up and down. Figures 25-1 and 25-5 illustrate this type, which is called the *tubular-run type.* As the gear on the crank or electric motor turns, it causes the gear segment to turn. This moves the lever and puts an up or down force on the channel in the glass bracket. The bracket and the glass attached to it are forced to move. The tube guides the glass so it moves in the proper direction. Figure 25-6 shows what a typical tube and guide look like.

○25-5 Servicing the Ford Dual U-Run Window Regulator

This regulator (Fig. 25-4) is used in many Ford-built cars. It is shown disassembled in Fig. 25-7. To remove the glass, proceed as follows:

REMOVING AND INSTALLING THE GLASS

1. Remove the trim panel and watershield.
2. Lower the glass until the glass retainers are visible at the access holes in the door inner panel. Remove the front and rear glass retainers by pushing the center pins from the retainers with a small drift punch.

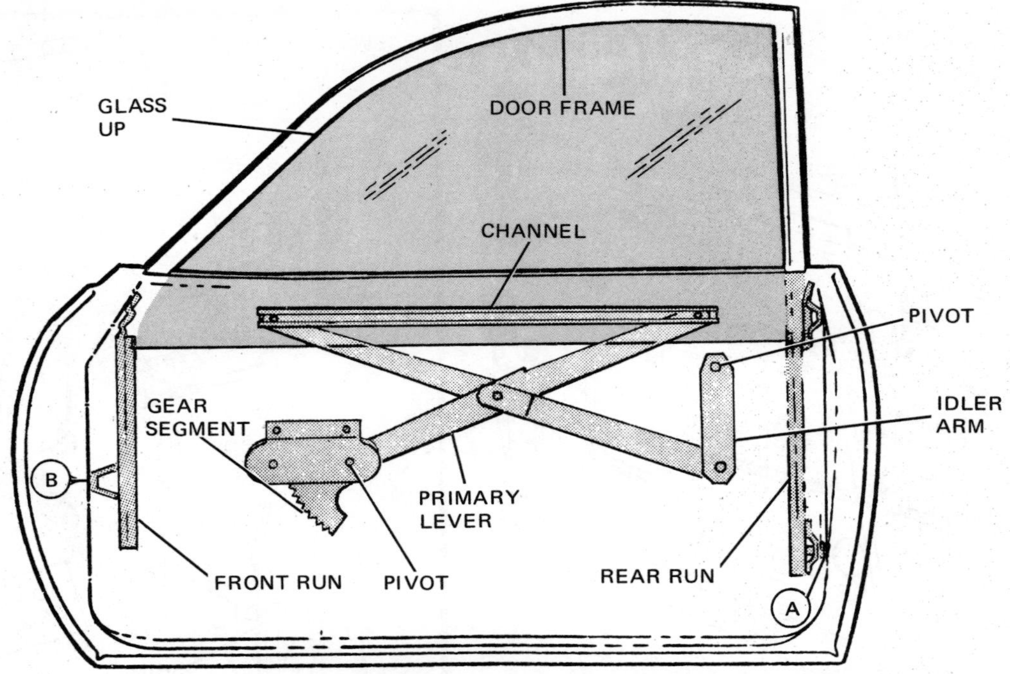

FIGURE 25-4. Window regulator in a front door with the glass rolled up. (*Ford Motor Company*)

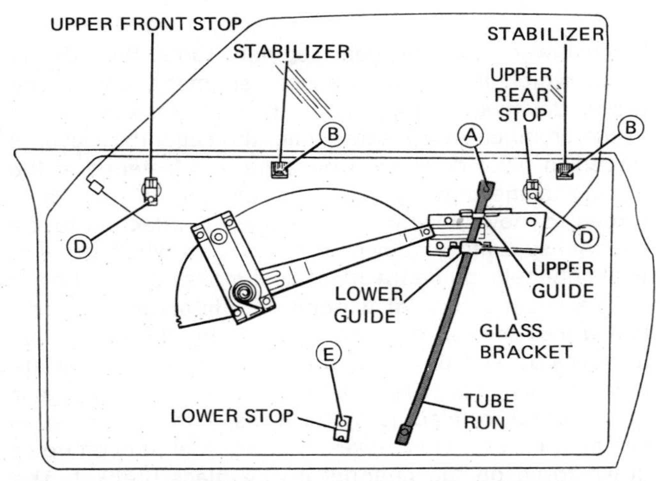

FIGURE 25-5. Window regulator using a tube run to guide the glass. (*Ford Motor Company*)

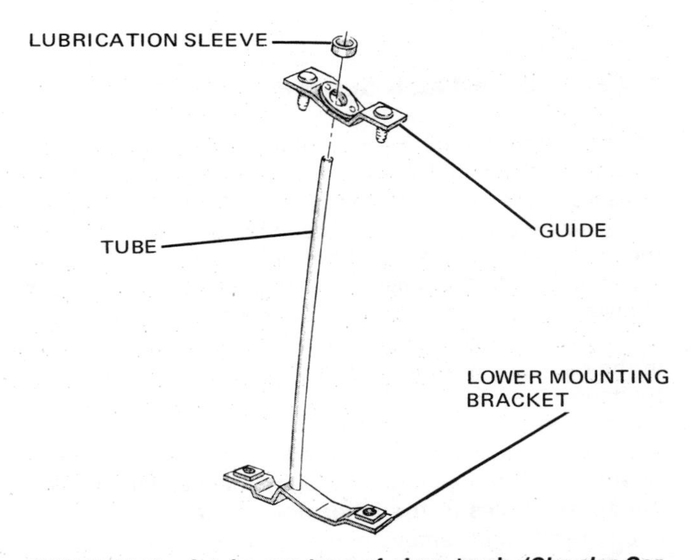

FIGURE 25-6. A tube-run type of glass track. (*Chrysler Corporation*)

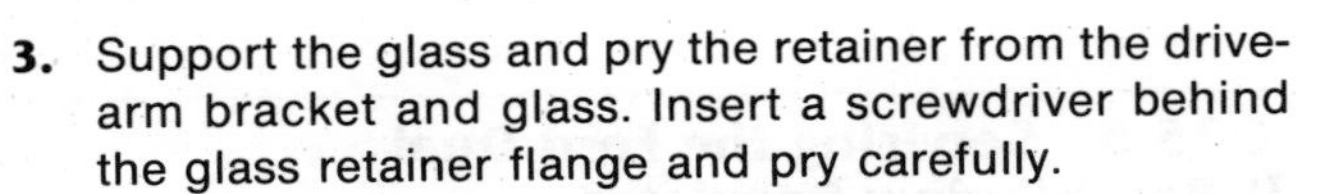

3. Support the glass and pry the retainer from the drive-arm bracket and glass. Insert a screwdriver behind the glass retainer flange and pry carefully.
4. Remove the front-run lower attaching screw.
5. Tip the front end of the glass downward, and lift the glass out of the door, working from the outside.
6. To reinstall the glass, insert it into the door and tip it into normal position. Hold the drive-arm bracket to the glass, and push the glass rear retainer into the hole. Then install the glass retainer pin by pushing it into the retainer hole until the end of the pin is flush with the retainer flange. Install the glass front retainer by the same procedure. Then, with the glass positioned in the two runs, install the run attaching screws. Adjust as indicated in step 7.
7. To adjust the glass, check the weatherstrip to make sure it is in good condition. Then raise the glass to the top. Loosen the two run-retaining screws (A and B in Fig. 25-4). Lower the glass until the top edge is about 4 inches [102 mm] above the belt line. Tighten the run retainer screws. Cycle the window up and down several times to make sure it works properly.

REMOVING AND INSTALLING THE WINDOW REGULATOR

1. Remove the trim panel and watershield.
2. Support the glass, and remove screw attaching window-regulator equalizer arm to door inner panel.

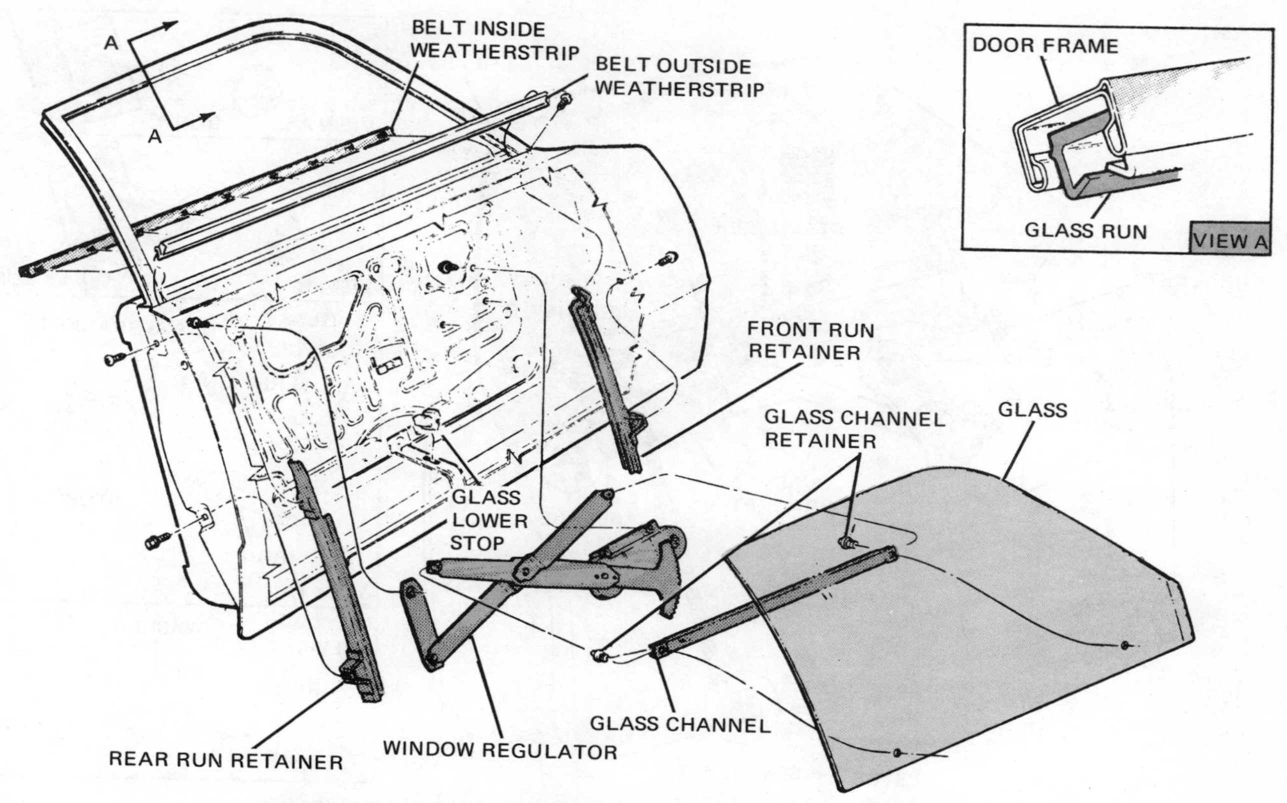

FIGURE 25-7. **Ford dual U-run window regulator.** *(Ford Motor Company)*

3. Remove four window-regulator attaching screws. Disengage the regulator from the channel, and remove the regulator through the lower access hole.
4. To reinstall the regulator, put the regulator in the door through the lower access hole. Engage the regulator arm rollers in the channel. Position the regulator and secure it with the attaching screws. Then attach the equalizer (idler) arm with a screw. Check the adjustment and, if it is satisfactory, install the watershield and trim panel.

○25-6 Servicing the Chrysler Dual U-Run Window Regulator

This regulator, shown in Fig. 25-8, is serviced in a similar manner to the Ford unit, covered in the previous section. However, it uses a pivot guide as shown in Fig. 25-8. Adjustment is made as follows.

Check the weatherstrip to make sure it is in good condition. Raise the glass almost all the way up so there is a gap of only about 1/8 inch [3 mm] between the top edge of the glass and the glass run at the top of the door frame. Loosen the pivot-guide attaching screws so the glass can be adjusted to make the top edge parallel to the door frame. Then tighten the fasteners.

○25-7 Adjusting Ford Tube-Run Window Regulator

This regulator is shown in Figs. 25-5 and 25-9. The glass must be repositioned if the glass has been replaced or

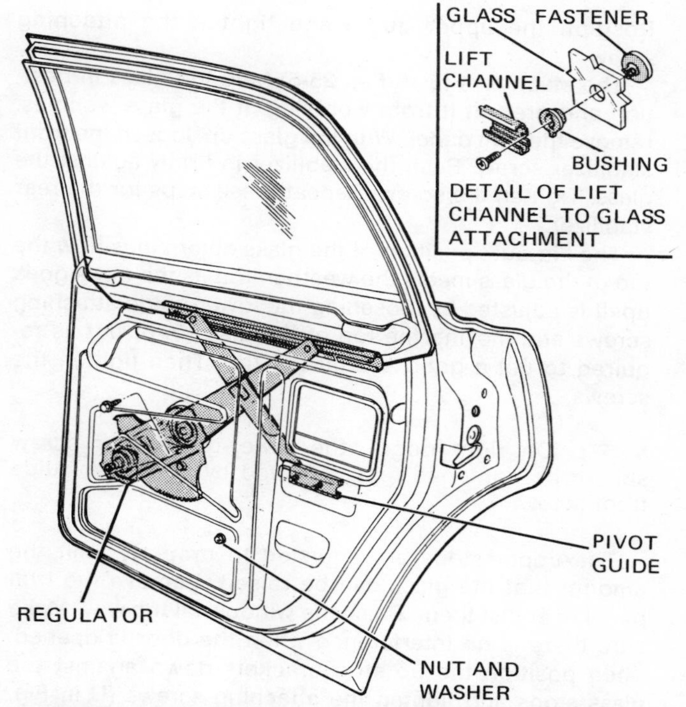

FIGURE 25-8. **Chrysler dual U-run window regulator.** *(Chrysler Corporation)*

if considerable fore-and-aft adjustment of the door hinges has been done. To adjust the glass, remove the trim panel and watershield. Loosen the upper-guide attaching screw (A in Fig. 25-5) and reposition the glass.

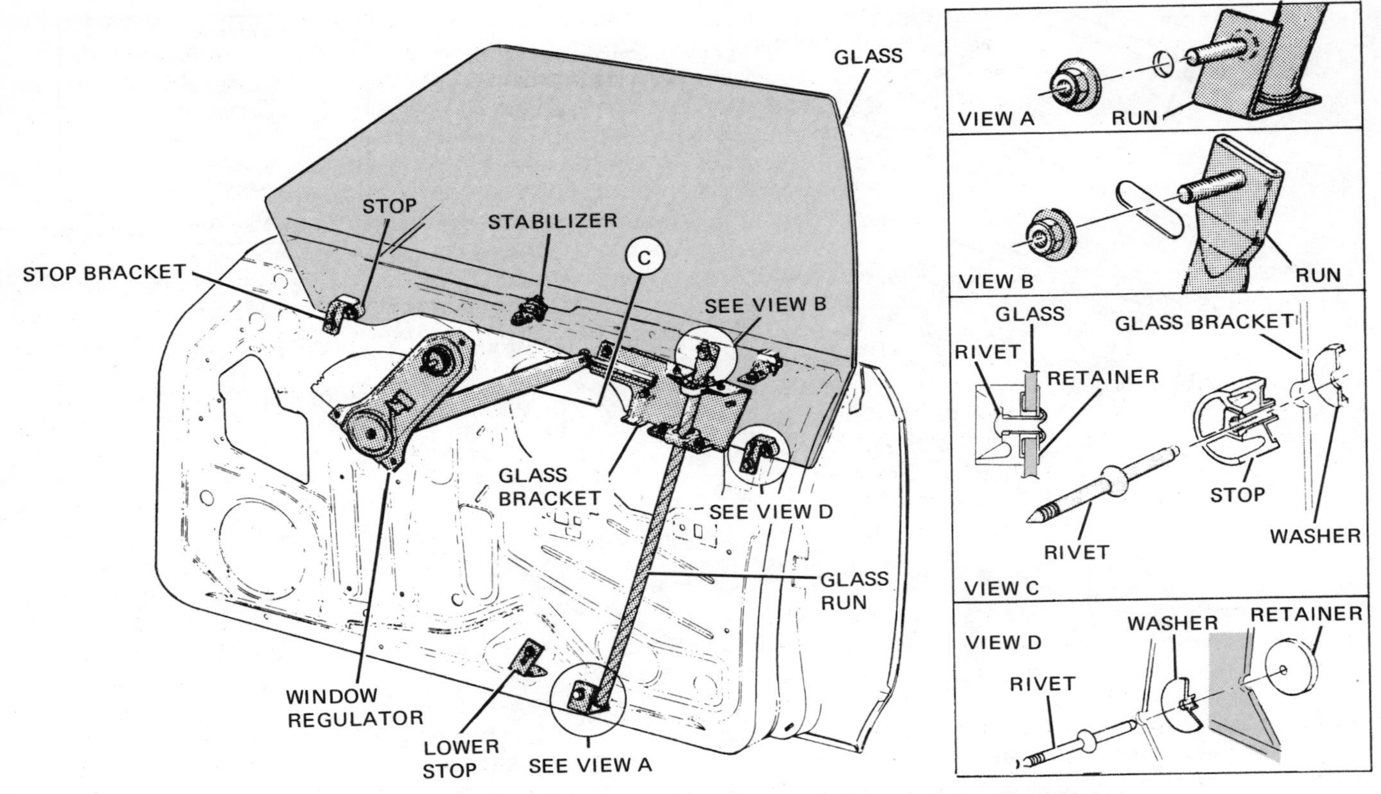

FIGURE 25-9. **Attachments of the Ford tube-run window regulator. (*Ford Motor Company*)**

Position the upper guide and tighten the attaching screw.

The stabilizers (B in Fig. 25-5) hold the glass in position and prevent it from wobbling. If the glass wobbles, remove the trim panel. With the glass up, loosen the front stabilizer screw. Push the stabilizer in firmly against the glass. Tighten the screw. Repeat these steps for the rear stabilizer.

The "in-out" position of the glass determines how the top of the glass meets the weatherstrip as the glass goes up. It is adjusted by loosening the lower-guide attaching screws and moving the top of the glass in or out as required to get a good seal at the top. Then tighten the screws.

NOTE: On right doors, the lower-guide rear screw should be tightened first, followed by the lower-guide front screw.

The upper stops are adjusted to properly limit the amount that the glass can be raised. Remove the trim panel to adjust them. Raise the window all the way. Make sure there is no interference when the door is opened. Then position the up stop brackets down against the glass stops and tighten the attaching screws (D in Fig. 25-5).

The lower stop (E in Fig. 25-5) is adjusted to prevent the glass from moving down too far when it is opened. To make the adjustment, remove the trim panel. Loosen the lower-stop screw and lower the glass until its top edge is flush to ¼ inch [6.35 mm] above the outer panel. Then raise the stop against the glass bracket and tighten the screw.

○25-8 Servicing the Ford Tube-Run Window Regulator

The services we cover now include removing and replacing the glass, the window regulator, the window motor, and the guides or run.

REMOVING AND REPLACING THE GLASS Remove the trim panel, watershield, glass stabilizers, and upper stops. Remove the center pins from the rivets attaching the glass bracket to the glass (Fig. 25-9) with a drift punch. Then drill out the rivet heads with a ¼-inch [6.35-mm] drill.

NOTE: Do not attempt to pry the rivets out. You can break the glass or bracket this way.

Push the rivets out. Move the glass forward until the rear upper stop aligns with the access notch in the inner panel of the belt line. Lift the rear of the glass up and out. Then move the glass rearward until the front upper stop is aligned with the access hole and remove the glass. To remove the stops from the glass, remove the rivets as explained above.

NOTE: The bolts and nuts recommended to install the glass are ¼-20 × 1 inch hex bolts and ¼-20 nuts, tightened to 6 to 11 lb-ft [0.83 to 1.38 kg-m] torque.

To install the glass, first attach the upper stops with bolts, washers, and nuts. Then insert the glass into the door, using the access notch to move the stops below the belt line. Position the glass on the glass bracket and secure with bolts, washers, and nuts.

Then install the upper front and rear stop brackets and the glass stabilizers. Adjust the stops and stabilizers as already explained in ○25-7. Install the watershield and trim panel.

REMOVING AND REPLACING THE WINDOW REGULATOR Remove the door trim panel and watershield. Support the glass in the up position. If the door has electric windows, remove the center pin from the motor bracket-to-inner-panel attaching rivets with a drift punch. Then drill the heads from the rivets with a ¼-inch [6.35-mm] drill.

Remove the center pin from the rivets attaching the window regulator. Drill the heads from the rivets as already explained. Disengage the regulator arm from the glass bracket and remove the regulator from the door.

If the motor is in good condition (electric windows) but the regulator is defective, remove the motor and install it on the new regulator. First drill a 5/16-inch [7.94-mm] hole through the regulator sector gear and the regulator plate. Install a ¼-inch [6.35-mm] bolt through the hole. This prevents the sector gear from moving (it is under spring tension) when the motor is removed.

To install the window regulator, first lubricate it (Fig. 25-10). Position the regulator in the door and insert the roller into the glass bracket channel. Secure the regulator to the panel with ¼-20 × ½ inch screws and washers. Attach the motor bracket to the inner panel (electric windows). Check the regulator operation. Install the watershield and trim panel.

MOTOR AND DRIVE REMOVAL AND REPLACEMENT (ELECTRIC WINDOWS) Remove the trim panel, watershield, and radio speaker. Many cars have holes punched in the door inner panel for motor and drive removal. On other cars, drill three ¾-inch [19.05-mm] holes with a hole saw in the door inner panel at the dimples. The pilot drill for the hole saw should not extend more than ¼ inch [6.35 mm] beyond the saw. This is to keep the drill from damaging the internal door parts.

Disconnect the motor wires at the connector. Working through the access holes, remove the three attaching screws and remove the motor and drive.

To install the motor and drive, attach it snug (but not tight) with the three screws. Connect the motor wires at the connector. Run the glass up and down to assure gear engagement. Then tighten the motor attaching screws. Install body tape over the drilled holes. Install the radio speaker. Recheck the window operation. Then install the watershield and trim panel.

REMOVING AND INSTALLING GUIDES AND RUNS Remove the door trim panel and watershield. Support the glass in the up position and remove the two attaching screws from the upper and lower guides. Remove the glass-run upper and lower attaching screws and remove the guides and run from the door. To replace them, first lubricate as shown in Fig. 25-10. Then reinstall the run and guides. Remove the glass support and adjust the glass as explained in ○ 25-7.

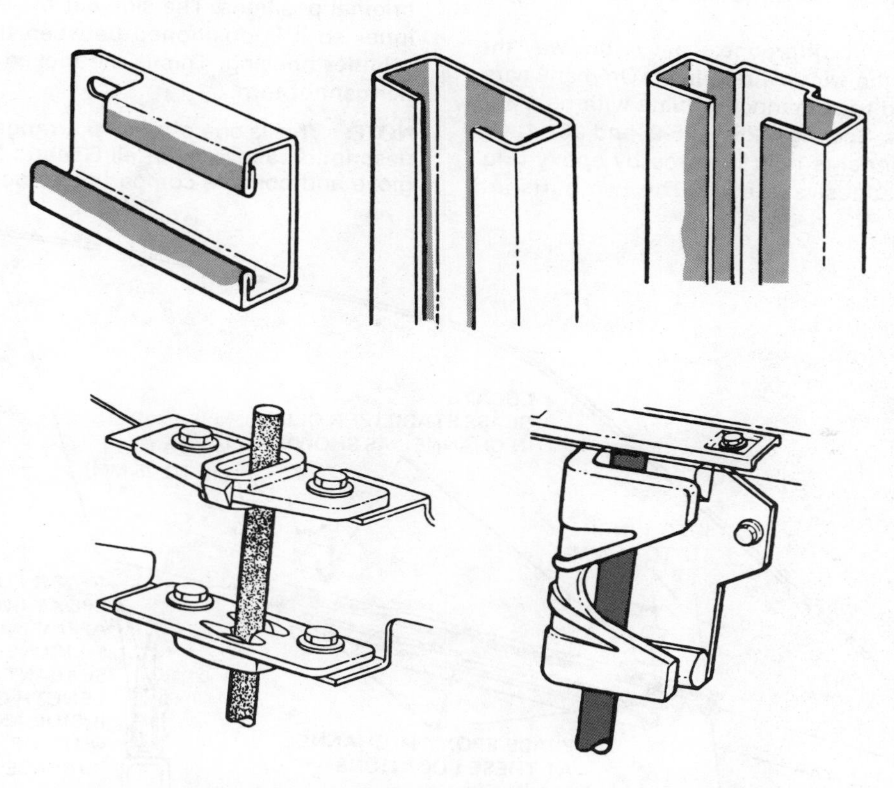

APPLY AN EVEN COATING OF POLYETHYLENE GREASE TO ALL WINDOW REGULATOR ROLLERS, SHAFTS AND THE ENTIRE LENGTH OF ROLLER GUIDES AS ILLUSTRATED BY THE SHADED AREAS.

FIGURE 25-10. Lubrication points for the window regulator. (*Ford Motor Company*)

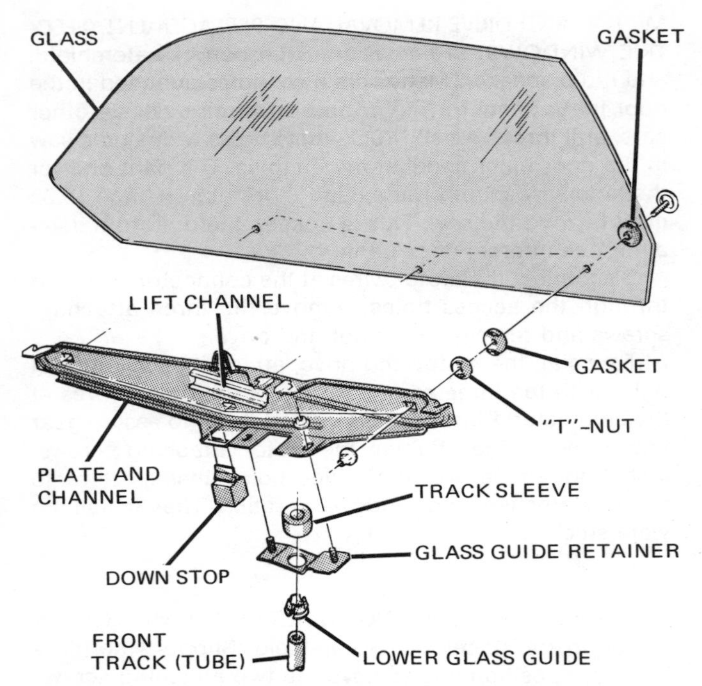

FIGURE 25-11. Attaching glass to channel. (*Ford Motor Company*)

○25-9 Adjusting and Servicing Other Window Regulators

The detailed step-by-step procedures given for Ford window regulators are typical of adjusting and servicing procedures for most cars.

There is one special difference. That is the way the glass is attached to the window regulator. On many cars, the glass is attached to a channel or plate with nuts and gaskets or bushings. See Figs. 25-8, 25-9, and 25-11. On other cars, the channel is held in place by epoxy (Fig. 25-12). A two-part adhesive is used. The two parts are mixed thoroughly and placed in the channel at three locations as shown in Fig. 25-12. Spacer clips are installed as shown. The channel is applied to the glass at the previously determined location and taped in place so it will not move until it is cured. (Curing takes about one hour.)

NOTE: Two types of adhesives have been used on original assembly to secure the channel to the glass: plastisol (which is tan) and urethane (which is black). If the adhesive is tan, it is permanent and the glass and channel are replaced as an assembly. If the adhesive is black, the channel can be removed from the glass by applying heat from a gas welding torch with a number 2 or 3 tip. Slowly pass the flame along the full bottom length of the channel for about 1 to 1½ minutes. This should soften the adhesive so the channel can be pulled off the glass with pliers.

CAUTION: Do not breathe the fumes which result from the burning out of the urethane. They are toxic!

○25-10 Locks and Keys

The key has a series of notches. When the key (Fig. 25-13) is inserted into the lock cylinder, a series of tumblers (Fig. 25-14) are raised to the correct height. This lines up the notches on all the tumblers. At the same time, a side bar is pushed into the notches by two small springs. When this side bar moves into the notches, it clears the space between the lock cylinder and the lock housing. This allows the key to turn the cylinder so that unlocking occurs. When the cylinder is turned to the locked position and the key withdrawn, the tumblers return to their original positions. The side bar moves back into the cylinder so it is positioned between the cylinder and the cylinder housing. This is the locked position. The cylinder cannot turn.

NOTE: This is one of several arrangements in locks. The description above is for all General Motors locks except glove and console compartment locks.

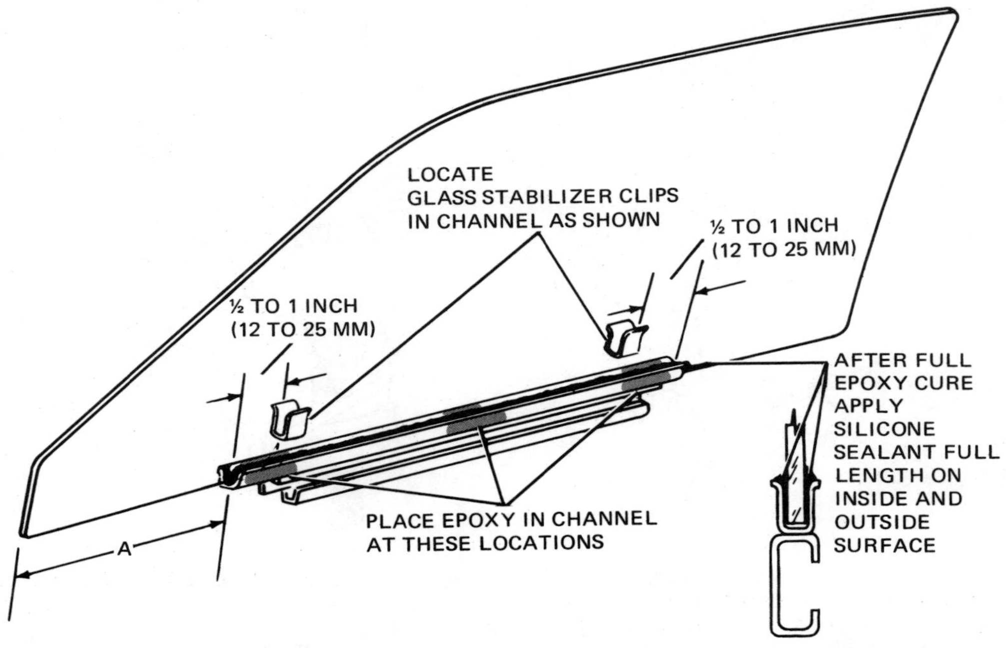

FIGURE 25-12. Glass channel held in place by epoxy. (*Fisher Body Division of General Motors Corporation*)

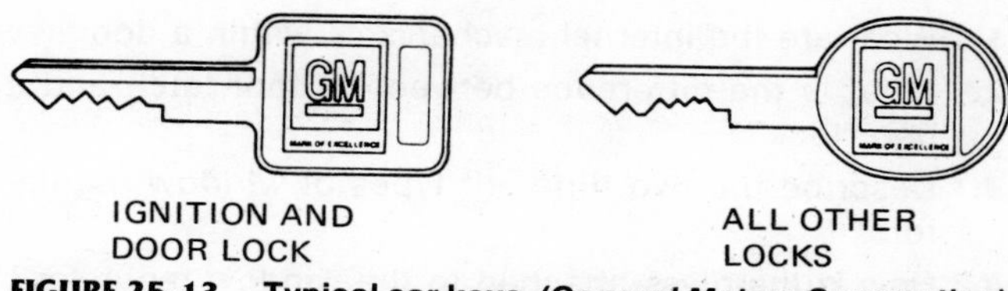

FIGURE 25-13. Typical car keys. (*General Motors Corporation*)

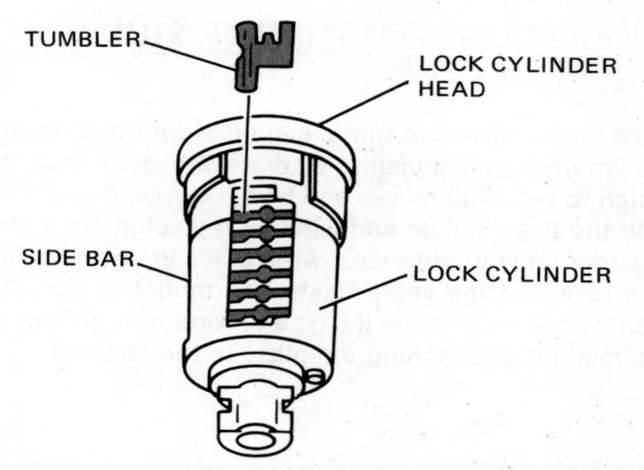

FIGURE 25-14. Location of tumblers in a lock cylinder. (*Fisher Body Division of General Motors Corporation*)

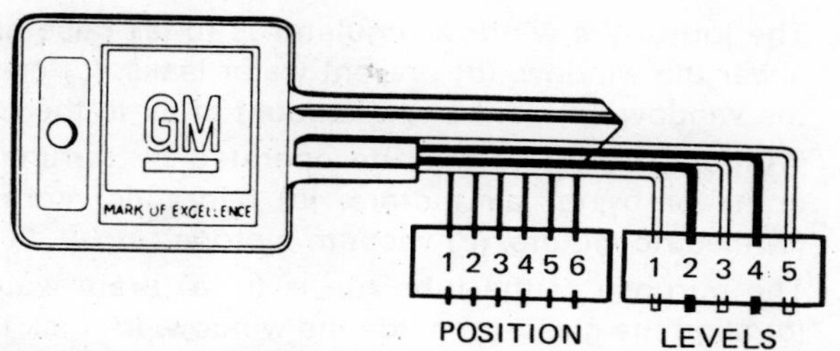

FIGURE 25-15. Using the key code diagram. (*Fisher Body Division of General Motors Corporation*)

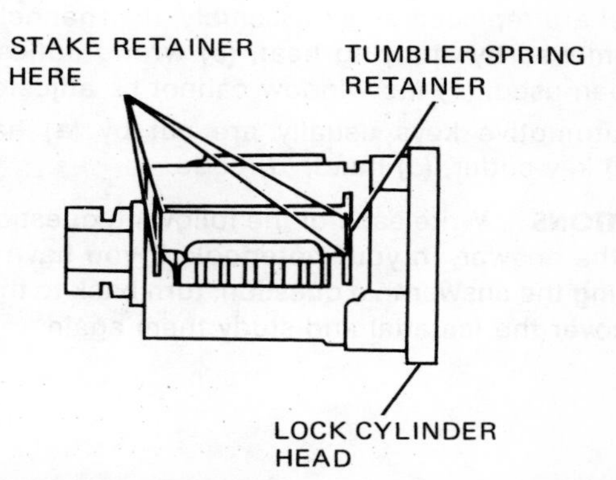

FIGURE 25-16. Installing the spring retainer. (*Fisher Body Division of General Motors Corporation*)

Locks do not normally require service. However, if a lock becomes defective, it will require replacement. The cylinders and tumblers are supplied separately, and you must assemble them properly so the key will work the lock. A special code, available to owners of key-cutting equipment, lists the parts numbers of the tumblers and their positions in the cylinder for every lock arrangement. This tells you what tumbler to put where in the cylinder. There are six tumblers in the cylinder shown in Fig. 25-14. They must be so arranged that when the key is inserted, the notches on the sides of the tumblers will line up. This allows the side bar to move out of the way so the cylinder can be rotated.

If the code is not available, you can still determine which tumblers to insert in which positions in the cylinder. Lay the key on the key code diagram in Fig. 25-15 so the key is outlined by the diagram. Start at the head of the key blade (position 1 in Fig. 25-15). Note and write down the lowest level (which is the tumbler number) that is visible in number 1 position. Repeat this for positions 2 through 6. You now have the tumbler numbers and positions that are to be inserted into the cylinder.

Pull out the side bar with your fingers so the tumblers will drop into place. Insert the properly numbered tumbler into its correct space in the cylinder. Insert a tumbler spring in the space provided above each tumbler. Install all tumblers in this manner.

NOTE: If the springs become entangled, do not pull them apart. Instead, unscrew them. Pulling them apart can stretch and ruin them.

Insert the end springs of the spring retainer into the slots at the ends of the cylinder (Fig. 25-16). Push the spring retainer down into place temporarily while you check the lock action. Insert the key into the cylinder. If the tumblers are properly installed, the side bar will drop down. If the bar does not drop, springs and tumblers are incorrectly installed.

NOTE: If improperly assembled, tumblers can be removed by holding the cylinder, tumbler slots down. Pull the side bar out with your fingers and jar the cylinder to shake the tumblers out.

When the key works as explained above, the tumblers are correctly installed and the spring retainer should be staked into place. Put the cylinder into a vise, using leather or wood at each vise jaw to prevent damage to the cylinder. Use a staking tool to lightly stake the spring retainer as shown in Fig. 25-16.

CHAPTER 25 CHECKUP

NOTE: Since the following is a chapter review test, you should review the chapter before taking the test.

In this chapter, we have discussed the mechanisms that are inside the door. These are the door latch, lock, and window regulator. Because these parts are not exposed, you must first learn how to get to them. These procedures were covered in the previous chapter (Chapter 24). Then after you have performed the service required, the trim panel and handles must be reinstalled on the door. Be sure to check and recheck that all of the door mechanisms work properly before reassembling the door.

COMPLETING THE SENTENCES The sentences below are incomplete. After each sentence there are several words or phrases, but only one of them correctly completes the sentence. Write each sentence in your notebook, ending the sentence with the one word or phrase that completes it correctly.

1. The job of the window regulator is to (*a*) raise and lower the window, (*b*) prevent water leaks, (*c*) clean the window, (*d*) control the amount of air in the car.
2. Window regulators may be operated by turning a crank or by (*a*) air motors, (*b*) hydraulic motors, (*c*) electric motors, (*d*) vacuum motors.
3. The purpose of the tube run is to (*a*) drain water, (*b*) align the glass, (*c*) guide the window, (*d*) lock the door.
4. When you see the channel secured to the glass with black adhesive, you know that the (*a*) glass and channel are replaced as an assembly, (*b*) channel can be removed by applying heat, (*c*) wrong adhesive has been used, (*d*) the window cannot be adjusted.
5. Automotive keys usually are cut by (*a*) hacksaw, (*b*) key cutter, (*c*) hand, (*d*) code.

QUESTIONS Write each of the following questions, and then the answer, in your notebook. If you have trouble recalling the answer to a question, turn back to the pages that cover the material and study them again.

1. What are the internal mechanisms within a door?
2. What is the difference between a door latch and a door lock?
3. Describe the two different types of window regulators.
4. How is the glass attached to the window regulator?
5. How often do door locks require service?

SUGGESTIONS FOR FURTHER STUDY

Take the handles and trim panel off a door and examine the internal mechanisms. Operate the door lock, and watch to see what moves and how it works. Do the same with the door handle and window regulator. On a sheet of paper for your notebook, write down the types of latch and lock and the year, make, and model of car. Then identify and write down the type of window regulator and the method of attaching the glass to the channel.

26 REAR-OPENING DOORS AND SUN ROOFS

In this chapter you will learn about the various rear openings in automotive vehicles and the types of gates and doors used to close them. Also, you will learn about the various types of sun roofs, their mechanisms, and their servicing procedures.

○26-1 Types of Rear-opening Doors

There are several different types of gates and doors which close the rear opening of automotive vehicles that do not have a separate luggage compartment. One type, often used on small station wagons, is called a lift gate (Fig. 26-1). It is hinged at the top and opens by swinging up. Many small coupes and sedans use this type of lift gate as a rear-compartment lid, as shown in Fig. 26-2. The body style frequently is called a *hatchback*.

A second type of rear-opening door is shown in Fig. 26-3. It is called a single-action tailgate. This tailgate swings down (as a drop gate) and is hinged at the bottom. A third type, called a dual-action tailgate, can swing down like the single-action tailgate, as shown in Fig. 26-3. In addition, the dual-action tailgate can swing to one side and open like a door, as shown in Fig. 26-4. The dual-action tailgate has two sets of hinges, one set along the bottom and one set at the side. The hinges can be selectively uncoupled, one set at a time. That is, the side hinges can be uncoupled so the tailgate can swing down (Fig. 26-3), or the bottom hinges can be uncoupled so the tailgate can be swung to the side like a door (Fig. 26-4).

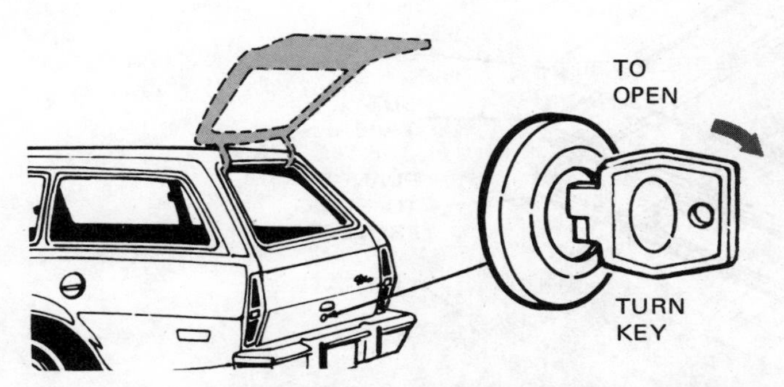

FIGURE 26.1 Small station wagons often use a lift gate, which is hinged at the top and opens by swinging up. (*Ford Motor Company*)

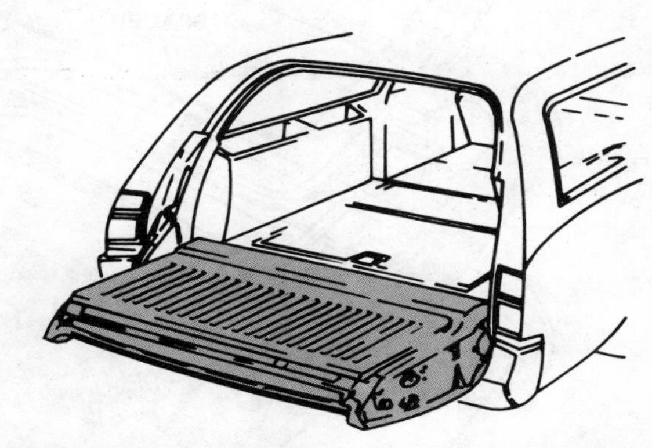

FIGURE 26-3. A single-action tailgate is hinged at the bottom. (*Chrysler Corporation*)

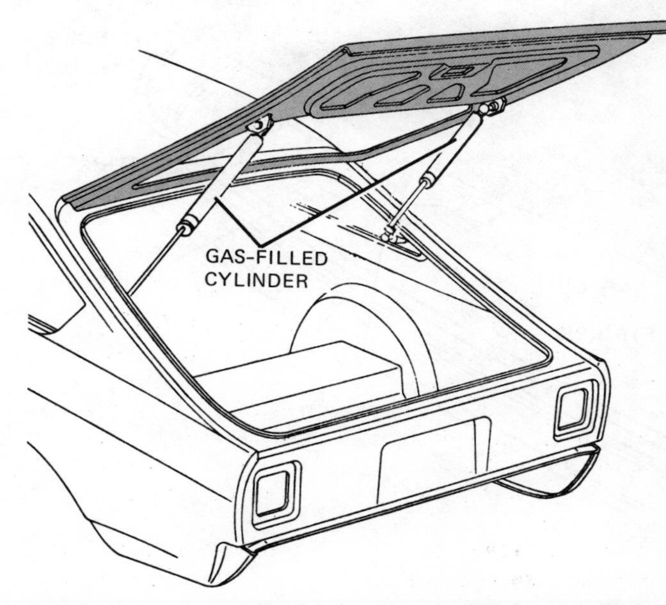

FIGURE 26-2. A rear lid on a hatchback. (*Fisher Body Division of General Motors Corporation*)

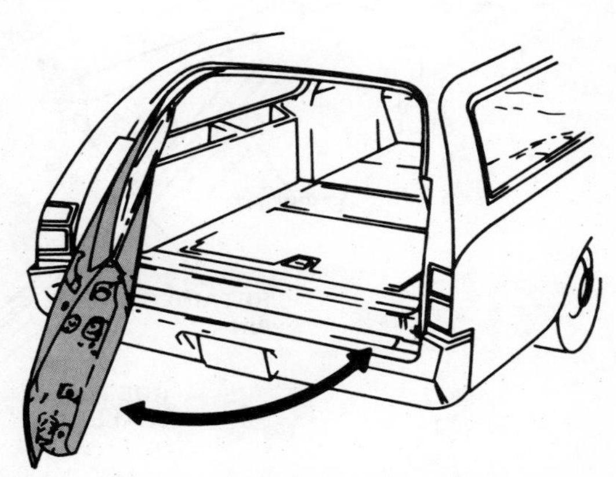

FIGURE 26-4. A double-action tailgate can open down as shown in Fig. 26-3 or swing open as a door. (*Chrysler Corporation*)

Some tailgates, such as the type that opens by swinging up (Fig. 26-1), have fixed glass. Others, which are hinged at the bottom (or bottom and side), have movable glass that can be raised or lowered by a window regulator. The regulator may be mechnically operated or, on some cars, operated by an electric motor.

○26-2 Lift Gate Service

The lift gate, or lid as it is also called, is hinged at the top and is swung up to gain access to the interior of the car (Fig. 26-1). It has a fixed glass and two supports. The supports act as springs to hold the lid up when it is raised. The support, in the model shown in Fig. 26-2, consists of a gas-filled cylinder with a piston in it. (Another type of support contains a strong spring.) The pressure of the gas pushes the piston outward when the lid is raised, and this holds the lid up.

Some lift gates have a solenoid, actuated by a switch controlled by the driver, to unlock them. This is similar to the electric door locks, described earlier. Also, some lift gates are equipped with an electric windshield wiper.

Figure 26-5 shows a lift gate, or lid, for a hatchback, disassembled so all components can be seen. Removing and replacing the parts does not require any special procedures. A defective support is removed and a new support is installed. However, you must be careful when working with either the gas-filled or spring-type support. Never try to detach the support with the lift gate closed.

CAUTION: The supports contain high-pressure gas (or a strong spring) and may injure you or damage the car if you try to detach them with the lift gate closed. Never try to repair or dismantle the supports.

Always wear eye protection while depressurizing a support. The support is filled with high-pressure gas, and when it is released, it can spurt out, carrying oil with it. If the gas or oil hits your eye, the eye can be injured.

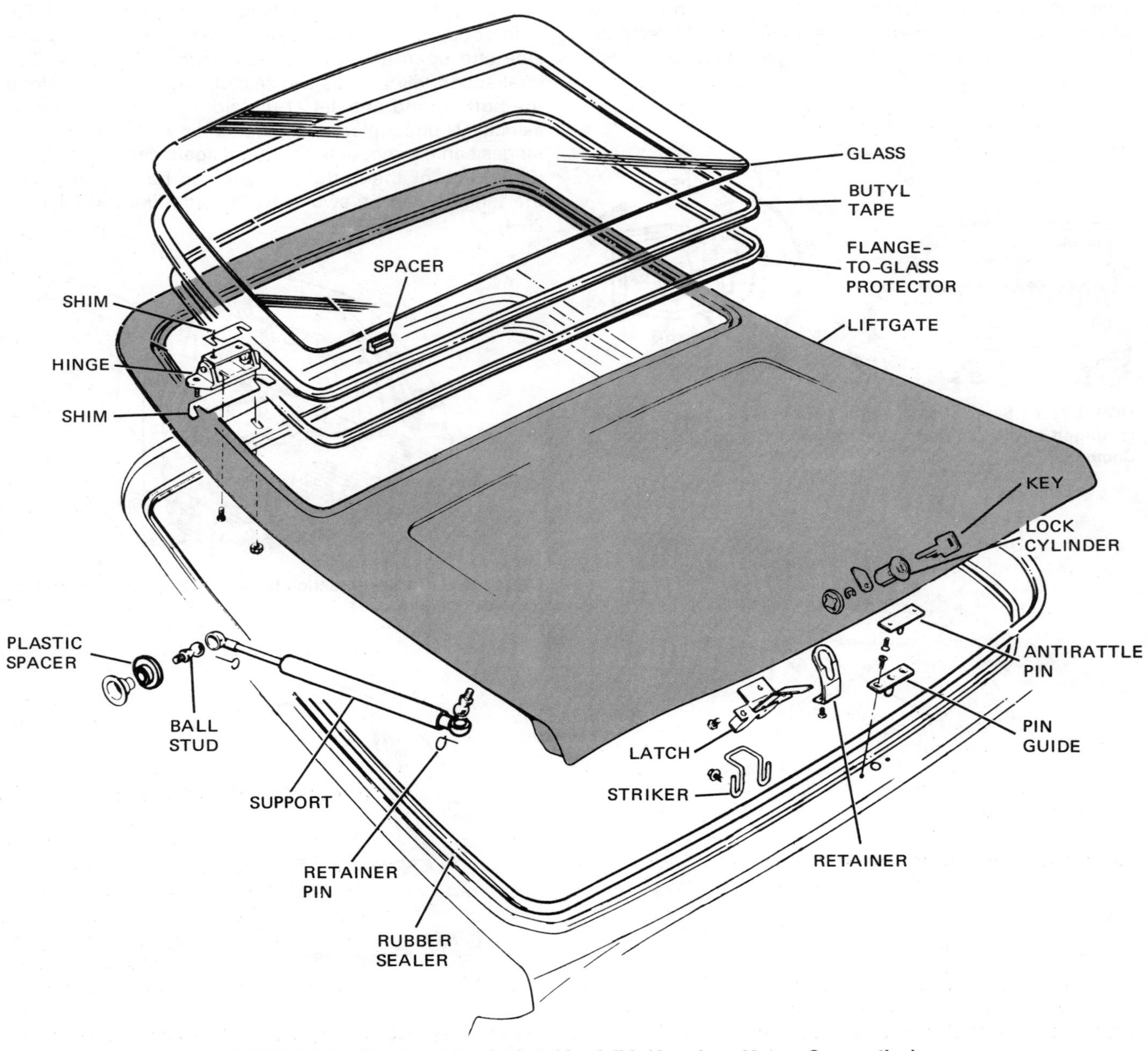

FIGURE 26-5. Components of a hatchback lid. (*American Motors Corporation*)

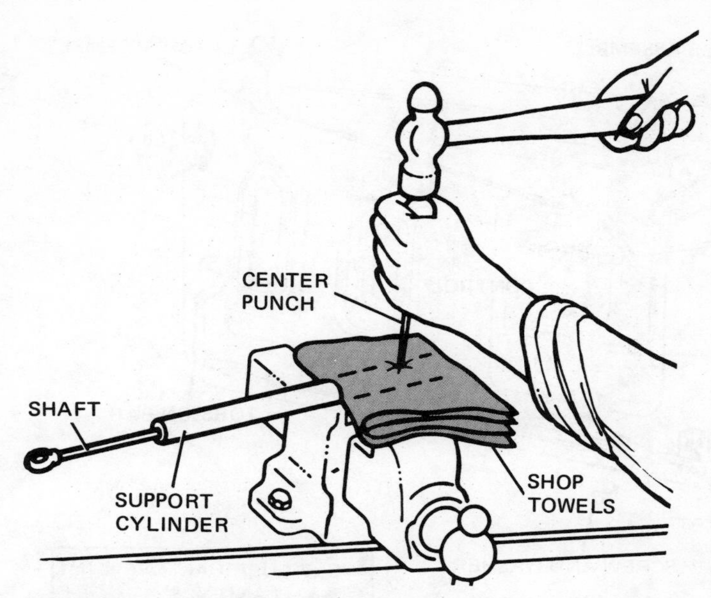

FIGURE 26-6. **Releasing the gas pressure in a support.** ***(American Motors Corporation)***

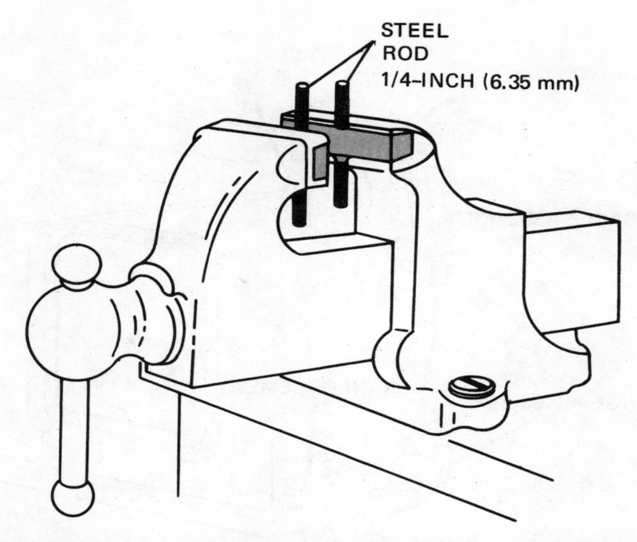

FIGURE 26-7. **To disable a spring-type support, first take two pieces of steel rod to the jaws of a vise.** ***(Fisher Body Division of General Motors Corporation)***

To dispose of a defective gas-filled support, you must first release the pressurized gas that is in it.

Clamp the support horizontally in a vise (Fig. 26-6). Put at least four layers of shop towels over the end of the cylinder. Measure about 1¼ inches [32 mm] from the end of the cylinder. Strike a sharp-pointed center punch with a hammer to drive a small hole into the cylinder so the gas can escape. Hold the towels and punch in place until all the gas has escaped. This takes several seconds. Then, still holding the towels over the support, push the shaft into the cylinder. This forces out the remaining oil. Remove the towels and discard them. Now you can safely throw away the support.

The spring-type support is made safe for disposal as follows: Tape two pieces of ¼-inch [6.35 mm] steel rods about 4 inches [102 mm] long to the jaws of a bench vise as shown in Fig. 26-7. Start at the back end of the support. Put the support in the vise, and tighten the jaws so as to put a crimp in the cylinder about 4 inches [102 mm] from the end (Fig. 26-8). Depth of the crimp should be about ¼ inch [6.35 mm]. Repeat the crimping operation at 6-inch [152.4-mm] intervals along the tube. Do not crimp closer than 2 inches [50.8 mm] from the end. The support can now be safely thrown away without danger of injury to someone trying to work on it.

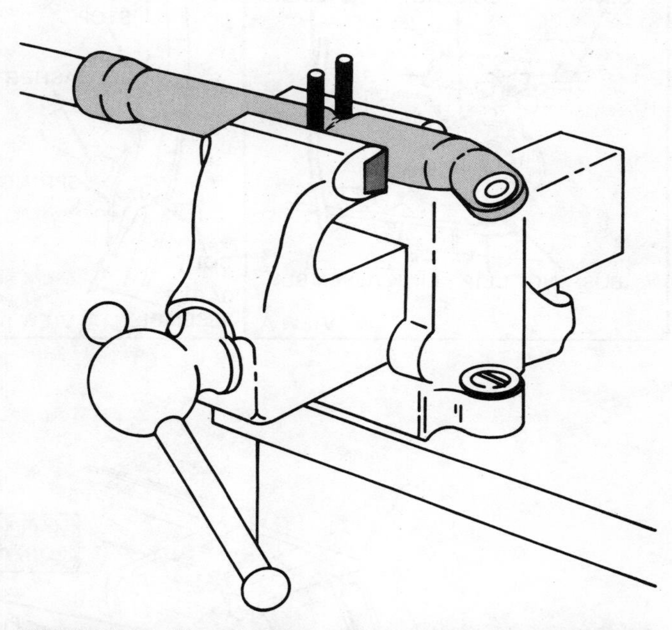

FIGURE 26-8. **Close the vise until each rod has made a crimp in the cylinder.** ***(Fisher Body Division of General Motors Corporation)***

○26-3 Single-Action Tailgate Service

This type of tailgate (Fig. 26-9) has hinges at the bottom only and swings down when opened so it is flush with the floor of the station wagon. When the handle is operated, the cables pull on the latches on the two sides of the tailgate, releasing the latches so the tailgate can be lowered. The assembly includes a torsion bar which is twisted when the tailgate is lowered. This makes it easier to close the tailgate, because the torsion in the twisted bar supplies much of the closing effort as the bar untwists.

Some single-action tailgates have a solenoid, actuated by the driver, to unlock them. This is similar to the electric door locks, discussed earlier.

The tailgate fit can be adjusted, on some station wagons, by loosening the hinge attaching screws and shifting the tailgate as required. Then, when the fit is corrected, the screws are tightened.

Figure 26-10 shows the weatherstrip and inside cover assembly for a dual-action tailgate. The weatherstrip and inside cover assembly for the single-action tailgate is similar. Several types of weatherstrip are used on tailgates, but all weatherstrips work the same way. They provide a seal around the sides and bottom of the tailgate and along the sides and top of the glass when it is raised.

Other services for the tailgate include replacing hinges and the latch and also replacing internal parts of the latching mechanism. Steps in these procedures are listed below.

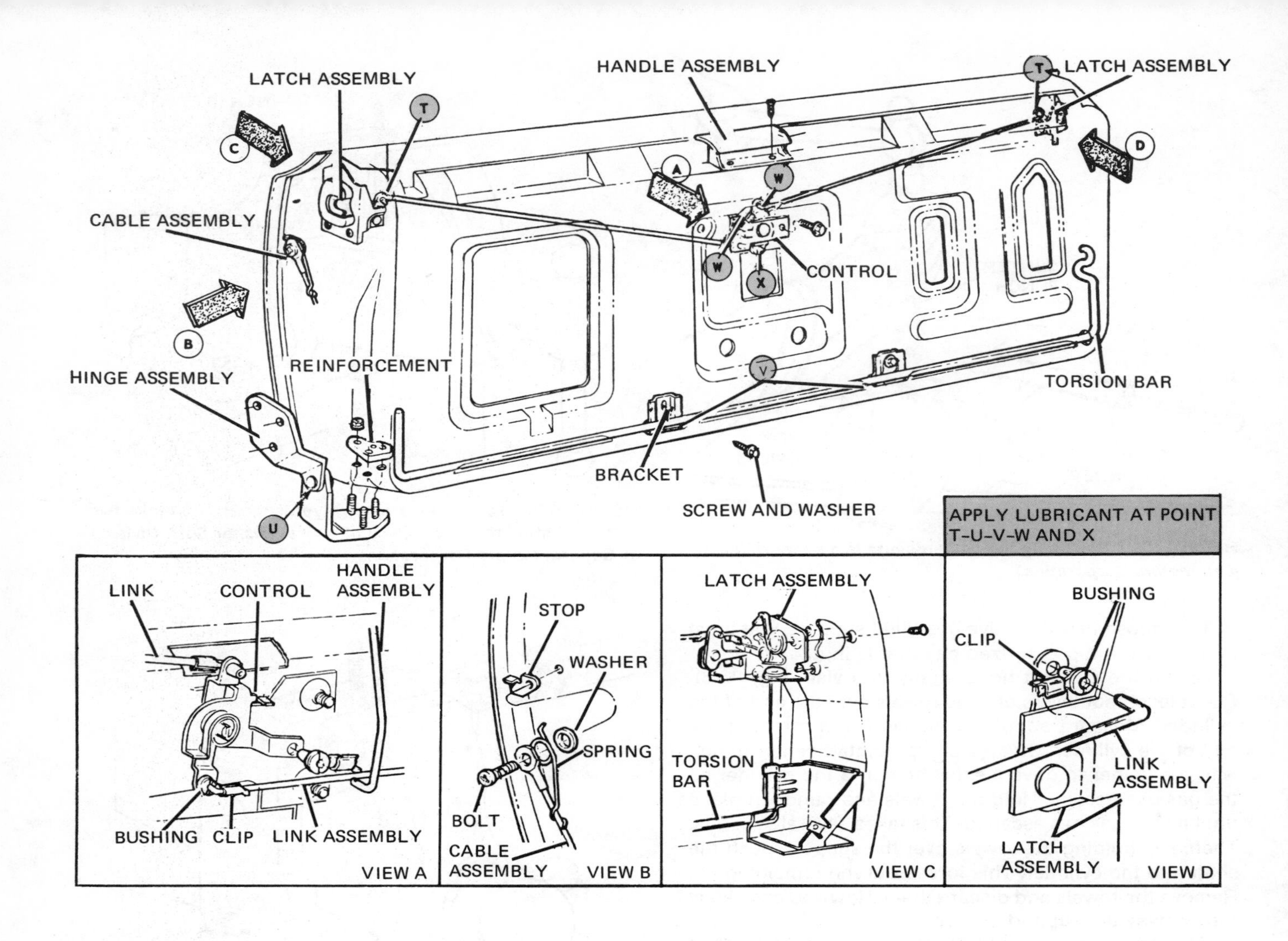

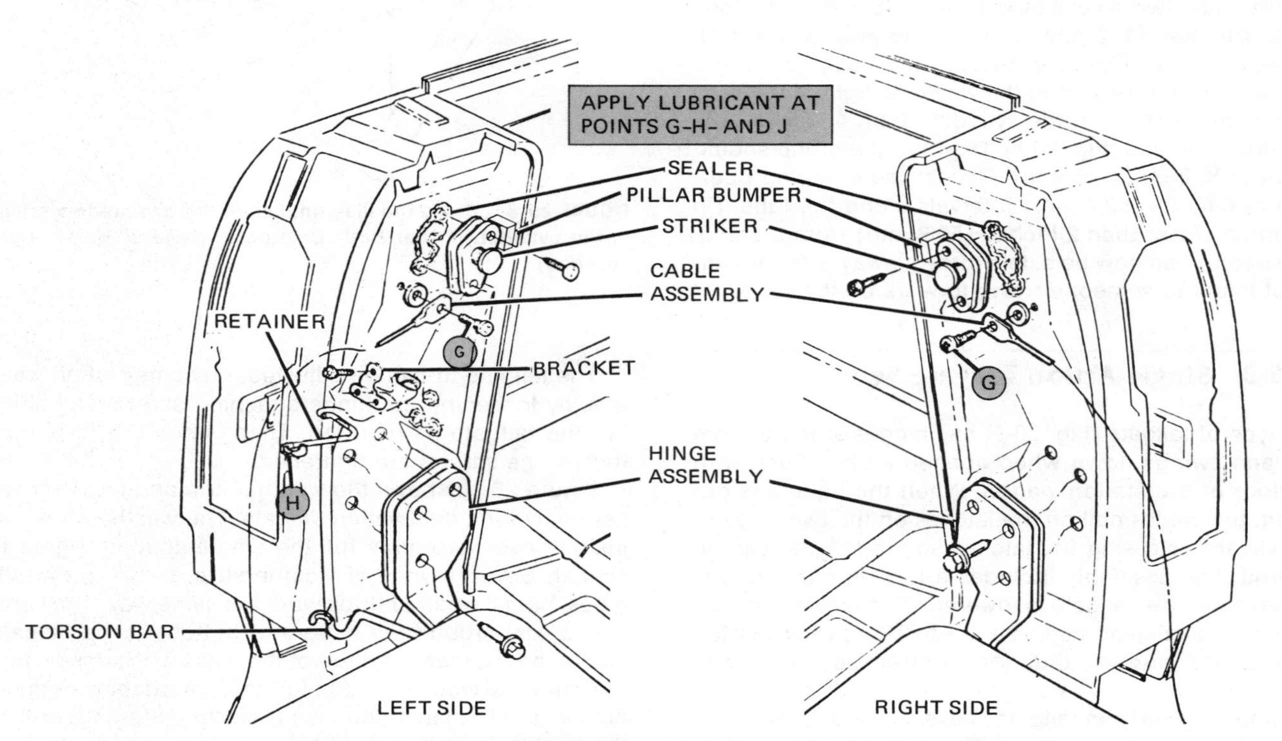

FIGURE 26-9. Single-action tailgate mechanism. (*Ford Motor Company*)

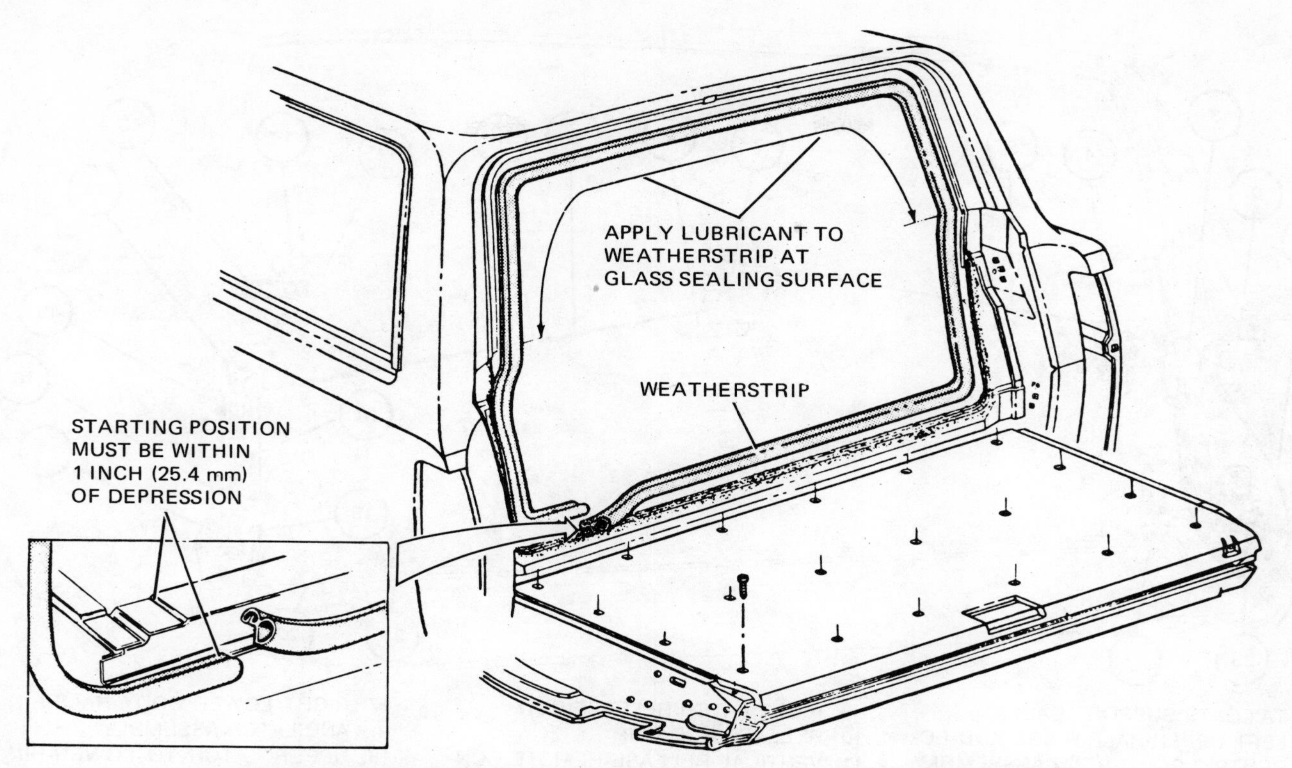

FIGURE 26-10. Weatherstrip around a dual-action tailgate. (*Ford Motor Company*)

REPLACING THE RIGHT-SIDE HINGE

1. Open the tailgate and remove the trim panel, watershield, and access cover. Mark the hinge location on the tailgate and body.
2. Support the tailgate with a suitable prop and remove the three hinge-to-body bolts. Then remove these hinge-to-tailgate nuts and remove the hinge.
3. To replace the hinge, install the hinge, bolts, and nuts. Align the tailgate and hinge with the marks previously made. Then tighten the bolts and nuts. Install the access cover, watershield, and trim panel.

REPLACING THE LEFT-SIDE HINGE

Replacing this hinge is a little more complicated because you must release the tension of the torsion bar.

1. Open the tailgate and mark the location of the hinge on the body and tailgate. Remove the trim panel, watershield, and access cover.
2. Hold the torsion bar in place with a deep socket and extension.
3. Remove the torsion-bar retainer-bracket screws. Then release the torsion bar and remove the bracket and retainer.
4. Support the tailgate with a suitable prop and remove the three hinge-to-body bolts. Disconnect one end of the cable assembly.
5. Remove the hinge-to-tailgate nuts and remove the hinge.
6. To install the hinge, position it on the tailgate and attach it with the nuts. Install the three hinge-to-body bolts. Align the tailgate and tighten the nuts and bolts.
7. Apply tension to the torsion bar and install the torsion-bar bracket and retainer.
8. Install the access cover, watershield, and trim panel.

LATCH SERVICE

1. To remove the latch, open the tailgate and remove the trim panel. Disconnect the latch release cable from the latch. Remove the three latch-attaching screws and take off the latch.
2. To install the latch, reverse the removal procedure.

○26-4 Dual-Action Tailgate Service

Figure 26-11 shows one arrangement of the mechanisms for the dual-action tailgate. All work in a similar manner. The tailgate is hinged along the bottom and also along one side. When the tailgate is lowered (as a drop gate), the bottom hinges are effective. The side hinges are disconnected. When the tailgate is opened as a door, the hinges along the bottom are disconnected. The glass can be raised or lowered, just as with side doors. In some tailgates, the glass is regulated by a mechanical crank. In others, a motor does the job. The motor can be actuated by a switch at the driver's seat or by the tailgate key, inserted into the tailgate lock. Figure 26-12 shows the circuit with the instrument-panel switch closed to cause the window to move up.

The adjustments of the dual-action tailgate are more

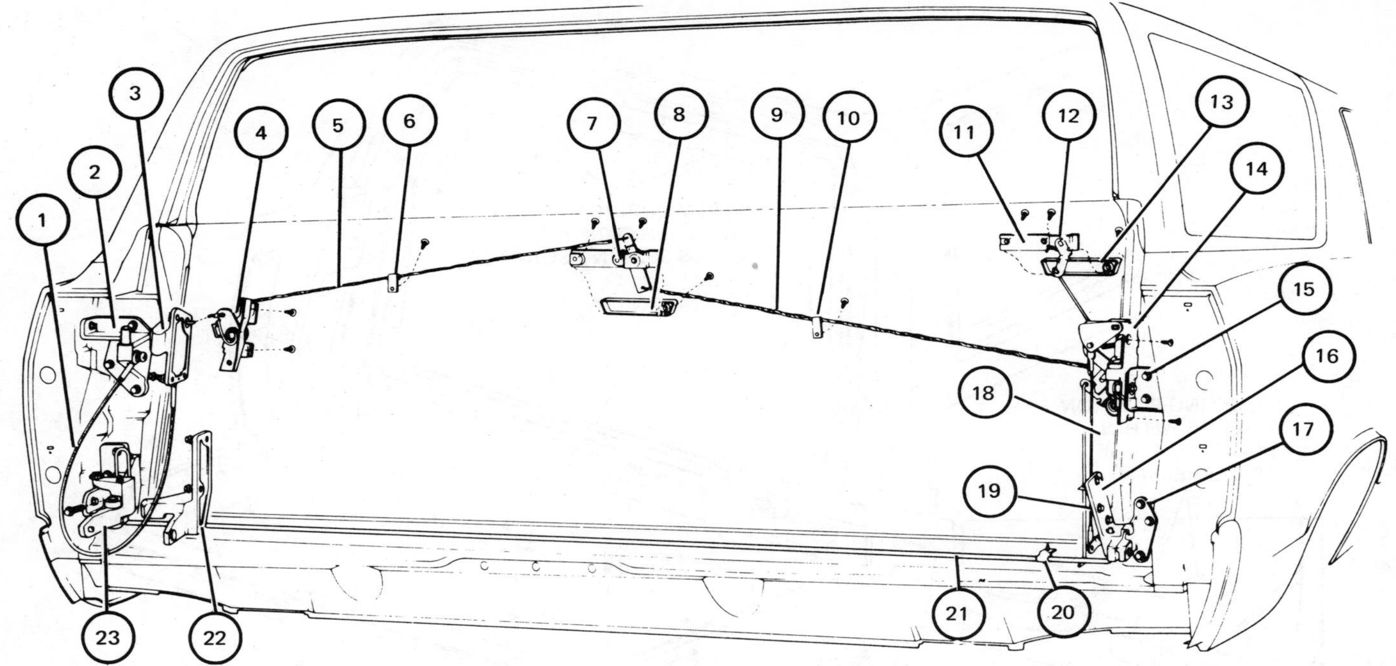

1. TAILGATE SUPPORT CABLE
2. LEFT UPPER-HALF HINGE AND ECCENTRIC ROLLER PIN ASSSEMBLY
3. LEFT UPPER BODY HALF HINGE AND LATCH ASSEMBLY
4. LEFT UPPER HINGE HORIZONTAL LATCH RELEASE BELL-CRANK
5. LEFT LATCH RELEASE ROD
6. RELEASE ROD CLIP
7. HORIZONTAL REMOTE CONTROL
8. HORIZONTAL RELEASE HANDLE
9. RIGHT LATCH RELEASE ROD
10. RELEASE ROD CLIP
11. VERTICAL RELEASE REMOTE CONTROL
12. VERTICAL RELEASE BELL-CRANK
13. VERTICAL RELEASE HANDLE
14. TAILGATE LATCH ASSEMBLY
15. LATCH STRIKER AND BRACKET ASSEMBLY
16. RIGHT LOWER-HALF HINGE AND LATCH ASSEMBLY
17. RIGHT LOWER BODY HALF HINGE AND LATCH ASSEMBLY
18. UPPER LATCH TO LOWER-HINGE RELEASE CABLE
19. GLASS OPERATED SAFETY RELEASE ROD
20. TORSION ROD RETAINER CLIP
21. TORSION ROD
22. LEFT LOWER-HINGE ASSEMBLY DOOR HALF
23. LEFT LOWER-HINGE ASSEMBLY BODY HALF

FIGURE 26-11. Dual-action tailgate mechanism. (*American Motors Corporation*)

complicated than for a side door. This is because the dual-action tailgate has two sets of hinges. Some adjustments are made by adding or removing shims. Other adjustments are made by shifting the hinges as shown in Fig. 26-13. The holes are enlarged to permit this. Figure 26-14 shows a typical method of adjusting the strikers, using shims and also taking advantage of the enlarged holes so the strikers can be shifted up or down, or fore or aft.

○26-5 Sun Roof Types

There are three basic types of sun roofs: the removable type, the manually operated type, and the electrically operated type. The manual and electric types are essentially the same except for the method of opening and closing them. All sun roofs have the same purpose. That is to provide an opening in the roof of the car over the driver and front-seat passenger (Fig. 26-15). This opening lets the sun and wind in. With the convertible body style no longer in production by the major automobile manufacturers, many people buy cars with a sun roof or have one installed.

NOTE: Ford calls their electrically operated clear sun roof a *moon roof*.

○26-6 Removable Sun Roof

This sun roof can be raised a small amount to serve as a vent. Forward movement of the car creates a draft which pulls air from the car. Figure 26-16 shows how to open the sun roof to the vent position. Move the release lever as far forward and upward as it will go. This raises the sun roof. The sun roof is closed by moving the lever back.

To remove the sun roof, move the release lever to its mid-position. Then squeeze the attaching links together to disengage the latching mechanism from the roof panel. From outside the car, raise the glass at the rear edge and remove it by lifting upward and pulling rearward.

There is a place to stow the sun roof in the car. On two-door models, the stowage bag rests against the rear seat back at the bottom edge. It clips to the drain trough beneath the weatherstrip at the top edge. On three-door models, the stowage bag is strapped to the rear floor on the passenger side of the car.

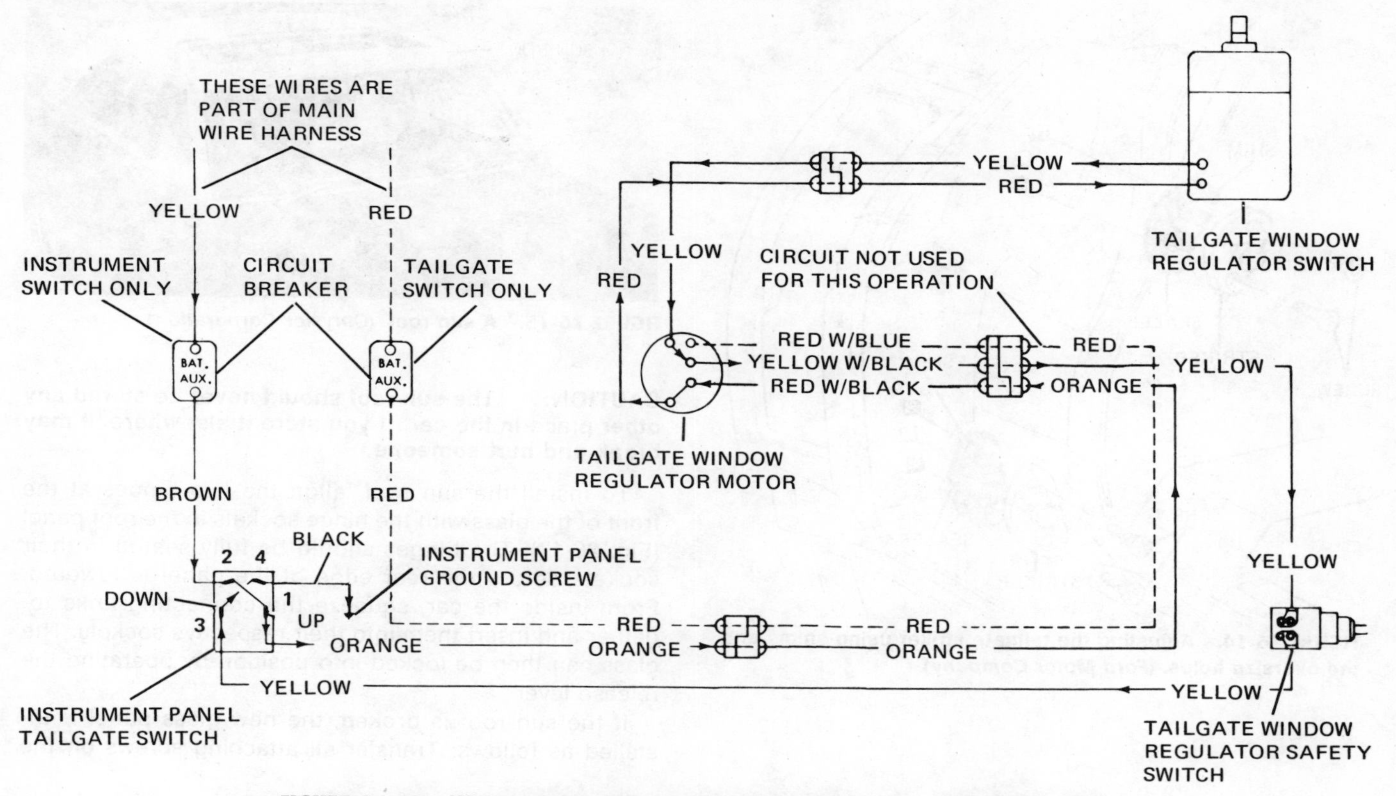

FIGURE 26-12. **Wiring circuit for an electrically operated glass in a tailgate. (*American Motors Corporation*)**

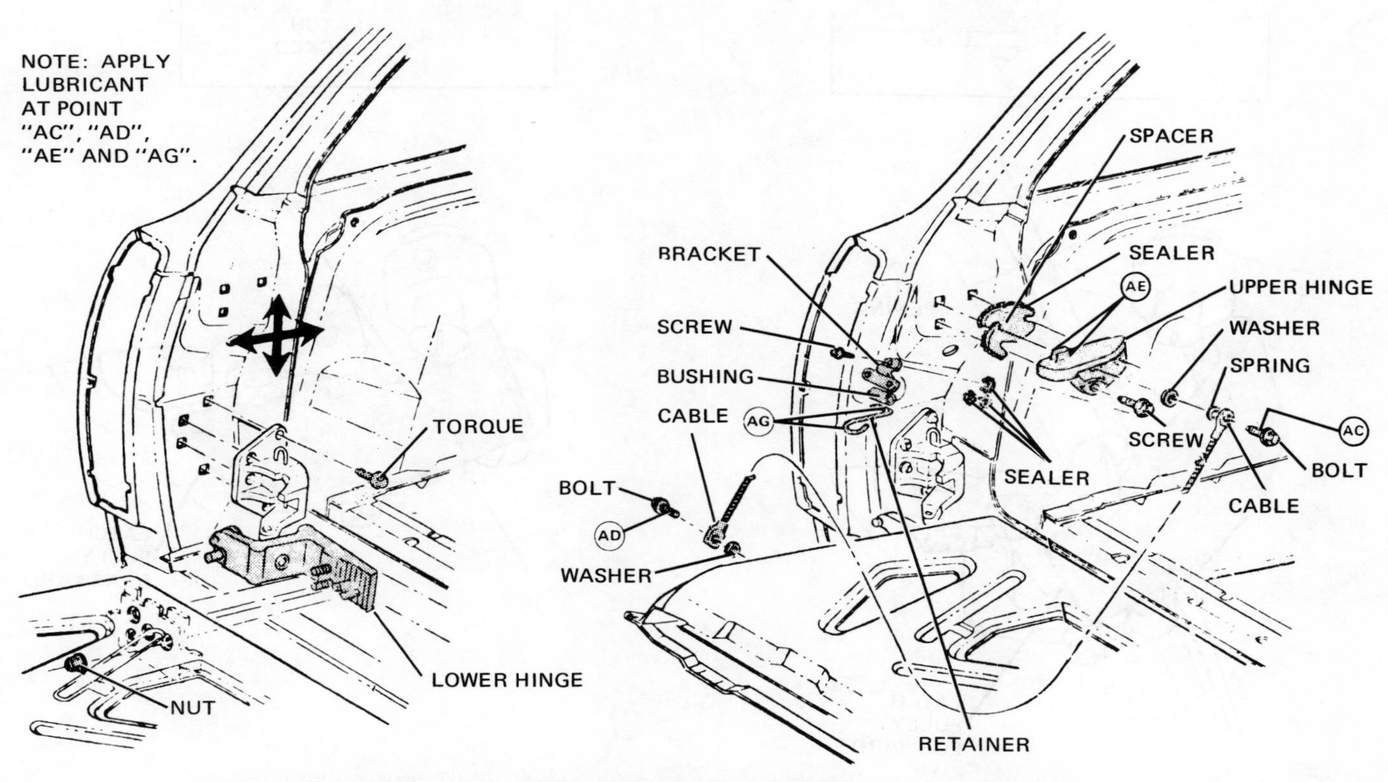

FIGURE 26-13. **Dual-action tailgate adjusted by shifting the hinges. (*Ford Motor Company*)**

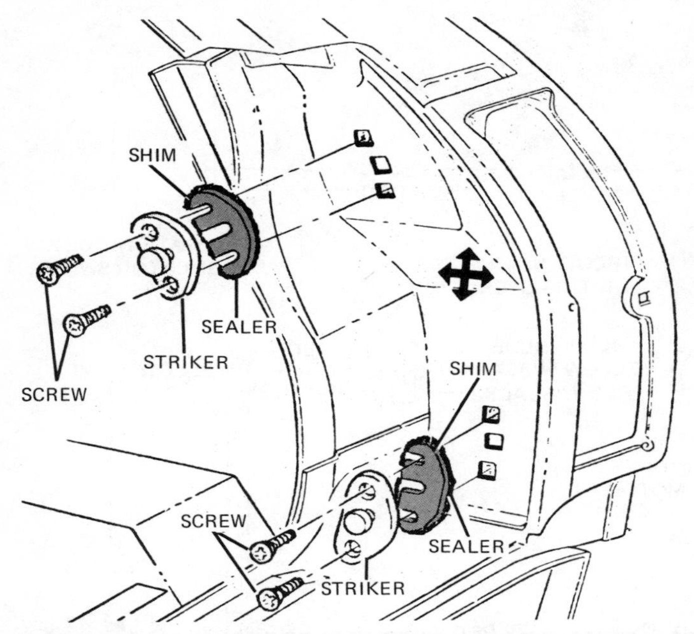

FIGURE 26-14. Adjusting the tailgate striker using shims and the oversize holes. (*Ford Motor Company*)

FIGURE 26-15. A sun roof. (*Chrysler Corporation*)

CAUTION: The sun roof should never be stored any other place in the car. If you store it elsewhere, it may break and hurt someone.

To install the sun roof, align the two hinges at the front of the glass with the hinge sockets in the roof panel (Fig. 26-17). The hinges should be fully seated in their sockets before the rear edge of the panel is lowered. From inside the car, squeeze the connecting links together and insert them into their respective sockets. The glass can then be locked into position by operating the release lever.

If the sun roof is broken, the new glass panel is installed as follows: Transfer all attaching screws on the

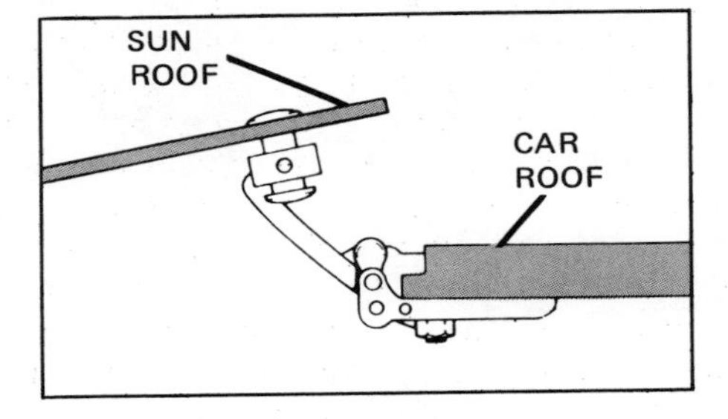

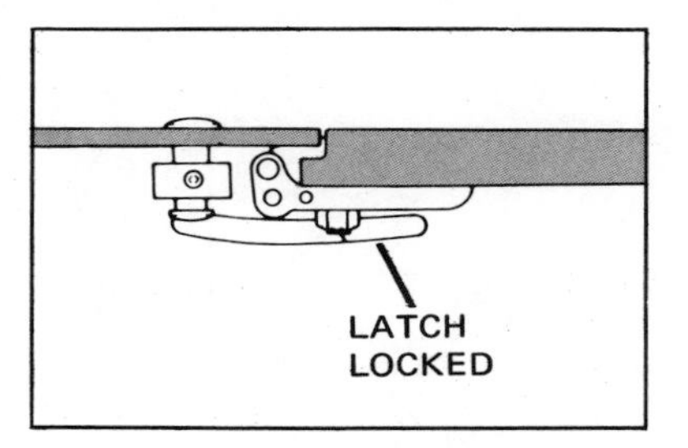

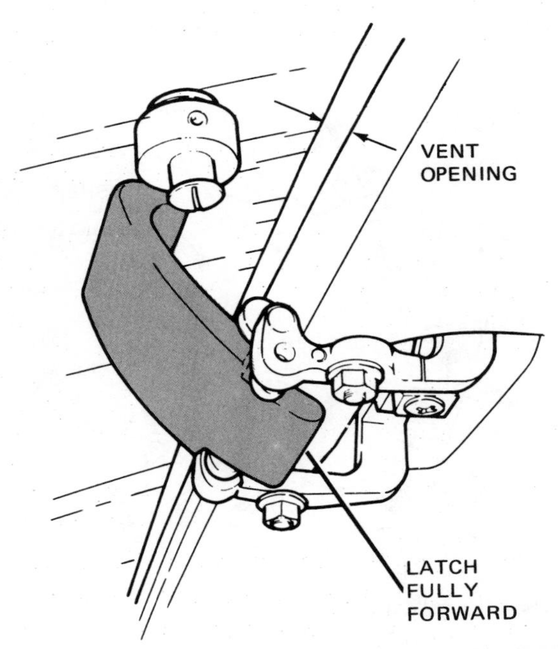

LATCH
FULLY
REARWARD

FIGURE 26-16. (Left) Sun roof in an open position. (Right) Sun roof closed. (*Ford Motor Company*)

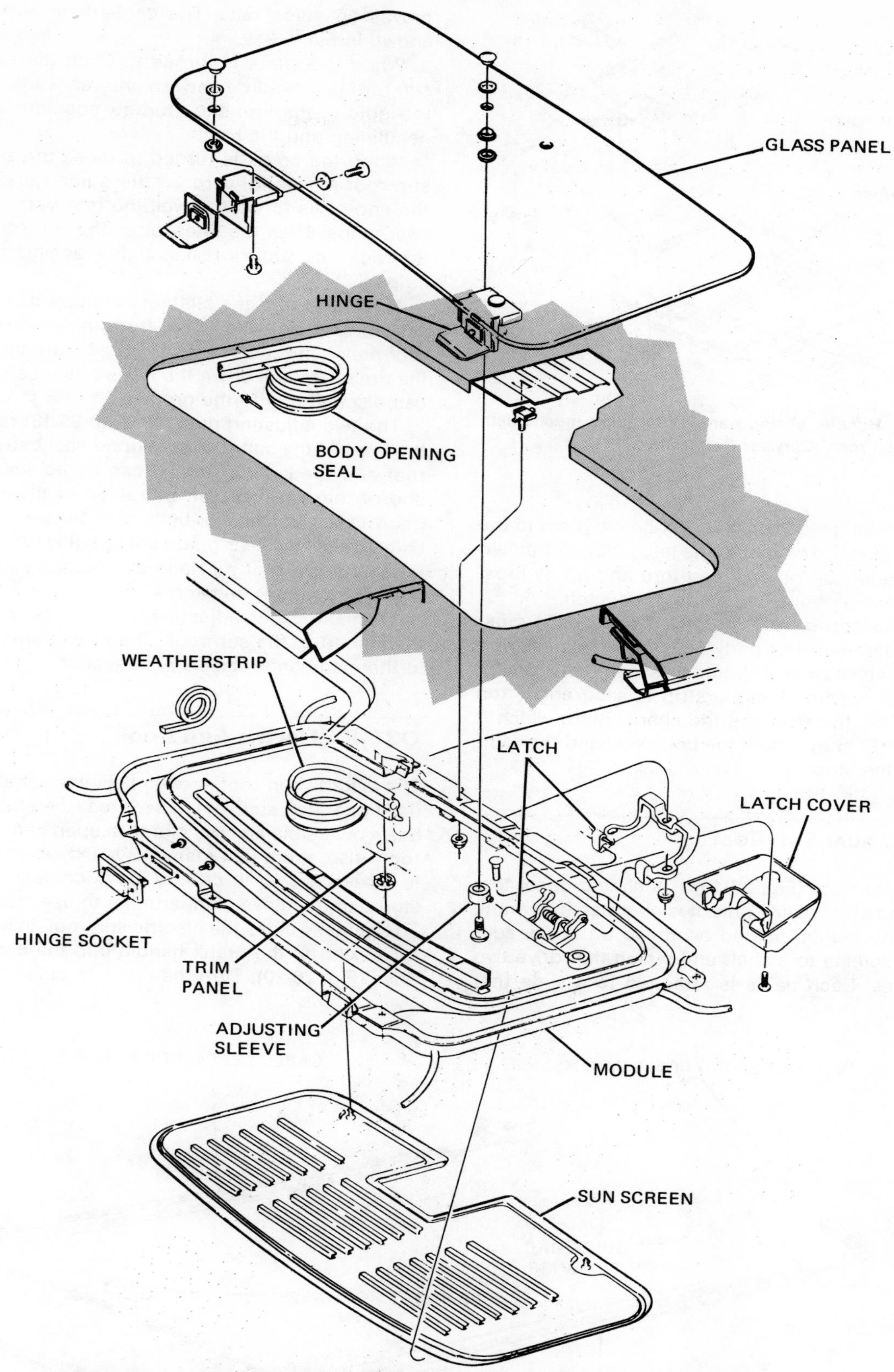

FIGURE 26-17. Exploded view of a manual sun roof that is removable. (*Ford Motor Company*)

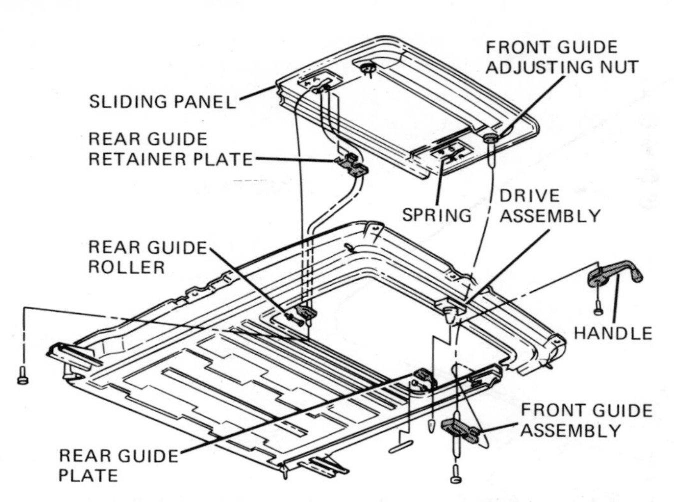

FIGURE 26-18. Handle, sliding panel, and guide mechanism for a manual sun roof. (*Chrysler Corporation*)

hinges and latching mechanism from the old glass to the new (see Fig. 26-17). The part of the latch that is attached to the roof panel can be adjusted fore and aft by loosening the attaching bolts and shifting the latch.

The weatherstrip is very important because it must seal tightly overhead. The body-opening seal is secured by Pop rivets. The new seal should be secured in a similar way. The roof-opening weatherstrip is secured by the shape of the weatherstrip and the channel into which it fits. Figure 26-17 shows both the body seal and the roof-opening weatherstrip.

○26-7 Manual Sun Roof

The manual sun roof (Fig. 26-18) is a sliding panel that slides fore and aft on guide rails. It is operated by a crank or handle. The crank, located overhead on the header assembly, is splined to a shaft and pinion that drive two flexible cables. Each cable is attached to a slide that moves on guide rails. The cable-drive arrangement is shown in Fig. 26-19.

When the crank is turned to open the sun roof, the sun roof is moved downward and rearward. It moves on the guide rails into the storage position between the headlining and the roof.

When the crank is turned to close the sun roof, the sun roof moves forward on the guide rails. As it nears the end of its forward travel, the rear part moves up on two ramps. Then the lifter raises the sun roof flush with the roof. The sun roof seals tightly against the weatherstrips.

Many sun-roof installations include a roof drainage system to drain water away from the seam between the roof panel and the sun roof. Tubes carry the water from the drain channel down the sides of the car so the water can discharge onto the ground.

The two adjusting nuts (see Fig. 26-18) raise or lower the front of the sun roof so a good seal between the sun roof and the car roof panel can be achieved. The rear end of the sun roof can be raised or lowered to get a good seal. On Chrysler-built cars, loosen the screw located under the rear guide linkage (Fig. 26-18). Raise or lower the sun-roof rear end as necessary to get a good seal. Then tighten the screw.

To make other adjustments, remove the trim panel (headliner) of the sun roof. The procedures are covered in the manufacturer's service manual.

○26-8 Electric Sun Roof

The electric sun roof is essentially the same as the manually operated sun roof except that the electric sun roof has a reversible electric motor to open and close the sun roof. Also, there is a manual system which can be used to close the roof in case of electrical failure. A crank is stored in the glove compartment to use for this purpose. To manually close the electric sun roof, insert the screwdriver end of the crank handle into the auxiliary socket drive (Fig. 26-20). Turn the crank to close the roof.

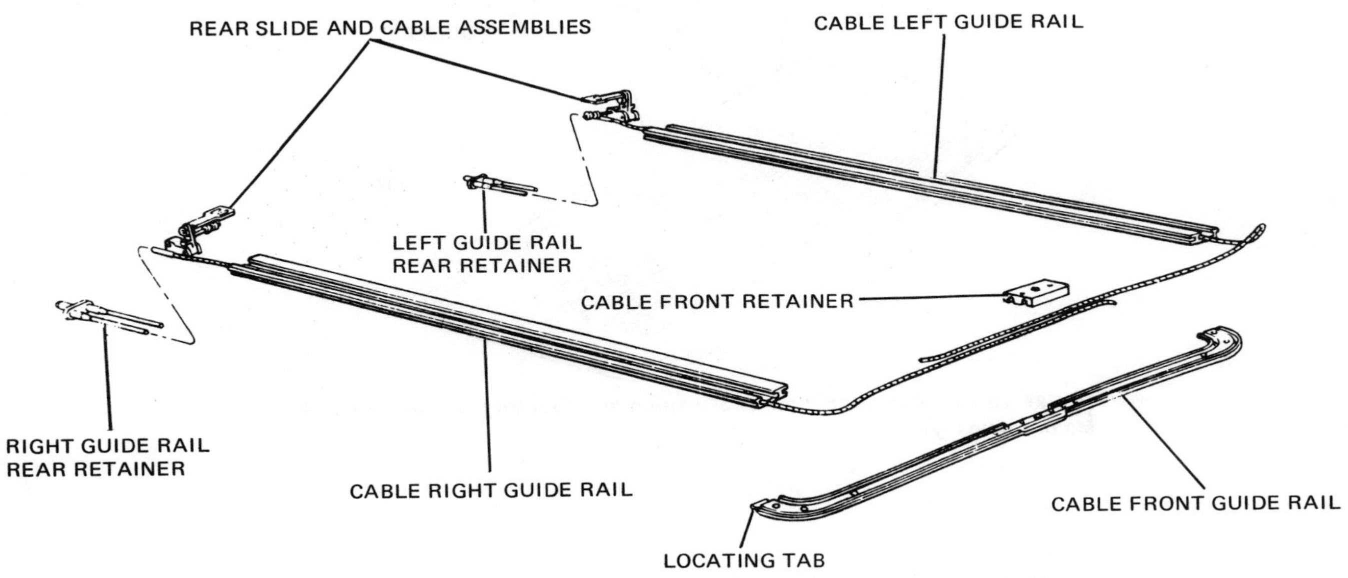

FIGURE 26-19. Guide rail and cable system for a manual sun roof. (*Ford Motor Company*)

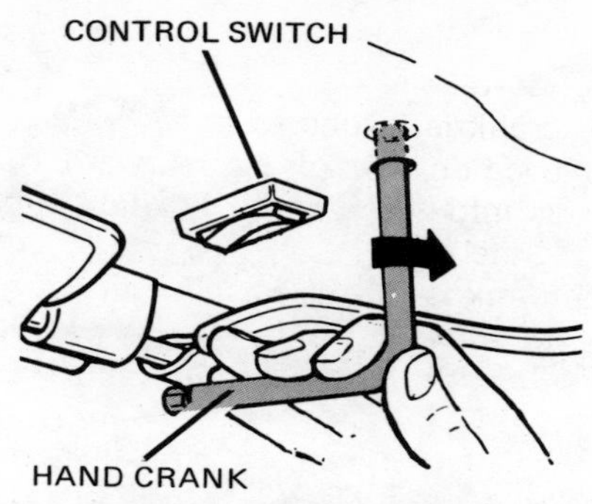

FIGURE 26-20. Using the hand crank to manually close an electric sun roof. (*Ford Motor Company*)

CHAPTER 26 CHECKUP

NOTE: Since the following is a chapter review test, you should review the chapter before taking the test.

Many repairs to tailgates and sun roofs are made by replacing the panel itself. Adjustments for fit are made in about the same way as those for hoods and trunk lids. However, water leaks may require additional work on the weatherstrip, water channels, and drain tubing. To find out how well you understand everything in this chapter, answer the questions that follow.

COMPLETING THE SENTENCES The sentences below are incomplete. After each sentence there are several words or phrases, but only one of them correctly completes the sentence. Write each sentence in your notebook, ending the sentence with the one word or phrase that completes it correctly.

1. Rear-opening doors are called (*a*) hoods and trunk lids, (*b*) lift gates and tailgates, (*c*) hatchbacks and sun roofs, (*d*) sun roofs and moon roofs.
2. A dual-action tailgate is hinged (*a*) at the top and at the bottom, (*b*) at the left side and at the right side, (*c*) in the middle and at the bottom, (*d*) at the bottom and at one side.
3. A lift gate is used on a (*a*) pickup truck, (*b*) large sedan, (*c*) van, (*d*) small station wagon.
4. In a tailgate, an electric motor can be used to (*a*) open and shut the tailgate, (*b*) lock and unlock the tailgate, (*c*) open and close the tailgate glass, (*d*) change from top opening to side opening.
5. The opening in the roof of the car that lets in the sun and wind is the (*a*) sun roof, (*b*) vinyl roof, (*c*) tailgate, (*d*) lift gate.

QUESTIONS Write each of the following questions, and then the answer, in your notebook. If you have trouble recalling the answer to the question, turn back to the pages that cover the material and study them again.

1. Name the types of rear-opening doors.
2. Why must a lift gate be open when removing a support?
3. How do you make a gas-filled lift-gate support safe for disposal?
4. How do you make a spring-loaded lift-gate support safe for disposal?
5. What can be done to close an electric sun roof stuck in the open position?

SUGGESTIONS FOR FURTHER STUDY

Go to a new car dealer near you and examine the various rear-opening doors. Note how each type is mounted and how it operates. Note also that there are several types of sun roofs installed in cars. Examine cars with different types, noting particularly how the roof panel is adjusted and how water is drained from around it.

PART 7

STATIONARY GLASS SERVICE

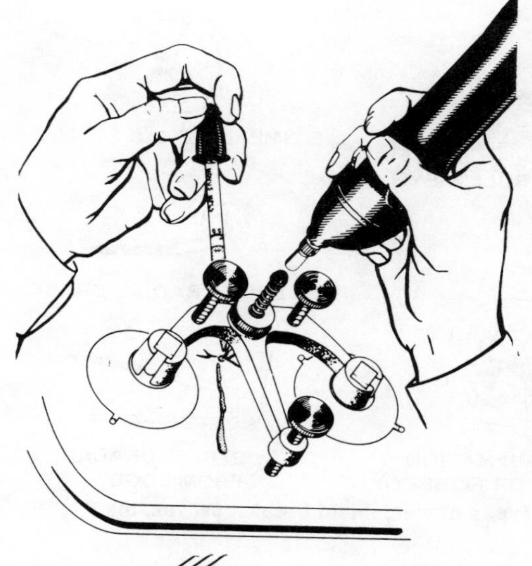

In this part, you will learn how to remove and replace stationary glass in a car. This includes the windshield, rear window, and stationary side windows. You will also learn how to repair small damaged spots in windshields, such as bull's-eyes and scratches.

There are two basic types of automotive glass: laminated safety glass, used for the windshield, and solid tempered plate glass, used for all side and back glass. The laminated safety glass consists of a layer of plastic material sandwiched between two layers of glass. The plastic material greatly reduces the possibility that the glass will shatter. If the glass does break, the plastic prevents the broken pieces from flying off. Tempered glass is less brittle than ordinary plate glass. When tempered glass is broken, it tends to crumble into very small pieces. There are no large pieces with sharp edges from the break that could cause injury to passengers.

There are two chapters in Part 7, as follows:

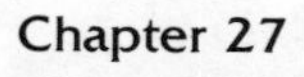

Chapter 27	Windshield Repair
Chapter 28	Stationary Glass Replacement

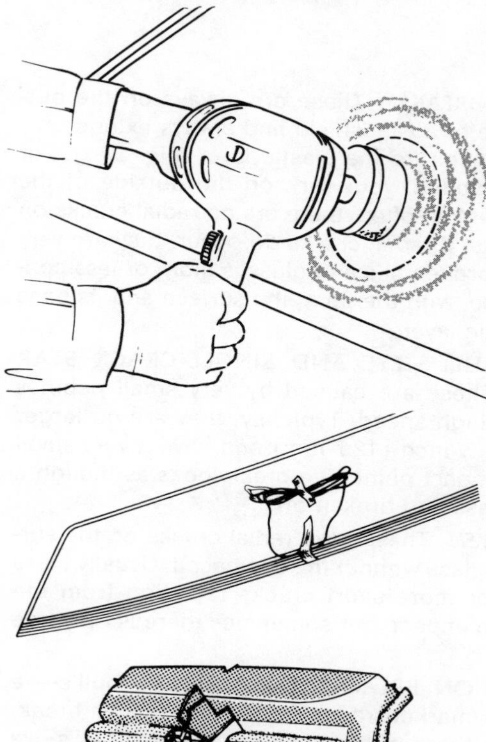

27 WINDSHIELD REPAIR

In this chapter, you will learn how to remove scratches and bull's-eyes from windshields. Bull's-eyes are caused by pebbles or other objects striking the windshield. Formerly, the only way to repair scratches, bull's-eyes, and similar damage was to replace the complete windshield. Today, however there are ways of repairing damage if it is not too severe.

○27-1 How a Windshield Breaks

The windshield is made of safety glass which consists of two layers of glass with a plastic center (Fig. 27-1). When the windshield is struck with a stone or pebble moving at high speed, an impact pit is formed, as shown. Actually, there are several kinds of damage that can occur. These are illustrated in Fig. 27-2.

The basic repair procedure requires the use of a clear resin liquid, similar to the plastic center layer of the windshield. This resin is injected into the damaged area, filling any voids all the way down to the plastic layer. The resin has the same optical properties as glass. Therefore, if the job is done properly, with the correct equipment, the break will no longer be visible.

If the damaged area is complicated or has long cracks, the resin may not be able to reach into all the voids. In such case, a second procedure is used. This procedure is to use a diamond drill to drill through the outside layer of glass, down to the plastic center layer. Resin can then be injected into this hole. We describe both procedures in the sections that follow.

○27-2 Types of Windshield Damage

Four types of windshield breaks that can usually be treated with the resin injection method are shown in Fig. 27-3. Note that the method is called the Novus Method©. Each of these types of break and one nonrepairable type of break are described below.

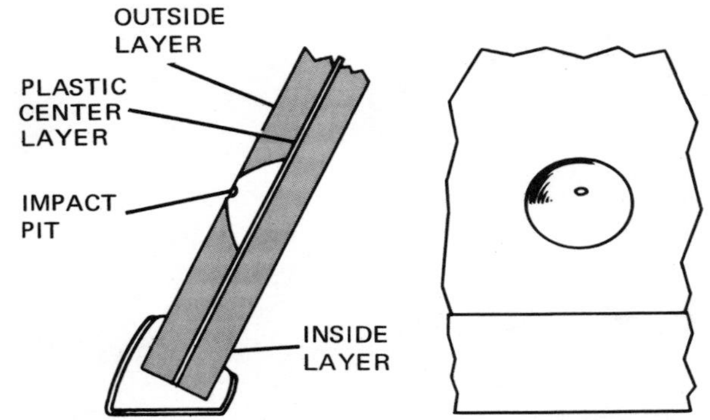

FIGURE 27-1. Construction of a windshield, showing how an impact pit is formed. (*Novus, Inc.*)

FIGURE 27-2. Types of windshield breaks. (*Novus, Inc.*)

1. BULL'S-EYE BREAKS These are always on the outside surface of a windshield and always extend only halfway through, to the plastic layer (Fig. 27-1). For bull's-eye repairs, you work on the outside of the windshield. Most often, there are no radial cracks on these breaks. If radial cracks do occur, they are very short. The broken piece of glass is more or less conical in shape, with the tip at the surface and its base at the plastic layer.
2. PARTIAL BULL'S-EYE AND SINGLE-CRACK STAR BREAKS These are caused by very small pebbles moving at high speed. Typically, they are no larger than about ½ inch [12.7 mm] and have a very small pit at the impact point. The break looks as though a sliver of glass had broken off.
3. STAR BREAKS These have radial cracks on the surface of the glass without the conical pit. Usually there are three or more short cracks radiating from the point of the impact, but sometimes there is only one crack.
4. COMBINATION BREAKS These have a bull's-eye break with marked radial cracks like a star break. Sometimes there will be a star break or a bull's-eye break on the outside of the windshield, with a star break on the inside layer of glass. This requires two repairs, one on the outside and one on the inside.

   Sometimes you may have trouble deciding whether the star break is on the outside or inside.

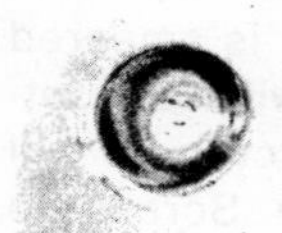

1. THE BULL'S-EYE
This is the type of break most often caused by a flying stone. At the point of impact there is a tiny pit. Behind it, a conical crack from 1/2 to 1 inch [12.7 to 25.4 mm] in diameter penetrates to the plastic inner layer. A typical bull's-eye is repairable by the Novus Method.

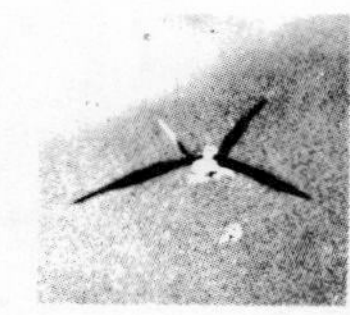

3. A STAR BREAK
Sometimes, where there are local stresses in the glass, a starbreak occurs with radial cracks emanating from the point of impact. These, too, if not larger than 2 inches [50.8 mm] in longest dimension, may be repaired by the Novus Method but may require patience to fill completely.

2. A PARTIAL BULL'S-EYE
When a stone produces an incomplete conical crack, the result is a partial bull's-eye. This type of break takes somewhat longer to repair because it takes longer for the material to penetrate to the very thin areas of the crack.

4. COMBINATION BREAK
Frequently a bull's-eye will also have radial cracks. This type is a combination break (see Fig. 27-2C). The ease with which it can be repaired depends on the amount of shattering that has occurred. Early repair will prevent the radial cracks from spreading.

FIGURE 27-3. Various types of repairable windshield breaks. (*Novus, Inc.*)

Bull's-eyes are always on the outside, but star breaks may also occur opposite bull's-eyes on the inside layer of glass. To check its location, hold a pencil point or fingernail exactly at the edge of the crack when viewed perpendicularly from the outside of the car. Move your head so as to view the crack and your fingernail or pencil as nearly parallel to the glass as possible. If the pointer appears to move away from the edge of the crack, then the crack is on the inside. If it stays put, the crack is on the outside.

NOTE: Don't get any dirt in the crack or pit. This would show up when the repair is done. The best repair is made as soon as possible after the damage. There is also the danger that a small crack may spread if it is not fixed quickly.

5. MISSING GLASS If the windshield received a hard blow, some of the glass may have broken away and be missing. Small chips may fall out from the inside layer of glass, opposite the point of impact. There is no suitable repair for such breaks. Even if such pieces are still in place, repair is not likely to succeed.

○27-3 Repairing Windshield Damage by Injecting Resin

Figure 27-4 shows the equipment needed to repair windshields by the injection method. To make the repair, the break should be as dry as possible. Water can get into the break from washing the car, from the windshield

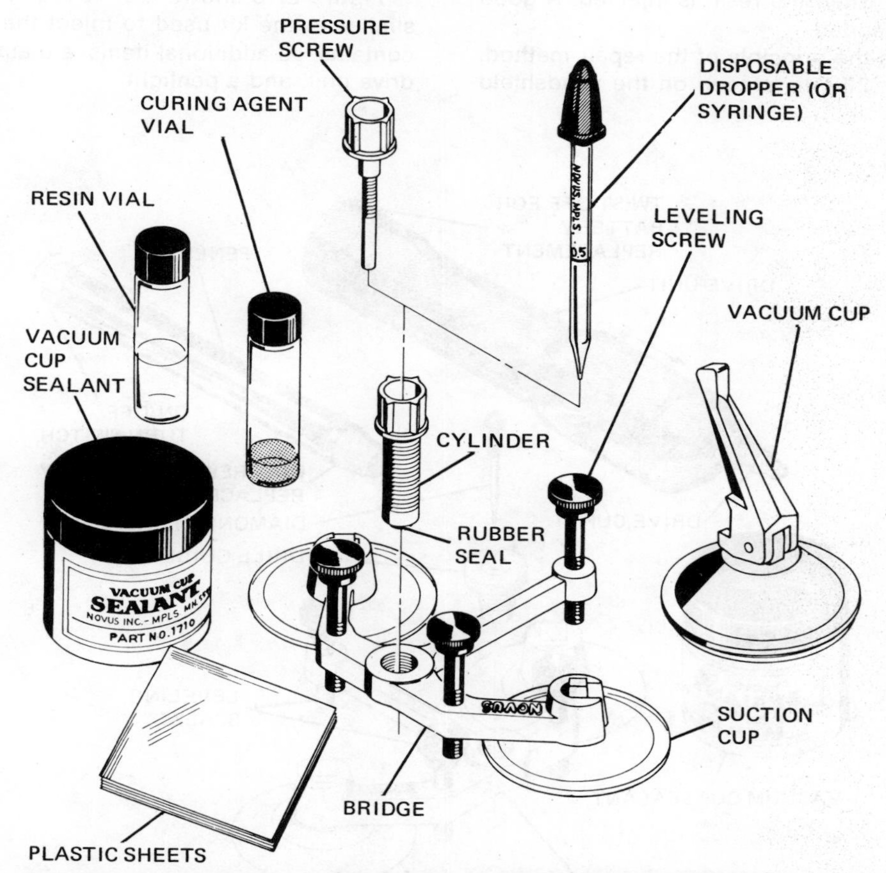

FIGURE 27-4. Equipment needed to repair windshield by the injection method. (*Novus, Inc.*)

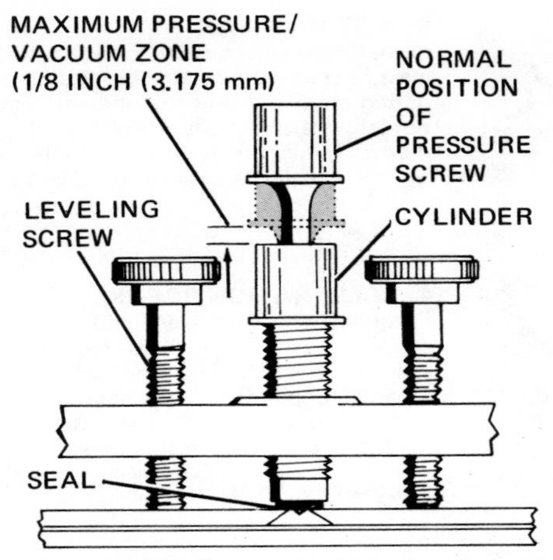

FIGURE 27-5. Applying pressure with the pressure screw. (*Novus, Inc.*)

washer, and from rain or snow. To remove the water, wipe the area with a dry towel. Press the vacuum cup (Fig. 27-4) over the break and push the vacuum cup lever down. Leave it in this position for about an hour. In cold weather run the car defroster to help the drying procedure.

Don't do the repair out of doors. Repair should be made with the temperature warmer than 50°F [10°C] and not hotter than 85°F [29.4°C]. If the windshield has been in direct sunlight, allow it to cool in the shade before starting the repair job. Good lighting is essential. You must be able to detect trapped air and water which will show up as bubbles when the resin is injected. A good flashlight is recommended.

Figure 27-5 shows the principle of the repair method. The bridge (see Fig. 27-4) is placed on the windshield with the tapped hole centered over the break. The windshield must be clean. Vacuum cup sealant is smeared thinly on the bridge vacuum cups, so they will hold better. The leveling screws are adjusted so the cylinder will be aligned perpendicular to the windshield. Screw the cylinder down until the rubber seal just touches the glass. Mix the resin and curing agent in the curing agent vial. Tip the vial back and forth several times to mix the two ingredients. Do not shake the vial. Then use the dropper to pick up the mixture and deposit it at the bottom of the cylinder hole. Reinstall the pressure screw and *very slowly* turn it down at a rate of about one-half turn every 20 to 30 seconds. Observe the break very closely during this time. Note that the increasing pressure compresses the air bubbles. When the largest is down to the size of a pinhead, enough pressure has been applied. Back off the pressure screw slowly. This forms a vacuum under the screw. You should be able to see the bubbles enlarging and leaving the break. After 1 to 2 minutes, reapply pressure until the remaining bubbles disappear.

◯27-4 Repairing a Windshield That Requires Drilling

Some windshield damage is too extensive to be repaired easily by the simple resin injection method. For example, the cracks radiating from the damage may go out too far to be filled with the resin when it is injected from the point of impact. However, if a hole is drilled out at the end of the crack, resin can be injected through the hole so the crack is filled.

Figure 27-6 shows the kit required for this job. It is similar to the kit used to inject the resin (Fig. 27-4). It contains, as additional items, a diamond bit assembly, a drive unit, and a penlight.

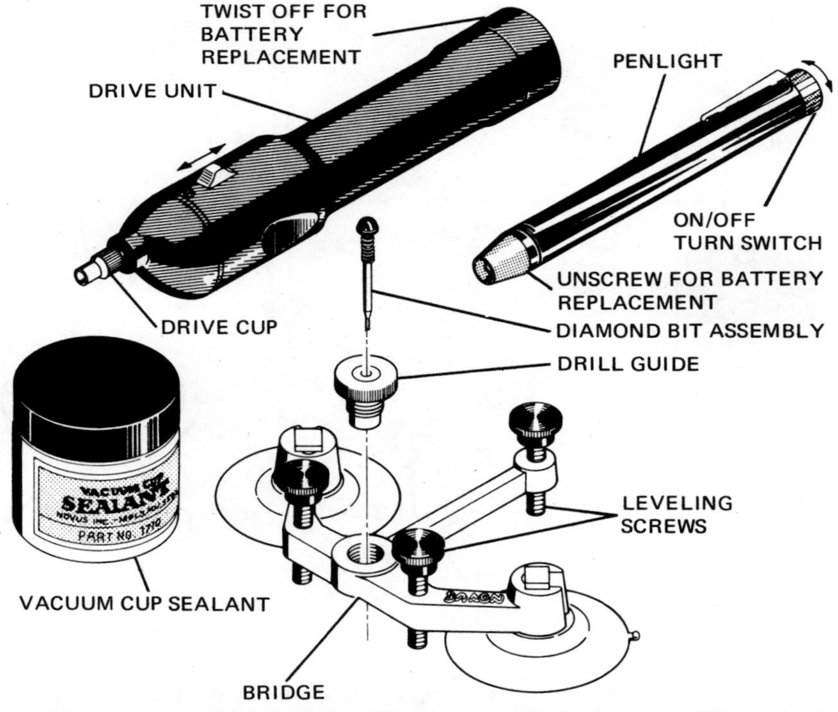

FIGURE 27-6. Equipment needed to drill a windshield for repair. (*Novus, Inc.*)

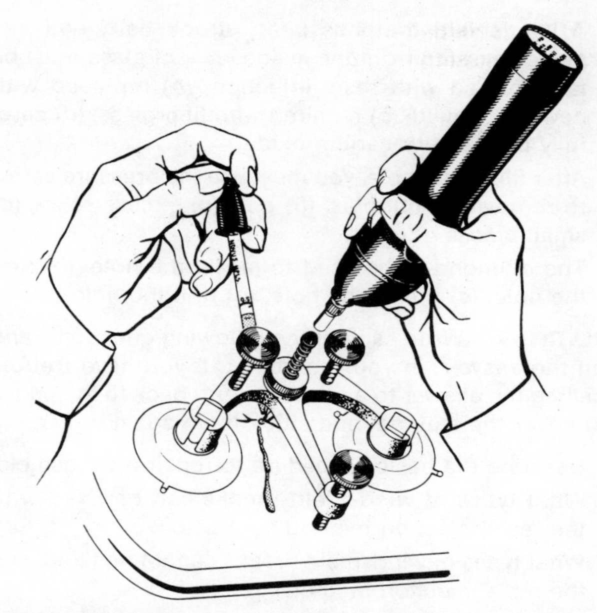

FIGURE 27-7. **Drilling a windshield.** (*Novus, Inc.*)

The diamond bit, which will drill through glass, is driven by the drive unit, which is powered by flashlight batteries. There are certain precautions to observe when using the diamond bit on glass. It must be lubricated. Figure 27-7 shows a dropper being used to apply a drop of the resin-curing-agent mixture at the point of the drilling. Then the drive cup of the drive unit is applied to the rubber tip of the diamond bit assembly, as shown. Apply light pressure to the glass for *only 2 seconds*. Lift the drive unit and allow the spring to raise the diamond bit so the diamond bit can cool. Continue to apply resin every time the bit is raised. Repeat the procedure, drilling for only 2 seconds at a time. Be patient; it will require about 3 minutes to drill down to the plastic layer. You can tell when you reach it because the drill resistance will suddenly become lighter.

After drilling to the plastic layer, use the injection equipment as described previously to complete the repair job.

○27-5 Removing Scratches from the Windshield

Minor scratches and abrasions in the glass can be removed or at least reduced by careful polishing. There is one possible problem that can develop if the polishing is not done correctly or if the polishing is carried too deeply into the glass: The polished area can develop a saucer shape which could cause double vision. Therefore, less polishing should be done on windshields in areas through which the driver or passenger normally looks.

The supplies and equipment required to polish glass include the following:

1. Powdered cerium oxide (No. 12 Rareox or equivalent)
2. Low-speed rotary polisher (600 to 1300 rpm)
3. Wool-felt rotary-type polishing pad, 3 inches [76.2 mm] in diameter and 2 inches [50.8 mm] thick
4. Wide-mouth container to hold the polish

The procedure is as follows:

1. Mix two parts of the polishing compound with one part of water to get a creamy consistency.
2. Agitate the mixture occasionally to keep the cerium oxide from settling out.
3. On the inside of the glass, draw a circle around the scratches with marking crayon. Draw other lines directly behind the scratches to serve as guide lines during the polishing procedure. See Fig. 27-8.
4. Cover the metal surfaces adjacent to the glass with masking tape and paper to keep the polish from dripping or splattering on the paint.
5. Attach the felt pad to the polisher and dip it into the mixture several times to make sure it is well saturated. But don't submerge the pad or allow it to stay in the mixture. This can loosen the bond between the pad and its metal back.
6. Use moderate but steady pressure and hold the pad flat against the glass. Use a feathering-out motion in all directions away from the scratch.

NOTE: Avoid heavy pressure. It will not speed up the job and can cause the glass to overheat. Also, never hold the pad in one spot and never work the pad on the glass longer than 30 to 45 seconds at a time. If the glass gets too hot to touch, allow it to air-cool. Never use cold water to cool the glass. This could crack it.

7. Dip the pad into the mixture about every 15 seconds to make sure the pad and glass are always wet with the polish. A dry pad can overheat the glass.
8. After the scratch is removed, wash the glass with water. Remove the masking tape and paper, and wash and wipe the paint to remove any traces of the polish.
9. Clean the polishing pad and put it away in a safe place if you expect to use it again. Don't let dirt or other materials get on the pad. These could add scratches to the glass.

NOTE: During the metal grinding of a front fender or hood, sparks fly. If these sparks hit the windshield, they can cause burns, or black spots. Never allow the sparks

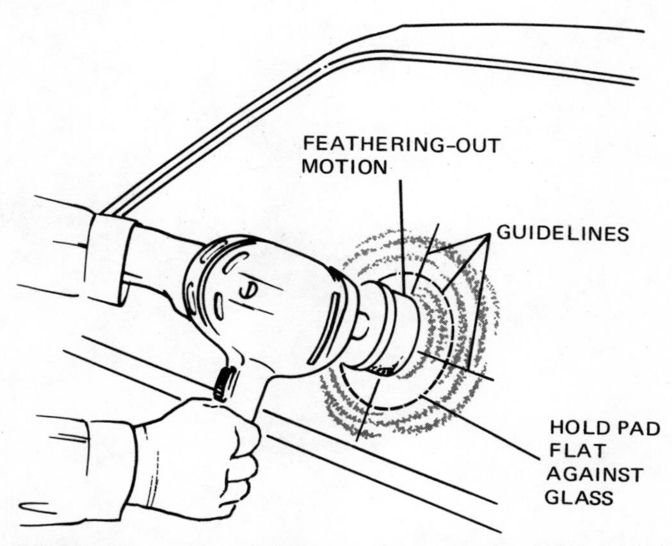

FIGURE 27-8. **Removing a minor scratch from glass.** (*Fisher Body Division of General Motors Corporation*)

from grinding to fly toward the windshield. However, if the windshield is pitted by sparks from grinding, treat the spots the same as scratches. The spots can be taken out by the polishing procedure outlined above. First, make sure that no particles of metal remain on the surface of the glass before you start polishing.

CHAPTER 27 CHECKUP

NOTE: Since the following is a chapter review test, you should review the chapter before taking the test.

For many years, the only repair possible on a windshield was to replace it. Now techniques have been developed for polishing away many surface problems. Also, several types of small cracks and damage can now be repaired. Because of the money savings to the customer, more body shops will probably be repairing some windshields. To find out how well you understand everything in this chapter, answer the questions that follow.

COMPLETING THE SENTENCES The sentences below are incomplete. After each sentence there are several words or phrases, but only one of them correctly completes the sentence. Write each sentence in your notebook, ending the sentence with the one word or phrase that completes it correctly.

1. A windshield is made of (*a*) solid sheet of clear plastic, (*b*) three layers of safety glass, (*c*) two layers of safety glass with a plastic center, (*d*) one layer of safety glass with plastic outer layers.
2. The windshield repair procedure outlined in this chapter is the (*a*) resin injection method, (*b*) water injection method, (*c*) glass injection method, (*d*) fuel injection method.
3. A windshield that has been struck hard and has pieces missing from the inside layer of glass must be (*a*) repaired with resin injection, (*b*) replaced with new windshield, (*c*) repaired with fiberglass, (*d*) carefully buffed with cerium oxide.
4. After filling the hole, you must use the pressure screw to remove (*a*) bubbles, (*b*) dirt, (*c*) excess resin, (*d*) small pieces of glass.
5. The diamond bit is used to (*a*) fill the hole, (*b*) find the hole, (*c*) polish the hole, (*d*) drill the hole.

QUESTIONS Write each of the following questions, and then the answer, in your notebook. If you have trouble recalling the answer to a question, turn back to the pages that cover the material and study them again.

1. Describe the basic procedure to repair a windshield.
2. What types of windshield breaks can be fixed with the resin injection method?
3. What types of windshield breaks cannot be fixed with the resin injection method?
4. How do you prepare the windshield for repair?
5. What is the procedure to drill a hole in the windshield, and when is it done?

SUGGESTIONS FOR FURTHER STUDY

Examine the illustrations in this chapter very carefully so you can recognize a repairable break and a nonrepairable break. On a page for your notebook, write down the types of breaks that can be repaired and a description of each. Write down the breaks that cannot be repaired and a description of each. Put this sheet in your notebook. Refer to it whenever you examine a car with a broken windshield. This will help you to quickly identify windshields that you can fix and those that must be replaced.

28 STATIONARY GLASS REPLACEMENT

In this chapter, you will learn how to remove and replace the stationary glass in automotive vehicles. This includes the windshield and the rear and quarter or opera windows. Often the glass is bonded to the body opening with a synthetic rubberlike adhesive. Other stationary glass, such as the windshield, is bonded to the body with a special polyvinyl chloride (PVC) tape, as shown in Fig. 28-1. Some station-wagon back windows and quarter windows are retained in rubber channels. The first step in removing a stationary glass is to take off all the trim and hardware surrounding the glass. This may include reveal moldings, garnish moldings or finishing lace, and windshield wiper arms.

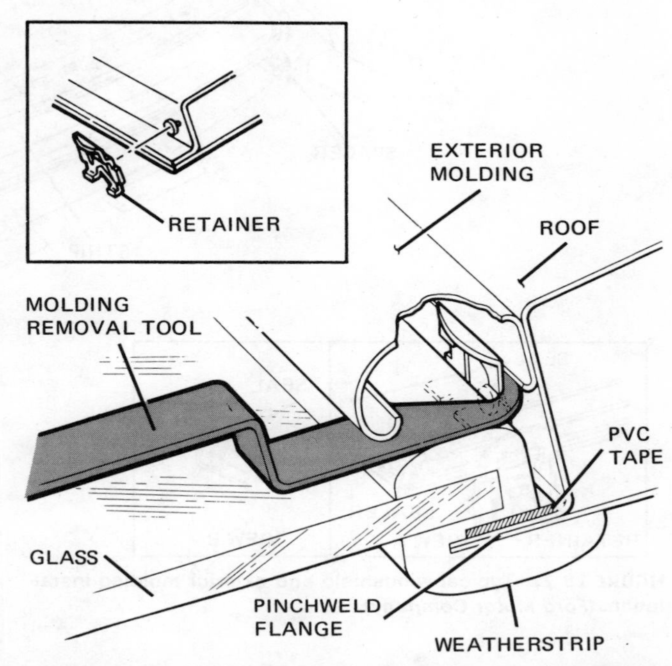

FIGURE 28-1. Using a special tool to remove the exterior molding from around the windshield. (*Ford Motor Company*)

○28-1 Types of Adhesive

An adhesive is a glue that is applied as a liquid or as a paste. After it cures, or hardens, the adhesive forms a rubberlike material. Dry adhesive sheet and tape also are available. Adhesives are used in many places on the automobile. They are used to join two materials together when mechanical fastening, such as rivets or nuts and bolts, is not possible or would impair the appearance. For many jobs, the use of liquid or paste adhesive lowers the assembling costs and at the same time seals the joint against water leaks.

In windshield installations, there are two basic types of adhesive caulking materials used to bond the glass to the glass opening. These are both synthetic, self-curing, rubberlike adhesives:

1. Polysulfide adhesive

2. Urethane tape

A special tape made of butyl polyvinyl chloride is used on some cars to bond the windshield or other glass to the opening (Fig. 28-1). Also, some glass, such as quarter windows, are set in rubber channels or gaskets and are not otherwise bonded to the opening.

In some cars, body strength is increased by using the stationary glass as an integral part of the body structure. Body rigidity is reduced when softer or noncuring adhesives are used to bond replacement windshields. Squeaks and rattles can develop when a windshield or back glass is not securely bonded to the body opening with adhesive of the proper strength.

General Motors recommends using its urethane adhesive caulking kit whenever a windshield is replaced in an older model vehicle. When you are replacing glass on other cars, use the same adhesive as was originally used.

NOTE: Before using a liquid or paste adhesive on a windshield installation, check that the windshield or the rubber gasket will not be damaged by the adhesive you are planning to use. Polysulfide adhesive, for example, may attack butyl rubber and cause or enlarge water leaks. Similarly, there is a problem with some sealants which are used to fill in areas and prevent water leaks. If the wrong sealant is used, it may attack the plastic center of the windshield around the edges. This will cloud the plastic, and bubbles may appear in it.

○28-2 Windshield Replacement—Short and Extended Methods

There are two methods of replacing the windshield. These are called the short method and the extended method.

The *short method* is recommended when the windshield is removed intact and the body opening does not require any repairs or straightening. After the glass is removed, a carefully controlled bead of adhesive is applied to the pinchweld flange. The pinchweld flange (Fig. 28-1) is the flange formed by the bent-down edge of the roof and the sheet metal welded to it. The bead of adhesive or adhesive tape laid down on this flange serves as a base for the glass when it is replaced.

The *extended method* is recommended where there is a considerable loss of adhesion between the original adhesive material and the body opening. It is also recommended in cars where the body opening requires repair. In these cars, all adhesive materials must be removed from the pinchweld flanges.

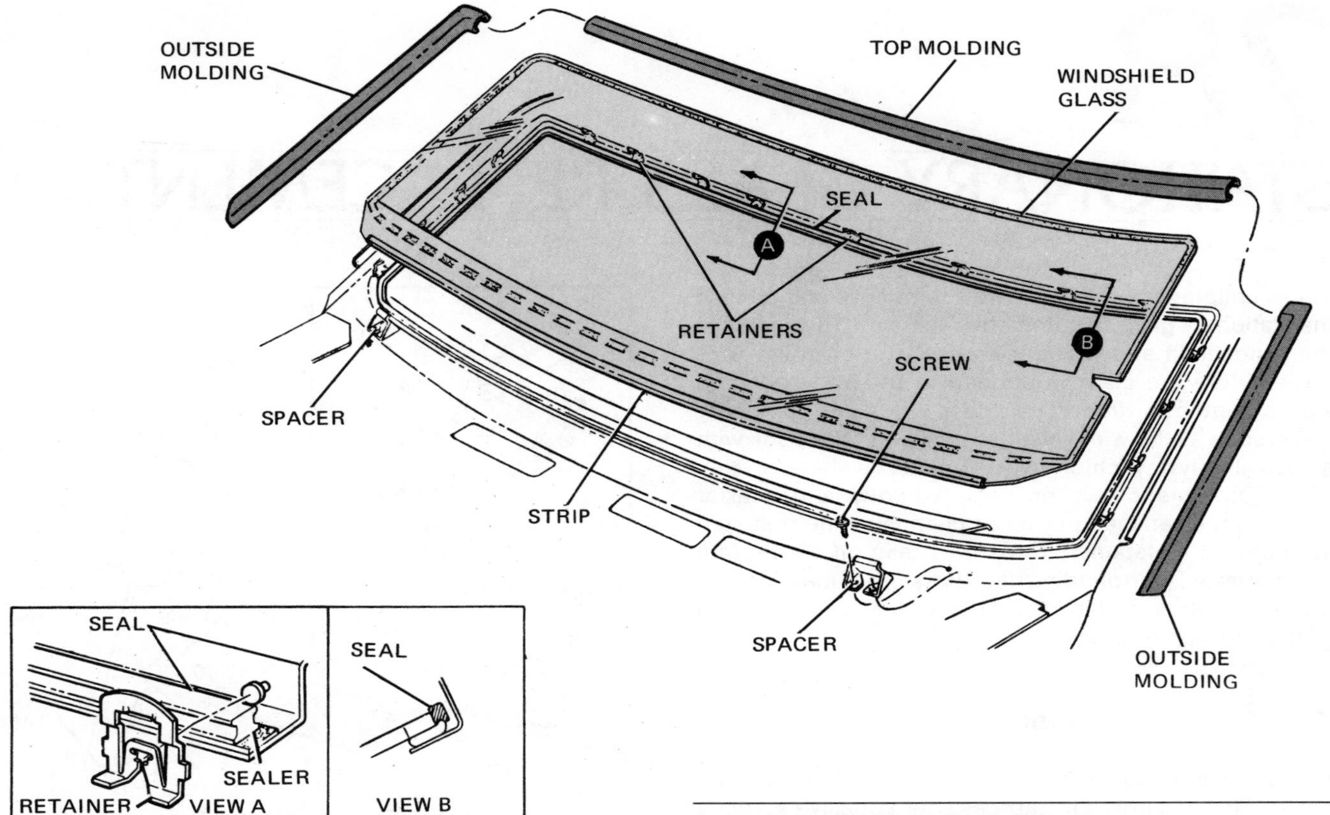

FIGURE 28-2. Typical windshield and exterior molding installation. (*Ford Motor Company*)

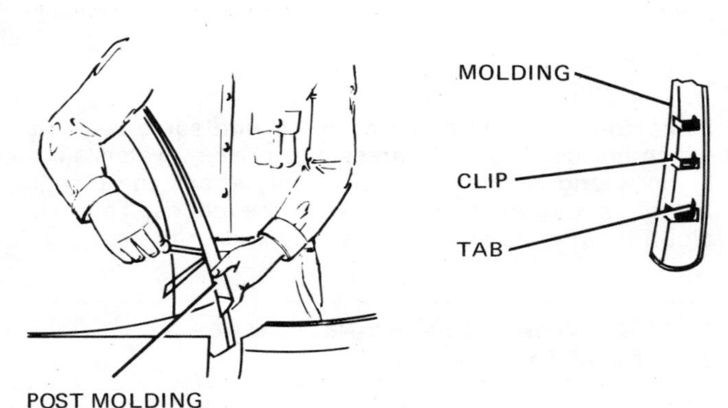

FIGURE 28-3. Removing a post molding. (*Chrysler Corporation*)

○28-3 Removing Trim and Hardware

The first step in windshield replacement is to remove all trim and hardware that could be in the way. Trim is any part that is attached to the body after it is painted. Some manufacturers refer to the molding that surrounds the glass and hides the joint as *reveal* molding. Others call it simply top, exterior, or outside molding. See Figs. 28-1 to 28-3. The molding is clipped in a variety of ways. A screwdriver or special tool (Figs. 28-1 and 28-3) is used to unclip it. If the molding is to be used again, be careful not to bend it as you take it off.

○28-4 Windshield Removal—Adhesive-Bonded type

First remove the trim and hardware as indicated in the previous section. Then put protective covering around the area where the glass is being removed so that the paint will not be damaged. Windshield removal is the same for the short and the extended installation methods. However, when the short installation method is used, extra care is required during windshield removal to make sure that an even, uniform bead of adhesive material remains on the window opening. This bead will serve as the base for the replacement glass.

If the windshield has a radio antenna built into it, disconnect the antenna lead at the lower center of the windshield. If the windshield is to be reused, fold and tape the lead wire onto the outer surface of the windshield so it won't be damaged during removal and installation of the glass.

Now, using the edge of the glass as a guide, cut adhesive material from the edge of the glass with a razor knife (Fig. 28-4). This is in preparation for the use of a cutting knife or steel music wire to complete the cutting of the adhesive from the glass.

Either a cutting knife or music wire can be used to cut the adhesive. There are two types of cutting knives: cold and hot. The procedure for cutting the adhesive and removing the glass is as follows:

1. USING THE KNIFE Figure 28-5 shows the use of the hot knife. It has an electric heating element in it that heats the blade hot enough to easily soften the adhesive. Note that two types of blades are shown. The standard blade is used where there is no adhesive on the back, or inside, of the glass. The special curved blade is used to cut through adhesive that is adhering to the back of the glass.

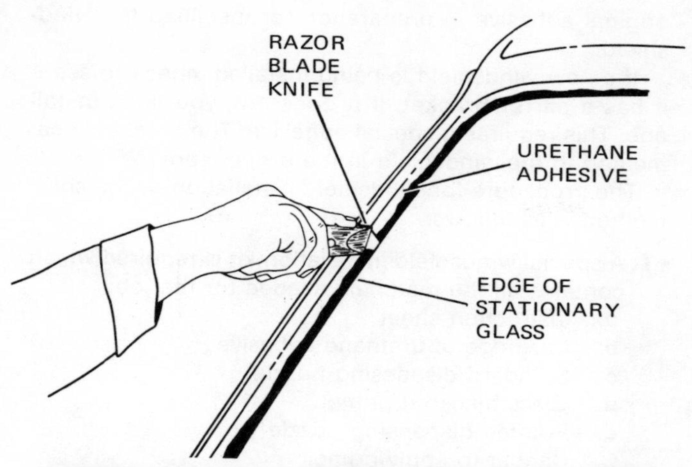

FIGURE 28-4. Cutting adhesive from the edge of the glass with a razor blade. (*American Motors Corporation*)

CAUTION: When using the hot knife, do not inhale the fumes of the burning material. Always have adequate ventilation in the work area.

Do not allow the hot knife blade to remain stationary at any one spot. This will overheat the adhesive so that it will become permanently soft.

The cold-knife method is similar to the hot-knife method. However, it requires a considerably greater pull—greater physical strength—to pull the knife through the adhesive. However, if the knife is kept sharp, it can be done satisfactorily.

In addition to keeping the hot-knife blade sharp, it should be cleaned immediately after use, while still hot, with steel wool. If the blade is cool, wash the adhesive off with a suitable solvent.

2. USING MUSIC WIRE Music wire can be used to cut through the adhesive as shown in Fig. 28-6. Note that the music wire has been wrapped around pieces of wood which serve as handles. With a helper working on the other side of the glass, carefully pull the wire through the adhesive material around the entire outside edge of the windshield. If the short method of installation is to be used, hold the wire as close to the inside of the glass as possible. This leaves a good bed of adhesive for the replacement glass. Keep tension on the wire throughout the cutting job to avoid kinking or breaking it. One person can do the job as shown in Fig. 28-7.

3. REMOVING THE WINDSHIELD After the adhesive is cut, have an assistant help you remove the glass from the car (Fig. 28-8). First push from the inside of the glass to make sure it is free. Then you and the as-

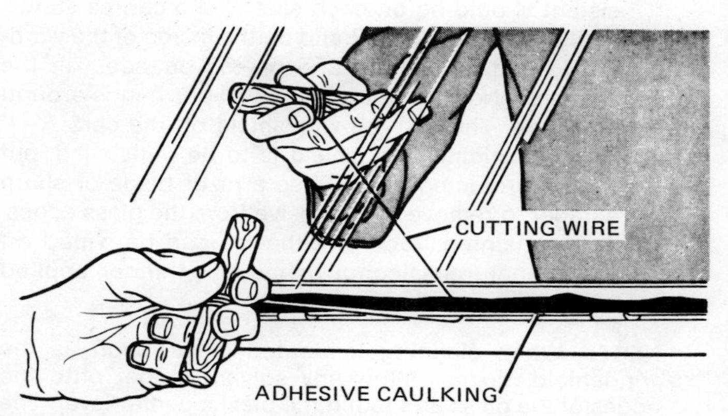

FIGURE 28-6. Using steel music wire to cut the adhesive in which the glass is set. (*Chrysler Corporation*)

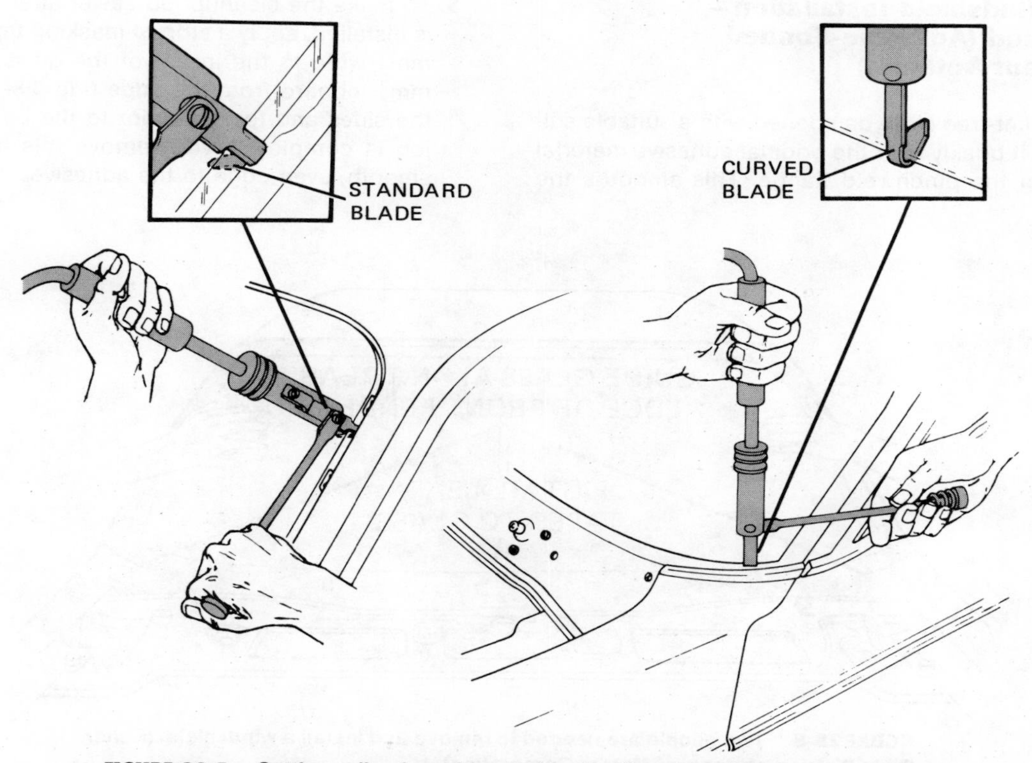

FIGURE 28-5. Cutting adhesive with a hot knife. (*American Motors Corporation*)

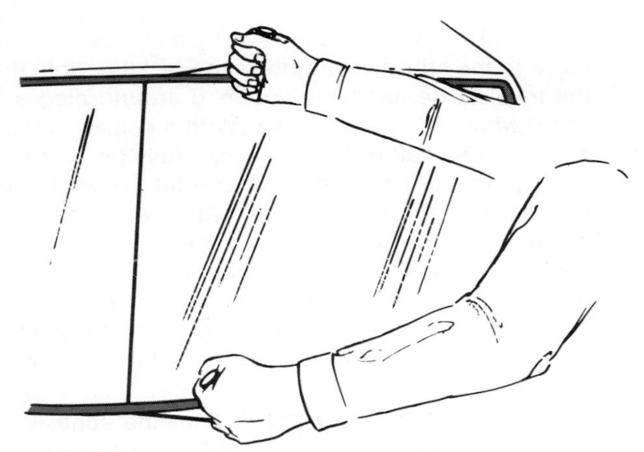

FIGURE 28-7. One person cutting the adhesive from the windshield with a music wire. (*Fisher Body Division of General Motors Corporation*)

sistant should be on each side of the car, as shown in Fig. 28-8. Place one hand on the inside of the windshield and the other hand on the outside. Tilt the windshield out so you can move your hands around the posts. Then lift the windshield off the car.

If the original windshield is to be reinstalled, put it on a protected bench. Use a razor blade or sharp scraper to remove old adhesive from the glass edges. Any remaining trace of adhesive can be wiped off with denatured alcohol or lacquer thinner applied with a clean cloth.

NOTE: When cleaning laminated glass, such as the windshield, do not allow any solvent to get onto the edges of the glass and touch the plastic center layer. The plastic will absorb the solvent and cause discoloration of the glass.

○28-5 Windshield Installation — Short Method (Adhesive-Bonded Type Without Antenna)

Use a clean, lint-free cloth dampened with a suitable solvent and rub it briskly over the original adhesive material remaining on the pinchweld flange. This smooths the original adhesive in preparation for installing the windshield.

If a new windshield is being installed, check to see if it has a mirror bracket. If it does not, you must install one. This requires a special adhesive. The bracket is cemented to the windshield in the proper spot.

The procedure for windshield installation by the short method is as follows:

1. A special windshield installation kit is required which contains all the materials needed for the job:
   a. Instruction sheet
   b. Cartridge of urethane adhesive
   c. Standard dispensing nozzle
   d. Glass blackout primer
   e. Pointed dispensing nozzle
   f. Dauber to apply primer
   g. Support spacers

   You will need, in addition, an adhesive dispensing gun, solvent, masking tape, and standoff spacers (for properly spacing the glass in the opening). In addition, when the pinchweld flange must be cleaned (and for the extended method), you will need paint primer to prime the flange.
2. Check the molding retaining clips and replace any that are broken or loose. Install the lower support spacers where used (Fig. 28-9).
3. Check the relationship of the glass to the adhesive material on the pinchweld flange. Gaps in excess of ⅛ inch [3.18 mm] must be corrected by applying more adhesive.
4. Put the glass in the proper position in the opening. Apply pieces of masking tape from the edge of the glass to the adjacent pillar or body part. Then slit the tape at the joint and remove the glass. The tape will serve as guides when you make the final installation of the windshield.
5. To make the cleanup job easier after the windshield is installed, apply a strip of masking tape 1 inch [25.4 mm] wide to the inside of the glass, ½ inch [12.7 mm] inboard from the edge (Fig. 28-10). Apply it to the sides and top only, not to the bottom. After the job is completed, you remove this tape, leaving a smooth, even edge to the adhesive.

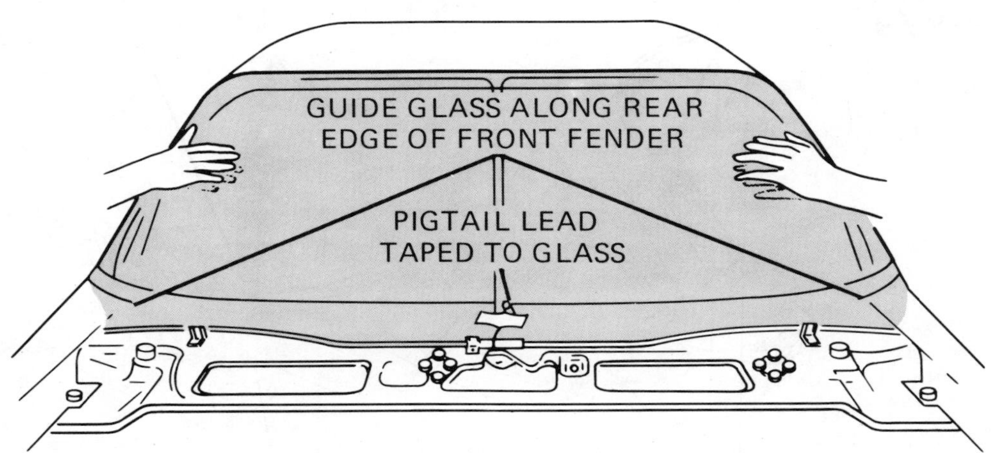

FIGURE 28-8. Two people are needed to remove and install a windshield. (*Fisher Body Division of General Motors Corporation*)

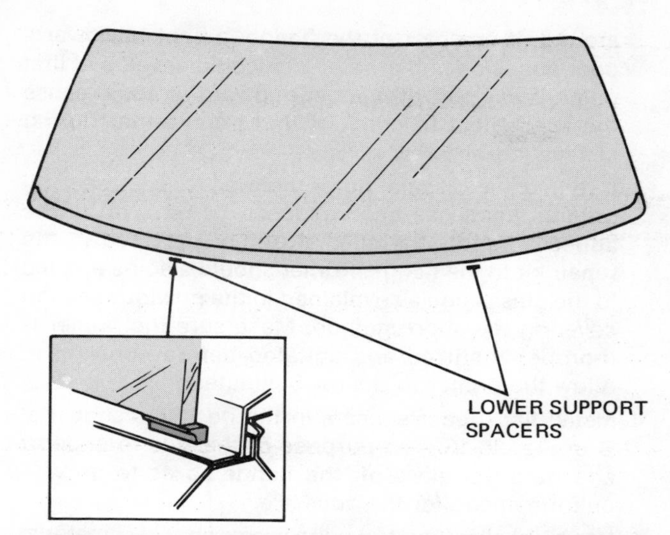

FIGURE 28-9. **Installation of the lower support spacers. (*American Motors Corporation*)**

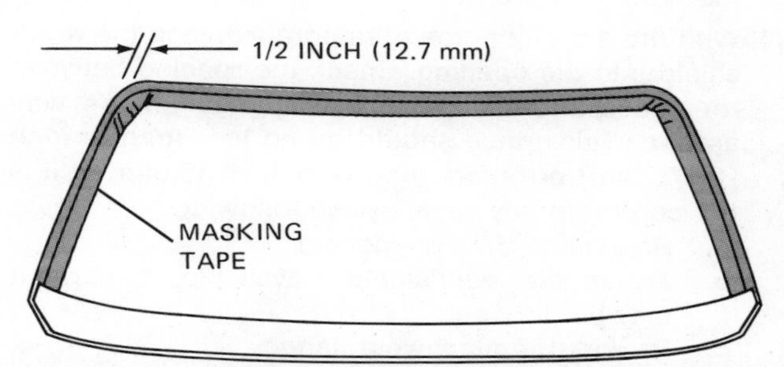

FIGURE 28-10. **Applying tape to make the cleanup job easier. (*American Motors Corporation*)**

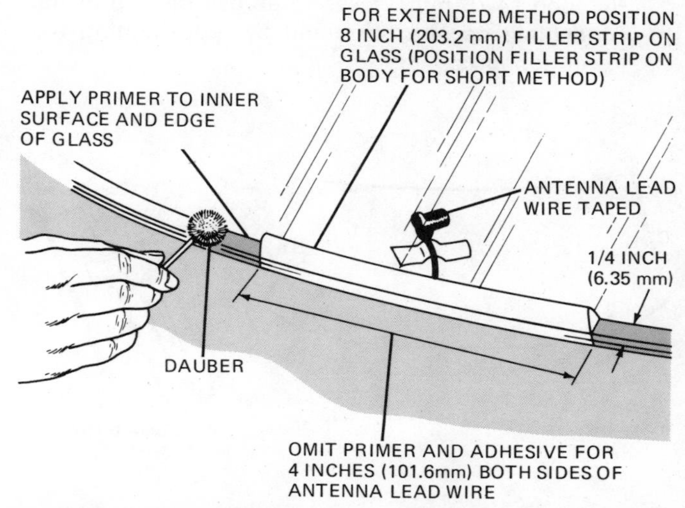

FIGURE 28-11. **Preparing for application of the adhesive. (*Fisher Body Division of General Motors Corporation*)**

6. Use a clean cloth, dampened with isopropyl alcohol, to wipe the surface of the glass between the masking tape and the outer edge. This is where a bead of adhesive will be applied.
7. Use the dauber to apply blackout primer around the entire inner surface and edge of the glass (Fig. 28-11).

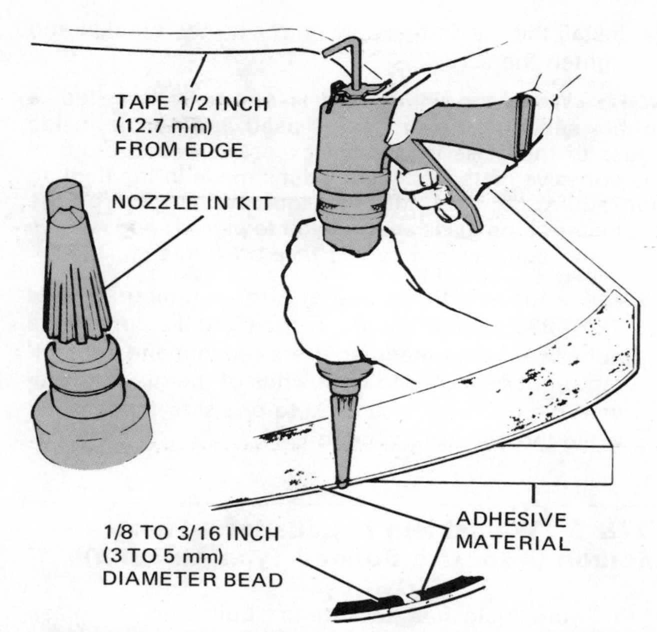

FIGURE 28-12. **Applying adhesive to the windshield. (*American Motors Corporation*)**

NOTE: Figure 28-11 shows a windshield with an antenna, but the general procedure of applying the primer is the same for any windshield. The purpose of the primer is to secure good sticking of the adhesive to the glass.

8. Use care in applying the primer, because it will damage trim and painted surfaces.
9. After waiting 10 minutes for the primer to dry, apply a smooth, continuous bead of adhesive around the entire inner edge of the glass (Fig. 28-12). The bead should be ⅛ to 3/16 inch [3 to 5 mm] in diameter.
10. Now, using the tape guides, carefully position the glass on the fenders next to the opening. To bring the glass to the opening, two technicians are required (Fig. 28-8). Each carries the glass with one hand inside and one hand outside the glass. At the window opening, put the glass in a horizontal position. One technician then reaches inside the car with the upper hand and brings it back on the glass. The other technician does the same. Now, with one hand inside and one hand outside the car, as shown, they can raise the glass to a vertical position and set it into the opening. With the tape guides aligned, and with the windshield on the lower support spacers, press the glass in against the adhesive on the pinchweld flange. Avoid excessive pressure, which could cause excessive squeeze-out of the adhesive.
11. Use a small disposable brush or a flat-bladed tool to paddle additional adhesive around the edge of the glass as necessary to fill voids and assure a good seal all around.
12. Water-test the windshield at once. Use a cold-water spray and allow the water to spill over the edge of the glass. Do not direct a hard stream of water at the adhesive because it has not set up yet. If you see any leaks, apply extra adhesive at the leaking points.
13. Install moldings and remove masking tape from the inner surface of the glass. Clean up the glass as necessary with a cloth dampened with solvent.

14. Install the inside rearview mirror on the bracket and tighten the screw.

NOTE: When the windshield is originally installed, a rubber sealing strip or dam is used around the inside edges of the glass to prevent excessive squeeze-out of the adhesive materials. Installations made in the field do not require the dam. Masking tape applied around the perimeter of the glass enables you to pick up and remove excessive squeeze-out as you take off the tape.

15. Leave the vehicle setting at a room temperature of 72°F [22.2°C] for 6 hours to complete the cure of the adhesive. Some manufacturers recommend cementing rubber spacers to both sides of the glass to prevent the glass from slipping to one side or the other while the adhesive is curing.

○28-6 Windshield Installation—Short Method (Adhesive-Bonded Type Antenna)

If the windshield has an antenna built into the glass, some additional steps and precautions are required during installation. Figure 28-8 shows how the antenna wire is taped up out of the way before the windshield is installed. When installing the windshield, note the following:

1. On the type with a butyl strip at the bottom center of the windshield (at antenna lead pigtail), mark the location of each end of the strip at the edge of the glass with tape or grease pencil. After glass removal, replace the original butyl strip with the new strip provided in the installation kit. Stretch or cut a new strip to fill the existing gap on the body.
2. On the type without the butyl strip at the bottom center of the windshield opening, measure 4 inches [101.6 mm] on both sides of the body centerline. Use tape or a grease pencil to mark the location on both the body and the glass. After the windshield removal, cut the original adhesive material from between the marks and insert the filler strip provided with the kit.
3. Apply primer around the outer edge of the glass as shown in Fig. 28-11, omitting the area between the two marks, or tape, established in steps 1 and 2 above. Also, when applying adhesive (Fig. 28-12), do not apply it in the area between the two marks.
4. To assure a good seal between the filler strips and the adjacent adhesive material, paddle additional material at the edges of the butyl strip.

○28-7 Windshield Installation—Extended Method (Adhesive-Bonded Type)

The windshield installation by the extended method is similar to the installation by the short method, with the following additional requirements:

1. Use a sharp scraper or chisel to remove old adhesive from the flanges on which the glass rests. Work all the way around the opening. If butyl or some other adhesive has been used, all traces of it must be removed.
2. Make whatever repairs are necessary to the opening and flanges. The flanges must be even all the way around. If any part of the flange is bent downward, poor adhesion and a water leak could develop at that point. If any part of it is bent upward, it could cause the windshield to crack at that point either during installation or later.
3. If refinishing or painting of the area is required, or if original paint has been exposed by removal of the adhesive, apply the special primer provided in the repair kit to the flange. Primer should also be applied to the glass edge as explained in the previous section covering the short method. Make sure the primer is thoroughly stirred and agitated before applying it. Allow the primer to dry for 5 minutes.
4. Install flat rubber spacers in the positions shown at B in Fig. 28-13. The purpose of these is to support and hold the glass off the flange so as to provide uniform space for the adhesive.
5. Use black weatherstrip adhesive or adhesive material to cement the rubber spacers into place.
6. Note the two spacers (A in Fig. 28-13) which support the bottom of the glass.
7. With the aid of a helper, temporarily place the windshield into the opening. Check the spacing between the glass and the pinchweld flange all the way around. This space should be no less than ⅛ inch [3.175 mm] nor more than ¼ inch [6.35 mm]. If it is not correct at any spot, try the following:
   a. Reposition the flat spacers.
   b. Try another windshield if available. Its contour may be different.
   c. Rework the pinchweld flange.
   d. Plan to add more adhesive at the areas where the spacing is excessive.
8. Check the location of the glass in the opening. The glass should overlap the pinchweld flange at least 3/16 inch [4.76 mm]. Overlap across the top of the windshield can be corrected by repositioning the lower supports.

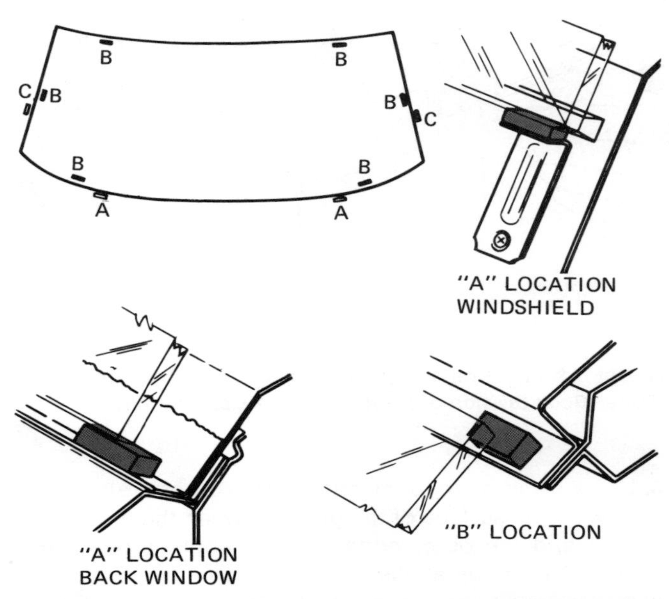

FIGURE 28-13. When installing the windshield, place the glass spacers in the positions shown at B. (*Fisher Body Division of General Motors Corporation*)

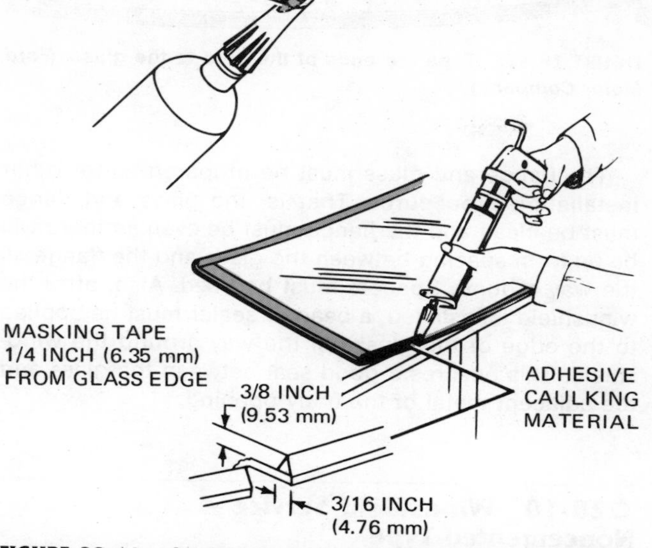

FIGURE 28-14. Applying adhesive in the extended method. (*Fisher Body Division of General Motors Corporation*)

9. After final adjustments have been made, apply strips of tape across the body and glass. Cut the tape at the joint between the two. The tape is lined up when the windshield is installed in the correct position.

10. The remainder of the installation job is the same as for the short method. That is, tape is applied around the inner surface of the windshield, ¼ inch [6.35 mm] inboard from the edge of the glass. The glass edge is then cleaned and primed (Fig. 28-11). Adhesive is then applied to the edge of the glass (Fig. 28-14). Note that the nozzle has been enlarged in order to lay down an extra heavy bead of adhesive. This is required for the extended method to replace the adhesive removed from the pinchweld.

11. After the adhesive is applied to the glass, the glass is then installed as for the short method and pressed down into place. Additional adhesive should be paddled into place as necessary in order to fill any gaps. Note the special precautions that must be taken if the windshield has an antenna embedded in it. See ○28-6.

12. Water-test the seal and apply additional adhesive if required to eliminate water leaks. Allow the seal to cure 6 hours before moving the car.

○28-8 Windshield Service – Tape-Sealed Weatherstrip Type

This type of installation (Fig. 28-1) uses adhesive tape to seal between the pinchweld flange and the glass weatherstrip. Removal and replacement of the windshield are described below. See Fig. 28-15.

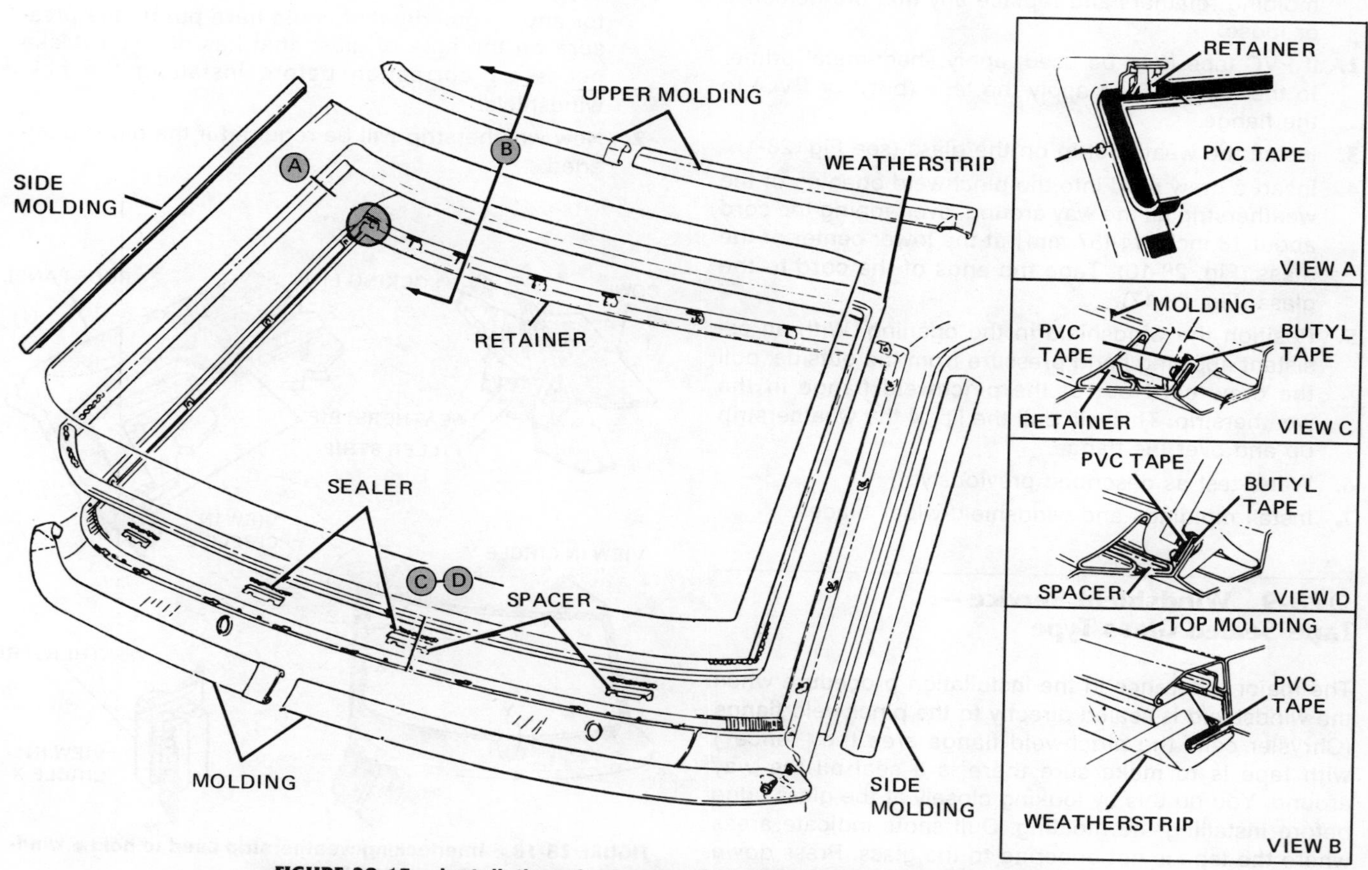

FIGURE 28-15. Installation of a tape-sealed windshield. (*Ford Motor Company*)

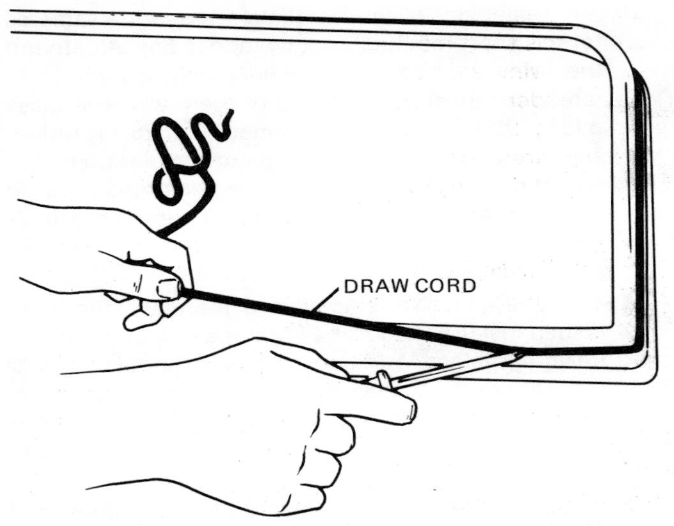

FIGURE 28-16. Working the draw cord into the pinchweld opening of the weatherstrip. (*Ford Motor Company*)

WINDSHIELD REMOVAL

1. Remove molding and windshield wiper blades as previously explained.
2. From inside the vehicle, push the windshield out of the opening.
3. Remove the weatherstrip from the glass.

WINDSHIELD INSTALLATION

1. Clean all adhesive from the pinchweld flange. Check molding retainers and replace any that are defective or loose.
2. If PVC tape is to be used, apply sheet-metal primer to the flange. Then apply the tape (butyl or PVC) to the flange.
3. Install the weatherstrip on the glass (see Fig. 28-1).
4. Insert a draw cord into the pinchweld opening of the weatherstrip all the way around, overlapping the cord about 18 inches [457 mm] at the lower center of the glass (Fig. 28-16). Tape the ends of the cord to the glass (Fig. 28-17).
5. Position the windshield in the opening. With an assistant applying hand pressure from the outside, pull the draw cord out of the pinchweld flange in the weatherstrip. This will pull the lip of the weatherstrip up and over the flange.
6. Water-test as described previously.
7. Install moldings and windshield-wiper blades.

○28-9 Windshield Service — Tape-Sealed Glass Type

The major difference in the installation procedure when the windshield is sealed directly to the pinchweld flange (Chrysler calls the pinchweld flange area the "fence") with tape is to make sure there is a seal all the way around. You do this by looking closely at the glass edge before installing the molding. Dull spots indicate areas where the tape is not adhering to the glass. Press down some more at these areas to get a good seal.

FIGURE 28-17. Tape the ends of the cord to the glass. (*Ford Motor Company*)

The flange and glass must be prepared as for other installation procedures. That is, the glass and flange must be clean and the flange must be even so there will be uniform spacing between the glass and the flange all the way around. Spacers must be used. Also, after the windshield is installed, a bead of sealer must be applied to the edge of the glass, all the way around the windshield. This ensures a good seal between the glass and the adjacent metal of the body opening.

○28-10 Windshield Service — Noncemented Type

This type of installation (Figs. 28-18 and 28-19) uses an interlocking weatherstrip. Before removing the windshield, you must unlock this weatherstrip from the glass. You do this by prying the lip away from the glass. Then insert a fiber wedge and work it all the way around the glass. Next, with the weatherstrip unlocked, have an assistant help you remove the glass.

The installation procedure is as follows:

1. If the glass has cracked, perhaps owing to some irregularity, check the fence, or pinchweld flange, for any irregularity that could have put undue pressure on the area of glass that has cracked. Make necessary correction before installing the new windshield.
2. New weatherstrip will be required if the old is damaged.

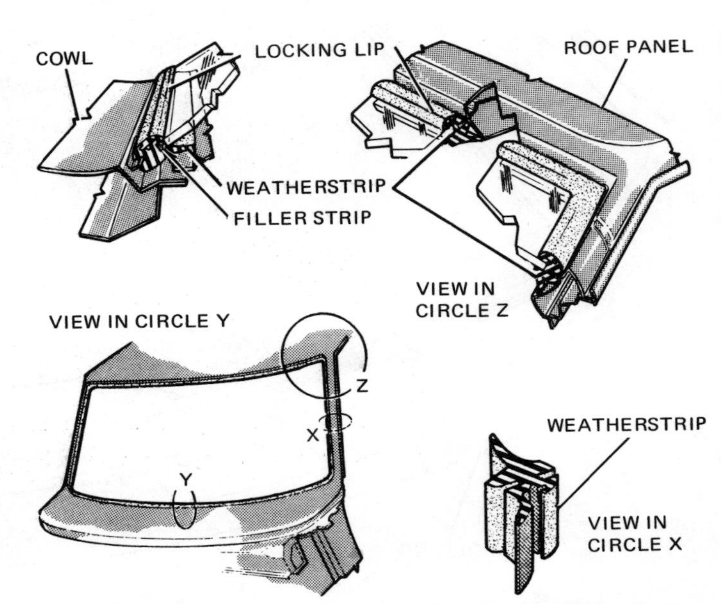

FIGURE 28-18. Interlocking weatherstrip used to hold a windshield. (*Chrysler Corporation*)

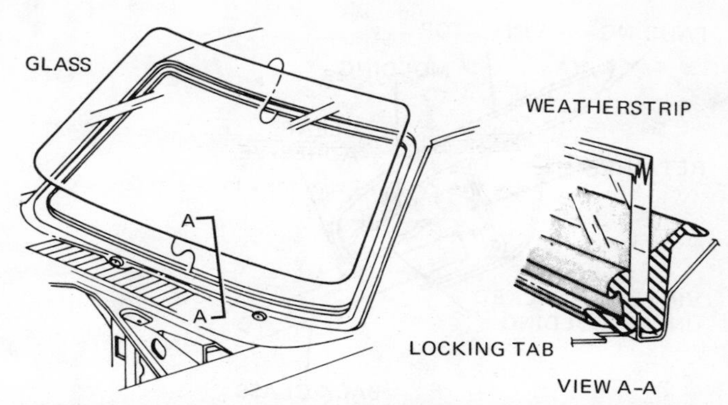

FIGURE 28-19. Windshield installation using an interlocking weatherstrip. (*Chrysler Corporation*)

3. To install the windshield, remove all old sealer and cement from the original weatherstrip. Apply sealer in fence and glass groove part of weatherstrip. Apply a ⅜-inch [9.5-mm] bead of sealer completely across the cowl top panel where the windshield weatherstrip will rest.
4. Position weatherstrip lower section at the tab area, starting at corners and installing it over the tab. Work toward the center.
5. Install weatherstrip all the way around the opening. Seat it with hand pressure.
6. With an assistant, slide the upper edge of the glass into the channel of the weatherstrip (Figs. 28-18 and 28-19). Use a fiber tool to force the weatherstrip lip over the glass.
7. Seat the glass in the weatherstrip, pounding the glass with the palm of the hand, using an upward motion.
8. Insert a fiber tool between the weatherstrip and the glass at either corner. Slide the tool along the top, sides, and bottom of the glass, forcing the lip over the glass.
9. Using the fiber tool, force the weatherstrip locking tab into the locked position in the fence.
10. Water-test the seal. Install moldings and windshield wiper blades.

○28-11 Rear Window Services

There are about 3000 different sizes and shapes of side and rear windows used in automobiles. Rear windows are installed in a variety of ways, similar to those used to install windshields. The removal and replacement procedures are also similar. With rear windows, however, you may need vacuum cups as shown in Fig. 28-20. In some cars, you and an assistant can remove the rear window by working partly on the inside and partly on the outside.

Figure 28-21 shows a typical installation arrangement for rear windows. The procedures of removing and replacing rear windows have, in effect, already been covered. As we mentioned previously, the installation procedures for windshields and rear windows are very similar.

There is one special design, however, that we describe here. This is the "frenched" back window (Fig. 28-20), in which the vinyl roof covering is carried to the glass and tucked under the molding. This is shown to the upper right in Fig. 28-20, which also shows the special procedures required to remove and replace the glass. With the vinyl pulled out from under the molding and taped back, as shown, the window can be removed. Then, when the window has been reinstalled, the ground-off putty knife is used to tuck the vinyl back in under the molding. Note, to upper right, that a thin bead of clear adhesive is used to seal between the vinyl and the glass.

○28-12 Heated Rear Window Service

Some cars have a heated rear window (Fig. 28-22). These windows have a heating element embedded in the glass. The heating element is connected to wiring harnesses on the two sides of the window. On some cars, the window is supplied with high voltage from a special alternator. On other cars, the heating current is supplied from the 12-volt alternator.

CAUTION: The engine must be off when you work on a rear window which has a heating element. The voltage is high enough to give you an extremely severe shock.

The only additional action required on the heated rear window is to disconnect the wiring from the window. If the same window is to be reinstalled, tape the leads to the glass so they will not be damaged.

○28-13 Side Window Service

These windows are fixed glass windows back of the rear door, above the quarter panel (Fig. 28-23). They are retained in place either by adhesive, such as butyl rubber tape, or by rubber channels. Their removal and installation are very similar to the procedures previously described for windshields and rear windows. Other installation methods using nuts, or brackets, also are employed.

○28-14 Back Windows for Three-Door Cars

These cars have a lift window at the rear that serves as a third door. Figure 28-24 shows two versions and their installation methods. Refer to these illustrations if you are required to replace the glass.

○28-15 Quarter Window for Station Wagon

Figure 28-25 shows the installation of a quarter window on a station wagon. Note that this installation requires spacers, sealers, and molding similar to that used in installing other stationary glass previously discussed in the chapter.

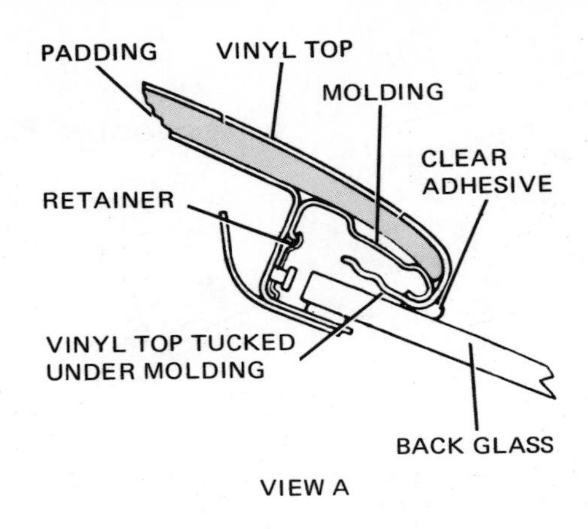

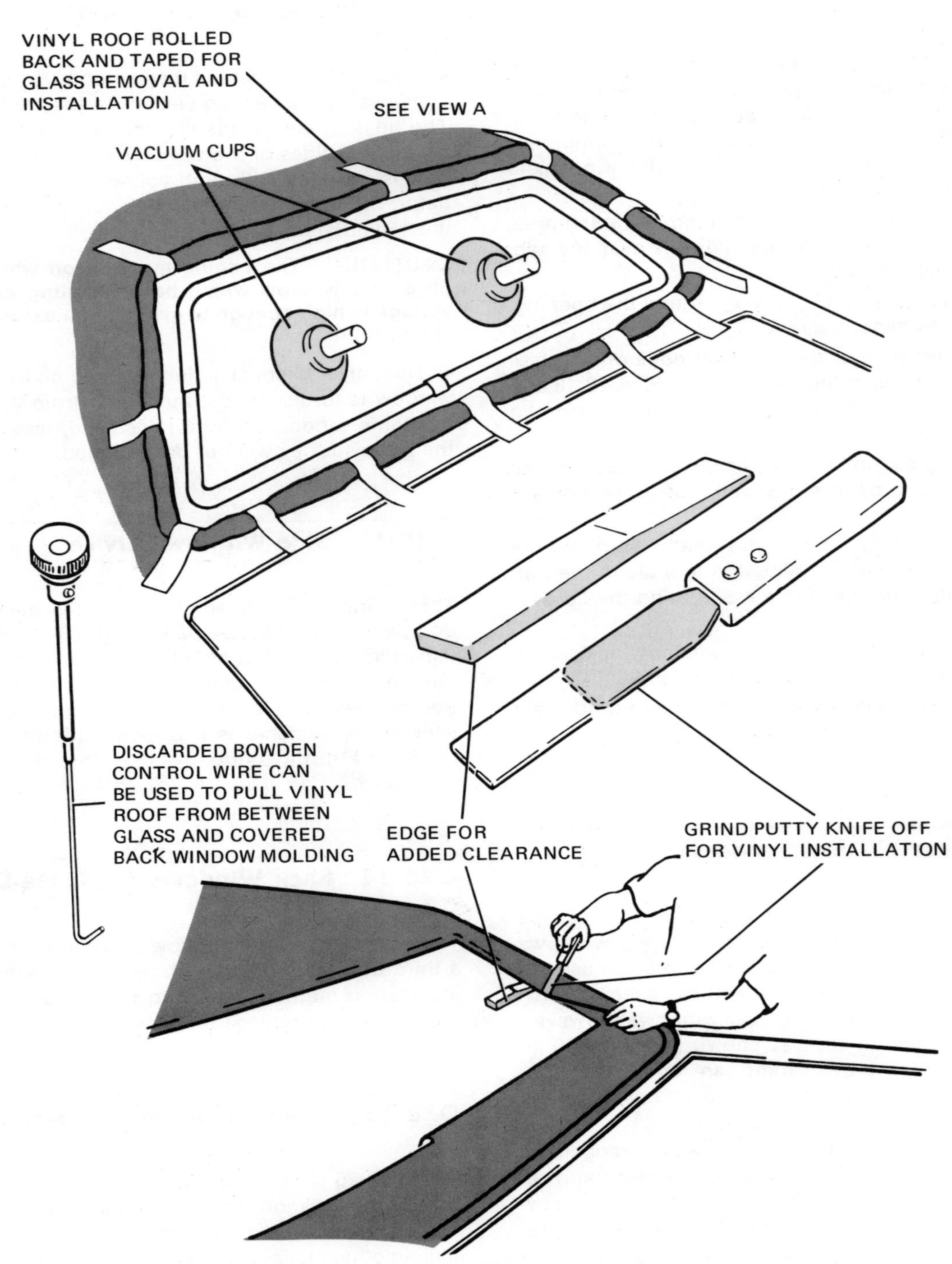

FIGURE 28-20. Servicing the frenched back window. (*Ford Motor Company*)

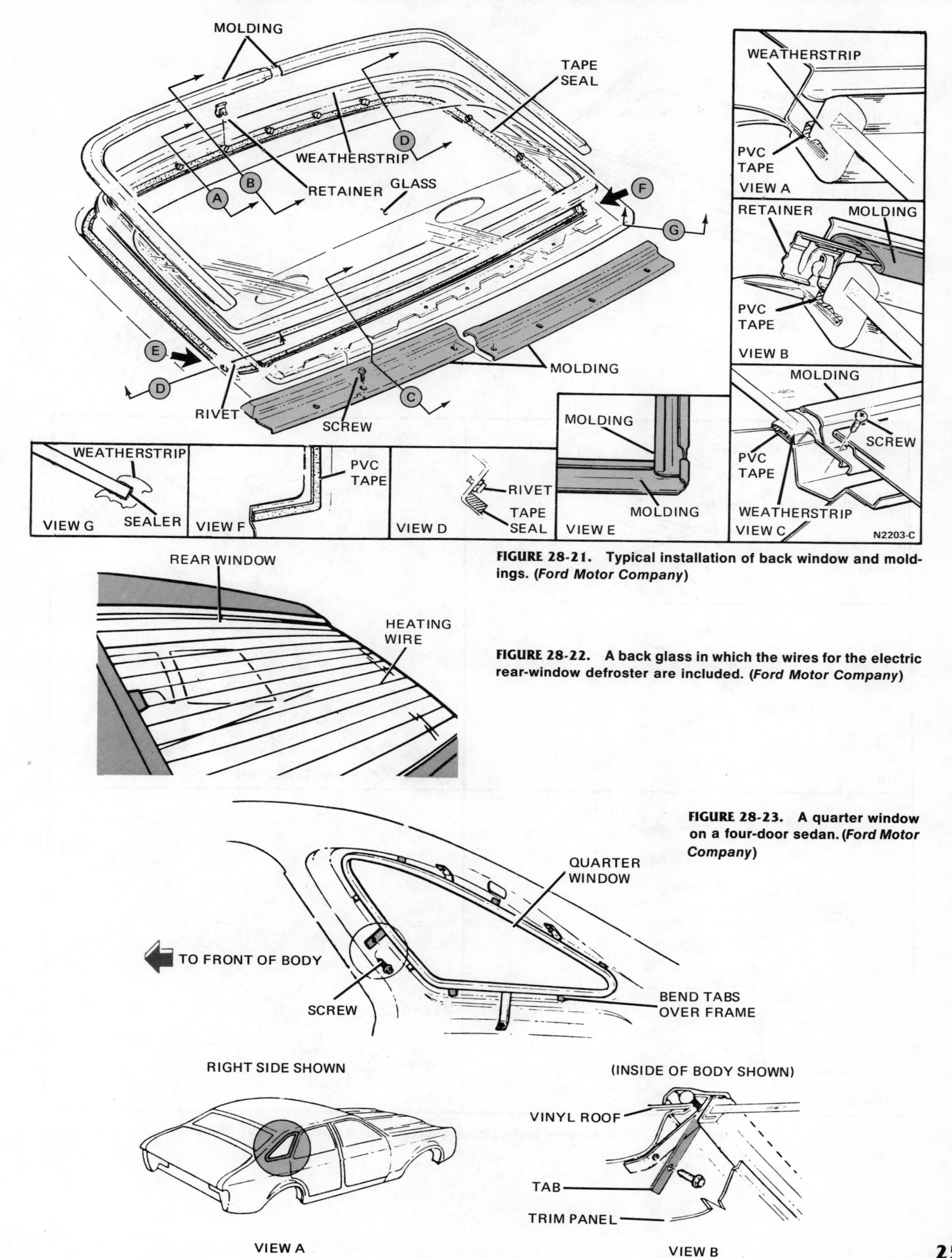

FIGURE 28-21. Typical installation of back window and moldings. (*Ford Motor Company*)

FIGURE 28-22. A back glass in which the wires for the electric rear-window defroster are included. (*Ford Motor Company*)

FIGURE 28-23. A quarter window on a four-door sedan. (*Ford Motor Company*)

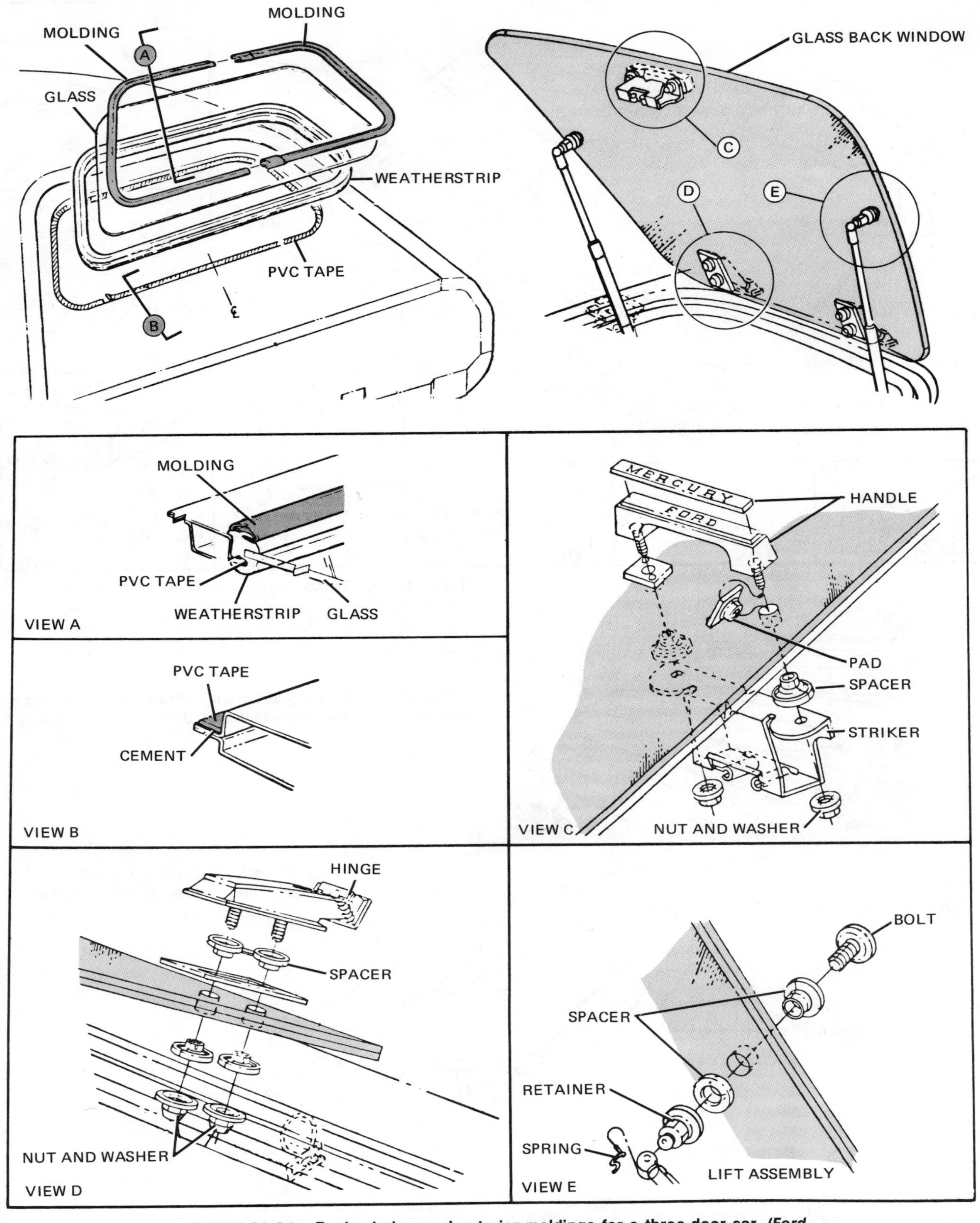

FIGURE 28-24. Back window and exterior moldings for a three-door car. (*Ford Motor Company*)

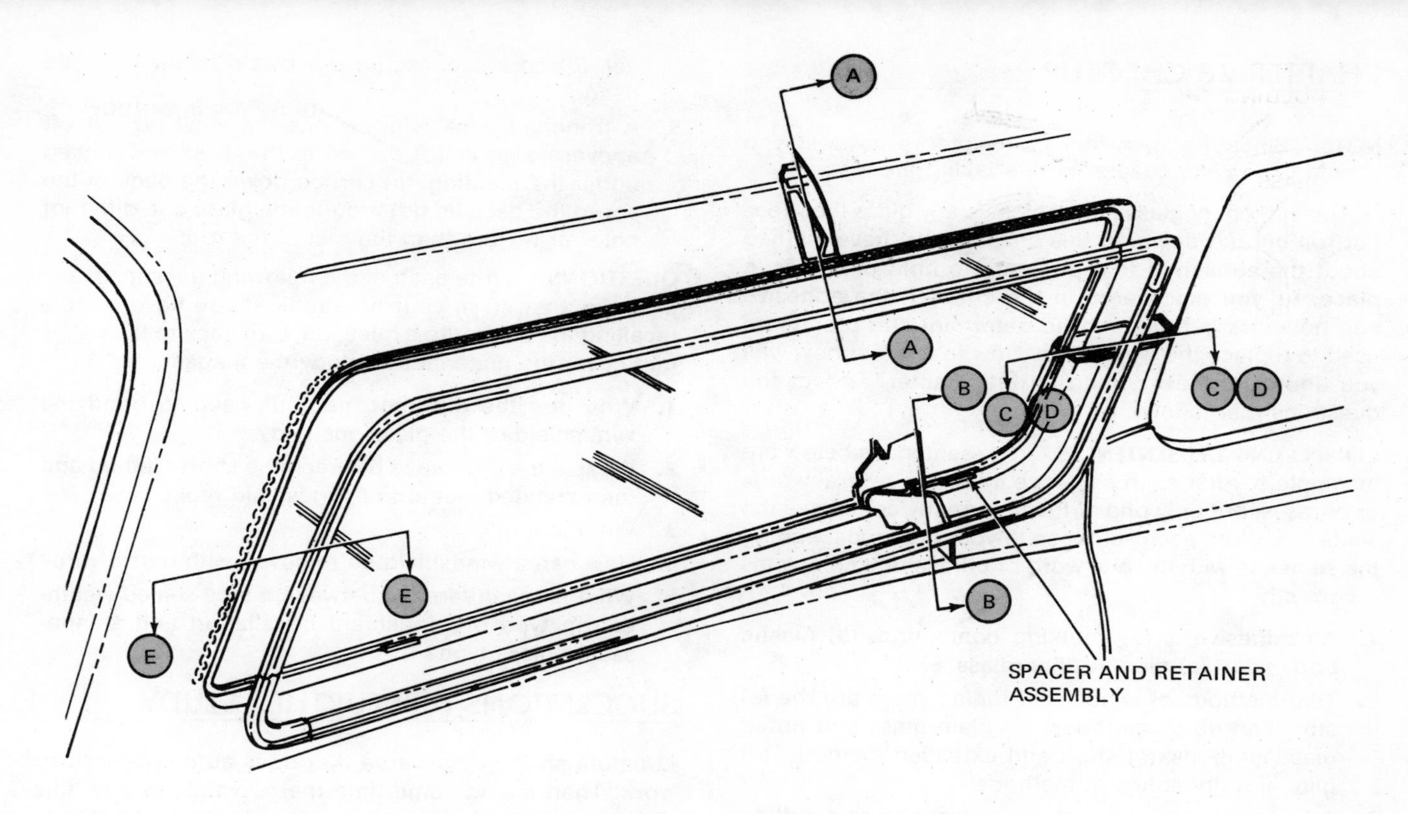

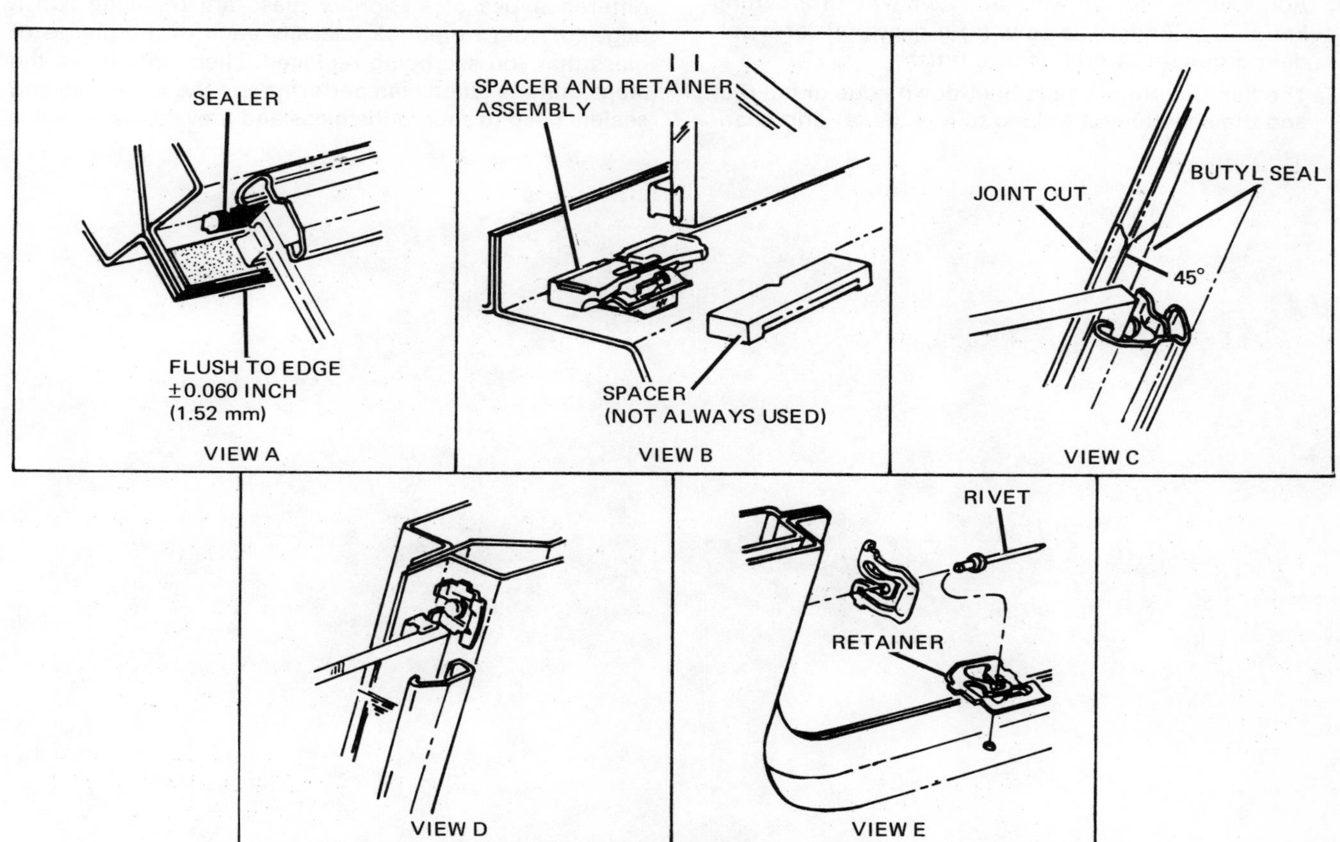

FIGURE 28-25. Quarter window and molding installation on a station wagon. ***(Ford Motor Company)***

CHAPTER 28 CHECKUP

NOTE: Since the following is a chapter review test, you should review the chapter before taking the test.

The stationary glass in a vehicle is any glass that does not roll up and down. In this chapter, you have learned about the adhesives that are used to hold the glass in place. As you discovered in the chapter, the adhesive and how it is cut or removed determine the procedure used to replace the windshield. Now to find out how well you understand everything in this chapter, answer the questions that follow.

COMPLETING THE SENTENCES The sentences below are incomplete. After each sentence there are several words or phrases, but only one of them correctly completes the sentence. Write each sentence in your notebook, ending the sentence with the one word or phrase that completes it correctly.

1. An adhesive is (*a*) caulking compound, (*b*) plastic body filler, (*c*) glue, (*d*) fiberglass.
2. Two methods of windshield replacement are the (*a*) slow and quick methods, (*b*) plain glass and tinted glass methods, (*c*) short and extended methods, (*d*) glue and dry adhesive methods.
3. Adhesive can be cut with (*a*) music wire or a cutting knife, (*b*) a knife or a saw, (*c*) a gas torch or a soldering gun, (*d*) a drill or wire brush.
4. The flange formed by the bent-down edge of the roof and the sheet metal welded to it is the (*a*) drip channel, (*b*) core support, (*c*) pinchweld flange, (*d*) axle flange.
5. A frenched back window has the vinyl (*a*) cut off above the glass, (*b*) carried to the glass and tucked under the molding, (*c*) carried down the back of the car to the deck lid, (*d*) around the glass of a different color or texture than the rest of the roof.

QUESTIONS Write each of the following questions, and then the answer, in your notebook. If you have trouble recalling the answer to a question, turn back to the pages that cover the material and study them again.

1. What are the different methods used to bond the windshield to the glass opening?
2. What is the difference between the short method and the extended method of windshield replacement?
3. What is trim?
4. How can a windshield be removed with music wire?
5. What is the difference between a tape-sealed weatherstrip type of windshield installation and a tape-sealed glass type?

SUGGESTIONS FOR FURTHER STUDY

Locate a shop in your area that does automotive glass work. Then spend some time there, watching how the different types of stationary glass are replaced. On a page for your notebook, classify each of the pieces of glass that you see being replaced. Then write down the steps that the technician performs and the adhesives and sealers used to secure the glass and prevent water leaks.

PART 8

SEATS, INTERIOR TRIM, SEAT BELTS, AND AIR BAGS

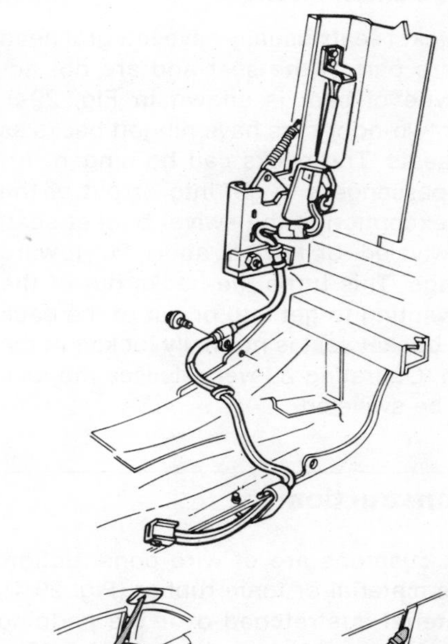

In this part, you will learn about the various kinds of seats used in automotive vehicles and how to service them. In addition, you will learn about interior trim, including headliner, carpet, and trim panels. This part also discusses safety belts and air bags. There are three chapters in Part 8, as follows:

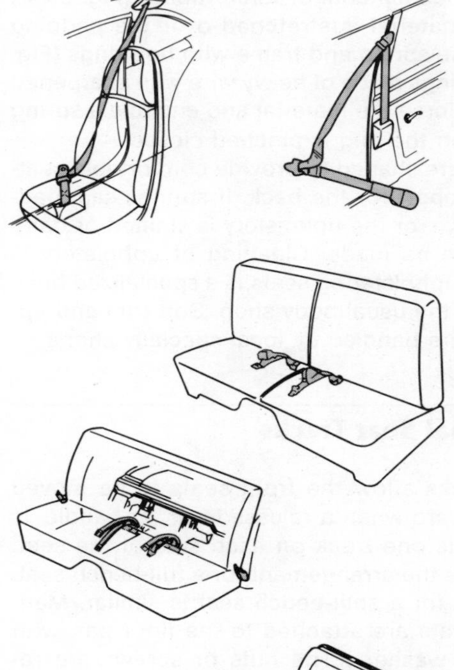

29 AUTOMOTIVE SEATS

In this chapter, you will learn how automotive seats are constructed, how they work, and how to service them. There are various kinds of seats (Figs. 2-27, 2-28, and 29-1). Front seats have an arrangement which permits them to be moved forward or backward. This adjustment is made manually on some seats, by operating a release handle. On others, the adjustment is made electrically, by means of an electric motor. The electrically operated seats can also be raised or lowered. These are four-way seats that can be moved back and forth and up and down. In addition, some models, called six-way seats, have an additional control that changes the tilt of the seat.

◯29-1 Types of Seat

Figure 29-1 shows various kinds of seats used in cars. The various types are discussed below.

1. Front seats. All front seats (Fig. 29-1) except the bucket type are equipped with head restraints. The head restraints can be raised or lowered to suit the person using the seat. The purpose of the head restraints is to prevent neck backlash if the car is hit from the rear. Without a head restraint, when the car is struck from the rear, the head may be snapped back. This can cause severe neck injury from the backlash. With a properly adjusted head restraint, the back of the person's head hits the restraint, which prevents the head from being snapped back so far as to cause a neck injury.

   All bench-type front seats used in two-door cars have hinged backs that enable them to be folded forward as shown in Fig. 2-27, so passengers can get into and out of the rear seat. The hinges have positive locks which prevent folding forward unless the control lever is operated. A typical latch and release mechanism is shown in Fig. 29-2.

   On the full-width bench seats, the bench can be moved forward or backward. This moves both seats together, so there is no individual choice of seat position. On the 60-40, 50-50, and 40-40 seats, the bench is in two parts and each seat can be individually controlled. The "60-40" means the passenger has 60 percent of the front seat width and the driver has 40 percent. The "50-50" means the width is split evenly. The "40-40" means that each seat takes 40 percent of the total width, with the remaining 20 percent being taken up by a console in the center between the two seats.

   Many front seats have reclining backs which can be tilted rearward about 30 degrees, as shown in Fig. 29-3. The back is operated by lifting a lever and pressing back on the seat back. The back then reclines. To restore the back to an upright position, the pressure is released and the lever operated. The spring incorporated in the mechanism then brings the back upright again.

NOTE: Front seat movement is manually controlled in some cars. In other cars, the movement is produced by electric motors, as we explain later.

2. Bucket seats. Bucket seats usually have integral head restraints that are part of the seat and are not adjustable. This type of seat is shown in Fig. 29-3. Bucket seats for two-door cars have hinged backs as for bench-type seats. The backs can be hinged forward to permit passengers to get into or out of the back seat. The exception is the swivel bucket seat, which can be swiveled, or turned, about 90° toward the door openings. This turns the backs out of the way of anyone wanting to get into or out of the back seat. The swivel bucket seat is normally locked in the forward position. Operating a lever releases the lock so the seat can be swiveled.

◯29-2 Seat Construction

The seat and back cushions are of wire construction, padded with fibrous material or foam rubber (Fig. 29-4). The upholstery material is stretched over the padding and secured to the spring and frame with hog rings (Fig. 29-5). These are rings made of heavy wire with sharpened ends. The ends pierce the material and encircle a spring or the frame. Then the ring is pinched closed.

The cushions are shaped to provide comfortable seating and good support for the back. If springs sag, padding crushes down, or the upholstery is stained or damaged, repairs can be made. Cleaning of upholstery is covered later. Reupholstering seats is a specialized business not done in the usual body shop. Soft trim and upholstery usually are handled by local specialty shops.

◯29-3 Manual Seat Tracks

Manual seat tracks allow the front seats to be moved forward or backward when a release lever, or handle, is operated. There is one track on each side of the seat. Figure 29-6 shows the arrangement for a full-bench seat. The arrangement for a split-bench seat is similar. Manually adjusted seats are attached to the floor pan with studs, nuts, and washers. The nuts or screws are removed from inside the vehicle on some cars and from underneath on others. When they are removed, the seat can be taken out of the car and carried to a clean area where it can be worked on.

The track on which the seat rides may be level or may be inclined and also curved. These tracks are shown in

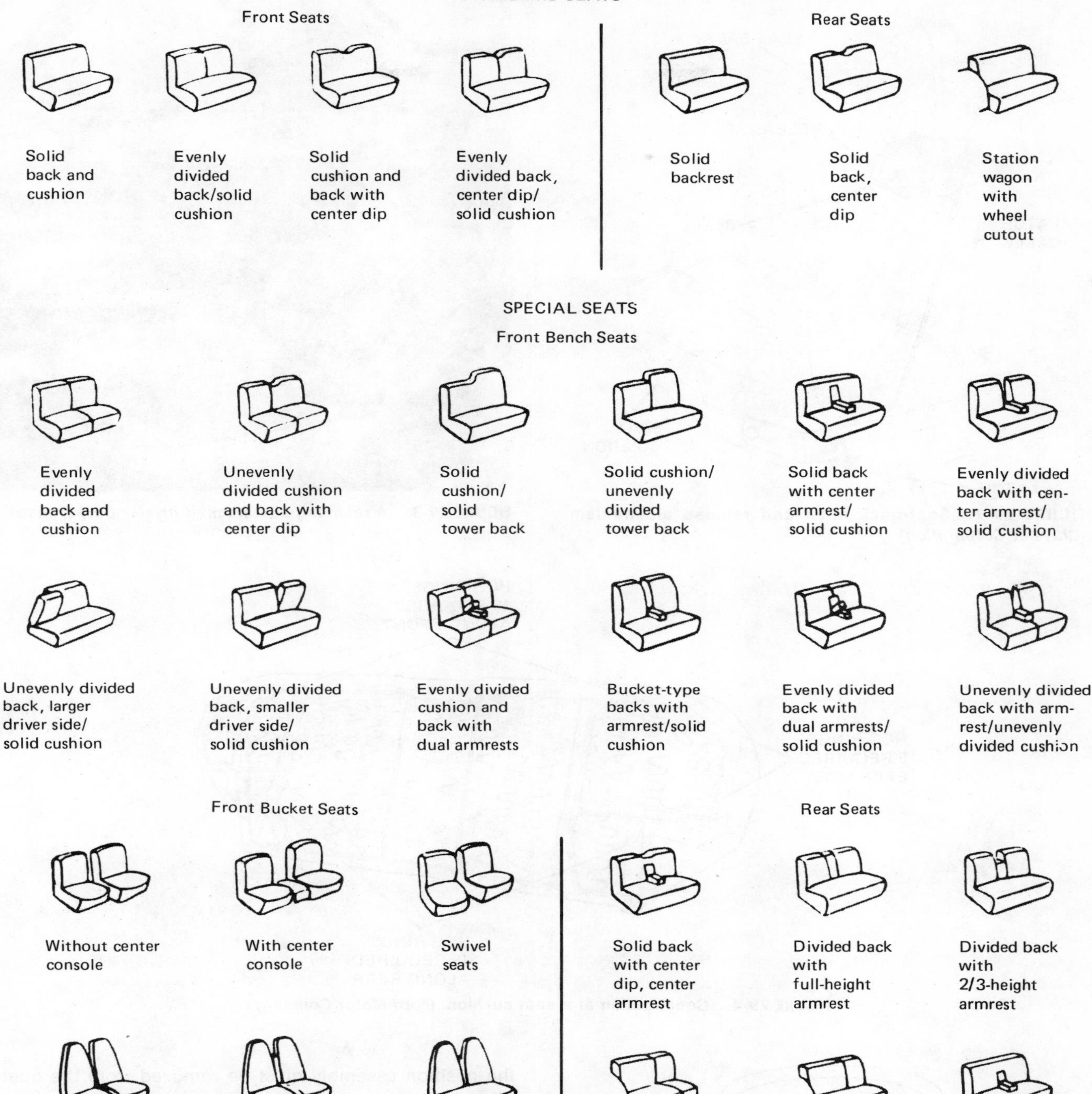

FIGURE 29-1. Types of seats.

Fig. 29-7, along with the seat action that each provides.

Mechanical seat tracks have an adjustment for the release mechanism. This adjustment coordinates the release for the two tracks. The adjustment affects only the track farthest away from the release handle or lever. Figure 29-8 shows one type of adjustment for a full-bench seat. If the right locking lever will not release, tighten the turnbuckle one turn at a time. Test the release each turn, until proper adjustment is reached. If the right side will not lock, loosen the turnbuckle one turn at a time until the proper operation is obtained.

Figure 29-9 shows the adjustment on full-width seats used in many General Motors cars. Use a pick, awl, or small screwdriver to disengage the locking wire from the locking wire retainer, as shown. If the right (passenger side) adjuster does not lock, reposition the locking wire

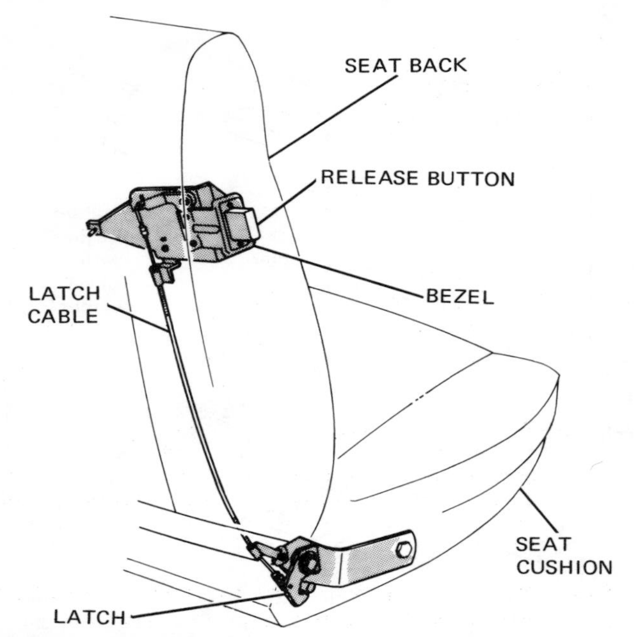

FIGURE 29-2. Seat-back latch and release mechanism. (*Chrysler Corporation*)

FIGURE 29-3. A reclining seat back. (*Chrysler Corporation*)

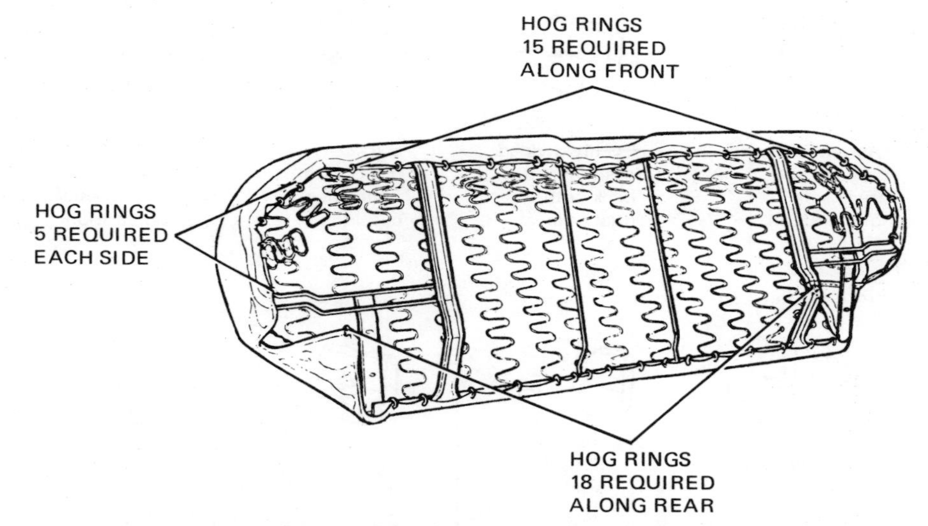

FIGURE 29-4. Construction of a seat cushion. (*Ford Motor Company*)

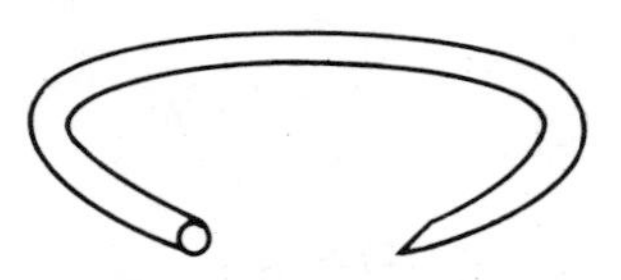

FIGURE 29-5. A hog ring.

coil so as to loosen the tension. If the right adjuster does not unlock, tighten the tension.

If a seat is not level or at the right height, spacers can be added to or removed from under the tracks.

○29-4 Four-way Power Seat

The four-way power seat has two motors, one for moving the seat forward and backward and the other for moving the seat up and down. To get to the track and motors, the cushion assembly must be removed from the operating mechanism and the operating mechanism detached from the floor pan. Figure 29-10 shows the track assembly in exploded view. The assembly is removed from the car in the same way that the manual seat is removed: by taking out the attaching bolts and nuts. There is one additional step, and this is disconnecting the electrical connector to the motors. The actions of the four-way power seat are shown in Fig. 29-11.

○29-5 Six-way Power Seat

The six-way power seat has three motors. One moves the seat forward and backward. The second moves the seat up and down. The third tilts the seat backward and forward. The three motors drive through cables. Figure 29-11 shows the various movements the six-way power seat can provide.

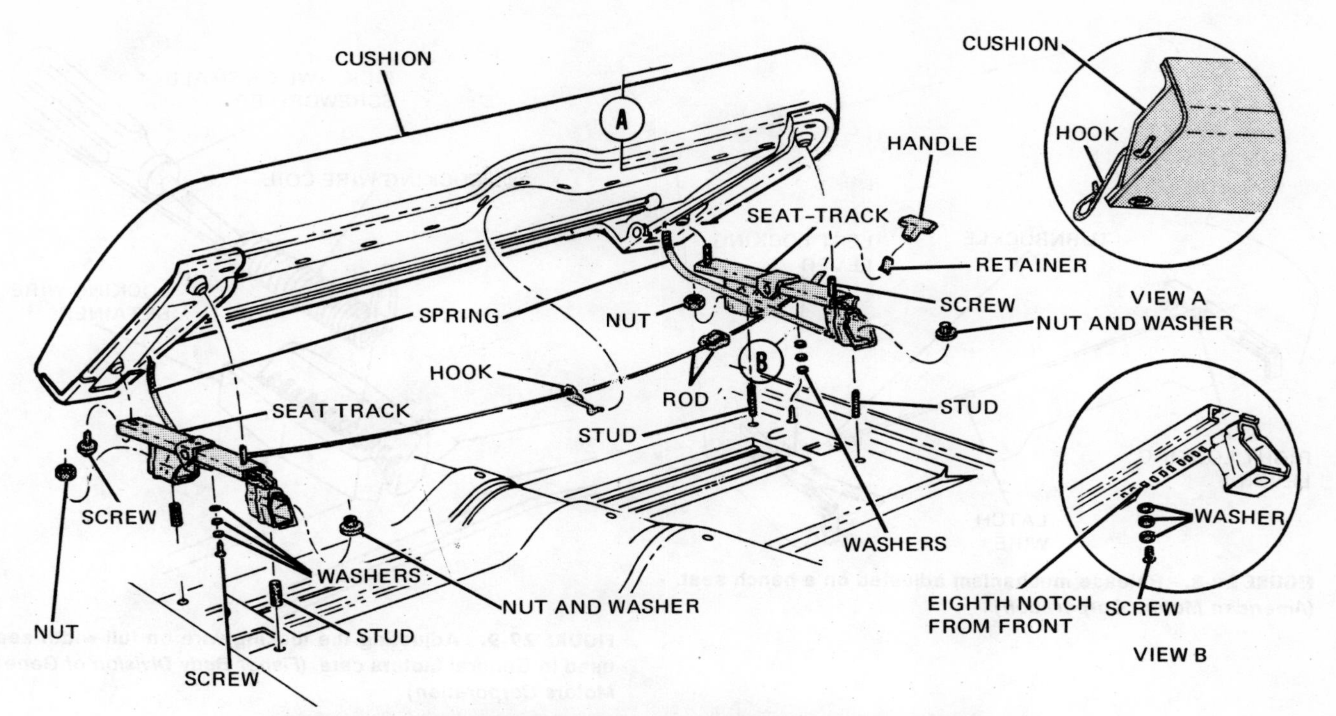

FIGURE 29-6. Manual seat track for a full-bench seat. (*Ford Motor Company*)

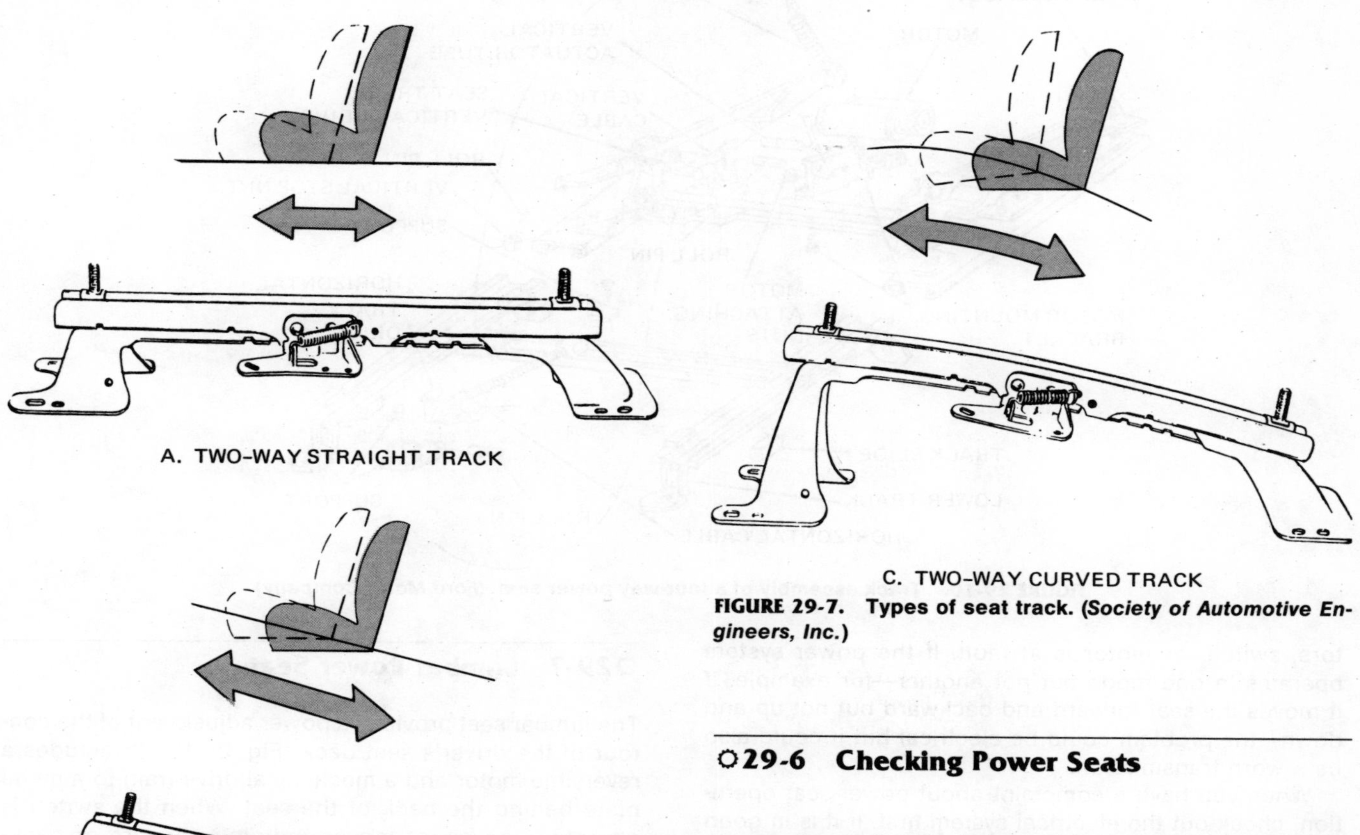

FIGURE 29-7. Types of seat track. (*Society of Automotive Engineers, Inc.*)

○29-6 Checking Power Seats

If a power seat malfunctions, the trouble could be in the electrical switches, wiring, motor, or transmission. In addition, the seat cushion or track could be loose. Also, the carpet or some object under the seat may be interfering with its operation.

The type of trouble should give you some clue as to the cause. For example, if nothing happens when any of the switches is operated, the trouble probably is in the electrical system and either the circuit breaker, connec-

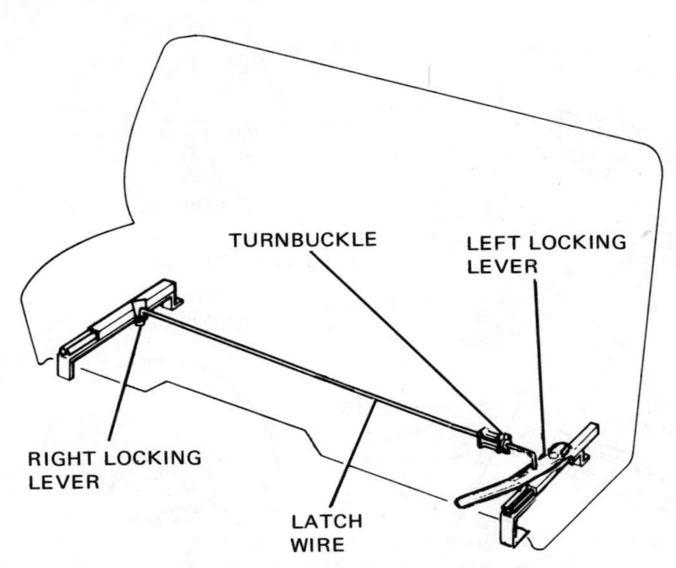

FIGURE 29-8. Release mechanism adjusted on a bench seat. (*American Motors Corporation*)

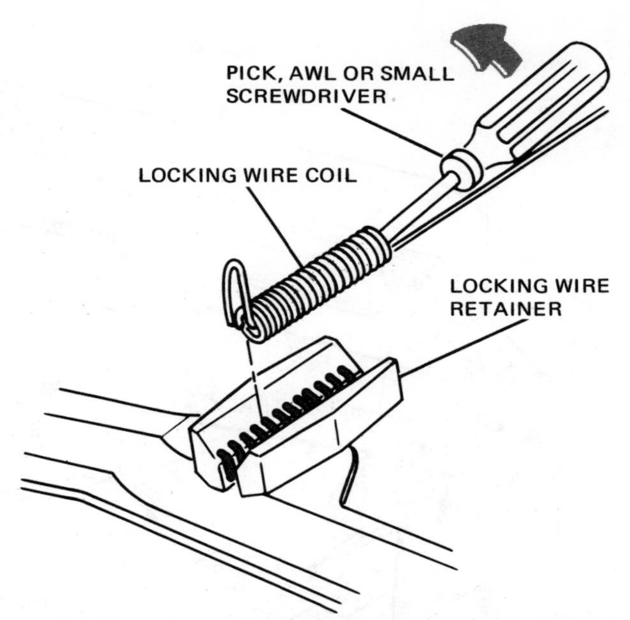

FIGURE 29-9. Adjusting the locking wire on full-width seats used in General Motors cars. (*Fisher Body Division of General Motors Corporation*)

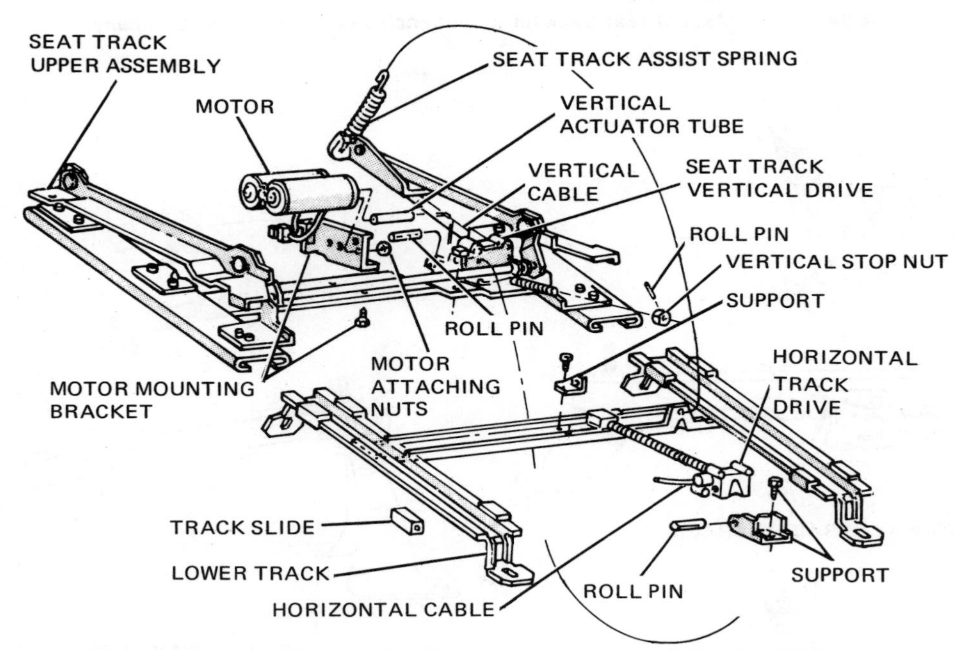

FIGURE 29-10. Track assembly of a four-way power seat. (*Ford Motor Company*)

tors, switch, or motor is at fault. If the power system operates in one mode but not another—for example, if it moves the seat forward and backward but not up and down—the problem could be electrical but it could also be a worn transmission.

When you have a complaint about power-seat operation, check out the electrical system first. If it is in good working order, suspect the transmission, loose drive cables, lack of lubrication, loose attaching bolts or nuts, or missing springs.

Each motor can be checked as follows. Disconnect the motor leads from the circuit. Connect the motor to the battery with jumper wires. The motor should run. Reverse the leads at the motor. It should run in the opposite direction. If the motor runs satisfactorily, check the tracks and drive mechanisms for binding.

○29-7 Lumbar Power Seat

The lumbar seat provides a power adjustment of the contour of the driver's seat back (Fig. 29-12). It includes a reversible motor and a mechanical drive train to a metal plate behind the back of the seat. When the switch is operated, the motor moves the plate forward or backward to change the contour of the back. The range of adjustment is about 2 inches [51 mm].

○29-8 Seat-Back Latch

This is a latch which, when released, permits a front seat to be folded forward so that a passenger can enter the

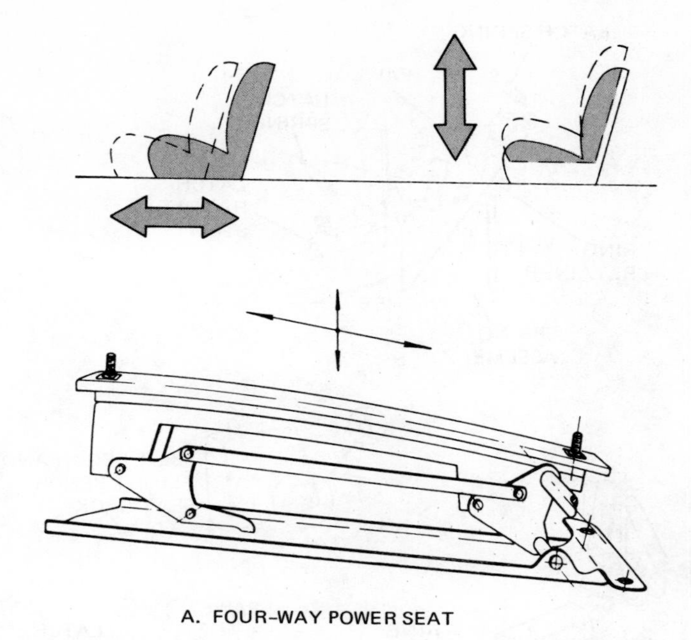

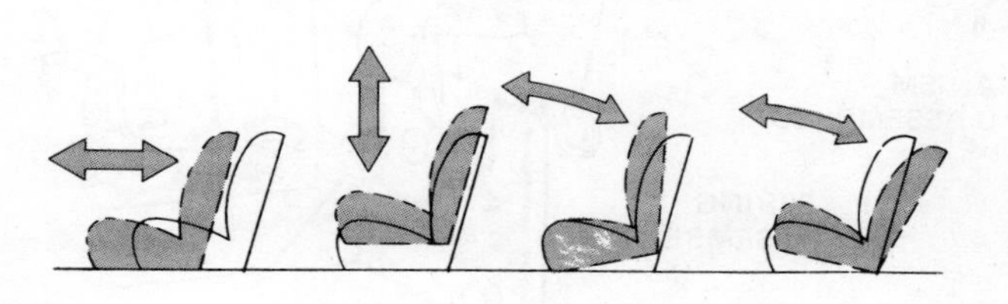

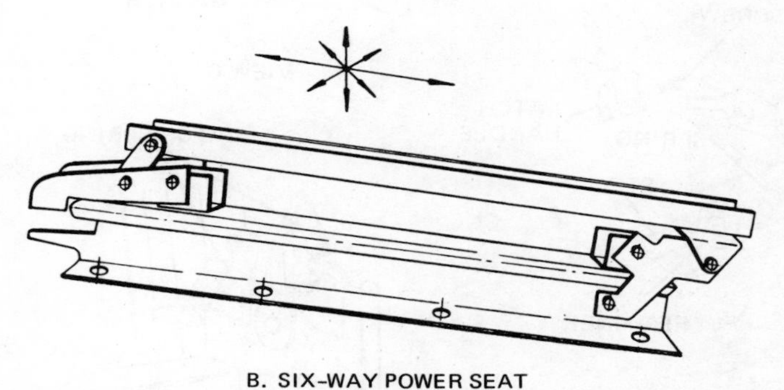

FIGURE 29-11. Actions of the four-way and six-way power seats. (*Society of Automotive Engineers, Inc.*)

rear seat. All two-door cars with rear seats have such a latch on each front seat. Figure 29-13 shows details of various latches used on Ford-built cars. Latches for other cars are similar.

○29-9 Automatic Seat-Back Latch

Some cars are equipped with an arrangement which automatically releases both front-seat-back latches when either front door is opened. There is a switch in each front-door hinge pillar that operates when the door is opened. This connects a relay switch to the battery. The relay switch then closes, connecting two solenoids, one in the back of each seat, to the battery. The solenoids operate the releases so the latches are released and the seats can be folded forward. Figure 29-14 shows the arrangements for Ford and Mercury two-door cars.

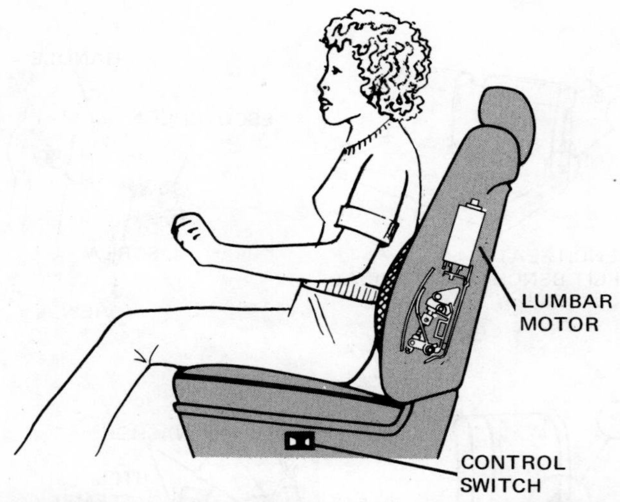

FIGURE 29-12. A power lumbar seat. The cross-hatched area of the cushion shows the amount of movement. (*Ford Motor Company*)

○29-10 Reclining Seat Back

Some cars have passenger-side seats with reclining backs. That is, the backs can be tilted backward. Figure 29-15 shows the arrangement used in some cars. Some models have a mechanical release lever. To operate it, turn the release handle and push back on the seat to get the desired tilt. Then release the lever, and the seat back will lock in that position. Some cars are equipped with an electric motor which drives a tilt-back mechanism. When the switch is closed in the one direction, the motor runs in one direction, driving a screw that causes the seat back to move backward. When the switch is closed in the other direction, the motor runs in the opposite direction, bringing the seat back upward toward an upright position.

○29-11 Head Restraints

Head restraints are positioned back of the heads of the driver and passenger in the front seat. They consist of a pad set on one or two posts (Fig. 29-16). The pad should be adjusted in height so that it would center on the head of the driver or passenger. In case of a rear-end crash, the head restraint allows only a limited backward movement of the head. This prevents neck backlash, a severe injury resulting from an unrestrained backward snapping of the head.

Some head restraints have a friction spring that allows the restraint to be moved up or down to the desired position. The spring holds the restraint in that position. It prevents the head restraint from being completely removed, however, without the use of a special tool to unlock the spring.

○29-12 Rear Seats

In standard passenger cars, the rear seats are fixed. However, in station wagons and similar vehicles, the rear seat can fold down to provide additional space for hauling. Figure 29-17 shows typical rear-seat arrangements. In the

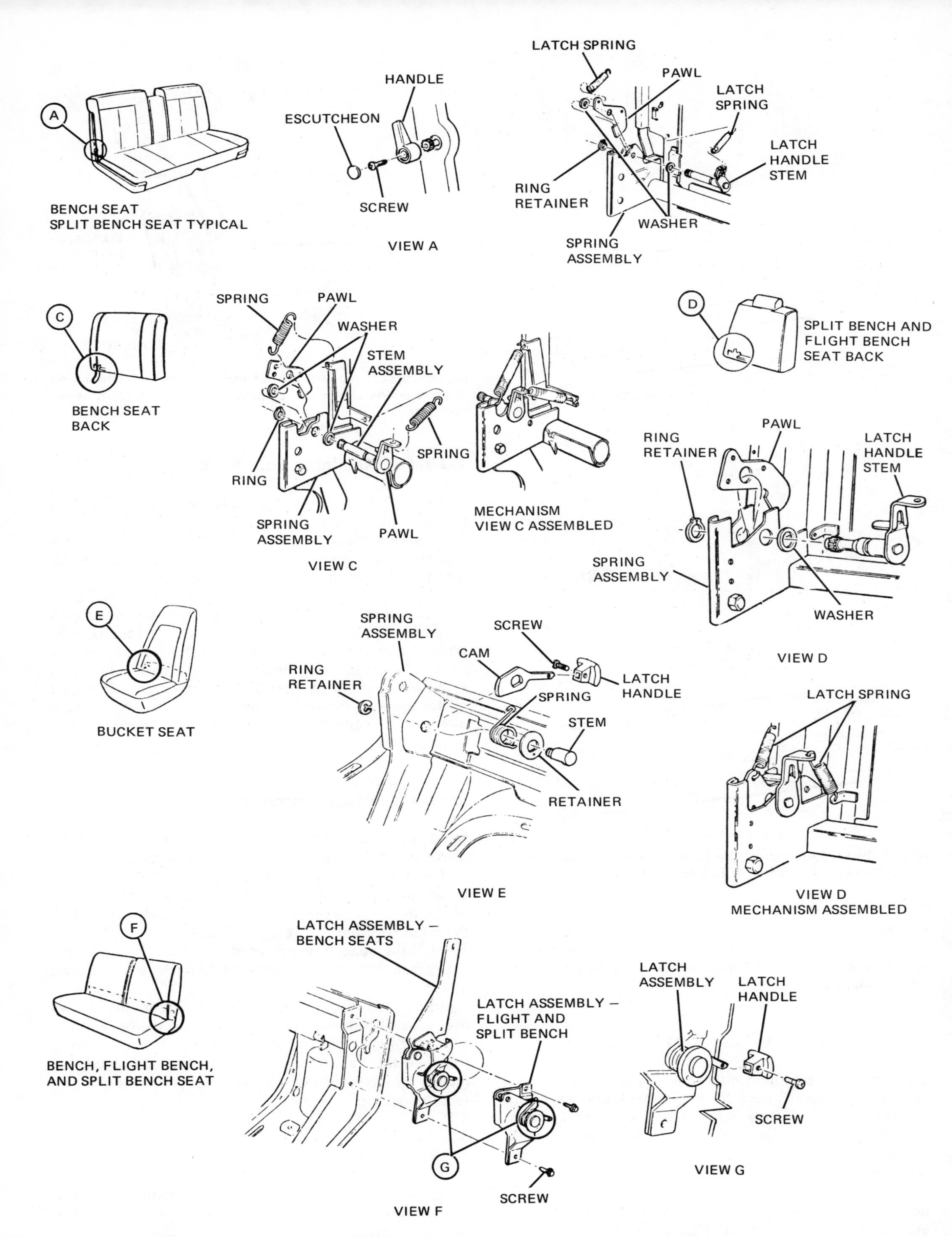

FIGURE 29-13. Various types of seat-back latches. ***(Ford Motor Company)***

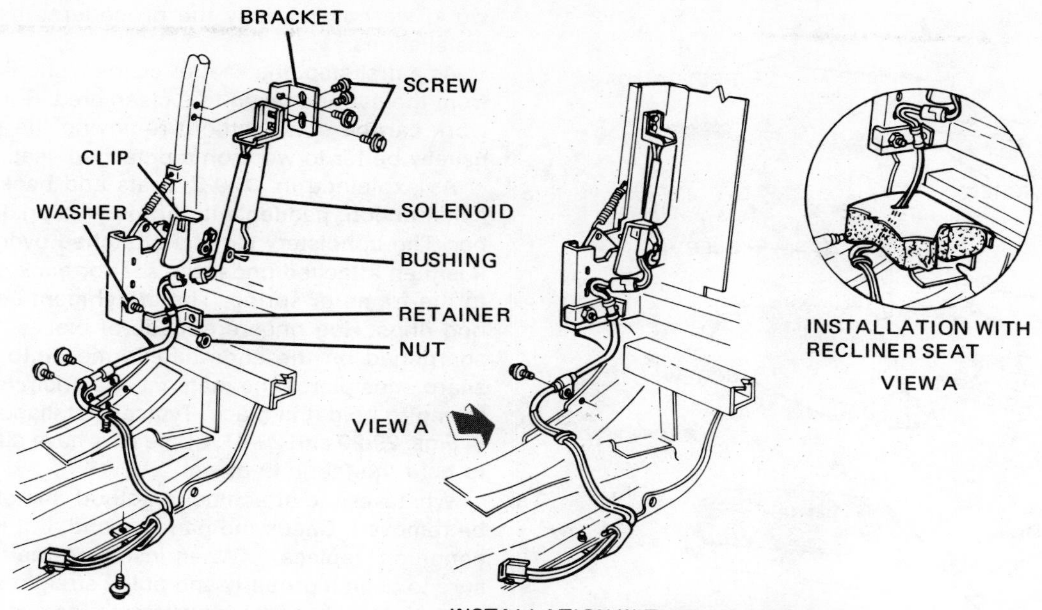

FIGURE 29-14. Automatic seat-back latch mechanism. (*Ford Motor Company*)

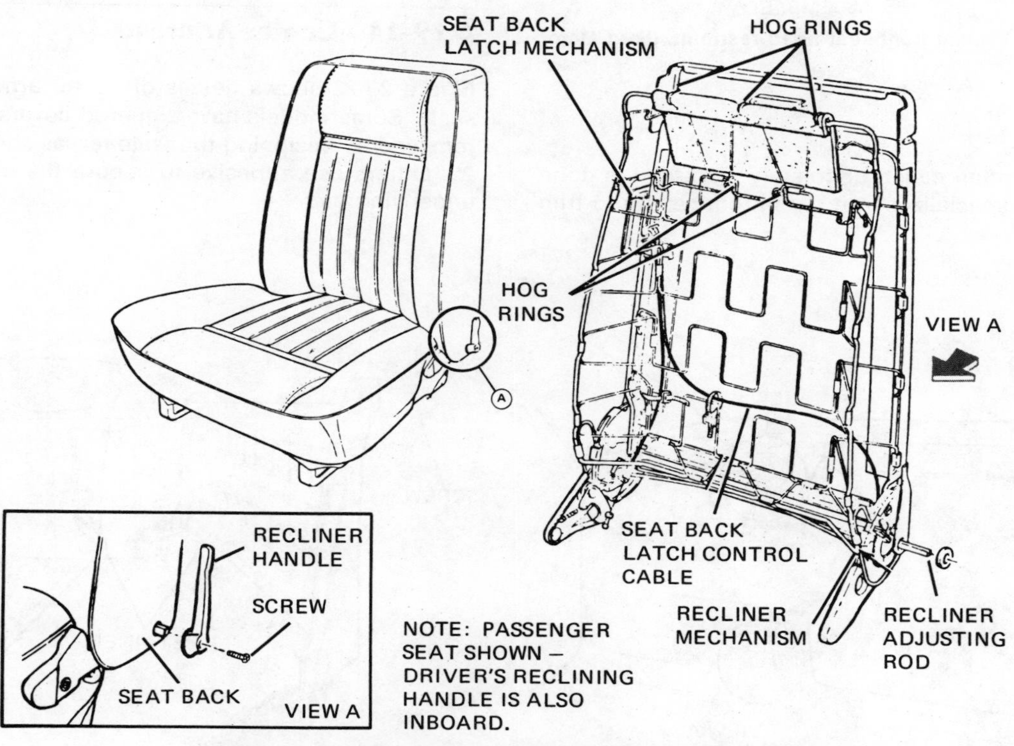

FIGURE 29-15. Reclining seat back. (*Ford Motor Company*)

type shown, the seat can be removed by applying knee pressure to the rear of the seat cushion. This unlocks the cushion so it can be removed. Then, to take off the back, remove the attaching screws at the bottom brackets and lift the back up to disengage the wire hangers.

Many station wagons have fold-down rear seats. Figure 29-18 shows an arrangement which includes a folding second seat and filler panel, as well as a folding third seat and panel. The panels are used to level the floor so that the load to be carried can be slid into place and removed with greater ease. Another arrangement is shown in Fig. 29-19. Two panels can be raised here to uncover a stowage compartment that is beneath the floor of the station wagon. Several other arrangements have been used to utilize the rear of the station wagon in various ways.

○29-13 Seat Trim

Seat trim includes the leather, fabric, or plastic covering the padding. Not all shops handle replacement of this

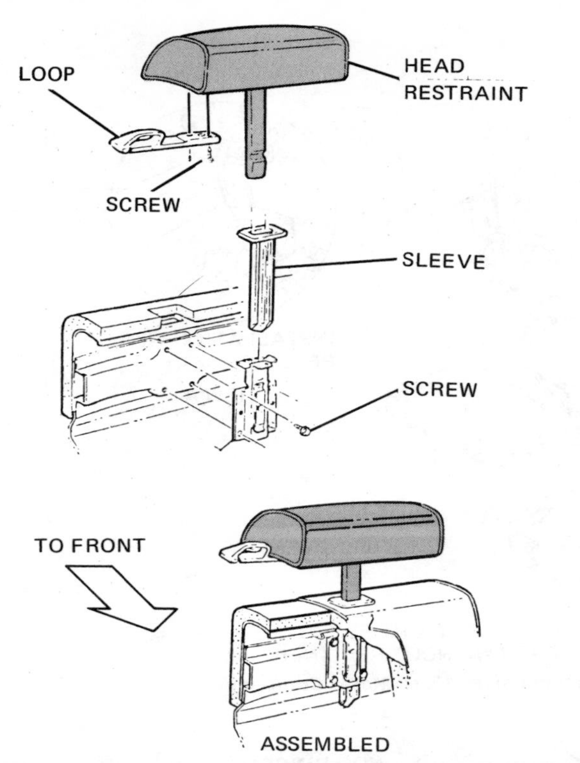

FIGURE 29-16. Typical front-seat head restraint. (*Ford Motor Company*)

covering. It is often called upholstery work and is done in a shop that specializes in it. To introduce you to trim work, we cover briefly the procedures used in typical installations.

As a first step, the seat or cushion should be removed from the car and taken to a clean area. Some upholstery work can be done without removing the seat, but it is usually better to work on a detached seat.

As explained in ○29-2, seats and backs are of wire construction, padded with fibrous material or foam rubber. The upholstery cloth is stretched over the padding. It is then attached under the seat or back of the cushion to the frame or spring. The attachment uses wires and hog rings. Hog rings are made of pieces of heavy wire, sharpened on the ends and formed into a circle. The sharp ends pierce the material and encircle the frame or spring to hold it in place. Typical installations are shown in Figs. 29-20 and 29-21. Some cars have plastic retainers to hold the fabric in place.

Whatever the attachment method, the old cover must be removed. Check the padding and, if it is not in good condition, replace it. When installing the new cover, be sure to align it properly and pull it straight so that it does not wrinkle. On some installations, cementing the fabric to the padding is recommended in order to do a neat job.

○29-14 Center Armrests

Figure 29-22 shows details of center armrests for front seats. Some models have zippered covers which can be removed by unzipping the fastener, as shown in Fig. 29-22. Others use adhesive to secure the covering to the underlying pad.

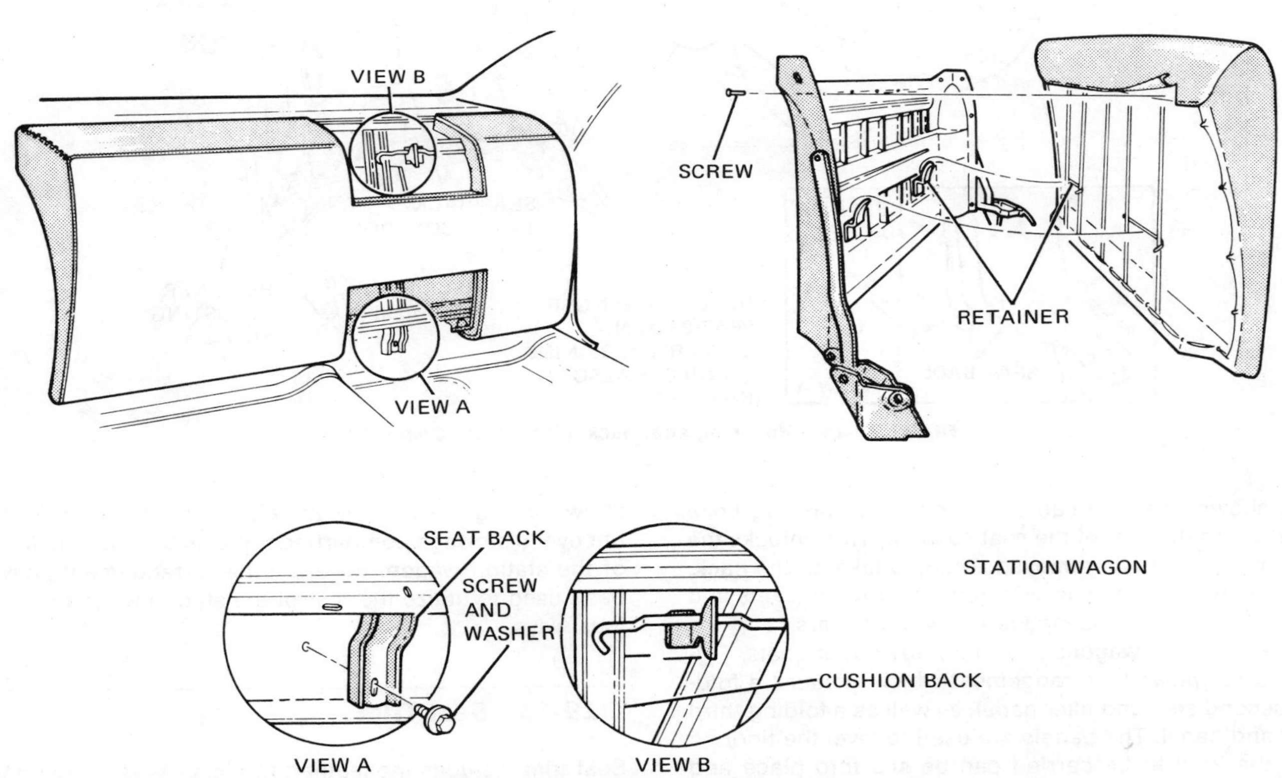

FIGURE 29-17. Removing a conventional rear seat. (*Ford Motor Company*)

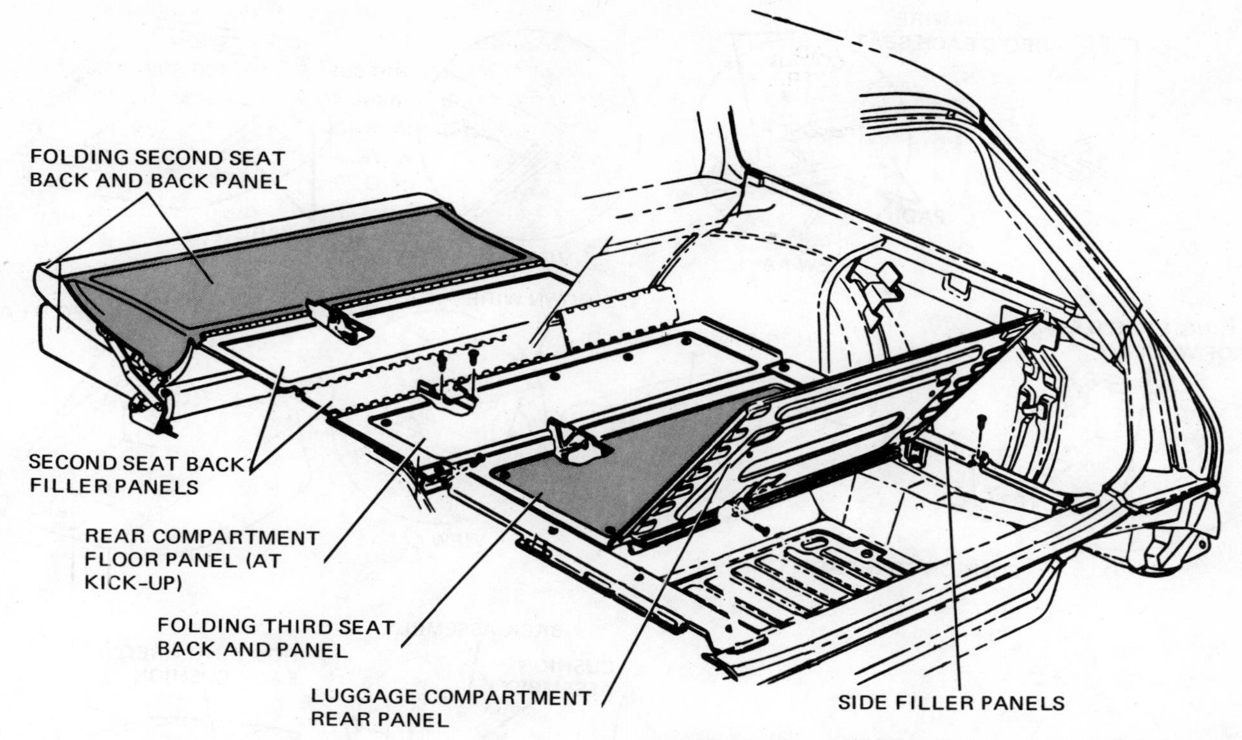

FIGURE 29-18. Folding seats and load panels in a three-seat station wagon. (*Fisher Body Division of General Motors Corporation*)

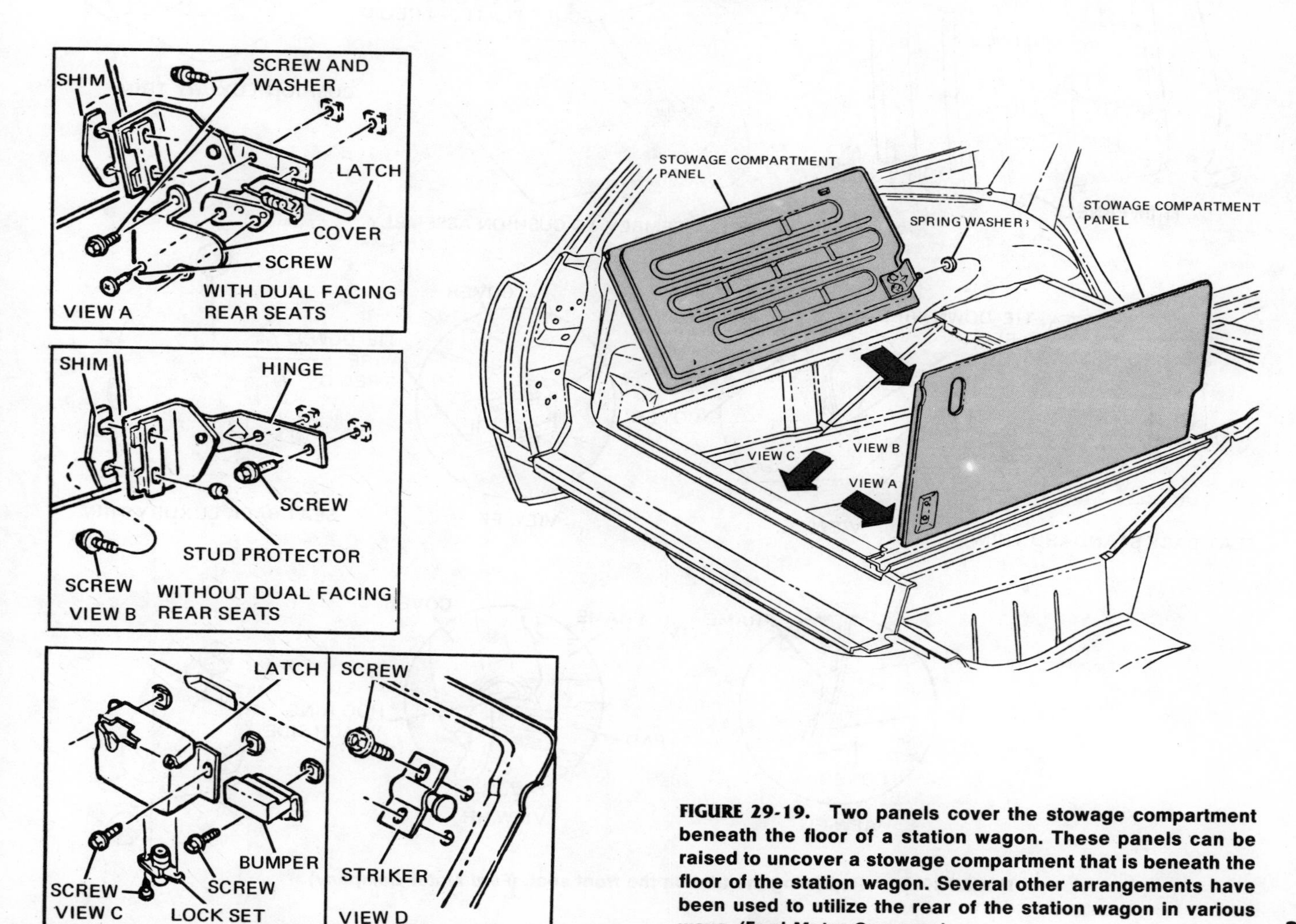

FIGURE 29-19. Two panels cover the stowage compartment beneath the floor of a station wagon. These panels can be raised to uncover a stowage compartment that is beneath the floor of the station wagon. Several other arrangements have been used to utilize the rear of the station wagon in various ways. (*Ford Motor Company*)

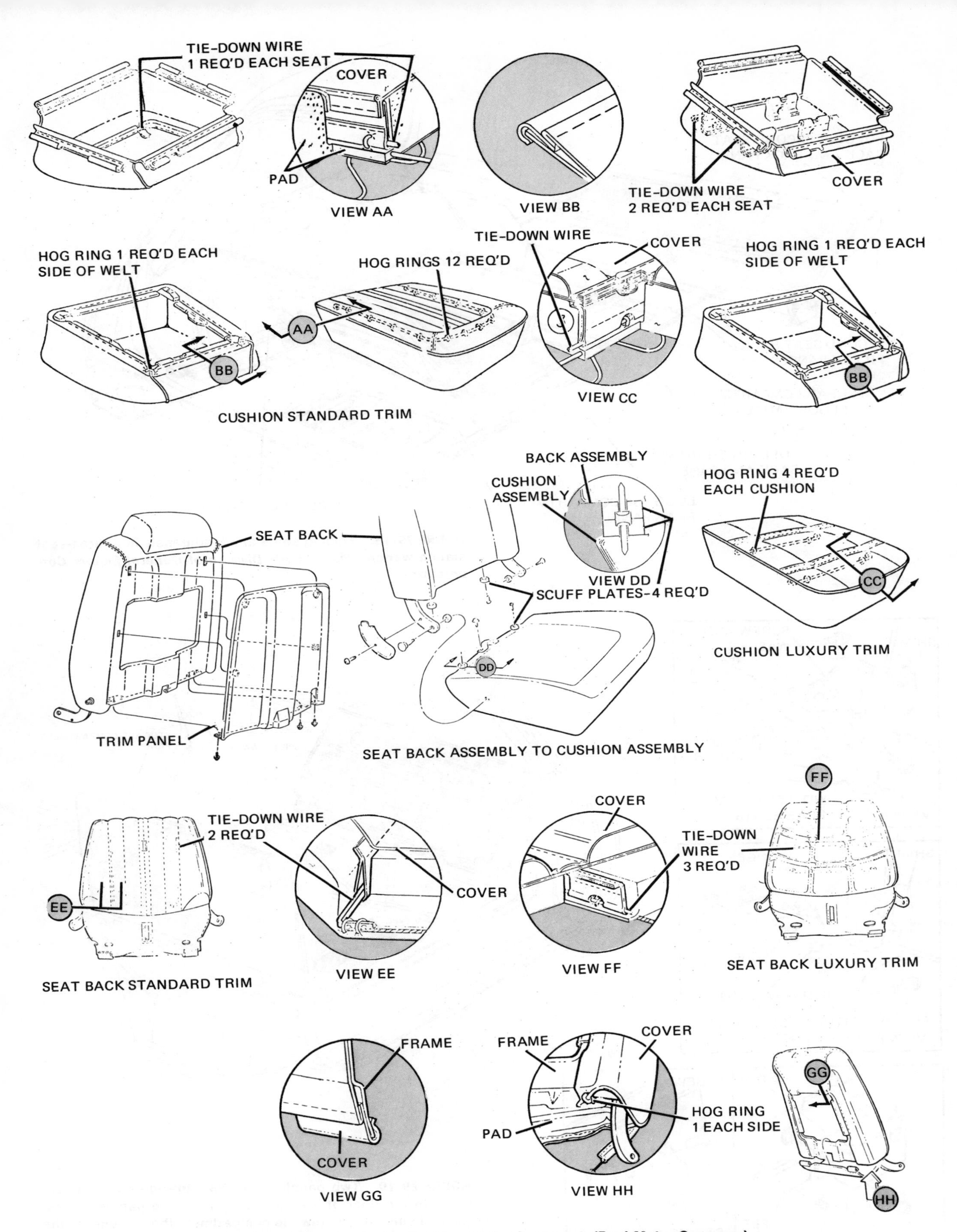

FIGURE 29-20. Replacing the trim on the front seat. (*Ford Motor Company*)

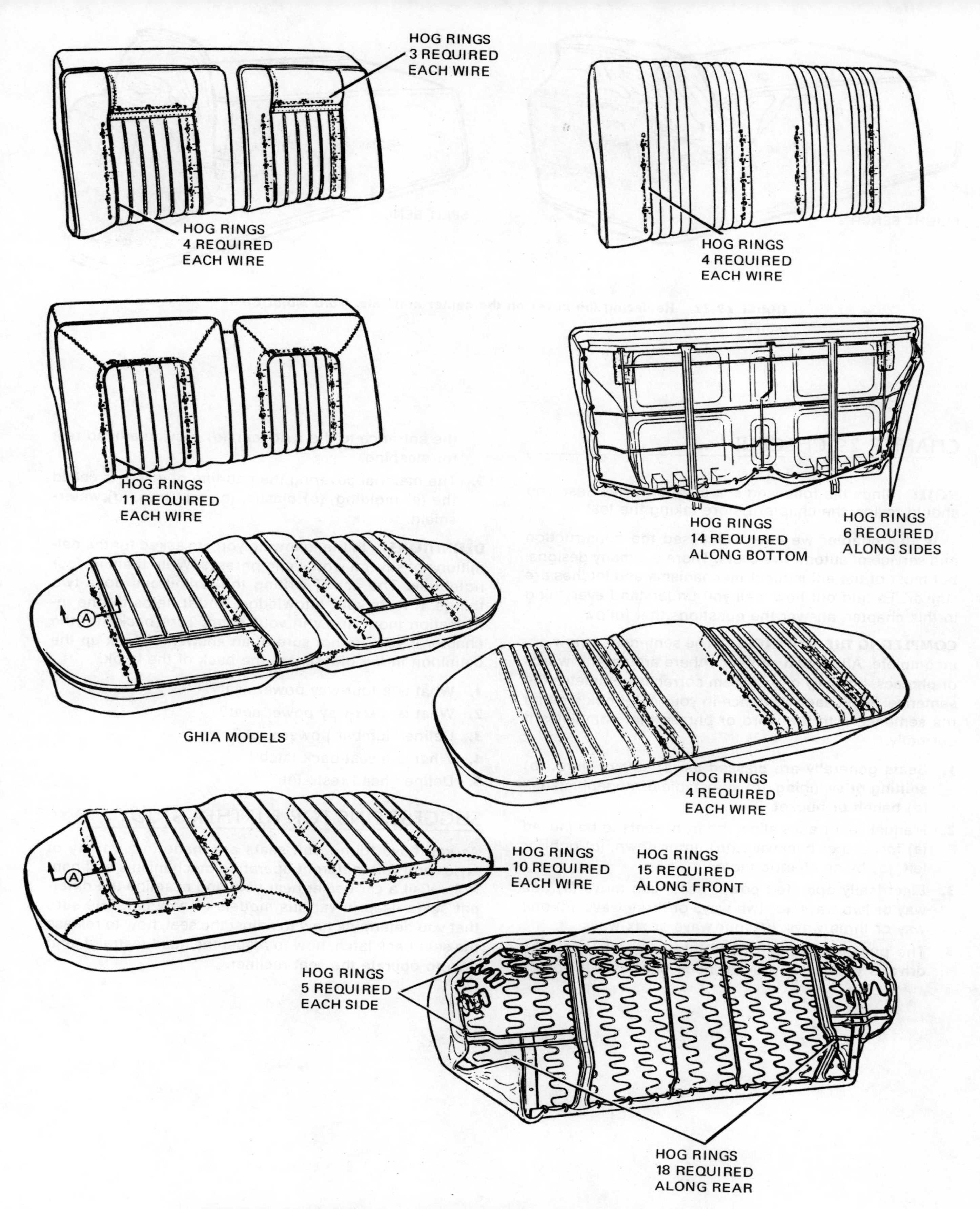

FIGURE 29-21. Installing new cover on the rear seat cushion and seat back. ***(Ford Motor Company)***

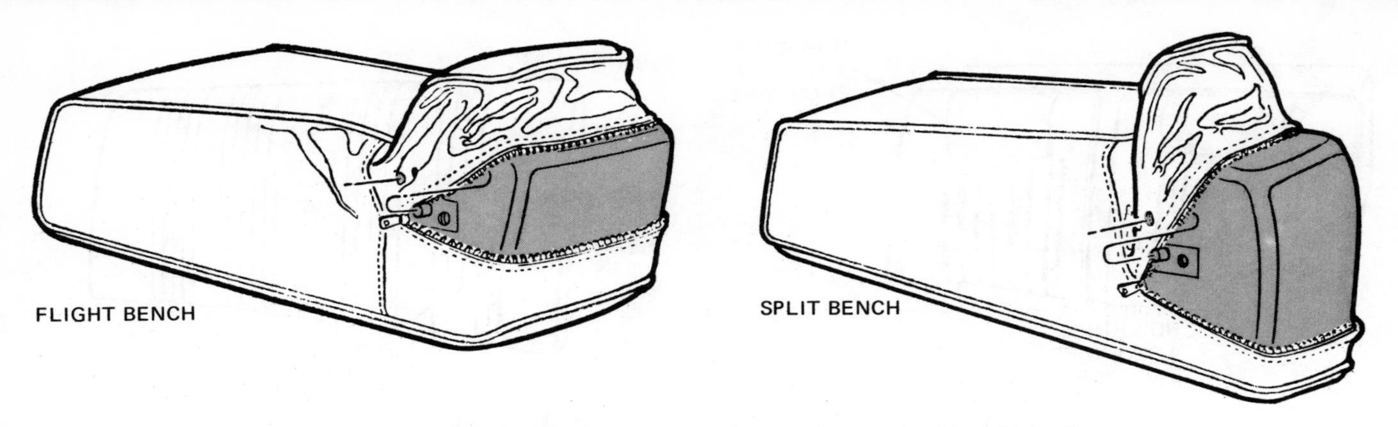

FIGURE 29-22. **Replacing the cover on the center armrests. (*Ford Motor Company*)**

CHAPTER 29 CHECKUP

NOTE: Since the following is a chapter review test, you should review the chapter before taking the test.

In this chapter we have discussed the construction and service of automotive seats. There are many designs, but most of the adjustment mechanisms and latches are similar. To find out how well you understand everything in this chapter, answer the questions that follow.

COMPLETING THE SENTENCES The sentences below are incomplete. After each sentence there are several words or phrases, but only one of them correctly completes the sentence. Write each sentence in your notebook, ending the sentence with the word or phrase that completes it correctly.

1. Seats generally are classed as (*a*) soft or hard, (*b*) shifting or swinging, (*c*) adjustable or nonadjustable, (*d*) bench or bucket.
2. Manual seat tracks allow the front seats to be moved (*a*) forward or backward, (*b*) up or down, (*c*) right or left, (*d*) by an electric motor.
3. Electrically operated power seats can move (*a*) one way or two ways, (*b*) two ways or three ways, (*c*) one way or three ways, (*d*) four ways or six ways.
4. The purpose of head restraints is to (*a*) block the driver's vision, (*b*) prevent neck backlash, (*c*) block the entrance to the rear seat, (*d*) provide a head rest for sleeping.
5. The material covering the padding of a seat is called the (*a*) molding, (*b*) plastic, (*c*) seat trim, (*d*) watershield.

DEFINITIONS In the following you are asked for the definitions of several words and phrases. Write them in your notebook. The act of writing the definitions does two things. It tests your knowledge, and it helps fix the information more firmly in your mind. Turn back into the chapter if you are not sure of an answer, or look up the definition in the glossary at the back of the book.

1. What is a four-way power seat?
2. What is a six-way power seat?
3. Define "lumbar power seat."
4. What is a seat-back latch?
5. Define "head restraint."

SUGGESTIONS FOR FURTHER STUDY

As you have found out, seats are made in a variety of styles and with different operating mechanisms and controls. Visit a car dealer near you, and examine the different seats used in various models of new cars. Be sure that you determine how to adjust the seat, how to release the seat-back latch, how to adjust the head restraint, and how to operate the seat recliner.

30
INTERIOR TRIM

In this chapter, you will learn how to service and care for interior trim. Interior trim includes seat covering (discussed in Chapter 29), quarter trim panels, trim panels on doors and front-seat backs, headliner, and carpet. It also includes interior molding. The removal and installation of door trim panels have already been discussed in Chapter 25. In this chapter, we discuss the servicing of the other interior trim.

○30-1 Quarter Trim Panel

This panel is shaped to fit over the quarter panel interior. Figure 30-1 shows a typical installation of a quarter trim panel.

To remove a quarter trim panel, first take out the rear seat cushion and seat back. Remove the window-regulator handle, if present. Then remove any screws, garnish molding retaining screws, and the door-sill step-plate rear screw. Then unclip the trim panel retaining clips and pull the trim panel from the quarter panel. Disconnect the power-window switch wires (if present). To reinstall the trim panel, reverse the procedure.

○30-2 Quarter Upper Trim Panel

This type of trim panel (Fig. 30-2) covers the upper quarter-panel area and includes the opening for any quarter or opera window. As you can see in Fig. 30-2, the quarter upper trim is attached by clips and screws in a manner similar to that used to attach the lower quarter trim panel. General Motors calls this panel the quarter upper trim. Ford calls it the roof side trim panel. The panel is removed and replaced in the same way as the quarter trim panel.

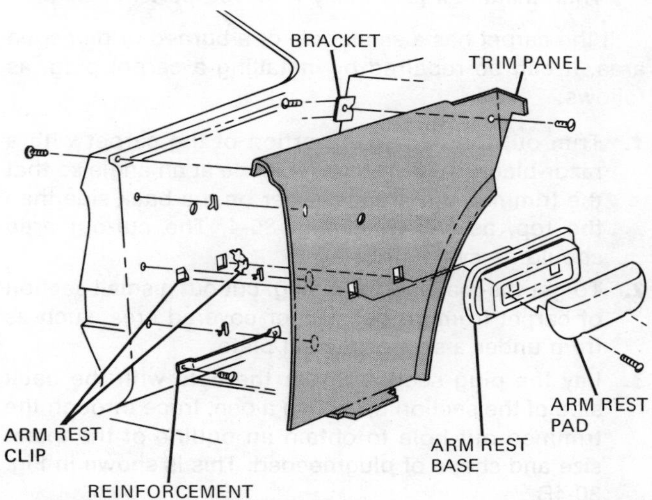

FIGURE 30-1. Typical installation of a quarter trim panel. ***(Ford Motor Company)***

○30-3 Floor-Pan Insulators

Floor-pan insulators are required on many cars owing to the use of catalytic converters in the exhaust system. Catalytic converters produce considerable heat, requiring some form of insulation in between the floor pan and the carpet. Figure 30-3 shows the typical installation of insulation in various cars produced by General Motors. Materials used for insulators include aluminum silica, resinated fiber, and fiberglass.

NOTE: When doing any carpet work or repairing any vehicle that has been damaged in an accident, any insulator that has been damaged or removed must be reinstalled. The proper material must be used, and it must be installed in the correct position.

Here are special points to observe when replacing a floor-pan insulator:

Use the original insulator as a template for cutting out the new insulator. The new material must be the type specified for that location in the vehicle. The new insulator must have the same shape as the old, and it must be installed in the same position. Do not enlarge any holes or cutouts in the insulator.

Electrical harness must be routed over the insulators, not under them. Do not use spray-on sound deadeners and trim adhesives on the floor pan in any area that is directly over the catalytic converter or muffler.

○30-4 Carpet

The floor carpet for some cars comes in two pieces, one for the front and one for the rear. Other cars have a one-piece carpet molded to fit over any irregularities, such as the drive-line channel in the floor pan. To remove the old one-piece carpet and install a new carpet, everything in the way must be removed. This includes seats, console (if supplied), and seat belts. Also, the door-sill scuff plates will require removal. Two-piece carpets usually have cutouts that allow them to be removed and installed with the seats in place.

Some floors are covered with heavy rubber floor mats. These are replaced like sections of floor carpet. Another type of floor covering is carpet, with rubber mats in the heavy wear areas.

Carpet with small cuts, tears, burns, or other minor damage often can be repaired by patching. This usually can be done without removing the carpet from the vehicle.

When the carpet has a straight cut or tear, it can be repaired without additional trimming around the damaged area. Here is the procedure to follow:

1. Remove all parts required to gain access to the back side of the carpet at the area to be repaired.

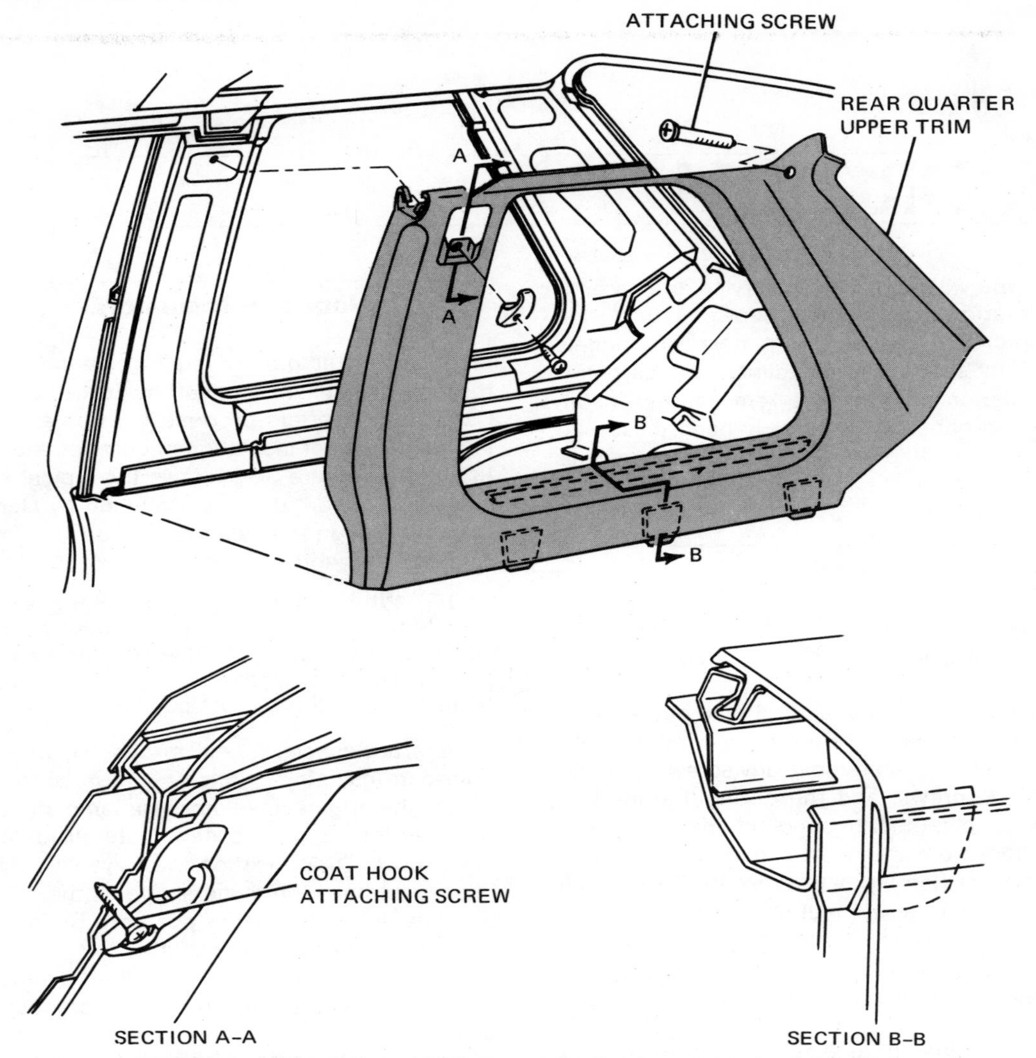

FIGURE 30-2. The quarter upper trim includes the opening for any quarter or opera window. (*Fisher Body Division of General Motors Corporation*)

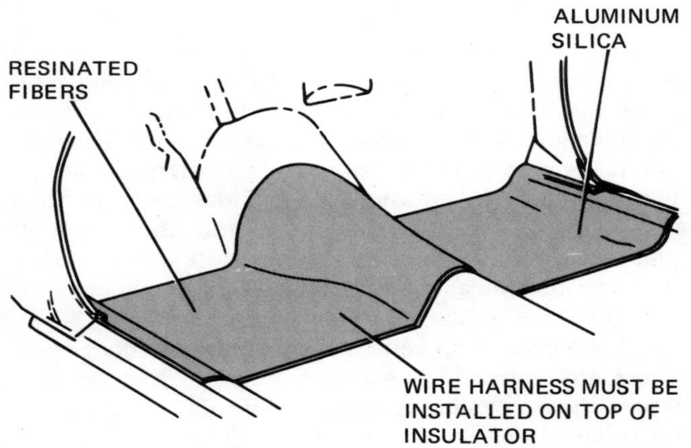

FIGURE 30-3. Front floor-pan insulator. (*Fisher Body Division of General Motors Corporation*)

2. With the carpet supported from the front side, apply fast-tack adhesive to the back side of the carpet over the cut or torn area.
3. Place a piece of waterproof cloth-back tape over the cut or torn area. Heat the tape with a heat gun until the tape begins to soften. Then, while the repair area and tape are still warm, press the tape firmly in place with a flat tool. This will fuse the carpet backing to the tape.
4. Allow the repaired area to cool for about 5 minutes. Then install all previously removed parts.

If the carpet has a small hole or a burned or damaged area, it can be repaired by installing a carpet plug, as follows:

1. Trim out the damaged portion of the carpet with a razor-blade knife. The cut is made at an angle so that the trimmed-out area is larger on the back side than the top, as shown in Fig. 30-4. The cut-out area should be symmetrical.
2. To get the material for a plug, cut out a small section of carpet from an obscure or covered area, such as from under a seat or the sill plate.
3. Lay the plug section under the hole with the back side of the section up. Using a pen, trace through the trimmed out hole to obtain an outline of the exact size and shape of plug needed. This is shown in Fig. 30-4B.
4. Cut out the new plug to the exact size by following the line you marked on it.

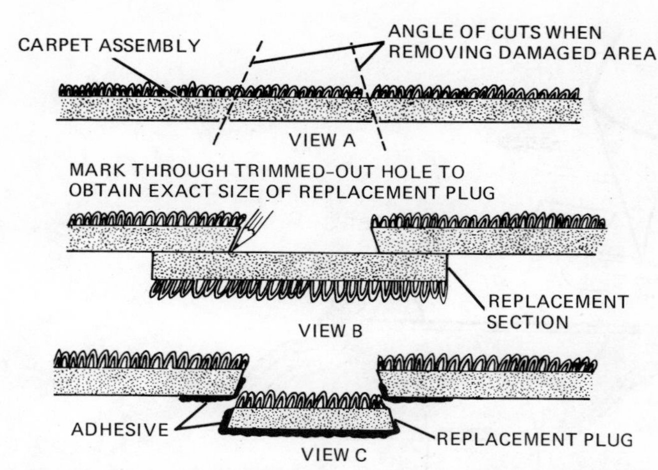

FIGURE 30-4. Repairing small damage to the carpet by installing a plug. (*Cadillac Motor Car Division of General Motors Corporation*)

5. Brush pile on both the carpet and plug to match the direction of pile.
6. Coat the back side of the carpet and the plug with fast-tack adhesive around the repair area, as shown in Fig. 30-4C. Place the plug into the trimmed-out hole. Tape it in place with waterproof cloth-back tape. Heat the tape with a heat gun until the tape begins to soften. Then, while the repaired area and tape are still warm, press the carpet firmly in place with a flat tool. This fuses the carpet backing to the tape.
7. Work carpet pile so that the plug blends into the adjacent carpet. Allow the repaired area to cool for about 5 minutes.
8. Then reinstall all previously removed parts.

○30-5 Floor Console

The console is attached to floor brackets with screws as shown in Fig. 30-5. To remove a console, take out the screws, disconnect any wiring, and the console is free.

○30-6 Sun Visor

The sun visor is attached by screws, as shown in Fig. 30-6, to roof brackets. Note how the center clip is attached to a bracket at the roof. Some sun visors have vanity mirrors, as shown in Fig. 30-6, and others have lighted vanity mirrors.

○30-7 Headlining Types

Headlining is of two types: soft (cloth and vinyl-coated) and formed (molded). Typical installation procedures for the two are described in following sections. First, we describe the methods of attachment of the two types.

1. Soft (cloth or vinyl-coated) headlining. This headlining assembly is attached to the roof inner panel by concealed plastic retaining strips. The retaining strips are sewed to the headlining assembly and contain rectangular lugs that fit into T slots in the roof inner panel (Fig. 30-7). In addition, the headlining is cemented into place along the sides. Garnish molding or finishing lace also helps to hold the headlining in place. Garnish molding along the side roof rail is secured to a headlining retainer or to the side roof rail by clips located in the molding.

   When finishing lace is used at the windshield and back window or rear body opening, the headlining is secured at these places with nonstaining adhesive.

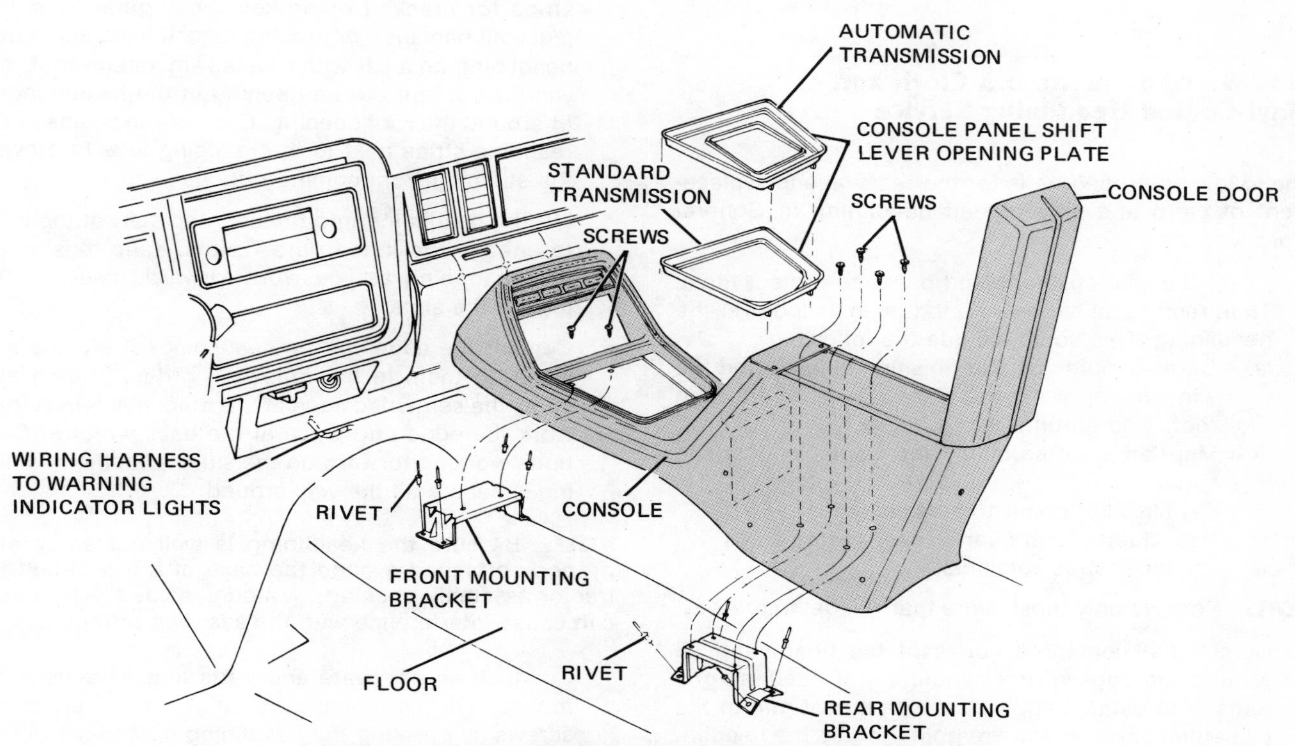

FIGURE 30-5. Floor console installation. (*Ford Motor Company*)

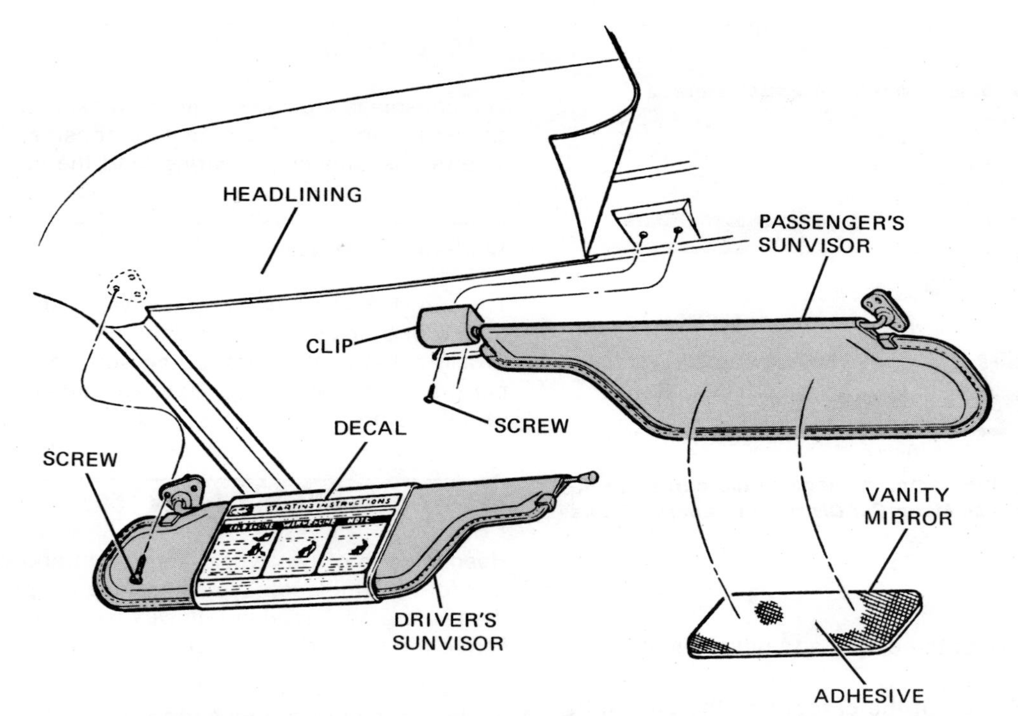

FIGURE 30-6. Mounting of sun visors above the front seat. (*Ford Motor Company*)

Removal and replacement of the cloth or vinyl headlining is covered in Sections 30-8 and 30-9.

2. Molded or formed headlining. This headlining is made of molded hardboard covered with foam and cloth or vinyl facing. It may be of either the one-piece type or the two-piece type. Formed headlining is used in station wagons and utility vehicles. Removal and replacement of the formed headlining is covered in ◯30-10.

◯30-8 General Motors Cloth and Vinyl-Coated Headlining Service

The following procedure is for the removal and replacement of cloth and vinyl-coated headlining in General Motors cars:

1. Cover the seat cushions and backs to protect them. Then remove all hardware and trim installed over the headlining. This could include the following:
   a. Garnish moldings and finishing lace around the windshield, along the sides, at vista vent (sun roof), and around back window.
   b. Map lamp, dome lamp, and visor or sunshade supports.
   c. Center pillar upper trim assembly.
   d. Rear quarter and quarter upper trim panels.
   e. Shoulder strap retainers.

NOTE: Remove only those parts that will get in the way.

2. Detach the cemented edges of the headlining all around the edge of the headlining. If headlining is difficult to detach, apply heat with a heat gun to the cemented areas. If you are going to use the headlining again, use care to avoid tearing it. Also, gather or fold the assembly with retaining strips on the outside of the material to keep the headlining from getting dirty.
3. Start at the front and carefully detach the retaining strips by pulling toward the rear to detach the rectangular lugs from the T slots in the inner roof (Fig. 30-7). Fold the headlining as you detach it.
4. Before installing the headlining, check the retaining strips for cracked or broken rectangular lugs. Replace all damaged or missing lugs. If installing a new headlining on a car with a vista vent, or sun roof, you will have to cut out an opening in the headlining to fit around the roof opening. Cement the seams at the retaining strips next to the retaining lugs to prevent the stitching from coming out.
5. Lift the headlining into the car, and start at the back to engage the lugs in the T slots. Keep tension on the headlining as you work forward, inserting the lugs in the slots.
6. Cement the edges of the headlining, stretching and securing them in the following order: Stretch and apply the cemented edge at the windshield first. Then work the edge into place at the back window. Continue working forward on the sides until the headlining is secure all the way around.

NOTE: Be sure the headlining is well cemented and properly attached around the base of the seat-belt retractor assembly openings. Material inside the trim area can cause interference with the seat-belt retractor.

7. Reattach all hardware and parts that have been removed. You can locate the holes for the attaching screws by pressing the headlining up against the inner roof panel.

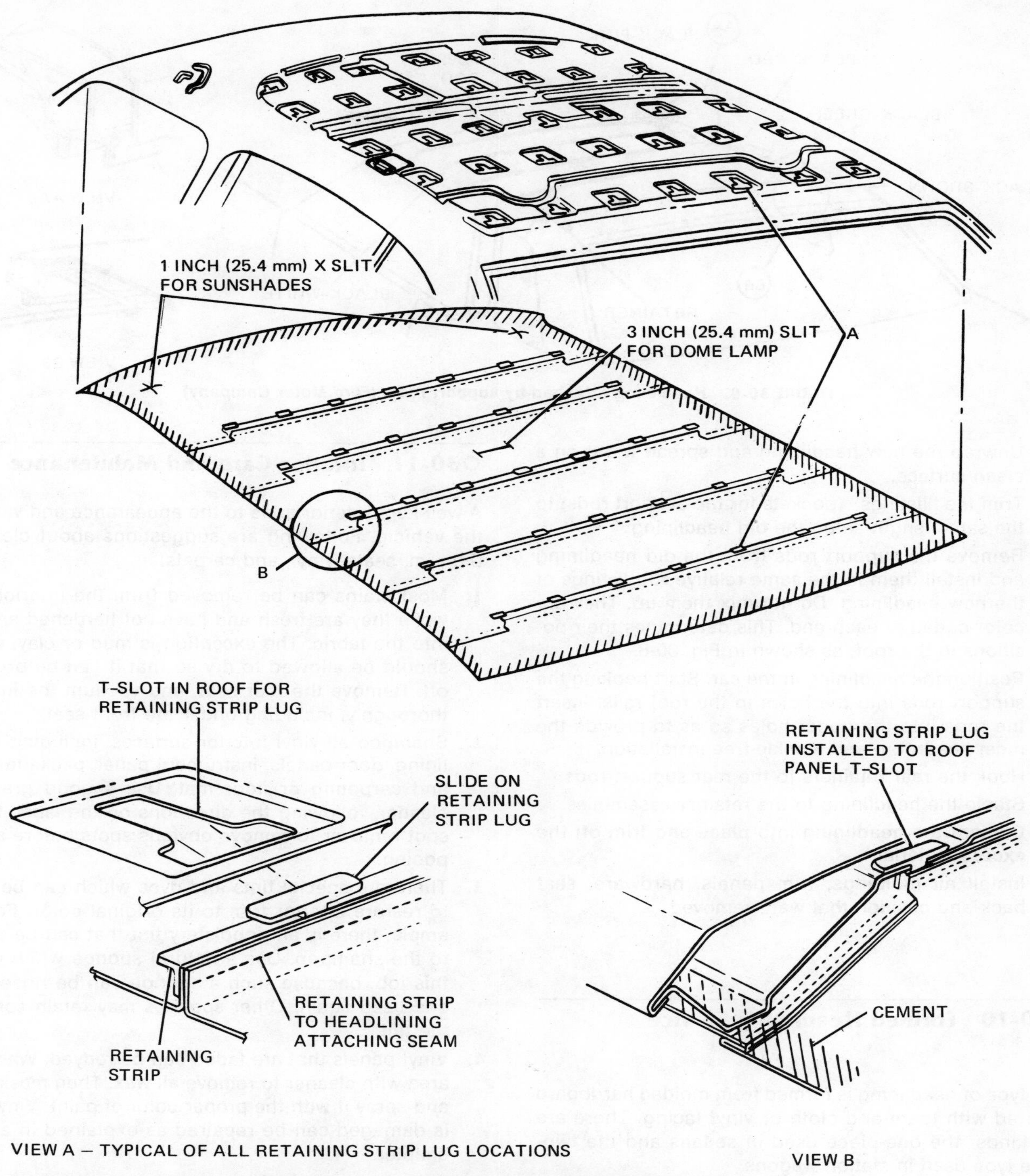

FIGURE 30-7. Headlining attached by lugs and T-slots. ***(Fisher Body Division of General Motors Corporation)***

○30-9 Ford Cloth Headlining Service

The following is a typical headlining removal and replacement procedure for Ford-built cars. Instead of employing rectangular lugs and T slots, Ford uses support rods that span the roof area from side to side, as shown in Fig. 30-8.

1. Remove all hardware and trim that would interfere with headlining removal. This includes sun visor and brackets, moldings, shoulder belts, and coat hooks. Then remove the rear seat cushion and back and quarter-panel lower- and upper-panel trim assemblies.
2. Also remove the dome light and package tray.
3. Then take out the staples that fasten the headlining to the roof side retainer assemblies. Pull the headlining loose from all cemented areas.
4. Unhook the right and left retainers from the headlining rear support rod. Unhook all support rods from the holes in the left and right roof rails and remove the headlining from the car.

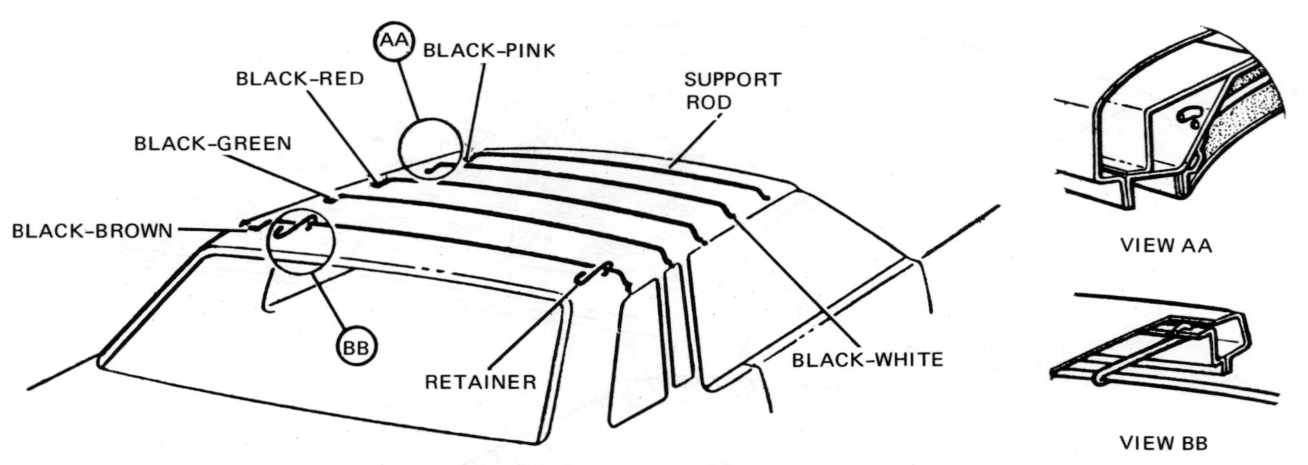

FIGURE 30-8. Headlining attached by support rods. (*Ford Motor Company*)

5. Unwrap the new headlining and spread it out on a clean surface.
6. Trim the "listings" (pockets for the support rods) to the same length as on the old headlining.
7. Remove the support rods from the old headlining and install them in the same relative rod listings of the new headlining. Do not mix them up. They are color-coded at each end. This determines their positions in the roof, as shown in Fig. 30-8.
8. Position the headlining in the car. Start hooking the support rods into the holes in the roof rails. Insert the rods into the upper holes so as to provide the most headroom and wrinkle-free installation.
9. Hook the rear retainers to the rear support rods.
10. Staple the headlining to the retainer assemblies.
11. Cement the headlining into place and trim off the excess material.
12. Install all moldings, trim panels, hardware, seat back and cushion that were removed.

○30-10 Formed Headlining Service

This type of headlining is formed from molded hardboard covered with foam and cloth or vinyl facing. There are two kinds: the one-piece used in sedans and the two-piece type used in station wagons.

To remove the headlining, first remove all hardware, moldings, and trim panels that would interfere. Then disengage the tabs or clips on each side of the headlining assembly. Move the assembly rearward enough to provide sufficient clearance to remove it. Take it out through the front door opening.

On reassembly be careful not to bend the headlining too much, because this could crack it. If the new headlining does not have an insulator cemented to the upper surface, remove the insulator from the old assembly and cement it onto the new. Use just enough cement in spots to hold it in place during assembly.

Raise the headlining up into position, and engage the tabs or clips on each side of the headlining. Reinstall all hardware and other parts that were removed.

○30-11 Interior Care and Maintenance

A well-kept interior adds to the appearance and value of the vehicle. Following are suggestions about cleaning the trim, seats, vinyl, and carpets:

1. Most stains can be removed from the interior trim while they are fresh and have not hardened and set into the fabric. The exception is mud or clay, which should be allowed to dry so that it can be brushed off. Remove the rear seat, and vacuum the interior thoroughly, including under the front seat.
2. Shampoo all vinyl interior surfaces, including headlining, door panels, instrument panel, package shelf, and carpeting or floor mat. Use a good grade of cleaner, following the directions on the label. Use a spot remover to remove obvious spots before shampooing.
3. There are special tints and dyes which can be used to restore interior trim to its original color. For example, there is an upholstery tint that can be added to the shampoo. Use a natural sponge when doing this job, because such a sponge can be rinsed out and used again. Other sponges may retain some of the tint.
4. Vinyl panels that are faded can be redyed. Wash the area with cleaner to remove all wax. Then mask it off and spray it with the proper color of paint. Vinyl that is damaged can be repaired as explained in a later chapter.
5. If the package shelf needs attention, remove it. Wipe it down with a cloth saturated with lacquer thinner. Then spray-paint it.

CHAPTER 30 CHECKUP

NOTE: Since the following is a chapter review test, you should review the chapter before taking the test.

Repairing or replacing the interior trim of a car is a very different job from metalworking or painting. To the car owner, it is no less important. Many interior trim jobs, such as installing a new cloth headlining, are usually performed by an upholstery shop. However, new trim panels and floor carpets may be ordered for some cars.

The auto body technician must know how to install these parts. To find out how well you understand everything in this chapter, answer the questions that follow.

COMPLETING THE SENTENCES The sentences are incomplete. After each sentence there are several words or phrases, but only one of them correctly completes the sentences. Write each sentence in your notebook, ending the sentence with the one word or phrase that completes it correctly.

1. You must remove the window-regulator handle to remove (*a*) a quarter trim panel, (*b*) a quarter upper trim panel, (*c*) the floor-pan insulator, (*d*) the carpet.
2. Cars with catalytic converters must be equipped with (*a*) floor carpet, (*b*) floor-pan insulators, (*c*) vinyl seat covers, (*d*) a solid headlining.
3. A cigarette burn in a carpet can be repaired with (*a*) a complete new carpet, (*b*) a rubber floor mat, (*c*) a piece of tape, (*d*) a carpet plug.
4. Sun visors may have a (*a*) map case, (*b*) rearview mirror, (*c*) vanity mirror, (*d*) dome light.
5. Two widely used types of headlining are (*a*) cut and sewn, (*b*) soft and formed, (*c*) riveted and stapled, (*d*) insulating and sound-deadening.

QUESTIONS Write each of the following questions, and then the answer, in your notebook. If you have trouble recalling the answer to a question, turn back to the pages that cover the material and study them again.

1. How is a quarter trim panel installed?
2. Why is it important to replace damaged or missing floor-pan insulators?
3. How do you repair a carpet with a small cut?
4. How do you repair a carpet with a small hole in it?
5. What is the procedure for installing a soft headlining?

SUGGESTIONS FOR FURTHER STUDY

Probably you have spent hundreds of hours riding in a car, with the headlining just inches over your head. You may never have stopped to think about the headlining and how it was installed. Get in several different cars and determine the types of headlining that you find. Then carefully examine each type of headlining to determine how it was fastened in place and how you would remove and replace it.

31

SAFETY BELTS AND AIR BAGS

In this chapter, you will learn about the various kinds of seat and shoulder belts that have been installed on cars and how to service them. Then you will learn more about air bags and how they operate.

○31-1 Purpose of Safety Belts

Safety belts are of two types: lap or seat belts and shoulder belts. The purpose of seat and shoulder belts is to restrain the driver and passengers if there is an accident. During a front-end crash, the car comes to a rapid stop. But every movable object inside the car, including the people, continues to move forward until it hits something solid. An unrestrained passenger would continue to move forward until he or she hit the windshield or the instrument panel, for example. It is these so-called second collisions that hurt and kill people. However, if the occupants of the car are wearing seat and shoulder belts, they will not continue forward and will not hit a solid object in the car. This greatly reduces the chances of their getting hurt.

○31-2 Kinds of Safety Belts

There are two types of safety belts: the seat or lap belt and the shoulder belt. The lap belt has been credited with saving many lives and preventing many injuries. The lap belt plus the shoulder belt is even more effective. A lap belt prevents the person from being thrown forward. The shoulder belt prevents jackknifing. That is, the upper body is kept from bending at the waist and moving forward. A driver who jackknifes is thrown into the steering column. A front-seat passenger who jackknifes is thrown into the instrument panel, striking it with his or her head.

The first laws requiring seat belts for the driver and right front-seat passenger became effective in January 1964. These early seat belts had no automatic retractors and required individual adjustment. The belts were often in the way, underfoot, and seldom used.

Shoulder belts for the driver and right front-seat passenger were built into cars manufactured after January 1968.

Seat belts installed on earlier-model cars were optional. The driver and passengers did not have to use them. On later-model cars, a warning buzzer was incorporated which sounded if the seat belts were not fastened. A later arrangement called the seat-belt–starter interlock system was used for a brief time. It required the driver and any front-seat passengers to buckle their seat belts before the engine could be started. The purpose of the interlock was to require the driver and front-seat passengers to use their seat belts. This protected them from injury or death in case the car was involved in an accident. However, there was so much objection from the driving public to this system that the law requiring it was repealed. You may still find cars containing these systems, but most of the owners of such cars have had the systems deactivated.

○31-3 Front-Seat-Belt Warning System

There have been several variations of this system. An early system is shown in Fig. 31-1. It included an electrical hookup with the front-seat-belt retractors (which contained switches), and a sensing switch under the passenger seat. With this system, the buzzer would sound continuously if the driver and passenger failed to buckle up. The system included a warning light on the instrument panel that came on when the buzzer sounded.

The latest version is much simplified and is electrically connected to the seat-belt retractor on the driver's side only. Also, the buzzer will sound (or a bell will tinkle) for only a few seconds if the driver fails to buckle the seat belt. The warning lamp will light whenever the ignition is turned to ON or START, whether or not the driver has buckled up. The lamp goes off automatically after 4 to 8 seconds. The warning buzzer will not sound if the driver buckles up before the ignition is turned to ON or START. However, if the driver does not buckle the belt, the buzzer will sound for 4 to 8 seconds and then go off automatically. In either case, the lamp will light and then go off after 4 to 8 seconds, since it works independently of the buzzer.

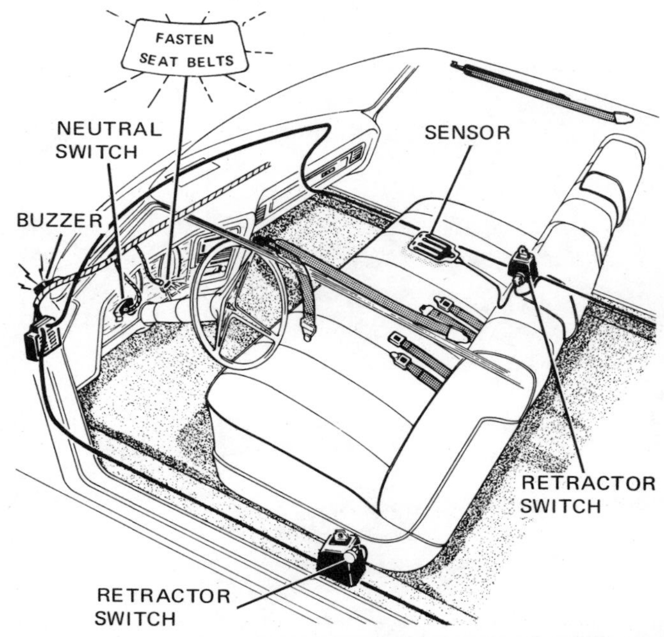

FIGURE 31-1. A front-seat-belt warning system. ***(Pontiac Motor Division of General Motors Corporation)***

○31-4 Seat-Belt—Starter Interlock System

The seat-belt–starter interlock system makes it necessary to buckle the front seat belts before the engine can be started. The sequence required of the driver is as follows:

1. Get in the car and sit down.
2. Buckle the seat belt. If a passenger gets in, the passenger must also buckle up.
3. Insert the ignition key and turn the switch to START.

This is the only sequence that will start the engine. Figure 31-2 shows how the shoulder belt, lap belt, and other parts in the system are arranged.

If the seat belts are not buckled, or are buckled before the occupants are seated, a relay operates to activate the warning light and buzzer. The light and buzzer will also come on if any front-seat occupant unbuckles after the transmission has been shifted to a forward-drive position.

The light and buzzer will not come on if a front seat belt is unbuckled and the engine is running with the transmission in PARK or NEUTRAL (automatic and column shift) or if the parking brake is engaged (floor-shift transmission).

1. BOUNCE The logic module is under the front seat. It has a time delay that deactivates the interlock system for a few seconds if a buckled-in occupant momentarily rises from the seat. Without this feature, the logic module would sense that the occupant had left the car and then buckled the seat belt before being reseated; that would prevent starting. However, the time delay allows the system to ignore the momentary rising of the occupant from the seat. But if the occupant is off the seat for more than 5 to 10 seconds, the seat belts must be unbuckled and then rebuckled before the engine will start.
2. RESTARTING Once the car has been started, if the correct sequence is followed as noted above, it can be restarted with the seat belts unbuckled as long as the driver remains seated. If the driver leaves the seat, the three-step sequence must be repeated to start the engine.
3. MECHANIC'S START The engine can be started with the seat belts in any position when the front seats are unoccupied. Simply reach inside the car and turn the ignition key to START without sitting on the front seat. The light and buzzer will come on if the front seat is then occupied and the transmission is shifted to DRIVE, but they will turn off as soon as the seat belts at the occupied positions are buckled up.
4. OVERRIDE RELAY An override or bypass relay is located on the fire wall under the hood (Fig. 31-2). This relay can be used to start the engine when the interlock system has failed and is preventing starting. To use the relay, turn the ignition switch to ON. Then open the hood and press and release the button on the relay. Holding the button in will damage the override mechanism. The engine can now be started by turning the ignition key to START. The relay will remain engaged until the ignition key is turned to OFF or LOCK.

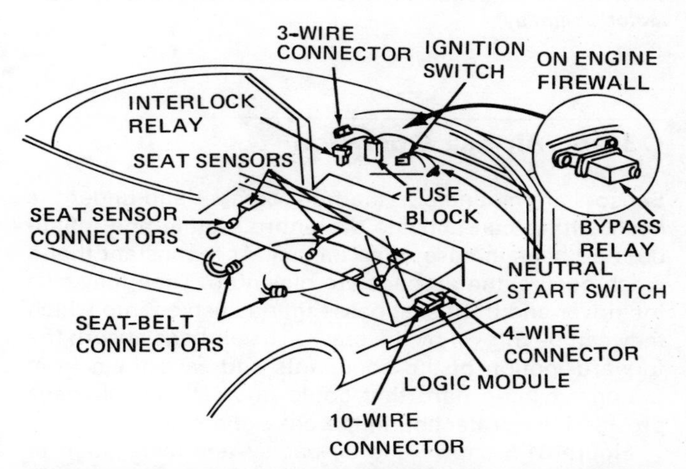

FIGURE 31-2. Location of components in the seat-belt-starter interlock system. *(Chevrolet Motor Division of General Motors Corporation)*

NOTE: Because so many people objected to the seat-belt–starter interlock system, federal law was changed so that the system is no longer required. It is legal to deactivate the system in cars now in operation.

○31-5 Seat-Belt Installations

Figure 31-3 shows different seat-belt installations. There are two types: the three-point system (Fig. 31-1) and the continuous loop system. The three-point system has a fixed tongue on the end of the lap belt and shoulder belt, where they are fastened together. It includes two retractors. The retractors pull the belts back when released. The continuous loop system has a movable tongue on the front lap-shoulder belt and only one retractor.

CAUTION: If a component part of a safety belt, such as the buckle or retractor, requires replacement, then the complete safety-belt assembly (buckle, tongue, and lap-and-shoulder belts) must be replaced. Individual components must not be replaced separately if the strength of the safety-belt system is to be maintained.

Both types of seat belts may be equipped with a shoulder-belt retractor (Fig. 31-4) that has one end of the shoulder belt fastened in it. The purpose of the shoulder-belt retractor is to allow the belt to move freely in or out. This avoids the necessity that each person adjust the shoulder belt for proper fit. Then when the vehicle decelerates rapidly, an inertia sensor or pendulum inside the retractor automatically locks the reel. This action stops belt travel, and it prevents jackknifing by the restrained person.

When the safety belt is fastened and the shoulder belt has a retractor, the shoulder belt adjusts automatically to a snug position. During normal movement, the inertia reel is in the free position. This allows the restrained person to move around freely, but within limits. When the vehicle is braked hard, or has an impact at about 5 mph [8 kmph] or more, the reel locks tightly.

The reel cannot be made to lock up by jerking on the belt. As you can see in Fig. 31-4 (left), the inertia reel is locked by upward movement of the pendulum, or inertia sensor, as it is also called. With the vehicle at rest, no matter how hard the belt is jerked, the pendulum cannot lock the reel.

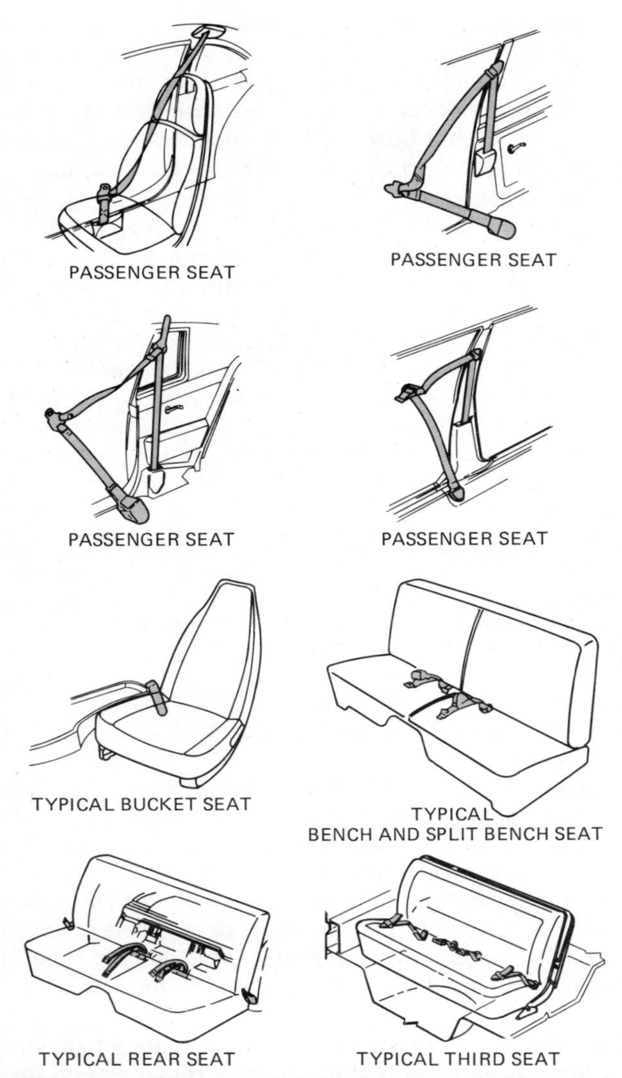

FIGURE 31-3. Various seat-belt and shoulder-belt installations. ***(Chrysler Corporation)***

○13-6 Checking Safety Belts

To check the seat belts, look for split webbing, frayed fabric, tears, buckles that don't work, loose or damaged anchorage. Also, check the operation of the seat-belt retractors, if the belts are equipped with them. As we mentioned, several types of safety-belt systems have been used. Refer to the shop manual for the car for the specific testing procedure.

○31-7 Purpose of Air Bags

"Air bags" is the term used for the air-cushion restraint system, which has been installed on some cars. Air bags are a passive safety device to protect the driver and passenger in an accident. "Passive" means that the driver and passenger do not have to do anything to be protected by the air bags. This is in contrast to seat belts, with which you are required to take some action. That is, you must buckle seat belts to be protected.

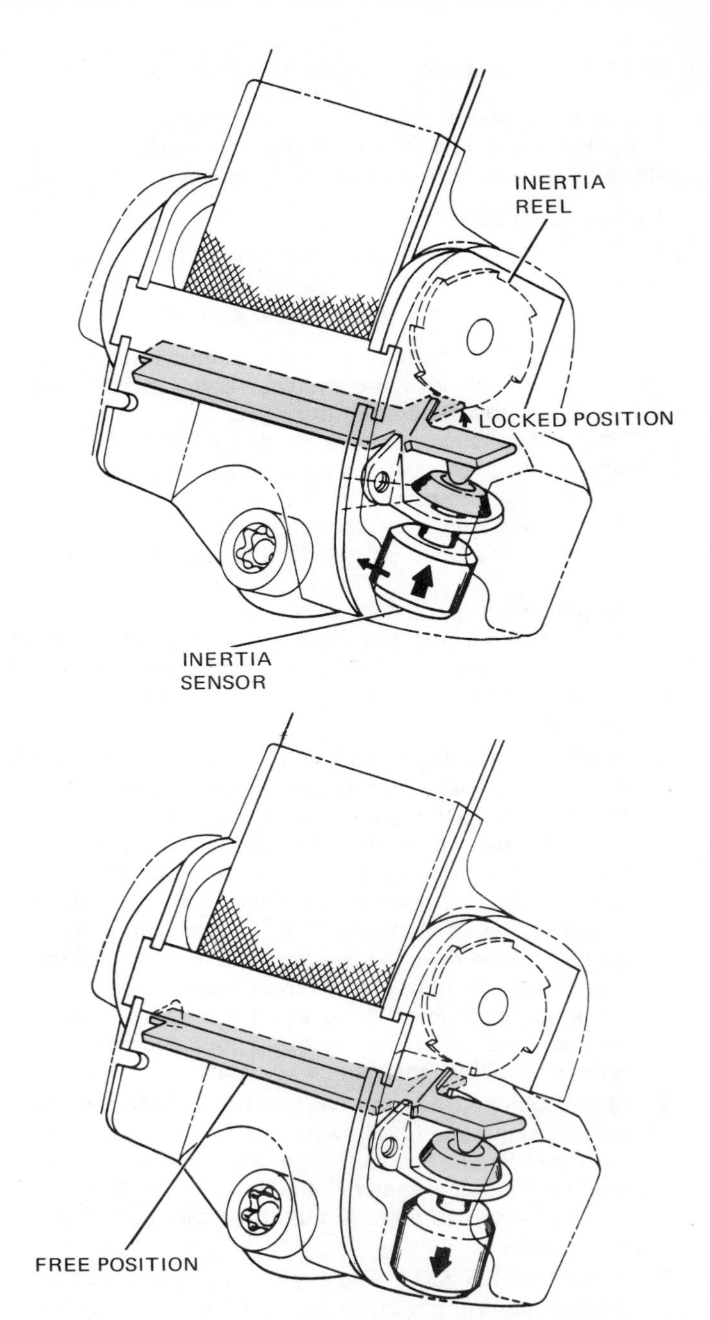

FIGURE 31-4. A pendulum-type shoulder-belt retractor. ***(Ford Motor Company)***

○31-8 Air-Bag Operation

Sensors are mounted in the front bumper and under the dash. Either can activate the entire system and inflate both air bags in case of an impact. At the instant that a crash occurs, the air bags are blown up. Then they give the driver and front-seat passenger a cushion into which they can be thrown by the crash. The air bags absorb the forward motion of the occupants and save them from hitting anything hard that could injure them. Air bags provide little protection in the case of a side impact.

Figure 31-5 shows one air-bag-system installation to protect the passengers in the front seat. Figure 31-6 shows how the system operates. At impact, the driver is sitting back in the seat in a normal position (Fig. 31-6A).

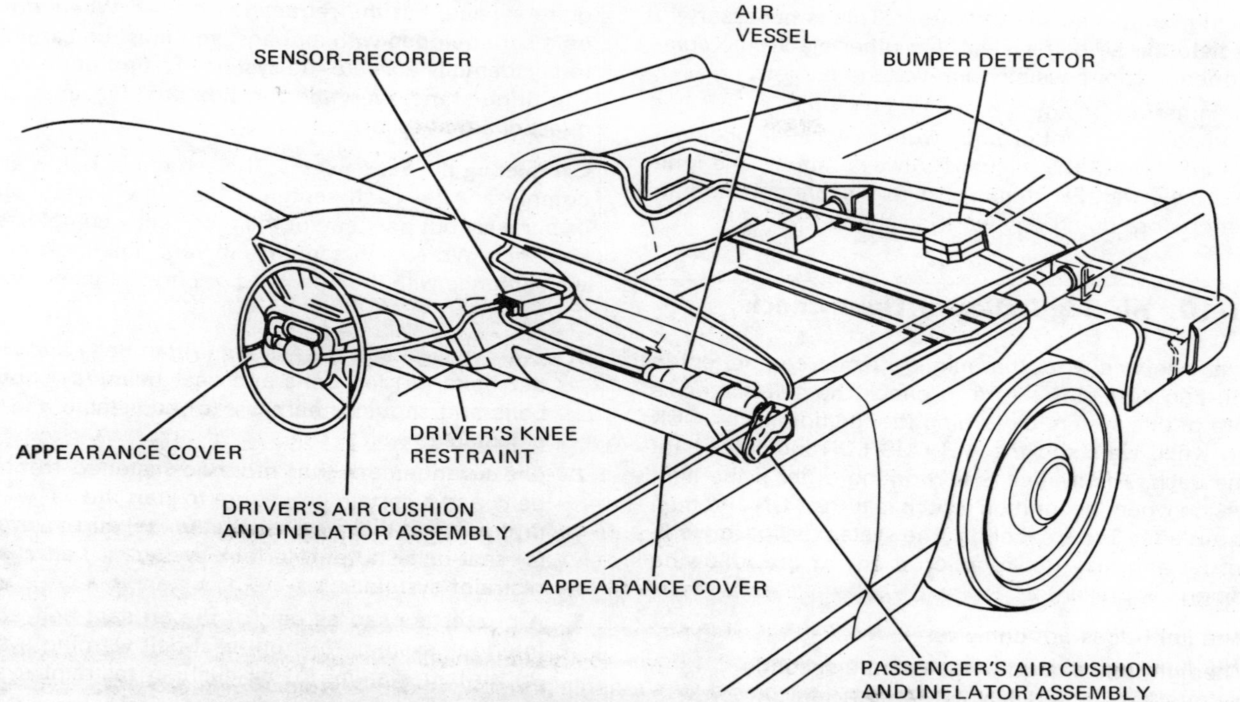

FIGURE 31-5. Air-bag restraint system for front-seat passengers. ***(General Motors Corporation)***

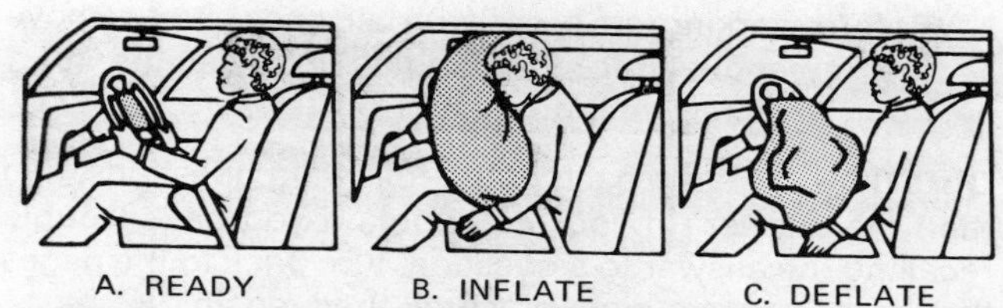

FIGURE 31-6. Air-bag operation in a front-end collision. ***(Allstate)***

At 1/30 second after the crash starts, the air-bag system has been actuated. The bag is already pushing out from its position in the instrument panel.

The system is actuated by a bumper detector. This detector contains a switch that is closed when the car is suddenly decelerated (as when it is brought to a quick stop in a collision). When the switch closes, the air-vessel-and-inflater assembly is actuated. The air vessel (Fig. 31-5) is filled with compressed gas. When it is triggered, this gas is released and it flows into the air bag. The action is almost instantaneous. Now see B at the center in Fig. 31-6. This is the condition 2/30 second after the impact. Note that the air bag is almost fully inflated and that the driver has been thrown forward into it. Now, a fraction of a second later, when the force of the driver's forward motion has been completely absorbed, the air bag begins to deflate through relief holes (C in Fig. 31-6). This allows quick deflation, after the air bag has done its job, so the passenger can get out of the car.

The air bag on the driver's side is located in the steering wheel (see Fig. 2-30). Figure 31-5 shows the complete air-bag system installation for the driver and passengers. The air bag for the front-seat passenger is in the right side of the instrument panel.

○31-9 Air-Bag Service Precautions

There are several service precautions that must be observed when working on a car equipped with air bags. Disregarding these precautions may damage the sensor-recorder or accidentally activate the system and inflate the bags. This requires an expensive replacement of the air bags and air vessel. Listed below are the safety precautions issued by General Motors that technicians must follow:

1. Always remove the ignition key and wait at least 2½ minutes before servicing or disconnecting *any* electrical or other component in the area of the instrument panel or under the dash. If electrical work is required, disconnect the battery, except when it is needed for diagnosis.
2. Never touch an air-bag electrical harness or connector with the leads from an ohmmeter, test light, or any other self-powered electrical device. If electrical diagnosis is needed on wiring under the dash, make certain to identify the wiring harness you are working on.
3. Diagnosis of the air-cushion restraint system itself should be done only by a trained technician, using the special analyzer and following the procedures specified by the Fisher Body Division of General Motors Corporation. These procedures are contained in a special air-bag service manual, which is available from General Motors Service Information.
4. To remove the steering wheel, steering column, or the front bumper, follow the procedures outlined in the special air-bag service manual.
5. Make certain that the ignition switch is in the LOCK position while jumper or battery-charger cables are

being connected to the battery. This is necessary to isolate the air-bag system and other electronic components from possible high-voltage surges.

6. Hammering or any type of impact such as in front bumper alignment or body work may cause accidental inflation of the air bags. Always remove the ignition key, wait 2½ minutes, then disconnect the battery before doing any work on the car.

○31-10 Air-Bag Indicator Light Check

After any service work that might affect a component in the air-bag system, be sure to check the self-diagnosis feature of this system by turning the ignition from LOCK to ON while watching the AIR CUSHION indicator light on the dash. The system is in working order if the light comes on when the ignition switch is turned ON and then goes out after 3 to 9 seconds. The system is *not* in working order and may not function if any of the following conditions is present:

a. The light does not come on.
b. The light remains on longer than 9 seconds.
c. The light goes on while you are driving.
d. The light goes on and off while you are driving.

○31-11 Air-Bag Inflator Assembly Disposal

If a vehicle is to be scrapped, the driver and passenger inflators should be made harmless before disposal. An inflator that has been removed for replacement must be made harmless before disposal. There is a method for rendering the inflator harmless. It is drilling and burning, as outlined in the *Fisher Body Air Cushion Restraint System Service Manual.* Only this recommended procedure should be followed by qualified technicians.

NOTE: If local ordinances prevent burning, or if you are unable to follow the instructions in the air-cushion restraint manual, you may contact General Motors for advice. Call the car divisional zone office which is listed in the back of the owner's manual for the vehicle. This phone number should not be called except when you need inflator assembly deactivation and disposal information for cars built by General Motors.

CHAPTER 31 CHECKUP

NOTE: Since the following is a chapter review test, you should review the chapter before taking the test.

Seat belts and air bags are safety devices located inside the passenger compartment. The belts seldom require service, but the retractors can fail. When working on a car equipped with air bags, you must be careful not to accidentally activate the system. To find out how well you understand everything in this chapter, answer the questions that follow.

Completing the Sentences The sentences below are incomplete. After each sentence there are several words or phrases, but only one of them correctly completes the sentence. Write each sentence in your notebook, ending the sentence with the one word or phrase that completes it correctly.

1. Two types of safety belts are (*a*) lap belts and shoulder belts, (*b*) lap belts and seat belts, (*c*) shoulder belts and shoulder harness, (*d*) adjustable and nonadjustable.
2. The arrangement that required fastened front-seat belts and a certain procedure to start the car was the (*a*) front-seat-belt warning system, (*b*) air-bag system, (*c*) seat-belt–starter interlock system, (*d*) air-cushion restraint system.
3. A buzzer is used as part of the (*a*) seat-belt–starter interlock system, (*b*) front-seat-belt warning system, (*c*) air-bag system, (*d*) air-cushion restraint system.
4. Pounding on the front bumper could cause the (*a*) seat belts to retract, (*b*) shoulder belts to disconnect, (*c*) front-seat-belt warning light to light, (*d*) air bags to inflate.
5. Before working on a car with air bags, first remove the key and wait (*a*) 2½ minutes, (*b*) 1 minute, (*c*) 1 hour, (*d*) a few seconds.

QUESTIONS Write each of the following questions, and then the answer, in your notebook. If you have trouble recalling the answer to a question, turn back to the pages that cover the material and study them again.

1. Which cars are required to have safety belts?
2. What is the front-seat-belt warning system?
3. What is a seat-belt retractor?
4. How are seat belts checked?
5. What service precautions must be followed when working on a car with air bags?

SUGGESTIONS FOR FURTHER STUDY

Sit in several cars and examine the complete safety-belt assembly. Determine the difference between the three-point belt and the continuous-loop belt. Then locate the anchors for each belt and then the retractors. If retractors are not used, figure out how to properly adjust the belts. Be sure you locate all the belts. For example, in a late-model full-size car with bench seats, you should locate six seat belts.

PART 9

VINYL ROOFS, OVERLAYS, AND DECALS

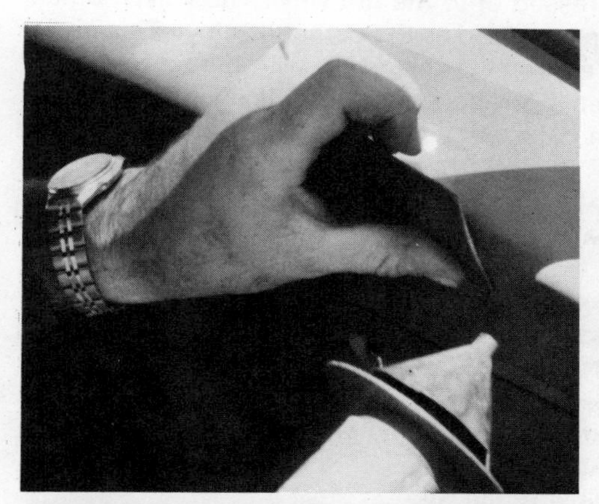

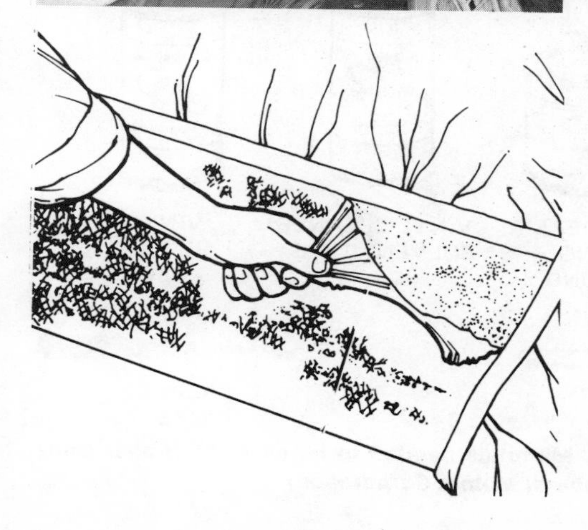

In this part, you will learn how to make repairs to vinyl roofs and padded dashes, how to apply wood-grain overlays and decals, and how to replace a vinyl roof cover.

Vinyl is extensively used today in cars. Many cars have grain-textured vinyl roof covers in various colors. Inside, the instrument panel and other interior surfaces are covered with vinyl. Vinyl is easily repaired if it is torn or damaged. Wood grain, used extensively on station wagons, is a thin vinyl film with an adhesive on the back.

There are two chapters in Part 9, as follows:

32 VINYL REPAIR AND ROOF REPLACEMENT

In this chapter, you will learn how to repair damage to vinyl, either on the outside or inside of the car. Also, you will learn how to remove a damaged vinyl roof and replace it with new material.

○32-1 Vinyl Repair Procedure

When vinyl was first used in cars, damaged vinyl had to be replaced if the appearance of the car was to be restored. However, in recent years repair techniques have been developed for certain types of damage. When damaged vinyl can be repaired, repair is much less expensive and often requires less time than installing new vinyl material. The basic repair technique was made possible by the availability of liquid vinyl.

So-called *liquid vinyl* actually is a paste that can be used to fill small holes in vinyl material. Then, with the application of heat, the liquid vinyl cures or hardens. In curing, the liquid vinyl fuses to the original material. Most vinyl has a grain or pattern in it. The original grain can be given to the patched area. This is done by using graining paper, or another piece of the original material, as a die to press against the liquid vinyl as it cures.

Liquid vinyl is available in a variety of colors, which can be mixed like paint to match the original color. Or, after the vinyl patch has cured, it can be painted to match the color of the original material.

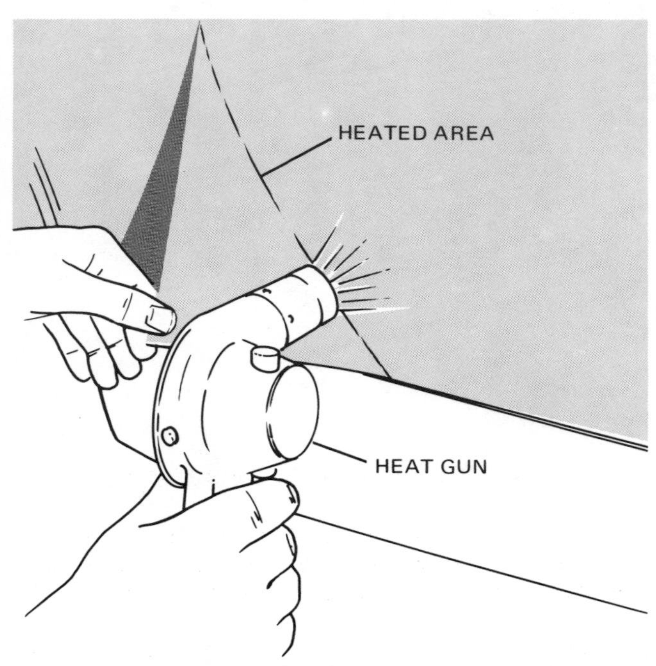

FIGURE 32-1. A heat gun, used in vinyl repair. ***(American Motors Corporation)***

To repair vinyl that is damaged, first trim back the damaged area until you leave only original material that is in good condition. New liquid vinyl is applied to the cut-out area and heated with a heat gun. During this process, a piece of the original vinyl is used as a die. That is, it is pressed onto the hot vinyl. The vinyl die has the same grain structure as the damaged vinyl. This gives the new vinyl a grain that blends in with the surrounding old vinyl. After the repair has dried, it is spray-painted with the same color paint to match the old vinyl.

○32-2 Materials for Vinyl Repair

In addition to the liquid vinyl patching compound, other materials needed to repair vinyl include vinyl dies, a heat gun (Fig. 32-1), a razor knife, a pallet knife, vinyl cleaner, scissors, and vinyl repair paint. For any specific repair job, the vinyl die used must match the surrounding grain. Also, the paint used must match. Figure 32-2 shows materials for a vinyl repair kit.

○32-3 Patching a Vinyl Roof

Figure 32-3 shows a vinyl roof which has a small hole rubbed in it. This is a new car, and the damage occurred during transportation of the car to the dealership. A retaining chain rubbed on the vinyl roof, causing the damage. Before repair started, the area was cleaned with vinyl cleaner (Fig. 32-2). Figure 32-4 shows the size of the damage in comparison with a hand. This illustration shows the technician applying vinyl from a dispensing can to the damage. Figure 32-5 shows a pallet knife being

FIGURE 32-2. Materials needed to repair vinyl. ***(Fisher Body Division of General Motors Corporation)***

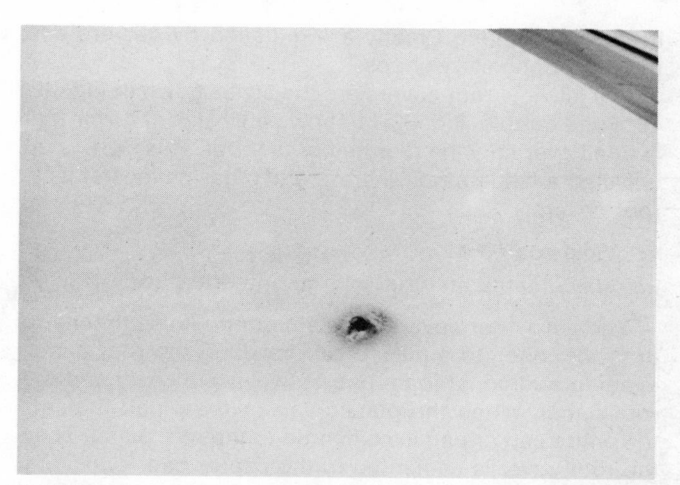

FIGURE 32-3. A hole rubbed in the vinyl roof of a new car by a loose chain on the car carrier.

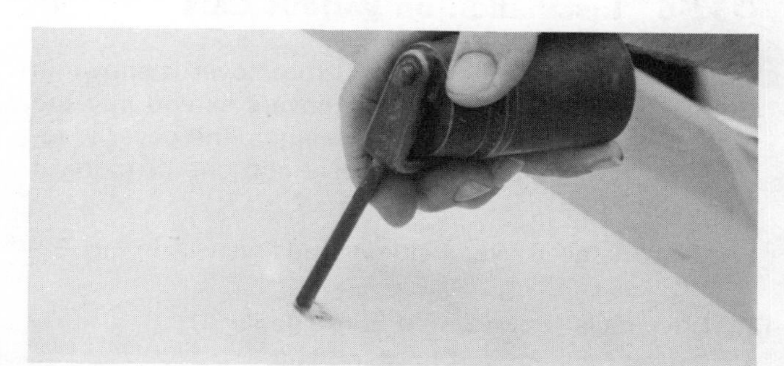

FIGURE 32-4. Applying liquid vinyl to the damaged area with a dispensing can.

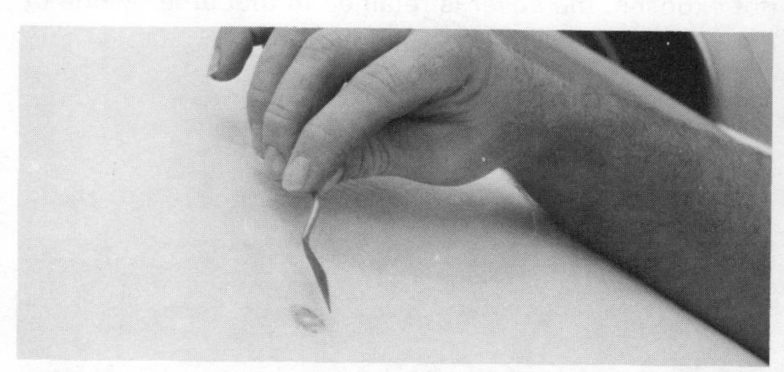

FIGURE 32-5. Using a pallet knife to smooth the vinyl into the hole.

used to smooth the vinyl into the hole. Figure 32-6 shows a heat gun being used to heat and cure the vinyl. Note that the technician is holding a vinyl die near the damaged area. When the vinyl is almost hard, the technician will press the die onto it. This imparts a grain to the vinyl. When the vinyl is cured, it is spray-painted. The resulting repair is almost impossible to detect.

○32-4 Repairing a Padded Dash

Figure 32-7 shows the instrument panel of a car which has been damaged. There is a crack in the vinyl at one place. At another, the vinyl material is completely missing.

As a first step in the repair, the area was cleaned. Figure 32-8 shows the repair job in process. The technician has filled the damaged area, which had material

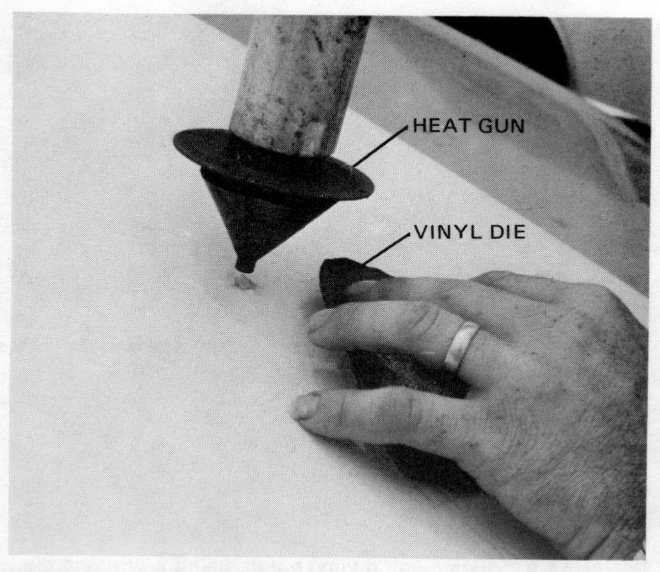

FIGURE 32-6. Heat gun being used to heat and cure the liquid vinyl.

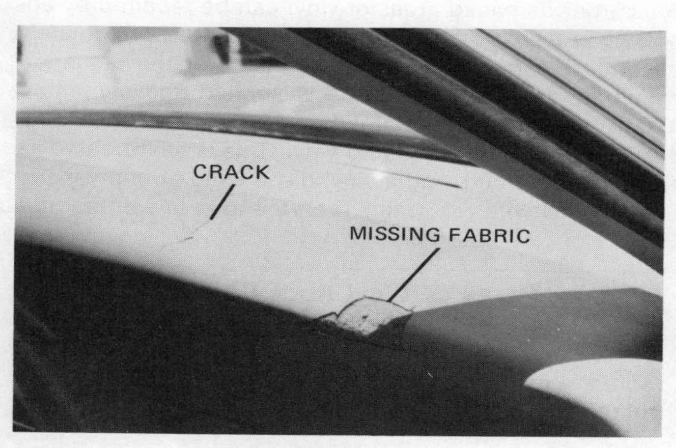

FIGURE 32-7. A damaged padded dash.

FIGURE 32-8. Curing a vinyl patch in a padded dash.

missing, with several thin coats of vinyl, smoothed in with a pallet knife. Each coat was heated to cure it. Finally, after the patched area is built up so that it is level with the surrounding vinyl, the technician uses a vinyl die to impress a grain on the vinyl (Fig. 32-9). Lastly, the technician spray-paints the patched area so that it matches the rest of the padded dash.

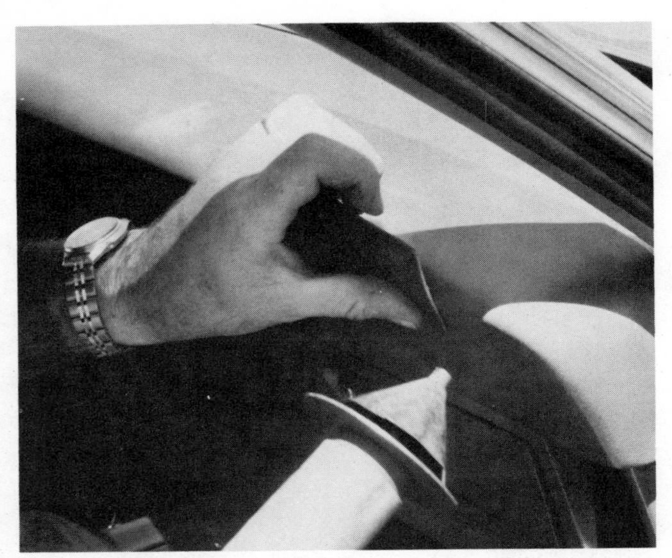

FIGURE 32-9. **"Graining" a vinyl patch, using a graining die.**

Larger damaged areas of vinyl can be repaired by applying patches of matching vinyl cut out to approximately fit the damage. Then, after the edges of the damaged vinyl are trimmed, the patch is applied and cemented into place. Finally, the joint between the patch and original vinyl is filled with liquid vinyl. This is heat-treated as already explained, and a vinyl die is used to impress the liquid vinyl with the grain. Then the area is painted.

○32-5 Types of Vinyl Roof Cover

Figure 32-10 shows a car with a full vinyl roof cover. Vinyl roofs are installed primarily to enhance the appearance of the car. They usually are installed on new cars during assembly, although many are installed by dealers and trim and upholstery shops.

Not all vinyl roof covers are the style shown in Fig. 32-10. For example, Fig. 32-11 shows a vinyl roof cover that is fitted over only the rear half of the roof. This style often is called a landau top. There are two basic types of vinyl roof covers:

1. Vinyl-coated fabric
2. Vinyl-coated material with an integral pad

The vinyl roof covers are cemented either directly to the roof panel, to a plastic cap covering the roof panel, or to an additional foam pad between the cover and the roof panel. When the plastic cap or foam pad is used, the entire cap or pad is cemented to the roof panel. Then the roof cover is cemented to the cap or pad.

○32-6 Installation on Various Cars

The installation of a typical vinyl roof cover is shown in Fig. 32-12. On styles where the covers extend into the windshield and back window openings, the cover is retained in the opening by adhesive and one or more of the following:

1. Clips installed over weld-on studs (view A in Fig. 32-12)
2. Drive nails (views D and E in Fig. 32-12)
3. Reveal molding and finishing lace

On styles where the back window reveal moldings are not exposed, the cover is retained in that area by one or more of the following:

1. Cement
2. Tabbed retainers
3. Finishing lace

FIGURE 32-10. **A car with a vinyl top, or roof cover.** ***(Oldsmobile Division of General Motors Corporation)***

FIGURE 32-11. **Car with a vinyl half-roof.** ***(Oldsmobile Division of General Motors Corporation)***

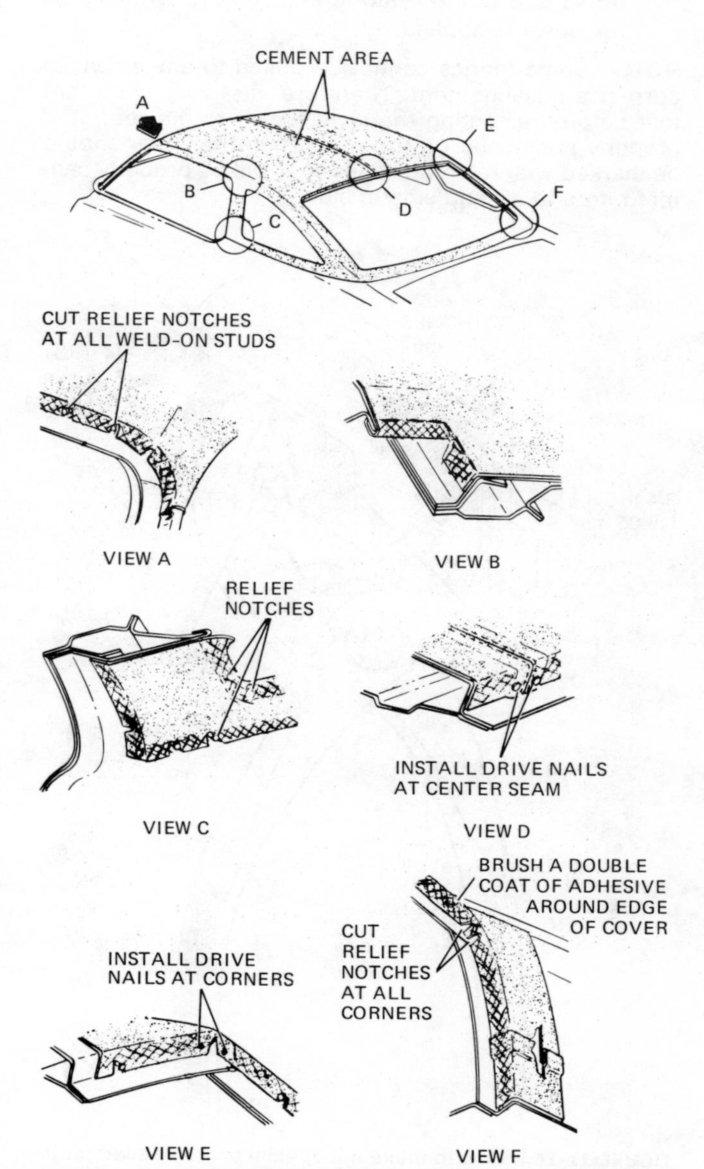

FIGURE 32-12. **Typical vinyl roof cover installation.** ***(Fisher Body Division of General Motors Corporation)***

Where the cover extends in and around drop moldings, or folds around the roof-panel flange, it is retained by one or more of the following:

1. Adhesive and drip scalp moldings
2. Weatherstrip retainers
3. Finish moldings

On styles with roof-panel moldings, the cover is retained under the moldings by adhesive and clips installed over weld-on studs. Examine various car roofs to note the methods used to retain the cover.

○32-7 Preparing to Remove the Vinyl Roof

Two removal and installation methods are required for the two different installation designs. One method is required for the type which is simply a vinyl-coated fabric. Another method is required for the type which has a foam pad that is integral with the fabric.

Regardless of the type of roof cover and the method required to remove and replace it, the following are removed:

1. Windshield and back window reveal moldings (where present) except where the cover does not extend into the windshield or back window openings.
2. Roof drip scalp moldings, weatherstrip retainers, or finish moldings (where cover extends into the drip moldings or folds around roof panel flange).
3. Rear quarter belt reveal moldings and rear end belt reveal moldings.
4. The following items if present:
   a. Roof cover retainer-to-rear-body lock pillar.
   b. Roof extension panel emblem, name plate assembly, or opera lights.
   c. Roof panel moldings and finishing trim lace.
   d. Quarter window reveal moldings.
   e. Stationary quarter window (if required).
   f. Louver quarter stationary windows.

g. Sliding sun roof panel (if cover for panel is being replaced).
h. Louver in quarter sail area.
i. Vista vent glass and weatherstrips.

5. Reveal molding clips across the top and sides of the windshield, quarter, and back glass openings. On styles where fabric cover extends below the back window, remove the reveal molding clips along the bottom of the back window. Clean off excessive adhesive.
6. Vinyl on the center post, fastened with four rivets and retainers (on some styles). To remove the vinyl from the post, drill out the rivets and remove the retainers.

○32-8 Directly Cemented Vinyl Roof Cover Removal

This is the roof covering that is directly cemented to the roof panel. It is removed as follows after all the preliminary work is done as outlined in the previous section:

1. Remove all drive nails around windshield and back window. On styles that do not have back window and quarter glass reveal moldings, carefully work cover from under covered retainer in those areas. Use a special reveal molding tool. Make sure that any tabs present on retainers around the back window opening are not damaged.

NOTE: When removing drive nails, protect the edge of the glass by applying several layers of cloth body tape. Drive nails can best be removed by first driving a screwdriver under the nail heads. Then use diagonal cutters to twist them out. Don't enlarge the holes more than you have to.

2. Mask off areas of the roof panel not covered by the fabric. Mask the upper windshield, back window, roof opening around the sun roof, doors, and flat-painted areas such as the hood and trunk lid. This will protect them from the cement you will use in applying the new roof covering.
3. Apply heat with a hot-air gun to the edges of the roof cover to loosen them. A hand-held heat lamp can also be used, as shown in Fig. 32-13. Avoid excessive heat.
4. After loosening the edges of the cover all around, carefully remove the cover.

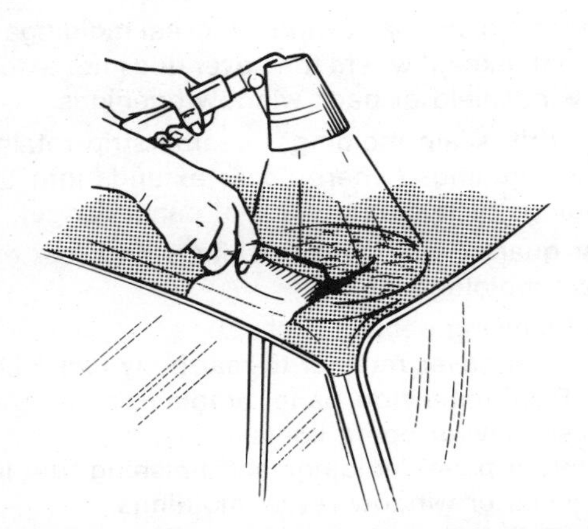

FIGURE 32-13. Using a hand-held heat lamp to loosen the edges of the vinyl roof.

5. Examine the cemented surfaces on the roof panel. Wire-brush by hand all areas where excessive padding from the cover backing or adhesive buildup is evident. If any metal finishing has been done on the roof panel, paint the repaired area.
6. To avoid "show-through" bumps or unevenness when the new cover is applied, the roof panel must be reasonably smooth.

○32-9 Directly Cemented Vinyl Roof Cover Installation

The recommended cement adhesive must be used to assure a good job. General Motors recommends Hughes HC 4183 or 3M 8064 or the equivalent. The preferred application method is to spray it on with a compressed-air spray gun.

1. The new cover should be installed at room temperature. It is harder to get a smooth job when the car and cover are cold. Use special pliers (Fig. 32-14) to grasp and pull the fabric and remove wrinkles as the cover is applied.

NOTE: Some fabrics cannot be pulled to any extent to correct a misalignment. Therefore, it is very important that before cementing the cover down to the roof, it is properly positioned on the roof. Then the cover should be marked with reference lines so it will be properly centered, fore to aft and side to side.

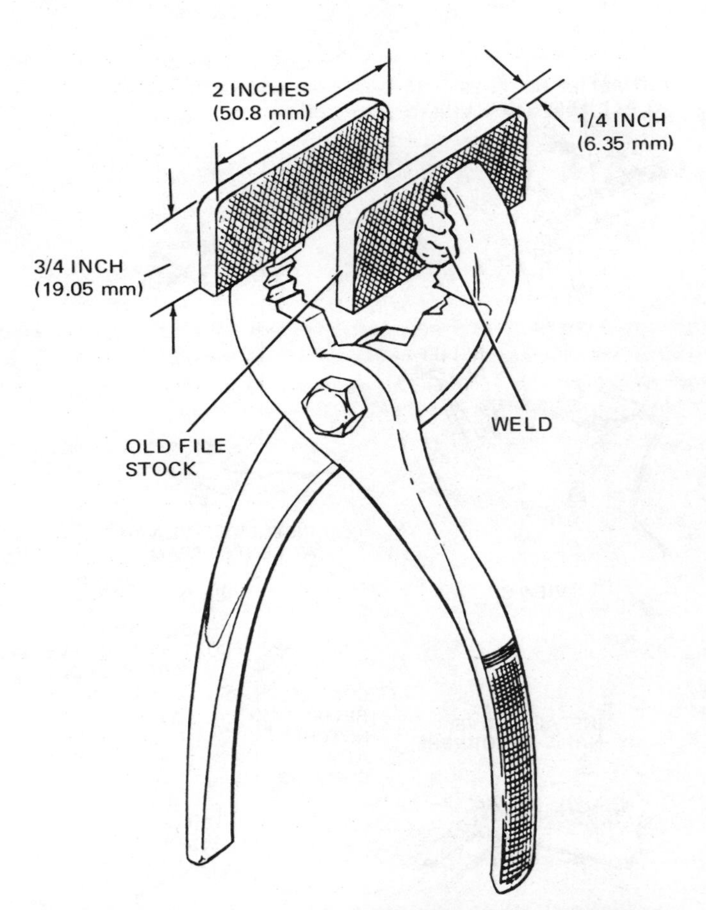

FIGURE 32-14. How to make the special pliers needed for installing vinyl roof covers. ***(Fisher Body Division of General Motors Corporation)***

2. If the old roof cover was properly aligned, you may be able to use the seam marks on the roof (which can usually be seen) as reference points to align the new cover.
3. Mark the center lines of the roof panel on the windshield and rear window with tape.
4. If no seam marks are available to help align the new cover, lay the cover on the roof. Fold it lengthwise at the center location. Mark the center at the front and rear of the cover.
5. With cover folded lengthwise, brush on or spray on adhesive along the center line of the cover and roof panel. Allow it to dry for 3 to 5 minutes, or until it becomes tacky. Do not use too much adhesive. This can cause the vinyl to come loose from its pad or underlining.
6. Make certain that the cover is free of wrinkles and properly aligned as you press it down into place. Do not pull too hard on the fabric to smooth it. Use pliers (Fig. 32-14) to help remove wrinkles. Pulling too hard can separate the backing from the vinyl and cause wrinkles or highlights (shiny areas from bumps or stretched vinyl). Use a plastic squeegee to "slick" down the cover as shown in Fig. 32-15.
7. Once the cover is centered and the center portion is cemented and slicked down, work away from the center on one side of the cover. Apply cement to the back of one side of the cover and to the adjacent roof panel. Do not include the quarter upper area at this time.
8. Then, starting along the center area, slick down the roof covering. Have an assistant help you by pulling and holding the cover away from the roof panel until you actually get to the area you want to press and slick down. Make sure the cover goes down free of wrinkles.
9. If the roof has a multiple-piece "plastic cap," make sure the cover seams align with the plastic cap seams.
10. Repeat the operation on the other side.
11. On models which have the vinyl running down the center pillars, cement these down next.
12. Now work on the quarter upper area as shown in Fig. 32-15. Apply cement to the cover and quarter upper area. Make the initial pull as shown to fit the quarter. Then slick it all down. If the vinyl extends below the back window, cement and apply the cover at this point.
13. Brush a double coat of adhesive on the edge of the cover to assure good adhesion.
14. Where the vinyl has to be worked down around the sun-roof opening, up to roof-panel moldings, or up to halo moldings, refer to Figs. 32-12 and 32-16 for details of how to do the job. In Fig. 32-12, note the use of nails to hold the center seam in place. Also note how the cover is notched out at all weld-on studs. This notching out should be done with sharp scissors at the time that the cover is being slicked down in place.
15. Finally, when the cover has been installed and is completely down all around, remove the protective masking from the car. Install all hardware and parts removed.

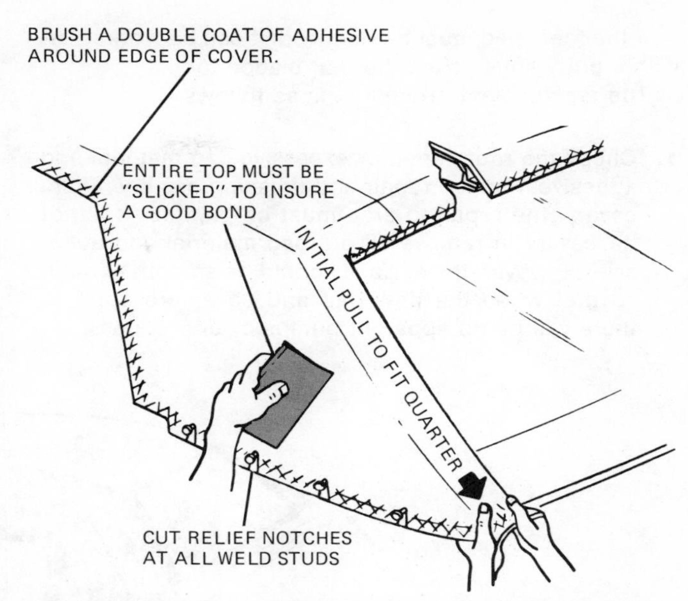
BRUSH A DOUBLE COAT OF ADHESIVE
AROUND EDGE OF COVER.
ENTIRE TOP MUST BE
"SLICKED" TO INSURE
A GOOD BOND
INITIAL PULL TO FIT QUARTER
CUT RELIEF NOTCHES
AT ALL WELD STUDS

FIGURE 32-15. Cementing cover to upper quarter. ***(Fisher Body Division of General Motors Corporation)***

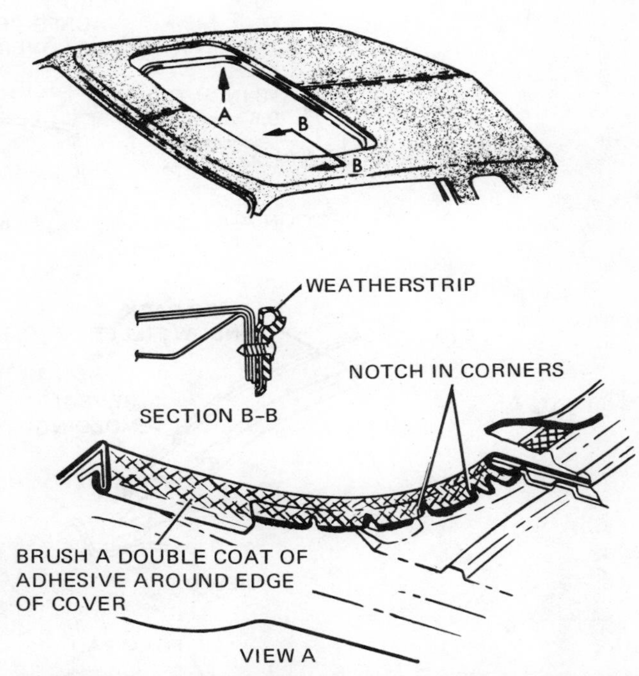
A
B
B
WEATHERSTRIP
NOTCH IN CORNERS
SECTION B–B
BRUSH A DOUBLE COAT OF
ADHESIVE AROUND EDGE
OF COVER
VIEW A

FIGURE 32-16. Installing vinyl roof cover on a car with a sun roof. ***(Fisher Body Division of General Motors Corporation)***

○32-10 Removing and Replacing Vinyl Roof Covering with Foam Pad

This is the roof covering that has a foam pad under it. The vinyl fabric is removed from the foam pad in the same way as the directly cemented type is removed from the roof panel. That is: First, all parts that would interfere should be removed. Then all areas that might be damaged should be masked with masking tape and paper. Then heat is applied around the edges to loosen the roof cover, as explained on ○32-8. Finally, the cover can be removed from the foam pad.

If the foam pad must be removed, it can be worked off with a putty knife or another flat-bladed tool.

The replacement procedure is as follows:

1. Check the roof panel for excessive pad material and adhesive. If metal repair and finishing has been necessary, the repaired area must be painted. It is not necessary to remove all old pad material and adhesive. However, the surface should be smooth enough so that when the new pad and cover are applied, there will be no apparent bumps or unevenness.

2. The pad is installed and cemented down onto the roof panel in the same way that the directly cemented vinyl roof covering is installed (Fig. 32-17). That is: First lay the pad on the roof panel, getting it accurately centered fore to aft and side to side. Then cement down the center area. After that, work from the center to one side, slicking down the pad. Then repeat the procedure for the other side.

NOTE: Work accurately. If you cement the pad down in a misaligned position, you may have to cut out some of the pad and patch in the needed material.

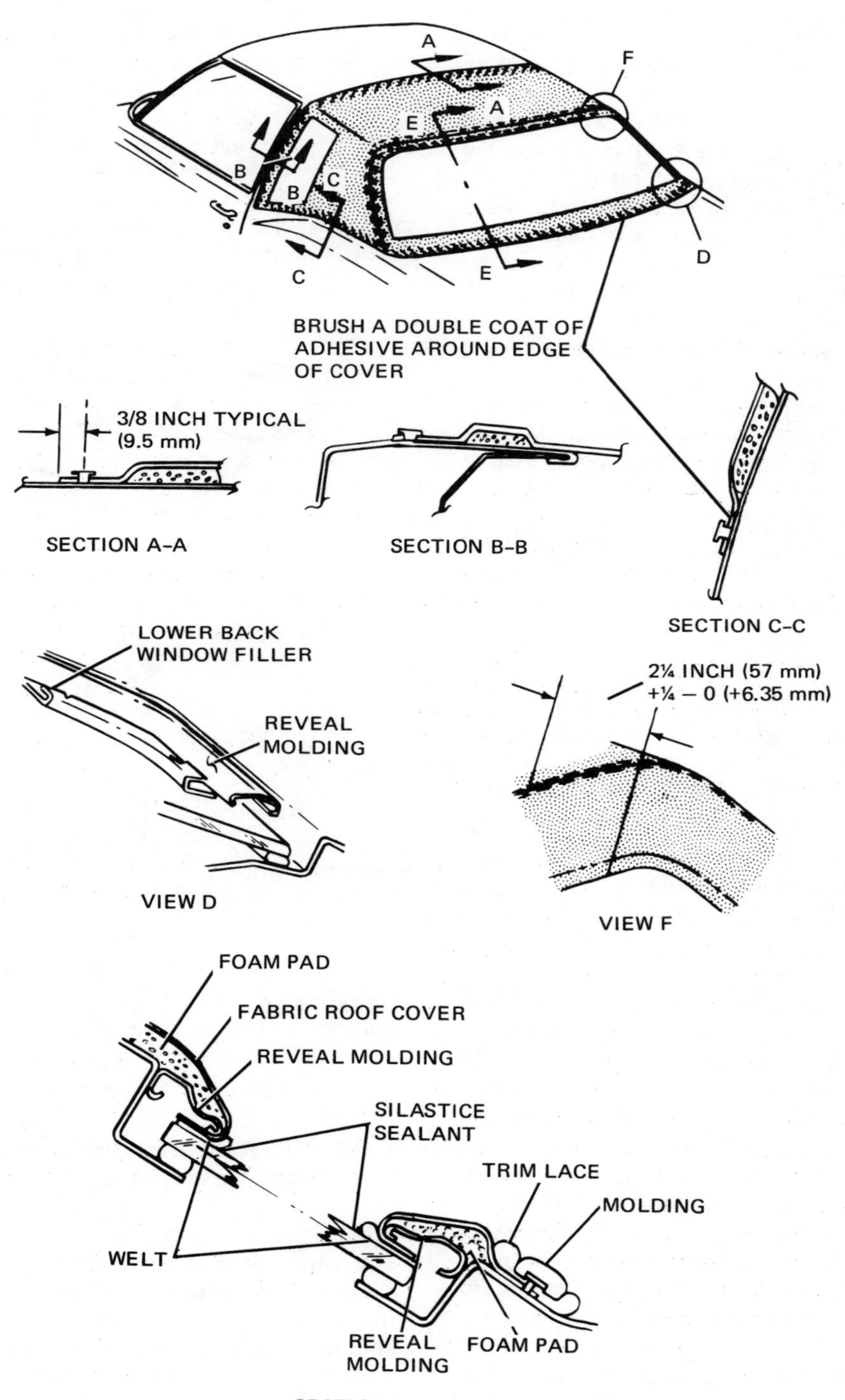

FIGURE 32-17. Installing a landau roof cover that has a foam pad under it. ***(Fisher Body Division of General Motors Corporation)***

3. Be sure to slick down the pad so as to avoid bubbles or wrinkles as you work out from the center.
4. Trim off excessive padding. Be sure the padding is cemented down well along all edges that have been trimmed.
5. The procedure of installing the vinyl roof covering over the foam pad is very similar to the procedure used to install the directly cemented vinyl roof covering. That is: First center the cover on the pad, fore to aft and side to side. Then cement down the center area, slicking it down to make sure it is smooth and without wrinkles and bubbles. Next work one side down, moving away from the center, cementing and slicking the cover down. Then repeat the procedure for the other side. Finally, remove all masking tape and paper. Install all parts that were removed.

○32-11 Removing Wrinkles from Roof Cover

Fabric roof cover wrinkles that do not disappear after several days exposure to sunlight can be corrected as follows:

1. Use a household iron applied over a dampened shop cloth, as shown in Fig. 32-18. Set the iron for medium heat (cotton or lower). Continue to iron until the wrinkles come out or until it is obvious that this method is not going to work.
2. The next step, if ironing does not work, is to remove the moldings adjacent to the wrinkled area. Apply heat to the wrinkled area with a heat gun, at the same time pulling on the edge of the fabric to raise it from the roof panel.

NOTE: Overheating the fabric—that is, applying heat above 200°F [93.9°C]—may cause the vinyl to lose its grain, become shiny, or blister.

3. Once the wrinkled area has been pulled clear of the roof panel, brush on adhesive. After the adhesive has become sticky, press the cover down into place, slicking it down to make sure the wrinkles do not reappear.

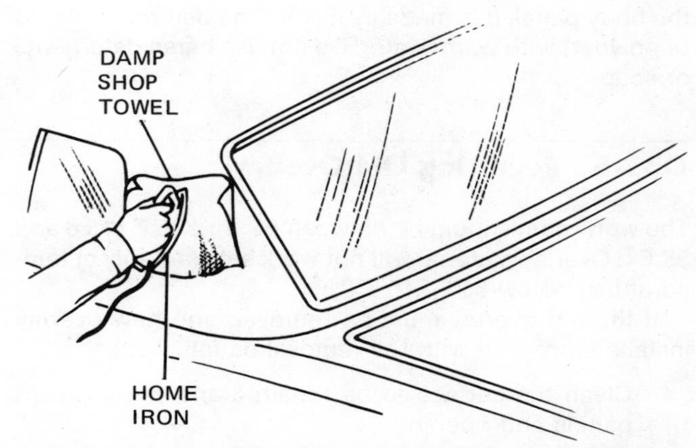

FIGURE 32-18. Removing wrinkles from a vinyl top with a household iron. ***(Fisher Body Division of General Motors Corporation)***

CHAPTER 32 CHECKUP

NOTE: Since the following is a chapter review test, you should review the chapter before taking the test.

With the widespread use of plastic materials, and particularly vinyl, the padded dash became standard equipment and the vinyl roof cover became a popular option. At first, damage to any piece of vinyl usually required that section of material to be replaced. Now many types of vinyl damage can be repaired. But when a large area is damaged—for example, when major damage to the vinyl roof has occurred—the entire roof cover still must be replaced. To find out how well you understand everything in this chapter, answer the questions that follow.

COMPLETING THE SENTENCES The sentences below are incomplete. After each sentence there are several words or phrases, but only one of them correctly completes the sentence. Write each sentence in your notebook, ending the sentence with the one word or phrase that completes it correctly.

1. The material used to fill a hole in vinyl is (*a*) vinyl repair kit, (*b*) liquid vinyl patching compound, (*c*) caulking compound, (*d*) vinyl cleaner.
2. A heat gun is used in vinyl repair to (*a*) soften the liquid vinyl, (*b*) cure the liquid vinyl, (*c*) warm the technician's hands, (*d*) heat the surrounding good vinyl so the patch will stick to it.
3. A vinyl die is used to (*a*) grain the patch, (*b*) stamp out the damaged area, (*d*) identify the damaged area, (*d*) color the patch.
4. Deep holes or long cuts in vinyl must be (*a*) filled with one thick layer, (*b*) sanded smooth before filling, (*c*) filled in several layers, (*d*) enlarged before they can be filled.
5. Large damaged areas should be patched with (*a*) several layers of liquid vinyl, (*b*) sewing, (*c*) one thick layer of liquid vinyl, (*d*) a matching patch cut from the same material.

QUESTIONS Write each of the following questions, and then the answer, in your notebook. If you have trouble recalling the answer to a question, turn back to the pages that cover the material and study them again.

1. What are the steps in the vinyl repair procedure?
2. How do you apply several layers of liquid vinyl?
3. How is a matching grain given to the patched area?
4. What are the types of roof cover?
5. What are the steps in the procedure to replace a vinyl roof cover?

SUGGESTIONS FOR FURTHER STUDY

Repairing vinyl and replacing vinyl roof covers are jobs that not every body technician performs. Find a shop that does do vinyl repair and vinyl roof installation. Watch the technicians at work. In a page for your notebook write down the types of damage that you see repaired and list each step that the technician performs to make the repair.

33
SERVICING WOOD-GRAIN OVERLAYS AND DECALS

In this chapter, you will learn how to remove and replace wood-grain overlays (or transfers, as they also are called) used on the panels of station wagons and some cars. These overlays are of vinyl material. Some of the wood-grain overlays are translucent (partly transparent) and allow some of the paint color underneath to show through. Replacement wood-grain-overlay material is available in rolls of various sizes. You will also learn in this chapter how to remove and apply decals and stripes. These are decorative stripes that enhance the appearance of the car.

○33-1 Wood-Grain-Overlay Material

Figure 33-1 shows a car that has wood-grain overlays on it. This material is made of vinyl with a wood-grain design. The vinyl has a pressure-sensitive adhesive back which is protected by paper backing in the roll. When the vinyl is to be applied, the paper backing is removed. The vinyl is applied to a previously prepared surface with a special wetting solution. Preparation of the surface, the wetting solution, and how to apply the vinyl are covered in following sections.

○33-2 Repairing Small Damages

Small nicks, bruises, or scratches in wood-grain overlays can be touched up with paint in much the same manner as painted surfaces. First, blend the paint to get the proper color. Then carefully touch up the damaged area.

Blisters or air bubbles can be removed as follows: Pierce them with a sharp needle. Work the trapped air out through the pinhole, and press the overlay firmly against the panel. You may have to heat the panel with a lamp or heat gun (Fig. 32-1) to soften the adhesive so the vinyl will stick. Heat may also be used to remove small wrinkles or bulges around the fuel-tank opening or other areas where the vinyl fits around a corner or opening.

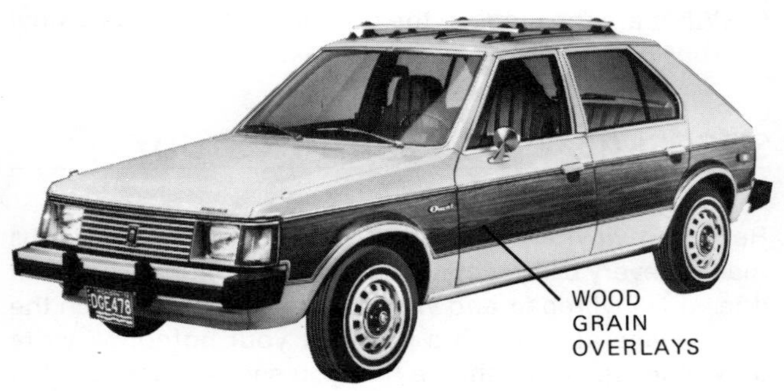

FIGURE 33-1. A car that has wood-grain overlays along the sides. *(Chrysler Corporation)*

○33-3 Materials Required to Remove and Replace Overlays

The following materials are required to remove and replace overlays:

1. Wood-grain and stripe remover—3M or equivalent
2. Adhesive remover—3M or equivalent
3. Detergent such as Joy or Vel (Chrysler recommends a powdered detergent)
4. Wax or silicone remover—3M General Purpose Adhesive Cleaner or equivalent
5. Isopropyl alcohol (rubbing alcohol)
6. Squeegee 4 to 5 inches [102 to 127 mm] wide, of plastic or rubber
7. Water bucket and sponge
8. Sandpaper (360 to 400, wet-or-dry type)
9. Heat gun or lamp
10. Wiping rags or paper towels
11. Sharp razor knife
12. Scissors
13. Sharp needle
14. Grease pencil

○33-4 Wetting Solution

The wetting solution is required to work the transfer onto the body panel. It is made by mixing the detergent (liquid or powder) with warm water. Do not use harsh detergents or soap.

○33-5 Removing Old Overlay

The workroom should be between 65° and 95°F [15.6 and 35°C]. Overlay material will not work satisfactorily at temperatures below 65°F [15.6°C].

If the old overlay must be removed and new overlay installed, proceed with the removal as follows:

1. Clean the surface to be repaired and the adjacent panels and openings.
2. Remove overlay reveal moldings, door handles, lock assembly, side-marker lamps, and other parts that overlap the transfer.

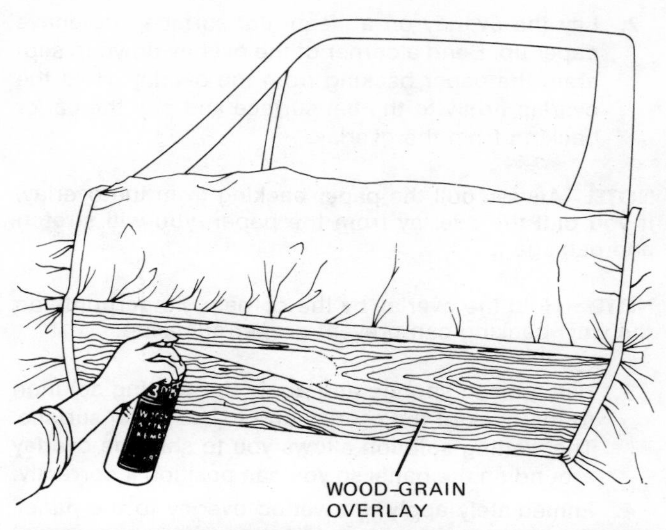

FIGURE 33-2. Spraying wood-grain remover on the overlay. ***(American Motors Corporation)***

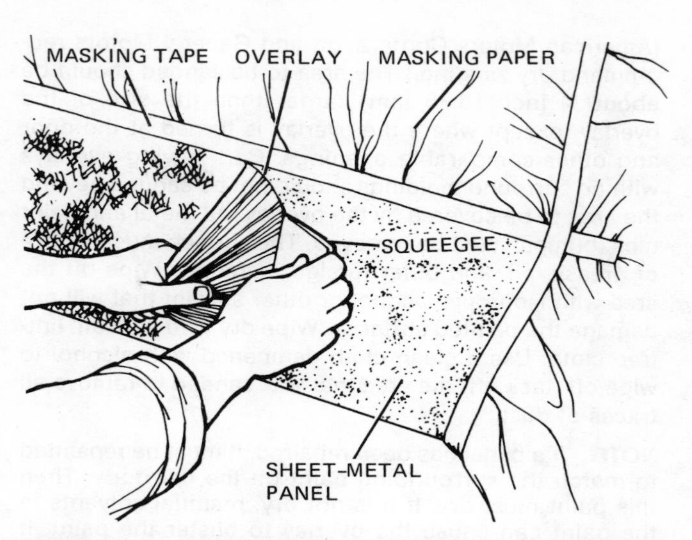

FIGURE 33-4. Using a squeegee to assist in removing the overlay. ***(American Motors Corporation)***

3. Mask off the surrounding area so that paint or chrome will not be damaged by the chemicals used to remove the transfer.
4. Spray wood-grain remover on a flange area first. Then spray the entire overlay to be removed (Fig. 33-2). Move the spray can back and forth across the entire overlay smoothly so as to get even application of the remover. Make sure the entire overlay is covered.

CAUTION: Use the wood-grain remover only in a well-ventilated area. The vapors from this preparation are toxic. Observe the manufacturer's warning printed on the label. Note that this material is for use on acrylic enamel only.

5. Spray the entire panel again. This time move the can up and down.
6. Wait for 20 minutes for the remover to work.
7. Then start peeling the overlay off. Begin at a flange area. Start at one corner and peel the overlay away from the panel (Fig. 33-3). If you have any trouble peeling it off, use the squeegee (Fig. 33-4).
8. Scrape all wood-grain remover from the panel. Then spray the panel with adhesive remover to remove any remaining adhesive. Use a slow spray application and apply the remover uniformly over the panel. The adhesive remover must be left on from 3 to 5 minutes.
9. After 5 minutes, squeegee the adhesive residue off (Fig. 33-5). If some adhesive is hard to remove, spray on more remover. Wait 2 minutes, and then use the squeegee again.
10. Remove the masking tape and paper.
11. Wash the panel with general-purpose adhesive cleaner. If any spots of adhesive remain on the panel, hard rubbing will remove it.

○33-6 Preparing Surface for Overlay Application

Sand all areas to be covered with the overlay, using 360 to 400 sandpaper soaked in water or mineral spirits.

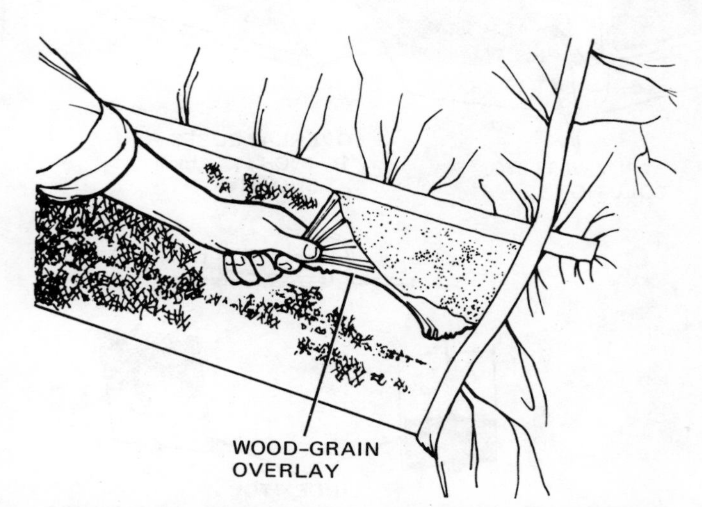

FIGURE 33-3. Peeling overlay from panel. ***(American Motors Corporation)***

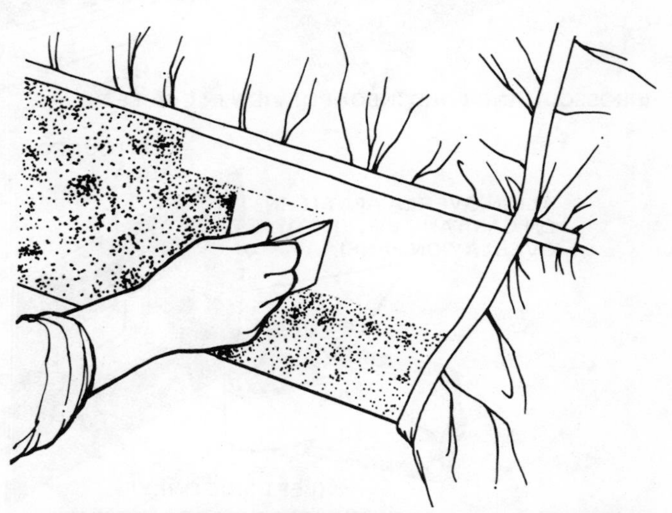

FIGURE 33-5. Removing the adhesive residue from the panel. ***(American Motors Corporation)***

(American Motors Corporation and General Motors recommend dry sanding.) The area to be sanded should be about ¼ inch [6.35 mm] larger than the size of the overlay, except where the overlay is turned at the door and other comparable openings. Cars having overlays with no surround moldings should not be sanded beyond the area to be covered by the overlay. All metal and paint nibs (bumps) must be removed. The surface must be free of grease, oil, and other foreign materials. Wipe off the area with isopropyl alcohol or other solvent that will not damage the painted surfaces. Wipe dry with a clean, lint-free cloth. Use a clean cloth dampened with alcohol to wipe off (tack off) the area that was sanded to remove all traces of dust.

NOTE: If a panel has been repaired, it must be repainted to match the surrounding paint on the car body. Then this paint must dry. If it is not dry, residual solvents in the paint can cause the overlay to blister the paint. It must be sanded in preparation for the application of the overlay, as explained above.

○33-7 Installing Overlay

After the area has dried, proceed as follows:

1. Position the overlay material, with paper backing still attached, on the panel surface. Mark the approximate outline of the overlay on the material with a grease pencil. Make sure that you allow enough excess material—½ inch [12.7 mm]—so it can be wrapped around edges. Use scissors to cut out the overlay. Make sure that you allow enough extra at the top and bottom so the material will extend halfway into the area to be covered by moldings (or to the molding studs, as shown in Fig. 33-6).
2. Lay the overlay on a clean, flat surface, protective paper up. Bend a corner of the overlay down to separate the paper backing from the overlay. Hold the overlap firmly to the flat surface and pull the paper backing from the overlay.

NOTE: Always pull the paper backing from the overlay. If you pull the overlay from the paper, you will stretch and damage it.

NOTE: Hold the overlay by the corners. Fingerprints on the vinyl backing can prevent proper adhesion.

3. Use a clean sponge and apply the wetting solution to the back of the overlay and to the panel surface. The wetting solution allows you to shift the overlay around on the panel so you can position it correctly.
4. Immediately apply the wetted overlay to the panel. Position it in the center of the area to be covered with at least ½ inch [12.7 mm] extending beyond the edges (Fig. 33-7). Apply wetting solution to the grain surface of the overlay so you can use the squeegee effectively.
5. Squeegee from the center to edges of the overlay (Fig. 33-8) with firm strokes to remove all air bubbles and wetting solution and to assure bonding of overlay to the painted surface. On large overlays, the following steps will help:
   a. Squeegee a short, 3- to 6-inch [101.6- to 152.4-mm] horizontal section of the overlay at the center of the panel. Lift right or left side of overlay, position it straight and close to the panel, and squeegee toward the lifted edge. Avoid stretching the overlay at the lifted end. Squeegee from the middle with firm, overlapping strokes.

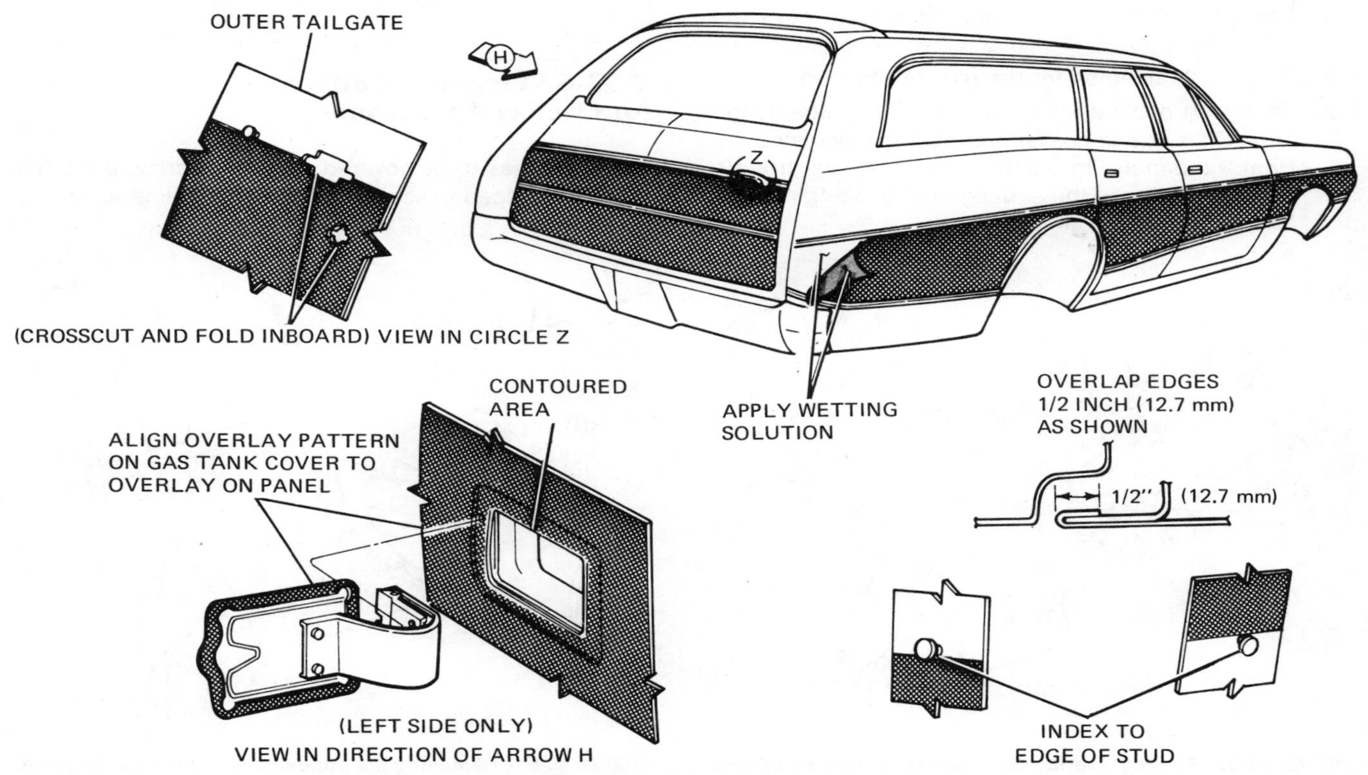

FIGURE 33-6. Installation of wood-grain overlay. *(Chrysler Corporation)*

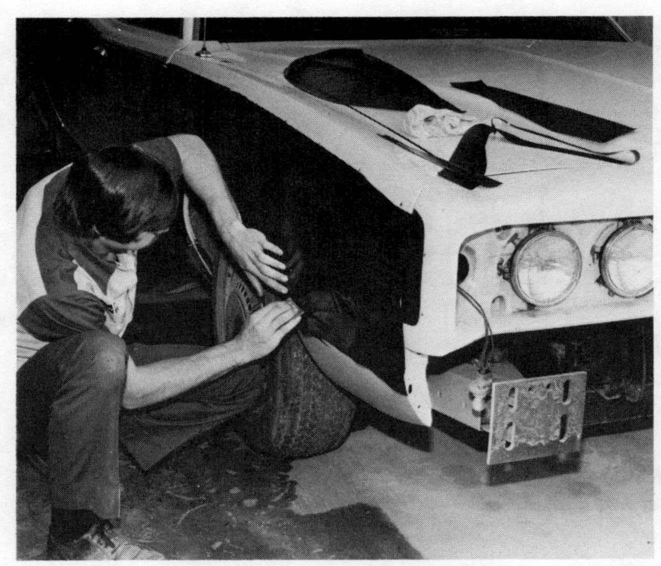

FIGURE 33-7. Working overlay down into area to be covered with molding.

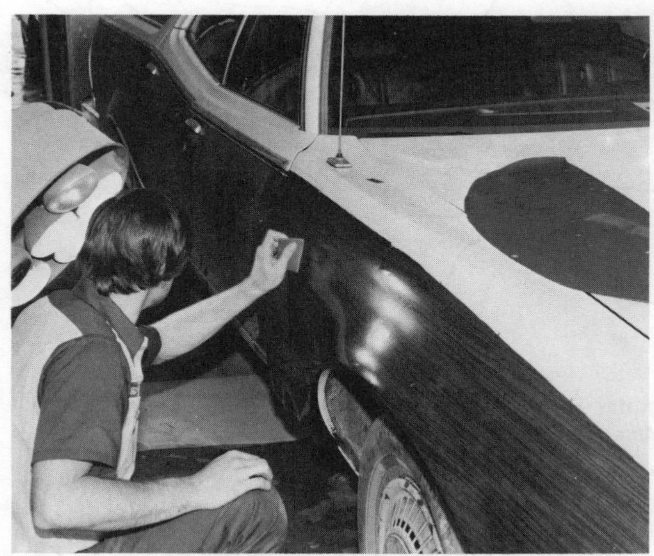

FIGURE 33-8. Squeegee from the center to the edges of the overlay. Note use of heat lamp.

b. Lift the upper area of the overlay down to the bonded area and work upward from the bonded area at the center, squeegeeing the overlay into place.

c. Lift the lower area of overlay (up to the bonded area) and work downward, squeegeeing the overlay into place.

NOTE: If a wrinkle or bubble is trapped during the squeegee operation, stop at once. Carefully lift the affected section. Realign the section to the panel and work outward to remove the wrinkle. Don't worry if a few small air or solution bubbles are trapped. They can be removed later.

6. Notch the corner or curved edges of the overlay where necessary and trim off excessive material. Allow ½ inch [12.7 mm] of extra material beyond the edges so it can be wrapped around the flange areas. To activate the adhesive at the edges, wipe it with isopropyl alcohol. Then use a heat gun or lamp to warm the edges. Firmly press the edges into place with fingertips, a cloth, and finally a squeegee. Alternately warm the edge and press until good adhesion is obtained.

NOTE: Avoid excessive pulling or stretching at the ends of the overlay. You could tear the overlay.

7. Apply heat to the overlay at door-handle holes, side-marker lamps, and other depressions, using a heat gun. Press overlay uniformly into the depressions to get a good bond, as shown in Fig. 33-9. Note the use of a piece of plastic or metal scale placed from the edge of the overlay to the depression. This allows trapped air to escape when the overlay is pressed down into the depression.
8. With a sharp knife, cut out excessive overlay material from the door handle, side-marker lamp, and other areas.
9. Inspect the overlay, using a side light to detect any irregularities. Remove all air or moisture bubbles as already described.
10. Install all parts previously removed.

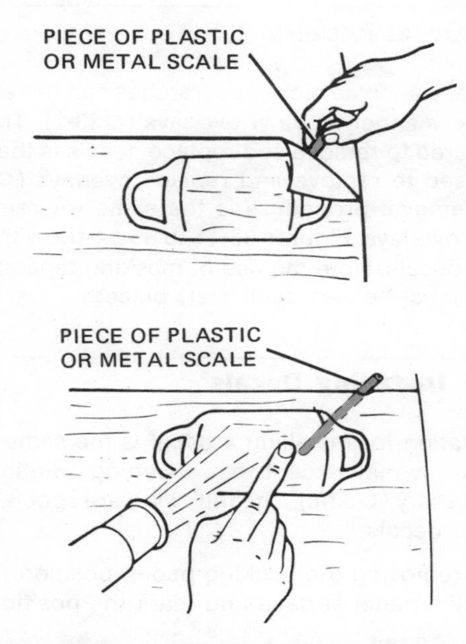

1. INSURE THE DEPRESSION IS FREE OF MOISTURE.
2. HEAT SHEET METAL IN DOOR DEPRESSION AREA TO APPROXIMATELY 200°F (93.8°C) AND APPLY TRANSFER IN NORMAL MANNER.
3. WITH A PIECE OF PLASTIC OR METAL SCALE IN PLACE, ALLOW THE TRAPPED AIR TO ESCAPE, SO A VACUUM IS CREATED TO HOLD TRANSFER FIRMLY IN DEPRESSION (DO NOT PUNCH HOLES IN TRANSFER). SQUEEGEE THE TRANSFER FILM INTO PLACE AROUND THE HANDLE.
4. PRESS THE FILM SECURELY INTO THE SHALLOW DEPRESSIONS.
5. USING HOT AIR TO MAKE THE FILM PLIABLE, CAREFULLY PRESS THE FILM INTO THE DEEP DEPRESSION, EXHAUSTING THE TRAPPED AIR TOWARD THE PIECE OF PLASTIC. WITH THE AIR EXHAUSTED, REMOVE THE PLASTIC TOOL AND SMOOTH THE FILM.

FIGURE 33-9. To stick permanently, the overlay must have a good bond. Work the overlay into any depression in the car body with your finger. *(Fisher Body Division of General Motors Corporation)*

FIGURE 33-10. A car with side decal and stripes. *(Chrysler Corporation)*

○33-8 Decals

Figure 33-10 shows a car that has side stripes and decals. Decals and stripes are made of tough, durable, weather-resistant solid vinyl. They have a pressure-sensitive back which is protected by a paper backing. The backing is removed when the decal is applied to the car body. The front face of the decal may be covered with an easy-release paper to protect it during storage and shipping.

○33-9 Decal Repairs

Decal damage such as nicks or scratches can be repaired in the same manner as vinyl overlays (○33-2). The materials required to remove and replace decals is the same as those used to remove and replace overlays (○33-3). Also, the removal procedure is the same for removing decals and overlays. Figures 33-11 to 33-14 show the procedure for decals. Note the use of masking tape and paper, which must be very accurately placed.

○33-10 Installing Decals

The preparation for installing a decal is the same as for installing an overlay except that a wetting solution may not be necessary (○33-6). The following are special steps required for decals:

1. Before removing the backing paper, position the decal on the panel surface and mark the position with a grease pencil (Fig. 33-15). Make sure to leave ½ inch [12.7 mm] to be wrapped around the door and fender areas. Cut decal to approximate length.
2. Position the decal, with paper still on the back, on the panel. Secure the decal in place with small strips

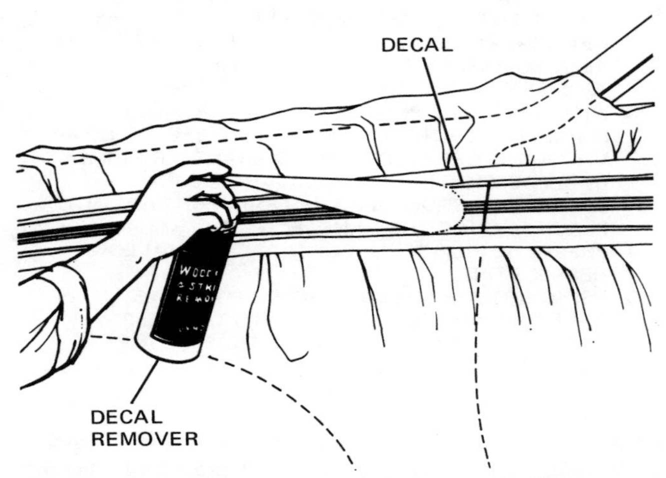

FIGURE 33-11. To remove a decal, first spray it with remover. *(American Motors Corporation)*

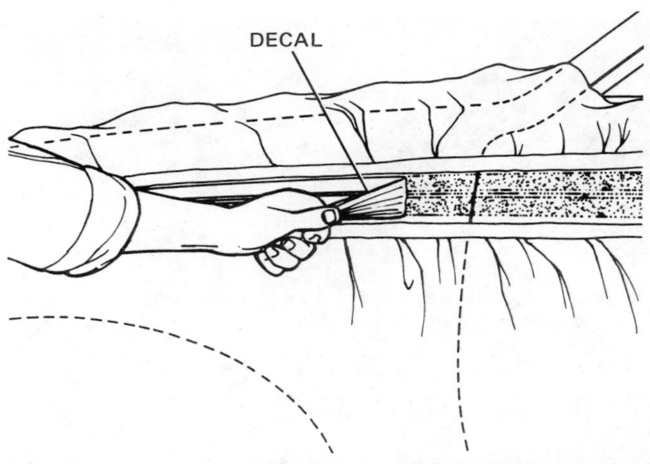

FIGURE 33-12. Peeling decal from a panel. *(American Motors Corporation)*

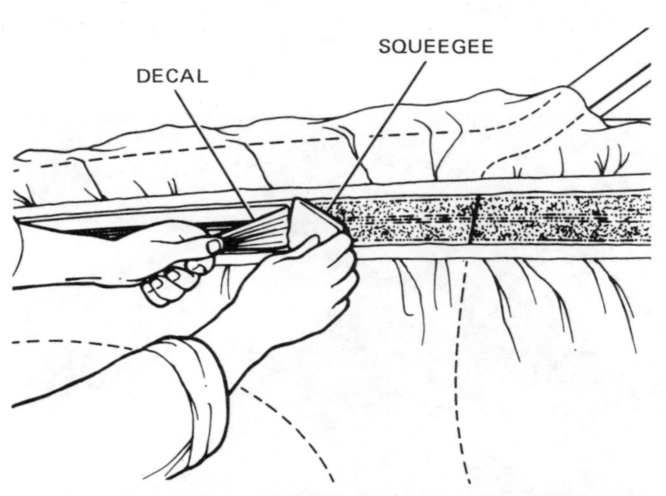

FIGURE 33-13. Use a squeegee to assist in removing a decal. *(American Motors Corporation)*

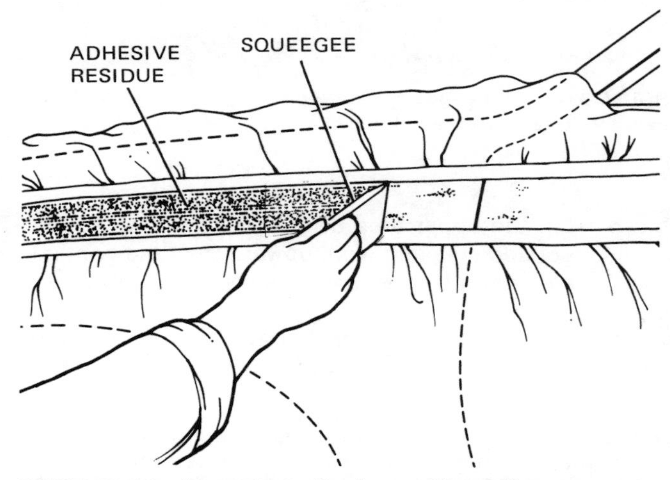

FIGURE 33-14. Removing adhesive residue with a squeegee. *(American Motors Corporation)*

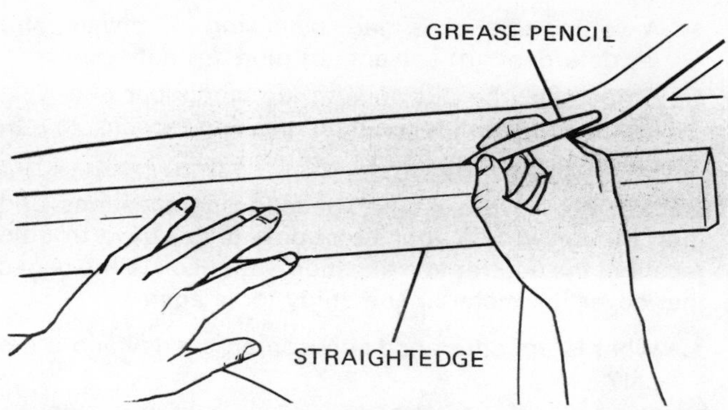

FIGURE 33-15. Marking position of decal. ***(American Motors Corporation)***

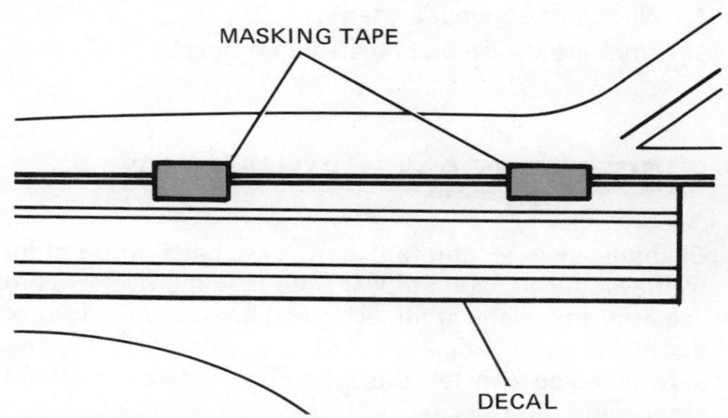

FIGURE 33-16. Positioning the decal with masking tape. ***(American Motors Corporation)***

of masking tape (Fig. 33-16). Be sure the decal is aligned with decals on adjacent panels.

3. Lift the decal, using the masking tape as hinges (Fig. 33-17). Strip off about 6 inches [152.4 mm] of backing paper from one end (Fig. 33-18).

NOTE: To avoid stretching the decal or getting it stuck on the panel in the wrong position, do not remove more than about 6 inches [152.4 mm] of paper at a time.

4. Fold the decal back into the aligned position. With firm strokes, squeegee the decal to the panel with one hand while removing the paper with the other (Fig. 33-19).
5. Wrap the end of the decal, where possible, around the corner or edge (Fig. 33-20) of the panel. Be careful not to trap air when you do this.

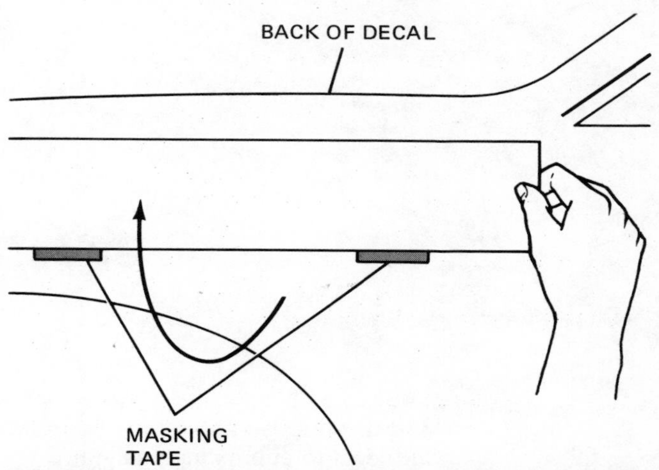

FIGURE 33-17. Lifting the decal. ***(American Motors Corporation)***

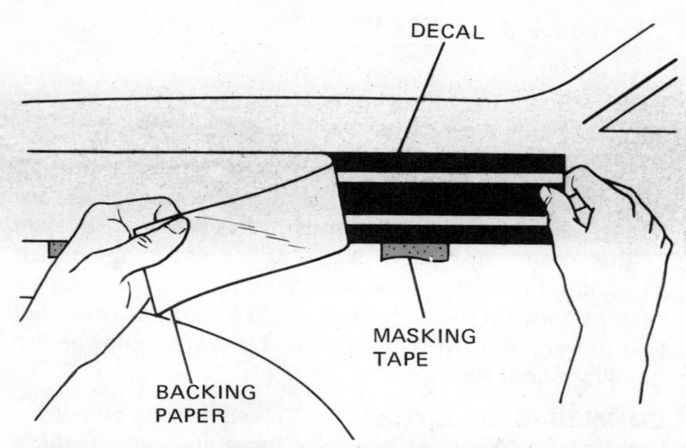

FIGURE 33-18. Removing backing paper from decal. ***(American Motors Corporation)***

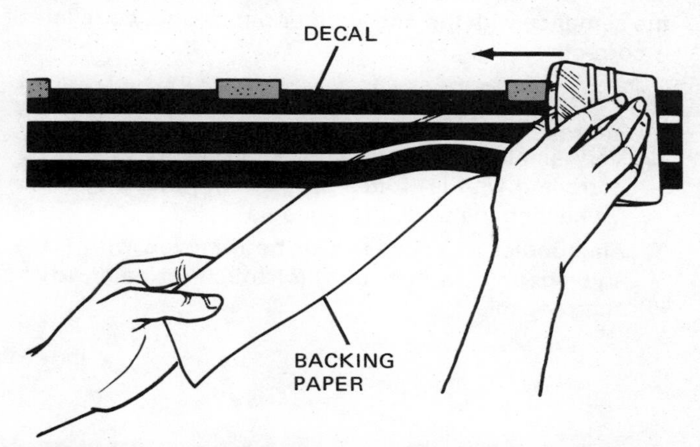

FIGURE 33-19. Installing decal with a squeegee. ***(American Motors Corporation)***

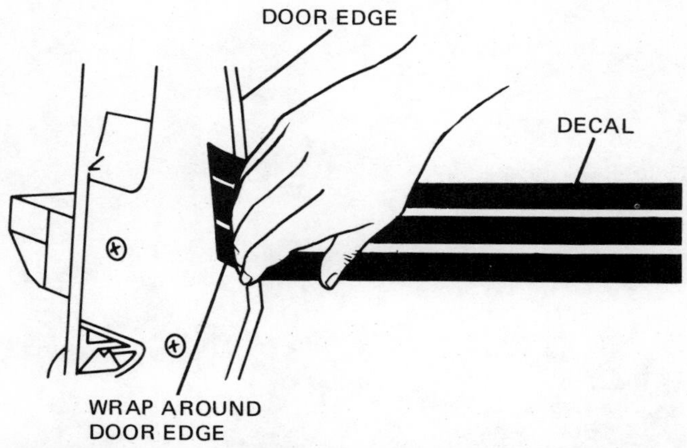

FIGURE 33-20. Working the decal around the edge of a door. ***(American Motors Corporation)***

6. Remove the easy-release paper from the front of the decal (if used).
7. Inspect the decal for irregularities, using side light. Remove all air or moisture bubbles.
8. Reinstall all parts that were removed.

NOTE: For large, intricately shaped decals, you may find it easier to use a wetting solution and treat the decal as the overlay was treated. See Chapter 32.

NOTE: Some technicians will paint on stripes, rather than install decals, if they are not too complex. Painting on stripes is quick and easy if careful masking is done.

CHAPTER 33 CHECKUP

NOTE: Since the following is a chapter review test, you should review the chapter before taking the test.

Decals and stripes are other uses of vinyl material. Just like wood-grain overlays, these applications are solely to benefit the appearance of the vehicle. Because of this, many car owners want service and replacement of damaged exterior vinyl. In this chapter, you learned how to perform these procedures. To find out how well you understand everything in this chapter, answer the questions that follow.

COMPLETING THE SENTENCES The sentences below are incomplete. After each sentence there are several words or phrases, but only one of them correctly completes the sentence. Write each sentence in your notebook, ending the sentence with the one word or phrase that completes it correctly.

1. Vinyl material that has a wood grain in it is called (*a*) a stripe, (*b*) a strip, (*c*) an overlay, (*d*) a decal.
2. Very small damage to wood-grain overlays can be corrected with (*a*) touch-up paint, (*b*) masking tape, (*c*) cellophane tape, (*d*) a needle.
3. Air bubbles in overlays can be removed with (*a*) a squeegee, (*b*) a heat gun, (*c*) touch-up paint, (*d*) a sharp needle.
4. A wetting solution is made by mixing warm water and (*a*) detergent, (*b*) solvent, (*c*) glue, (*d*) adhesive.
5. Stripes may be put on with (*a*) sandpaper and wax, (*b*) tape or paint, (*c*) painted masking tape, (*d*) touch-up paint or spray paint.

QUESTIONS Write each of the following questions, and then the answer, in your notebook. If you have trouble recalling the answer to a question, turn back to the pages that cover the material and study them again.

1. What is the difference between an overlay and a decal?
2. How do you remove an overlay?
3. How do you install an overlay?
4. When is a squeegee used?
5. What are the steps in installing a decal?

SUGGESTIONS FOR FURTHER STUDY

Examine several different cars that have wood-grain overlays, decals, and stripes. Note how the overlays are secured, especially at the ends and around the edges of doors and body panels. Look at stripes carefully, making sure that you can tell the difference between painted stripes and tape stripes.

PART 10

PAINTING AND REFINISHING

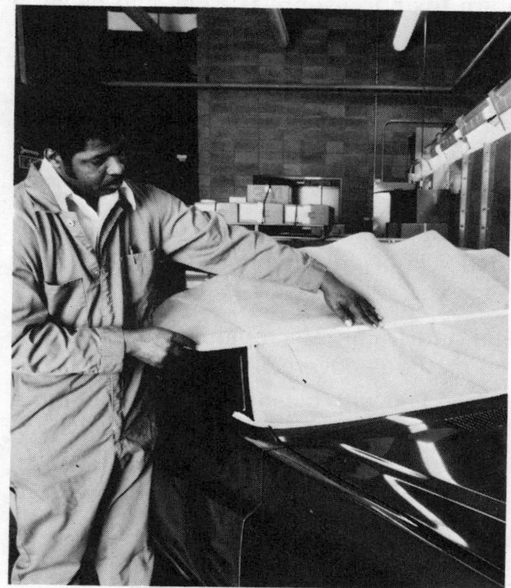

In this part, you will learn how to paint and refinish the car body and the interior and exterior parts attached to it. When a car body is to be painted, the surface must first be prepared as described in earlier chapters. Then the parts that are not to be painted must be masked, or covered with tape and paper. Finally, the paint is selected and the surface is primed and painted with a spray gun.

There are six chapters in Part 10, as follows:

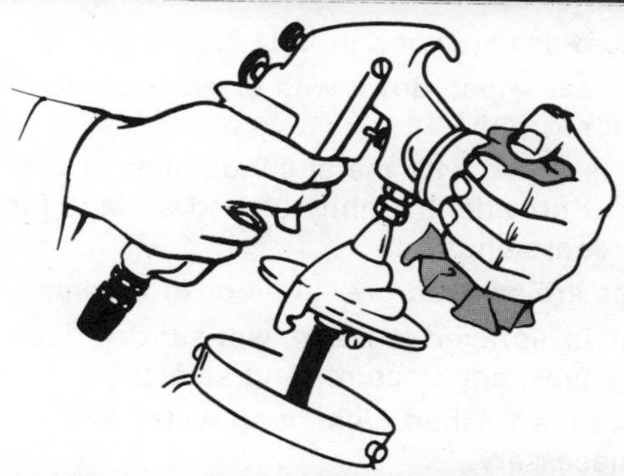

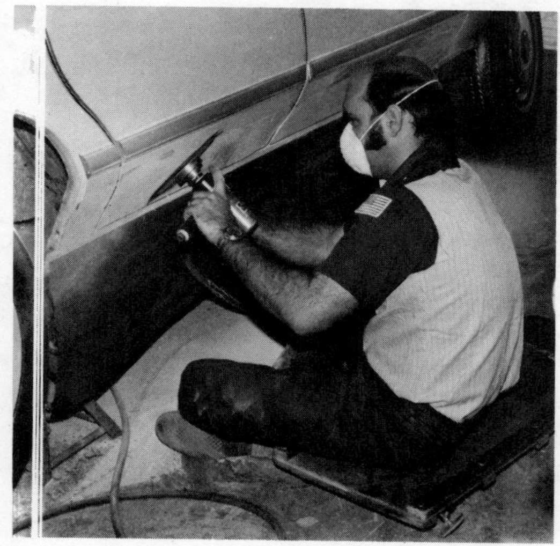

34 PAINTING SUPPLIES AND EQUIPMENT

In this chapter, you will learn about the various supplies and items of equipment that are used in the paint shop. We have already covered some of the equipment in previous chapters. These include electric and air-powered sanders and the compressed-air equipment for the paint spray guns (Chapters 6 and 7).

Also in this chapter, you will learn the principles of masking. Masking requires special paper and tape, which are applied to all parts of a car body not being worked on when painting is to be done.

○34-1 Safety in the Paint Shop

Earlier in the book, in Chapter 3, we discussed the general safety rules for the shop. You should review these rules perodically to make sure that you have not forgotten any of them. A single forgetful moment can get you into trouble and lead to an accident. Go back to Chapter 3 now and review the rules. In addition to these general rules, there are certain special safety precautions you should follow in the paint shop.

Almost all paint materials, including lacquers, enamels, varnishes, thinners, reducers, and solvents, are potential fire hazards. These materials can catch fire very easily. When they do catch fire, they will burn violently and can very quickly get out of control. Vapors from thinners and other such solvents can spread quickly through an enclosed area and become ignited by sparking motors, lighted cigarettes, welding torches, even the spark from turning off an electrical switch. For this reason, adequate ventilation in the paint shop is a *must!*

1. Make sure the ventilation system is adequate and is working properly.
2. Make sure the No Smoking signs are prominently displayed and are being obeyed.
3. Make sure fire extinguishers are in good working order and are prominently displayed.
4. Do not drive a car into or out of the spray booth. Push it in or out by hand. A running engine can ignite any vapors in the paint booth.
5. Don't try to connect extra electrical equipment to a circuit by using three-way plugs. This can overload the circuit and cause sparking if something burns out.
6. Check all electrical equipment regularly. Make sure the ground wires are connected properly.
7. Keep the area clean. Do not allow rags and shop towels to accumulate in piles on the floor. They can ignite spontaneously and burst into flames. Make sure they are removed from the area periodically—at least once a day and especially before you go home in the evening. Dispose of them as you would oily rags—by putting them into the special container set aside for this purpose. The container should have an airtight lid, and it should be emptied frequently.
8. Always wear a respirator when in the paint shop. The fumes from the paint and other materials used in the paint shop are toxic (poisonous). They can cause a variety of diseases if inhaled over a period of time. Protect yourself; wear a respirator!

○34-2 Steps in Painting a Car Body

The metal must be straightened, filled with plastic filler, and sanded. Then it is given additional treatment. Here are the various steps:

1. Sheet metal and frame are repaired and straightened by the methods covered in Part 3.
2. Sheet metal is filled with plastic filler (as covered in Part 4) and sanded down to contour.
3. Dust is wiped off. The car is washed and dried. All crevices where dust might collect are blown out with compressed air.
4. Repaired area is smoothed with fine sandpaper and blown clean.
5. Car is masked as explained in ○34-7.
6. Repaired area is wiped down with clean paper towels and tack rag (○34-4).
7. Bare metal is wiped with metal conditioner to prevent rust and provide a slightly etched surface for good undercoat adhesion.
8. Primer coats are sprayed on—three or four coats.
9. Guide coat is sprayed on and wet-sanded (see ○37-8) to remove any trace of sand scratches.
10. Repaired area is washed clean with water and remasked if necessary.
11. Final color coats are sprayed on.

We describe these various steps in the following chapter. In this chapter we discuss the painting materials and equipment not covered earlier in the book.

○34-3 Cloth and Paper Towels

The areas on the vehicle to be painted must be clean. Disposable paper towels are best for this purpose. Shop cloths, even if clean, can leave lint. No matter how well laundered, they can still contain foreign material that would ruin a paint job.

NOTE: The paper towels used for this purpose are not the type that come in a roll for home use. These are special no-lint shop paper towels.

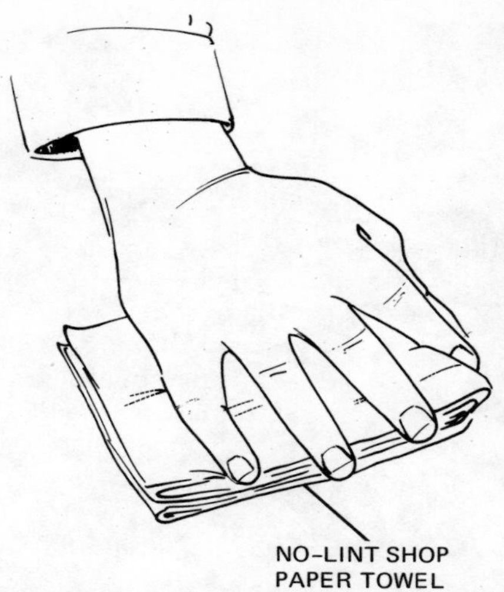

FIGURE 34-1. Wiping area to be painted with a clean towel.

Here are some hints on how to use paper or cloth towels:

1. Fold the towel into a pad. Refold it frequently so you will always be wiping with a clean section of the towel (Fig. 34-1).
2. When using cleaning solvent, wet the towel thoroughly.
3. Use a second dry towel to wipe away the solvent. Don't try to use the first towel, even if it feels dry.
4. Use plenty of towels. You must get the area to be painted clean and free of all traces of grease and oil.

NOTE: Don't touch the cleaned area with your fingers. Even if you have just washed your hands, you will leave traces of skin oil that will show up later in the paint job.

○ 34-4 Tack Rag

The tack rag is a cheesecloth pad that has been soaked in a sticky nondrying varnish. It is used to pick up lint, dust, and dirt. Just before the primer is applied, the repaired area is wiped off with a tack rag to make sure that it is clean (Fig. 34-2). The tiniest particles of dust will show up and spoil an otherwise good paint job.

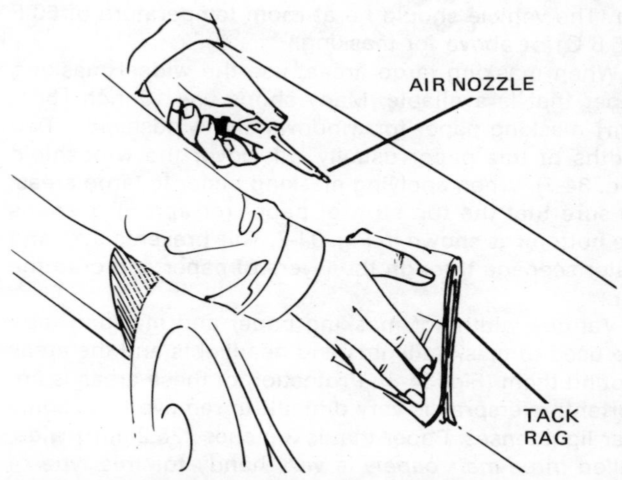

FIGURE 34-2. Wiping up lint and dust with a tack rag.

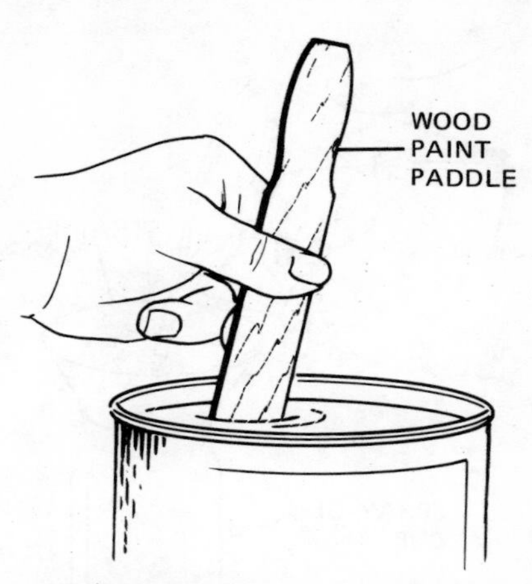

FIGURE 34-3. Stirring paint with a paint paddle.

○ 34-5 Paint Paddle

The paint paddle, made of wood or metal (Fig. 34-3), is used to stir the paint in the container before it is poured into the spray gun. A good paint paddle should have sharp edges so as to get down into the corners of the container and stir up any pigment that has settled there. If the paint container has been thoroughly shaken by a commercial shaker before it is opened (see Fig. 6-15), it will not be necessary to use a paint paddle. Nevertheless, it is a good idea to stir the paint with the paddle after you open the container. You will need a paddle in any event to mix the paint with thinner, or catalyst, as we explain later.

○ 34-6 Strainer

Strainers are funnel-shaped and are used to strain out any dirt, lumps, or scum in the paint as it is poured into the spray-gun cup (Fig. 34-4). Any foreign material in the spray gun will cause trouble. Impurities either will clog the gun so it throws an irregular pattern or will show up in the final paint job as raised specks on the paint that would have to be removed. Strainers are made of mesh, fiber or wire, or disposable filter paper.

NOTE: If you strain metallic paints through too fine a filter, you will remove the metal flakes in the paint.

○ 34-7 Masking Tape and Paper

Masking is a simple job, but it must be done correctly if the car is to come out of the paint shop with the best possible paint job. The basic principles of masking are discussed in this section, along with the type of paper and tape used.

Figure 34-5 shows a car completely masked and ready for painting. Masking has two purposes: First, it greatly reduces the time necessary to clean up the car after it is

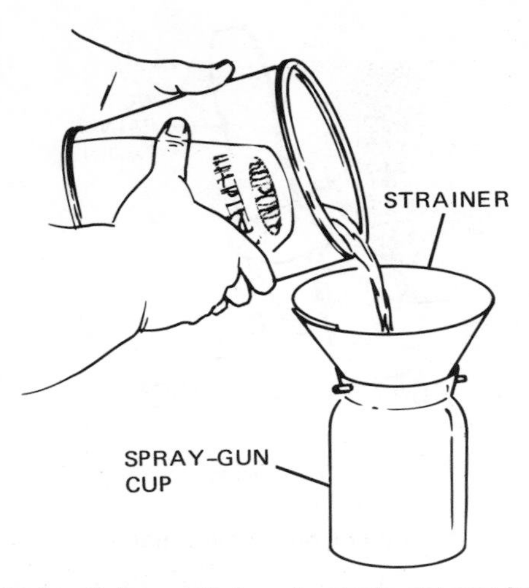

FIGURE 34-4. Using a strainer to strain out any impurities in the paint.

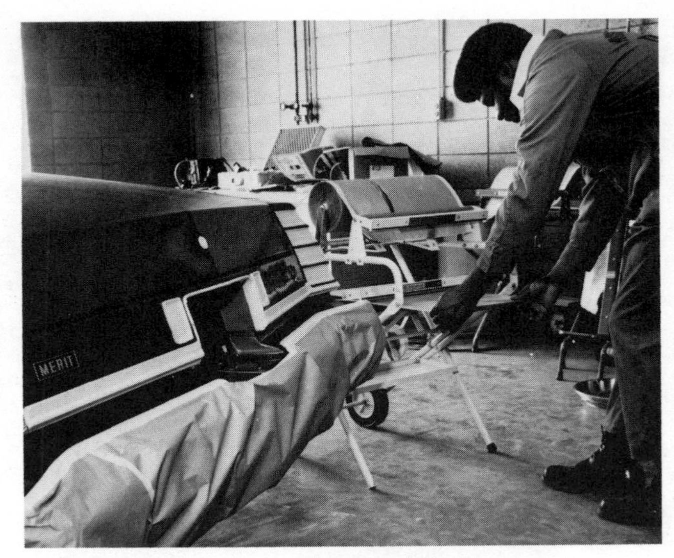

FIGURE 34-6. Using a masking stand. ***(3M Company)***

FIGURE 34-5. A masking stand makes masking a car quicker and easier. ***(3M Company)***

FIGURE 34-7. Two widths of 15-inch [381-mm] masking paper usually will cover the windshield. ***(3M Company)***

painted. Second, by catching any overspray, the masking tape and paper prevent primer and paint from getting on any surfaces other than those you intend to paint. This avoids hard-to-remove paint spray on adjacent glass and chrome trim.

There really is no special way that a car has to be masked. Probably the secret of good, fast masking is the use of a masking stand, as shown in Fig. 34-6. This device dispenses various widths of paper with a strip of masking tape stuck to one edge. Special wheel covers that quickly slip over the complete wheel assembly are sometimes used. Some technicians tape newspaper (rather than masking paper) over the glass and wheels. However, newspaper must not be taped over a painted surface, as the newspaper ink may dissolve and stain the paint. There are some water-soluble masking compounds available. These are brushed on, and then later washed off.

Masking tape should be applied to a clean, dry surface that is free of dust, dirt, and lubricants. On weatherstrip and rubber seals, apply a thin coat of clear lacquer with a cloth. Allow the lacquer to dry, and then apply the tape. Masking tape should not be stretched, except where you have to stretch it on curves. Position the tape, lay it down, and then press it in place with your fingers. Never apply masking tape to, or remove masking tape from, a cold car. The vehicle should be at room temperature of 60°F [15.6°C] or above for masking.

When masking large areas, use the widest masking paper that is available. Many shops use 15-inch [381-mm] masking paper for windows and windshields. Two widths of this paper usually will cover the windshield (Fig. 34-7). When applying masking paper to large areas, be sure that the top strip of paper (or apron) overlaps the bottom, as shown in Fig. 34-7. This prevents dust and water seepage through the layers of paper and onto the car.

Various widths of masking paper and masking tape are used to mask taillights and headlights and the areas around them (Fig. 34-8). Protection of these areas is important; overspray is very difficult to remove from some rear light lenses. Paper that is 3 inches [76.2 mm] wide, called *three-inch paper,* is very handy for this type of masking. Six-inch paper also is used frequently. In gen-

FIGURE 34-8. Various widths of masking tape are used to cover the rear lights and the areas around them. ***(3M Company)***

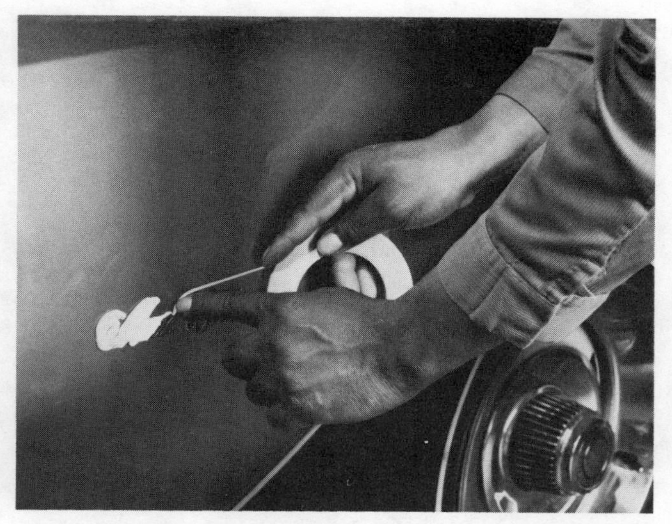

FIGURE 34-9. Narrow masking tape, ¼ inch [6.35 mm] wide, is used to mask letters. ***(3M Company)***

eral, the widest paper possible should be used, to keep down the cost of paper and labor to mask a car.

When spraying door jambs, sills, and pillars, you must be very careful to prevent overspray from hitting the interior of the car. Although too much masking paper spread about is wasteful, you must be sure that enough masking paper is used to protect all other areas, especially the interior of the car.

If you are spraying acrylic lacquer on a fender, hood, or trunk lid, use a double layer of masking paper. This will prevent dulling of the protected paint surface caused by solvent penetrating through the paper and contacting the paint.

Rubber and weatherstrip around doors, trunks, and windows often are coated with silicone lubricant. It is difficult to get masking tape to stick to coated rubber. To overcome this problem, apply a thin coat of clear lacquer to the rubber with a cloth or brush. Allow a few minutes for the lacquer to dry before applying the masking tape. The tape will stick more easily to the rubber. Also, the tape can be removed without tearing the rubber or transferring the adhesive. Do not use thinners or solvents to remove silicone from the rubber. Such materials can cause the adhesive from the tape to stick to the rubber.

When masking a car for a spot repair, reverse masking is often used. In this technique, the apron, or strip of paper, is folded back over the area to be protected. This exposes the adhesive side of the tape. The result is a less definite line and easier blending of the paint. The fold in the paper gives added protection against solvent and paint bleeding, a condition that occurs with acrylic paints.

Very narrow masking tape, usually ¼ inch [6.35 mm] wide, is used to mask letters and emblems (Fig. 34-9). This is usually less costly than removing the letters and emblems. Also, it eliminates the possibility of breaking the letters or emblems during removal and installation. Other masking tape widths, such as ½ inch [12.7 mm] and 1 inch [25.4 mm], can sometimes be used to quickly cover large emblems, molding, and trim (Fig. 34-10).

Remove the masking tape as soon as the paint is no longer sticky. To remove the tape, pull it at a 90° angle

FIGURE 34-10. Use ½-inch [12.7-mm] masking tape to cover body trim. ***(3M Company)***

to the surface. This procedure lessens the chances that the tape will pull paint from the body. The masking tape should be stored in a cool place, never on radiators, solvent cans, or in sunlight.

○34-8 Sandpaper

Sandpaper comes in many grit sizes, as explained in an earlier chapter. The grit size refers to the coarseness or fineness of the cutting edge of the sandpaper. Each grit size has a number, and sandpaper is ordered by this grit number. The greater the number, the finer the grit. A coarse sandpaper, such as 24 or 50, is used to remove old paint and prepare the metal surface for fine sanding. Fine sandpaper, such as 360 or 400, is used to featheredge (see ○34-9) from painted areas into metal to be painted and to get rid of sand scratches from coarser sandpaper.

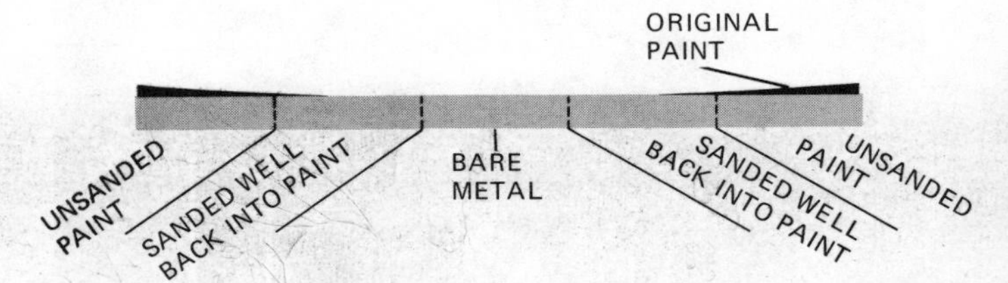

FIGURE 34-11. Sectional view of featheredging. *(Rinshed-Mason Company)*

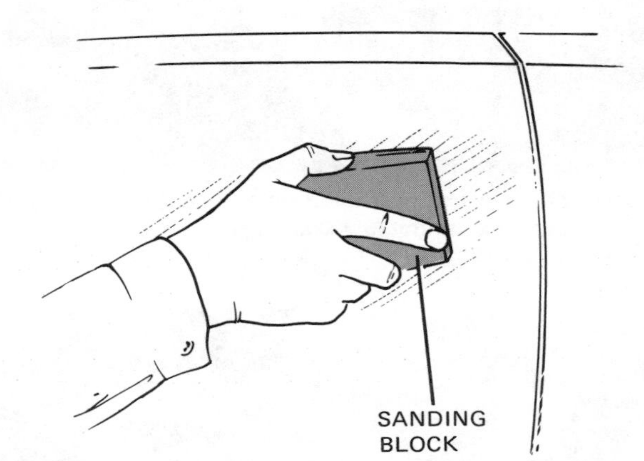

FIGURE 34-12. A sanding block.

○34-9 Featheredging

It is very important for you to know what featheredging means and how it is produced. When a spot repair is being done, the old paint is featheredged out into the raw metal. That is, the paint is sanded so that it tapers off from full thickness to no thickness. Figure 34-11 shows what this means. The thickness of the paint gradually slopes off into the bare metal. This is important, because the slightest ridge of paint would show up when the area is repainted. Featheredging is done with fine sandpaper (400 or finer). The surface then is cleaned before painting, as explained later.

○34-10 Sanding Blocks

When sanding flat surfaces by hand, always use a sanding block (Fig. 34-12). The block usually is made of wood with a rubber face. By using the block, the sandpaper is applied to the metal surface evenly. If you try to sand by holding the sandpaper to the metal with your fingers or hand, a very uneven sanding job can result.

For curved surfaces, a sanding block backed with a sponge-rubber pad can be used. The sponge rubber adjusts to the shape of the curve. For fairly sharp curves, you can use a short length of radiator hose with the sandpaper wrapped around it.

○34-11 Power Sanders

Power sanders of various types—disk, orbital, reciprocating—were discussed earlier in Chapters 6 and 7.

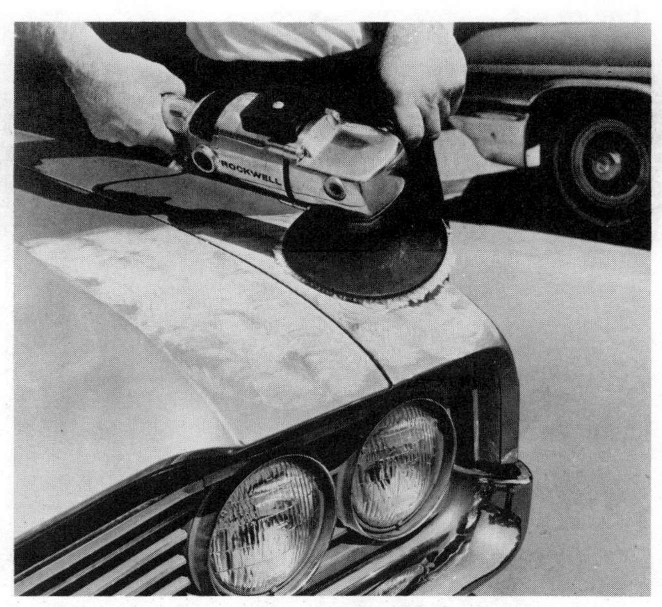

FIGURE 34-13. Using rubbing compound and a power polisher to finish a spot paint job. *(Rockwell International)*

○34-12 Power Polisher

The power polisher is similar in construction to the disk power sander. It is usually lighter and has a lower rpm (Fig. 34-13). The power polisher is used to rub down, or compound, a paint finish and also to polish the finish. Compounding is done with a very fine abrasive material in liquid or paste form. Its purpose is to improve the gloss of a new paint job.

NOTE: Compounding is also done to remove sand scratches around a repair area, or to prepare an acrylic enamel finish area which is to be spot-repaired with acrylic lacquer. This is discussed later.

When compounding, or polishing, do not apply too much pressure. Keep the polisher moving. If you let it stay in one spot too long, it will burn or cut through the finish. To avoid cutting through styling edges, mask them with masking tape.

CHAPTER 34 CHECKUP

NOTE: Since the following is a chapter review test, you should review the chapter before taking the test.

Painting a car requires more than a spray gun and paint. It requires several different types of painting supplies and the use of some special equipment. In this chapter, we have brought together a discussion of each of these, along with references to other chapters in the book that cover them also. To find out how well you understand everything in this chapter, answer the questions that follow.

COMPLETING THE SENTENCES The sentences below are incomplete. After each sentence there are several words or phrases, but only one of them correctly completes the sentence. Write each sentence in your notebook, ending the sentence with the one word or phrase that completes it correctly.

1. Almost all paint materials are (*a*) water-soluble, (*b*) mixed with oil, (*c*) potential fire hazards, (*d*) black in color.
2. Before painting, the purpose of wiping bare metal with a metal conditioner is to (*a*) prevent rust, (*b*) make the paint stick, (*c*) make the paint dry, (*d*) prevent runs in the paint.
3. A tack rag is used to (*a*) polish the car, (*b*) dissolve the old paint, (*c*) pick up lint, dust, and dirt, (*d*) make the masking tape tacky.
4. Before painting a spot on the car, first you must (*a*) wash the car, (*b*) grind off the old paint, (*c*) mask the area, (*d*) wipe the area with solvent.
5. Featheredging is used to prevent the appearance of (*a*) ripples in the paint, (*b*) a ridge line in the paint, (*c*) dirt in the paint, (*d*) scratch marks in the paint.

DEFINITIONS In the following, you are asked to define certain terms. Write the definitions in your notebook. This will help you remember them. It will also provide you with a quick way to locate meanings when you need the information again. If you do not know the meanings of the terms, look them up in the text or in the glossary at the back of the book.

1. In the paint shop, what is a disposable paper towel?
2. What is a paint paddle?
3. What is a strainer?
4. Define "featheredging."
5. What is a power polisher?

SUGGESTIONS FOR FURTHER STUDY

In a page for your notebook, write the heading "Paint Supplies." Then make an inventory of each of the various paint supplies that are available in your shop. For example, under "Masking Tape," write down the widths available. Under the heading "Sandpaper," list the various types, sizes, and grits available. Also, after each item, note its location. In this way, when you need any paint supplies, you will know what is available and where to look for it.

35 SPRAY GUNS

In this chapter, you will learn how paint spray guns are constructed and how they work. You will also learn how to clean and use them.

There are two types of spray gun, as explained in Chapter 7: the suction-feed type and the pressure-feed type. The suction-feed type is the one generally used in the automotive paint shop. Both types are discussed below. The purpose of the spray gun (both types) is to turn the liquid paint material into tiny droplets, or spray, and throw this spray uniformly onto the surface to be painted. The process of turning the liquid into fine droplets is called atomization. The spray gun operates on compressed air.

NOTE: Before using a spray gun, read the safety cautions at the beginning of Chapter 34.

○35-1 Suction-Feed Spray Gun

Figure 35-1 shows a suction-feed spray gun. In this gun, compressed air flows through a small opening around a fluid tip in the gun cap. This produces a slight vacuum which, in effect, "pulls" paint up from the cup. The paint flows up and out past the fluid tip. The stream of compressed air is also directed through the two side portholes of the cap (Fig. 35-1). Without any air flowing through the side portholes, the spray would be round (Fig. 35-2) and it would be hard to get an even layer of paint when spraying a panel, for example. With the air flowing through the two side portholes, the spray is reshaped, or fanned out, into an oval pattern (Fig. 35-3).

Figures 35-4 to 35-7 show the principle parts of the spray gun and how they work. Let us look at Fig. 35-4 first. The fan adjustment screw changes the amount of air flowing through the two side portholes in the air cap. If this screw is backed off, more air flows and the oval spray pattern is elongated. If it is turned in, the pattern changes toward a rounder shape. The fluid adjustment screw adjusts the amount of paint that flows out past the fluid needle. If this screw is backed out, more paint flows. If it is turned in, less paint flows. The two screws must be adjusted just right, so that the right amount of paint flows and the right amount of air flows to produce the desired pattern. The adjustments are different for different paints and mixtures of paint and thinner. Also, adjustments vary according to the type of paint job (spot repair or complete car paint job).

In Fig. 35-5, we see conditions with the air and fluid valves closed. Figure 35-6 shows the conditions with the trigger at the halfway point. The air valve is opened, allowing compressed air to flow out through the two side portholes in the air cap and also around the fluid tip. No paint can flow, because the fluid needle valve is closed at the half-trigger position.

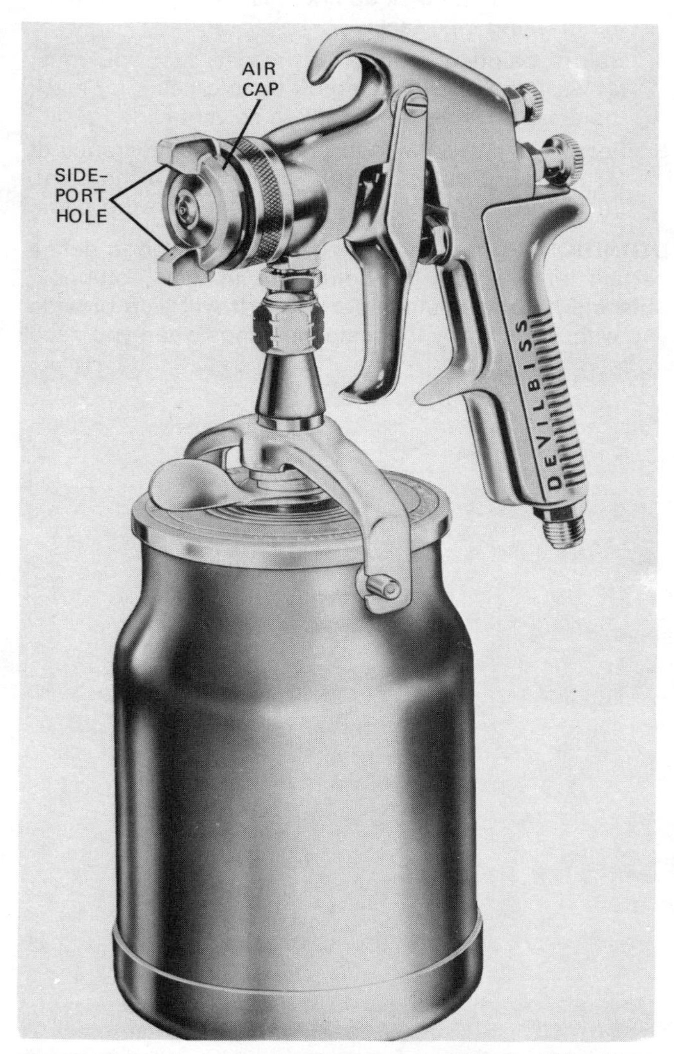

FIGURE 35-1. **A suction-feed spray gun. *(The Devilbiss Company)***

Figure 35-7 shows the conditions when the trigger is pulled all the way back, to the spraying position. This pulls the needle valve back so the paint can flow up from the cup and out past the paint of the needle valve. The compressed air breaks the paint up into tiny droplets (atomizes it) so the paint emerges as a fine spray. The compressed air from the two side portholes in the air cap shape this into an oval pattern, as already explained.

NOTE: There are three trigger positions: OFF, AIR ON, and AIR AND FLUID ON. You do not pull the trigger back only part way past the AIR ON position to partly open the fluid needle valve. The trigger is always pulled all the way back to fully open the needle valve.

We mentioned previously that the vacuum formed by the compressed air flowing past the fluid tip "pulled"

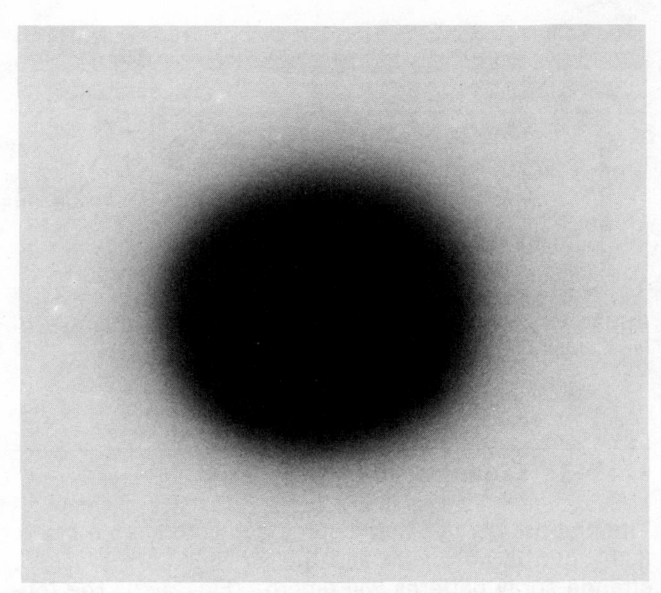

FIGURE 35-2. When no air flows through the side portholes, the spray pattern is round.

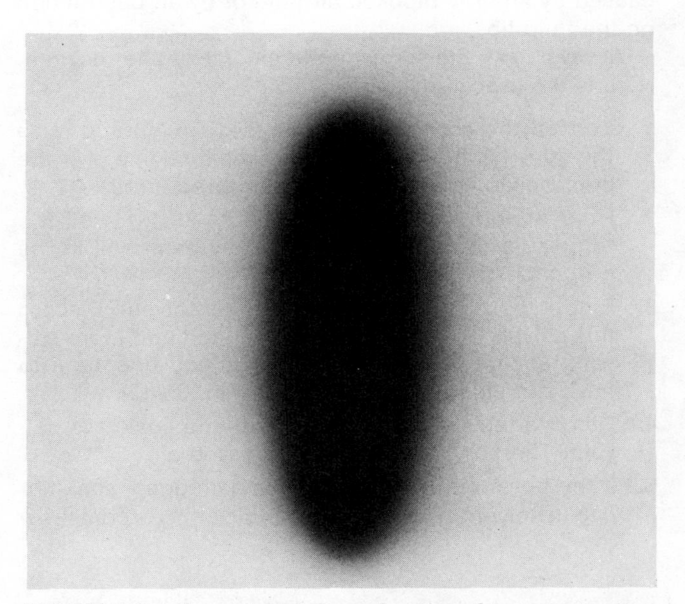

FIGURE 35-3. Normal oval-shaped pattern from a spray gun.

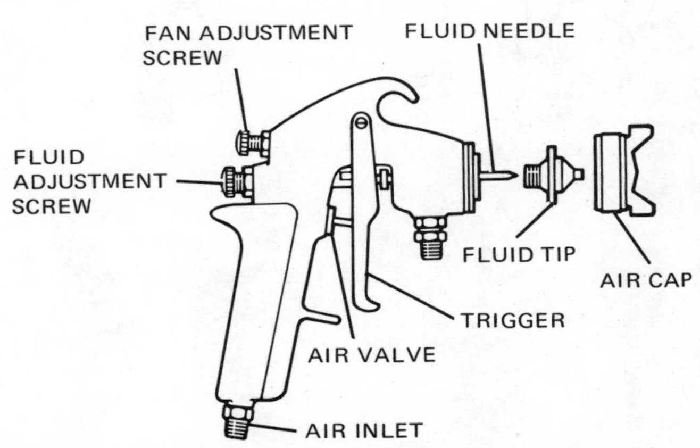

FIGURE 35-4. Main parts of a spray gun. ***(Ford Motor Company)***

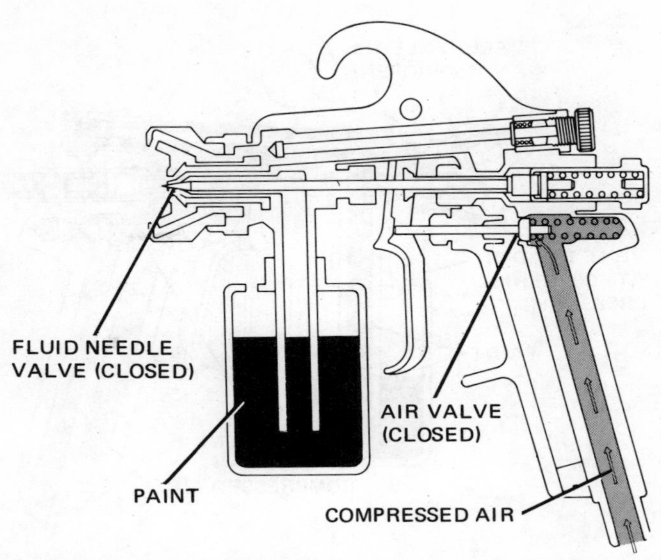

FIGURE 35-5. Conditions in the spray gun with the air and fluid valves closed. ***(Ford Motor Company)***

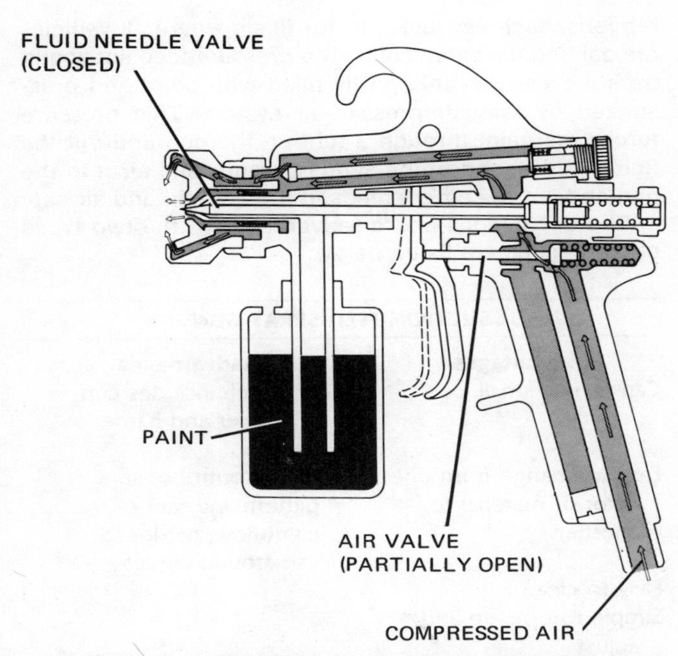

FIGURE 35-6. Air flows from the side portholes and around the fluid tip at the half-trigger position. ***(Ford Motor Company)***

paint up from the cup. Actually, atmospheric pressure, acting on the paint in the cup, pushes the paint up (Fig. 35-7). The vacuum at the fluid tip means there is less pressure at that point than atmospheric pressure. The difference in pressure, therefore, pushes the paint up and out past the needle-valve tip. The vent to admit atmospheric pressure to the cup is shown in Fig. 35-7.

○35-2 Pressure-Feed Spray Gun

The pressure-feed spray gun (Fig. 35-8) is not often found in the typical auto paint shop, because it is less convenient for small jobs. This type of gun is more useful for

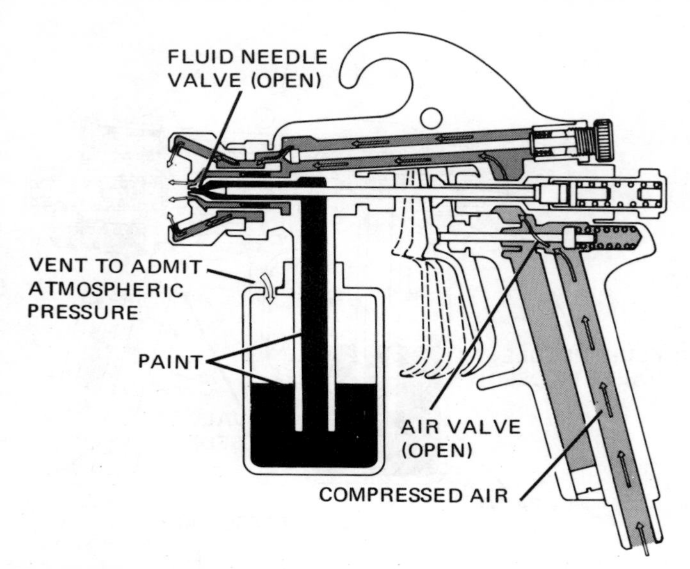

FIGURE 35-7. Full-trigger position with air and fluid valves open. ***(Ford Motor Company)***

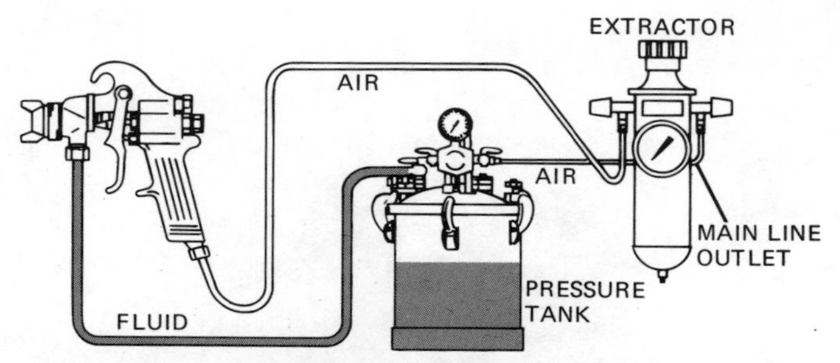

FIGURE 35-8. A pressure-feed spray gun. ***(Binks Manufacturing Company)***

big jobs, such as trucks, or for fleets where all vehicles are painted the same color. The pressure-feed spray gun uses a pressure tank, partly filled with paint and pressurized by the compressed-air system. This pressure forces the paint through a tube to the gun and out the fluid tip. A second tube sends compressed air into the gun and out the air openings in the fluid tip and air cap.

The advantages and disadvantages of the two types of spray guns are listed below:

SUCTION-FEED SPRAY GUN

Advantages	Disadvantages
Can handle small jobs	Gun, which includes cup, is heavier and harder to handle
Easy to change from one color or material to another	Limited control of spray pattern and rate of paint flow; harder to use around curves
Easy to clean	
Simple to operate and adjust	

PRESSURE-FEED SPRAY GUN

Advantages	Disadvantages
Can handle large amounts of paint and big jobs	Not suitable for small jobs requiring small amounts of paint
Provides constant flow of paint at uniform pressure	Frequent changes of color and material not practical
Will handle heavy materials such as spray-on vinyl	Difficult to clean
Lightweight and easy to handle	
Working angles of nozzle are unlimited	

○35-3 Cleaning the Spray Gun

The first priority in using a spray gun is to keep it clean. If the gun is not clean and the air holes are blocked, strange spray patterns will emerge (Fig. 35-9). The top-heavy or bottom-heavy spray is due to clogged side port-holes in the air cap. The crescent-shaped pattern is caused by a partly blocked air hole or by an obstruction on the fluid tip.

Always clean the spray gun immediately after using it. Here is the procedure:

1. Loosen the cup from the gun (Fig. 35-10) and raise the gun, still holding the end of the fluid line over the cup. Unscrew the air cap two or three turns.
2. Hold a cloth over the air cap (Fig. 35-11). Pull the trigger on the gun. This forces any paint still in the gun back into the cup.
3. Empty the cup and rinse it out with solvent. Discard this solvent after the cup is clean, and add more solvent. Put the cup back on the gun and operate it to flush out all paint from the gun (Fig. 35-12).
4. Remove the air cap from the gun and soak it in solvent. Then dry it off with compressed air.
5. If the holes in the air cap become clogged, soak the cap in solvent. Then use a toothpick or a broomstraw

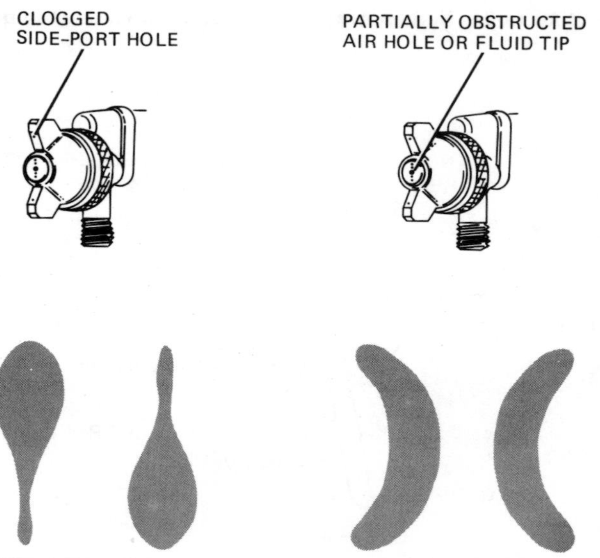

FIGURE 35-9. Faulty spray patterns. ***(Binks Manufacturing Company)***

to clean out the holes (Fig. 35-13). Never use a metal object such as a drill or wire to clean out the holes. This can enlarge the holes and completely destroy the proper spray pattern.

6. After the spray gun is cleaned, reassemble it in readiness for future use.
7. Lubricate the spray gun periodically with the type of oil recommended by the spray-gun manufacturer (Fig. 35-14).

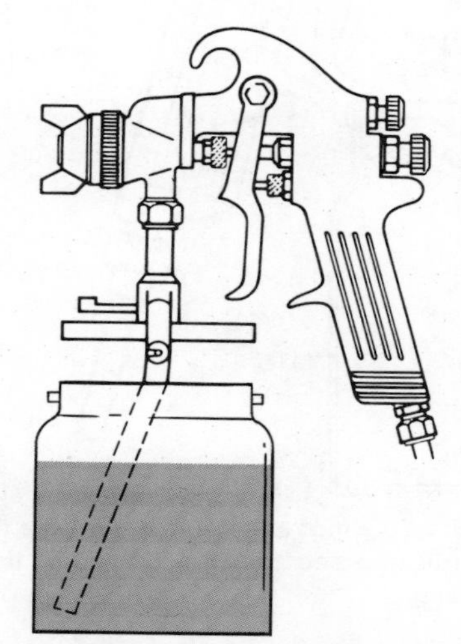

FIGURE 35-10. To clean a spray gun, first remove the cup. ***(Binks Manufacturing Company)***

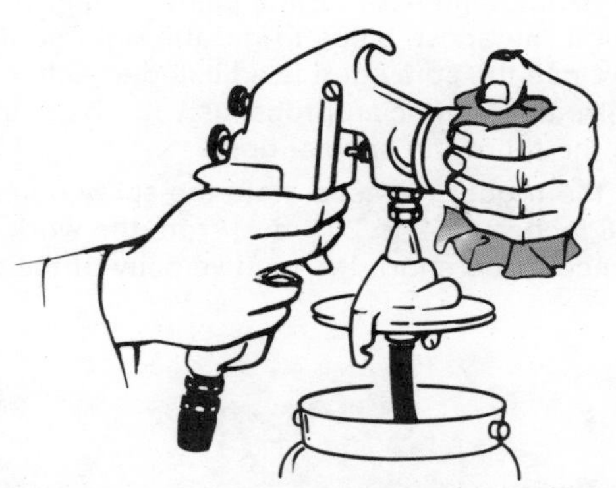

FIGURE 35-11. Hold a cloth over the air cap, and pull the trigger to force any paint in the gun back into the cup.

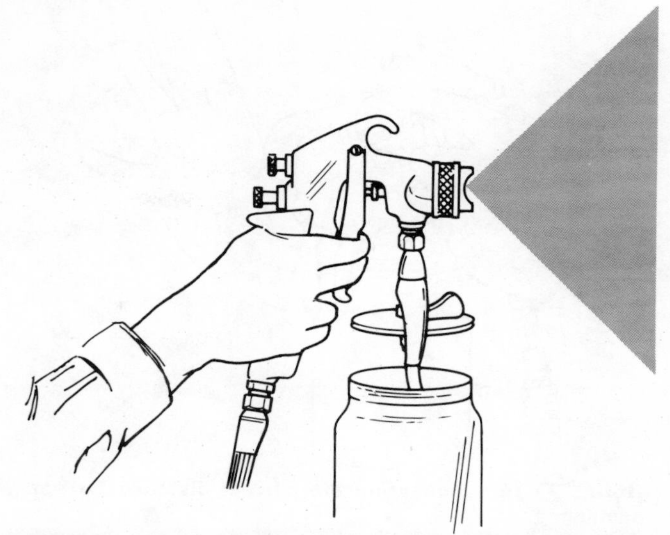

FIGURE 35-12. Spraying solvent to flush all paint from the gun.

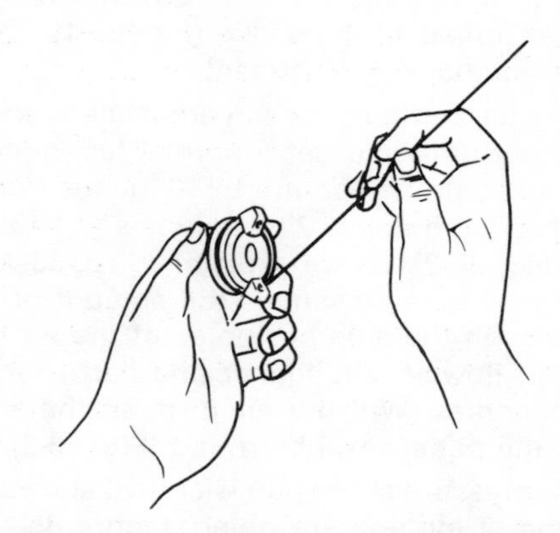

FIGURE 35-13. Use a toothpick or broomstraw to clean the holes in the air cap.

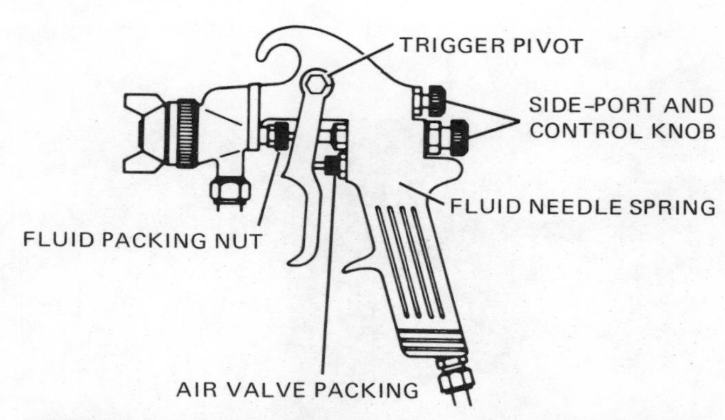

FIGURE 35-14. Lubrication points for a spray gun. ***(Binks Manufacturing Company)***

○35-4 Using the Spray Gun

When using the spray gun, temperature is important—both the temperature of the paint and the temperature of the object being sprayed. If the temperature is too low, the paint will go on sluggishly and dry slowly. This can be helped by adding more thinner. If the temperature is too high, the thinner may evaporate too fast and the paint will not smooth out, or flow, to provide a good job. The ideal temperature for spray painting is around 75°F [23.9°C].

The paint thinner, and other ingredients, should be properly mixed, agitated, strained, and poured into the spray-gun cup. Then attach the cup to the gun and connect the air hose to the gun. Open the air outlet valve leading to the air hose. Adjust the regulator valve (on the air transformer) to the recommended air pressure. Then proceed as follows:

1. Hold the spray gun about 6 to 8 inches [152 to 203 mm] from a test panel. An easy way to measure the correct distance is to stretch your fingers and touch the surface with your little finger and the tip of the spray gun with your thumb (Fig. 35-15). This puts the gun at the right distance from the work.

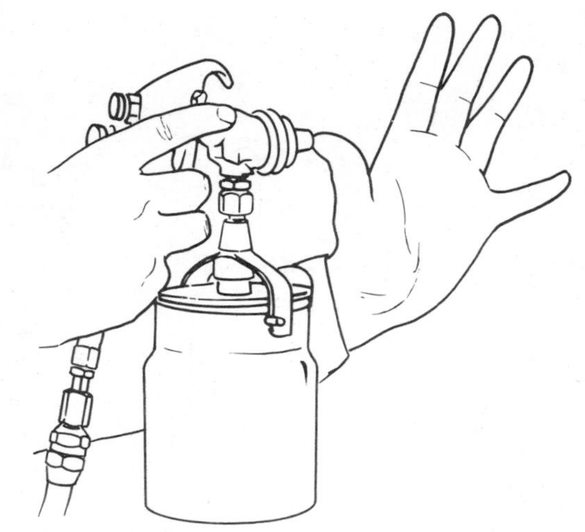

FIGURE 35-15. Measuring the correct distance for spray painting.

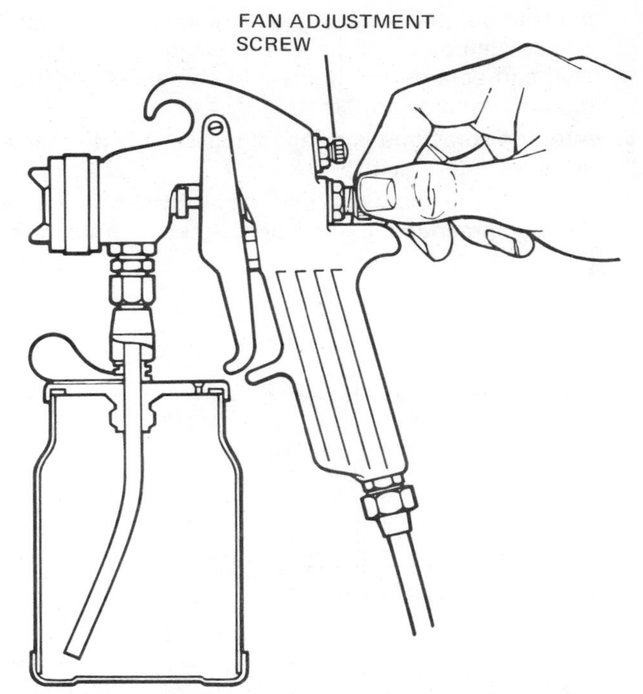

FIGURE 35-16. To shoot a test panel, turn the fluid adjustment screw out until you see the first thread of the screw. *(Ford Motor Company)*

2. Turn the fluid adjustment screw out until you see the first thread of the screw (Fig. 35-16). You now have a wide-open adjustment.
3. Pull trigger and turn the fan adjustment screw (Fig. 35-16) out until you get a normal test pattern. The pattern should be about 8 to 10 inches [203 to 254 mm] high and about 2 to 3 inches [51 to 76 mm] wide (Fig. 35-3). As we explained in ○35-1, the fan adjustment screw changes the amount of air flowing through the side portholes of the air cap. The more air flowing, the higher and narrower the pattern becomes. With no air through the side portholes, the pattern will be round (Fig. 35-2).
4. The air pressure at the gun is critical and varies with the type of job you are doing. Figure 35-17 shows the results of low and excessive air pressures. The air pressure is adjusted at the air transformer and is controlled by the regulator valve on the transformer.
5. It takes but a moment for the paint technician to go through the above steps to get the right spray pattern. Once the spray gun is adjusted to achieve this pattern, the technician proceeds with the paint job. Note the following special tips.
6. With the trigger released, hold the spray gun about 6 to 8 inches [152 to 203 mm] from the work. If the distance is too short, the high velocity of the spray-

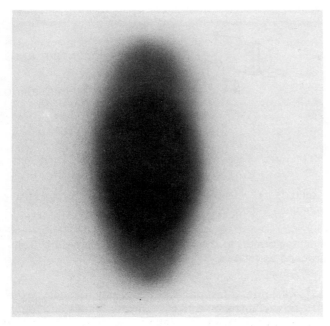

(A) LOW AIR PRESSURE

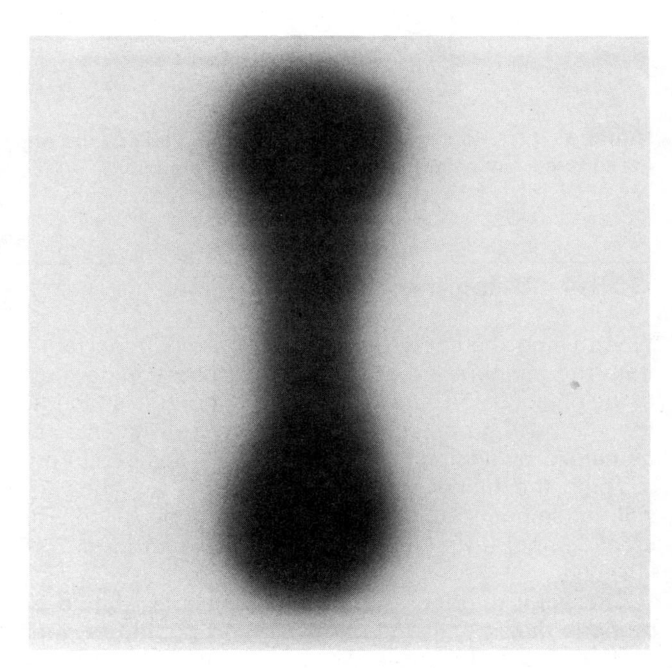

(B) HIGH AIR PRESSURE

FIGURE 35-17. Spray patterns with low and high air pressure.

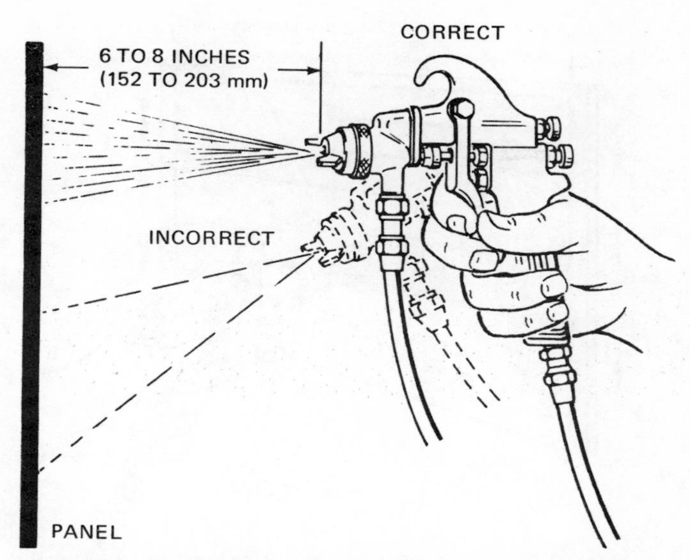

FIGURE 35-18. **Hold the spray gun level with and perpendicular to the panel.** ***(Binks Manufacturing Company)***

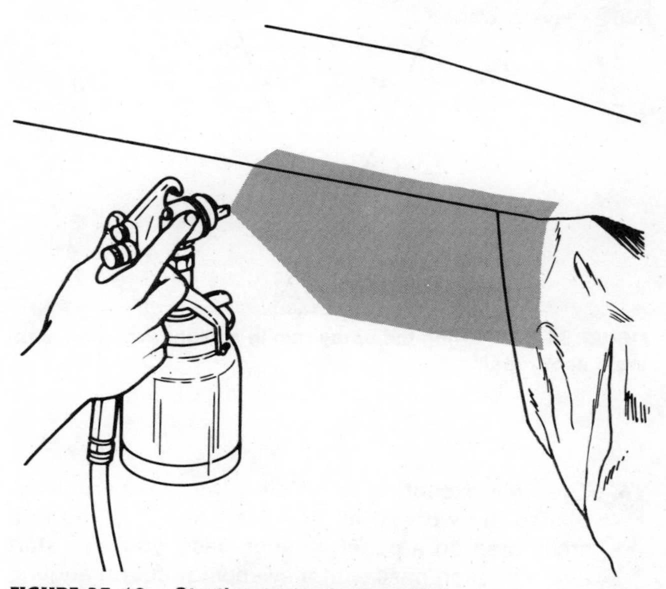

FIGURE 35-19. **Starting to apply the paint.**

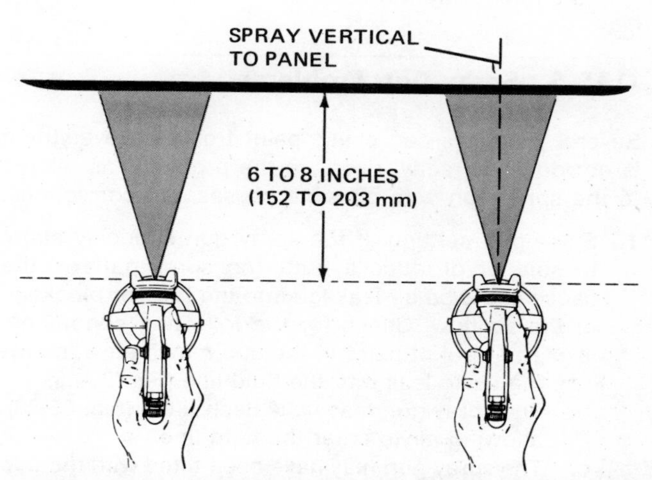

FIGURE 35-20. **Keep the spray gun at the same distance from and aimed vertically at the panel.** ***(Ford Motor Company)***

ing air tends to ripple the wet film. If the distance is too great, too much of the thinner will evaporate on the way to the work. This can result in orange peel, or a dry film.

7. Hold the gun level and at right angles (Fig. 35-18) to the work. Keep your wrist stiff, and use your arm and shoulder to move the spray gun across the surface to be painted. Keep the gun pointing vertically at the work. Before you actually press the trigger, practice moving the gun in steady, sweeping strokes, across the panel you are about to paint.

NOTE: We assume the panel has been properly prepared for painting and the car has been properly masked.

8. Now get ready to apply the paint. Aim the gun nozzle at the top of the panel and several inches to one side. Note, in Fig. 35-19, that the spray pattern is centered vertically on the mask. This means that part of the paint will spray off into space or onto the mask, which is all right. But it is important to get the center part of the pattern, where the larger amount of paint is being applied, to cover the top part of the panel.
9. Now, with the gun aimed at the top of the panel and to one side, pull the trigger and at the same time start the gun moving sideways across the panel. Move the gun smoothly and at a constant speed of about 1 foot [0.3 m] per second. Keep the gun at the same distance from and aimed vertically at the panel (Fig. 35-20). Never stop the motion of the gun across the work. It must be moved with uniform speed. If you move the gun too fast, the film will be too thin. If you move it too slowly, too much paint will get on the work and the paint will sag or run.
10. As you reach the end of the first pass across the panel, release the trigger just enough to close the fluid needle valve and stop the flow of paint. The air valves remain open. This action, known as *triggering,* prevents paint buildup at the edge of the panel, reduces paint waste caused by overspray and makes the job easier. Relaxing your hand muscles at the end of each pass reduces muscle fatigue so you can do a better and more accurate job.
11. As you move the gun out past the end of the panel, shift the aim downward one-half of the height of the spray pattern. That is, aim at the bottom of the previous pass. Now, on the second pass, the upper half of the pattern that is sprayed on will overlap the lower half of the spray pattern of the previous pass (Fig. 35-21).
12. In making the second pass, if the first pass was from right to left, the second pass must be from left to right. Just before the gun moves onto the panel, trigger it. Keep the gun moving across the panel at a steady speed, holding the gun perpendicular to the panel and at the correct distance from it. Aiming the gun at the bottom of the previous pass as described above will give a 50 percent overlap, which is the ideal overlap for a good paint job.
13. Continue to move the gun back and forth as previously described until the complete panel is covered with paint.
14. If you have a panel to paint that is longer than about 3 feet [914 mm], handle the job by spraying it in

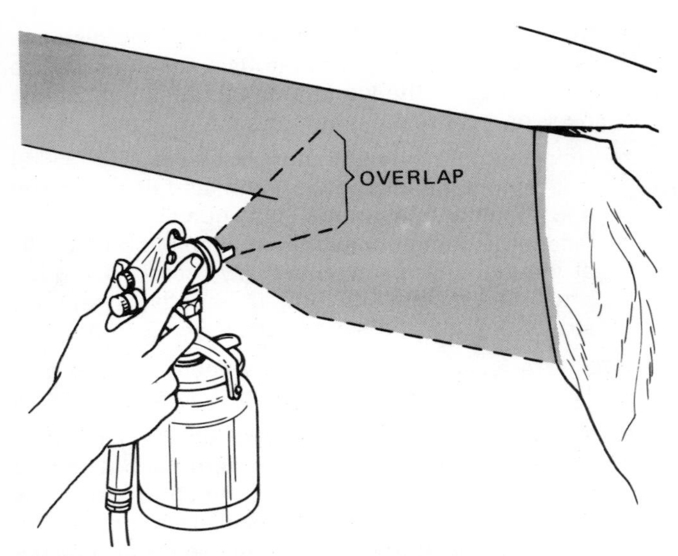

FIGURE 35-21. How to overlap the spray pattern.

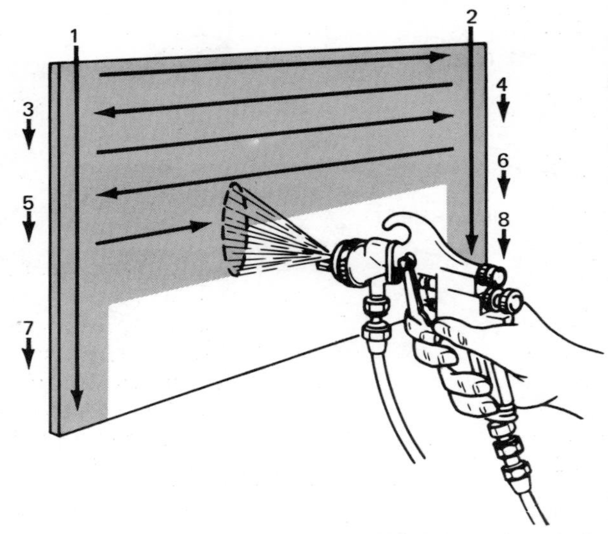

FIGURE 35-23. Banding a panel. *(Binks Manufacturing Company)*

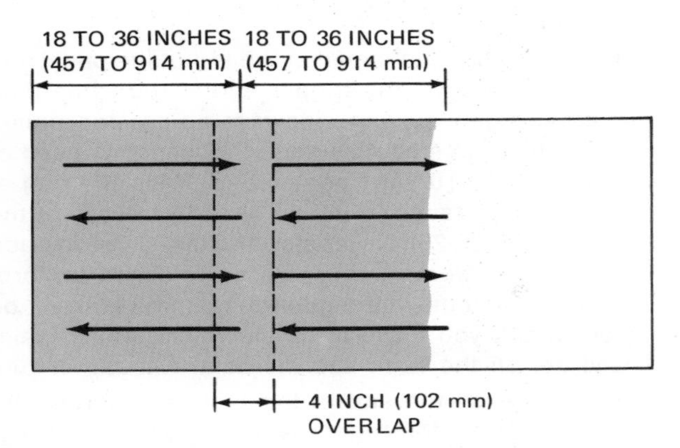

FIGURE 35-22. Spray a long panel in overlapping sections. *(Binks Manufacturing Company)*

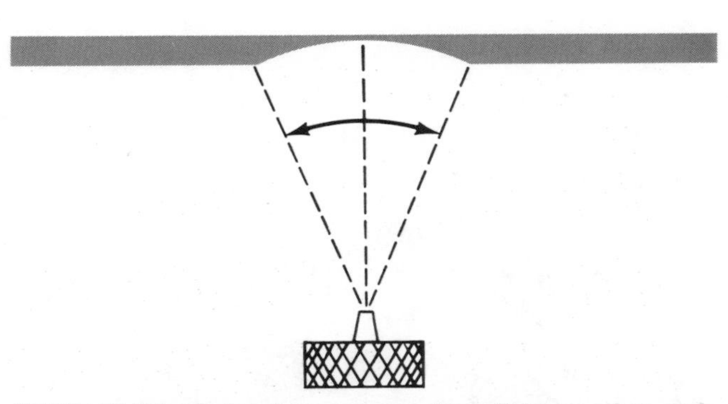

FIGURE 35-24. Swing the spray gun in a slight arc when making a spot repair.

overlapping sections (Fig. 35-22). Divide the panel up into two or three equal widths. Handle the first section as though it were a complete panel. As quickly as you finish the first section, move to the second section, overlapping the passes, as shown in Fig. 35-22. Then paint the third section. Properly done, the completed paint job will reveal no signs of the overlap. The secret here is that as you near the inner end of the first strokes, let up on the trigger (just as though it were actually the other edge of a panel). This causes the last part of the pass to fade off into nothing. Now, as soon as the first section of the panel is painted, move on to the second section. The first pass there should start at the point where the "fade-off" began on the adjacent pass (in the first section). This will fill in the fade-off area as the pass in the second section starts.

15. Banding is used on panels to assure good coverage at the start and end of the passes and to prevent overspraying. Figure 35-23 shows the procedure. The first two passes are vertical at the two sides of the panel (1 and 2 in Fig. 35-23). Then the panel is covered with horizontal, overlapping strokes, as shown at 3 to 8.

16. The only exception to holding the gun perpendicular to the work at all times is when spotting in a small area on a panel. In such case, you may start and end each pass with a sweeping motion angling away from the work as shown in Fig. 35-24. This fades the paint off on the two sides and helps blend the new paint into the old.

○35-5 Spray-Gun Problems

Several problems can cause paint trouble if everything is not done correctly. Here are the problems as related to the spray gun with possible causes and corrections.

1. Spray-gun spitting. If the spray gun suddenly starts to spit, or produce a fluttering spray pattern, the cause could be air leakage into the fluid or blockage of the air flow. Check for the following conditions:
   a. The level of paint in the cup may be low, allowing air to leak into the fluid line (Fig. 35-25).
   b. The spray gun may have been tilted (Fig. 35-26), allowing air to enter the fluid line.
   c. The spray gun may have been tilted with the cup full, causing the paint to block the air vent (Fig. 35-27). When this happens, air cannot enter, and

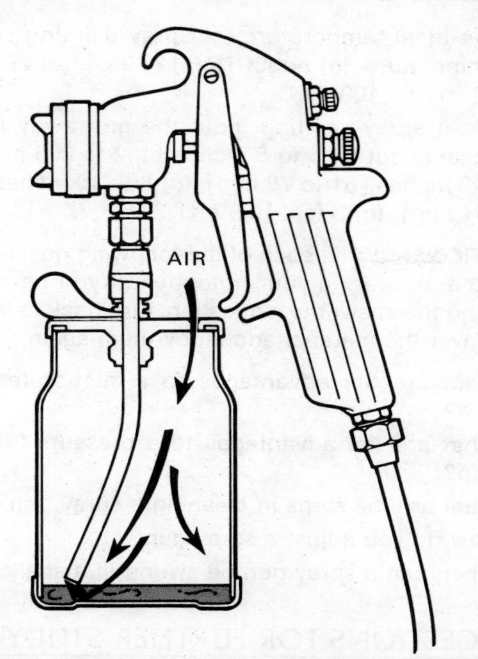

FIGURE 35-25. Running out of paint in the cup can cause the spray gun to spit. *(Ford Motor Company)*

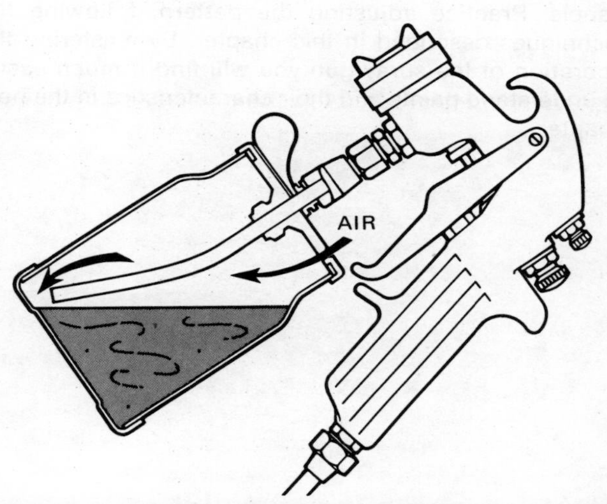

FIGURE 35-26. Tilting the spray gun may allow air to enter the fluid line. *(Ford Motor Company)*

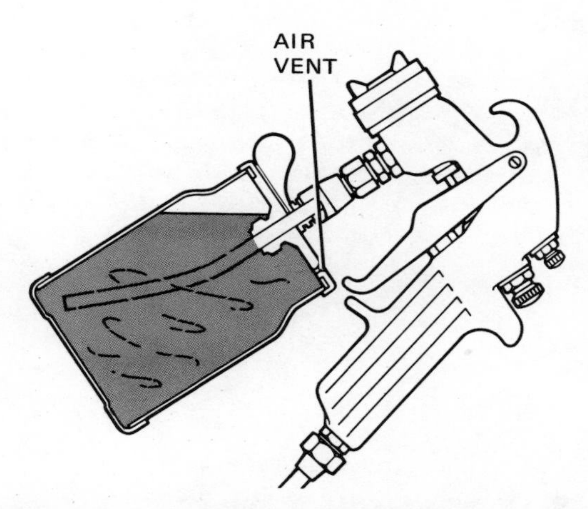

FIGURE 35-27. Tilting a spray gun with a full cup can clog the air vent. *(Ford Motor Company)*

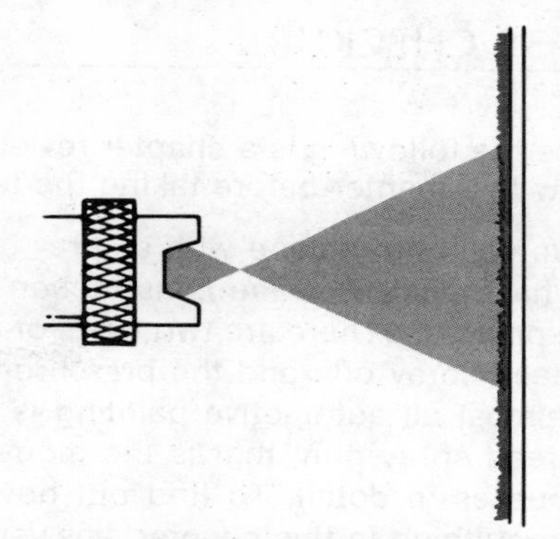

FIGURE 35-28. Spray gun delivering a thin coat. *(Ditzler)*

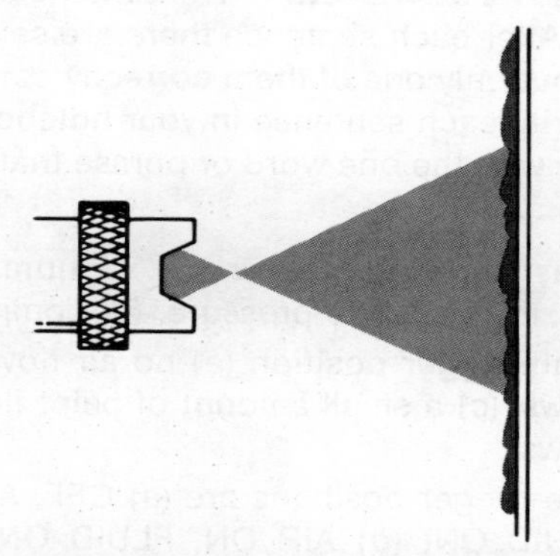

FIGURE 35-29. Spray gun delivering a heavy coat. *(Ditzler)*

therefore, the paint will not be pushed up to the fluid needle valve by atmospheric pressure.

d. Other causes could be a loose or cracked fluid tube, a loose cup lid, dry packing in the gun or a loose fluid needle packing nut, material too thick to flow freely, or material not properly strained and thus containing particles that clog the fluid needle valve.

2. Thin coat that is rough, dry, and has no luster (Fig. 35-28). This can be caused by any of the following:

a. Fluid adjustment screw not opening enough to feed sufficient paint
b. Gun held too far away
c. Paint too thin
d. Too much air
e. Gun moved too fast across panel
f. Not enough overlap of the various passes

3. Heavy coat with sags, ripples, or orange peel (Fig. 35-29). Orange-peel finish is a finish that is rough, like the peel of an orange. Orange peel, sags, or ripples can be caused by any of the following:

a. Dirty air nozzle
b. Gun held too close to panel
c. Paint too thin or too thick
d. Low air pressure
e. Stroke too slow
f. Too much overlap

NOTE: In Chapter 39 we describe and illustrate various faulty paint jobs and explain what caused them to go wrong. Several conditions not related to the spray gun or how it is used can cause paint troubles. We describe them all in Chapter 39.

CHAPTER 35 CHECKUP

NOTE: Since the following is a chapter review test, you should review the chapter before taking the test.

Automotive painting is done with a spray gun. In this chapter, we have discussed the construction and operation of the spray gun. There are two types of spray gun: the suction-feed spray gun and the pressure-feed spray gun. Since almost all automotive painting is done with the suction-feed spray gun, that is the model that this chapter discusses in detail. To find out how well you understand everything in this chapter, answer the questions that follow.

COMPLETING THE SENTENCES The sentences below are incomplete. After each sentence there are several words or phrases, but only one of them correctly completes the sentence. Write each sentence in your notebook, ending the sentence with the one word or phrase that completes it correctly.

1. The spray gun operates on (*a*) vacuum, (*b*) water pressure, (*c*) hydraulic pressure, (*d*) compressed air.
2. In the half-trigger position (*a*) no air flows, (*b*) only paint flows, (*c*) a small amount of paint flows, (*d*) no paint flows.
3. The three trigger positions are (*a*) OFF, AIR ON, AIR AND FLUID ON; (*b*) AIR ON, FLUID ON, AIR AND FLUID ON; (*c*) OFF, AIR ON, FLUID ON; (*d*) AIR OFF, FLUID ON, AIR AND FLUID ON.
4. The ideal temperature for spray painting is (*a*) any temperature, (*b*) about 75°F [23.9°C], (*c*) 32°F [0°C], (*d*) 212°F [100°C].
5. When spray-painting, hold the gun away from the panel about (*a*) 6 to 8 inches [152 to 203 mm], (*b*) 2 to 3 inches [51 to 76 mm], (*c*) 8 to 10 inches [203 to 254 mm], (*d*) 3 feet [0.9 m].

QUESTIONS Write each of the following questions, and then the answer, in your notebook. If you have trouble recalling the answer to a question, turn back to the pages that cover the material and study them again.

1. What are the advantages to a suction-feed spray gun?
2. What are the advantages to a pressure-feed spray gun?
3. What are the steps in cleaning a spray gun?
4. How do you adjust a spray gun?
5. When can a spray gun be swung in a shallow arc?

SUGGESTIONS FOR FURTHER STUDY

Learning to be a good painter requires practice and patience. Get a spray gun and begin to practice spraying panels. Practice adjusting the pattern, following the techniques described in this chapter. By mastering the operation of the spray gun you will find it much easier to understand paints and their characteristics in the next chapter.

36

AUTOMOTIVE BODY PAINTS

In this chapter, you will learn about the various kinds of paint used on automotive bodies and cautions regarding their uses and applications. A great variety of body paints have been used in the past, including numerous kinds of enamels and lacquers. Today, however, the original finishes on new cars produced in the United States are of two types: acrylic enamel and acrylic lacquer. The word "acrylic" pertains to a type of chemical—a liquid plastic—used in the manufacture of enamel or lacquer.

○36-1 Mr. Ford's "Black"

Cars produced early in this century were usually painted black. Henry Ford was supposed to have said he would supply cars in any color—"so long as they're black." The reason for this was that in those days it was difficult enough to get one color right—black—without having to be concerned with other colors. It took up to a month to paint a car in the early days. The paint was applied with a brush. After each coat dried, it was hand-sanded and rubbed and then repainted. Several coats were applied. The final coat was then waxed. You can see that painting the bodies was a real bottleneck to fast production.

In the early 1920s DuPont came out with a product that changed all this: Duco (for *DU*Pont *CO*mpany). This was a synthetic lacquer. It could be applied with a spray gun (and it dried in a few hours). Duco could be made in many colors, so colors other than black became popular. Still later, other types of lacquer and enamel appeared. By 1959, General Motors was using a form of acrylic lacquer on all its cars. This type of finish is used on GM cars today. American Motors Corporation, Chrysler Corporation, and Ford Motor Company used baking enamel before about 1955, but in the early 1960s switched to acrylic enamel, similar to the enamel used by these companies today.

Research continues on paints for automotive bodies, and improvements appear from time to time. For example, in 1975, Chevrolet Vega bodies from GM's Southgate, California, assembly plant were painted with a new type of enamel, called *water-based* acrylic. This enamel is said to have superior wearing qualities and holds its color longer (does not fade or streak). However, it does require some special care if a spot repair is required. We will come back to this later, when we discuss repairs of body paint.

There is one aspect of developing new paints that the paint scientists must keep in mind. Whatever new paint they come up with must be repairable with the equipment and skills available in the field. Therefore, you need not worry that the cars produced next year or the year after will have strange new paint jobs that require some new kind of equipment or painting procedures. In spite of the great variety of paints that have been used on cars in the past, the same general repair and painting procedures have not changed. You will use different materials on enamel and lacquer, but the general procedures are still the same. We will refer to this again when we talk about specific paints and materials.

○36-2 Paint Ingredients

All paints, regardless of the type or who manufactures them, have three basic ingredients:

1. Pigment
2. Binder
3. Vehicle

Let us look at each of these in detail.

○36-3 Pigments

Pigments give the paint its color. They come in all sorts of colors, from white to black. If you saw a white pigment all by itself, you'd say it looks like talcum powder. Pigments are finely ground powder. The materials from which the pigment is ground determines its color and the color of the paint job on the car.

The so-called "glamour" paints—the paints with a metallic sheen—have tiny chips of metal, such as aluminum, mixed in with the pigment. These chips are shiny and impart an iridescent, or sparkling, appearance to the paint. See ○36-16.

○36-4 Binder

The binder does what its name implies. It binds the pigment together and to the metal of the car body. By itself, the binder looks like syrup for pancakes. Adding the pigment gives the binder its color. Many different kinds of binders have been used, with many different chemical formulas. The binder in general use today is the liquid plastic called acrylic. There are different kinds of acrylic. One is used in acrylic enamel, another in acrylic lacquer. We describe these two paints later.

○36-5 Vehicle

A binder mixed with pigment would be too heavy to spray. It must be thinned out. The chemical used to thin the mixture is called the vehicle. Adding the vehicle to the binder and pigment mix results in a paint thin enough to be sprayed. The vehicle is highly volatile. That is, it evaporates very easily. Actually, part of the vehicle evaporates from the paint on the way from the gun to the surface being painted. The rest of the vehicle, once it carries the paint to the surface and flows it out to a smooth surface, also evaporates. At that point, the vehicle has done its job.

There are two kinds of vehicle, one for enamel and another for lacquer:

1. Lacquer vehicle. This vehicle is called a *thinner.* It has the correct chemical composition to work with the other chemicals in the paint—the acrylic and pigment.
2. Enamel vehicle. This vehicle is called a *reducer.* It has the correct chemical composition to work with the other chemicals in the paint—the acrylic and pigment.

Note that, while both are *vehicles,* the lacquer vehicle is called a *thinner* while the enamel vehicle is called a *reducer.* The reason for this difference in name is to guard against using the wrong vehicle. A lacquer vehicle (a thinner) will not work with enamel. Nor will an enamel vehicle (a reducer) work with lacquer.

NOTE: There are several varieties of thinners and reducers, differing in the speed with which they evaporate. You should always choose the slowest-drying thinner or reducer that you can safely handle without sags or runs. This assures a smooth surface.

So-called universal vehicles are available which the manufacturers state can be used with either lacquer or enamel. The advantage of these is that the paint shop using a universal vehicle has one less chemical to stock. However, many painting technicians say they cannot get as good results with this type of product as they can with vehicles designed specifically for the enamel or lacquer they are using.

○36-6 Difference Between Enamel and Lacquer

As we mentioned previously, two kinds of paint are used today in automotive factories: acrylic enamel and acrylic lacquer. They are different in chemical composition, are different in the vehicle used to thin them, and are different in the way they are applied and finished. However,

FIGURE 36-1. Car body being spray-painted on the assembly line. *(Fisher Body Division of General Motors Corporation)*

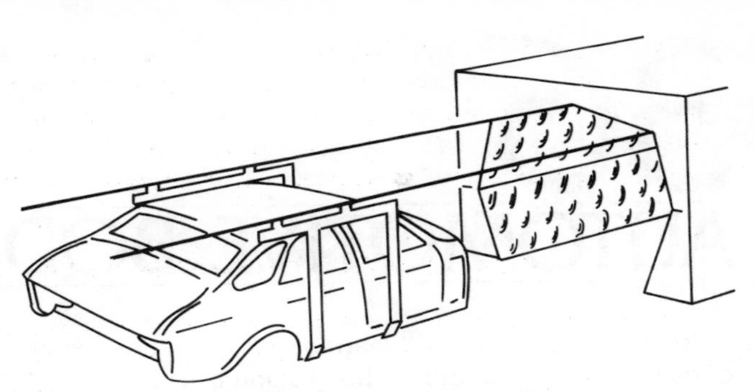

FIGURE 36-2. After painting, the car body is baked to dry the paint. *(Fisher Body Division of General Motors Corporation)*

these differences are not so great as to cause you trouble. Their similarities are much greater than their differences.

The main difference between lacquer and enamel, so far as the paint technician is concerned, is what happens to the paint after it is sprayed onto the car body. With lacquer, the paint dries as the vehicle (thinner) evaporates to form the final paint coat. With enamel, the paint also dries as the vehicle (reducer) evaporates to form the paint coat. However, the enamel binder, having a different chemical composition, gradually oxidizes over a period of weeks to produce the final hard finish. It is this difference that requires the paint technician to handle the two jobs—acrylic lacquer finishing and acrylic enamel finishing—in different ways, as we will explain later in the chapter.

○36-7 Lacquer

As previously mentioned, the first synthetic lacquer, Duco, was brought out by DuPont. Later developments brought improved lacquers, leading up to the presently used acrylic lacquer. At the automotive factory, the lacquer is sprayed on and then the car body is baked at high temperature (Figs. 36-1 and 36-2). Note that all this is done before any glass, rubber, or plastic is applied to the car body. Therefore, high temperature can be used to make the lacquer flow out smoothly to produce a high-luster shine.

In the body shop, such high temperatures are not possible, and so another method of getting the high gloss is required. The reason that the lacquer cannot be subjected to high temperatures in the body shop is that the heat would damage the rubber and plastic attached to the body sheet metal. Also, it could damage the glass and interior trim of the car.

To achieve the high gloss that is so desirable, the lacquer finish must be "rubbed out," a process called *compounding*, in the body paint shop. After the lacquer has dried sufficiently, a technician applies the "compound" either by hand or with a power polisher (sometimes called a *wheel*). The compound is a very fine abrasive material in paste form. When it is rubbed on, it removes any surface irregularities, and so the final job is smooth and glossy. After the lacquer has had time to cure or dry completely (a time of up to 3 months' duration), the lacquer should be waxed. We described compounding in ○34-12.

Because some of the lacquer is removed during compounding, and also because the lacquer coats go on more thinly than enamel, more lacquer coats are required—four or more, as compared with enamel, which requires only two or three at most. This and other differences in using lacquer and enamel are described in a following section (○36-15).

○36-8 Enamels

Acrylic enamel sets up (that is, the paint film forms) by both evaporation of the vehicle (reducer) and by oxidation of the binder. Three of the major companies manufacturing automobiles in the United States have been using acrylic enamel in recent years. These are American Motors Corporation, Chrysler Corporation, and Ford Motor Company. However, General Motors uses acrylic lacquer on its cars.

Enamels are baked at high temperatures on the car bodies at the car factory. Such high temperatures cannot be used in the body shop. However, the enamels supplied to body shops today are properly compounded to flow out smoothly if properly mixed with reducer and properly sprayed onto the car body. Acrylic enamels are slow drying as compared with acrylic lacquers. However, they dry to a high gloss, if properly used, and do not require compounding. In fact, because it takes up to a month for the binder in the acrylic enamel to oxidize, the enamel should not be rubbed or polished during that time. It is fairly soft at first, gradually hardening as it oxidizes.

○36-9 Polyurethane Enamel

A recently introduced enamel uses a special plastic binder which sets up chemically when an activator is added to the paint. That is, the paint materials come in two containers. One is a regular paint can which contains the mix of pigment, binder, and vehicle. The other is a small container which holds an activating chemical. Just before the enamel is to be used, the two are mixed and poured into the spray-gun cup. No thinner or reducer is required. The activator causes the binder to set up chemically to form a hard, smooth finish.

NOTE: This paint, with the activator mixed in, may set up, or jell, in the spray gun within a short time—in as little as 2 hours if the temperature is high. Therefore, the spray gun should be cleaned immediately after it is used to spray polyurethane enamel.

○36-10 Water-Based Acrylic Enamel

In recent years, some vehicles have been finished at the factory with water-based enamel. That is, the solvent used is water instead of a chemical vehicle. Use of this type of paint cuts atmospheric pollution, because during the baking process following the application of the paint, only water evaporates, not a chemical thinner or reducer. The process uses more energy, however, because it takes more heat to cure the paint after it is applied. The paint is repaired in the usual manner with one exception. This is that the finish must be sanded and a sealer applied before the repair paint is sprayed on. You cannot do a spot repair job on water-based enamel. Instead, you must repair the complete panel, out to its nearest definition lines. See Fig. 37-2, which shows part of a fender masked to its nearest definition lines. ○38-5 describes the procedure of repairing water-based acrylic paint.

○36-11 Basecoat/Clearcoat Finish

A recently developed two-step paint process is now being used on some top-line cars, such as the Lincoln Versailles. The finish is made up of two coats of a highly pigmented enamel, followed by two coats of clear acrylic. This provides a brighter, more reflective surface which has a high degree of luster. Tests with a special light-reflective meter shows that this finish has almost the same reflective ability as a mirror. The new finish is also said to have greater resistance to discoloration or spotting from industrial fallout. In addition, minor scratches that do not penetrate to the color coats can be buffed out of the clear acrylic surface.

○36-12 Urethane Paint for Urethane Body Parts

Urethane is a special type of plastic that is flexible, like rubber. Several body parts are made of urethane in modern cars, including the bumpers. Ordinary lacquer or enamel will not work very well on these parts, because lacquer and enamel do not form a sufficiently flexible film. Special urethane paint is required for such parts. Also, there are special urethane additives that can be mixed with regular lacquer or enamel to give the resulting paint film sufficient flexibility. You must follow the directions on the container to achieve the results necessary.

○36-13 Chassis Paint

Chassis parts are painted with a tough black enamel. This protects them against rust. New chassis parts that come from the factory are painted. If the paint on chassis parts has been damaged, either by an accident or by the metal-straightening procedure, the parts should be repainted. Any place the paint film has been broken should be sanded clean and repainted.

○36-14 Trunk Paint

This type of paint produces a spatter appearance when sprayed on. That is, it is not a single color, but contains small droplets of a second color, which show up in the finished job as specks of a different color. This provides a pleasing finish without the necessity of careful preparation of the panels that form the trunk. However, many paint technicians prefer to use the same color in the trunk as for the body. Normally, the trunk is painted only when a complete body paint job is being done.

○36-15 Comparing Acrylic Lacquer and Acrylic Enamel

Some shops prefer lacquer over enamel. Other shops prefer enamel. There are advantages and disadvantages to each. We mention some of these here.

Lacquer is fast drying. It can be used over old lacquer and enamel. Small nicks such as on door edges can be touched up with a small brush dipped in lacquer of the correct color. Disadvantages are that lacquer requires more coats (four or five) and needs polishing to bring out the high gloss. Also, it will not hide small imperfections, such as sand scratches or chips, as well as enamel.

Enamel covers better with fewer coats (two or three) and needs no compounding to bring out the gloss. It covers well and can hide small surface imperfections. Disadvantages are that it is slower drying, which means the paint booth must be more dust-free. An enamel job may come out less glossy with some orange peel (a surface finish slightly rough like the peel of an orange). Enamel also is considered to be more sensitive to spraying techniques. That is, the air pressure used, the adjustments of the spray gun, and the distance the gun is held from the work, must all be more carefully controlled when spraying enamel. This is the reason that, in many body shops, the new paint technician is started out spraying lacquer. When this is mastered, the technician can then move on to spraying enamel.

○36-16 Metallic Paint

Metallic paints (sometimes called the "glamour" paints) contain a large number of tiny metallic chips, usually of aluminum, which impart a metallic sheen to the finish. They reflect the light that hits the surface, to give the surface a sparkling appearance. Figure 36-3 shows this effect. The light comes to the entire surface uniformly at the same angle. But since the chips are oriented in all directions, the light rays are reflected at all angles from the surface. This is what gives the surface its iridescent, or sparkling, appearance.

When metallic paint requires repair, a special problem comes up for the paint technician. This is that the ultimate appearance of the repair job will depend not only on matching the new paint color correctly with the old, but also on the special way the new paint is sprayed onto the surface.

If the new paint goes on comparatively dry, the metallic chips will be scattered throughout the paint film as shown in Fig. 36-3. The reason for this is that the metallic chips do not have time to sink down, because the paint is almost dry when it hits the surface. If the paint is sprayed on wet, the wetness of the film gives the metallic chips enough time to settle to the bottom of the film, as shown in Fig. 36-3A. Now, when light hits the paint, it will be reflected basically in one direction. The paint is duller and darker. It has lost its iridescence.

The paint technician must control the variables during the spraying job to get the same orientation of the metallic chips in the new paint as the old paint had. That is, the following must be properly controlled:

1. Amount and type of thinner used
2. Adjustment of the paint flow from the gun
3. Adjustment of the air flow to get the proper dispersion of paint
4. Distance of the gun from the surface
5. Speed of the stroke—that is, how fast the gun is carried across the panel
6. Time between coats

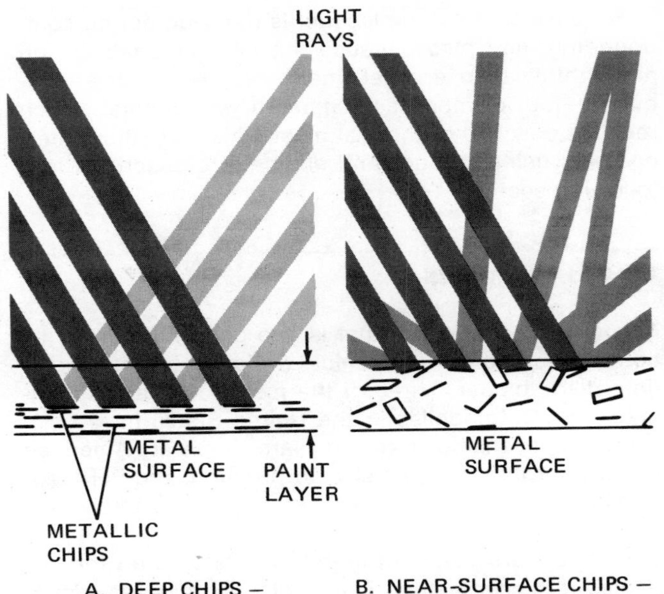

FIGURE 36-3. (Left) Metallic flakes deep in the paint create a dark metallic color. (Right) Flakes near the surface create a light metallic color.

For example, if more thinner is used, the paint will still be wet when it hits the surface. The same result can be achieved by holding the gun closer to the surface or moving the gun more slowly across the surface. Also, if less time elapses between coats, the thinner will not have time to evaporate, or to "flash-off."

We will come back to the technique of spraying metallic paint in a later section.

○36-17 Buying Paint

Only the larger paint shops blend their own paints, and they do this for two reasons. One is cost. It is cheaper to buy the basic ingredients (premixed binder and vehicle and tints to color the paint) than to buy the paint ready-mixed. Second, if a particular color is needed, blending it with ingredients on hand eliminates the necessity of waiting for a paint shop to deliver it.

However, most shops buy their paint from an automotive paint dealer ready-mixed to match the old paint, or if the customer wants something different, the new color the customer selects. Of basic importance is to properly match the new paint with the old. All cars carry a body identification plate (Fig. 36-4) which has the numbers and letters indicating the type and color of paint used on the car body. Figure 36-5 shows the location of the identification plates on 1978 cars made in the United States. Figure 36-6 shows lists of colors and their paint codes, as well as the Ditzler code numbers for some car models.

The average paint shop has two choices. It can buy a can of factory-mixed paint (Fig. 36-7) or a can of custom-mixed paint (Fig. 36-8). The factory-mixed paint is packaged at the paint factory. However, it is not the same as the paint used in the factory to paint the car body. Recall that the paint that is applied to the car body at the factory

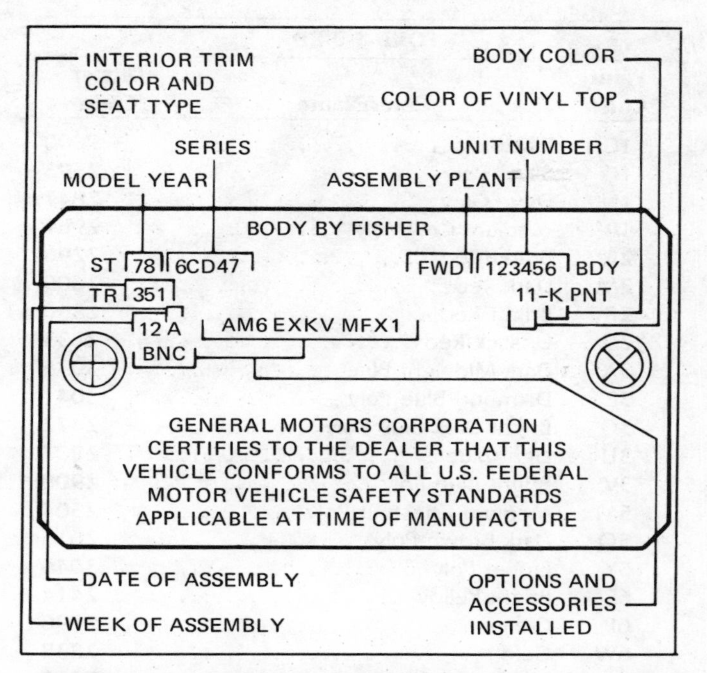

FIGURE 36-4. Body identification plate, showing the paint number.

is baked on. It therefore has a special formulation that permits it to be finished in this manner. The paint used in the body shop is applied and dried in a different manner. Therefore, it must have a different formulation. The main point is that the factory-mixed paint, even though differently formulated, will come out looking the same as the factory job.

If you are repairing the paint job on a recent model car, it is usually best to get the *factory-mixed* paint. However, after a number of years the factory stops supplying paints (for the older models). Thus, if you get an older model car, you will have to use a *custom-mixed* paint. This becomes more complicated with older cars, because the old paint may have faded. Also, an older car may already have had a paint job. In either case, you would not know what color code to use to order your custom-mixed paint. What you do then is to use the color-chip book (Fig. 36-9) found in all body paint shops. Compare the chips in the book with the car paint until you find a color that matches the car paint color exactly. Wetting the car surface and the chip will help you more accurately make the match. The surface of the car you are trying to match should be clean.

When you find the chip that matches, note its code number so you can order the color paint you need. Sometimes you will be unable to find a chip that matches. This is possible if the owner had an unusual blend of colors used in the previous paint job. If you are not mixing your own paint, either drive the car to the paint supply shop or take off some small part as a color sample and send it to the shop. With the actual paint sample before them the specialists in the paint supply shop can make a blend that will accurately match the old paint. This may take a while, because several tints might be required. Every time a paint sample is prepared, it should be sprayed on a panel and then dried. The paint color changes as it dries. Eventually you should have the exact match you need. Then prepare the car body for painting, and apply the paint correctly to get the matching color that you need.

The next chapters describe how to prepare the surface for painting, typical paint repair jobs, and complete paint jobs.

○36-18 Metal Conditioner

Bare metal should be given a special treatment with a metal conditioner. Sanding a surface down to bare metal does not make the surface chemically clean. The disk may grind some of the impurities into the pores of the metal. If paint is applied over the impurities, problems may soon develop. The purpose of the metal conditioner is to make sure that the bare metal is chemically clean before any coating or paint is sprayed on.

The metal conditioner is a liquid that is applied to the raw metal and then wiped off. It does two jobs. It prevents any rusting during the time that the raw metal is exposed to the air before it is painted. Second, the metal conditioner lightly etches the surface. The etching produces a very fine irregularity which provides more area for the undercoat to grip when it is sprayed on. The undercoat cannot grip a perfectly smooth surface as effectively as it grips the etched surface. Always use the metal conditioner on a bare metal panel after plastic body filler has been applied to it.

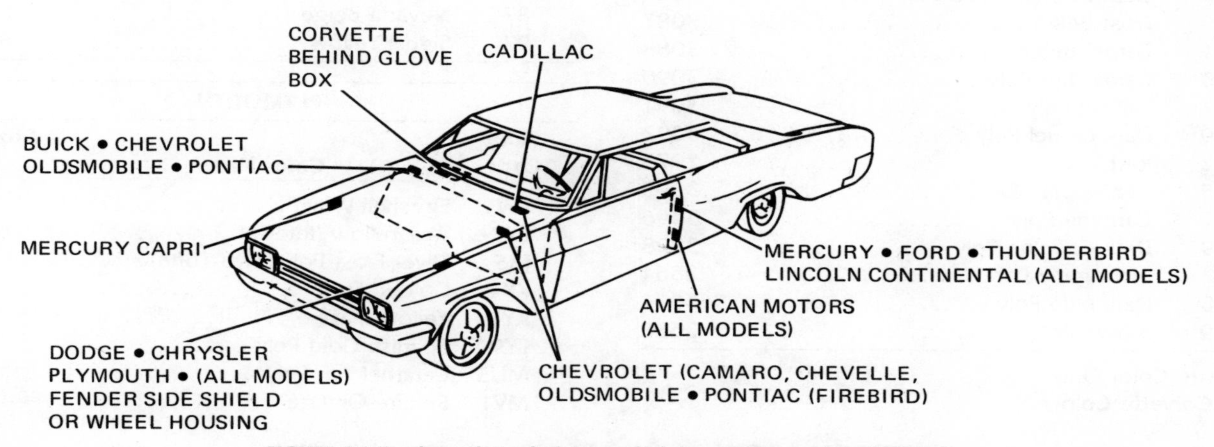

FIGURE 36-5. Location of plate containing paint number. ***(Ditzler)***

AMERICAN MOTORS

Paint Code	Color Name	Ditzler Code
P1	Classic Black	9000,9300
•J1	Pewter Gray Poly	33160
G7	Alpine White	2702
6D	Sand Tan	2820
6P	Firecracker Red	2824
•6R	Brilliant Blue	2825
6V	Sunshine Yellow	2827
7B	Mocha Brown Poly	2895
7C	Autumn Red Poly	2992
7D	Powder Blue	2896
•7E	Oak Leaf Brown (Intermix Only)	24443
7K	Midnight Blue Poly	2897
7L	Loden Green Poly	2898
7M	Golden Ginger Poly	2899
7W	Captain Blue Poly	2901
7Z	Sun Orange	2903
8A	Khaki	3028
8B	British Bronze Poly	3029
8C	Quicksilver Poly	3030
8D	Claret Poly	3022

•Jeep Color Only

CHEVROLET

Paint Code	Color Name	Ditzler Code
*07	Dark Gray Poly (Two-Tone)	2862
*10	Classic White	8631
11	Antique White	2058
*13	Silver Poly	2953
15	Silver Poly	3076
16	Gray Poly (Two-Tone)	3077
•19	Black	9300
21	Pastel Blue	3078
22	Light Blue Poly	2955
24	Ultramarine Blue Poly	3079
*26	Frost Blue	3080
29	Dark Blue Poly	2959
34	Orange	3070
44	Medium Green Poly	3081
45	Dark Green Poly	3082
48	Dark Blue Green Poly	2965
51	Bright Yellow	3084
*52	Yellow	3072
56	Gold Poly (Two-Tone)	3086
*59	Frost Beige	3087
61	Camel Beige	3088
63	Camel Tan Poly	3090
67	Saffron Poly	3091
69	Dark Camel Poly	3092
*72	Red	2973
75	Red	3095
77	Carmine Poly	3096
79	Dark Carmine Poly	3098
*82	Mahogany Poly	2864
*83	Dark Blue Poly	3074
*89	Brown Poly	2656

*Corvette Color Only
•Also Corvette Color

FORD-T-BIRD

Paint Code	Color Name	Ditzler Code
1C	Black	9000
1G	Silver Poly	2593
1N	Dove Gray	2847
1P	Medium Gray Poly	2967
2B	Bright Red	2296
2M	Dark Red	2609
2R	Bright Red	2830
2U	Lipstick Red	2833
3A	Dark Midnight Blue	3035
3E	Diamond Blue Poly	3041
3G	Bright Dark Blue Poly	2472
3U	Light Blue	2907
3V	Bright Blue Poly	2908
5M	Medium Chestnut Poly	2504
5Q	Dark Brown Poly	2616
5Y	Ember Poly	3046
6E	Bright Yellow	2414
6P	Cream	2790
6W	Gold	2838
7H	Bright Aqua Poly	2910
7L	Medium Jade Poly	2911
7Q	Light Aqua Poly	2887
7W	Medium Jade	3044
8J	Medium Tan Poly	2917
8N	Dark Cordovan Poly	2920
8W	Champois Poly	2923
8Y	Champagne Poly	2924
9D	White	2684
9E	White (Special)	8321
21	Red	3060
34	Medium Blue	3048
46	Dark Jade Poly	2725
62	Antique Cream	3051
81	Russet Poly	3056
83	Light Chamois	3057
85	Tangerine	3058
86	Pastel Beige	2999

FIESTA

Paint Code	Color Name	Ditzler Code
B7	Diamond White	W8101
C7	Oyster Gold Poly (Clear Coat)	24567
H7	Signal Orange	60897
R7	Venetian Red	72264
V7	Strato Silver Poly (Clear Coat)	8987
37	Jupiter Red Poly (Clear Coat)	72289
87	Nevada Beige	24489
97	Signal Yellow	82349

PLYMOUTH

Paint Code	Color Name	Ditzler Code
EW1	Eggshell White	2033
EY7	Taxi Yellow (Intermix only)	81746
JA5	Silver Frost Poly (Two-Tone)	2513
KY4	Golden Fawn	2635
KY5	Yellow Blaze	2636
LY9	Spanish Gold Poly	2739
MU3	Caramel Tan Poly	2856
MV1	Spitfire Orange	2858

FIGURE 36-6. **Ditzler paint codes for some car models.** ***(Ditzler)***

PB2	Wedgewood Blue	2934
PB3	Cadet Blue Poly	2935
PB6	Regatta Blue Poly	2937
PB9	Starlight Blue "Sunfire" Poly	2938
PT2	Light Mocha Tan	2943
PY1	Jasmine Yellow	2946
RA1	Dove Grey	3015
RA2	Pewter Grey Poly	3016
RA9	Charcoal Grey "Sunfire" Poly	3017
RF3	Mint Green Poly	3019
RF9	Augusta Green "Sunfire" Poly	3018
RJ3	Citron Poly	3066
RK2	Sunrise Orange	3067
RR4	Brite Canyon Red	3068
RR7	Tapestry Red "Sunfire" Poly	3020
RR9	Crimson Red "Sunfire" Poly (Two-Tone)	3064
RT9	Sable "Sunfire" Poly	3014
RY3	Classic Cream	3021

TX9	Black	9000-9300
ARROW AND SAPPORO		
006	Green	45315
015	Black	9000-9300
022	Bright Blue Poly	14932
061	Warm White	90071
063	Tan Poly	24438
073	Orange	60915
074	Flat Back On "Arrow Jet Package"	9437
090	Bright Yellow	82234
093	Bright Silver Poly	33293
094	Medium Red Poly	72307
095	Brown Poly	24550
096	Medium Gray Poly	33294
	Bumpers—Painted	DEE671

FIGURE 36-6, continued.

FIGURE 36-7. A can of factory-mixed paint.

FIGURE 36-8. A can of custom-mixed paint.

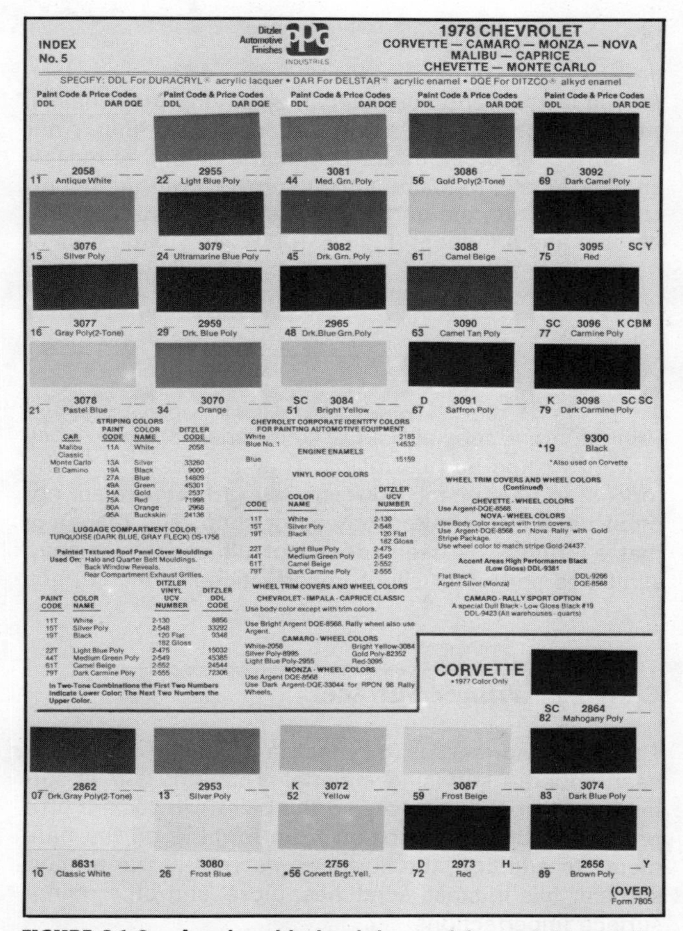

FIGURE 36-9. A color-chip book is used for matching paint when you do not know the paint number.

CAUTION: Wear rubber gloves and goggles when working with metal conditioner. It is an acid that could damage your eyes and attack your skin if safety precautions are not followed. Always read and follow the safety instructions printed on the container label.

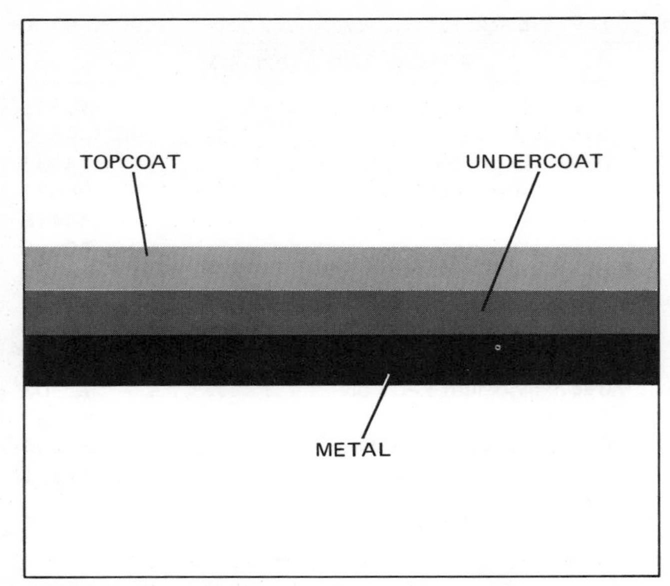

FIGURE 36-10. The layers in a completely painted surface.

○36-19 Undercoats

Acrylic lacquer and acrylic enamel, among other paints, will not stick on metal, old paint, or plastic filler. After the surface is prepared for painting, it must first receive an undercoat. The paint is then sprayed onto the undercoat. Therefore, the finish consists of two layers: an undercoat and a topcoat (Fig. 36-10). When you do a paint repair job or a complete repaint job, you will always spray on an undercoat before you put on the finish or topcoat.

○36-20 Primer

Primers are a special type of undercoat material. They prevent rusting and corrosion. They also help bond the topcoat to bare metal. However, straight primers are not often used in the auto body paint shop. The reason is that a primer, by itself, does not fill and cover sand scratches and other slight imperfections in the surface to be painted.

○36-21 Primer-Surfacer

The primer-surfacer is, in effect, a primer to which has been added a surfacing material. Thus, the primer-surfacer prepares the surface so the paint will stick. It also prevents rust and corrosion from forming on the bare metal. In addition, the surfacer material in the primer-surfacer fills in small scratches, nicks, and other minor surface imperfections.

The type of primer-surfacer that is used depends on the type of topcoat and also the type of surface to be painted. The usual recommendation is to use a lacquer primer-surfacer if the topcoat is to be lacquered. For an enamel topcoat, an enamel primer-surfacer should be used. Some companies put out an all-purpose primer-surfacer which can be used with either enamel or lacquer. In addition, there are special primer-surfacers for aluminum and galvanized steel surfaces.

Primer-surfacers come in several colors. You would normally use a dark primer-surfacer if the topcoat is to be a dark paint. You would normally use a light primer-surfacer if the topcoat is to be a light paint. The color of the last coat of primer-surfacer should match, as nearly as possible, the color of the topcoat to be applied. Several coats of primer-surfacer may be required on some jobs.

○36-22 Putty

The putty, or spot putty, used on the car body, is a special paste that comes in tubes (Fig. 36-11). It is about the same material as that added to primer to make the primer-surfacer. The purpose of the putty is to fill in small flaws that are not filled with the primer-surfacer. Putty should not be used to fill deep gouges or dents. These require body work: straightening metal and filling with plastic body filler. Also, spot putty should not be applied directly to bare metal before priming. Poor adhesion would result.

○36-23 Guide Coat

At many body paint shops guide coat is sprayed on after the primer-surfacer coats have been applied. The purpose of the guide coat is to help the paint technician detect and eliminate sand scratches. If the primer-surfacer that has been applied is of a dark color, then the guide coat should be of a light color. If the primer-surfacer is of a light color, then the guide coat should be dark. The purpose here is to provide some contrast which will show up any imperfections in the surface. The guide coat is a light mist coat. After it has flashed off, the surface is wet-sanded with a very fine sandpaper (400, for example). (Wet sanding is described in ○37-8.) This sands off the guide coat. If there are any sand scratches, they will show up during the sanding, because traces of the guide coat will lie in these scratches. When scratches show up, sanding is continued until they are sanded out. We refer to this procedure again in a later chapter.

Figure 36-12 shows the paint technician wet-sanding a car hood that has had a guide coat sprayed on it. Note

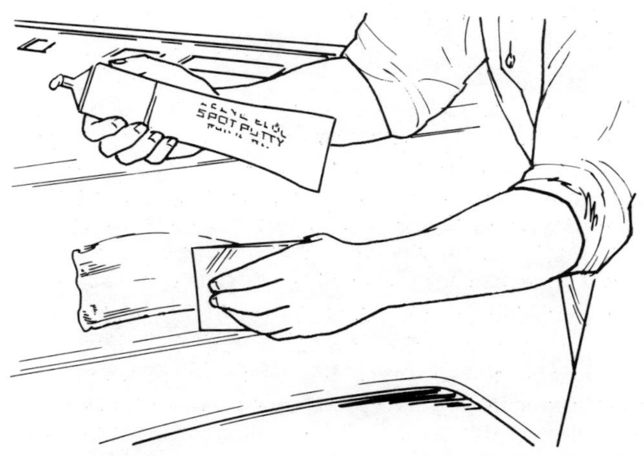

FIGURE 36-11. Spot putty used to fill small flaws that are not filled by the primer-surfacer.

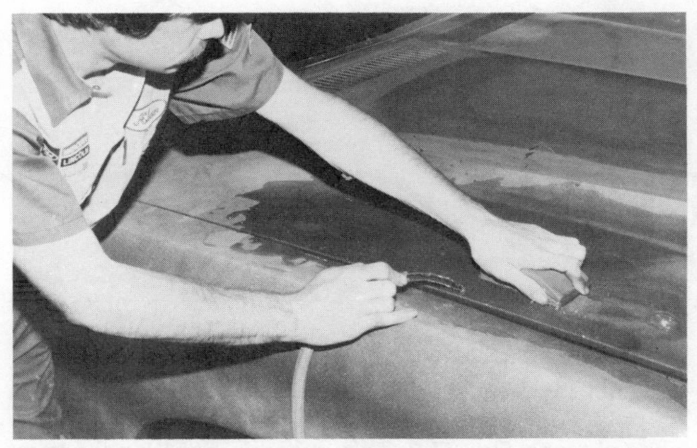

FIGURE 36-12. Wet-sanding the guide coat from a car hood.

FIGURE 36-13. Close-up of an area that has had the guide coat sanded off and is ready for painting.

the rough, misty appearance of the surfaces around the area being sanded. This is due to the guide coat, which goes on almost dry. Figure 36-13 is a close-up of an area that has been sanded to remove the guide coat. It is very smooth and ready to take the topcoat.

○36-24 Sealer

The sealer has the purpose of providing a sealing film between the primer-surfacer and the top coats. Sealers are desirable for some jobs and are not used for others. For example, if you apply enamel over lacquer, use a sealer first. This prevents the lacquer from bleeding through the enamel and giving the topcoats a spotty appearance.

If you apply lacquer over enamel, sealer is also recommended (Fig. 36-14). However, if you apply enamel over enamel, or lacquer over lacquer, a sealer is not generally required. But, if there are sand scratches present and they are not wet-sanded away (using a guide coat as noted previously), then a sealer often is used. In this case, it tends to prevent the sand scratches from showing through the topcoats. The reason is that it prevents the thinner from getting to the undercoat covering the scratches. If thinner gets to the undercoat, it causes the primer-surfacer embedded in the scratches to swell. Since this undercoat is thicker than the undercoat on the

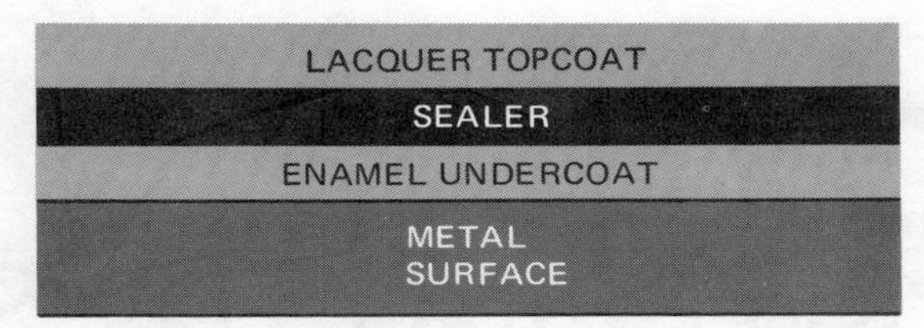

FIGURE 36-14. When a surface painted with enamel is to be covered with lacquer, a sealer must be used between the two different paints. *(DuPont)*

surrounding unscratched surface, it swells more and will show through the topcoats.

Whether you use a sealer or not depends on the type and quality of the job you are doing.

CHAPTER 36 CHECKUP

NOTE: Since the following is a chapter review test, you should review the chapter before taking the test.

COMPLETING THE SENTENCES The sentences below are incomplete. After each sentence there are several words or phrases, but only one of them correctly completes the sentence. Write each sentence in your notebook, ending the sentence with the one word or phrase that completes it correctly.

1. General Motors cars are painted with (*a*) acrylic enamel, (*b*) acrylic lacquer, (*c*) Duco, (*d*) reducer.
2. AMC, Chrysler, and Ford cars are painted with (*a*) polyurethane enamel, (*b*) acrylic lacquer, (*c*) pigment, (*d*) acrylic enamel.
3. The three basic ingredients of paint are (*a*) metal chips, enamel, and lacquer; (*b*) reducer, thinner, and compound; (*c*) pigment, binder, and vehicle; (*d*) polyurethane, activator, and water-base.
4. At the factory, lacquer is sprayed on and the car is (*a*) sand-blasted, (*b*) baked at high temperature, (*c*) rubbed out with compound, (*d*) stored for 3 weeks to dry.
5. A paint that requires addition of a chemical activator is (*a*) polyurethane, (*b*) acrylic enamel, (*c*) acrylic lacquer, (*d*) Duco.

QUESTIONS Write each of the following questions, and then the answer, in your notebook. If you have trouble recalling the answer to a question, turn back to the pages that cover the material and study them again.

1. What is the job of each of the ingredients in paint?
2. What is the difference between acrylic enamel and acrylic paint?
3. What gives metallic paint its sparkling appearance?

SUGGESTIONS FOR FURTHER STUDY

Take your notebook into the paint room and make an inventory of the paints and supplies. Copy the important points from the "Directions" label on each type of can. Note carefully, for example, the precautions that you must follow to handle some metal conditioners safely. Also, write down the procedures to follow in mixing and using each type of paint.

37 PREPARING THE SURFACE FOR PAINTING

In this chapter, you will learn how to prepare the surface requiring painting so that it will take the undercoats and topcoats. Unless the surface is properly prepared, the paint job will be a failure. The auto paint shop handles vehicles that have been repaired in the body shop and also vehicles that need only paint work. Some paint jobs involve painting a panel or spot-painting only part of a panel. Other vehicles require complete repainting. In addition to handling on-vehicle paint jobs, the paint shop technicians may also paint detached parts. For example, a new fender might be painted before it is installed on a car. Or a detached door might have a new skin (outer panel) installed. It might be more convenient for the new panel to be painted before the door is reinstalled on the car.

○37-1 Types of Paint Job

There are three basic types of paint job. These are spot repair, panel repair, and complete repainting. In the spot-repair job, only the immediate area around the damage is repainted, not a complete panel. Figure 37-1 shows the preparation for a spot-repair job. Note that only the area around the panel has been masked. The painting will be confined to a small area arrowed in Fig. 37-1. To make this type of repair, the painter must be skilled in blending new paint into old. Further, the paint color must match accurately. Otherwise, the repair would show up a spot of a different color on the panel.

In the panel-repair job, a complete panel is painted. A panel in this case would be a surface which has a stopping point at the top, bottom, front, and rear. For example, see Fig. 37-2. This shows a right fender paint job, masked in readiness for the undercoats and topcoats. The stopping places (where the masking is applied) are called the definition lines. At the top, the definition line is the line where the upper trim is attached. At the front, the definition line is where the front end of the fender stops. At the bottom, the definition line is the line where the lower trim is attached. At the rear, the definition line is where the fender ends. Note that, at this point, the masking paper is tucked into the joint between the fender and the front of the door.

It is easier to paint a panel than to make a spot repair. The entire panel between the definition lines is painted uniformly. You don't have to be particularly careful about the stopping points where you trigger the spray gun, but these are important in a spot-repair job.

In the complete repainting job, you do the complete vehicle. In many shops, this includes painting the trunk area, door jambs, and other interior surfaces that were originally painted.

○37-2 Steps in Surface Preparation

To prepare the surface for painting, several steps are required. The actual procedure will vary with the kind of paint-repair job and also with the type of paint already

FIGURE 37-1. Preparing to paint a spot repair.

FIGURE 37-2. Preparing a panel for repair.

on the vehicle. Here are the steps in surface preparation. We describe them in detail later.

1. Blow the dust off, including the dust between joints.
2. Wash the car. Dry it completely.
3. Clean the area to be repaired, using a precleaning solvent to remove all traces of wax, tar, and polish.
4. Examine the type of damage and the condition of the paint. In some cases you will grind off the paint and featheredge out to good paint surrounding the damage. In other cases you will remove all the paint from the panel and paint the complete panel instead of trying a spot repair. A third alternative would be to treat the old paint as necessary and spray the new paint over it. We discuss these alternatives later.

NOTE: We are assuming that, if metal damage has occurred, the vehicle has gone through the body shop, where the metal was straightened and filled in preparation for painting.

○37-3 Dusting Off the Vehicle

Use the air hose to blow the dust off the car. Blow into all joints and crevices to remove any dust that might have accumulated. This includes the joints between the hood and surrounding metal, the trunk lid and surrounding metal, and the joints around the doors. Unless this is done, some of the dust in these joints could blow out while you are spray-painting the car and could get on the wet paint. You would then have an extra paint-repair job to do.

○37-4 Wash the Car

Use a mild detergent and water to wash off the car, or at least the area you must repair (Fig. 37-3). Washing removes all dust and dirt on the paint that compressed air will not remove. Also, getting all the dust off gives you a clear picture of the paint color. Then, if you have to match paint chips from the paint book, you can make a more accurate match. Also, when masking, you will find the tape will stick better to the clean surface.

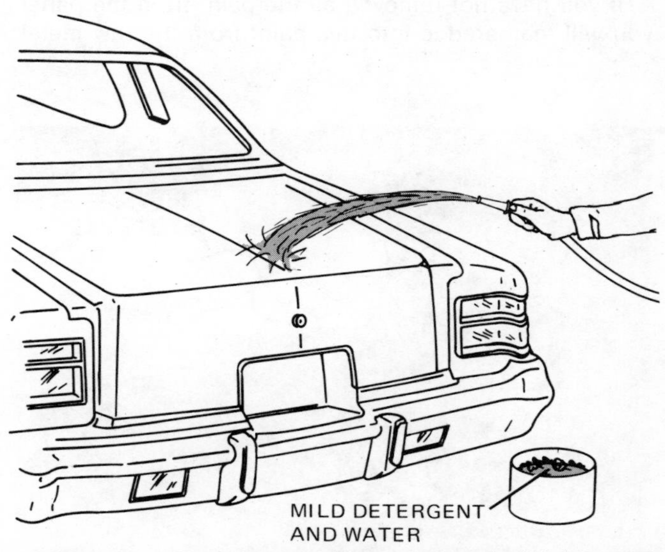

FIGURE 37-3. Wash the car with a solution of mild detergent and water.

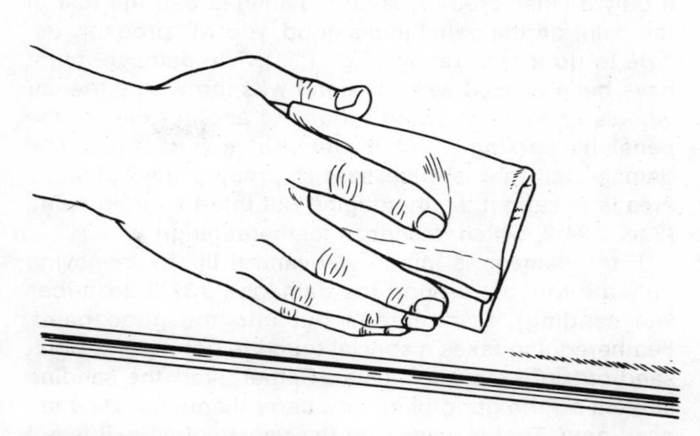

FIGURE 37-4. Remove all remaining contaminants from the paint by cleaning it with a precleaning solution.

○37-5 Using a Precleaning Solvent

Clean the area to be repaired with precleaning solvent (Fig. 37-4). Use new, clean shop towels, or special paint-shop towels. Do not use cloths that have been laundered, because they may still have traces of grease or other materials. These could wipe onto the car surface and cause a paint failure.

The precleaning solution must be used regardless of whether or not the paint is to be ground off. If the painted area is sanded down before the wax or polish is removed, some of this material could be ground into the metal. Wherever there is a trace of grease, wax, or polish on the metal, the undercoat will not adhere. As a result, you would end up with a defective paint job. Even touching the cleaned surface with your fingers can leave oil on the surface which will cause a paint failure. This can happen even after you have washed your hands.

The proper way to use the precleaner is to fold a clean shop cloth into a pad (Fig. 37-4) and wet it with cleaner. Then rub the cloth on the area to be cleaned, rubbing hard enough to loosen the wax or polish. Immediately take a dry shop cloth and wipe the area. Repeat as necessary to make sure the area to be repaired is clean. Use plenty of shop cloths. (See also ○34-3.)

○37-6 Deciding on the Type of Repair

If you have taken the preceding steps, you probably already know just about what has to be done to the damaged area. If it is a small damaged area in a panel, probably all that is needed is a spot-repair job. If the damage is fairly extensive, you may decide to redo the whole panel. In this case, you would examine the undamaged paint and decide whether it should all be removed or whether you can paint on top of it. Let's look at each of these possibilities and see what has to be done for surface preparations.

○37-7 Preparing for a Spot Repair

If only a small area of paint is damaged and the rest of the paint on the panel looks good, you will probably decide to do a spot repair (Fig. 37-1). The damage might have been caused when a stone was thrown by the car wheels or perhaps when a door of another car hit the panel in a parking lot. At any rate, since there is no metal damage, all that is necessary to prepare the damaged area is to sand it, featheredging out into the good paint. (See ○34-9, which describes featheredging.)

If the damage is minor, wet-sand it lightly, removing only the topcoat around the damage (○37-8 describes wet sanding). Featheredge out into the good paint. Featheredging takes a special touch to get it right. Don't sand *out* into the good paint. Rather, start the sanding strokes on the good paint and carry them into the damaged area. That is, sand *into* the damaged area. It is not necessary to cut through the undercoat if it is intact. In fact, if you do cut through the undercoat and expose raw metal, you will have to condition the raw metal with metal conditioner and then coat it with primer-surfacer.

○37-8 Wet Sanding

Wet sanding requires the use of very fine sandpaper (400, for example) and plenty of water. Figure 36-12 shows a paint technician wet-sanding the hood of a car. The purpose of the sanding operation is to produce a smooth surface and to remove sand scratches left by the use of a coarser sandpaper. The water continuously washes away the products of sanding that could otherwise cause other scratches. Wet sanding is used on both raw metal and on the undercoats to smooth them before the application of the topcoats. Wet sanding is used after the guide coat has been sprayed on (Figs. 36-12 and 36-13). Use 400-grit paper for wet-sanding primer-surfaces when acrylic lacquer is to be the topcoat.

○37-9 Determining Type of Old Paint

Before selecting the type of paint you will use to make the spot repair, you must determine what the old finish is. Also, you must select the right color of new paint to match the old, as already discussed.

If the vehicle has not been repainted, you can check the body identification plate (Figs. 36-4 and 36-5) to determine the code numbers and letters identifying the type and color of paint used originally (○36-17). If the vehicle has been repainted and you cannot identify the type of material used, there is another method of determining whether the old paint is lacquer or enamel. A container of special compound supplied by the paint manufacturers is required for the test. Put a little of the compound on a shop cloth and rub a small area of the old paint with it. If the paint is lacquer, it will dissolve and come off on the cloth. Enamel will not dissolve.

There are two types of lacquer that you might find on cars: nitrocellulose lacquer, which has been little used in recent years, and acrylic lacquer, which we discussed in ○36-7. If you have doubts as to which kind of lacquer was used to paint the vehicle, rub a small area with silicone polish remover. This remover will rub off acrylic lacquer but will not remove nitrocellulose lacquer.

Once you have determined the type and color of paint, you can mix it or order it from the paint supplier. The paint supplier will then deliver the paint, either factory-mixed or custom-mixed.

○37-10 Panel Repainting

If the damage to the panel has been rather extensive, then the whole panel should be repainted. If the sheet metal has been straightened or patched, there will be areas which have been filled with plastic body filler. However, some parts of the panel still may have the original paint on them. This paint can be removed so that you start with the raw metal and recover the complete panel. Or you can featheredge into this paint. Either way, you will paint the complete panel.

There are two basic methods of removing the paint from the panel: by using a power sander and by using a chemical paint remover which strips the paint off. The chemical, which is a liquid, is brushed on and allowed to stand for a short time. The paint bubbles, and then it is scraped off with a putty knife (Fig. 37-5) or washed off with water. Many paint technicians prefer to use the power sander if paint is to be removed, because they find it more convenient and less messy. The paint remover will soften any plastic body filler, which will therefore have to be replaced.

We described in earlier chapters how to use the power sander. Even though the sanding job is finished with an orbital sander using a fine grade of sandpaper, further sanding will be required. This will be done by hand, using a fine grade of sandpaper and water. That is, the area that is cleaned of paint should be wet-sanded. While the bare metal is being wet-sanded, the sanding operation should also move into any area where there is still paint. While power-sanding or even wet-sanding a panel, you probably should mask off adjacent panels to protect them from accidental damage. Figure 37-6 shows a technician power-sanding a door panel. Note that the rocker panel below has been masked off to prevent damage to it.

If you have not removed all the paint from the panel, you will featheredge into this paint from the raw metal.

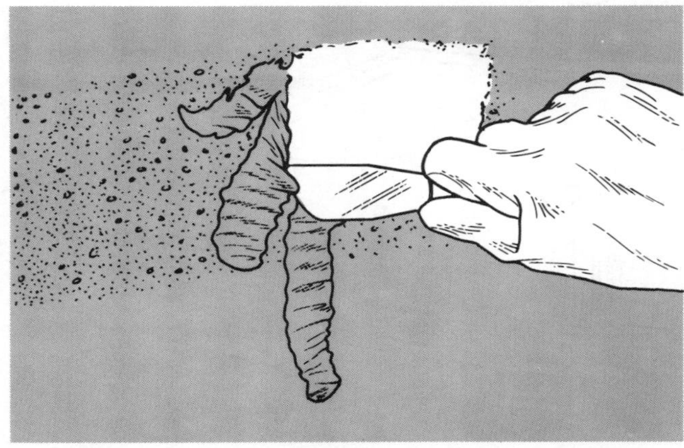

FIGURE 37-5. Removing paint that has been treated with a chemical paint remover.

FIGURE 37-6. Power-sanding a door. Note that the rocker panel below the door is masked.

Then, when wet-sanding the panel, you will include the old paint. The old paint should be scuffed slightly so that the new paint will have something to "hang" onto.

After the wet sanding has been completed, the panel should be washed off with water and dried. Then the bare metal should be treated with metal conditioner, as already described. Next the entire panel should be washed with a chemical cleaner recommended for the job. Some technicians recommend using an enamel reducer which will not damage the old paint but will remove any trace of wax or grease.

Apply primer-surfacer to any bare metal or areas where the original paint and primer have been sanded thin. Allow the primer-surfacer coats to dry. If you see any small nicks or scratches that the primer-surfacer has not filled, fill them with spot putty. Now wet-sand the panel again, with special attention to the areas where primer-surfacer has been applied. A guide coat, applied before this final sanding, will help you locate any sand scratches that should be sanded out (see ○36-23).

NOTE: Some technicians recommend different grades of sandpaper for final wet sanding, depending on the type of topcoat to be applied. For enamel, they recommend 320 sandpaper. For lacquer, they recommend 400 sandpaper. Also, if enamel primer-surfacer was used and the topcoat is to be lacquer, then a sealer should be applied before the lacquer topcoat is sprayed on.

Finally, after the panel has been washed with water and dried, it should be wiped off with a tack cloth.

The panel should then be masked out. That is, the surfaces around it—glass and metal—should be covered with masking tape and paper, as explained in ○34-7. Then the panel is ready for undercoating and painting.

○37-11 Painting a Detached Panel

Replacement panels from the factory, such as fenders, door skins, quarter panels, hoods, and trunk lids, are given a primer coat at the factory. This protects them from rusting. The primer coat, however, is not a very good base for the topcoat. It will require wet sanding and additional treatment.

As a first step, note the method to be used to attach the panel. If the panel is to be bolted into place (like a fender, for example), then the best procedure usually is to treat and paint the panel off the car. If the panel is to be spot-welded into place, it should be installed on the vehicle first and then painted. The spot welding probably is going to create some sheet-metal damage, which must be repaired in the body shop, so this must be taken care of before the paint job.

There is one refinement here that is recommended but that is often overlooked. This is drilling holes in the panel for the trim. Fenders, for example, usually come without trim holes drilled. If these holes are drilled before the fender is painted, the raw metal exposed by the drilling will also be painted. A small point, perhaps, but attention to small points is what produces the best job. Any raw metal provides a starting point for rust.

The painting of the detached panel proceeds in the same manner as the repainting of a panel on the car. That is, the entire panel should be wet-sanded with 360 or 400 sandpaper. The panel should be washed off with water and dried. Any spots which are sanded down to bare metal should be treated with metal conditioner. Then the panel should be washed with a chemical cleaner such as enamel reducer. Primer-surfacer should be applied to any bare spots or areas where the original primer has been sanded almost to the metal. If there are small imperfections such as nicks, they should be filled with paint putty.

After the primer-surfacer coats have dried, wet-sand the panel. One recommendation is to use 320 sandpaper if the topcoat is to be enamel, 400 sandpaper if the topcoat is to be lacquer. After the panel has dried, wipe it with a tack cloth. It is now ready for the topcoat.

○37-12 Preparing a Vehicle for Complete Repainting

It sometimes happens that the owner of a car which has been in a collision will want a complete repaint job. There are also other reasons for a complete repaint job: The owner may want a different color. The original paint on the car may have begun to deteriorate, so it looks bad. There may be rust spots which the owner wants repaired, so an extensive repair and complete repaint job are in order. At any rate, it is assumed that the car comes to the body shop after all repairs on the sheet metal have been made. All trim is removed.

The next step is a careful examination of the original paint to determine its condition. If it is in good condition, it can serve as a base for the new paint. If it is in poor condition, then it will have to be removed either by sanding or by the use of a chemical paint remover.

One method of checking the adhesion of the paint to the metal is to sand through the paint in one spot and featheredge from the raw metal out to the original paint. Examine the featheredge. If the thin edge of the paint does not flake off, it is binding well to the metal. Make this check in several places, especially along the lower edges of the doors, along the rocker panels, and along the lower edge of the quarter panels. These are places where rust might start. Sometimes the lower edge of a panel starts to rust from the inside. Rust may be well advanced before it shows through the paint. Sanding through the paint in any spot where rust has started will usually show up the damage. If there are rusted areas, they should be patched as described previously.

The preparation of the body for repainting is the same as the preparation of a panel for repainting, as covered in previous sections. The major difference is that there is more surface to work on. However, the steps in the process are the same. Wherever you get down to bare metal, use a metal conditioner and then a primer-surfacer as previously described. Follow the various steps as outlined in earlier sections.

○37-13 Preparing Other Metals for Painting

Aluminum panels are often used on truck bodies because they are lighter than steel. They also are used for some car hoods. Galvanized metal panels are used on some vehicles, such as school buses. These require special prepainting preparation and special chemicals. If you go into a shop specializing in the painting of such vehicles, you will be given special instructions and supplied with the special materials required for the jobs.

CHAPTER 37 CHECKUP

NOTE: Since the following is a chapter review test, you should review the chapter before taking the test.

Paint will not stick unless the surface is properly prepared. In this chapter, we have discussed the steps necessary to properly prepare the surface for painting. Also, we have discussed the various types of paint job that you may have to do. To find out how well you understand everything in this chapter, answer these questions.

COMPLETING THE SENTENCES The sentences below are incomplete. After each sentence there are several words or phrases, but only one of them correctly completes the sentence. Write each sentence in your notebook, ending the sentence with the one word or phrase that completes it correctly.

1. The three basic types of paint job are (*a*) spot repair, panel repair, and complete repainting; (*b*) enamel, lacquer, and metal flake; (*c*) precleaning, metal conditioning and sealing; (*d*) car, trunk, and van painting.
2. The chemical used to remove any traces of wax or polish is called a (*a*) metal conditioner, (*b*) sealer, (*c*) primer, (*d*) precleaning solvent.
3. Wet sanding requires the use of (*a*) very fine sandpaper, (*b*) very coarse sandpaper, (*c*) a wire brush, (*d*) plenty of oil.
4. You can remove paint from a panel with a power sander or with (*a*) paint remover, (*b*) a putty knife, (*c*) sealer, (*d*) primer.
5. Small nicks and scratches that the primer-surfacer has not filled should be filled with (*a*) spot putty, (*b*) caulking compound, (*c*) extra layers of paint, (*d*) reducer.

QUESTIONS Write each of the following questions, and then the answers, in your notebook.

1. How do you make a spot repair?
2. How do you make a panel repair?
3. What are the steps in completely repainting a vehicle?
4. What are the steps in preparing the surface for painting?
5. How can you check the adhesion of paint to metal?

SUGGESTIONS FOR FURTHER STUDY

Determining the type of paint repair to make is a very important decision for the painter. On a sheet for your notebook, make three columns, with the headings "Spot Repair," "Panel Repair," and "Complete Repainting." Then visit a busy paint shop and watch the work taking place. List each job that you see performed under the appropriate heading. Then write down the conditions that caused the painter to make the type of repair that you saw performed.

38 TYPICAL PAINT JOBS

In this chapter, you will learn how typical paint jobs are done. These include spot repairs, painting a panel on the car, and doing a complete repainting job. We have already covered, in previous chapters, the use of the spray gun and the preparation of the surface to receive the topcoat. We have also covered compounding, or the "rubbing out" of the lacquer-type topcoat to give it the desired polish. Now let us look at typical repaint jobs.

○38-1 Doing a Spot Repair

Figure 38-1 shows the paint technician pointing to a small nick in the paint of a door. This probably was caused when the door was hit by the door of another car. As a first step in this minor repair job, the immediate area is sanded (Fig. 38-2). Figure 38-3 shows the technician feeling the featheredging from the raw metal to the original good paint. Note that this minor repair job does not require all the steps listed in ○37-7, which covers preparing an area for a spot repair. That is, with the minor job shown in Fig. 38-1, wet sanding is not always needed. However, metal conditioner should be used on bare metal, followed by primer-surfacer. Then the technician uses the spray gun to topcoat the area being repaired, feathering the paint out on both sides of the repair. The paint used matches the color of the original and is of the same type as the original. If the paint is lacquer, it is compounded after it has dried.

○38-2 Painting a Panel

We have already covered the various steps required to prepare a body panel for painting. After these steps have been taken, the car is masked to protect surrounding metal and glass from the spray. Then the proper paint of the proper color is sprayed onto the panel. We have already described these various steps in previous chapters. Note particularly the chapter on spray guns (Chapter 35) and ○35-4 on how to use the spray gun to spray-paint a panel.

Wait long enough between coats for the paint to flash off (for the thinner or reducer to largely evaporate). This is important, because if you don't wait long enough, the paint could sag or run. If you wait too long, the new coat will not blend properly with the old. It is a matter of judgment how long to wait, and this judgment comes from experience.

FIGURE 38-2. Dry-sanding small paint damage.

FIGURE 38-3. Feeling the featheredge.

FIGURE 38-1. A small nick in the paint.

You can test the paint after you have sprayed on a coat and waited for a few minutes. Touch the masking tape adjacent to a sprayed area. If the paint is still slippery, wait longer. if the paint is tacky or sticky, but not wet, it is time to spray on another coat.

Remember that if lacquer is applied, it will require compounding after it has dried. Enamel should not be compounded or polished for a month after it has been put on.

○38-3 The Complete Repainting Job

You must have a plan in mind when you start to paint a vehicle. That is, you must know where you will start, where you go from there, and the sequence in which the body panels will be painted. Figure 38-4 shows two sequences. Whatever sequence you select, follow it carefully. By the time you have circled the car once, the paint where you started should be flashed off, so you can start again with the second coat. The experienced body painter knows how long it will take to circle the car and arrive back at the starting point. The experienced technician will adjust the amount of thinner or reducer in the paint mix to match this time. That is, if the paint is flashing off too fast, more thinner or reducer can be added. If it is flashing off too slowly, less thinner or reducer can be used in the mix.

Before starting on the main sequence, paint the hidden edges such as the door jambs, trunk-lid edges, and hood edges. Use low air pressure to spray these to prevent overspray. Weatherstripping and the car interior should be adequately masked to prevent paint from getting to the wrong places. Leave the doors, trunk lid, and hood slightly ajar to permit them to dry without sticking.

Most painters prefer to do half the roof to start with and then come back to the other half after they have partly circled the car. Whatever the sequence used, the plan should minimize the blending required on a panel between coats. That is, you should try to paint complete panels with each coat and not do half a panel later. ○35-4 explains how to paint a large panel in sections.

○38-4 Spraying Metallic Paints

We discussed metallic paints in ○36-16. We explained that the way the paint is sprayed on determines how light or dark the paint will be, and also how iridescent, or sparkling, the paint will appear. See Fig. 36-3. If you have the job of matching the original paint, you must not only match the color of the pigment, but you must also spray the paint on correctly. This means careful attention to the amount of thinner used, the adjustment of the spray gun, and the manner in which you manipulate the gun.

The first step is getting a can of the right paint. Usually this would be a can of factory-mixed paint of the proper code number or letters. The code is found on the body identification plate as previously noted (○36-17 and see also Fig. 36-4). The paint can must be agitated on a shaker for at least 10 minutes to make sure the pigment and metallic particles are well mixed. After the can is opened, the paint should be stirred with a paint paddle to make certain it is thoroughly mixed. Then add the proper amount of thinner or reducer as recommended on the can.

NOTE: Straining metallic paint through an excessively fine strainer can remove metallic flakes and change the character of the paint.

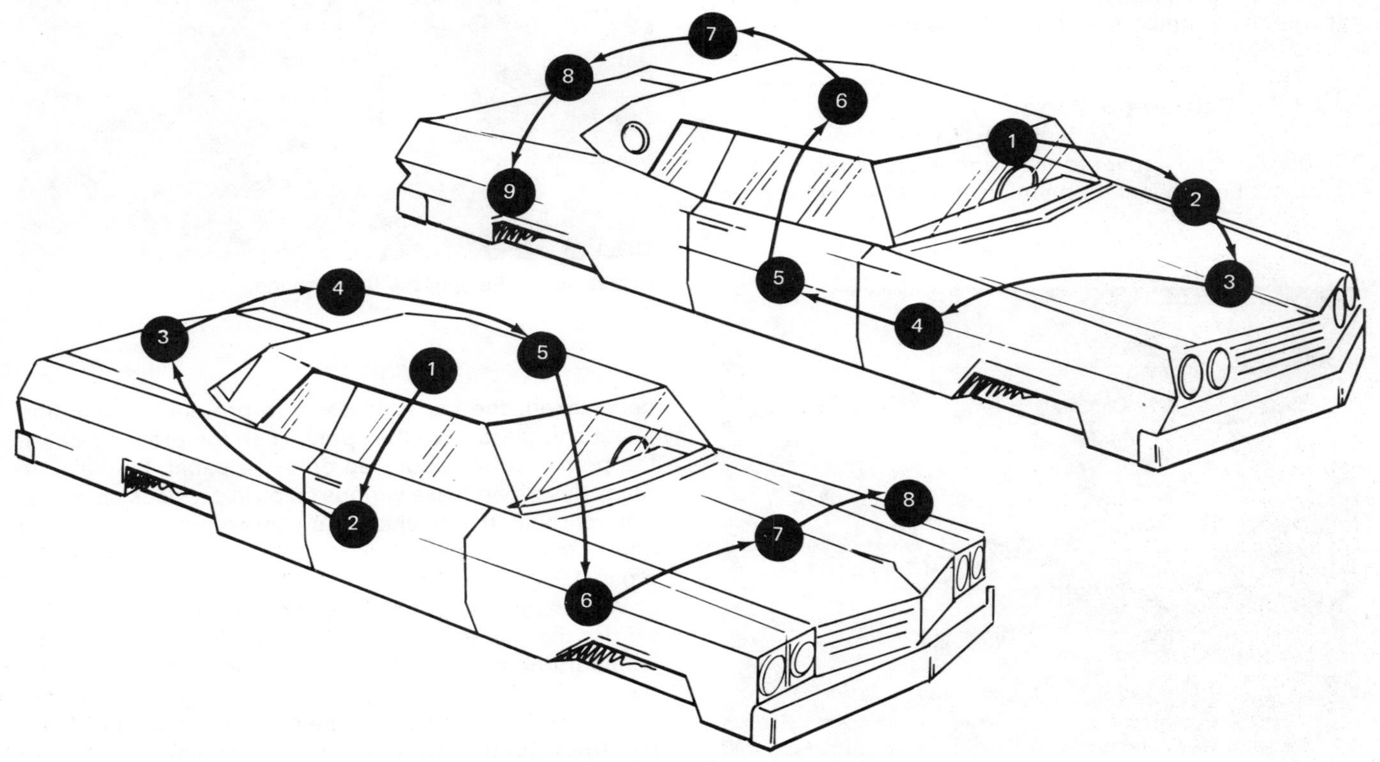

FIGURE 38-4. Spraying sequences for the complete paint job.

Next spray a scrap panel and allow it to dry. Wash a small area of the original paint on the car and polish it, if necessary, to remove any chalk and bring up the gloss. Polish the panel if its gloss is low after it has dried. This is necessary, because a low-gloss finish will reflect the light differently from a high-gloss finish and this changes the color effect.

Now compare the test panel with the original finish. If the color on the test panel is too light (dry), make one or more of the following adjustments to darken the metallic color:

1. Open the fluid adjustment on the spray gun.
2. Decrease the fan pattern on the spray gun by adjusting the fan adjustment screw.
3. Decrease the air pressure to the gun.
4. Slow down the speed with which you move the spray gun across the panel.
5. Decrease the distance between the gun and the work.
6. Use a thinner or reducer that evaporates more slowly.
7. Decrease the time between coats.

Code	Color
A	White
B	Gold
C	Indo Orange
D	Moly Orange
E	Aluminum
F	Mono Red
G	Indo Maroon
H	Green Toner
J	Yellow Green Toner
K	Blue Toner
L	Black

FIGURE 38.5. Tint color code letters for acrylic enamel and acrylic lacquer shading chart. *(Ford Motor Company)*

If the color on the test panel is too dark (wet), make one or more of the following adjustments to lighten the metallic color:

1. Close the fluid adjustment on the spray gun.
2. Increase the fan pattern of the gun.
3. Increase the air pressure to the gun.
4. Speed up the spray stroke. That is, move the gun across the panel more rapidly.
5. Increase the distance between the gun and the work.
6. Use a thinner or reducer that evaporates more rapidly.
7. Increase the time between coats.

If you cannot get a good match despite taking the steps listed above, it may be that the original finish has changed color. This can result from exposure to weather over a period of time. In such case, you can use special tints to change the color of the new paint. If the paint is enamel, be sure to use an enamel tinting color. If the paint is lacquer, use a lacquer tinting color. Figure 38-5 is a shading chart for acrylic enamel and acrylic lacquer and also indicates the tint-color code letters and their meaning.

The specialty paint dealer can probably do a quicker and more accurate job of tinting the paint to match the old finish. To get the match, you would have to take the car to the paint dealer or send a chip from the car to the dealer.

○ 38-5 Repairing Water-Based Acrylic Paint

In recent years, some cars have been painted with a water-based enamel. The body identification plate identifies this type of paint job with the letter W prefixing the paint code number. This paint is repairable with acrylic lacquer in the usual manner. However, it is necessary to

ACRYLIC ENAMEL AND ACRYLIC LACQUER SHADING CHART

Fresh Color	If Too Dark Add:	If Too Light Add:	If Too Green Add:	If Too Red Add:	If Too Yellow Add:	If Too Blue Add:	If Too Gray Add:
Gray Metallic	E	L	F	H	K	F	–
Blue Metallic	E	K	G	H	–	H	K
Green Metallic	E	H	K	H	K	J	H
Red	D	F	–	–	F	D	–
Maroon Metallic	E	G	–	B	G	C	–
Yellow	A	J	A&C	H	–	–	–
Ivory or White	A	–	C	H	A&K	–	A
Tan or Brown Metallic	E	B	G	B	G	–	–
Pastel Blue	A	K	G&A	H&A	–	H&A	K
Pastel Green	A	H	K&A	H&A	K	J	H
Pastel Tan or Brown	A	B	G	B	G&A	–	–

FIGURE 38-6. Shading chart for acrylic enamel and acrylic lacquer. *(Ford Motor Company)*

sand the finish and apply a sealer before the lacquer is sprayed on. This means that spot repairs are not possible. If a paint repair must be made, the complete panel, to the nearest definition lines, must be painted. (See Fig. 37-2, which shows part of a fender masked to its nearest definition lines.)

The procedure recommended is to clean the complete panel with paint-finishing solvent. Then wet-sand it with 400 sandpaper, wash and dry the car. Apply the sealer recommended by the manufacturer. Paint the panel with acrylic lacquer in the usual manner. After the lacquer has dried, compound it.

CHAPTER 38 CHECKUP

NOTE: Since the following is a chapter review test, you should review the chapter before taking the test.

For the painter, no two jobs are exactly alike. However, many of the jobs can be classed into one of several types. In this chapter, we have discussed each of the typical paint jobs and provided you with a guide to follow in painting the complete car. To find out how well you understand everything in this chapter, answer the questions that follow.

COMPLETING THE SENTENCES The sentences below are incomplete. After each sentence there are several words or phrases, but only one of them correctly completes the sentence. Write each sentence in your notebook, ending the sentence with the one word or phrase that completes it correctly.

1. Metal conditioner is used on (*a*) primer-surfacer, (*b*) paint, (*c*) bare metal, (*d*) sealer.
2. The type of paint that requires compounding after it dries is (*a*) lacquer, (*b*) enamel, (*c*) pigment, (*d*) binder.
3. When the thinner or reducer has largely evaporated, the paint is said to (*a*) have dried, (*b*) be wet, (*c*) flashed off, (*d*) turned chalky.
4. If the paint is flashing off too fast, (*a*) use less thinner or reducer, (*b*) turn on the heat lamps, (*c*) use more thinner or reducer, (*d*) move the car into the sun.
5. Straining metallic paint through a very fine strainer can (*a*) improve the finish, (*b*) prevent the paint from drying properly, (*c*) break up the metal flakes, (*d*) remove the metal flakes from the paint.

QUESTIONS Write each of the following questions, and then the answer, in your notebook.

1. What are the steps in repainting a spot repair?
2. How is a complete panel masked off for painting?
3. What is the sequence for painting body panels when doing a complete paint job?
4. What are the steps in spraying metallic paints?
5. How do you identify a car that is factory-painted with water-based acrylic paint?

SUGGESTIONS FOR FURTHER STUDY

An illustration in this chapter shows two sequences that can be followed in doing a complete paint job. Visit a professional paint shop, and watch the procedure followed by the painter in doing a complete paint job. If the procedure varies from those shown in this chapter, on a page for your notebook write down the panel sequence that the painter followed.

39 PAINT PROBLEMS

In this chapter, you will learn the various possible troubles that you might have with paint jobs. Some of these troubles come from using the wrong materials or from using the right materials in the wrong way. Some come from improper preparation of the surface for painting. Whatever the cause, this chapter describes paint troubles and their causes. In addition, it explains the things to do to prevent or correct the troubles that are discussed. For convenience of locating specific troubles, we discuss the conditions in alphabetical order, starting with ○39-1 Bleeding.

The following paint problems are covered in this chapter:

1. Bleeding
2. Blisters, Bubbles, Pop-ups
3. Chalking, Dulling
4. Chipping
5. Color Mismatch, Mottle
6. Cracking, Checking
7. Craters, Fisheyes
8. Dirt in Paint
9. Foreign Material on Surface
10. Industrial Fallout
11. Lifting
12. Metal-Finishing Marks or Sand Scratches
13. Molding Installation Damage or Rust
14. Orange Peel
15. Overspray
16. Peeling
17. Poor Drying, Hardness
18. Rusting
19. Sags, Runs
20. Scratches
21. Sealer, Deadener under Paint
22. Stains, Tarnish, Fading
23. Thin Paint, No Paint
24. Water Spotting
25. Wrinkling

○39-1 Bleeding

Bleeding is the result of colored soluble hues or pigments in the old finish, or undercoat, which dissolve in the solvents of the refinish paint, causing it to go off color. This is usually a problem only when a color change is involved in repainting. It also usually occurs only with maroon or red original finishes (Fig. 39-1).

NOTE: The material that follows was adapted from the Ford Motor Company publication *Automotive Paint Refinishing,* which provides complete and comprehensive coverage of paint problems and their possible causes, prevention, and repair.

FIGURE 39-1. Bleeding paint. ***(Ford Motor Company)***

CAUSE Bleeding is caused by the solubility of the dyes or pigments used in previous paint applications. Obviously there is nothing a refinisher can do to change the solubility of an old paint coat. There are, however, a few precautions refinishers can use to reduce bleeding problems.

PREVENTION 1. Before repainting over a color suspected of being a bleeder, spray a small area of the unit with the new color. Bleeding will generally appear in a few minutes if the old finish is a bleeder. If it is a bleeder, either remove the old finish or use a "bleeder sealer" before applying the finish coats. 2. When using refinish materials which are known to be bleeders, never allow overspray to fall on any other vehicles. Also, thoroughly clean your equipment after spraying a bleeder to avoid contaminating subsequent colors.

REPAIR The best way to repair a bleeding paint job is to remove the paint and refinish. Mild cases of bleeding can often be corrected by spraying a "bleeder sealer" followed by additional finish coats.

○39-2 Blisters, Bubbles, Pop-ups

Blistering is the formation of many small eruptions in the finish and may occur between the metal and the undercoats or between the undercoats and the enamel topcoat. Blisters usually follow one of two distribution patterns: usually they are either uniformly distributed over a comparatively large area or concentrated in a localized area in the shape of a water spot or drip streak. Sometimes they are so small that they are difficult to identify without using a magnifying glass. In some instances, blisters may be confused with dirt. To verify the condition, prick the suspected area with a sharp point, and note whether a void (hole) or water exists. If so, blistering is confirmed. As the problem progresses, it may be accompanied by peeling if the eruption flakes off and by rusting if the blister extends down to the metal. Figure 39-2 shows blisters near the rear edge of a door.

A pit has the appearance of a void in the base metal or undercoat that is not filled or covered with paint. A pop-up is the term applied to a problem in the paint film around a pit. It results from the formation of a bubble in wet paint over the pit. If the bubble does not break, it is called a pop-up. If the bubble does break while the paint is still wet, a craterlike ring is formed.

The causes, prevention, and repair of blisters, bubbles, and pop-ups are indicated below.

CAUSES

1. Moisture or contamination on the surface such as water, oil, grease, tar, silicone, etc.
2. Moisture in the spray lines
3. Rust under the surface
4. Not enough drying time of undercoat

PREVENTION

1. Clean the surface thoroughly. Use a metal conditioner on bare metal. Use wax and silicone remover on old finishes. Keep bare hands off bare metal and primed surface.
2. Make sure all the water is wiped off the surface after wet sanding.
3. Drain air compressers, transformers, and lines daily.
4. Make sure the undercoat is dry before applying either more undercoat or topcoats. Failure to do this can trap solvents under the film and cause blisters.

REPAIR

The only way to repair a blistered finish is to remove the blisters to their full depth and repaint.

Pop-ups found in factory finishes sometimes can be repaired by sanding, polishing, and buffing.

If the pop-up is so large that it cannot be removed by light sanding, polishing, and buffing, it will be necessary to fill the defect with air dry lacquer applied with a fine-tipped brush.

An excess of lacquer should be applied to completely fill the void after drying (drying time can be accelerated by using a heat gun). After the lacquer is dry, lightly sand it to level it out to the depth of the original surface, and then polish and buff. In extreme cases, it may be necessary to remove the blemish and repaint.

○39-3 Chalking, Dulling

This condition may be called poor gloss or no luster. The terms describe a paint durability problem which may show up in extended service (6 to 24 months). Chalking or dulling is usually confined to the horizontal surfaces of the vehicle such as the hood, tops of fenders, roof, tops of quarter panels and deck lid. Chalking is the presence of loose, nonadherent pigment on the finish. Dulling is a loss of luster (Fig. 39-3).

CAUSES

1. Dry-spray resulting from improper spray techniques (high air pressure, low paint flow, wide air fan, gun distance too great, etc.) or poor reducing solvent (evaporation too fast, low solvency, etc.) or an excessive amount of reducer or thinner.
2. Poor holdout of undercoat system and resulting absorption of topcoats, which may also be accompanied by sand scratches showing excessively.
3. Dry overspray falling on incompletely masked surfaces adjacent to the one being repainted.
4. Application of paint to a surface contaminated with wax, oil, grease, soap, etc.
5. Use of abrasives which are too coarse when sanding the undercoat.
6. Application of topcoat to a heavily chalked or checked finish without adequate sanding.

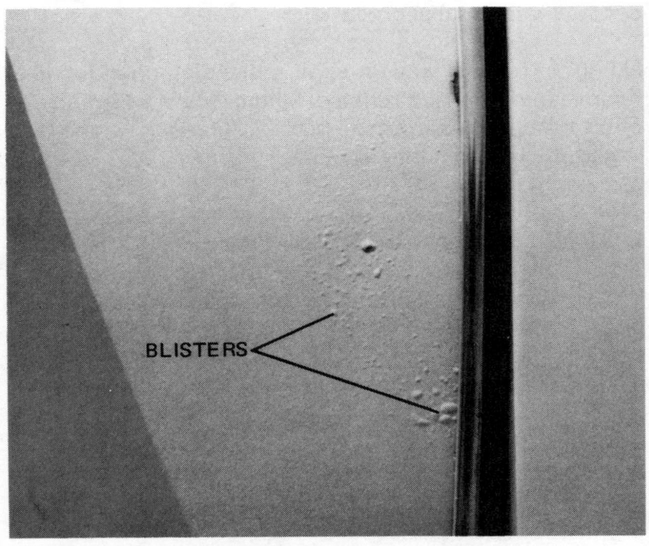

FIGURE 39-2. Bubbles, blisters, and pop-ups.

FIGURE 39-3. Chalking and dull paint. *(Ford Motor Company)*

7. Applying material from a can which had been previously opened and used but which had been improperly mixed. The remaining material would have an excess of pigment in proportion to the vehicle remaining and therefore would have low gloss.
8. Mixing improper additives, such as flatting agents, with the finishes.
9. Applying topcoat to primer, primer-surfacer, putty or glaze which is not sufficiently dried.
10. Insufficient topcoat film thickness.

PREVENTION

1. Use spray techniques and reducing solvents which will provide a wet film and good flow-out.
2. Use undercoats (primer, primer-surfacer, sealer, glazes, and putties) which are formulated for the particular refinishing material employed—lacquer or enamel. Also, if possible, use all materials from the same source of manufacture. Using a sealer coat is good insurance against poor holdout.
3. Carefully mask adjacent surfaces. If refinish paint overspray should get on old finish, remove the overspray before it dries with enamel reducer or lacquer thinner.
4. Thoroughly clean all surfaces to be painted, using a good wax and silicone remover.
5. Use fine abrasive, such as 400-grit, in all final sanding of the old finish or undercoats before applying refinish coats.
6. Completely sand off all old chalked or checked original finish.
7. Always be sure that all materials are completely mixed in the original package before using.
8. Do not use unknown additives. Use only those recommended by the manufacturer.
9. Be sure undercoats have been sufficiently air- or force-dried in line with supplier's recommendations, before applying finish coats.
10. Always apply sufficient undercoat and topcoat to provide a full, glossy finish. Low film thickness of either can lead to a dull coating.

REPAIR

Poor gloss encountered in original finishes or refinishing can usually be improved by polishing with a fine compound and buffing. However, the polishing and buffing should take place only after the finish has become thoroughly dry and hard. If this does not produce the desired gloss, refinishing will be necessary.

○ 39-4 Chipping

This condition may also be called stone bruise. The problem represents damage resulting from the impact of a sharp object which removes some of the finish. It may be caused from such things as road gravel, misaligned door, deck lid, tailgate or hood edges, or a sharp tool striking a painted surface. If the impact is light, only the topcoat will be removed and the red or gray primer will show. If the impact is severe, the entire finish will be removed, exposing bare metal, and early rusting will result (Fig. 39-4).

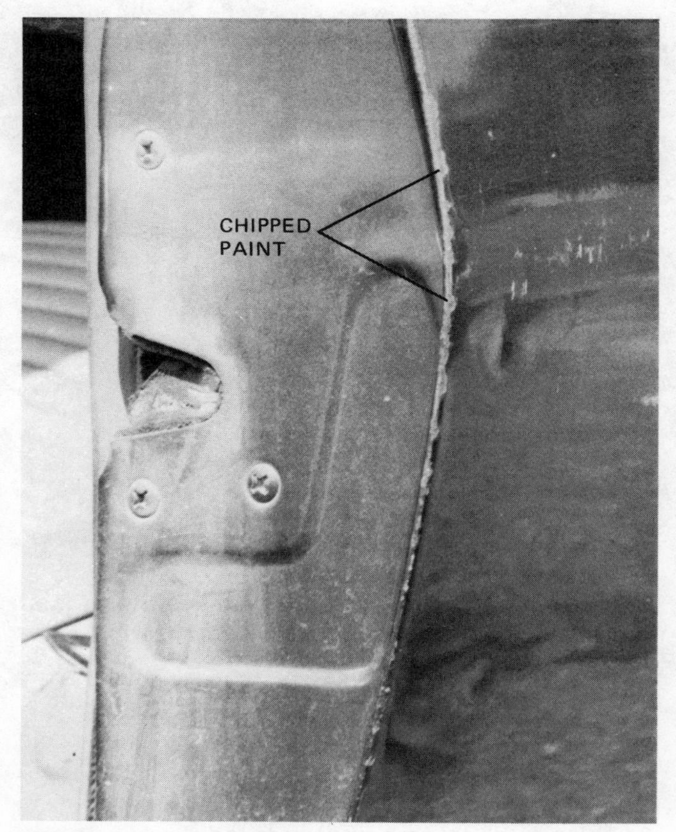

FIGURE 39-4. Chipped paint.

REPAIR

If the chipping is minor and confined to an edge or isolated location, it can be repaired by brush touch-up. If the chipping is centrally located in a highly visible area, it must be repaired by repainting.

○ 39-5 Color Mismatch, Mottle

This condition may also be called off color, wrong color, streaked, flooding, blotchy. "Color mismatch" is the term applied to the appearance of adjacent areas that do not match. Mismatch of two different panels can result under the following conditions:

1. If the panels were painted with two different batches of topcoat which were two different shades
2. If the color of the undercoat shows through on one panel
3. In the case of metallic colors, if the adjacent panels were not sprayed with the same degree of wetness

The terms "mottle," "flooding," "streaking," etc., are applied to metallic colors and describe the appearance of light and dark areas within a panel (Fig. 39-5). These differences depend on the wetness or dryness of the coating during application.

CAUSES

1. Improper spraying techniques
2. Refinish color not thoroughly agitated

FIGURE 39-5. Mottled paint. *(Ford Motor Company)*

3. Insufficient hiding
4. Applying the topcoat to a cold surface or in a cold room
5. Failure to use a mist coat on metallics
6. Using a solvent that evaporates too slowly

PREVENTION

1. Use good spraying techniques. Keep the gun a constant distance from the work, trigger the gun at the end of each stroke, and avoid "toeing" and "heeling" the gun. Spray a test panel to check color match before you apply color to the vehicle.
2. Thoroughly agitate topcoat materials before application. Failure to do this causes uneven pigment dispersion in the paint and results in mottling or off color.
3. Apply the required number of topcoats. Insufficient hiding is almost always caused by films that are too thin.
4. Never spray on a cold surface or in a cold room.
5. Spray a mist coat over metallic colors to obtain color uniformity.
6. Use solvents that are compatible with your shop conditions. Use of a slow-drying solvent where a regular-drying solvent would do can cause pigment particles to drift to uneven layers in the paint film.

REPAIR

In some cases of off color in metallics, a light area can be corrected by polishing and buffing, as this will tend to darken the appearance. If polishing and buffing does not correct the mismatch condition, the off-color area must be repainted.

○39-6 Cracking, Checking

This condition may also be called crazing, crow's-foot checking, spider-webbing, cobwebbing, alligatoring, hairline cracks, cold cracking. The terms "cracking" and "checking" describe durability problems which show up with extended service of 6 to 24 months after exposure to the weather. They are fractures in the paint film resulting from shrinkage which is caused by oxidation or extreme cold.

"Cracking" is the term applied to a fracture which extends down through the paint film to the surface painted. It may be accompanied by curling of the edges of the fracture and peeling, also rusting if the finish peels off bare metal. Cracking is often observed in excessively thick films (10 mils or more) which have been exposed to a low temperature (Fig. 39-6).

"Checking" is the term applied to the fractures if they occur only on the surface of the topcoat and do not extend down through the film. It may be observed in combination with chalking or dulling (Fig. 39-7).

CAUSES

1. Application of a new finish over an old finish which has already checked
2. Application of a new finish over a surface which is too soft or undercured
3. Application of a new finish over an undercoat that is either too thick or not dry
4. Insufficient stirring or mixing
5. Improper thinners, for example, using a lacquer thinner in an enamel
6. Application of extremely thick finish coats
7. Adding unproven additives, such as gloss improvers, with the color coat
8. Addition of excessive amounts of clear lacquer or enamel to a color

PREVENTION

1. Check the old finish carefully with a magnifying glass. If the old film shows any sign of checking, remove it completely.

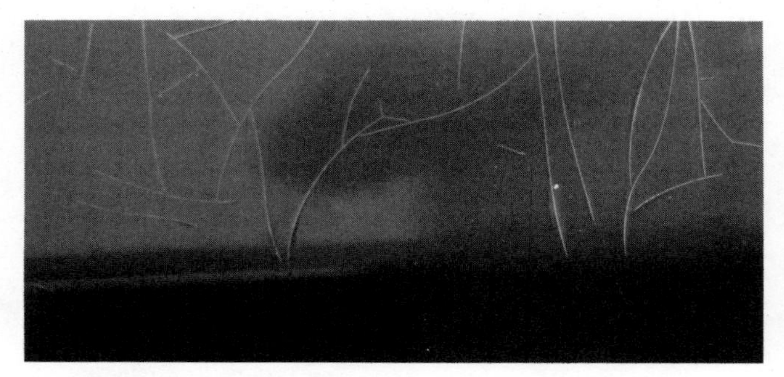

FIGURE 39-6. Cracked paint.

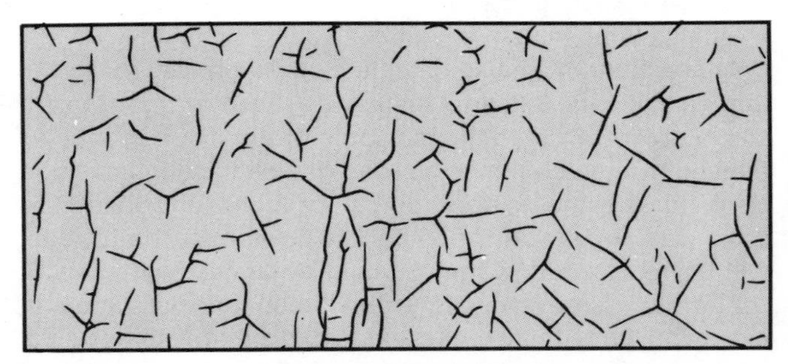

FIGURE 39-7. Checked paint. *(Ford Motor Company)*

2. Apply undercoats in medium thin coats, allowing plenty of time for each coat to flash off.
3. Make sure each coat is thoroughly dry before applying the next coat.
4. Stir all materials thoroughly. Remember that thinned materials settle faster. It is wise to occasionally agitate the material while it is in the spray cup.
5. Always use the solvents recommended by the paint manufacturer. Don't intermix solvents from one company with materials from another.
6. Don't apply the paint too thick.
7. Don't add anything to refinishing materials that is not specifically recommended by the manufacturer.
8. Don't shoot several coats of clear enamel over the color coat. Clear enamel has a tendency to check on prolonged exposure to sunlight or sudden changes in temperature.

REPAIR

Checking or cracking found in any type of paint film can be repaired only by stripping off the defective film and repainting.

○39-7 Craters, Fisheyes

This condition may also be known as crawling, poor wetting. Craters or fisheyes are surface conditions caused by paint flowing away from a contaminated spot before it dries. The contamination may be water, oil, grease, silicone, wax, soap, detergent, etc., and may affect a small localized area or extend over a complete panel. The contamination may exist on the surface before paint is applied, it may fall into the film while paint is being applied, or it may fall on the wet paint after the last coat has been applied (Figs. 39-8 and 39-9).

CAUSES

1. Silicone containing wax not completely removed from original paint surface
2. Oil or grease not cleaned from surface before repainting
3. Oil or water from air compressor sprayed into finish
4. Airborne dirt containing silicone falling into wet paint
5. Residue from dirty or contaminated shop towels remaining on surface before application of paint

PREVENTION

1. Clean the surface of the original finish thoroughly by using silicone and wax remover.
2. Use disposable paper towels for all cleanup operations.
3. Drain air compressors, air line pressure regulators, and blow-off air lines daily.
4. Confine topcoat painting to a spray booth supplied with clean tempered air.

REPAIR

Shallow craters in the original finish may be removed by sanding, polishing, and buffing. If the crater is deep or if the cratering is extensive, it will be necessary to sand out the defect and repaint the affected panel.

FIGURE 39-8. Craters in paint. *(Ford Motor Company)*

FIGURE 39-9. Fisheyes in paint.

○39-8 Dirt in Paint

This is also called foreign material, contamination, hair, lint, sand, grit, trash, etc. It is due to a foreign body under or in the finish. It is covered by paint so that it has the same color as the topcoat but becomes objectionable because it protrudes above the finished surface (Fig. 39-10).

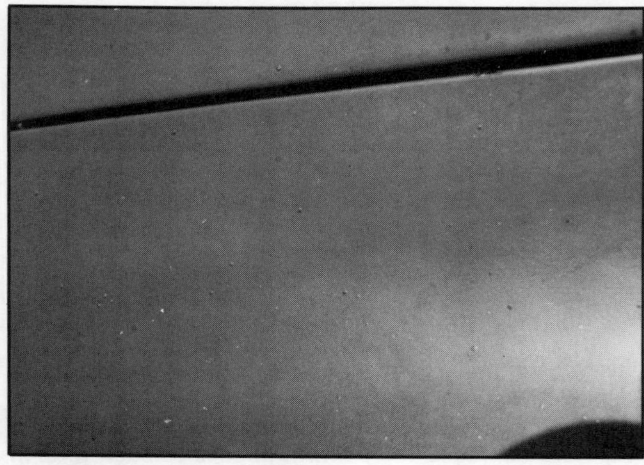

FIGURE 39-10. Dirt in paint.

CAUSES

1. Improper surface preparation techniques
2. Dirty spray booth
3. Dirty air lines or spray guns
4. Improper solvent, adding the paint to the solvent, or adding the solvent to the paint too quickly
5. Spraying in an open room
6. Dirty car or clothing
7. Improper straining of or not straining the paint

PREVENTION

1. Thoroughly clean the surface being painted. Wash the vehicle with warm water and a mild detergent. Rinse, and then apply wax and silicone remover. Make sure to blow out all cracks and body joints while the car is outside the spray booth. Once the vehicle is in the spray booth, always tack it off thoroughly with new tack rags immediately before the application of paint.
2. Make sure the spray area is clean. Wetting down the booth, frequently changing the air filters in the booth, and never sanding in the booth will help ensure jobs that are free from objectionable dirt.
3. Always use clean equipment. Dirty air regulators, air lines, and spray guns are frequently the cause of dirt in paint.
4. Always use the type and amount of solvent recommended by the paint manufacturer. Also, be careful how you mix the paint and the solvent. Adding the paint to the solvent or adding the solvent to the paint too quickly can result in "kick-out," which looks like dirt in the paint.
5. Never spray any paint in an open area where other work is being done. Confine spraying operations to the spray booth.
6. Make sure the car being painted is thoroughly blown off before it enters the spray booth. Seal the door jambs and edges with a thin wet coat of paint before painting the surface. Always wear clean, lint-free clothing and a cap to prevent dirt, oil, lint, hair, dandruff, etc., from falling on a freshly painted surface.
7. Always strain the reduced material through a fine strainer. It's a good idea to strain the material a second time through the same strainer.

REPAIR

In most cases, dirt found in original factory finishes can be repaired by polishing and buffing.

Dirt found in enamel paint sprayed by refinishers will usually have to be sanded out and repainted because of the long cure time required for refinishing enamels. Dirt found in acrylic lacquer used for refinishing can usually be removed by sanding and polishing.

○39-9 Foreign Material on Surface

This is also called fluid drippings, organic fallout, trim cement, glue. The term describes contamination on the paint film surface which is difficult to remove and which may have damaged the paint. It applies to such foreign materials as chemical sprays like insecticides and weed killers, alkaline water spots, brake fluid, oil, grease, road tar, carcasses of certain types of insects, etc., which if left on the finish will under certain conditions result in permanent damage.

All these substances can cause dulling, discoloration, pitting, crazing, and finally disintegration of the paint at the points of contact.

CAUSES

All the materials will seriously damage paint on horizontal surfaces, especially during hot, dry weather. Frequent heavy rainfall will either dilute or wash off these chemical substances and possibly prevent or greatly restrict the severity of paint damage. On the other hand, the cycling of hot sun and dew formation serves to extract and concentrate the destructive chemicals so as to accelerate the damage to the paint film (Fig. 39-11).

PREVENTION

1. In the more seriously affected areas, it is recommended that all vehicles be washed and inspected on arrival. Vehicles that are kept in outside storage should be inspected weekly and washed as required to remove all contaminants. This should aid considerably in preventing severe spotting that cannot be removed by ordinary polishing.
2. There are conditions, however, where insect control is not feasible during long intervals of storage. In such places, it would be far better to apply an approved protective wax coating on the cleaned cars as they are received. There are many protective wax products now being offered for this purpose. Several have been found to be most effective in reducing paint spotting by insects. The coating itself is not damaging to the paint. This coating should be applied as a medium wet continuous coat on horizontal surfaces with ordinary paint spray equipment in a sheltered area. A light film thickness is sufficient. (Heavier coats should be avoided as they are more difficult to remove). Cars so protected can remain in outside storage for as long as 90 days. Longer intervals are not recommended because of increasing trouble in removing the coating. Many solvent detergent cleaners are available for washing off wax coatings so that one technician can usually clean a car in about 20 minutes. This type of protection is certainly much less expensive than paint repairs.

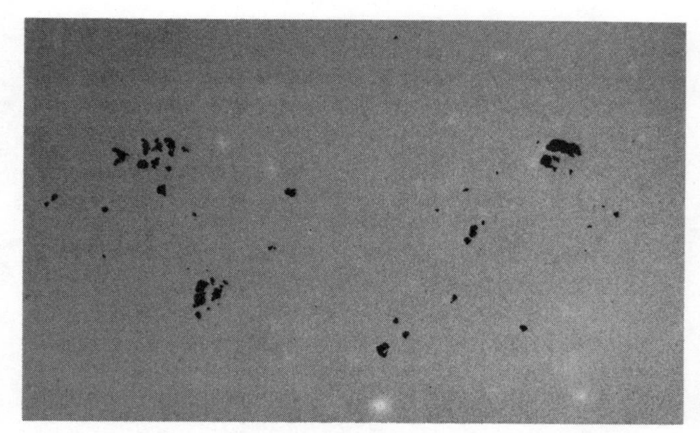

FIGURE 39-11. Foreign material on surface of paint.

3. Another approach to the insect problem is by special illumination at the storage lot. Many lots are equipped with ordinary white incandescent lights or floodlights. These all emit enough blue light to attract most insects. For that matter, most blue cars attract insects more than cars of other colors. Actually, red lights would be least attractive to bugs. But because of the many objections to this color, a yellow or an orange-yellow light is generally recommended. Actually, none of these colored lights are insect-repellent and only those high in blue content are capable of attracting insects. Hence, a blue light at some distance from the stored cars might serve as a decoy, causing the insects to detour around the lot.

REPAIR

In many cases, this contamination can be removed by washing the vehicle, using a mild detergent, and damage will not result. If, after washing, some contamination remains, it can usually be removed by a combination of sanding, hand or machine polishing, and buffing. In extreme cases, the damage will have penetrated the topcoat, and repainting will be required.

○39-10 Industrial Fallout

Industrial fallout is the result of particles being exhausted into the air by the various processes of heavy industry. Examples are fly ash, foundry dust, soot, etc.

Iron-base fallout particles, such as foundry dust, appear to the eye as tiny rust-colored dots on the paint film, and they cause the surface to feel rough to the touch. Some of the particles have excellent adhesion and are difficult to remove (Fig. 39-12).

PREVENTION

1. Wash the car regularly.
2. Use a wax protective coating.
3. Use covers.

REPAIR

A procedure that has proven effective in the removal of this fallout is listed below.

1. First, wash the car with a body-wash detergent compound to remove any loose soil. Rinse well and examine the painted surfaces for iron-base fallout particles. If there is a significant quantity of fallout not removed by ordinary washing, the following oxalic treatment should then be used. All cracks, ledges, grooves, etc., where fallout has accumulated should be cleaned by wiping or by air blow-off.
2. Apply industrial fallout remover (oxalic acid-water solution) liberally to all affected surfaces of the vehicle with a large sponge. Use a broad wiping stroke, and keep the work completely wet for about 15 minutes or until you can no longer feel any surface roughness or even isolated gritty particles with bare or gloved fingertips. If this is not done thoroughly, rust staining may soon develop. Again, it is most important that the work be kept wet, since a dry acid residue is not active in loosening fallout. Be sure that the entire acid cleaning procedure is performed in a sheltered area so that the work will be kept as cool as possible. This will prevent rapid evaporation of water and consequent surface drying. *Do not work in the sun.* Even a strong breeze makes it difficult to keep the job wet over a large area.
3. Rinse the area with clear water. This must be done very thoroughly in order to prevent possible corrosion.

No traces of acid should be left on any surface. Bright trim parts, particularly anodized aluminum and stainless steel, may be stained by prolonged contact with the cleaning solution. Even painted areas can be spotted by prolonged exposure. It is also important to keep the oxalic acid cleaner solution from leaking inboard, because some fabrics might be bleached or discolored by it.

If the fallout is not completely removed or is deeply embedded in the paint film, cleaning with the acid-detergent mixture must be repeated. This may be aided by using a fine nylon bristle type of scrub brush. Be sure that the light scrubbing required does not scratch the paint. Rubbing the work with a mixture of equal parts of the oxalic acid cleaner and body polish, using a piece of heavy towel, is also sometimes helpful. Again, thorough water rinsing is extremely important.

Small black spots may remain after the oxalic cleaning has removed all iron-based fallout. These deposits might be asphaltic or overspray from certain air-dry paints used in the engine compartment during assembly operations. They can usually be removed by rubbing vigorously with a cloth saturated with silicone and wax remover.

FIGURE 39-12. Industrial fallout in paint.

○39-11 Lifting

This is also called puckering, swelling, raising. Lifting describes the effect of a refinish paint on a previously applied paint coating in which the original coat will separate from the surface to which it was applied. It is usually caused by the solvents in the refinish paint which have attacked the original finish, causing it to swell and lose adhesion in a distorted pattern. It is a common occurrence when lacquer is sprayed over an undercured enamel. Lifting may also occur when air-dry enamels have been recoated within a critical time range without the use of a recoating sealer (Fig. 39-13).

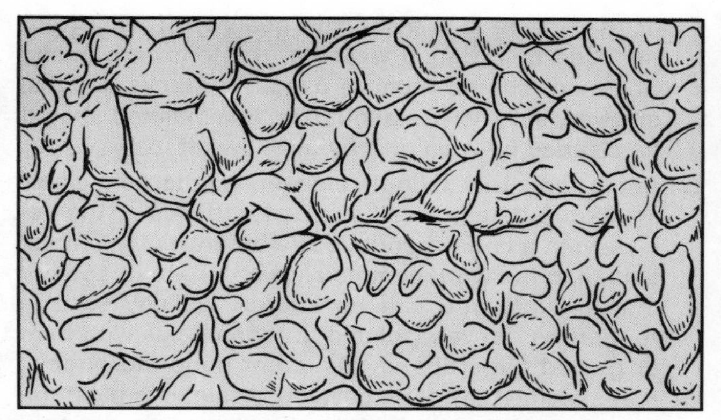

FIGURE 39-13. Paint that is lifting. ***(Ford Motor Company)***

CAUSES

1. Use of lacquer over undercured enamel
2. Use of lacquer thinner or "hot" solvents in reducing refinish enamels
3. Application of a color over an incompletely cured or incompatible undercoat
4. Application of a second coat of enamel over first enamel coat which has become partially cured (oxidized)

PREVENTION

1. Do not use lacquer thinner in enamels.
2. Do not recoat air-dried enamel with lacquer.
3. Use undercoats which are compatible with the topcoat used. A primer-surfacer designed for use with enamel will not necessarily work with lacquer color coats.
4. Don't apply color coats over undercoats which are not completely dry and hard.
5. Always apply a recoating sealer when recoating an air-dry enamel surface that has cured between 4 and 72 hours.

REPAIR

Remove the lifted film and repaint.

○39-12 Metal-Finishing Marks and Sand Scratches

Metal-finishing marks are the result of poor surface preparation techniques. Usually they are caused by gouging metal with coarse grinder disks or files. Sometimes, however, they are caused by shoddy sanding techniques or by the use of too coarse a grit of sandpaper on undercoats. These marks were not removed in the final metal finish operation or were not properly filled and surfaced with putty (Figs. 39-14 and 39-15).

CAUSES

1. Improper metal-finishing techniques
2. Too thin a coating of primer-surfacer
3. Failure to use putty when required
4. Failure to allow primer-surfacer or putty to dry long enough before sanding
5. Cross sanding

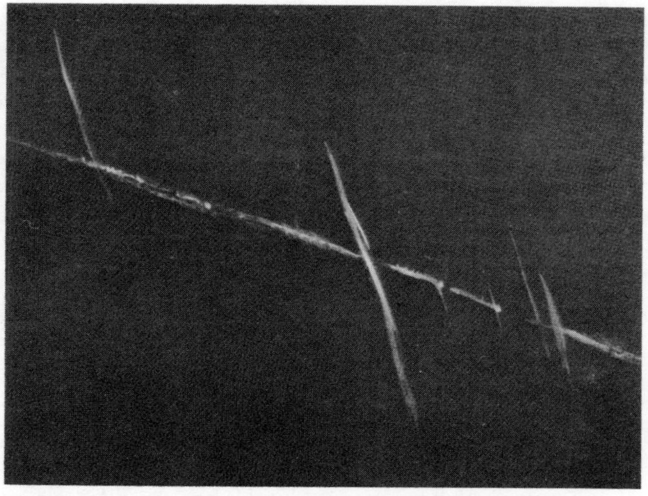

FIGURE 39-14. Sanding scratches in paint. ***(Ford Motor Company)***

FIGURE 39-15. Metal-finishing marks in paint. ***(Ford Motor Company)***

6. Poor sanding techniques
7. Use of too coarse a sandpaper
8. Use of poor or improper topcoat solvents

PREVENTION

1. Always finish off a stripping- or metal-finishing operation with a fine grit abrasive (No. 80 or finer).
2. Apply a good coating of primer-surfacer. Don't, however, apply it too heavily. Very heavy applications of primer-surfacer often lead to sand scratches.
3. Use a putty glaze to fill surface variations that primer-surfacer won't fill. Don't try to fill deep scratches with heavy applications of primer-surfacer. Apply the putty in thin layers.
4. Allow both primer-surfacer and putty to flash off before applying succeeding coats. Failure to do this results in crusting, a defect which eventually makes sand scratches show up more.
5. Use good sanding techniques. The best sanding jobs usually come from wet-sanding operations. If you do use dry sandpaper, tap it frequently to remove the sanding sludge. Never cross-sand. Use a sanding block or sand with the flat of the hand, never with the fingers.

6. Use the proper grit of sandpaper. Try to finish off all sanding operations with No. 400 grit paper or finer.
7. Use the solvent recommended by the topcoat manufacturer. Poor solvents usually lead to sand-scratch swelling.

REPAIR

Metal-finishing marks and sand scratches found on original factory finishes can usually be repaired by a combination of sanding, polishing, and buffing. In some extreme cases, the surface may have to be repainted.

The long cure time of refinishing enamels prevents polishing and buffing from being used on newly painted surfaces. Most cases of metal-finishing marks or sand scratches found on refinished cars will have to be repaired by repainting.

○39-13 Molding Installation Damage or Rust

This describes a specific kind of scratching or chipping of the paint finish adjacent to, or underneath, bright moldings, or ornaments. This damage occurs during the installation process and may not be apparent until after outdoor weathering has caused rust to form at the edges or rust stain to bleed out from underneath (Fig. 39-16).

REPAIR

Repair of this problem involves removing the molding or ornament, removing the rust, and repainting the affected area.

○39-14 Orange Peel

"Orange peel" is a term which indicates the uneven appearance of a paint film which has not flowed out to a smooth, glossy surface (Fig. 39-17).

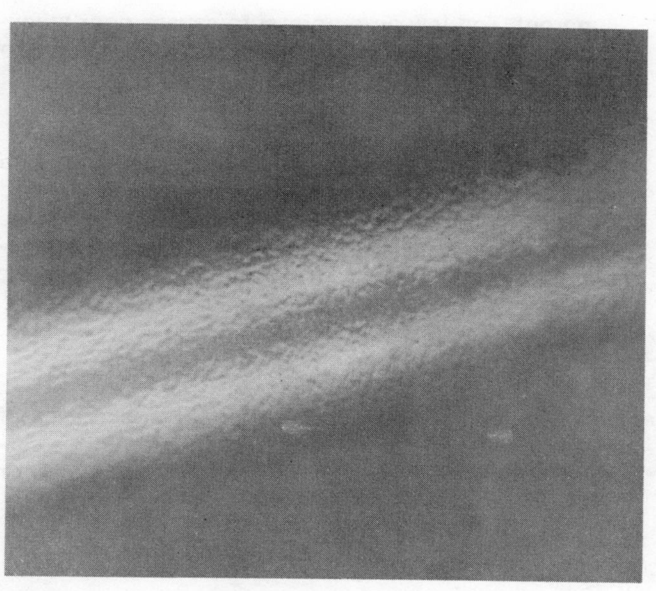

FIGURE 39-17. Paint that has orange peel.

CAUSES

1. Wrong solvent or improper reduction
2. Poor gun techniques
3. Improper air pressure

PREVENTION

1. Always reduce the paint with the amount and type of solvent specified by the paint manufacturer. Poor quality solvents, fast evaporating solvents, and underreduction are common causes of orange peel.
2. Use good gun techniques. Apply topcoats in wet coats, holding the gun 6 to 10 inches [152 to 254 mm] from the surface, keeping the gun at right angles to the area being painted.
3. Use the proper air pressure. Too high an air pressure causes a dry-spray and prevents the paint from flow-

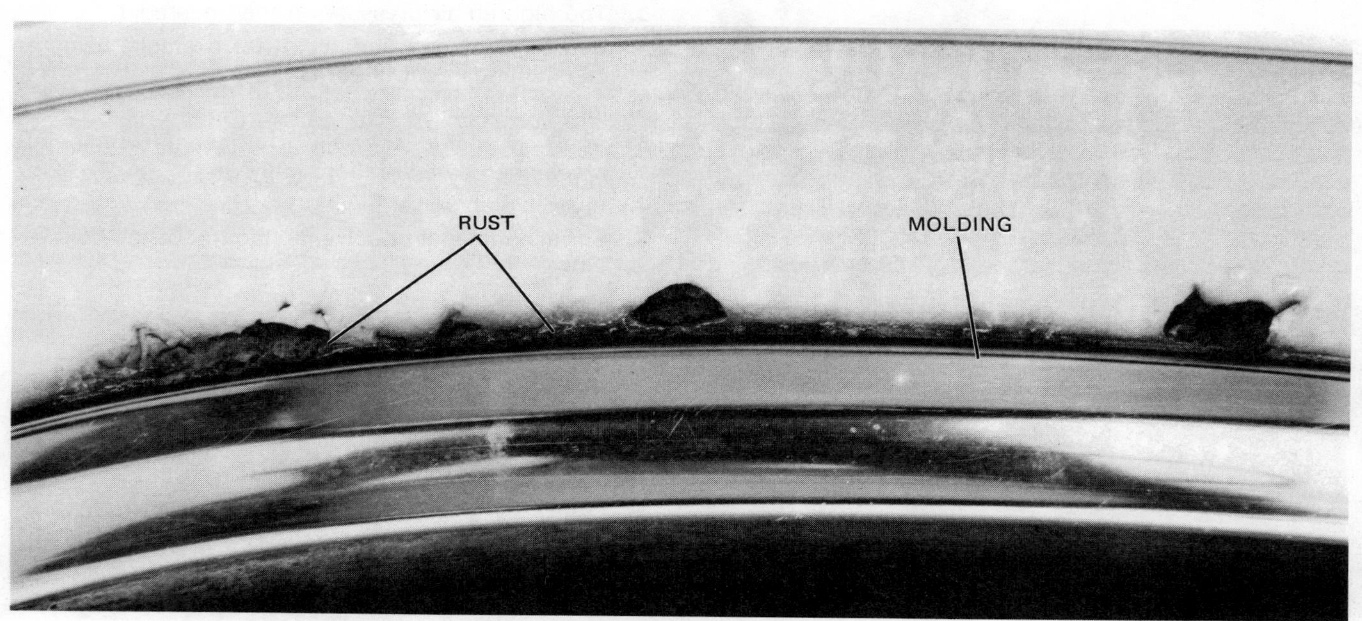

FIGURE 39-16. Damage or rust from molding installation.

ing out. Too low an air pressure causes poor atomization. Poor flow-out and atomization both result in orange peel.

REPAIR

Orange peel found in any painted surface can usually be repaired by a combination of sanding, polishing, and buffing as long as the film is completely cured. In some extreme cases, it may be necessary to sand out the orange peel and repaint.

○39-15 Overspray

Overspray is a term used to describe the appearance of small particles of paint of a contrasting color on the surface of the car. It is usually caused by poor masking or sloppy gun technique (Fig. 39-18).

CAUSES

1. Sloppy gun technique
2. Improper masking
3. Spraying onto a car near the car being painted

PREVENTION

1. Make sure adjacent surfaces are adequately covered with tape and masking paper before spraying.
2. Make sure all your masking tape and paper are properly stuck down.
3. Trigger the gun at the end of each stroke. Don't use such an excess of air pressure that you start to remove the masking tape.
4. Always spray in the spray booth. Keep the spray-booth doors closed and other cars out of the booth while you are spraying.
5. Don't blow paint all over the booth while making a spot repair.

REPAIR

Overspray found on original factory finishes can usually be repaired by wiping the surface with a good solvent. In some extreme cases, a combination of sanding, polishing, and buffing may have to be used.

Overspray caused by refinish operations over a factory finish usually can also be repaired by wiping the surface with a good solvent. However, if the overspray has aged and is insoluble in solvent, it will have to be compounded off.

Overspray caused by refinish operations over a refinished surface can sometimes be repaired by wiping the surface with a good solvent. If the solvent does not take all of the overspray off, it will probably have to be stripped off. (The long cure time of refinish enamels usually prevents a sanding and polishing operation.)

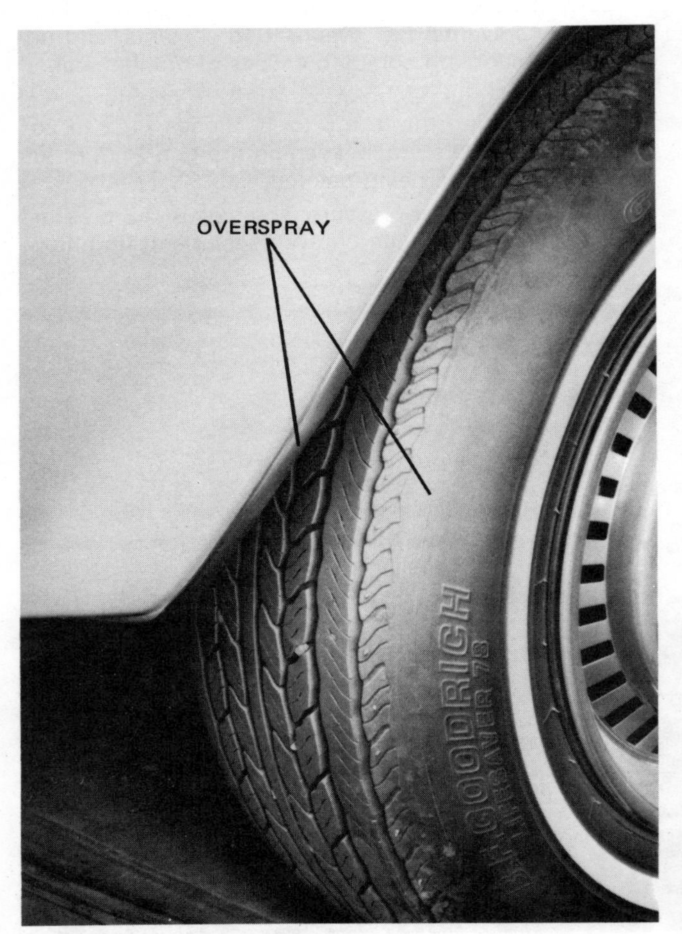

FIGURE 39-18. Overspray on paint.

○39-16 Peeling

This is also known as scaling or flaking. Peeling is the term applied to the separation of a paint film from the surface to which it has been applied. It includes peeling of the finish coats from the primer, separation of topcoat films (enamel from enamel or striping lacquer from enamel), or peeling of the finish from the metal, which may be accompanied by rusting (Fig. 39-19).

CAUSES

1. Presence of any foreign material such as wax, silicones, oil, etc., on the surface before painting
2. Improper or no use of metal conditioner on bare metal
3. Too high an air pressure on the undercoat
4. Use of the wrong undercoat; for example, using an enamel undercoat under lacquer
5. Insufficient sanding
6. Applying additional coats of primer-surfacer before preceding coats are thoroughly dry
7. Using cheap solvent
8. Surface material or solvents, too hot or too cold

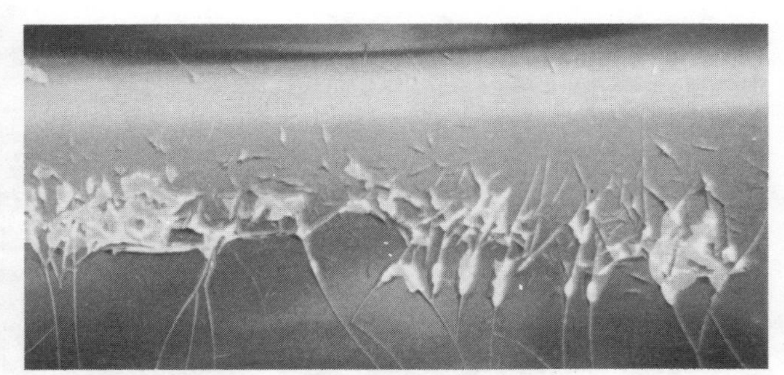

FIGURE 39-19. Peeling paint.

PREVENTION

1. Remove all dirt, wax, grease, etc., before sanding.
2. Use a metal conditioner on bare metal.
3. Thoroughly sand all surfaces where paint is to be applied.
4. Follow manufacturer's directions for thinning, applying, drying, and recoating all products.
5. Prime bare metal areas as soon as possible to prevent rusting.
6. Keep surface, paint, and thinners at room temperature.

REPAIR

Remove all of the paint having poor adhesion, and repaint as required.

○39-17 Poor Drying, Hardness

This condition is also termed softness, tackiness, slow drying. The drying of a paint film goes through several stages, or degrees of hardness, in progressing from a liquid to a solid coating. These may be described as follows:

Stage 1. *Dust-free* is the point at which dust or lint settling on the surface will not become embedded but can be wiped or blown off.

Stage 2. *Tack-free* is the point at which light finger pressure will not leave a print and the surface will no longer feel sticky.

Stage 3. *Dry to handle* is the point at which the painted part may be moved or handled without damaging the fresh paint. It is also the point at which taping and recoating can be accomplished.

Stage 4. *Hard dry* is the point at which optimum hardness is reached and the finish may be compounded, wheel-polished, buffed, waxed, washed, or otherwise treated.

The term "poor drying" or "hardness" can therefore apply to the result obtained at any of these four stages. In addition, the result obtained is related to the type of material used. For example, nitrocellulose and acrylic lacquers will dry harder, faster than enamels. Acrylic enamels will dry dust-free and tack-free faster than alkyd enamels. Differences in drying rate sometimes occur between colors with the same general type of formulation.

"Poor drying," then, describes the occurrence of softness in a film when experience indicates that it should be harder.

CAUSES

1. Use of slow reducing solvents
2. Use of excess amounts of retarders or other additives
3. Excessive film thickness
4. Painting over oil, grease, or other contamination
5. Oil in compressed air
6. Poor ventilation
7. Excess humidity in atmosphere
8. Low temperature—atmosphere, paint, solvent, or part
9. Dryer left out (if required by type of formulation)
10. Wet undercoat

PREVENTION

1. Do not use excessive slow reducing solvents or retarder. Use only as required in hot, dry weather in order to obtain flow-out.
2. Use only the additives prescribed by your paint supplier.
3. Avoid excessive undercoat and color coat film thickness by following the recommendation of the supplier regarding the amount and kind of reducing solvent used and the number of coats to be applied.
4. Clean surfaces to be painted with good silicone wax and oil remover.
5. Drain compressor and air lines frequently to prevent buildup of oil or water. Use a trap on all air lines used for blow-off or spray operations.
6. Spraying and drying of paint should be done only in a well-ventilated area.
7. Excess atmospheric humidity will retard drying. This can be partly compensated for through the use of faster solvents and higher air pressure. Further drying can be accelerated by the use of heat.
8. Maintain temperature in spray booth and drying room above 70°F [21.1°C]. Also, the temperature of the paint materials and solvents used should be at least 70°F [21.1°C]. The surface of the car to be painted should be at room temperature. Cars brought in from the outside in cold weather should be allowed to reach room temperature before painting. Steam, hot water, or hot air can be used to warm the surface if necessary.
9. Certain types of material require the addition of dryers if hardness is to be obtained with room-temperature air drying. Be sure the necessary dryers are added before attempting to use one of these types.
10. Make sure that the undercoats have thoroughly dried before applying color coats.

REPAIR

Air-dry the soft film for 24 hours or force-dry for ½ hour under radiant heat. If, after this, the film has still not reached sufficient hardness, it will be necessary to remove and repaint the defective area.

○39-18 Rusting

This may also be called corroding, rust stain, or rust bleed. This condition is the result of weathering (oxidation) of exposed or insufficiently protected or prepared metal. Either the metal was not painted, the metal was not painted enough, or the paint was applied over a rusted surface or was removed, with rusting the result. Accordingly, rusting may be the secondary effect of a primary problem, such as thin paint, chipping, scratching, peeling, etc. (Fig. 39-20).

CAUSES

1. Exterior damage to the paint film
2. Insufficient film thickness or incomplete coverage

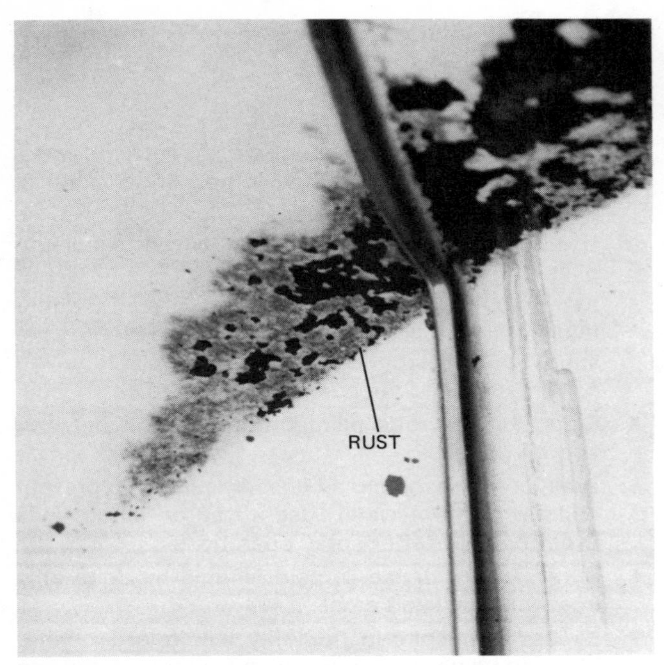

FIGURE 39-20. Metal rusting under paint.

3. Applying paint to a metal which contains rust not completely removed
4. Painting over metal touched by bare hands, or metal contaminated by chemical deposits from sanding water

PREVENTION

1. Apply the recommended number of coats to get adequate thickness.
2. Apply paint carefully to ensure complete coverage.
3. Thoroughly prepare metal for painting by sanding to remove all traces of rust from the surface.
4. Always use a metal conditioner on bare metal.
5. Don't touch bare metal with your hands after the metal conditioner is applied. Apply primer-surfacer within 30 minutes of the metal conditioner application.

REPAIR

Remove the affected paint film down to the metal, remove the rust, apply metal conditioner, and repaint.

○39-19 Sags, Runs

This condition may also be called drips, blobs, tears, curtains. All these terms describe a condition resulting from the application of an excessive amount of paint to a localized area so that it flows downward and accumulates in objectionable thickness (Fig. 39-21).

CAUSES

1. Spraying over a surface contaminated with wax, oil, grease, or silicone
2. Solvent, material, surface, or spray booth too cold
3. Using too much or too little solvent or a solvent that dries too slowly

FIGURE 39-21. Sags and runs in paint.

4. "Piling on" coats by recoating before preceding coats have flashed off
5. Using too low an air pressure
6. Improper spray gun adjustment
7. Improper spray gun technique

PREVENTION

1. Thoroughly clean the surface to be painted. Use a wax and silicone remover before applying paint to a previously painted surface.
2. Keep the surface, solvents, and material at room temperature. Delay spraying in a spray booth until the booth has reached normal room temperature.
3. Make sure the paint is properly reduced (per the paint manufacturer's recommendations). Runs can be caused by overreduction and use of a solvent which evaporates too slowly. Sags can be caused by underreduction which results in "piling on" in heavy coats.
4. Allow preceding coats to flash off before applying the next coat. Failure to do this can cause sags.
5. Make sure sufficient air pressure is used. Low air pressure can cause sags, because the paint will not properly atomize.
6. Properly adjust the fluid and fan controls on the spray gun. Too narrow a fan with too much paint will cause sags.
7. Keep the gun at the proper distance from the work. Holding the gun too close piles on the paint and invites sags. Also, avoid using a jerky spray stroke and moving the gun too slowly.

REPAIR

Sags found in original nonmetallic finishes can usually be corrected by cutting off the excess paint with a knife or razor blade followed by sanding, polishing, and buffing to remove the excess paint. Sags in metallic colors, when they are not accompanied by a change in color, can be repaired in the same way. However, when there is a change in color, the area will have to be repainted.

Runs or sags caused by refinishers in local paint shops will usually have to be sanded off or washed off (if the paint is still wet) and then repainted. In some instances, however, a sag that is still wet can be removed by picking up the excess paint with a wet finger or by flowing it off the panel by spraying it with solvent.

○39-20 Scratches

These may also be called marred paint. The term "scratch" describes the appearance of the finish when it has been damaged by the penetration of a sharp object. The result is a permanent scar or tear in the film which, in extreme cases, penetrates to the base metal and may be accompanied by rusting (Fig. 39-22).

REPAIR

If the scratch is in but not through the topcoat and the topcoat is thoroughly cured, the finish can usually be repaired by polishing and buffing. If the scratch is through the topcoat, but not through the undercoat, and is in an inconspicuous location, the finish can be repaired by brush touch-up. If the scratch has penetrated to the metal and the metal has corroded, it must be removed and the area repainted.

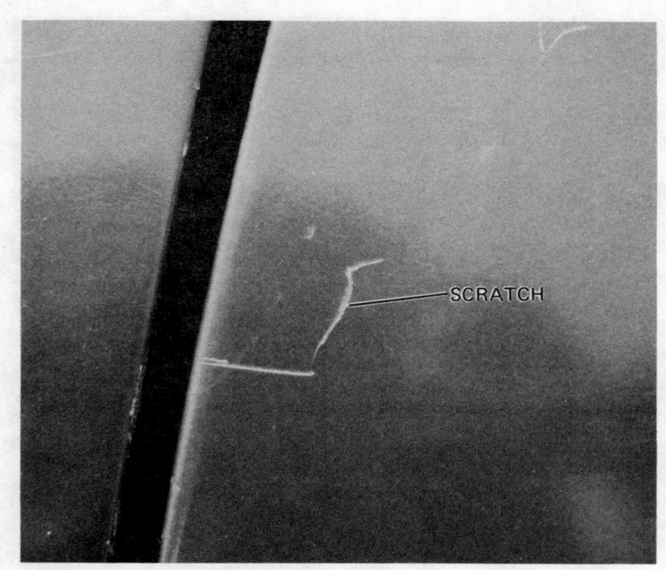

FIGURE 39-22. Scratches or marred paint.

○39-21 Sealer, Deadener under Paint

This condition is also caused by oil, grease, or other contamination. These terms describe specific types of dirt under paint resulting from poor repaint cleanup operations. Proper identification can therefore assist in the initiation of proper corrective action. Since these are usually substantial "gobs" of contamination, their removal will probably result in exposing primer or bare metal.

REPAIR

Remove the contamination and repaint.

FIGURE 39-23. Stained, tarnished, and faded paint.

○39-22 Stains, Tarnish, Fading

This condition may also be called off-color spots, discolored spots, bleeding. The terms "stains" and "off-color or discolored spots" describe the result of surface contamination which has affected the color of the finish. The term "fading" describes a change in color from the original, resulting from exposure to weathering in service.

Most of the comments listed above under ○39-9, Foreign Material on Surface, and ○39-10, Industrial Fallout, apply to stains and off-color spots. In many instances, these off-color spots are caused by acid containing industrial fallout or by battery acid.

Fading of the finish in extended service (6 to 24 months) represents a color change occurring in the paint pigment on exposure to sunlight (Fig. 39-23).

REPAIR

Off-color spots or stains on the surface can often be removed by sanding, polishing, and buffing. If the contamination has penetrated the topcoat and is not removed by polishing, repainting will be necessary.

Faded areas require repainting to restore the color.

○39-23 Thin Paint, No Paint

This condition may also be called skips, holidays, primer shows, no primer under topcoat.

The term "thin paint" describes a condition in which an insufficient amount of paint has been applied or an excessive amount has been removed by abrasion or erosion (Fig. 39-24). The result is that either bare metal is exposed (in which case rusting may be evident) or primer shows through the finish coats, causing an off-color condition.

CAUSES

1. Incomplete coverage
2. Insufficient film thickness
3. Abnormal polishing of color coat
4. Wrong color undercoat
5. Improper or overreduced materials

PREVENTION

1. Use care when applying paint to be sure all surfaces are coated.
2. Use normal coating thicknesses.

FIGURE 39-24. Thin paint. *(Ford Motor Company)*

3. Be careful not to overcompound or overpolish, especially on edges and corners where it is very easy to remove the color.
4. Use undercoats similar in color to the color of the topcoat being applied.
5. Follow the recommendations of the paint manufacturer regarding the amount and type of solvent used for reduction and the number of coats required.

REPAIR

Thin paint must be repaired by repainting.

○39-24 Water Spotting

Water spotting is usually caused by exposing the surface of a paint film that has not dried sufficiently to snow, rain, or dew. The effect of this water is magnified if the droplets are dried by sunlight. The damage may appear either as a roughening of the surface of the paint or as a circular, whitish water residue embedded in the surface (Fig. 39-25).

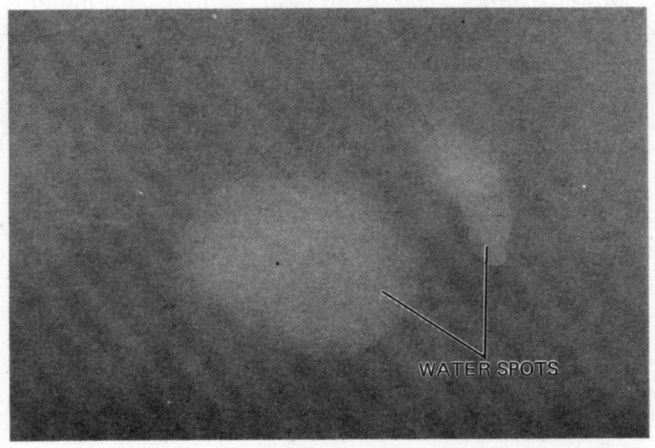

FIGURE 39-25. Water spotting in paint. *(Ford Motor Company)*

CAUSES

1. Allowing rain, snow, or dew to get on the surface or washing the surface before it is thoroughly dry
2. Applying excessively thick coats or using any techniques that cause poor drying

PREVENTION

1. Allow freshly painted vehicles sufficient air-dry or force-dry time before exposing them to the elements.
2. Use materials that have maximum resistance to water spotting.
3. See also preventions listed in ○39-17 Poor Drying, Hardness.

REPAIR

Minor water spotting may be removed by polishing and buffing after the finish has been allowed to harden. Severe water spotting requires sanding and repainting to correct.

○39-25 Wrinkling

Wrinkling is seldom encountered in today's original finishes. It does, however, occur in thick air-dry finishes and is the result of uneven drying between the top surface and undersurface of the finish coat material (Fig. 39-26).

CAUSES

1. Too heavy a coat or coats of paint; rapid drying of the top surface of the film while the film underneath remains soft
2. Force drying of enamels without using a baking converter when required
3. Use of lacquer thinner in enamel, which may cause wrinkling or lifting of the original finish or the primer-surfacer
4. Exposing enamel to sunlight before it is thoroughly dry
5. Any technique or condition that would produce sags or slow drying
6. Abnormally hot and humid weather

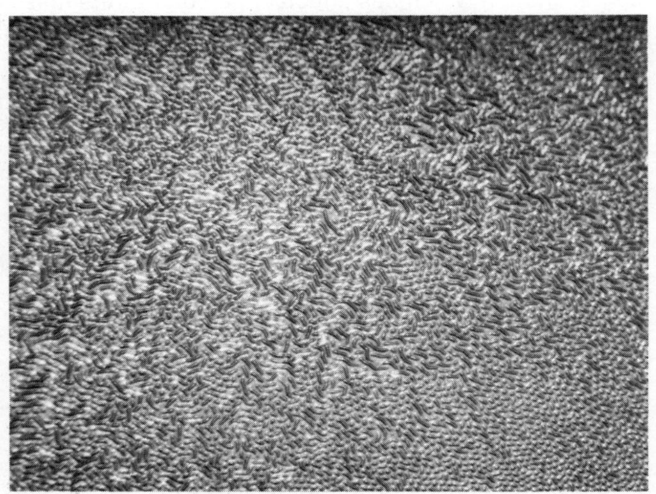

FIGURE 39-26. Wrinkled paint.

PREVENTION

1. Don't spray enamel too thick. Avoid piling on.
2. If you force-dry enamels, make sure you add a baking converter to the paint if it is recommended by the paint manufacturer.
3. Use the solvent recommended by the paint manufacturer.
4. Try to keep the spray booth and car at normal temperature.
5. Avoid spray-gun techniques that cause very heavy applications of paint (for example, holding the gun very close to the work and moving the gun very slowly).
6. Keep the car out of the sunshine until it has thoroughly dried.

REPAIR

The only way to repair a wrinkled surface is to remove the wrinkled film and to repaint.

CHAPTER 39 CHECKUP

NOTE: Since the following is a chapter review test, you should review the chapter before taking the test.

Paint problems can happen with almost any paint job. However, their possible causes are well known, and by following certain steps most paint problems can be prevented. In this chapter, we have reviewed in detail the various types of paint problems and their causes, prevention, and repair. To find out how well you understand everything in this chapter, answer the questions that follow.

COMPLETING THE SENTENCES The sentences below are incomplete. After each sentence there are several words or phrases, but only one of them correctly completes the sentence. Write each sentence in your notebook, ending the sentence with the one word or phrase that completes it correctly.

1. A paint problem that sometimes can be repaired by brush touch-up is (*a*) bleeding, (*b*) chalking, (*c*) orange peel, (*d*) chipped paint.
2. A paint problem caused by paint flowing away from a contaminated spot before it dries is (*a*) lifting, (*b*) peeling, (*c*) dulling, (*d*) craters or fisheyes.
3. Painting over a waxed finish may cause (*a*) bleeding, (*b*) bubbles, (*c*) peeling, (*d*) cracking.
4. Sags or runs in the paint may be caused by (*a*) too low an air pressure, (*b*) too high an air pressure, (*c*) waiting too long between coats, (*d*) heat lamps.
5. A freshly painted surface that gets wet may result in (*a*) wrinkling, (*b*) water spotting, (*c*) chalking, (*d*) orange peel.

DEFINITIONS In the following, you are asked to define certain terms. Write the definitions in your notebook. This will help you remember them. It will also provide you with a quick way to locate meanings when you need the information again. If you do not know the meanings of the terms, look them up in the text or in the glossary at the back of the book.

1. What is mottled paint?
2. Define "orange peel."
3. What is wrinkling?
4. What is the difference between lifting paint and peeling paint?
5. What are fisheyes?
6. Define "bleeding."
7. What is industrial fallout?
8. Define "sags."
9. What is thin paint?
10. What is faded paint?

SUGGESTIONS FOR FURTHER STUDY

In a page for your notebook, write down the 25 paint problems that are discussed in this chapter. Then after each problem, write down a short definition. It is very important that you know how to identify each type of paint problem. Until you know the paint problem and what caused it, you usually cannot proceed with repairing it.

PART 11

ESTIMATING

A written estimate is used by body and paint technicians as a "roadmap" to guide them through the repair of damaged vehicles. It is the job of the estimator to prepare this roadmap, which is called properly the written estimate or simply the estimate.

There are many things to consider in preparing an accurate estimate. This means that the estimator must be a person who knows automotive construction and repair procedures. In this part, we discuss some of the things the estimator must check and do to prepare the estimate.

There is one chapter in Part 11:

40

ESTIMATING THE DAMAGE

In this chapter, we describe the procedure of determining if a damaged car is worth repairing and, if it is, what needs to be done and how much it will cost. The body shop estimator has the responsibility of doing this.

○40-1 Duties of the Estimator

The job of the body-shop estimator is to keep a steady flow of work coming into the shop. ○1-5 discusses in detail the duties of the estimator and the importance of this job to successful body-shop operations. If the estimator makes mistakes and cannot accurately estimate how much repair jobs will cost, the body shop can be in serious trouble.

A person who is an estimator must have many skills. The major task, of course, is writing the estimate. Then, when approved by whoever is to pay the bill and accepted by the body shop, the written estimate becomes the roadmap to be followed by the body and paint technicians in restoring the vehicle. Preparation of the written estimate is covered later in ○40-4 to ○40-8.

In addition to estimating, the estimator usually is the only contact the car owner has with the body shop. This means that the estimator must be good at customer relations. Also, the estimator must work with the adjuster for the insurance company on many jobs. This requires skill at negotiating, flexibility, and an accurate knowledge of both parts and labor costs.

The insurance adjuster makes a separate estimate and compares it with the body-shop estimate. If the estimates are comparable, the body shop is given the go-ahead to do the repair job. Sometimes the insurance adjuster simply examines the damaged car with the estimator and does not make a detailed estimate.

○40-2 Frequency of Collisions

There are about 140 million cars, trucks, and buses operating on the streets and highways throughout the United States. Statistics indicate that there are about 17 million major and minor collisions each year. In other words, cars are damaged at a rate exceeding one car every other second of every hour each day!

As you know, before most of these damaged cars are repaired, an estimate of the cost of repair is prepared. Then a decision is made as to whether the vehicle is

FIGURE 40-1. A detailed written estimate is not always needed when the damage has obviously totaled the car.

economically repairable. This is a problem that arises frequently in major collisions and roll-overs. It is not often a problem when only one fender or panel must be repaired. However, written estimates usually are not prepared on a car that is obviously totaled. For example, a large tree falling on a car and crushing it probably will total the car (Fig. 40-1).

○40-3 After the Damage

After a minor collision, the car may still be drivable. If so, the owner drives the car to the body shop, where the estimator inspects the damage and prepares the written estimate. After a major collision, the car usually is towed away. It may be taken directly to the body shop or to a local storage lot designated by the police or the insurance company. Sometimes it takes a tow truck to move a wrecked car. In this case, the estimator travels to the car to inspect it so the estimate can be prepared. After the decision is made as to which body shop will do the repair job, arrangements are made for towing the car to that body shop.

○40-4 Inspecting the Damage

The first thing the estimator does when a damaged car is driven in or brought in by a wrecker (Fig. 40-2) is to inspect the car and decide what work is required, how many hours it will take, and what parts are needed and how much they will cost. In some cases, the car is so badly damaged it is not worth fixing up. Such a car is said to be *totaled,* as we have explained.

If the car is worth repairing, the estimator fills out a written estimate form such as shown in Fig. 40-3. On the form, the left columns list operations such as replacing parts, straightening panels, refinishing, and so on. The labor column lists the hours of labor required for each operation. The next column lists the costs of new or salvaged parts that are needed. The right column lists the costs of certain jobs that may be sublet. Sublet jobs are those that will be done by another shop. They may include such operations as straightening and rechroming a bumper, aligning the front wheels, adjusting headlights, and checking the charging or ignition system.

FIGURE 40-2. A written estimate is prepared on cars brought to the body shop by a wrecker.

When you inspect a vehicle for damage, the first question to answer is about the whole car. *Is the vehicle repairable?* If so, then you must ask another question about each damaged part. *How is this part to be repaired?* It may be replaced with a new one, straightened and refinished, or replaced with a used part from a salvaged vehicle. Sometimes a lack of parts availability helps answer the question for you.

To inspect damage, begin by standing directly in front of it. Carefully note each crushed part. Then work through the damaged area, analyzing each damaged part in terms of *"what's wrong?"* and *"how can it be fixed?"* Your biggest concern is that you see all of the damage. Many types of collision damage are not readily visible. For example, a car that has been struck hard on the side may have frame and drive-shaft damage. Also, the impact may have broken the engine mounts. To check for this type of damage, have the car placed on safety stands so you can get under the vehicle to make a thorough inspection. Detecting and correcting frame damage are covered in detail in Chapters 16 and 17.

A front-end collision also can cause damage that you can easily overlook. For example, a punctured air-conditioner condenser and engine radiator will have to be repaired or replaced. In addition, the air-conditioning system will have to be recharged with refrigerant, and the radiator will have to be refilled with antifreeze. Both of these chemicals are expensive. You must be sure to include their costs in preparing the estimate.

There are many types of hidden damage that only experience will teach you to find. When estimating any vehicle repair, remember always to check for the hidden damage.

○40-5 The Estimating Procedure

Start the estimating procedure on the outside of the vehicle in front of the damage. On the estimate form, list each damaged panel or major part, along with all other parts attached to it that also are damaged. Start outside the vehicle and work inward with your inspection until there is no more damage to be repaired.

When you finish inspecting each panel or major part, carefully take a second look at it. Make sure that you have included any emblems or moldings that must be replaced or reinstalled on the new panel. Next, carefully inspect all adjacent parts for damage and proper alignment. Check all doors, hood, and trunk lid for proper operation and locking, if any of these could have been affected by the collision. Check the bumpers and grill for damage, and all lights and the brakes for proper operation.

If the collision could have caused bent wheels or steering or suspension damage or affected front-end or rear-wheel alignment, then these items must be checked. By following the steps discussed above as you prepare the estimate, you will have written on the estimate form a complete list of all the damaged parts.

○40-6 Checking for Air-Conditioner Collision Damage

Figure 40-4 shows the location of the air-conditioning components in a car. If a car has been in a collision, the

UNISET THE REYNOLDS AND REYNOLDS COMPANY • CELINA, OHIO UNISET
BUSINESS FORMS □ ACCOUNTING SYSTEMS □ EDP SERVICES

RAY W. REYNOLDS COMPANY

2619 HEMSTEAD BLVD. TELEPHONE 224-2678

HOMETOWN, STATE 19787

BODY AND FENDER REPAIRS • EXPERT REFINISHING

NAME ____________________ DATE ____________

ADDRESS ____________________ PHONE ____________

DATE WANTED ____________

YEAR-MODEL-COLOR	MAKE OF CAR	BODY TYPE	LICENSE NO.	SERIAL NO.	MOTOR NO.	MILEAGE

REPAIR	REPLACE		LABOR	PARTS AND MATERIALS	SUBLET WORK
		TOTALS			

LABOR	
PARTS AND MATERIALS	
SUBLET WORK	
TAX	
GRAND TOTAL	

THIS ESTIMATE IS BASED ON OUR INSPECTION AND DOES NOT COVER ADDITIONAL PARTS OR LABOR WHICH MAY BE REQUIRED AFTER THE WORK HAS BEEN STARTED. AFTER THE WORK HAS STARTED, WORN OR DAMAGED PARTS WHICH ARE NOT EVIDENT ON FIRST INSPECTION MAY BE DISCOVERED. NATURALLY THIS ESTIMATE CANNOT COVER SUCH CONTINGENCIES. PARTS PRICES SUBJECT TO CHANGE WITHOUT NOTICE. THIS ESTIMATE IS FOR IMMEDIATE ACCEPTANCE.

THIS WORK AUTHORIZED BY ____________________

ESTIMATE SHEET AND REPAIR ORDER

FORM SA-87 THE REYNOLDS & REYNOLDS CO., CELINA, OHIO LITHO IN U.S.A.

FIGURE 40-3. **Form used to prepare an estimate.** ***(The Reynolds and Reynolds Company)***

air-conditioner system should be inspected as soon as possible. If the system has been opened by the impact, it should be repaired without delay. Leaving an air-conditioner system exposed to the atmosphere allows air, moisture, and dirt to enter. The longer the exposure, the greater the amount of air, moisture, and dirt that get in. Therefore, the greater the damage to the system.

You can often tell at a glance when components are damaged beyond repair or the whole system is useless. The inspection procedure recommended by Chevrolet follows. Note that the procedure is merely a general guide. Details of air-conditioner service are covered in *Automotive Air Conditioning,* another book in the McGraw-Hill *Automotive Technology Series.*

1. Remove the drive belt. Cut it off if necessary.
2. Look at the various components of the system—condenser, evaporator, VIR unit, compressor, mounting brackets, connecting lines, and controls—to determine if any have been damaged. The condenser, being in front of the engine radiator, is the most vulnerable and most apt to be damaged in a front-end collision.

NOTE: No repairs of any kind, including soldering, welding, or brazing, should be attempted on the condenser. If the vapor passages are bent or damaged in any way or if the fins are mashed together, discard the condenser and install a new one.

3. Inspect the VIR unit for cracks and other damage. If it appears to be intact, clean it with a suitable cleaner. Dry it thoroughly. Replace the desiccant bag.
4. If the evaporator shows any signs of damage, replace it.
5. Check the control system, connecting wires, vacuum hoses, and vacuum motors for damage. Install new parts as necessary.
6. Check all connecting lines and flexible hoses for damage. Inspect them along their full length. Make sure all connections are in good condition. Replace any lines or hoses that are damaged in any way.
7. Check the clutch pulley for proper operation.
8. Check the compressor (Fig. 40-4) for damage.
9. Install the charging station, and discharge the refrigerant system.
10. Remove the compressor from the engine. Unscrew the oil test fitting, and pour the oil into a clean glass container. Examine the oil for dirt, water, metal particles, etc. If any of these are present, discard the compressor and the desiccant bag in the VIR unit. Flush the other system components with liquid refrigerant.
11. If the compressor oil is clean and free of any harmful substance, discard it. Put the same amount of new, fresh oil into the compressor.

NOTE: If system components have been flushed, replace the full charge of oil. If not, add no more new oil than you poured out.

12. Use a can or supply tank of refrigerant to charge the compressor. Use the leak detector to check the compressor for leaks. If it has no leaks, reinstall it.
13. Evacuate the system. Put some refrigerant into the system, and leak-test it.
14. If the system passes the leak test, recharge it.

○40-7 Inspecting Energy-absorbing Bumpers

Energy-absorbing bumpers are required by law on late-model vehicles. Such bumpers will withstand collisions at low speed without damage to the bumper or vehicle. Most energy-absorbing bumpers are designed to assume their original position after the collision. There are several types, for both the front and rear of late-model cars. One uses a leaf-spring assembly which supports the bumper (see Fig. 2-31). On impact, the spring gives and absorbs the blow. It then returns to its original position if the impact is within the design limits. If the impact is greater than the design limits, damage may occur and repair may be required.

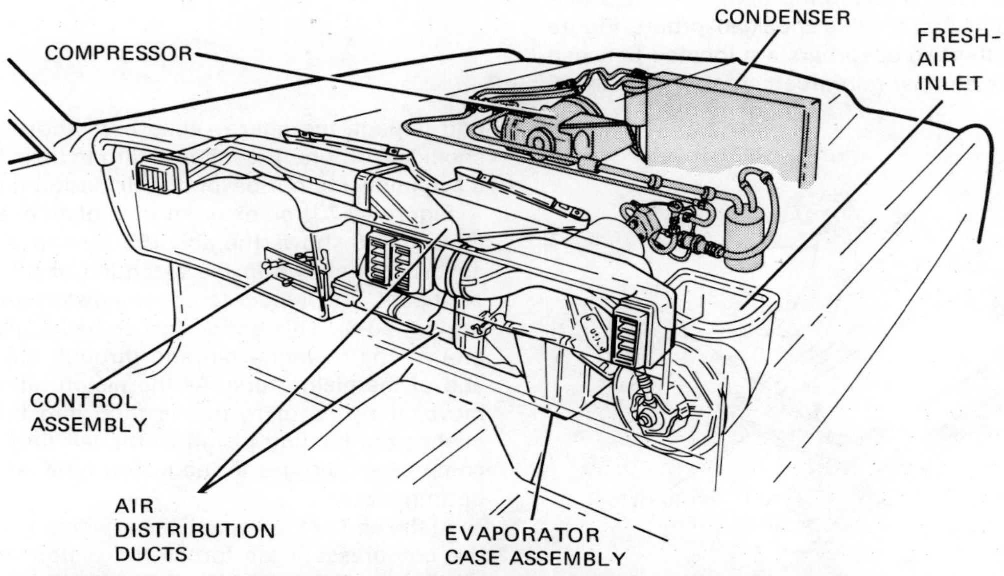

FIGURE 40-4. Location of air-conditioning components in car. ***(Ford Motor Company)***

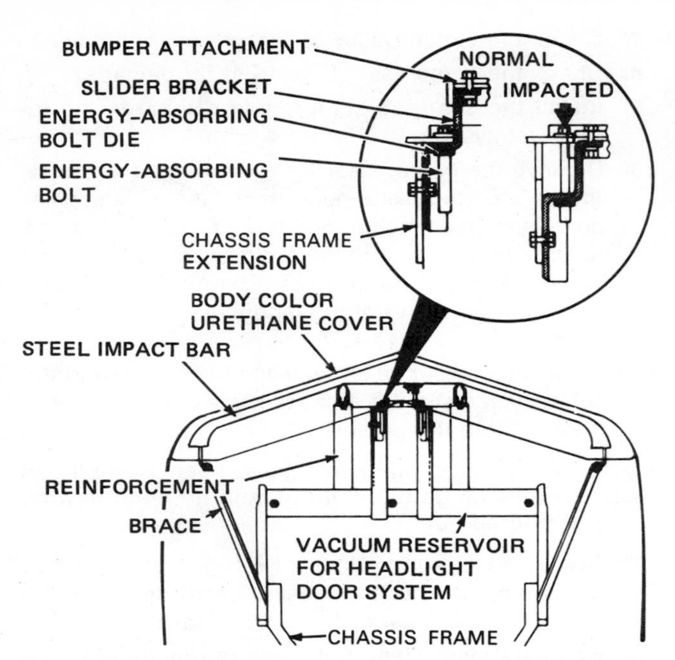

FIGURE 40-5. Front-bumper system using a pair of special bolts and dies. The dies draw the bolts to a smaller diameter to absorb the energy of a front-end impact. ***(Chevrolet Motor Division of General Motors Company)***

A second type uses a pair of special energy-absorbing bolts and two bolt dies (Fig. 40-5). The dies are steel rings with an inner diameter smaller than the special bolts. During impact, the dies are pushed along the bolts. This action reduces the diameter of the energy-absorbing bolts. In the system shown, the bolt diameters are reduced from 0.33 inch [8.38 mm] to 0.31 inch [7.87 mm]. The bolts are elongated about 1 inch [25 mm] during an impact that moves the bumper 3½ inches [8.9 mm]. If the impact is strong enough to elongate the bolts, the energy-absorbing-bolt assembly, dies, and related parts must be replaced. If the impact is greater than the design limit of the system, other damage may occur and require repair.

A third type of energy-absorbing bumper uses a pair of energy absorbers that are like shock absorbers. Figure 40-6 shows how the two absorbers are located between the frame and the bumper reinforcement. During a front-end impact, the energy absorbers shorten, similarly to shock absorbers. They then return to their original length if the impact is not beyond their design limits.

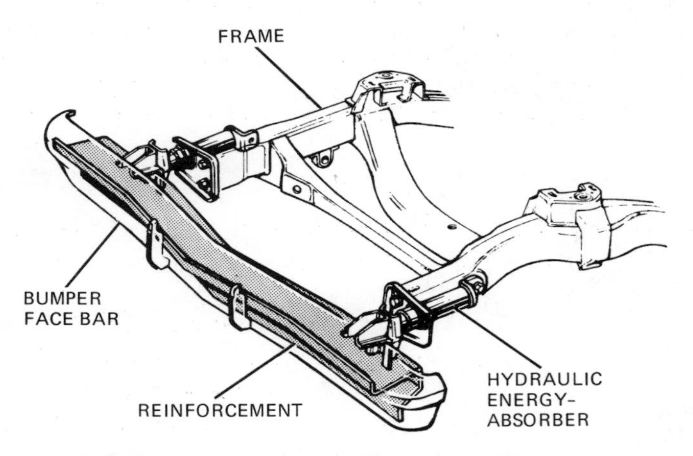

FIGURE 40-6. Location of components in a front-bumper system using two energy absorbers to absorb impacts up to 5 mph [8 kmph]. ***(Chrysler Corporation)***

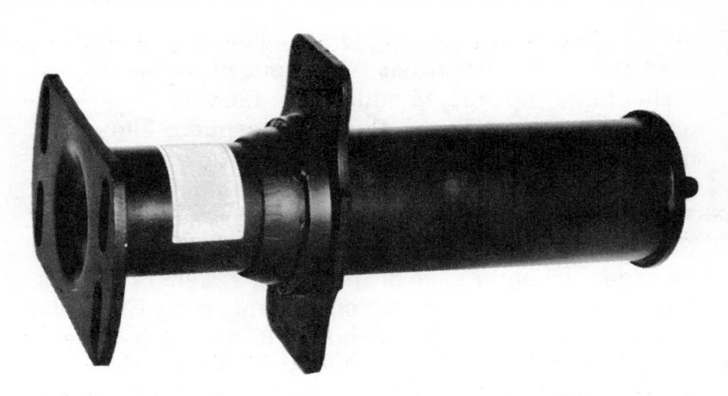

FIGURE 40-7. An energy absorber. ***(Chevrolet Motor Division of General Motors Corporation)***

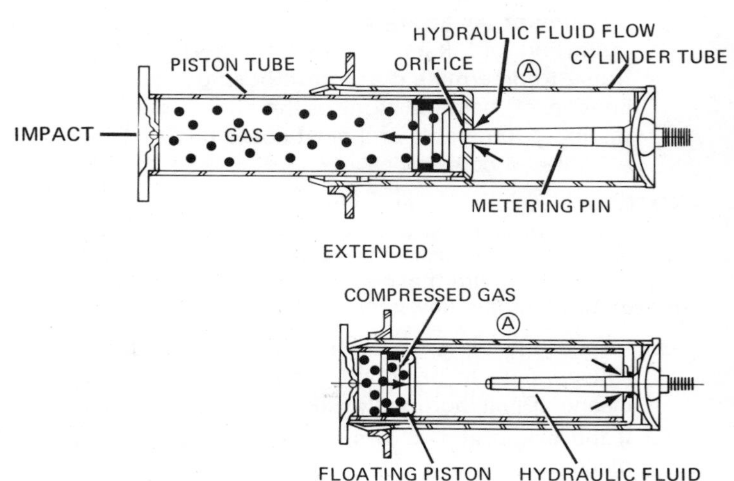

FIGURE 40-8. Operation of the energy absorber during a front-end impact. (Top) Action at the start of the impact; the piston tube starts to enter the cylinder tube, and hydraulic fluid flows through the orifice. (Bottom) The piston tube has reached the inner limit of motion; hydraulic fluid has flowed through the orifice, forcing the floating piston to compress the gas. ***(General Motors Corporation)***

Figure 40-7 is an external view of an energy absorber. Figure 40-8 shows the absorber action. At the top, the absorber is shown in the extended position at the start of impact. The impact forces the piston tube to the right (in Fig. 40-8). This action forces hydraulic fluid to flow around the metering pin and through the orifice in the end of the piston tube. As the piston tube continues to move, the flow of hydraulic fluid into the piston tube pushes the floating piston to the left (in Fig. 40-8). This compresses the gas in the piston tube, as shown in the bottom picture.

At the end of the impact, if it is within the design limits, the compressed gas forces the piston tube out to its original position. If the impact is greater than the design limits of the system, damage may occur and require repair.

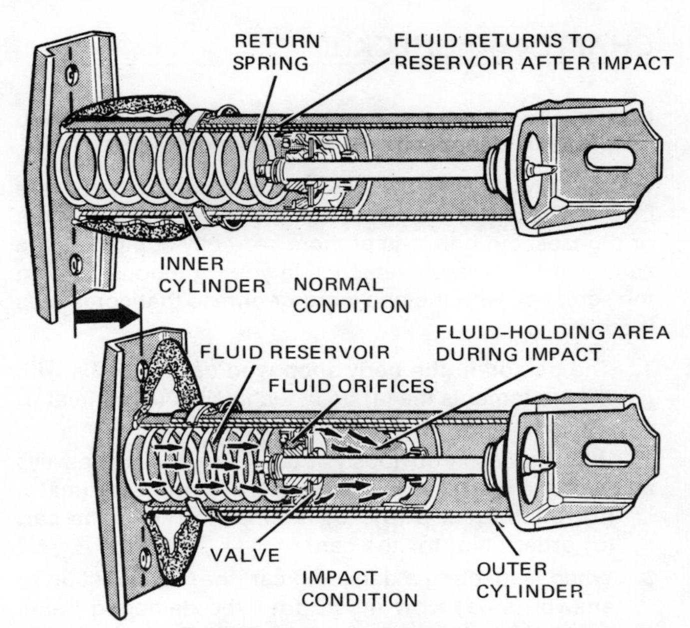

FIGURE 40-9. Bumper-impact energy absorber with spring return. ***(Chrysler Corporation)***

A somewhat different energy absorber is shown in Fig. 40-9. The energy absorber described above depends on a chamber filled with high-pressure gas for its action. The unit shown in Fig. 40-9 uses a heavy return spring. In this design, when bumper impact loads reach about 10,000 pounds [4536 kg], a valve in the absorber opens. This allows hydraulic fluid to be forced through a set of small holes. Then, if the impact causes no structural damage, the spring pushes the two ends of the absorber apart. They return to the normal position.

On all bumpers, energy-absorbing and otherwise, inspect for any conditions that could be hazardous. These include a loose or misplaced bumper, or a broken or torn part that sticks out. On energy-absorbing bumpers, check also to see if the bumper has impacted hard enough to retract. If so, note whether or not the bumper has returned to its original position. On the nonreturn type, such as that in Fig. 40-5, if the impact has actuated the energy absorber, it must be replaced.

Carefully inspect a vehicle with an energy-absorbing bumper that has been impacted and has not returned to its original position. You can check the types of energy absorber shown in Figs. 40-6 to 40-9, by noting whether the absorber looks damaged or has oil dripping from it. Either of these signs would indicate that internal damage has occurred.

The energy absorbers shown in Figs. 40-6 to 40-9 can be checked for normal operation with the bumper on the car as follows: Move the car close to a sturdy barrier such as a wall, pillar, or post (Fig. 40-10). Then turn the engine off, with the transmission in PARK and the parking brake on. Put a device, such as a tire jack, between the bumper and the barrier, just in front of where one of the energy absorbers is attached. Apply pressure to see if the energy absorber will move ⅜ inch [9.5 mm] or more. Then release the pressure to see if the energy absorber will move out to its original position. Check the other energy absorber, on the other side of the bumper, in the same way. If the energy absorber does not work as described, it is defective and must be replaced.

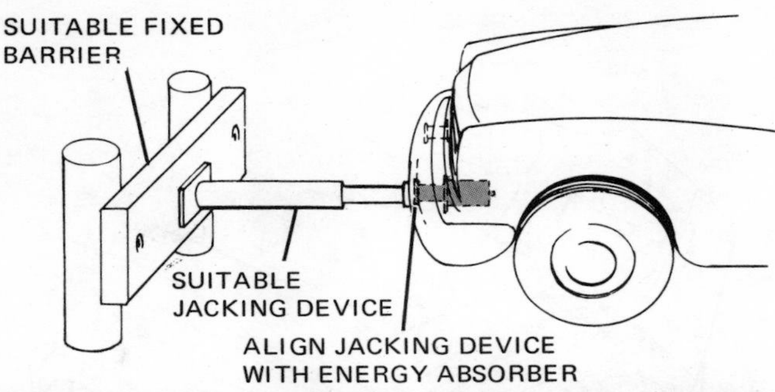

FIGURE 40-10. Testing an energy absorber on the car. ***(Buick Motor Division of General Motors Corporation)***

CAUTION: These energy absorbers are filled with gas at high pressure. They can explode if heat is applied to them. Under no condition should heat be applied, as, for example, to repair the unit by welding. The procedure for deactivating a damaged energy-absorber and disposing of it safely is covered in Chapter 13.

In addition to the energy-absorbing bumpers discussed above, there are other kinds in use. Figure 40-11 shows the molded rubber isolators that are used on many Ford cars. In this system, the energy-absorber or isolator is made of molded rubber bonded between two heavy stamped metal channels. One channel is attached to the car frame, and the other is attached to the bumper. On heavy impact, the rubber shears at the bond between the metal and the rubber. When this happens, the isolator must be replaced.

To check the energy absorber or isolator that is off the car, place it in an arbor press. Compress the energy absorber about ⅜ inch [9.5 mm], and then release the pressure. If the energy absorber is good, it will extend

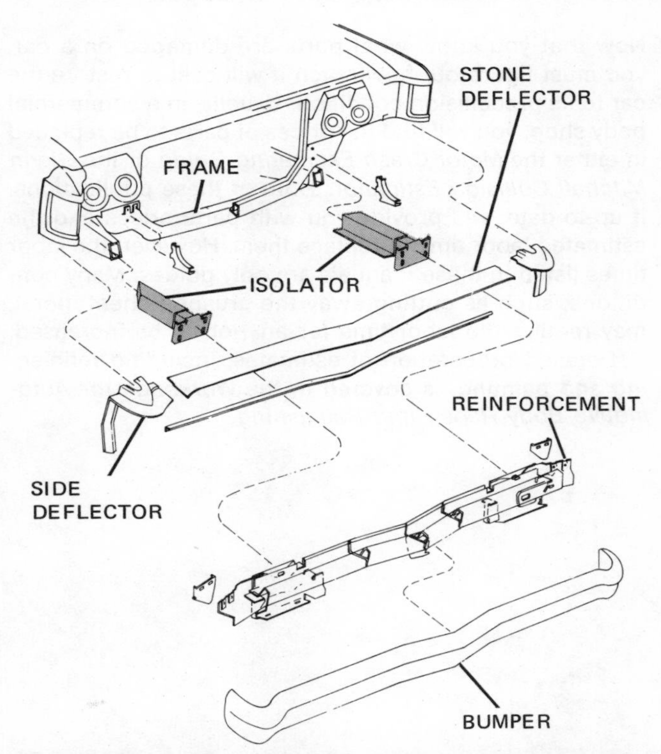

FIGURE 40-11. Bumper system using isolators made of molded rubber to absorb impact. ***(Ford Motor Company)***

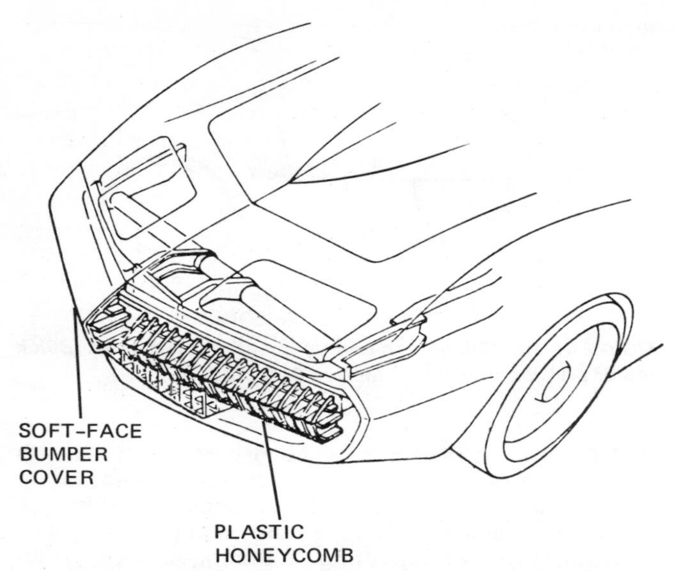

FIGURE 40-12. Soft-face bumper with plastic honeycomb inside. ***(Chevrolet Motor Division of General Motors Corporation)***

out to its original position. This energy absorber can be reinstalled. If it fails to extend, the unit must be replaced.

Figure 40-12 shows a flexible front bumper. It uses a plastic honeycomb to absorb the force of the impact. When a light impact occurs, the soft-face bumper cover and the honeycomb temporarily are compressed and deformed. Then they return to their original shape and position. If the bumper cover is cut or gouged, it often can be repaired by following procedures similar to those used in repairing other types of plastic material. These are discussed in Chapter 30.

○40-8 Determining Cost of Repair

Now that you know what parts are damaged on a car, you must figure out how much it will cost to restore the car to its precollision condition. Usually, in a commercial body shop, you will find the prices of parts to be replaced in either the *Motor Crash Estimating Guide* or the *Glenn Mitchell Collision Estimator.* Both of these publications, if up-to-date, will provide you with parts prices and the estimated labor time to replace them. However, the labor times listed in these manuals are only guides. Many conditions, such as cutting away the crushed sheet metal, may require the labor time for any job to be increased.

Detailed preparation of estimates, including refinishing and painting, is covered in the *Workbook for Automotive Body Repair and Refinishing*.

CHAPTER 40 CHECKUP

NOTE: Since the following is a chapter review test, you should review the chapter before taking the test.

COMPLETING THE SENTENCES The sentences below are incomplete. After each sentence there are several words or phrases, but only one of them correctly completes the sentence. Write each sentence in your notebook, ending the sentence with the one word or phrase that completes it correctly.

1. The person in the body shop who usually deals with the customer is the (*a*) body technician, (*b*) estimator, (*c*) paint technician, (*d*) wrecker operator.
2. When a car is obviously totaled, you do not always need to (*a*) prepare a detailed written estimate, (*b*) tow the car away, (*c*) attempt to repair the car, (*d*) order paint for the car.
3. When inspecting a damaged car, the first question to answer is: (*a*) How much does the damaged panel cost? (*b*) Is the car repairable? (*c*) Can the car be towed? (*d*) How much paint time is required?
4. When a car has been in a front-end collision, you should check for (*a*) transmission damage, (*b*) rear-end damage, (*c*) damage to the headliner, (*d*) damage to the air conditioner.
5. The device used between the bumper and the frame to absorb shocks of light impacts is the (*a*) shock absorber, (*b*) bumper bracket, (*c*) energy absorber, (*d*) bumper guard.

QUESTIONS Write each of the following questions, and then the answer in your notebook. If you have trouble recalling the answer to a question, turn back to the pages that cover the material and study them again.

1. What are the duties of the estimator?
2. What is an estimate?
3. What is hidden damage, and how do you detect it?
4. What are the steps in the estimating procedure?
5. How do you inspect energy-absorbing bumpers?

SUGGESTIONS FOR FURTHER STUDY

Visit a body shop near you and watch the estimator at work. As the estimate is prepared, ask the estimator why certain parts were marked "straighten" and why other parts were to be replaced. Note carefully how the estimator determines metal-straightening times, and note the costs of paint, material, and refinishing times.

GLOSSARY

A/C–Abbreviation for air conditioning.
abrasive–A substance used for cutting, grinding, lapping, or polishing metals.
accessories–Devices not considered essential to the operation of a vehicle, such as the radio, car heater, and electric window lifts.
acrylic–A clear chemical compound used in lacquer and enamel paint binder. Gives paint durability, and helps retain the original color and gloss.
adhesion–Ability of a substance to stick to a surface.
adjust–To bring the parts of a component system to the specified relationship, dimension, or pressure.
adjustments–Necessary to desired changes in clearances, fit, or settings.
absorb–To collect in a very thin layer on another surface.
aerosol spray–Small metal container that sprays paint in a mist.
aiming screws–Horizontal and vertical self-locking adjusting screws, used to aim a headlight and retain it in position.
air bags–A passive restraint system consisting of balloon-type passenger-safety devices that inflate automatically on vehicle impact.
air compressor–A mechanical device used to compress air from normal atmospheric pressure to the pressures required to operate various air-operated equipment.
air conditioning–An accessory system that conditions passenger-compartment air by cleaning, cooling, and drying it.
air dry–Allowing a finish, such as paint, to harden completely under normal atmospheric conditions.
air filter–A screen that traps any dust and dirt particles in the air flowing through.
air line–A hose, pipe, or tube through which air passes.
air pressure–Atmospheric pressure; also the pressure produced by an air pump or by compression of air in a cylinder.
air pump–Any device for compressing air.
air suspension–A suspension system that uses contained air, such as in air bags, for vehicle springing.
air transformer–A device used to reduce and control the pressure of air coming from the air compressor. Transformers also contain filters which clean the air as it passes through.
alignment–The act of lining up, the state of being in a true line.
alkyd–A chemical compound used in paint binder.
alloy–A mixture of two or more metals.
ambient temperature–The temperature of the air surrounding the car.
antifreeze–A chemical, usually ethylene glycol, that is added to the engine coolant to raise the coolant boiling point and lower its freezing point.
atomization–The spraying of a liquid through a nozzle so that the liquid is broken into a very fine mist.
automatic level control–A suspension system which compensates for variations in load in the rear of the car; positions the rear at a predesigned level regardless of load.
axle–A cross bar supporting a vehicle and on which one or more wheels turn.

back light–The back window, usually located in the roof panel.
base metal–The metal to be welded or cut.
battery–An electrochemical device for storing energy in chemical form so that it can be released as electricity; a group of electric cells connected together.
battery acid–The electrolyte used in a battery, a mixture of sulfuric acid and water.
battery charging–Restoration of chemical energy to a battery by supplying a measured flow of electric current to it over a specified period of time.
bead weld–A type of weld by one passage of electrode or rod.
belt tension–Tightness of a drive belt.
bevel angle–The angle of bevel on the prepared edge of a part to be welded.
binder–One of the substances in paint which acts as a glue to bond the pigment particles together and to the painted surface to form a paint film.
bleeding–An old color which comes through and colors a fresh topcoat of paint.
blistering–Small bubbles that form in a paint film.
Bloc-Chek–A tester that is inserted in the radiator filler neck of a running engine to detect the leakage of exhaust gas into the cooling system.
blushing–A topcoat with a milky or misty appearance.
body–On a vehicle, the self-contained unit that provides enclosures for the passengers, engine, and luggage.
body hardware–Includes the door handles, window cranks, and other appearance and functional parts, both inside and outside of the body.
body lock pillar–The body pillar that contains the lock striker plate; usually part of the center pillar or rear quarter assembly.
body mounting–Putting a car body onto a car chassis. Also, the placing of rubber cushions along the chassis to soak up noise and vibration.
body panels–Sheets of metal or plastic which are fastened together to form the car body.
body side molding–The principal trim molding used around the exterior of the body, approximately horizontal to the ground.
body trim–Material used to upholster and line the interior of the body and rear luggage compartment.
brake lines–The tubes or hoses connecting the master cylinder to the wheel cylinders, or calipers, in a hydraulic brake system.
brazing–A welding process in which the filler metal is a nonferrous metal or alloy whose melting point is higher than 800°F [427°C] but lower than that of the metals or alloys to be joined.
bronzing–The formation of a metallic-appearing haze on a paint film.
build–The depth or thickness of the paint film deposited, measured in mils (thousandths of an inch).
bulb–An assembly which contains a source of light, normally used in a lamp.
burr–A feather edge of metal left on a part being cut with a file or other cutting tool.
butt joint–A welded joint between two abutting parts lying in approximately the same plane.

cables–Stranded conductors, usually covered with insulating material, used for connections between electrical devices.
calibrate–To check or correct the initial setting of a test instrument.
carburizing flame–A gas flame having the property of introducing carbon into the metal heated.
catalytic converter–A mufflerlike device for use in an exhaust system; it converts harmful exhaust gases into harmless gases by promoting a chemical reaction between a catalyst and the pollutants.
Celsius–A thermometer scale on which water boils at 100° and freezes at 0°. The formula $°C = 5/9\ (°F - 32)$ converts Fahrenheit readings to Celsius. Formerly called centrigrade.
CENTARI–DuPont's name for acrylic enamel; introduced in 1969.

center pillar–A box-type construction used on four-door bodies. The center pillar forms the front-door body lock pillar and the rear-door body hinge pillar.

centrigrade–See Celsius.

centimeter (cm)–A unit of linear measure in the metric system; equal to approximately 0.390 inch.

chalking–The presence of loose, powdery pigment which is no longer held to the surface by the binder. Finish looks dull.

change of state–Transformation of a substance from solid to liquid, from liquid to vapor, or vice versa.

charcoal canister–A container filled with activated charcoal, used to trap gasoline vapor from the fuel tank and carburetor while the engine is off.

chassis–The assembly of mechanisms that makes up the major operating part of the vehicle; usually assumed to include everything except the car body.

check–To verify that a component, system, or measurement complies with specifications.

check (paint)–A break on the surface of the topcoat caused by shrinkage, due to oxidation or extreme cold.

check valve–A valve that opens to permit the passage of air or fluid in one direction only, or operates to prevent some undesirable action.

chemical instability–An undesirable condition caused by the presence of contaminants in a refrigeration system. Refrigerants are stable chemicals, but in contact with contaminants they may break down into harmful chemicals.

chemical reaction–The formation of one or more new substances when two or more substances are brought together.

chipping–Damage resulting from the impact of a sharp object, such as a stone, which removes some of the finish. Also called stone bruise.

circuit–The complete path of an electric current, including the current source. When the path is continuous, the circuit is closed and current flows. When the path is broken, the circuit is open and no current flows. Also used to refer to fluid paths, as in refrigerant and hydraulic systems.

clear–A finish having no pigments (color) or transparent pigments only.

clearance–The space between two moving parts, or between a moving and a stationary part.

coach joint–Pinchweld joint on the exterior surface of the body.

coalescence–Fusion or flowing together, as atomized paint droplets.

coat: double–Two single coats of paint, one followed by the other with little or no flash time between each coat.

coat: single–A coat produced by two passes of the spray gun, one pass overlapping the other by 50 percent.

cold–The absence of heat. An object is considered cold to the touch if its temperature is less than body temperature of 98.6°F [37°C].

cold welding–Repairing a crack in metal by drilling a hole through the crack, threading the hole, and screwing in a section of threaded rod to form a seal.

collapsible steering column–An energy-absorbing steering column designed to collapse if the driver is thrown into it by a severe collision.

compartment shelf panel–The horizontal panel located between the rear seat-back and the back window.

compatibility–The ability of two or more materials to work with each other. Oil and water are not compatible.

compounding–See Polishing.

compressor–The pump in an air-conditioning system that compresses refrigerant vapor to increase its pressure and temperature.

condensate–Water that is removed from air. It forms on the exterior surface of the air-conditioner evaporator.

condensation–A change of state during which a gas turns to liquid, usually because of temperature or pressure changes. Also, moisture from the air, deposited on a cool surface.

condenser–In an air-conditioning system, the radiatorlike heat exchanger in which refrigerant vapor loses heat and returns to the liquid state.

conductor–Any material or substance that allows current or heat to flow easily.

cone–The conical part of a gas flame that is next to the original orifice of the tip.

contaminants (air-conditioning)–Anything other than refrigerant and refrigerant oil in a refrigeration system; includes rust, dirt, moisture, and air.

contaminants (painting)–Anything on the surface to be painted that might harm the finish. Examples are polishes, waxes, dirt, tree sap, and tar.

convex fillet weld–A fillet weld having a convex face.

coolant–The liquid mixture of about 50 percent antifreeze and 50 percent water used to carry heat out of the engine.

core–In a radiator, a number of coolant passages surrounded by fins through which air flows to carry away heat.

corrosion–A chemical reaction which results in deterioration of a metal. Rust is an example of corrosion.

coverage–The surface area a given amount of paint will cover.

cracking–A break in the paint film which extends down to the metal surface or undercoat.

craters–Holes in the paint film caused by paint flowing away from contaminated spots before it dries.

crazing–A breakdown of the finish in the form of small cracks in all directions. Similar to crow's-feet.

crease line–A line on the body caused by a crease or break in the body surface.

cubic centimeter (cu cm, cm^3, or cc)–A unit of volume in the metric system; equal to approximately 0.061 cubic inch.

curb weight–The weight of an empty vehicle without payload or driver but including fuel, coolant, oil, and all items of standard equipment.

curing–The complete or final drying stage in which the paint reaches its full strength owing to solvent evaporation and chemical change.

cutting attachment–A device that is attached to a welding torch to convert it to a cutting torch.

cutting tip–A torch tip especially adapted for cutting.

cylinder–A portable container used for storage of a compressed gas.

dash panel–A panel in the body front-end assembly forming the front vertical plane of the body.

defroster–The part of the car heater system designed to melt frost or ice on the inside or outside of the windshield; includes the required ductwork.

degree–Part of a circle. One degree is 1/360 of a complete circle.

deposited metal–Metal that has been added by a welding process.

desiccant–A drying agent. In an air conditioner, desiccant is placed in the receiver-dehydrator to remove moisture from the refrigerant.

detent–A small depression in a shaft, rail, or rod into which a pawl or ball drops when the shaft, rail, or rod is moved; this provides a locking effect.

device–A mechanism, tool, or other piece of equipment designed to serve a special purpose or perform a special function.

diagnosis–A procedure followed in locating the cause of a malfunction.

diaphragm–A thin dividing sheet or partition which separates an area into compartments.

dimmer switch–A two-position switch, usually mounted on the car floor; operated by the driver to select the high or low headlight beam.

directional signal–A device on the car that flashes lights to indicate the direction in which the driver intends to turn.

dirt in paint–Foreign material under or in a paint finish.

disassemble–To take apart.

discharge–To depressurize; to crack a valve to allow refrigerant to escape from an air conditioner; to bleed.
discharge air–Conditioned air leaving the refrigeration unit of an air conditioner.
discharge line–In an air conditioner, the tube that connects the compressor outlet and the condenser inlet. High-pressure refrigerant vapor flows through the line.
discharge pressure–In an air conditioner, the pressure of refrigerant being discharged from the compressor; also called the high pressure.
dolly blocks–Blocks of metal, variously shaped and contoured, used to straighten body panels and fenders. The dolly block is held on one side of the panel while the other side is struck with a special hammer.
dowel–A metal pin attached to one object which, when inserted into a hole in another object, ensures proper alignment.
drier–A catalyst added to paint to speed up the curing or drying time.
drip molding–A channel molding over the door and quarter openings to drain the water from the roof away from the openings.
drive shaft–An assembly of one or two universal joints and slip joints connected to a heavy metal tube; used to transmit power from the transmission to the differential. Also called the propeller shaft.
drop light–A portable light, with a long electric cord, used in the shop to illuminate the immediate work area.
drop-center wheel–The conventional passenger-car wheel, which has a space (drop) in the center for one bead to fit into while the other bead is being lifted over the rim flange.
dry-spray–A small amount of paint in relation to the spray-gun air pressure, resulting in a light, thin dry film of paint.
DUCO–DuPont's name for nitrocellulose lacquer, the original modern automotive finish developed first by DuPont in 1924.
duct–A tube or channel used to convey air or liquid from one point to another.
DULUX–Dupont's name for alkyd enamel; introduced first by DuPont in 1928.
durability–Length of life of a paint film.

eccentric–An offset section of a shaft used to convert rotary to reciprocating motion. Also called a cam.
electric system–In the automobile, the system that electrically cranks the engine for starting; furnishes high-voltage sparks to the engine cylinders to fire the compressed air-fuel charges; lights the lights; and powers the heater motor, radio, and other accessories. Consists, in part, of the starting motor, wiring, battery alternator, regulator, ignition distributor, and ignition coil.
electrolyte–The mixture of sulfuric acid and water used in lead-acid storage batteries. The acid enters into chemical reaction with active material in the plates to produce voltage and current.
enamel–A type of finish which dries or cures through evaporation of solvents and through a chemical change called oxidation.
epoxy–A plastic compound that can be used to repair some types of cracks in metal.
ethylene glycol–Chemical name of a widely used type of permanent antifreeze.
evacuate–To use a vacuum pump to pump any air and moisture out of an air-conditioner refrigerant system; required whenever any component in the refrigerant system has been removed and replaced.
evaporation–To change from a liquid to a gas. In painting, the process during which the solvent in paint changes to a gas and evaporates.
evaporator–The heat exchanger in an air conditioner in which refrigerant changes from a liquid to a gas (evaporates), taking heat from the surrounding air as it does so.
exhaust pipe–The pipe connecting the exhaust manifold with the muffler.
expansion tank–A tank at the top of an automobile radiator which provides room for heated coolant to expand and to give off any air that may be trapped in the coolant. Also, a similar tank used in some fuel tanks to prevent fuel from spilling out of the tank through expansion.

fading–A change in color from the original, usually resulting from exposure to weathering during use.
fan–The bladed device on the front of the engine that rotates to draw cooling air through the radiator, or around the engine cylinders; an air blower such as the heater fan and the A/C blower.
fanning–Use of pressurized air through spray gun or dusting gun to speed up the drying time of a finish. Not a recommended procedure.
fatigue failure–A type of metal failure resulting from repeated stress which finally alters the character of the metal so that it cracks.
featheredge–A tapered paint edge from base metal to topcoat.
filler metal–Metal to be added in making a weld.
filter–A device through which air, gases, or liquids are passed to remove impurities.
finish–A protective or decorative coating; to apply such as coating.
fisheyes–See Craters.
flash–The first stage of drying during which some of the solvents evaporate, dulling the paint from a very high gloss.
flasher–An automatic-reset circuit breaker used in the directional-signal and emergency-signal circuits.
floor pan–The main stamping in the underbody assembly; forms the floor of the body in the passenger compartment.
flow–The ability of the droplets of paint sprayed to merge or melt together to form a smooth film. Also called flow-out.
fluid–Any liquid or gas.
flush–In an air conditioner, to wash out the refrigerant passages with refrigerant to remove contaminants; in a brake system, to wash out the hydraulic system and the master cylinder and wheel cylinders, or calipers, with clean brake fluid to remove any dirt or impurities in the system.
flux–A fusible material or gas used to dissolve and prevent the formation of oxides, nitrides, or other undesirable inclusions formed in welding.
fog coat–A coat of regularly reduced enamel or lacquer, sprayed at slightly higher pressure and greater distance with the gun set for reduced fluid flow.
force dry–Accelerated drying of finishes by means of heat or air.
foreign material on surface–Contamination, such as oil, grease, road tar, insecticides, on the paint film surface. This condition is often difficult to remove and may damage the paint.
frame–The assembly of metal structural parts and channel sections that supports the car engine and body and is supported by the wheels.
frame gauges–Gauges hung from the car frame to check its alignment.
Freon-12–Refrigerant used in automobile air conditioners. Also known as Refrigerant-12 and R-12.
friction–The resistance to motion between two bodies in contact with each other.
front body hinge pillar–A structural member on which the front door is hung.
fuel gauge–A gauge that indicates the amount of fuel in the fuel tank.
fuel line–The pipe or tubes through which fuel flows from the fuel tank to the carburetor.
fuel tank–The storage tank for fuel on the vehicle.
fuse–A device designed to open an electric circuit when the current is excessive, to protect equipment in the circuit. An open, or "blown," fuse must be replaced after the circuit problem is corrected.

fuse block–A boxlike unit that holds the fuses to the various electric circuits in an automobile.

fusible link–A type of fuse in which a special wire melts to open the circuit when the current is excessive. An open, or "blown," fusible link must be replaced after the circuit problem is corrected.

fusion–Melting; conversion from the solid to the liquid state.

fusion welding–A group of processes in which metals are welded together by bringing them to the molten state at the surface to be joined, with or without the addition of mechanical pressure of force.

gas pocket–A cavity in a weld caused by gas inclusion.

gas welding–A nonpressure (fusion) welding process in which the welding heat is obtained from a gas flame.

gasket–A layer of material, such as cork or metal or both, placed between two surfaces to provide a tight seal between them.

gasket cement–A liquid adhesive material, or sealer, used to install gaskets; in some applications, a layer of gasket cement is used as a gasket.

gauge set–One or more instruments attached to a manifold (a pipe fitted with several outlets for connecting pipes) and used for measuring pressures in the air conditioner.

GVW–Abbreviation for gross vehicle weight; the total weight of a vehicle, including the body, payload, fuel, driver, etc.

gloss–The shininess of a paint film, caused by the paint's ability to reflect light.

goggles–Special safety glasses worn over the eyes to protect them from flying chips, dirt, dust, spraying refrigerant, and splashing liquids.

grommet–A device, usually made of hard rubber or plastic, used to encircle or support a part.

ground-return system–Common system of electric wiring in which the chassis and frame of a vehicle are used as part of the electric return circuit to the battery or alternator; also known as the single-wire system.

gutter–A trough following the contour of a body opening which provides a water drain and also aids in sealing the opening.

hardness–That quality which gives a dry paint film resistance to surface damage or deformation.

hazard system–Also called the emergency signal system; a driver-controlled system of flashing front and rear lights, used to warn approaching motorists when a car has made an emergency stop.

headlights–Lights at the front of a vehicle; designed to illuminate the road ahead of the vehicle.

headlining–Interior trim which covers the underside of the roof panel.

heater core–A small radiator, mounted under the dash, through which hot coolant circulates. When heat is needed in the passenger compartment, a fan is turned on to circulate air through the hot core.

Heli-Coil–A thread insert used when original threads are worn or damaged. The insert is installed in a retapped hole to reduce the thread size to the original size.

hem flange–A finished edge for a metal assembly, such as a door assembly. It is formed by folding the outer panel over the inner panel.

hiding–The degree to which a paint obscures the surface to which it is applied. Also called hiding ability.

high-pressure lines–The lines from the air-conditioner compressor outlet to the thermostatic-expansion-valve inlet that carry high-pressure refrigerant. The two longest high-pressure lines are the discharge and liquid lines.

hold-out–Ability of the surface to keep topcoat from sinking in.

hood–The part of the car body that fits over and protects the engine.

hub–The center part of a wheel.

humidity–Amount of moisture in the air. Relative humidity is the ratio of the amount of moisture present to the greatest amount possible at the given temperature.

hydraulic brakes–A braking system that uses hydraulic pressure to force the brake shoes against the brake drums, or rotors, as the brake pedal is depressed.

hydraulic pressure–Pressure exerted through the medium of a liquid.

hydraulics–The use of a liquid under pressure to transfer force or motion, or to increase an applied force.

hydrometer–A device used to measure specific gravity. In automotive servicing, a device used to measure the specific gravity of battery electrolyte to determine the state of the battery charge; also a device used to measure the specific gravity of coolant to determine its freezing temperature.

idler arm–In the steering system, a link that supports the tie rod and transmits steering motion to both wheels through the tie-rod ends.

independent front suspension–The conventional front-suspension system in which each front wheel is independently supported by a spring.

indicator–A device used to make some condition known by use of a light or a dial and pointer; for example, the temperature indicator or oil-pressure indicator.

industrial fallout–A condition caused by particles being blown into the air by the various processes of heavy industry and then being deposited on a vehicle's surface. The particles often cause rust- or off-color spots in the finish which require repair.

inertia–Property of an object that causes it to resist any change in its speed or the direction of its travel.

inspect–To examine a component or system for correct surface, condition, or function.

install–The installation of any part, accessory, option, or kit which has not previously been part of, or attached to the vehicle.

instrument panel–An interior body panel carrying such components as the instrument cluster, glove compartment, and radio speaker grille.

insulation–Material that stops the travel of electricity (electrical insulation) or heat (heat insulation).

insulator–A poor conductor of electricity or of heat.

integral–Built into, as part of the whole.

interchangeability–The manufacture of similar parts to close tolerance so that any one of the parts can be substituted for another in a device, and the part will fit and operate properly; the basis of mass production.

kerf–The space from which the metal has been removed by a cutting process.

kilogram (kg)–In the metric system, a unit of weight and mass; approximately equal to 2.2 pounds.

kilometer (km)–In the metric system, a unit of linear measure equal to 0.621 mile.

kinetic energy–The energy of motion; the energy stored in a moving body through its momentum; for example, the kinetic energy stored in a rotating flywheel.

kingpin–In older cars and trucks, the steel pin on which the steering knuckle pivots; attaches the steering knuckle to the knuckle support or axle.

knuckle–A steering knuckle; a front-suspension part that acts as a hinge to support a front wheel and permits it to be turned to steer the car. The knuckle pivots on ball joints or, in earlier models, on kingpins.

knurl–A series of ridges, formed on the outer surface of a material.

lacquer–A type of paint that dries or cures through evaporation of solvents only, without chemical reaction. In a lacquer, the binder is made up of solid particles.

lamb's-wool bonnet–A round pad of lamb's wool used for final polishing.

laminated–Made up of several thin sheets or layers.

lamp–A divisible assembly that provides a light; contains a bulb or other light source and sometimes a lens and reflector.

lap joint–A welded joint in which two overlapping parts are connected by means of fillet, plug, slot, spot, projection, or seam welds.

leak detector–Any device used to locate an opening where refrigerant may escape from an air conditioner. Common types are flame, electronic, dye, and soap bubbles.

lifting–A condition in which a refinish paint is applied over a paint coating, causing the original coat to separate from the surface to which it was applied.

light–A gas-filled bulb enclosing a wire that flows brightly when an electric current passes through it; a lamp. Also, any visible radiant energy.

linkage-type power steering–A type of power steering in which the power-steering units (power cylinder and valve) are part of the steering linkage; frequently a bolt-on type of unit.

liquid line–In an air conditioner, hose that connects the receiver-dehydrator outlet and the thermostatic-expansion-valve inlet. High-pressure liquid refrigerant flows through the line.

liter (L)–In the metric system, a measure of volume; approximately equal to 0.26 gallons (U.S.) or about 61 cubic inches. Used as a metric measure of engine-cylinder displacement; 33.8 fluid ounces.

low-pressure line–see Suction line.

low-pressure vapor line–see Suction line.

lower beam–A headlight beam intended to illuminate the road ahead of the vehicle when meeting or following another vehicle.

LUCITE–DuPont's name for acrylic lacquer; introduced in 1956.

machining–The process of using a machine to remove metal from a metal part.

mag wheel–Any chromed, aluminum, offset, or wide-rim wheel of spoke design.

Magna-Flux–A process in which an electromagnet and a special magnetic powder are used to detect cracks in iron and steel which might otherwise be invisible to the naked eye.

make–A distinctive name applied to a group of vehicles produced by one manufacturer; may be further subdivided into car lines, body types, etc.

malfunction–Improper or incorrect operation.

manifold gauge set–A high-pressure and a low-pressure gauge mounted together as a set, used for checking pressure in the air-conditioning system.

manufacturer–Any person, firm, or corporation engaged in the production or assembly of motor vehicles or other products.

masking–Covering of areas not to be painted.

mass production–The manufacture of interchangeable parts and similar products in large quantities.

master cylinder–The liquid-filled cylinder in the hydraulic braking system or clutch where hydraulic pressure is developed when the driver depresses a foot pedal.

matter–Anything that has weight and occupies space.

measuring–The act of determining the size, capacity, or quantity of an object.

mechanism–A system of interrelated parts that make up a working assembly.

member–Any essential part of a machine or assembly.

metal conditioner–An acid-type cleaner that removes rust and corrosion from bare metal and etches it for better adhesion. Also forms a film which somewhat inhibits further corrosion.

metal-finishing marks (sand scratches)–The result of poor surface preparation techniques, such as gouging by coarse grinder disks or files, poor sanding, or the use of too coarse a sandpaper. These marks were not removed in the metal-finish operation or properly filled and surfaced with putty glaze.

metallic paints–Lacquers or enamels in which small metal flakes (usually aluminum) are added to the color pigment to give a metallic effect.

meter (m)–A unit of linear measure in the metric system, equal to 39.37 inches. Also, the name given to any test instrument that measures a property of substance passing through it, as an ammeter measures electric current. Also, any device that measures and controls the flow of a substance passing through it.

millimeter (mm)–In the metric system, a unit of linear measure, approximately equal to 0.039 inch.

mineral spirits–A petroleum product commonly used as a lubricant for wet sanding.

mist coat–A coat of rich, slow evaporating thinner with little or no color added.

model year–The production period for new motor vehicles or new engines, designated by the calendar year in which the period ends.

modification–An alteration; a change from the original.

moisture–Humidity, dampness, wetness, or very small drops of water.

mold–A hollow form into which molten metal or plastic is poured and allowed to harden.

molecule–The smallest particle into which a substance can be divided and still retain the properties of the substance.

motor–A device that converts electric energy into mechanical energy; for example, the starting motor.

motor vehicle–A vehicle propelled by a means other than muscle power, usually mounted on rubber tires, which does not run on rails or tracks.

mottling–A painting problem with metallics in which the coat is so wet that the metal flakes float together to form a spotty or dappled effect.

mph–Abbreviation for miles per hour, a unit of speed.

muffler–In the engine exhaust system, a device through which the exhaust gases must pass and which reduces the exhaust noise. In an air-conditioning system, a device to minimize pumping sounds from the compressor.

neoprene–A synthetic rubber that is not affected by chemicals harmful to natural rubber.

neutral–In a transmission, the setting in which all gears are disengaged and the output shaft is disconnected from the drive wheels.

neutral flame–A gas flame wherein the portion used is neither oxidizing nor carburizing.

neutral-start switch–A switch wired into the ignition switch to prevent engine cranking unless the transmission shift lever is in NEUTRAL.

NHTSA–Abbreviation for National Highway Traffic Safety Administration.

noble metals–Metals (such as gold, silver, platinum, and palladium) which do not readily oxidize or enter into other chemical reactions, but do promote reactions between other substances. Platinum and palladium are used as catalysts in catalytic converters.

normal surface of metal–The general contour of the part excluding any local deformations.

nut–A removable fastener used with a bolt to lock pieces together; made by threading a hole through the center of a piece of metal which has been shaped to a standard size.

O ring–A type of sealing ring, made of a special rubberlike material; in use, the O ring is compressed into a groove to provide the sealing action.

odometer–The meter that indicates the total distance a vehicle has traveled, in miles or kilometers; usually located in the speedometer.

oil pan–The detachable lower part of the engine, made of sheet metal, which encloses the crankcase and acts as an oil reservoir.

oil-pressure indicator–A gauge that indicates to the driver that there is adequate oil pressure in the engine lubricating system.

one-wire system–On autombiles, use of the car body, engine, and frame as a path for the grounded side of the electric circuits; eliminates the need for a second wire as a return path to the battery or alternator.

open circuit–In an electric circuit, break, or opening, which prevents the passage of current.

orange peel–A rough texture in the paint resembling the skin of an orange, caused by failure of the sprayed paint film to flow out smoothly.

original finish–The finish applied to the vehicle at time of manufacture.

overflow–Spilling of the excess of a substance; also, to run or spill over the sides of a container, usually because of overfilling.

overflow tank–see Expansion tank.

overhaul–To completely disassemble a unit, clean and inspect all parts, reassemble it with the original or new parts, and make all adjustments necessary for proper operation.

overheat–To heat excessively; also, to become excessively hot.

overlap–Protrusion of weld metal at the toe of a weld beyond the limits of fusion.

overspray–Droplets of paint from a spray gun which fall on areas where they are not wanted.

oxidation–The combining of a material with oxygen; rusting is slow oxidation, and combustion is rapid oxidation. A chemical reaction, between the oxygen in the air and a substance in the paint, during which oxygen is absorbed from the air by the paint.

oxidizing flames–A gas flame with excess oxygen having an oxidizing effect on weld area.

oxy-acetylene welding–A gas-welding process wherein the welding heat is obtained from the combustion of oxygen and acetylene.

oxygen (O)–A colorless, tasteless, odorless, gaseous element which makes up about 21 percent of air. Capable of combining rapidly with all elements except the inert gases in the oxidation process called burning. Combines very slowly with many metals in the oxidation process called rusting.

oxygen cutting–A process of severing ferrous metals by means of the chemical action of oxygen on elements in the base metal at high temperatures.

paint remover–A chemical which breaks down an old finish by liquefying it.

paint remover–A chemical which reacts with the old finish to lift it from a base surface or to form a liquid. The old finish can then be easily wiped off. Also called stripper.

parking brake–Mechanically operated brake that is independent of the foot-operated service brakes on the vehicle; set when the vehicle is parked.

particle–A very small piece of metal, dirt, or other impurity.

pass–The weld metal deposited by one general progression along the axis of a weld.

passenger car–Any four-wheeled motor vehicle manufactured primarily for use on streets and highways and carrying 10 passengers or fewer.

pawl–An arm, pivoted so that its free end can fit into a detent, slot, or groove at certain times to hold a part stationary.

peeling–The separation of a paint film from the surface to which it has been applied.

peen–To mushroom or spread the end of a pin or rivet.

penetration–The penetration, or depth of fusion, of a weld is the distance from the original surface of the base metal to that point at which fusion ceases.

pigment–Finely ground particles in the paint which give it its color, durability, and hiding ability.

pilot shaft–A shaft that is used to align parts and that is removed before final installation of the parts; a dummy shaft.

pinchweld–Two metal flanges pointing in the same direction and spot-welded together.

pinholing–Tiny holes that form in the topcoat or undercoat.

pivot–A pin or shaft upon which another part rests or turns.

plastic gasket compound–A plastic paste which can be squeezed out of a tube to make a gasket in any shape.

polisher–A portable electric or air-driven motor used with various pads and bonnets to polish a paint film; usually operates at 1700 to 1800 rpm.

polishing–Rubbing action using a fine abrasive compound, which helps make a surface smooth and lustrous.

polishing compound–Fine abrasive paste for smoothing and polishing a paint film.

polishing pad–A round tufted cotton pad made to fit a polisher.

poor drying (hardness)–Softness in a paint film when it should be harder.

porosity–The presence of gas pockets or inclusions in a weld.

postheating–Heat applied after welding or cutting operations.

power brakes–A brake system that uses vacuum and atmospheric pressure to provide most of the effort required for braking.

power cylinder–An operating cylinder which produces the power to actuate a mechanism. Both power brakes and power-steering units contain power cylinders.

power plant–The engine or power source of a vehicle.

power steering–A steering system that uses hydraulic pressure (from a pump) to multiply the driver's steering effort.

power tool–A tool whose power source is not muscle power; a tool powered by air or electricity.

power train–The mechanisms that carry the rotary motion developed in the engine to the car wheels; includes the clutch, transmission, drive shaft, differential, and axles.

PR–Abbreviation for ply rating; a measure of the strength of a tire, based on the strength of a single ply of designated construction.

preheating–Heat applied before welding or cutting operations.

press fit–A fit (between two parts) so tight that one part has to be pressed into the other, usually with an arbor press or hydraulic press.

pressure–Force per unit area, or force divided by area. Usually measured in pounds per square inch (psi) and kilograms per square centimeter (kg/cm^2).

pressure bleeder–A piece of shop equipment that uses air pressure to force brake fluid into the brake system for bleeding.

pressure cap–A radiator cap, with valves, which causes the cooling system to operate under pressure at a somewhat higher and more efficient temperature.

pressure regulator–A device which operates to prevent excessive pressure from developing.

pressure-relief valve–A valve in the line that opens to relieve excessive pressures.

pressure-sensing line–In an air conditioner, a line that prevents the compressor suction pressure from dropping below a predetermined pressure. It opens the thermostatic expansion valve, allowing liquid refrigerant to flood the evaporator.

pressure tester–An instrument that clamps in the radiator filler neck; used to pressure-test the cooling system for leaks.

pressurize–To apply more than atmospheric pressure to a gas or liquid.

preventive maintenance–The systematic inspection of a vehicle to detect and correct failures, either before they occur or before they develop into major defects. A procedure for economically maintaining a vehicle in a satisfactory and dependable operating condition.

primer–A base or undercoat next to the metal or substrate which improves adhesion of the topcoat.

primer-surfacer–A primer with solids in it to promote adhesion of the topcoat and fill minor surface imperfections to provide a smooth level surface.

printed circuit–An electric circuit made by applying a conductive material to an insulating board in a pattern that provides current paths between components mounted on or connected to the board.

prussian blue–A blue pigment; in solution, useful in determining the area of contact between two surfaces.

psi–Abbreviation for pounds per square inch; a unit of pressure.

psig–Abbreviation for pounds per square inch of gauge pressure.

puller–Generally, a shop tool used to separate two closely fitted parts without damage. Often contains a screw, or several screws, which can be turned to apply gradual pressure.

pulley–A metal wheel with a V-shaped groove around the rim; drives, or is driven by, a belt.

pump–A device that transfers gas or liquid from one place to another.

punch–A hand-held tool that is struck with a hammer to drive one piece of metal from inside another.

purge–To remove, evacuate, or empty trapped substances from a space. In an air conditioner, to remove moisture and air from the refrigerant system by flushing with nitrogen or refrigerant.

putty–A thick material used to fill flaws in the metal surface that are too large to be filled by primer-surfacer.

quarter panel–A major panel forming the rear corner sections of the body. The front edge of the panel forms the rear body lock pillar.

quick charger–A battery charger that produces a high charging current and substantially charges, or boosts, a battery in a short time.

R&I–Remove a part or assembly from a vehicle to facilitate other work and reinstall the same part or assembly on the vehicle. Includes alignment that can be done by shifting the part or assembly.

R&R–Remove a part or assembly from a vehicle; transfer bolted, riveted, or clipped-on parts to new part; and install part or assembly on the vehicle. Includes alignment or adjustment that can be done by shifting the part or assembly.

radiator–In the cooling system, the device that removes heat from coolant passing through it; takes hot coolant from the engine and returns the coolant to the engine at a lower temperature.

radiator pressure cap–see Pressure cap.

ratio–Proportion; the relative amounts of two or more substances in a mixture. Usually expressed as a numerical relationship, as in 2:1.

reamer–A round metal-cutting tool with a series of sharp cutting edges; enlarges a hole when turned in it.

rear compartment lid–A door, made up of an inner and outer panel, located over the rear luggage compartment.

rear compartment pan–That part of the underbody forming the floor in the luggage compartment.

rear end panel–A body panel running across the rearmost part of the body immediately under the rear compartment opening.

rear quarter window–The rearmost side window located in the rear quarter panel. Not used in all body styles.

rear seat pan–A part of the underbody assembly located under the rear seat.

reassembly- Putting the parts of a device back together.

recapping–A form of tire repair in which a cap of new tread material is placed on the old casing and vulcanized into place.

reciprocating motion–Motion of an object between two limiting positions; motion in a straight line back and forth or up and down.

reducer–A solvent used to reduce or dilute enamels.

refrigerant–A substance used to transfer heat in an air conditioner through a cycle of evaporation and condensation.

relative humidity–The actual moisture content of the air, as a percentage of the total moisture that the air can hold at a given temperature.

relay–An electrical device that opens or closes a circuit or circuits in response to a voltage signal.

relief valve–A valve that opens when a preset pressure is reached. This relieves or prevents excessive pressures.

remove and install (R&I)–The removal of a part and the reinstallation of the same part in its original position, and any inspection, adjustment, cleaning, and lubrication operations which may be required.

remove and reinstall (R&R)–To perform a series of servicing procedures on an original part or assembly; includes removal, inspection, lubrication, all necessary adjustments, and reinstallation.

replace–To remove a used part or assembly and install a new part or assembly in its place; includes cleaning, lubricating, and adjusting as required.

respirator–A breathing mask used to filter particles out of the air being breathed.

retarder–A very slow-drying solvent that slows paint drying time by reducing the rate of solvent evaporation. An additive; opposite of drier.

return spring–A "pull-back" spring, often used in brake systems.

rivet–A semipermanent fastener used to hold two pieces together.

rocker panel–The inner panel and outer panel which form a box located at the outer edge of the floor pan, immediately below the doors. It extends from the front body hinge pillar to the rear body lock pillar.

roof panel–The body upper closure.

roof rail–A box consisting of an inner and outer panel. It extends from the front end frame to the rear quarter side panel forming the upper line of the door body openings.

rotary–The motion of a part that continually rotates or turns.

rpm–Abbreviation for revolutions per minute, a measure of rotational speed.

rubbing compound–An abrasive paste (coarser than polishing compound) that smoothes the paint film.

ruler–A graduated straightedge used for measuring distances, usually up to 1 foot.

runout–Wobble.

rust–A condition resulting from weathering (oxidation) of exposed or insufficiently protected or prepared metal.

rust inhibiting–Slows down rusting or oxidation of metals.

SAE–Abbreviation for Society of Automotive Engineers.

safety–Freedom from injury or danger.

safety rim–A wheel rim with a hump on the inner edge of the ledge on which the tire bead rides. The hump helps hold the tire on the rim in case of a blowout.

safety stand–A pinned or locked device placed under a car to support its weight after the car has been raised with a floor jack or lift. Also called a car stand or jack stand.

sags–A paint film that drips or runs because of applying too much paint.

sander–A power tool designed to sand finishes. May be powered by electricity or air and can be straight-line reciprocal, orbital, or rotary-type.

sanding–A scrubbing action using an abrasive material to remove defects, smooth surfaces to be painted, and improve adhesion of paint coats.

sanding block–A hard, flexible block to provide a smooth backing for hand sanding.

sanding sludge–Particles of paint which have been loosened during sanding and mixed with water or mineral spirits to form a mudlike substance.

sand-scratch swelling–Swelling in sandscratches in the old finish caused by solvents in the topcoat being applied.

sand-scratches–Metal-finish marks or scratches, usually caused by poor surface preparation techniques.

Schrader valve–A spring-loaded valve through which a connection can be made to a refrigeration system; also used in tires.

scratched–The appearance of the finish when it has been damaged by the penetration of a sharp object.

screens–Pieces of fine-mesh metal fabric; used to prevent solid particles from circulating through any liquid or vapor system and damaging vital moving parts. In an air conditioner, screens are located in the receiver-dehydrator, thermostatic expansion valve, and compressor.

screw–A metal fastener with threads that can be turned into a threaded hole, usually with a screwdriver. There are many different types and sizes of screws.

screwdriver–A hand tool used to loosen or tighten screws.

seal–A material shaped around a part, used to close off a compartment.

sealed-beam headlight–A headlight that contains the filament, reflector, and lens in a single sealed unit.

sealer–An intercoat between the topcoat and primer-surfacer or old topcoat. Promotes adhesion and helps prevent sand-scratch swelling.

sealer under paint–Types of dirt under paint resulting from poor prepaint cleanup operations.

seat–The surface upon which another part rests, as a valve seat.

seat adjuster–A device that permits forward and backward (and sometimes upward and downward) movement of the front seat of a vehicle.

self-locking screw–A screw that locks itself in place, without the use of a separate nut or lock washer.

self-tapping screw–A screw that cuts its own threads as it is turned into an unthreaded hole.

service manual–A book published annually by each vehicle manufacturer, listing the specifications and service procedures for each make and model of vehicle. Also called a shop manual.

setscrew–A type of metal fastener that holds a collar or gear on a shaft when its point is turned down into the shaft.

settling–The tendency of solids (pigment and binder) in a paint to drop to the bottom of the container.

shackle–The swinging support by which one end of a leaf spring is attached to the car frame.

sheet metal–Parts that are not integral with the body, such as bumpers, grille, hood, front fenders, and gravel guards.

shift lever–The lever used to change gears in a transmission.

shim–A slotted strip of metal used to make small front-end alignment on many cars; also used to make small corrections in the position of body sheet metal and other parts.

shimmy–Rapid oscillation. In wheel shimmy, for example, the front wheel turns in and out alternately and rapidly; this causes the front end of the car to oscillate, or shimmy.

shock absorber–A device placed at each vehicle wheel to regulate spring rebound and compression.

shop layout–The locations of aisles, work areas, machine tools, etc., in a shop.

shrink fit–A tight fit of one part into another, achieved by heating or cooling one part and then assembling it to the other part. A heated part will shrink on cooling to provide the tight fit; a cooled part will expand on warming to provide the tight fit.

shroud–A hood placed around an engine fan to improve fan action.

sight glass–In a car air conditioner a viewing glass or window set in the refrigerant line, usually in the top of the receiver-dehydrator; the sight glass allows a visual check of the refrigerant passing from the receiver to the evaporator.

silicone–An ingredient in waxes and polishes which makes them smooth and slippery to the touch. The primary cause of fisheyes in refinish coatings if not removed.

silicone and wax remover–A chemical solution used to remove grease, tar, and wax from a paint during surface preparation.

skinning–Formation of a film on the top of the liquid in a container of paint. Also the formation of a film on heavy or thick topcoats before the solvents in the underlayer of the topcoat have evaporated.

socket wrench–A wrench that fits entirely over or around the head of a bolt.

soldering–Joining pieces of metal with solder, flux, and heat.

solids–The percentage, on a weight basis, of solid material in a paint after the solvents have evaporated.

solvent–A chemical liquid that dissolves, dilutes, or liquefies another liquid or solid. Reducers, thinners, and cleaners are solvents.

solvent popping–Bubbles which form in a paint film.

solvent tank–In the shop, a tank of cleaning fluid, in which most parts are brushed and washed clean.

specific gravity–The weight per unit volume of a substance as compared with the weight per unit volume of water.

specifications–Information provided by the manufacturer that describes each automotive system and its components, operation, and clearances. Also, the service procedures that must be followed for a system to operate properly.

specs–Short for specifications.

speed–The rate of motion; for vehicles, measured in miles per hour or kilometers per hour.

speedometer–An instrument that indicates vehicle speed; usually driven from the transmission.

spray booth–A room which provides the proper lighting and ventilation required to properly spray paint.

spray gun–A tool which uses air pressure to atomize paint.

spring–A device that changes shape under stress or pressure, but returns to its original shape when the stress or pressure is removed; the component of the automotive suspension system that absorbs road shocks by flexing and twisting.

sprung weight–That part of the car which is supported on springs (includes the engine, frame, and body).

squeak–A high-pitched noise of short duration.

squeal–A continuous, high-pitched, low-volume noise.

squeegee–A flexible rubber or plastic block used to wipe off wet-sanded areas and apply putty.

stabilizer bar–An interconnecting shaft between the two lower suspension arms; reduces body roll on turns.

stains–The result of surface contamination which has affected the color of the finish.

steam cleaner–A machine used for cleaning large parts with a spray of steam, often mixed with soap.

steering-and-ignition lock–A device that locks the ignition switch in the OFF position and locks the steering wheel so it cannot be turned.

steering gear–That part of the steering system that is located at the lower end of the steering shaft; carries the rotary motion of the steering wheel to the car wheels for steering.

steering knuckle–The front-wheel spindle which is supported by upper and lower ball joints and by the wheel; the part on which a front wheel is mounted and which is turned for steering.

steering system–The mechanism that enables the driver to turn the wheels for changing the direction of vehicle movement.

steering wheel–The wheel, at the top of the steering shaft, which is used by the driver to guide, or steer, the car.

stepped feeler gauge–A feeler gauge which has a thin tip, of a known dimension and is thicker along the rest of the gauge; a "go–no-go" feeler gauge.

stoplight switch–The switch that turns the stoplights on and off as the brakes are applied and released.

stoplights–Lights at the rear of a vehicle which indicate that the brakes are being applied to slow or stop the vehicle.

storage battery–A device that changes chemical energy into electrical energy; that part of the electric system which acts as a reservoir for electric energy, storing it in chemical form.

strainer–A fine screen used to filter out undesirable particles in paint before spraying.
streamlining–The shaping of a car body or truck cab so that it minimizes air resistance and can be moved through the air with less energy.
stripper–see Paint remover.
strut–A bar that connects the lower control arm to the car frame; used when the lower control arm is of the type that is attached to the frame at only one point. Also called a brake reaction rod.
stud–A headless bolt that is threaded on both ends.
stud extractor–A special tool used to remove a broken stud or bolt.
substrate–The surface of the material to be painted. May be an old finish or an unpainted surface.
suction line–In an air conditioner, the tube that connects the evaporator outlet and the compressor inlet. Low-pressure refrigerant vapor flows through this line.
suction throttling valve–In an air conditioner, a valve located between the evaporator and the compressor; controls the temperature of the air flowing from the evaporator, to prevent freezing of moisture on the evaporator.
suspension–The system of springs and other parts which supports the upper part of a vehicle on its axles and wheels.
suspension arm–In the front suspension, one of the arms pivoted on the frame at one end, and on the steering-knuckle support at the other end.
sway bar–see Stabilizer bar.
switch–A device that opens and closes an electric circuit.

tachometer–A device for measuring engine speed, or revolutions per minute.
tack rag–A cloth saturated with diluted varnish to make it sticky so it will pick up dust and dirt particles.
taillights–Steady-burning low-intensity lights used on the rear of a vehicle.
tank unit–The part of the fuel-indicating system that is mounted in the fuel tank.
tap–A tool used for cutting threads in a hole.
temperature–The measure of heat intensity or concentration, in degrees. Temperature is not a measure of heat quantity.
temperature gauge–A gauge that indicates to the driver the temperature of the coolant in the engine cooling system.
temperature indicator–see Temperature gauge.
temperature-sending unit–A device in contact with the engine coolant whose electrical resistance changes as the coolant temperature increases or decreases; these changes control the movement of the indicator needle of the temperature gauge.
template–A gauge or pattern, commonly a thin metal plate or board, used as a guide to establish the form of the work to be done.
thermal–Of or pertaining to heat.
thermometer–An instrument which measures heat intensity (temperature) via the thermal expansion of a liquid.
thermostat–A device for the automatic regulation of temperature; usually contains a temperature-sensitive element that expands or contracts to open or close off the flow of air, gas, or liquid
thin paint–A condition in which not enough paint has been applied or an excessive amount has been removed by abrasion or erosion.
thinner–A solvent used to thin or dilute lacquers.
thread chaser–A device similar to a die that is used to clean threads.
thread class–A designation indicating the closeness of fit between a pair of threaded parts, such as a nut and bolt.
thread series–A designation indicating the pitch, or number of threads per inch, on a threaded part.
threaded insert–A threaded coil that is used to restore the original thread size to a hole with damaged threads; the hole is drilled oversize and tapped, and the insert is threaded into the tapped hole.
tie rods–In the steering system, the rods that link the pitman arm to the steering-knuckle arms; small steel components that connect the front wheels to the steering mechanism.
tilt steering wheel–A type of steering wheel that can be tilted at various angles, through a flex joint in the steering shaft.
tire–The casing-and-thread assembly (with or without a tube) that is mounted on a car wheel to provide pneumatically cushioned contact and traction with the road.
topcoats–The final layers of paint material such as lacquers or enamels used to give the vehicle color and resistance to corrosion.
torque–Turning or twisting effort; usually measured in pound-feet or kilogram-meters. Also, a turning force such as that required to tighten a connection.
torque wrench–A wrench that indicates the amount of torque being applied.
touch-up paint–A pastelike topcoat that comes in a tube. Used for touching up minor surface damage.
tracking–Rear wheels following directly behind (in the tracks of) the front wheels.
tramp–Up-and-down motion (hopping) of the front wheels at higher speeds, due to unbalanced wheels or excessive wheel runout. Also called high-speed shimmy.
transmission–An assembly of gears that provides the different gear ratios, as well as neutral and reverse, through which engine power is transmitted to the differential to rotate the drive wheels.
tread–That part of the tire that contacts the road. It is the thickest part of the tire, and is cut with grooves to provide traction for driving and stopping.
trim–Any part that is attached to the body after it is painted. Usually, divided into hard trim, such as moldings, and soft trim, such as upholstery.
trim finishing molding–A decorative molding used on the interior trim of the doors and quarters.
trouble diagnosis–The detective work necessary to find the cause of a trouble.
turn signal–see Directional signal.
turn under–The portion of the body surface below the widest part of the body that sweeps down and toward the center line of the body.
twist drill–A conventional drill bit.
two-tone–Two different colors on a paint job; to apply two colors on the same paint job.

U bolt–An iron rod with threads on both ends bent into the shape of a U and fitted with a nut at each end.
under-dash unit–The hang-on type air-conditioning system installed under the dash after the vehicle leaves the factory. Air outlets are in the evaporator case, and the system normally uses only recirculated air. The discharge air temperature is controlled by a cycling thermostatic expansion switch or a suction throttling valve.
underbody assembly–A welded assembly of metal stampings consisting mainly of a floor pan, rear seat pan, and rear compartment pan. It forms the body closure next to the chassis.
undercoats–Layers of paint material such as primer-surfacer, putty glaze, and sealer used to provide a smooth base for the topcoats. They help the topcoat stick to the surface and prevent rust and corrosion.
unit–An assembly or device that can perform its function only if it is not further divided into its components.
unitized construction–A type of automotive construction in which the frame and body parts are welded together to form a single unit.
universal joint–In the power train, a jointed connection in the drive shaft that permits the driving angle to change.
unsprung weight–The weight of that part of the car which is not supported on springs; for example, the wheels and tires.

upper beam–A headlight beam intended primarily for distant illumination; not for use when meeting or following other vehicles.

vacuum–Negative gauge pressure, or a pressure less than atmospheric pressure. Vacuum can be measured in psi, but is usually measured in inches or millimeters of mercury (Hg); a reading of 30 inches [762 mm] Hg would indicate a perfect vacuum.
vacuum motor–A small motor, powered by intake-manifold vacuum; used for jobs such as raising and lowering headlight doors.
vacuum pump–A mechanical device used to evacuate the refrigerant system of an air conditioner.
vacuum switch–A switch that closes or opens its contacts in response to changing vacuum conditions.
valve–A device that can be opened or closed to allow or stop the flow of a liquid or gas.
vapor–A gas; any substance in the gaseous state, as distinguished from the liquid or solid state.
vaporization–A change of state from liquid to vapor or gas, by evaporation or boiling; a general term including both evaporation and boiling.
vehicle–All of a paint except the pigment. This includes solvents, diluents, resins, gums, driers, etc.
vehicle identification number (VIN)–The number assigned to each vehicle by its manufacturer, primarily for registration and identification purposes.
vent–An opening through which air can leave an enclosed chamber.
ventilation–The circulating of fresh air through any space, to replace impure air.
vibration–A rapid back-and-forth motion; an oscillation.
VIN–Abbreviation for Vehicle identification number.
vinyl tape–A plastic tape which has a pressure-sensitive adhesive and which is used as an accent stripe.
viscous–Thick; tending to resist flowing.
vise–A gripping device; used to hold a part steady while it is being worked on.
volatile–Evaporating readily. For example, Refrigerant-12 is volatile (evaporates quickly) at room temperature.
volatility–A measure of the ease with which a liquid evaporizes; has a direct relationship to the flammability of a fuel.

water spotting–Damage caused by exposing to snow, rain, or dew a new paint film that has not completely dried. Appears as a rough area in the paint or as a circular, whitish water residue embedded in the surface.
weight distribution–The percentage of a vehicle's total weight that rests on each axle.
weld–A localized consolidation of metals by a welding process.
weld metal–The metal resulting from the fusion of the base metal or the base metal and the filler metal.
welding–The process of joining pieces of metal by fusing them together with heat.
welding procedure–The detailed methods and practices involved in the production of a welded structure.
welding rod–Filler metal, in wire or rod form, used in the welding process.
welding tip–A gas-torch tip especially adapted for welding.
welding torch–A device used in gas welding for mixing and controlling the gases.
wet spots–Areas where the paint fails to dry and adhere uniformly; generally caused by grease spots, finger marks, etc.
wheel alignment–A series of tests and adjustments to ensure that wheels and tires are properly positioned on the vehicle.
wheel tramp–Tendency for a wheel to move up and down so it repeatedly bears down hard, or "tramps" on the road. Sometimes called high-speed shimmy.
wheelbase–The distance between the center lines of the front and rear axles. For trucks with tandem rear axles, the rear center line is considered to be midway between the two rear axles.
wheelhouse–An inner body housing over the rear wheel.
window regulator–A device for opening and closing a window; usually operated by a crank.
windshield pillar–The structural member joining the shroud assembly to the roof panel and defining the sides of the windshield opening.
windshield wiper–A mechanism which moves a rubber blade back and forth to wipe the windshield; operated electrically.
wire feeler gauge–A set of round wires of known diameters; used to check clearances between electrical contacts.
wiring harness–A group of individually insulated wires, wrapped together to form a neat, easily installed bundle.
work–The changing of the position of an object against an opposing force; measured in foot-pounds or meter-kilograms. The product of a force and the distance through which it acts.
wrench–A tool designed for tightening and loosening nuts and bolts.
wrinkling–Skinning of a thick or heavy coat of paint before the underpart of the film has properly dried, resulting in wrinkling.

Zip gun–An air-powered cutting tool for sheet metal and tube.

INDEX

ANSWERS TO QUESTIONS

The answers to questions in the progress quizzes and chapter checkups are given below. In some questions, you are asked to list parts, describe the purpose and operation of components, define terms, and so on. The answers to such questions cannot be given here, since that would mean repeating most of the book. Therefore, you are asked to refer to the book and to the glossary to check those answers.

If you want to figure your grade on any quiz, divide 100 by the number of questions in the quiz. This gives you the value of each question. Suppose there are 8 questions. Since 100 divided by 8 is 12.5, each correct answer is worth 12.5 points. If you got 6 correct out of the 8, then your grade is 75 (that is, 6 × 12.5).

If you are not satisfied with your grade, restudy the chapter or section and take the quiz again.

CHAPTER 1

PROGRESS QUIZ 1-1 1. *d* 2. *b* 3. *a* 4. *a* 5. *c* 6. *d* 7. *a* 8. *c* 9. *b* 10. *b*

CHAPTER 1 CHECKUP

Matching

about 200,000	auto body technicians
foreman	runs the shop
dismantler	buys "totaled" cars
one out of every eight	self-employed body-repair technicians
body-repair technician	cuts out badly damaged parts
upholsterer	maintains and repairs interior
estimator	looks over wrecked car
painter	uses lots of sandpaper
manager	hires, trains, and fires
more than 30 million	paint and body repairs each year

CHAPTER 2

PROGRESS QUIZ 2-1 1. *c* 2. *a* 3. *d* 4. *b* 5. *b* 6. *d* 7. *a* 8. *c* 9. *c* 10. *a*

CHAPTER 2 CHECKUP

Correcting Parts Lists 1. Windshield 2. Ignition switch 3. Backup lights 4. Air bags

Completing the Sentences 1. *b* 2. *a* 3. *b* 4. *d* 5. *c*

CHAPTER 3 CHECKUP

Completing the Sentences 1. *b* 2. *a* 3. *c* 4. *c* 5. *b* 6. *a* 7. *b* 8. *d* 9. *d* 10. *a*

CHAPTER 4 CHECKUP

Completing the Sentences 1. *a* 2. *c* 3. *c* 4. *d* 5. *b*

CHAPTER 5 CHECKUP

Completing the Sentences 1. *d* 2. *b* 3. *b* 4. *d* 5. *a*

CHAPTER 6 CHECKUP

Completing the Sentences 1. *c* 2. *c* 3. *b* 4. *d* 5. *d*

CHAPTER 7 CHECKUP

Completing the Sentences 1. *a* 2. *b* 3. *a* 4. *d* 5. *b*

Matching Tools and Uses

TOOL	USE
air chisel	cuts rusted nuts
air nibbler	cuts thin ribbon of metal
impact wrench	turns bolts and nuts
air drill	stalls without damage
air sander	spins a rotating disk

CHAPTER 8 CHECKUP

Completing the Sentences 1. *c* 2. *c* 3. *a* 4. *b* 5. *d*

CHAPTER 9 CHECKUP

Completing the Sentences 1. *b* 2. *a* 3. *d* 4. *a* 5. *c*

CHAPTER 10 CHECKUP

Completing the Sentences 1. *a* 2. *c* 3. *a* 4. *c* 5. *c*

CHAPTER 11 CHECKUP

Completing the Sentences 1. *c* 2. *b* 3. *d* 4. *d* 5. *c*

CHAPTER 12 CHECKUP

Completing the Sentences 1. *d* 2. *c* 3. *a* 4. *b* 5. *a*

CHAPTER 13 CHECKUP

Completing the Sentences 1. *d* 2. *b* 3. *c* 4. *b* 5. *d*

CHAPTER 14 CHECKUP

Completing the Sentences 1. *a* 2. *b* 3. *c* 4. *d* 5. *b*

CHAPTER 15 CHECKUP

Completing the Sentences 1. *c* 2. *c* 3. *b* 4. *d* 5. *d*

CHAPTER 16 CHECKUP

Completing the Sentences 1. *a* 2. *d* 3. *b* 4. *c* 5. *b*

CHAPTER 17 CHECKUP

Completing the Sentences 1. *a* 2. *d* 3. *a* 4. *c* 5. *a*

CHAPTER 18 CHECKUP

Completing the Sentences 1. *d* 2. *d* 3. *c* 4. *a* 5. *b*

CHAPTER 19 CHECKUP

Completing the Sentences 1. *b* 2. *c* 3. *b* 4. *d* 5. *c*

CHAPTER 20 CHECKUP

Completing the Sentences 1. *d* 2. *a* 3. *c* 4. *a* 5. *c*

CHAPTER 21 CHECKUP

Completing the Sentences 1. *b* 2. *d* 3. *c* 4. *b* 5. *a*

CHAPTER 22 CHECKUP

Completing the Sentences 1. *c* 2. *b* 3. *d* 4. *c* 5. *b*

CHAPTER 23 CHECKUP

Completing the Sentences 1. *b* 2. *a* 3. *d* 4. *b* 5. *c*

CHAPTER 24 CHECKUP

Completing the Sentences 1. *c* 2. *a* 3. *c* 4. *c* 5. *b*

CHAPTER 25 CHECKUP

Completing the Sentences 1. *a* 2. *c* 3. *c* 4. *b* 5. *d*

CHAPTER 26 CHECKUP

Completing the Sentences 1. *b* 2. *d* 3. *d* 4. *c* 5. *a*

CHAPTER 27 CHECKUP

Completing the Sentences 1. *c* 2. *a* 3. *b* 4. *a* 5. *d*

CHAPTER 28 CHECKUP

Completing the Sentences 1. *c* 2. *c* 3. *a* 4. *c* 5. *b*

CHAPTER 29 CHECKUP

Completing the Sentences 1. *d* 2. *a* 3. *d* 4. *b* 5. *c*

CHAPTER 30 CHECKUP

Completing the Sentences 1. *a* 2. *b* 3. *d* 4. *c* 5. *b*

CHAPTER 31 CHECKUP

Completing the Sentences 1. *a* 2. *c* 3. *b* 4. *d* 5. *a*

CHAPTER 32 CHECKUP

Completing the Sentences 1. *b* 2. *b* 3. *a* 4. *c* 5. *d*

CHAPTER 33 CHECKUP

Completing the Sentences 1. *c* 2. *a* 3. *d* 4. *a* 5. *b*

CHAPTER 34 CHECKUP

Completing the Sentences 1. *c* 2. *a* 3. *c* 4. *c* 5. *b*

CHAPTER 35 CHECKUP

Completing the Sentences 1. *d* 2. *d* 3. *a* 4. *b* 5. *a*

CHAPTER 36 CHECKUP

Completing the Sentences 1. *b* 2. *d* 3. *c* 4. *b* 5. *a*

CHAPTER 37 CHECKUP

Completing the Sentences 1. *a* 2. *d* 3. *a* 4. *a* 5. *a*

CHAPTER 38 CHECKUP

Completing the Sentences 1. *c* 2. *a* 3. *c* 4. *c* 5. *d*

CHAPTER 39 CHECKUP

Completing the Sentences 1. *d* 2. *d* 3. *c* 4. *a* 5. *b*

CHAPTER 40 CHECKUP

Completing the Sentences 1. *b* 2. *a* 3. *b* 4. *d* 5. *c*